PROFESSIONAL
C# AND .NET

T0188508

Continues

This book is dedicated to my family—Angela, Stephanie, Matthias, and Katharina—I love you all!

ABOUT THE AUTHOR

CHRISTIAN NAGEL is a Microsoft MVP for Visual Studio and Development Technologies and has been Microsoft Regional Director for more than 15 years. Christian is the founder of CN innovation, where he offers coaching, training, code reviews, and assistance with architecting and developing solutions using Microsoft technologies. He draws on more than 25 years of software development experience.

Christian started his computing career with PDP 11 and VAX/VMS systems at Digital Equipment Corporation, covering a variety of languages and platforms. Since 2000, when .NET was just a technology preview, he has been working with various technologies to build .NET solutions. Currently, he mainly coaches people on developing and architecting solutions based on .NET and Microsoft Azure technologies, including Windows apps, ASP.NET Core, and .NET MAUI. A big part of his job is helping companies move their solutions to Microsoft Azure.

Even after many years in software development, Christian still loves learning and using new technologies and teaching others how to use them. Using his profound knowledge of Microsoft technologies, he has written numerous books and is certified as a Microsoft Certified Trainer, Azure Developer Associate, DevOps Engineer Expert, and Certified Solution Developer. Christian speaks at international conferences such as Microsoft Ignite (previously named TechEd), BASTA!, and TechDays. You can contact Christian via his website at www.cninnovation.com, read his blog at csharp.christiannagel.com, and follow his tweets at @christiannagel.

ABOUT THE TECHNICAL EDITOR

ROD STEPHENS is a long-time developer and author who has written more than 250 magazine articles and 35 books that have been translated into languages around the world. During his career, Rod has worked on an eclectic assortment of applications in such fields as telephone switching, billing, repair dispatching, tax processing, wastewater treatment, concert ticket sales, cartography, and training for professional football teams.

Rod's popular C# Helper website (www.csharphelper.com) receives millions of hits per year and contains tips, tricks, and example programs for C# programmers. His VB Helper website (www.vb-helper.com) contains similar material for Visual Basic programmers.

You can contact Rod at RodStephens@csharphelper.com or RodStephens@vb-helper.com.

ACKNOWLEDGMENTS

I WANT TO THANK Charlotte Kughen. For many years and many editions of this book, she has made my text so much more readable. Often, I completed chapters late in the evening, when I miss things as I turn sentences around. Charlotte was of enormous help in changing my ideas into great readable text. Charlotte, big thanks for your continued support with these editions; I'm looking forward to working together in the future as well.

Special thanks also go to Rod Stephens, the technical editor of this edition. Rod had great comments on my source code and induced some changes that helped with the quality of the source code. Rod is also the author of some great books, for example *Essential Algorithms: A Practical Approach to Computer Algorithms Using Python and C#* and *WPF 3d: Three-Dimensional Graphics with WPF and C#*. These books can be a great addition for your C# bookshelf.

My thanks also go to the complete team working on the book. In particular, I want to thank István Novak, technical editor of several previous editions of this book. Now István had the role as technical proofreader to solve some final issues. I also want to thank Kim Wimpsett, who fixed some more text issues during the production phase, and Barath Kumar Rajasekaran, who helped the flow during production.

I would also like to thank all the people working on C# and .NET, especially Mads Torgersen, who has worked with his team and the community to bring new features to C#; Richard Lander from the .NET Core team, with whom I had great discussions on the content and the direction of the book; and David Fowler, who enhances .NET not only with performance improvements but also usability. Thanks go to Scott Hanselman—who I have known for many years from our time together as Microsoft RDs—for his great ideas and continuously working with the community. Thanks go to Don Box, who influenced me in the times before .NET was available about love and freedom (COM and XML).

This edition of the book was born during the COVID-19 crisis, which changed the business landscape faster than everyone thought would have been possible. I didn't have less business during this time as I worked online from my home office, but during my career, I'd never had less travel. This available time was completely spent working on the book. On the other hand, for previous editions of this book, I remember working many hours while waiting at the airport. This time, I wrote the entire book in my home office. I want to give a big thanks to my wife and my children for supporting my writing. You've been enormously helpful and understanding while I was working on the book for many nights, weekends, and without a vacation (not only because of the coronavirus crisis). Angela, Stephanie, Matthias, and Katharina—you are my loved ones. This would not have been possible without you.

CONTENTS

PART II: LIBRARIES

CHAPTER 14: LIBRARIES, ASSEMBLIES, PACKAGES, AND NUGET   377

PART IV: APPS

INTRODUCTION

EVEN THOUGH .NET was announced in the year 2000, it is not becoming a grandfather technology. Instead, .NET keeps increasing developer traction since it has become open source and is available not only on Windows but also on Linux platforms. .NET can also run within the browser on the client—without the need to install a plugin—by using the WebAssembly standard.

As new enhancements for C# and .NET are coming, a focus lies not only on performance gains but also on ease of use. .NET more and more is a choice for new developers.

C# is also attractive for long-term developers. Every year, Stack Overflow asks developers about the most loved, dreaded, and wanted programming languages and frameworks. For several years, C# has been within the top 10 of the most loved programming languages. ASP.NET Core now holds the top position as the most loved web framework. .NET Core is number one in the most loved other frameworks/libraries/tools category. See `https://insights.stackoverflow.com/survey/2020` for details.

When you use C# and ASP.NET Core, you can create web applications and services (including microservices) that run on Windows, Linux, and Mac. You can use the Windows Runtime to create native Windows apps using C#, XAML, and .NET. You can create libraries that you share between ASP.NET Core, Windows apps, and .NET MAUI. You can also create traditional Windows Forms and WPF applications.

Most of the samples of this book are built to run on a Windows or Linux system. Exceptions are the Windows app samples that run only on the Windows platform. You can use Visual Studio, Visual Studio Code, or Visual Studio for the Mac as the developer environment; only the Windows app samples require Visual Studio.

THE WORLD OF .NET

.NET has a long history; the first version was released in the year 2002. The new .NET generation with a complete rewrite of .NET (.NET Core 1.0 in the year 2016) is very young. Recently, many features from the old .NET version have been brought to .NET Core to ease the migration experience.

When creating new applications, there is no reason not to move to the new .NET versions. Whether old applications should stay with the old version of .NET or be migrated to the new one depends on the features used, how difficult the migration is, and what advantages you gain after the application is migrated. The best options here need to be considered with an application-by-application analysis.

The new .NET provides easy ways to create Windows and web applications and services. You can create microservices running in Docker containers in a Kubernetes cluster; create web applications; use the new OpenTelemetry standard to analyze distributed traces in a vendor-independent manner; create web applications returning HTML, JavaScript, and CSS; and create web applications returning HTML, JavaScript, and .NET binaries that run in the client's browser in a safe and standard way using WebAssembly. You can create Windows applications in traditional ways using WPF and Windows Forms and make use of modern XAML features and controls that support the fluent design with WinUI and mobile applications with .NET MAUI.

.NET uses modern patterns. Dependency injection is built into core services, such as ASP.NET Core and EF Core, which not only makes unit testing easier but also allows developers to easily enhance and change features from these technologies.

.NET runs on multiple platforms. Besides Windows and macOS, many Linux environments are supported, such as Alpine, CentOS, Debian, Fedora, openSUSE, Red Hat, SLES, and Ubuntu.

.NET is open source (`https://github.com/dotnet`) and freely available. You can find meeting notes for the C# compiler (`https://github.com/dotnet/csharplang`), the source code for the C# compiler (`https://github.com/dotnet/Roslyn`), the .NET runtime and libraries (`https://github.com/dotnet/runtime`), and ASP.NET Core (`https://github.com/dotnet/aspnetcore`) with Razor Pages, Blazor, and SignalR.

Here's a summary of some of the features of the new .NET:

➤ .NET is open source.

➤ .NET uses modern patterns.

➤ .NET supports development on multiple platforms.

➤ ASP.NET Core can run on Windows and Linux.

THE WORLD OF C#

When C# was released in the year 2002, it was a language developed for the .NET Framework. C# was designed with ideas from C++, Java, and Pascal. Anders Hejlsberg had come to Microsoft from Borland and brought experience from the language development of Delphi. At Microsoft, Hejlsberg worked on Microsoft's version of Java, named J++, before creating C#.

> **NOTE** *Today, Anders Hejlsberg has moved to TypeScript (although he still influences C#), and Mads Torgersen is the project lead for C#. C# improvements are discussed openly at* `https://github.com/dotnet/csharplang`, *and you can read C# language proposals and event meeting notes. You can also submit your own proposals for C#.*

C# started not only as an object-oriented general-purpose programming language but was a component-based programming language that supported properties, events, attributes (annotations), and building assemblies (binaries including metadata).

Over time, C# was enhanced with generics, Language Integrated Query (LINQ), lambda expressions, dynamic features, and easier asynchronous programming. C# is not an easy programming language because of the many features it offers, but it's continuously evolving with features that are practical to use. With this, C# is more than an object-oriented or component-based language; it also includes ideas of functional programming—things that are of practical use for a general-purpose language developing all kinds of applications.

Nowadays, a new version of C# is released every year. C# 8 added nullable reference types, and C# 9 added records and more. C# 10 is releasing with .NET 6 in 2021 and C# 11 will be released with .NET 7 in 2022. Because of the frequency of changes nowadays, check the GitHub repository for the book (read more in the section "Source Code") for continuous updates.

WHAT'S NEW IN C#

Every year, a new version of C# is released, with many new features available in each version. The latest versions include features such as nullable reference types to reduce exceptions of type `NullableReferenceException` and instead let the compiler help more; features to increase productivity such as indices and ranges; `switch` expressions that make the `switch` statement look old; features for using declarations;

and enhancements with pattern matching. Top-level statements allow reducing the number of source code lines with small applications and records—classes where the compiler creates boilerplate code for equality comparison, deconstruction, and `with` expressions. Code generators allow creating code automatically while the compiler runs. All these new features are covered in this book.

WHAT'S NEW IN ASP.NET CORE

ASP.NET Core now contains new technology for creating web applications: Blazor Server and Blazor WebAssembly. With Blazor, you have a full-stack option to write C# code both for the client and for the server. With Blazor Server, the Razor components you create containing HTML and C# code run on the server. With Blazor WebAssembly, Razor components written with C# and HTML run on the client using the HTML 5 standard WebAssembly that allows you to run binary code in the browser, which is supported by all modern web browsers.

For creating services, you can now use gRPC with ASP.NET Core for binary communication between services. This is a great option for service-to-service communication to reduce the bandwidth needed, as well as CPU and memory usage if a lot of data transfer is needed.

WHAT'S NEW WITH WINDOWS

For developing applications for Windows, a new technology combines the features of the Universal Windows Platform and desktop applications: WinUI 3. WinUI is the native UI platform for Windows 10 applications. With WinUI 3, you can use modern XAML code that includes compiled binding to create desktop applications. New controls with Microsoft's fluent design system are available. These controls are not delivered with the Windows Runtime as was previously the case with the Universal Windows Platform (UWP). These controls are developed independently of the Windows 10 version that allows you to use the newest controls with Windows 10 versions 1809 and above. As the roadmap available with WinUI shows, these new controls will be usable from WPF applications as well.

WHAT YOU NEED TO WRITE AND RUN C# CODE

.NET runs on Windows, Linux, and Mac operating systems. You can create and build your programs on any of these operating systems using Visual Studio Code (`https://code.visualstudio.com`). You can build and run most of the samples on Windows or Linux and use the .NET development tools of your choice. Only the WinUI applications require you to use the Windows platform, and here, Visual Studio is the best option to use. The minimum version required to build and run the WinUI application is version 16.10.

The command line plays an important part when using the .NET CLI and the Azure CLI; you can use the new Windows Terminal. With the newest Windows 10 versions, this terminal is delivered as part of Windows. With older versions, you can download it from the Microsoft Store.

Most .NET developers use the Windows platform as their development machine. When using the Windows Subsystem for Linux (WSL 2), you can build and run your .NET applications in a Linux environment, and you can install different Linux distributions from your Windows environment and access the same files. Visual Studio even allows debugging your .NET applications while they run in a Linux environment on WSL 2.

With some samples of the book, Microsoft Azure is shown as an optional hosting environment to run your web applications, use Azure Functions, and use Entity Framework Core to access SQL Server and Azure Cosmos DB. For this, you can use a free trial offering from Microsoft Azure; visit `https://azure.microsoft.com/free` to register.

WHAT THIS BOOK COVERS

This book covers these four major parts:

➤ The C# language

➤ Using base class libraries from .NET

➤ Developing web applications and services

➤ Developing Windows applications

Let's get into the different parts and all the chapters in more detail.

Part I, "The C# Language"

The first part of this book covers all the aspects of the C# programming language. You learn the syntax options and see how the C# syntax integrates with classes and interfaces from .NET. This part gives good grounding in the C# language. This section doesn't presume knowledge of any particular programming language, but it's assumed you are an experienced programmer. You start looking at C#'s basic syntax and data types before getting into advanced C# features.

➤ Chapter 1, ".NET Applications and Tools," covers what you need to know to create .NET applications. You learn about the .NET CLI and create a Hello World application using C# 9 top-level statements.

➤ Chapter 2, "Core C#," dives into core C# features and gives you details on top-level statements and information on declaration of variables and data types. The chapter covers target-typed new expressions, explains nullable reference types, and defines a program flow that includes the new `switch` expressions.

➤ Chapter 3, "Classes, Records, Structs, and Tuples," gives you information to create reference or value types, create and use tuples, and make use of the C# 9 enhancement to create and use records.

➤ Chapter 4, "Object-Oriented Programming in C#," goes into details of object-oriented techniques with C# and demonstrates all the C# keywords for object orientation. It also covers using inheritance with C# 9 records.

➤ Chapter 5, "Operators and Casts," explains the C# operators, and you also learn how to overload standard operators for custom types.

➤ Chapter 6, "Arrays," doesn't stop with simple arrays; you learn using multidimensional and jagged arrays, use the `Span` type to access arrays, and use the new index and range operators to access arrays.

➤ Chapter 7, "Delegates, Lambdas, and Events," covers .NET pointers to methods, lambda expressions with closures, and .NET events.

➤ Chapter 8, "Collections," dives into the different kind of collections, such as lists, queues, stacks, dictionaries, and immutable collections. The chapter also gives you the information you need to decide which collection to use in what scenario.

➤ Chapter 9, "Language Integrated Query," gives you the C# language integrated query features to query data from your collections. You also learn how to use multiple CPU cores with a query and what's behind expression trees that are used when you use LINQ to access your database with Entity Framework Core.

➤ Chapter 10, "Errors and Exceptions," covers how you should deal with errors, throw and catch exceptions, and filter exceptions when catching them.

➤ Chapter 11, "Tasks and Asynchronous Programming," shows the C# keywords `async` and `await` in action— not only with the task-based async pattern but also with async streams, which is a new feature since C# 8.

➤ Chapter 12, "Reflection, Metadata, and Source Generators," covers using and reading attributes with C#. The attributes will not just be read using reflection, but you'll also see the functionality of source generators that allow creating source code during compile time.

➤ Chapter 13, "Managed and Unmanaged Memory," is the last chapter of Part I, which not only shows using the `IDisposable` interface with the `using` statement and the new `using` declaration but also demonstrates using the `Span` type with managed and unmanaged memory. You can read about using Platform Invoke both with Windows and with Linux environments.

Part II, "Libraries"

Part II starts with creating custom libraries and NuGet packages, but the major topics covered with Part II are for using .NET libraries that are important for all application types.

➤ Chapter 14, "Libraries, Assemblies, Packages, and NuGet," explains the differences between assemblies and NuGet packages. In this chapter, you learn how to create NuGet packages and are introduced to a new C# feature, module initializers, which allow you to run initial code in a library.

➤ Chapter 15, "Dependency Injection and Configuration," gives detail about how the `Host` class is used to configure a dependency injection container and the built-in options to retrieve configuration information from a .NET application with different configuration providers, including Azure App Configuration and user secrets.

➤ Chapter 16, "Diagnostics and Metrics," continues using the `Host` class to configure logging options. You also learn about reading metric information that's offered from some NET providers, using Visual Studio App Center, and extending logging for distributed tracing with OpenTelemetry.

➤ Chapter 17, "Parallel Programming," covers myriad features available with .NET for parallelization and synchronization. Chapter 11 shows the core functionality of the `Task` class. In Chapter 17, more of the `Task` class is shown, such as forming task hierarchies and using value tasks. The chapter goes into issues of parallel programming such as race conditions and deadlocks, and for synchronization, you learn about different features available with the `lock` keyword, the `Monitor`, `SpinLock`, `Mutex`, `Semaphore` classes, and more.

➤ Chapter 18, "Files and Streams," not only covers reading and writing from the file system with new stream APIs that allow using the `Span` type but also covers the new .NET JSON serializer with classes in the `System.Text.Json` namespace.

➤ In Chapter 19, "Networking," you learn about foundational classes for network programming, such as the `Socket` class and how to create applications using TCP and UDP. You also use the `HttpClient` factory pattern to create `HttpClient` objects with automatic retries if transient errors occur.

➤ Chapter 20, "Security," gives you information about cryptography classes for encrypting data, explains how to use the new `Microsoft.Identity` platform for user authentication, and provides information on web security and what you need to be aware of with encoding issues as well as cross-site request forgery attacks.

➤ Chapter 21, "Entity Framework Core," covers reading and writing data from a database—including the many features offered from EF Core, such as shadow properties, global query filters, many-to-many relations, and what metric information is now offered by EF Core—and reading and writing to Azure Cosmos DB with EF Core.

➤ In Chapter 22, "Localization," you learn to localize applications using techniques that are important both for Windows and web applications.

➤ Chapter 23, "Tests," covers creating unit tests, analyzing code coverage with the .NET CLI, using a mocking library when creating unit tests, and what features are offered by ASP.NET Core to create integration tests.

Part III, "Web Applications and Services"

Part III of this book is dedicated to ASP.NET Core technologies for creating web applications and services, no matter whether you run these applications and services in your on-premises environment or in the cloud making use of Azure App Services, Azure Static Web Apps, or Azure Functions.

➤ Chapter 24, "ASP.NET Core," gives you the foundation of ASP.NET Core. Based on the dependency injection container you learned about in Part II, this chapter shows how ASP.NET Core makes use of middleware to add functionality to every HTTP request and define routes with ASP.NET Core endpoint routing.

➤ Chapter 25, "Services," dives into creating microservices using different technologies such as ASP.NET Core as well as using Azure Functions and gRPC for binary communication.

➤ Chapter 26, "Razor Pages and MVC," is about interacting with users with ASP.NET Core technologies. It covers Razor pages, Razor views, and functionality such as tag helpers and view components.

➤ Chapter 27, "Blazor," is about the newest enhancement of ASP.NET Core with Razor components, which allows you to implement C# code running either on the server or in the client using WebAssembly. You learn about the differences between Blazor Server and Blazor WebAssembly, what the restrictions are with these technologies, and the built-in components available.

➤ Chapter 28, "SignalR," covers the real-time functionality available with ASP.NET Core to send information to a group of clients and how you can use C# async streams with SignalR.

Part IV, "Apps"

Part IV of this book is dedicated to XAML code and creating Windows applications with the native UI platform for Windows 10: WinUI. Much of the information you get here can also be applied to WPF applications and to .NET MAUI and developing XAML-based applications for mobile platforms.

➤ Chapter 29, "Windows Apps," gives you foundational information on XAML, including dependency properties and attached properties. You learn how to create custom markup extensions and about the control categories available with WinUI, including advanced techniques such as adaptive triggers and deferred loading.

➤ Chapter 30, "Patterns with XAML Apps," gives you the information you need to use the MVVM pattern and how you can share as much code as possible between different XAML-based technologies such as WinUI, WPF, and .NET MAUI.

➤ Chapter 31, "Styling Windows Apps," explains XAML shapes and geometry elements, dives into styles and control templates, gives you information on creating animations, and explains how you can use the Visual State Manager with your XAML-based applications.

CONVENTIONS

To help you get the most from the text and keep track of what's happening, I use some conventions through-out the book.

> **WARNING** *Warnings hold important, not-to-be-forgotten information that is directly relevant to the surrounding text.*

> **NOTE** *Notes indicate notes, tips, hints, tricks, and/or asides to the current discussion.*

As for styles in the text:

➤ We *highlight* new terms and important words when we introduce them.

➤ We show keyboard strokes like this: Ctrl+A.

➤ We show filenames, URLs, and code within the text like so: `persistence.properties`.

We present code in two different ways:

```
We use a monofont type with no highlighting for most code examples.
We use bold to emphasize code that's particularly important in the present context or to
show changes from a previous code snippet.
```

SOURCE CODE

As you work through the examples in this book, you may choose either to type all the code manually or to use the source code files that accompany the book. All the source code used in this book is available for download at `www.wiley.com`. When at the site, simply locate the book's title (either by using the Search box or by using one of the title lists) and click the Download Code link on the book's detail page to obtain all the source code for the book.

> **NOTE** *Because many books have similar titles, you may find it easiest to search by ISBN; this book's ISBN is 978-1-119-79720-3.*

After you download the code, just decompress it with your favorite compression tool.

The source code is also available on GitHub at `https://www.github.com/ProfessionalCSharp/ProfessionalCSharp2021`. With GitHub, you can also open each source code file with a web browser. When you use the website, you can download the complete source code in a zip file. You can also clone the source code to a local directory on your system. Just install the Git tools, which you can do with Visual Studio or by downloading the Git tools from `https://git-scm.com/downloads` for Windows, Linux, and Mac. To clone the source code to a local directory, use `git clone`:

```
> git clone https://www.github.com/ProfessionalCSharp/ProfessionalCSharp2021
```

With this command, the complete source code is copied to the subdirectory `ProfessionalCSharp2021`. From there, you can start working with the source files.

As updates of .NET become available (until the next edition of the book will be released), the source code will be updated on GitHub. Check the `readme.md` file in the GitHub repo for updates. If the source code changes after you cloned it, you can pull the latest changes after changing your current directory to the directory of the source code:

```
> git pull
```

In case you've made some changes on the source code, `git pull` might result in an error. If this happens, you can stash away your changes and pull again:

```
> git stash
> git pull
```

The complete list of git commands is available at `https://git-scm.com/docs`.

In case you have questions on the source code, use discussions with the GitHub repository. If you find an error with the source code, create an issue. Open `https://github.com/ProfessionalCSharp/ProfessionalCSharp2021` in the browser, click the Issues tab, and click the New Issue button. This opens an editor. Just be as descriptive as possible to describe your issue.

For reporting issues, you need a GitHub account. If you have a GitHub account, you can also fork the source code repository to your account. For more information on using GitHub, check `https://guides.github.com/activities/hello-world`.

> **NOTE** *You can read the source code and issues and clone the repository locally without joining GitHub. For posting issues and creating your own repositories on GitHub, you need your own GitHub account. For basic functionality, GitHub is free (see* `https://github.com/pricing`*).*

ERRATA

We make every effort to ensure that there are no errors in the text or in the code. However, no one is perfect, and mistakes do occur. If you find an error in one of our books, like a spelling mistake or faulty piece of code, we would be grateful for your feedback. By sending in errata, you may save another reader hours of frustration, and at the same time you can help provide even higher-quality information.

To find the errata page for this book, go to `www.wiley.com` and locate the title using the Search box or one of the title lists. Then, on the book details page, click the Book Errata link. On this page, you can view all errata that have been submitted for this book and posted by the book's editors.

If you don't spot "your" error on the Book Errata page, go to `https://support.wiley.com/s/article/reporting-a-wiley-book-error` for information about how to send us the error you have found. We'll check the information and, if appropriate, post a message to the book's errata page and fix the problem in subsequent editions of the book.

PART I
The C# Language

Common Language Runtime

The C# compiler compiles C# code to Microsoft Intermediate Language (IL) code. This code is a little bit like assembly code, but it has more object-oriented features. The IL code is run by the Common Language Runtime (CLR). What's done by a CLR?

The IL code is compiled to native code by the CLR. The IL code available in .NET assemblies is compiled by a Just-In-Time (JIT) compiler. This compiler creates platform-specific native code. The runtime includes a JIT compiler named RyuJIT. This compiler is not only faster than the previous one, but it also has better support for using Edit & Continue while you're debugging the application with Visual Studio.

The runtime also includes a type system with a type loader that is responsible for loading types from assemblies. Security infrastructure with the type system verifies whether certain type system structures are permitted—for example, with inheritance.

After instances of types are created, they also need to be destroyed, and memory needs to be recycled. Another feature of the runtime is the garbage collector. The garbage collector cleans up memory from objects that are no longer referenced in the managed heap.

The runtime is also responsible for threading. When you are creating a managed thread from C#, it is not necessarily a thread from the underlying operating system. Threads are virtualized and managed by the runtime.

> **NOTE** *How you can create and manage threads from C# is covered in Chapter 17, "Parallel Programming." Chapter 13, "Managed and Unmanaged Memory," gives information about the garbage collector and how to clean up memory.*

.NET Compiler Platform

The C# compiler that's installed as part of the SDK belongs to the .NET Compiler Platform, which is also known by the code name Roslyn. Roslyn allows you to interact with the compilation process, work with syntax trees, and access the semantic model that is defined by language rules. You can use Roslyn to write code analyzers and refactoring features. You also can use Roslyn with a new feature of C# 9, code generators, which are discussed in Chapter 12, "Reflection, Metadata, and Source Generators."

.NET Framework

The .NET Framework is the name of the old .NET. The last version available is .NET Framework 4.8. It's not that useful to create new applications with this framework, but of course you can maintain existing applications because this technology will still be supported for many years to come. If existing applications don't get any advantages by moving to new technologies and there's not a lot of maintenance going on, there's no need to switch in the short term.

Depending on the technologies used with existing applications, the switch to .NET can be easy. WPF and Windows Forms have been offered with newer technologies since .NET Core 3. However, WPF and Windows applications could have used features where the application architecture might need a change.

Examples of technologies that are no longer offered with new versions of .NET are ASP.NET Web Forms, Windows Communication Foundation (WCF), and Windows Workflow Foundation (WF). Instead of ASP.NET Web Forms, you can rewrite applications using ASP.NET Blazor. Instead of WCF, you can use ASP.NET Core Web API or gRPC. Instead of WF, moving to Azure Logic Apps might be useful.

.NET Core

.NET Core is the new .NET that is used by all new technologies and is a main focus of this book (with the new name .NET). This framework is open source, and you can find it at http://www.github.com/dotnet.

templates, restore packages, build and test the application, and create deployment packages. Later in this chapter in the section ".NET CLI," you will see how to create and build applications.

If you use Visual Studio 2019, the .NET SDK is installed as part of Visual Studio. If you don't have Visual Studio, you can install the SDK from `https://dot.net`. Here, you can find instructions on how to install the SDK on Windows, Mac, and Linux systems.

You can install multiple versions of the .NET SDK in parallel. The command

```
> dotnet --list-sdks
```

shows all the different SDK versions that are installed on the system. By default, the latest version is used.

> **NOTE** *To run the command, you have many different options to start a command prompt. One is the Windows built-in Command Prompt; you can install the new Windows Terminal; if Visual Studio is installed, you can start the Developer Command Prompt; or you can use the bash shell. Read more on the Windows Terminal later in this chapter in the section "Developer Tools."*

You can create a `global.json` file if you do not want to use the latest version of the SDK. The command

```
> dotnet new globaljson
```

creates the file `global.json` in the current directory. This file contains the version element with the version number currently used. You can change the version number to one of the other SDK versions that is installed:

```
{
  "sdk": {
    "version": "5.0.202"
  }
}
```

In the directory of `global.json` and its subdirectories, the specified SDK version is used. You can verify this with

```
> dotnet --version
```

.NET Runtime

On the target system, the .NET SDK is not required. Here you just need to install the .NET runtime. The runtime includes all the core libraries and the dotnet driver.

The dotnet driver is used to run the application—for example, the Hello, World application with

```
> dotnet hello-world.dll
```

At `https://dot.net`, you can find not only instructions to download and install the SDK on different platforms but also the runtime.

Instead of installing the runtime on the target system, you also can deliver the runtime as part of the application (which is known as *self-contained deployment*). This technique is very different from older .NET Framework applications and is covered later in the chapter in the "Using the .NET CLI" section.

To see which runtimes are installed, you can use

```
> dotnet --list-runtimes
```

and Web Forms to create web applications. This version of .NET was available only for Microsoft Windows. At that time, Microsoft also invented a standard for C# at ECMA (`https://www.ecma-international.org/publications/standards/Ecma-334.htm`).

Later, Silverlight used a subset of this technology with a limited library and runtime running in browsers using a browser add-in. At that time, the company Ximian developed the Mono runtime. This runtime was available for Linux and Android and offered a subset of Microsoft .NET's functionality. Later, Novell bought Ximian, and Novell was later bought by The Attachmate Group. As the new organization lost interest in .NET, Miguel de Icaza (the founder of Ximian) started Xamarin and took the interesting .NET parts into his new organization to start .NET for Android and iOS. Nowadays, Xamarin belongs to Microsoft, and the Mono runtime is part of the dotnet runtime repo (`https://github.com/dotnet/runtime`).

Silverlight started .NET development for other devices with different form factors, which have different needs for .NET. Silverlight was not successful in the long term because HTML5 offered features that previously only were available by using browser add-ins. However, Silverlight started moving .NET in other directions that resulted in .NET Core.

.NET Core was the biggest change to .NET since its inception. .NET code became open-source, you could create apps for other platforms, and the new code base of .NET is using modern design patterns. The next step is a logical move: the version of .NET after .NET Core 3.1 is *NET 5*. The *Core* name is removed, and version 4 was skipped to send a message to .NET Framework developers that there's a higher version than .NET Framework 4.8, and it's time to move to .NET 5 for creating new applications.

For developers using .NET Core, the move is an easy one. With existing applications, usually all that needs to be changed is the version number of the target framework. Moving applications from the .NET Framework is not that easy and might require bigger changes. Depending on the application type, more or less change is needed. .NET Core 3.x supports WPF and Windows Forms applications. With these application types, the change can be easy. However, existing .NET Framework WPF applications may have features that cannot be moved that easily to the new .NET. For example, application domains are not supported with .NET Core and .NET 5. Moving Windows Communication Foundation (WCF) services to .NET 5 is not at all easy. The server part of WCF is not supported in the new .NET era. The WCF part of the application needs to be rewritten to ASP.NET Core Web API, gRPC, or another communication technology that fulfills the needs.

With existing applications, it can be useful to stay with the .NET Framework instead of changing to the new .NET because the old framework will still be maintained for many years to come. The .NET Framework is installed with Windows 10, and support for the .NET Framework has a long target that is bound to the support of the Windows 10 versions.

The new .NET and NuGet packages allow Microsoft to provide faster update cycles for delivering new features. It's not easy to decide what technology should be used for creating applications. This chapter helps you with that decision. It gives you information about the different technologies available for creating Windows and web apps and services, offers guidance on what to choose for database access, and helps with moving from old technologies to new ones. You'll also read about the .NET tooling that you can use with the code samples through all the chapters of this book.

.NET TERMS

Before digging deeper, you should understand concepts and some important .NET terms, such as what's in the .NET SDK and what the .NET runtime is. You also should get a better understanding of the .NET Framework and .NET, when to use the .NET Standard, and the NuGet packages and .NET namespaces.

.NET SDK

For developing .NET applications, you need to install the .NET SDK. The SDK contains the .NET command-line interface (CLI), tools, libraries, and the runtime. With the .NET CLI, you can create new applications based on

1

.NET Applications and Tools

WHAT'S IN THIS CHAPTER?

- ➤ From .NET Framework to .NET Core to .NET
- ➤ .NET terms
- ➤ .NET support length
- ➤ Application types and technologies
- ➤ Developer tools
- ➤ Using the .NET command-line interface
- ➤ Programming "Hello World!"
- ➤ Technologies for creating web apps

CODE DOWNLOADS FOR THIS CHAPTER

The source code for this chapter is available on the book page at www.wiley.com. Click the Downloads link. The code can also be found at https://github.com/ProfessionalCSharp/ ProfessionalCSharp2021 in the directory 1_CS/HelloWorld.

The code for this chapter is divided into the following major examples:

- ➤ HelloWorld
- ➤ WebApp
- ➤ SelfContainedHelloWorld

FROM .NET FRAMEWORK TO .NET CORE TO .NET

The first version of .NET was released in 2002. Since the first version, many things have changed. The first era of .NET was the .NET Framework that offered Windows Forms for Windows desktop development

Software as a Service

SaaS offers complete software; you don't have to deal with management of servers, updates, and so on. Office 365 is one of the SaaS offerings for using email and other services via a cloud offering. A SaaS offering that's relevant for developers is *Azure DevOps Services*. Azure DevOps Services is the cloud version of Azure DevOps Server (previously known as Team Foundation Server) that can be used for private and public code repository, for tracking bugs and work items, and for building and testing services. Another offering from Microsoft in this category is GitHub, which is just enhanced to receive many features from Azure DevOps.

Infrastructure as a Service

Another service offering is IaaS. Virtual machines are included in this service offering. You are responsible for managing the operating system and maintaining updates. When you create virtual machines, you can decide between different hardware offerings starting with shared cores up to 416 cores (at the time of this writing, but things change quickly). The M-Series of machines include 416 cores, 11.4TB RAM, and 8TB local SSD.

With preinstalled operating systems, you can decide between Windows, Windows Server, Linux, and operating systems that come preinstalled with SQL Server, BizTalk Server, SharePoint, Oracle, and many other products.

I use virtual machines often for environments that I need only for several hours a week because the virtual machines are paid on an hourly basis. If you want to try compiling and running .NET Core programs on Linux but don't have a Linux machine, installing such an environment on Microsoft Azure is an easy task.

Platform as a Service

For developers, the most relevant part of Microsoft Azure is platform as a service (PaaS). You can access services for storing and reading data, use computing and networking capabilities of app services, and integrate developer services within the application.

For storing data in the cloud, you can use a relational data store SQL Database. SQL Database is nearly the same as the on-premise version of SQL Server. There are also some NoSQL solutions, such as Cosmos DB, with different store options such as JSON data, relationships, or table storage, and Azure Storage that stores blobs (for example, for images or videos).

App Services can be used to host your web apps and API apps that you create with ASP.NET Core.

Along with the previously introduced Visual Studio Team Services, another part of the Developer Services in Microsoft Azure is Application Insights. With faster release cycles, it's becoming more and more important to get information about how the user uses the app. What menus are never used because the users probably can't find them? What paths in the app does the user take to accomplish tasks? With Application Insights, you can get good anonymous user information to find out the issues users have with the application, and, with DevOps in place, you can do quick fixes.

You can also use Cognitive Services that offer functionality to process images, use Bing Search APIs, understand what users say with Language services, and more.

Functions as a Service

FaaS, also known with the category name *Azure serverless*, is a new concept for cloud service. Of course, behind the scenes there's always a server. You just don't pay for reserved CPU and memory because they're handled with AppServices that are used from web apps. Instead, you pay based on consumption—the number of calls done with some limitations on the memory and time needed for the activity. Azure Functions is one technology that can be deployed using FaaS.

> **NOTE** *Chapter 15, "Dependency Injection and Configuration," not only describes the architecture to define configuration with .NET applications, but it also covers what you need to use this configuration approach to access Microsoft Azure App Configuration and the Azure Key Vault. Chapter 16, "Diagnostics and Metrics," covers using Azure Monitor, and Chapter 21 shows how to access relational databases both with the on-premises SQL database and with Azure SQL. It also shows how you can use EF Core to access the Azure Cosmos NoSQL database. Chapter 25 uses Azure App Services and Azure Functions for deployment options.*

DEVELOPER TOOLS

For development, you need an SDK to build your applications and test them, and you need a code editor. Some other tools can help, such as a Linux environment on your Windows system and an environment to run Docker images. Let's get into some practical tools.

.NET CLI

For development, you need the .NET SDK. If you're using Visual Studio for development, the .NET SDK is installed with Visual Studio. If you're using a different environment or you want to install different versions that are not part of the Visual Studio installation, you can get downloads for the SDK from `https://dot.net`. Here you can download and install distributions of the SDK for different platforms.

Part of the SDK is the .NET CLI—the command-line interface to develop .NET applications. You can use the .NET CLI to create new applications, compile applications, run unit tests, create NuGet packages, and create the files you need for publishing. Other than that, you can use any editor such as Notepad to write the code. Of course, if you have access to other tools that offer IntelliSense, using them makes it easier to run and debug your applications.

A tour of the .NET CLI is given later in this chapter in the section "Using the .NET CLI."

Visual Studio Code

Visual Studio Code is a lightweight editor available not only on Windows but also on Linux and macOS. The community created a huge number of extensions that make Visual Studio Code the preferred environment for many technologies.

With many chapters of this book, you can use Visual Studio Code as your development editor. What you currently can't do is create WinUI and Xamarin applications. You can use Visual Studio Code for .NET Core console applications and ASP.NET Core web applications.

You can download Visual Studio Code from `http://code.visualstudio.com`.

Visual Studio Community

This edition of Visual Studio is a free edition with features that the Professional edition previously had, but there's a license restriction for when it can be used. It's free for open-source projects and training and to academic and small professional teams. Unlike the Express editions of Visual Studio that previously have been the free editions, this product allows using extensions with Visual Studio.

Visual Studio Professional

Visual Studio Professional includes more features than the Community edition, such as the CodeLens and Team Foundation Server for source code management and team collaboration. With this edition, you also get a subscription that includes several server products from Microsoft for development and testing, as well as a free amount that you can use with Microsoft Azure for development and testing.

Visual Studio Enterprise

Unlike the Professional edition, Visual Studio Enterprise contains a lot of tools for testing, such as Live Unit Testing, Microsoft Fakes (unit test isolation), and IntelliTest (unit testing is part of all Visual Studio editions). With Code Clone you can find similar code in your solution. Visual Studio Enterprise also contains architecture and modeling tools to analyze and validate the solution architecture.

> **NOTE** *Be aware that with a Visual Studio subscription you're entitled to free use of Microsoft Azure up to a specific monthly amount that is contingent on the type of the Visual Studio subscription you have.*

> **NOTE** *For some of the features in this book—for example, live unit testing that is briefly explained—you need Visual Studio Enterprise. However, you can work through most parts of the book with the Visual Studio Community edition.*

Visual Studio for Mac

Visual Studio for Mac originated in the Xamarin Studio, but now it has a lot more than the earlier product. The actual version of Visual Studio for Mac is using the same source code for the editor that is available with the Windows version of Visual Studio. With Visual Studio for Mac, you can create not only Xamarin apps but also ASP.NET Core apps that run on Windows, Linux, and Mac. With many chapters of this book, you can use Visual Studio for Mac. Exceptions are the chapters that cover WinUI (Chapters 29 through 31), which require Windows to run and develop the app.

Windows Terminal

After so many years without changes to the Windows command prompt, now there's a completely new one. The source code is public at `https://github.com/Microsoft/terminal`, and it offers many features that are useful for development. This terminal offers multiple tabs and different shells, such as the Windows PowerShell, a command prompt, the Azure Cloud Shell, and WSL 2 environments. You can have the terminal full screen, open different tabs to keep different folders easily accessible, and also split panes to have different folders open in a single screen for easy comparison. New features are added on a monthly basis, and you can install the terminal from the Microsoft Store.

WSL 2

WSL 2 is the second generation of the Windows Subsystem for Linux. With this, the subsystem to run Linux is not only faster, but it also offers practically all Linux APIs.

Using WSL 2, you can install different Linux distributions from the Microsoft Store. If you use the Windows Terminal, different tabs can be opened for every Linux distribution installed.

WSL 2 gives you an easy way to build and run .NET applications on a Linux environment from your Windows system. You can even use Visual Studio to debug your .NET applications while they run in the Linux environment. You just need to install the extension .NET Core Debugging with WSL 2. When you run a debug session from Visual Studio, the .NET SDK gets automatically installed in your WSL 2 environment.

Docker Desktop

The Docker Desktop for Linux (which you can install from `https://hub.docker.com/editions/community/docker-ce-desktop-windows`) allows running Docker containers for Linux or Windows. Using Docker allows creating images that include your application code based on images containing the .NET runtime. The .NET runtime itself is based on Linux or Windows images.

You can use Docker to create a solution using many .NET services running in multiple Docker containers. Docker containers are running instances of Docker images that you can built with support from Visual Studio or dotnet tools such as tye (`https://github.com/dotnet/tye`).

> **NOTE** *Creating microservices and running them in Docker containers is covered in Chapter 25.*

USING THE .NET CLI

With many chapters in this book, you don't need Visual Studio. Instead, you can use any editor and a command line, such as the .NET CLI. Let's take a look at how to set up your system and how you can use this tool. This works the same on all platforms.

Nowadays, having a focus on the command line is also due to CI/CD. You can create a pipeline in which compiling, testing, and deployment happens automatically in the background.

If you install .NET CLI tools, you have what you need as an entry point to start all these tools. Use the command

```
> dotnet --help
```

to see all the different options of the dotnet tools available. Many of the options have a shorthand notation. For help, you can also type

```
> dotnet -h
```

Creating the Application

The dotnet tools offer an easy way to create a "Hello World!" application. Just enter this command to create a console application:

```
> dotnet new console --output HelloWorld
```

This command creates a new `HelloWorld` directory and adds the source code file `Program.cs` and the project file `HelloWorld.csproj`. The command `dotnet new` also includes the functionality of `dotnet restore` where all needed NuGet packages are downloaded. To see a list of dependencies and versions of libraries used by the application, you can check the file `project.assets.json` in the `obj` subdirectory. Without using the option `--output` (or `-o` as shorthand), the files would be generated in the current directory.

The generated source code looks like the following code snippet:

```
using System;

namespace HelloWorld
{
  class Program
  {
    static void Main(string[] args)
    {
      Console.WriteLine("Hello World!");
    }
  }
}
```

> **NOTE** *Since the 1970s, when Brian Kernighan and Dennis Ritchie wrote the book* The C Programming Language, *it's been a tradition to start learning programming languages using a "Hello World!" application. With the .NET CLI, this program is automatically generated.*

Let's get into the syntax of this program. The `Main` method is the entry point for a .NET application. The CLR invokes a static `Main` method on startup. The `Main` method needs to be put into a class. Here, the class is named `Program`, but you could call it by any name.

`Console.WriteLine` invokes the `WriteLine` method of the `Console` class. The `Console` class can be found in the `System` namespace. To avoid writing `System.Console.WriteLine` to invoke this method, the `System` namespace is opened with the `using` declaration on top of the source file.

After writing the source code, you need to compile the code to run it. How you can do this is explained soon in the section "Building the Application."

The created project configuration file is named `HelloWorld.csproj`. This file contains the project configuration, such as the target framework, and the type of binary to create. An important piece of information in this file is the reference to the SDK (project file `HelloWorld/HelloWorld.csproj`):

```
<Project Sdk="Microsoft.NET.Sdk">
  <PropertyGroup>
    <OutputType>Exe</OutputType>
    <TargetFramework>net5.0</TargetFramework>
  </PropertyGroup>
</Project>
```

Top-Level Statements

C# 9 allows you to simplify the code for the "Hello World!" application. With *top-level statements*, the namespace, class, and `Main` method declarations can be removed to write only top-level statements. The application can look like the "Hello World!" application code shown here (code file `HelloWorld/Program.cs`):

```
using System;

Console.WriteLine("Hello World!");
```

If you prefix the invocation of the `WriteLine` method to add the namespace, you can write the program in a single code line:

```
System.Console.WriteLine("Hello World!");
```

> **NOTE** *Behind the scenes, with top-level statements, a class and a* Main *method are still created. Looking into the generated IL code, a class named* <Program>$, *and a main method named* <Main>$ *are generated to contain the top-level statements. You just don't have to write this code on your own.*
>
> *With small applications like sample applications, top-level statements reduce the required code. When C# is used in a script-like environment, top-level statements are practical as well. Top-level statements are discussed in more detail in Chapter 2, "Core C#."*

Selecting the Framework and Language Versions

Instead of building a binary for just one framework version, you can replace the `TargetFramework` element with `TargetFrameworks`, and you can specify multiple frameworks as shown with .NET 5 and .NET Framework 4.8. The `LangVersion` element is added because the sample application uses the C# 9 code (top-level statements). Without using this attribute, the C# version is defined by the framework version. .NET 5 by default is using C# 9, and .NET Framework 4.8 is using C# 7.3
(project file `HelloWorld/HelloWorld.csproj`):

```
<Project Sdk="Microsoft.NET.Sdk">
  <PropertyGroup>
    <OutputType>Exe</OutputType>
    <TargetFrameworks>net5.0;net48</TargetFrameworks>
    <LangVersion>9.0</LangVersion>
  </PropertyGroup>
</Project>
```

The `Sdk` attribute specifies the SDK that is used by the project. Microsoft ships different SDKs: `Microsoft.NET.Sdk` for console applications, `Microsoft.NET.Sdk.Web` for ASP.NET Core web applications, and `Microsoft.NET.Sdk.BlazorWebAssembly` for web applications with Blazor and WebAssembly.

You don't need to add source files to the project. Files with the `.cs` extension in the same directory and subdirectories are automatically added for compilation. Resource files with the `.resx` extension are automatically added for embedding resources. You can change the default behavior and exclude/include files explicitly.

You also don't need to add the .NET Core package. When you specify the target framework `net5.0`, the metapackage `Microsoft.NETCore.App` that references many other packages is automatically included.

Building the Application

To build the application, you need to change the current directory to the directory of the application and start `dotnet build`. You can see output like the following, which is compiled for .NET 5.0 and .NET Framework 4.8:

```
> dotnet build
Microsoft (R) Build Engine version 16.8.0 for .NET Copyright (C)
Microsoft Corporation. All rights reserved.

Determining projects to restore...
Restored C:\procsharp\Intro\HelloWorld\HelloWorld.csproj (in 308 ms).
HelloWorld -> C:\procsharp\Intro\HelloWorld\bin\Debug\net48\HelloWorld.exe
HelloWorld -> C:\procsharp\Intro\HelloWorld\bin\Debug\net5.0\HelloWorld.dll
```

```
    win10-x64;ubuntu-x64;osx.10.11-x64;
  </RuntimeIdentifiers>
  <PublishTrimmed>true</PublishTrimmed>
  <TrimMode>link</TrimMode>
 </PropertyGroup>
</Project>
```

You use the following command and the previous project configuration to create a single file executable that is trimmed. At the time of this writing, the size of the binary for "Hello, World!" is reduced from 54MB to 2.8MB. That's quite impressive. As the feature is improved continuously, more savings can be expected in the future.

```
> dotnet publish -o publishtrimmed -p:PublishSingleFile=true --self-contained
-r win10-x64
```

There is a risk with trimming. For example, if the application makes use of reflection, the trimmer is not aware that the reflected members are needed during runtime. To deal with such issues, you can specify what assemblies, types, and type members should not be trimmed. To configure such options, read the detailed documentation at https://docs.microsoft.com/dotnet/core/deploying/trimming-options.

SUMMARY

This chapter covered a lot of ground to review important technologies and changes with .NET. With new applications you should use .NET Core (now renamed to just .NET) for future development. With existing applications, it depends on the state of the application if you prefer to stay with older technologies or migrate to new ones. For moving to .NET, you now know about frameworks that you can use to replace older frameworks.

You read about tools you can use for development and dived into the .NET CLI to create, build, and publish applications.

You looked at technologies for accessing the database and creating Windows apps, and you read about different ways to create web applications.

Whereas this chapter laid the foundation with a "Hello World!" example, Chapter 2 dives fast into the syntax of C#. It covers variables, how to implement program flows, how to organize your code into namespaces, and more.

2

Core C#

WHAT'S IN THIS CHAPTER?

- ➤ Top-level statements
- ➤ Declaring variables
- ➤ Target-typed new expressions
- ➤ Nullable types
- ➤ Predefined C# data types
- ➤ Program flow
- ➤ Namespaces
- ➤ Strings
- ➤ Comments and documentation
- ➤ C# preprocessor directives
- ➤ Guidelines and coding conventions

CODE DOWNLOADS FOR THIS CHAPTER

The source code for this chapter is available on the book page at www.wiley.com. Click the Downloads link. The code can also be found at https://github.com/ProfessionalCSharp/ProfessionalCSharp2021 in the directory 1_CS/CoreCSharp.

The code for this chapter is divided into the following major examples:

- ➤ TopLevelStatements
- ➤ CommandLineArgs
- ➤ VariableScopeSample
- ➤ NullableValueTypes

➤ NullableReferenceTypes

➤ ProgramFlow

➤ SwitchStatement

➤ SwitchExpression

➤ ForLoop

➤ StringSample

All the sample projects have nullable reference types enabled.

FUNDAMENTALS OF C#

Now that you understand more about what C# can do, you need to know how to use it. This chapter gives you a good start in that direction by providing a basic understanding of the fundamentals of C# programming, which subsequent chapters build on. By the end of this chapter, you will know enough C# to write simple programs (though without using inheritance or other object-oriented features, which are covered in later chapters).

The previous chapter explained how to create a "Hello, World!" application using the .NET CLI tools. This chapter focuses on C# syntax. First, here's some general information on the syntax:

➤ Statements end in a semicolon (;) and can continue over multiple lines without needing a continuation character.

➤ Statements can be joined into blocks using curly braces ({ }).

➤ Single-line comments begin with two forward slash characters (//).

➤ Multiline comments begin with a slash and an asterisk (/*) and end with the same combination reversed (*/).

➤ C# is case-sensitive. Variables named `myVar` and `MyVar` are two different variables.

Top-Level Statements

A new feature of C# 9 is top-level statements. You can create simple applications without defining a namespace, declaring a class, and defining a `Main` method. A one-line "Hello, World!" application can look like this:

```
System.Console.WriteLine("Hello World!");
```

Let's enhance this one-line application to open the namespace where the `Console` class is defined first. With the `using` directive to import the `System` namespace, you can use class `Console` without prefixing it with the namespace:

```
using System;
Console.WriteLine("Hello World!");
```

Because `WriteLine` is a static method of the `Console` class, it's even possible to open the `Console` class with the `using static` directive:

```
using static System.Console;
WriteLine("Hello World!");
```

Behind the scenes, with top-level statements, the compiler creates a class with a `Main` method and adds the top-level statements to the `Main` method:

```
using System;

class Program
{
```

```
  static void Main()
  {
    Console.WriteLine("Hello, World!");
  }
}
```

> **NOTE** *Many of the samples of this book use top-level statements because this feature is extremely useful with small sample applications. This feature can also be of practical use with small microservices that you now can write in a few code lines and when you use C# in a scripting-like environment.*

Variables

C# offers different ways to declare and initialize variables. A variable has a type and a value that can change over time. In the next code snippet, the variable s1 is of type `string` as defined with the type declaration at the left of the variable name, and it is initialized to a new string object where the string literal `"Hello, World!"` is passed to the constructor. Because the `string` type is commonly used, instead of creating a new string object, the string `"Hello, World!"` can be directly assigned to the variable (shown with the variable s2).

C# 3 invented the `var` keyword with *type inference*, which can be used to declare a variable as well. Here, the type is required on the right side, and the left side would infer the type from it. As the compiler creates a string object from the string literal `"Hello, World"`, s3 is in the same way a type-safe strongly defined string like s1 and s2.

C# 9 provides another new syntax to declare and initialize a variable with the *target-typed new expression*. Instead of writing the expression `new string("Hello, World!")`, if the type is known at the left side, using just the expression `new("Hello, World!")` is sufficient; you don't have to specify the type on the right side (code file `TopLevelStatements/Program.cs`):

```
using System;

string s1 = new string("Hello, World!");
string s2 = "Hello, World!";
var s3 = "Hello, World!";
string s4 = new("Hello, World!");

Console.WriteLine(s1);
Console.WriteLine(s2);
Console.WriteLine(s3);
Console.WriteLine(s4);
//...
```

> **NOTE** *Declaring the type on the left side using the var keyword or the target-typed new expression often is just a matter of taste. Behind the scenes, the same code gets generated. The var keyword has been available since C# 3 and reduced the amount of code you needed to write by defining the type both on the left side to declare the type and on the right side when instantiating the object. With the var keyword, you only have to have the type on the right side. However, the var keyword cannot be used with members of types. Before C# 9, you had to write the type two times with class members; now you can use target-typed new. Target-typed new can be used with local variables, which you can see in the preceding code snippet with variable s4. This doesn't make the var keyword useless; it still has its advantages—for example, on receiving values from a method.*

Command-Line Arguments

When you're passing values to the application when starting the program, the variable args is automatically declared with top-level statements. In the following code snippet, with the foreach statement, the variable args is accessed to iterate through all the command-line arguments and display the values on the console (code file CommandLineArgs/Program.cs):

```
using System;

foreach (var arg in args)
{
  Console.WriteLine(arg);
}
```

Using the .NET CLI to run the application, you can use dotnet run followed by -- and then pass the arguments to the program. The -- needs to be added so as not to confuse the arguments of the .NET CLI with the arguments of the application:

```
> dotnet run -- one two three
```

When you run this, you see the strings one two three on the console.

When you create a custom Main method, the method needs to be declared to receive a string array. You can choose a name for the variable, but the variable named args is commonly used, which is the reason this name was selected for the automatically generated variable with top-level statements:

```
using System;

class Program
{
  static void Main(string[] args)
  {
    foreach (var arg in args)
    {
      Console.WriteLine(arg);
    }
  }
}
```

Understanding Variable Scope

The *scope* of a variable is the region of code from which the variable can be accessed. In general, the scope is determined by the following rules:

➤ A *field* (also known as a member variable) of a class is in scope for as long as its containing class is in scope.

➤ A *local variable* is in scope until a closing brace indicates the end of the block statement or method in which it was declared.

➤ A local variable that is declared in a for, while, or similar statement is in scope in the body of that loop.

It's common in a large program to use the same variable name for different variables in different parts of the program. This is fine as long as the variables are scoped to completely different parts of the program so that there is no possibility for ambiguity. However, bear in mind that local variables with the same name can't be declared twice in the same scope. For example, you can't do this:

```
int x - 20;
// some more code
int x = 30;
```

Consider the following code sample (code file `VariableScopeSample/Program.cs`):

```
using System;

for (int i = 0; i < 10; i++)
{
  Console.WriteLine(i);
} // i goes out of scope here

// We can declare a variable named i again, because
// there's no other variable with that name in scope
for (int i = 9; i >= 0; i--)
{
  Console.WriteLine(i);
} // i goes out of scope here.
```

This code simply prints out the numbers from 0 to 9, and then from 9 to 0, using two `for` loops. The important thing to note is that you declare the variable i twice in this code, within the same method. You can do this because i is declared in two separate loops, so each i variable is local to its own loop.

Here's another example (code file `VariableScopeSample2/Program.cs`):

```
int j = 20;
for (int i = 0; i < 10; i++)
{
  int j = 30; // Can't do this — j is still in scope
  Console.WriteLine(j + i);
}
```

If you try to compile this, you get an error like the following:

```
error CS0136: A local or parameter named 'j' cannot be declared in this scope because
that name is used in an enclosing local scope to define a local or
parameter
```

This occurs because the variable j, which is defined before the start of the `for` loop, is still in scope within the `for` loop and won't go out of scope until the `Main` method (which is created from the compiler) has finished executing. The compiler has no way to distinguish between these two variables, so it won't allow the second one to be declared.

It even doesn't help to put the variable j declared outside of the `for` loop after the end of the `for` loop. The compiler moves all variable declarations at the beginning of a scope no matter where you declare it.

Constants

For values that never change, you can define a constant. For constant values, you can use the `const` keyword.

With variables declared with the `const` keyword, the compiler replaces the variable in every occurrence with the value specified with the constant.

A constant is specified with the `const` keyword before the type:

```
const int a = 100; // This value cannot be changed.
```

The compiler replaces every occurrence of the local field with the value. This behavior is important in terms of versioning. If you declare a constant with a library and use the constant from an application, the application needs to be recompiled to get the new value; otherwise, the library could have a different value from the application. Because of this, it's best to use `const` only with values that never change, even in future versions.

Constants have the following characteristics:

➤ They must be initialized when they are declared. After a value has been assigned, it can never be overwritten.

➤ The value of a constant must be computable at compile time. You can't initialize a constant with a value taken from a variable. If you need to do this, you must use a read-only field.

➤ Constants are always implicitly static. Notice that you don't have to (and, in fact, are not permitted to) include the static modifier in the constant declaration.

The following are the advantages of using constants in your programs:

➤ Constants make your programs easier to read by replacing magic numbers and strings with readable names whose values are easy to understand.

➤ Constants help prevent mistakes in your programs. If you attempt to assign another value to a constant somewhere in your program other than at the point where the constant is declared, the compiler flags the error.

> **NOTE** *If multiple instances could have different values but the value never changes after initialization, you can use the* readonly *keyword. This is discussed in Chapter 3, "Classes, Records, Structs, and Tuples."*

Methods and Types with Top-Level Statements

You can also add methods and types to the same file with top-level statements. In the following code snippet, the method named Method is defined and invoked after the method declaration and implementation (code file TopLevelStatements/Program.cs):

```
//...
void Method()
{
    Console.WriteLine("this is a method");
}

Method();
//...
```

The method can be declared before or after it is used. Types can be added to the same file, but these need to be specified following the top-level statements. With the following code snippet, the class Book is specified to contain a Title property and the ToString method. Before the declaration of the type, a new instance is created and assigned to the variable b1, the value of the Title property is set, and the instance is written to the console. When the object is passed as an argument to the WriteLine method, in turn the ToString method of Book class is invoked:

```
Book b1 = new();
b1.Title = "Professional C#";
Console.WriteLine(b1);


class Book
{
```

```
    public string Title { get; set; }
    public override string ToString() => Title;
}
```

> **NOTE** *Creating and invoking methods and defining classes are explained in detail in Chapter 3.*

> **NOTE** *All the top-level statements need to reside in one file. Otherwise, the compiler wouldn't know where to start. If you use top-level statements, make them easy to find, such as by adding them to the* Program.cs *file. You don't want to search for the top-level statements in a list of multiple files.*

NULLABLE TYPES

With the first version of C#, a value type couldn't have a null value, but it was always possible to assign null to a reference type. The first change happened with C# 2 and the invention of the *nullable value type*. C# 8 brought a change with reference types because most exceptions occurring with .NET are of type NullReferenceException. These exceptions occur when a member of a reference is invoked that has null assigned. To reduce these issues and get compiler errors instead, *nullable reference types* were introduced with C# 8.

This section covers both nullable value types and nullable reference types. The syntax looks similar, but it's very different behind the scenes.

Nullable Value Types

With a value type such as int, you cannot assign null to it. This can lead to difficulties when mapping to databases or other data sources, such as XML or JSON. Using a reference type instead results in additional overhead: an object is stored in the heap, and the garbage collection needs to clean it up when it's not used anymore. Instead, the ? can be used with the type definition, which allows assigning null:

```
int? x1 = null;
```

The compiler changes this to use the Nullable<T> type:

```
Nullable<int> x1 = null;
```

Nullable<T> doesn't add the overhead of a reference type. This is still a struct (a value type) but adds a Boolean flag to specify if the value is null.

The following code snippet demonstrates using nullable value types and assigning non-nullable values. The variable n1 is a nullable int that has been assigned the value null. A nullable value type defines the property HasValue, which can be used to check whether the variable has a value assigned. With the Value property, you can access its value. This can be used to assign the value to a non-nullable value type. A non-nullable value can always be assigned to a nullable value type; this always succeeds (code file NullableValueTypes/Program.cs):

```
int? n1 = null;
if (n1.HasValue)
{
  int n2 = n1.Value;
}
int n3 = 42;
int? n4 = n3;
```

Nullable Reference Types

Nullable reference types have the goal of reducing exceptions of type `NullReferenceException`, which is the most common exception that occurs with .NET applications. There always has been a guideline that an application should not throw such exceptions and should always check for `null`, but without the help of the compiler, such issues can be missed too easily.

To get help from the compiler, you need to turn on nullable reference types. Because this feature has breaking changes with existing code, you need to turn it on explicitly. You specify the `Nullable` element and set the `enable` value in the project file (project file `NullableReferenceTypes.csproj`):

```
<Project Sdk="Microsoft.NET.Sdk">
  <PropertyGroup>
    <OutputType>Exe</OutputType>
    <TargetFramework>net5.0</TargetFramework>
    <Nullable>enable</Nullable>
  </PropertyGroup>
</Project>
```

Now, `null` cannot be assigned to reference types. When you write this code with nullable enabled,

```
string s1 = null; // compiler warning
```

you get the compiler warning "CS8600: Converting a null literal or a possible null value to non-nullable type."

To assign null to the string, the type needs to be declared with a question mark—like nullable value types:

```
string? s1 = null;
```

When you're using the nullable `s1` variable, you need to make sure to verify for not `null` before invoking methods or assigning it to non-nullable strings; otherwise, compiler warnings are generated:

```
string s2 = s1.ToUpper(); // compiler warning
```

Instead, you can check for `null` before invoking the method with the *null-conditional operator* `?.`, which invokes the method only if the object is not `null`. The result cannot be written to a non-nullable string. The result of the right expression can be `null` if `s1` is `null`:

```
string? s2 = s1?.ToUpper();
```

You can use the *coalescing operator* `??` to define a different return value in the case of `null`. With the following code snippet, an empty string is returned in case the expression to the left of `??` returns `null`. The complete result of the right expression is now written to the variable `s3`, which can never be `null`. It's either the uppercase version of the `s1` string if `s1` is not `null`, or an empty string if `s1` is `null`:

```
string s3 = s1?.ToUpper() ?? string.Empty;
```

Instead of using these operators, you can also use the `if` statement to verify whether a variable is not `null`. With the `if` statement in the following code snippet, the C# pattern `is not` is used to verify that `s1` is not `null`. The block covered by the `if` statement is invoked only when `s1` is not `null`. Here it is not necessary to use the null-conditional operator to invoke the method `ToUpper`:

```
if (s1 is not null)
{
  string s4 = s1.ToUpper();
}
```

Of course, it's also possible to use the *not equals operator* `!=`:

```
if (s1 != null)
{
  string s5 = s1.ToUpper();
}
```

> **NOTE** *Operators are covered in detail in Chapter 5, "Operators and Casts."*

Using nullable reference types is also important with members of types, as shown in the Book class with the Title and Publisher properties in the following code snippet. The Title is declared with a non-nullable string type; thus, it needs to be initialized when creating a new object of the Book class. It's initialized with the constructor of the Book class. The Publisher property is allowed to be null, so it doesn't need initialization (code file NullableReferenceTypes/Program.cs):

```
class Book
{
  public Book(string title) => Title = title;

  public string Title { get; set; }
  public string? Publisher { get; set; }
}
```

When you're declaring a variable of the Book class, the variable can be declared as nullable (b1), or it needs a Book object with the declaration using the constructor (b2). The Title property can be assigned to a non-nullable string type. With the Publisher property, you can assign it to a nullable string or use the operators as shown earlier:

```
Book? b1 = null;
Book b2 = new Book("Professional C#");
string title = b2.Title;
string? publisher = b2.Publisher;
```

Behind the scenes with nullable value types, the type Nullable<T> is used behind the scenes. This is not the case with nullable reference types. Instead, the compiler adds annotation to the types. Nullable reference types have Nullable attributes associated. With this, nullable reference types can be used with libraries to annotate parameters and members with nullability. When the library is used with new applications, IntelliSense can give information regarding whether a method or property can be null, and the compiler acts accordingly with compiler warnings. Using an older version of the compiler (earlier than C# 8), the library can still be used in the same way nonannotated libraries are used. The compiler just ignores the attributes it doesn't know.

> **NOTE** *Nearly all the samples of this book are configured to have nullable reference types turned on. With .NET 5, nearly all the base class libraries have been fully annotated with nullable reference types. This helps getting information about what is required with parameters and what is returned. An interesting aspect here is the choices Microsoft made in deciding nullability. The string returned from the* object.ToString *method was originally documented that overriding this method should never return null. The .NET team reviewed different implementations: some Microsoft teams overriding this method returned null. Because the usage was different than the documentation, Microsoft decided to declare the* object.ToString *method to return* string?, *which allows it to return* null. *Overriding this method, you can be stricter and return* string. *Overriding methods is explained in detail in Chapter 4, "Object-Oriented Programming in C#."*
>
> *Because nullable reference types is a breaking change when turning this feature on with existing applications, to allow for a slow migration to this new feature, you can use the preprocessor directive* #nullable *to turn it on or off and to restore it to the setting from the project file. This is discussed in the section "C# Preprocessor Directives."*

USING PREDEFINED TYPES

Now that you have seen how to declare variables and constants and know about an extremely important enhancement with nullability, let's take a closer look at the data types available in C#.

The C# keywords for data types—such as `int`, `short`, and `string`—are mapped from the compiler to .NET data types. For example, when you declare an `int` in C#, you are actually declaring an instance of a .NET struct: `System.Int32`. All the primitive data types offer methods that can be invoked. For example, to convert `int i` to a `string`, you can write the following:

```
string s = i.ToString();
```

I should emphasize that behind this syntactical convenience, the types really are stored as primitive types, so absolutely no performance cost is associated with the idea that the primitive types are represented by .NET structs.

The following sections review the types that are recognized as built-in types in C#. Each type is listed along with its definition and the name of the corresponding .NET type. I also show you a few exceptions—some important data types that are available only with their .NET type and don't have a specific C# keyword.

Let's start with predefined value types that represent primitives, such as integers, floating-point numbers, characters, and Booleans.

Integer Types

C# supports integer types with various numbers of bits used and differs between types that support only positive values or types with a range of negative and positive values. Eight bits are used by the `byte` and `sbyte` types. The `byte` type allows values from 0 to 255—only positive values—whereas the s in `sbyte` means to use a sign; that type supports values from –128 to 127, which is what's possible with 8 bits.

The `short` and `ushort` types make use of 16 bits. The `short` type covers the range from –32,768 to 32,767. With the `ushort` type, the u is for unsigned, and it covers 0 to 65,535. Similarly, the `int` type is a signed 32-bit integer, and the `uint` type is an unsigned 32-bit integer. `long` and `ulong` have 64 bits available. Behind the scenes, the C# keywords `sbyte`, `short`, `int`, and `long` map to `System.SByte`, `System.Int16`, `System.Int32`, and `System.Int64`. The unsigned versions map to `System.Byte`, `System.UInt16`, `System.UInt32`, and `System.UInt64`. The underlying .NET types clearly list the number of bits used in the name of the type.

To check for the maximum and minimum values from the type, you can use the `MaxValue` and `MinValue` properties.

Big Integer

In case you need a number representation that has a bigger value than the 64 bits available in the `long` type, you can use the `BigInteger` type. This struct doesn't have a limit on the number of bits and can grow until there's not enough memory available. There's not a specific C# keyword for this type, and you need to use `BigInteger`. Because this type can grow endlessly, `MinValue` and `MaxValue` properties are not available. This type offers built-in methods for calculation such as `Add`, `Subtract`, `Divide`, `Multiply`, `Log`, `Log10`, `Pow`, and others.

Native Integer Types

With `int`, `short`, and `long`, the number of bits and available sizes are independent if the application is a 32- or 64-bit application. This is different from the integer definitions as defined with C++. C# 9 has new keywords for platform-specific values: `nint` and `nuint` (native integer and native unsigned integer, respectively). In a 64-bit application, these integer types make use of 64 bits, whereas in a 32-bit application just 32 bits are used. These types are important with direct memory access, which is covered in Chapter 13, "Managed and Unmanaged Memory."

Digit Separators

For better readability of numbers, you can use digit separators. You can add underscores to numbers, as shown in the following code snippet. In this code snippet, also the `0x` prefix is used to specify hexadecimal values (code file `DataTypes/Program.cs`):

```
long l1 = 0x_123_4567_89ab_cedf;
```

The underscores used as separators are just ignored by the compiler. These separators help with readability and don't add any functionality. With the preceding sample, reading from the right, every 16 bits (or 4 hexadecimal characters) a digit separator is added. This is a lot more readable compared to this:

```
long l2 = 0x123456789abcedf;
```

Of course, because the compiler ignores the underscores, you are responsible for readability yourself. You can put the underscores at any position, which may not really help with readability:

```
long l3 = 0x_12345_6789_abc_ed_f;
```

It's useful that any position can be used, which allows for different use cases such as to work with hexadecimal or octal values or to separate different bits needed for a protocol, as shown in the next section.

Binary Values

Besides offering digit separators, C# also makes it easy to assign binary values to integer types. Using the `0b` literal, it's only allowed to assign values of 0 and 1, such as the following (code file `DataTypes/Program.cs`):

```
uint binary1 = 0b_1111_1110_1101_1100_1011_1010_1001_1000;
```

The preceding code snippet uses an unsigned int with 32 bits available. Digit separators help with readability for using binary values. This snippet makes a separation every 4 bits. Remember, you can write this in the hex notation as well:

```
uint hex1 = 0xfedcba98;
```

Using the separator every 3 bits helps in working with the octal notation, where characters are used between 0 (000 binary) and 7 (111 binary).

```
uint binary2 = 0b_111_110_101_100_011_010_001_000;
```

If you need to define a binary protocol—for example, where 2 bits define the rightmost part followed by 6 bits in the next section, and two times 4 bits to complete 16 bits—you can put separators per this protocol:

```
ushort binary3 = 0b1111_0000_101010_11;
```

> **NOTE** *Read Chapter 5 for additional information on working with binary data.*

Floating-Point Types

C# also specifies floating-point types with different numbers of bits based on the IEEE 754 standard. The `Half` type (new as of .NET 5) uses 16 bits, `float` (`Single` with .NET) uses 32 bits, and `double` (`Double`) uses 64 bits. With all of these data types, 1 bit is used for the sign. Depending on the type, 10 through 52 bits are used for the significand, and 5 through 11 bits for the exponent. The following table shows the details:

C# KEYWORD	.NET TYPE	DESCRIPTION	SIGNIFICAND BIT	EXPONENT BIT
	`System.Half`	16-bit, single-precision floating point	10	5
`float`	`System.Single`	32-bit, single-precision floating point	23	8
`double`	`System.Double`	64-bit, double-precision floating point	52	11

When you assign a value, if you hard-code a noninteger number (such as 12.3), the compiler assumes that's a double. To specify that the value is a `float`, append the character F (or f):

```
float f = 12.3F;
```

With the `decimal` type (.NET struct `Decimal`), .NET has a high-precision floating-point type that uses 128 bits and can be used for financial calculations. With the 128 bits, 1 is used for the sign, and 96 for the integer number. The remaining bits specify a scaling factor. To specify that your number is a `decimal` type rather than a `double`, a `float`, or an integer, you can append the M (or m) character to the value:

```
decimal d = 12.30M;
```

The Boolean Type

You use the C# `bool` type to contain Boolean values of either `true` or `false`.

You cannot implicitly convert `bool` values to and from integer values. If a variable (or a function return type) is declared as a `bool`, you can only use values of `true` and `false`. You get an error if you try to use zero for `false` and a nonzero value for `true`.

The Character Type

The .NET string consists of two-byte characters. The C# keyword `char` maps to the .NET type `Char`. Using single quotation marks, for example, `'A'`, creates a char. With double quotation marks, a string is created.

As well as representing chars as character literals, you can represent them with four-digit hex Unicode values (for example, `'\u0041'`), as integer values with a cast (for example, `(char) 65`), or as hexadecimal values (for example, `'\x0041'`). You can also represent them with an escape sequence, as shown in the following table:

ESCAPE SEQUENCE	CHARACTER
`\'`	Single quotation mark
`\"`	Double quotation mark
`\\`	Backslash
`\0`	Null
`\a`	Alert
`\b`	Backspace
`\f`	Form feed

ESCAPE SEQUENCE	CHARACTER
\n	Newline
\r	Carriage return
\t	Tab character
\v	Vertical tab

Literals for Numbers

In the preceding sections, literals have been shown for numeric values. Let's summarize them here in the following table:

LITERAL	POSITION	DESCRIPTION
U	Postfix	unsigned int
L	Postfix	long
UL	Postfix	unsigned long
F	Postfix	float
M	Postfix	decimal (money)
0x	Prefix	Hexadecimal number; values from 0 to F are allowed
0b	Prefix	Binary number; only 0 and 1 are allowed
true	NA	Boolean value
false	NA	Boolean value

The object Type

Besides value types, with C# keywords, two reference types are defined: the object keyword that maps to the Object class and the string keyword that maps to the String class. The string type is discussed later in this chapter in the section "Working with Strings." The Object class is the ultimate base class of all reference types and can be used for two purposes:

➤ You can use an object reference to bind to an object of any particular subtype. For example, in Chapter 5, you'll see how you can use the object type to box a value object on the stack to move it to the heap; object references are also useful in reflection, when code must manipulate objects whose specific types are unknown.

➤ The object type implements a number of basic, general-purpose methods, which include Equals, GetHashCode, GetType, and ToString. User-defined classes might need to provide replacement implementations of some of these methods using an object-oriented technique known as *overriding*, which is discussed in Chapter 4. When you override ToString, for example, you equip your class with a method for intelligently providing a string representation of itself. If you don't provide your own implementations for these methods in your classes, the compiler picks up the implementations of the object type, which returns the name of the class.

CONTROLLING PROGRAM FLOW

This section looks at the real nuts and bolts of the language: the statements that allow you to control the *flow* of your program rather than execute every line of code in the order it appears in the program. With conditional statements like the `if` and `switch` statements, you can branch your code depending on whether certain conditions are met. You can repeat statements in loops with `for`, `while`, and `foreach` statements.

The if Statement

With the `if` statement, you can specify an expression within parentheses. If the expression returns `true`, the block that's specified with curly braces is invoked. In case the condition is not `true`, you can check for another condition to be true using `else if`. The `else if` can be repeated to check for more conditions. If neither the expressions specified with the `if` nor all the `else if` expressions evaluate to `true`, the block specified with the `else` block is invoked.

With the following code snippet, a string is read from the console. If an empty string is entered, the code block following the `if` statement is invoked. The `string` method `IsNullOrEmpty` returns `true` if the `string` is either `null` or empty. The block specified with the `else if` statement is invoked when the length of the input is smaller than five characters. In all other cases—for example, with an input length of five or more characters—the `else` block is invoked (code file `ProgramFlow/Program.cs`):

```
Console.WriteLine("Type in a string");
string? input = Console.ReadLine();

if (string.IsNullOrEmpty(input))
{
  Console.WriteLine("You typed in an empty string.");
}
else if (input?.Length < 5)
{
  Console.WriteLine("The string had less than 5 characters.");
}
else
{
  Console.WriteLine("Read any other string");
}
Console.WriteLine("The string was " + input);
```

> **NOTE** *If there's just a single statement with the* if/else if/else *blocks, the curly braces are not necessary. They are necessary only with multiple statements. However, the curly braces also help with readability with single code lines.*

With the `if` statement, `else if` and `else` are optional. If you just need to invoke a code block based on a condition and don't invoke a code block if this condition is not met, you can use the `if` without `else`.

Pattern Matching with the is Operator

One of the C# features is *pattern matching*, which you can use with the `if` statement and the `is` operator. The earlier section "Nullable Reference Types" included an example that used an `if` statement and the pattern `is not null`.

The following code snippet compares the argument received that is of type `object` with `null`, using a *const pattern* to compare the argument with null and throw the `ArgumentNullException`. With the expression used in else if, the *type pattern* is used to check whether the variable o is of type Book. If this is the case, the variable o is assigned to the variable b. Because variable b is of type Book, with b the Title property that is specified by the Book type can be accessed (code file ProgramFlow/Program.cs):

```
void PatternMatching(object o)
{
  if (o is null) throw new ArgumentNullException(nameof(o));
  else if (o is Book b)
  {
    Console.WriteLine($"received a book: {b.Title}");
  }
}
```

> **NOTE** *In this example, for throwing the* ArgumentNullException, *the* nameof *expression is used. The* nameof *expression is resolved from the compiler to take the name of the argument—for example, the variable o—and pass it as a string.* throw new ArgumentNullException(nameof(o)); *resolves to the same code as* throw new ArgumentNullException("o");. *However, if the variable o is renamed to a different value, refactoring features can automatically rename the variable specified with the* nameof *expression. If the parameter of* nameof *is not changed when the variable is renamed, a compiler error will be the result. Without the* nameof *expression, the variable and the string can easily get out of sync.*

A few more samples for const and type patterns are shown in the following code snippet:

```
if (o is 42) // const pattern
if (o is "42") // const pattern
if (o is int i) // type pattern
```

> **NOTE** *You can use pattern matching with the* is *operator, the* switch *statement, and the* switch *expression. You can use different categories of pattern matching. This chapter only covers const, type, relational patterns, and pattern combinators. More patterns, such as property patterns, patterns with tuples, and recursive patterns, are covered in Chapter 3.*

The switch Statement

The switch/case statement is good for selecting one branch of execution from a set of mutually exclusive ones. It takes the form of a switch argument followed by a series of case clauses. When the expression in the switch argument evaluates to one of the values specified by a case clause, the code immediately following the case clause executes. This is one example for which you don't need to use curly braces to join statements into blocks; instead, you mark the end of the code for each case using the break statement. You can also include a default case in the switch statement, which executes if the expression doesn't evaluate to any of the other cases. The following switch statement tests the value of the x variable (code file SwitchStatement/Program.cs):

```
void SwitchSample(int x)
{
  switch (x)
  {
    case 1:
      Console.WriteLine("integerA = 1");
```

In such a scenario, if you need to return a value based on different options, you can use the *switch expression* that is new as of C# 8. The method `NextLight` receives and returns a `TrafficLight` value similar to the previously shown method. The implementation is now done with an expression bodied member because the implementation is done in a single statement. Curly braces and the `return` statement are unnecessary in this case. When you use a `switch` expression instead of the `switch` statement, the variable and `switch` keyword are reversed. With the `switch` statement, the value on the switch follows in braces after the `switch` keyword. With the `switch` expression, the variable is followed by the `switch` keyword. A block with curly braces defines the different cases. Instead of using the `case` keyword, the `=>` token is used to define what's returned. The functionality is the same as before, but you need fewer lines of code:

```
TrafficLight NextLight(TrafficLight light) =>
  light switch
  {
    TrafficLight.Green => TrafficLight.Amber,
    TrafficLight.Amber => TrafficLight.Red,
    TrafficLight.Red => TrafficLight.Green,
    _ => throw new InvalidOperationException()
  };
```

If the `enum` type `TrafficLight` is imported with the `using static` directive, you can simplify the implementation even more by just using the `enum` value definitions without the type name:

```
using static TrafficLight;

TrafficLight NextLight(TrafficLight light) =>
  light switch
  {
    Green => Amber,
    Amber => Red,
    Red => Green,
    _ => throw new InvalidOperationException()
  };
```

> **NOTE** *In the United States, the switch on the traffic light is simple compared to many other countries. In many countries, the light switches from red back to amber. Here you could use multiple amber states such as* `AmberAfterGreen` *and* `AmberAfterRed`*. But there are other options that require the property pattern or pattern matching based on tuples. This is covered in Chapter 3.*

With the next example, a pattern combinator is used to combine multiple patterns. First, input is retrieved from the console. If string `one` or `two` is entered, the same match applies, using the `or` combinator pattern (code file `SwitchExpression/Program.cs`):

```
string? input = Console.ReadLine();

string result = input switch
{
  "one" => "the input has the value one",
  "two" or "three" => "the input has the value two or three",
  _ => "any other value"
};
```

With pattern combinators, you can combine patterns using the `and`, `or`, and `not` keywords.

The for Loop

C# provides four different loops (for, while, do-while, and foreach) that enable you to execute a block of code repeatedly until a certain condition is met. With the for keyword, you iterate through a loop whereby you test whether a particular condition holds true before you perform another iteration:

```
for (int i = 0; i < 100; i++)
{
    Console.WriteLine(i);
}
```

The first expression of the for statement is the *initializer*. It is evaluated before the first loop is executed. Usually you use this to initialize a local variable as a loop counter.

The second expression is the *condition*. This is checked before every iteration of the for block. If this expression evaluates to true, the block is executed. If it evaluates to false, the for statement ends, and the program continues with the next statement after the closing curly brace of the for body.

After the body is executed, the third expression, the *iterator*, is evaluated. Usually, you increment the loop counter. With i++, a value of 1 is added to the variable i. After the third expression, the condition expression is evaluated again to check whether another iteration with the for block should be done.

The for loop is a so-called pretest loop because the loop condition is evaluated before the loop statements are executed; therefore, the contents of the loop won't be executed at all if the loop condition is false.

It's not unusual to nest for loops so that an inner loop executes once completely for each iteration of an outer loop. This approach is typically employed to loop through every element in a rectangular multidimensional array. The outermost loop loops through every row, and the inner loop loops through every column in a particular row. The following code displays rows of numbers. It also uses another Console method, Console.Write, which does the same thing as Console.WriteLine but doesn't send a carriage return to the output (code file ForLoop/Program.cs):

```
// This loop iterates through rows
for (int i = 0; i < 100; i += 10)
{
    // This loop iterates through columns
    for (int j = i; j < i + 10; j++)
    {
        Console.Write($" {j}");
    }
    Console.WriteLine();
}
```

This sample results in this output:

```
0 1 2 3 4 5 6 7 8 9
10 11 12 13 14 15 16 17 18 19
20 21 22 23 24 25 26 27 28 29
30 31 32 33 34 35 36 37 38 39
40 41 42 43 44 45 46 47 48 49
50 51 52 53 54 55 56 57 58 59
60 61 62 63 64 65 66 67 68 69
70 71 72 73 74 75 76 77 78 79
80 81 82 83 84 85 86 87 88 89
90 91 92 93 94 95 96 97 98 99
```

> **NOTE** *It is technically possible to evaluate something other than a counter variable in a* `for` *loop's test condition, but it is certainly not typical. It is also possible to omit one (or even all) of the expressions in the* `for` *loop. In such situations, however, you should consider using the* `while` *loop.*

The while Loop

Like the `for` loop, `while` is a pretest loop. The syntax is similar, but `while` loops take only one expression:

```
while(condition)
    statement(s);
```

Unlike the `for` loop, the `while` loop is most often used to repeat a statement or a block of statements for a number of times that is not known before the loop begins. Usually, a statement inside the `while` loop's body sets a Boolean flag to `false` on a certain iteration, triggering the end of the loop, as in the following example:

```
bool condition = false;
while (!condition)
{
  // This loop spins until the condition is true.
  DoSomeWork();
  condition = CheckCondition(); // assume CheckCondition() returns a bool
}
```

The do-while Loop

The `do-while` loop is the post-test version of the `while` loop. This means that the loop's test condition is evaluated after the body of the loop has been executed. Consequently, `do-while` loops are useful for situations in which a block of statements must be executed at least one time, as in this example:

```
bool condition;
do
{
  // This loop will at least execute once, even if the condition is false.
  MustBeCalledAtLeastOnce();
  condition = CheckCondition();
} while (condition);
```

The foreach Loop

The `foreach` loop enables you to iterate through each item in a collection. For now, don't worry about exactly what a collection is (it is explained fully in Chapter 6, "Arrays"); just understand that it is an object that represents a list of objects. Technically, for an object to count as a collection, it must support an interface called `IEnumerable`. Examples of collections include C# arrays, the collection classes in the `System.Collections` namespaces, and user-defined collection classes. You can get an idea of the syntax of `foreach` from the following code, if you assume that `arrayOfInts` is (unsurprisingly) an array of `int`s:

```
foreach (int temp in arrayOfInts)
{
  Console.WriteLine(temp);
}
```

Here, `foreach` steps through the array one element at a time. With each element, it places the value of the element in the `int` variable called `temp` and then performs an iteration of the loop.

Here is another situation where you can use type inference. The `foreach` loop would become the following:

```
foreach (var temp in arrayOfInts)
{
  // ...
}
```

`int` would infer from `temp` because that is what the collection item type is.

An important point to note with `foreach` is that you can't change the value of the item in the collection (`temp` in the preceding code), so code such as the following will not compile:

```
foreach (int temp in arrayOfInts)
{
  temp++;
  Console.WriteLine(temp);
}
```

If you need to iterate through the items in a collection and change their values, you must use a `for` loop instead.

Exiting Loops

Within a loop, you can stop the iterations with the `break` statement or end the current iteration and continue with the next iteration with the `continue` statement. With the `return` statement, you can exit the current method and thus also exit a loop.

ORGANIZATION WITH NAMESPACES

With small sample applications, you don't need to specify a namespace. When you create libraries where classes are used in applications, to avoid ambiguities, you must specify namespaces. The `Console` class used earlier is defined in the `System` namespace. To use the class `Console`, you either have to prefix it with the namespace or import the namespace from this class.

Namespaces can be defined in a hierarchical way. For example, the `ServiceCollection` class is specified in the namespace `Microsoft.Extensions.DependencyInjection`. To define the class `Sample` in the namespace `Wrox.ProCSharp.CoreCSharp`, you can specify this namespace hierarchy with the `namespace` keyword:

```
namespace Wrox
{
  namespace ProCSharp
  {
    namespace CoreCSharp
    {
      public class Sample
      {
      }
    }
  }
}
```

You can also use the dotted notation to specify the namespace:

```
namespace Wrox.ProCSharp.CoreCSharp
{
```

```
public class Sample
{
}
}
```

A namespace is a logical construct and completely independent of physical files or components. One assembly can contain multiple namespaces, and a single namespace can be spread across multiple assemblies. It's a logical construct to group different types together.

Each namespace name is composed of the names of the namespaces it resides within, separated with periods, starting with the outermost namespace and ending with its own short name. Therefore, the full name for the `ProCSharp` namespace is `Wrox.ProCSharp`, and the full name of the `Sample` class is `Wrox.ProCSharp.CoreCSharp.Sample`.

The using Directive

Obviously, namespaces can grow rather long and tiresome to type, and the capability to indicate a particular class with such specificity may not always be necessary. Fortunately, as noted earlier in this chapter, C# allows you to abbreviate a class's full name. To do this, list the class's namespace at the top of the file, prefixed with the `using` keyword. Throughout the rest of the file, you can refer to the types in the namespace by their type names.

If two namespaces referenced by `using` declarations contain a type of the same name, you need to use the full (or at least a longer) form of the name to ensure that the compiler knows which type to access. For example, suppose classes called `Test` exist in both the `ProCSharp.CoreCSharp` and `ProCSharp.OOP` namespaces. If you then create a class called `Test` and both namespaces are imported, the compiler reacts with an ambiguity compilation error. In this case, you need to specify the namespace name for the type.

Namespace Aliases

Instead of specifying the complete namespace name for the class to resolve ambiguity issues, you can specify an alias with the `using` directive, as shown with different `Timer` classes from two namespaces:

```
using TimersTimer = System.Timers.Timer;
using Webtimer = System.Web.UI.Timer;
```

WORKING WITH STRINGS

The code in this chapter has already used the `string` type several times. `string` is an important reference type that offers many features. Although it's a reference type, it's immutable—it can't be changed. All the methods this type offers don't change the content of the string but instead return a new string. For example, to concatenate strings, the + operator is overloaded. The expression `s1 + " " + s2` first creates a new string combining `s1` and the string containing the space character. Another new string is created by combining the result string with `s2` to create another new string. Finally, the result string is referenced from the variable `s3`:

```
string s1 = "Hello";
string s2 = "World";
string s3 = s1 + " " + s2;
```

With many strings created, you need to be aware that the objects that are no longer necessary need to be cleaned up by the garbage collector. The garbage collector frees up memory in the managed heap from objects that are no longer needed. This doesn't happen when the reference is not used anymore; it's based on certain memory limits. Read Chapter 13 for more information on the garbage collector. It's best to avoid object allocation, which can be done when dynamically working with strings by using the `StringBuilder` class.

Using the StringBuilder

The `StringBuilder` allows a program to dynamically work with strings using `Append`, `Insert`, `Remove`, and `Replace` methods without creating new objects. Instead, the `StringBuilder` uses a memory buffer and modifies this buffer as the need arises. When you're creating a `StringBuilder`, the default capacity is 16 characters. If strings are appended as shown in the following code snippet and more memory is needed, the capacity is doubled to 32 characters (code file `StringSample/Program.cs`):

```
void UsingStringBuilder()
{
  StringBuilder sb = new("the quick");
  sb.Append(' ');
  sb.Append("brown fox jumped over ");
  sb.Append("the lazy dogs 1234567890 times");
  string s = sb.ToString();
  Console.WriteLine(s);
}
```

If the capacity is too small, the buffer size always doubles—for example, from 16 to 32 to 64 to 128 characters. The length of the string can be accessed with the `Length` property. The capacity of the `StringBuilder` is returned from the `Capacity` property. After creating the necessary string, you can use the `ToString` method, which allocates a new string containing the content of the `StringBuilder`.

String Interpolation

Code snippets in this chapter have already included strings with the `$` prefix. This prefix allows evaluating expressions within the string and is known as *string interpolation*. For example, with string s2, the content of string s1 is embedded within s2 to have the final result of `Hello, World!`:

```
string s1 = "World";
string s2 = $"Hello, {s1}!";
```

You can write code expressions within the curly braces to get the expression evaluated and the result added into the string. In the following code snippet, a string is specified with three placeholders where the value of x, the value of y, and the result of the addition of x and y are put into the string:

```
int x = 3, y = 4;
string s3 = $"The result of {x} and {y} is {x + y}";
Console.WriteLine(s3);
```

The resulting string is `The result of 3 and 4 is 7`.

The compiler translates the interpolated string to invoke the `Format` method of the string, passes a string with numbered placeholders, and passes additional arguments following the string. The result of the additional arguments is from the implementation of the `Format` method passed to the placeholders based on the numbers. The first argument following the string is passed to the 0 placeholder, the second argument to the 1 placeholder, and so on:

```
string s3 = string.Format("The result of {0} and {1} is {2}", x, y, x + y);
```

> **NOTE** *To escape curly braces in an interpolated string, you can use double curly braces:* {{}}.

FormattableString

What the interpolated string gets translated to can easily be seen by assigning a string to a `FormattableString`. The interpolated string can be directly assigned to this type because it's a better match than the normal string. This type defines the `Format` property that returns the resulting format string, an `ArgumentCount` property, and the method `GetArgument` that returns the argument values (code file `StringSample/Program.cs`):

```
void UsingFormattableString()
{
  int x = 3, y = 4;
  FormattableString s = $"The result of {x} + {y} is {x + y}";
  Console.WriteLine($"format: {s.Format}");
  for (int i = 0; i < s.ArgumentCount; i++)
  {
    Console.WriteLine($"argument: {i}:{s.GetArgument(i)}");
  }
  Console.WriteLine();
}
```

Running this code snippet results in this output:

```
format: The result of {0} + {1} is {2}
argument 0: 3
argument 1: 4
argument 2: 7
```

> **NOTE** *In Chapter 22, "Localization," you can read about using string interpolation with different cultures. By default, string interpolation makes use of the current culture.*

String Formats

With an interpolated string, you can add a string format to the expression. .NET defines default formats for numbers, dates, and time based on the computer's locale. The following code snippet shows a date, an `int` value, and a `double` with different format representations. D is used to display the date in the long date format, d in the short date format. The number is shown with integral and decimal digits (n), using an exponential notation (e), a conversion to hexadecimal (x), and a currency (c). With the double value, the first result is shown rounded after the decimal point to three digits (###.###); with the second version, the three digits before the decimal point are shown as well (000.000):

```
void UseStringFormat()
{
  DateTime day = new(2025, 2, 14);
  Console.WriteLine($"{day:D}");
  Console.WriteLine($"{day:d}");

  int i = 2477;
  Console.WriteLine($"{i:n} {i:e} {i:x} {i:c}");

  double d = 3.1415;
  Console.WriteLine($"{d:###.###}");
  Console.WriteLine($"{d:000.000}");
  Console.WriteLine();
}
```

When you run the application, this is shown:

```
Friday, February 14, 2025
2/14/2025
2,477.00 2.477000e+003 9ad $2,477.00
3.142
```

> **NOTE** *See the Microsoft documentation for all the different format strings for numbers at* https://docs.microsoft.com/en-us/dotnet/standard/base-types/standard-numeric-format-strings *and for date/time at* https://docs.microsoft.com/en-us/dotnet/standard/base-types/standard-date-and-time-format-strings. *To define custom formats with a custom type, see the sample in Chapter 9, "Language Integrated Query."*

Verbatim Strings

Code snippets in the section "The Character Type" earlier in this chapter included special characters such as \t for a tab or \r\n for carriage return newline. You can use these characters in a complete string to get the specific meaning. If you need a backslash in the output of the string, you can escape this with a double backslash \\. This can be annoying if backslashes are needed multiple times because they can make the code unreadable. For such scenarios, such as when using regular expressions, you can use verbatim strings. A verbatim string is prefixed with the @ character:

```
string s = @"a tab: \t, a carriage return: \r, a newline: \n";
Console.WriteLine(s);
```

Running the preceding code results in this output:

```
a tab: \t, a carriage return: \r, a newline: \n
```

Ranges with Strings

The `String` type offers a `Substring` method to retrieve a part of a string. Instead of using the `Substring` method, as of C# 8 you can use the *hat* and the *range* operators. The range operator uses the `..` notation to specify a range. With the string, you can use the indexer to access one character or use it with the range operator to access a substring. The numbers left and right of the `..` operator specify the range. The left number specifies the 0-indexed first value from the string, which is included from the string up to the 0-indexed last value that is excluded. The range `0..3` would span the string `The`. To start from the first character in the string, the `0` can be omitted as shown with the following code snippet. The range `4..9` starts with the fifth character and goes up to the eighth character. To count from the end, you can use the hat operator `^` (code file `StringSample/Program.cs`):

```
void RangesWithStrings()
{
  string s = "The quick brown fox jumped over the lazy dogs down " +
    "1234567890 times";
  string the = s[..3];
  string quick = s[4..9];
  string times = s[^5..^0];
  Console.WriteLine(the);
  Console.WriteLine(quick);
  Console.WriteLine(times);
  Console.WriteLine();
}
```

> **NOTE** *For more information about the indices, ranges, and the hat operator, read Chapter 6, "Arrays."*

COMMENTS

The next topic—adding comments to your code—looks simple on the surface, but it can be complex. Comments can be beneficial to other developers who may look at your code. Also, as you will see, you can use comments to generate documentation for your code that other developers can use.

Internal Comments Within the Source Files

C# uses the traditional C-type single-line (// . .) and multiline (/* .. */) comments:

```
// This is a single-line comment
/* This comment
spans multiple lines. */
```

Everything in a single-line comment, from the // to the end of the line, is ignored by the compiler, and everything from an opening /* to the next */ in a multiline comment combination is ignored. It is possible to put multiline comments within a line of code:

```
Console.WriteLine(/* Here's a comment! */ "This will compile.");
```

Inline comments can be useful when debugging if, for example, you temporarily want to try running the code with a different value somewhere, as in the following code snippet. However, inline comments can make code hard to read, so use them with care.

```
DoSomething(Width, /*Height*/ 100);
```

XML Documentation

In addition to the C-type comments illustrated in the preceding section, C# has a very neat feature: the capability to produce documentation in XML format automatically from special comments. These comments are single-line comments, but they begin with three slashes (///) instead of two. Within these comments, you can place XML tags containing documentation of the types and type members in your code.

The tags in the following table are recognized by the compiler:

TAG	DESCRIPTION
`<c>`	Marks up text within a line as code—for example, `<c>int i = 10;</c>`.
`<code>`	Marks multiple lines as code.
`<example>`	Marks up a code example.
`<exception>`	Documents an exception class. (Syntax is verified by the compiler.)
`<include>`	Includes comments from another documentation file. (Syntax is verified by the compiler.)
`<list>`	Inserts a list into the documentation.
`<para>`	Gives structure to text.

TAG	DESCRIPTION
`<param>`	Marks up a method parameter. (Syntax is verified by the compiler.)
`<paramref>`	Indicates that a word is a method parameter. (Syntax is verified by the compiler.)
`<permission>`	Documents access to a member. (Syntax is verified by the compiler.)
`<remarks>`	Adds a description for a member.
`<returns>`	Documents the return value for a method.
`<see>`	Provides a cross-reference to another parameter. (Syntax is verified by the compiler.)
`<seealso>`	Provides a "see also" section in a description. (Syntax is verified by the compiler.)
`<summary>`	Provides a short summary of a type or member.
`<typeparam>`	Describes a type parameter in the comment of a generic type.
`<typeparamref>`	Provides the name of the type parameter.
`<value>`	Describes a property.

The following code snippet shows the `Calculator` class with documentation specified for the class, and documentation for the `Add` method (code file `Math/Calculator.cs`):

```
namespace ProCSharp.MathLib
{
  ///<summary>
  /// ProCsharp.MathLib.Calculator class.
  /// Provides a method to add two doubles.
  ///</summary>
  public static class Calculator
  {
    ///<summary>
    /// The Add method allows us to add two doubles.
    ///</summary>
    ///<returns>Result of the addition (double)</returns>
    ///<param name="x">First number to add</param>
    ///<param name="y">Second number to add</param>
    public static double Add(double x, double y) => x + y;
  }
}
```

To generate the XML documentation, you can add the `GenerateDocumentationFile` to the project file (project configuration file `Math/Math.csproj`):

```
<Project Sdk="Microsoft.NET.Sdk">

  <PropertyGroup>
    <OutputType>exe</OutputType>
    <TargetFramework>net5.0</TargetFramework>
    <Nullable>enable</Nullable>
    <GenerateDocumentationFile>true</GenerateDocumentationFile>
  </PropertyGroup>

</Project>
```

With this setting, the documentation file is created in the same directory where the program binary will show up as you compile the application. You can also specify the `DocumentationFile` element to define a name that's different from the project file, and you can also specify an absolute directory where the documentation should be generated.

Using tools like Visual Studio, IntelliSense will show tooltips with the information from the documentation as the classes and members are used.

C# PREPROCESSOR DIRECTIVES

Besides the C# keywords, most of which you have now encountered, C# includes a number of commands that are known as *preprocessor directives*. These commands are never actually translated to any commands in your executable code, but they affect aspects of the compilation process. For example, you can use preprocessor directives to prevent the compiler from compiling certain portions of your code. You might do this if you target different frameworks and deal with the differences. In another scenario, you might want to turn nullable reference types on or off because changing existing codebases cannot be fixed in the short term.

The preprocessor directives are all distinguished by beginning with the # symbol.

The following sections briefly cover the purposes of the preprocessor directives.

#define and #undef

`#define` is used like this:

```
#define DEBUG
```

This tells the compiler that a symbol with the given name (in this case `DEBUG`) exists. It is a little bit like declaring a variable, except that this variable doesn't really have a value—it just exists. Also, this symbol isn't part of your actual code; it exists only for the benefit of the compiler, whereas the compiler is compiling the code and has no meaning within the C# code itself.

`#undef` does the opposite and removes the definition of a symbol:

```
#undef DEBUG
```

If the symbol doesn't exist in the first place, then `#undef` has no effect. Similarly, `#define` has no effect if a symbol already exists.

You need to place any `#define` and `#undef` directives at the beginning of the C# source file, before any code that declares any objects to be compiled.

`#define` isn't of much use on its own, but when combined with other preprocessor directives, especially `#if`, it becomes powerful.

By default, with a Debug build, the `DEBUG` symbol is defined, and with the Release code, the `RELEASE` symbol is defined. To define different code paths on debug and release builds, you don't need to define these symbols; all you have to do is to use the preprocessor directives shown in the next section to define the code paths the compiler should take.

> **NOTE** *Preprocessor directives are not terminated by semicolons, and they normally constitute the only command on a line. If the compiler sees a preprocessor directive, it assumes that the next command is on the next line.*

#if, #elif, #else, and #endif

These directives inform the compiler whether to compile a block of code. Consider this method:

```
int DoSomeWork(double x)
{
  // do something
  #if DEBUG
  Console.WriteLine($"x is {x}");
  #endif
}
```

This code compiles as normal except for the `Console.WriteLine` method call contained inside the `#if` clause. This line is executed only if the symbol `DEBUG` has been defined. As previously mentioned, it's defined with a Debug build—or you defined it with a previous `#define` directive. When the compiler finds the `#if` directive, it checks to see whether the symbol concerned exists and compiles the code inside the `#if` clause only if the symbol does exist. Otherwise, the compiler simply ignores all the code until it reaches the matching `#endif` directive. Typical practice is to define the symbol `DEBUG` while you are debugging and have various bits of debugging-related code inside `#if` clauses. Then, when you are close to shipping, you simply comment out the `#define` directive, and all the debugging code miraculously disappears, the size of the executable file gets smaller, and your end users don't get confused by seeing debugging information. (Obviously, you would do more testing to ensure that your code still works without `DEBUG` defined.) This technique is common in C and C++ programming and is known as *conditional compilation*.

The `#elif` (=else if) and `#else` directives can be used in `#if` blocks and have intuitively obvious meanings. It is also possible to nest `#if` blocks:

```
#define ENTERPRISE
#define W10
// further on in the file
#if ENTERPRISE
// do something
#if W10
// some code that is only relevant to enterprise
// edition running on W10
#endif
#elif PROFESSIONAL
// do something else
#else
// code for the leaner version
#endif
```

`#if` and `#elif` support a limited range of logical operators, too, using the operators `!`, `==`, `!=`, `&&`, and `||`. A symbol is considered to be `true` if it exists and `false` if it doesn't. Here's an example:

```
#if W10 && !ENTERPRISE // if W10 is defined but ENTERPRISE isn't
```

#warning and #error

Two other useful preprocessor directives, `#warning` and `#error`, cause a warning or an error, respectively, to be raised when the compiler encounters them. If the compiler sees a `#warning` directive, it displays whatever text appears after the `#warning` to the user, after which compilation continues. If it encounters an `#error` directive, it displays the subsequent text to the user as if it is a compilation error message and then immediately abandons the compilation, so no IL code is generated.

You can use these directives as checks that you haven't done anything silly with your `#define` statements; you can also use the `#warning` statements to remind yourself to do something:

```
#if DEBUG && RELEASE
#error "You've defined DEBUG and RELEASE simultaneously!"
#endif

#warning "Don't forget to remove this line before the boss tests the code!"
Console.WriteLine("*I love this job.*");
```

#region and #endregion

The `#region` and `#endregion` directives are used to indicate that a certain block of code is to be treated as a single block with a given name, like this:

```
#region Member Field Declarations
int x;
double d;
decimal balance;
#endregion
```

The region directives are ignored by the compiler and used by tools such as the Visual Studio code editor. The editor allows you to collapse region sections, so only the text associated with the region shows. This makes it easier to scroll through the source code. However, you should prefer to write shorter code files instead.

#line

You can use the `#line` directive to alter the filename and line number information that is output by the compiler in warnings and error messages. You probably won't want to use this directive often. It's most useful when you are coding in conjunction with another package that alters the code you are typing before sending it to the compiler. In this situation, line numbers, or perhaps the filenames reported by the compiler, don't match up to the line numbers in the files or the filenames you are editing. The `#line` directive can be used to restore the match. You can also use the syntax `#line default` to restore the line to the default line numbering:

```
#line 164 "Core.cs" // We happen to know this is line 164 in the file
// Core.cs, before the intermediate
// package mangles it.
// later on
#line default // restores default line numbering
```

#pragma

The `#pragma` directive can either suppress or restore specific compiler warnings. Unlike command-line options, the `#pragma` directive can be implemented on the class or method level, enabling fine-grained control over what warnings are suppressed and when. The following example disables the "field not used" warning and then restores it after the `MyClass` class compiles:

```
#pragma warning disable 169
public class MyClass
{
    int neverUsedField;
}
#pragma warning restore 169
```

#nullable

With the `#nullable` directive, you can turn on or off nullable reference types within a code file. `#nullable enable` turns nullable reference types on, no matter what the setting in the project file. `#nullable disable` turns it off. `#nullable restore` switches the settings back to the settings of the project file.

How do you use this? If nullable reference types are enabled with the project file, you can temporarily turn them off in code sections where you have issues with this compiler behavior and restore it to the project file settings after the code with nullability issues.

C# PROGRAMMING GUIDELINES

This final section of the chapter supplies the guidelines you need to bear in mind when writing C# programs. These are guidelines that most C# developers use. When you use these guidelines, other developers will feel comfortable working with your code.

Rules for Identifiers

This section examines the rules governing what names you can use for variables, classes, methods, and so on. Note that the rules presented in this section are not merely guidelines: they are enforced by the C# compiler.

Identifiers are the names you give to variables, user-defined types such as classes and structs, and members of these types. Identifiers are case sensitive, so, for example, variables named `interestRate` and `InterestRate` would be recognized as different variables. The following are a few rules determining what identifiers you can use in C#:

➤ They must begin with a letter or underscore, although they can contain numeric characters.

➤ You can't use C# keywords as identifiers.

See the list of C# reserved keywords at `https://docs.microsoft.com/en-us/dotnet/csharp/language-reference/keywords/`.

If you need to use one of these words as an identifier (for example, if you are accessing a class written in a different language), you can prefix the identifier with the `@` symbol to indicate to the compiler that what follows should be treated as an identifier, not as a C# keyword (so `abstract` is not a valid identifier, but `@abstract` is).

Finally, identifiers can also contain Unicode characters, specified using the syntax `\uXXXX`, where XXXX is the four-digit hex code for the Unicode character. The following are some examples of valid identifiers:

➤ `Name`

➤ `Überfluß`

➤ `_Identifier`

➤ `\u005fIdentifier`

The last two items in this list are identical and interchangeable (because `005f` is the Unicode code for the underscore character), so, obviously, both these identifiers couldn't be declared in the same scope.

Usage Conventions

In any development language, certain traditional programming styles usually arise. The styles are not part of the language itself but rather are conventions—for example, how variables are named or how certain classes, methods, or functions are used. If most developers using that language follow the same conventions, it's easier for different developers to understand each other's code—which in turn generally helps program maintainability. Conventions do, however, depend on the language and the environment. For example, C++ developers programming on the Windows platform have traditionally used the prefixes psz or lpsz to indicate strings—char *pszResult; char *lpszMessage;—but on Unix machines it's more common not to use any such prefixes: char *Result; char *Message;.

> **NOTE** *The convention by which variable names are prefixed with letters that represent the data type is known as Hungarian notation. It means that other developers reading the code can immediately tell from the variable name what data type the variable represents. Hungarian notation is widely regarded as redundant in these days of smart editors and IntelliSense.*

Whereas many languages' usage conventions simply evolved as the language was used, for C# and the whole of the .NET Framework, Microsoft has written comprehensive usage guidelines that are detailed in the .NET/C# documentation. This means that, right from the start, .NET programs have a high degree of interoperability in terms of developers being able to understand code. The guidelines have also been developed with the benefit of some 20 years' hindsight in object-oriented programming. Judging by the relevant newsgroups, the guidelines have been carefully thought out and are well received in the developer community. Hence, the guidelines are well worth following.

Note, however, that the guidelines are not the same as language specifications. You should try to follow the guidelines when you can. Nevertheless, you won't run into problems if you have a good reason for not doing so—for example, you won't get a compilation error because you don't follow these guidelines. The general rule is that if you don't follow the usage guidelines, you must have a convincing reason. When you depart from the guidelines, you should be making a conscious decision rather than simply not bothering. Also, if you compare the guidelines with the samples in the remainder of this book, you'll notice that in numerous examples I have chosen not to follow the conventions. That's usually because the conventions are designed for much larger programs than the samples; although the guidelines are great if you are writing a complete software package, they're not really suitable for small 20-line stand-alone programs. In many cases, following the conventions would have made the samples harder, rather than easier, to follow.

The full guidelines for good programming style are quite extensive. This section is confined to describing some of the more important guidelines, as well as those most likely to surprise you. To be absolutely certain that your code follows the usage guidelines completely, you need to refer to the Microsoft documentation.

Naming Conventions

One important aspect of making your programs understandable is how you choose to name your items—and that includes naming variables, methods, classes, enumerations, and namespaces.

It is intuitively obvious that your names should reflect the purpose of the item and should not clash with other names. The general philosophy in the .NET Framework is also that the name of a variable should reflect the purpose of that variable instance and not the data type. For example, height is a good name for a variable, whereas integerValue isn't. However, you are likely to find that principle is an ideal that is hard to achieve. Particularly when you are dealing with controls, in most cases you'll probably be happier sticking with variable names such as confirmationDialog and chooseEmployeeListBox, which do indicate the data type in the name.

The following sections look at some of the things you need to think about when choosing names.

Casing of Names

In many cases, you should use *Pascal casing* for names. With Pascal casing, the first letter of each word in a name is capitalized: EmployeeSalary, ConfirmationDialog, PlainTextEncoding. Notice that nearly all the names of namespaces, classes, and members in the base classes follow Pascal casing. In particular, the convention of joining words using the underscore character is discouraged. Therefore, try not to use names such as `employee_salary`. It has also been common in other languages to use all capitals for names of constants. This is not advised in C# because such names are harder to read—the convention is to use Pascal casing throughout:

```
const int MaximumLength;
```

The only other casing convention that you are advised to use is *camel casing*. Camel casing is similar to Pascal casing, except that the first letter of the first word in the name is not capitalized: `employeeSalary`, `confirmationDialog`, `plainTextEncoding`. The following are three situations in which you are advised to use camel casing:

➤   For names of all private member fields in types.

➤   For names of all parameters passed to methods.

➤   To distinguish items that would otherwise have the same name. A common example is when a property wraps around a field:

```
private string employeeName;
public string EmployeeName
{
  get
  {
    return employeeName;
  }
}
```

> **NOTE** *Since .NET Core, the .NET team has been prefixing names of private member fields with an underscore. This is also used as a convention with this book.*

If you are wrapping a property around a field, you should always use camel casing for the private member and Pascal casing for the public or protected member so that other classes that use your code see only names in Pascal case (except for parameter names).

You should also be wary about case sensitivity. C# is case sensitive, so it is syntactically correct for names in C# to differ only by the case, as in the previous examples. However, bear in mind that your assemblies might at some point be called from Visual Basic applications—and *Visual Basic is not case sensitive*. Hence, if you do use names that differ only by case, it is important to do so only in situations in which both names will never be seen outside your assembly. (The previous example qualifies as okay because camel case is used with the name that is attached to a `private` variable.) Otherwise, you may prevent other code written in Visual Basic from being able to use your assembly correctly.

Name Styles

Be consistent about your style of names. For example, if one of the methods in a class is called `ShowConfirmationDialog`, then you should not give another method a name such as `ShowDialogWarning` or `WarningDialogShow`. The other method should be called `ShowWarningDialog`.

Namespace Names

It is particularly important to choose namespace names carefully to avoid the risk of ending up with the same name for one of your namespaces as someone else uses. Remember, namespace names are the *only* way that .NET distinguishes names of objects in shared assemblies. Therefore, if you use the same namespace name for your software package as another package and both packages are used by the same program, problems will occur. Because of this, it's almost always a good idea to create a top-level namespace with the name of your company and then nest successive namespaces that narrow down the technology, group, or department you are working in or the name of the package for which your classes are intended. Microsoft recommends namespace names that begin with `<CompanyName>.<TechnologyName>`.

Names and Keywords

It is important that the names do not clash with any keywords. In fact, if you attempt to name an item in your code with a word that happens to be a C# keyword, you'll almost certainly get a syntax error because the compiler will assume that the name refers to a statement. However, because of the possibility that your classes will be accessed by code written in other languages, it is also important that you don't use names that are keywords in other .NET languages. Generally speaking, C++ keywords are similar to C# keywords, so confusion with C++ is unlikely, and those commonly encountered keywords that are unique to Visual C++ tend to start with two underscore characters. As with C#, C++ keywords are spelled in lowercase, so if you hold to the convention of naming your public classes and members with Pascal-style names, they will always have at least one uppercase letter in their names, and there will be no risk of clashes with C++ keywords. However, you are more likely to have problems with Visual Basic, which has many more keywords than C# does, and being non-case-sensitive means that you cannot rely on Pascal-style names for your classes and methods.

Check the Microsoft documentation at `docs.microsoft.com/dotnet/csharp/language-reference/keywords`. Here, you find a long list of C# keywords that you shouldn't use with classes and members.

Use of Properties and Methods

One area that can cause confusion regarding a class is whether a particular quantity should be represented by a property or a method. The rules are not hard and strict, but in general you should use a property if something should look and behave like a variable. (If you're not sure what a property is, see Chapter 3.) This means, among other things, that

➤   Client code should be able to read its value. Write-only properties are not recommended, so, for example, use a `SetPassword` method, not a write-only `Password` property.

➤   Reading the value should not take too long. The fact that something is a property usually suggests that reading it will be relatively quick.

➤   Reading the value should not have any observable and unexpected side effect. Furthermore, setting the value of a property should not have any side effect that is not directly related to the property. Setting the width of a dialog has the obvious effect of changing the appearance of the dialog on the screen. That's fine, because it's obviously related to the property in question.

➤   It should be possible to set properties in any order. In particular, it is not good practice when setting a property to throw an exception because another related property has not yet been set. For example, to use a class that accesses a database, you need to set `ConnectionString`, `UserName`, and `Password`, and then the author of the class should ensure that the class is implemented such that users can set them in any order.

➤   Successive reads of a property should give the same result. If the value of a property is likely to change unpredictably, you should code it as a method instead. `Speed`, in a class that monitors the motion of an automobile, is not a good candidate for a property. Use a `GetSpeed` method here; but `Weight` and `EngineSize` are good candidates for properties because they will not change for a given object.

If the item you are coding satisfies all the preceding criteria, it is probably a good candidate for a property. Otherwise, you should use a method.

Use of Fields

The guidelines are pretty simple here. Fields should almost always be private, although in some cases it may be acceptable for constant or read-only fields to be public. Making a field public may hinder your ability to extend or modify the class in the future.

The previous guidelines should give you a foundation of good practices, and you should use them in conjunction with a good object-oriented programming style.

A final helpful note to keep in mind is that Microsoft has been relatively careful about being consistent and has followed its own guidelines when writing the .NET base classes, so a good way to get an intuitive feel for the conventions to follow when writing .NET code is to simply look at the base classes—see how classes, members, and namespaces are named, and how the class hierarchy works. Consistency between the base classes and your classes will facilitate readability and maintainability.

> **NOTE** *The* `ValueTuple` *type contains public fields, whereas the old* `Tuple` *type used properties instead. Microsoft broke a guideline it defined for fields. Because variables of a tuple can be as simple as a variable of an* `int` *and because performance is paramount, it was decided to have public fields for value tuples. No rules without exceptions. Read Chapter 3 for more information on tuples.*

SUMMARY

This chapter examined the basic syntax of C#, covering the areas needed to write simple C# programs. Much of the syntax is instantly recognizable to developers who are familiar with any C-style language (or even JavaScript). C# has its roots with C++, Java, and Pascal (Anders Hejlsberg, the original lead architect of C# was the original author of Turbo Pascal, and also created J++, Microsoft's version of Java).

Over time, some new features have been invented that are also available with other programming languages, and C# also has gotten more enhancements already available with other languages. The next chapter dives into creating different types; differences between classes, structs, and the new records; and an explanation about the members of types such as properties and more about methods.

3

Classes, Records, Structs, and Tuples

WHAT'S IN THIS CHAPTER?

- ➤ Pass by value and by reference
- ➤ Classes and members
- ➤ Records
- ➤ Structs
- ➤ Enum types
- ➤ ref, in, and out keywords
- ➤ Tuples
- ➤ Deconstruction
- ➤ Pattern Matching
- ➤ Partial Types

CODE DOWNLOADS FOR THIS CHAPTER

The source code for this chapter is available on the book page at www.wiley.com. Click the Downloads link. The code can also be found at https://github.com/ProfessionalCSharp/ ProfessionalCSharp2021 in the directory 1_CS/Types.

The code for this chapter is divided into the following major examples:

- ➤ TypesSample
- ➤ ClassesSample
- ➤ MathSample
- ➤ MethodSample

➤ ExtensionMethods

➤ RecordsSample

➤ StructsSample

➤ EnumSample

➤ RefInOutSample

➤ TuplesSample

➤ PatternMatchingSample

All the projects have nullable reference types enabled.

CREATING AND USING TYPES

So far, you've been introduced to some of the building blocks of the C# language, including variables, data types, and program flow statements, and you have seen a few short but complete programs that contain little more than top-level statements and a few methods. What you haven't seen yet is how to put all these elements together to form a longer program. The key to this lies in working with the types of .NET—classes, records, structs, and tuples, which are the subject of this chapter.

> **NOTE** *This chapter introduces the basic syntax associated with types. However, I assume that you are already familiar with the underlying principles of using classes—for example, that you know what a constructor or a property is. This chapter is largely confined to applying those principles in C# code.*

PASS BY VALUE OR BY REFERENCE

The types available with .NET can be categorized as pass by reference or pass by value.

Pass by value means that if you assign a variable to another variable, the value is copied. If you change the new value, the original value does not change. The content of the variable is copied on assignment. With the following code sample, a struct is created that contains a public field A. x1 and x2 are variables of this type. After creating x1, x2 is assigned to x1. Because struct is a value type, the data from x2 is copied to x1. Changing the value of the public field with x2 doesn't influence x1 at all. The x1 variable still lists the original value; the value was copied (code file TypesSample/Program.cs):

```
AStruct x1 = new() { A = 1 };
AStruct x2 = x1;
x2.A = 2;
Console.WriteLine($"original didn't change with a struct: {x1.A}");

//...

public struct AStruct
{
  public int A;
}
```

> **NOTE** *Usually, you should not create public fields; instead, you should use other members such as properties. To give you an easy view of major differences with the .NET types, public fields are used.*

This behavior is very different with classes. If you change the public member of A within the y2 variable, using the reference y1, the new value assigned from y2 can be read. *Pass by reference* means that the variables y1 and y2 after assignment reference the same object (code file TypesSample/Program.cs):

```
AClass y1 = new() { A = 1 };
AClass y2 = y1;
y2.A = 2;
Console.WriteLine($"original changed with a class: {y1.A}");

//...

public class AClass
{
  public int A;
}
```

Another difference between the types that's worth mentioning is where the data is stored. With a reference type like the class, the memory where the data is stored is the managed heap. The variable itself is on the stack and references the content on the heap. A value type like the struct is usually stored on the stack. This is important with regard to garbage collection. The garbage collector needs to clean up objects in the heap if they are no longer used. Memory on the stack is automatically released at the end of the method, when the variable is outside of its scope.

> **NOTE** *The value of a struct typically is stored on the stack. However, with boxing—that is, when a struct is passed as an object or object methods are invoked with the struct—the data of the struct is moved to the heap. Boxing moves a struct to the heap; unboxing moves it back. C# also has a type where the data can never be stored on the heap; this is the ref struct. With a ref struct, you get a compilation error if operations are used that would move the data to the heap. This is discussed in Chapter 13, "Managed and Unmanaged Memory."*

Let's take a look at the record type that's new with C# 9. Using the record keyword, a record is created. Similar to our previous example when the class keyword was used to create a reference type, with the record keyword a reference type is created as well. A C# 9 record is a class. This C# keyword is just "syntax sugar": the compiler creates a class behind the scenes. There's no functionality needed from the runtime; you could create the same generated code without using this keyword, you just would need a lot more code lines (code file TypesSample/Program.cs):

```
ARecord z1 = new() { A = 1 };
ARecord z2 = z1;
z2.A = 2;
Console.WriteLine($"original changed with a record: {z1.A}");

//...
```

```
public record ARecord
{
  public int A;
}
```

> **NOTE** *A record supports value semantics like a struct, but it's implemented as a class. This comes from the fact that a record offers easy creation of immutable types and has members that cannot be changed after initialization. Read more about records later in this chapter.*

What about tuples? With tuples, you combine multiple types into one type without needing to create a class, struct, or record. How does this type behave?

In the following code snippet, t1 is a tuple that combines a number and a string. The tuple t1 is then assigned to the variable t2. If you change the value of t2, t1 is not changed. The reason is that behind the scenes, using the C# syntax for tuples, the compiler makes use of the ValueTuple type—which is a struct—and copies values (code file TypesSample/Program.cs):

```
var t1 = (Number: 1, String: "a");
var t2 = t1;
t2.Number = 2;
t2.String = "b";
Console.WriteLine($"original didn't change with a tuple: {t1.Number} {t1.String}");
```

> **NOTE** *.NET offers the* Tuple<T> *type as well as the* ValueTuple<T> *type.* Tuple<T> *is the older one that is implemented as a class. With the built-in C# syntax for tuples, the* ValueTuple *is used. This* ValueTuple *contains public fields for all the members of the tuple. The old* Tuple<T> *type contains public read-only properties where the values cannot be changed. Today, there's no need to use the* Tuple<T> *type in your applications because there's better built-in support for* ValueTuple<T>.

Now that you've been introduced to the main differences between classes, structs, records, and tuples, let's dive deeper into the classes, including the members of classes. Most of the members of classes you learn about also apply to records and structs. I discuss the differences between records and structs after I introduce the members of classes.

CLASSES

A class contains members, which can be static or instance. A *static member* belongs to the class; an *instance member* belongs to the object. With static fields, the value of the field is the same for every object. With instance fields, every object can have a different value. Static members have the static modifier attached.

The kinds of members are explained in the following table:

MEMBER	DESCRIPTION
Fields	A field is a data member of a class. It is a variable of a type that is a member of a class.
Constants	Constants are associated with the class (although they do not have the static modifier). The compiler replaces constants everywhere they are used with the real value.

MEMBER	DESCRIPTION
Methods	Methods are functions associated with a particular class.
Properties	Properties are sets of functions that can be accessed from the client in a similar way to the public fields of the class. C# provides a specific syntax for implementing read and write properties on your classes, so you don't have to use method names that are prefixed with the words Get or Set. Because there's a dedicated syntax for properties that is distinct from that for normal functions, the illusion of objects as actual things is strengthened for client code.
Constructors	Constructors are special functions that are called automatically when an object is instantiated. They must have the same name as the class to which they belong and cannot have a return type. Constructors are useful for initialization.
Indexers	Indexers allow your object to be accessed the same way as arrays. Indexers are explained in Chapter 5, "Operators and Casts."
Operators	Operators, at their simplest, are actions such as + or –. When you add two integers, you are, strictly speaking, using the + operator for integers. C# also allows you to specify how existing operators will work with your own classes (operator overloading). Chapter 5 looks at operators in detail.
Events	Events are class members that allow an object to notify a subscriber whenever something noteworthy happens, such as a field or property of the class changing, or some form of user interaction occurring. The client can have code, known as an *event handler*, that reacts to the event. Chapter 7, "Delegates, Lambdas, and Events," looks at events in detail.
Destructors	The syntax of destructors or finalizers is similar to the syntax for constructors, but they are called when the CLR detects that an object is no longer needed. They have the same name as the class, preceded by a tilde (~). It is impossible to predict precisely when a finalizer will be called. Finalizers are discussed in Chapter 13.
Deconstructors	Deconstructors allow you to deconstruct the object into a tuple or different variables. Deconstruction is explained later in the section "Deconstruction."
Types	Classes can contain inner classes. This is interesting if the inner type is used only in conjunction with the outer type.

Let's get into the details of class members.

Fields

Fields are any variables associated with the class. In the class Person, the fields _firstName and _lastName of type string are defined. It's a good practice to declare fields with the private access modifier, which only allows accessing fields from within the class (code file ClassesSample/Person.cs):

```
public class Person
{
```

```
//...
private string _firstName;
private string _lastName;
//...
}
```

> **NOTE** *Members declared with the* `private` *access modifier only allow members of the class to invoke this member. To allow access from everywhere, use the* `public` *access modifier. Besides these two modifiers, C# also defines* `internal` *and* `protected` *to be used with access modifiers. All the different access modifiers are explained in detail in Chapter 4, "Object-Oriented Programming in C#."*

In the class `PeopleFactory`, the field `s_peopleCount` is of type `int` and has the `static` modifier applied. With the `static` modifier, the field is used with all instances of the class. Instance fields (without the `static` modifier) have different values for every instance of the class. Because this class only has static members, the class itself can have the `static` modifier applied. The compiler than makes sure that instance members are not added (code file `ClassesSample/PeopleFactory.cs`):

```
public static class PeopleFactory
{
  //...
  private static int s_peopleCount;
  //...
}
```

Readonly Fields

To guarantee that fields of an object cannot be changed, fields can be declared with the `readonly` modifier. Fields with the `readonly` modifier can be assigned only values from constructors. This is different from the `const` modifier shown in Chapter 2, "Core C#." With the `const` modifier, the compiler replaces the variable by its value everywhere it is used. The compiler already knows the value of the constant. Read-only fields are assigned during runtime from a constructor. The following `Person` class specifies a constructor where values for both `firstName` and `lastName` need to be passed.

Contrary to const fields, read-only fields can be instance members. With the following code snippet, the `_firstName` and `_lastName` fields are changed to add the `readonly` modifier. The compiler complains with errors if this field is changed after initializing it in the constructor (code file `ClassesSample/Person.cs`):

```
public class Person
{
  //...
  public Person(string firstName, string lastName)
  {
    _firstName = firstName;
    _lastName = lastName;
  }

  private readonly string _firstName;
  private readonly string _lastName;
  //...
}
```

Properties

Instead of having a method pair to set and get the values of a field, C# defines the syntax of a property. From outside of the class, a property looks like a field with typically used uppercase names. Within the class, you can write a custom implementation to set not just fields and get the value of fields, but you can add some programming logic to validate the value before assigning it to a variable. You can also define a purely computed property without any variable that is accessed by the property.

The class `Person` as shown in the following code snippet defines a property with the name `Age` accessing the private field `_age`. With the `get` accessor, the value of the field is returned. With the `set` accessor, the variable `value`, which contains the value passed when setting the property, is automatically created. In the code snippet, the value variable is used to assign the value to the `_age` field (code file `ClassesSample/Person.cs`):

```
public class Person
{
  //...

  private int _age;
  public int Age
  {
    get => _age;
    set => _age = value;
  }
}
```

In case more than one statement is needed with the implementation of the property accessor, you can use curly brackets as shown in the following code snippet:

```
private int _age;
public int Age
{
  get
  {
    return _age;
  }
  set
  {
    _age = value;
  }
}
```

To use the property, you can access the property from an object instance. Setting a value to the property invokes the `set` accessor. Reading the value invokes the `get` accessor:

```
person.Age = 4; // setting a property value with the set accessor
int age = person.Age; // accessing the property with the get accessor
```

Auto-Implemented Properties

If there isn't going to be any logic in the property accessors `set` and `get`, then auto-implemented properties can be used. Auto-implemented properties implement the backing member variable automatically. The code for the earlier `Age` example would look like this:

```
public int Age { get; set; }
```

The declaration of a private field is not needed. The compiler creates this automatically. With auto-implemented properties, you cannot access the field directly because you don't know the name the compiler generates. If all you need to do with a property is read and write a field, the syntax for the property using auto-implemented properties is shorter than using expression-bodied property accessors.

By using auto-implemented properties, validation of the property cannot be done at the property set. Therefore, with the Age property, you could not have checked to see whether an invalid age is set.

Auto-implemented properties can be initialized using a property initializer. The compiler moves this initialization to the created constructor, and the initialization is done before the constructor body.

```
public int Age { get; set; } = 42;
```

Access Modifiers for Properties

C# allows the set and get accessors to have differing access modifiers. This would allow a property to have a public get and a private or protected set. This can help control how or when a property can be set. In the following code example, notice that the set has a private access modifier, but the get does not. In this case, the get takes the access level of the property. One of the accessors must follow the access level of the property. A compile error is generated if the get accessor has the protected access level associated with it because that would make both accessors have a different access level from the property.

```
private string _name;
public string Name
{
  get => _name;
  private set => _name = value;
}
```

Different access levels can also be set with auto-implemented properties:

```
public int Age { get; private set; }
```

Readonly Properties

It is possible to create a read-only property by simply omitting the set accessor from the property definition. Thus, to make FirstName a read-only property, you can do this by just defining the get accessor:

```
private readonly string _firstName;
public string FirstName
{
  get => _firstName;
}
```

Declaring the field with the readonly modifier only allows initializing the value of the property in the constructor.

> **NOTE** *Similar to properties that only make use of a get accessor, you can also specify a property with just a set accessor. This is a write-only property. However, this is regarded as poor programming practice and could be confusing to the developers who access this property. It's recommended that you define methods instead of using write-only properties.*

Expression-Bodied Properties

With properties that only implement a get accessor, you can use a simplified syntax with the => token and assign an expression-bodied member. There's no need to write the get accessor to return a value. Behind the scenes, the compiler creates an implementation with a get accessor.

In the following code snippet, a `FirstName` property is defined that returns the field `_firstName` using an expression-bodied property. The `FullName` property combines the `_firstName` field and the value from the `LastName` property to return the full name (code file `ClassesSample/Person.cs`):

```
private readonly string _firstName;
public string FirstName => _firstName;
private readonly string _lastName;
public strign LastName => _lastName;
public string FullName => $"{FirstName} {LastName}";
```

Auto-Implemented Read-Only Properties

C# offers a simple syntax with auto-implemented properties to create read-only properties that access read-only fields. These properties can be initialized using property initializers:

```
public string Id { get; } = Guid.NewGuid().ToString();
```

Behind the scenes, the compiler creates a read-only field and a property with a `get` accessor to this field. The code from the initializer moves to the implementation of the constructor and is invoked before the constructor body is called.

Read-only properties can also explicitly be initialized from the constructor, as shown with this code snippet:

```
public class Book
{
  public Book(string title) => Title = title;

  public string Title { get; }
}
```

Init-Only Set Accessors

C# 9 allows you to define properties with `get` and `init` accessors by using the `init` keyword instead of the `set` keyword. This way the property value can be set only in the constructor or with an object initializer (code file `ClassesSample/Book.cs`):

```
public class Book
{
  public Book(string title)
  {
    Title = title;
  }

  public string Title { get; init; }
  public string? Publisher { get; init; }
}
```

C# 9 offers a new option with properties that should only be set with constructors and object initializers. A new `Book` object can now be created by invoking the constructor and using an object initializer to set the properties as shown in the following code snippet (code file `ClassesSample/Program.cs`):

```
Book theBook = new("Professional C#")
{
  Publisher = "Wrox Press"
};
```

You can use object initializers to initialize properties on creation of the object. The constructor defines the required parameters that the class needs for initialization. With the object initializer, you can assign all properties with a `set` and an `init` accessor. The object initializer can be used only when creating the object, not afterward.

Methods

With the C# terminology, there's a distinction between functions and methods. The term *function member* includes not only methods, but also other nondata members such as indexers, operators, constructors, destructors, and properties—all members that contain executable code.

Declaring Methods

In C#, the definition of a method consists of any method modifiers (such as the method's accessibility), followed by the type of the return value, followed by the name of the method, followed by a list of parameters enclosed in parentheses, followed by the body of the method enclosed in curly brackets.

Each parameter consists of the name of the type of the parameter and the name by which it can be referenced in the body of the method. Also, if the method returns a value, a return statement must be used with the return value to indicate each exit point, as shown in this example:

```
public bool IsSquare(Rectangle rect)
{
    return (rect.Height == rect.Width);
}
```

If the method doesn't return anything, specify a return type of void because you can't omit the return type altogether. If the method takes no parameters, you need to include an empty set of parentheses after the method name. With a void return, using a return statement in the implementation is optional—the method returns automatically when the closing curly brace is reached.

Expression-Bodied Methods

If the implementation of a method consists just of one statement, C# gives a simplified syntax to method definitions: *expression-bodied methods*. You don't need to write curly brackets and the return keyword with this syntax. The => token is used to distinguish the declaration of the left side of this operator to the implementation that is on the right side.

The following example is the same method as before, IsSquare, implemented using the expression-bodied method syntax. The right side of the => token defines the implementation of the method. Curly brackets and a return statement are not needed. What's returned is the result of the statement, and the result needs to be of the same type as the method declared on the left side, which is a bool in this code snippet:

```
public bool IsSquare(Rectangle rect) => rect.Height == rect.Width;
```

Invoking Methods

The following example illustrates the syntax for definition and instantiation of classes and for definition and invocation of methods. The class Math defines instance and static members (code file MathSample/Math.cs):

```
public class Math
{
    public int Value { get; set; }
    public int GetSquare() => Value * Value;
    public static int GetSquareOf(int x) => x * x;
}
```

The top-level statements in the Program.cs file uses the Math class, calls static methods, and instantiates an object to invoke instance members (code file MathSample/Program.cs):

```
using System;
```

```
// Call static members
int x = Math.GetSquareOf(5);
Console.WriteLine($"Square of 5 is {x}");

// Instantiate a Math object
Math math = new();

// Call instance members
math.Value = 30;
Console.WriteLine($"Value field of math variable contains {math.Value}");
Console.WriteLine($"Square of 30 is {math.GetSquare()}");
```

Running the `MathSample` example produces the following results:

```
Square of 5 is 25
Value field of math variable contains 30
Square of 30 is 900
```

As you can see from the code, the `Math` class contains a property that contains a number, as well as a method to find the square of this number. It also contains one static method to find the square of the number passed in as a parameter.

Method Overloading

C# supports method overloading—several versions of the method that have different signatures (that is, the same name but a different number of parameters and/or different parameter data types). To overload methods, simply declare the methods with the same name but different numbers of parameter types:

```
class ResultDisplayer
{
  public void DisplayResult(string result)
  {
    // implementation
  }

  public void DisplayResult(int result)
  {
    // implementation
  }
}
```

It's not just the parameter types that can differ; the number of parameters can differ too, as shown in the next example. One overloaded method can invoke another:

```
class MyClass
{
  public int DoSomething(int x) => DoSomething(x, 10);

  public int DoSomething(int x, int y)
  {
    // implementation
  }
}
```

> **NOTE** *With method overloading, it is not sufficient to differ overloads only by the return type. It's also not sufficient to differ them by parameter names. The number of parameters and/or types needs to differ.*

Named Arguments

When invoking methods, the variable name need not be added to the invocation. However, if you have a method signature like the following to move a rectangle:

```
public void MoveAndResize(int x, int y, int width, int height)
```

and you invoke it with the following code snippet, it's not clear from the invocation what numbers are used for what:

```
r.MoveAndResize(30, 40, 20, 40);
```

You can change the invocation to make it immediately clear what the numbers mean:

```
r.MoveAndResize(x: 30, y: 40, width: 20, height: 40);
```

Any method can be invoked using named arguments. You just need to write the name of the variable followed by a colon and the value passed. The compiler gets rid of the name and creates an invocation of the method just as if the variable name is not there—so there's no difference within the compiled code.

You can also change the order of variables this way, and the compiler rearranges it to the correct order. The real advantage to this is shown in the next section with optional arguments.

Optional Arguments

Parameters can also be optional. You must supply a default value for optional parameters, which must be the last ones defined:

```
public void TestMethod(int notOptionalNumber, int optionalNumber = 42)
{
    Console.WriteLine(optionalNumber + notOptionalNumber);
}
```

This method can now be invoked using one or two parameters. When you pass one parameter, the compiler changes the method call to pass 42 with the second parameter:

```
TestMethod(11);
TestMethod(11, 42);
```

> **NOTE** *Because the compiler changes methods with optional parameters to pass the default value, the default value should never change with newer versions of the library. This is a breaking change because the calling application can still have the previous value without recompilation.*

You can define multiple optional parameters, as shown here:

```
public void TestMethod(int n, int opt1 = 11, int opt2 = 22, int opt3 = 33)
{
    Console.WriteLine(n + opt1 + opt2 + opt3);
}
```

This way, the method can be called using one, two, three, or four parameters. The first line of the following code leaves the optional parameters with the values 11, 22, and 33. The second line passes the first three parameters, and the last one has a value of 33:

```
TestMethod(1);
TestMethod(1, 2, 3);
```

With multiple optional parameters, the feature of named arguments shines. When you use named arguments, you can pass any of the optional parameters. For example, this example passes just the last one:

```
TestMethod(1, opt3: 4);
```

> **WARNING** *Pay attention to versioning issues when using optional arguments. One issue is changing default values in newer versions; another issue is changing the number of arguments. It might be tempting to add another optional parameter because it is optional anyway. However, the compiler changes the calling code to fill in all the parameters, and that's the reason why earlier compiled callers fail if another parameter is added later.*

Variable Number of Arguments

When you use optional arguments, you can define a variable number of arguments. However, there's also a different syntax that allows passing a variable number of arguments—and this syntax doesn't have versioning issues.

When you declare the parameter of type array—the sample code uses an int array—and add the params keyword, the method can be invoked using any number of int parameters.

```
public void AnyNumberOfArguments(params int[] data)
{
  foreach (var x in data)
  {
    Console.WriteLine(x);
  }
}
```

> **NOTE** *Arrays are explained in detail in Chapter 6, "Arrays."*

Because the parameter of the method AnyNumberOfArguments is of type int[], you can pass an int array, or because of the params keyword, you can pass zero or more int values:

```
AnyNumberOfArguments(1);
AnyNumberOfArguments(1, 3, 5, 7, 11, 13);
```

If arguments of different types should be passed to methods, you can use an object array:

```
public void AnyNumberOfArguments(params object[] data)
{
  // ...
```

Now it is possible to use any type for the parameters calling this method:

```
AnyNumberOfArguments("text", 42);
```

If the params keyword is used with multiple parameters that are defined with the method signature, params can be used only once, and it must be the last parameter:

```
Console.WriteLine(string format, params object[] arg);
```

> **NOTE** *In case you've overloaded methods, and one of these methods is using the* `params`
> *keyword, the compiler prefers fixed parameters rather than the* `params` *keyword. For*
> *example, if a method is declared with two* `int` *parameters (*`Foo(int, int)`*), and another*
> *method is using the* `params` *keyword (*`Foo(int[] params)`*), when invoking this method with*
> *two* `int` *arguments, the method* `Foo(int, int)` *wins because it has a better match.*

Now that you've looked at the many aspects of methods, let's get into constructors, which are a special kind of method.

Constructors

The syntax for declaring basic constructors is a method that has the same name as the containing class and that does not have any return type:

```
public class MyClass
{
  public MyClass()
  {
  }

  //...
}
```

It's not necessary to provide a constructor for your class. If you don't supply any constructor, the compiler generates a default behind the scenes. This constructor initializes all the member fields to the default values, which is 0 for numbers, `false` for `bool`, and `null` for reference types. When you're using nullable reference types and don't declare your reference types to allow `null`, you'll get a compiler warning if these fields are not initialized.

Constructors follow the same rules for overloading as other methods—that is, you can provide as many overloads to the constructor as you want, provided they are clearly different in signature:

```
public MyClass() // parameterless constructor
{
  // construction code
}

public MyClass(int number) // constructor overload with an int parameter
{
  // construction code
}
```

If you supply any constructors, the compiler does not automatically supply a default one. The default constructor is created only if other constructors are not defined.

Note that it is possible to define constructors as `private` or `protected` so that they are invisible to code in unrelated classes, too:

```
public class MyNumber
{
  private int _number;
  private MyNumber(int number) => _number = number;
  //...
}
```

An example in which this is useful is to create a singleton where an instance can be created only from a static factory method.

Expression Bodies with Constructors

If the implementation of a constructor just consists of a single expression, the constructor can be implemented with an expression-bodied implementation:

```
public class Singleton
{
  private static Singleton s_instance;
  private int _state;
  private Singleton(int state) => _state = state;

  public static Singleton Instance => s_instance ??= new Singleton(42);
}
```

You can also initialize multiple properties with a single expression. You can do this using the tuple syntax as shown in the following code snippet. With the Book constructor, two parameters are required. Putting these two variables in parentheses creates a tuple. This tuple is then deconstructed and put into the properties specified with the left side of the assignment operator. Behind the scenes, the compiler detects that tuples are not needed for the initialization and creates the same code whether you initialize the properties within curly brackets or with the tuple syntax shown:

```
public class Book
{
  public Book(string title, string publisher) =>
    (Title, Publisher) = (title, publisher);

  public string Title { get; }
  public string Publisher { get; }
}
```

Calling Constructors from Other Constructors

When you're creating multiple constructors in a class, you shouldn't duplicate the implementation. Instead, one constructor can invoke another one from a constructor initializer.

Both constructors initialize the same fields. It would clearly be tidier to place all the code in one location. C# has a special syntax known as a *constructor initializer* to enable this:

```
class Car
{
  private string _description;
  private uint _nWheels;
  public Car(string description, uint nWheels)
  {
    _description = description;
    _nWheels = nWheels;
  }
  public Car(string description): this(description, 4)
  {
  }
}
```

In this context, the this keyword simply causes the constructor with the matching parameters to be called. Note that any constructor initializer is executed before the body of the constructor.

Static Constructors

Static members of a class can be used before any instance of this class is created (if any instance is created at all). To initialize static members, you can create a static constructor. The static constructor has the same name as the class (similar to an instance constructor), but the `static` modifier is applied. This constructor cannot have an access modifier applied because it isn't invoked from the code using the class. This constructor is automatically invoked before any other member of this class is called or any instance is created:

```
class MyClass
{
  static MyClass()
  {
    // initialization code
  }
  //...
}
```

The .NET runtime makes no guarantees about when a static constructor will be executed, so you should not place any code in it that relies on it being executed at a particular time (for example, when an assembly is loaded). Nor is it possible to predict in what order static constructors of different classes will execute. However, what is guaranteed is that the static constructor will run at most once, and it will be invoked before your code makes any reference to the class. In C#, the static constructor is usually executed immediately before the first call to any member of the class.

Local Functions

Methods with a `public` access modifier can be invoked from outside of the class. Methods with a `private` access modifier can be invoked from anywhere within the class (from other methods, property accessors, constructors, and so on). To restrict this further, a *local function* can be invoked only from within the method where the local function is declared. The local function has the scope of the method and cannot be invoked from somewhere else.

Within the method `IntroLocalFunctions`, the local function `Add` is defined. Parameters and return types are implemented in the same way as a normal method. Similarly to a normal method, a local function can be implemented by using curly brackets or with an expression-bodied implementation as shown in the following code. Since C# 8, the local function can have the `static` modifier associated if the implementation doesn't access instance members defined with the class or local variables of the method. With the `static` modifier, the compiler makes sure this does not happen and can optimize the generated code. The local function is invoked in the method itself; it cannot be invoked anywhere else in the class. Whether the local function is declared before or after its use is just a matter of taste (code file `MethodSample/LocalFunctionsSample.cs`):

```
public static void IntroLocalFunctions()
{
  static int Add(int x, int y) => x + y;

  int result = Add(3, 7);
  Console.WriteLine("called the local function with this result: {result}");
}
```

With the next code snippet, the local function `Add` is declared without the `static` modifier. In the implementation, this function not only uses the variables specified with the arguments of the function but also variable z, which is specified in the outer scope of the local function, within the scope of the method. When accessing the variable outside of its scope (known as *closure*), the compiler creates a class where the data used within this function is passed in a constructor. Here, the local function needs to be declared after the variables used within the local function. That's why the local function is put at the end of the method `LocalFunctionWithClosure`:

```
public static void LocalFunctionWithClosure()
{
  int z = 3;
```

```
int result = Add(1, 2);
Console.WriteLine("called the local function with this result: {result}");

int Add(int x, int y) => x + y + z;
}
```

> **NOTE** *Local functions can help with error handling when using deferred execution with the* yield *statement. This is shown in Chapter 9, "Language Integrated Query." With C# 9, local functions can have the* extern *modifier. This is shown for invoking native methods in Chapter 13.*

Generic Methods

If you need implementations of methods that support multiple types, you can implement generic methods. The method Swap<T> defines T as a generic type that is used for two arguments and a local variable temp (code file MeethodSample/GenericMethods.cs):

```
class GenericMethods
{
  public static void Swap<T>(ref T x, ref T y)
  {
    T temp;
    temp = x;
    x - y;
    y = temp;
  }
}
```

> **NOTE** *It's a convention to use* T *for the name of the generic type. In case you need multiple generic types, you can use* T1, T2, T3, *and so on. For specific generic types, you can also add a name—for example,* TKey *and* TValue *for generic types representing the type of the key and the type of the value.*

> **NOTE** *With generic methods, you can also invoke members of the generic type other than members of the object class if you define constraints and define that the generic type needs to implement an interface or derive from a base class. This is explained in Chapter 4 where generic types are covered.*

Extension Methods

With extension methods, you can create methods that extend other types.

The following code snippet defines the method GetWordCount that is used to extend the string type. An extension method is not defined by the name of the class but instead by using the this modifier with the parameter.

`GetWordCount` extends the string type because the parameter with the `this` modifier (which needs to be the first parameter) is of type string. Extension methods need to be static and declared in a static class (code file `ExtensionMethods/StringExtensions.cs`):

```
public static class StringExtensions
{
  public static int GetWordCount(this string s) => s.Split().Length;
}
```

To use this extension method, the namespace of the extension class needs to be imported; then the method can be called in the same way as an instance method (code file `ExtensionMethods/Program.cs`):

```
string fox = "the quick brown fox jumped over the lazy dogs";
int wordCount = fox.GetWordCount();
Console.WriteLine($"{wordCount} words");
Console.ReadLine();
```

It might look like extension methods break object-oriented rules in regard to inheritance and encapsulation because methods can be added to an existing type without inheriting from it and without changing the type. However, you can only access public members. Extension methods are really just "syntax sugar" because the compiler changes the invocation of the method to call a static method that's passing the instance as the parameter, as shown here:

```
int wordCount = StringExtensions.GetWordCount(fox);
```

Why would you create extension methods instead of calling static methods? The code can become a lot easier to read. Just check into the extension methods implemented for LINQ (see Chapter 9) or the extension methods used to configure configuration and logging providers (see Chapter 15, "Dependency Injection and Configuration").

Anonymous Types

Chapter 2 discusses the `var` keyword in reference to implicitly typed variables. When used with the `new` keyword, you can create anonymous types. An *anonymous type* is simply a nameless class that inherits from `object`. The definition of the class is inferred from the initializer, just as with implicitly typed variables.

For example, if you need an object that contains a person's first, middle, and last name, the declaration would look like this:

```
var captain = new
{
  FirstName = "James",
  MiddleName = "Tiberius",
  LastName = "Kirk"
};
```

This would produce an object with `FirstName`, `MiddleName`, and `LastName` read-only properties. If you were to create another object that looked like this:

```
var doctor = new
{
  FirstName = "Leonard",
  MiddleName = string.Empty,
  LastName = "McCoy"
};
```

then the types of `captain` and `doctor` are the same. You could set `captain = doctor`, for example. This is possible only if all the properties match.

The names for the members of anonymous types can be inferred if the values that are being set come from another object. This way, the initializer can be abbreviated. If you already have a class that contains the properties FirstName, MiddleName, and LastName and you have an instance of that class with the instance name person, then the captain object could be initialized like this:

```
var captain = new
{
  person.FirstName,
  person.MiddleName,
  person.LastName
};
```

The property names from the person object are inferred in the new object named captain, so the object named captain has FirstName, MiddleName, and LastName properties.

The actual type name of anonymous types is unknown, which is where the name comes from. The compiler "makes up" a name for the type, but only the compiler is ever able to make use of it. Therefore, you can't and shouldn't plan on using any type reflection on the new objects because you will not get consistent results.

RECORDS

So far in this chapter, you've seen that records are reference types that support value semantics. This type allows reducing the code you need to write because the compiler automatically implements comparing records by value and gives some more features, which are explained in this section.

Immutable Types

A main use case for records is to create immutable types (although you can also create mutable types with records). An immutable type just contains members where the state of the type cannot be changed. You can initialize such a type in a constructor or with an object initializer, but you can't change any values afterward.

Immutable types are useful with multithreading. When you're using multiple threads to access the immutable object, you don't need to worry with synchronization because the values cannot change.

An example of an immutable type is the String class. This class does not define any member that is allowed to change its content. Methods such as ToUpper (which changes the string to uppercase) always return a new string, but the original string passed to the constructor remains unchanged.

Nominal Records

Records can be created in two kinds: nominal and positional records. A nominal record looks like a class just using the record keyword instead of the class keyword, as shown with the type Book1. Here, init-only set accessors are used to forbid state changes after an instance has been created (code file RecordsSample/Program.cs):

```
public record Book1
{
    public string Title { get; init; } = string.Empty;
    public string Publisher { get; init; } = string.Empty;
}
```

You can add constructors and all the other members you learned about in this chapter. The compiler just creates a class with the record syntax. What's different from classes is that the compiler creates some more functionality inside this class. The compiler overrides the GetHashCode and ToString methods of the base class object, creates methods and operator overloads to compare different values for equality, and creates methods to clone existing objects and create new ones where object initializers can be used to change some property values.

> **NOTE** *See Chapter 5 for information about operator overloads.*

Positional Records

The second way to implement a record is to use the positional record syntax. With this syntax, parentheses are used after the name of the record to specify the members. This syntax has the name *primary constructor*. The compiler creates a class from this code as well, with init-only set accessors for the types used with the primary constructor and a constructor with the same parameters to initialize the properties (code file `RecordsSample/Program.cs`):

```
public record Book2(string Title, string Publisher);
```

You can use curly brackets to add what you need to the already existing implementation—for example, by adding overloaded constructors, methods, or any other members you've seen earlier in this chapter:

```
public record Book2(string Title, string Publisher)
{
  // add your members, overloads
}
```

As the compiler creates a constructor with parameters, you can instantiate an object as you're used to—by passing the values to the constructor (code file `RecordsSample/Program.cs`):

```
Book2 b2 = new("Professional C#", "Wrox Press");
Console.WriteLine(b2);
```

Because the compiler creates a `ToString` method that is implicitly invoked by passing the variable to the `WriteLine` method, this is what's shown on the console: the name of the class followed by the property names with their values in curly brackets:

```
Book2 { Title = Professional C#, Publisher = Wrox Press }
```

With positional records, the compiler creates the same members as with nominal records and adds methods for deconstruction. Deconstruction is explained later in this chapter in the section "Deconstruction."

Equality Comparison with Records

With classes, the default implementation for equality is to compare the reference. Creating two new objects of the same type that are initialized to the same values are different because they reference different objects in the heap. This is different with records. With the equality implementation of records, two records are equal if their property values are the same.

In the following code snippet, two records that contain the same values are created. The `object` `.ReferenceEquals` method returns `false`, because these are two different references. Using the equal operator `==` returns `true` because this operator is implemented with the record type (code file `RecordsSample/Program.cs`):

```
Book1 book1a = new() { Title = "Professional C#", Publisher = "Wrox Press" };
Book1 book1b = new() { Title = "Professional C#", Publisher = "Wrox Press" };
if (!object.ReferenceEquals(book1a, book1b))
  Console.WriteLine("Two different references for equal records");

if (book1a == book1b)
  Console.WriteLine("Both records have the same values");
```

The record type implements the `IEquality` interface with the `Equals` method, as well as the equality `==` and the inequality `!=` operators.

With Expressions

Records make it easy to create immutable types, but there's a new feature with records for easily creating new record instances. The .NET Compiler Platform (also known by the name Roslyn) is built with immutable objects and many `With` methods to create new objects from existing ones. With the C# 9 enhancement, the `with` expressions, there's a lot of simplification that can be used by the Roslyn team. The code created with the record syntax includes a copy constructor and a Clone method with a hidden name where all the values of the existing object are copied to a new instance that's returned from this method. The `with` expression now makes use of this Clone method, and with the init-only set accessors, you can use object initialization to set the values that should be different.

```
var aNewBook = book1a with { Title = "Professional C# and .NET - 2024" };
```

> **NOTE** *See Chapter 4 for inheritance not only with classes but also with records.*

STRUCTS

So far, you have seen how classes and records offer a great way to encapsulate objects in your program. You have also seen how they are stored on the heap in a way that gives you much more flexibility in data lifetime but with a slight cost in performance. Objects stored in the heap require work from the garbage collector to remove the memory of the objects that are no longer needed. To reduce the work needed by the garbage collector, you can use the stack for smaller objects.

Chapter 2 discusses predefined value types such as `int` and `double`, which are represented as a struct type. You can create such structs on your own.

Just by using the `struct` keyword instead of the `class` keyword, the type is by default stored in the stack instead of the heap.

The following code snippet defines a struct called `Dimensions`, which simply stores the length and width of an item. Suppose you're writing a furniture-arranging program that enables users to experiment with rearranging their furniture on the computer, and you want to store the dimensions of each item of furniture. All you have is two numbers, which you'll find convenient to treat as a pair rather than individually. There is no need for a lot of methods, or for you to be able to inherit from the class, and you certainly don't want to have the .NET runtime go to the trouble of bringing in the heap, with all the performance implications, just to store two `doubles` (code file `StructsSample/Dimensions.cs`):

```
public readonly struct Dimensions
{
  public Dimensions(double length, double width)
  {
    Length = length;
    Width = width;
  }

  public double Length { get; }
  public double Width { get; }
  //...
}
```

> **NOTE** *If the members of a struct don't change any state (other than the constructors), the struct can be declared with the* `readonly` *modifier. The compiler will make sure you don't add any members that change state.*

Defining members for structs is done in the same way as defining them for classes and records. You've already seen a constructor with the `Dimensions` struct. The following code demonstrates adding the property `Diagonal` invoking the `Sqrt` method of the `Math` class (code file `StructsSample/Dimensions.cs`):

```
public struct Dimensions
{
  //...
  public double Diagonal => Math.Sqrt(Length * Length + Width * Width);
}
```

Structs make use of the previously discussed pass by value semantics, where values are copied. This is not the only difference with classes and records:

➤ Structs do not support inheritance. You can implement interfaces with structs but not derive from another struct.

➤ Structs always have a default constructor. With a class, if you define a constructor, the default constructor no longer gets generated. The struct type is different than a class. A struct always has a default constructor, and you cannot create a custom parameterless constructor.

➤ With a struct, you can specify how the fields are laid out in memory. This is examined in Chapter 13.

➤ Structs are stored on the stack or inline (if they are part of another object that is stored on the heap). When a struct is used as an object (for example, passed to an object parameter or an object-based method is invoked), boxing occurs, and the value is copied to the heap as well.

ENUM TYPES

An enumeration is a value type that contains a list of named constants, such as the `Color` type shown here. The enumeration type is defined by using the `enum` keyword:

```
public enum Color
{
  Red,
  Green,
  Blue
}
```

You can declare variables of `enum` types, such as the variable `c1`, and assign a value from the enumeration by setting one of the named constants prefixed with the name of the `enum` type (code file `EnumSample/Program.cs`):

```
void ColorSamples()
{
  Color c1 = Color.Red;
  Console.WriteLine(c1);

  //...
}
```

When you run the program, the console output shows `Red`, which is the constant value of the enumeration.

By default, the type behind the enum type is an `int`. You can change the underlying type to other integral types (`byte`, `short`, `int`, `long` with signed and unsigned variants). The values of the named constants are incremental values starting with 0, but you can change them to other values (code file `EnumSample/Color.cs`):

```
public enum Color : short
{
  Red = 1,
  Green = 2,
  Blue = 3
}
```

You can change a number to an enumeration value and back using casts.

```
Color c2 = (Color)2;
short number = (short)c2;
```

You can also use an enum type to assign multiple options to a variable and not just one of the enum constants. To make exclusive enum values, the numbers assigned to the values should each set a single different bit.

The enum type `DaysOfWeek` defines different values for every day. Setting different bits can be done easily using hexadecimal values that are assigned using the `0x` prefix. The `Flags` attribute is information for the compiler for creating a different string representation of the values—for example, setting the value 3 to a variable of `DaysOfWeek` results in `Monday, Tuesday` when you use the `Flags` attribute (code file `EnumSample/DaysOfWeek.cs`):

```
[Flags]
public enum DaysOfWeek
{
  Monday = 0x1,
  Tuesday = 0x2,
  Wednesday = 0x4,
  Thursday = 0x8,
  Friday = 0x10,
  Saturday = 0x20,
  Sunday = 0x40
}
```

With such an enum declaration, you can assign a variable multiple values using the logical OR operator (code file `EnumSample/Program.cs`):

```
DaysOfWeek mondayAndWednesday = DaysOfWeek.Monday | DaysOfWeek.Wednesday;
Console.WriteLine(mondayAndWednesday);
```

When you run the program, the output is a string representation of the days:

```
Monday, Wednesday
```

When you set different bits, you also can combine single bits to cover multiple values, such as `Weekend` with a value of `0x60`. The value `0x60` is created by combining `Saturday` and `Sunday` with the logical OR operator. `Workday` is set to `0x1f` to combine all days from `Monday` to `Friday`, and `AllWeek` to combine `Workday` and `Weekend` with the logical OR operator (code file `EnumSample/DaysOfWeek.cs`):

```
[Flags]
public enum DaysOfWeek
{
  Monday = 0x1,
  Tuesday = 0x2,
  Wednesday = 0x4,
  Thursday = 0x8,
  Friday = 0x10,
```

```
      Saturday = 0x20,
      Sunday = 0x40,
      Weekend = Saturday | Sunday,
      Workday = 0x1f,
      AllWeek = Workday | Weekend
   }
```

With this in place, you can assign `DaysOfWeek.Weekend` directly to a variable, but assigning the separate values `DaysOfWeek.Saturday` and `DaysOfWeek.Sunday` combined with the logical OR operator gives the same result. The output shown is the string representation of `Weekend`:

```
   DaysOfWeek weekend = DaysOfWeek.Saturday | DaysOfWeek.Sunday;
   Console.WriteLine(weekend);
```

When you're working with enumerations, the class `Enum` is sometimes a big help for dynamically getting some information about enum types. `Enum` offers methods to parse strings to get the corresponding enumeration constant and to get all the names and values of an enum type.

The following code snippet uses a string to get the corresponding `Color` value using `Enum.TryParse` (code file `EnumSample/Program.cs`):

```
   if (Enum.TryParse<Color>("Red", out Color red))
   {
      Console.WriteLine($"successfully parsed {red}");
   }
```

> **NOTE** `Enum.TryParse` *is a generic method where* `T` *is a generic parameter type. The return value is a Boolean to return* `true` *when parsing succeeded. To return the parsed enum result, the* `out` *keyword is used as a modifier of the parameter. With the* `out` *keyword, you can specify to return multiple values from a method. This keyword is discussed in the next section.*

The `Enum.GetNames` method returns a string array of all the names of the enumeration:

```
   foreach (var color in Enum.GetNames(typeof(Color)))
   {
      Console.WriteLine(color);
   }
```

When you run the application, this is the output:

```
   Red
   Green
   Blue
```

To get all the values of the enumeration, you can use the method `Enum.GetValues`. To get the integral value, it needs to be cast to the underlying type of the enumeration, which is done by the `foreach` statement:

```
   foreach (short color in Enum.GetValues(typeof(Color)))
   {
      Console.WriteLine(color);
   }
```

REF, IN, AND OUT

A *value type* is passed by value; thus, the value of a variable is copied when assigned to another variable, such as when it's passed to a method. There's a way around that. If you use the `ref` keyword, a value type is passed by reference. In this section, you learn about the parameter and return type modifiers `ref`, `in`, and `out`.

ref Parameters

The following code snippet defines the method `ChangeAValueType`, where an int is passed by reference. Remember, the int is declared as struct, so this behavior is valid with custom structs as well. By default, the int would be passed by value. Because of the `ref` modifier, the int is passed by reference (using an address of the int variable). Within the implementation, now the variable named x references the same data on the stack as the variable a does. Changing the value of x also changes the value of a, so after the invocation, the variable a contains the value 2 (code file `RefInOutSample/Program.cs`):

```
int a = 1;
ChangeAValueType(ref a);
Console.WriteLine($"the value of a changed to {a}");

void ChangeAValueType(ref int x)
{
  x = 2;
}
```

Passing a value type by reference requires the `ref` keyword with the method declaration and when calling the method. This is important information for the caller; knowing the method receiving this value type can change the content.

Now you might wonder if it could be useful to pass a reference by using the `ref` keyword. Passing a reference allows the method to change the content anyway. Indeed, it can be useful, as the following code snippet demonstrates. The method `ChangingAReferenceByReference` specifies the `ref` modifier with the argument of type `SomeData`, which is a class. In the implementation, first the value of the `Value` property is changed to 2. After this, a new instance is created, which references an object with a `Value` of 3. If you try to remove the `ref` keyword from the method declaration, as well as the invocation of this method, after the invocation `data1.Value` has the value 2. Without the `ref` keyword, the `data1` variable references the object on the heap and the `data` variable at the beginning of the method. After creating a new object, the `data` variable references a new object on the heap, which then contains the value 3. With the `ref` keyword used as in the sample, the `data` variable references the `data1` variable; it's a pointer to a pointer. This way, a new instance can be created within the `ChangingAReferenceByRef` method, and the variable `data1` references this new object instead of the old one:

```
SomeData data1 = new() { Value = 1 };
ChangingAReferenceByRef(ref data1);
Console.WriteLine($"the new value of data1.Value is: {data1.Value}");

void ChangingAReferenceByRef(ref SomeData data)
{
  data.Value = 2;
  data = new SomeData { Value = 3 };
}

class SomeData
{
  public int Value { get; set; }
}
```

in Parameters

If you want to avoid the overhead of copying a value type when passing it to a method but don't want to change the value within the method, you can use the `in` modifier.

For the next sample code, the `SomeValue` struct, which contains four `int` values, is defined (code file `RefInOutSample/Program.cs`):

```
struct SomeValue
{
  public SomeValue(int value1, int value2, int value3, int value4)
  {
    Value1 = value1;
    Value2 = value2;
    Value3 = value3;
    Value4 = value4;
  }
  public int Value1 { get; set; }
  public int Value2 { get; set; }
  public int Value3 { get; set; }
  public int Value4 { get; set; }
}
```

If you declare a method where the `SomeValue` struct is passed as an argument, the four `int` values need to be copied on method invocation. When you use the `ref` keyword, you don't need a copy, and you can pass a reference. However, with the `ref` keyword, the caller might not want the called method to make any change. To guarantee that changes are not happening, you use the `in` modifier. With this modifier, a pass by reference is happening, but the compiler does not allow change to any value when the data variable is used. Data is now a read-only variable:

```
void PassValueByReferenceReadonly(in SomeValue data)
{
  // data.Value1 = 4; - you cannot change a value, it's a read-only variable!
}
```

ref return

To avoid copying the value on return of a method, you can declare the return type with the `ref` keyword and use `return ref`. The `Max` method receives two `SomeValue` structs with the parameters and returns the larger of these two. With the parameters, the values are not copied using the `ref` modifier, as shown here:

```
ref SomeValue Max(ref SomeValue x, ref SomeValue y)
{
  int sumx = x.Value1 + x.Value2 + x.Value3 + x.Value4;
  int sumy = y.Value1 + y.Value2 + y.Value3 + y.Value4;

  if (sumx > sumy)
  {
    return ref x;
  }
  else
  {
    return ref y;
  }
}
```

Within the implementation of the Max method, you can replace the if/else statement with a *conditional ref expression*. With this, the ref keyword needs to be used with the expression to compare sumx and sumy. Based on the result, a ref to x or to y is written to a ref local, which is then returned:

```
ref SomeValue Max(ref SomeValue x, ref SomeValue y)
{
  int sumx = x.Value1 + x.Value2 + x.Value3 + x.Value4;
  int sumy = y.Value1 + y.Value2 + y.Value3 + y.Value4;

  ref SomeValue result = ref (sumx > sumy) ? ref x : ref y;
  return ref result;
}
```

Whether the returned value should be copied or a reference should be used is a decision from the caller. In the following code snippet, with the first invocation of the Max method, the result is copied to the bigger1 variable, although the method is declared to return a ref. There's not a compiler error with the first version (contrary to the ref parameters). You will not have any issues when the value is copied—other than the performance hit. With the second invocation, the ref keyword is used to invoke the method to get a ref return. With this invocation, the result needs to be written to a ref local. The third invocation writes the result into a ref readonly local. With the Max method, there's no change needed. The readonly used here is only to specify that the bigger3 variable will not be changed, and the compiler complains if properties are set to change its values:

```
SomeValue one = new SomeValue(1, 2, 3, 4);
SomeValue two = new SomeValue(5, 6, 7, 8);

SomeValue bigger1 = Max(ref one, ref two);
ref SomeValue bigger2 = ref Max(ref one, ref two);
ref readonly SomeValue bigger3 = ref Max(ref one, ref two);
```

The Max method doesn't change any of its inputs. This allows using the in keyword with the parameters as shown with the MaxReadonly method. However, here the declaration of the return must be changed to ref readonly. If this change wouldn't be necessary, the caller of this method would be allowed to change one of the inputs of the MaxReadonly method after receiving the result:

```
ref readonly SomeValue MaxReadonly(in SomeValue x, in SomeValue y)
{
  int sumx = x.Value1 + x.Value2 + x.Value3 + x.Value4;
  int sumy = y.Value1 + y.Value2 + y.Value3 + y.Value4;

  return ref (sumx > sumy) ? ref x : ref y;
}
```

Now the caller is required to write the result to a ref readonly or to copy the result into a new local. With bigger5, readonly is not required because the original value received is copied:

```
ref readonly SomeValue bigger4 = ref MaxReadonly(in one, in two);
SomeValue bigger5 = MaxReadonly(in one, in two);
```

out Parameters

If a method should return multiple values, there are different options. One option is to create a custom type. Another option is to use the ref keyword with parameters. Using the ref keyword, the parameter needs to be initialized before invoking the method. With the ref keyword, data is passed into and returned from the method. If the method should just return data, you can use the out keyword.

The int.Parse method expects a string to be passed and returns an int—if the parsing succeeds. If the string cannot be parsed to an int, an exception is thrown. To avoid such exceptions, you can instead use the `int.TryParse` method. This method returns a Boolean whether the parsing is successful or not. The result of the parse operation is returned with an `out` parameter.

This is the declaration of the `TryParse` method with the `int` type:

```
bool TryParse(string? s, out int result);
```

To invoke the `TryParse` method, an `int` is passed with the `out` modifier. Using the `out` modifier, the variable doesn't need to be declared before invoking the method and doesn't need to be initialized:

```
Console.Write("Please enter a number: ");
string? input = Console.ReadLine();
if (int.TryParse(input, out int x))
{
  Console.WriteLine();
  Console.WriteLine($"read an int: {x}");
}
```

TUPLES

With arrays, you can combine multiple objects of the same type into one object. When you're using classes, structs, and records, you can combine multiple objects into one object and add properties, methods, events, and all the different members of types. Tuples enable you to combine multiple objects of different types into one without the complexity of creating custom types.

To better understand some advantages of tuples, let's take a look at what a method can return. To return a result from a method that returns multiple results, you need to either create a custom type where you can combine the different result types or use the `ref` or `out` keywords with parameters. Using `ref` and `out` has an important restriction: you cannot use this with asynchronous methods. Creating custom types has its advantages, but in some cases, this is not needed. You have a simpler path with tuples and can return a tuple from a method. As of C# 7, tuples are integrated with the C# syntax.

Declaring and Initializing Tuples

A tuple can be declared using parentheses and initialized using a tuple literal that is created with parentheses as well. In the following code snippet, on the left side, a tuple variable `tuple1` that contains a `string`, an `int`, and a `Book` is declared. On the right side, a tuple literal is used to create a tuple with the string `magic`, the number `42`, and a `Book` object initialized using the primary constructor of the `Book` record. The tuple can be accessed using the variable `tuple1` with the members declared in the parentheses (`AString`, `Number`, and `Book` in this example; code file `TuplesSample/Program.cs`):

```
void IntroTuples()
{
  (string AString, int Number, Book Book) tuple1 =
    ("magic", 42, new Book("Professional C#", "Wrox Press"));
    Console.WriteLine($"a string: {tuple1.AString}, " +
      $"number: {tuple1.Number}, " +
      $"book: {tuple1.Book}");
  //...
}

public record Book(string Title, string Publisher);
```

When you run the application (the top-level statements invoke `IntroTuples`), the output shows the values of the tuple:

```
a string: magic, number: 42, book: Book { Title = Professional C#, Publisher =
Wrox Press }
```

NOTE *There was some discussion on naming tuples using camelCase or PascalCase. Micro-soft doesn't give a guideline on naming internal and private members, but with public APIs it was decided to name tuple members using PascalCase. After all, the names you specify with the tuple are public members, and these are usually PascalCase. See* https://github.com/dotnet/runtime/issues/27939 *if you are interested in this discussion between different teams at Microsoft and the community.*

The tuple literal also can be assigned to a tuple variable without declaring its members. This way the members of the tuple are accessed using the member names of the ValueTuple struct: Item1, Item2, and Item3:

```
var tuple2 = ("magic", 42, new Book("Professional C#", "Wrox Press"));
Console.WriteLine($"a string: {tuple2.Item1}, number: {tuple2.Item2}, " +
  $"book: {tuple2.Item3}");
```

You can assign names to the tuple fields in the tuple literal by defining the name followed by a colon, which is the same syntax as with object literals:

```
var tuple3 = (AString: "magic", Number: 42,
  Book: new Book("Professional C#", "Wrox Press"));
```

With all this, names are just a convenience. You can assign one tuple to another one when the types match; the names do not matter:

```
(string S, int N, Book B) tuple4 = tuple3;
```

The name of the tuple members can also be inferred from the source. With the variable tuple5, the second member is a string with the title of the book. A name for this member is not assigned, but because the property has the name Title, Title is automatically taken for the tuple member name:

```
Book book = new("Professional C#", "Wrox Press");
var tuple5 = (ANumber: 42, book.Title);
Console.WriteLine(tuple5.Title);
```

Tuple Deconstruction

Tuples can be deconstructed into variables. To do this, you just need to remove the tuple variable from the previous code sample and define variable names in parentheses. The variables that contain the values of the tuple parts can then be directly accessed. In case some variables are not needed, you can use *discards*. Discards are C# placeholder variables with the name _. Discards are meant to just ignore the results, as shown with the second deconstruction in the following code snippet (code file TuplesSample/Program.cs):

```
void TuplesDeconstruction()
{
  var tuple1 = (AString: "magic",
    Number: 42, Book: new Book("Professional C#", "Wrox Press"));
  (string aString, int number, Book book) = tuple1;

  Console.WriteLine($"a string: {aString}, number: {number}, book: {book}");

  (_, _, var book1) = tuple1;
  Console.WriteLine(book1.Title);
}
```

Returning Tuples

Let's get into a more useful example: a method returning a tuple. The method `Divide` from the following code snippet receives two parameters and returns a tuple consisting of two `int` values. Tuple results are created by putting the methods return group within parentheses (code file `Tuples/Program.cs`):

```
static (int result, int remainder) Divide(int dividend, int divisor)
{
  int result = dividend / divisor;
  int remainder = dividend % divisor;
  return (result, remainder);
}
```

The result is deconstructed into the `result` and `remainder` variables:

```
private static void ReturningTuples()
{
  (int result, int remainder) = Divide(7, 2);
  Console.WriteLine($"7 / 2 - result: {result}, remainder: {remainder}");
}
```

> **NOTE** *When you're using tuples, you can avoid declaring method signatures with* out *parameters.* out *parameters cannot be used with* async *methods; this restriction does not apply with tuples.*

VALUETUPLE

When you're using the C# tuple syntax, the C# compiler creates `ValueTuple` structures behind the scenes. .NET defines seven generic `ValueTuple` structures for one to seven generic parameters and another one where the eighth parameter can be another tuple. Using a tuple literal results in an invocation of `Tuple.Create`. The tuple structure defines public fields named `Item1`, `Item2`, `Item3`, and so on to access all the items.

For the names of the elements, the compiler uses the attribute `TupleElementNames` to store the custom names of the tuple members. This information is read from the compiler to invoke the correct members.

> **NOTE** *Attributes are covered in detail in Chapter 12, "Reflection, Metadata, and Source Generators."*

DECONSTRUCTION

You've already seen deconstruction with tuples—writing tuples into simple variables. You also can do deconstruction with any custom type: deconstructing a class or struct into its parts.

For example, you can deconstruct the previously shown `Person` class into first name, last name, and age. In the sample code, the age returned from the deconstruction is ignored using discard (code file `Classes/Program.cs`):

```
//...
(var first, var last, _) = katharina;
Console.WriteLine($"{first} {last}");
```

All you need to do is create a `Deconstruct` method (also known by the name *deconstructor*) that fills the separate parts into parameters with the `out` modifier (code file `Classes/Person.cs`):

```
public class Person
{
  //...
  public void Deconstruct(out string firstName, out string lastName,
    out int age)
  {
    firstName = FirstName;
    lastName = LastName;
    age = Age;
  }
}
```

Deconstruction is implemented with the method name `Deconstruct`. This method is always of type `void` and returns the parts with multiple `out` parameters. Instead of creating a member of a class, for deconstruction you can also create an extension method as shown here:

```
public static class PersonExtensions
{
  public static void Deconstruct(this Person person, out string firstName,
    out string lastName, out int age)
  {
    firstName = person.FirstName;
    lastName = person.LastName;
    age = person.Age;
  }
}
```

> **NOTE** *With positional records, the* `Deconstruct` *method is implemented from the compiler. When you're defining a primary constructor, the compiler knows about the ordering of the parameters for the* `Deconstruct` *method and can create it automatically. With nominal records, you can create a custom implementation of the* `Deconstruct` *method similar to classes you've seen. In any case (with positional or nominal records, or with classes), you can define overloads with different parameter types as needed.*

PATTERN MATCHING

Chapter 2 covers basic functionality with pattern matching using the `is` operator and the `switch` statement. This can now be extended with some more features on pattern matching, such as using tuples and property patterns.

Pattern Matching with Tuples

The previous chapter included a sample of simple pattern matching with traffic lights. Now let's extend this sample with not just a simple flow from red to green to amber to red. . . but to change to different states after amber depending on what the previous light was. Pattern matching can be based on tuple values.

> **NOTE** *The traffic light sequences are different in many countries worldwide. With a change from amber (or yellow) to red in Canada and a few other countries, amber and red appear together to indicate a change. In most European countries, changing from red to green, the red and amber lights are displayed together for one, two, or three seconds. In Austria, China, Russia, Israel, and more, the green light starts flashing at the end of the go phase. If you are interested in the details, read* `https://en.wikipedia.org/wiki/Traffic-light_signal-ling_and_operation.`

The method `NextLightUsingTuples` receives enum values for the current and previous traffic light in two parameters. The two parameters are combined to a tuple with `(current, previous)` to define the switch expression based on this tuple. With the switch expression, tuple patterns are used. The first case matches when the current light has the value `Red`. The value of the previous light is ignored using a discard. The `NextLightUsingTuples` method is declared to return a tuple with `Current` and `Previous` properties. In the first match, a tuple that matches this return type is returned with `(Amber, current)` to specify the new value `Amber` for the current light. In all the cases, the previous light is set from the current light that was received. When the current light is `Amber`, now the tuple pattern results in different outcomes depending on the previous light. If the previous light was `Red`, the new light returned is `Green`, and vice versa (code file `PatternMatchingSample/Program.cs`):

```
(TrafficLight Current, TrafficLight Previous)
  NextLightUsingTuples(TrafficLight current, TrafficLight previous) =>
    (current, previous) switch
    {
      (Red, _) => (Amber, current),
      (Amber, Red) => (Green, current),
      (Green, _) => (Amber, current),
      (Amber, Green) => (Red, current),
      _ => throw new InvalidOperationException()
    };
```

With the following code snippet, the method `NextLightUsingTuples` is invoked in a `for` loop. The return value is deconstructed into `currentLight` and `previousLight` variables to write the current light information to the console and to invoke the `NextLightUsingTuples` method in the next iteration:

```
var previousLight = Red;
var currentLight = Red;
for (int i = 0; i < 10; i++)
{
  (currentLight, previousLight) = NextLightUsingTuples(currentLight,
    previousLight);
  Console.Write($"{currentLight} - ");
  await Task.Delay(1000);
}
Console.WriteLine();
```

> **NOTE** *With the statement* `await Task.Delay(1000);` *the application just waits for one second before the next statement is invoked. With top-level statements, you can directly add* `async` *methods as shown. In case you want to add this statement to a method, the method needs to have the async modifier and it is best to return a* `Task`. *This is covered in detail in Chapter 11, "Tasks and Asynchronous Programming."*

Property Pattern

Let's extend the traffic light sample again. When you're using tuples, additional values and types can be added to extend the functionality. However, at some point this doesn't help with readability, and using classes or records is helpful.

One extension to the traffic light is having different timings for the different light phases. Another extension is used in some countries: before the light changes from the green to the amber light, another phase is introduced: the green light blinks three times. To keep up with the different states, the record `TrafficLightState` is introduced (code file `PatternMatchingSample/Program.cs`):

```
public record TrafficLightState(TrafficLight CurrentLight,
    TrafficLight PreviousLight, int Milliseconds, int BlinkCount = 0);
```

The enum type `TrafficLight` is extended to include `GreenBlink` and `AmberBlink`:

```
public enum TrafficLight
{
  Red,
  Amber,
  Green,
  GreenBlink,
  AmberBlink
}
```

The new method `NextLightUsingRecords` receives a parameter of type `TrafficLightState` with the current light state and returns a `TrafficLightState` with the new state. In the implementation, a `switch` expression is used again. This time, the cases are selected using the *property pattern*. If the property `CurrentLight` of the variable `trafficLightState` has the value `AmberBlink`, a new `TrafficLightState` with the current red light is returned. When the `CurrentLight` is set to `Amber`, the `PreviousLight` property is verified as well. Depending on the `PreviousLight` value, different records are returned. Another pattern is used in this scenario—the *relational pattern* that is new with C# 9. `BlinkCount: < 3` references the `BlinkCount` property and verifies whether the value is smaller than 3. If this is the case, the returned `TrafficLightState` is cloned from the previous state using the `with` expression, and the `BlinkCount` is incremented by 1:

```
TrafficLightState NextLightUsingRecords(TrafficLightState trafficLightState)
    => trafficLightState switch
    {
      { CurrentLight: AmberBlink } =>
        new TrafficLightState(Red, trafficLightState.PreviousLight, 3000),
      { CurrentLight: Red } =>
        new TrafficLightState(Amber, trafficLightState.CurrentLight, 200),
      { CurrentLight: Amber, PreviousLight: Red} =>
        new TrafficLightState(Green, trafficLightState.CurrentLight, 2000),
      { CurrentLight: Green } =>
        new TrafficLightState(GreenBlink, trafficLightState.CurrentLight,
          100, 1),
      { CurrentLight: GreenBlink, BlinkCount: < 3 } =>
        trafficLightState with
          { BlinkCount = trafficLightState.BlinkCount + 1 },
      { CurrentLight: GreenBlink } =>
        new TrafficLightState(Amber, trafficLightState.CurrentLight, 200),
      { CurrentLight: Amber, PreviousLight: GreenBlink } =>
        new TrafficLightState(Red, trafficLightState.CurrentLight, 3000),
      _ => throw new InvalidOperationException()
    };
```

The method `NextLightUsingRecords` is invoked in a `for` loop similar to the sample before. Now, an instance of `TrafficLightState` is passed as an argument to the method `NextLightUsingRecords`. The new value is received from this method, and the current state is shown on the console:

```
TrafficLightState currentLightState = new(AmberBlink, AmberBlink, 2000);

for (int i = 0; i < 20; i++)
{
  currentLightState = NextLightUsingRecords(currentLightState);
  Console.WriteLine($"{currentLightState.CurrentLight},
    {currentLightState.Milliseconds}");
  await Task.Delay(currentLightState.Milliseconds);
}
```

PARTIAL TYPES

The `partial` keyword allows a type to span multiple files. Typically, a code generator of some type is generating part of a class, and having the class in multiple files can be beneficial. Let's assume you want to make some additions to the class that is automatically generated from a tool. If the tool reruns, your changes are lost. The `partial` keyword is helpful for splitting the class into two files and making your changes to the file that is not defined by the code generator.

To use the `partial` keyword, simply place `partial` before `class`, `struct`, or `interface`. In the following example, the class `SampleClass` resides in two separate source files: `SampleClassAutogenerated.cs` and `SampleClass.cs`:

```
//SampleClassAutogenerated.cs
partial class SampleClass
{
  public void MethodOne() { }
}

//SampleClass.cs
partial class SampleClass
{
  public void MethodTwo() { }
}
```

When the project that contains the two source files is compiled, a single type called `SampleClass` will be created with two methods: `MethodOne` and `MethodTwo`.

Nested partials are allowed as long as the `partial` keyword precedes the `class` keyword in the nested type. Attributes, XML comments, interfaces, generic-type parameter attributes, and members are combined when the partial types are compiled into the type. Given these two source files:

```
// SampleClassAutogenerated.cs
[CustomAttribute]
partial class SampleClass: SampleBaseClass, ISampleClass
{
  public void MethodOne() { }
}

// SampleClass.cs
[AnotherAttribute]
partial class SampleClass: IOtherSampleClass
```

```
{
  public void MethodTwo() { }
}
```

the equivalent source file would be as follows after the compile:

```
[CustomAttribute]
[AnotherAttribute]
partial class SampleClass: SampleBaseClass, ISampleClass, IOtherSampleClass
{
  public void MethodOne() { }
  public void MethodTwo() { }
}
```

> **NOTE** *Although it may be tempting to create huge classes that span multiple files and possibly have different developers working on different files but the same class, the* partial *keyword was not designed for this use. With such a scenario, it would be better to split the big class into several smaller classes to have a class just for one purpose.*

Partial classes can contain partial methods. This is extremely useful if generated code should invoke methods that might not exist at all. The programmer extending the partial class can decide to create a custom implementation of the partial method or do nothing. The following code snippet contains a partial class with the method `MethodOne` that invokes the method `APartialMethod`. The method `APartialMethod` is declared with the `partial` keyword; thus, it does not need any implementation. If there's not an implementation, the compiler removes the invocation of this method:

```
//SampleClassAutogenerated.cs
partial class SampleClass
{
  public void MethodOne()
  {
    APartialMethod();
  }
  public partial void APartialMethod();
}
```

An implementation of the partial method can be done within any other part of the partial class, as shown in the following code snippet. With this method in place, the compiler creates code within `MethodOne` to invoke this `APartialMethod` declared here:

```
// SampleClass.cs
partial class SampleClass: IOtherSampleClass
{
  public void APartialMethod()
  {
    // implementation of APartialMethod
  }
}
```

> **NOTE** *Prior to C# 9, partial methods had to be declared* void. *This is no longer necessary. However, with partial methods that do not return* void, *an implementation is required. This is an extremely useful enhancement, such as when using code generators. Code generators are covered in Chapter 12.*

SUMMARY

This chapter examined C# syntax for creating custom types with classes, records, structs, and tuples. You've seen how to declare static and instance fields, properties, methods, and constructors, both with curly brackets and with expression-bodied members.

In a continuation of Chapter 2, you've also seen more features with pattern matching, such as tuple, property, and relational patterns.

The next chapter extends the types with inheritance, adding interfaces, and using inheritance with classes, records, and interfaces.

Object-Oriented Programming in C#

CODE DOWNLOADS FOR THIS CHAPTER

The source code for this chapter is available on the book page at www.wiley.com. Click the Downloads link. The code can also be found at https://github.com/ProfessionalCSharp/ ProfessionalCSharp2021 in the directory 1_CS/ObjectOrientation.

The code for this chapter is divided into the following major examples:

➤ VirtualMethods

➤ AbstractClasses

➤ InheritanceWithConstructors

➤ RecordsInheritance

➤ UsingInterfaces

➤ DefaultInterfaceMethods

➤ GenericTypes

➤ GenericTypesWithConstraints

All the projects have nullable reference types enabled.

OBJECT ORIENTATION

C# is not a pure object-oriented programming language because it offers multiple programming paradigms. However, object orientation is an important concept with C#; it's a core principle of all the libraries offered by .NET.

The three most important concepts of object orientation are *inheritance*, *encapsulation*, and *polymorphism*. Chapter 3, "Classes, Records, Structs, and Tuples," talks about creating individual types to arrange properties, methods, and fields. When members of a type are declared `private`, they cannot be accessed from the outside. They are *encapsulated* within the type. This chapter covers inheritance and polymorphism and extends encapsulation features with inheritance.

The previous chapter explained all the members of a type. This chapter explains how to use inheritance to enhance base types, how to create a hierarchy of classes, and how polymorphism works with C#. It also describes all the C# keywords related to inheritance, shows how to use interfaces as contracts for dependency injection, and covers default interface methods that allow implementations with interfaces.

INHERITANCE WITH CLASSES

If you want to declare that a class derives from another class, use the following syntax:

```
class MyDerivedClass: MyBaseClass
{
  // members
}
```

> **NOTE** *If you do not specify a base class in a class definition, the base class will be* `System.Object`.

Let's get into an example to define a base class `Shape`. Something that's common with shapes—no matter whether they are rectangles or ellipses—is that they have position and size. For position and size, corresponding records are defined that are contained within the `Shape` class. The `Shape` class defines read-only properties `Position` and `Size` that are initialized using auto properties with property initializers (code file `VirtualMethods/Shape.cs`):

```
public class Position
{
  public int X { get; set; }
  public int Y { get; set; }
}

public class Size
{
  public int Width { get; set; }
  public int Height { get; set; }
}

public class Shape
{
  public Position Position { get; } = new Position();
  public Size Size { get; } = new Size();
}
```

> **NOTE** *With the shapes sample, the* Position *and* Size *objects are contained within an object of the* Shape *class. This is the concept of composition. The* Rectangle *and* Ellipse *classes derive from the base class* Shape. *This is inheritance.*

Virtual Methods

By declaring a base class method as virtual, you allow the method to be overridden in any derived classes.

The following code snippet shows the DisplayShape method that is declared with the virtual modifier. This method is invoked by the Draw method of the Shape. Virtual methods can be public or protected. The access modifier cannot be changed when overriding this method in a derived class. Because the Draw method has a public access modifier, this method can be used from the outside when using the Shape or when using any class deriving from Shape. The Draw method cannot be overridden as it doesn't have the virtual modifier applied (code file VirtualMethods/Shape.cs):

```
public class Shape
{
  public void Draw() => DisplayShape();

  protected virtual void DisplayShape()
  {
    Console.WriteLine($"Shape with {Position} and {Size}");
  }
}
```

> **NOTE** *All the C# access modifiers are discussed later in this chapter in detail.*

You also may declare a property as virtual. For a virtual or overridden property, the syntax is the same as for a nonvirtual property, with the exception of the keyword virtual, which is added to the definition:

```
public virtual Size Size { get; set; }
```

For simplicity, the following discussion focuses mainly on methods, but it applies equally well to properties.

Methods that are declared virtual can be overridden in a derived class. To declare a method that overrides a method from a base class, use the override keyword (code file VirtualMethods/ConcreteShapes.cs):

```
public class Rectangle : Shape
{
  protected override void DisplayShape()
  {
    Console.WriteLine($"Rectangle at position {Position} with size {Size}");
  }
}
```

Virtual functions offer a core feature of OOP: *polymorphism*. With virtual functions, the decision of which method to invoke is delayed during runtime. The compiler creates a *virtual method table* (vtable) that lists the methods that can be invoked during runtime, and it invokes the method based on the type at runtime.

For performance reasons, in C#, functions are not virtual by default. For nonvirtual functions, the vtable is not needed, and the compiler directly addresses the method that's invoked.

The `Size` and `Position` types override the `ToString` method. This method is declared as `virtual` in the base class `Object` (code file `VirtualMethods/ConcreteShapes.cs`):

```
public class Position
{
  public int X { get; set; }
  public int Y { get; set; }

  public override string ToString() => $"X: {X}, Y: {Y}";
}

public class Size
{
  public int Width { get; set; }
  public int Height { get; set; }

  public override string ToString() => $"Width: {Width}, Height: {Height}";
}
```

Before C# 9, there was the rule that, when overriding methods of the base class, the signature (all parameter types and the method name) and the return type must match exactly. If you want different parameters, you need to create a new member that does not override the base member.

With C# 9, there's a small change to this rule: when overriding methods, the return type might differ, but only to return a type that derives from the return type of the base class. One example where this can be used is to create a type-safe `Clone` method. The `Shape` class defines a virtual `Clone` method that returns a `Shape` (code file `VirtualMethods/Shape.cs`):

```
public virtual Shape Clone() => throw new NotImplementedException();
```

The `Rectangle` class overrides this method to return a `Rectangle` type instead of the base class `Shape` by creating a new instance and copying all the values from the existing instance to the newly created one:

```
public override Rectangle Clone()
{
  Rectangle r = new();
  r.Position.X = Position.X;
  r.Position.Y = Position.Y;
  r.Size.Width = Size.Width;
  r.Size.Height = Size.Width;
  return r;
}
```

In the top-level statements of the `Program.cs` file, a rectangle and an ellipse are instantiated, properties are set, and the rectangle is cloned by invoking the virtual `Clone` method. Finally, the `DisplayShapes` method is invoked passing all the different created shapes. The `Draw` method of the `Shape` class is invoked to, in turn, invoke the overridden methods of the derived types. In this code snippet, you also see the `Ellipse` class used; this is similar to the `Rectangle` type, deriving from `Shape` (code file `VirtualMethods/Program.cs`):

```
Rectangle r1 = new();
r1.Position.X = 33;
r1.Position.Y = 22;
r1.Size.Width = 200;
r1.Size.Height = 100;
```

```
Rectangle r2 = r1.Clone();
r2.Position.X = 300;

Ellipse e1 = new();
e1.Position.X = 122;
e1.Position.Y = 200;
e1.Size.Width = 40;
e1.Size.Height = 20;

DisplayShapes(r1, r2, e1);

void DisplayShapes(params Shape[] shapes)
{
  foreach (var shape in shapes)
  {
    shape.Draw();
  }
}
```

Run the program to see the output of the Draw method coming from the implementation of the overridden Rectangle and Shape DisplayShape methods:

```
Rectangle at position X: 33, Y: 22 with size Width: 200, Height: 100
Rectangle at position X: 300, Y: 22 with size Width: 200, Height: 200
Ellipse at position X: 122, Y: 200 with size Width: 40, Height: 20
```

> **NOTE** *Neither member fields nor static methods can be declared as virtual. The concept of virtual members doesn't make sense for anything other than instance function members.*

Hiding Methods

If a method with the same signature is declared in both base and derived classes, but the methods are not declared with the modifiers virtual and override, respectively, then the derived class version is said to *hide* the base class version.

For hiding methods, you can use the new keyword as a modifier with the method declaration. In most cases, you would want to override methods rather than hide them. By hiding them, you risk calling the wrong method for a given class instance. However, as shown in the following example, C# syntax is designed to ensure that the developer is warned at compile time about this potential problem, thus making it safer to hide methods if that is your intention. This also has versioning benefits for developers of class libraries.

Suppose that you have a class called Shape in a class library:

```
public class Shape
{
  // various members
}
```

At some point in the future, you write a derived class Ellipse that adds some functionality to the Shape base class. In particular, you add a method called MoveBy, which is not present in the base class:

```
public class Ellipse: Shape
{
  public void MoveBy(int x, int y)
```

```
  {
    Position.X += x;
    Position.Y += y;
  }
}
```

At some later time, the developer of the base class decides to extend the functionality of the base class and, by coincidence, adds a method that is also called MoveBy and that has the same name and signature as yours; however, it probably doesn't do the same thing. This new method might be declared virtual or not.

If you recompile the derived class, you get a compiler warning because of a potential method clash. The application is still working, and where you've written code to invoke the MoveBy method using the Ellipse class, the method you've written is invoked. Hiding a method is the default behavior to avoid breaking changes when adding methods to a base class.

To get rid of the compilation error, you need to add the new modifier to the MoveBy method. The code the compiler is creating with or without the new modifier is the same; you just get rid of the compiler warning and flag this as a new method—a different one from the base class:

```
public class Ellipse: Shape
{
  new public void MoveBy(int x, int y)
  {
    Position.X += x;
    Position.Y += y;
  }
  //...
}
```

Instead of using the new keyword, you can also rename the method or override the method of the base class if it is declared virtual and serves the same purpose. However, if other methods already invoke this method, a simple rename can lead to breaking other code.

> **NOTE** *You shouldn't use the* new *method modifier to hide members of the base class deliberately. The main purpose of this modifier is to deal with version conflicts and react to changes on base classes after the derived class was done.*

Calling Base Versions of Methods

If a derived class overrides or hides a method in its base class, then it can invoke the base class version of the method by using the base keyword. For example, in the base class Shape, the virtual Move method is declared to change the actual position and write some information to the console. This method should be called from the derived class Rectangle to use the implementation from the base class (code file VirtualMethods/Shape.cs):

```
public class Shape
{
  public virtual void Move(Position newPosition)
  {
    Position.X = newPosition.X;
    Position.Y = newPosition.Y;
    Console.WriteLine($"moves to {Position}");
  }
  //...
}
```

The Move method is overridden in the Rectangle class to add the term Rectangle to the console. After this text is written, the method of the base class is invoked using the base keyword (code file VirtualMethods/ConcreteShapes.cs):

```
public class Rectangle: Shape
{
  public override void Move(Position newPosition)
  {
    Console.Write("Rectangle ");
    base.Move(newPosition);
  }
  //...
}
```

Now move the rectangle to a new position (code file VirtualMethods/Program.cs):

```
r1.Move(new Position { X = 120, Y = 40 });
```

Run the application to see output that is a result of the Move method in the Rectangle and the Shape classes:

```
Rectangle moves to X: 120, Y: 40
```

> **NOTE** *Using the* base *keyword, you can invoke any method of the base class—not just the method that is overridden.*

Abstract Classes and Methods

C# allows both classes and methods to be declared as abstract. An abstract class cannot be instantiated, whereas an *abstract* method does not have an implementation and must be overridden in any nonabstract derived class. Obviously, an abstract method is *automatically* virtual. If any class contains any abstract methods, that class is also abstract and must be declared as such.

Let's change the Shape class to be abstract. Instead of throwing a NotImplementedException, the Clone method is now declared abstract, and thus it can't have any implementation in the Shape class (code file AbstractClasses/Shape.cs):

```
public abstract class Shape
{
  public abstract Shape Clone(); // abstract method
}
```

When deriving a type from the abstract base class that itself is not abstract, it's a concrete type. With a concrete class it is necessary to implement all abstract members. Otherwise, the compiler complains (code file AbstractClasses/ConcreteShapes.cs):

```
public class Rectangle : Shape
{
  //...
  public override Rectangle Clone()
  {
    Rectangle r = new();
    r.Position.X = Position.X;
    r.Position.Y = Position.Y;
    r.Size.Width = Size.Width;
    r.Size.Height = Size.Width;
    return r;
  }
}
```

Using the abstract `Shape` class and the derived `Ellipse` class, you can declare a variable of a `Shape`. You cannot instantiate it, but you can instantiate an `Ellipse` and assign it to the `Shape` variable (code file `AbstractClasses/Program.cs`):

```
Shape s1 = new Ellipse();
s1.Draw();
```

Sealed Classes and Methods

If you don't want to allow other classes to derive from your class, your class should be sealed. Adding the `sealed` modifier to a class doesn't allow you to create a subclass of it. Sealing a method means it's not possible to override this method.

```
sealed class FinalClass
{
  //...
}

class DerivedClass: FinalClass // wrong. Cannot derive from sealed class.
{
  //...
}
```

The most likely situation in which you'll mark a class or method as `sealed` is if the class or method is internal to the operation of the library, class, or other classes that you are writing. Overriding methods could lead to instability of the code. When you seal the class, you make sure that overriding is not possible.

There's another reason to seal classes. With a sealed class, the compiler knows that derived classes are not possible, and thus the virtual table used for virtual methods can be reduced or eliminated, which can increase performance. The `string` class is sealed. I haven't seen a single application that doesn't use strings, so it's best to have this type as performant as possible. Making the class sealed is a good hint for the compiler.

Declaring a method as `sealed` serves a purpose similar to that for a class. The method can be an overridden method from a base class, but in the following example, the compiler knows another class cannot extend the virtual table for this method; it ends here.

```
class MyClass: MyBaseClass
{
  public sealed override void FinalMethod()
  {
    // implementation
  }
}

class DerivedClass: MyClass
{
  public override void FinalMethod() // wrong. Will give compilation error
  {
  }
}
```

To use the `sealed` keyword on a method or property, the member must have first been overridden from a base class. If you do not want a method or property in a base class overridden, then don't mark it as virtual.

Constructors of Derived Classes

Chapter 3 discusses how constructors can be applied to individual classes. An interesting question arises as to what happens when you start defining your own constructors for classes that are part of a hierarchy, inherited from other classes that may also have custom constructors.

In the sample application that uses shapes, so far, custom constructors have not been specified. The compiler creates a default constructor automatically to initialize all members to `null` or `0` (depending on whether the types are reference or value types) or uses the code from specified property initializers to add these to the default constructor. Now, let's change the implementation to create immutable types and define custom constructors to initialize their values. The `Position`, `Size`, and `Shape` classes are changed to specify read-only properties, and the constructors are changed to initialize the properties. The `Shape` class is still abstract, which doesn't allow creating instances of this type (code file `InheritanceWithConstructors/Shape.cs`):

```
public class Position
{
  public Position(int x, int y) => (X, Y) = (x, y);

  public int X { get; }
  public int Y { get; }

  public override string ToString() => $"X: {X}, Y: {Y}";
}

public class Size
{
  public Size(int width, int height) => (Width, Height) = (width, height);

  public int Width { get; }
  public int Height { get; }

  public override string ToString() => $"Width: {Width}, Height: {Height}";
}

public abstract class Shape
{
  public Shape(int x, int y, int width, int height)
  {
    Position = new Position(x, y);
    Size = new Size(width, height);
  }

  public Position Position { get; }
  public virtual Size Size { get; }

  public void Draw() => DisplayShape();

  protected virtual void DisplayShape()
  {
    Console.WriteLine($"Shape with {Position} and {Size}");
  }

  public abstract Shape Clone();
}
```

Now the `Rectangle` and `Ellipse` types need to be changed as well. Because the `Shape` class doesn't have a parameterless constructor, the compiler complains because it cannot automatically invoke the constructor of the base class. A custom constructor is required here as well.

With the new implementation of the `Ellipse` class, a constructor is defined to supply the position and size for the shape. To invoke the constructor from the base class, such as invoking methods of the base class, you use the `base` keyword, but you just can't use the `base` keyword in the block of the constructor body. Instead, you need to use the `base` keyword in the constructor initializer and pass the required arguments. The `Clone` method can now be simplified to invoke the constructor to create a new `Ellipse` object by forwarding the values from the existing object (code file `InheritanceWithConstructors/ConcreteShapes.cs`):

```csharp
public class Ellipse : Shape
{
  public Ellipse(int x, int y, int width, int height)
    : base(x, y, width, height) { }

  protected override void DisplayShape()
  {
    Console.WriteLine($"Ellipse at position {Position} with size {Size}");
  }

  public override Ellipse Clone() =>
    new(Position.X, Position.Y, Size.Width, Size.Height);
}
```

> **NOTE** *Chapter 3 covers constructor initializers with the* `this` *keyword to invoke other constructors of the same class. To invoke constructors of the base class, you use the* `base` *keyword.*

MODIFIERS

You have already encountered quite a number of so-called modifiers—keywords that can be applied to a type or a member. Modifiers can indicate the visibility of a method, such as `public` or `private`, or the nature of an item, such as whether a method is `virtual` or `abstract`. C# has a number of modifiers, and at this point it's worth taking a minute to provide the complete list.

Access Modifiers

Access modifiers indicate which other code items can access an item.

You can use all the access modifiers with members of a type. The `public` and `internal` access modifiers can also be applied to the type itself. With nested types (types that are specified within types), you can apply all access modifiers. In regard to access modifiers, nested types are members of the outer type, such as those shown in the following code snippet where the `OuterType` is declared with the `public` access modifier, and the type `InnerType` has the `protected` access modifier applied. With the `protected` access modifier, the `InnerType` can be accessed from the members of the `OuterType`, and all types that derive from the `OuterType`:

```csharp
public class OuterType
{
  protected class InnerType
  {
    // members of the inner type
  }
  // more members of the outer type
}
```

The `public` access modifier is the most open one; everyone has access to a class or a member that has the `public` access modifier applied. The private access modifier is the most restrictive one. Members with this access modifier can be used only within the class where the modifier is used. The `protected` access modifier is in between these access restrictions. In addition to the `private` access modifier, it allows access to all types that derive from the type where the `protected` access modifier is used.

The `internal` access modifier is different. This access modifier has the scope of the assembly. All the types defined within the same assembly have access to members and types where the internal access modifier is used.

If you do not supply an access modifier with a type, by default `internal` access is specified. You can use this type only within the same assembly.

The `protected internal` access modifier is a combination of `protected` and `internal`—combining these access modifiers with OR. `protected internal` members can be used from any type in the same assembly or from types from another assembly if an inheritance relationship is used. With the intermediate language (IL) code, this is known as `famorassem` (family or assembly)—family for the `protected` C# keyword and assembly for the `internal` keyword. `famandassem` is also available with the IL code. Because of the demand for an AND combination, the C# team had some issues finding a good name for this, and finally it was decided to use `private protected` to restrict access from within the assembly to types that have an inheritance relationship but no types from any other assembly.

The following table lists all the access modifiers and their uses:

MODIFIER	APPLIES TO	DESCRIPTION
`public`	Any types or members	The item is visible to any other code.
`protected`	Any member of a type and any nested type	The item is visible only to the type and any derived type.
`internal`	Any types or members	The item is visible only within its containing assembly.
`private`	Any member of a type, and any nested type	The item is visible only inside the type to which it belongs.
`protected internal`	Any member of a type and any nested type	The item is visible to any code within its containing assembly and to any code inside a derived type.
`private protected`	Any members of a type and any nested type	The item is visible to the type and any derived type that is specified within the containing assembly.

Other Modifiers

The modifiers in the following table can be applied to members of types and have various uses. A few of these modifiers also make sense when applied to types:

MODIFIER	APPLIES TO	DESCRIPTION
`new`	Function members	The member hides an inherited member with the same signature.
`static`	All members	The member does not operate on a specific instance of the class. This is also known as *class member* instead of instance member.
`virtual`	Function members only	The member can be overridden by a derived class.

continues

(continued)

MODIFIER	APPLIES TO	DESCRIPTION
abstract	Function members only	A virtual member that defines the signature of the member but doesn't provide an implementation.
override	Function members only	The member overrides an inherited virtual or abstract member.
sealed	Classes, methods, and properties	For classes, the class cannot be inherited from. For properties and methods, the member overrides an inherited virtual member but cannot be overridden by any members in any derived classes. This must be used in conjunction with override.
extern	Static [DllImport] methods only	The member is implemented externally, in a different language. The use of this keyword is explained in Chapter 13, "Managed and Unmanaged Memory."

INHERITANCE WITH RECORDS

Chapter 3 discusses a new feature with C# 9: records. Behind the scenes, records are classes. However, you cannot derive a record from a class (other than the object type), and a class cannot derive from a record. However, records can derive from other records.

Let's change the shapes sample to use positional records. With the following code snippet, Position and Size are records that contain X, Y, Width, and Height properties with set init-only accessors as specified by the primary constructor. Shape is an abstract record with Position and Size properties, a Draw method, and a virtual DisplayShape method. As with classes, you can use modifiers with records, such as abstract and virtual. The previously specified Clone method is not needed with records because this is created automatically using the record keyword (code file RecordsInheritance/Shape.cs):

```
public record Position(int X, int Y);

public record Size(int Width, int Height);

public abstract record Shape(Position Position, Size Size)
{
  public void Draw() => DisplayShape();

  protected virtual void DisplayShape()
  {
    Console.WriteLine($"Shape with {Position} and {Size}");
  }
}
```

The Rectangle record derives from the Shape record. With the primary constructor syntax used with the Rectangle type, derivation from Shape passes the same values to the primary constructor of the Shape. Similar to the Rectangle class created earlier, in the Rectangle record, the DisplayShape method is overridden (code file RecordsInheritance/ConcreteShapes.cs):

```
public record Rectangle(Position Position, Size Size) : Shape(Position, Size)
{
  protected override void DisplayShape()
```

```
  {
    Console.WriteLine($"Rectangle at position {Position} with size {Size}");
  }
}
```

With the top-level statements in the `Program.cs` file, a `Rectangle` and an `Ellipse` are created using primary constructors. The implementation of the `Ellipse` record is similar to the `Rectangle` record. The first rectangle created is cloned by using the built-in functionality, and with the new `Rectangle`, the `Position` property is set to a new value using the `with` expression. The `with` expression makes use of the init-only set accessors created from the primary constructor (code file `RecordsInheritance/Program.cs`):

```
Rectangle r1 = new(new Position(33, 22), new Size(200, 100));
Rectangle r2 = r1 with { Position = new Position(100, 22) };
Ellipse e1 = new(new Position(122, 200), new Size(40, 20));

DisplayShapes(r1, r2, e1);

void DisplayShapes(params Shape[] shapes)
{
  foreach (var shape in shapes)
  {
    shape.Draw();
  }
}
```

> **NOTE** *With future C# versions, the inheritance with records might be relaxed to allow inheritance from classes.*

USING INTERFACES

A class can derive from one class, and a record can derive from one record; you cannot use multiple inheritance with classes and records. You can use interfaces to bring multiple inheritance into C#. Both classes and records can implement multiple interfaces. Also, one interface can inherit from multiple interfaces.

Before C# 8, an interface never had any implementation. In the versions since C# 8, you can create an implementation with interfaces, but this is very different from the implementation with classes and records; interfaces cannot keep state, so fields or automatic properties are not possible. Because method implementation is only an additional feature of interfaces, let's keep this discussion for later in this chapter and first focus on the contract aspect of interfaces.

Predefined Interfaces

Let's take a look at some predefined interfaces and how they are used with .NET. Some C# keywords are even designed to work with particular predefined interfaces. The `using` statement and the `using` declaration (covered in detail in Chapter 13) use the `IDisposable` interface. This interface defines the method `Dispose` without any arguments and without return type. A class deriving from this interface needs to implement this `Dispose` method:

```
public IDisposable
{
  void Dispose();
}
```

The using statement uses this interface. You can use this statement with any class (here, the Resource class) implementing this interface:

```
using (Resource resource = new())
{
    // use the resource
}
```

The compiler converts the using statement to this code to invoke the Dispose method in the finally block of the try/finally statement:

```
Resource resource = new();
try
{
    // use the resource
}
finally
{
    resource.Dispose();
}
```

> **NOTE** *The* try/finally *block is covered in Chapter 10, "Errors and Exceptions."*

Another example where an interface is used with a language keyword is the foreach statement that's using the IEnumerator and IEnumerable interfaces. This code snippet

```
string[] names = { "James", "Jack", "Jochen" };
foreach (var name in names)
{
    Console.WriteLine(name);
}
```

is converted to access the GetEnumerator method of the IEnumerable interface and uses a while loop to access the MoveNext method and the Current property of the IEnumerator interface:

```
string[] names = { "James", "Jack", "Jochen" };
var enumerator = names.GetEnumerator();
while (enumerator.MoveNext())
{
    var name = enumerator.Current;
    Console.WriteLine(name);
}
```

> **NOTE** *Creating a custom implementation of the* IEnumerable *and* IEnumerator *interfaces with the help of the* yield *statement is covered in Chapter 6, "Arrays."*

Let's look at an example where an interface is used from a .NET class, and you can easily implement this interface. The interface IComparable<T> defines the CompareTo method to sort objects of the type you need to specify with the generic parameter T. This interface is used by various classes in .NET to order objects of any type:

```
public interface IComparable<in T>
```

```
{
    int CompareTo(T? other);
}
```

With the following code snippet, the record `Person` implements this interface specifying `Person` as a generic parameter. `Person` specifies the properties `FirstName` and `LastName`. The `CompareTo` method is defined to return 0 if both values (`this` and `other`) are the same, a value lower than 0 if `this` object should come before the `other` object, and a value greater than 0 if `other` should be first. Because the `string` type also implements `IComparable`, this implementation is used to compare the `LastName` properties. If the comparison on the last name returns `0`, a comparison is done on the `FirstName` property as well (code file `UsingInterfaces/Person.cs`):

```
public record Person(string FirstName, string LastName) : IComparable<Person>
{
  public int CompareTo(Person? other)
  {
    int compare = LastName.CompareTo(other?.LastName);
    if (compare is 0)
    {
      return FirstName.CompareTo(other?.FirstName);
    }
    return compare;
  }
}
```

With the top-level statements in `Program.cs`, three `Person` records are created within an array, and the array's `Sort` method is used to sort the elements in the array (code file `UsingInterfaces/Program.cs`):

```
Person p1 = new("Jackie", "Stewart");
Person p2 = new("Graham", "Hill");
Person p3 = new("Damon", "Hill");

Person[] people = { p1, p2, p3 };
Array.Sort(people);
foreach (var p in people)
{
  Console.WriteLine(p);
}
```

Running the application shows the `ToString` output of the record type in a sorted order:

```
Person { FirstName = Damon, LastName = Hill }
Person { FirstName = Graham, LastName = Hill }
Person { FirstName = Jackie, LastName = Stewart }
```

Interfaces can act as a contract. The record `Person` implements the `IComparable` contract that is used by the `Sort` method of the `Array` class. The `Array` class just needs to know the contract definition (the members of the interface) to know what it can use.

Dependency Injection with Interfaces

Let's create a custom interface. With the shapes sample, the `Shape` and `Rectangle` types used the `Console.WriteLine` method to write a message to the console:

```
protected virtual void DisplayShape()
{
  Console.WriteLine($"Shape with {Position} and {Size}");
}
```

This way, the method `DisplayShape` has a strong dependency on the `Console` class. To make this implementation independent of the `Console` class and to write to either the console or a file, you can define a contract such as the `ILogger` interface in the following code snippet. This interface specifies the `Log` method where a string can be passed as an argument (code file `UsingInterfaces/ILogger.cs`):

```
public interface ILogger
{
  void Log(string message);
}
```

A new version of the `Shape` class uses *constructor injection* where the interface is injected into an object of this class. In the constructor, the object passed with the parameter is assigned to the read-only property `Logger`. With the implementation of the `DisplayShape` method, the property of type `ILogger` is used to write a message (code file `UsingInterfaces/Shape.cs`):

```
public abstract class Shape
{
  public Shape(ILogger logger)
  {
    Logger = logger;
  }

  protected ILogger Logger { get; }
  public Position? Position { get; init; }
  public Size? Size { get; init; }

  public void Draw() => DisplayShape();

  protected virtual void DisplayShape()
  {
    Logger.Log($"Shape with {Position} and {Size}");
  }
}
```

With a concrete implementation of the abstract `Shape` class, in the constructor, the `ILogger` interface is forwarded to the constructor of the base class. With the `DisplayShape` method, the protected property `Logger` is used from the base class (code file `UsingInterfaces/ConcreteShapes.cs`):

```
public class Ellipse : Shape
{
  public Ellipse(ILogger logger) : base(logger) { }

  protected override void DisplayShape()
  {
    Logger.Log($"Ellipse at position {Position} with size {Size}");
  }
}
```

Next, a concrete implementation of the `ILogger` interface is required. One way you can implement writing a message to the console is with the `ConsoleLogger` class. This class implements the `ILogger` interface to write a message to the console (code file `UsingInterfaces/ConsoleLogger.cs`):

```
public class ConsoleLogger : ILogger
{
  public void Log(string message) => Console.WriteLine(message);
}
```

> **NOTE** *Using the* ILogger *interface from the* Microsoft.Extensions.Logging *namespace is discussed in Chapter 16, "Diagnostics and Metrics."*

For creating a `Rectangle`, the `ConsoleLogger` can be created on passing an instance to implement the `ILogger` interface (code file `UsingInterfaces/Program.cs`):

```
Ellipse e1 = new(new ConsoleLogger())
{
  Position = new(20, 30),
  Size = new(100, 120)
};
r1.Draw();
```

> **NOTE** *With dependency injection, the responsibility is turned over. Instead of having a strong dependency with the implementation of the shape for the* Console *class, the responsibility for what is used is turned over outside of the* Shape *type. This way what is used can be specified from the outside. This is also known as the Hollywood Principle—"Don't call us, we call you." Dependency injection makes unit testing easier because dependencies can be easily replaced with mock types. Another advantage when using dependency injection is that you can create platform-specific implementations. For example, showing a message box is different with the Universal Windows Platform* (MessageDialog.ShowAsync)*, WPF* (MessageBox.Show)*, and Xamarin.Forms* (Page.Alert)*. With a common view model, you can use the interface* IDialogService *and define different implementations with the different platforms. Read more about dependency injection using a dependency injection container in Chapter 15, "Dependency Injection and Configuration." Unit testing is covered in Chapter 23, "Tests."*

Explicit and Implicit Implemented Interfaces

Interfaces can be explicitly or implicitly implemented. With the example so far, you've seen implicitly implemented interfaces, such as with the `ConsoleLogger` class:

```
public class ConsoleLogger : ILogger
{
  public void Log(string message) => Console.WriteLine(message);
}
```

With an explicit interface implementation, the member implemented doesn't have an access modifier and has the interface prefixed to the method name:

```
public class ConsoleLogger : ILogger
{
  void ILogger.Log(string message) => Console.WriteLine(message);
}
```

With an explicit interface implementation, the interface is not accessible when you use a variable of type `ConsoleLogger` (it's not public). If you use a variable of the interface type (`ILogger`), you can invoke the `Log` method; the contract of the interface is fulfilled. You can also cast the `ConsoleLogger` variable to the interface `ILogger` to invoke this method.

Why would you want to do this? One reason is to resolve a conflict. If different interfaces define the same method signature, your class needs to implement all these interfaces, and the implementations need to differ, you can use explicit interface implementation.

Another reason to use explicit interface implementation is to hide the interface method from code outside of the class but still fulfill the contract from the interface. An example is the `StringCollection` class from the `System .Collections.Specialized` namespace and the `IList` interface. One of the members that's defined by the `IList` interface is the `Add` method:

```
int Add(object? value);
```

The `StringCollection` class is optimized for strings and thus prefers to use the string type with the `Add` method:

```
public int Add(string? value);
```

The version to pass an object is hidden from the `StringCollection` class because the `StringCollection` class has an explicit interface implementation with this method. To use this type directly, you just pass a string parameter. If a method uses `IList` as a parameter, then you can use any object that implements `IList` for that parameter. In particular, you can use a `StringCollection` for the parameter because that class still implements that interface.

Comparing Interfaces and Classes

Now that you've seen the foundations of interfaces, let's compare interfaces, classes, records, and structs with regard to object orientation:

➤ You can declare a variable of the type of all these C# constructs. You can declare a variable of a class, an interface, a record, or a struct.

➤ You can instantiate a new object with classes, records, and structs. You cannot instantiate a new object with an abstract class or an interface.

➤ With a class, you can derive from a base class. With a record, you can derive from a base record. Both with classes and records, implementation inheritance is supported. Structs don't support inheritance.

➤ Classes, records, and structs can implement multiple interfaces. Implementing interfaces is not possible with ref structs.

Default Interface Methods

Before C# 8, changing an interface was always a breaking change. Even just adding a member to an interface is a breaking change. The type implementing this interface needs to implement this new interface member. Because of this, many .NET libraries are built with abstract base classes. When you add a new member to an abstract base class, if it's not an abstract member, it is not a breaking change. With Microsoft's Component Object Model (COM), which is based on interfaces, always a new interface was defined when a breaking change was introduced—for example, `IViewObject`, `IViewObjectEx`, `IViewObject2`, `IViewObject3`.

As of C# 8, interfaces can have implementations. However, you need to be aware where you can use this feature. C# 8 is supported by .NET Core 3.x. With older technologies, you can change the compiler version at your own risk. To support default interface members, a runtime change is required. This runtime change is available only with .NET Core 3.x+ and .NET Standard 2.1+. You cannot use default interface members with .NET Framework applications or UWP applications without .NET 5 support.

Avoiding Breaking Changes

Let's get into the main feature of default interface members to avoid breaking changes. In a previous code sample, the `ILogger` interface has been specified:

```
public interface ILogger
{
```

```
    void Log(string message);
}
```

If you add any member without implementation, the `ConsoleLogger` class needs to be updated. To avoid a breaking change, an implementation to the new `Log` method with the `Exception` parameter is added. With the implementation, the previous `Log` method is invoked by passing a `string` (code file `DefaultInterfaceMethods/ILogger.cs`):

```
public interface ILogger
{
    void Log(string message);
    public void Log(Exception ex) => Log(ex.Message);
}
```

> **NOTE** *The implementation of the* `Log` *method has the* `public` *access modifier applied. With interface members,* `public` *is the default, so this access modifier is not required. However, with implementations in the interface, you can use the same modifiers you've seen with classes, including* `virtual`, `abstract`, `sealed`, *and so on.*

The application can be built without changing the implementation of the `ConsoleLogger` class. If a variable of the interface type is used, both `Log` methods can be invoked: the `Log` method with the string parameter and the `Log` method with the `Exception` parameter (code file `DefaultInterfaceMethods/Program.cs`):

```
ILogger logger = new ConsoleLogger();
logger.Log("message");
logger.Log(new Exception("sample exception"));
```

With a new implementation of the `ConsoleLogger` class, a different implementation of the new `Log` method defined with the `ILogger` interface can be created. In this case, using the `ILogger` interface invokes the method implemented with the `ConsoleLogger` class. The method is implemented with explicit interface implementation but could be implemented with implicit interface implementation as well (code file `DefaultInterfaceMethods/ConsoleLogger.cs`):

```
public class ConsoleLogger : ILogger
{
    public void Log(string message) => Console.WriteLine(message);

    void ILogger.Log(Exception ex)
    {
        Console.WriteLine(
            $"exception type: {ex.GetType().Name}, message: {ex.Message}");
    }
}
```

Traits with C#

Default interface members can be used to implement traits with C#. *Traits* allow you to define methods for a group of types. One way to implement traits is with extension methods; the other option is using default interface methods.

With Language Integrated Query (LINQ), many LINQ operators have been implemented with extension methods. With this new feature, it would be possible to implement these methods with default interface members instead.

> **NOTE** *Extension methods are introduced in Chapter 3. Chapter 9, "Language Integrated Query," covers all the extension methods implemented with LINQ.*

To demonstrate this, the `IEnumerableEx<T>` interface is defined that derives from the interface `IEnumerable<T>`. Deriving from this interface, `IEnumerableEx<T>` specifies the same contract as the base interface, but the `Where` method is added. This method receives a delegate parameter to pass a predicate method that returns a Boolean value, iterates through all the items, and invokes the method referenced by the predicate. If the predicate returns true, the Where method returns the item with `yield return`.

```
using System;
using System.Collections.Generic;

public interface IEnumerableEx<T> : IEnumerable<T>
{
  public IEnumerable<T> Where(Func<T, bool> pred)
  {
    foreach (T item in this)
    {
      if (pred(item))
      {
        yield return item;
      }
    }
  }
}
```

> **NOTE** *The `yield` statement is covered in detail in Chapter 6.*

Now you need a collection to implement the interface `IEnumerableEx<T>`. You can do this easily by creating a new collection type, `MyCollection`, that derives from the `Collection<T>` base class defined in the `System.Collections.ObjectModel` namespace. Because the `Collection<T>` class already implements the interface `IEnumerable<T>`, no additional implementation is needed to support `IEnumerableEx<T>` (code file `DefaultInterfaceMethods/MyCollection.cs`):

```
class MyCollection<T> : Collection<T>, IEnumerableEx<T>
{
}
```

With this in place, a collection of type `MyCollections<string>` is created that's filled with names. A lambda expression that returns a Boolean value and receives a string is passed to the `Where` method that's defined with the interface. The `foreach` statement iterates through the result and only displays the names starting with J (code file `DefaultInterfaceMethods/Program.cs`):

```
IEnumerableEx<string> names = new MyCollection<string>
  { "James", "Jack", "Jochen", "Sebastian", "Lewis", "Juan" };

var jNames = names.Where(n => n.StartsWith("J"));
foreach (var name in jNames)
{
  Console.WriteLine(name);
}
```

> **NOTE** *When you invoke default interface members, you always need a variable of the interface type, similar to explicitly implemented interfaces.*
>
> *What cannot be done with interfaces and default interface members is to add members that keep state. Fields, events (with delegates), and auto properties add state—these members are not allowed. If state is required, you should use abstract classes instead.*

GENERICS

One way to reduce the code you need to write is by using inheritance and adding functionality to base classes. Another way is to create generics where a type parameter is used, which allows specifying the type when instantiating the generic (which can also be combined with inheritance).

Let's get into an example to create a linked list of objects where every item references the next and previous items. The first generic type created is a record. The generic type parameter is specified using angle brackets. `T` is the placeholder type parameter name. With the primary constructor, a property with an init-only set accessor is created. The record has two additional properties, `Next` and `Prev`, to reference the next and previous items. With these additional properties, the `internal` access
modifier is used to allow calling the set accessor only from within the same assembly (code file `GenericTypes/LinkedListNode.cs`):

```
public record LinkedListNode<T>(T Value)
{
  public LinkedListNode<T>? Next { get; internal set; }
  public LinkedListNode<T>? Prev { get; internal set; }
  public override string? ToString() => Value?.ToString();
}
```

> **NOTE** *Because the* `LinkedListNode` *type is a record, it's important to override the* `ToString` *method. With the default implementation of the* `ToString` *method, the value of all property members is shown, which invokes* `ToString` *with every property value. Because the* `Next` *and* `Prev` *properties reference other objects, a stack overflow can occur.*

The generic class `LinkedList` contains the properties `First` and `Last` to access the first and last elements of the list, the method `AddLast` to add a new node at the end of the list, and an implementation of the `IEnumerable<T>` interface, which allows iterating through all elements (code file `GenericTypes/LinkedList.cs`):

```
public class LinkedList<T> : IEnumerable<T>
{
  public LinkedListNode<T>? First { get; private set; }
  public LinkedListNode<T>? Last { get; private set; }
  public LinkedListNode<T> AddLast(T node)
  {
    LinkedListNode<T> newNode = new(node);
    if (First is null || Last is null)
    {
      First = newNode;
```

```
      Last = First;
    }
    else
    {
      newNode.Prev = Last;
      LinkedListNode<T> previous = Last;
      Last.Next = newNode;
      Last = newNode;
    }
    return newNode;
  }

  public IEnumerator<T> GetEnumerator()
  {
    LinkedListNode<T>? current = First;
    while (current is not null)
    {
      yield return current.Value;
      current = current.Next;
    }
  }

  IEnumerator IEnumerable.GetEnumerator() => GetEnumerator();
}
```

In the generated Main method, the LinkedList is initiated by using the int type by using the string type, a tuple, and a record. LinkedList works with any type (code file GenericTypes/Program.cs):

```
LinkedList<int> list1 = new();
list1.AddLast(1);
list1.AddLast(3);
list1.AddLast(2);

foreach (var item in list1)
{
  Console.WriteLine(item);
}
Console.WriteLine();

LinkedList<string> list2 = new();
list2.AddLast("two");
list2.AddLast("four");
list2.AddLast("six");

Console.WriteLine(list2.Last);

LinkedList<(int, int)> list3 = new();
list3.AddLast((1, 2));
list3.AddLast((3, 4));
foreach (var item in list3)
{
  Console.WriteLine(item);
}
Console.WriteLine();
```

```
LinkedList<Person> list4 = new();
list4.AddLast(new Person("Stephanie", "Nagel"));
list4.AddLast(new Person("Matthias", "Nagel"));
list4.AddLast(new Person("Katharina", "Nagel"));

// show the first
Console.WriteLine(list4.First);

public record Person(string FirstName, string LastName);
```

Constraints

With the previous implementation of the LinkedListNode<T> and LinkedList<T> types there was not a special requirement on the generic type; any type can be used. This prevents you from using any nonobject members with the implementation. The compiler doesn't accept invoking any property or method on the generic type T.

Adding the DisplayAllTitles method to the LinkedList<T> class results in a compiler error. T does not contain a definition for Title, and no accessible extension method Title accepting a first argument of type T could be found (code file GenericTypesWithConstraints/LinkedList.cs):

```
public void DisplayAllTitles()
{
  foreach (T item in this)
  {
    Console.WriteLine(item.Title);
  }
}
```

To resolve this, the interface ITitle is specified that defines a Title property that needs to be implemented with the implementation of this interface:

```
public interface ITitle
{
  string Title { get; }
}
```

Defining the generic LinkedList<T>, now the constraint for the generic type T, can be specified to implement the interface ITitle. Constraints are specified with the where keyword followed by the requirement on the type:

```
public class LinkedList<T> : IEnumerable<T>
    where T : ITitle
{
  //...
}
```

With this change in place, the DisplayAllTitles method compiles. This method uses the members specified by the ITitle interface, and this is a requirement on the generic type. You can no longer use int and string for the generic type parameter, but the Person record can be changed to implement this constraint (code file GenericTypesWithConstraints/Program.cs):

```
public record Person(string FirstName, string LastName, string Title)
    : ITitle { }
```

The following table lists the constraints you can specify with a generic:

CONSTRAINT	DESCRIPTION
where T : struct	With a struct constraint, T must be a value type.
where T : class	With a class constraint, T must be a reference type.
where T : class?	T must be a nullable or a non-nullable reference type.
where T : notnull	T must be a non-nullable type. This can be a value or a reference type.
where T : unmanaged	T must be a non-nullable unmanaged type.
where T : IFoo	This specifies that the type T is required to implement interface IFoo.
where T : Foo	This specifies that the type T is required to derive from base class Foo.
where T : new()	A constructor constraint; this specifies that T must have a parameterless constructor. You cannot specify a constraint for constructors with parameters.
where T1 : T2	With constraints, it is also possible to specify that type T1 derives from a generic type T2.

SUMMARY

This chapter described how to code inheritance in C#. You saw the rich support for both implementing multiple interfaces and single inheritance with classes and records. You saw how C# provides a number of useful syntactical constructs designed to assist in making code more robust, which includes different access modifiers, and the concept of nonvirtual and virtual methods. You also saw the new feature for interfaces, which allows adding code implementation. Generics have been covered as another concept to reuse code.

The next chapter continues with all the C# operators and casts.

5

Operators and Casts

WHAT'S IN THIS CHAPTER?

➤ Operators in C#

➤ Implicit and explicit conversions

➤ Overloading standard operators for custom types

➤ Comparing objects for equality

➤ Implementing custom indexers

➤ User-defined conversions

CODE DOWNLOADS FOR THIS CHAPTER

The source code for this chapter is available on the book page at www.wiley.com. Click the Downloads link. The code can also be found at https://github.com/ProfessionalCSharp/ProfessionalCSharp2021 in the directory 1_CS/OperatorsAndCasts.

The code for this chapter is divided into the following major examples:

➤ OperatorsSample

➤ BinaryCalculations

➤ OperatorOverloadingSample

➤ EqualitySample

➤ CustomIndexerSample

➤ UserDefinedConversion

All the projects have nullable reference types enabled.

The preceding chapters have covered most of what you need to start writing useful programs using C#. This chapter continues the discussion with essential language elements and illustrates some powerful aspects of C# that enable you to extend its capabilities. This chapter also covers information about using operators and extending custom types with operator overloading and custom conversion.

OPERATORS

C# supports the operators and expressions listed in the following table. In the table, the operators start with the highest precedence and go down to the lowest.

CATEGORY	OPERATOR
Primary	`x.y x?.y f(x) a[x] x++ x-- x! x->y new typeof default checked unchecked delegate nameof sizeof delegate stackalloc`
Unary	`+x -x !x ~x ++x --x ^x (T)x await &x *x true false`
Range	`x..y`
Multiplicative	`x*y x/y x%y`
Additive	`x+y x-y`
Shift	`x<<y x>>y`
Relational	`x<y x>y x<=y x>=y`
Type testing	`is as`
Equality	`x==y x!=y`
Logical	`x&y x^y x|y`
Conditional logical	`x&&y x||y`
Null coalescing	`x??y`
Conditional operator	`c?t:f`
Assignment	`x=y x+=y x-=y x*=y x/=y x%=y x&=y x|=y x^=y x<<=y x>>=y x??=y`
Lambda expression	`=>`

> **NOTE** *Four specific operators (`sizeof`, `*`, `->`, and `&`) are available only in unsafe code (code that bypasses C#'s type-safety checking), which is discussed in Chapter 13, "Managed and Unmanaged Memory."*
>
> *Using the new range and hat operators with strings is covered in Chapter 2, "Core C#." Using these operators with arrays is covered in Chapter 6, "Arrays," where you also can read how to support custom collections with these operators.*

Compound Assignment Operators

Compound assignment operators are a shortcut to using the assignment operator with another operator. Instead of writing x = x + 2, you can use the compound assignment x += 2. Incrementing by 1 is required even more often, so there's another shortcut, x++:

```
int x = 1;
int x += 2; // shortcut for int x = x + 2;
x++; // shortcut for x = x + 1;
```

Shortcuts can be used with all the other compound assignment operators. A new compound assignment operator has been available since C# 8: the null-coalescing compound assignment operator. This operator is discussed later in this chapter.

You may be wondering why there are two examples for the ++ increment operator. Placing the operator *before* the expression is known as a *prefix*; placing the operator *after* the expression is known as a *postfix*. Note that there is a difference in the way they behave.

The increment and decrement operators can act both as entire expressions and within expressions. When used by themselves, the effect of both the prefix and postfix versions is identical and corresponds to the statement x = x + 1. When used within larger expressions, the prefix operator increments the value of x *before* the expression is evaluated; in other words, x is incremented, and the new value is used as the result of the expression. Conversely, the postfix operator increments the value of x *after* the expression is evaluated. The result of the expression returns the original value of x. The following example uses the increment operator (++) as an example to demonstrate the difference between the prefix and postfix behavior (code file OperatorsSample/Program.cs):

```
void PrefixAndPostfix()
{
  int x = 5;
  if (++x == 6) // true - x is incremented to 6 before the evaluation
  {
    Console.WriteLine("This will execute");
  }
  if (x++ == 6) // true - x is incremented to 7 after the evaluation
  {
    Console.WriteLine("The value of x is: {x}"); // x has the value 7
  }
}
```

The following sections look at some of the commonly used and new operators that you will frequently use within your C# code.

The Conditional-Expression Operator (?:)

The conditional-expression operator (?:), also known as the *ternary operator*, is a shorthand form of the if...else construction. It gets its name from the fact that it involves three operands. It allows you to evaluate a condition, returning one value if that condition is true or another value if it is false. The syntax is as follows:

```
condition ? true_value: false_value
```

Here, condition is the Boolean expression to be evaluated, true_value is the value that is returned if condition is true, and false_value is the value that is returned otherwise.

When used sparingly, the conditional-expression operator can add a dash of terseness to your programs. It is especially handy for providing one of a couple of arguments to a function that is being invoked. You can use it to quickly convert a Boolean value to a string value of `true` or `false`. It is also handy for displaying the correct singular or plural form of a word (code file `OperatorsSample/Program.cs`):

```
int x = 1;
string s = x + " ";
s += (x == 1 ? "man": "men");
Console.WriteLine(s);
```

This code displays `1 man` if x is equal to one but displays the correct plural form for any other number. Note, however, that if your output needs to be localized to different languages, you have to write more sophisticated routines to take into account the different grammatical rules of different languages. Read Chapter 22, "Localization," for globalizing and localizing .NET applications.

The checked and unchecked Operators

Consider the following code:

```
byte b = byte.MaxValue;
b++;
Console.WriteLine(b);
```

The `byte` data type can hold values only in the range 0 to 255. Assigning `byte.MaxValue` to a byte results in 255. With 255, all bits of the 8 available bits in the byte are set: 11111111. Incrementing this value by one causes an overflow and results in 0.

To get exceptions in such cases, C# provides the `checked` and `unchecked` operators. If you mark a block of code as `checked`, the CLR enforces overflow checking, throwing an `OverflowException` if an overflow occurs. The following changes the preceding code to include the `checked` operator (code file `OperatorsSample/Program.cs`):

```
byte b = 255;
checked
{
  b++;
}
Console.WriteLine(b);
```

Instead of writing a `checked` block, you also can use the `checked` keyword in an expression:

```
b = checked(b + 3);
```

When you try to run this code, the `OverflowException` is thrown.

You can enforce overflow checking for all unmarked code by adding the `CheckForOverflowUnderflow` setting in the `csproj` file:

```
<PropertyGroup>
  <OutputType>Exe</OutputType>
  <TargetFramework>net5.0</TargetFramework>
  <Nullable>enable</Nullable>
  <CheckForOverflowUnderflow>true</CheckForOverflowUnderflow>
</PropertyGroup>
```

With a project setting to be configured for overflow checking, you can mark code that should not be checked using the `unchecked` operator.

> **NOTE** *By default, overflow and underflow are not checked because enforcing checks has a performance impact. When you use checked as the default setting with your project, the result of every arithmetic operation needs to be verified regardless of whether the value is out of bounds. i++ is an arithmetic operation that's used a lot with* `for` *loops. To avoid having this performance impact, it's better to keep the default setting (Check for Arithmetic Overflow/Underflow) unchecked and use the* `checked` *operator where needed.*

The is and as Operators

You can use the `is` and `as` operators to determine whether an object is compatible with a specific type. This is useful with class hierarchies.

Let's assume a simple class hierarchy. The class `DerivedClass` derives from the class `BaseClass`. You can assign a variable of type `DerivedClass` to a variable of type `BaseClass`; all the members of the `BaseClass` are available with the `DerivedClass`. In the following example, an implicit conversion is taking place:

```
BaseClass = new();
DerivedClass = new();
baseClass = derivedClass;
```

If you have a parameter of the `BaseClass` and want to assign it to a variable of the `DerivedClass`, implicit conversion is not possible. To the `SomeAction` method, an instance of the `BaseClass` or any type that derives from this class can be passed. This will not necessarily succeed. Here, you can use the `as` operator. The `as` operator either returns a `DerivedClass` instance (if the variable is of this type) or returns `null`:

```
public void SomeAction(BaseClass baseClass)
{
  DerivedClass? derivedClass = baseClass as DerivedClass;
  if (derivedClass != null)
  {
    // use the derivedClass variable
  }
}
```

Instead of using the `as` operator, you can use the `is` operator. The `is` operator returns `true` if the conversion succeeds; otherwise, it returns `false`. With the `is` operator, a variable can be specified that is assigned if the `is` operator returns true:

```
public void SomeAction(BaseClass baseClass)
{
  if (baseClass is DerivedClass derivedClass)
  {
    // use the derivedClass variable
  }
}
```

> **NOTE** *Chapter 2 covers pattern matching with the* `is` *operator using const, type, and relational patterns.*

The sizeof Operator

You can determine the size (in bytes) required on the stack by a value type using the `sizeof` operator (code file `OperatorsSample/Program.cs`):

```
Console.WriteLine(sizeof(int));
```

This displays the number 4 because an `int` is 4 bytes long.

You can also use the `sizeof` operator with structs if the struct contains only value types—for example, the `Point` class as shown here (code file `OperatorsSample/Point.cs`):

```
public readonly struct Point
{
  public Point(int x, int y) => (X, Y) = (x, y);

  public int X { get; }
  public int Y { get; }
}
```

> **NOTE** *You cannot use* `sizeof` *with classes.*

When you use `sizeof` with custom types, you need to write the code within an unsafe code block (code file `OperatorsSample/Program.cs`):

```
unsafe
{
  Console.WriteLine(sizeof(Point));
}
```

> **NOTE** *By default, unsafe code is not allowed. You need to specify the* `AllowUnsafeBlocks` *in the* `csproj` *project file. Chapter 13 looks at unsafe code in more detail.*

The typeof Operator

The `typeof` operator returns a `System.Type` object representing a specified type. For example, `typeof(string)` returns a `Type` object representing the `System.String` type. This is useful when you want to use reflection to find information about an object dynamically. For more information, see Chapter 12, "Reflection, Metadata, and Source Generators."

The nameof Expression

The `nameof` operator is of practical use when strings are needed as parameters that are already known at compile time. This operator accepts a symbol, property, or method and returns the name.

One use example is when the name of a variable is needed, as in checking a parameter for null, as shown here:

```
public void Method(object o)
{
  if (o == null) throw new ArgumentNullException(nameof(o));
}
```

Of course, it would be similar to throw the exception by passing a string instead of using the `nameof` operator. However, using `nameof` prevents you from misspelling the parameter name when you pass it to the exception's constructor. Also, when you change the name of the parameter, you can easily miss changing the string passed to the `ArgumentNullException` constructor. Refactoring features also help changing all occurrences where `nameof` is used:

```
if (o == null) throw new ArgumentNullException("o");
```

Using the `nameof` operator for the name of a variable is just one use case. You can also use it to get the name of a property—for example, for firing a change event (using the interface `INotifyPropertyChanged`) in a property `set` accessor and passing the name of a property.

```
public string FirstName
{
  get => _firstName;
  set
  {
    _firstName = value;
    OnPropertyChanged(nameof(FirstName));
  }
}
```

The `nameof` operator can also be used to get the name of a method. This also works if the method is overloaded because all overloads result in the same value: the name of the method.

```
public void Method()
{
  Log($"{nameof(Method)} called");
}
```

The Indexer

You use the indexer (brackets) for accessing arrays in Chapter 6. In the following code snippet, the indexer is used to access the third element of the array named `arr1` by passing the number 2:

```
int[] arr1 = {1, 2, 3, 4};
int x = arr1[2]; // x == 3
```

Similarly to accessing elements of an array, the indexer is implemented with collection classes (discussed in Chapter 8, "Collections").

The indexer doesn't require an integer within the brackets. Indexers can be defined with any type. The following code snippet creates a generic dictionary where the key is a `string` and the value an `int`. With dictionaries, the key can be used with the indexer. In the following sample, the string `first` is passed to the indexer to set this element in the dictionary, and then the same string is passed to the indexer to retrieve this element:

```
Dictionary<string, int> dict = new();
dict["first"] = 1;
int x = dict["first"];
```

> **NOTE** *Later in this chapter in the "Implementing Custom Indexers" section, you can read how to create index operators in your own classes.*

The Null-Coalescing and Null-Coalescing Assignment Operators

The null-coalescing operator (`??`) provides a shorthand mechanism to cater to the possibility of `null` values when working with nullable and reference types. The operator is placed between two operands—the first operand must be a nullable type or reference type, and the second operand must be of the same type as the first or of a type that is implicitly convertible to the type of the first operand. The null-coalescing operator evaluates as follows:

➤   If the first operand is not `null`, then the overall expression has the value of the first operand.

➤   If the first operand is `null`, then the overall expression has the value of the second operand.

Here's an example:

```
int? a = null;
int b;
b = a ?? 10; // b has the value 10
a = 3;
b = a ?? 10; // b has the value 3
```

If the second operand cannot be implicitly converted to the type of the first operand, a compile-time error is generated.

The null-coalescing operator is not only important with nullable types but also with reference types. In the following code snippet, the property `Val` returns the value of the `_val` variable only if it is not null. In case it is null, a new instance of `MyClass` is created, assigned to the `_val` variable, and finally returned from the property. This second part of the expression within the `get` accessor only happens when the variable `_val` is null:

```
private MyClass _val;
public MyClass Val
{
  get => _val ?? (_val = new MyClass());
}
```

Using the null-coalescing assignment operator, the preceding code can now be simplified to create a new `MyClass` and assign it to `_val` if `_val` is null:

```
private MyClass _val;
public MyClass Val
{
  get => _val ??= new MyClass();
}
```

The Null-Conditional Operator

The *null-conditional operator*, is a feature of C# that reduces the number of code lines. A great number of code lines in production code verify null conditions. Before accessing members of a variable that is passed as a method parameter, the variable needs to be checked to determine whether it has a value of null. Otherwise, a `NullReferenceException` would be thrown. A .NET design guideline specifies that code should never throw exceptions of these types and should always check for null conditions. However, such checks could be missed easily. This code snippet verifies whether the passed parameter `p` is not null. In case it is null, the method just returns without continuing:

```
public void ShowPerson(Person? p)
{
  if (p is null) return;
  string firstName = p.FirstName;
  //...
}
```

Using the null-conditional operator to access the `FirstName` property (`p?.FirstName`), when `p` is `null`, only `null` is returned without continuing to the right side of the expression (code file `OperatorsSample/Program.cs`):

```
public void ShowPerson(Person? p)
{
  string firstName = p?.FirstName;
  //...
}
```

When a property of an `int` type is accessed using the null-conditional operator, the result cannot be directly assigned to an `int` type because the result can be `null`. One option to resolve this is to assign the result to a nullable `int`:

```
int? age = p?.Age;
```

Of course, you can also solve this issue by using the null-coalescing operator and defining another result (for example, `0`) in case the result of the left side is `null`:

```
int age1 = p?.Age ?? 0;
```

You also can combine multiple null-conditional operators. In the following example, the `Address` property of a `Person` object is accessed, and this property in turn defines a `City` property. Null checks need to be done for the `Person` object and, if it is not null, also for the result of the `Address` property:

```
Person p = GetPerson();
string city = null;
if (p != null && p.HomeAddress != null)
{
  city = p.HomeAddress.City;
}
```

When you use the null-conditional operator, the code becomes much simpler:

```
string city = p?.HomeAddress?.City;
```

You can also use the null-conditional operator with arrays. With the following code snippet, a `NullReferenceException` is thrown using the index operator to access an element of an array variable that is `null`:

```
int[] arr = null;
int x1 = arr[0];
```

Of course, traditional null checks could be done to avoid this exceptional condition. A simpler version uses `?[0]` to access the first element of the array. In case the result is `null`, the null-coalescing operator returns the value 0 for the `x1` variable:

```
int x1 = arr?[0] ?? 0;
```

USING BINARY OPERATORS

Working with binary values historically has been an important concept to understand when learning programming because the computer works with 0s and 1s. Many people who are newer to programming may have missed learning this because they start to learn programming with Blocks, Scratch, Python, and possibly JavaScript. If you are already fluent with 0s and 1s, this section might still help you as a refresher.

First, let's start with simple calculations using binary operators. The method `SimpleCalculations` first declares and initializes the variables `binary1` and `binary2` with binary values—using the binary literal and digit separators. Using the & operator, the two values are combined with the binary AND operator and written to the variable binaryAnd. In the following code, the | operator is used to create the binaryOr variable, the ^ operator for the binaryXOR variable, and the ~ operator for the reverse1 variable (code file BinaryCalculations/Program.cs):

```
void SimpleCalculations()
{
    Console.WriteLine(nameof(SimpleCalculations));
    uint binary1 = 0b1111_0000_1100_0011_1110_0001_0001_1000;
    uint binary2 = 0b0000_1111_1100_0011_0101_1010_1110_0111;
    uint binaryAnd = binary1 & binary2;
    DisplayBits("AND", binaryAnd, binary1, binary2);
    uint binaryOR = binary1 | binary2;
    DisplayBits("OR", binaryOR, binary1, binary2);
    uint binaryXOR = binary1 ^ binary2;
    DisplayBits("XOR", binaryXOR, binary1, binary2);
    uint reverse1 = ~binary1;
    DisplayBits("NOT", reverse1, binary1);
    Console.WriteLine();
}
```

To display uint and int variables in a binary form, the extension method ToBinaryString is created. Convert.ToString offers an overload with two int parameters, where the second int value is the toBase parameter. Using this, you can format the output string binary by passing the value 2 (for binary), 8 (for octal), 10 (for decimal), and 16 (for hexadecimal). By default, if a binary value starts with 0 values, these values are ignored and not printed. The PadLeft method fills up these 0 values in the string. The number of string characters needed is calculated by the sizeof operator and a left shift of four bits. The sizeof operator returns the number of bytes for the specified type, as discussed earlier in this chapter. For displaying the bits, the number of bytes needs to be multiplied by 8, which is the same as shifting three bits to the left. Another extension method is AddSeparators, which adds _ separators after every four digits using LINQ methods (code file BinaryCalculations/BinaryExtensions.cs):

```
public static class BinaryExtensions
{
    public static string ToBinaryString(this uint number) =>
        Convert.ToString(number, toBase: 2).PadLeft(sizeof(uint) << 3, '0');

    public static string ToBinaryString(this int number) =>
        Convert.ToString(number, toBase: 2).PadLeft(sizeof(int) << 3, '0');

    public static string AddSeparators(this string number) =>
        string.Join('_',
            Enumerable.Range(0, number.Length / 4)
                .Select(i => number.Substring(i * 4, 4)).ToArray());
}
```

> **NOTE** *The* AddSeparators *method makes use of LINQ. LINQ is discussed in detail in Chapter 9, "Language Integrated Query."*

The method `DisplayBits`, which is invoked from the previously shown `SimpleCalculations` method, makes use of the `ToBinaryString` and `AddSeparators` extension methods. Here, the operands used for the operation are displayed, as well as the result (code file `BinaryCalculations/Program.cs`):

```
void DisplayBits(string title, uint result, uint left,
  uint? right = null)
{
  Console.WriteLine(title);
  Console.WriteLine(left.ToBinaryString().AddSeparators());
  if (right.HasValue)
  {
    Console.WriteLine(right.Value.ToBinaryString().AddSeparators());
  }
  Console.WriteLine(result.ToBinaryString().AddSeparators());
  Console.WriteLine();
}
```

When you run the application, you can see the following output using the binary & operator. With this operator, the resulting bits are only 1 when both input values are also 1:

```
AND
1111_0000_1100_0011_1110_0001_0001_1000
0000_1111_1100_0011_0101_1010_1110_0111
0000_0000_1100_0011_0100_0000_0000_0000
```

When you apply the binary | operator, the result bit is set (1) if one of the input bits is set:

```
OR
1111_0000_1100 0011_1110_0001_0001_1000
0000_1111_1100_0011_0101_1010_1110_0111
1111_1111_1100_0011_1111_1011_1111_1111
```

With the ^ operator, the result is set if just one of the original bits is set, but not both:

```
XOR
1111_0000_1100_0011_1110_0001_0001_1000
0000_1111_1100_0011_0101_1010_1110_0111
1111_1111_0000_0000_1011_1011_1111_1111
```

And finally, with the ~ operator, the result is the negation of the original:

```
NOT
1111_0000_1100_0011_1110_0001_0001_1000
0000_1111_0011_1100_0001_1110_1110_0111
```

> **NOTE** *For working with binary values, read about using the* `BitArray` *class in Chapter 6.*

Shifting Bits

As you've already seen in the previous sample, shifting three bits to the left is a multiplication by 8. A shift by one bit is a multiplication by 2. This is a lot faster than invoking the multiply operator—in case you need to multiply by 2, 4, 8, 16, 32, and so on.

The following code snippet sets one bit in the variable s1, and in the for loop the bit always shifts by one bit (code file BinaryCalculations/Program.cs):

```
void ShiftingBits()
{
  Console.WriteLine(nameof(ShiftingBits));
  ushort s1 = 0b01;
  Console.WriteLine($"{"Binary",16} {"Decimal",8} {"Hex",6}");
  for (int i = 0; i < 16; i++)
  {
    Console.WriteLine($"{s1.ToBinaryString(),16} {s1,8} hex: {s1,6:X}");
    s1 = (ushort)(s1 << 1);
  }
  Console.WriteLine();
}
```

In the program output, you can see binary, decimal, and hexadecimal values with the loop:

```
          Binary  Decimal    Hex
0000000000000001        1      1
0000000000000010        2      2
0000000000000100        4      4
0000000000001000        8      8
0000000000010000       16     10
0000000000100000       32     20
0000000001000000       64     40
0000000010000000      128     80
0000000100000000      256    100
0000001000000000      512    200
0000010000000000     1024    400
0000100000000000     2048    800
0001000000000000     4096   1000
0010000000000000     8192   2000
0100000000000000    16384   4000
1000000000000000    32768   8000
```

Signed and Unsigned Numbers

One important thing to remember when working with binary numbers is that when using signed types, such as int, long, and short, the leftmost bit is used to represent the sign. When you use an int, the highest number available is 2147483647—the positive number of 31 bits or 0x7FFF_FFFF. With a uint, the highest number available is 4294967295 or 0xFFFF_FFFF. This represents the positive number of 32 bits. With the int, the other half of the number range is used for negative numbers.

To understand how negative numbers are represented, the following code snippet initializes the maxNumber variable to the highest positive number that fits into 15 bits using short.MaxValue. Then, in a for loop, the variable is incremented three times. In the results, binary, decimal, and hexadecimal values are shown (code file BinaryCalculations/Program.cs):

```
void SignedNumbers()
{
  Console.WriteLine(nameof(SignedNumbers));

  void DisplayNumber(string title, short x) =>
    Console.WriteLine($"{title,-11} " +
      $"bin: {x.ToBinaryString().AddSeparators()}, " +
      $"dec: {x,6}, hex: {x,4:X}");
```

```
    short maxNumber = short.MaxValue;
    DisplayNumber("max short", maxNumber);
    for (int i = 0; i < 3; i++)
    {
      maxNumber++;
      DisplayNumber($"added {i + 1}", maxNumber);
    }
    Console.WriteLine();
    //...
  }
```

With the output of the application, you can see all the bits—except the sign bit—are set to achieve the maximum integer value. The output shows the same value in different formats—binary, decimal, and hexadecimal. Adding 1 to the first output results in an overflow of the short type setting the sign bit, and all other bits are 0. This is the highest negative value for the int type. After this result, two more increments are done:

```
max short    bin: 0111_1111_1111_1111, dec:  32767, hex: 7FFF
added 1      bin: 1000_0000_0000_0000, dec: -32768, hex: 8000
added 2      bin: 1000_0000_0000_0001, dec: -32767, hex: 8001
added 3      bin: 1000_0000_0000_0010, dec: -32766, hex: 8002
```

With the next code snippet, the variable zero is initialized to 0. In the for loop, this variable is decremented three times:

```
short zero = 0;
DisplayNumber("zero", zero);
for (int i = 0; i < 3; i++)
{
  zero--;
  DisplayNumber($"subtracted {i + 1}", zero);
}
Console.WriteLine();
```

With the output, you can see 0 is represented with all the bits not set. Doing a decrement results in decimal -1, which is all the bits set, including the sign bit:

```
zero          bin: 0000_0000_0000_0000, dec:     0, hex:    0
subtracted 1 bin: 1111_1111_1111_1111, dec:    -1, hex: FFFF
subtracted 2 bin: 1111_1111_1111_1110, dec:    -2, hex: FFFE
subtracted 3 bin: 1111_1111_1111_1101, dec:    -3, hex: FFFD
```

Next, start with the largest negative number for a short. The number is incremented three times:

```
short minNumber = short.MinValue;
DisplayNumber("min number", minNumber);
for (int i = 0; i < 3; i++)
{
  minNumber++;
  DisplayNumber($"added {i + 1}", minNumber);
}
Console.WriteLine();
```

The highest negative number was already shown earlier when overflowing the highest positive number. Earlier you saw this same number when int.MinValue was used. This number is then incremented three times:

```
min number   bin: 1000_0000_0000_0000, dec: -32768, hex: 8000
added 1      bin: 1000_0000_0000_0001, dec: -32767, hex: 8001
added 2      bin: 1000_0000_0000_0010, dec: -32766, hex: 8002
added 3      bin: 1000_0000_0000_0011, dec: -32765, hex: 8003
```

TYPE SAFETY

The Intermediate Language (IL) enforces strong type safety upon its code. Strong typing enables many of the services provided by .NET, including security and language interoperability. As you would expect from a language compiled into IL, C# is also strongly typed. Among other things, this means that data types are not always seamlessly interchangeable. This section looks at conversions between primitive types.

> **NOTE** *C# also supports conversions between different reference types and allows you to define how data types that you create behave when converted to and from other types. Both of these topics are discussed later in this chapter.*
>
> *Generics, however, enable you to avoid some of the most common situations in which you would need to perform type conversions. See Chapter 4, "Object-Oriented Programming in C#", and Chapter 8 when using many generic collection classes.*

Type Conversions

Often, you need to convert data from one type to another. Consider the following code:

```
byte value1 = 10;
byte value2 = 23;
byte total = value1 + value2;
Console.WriteLine(total);
```

When you attempt to compile these lines, you get the following error message:

```
Cannot implicitly convert type 'int' to 'byte'
```

The problem here is that when you add 2 bytes together, the result is returned as an int, not another byte. This is because a byte can contain only 8 bits of data, so adding 2 bytes together could easily result in a value that cannot be stored in a single byte. If you want to store this result in a byte variable, you have to convert it back to a byte. The following sections discuss two conversion mechanisms supported by C#—*implicit* and *explicit*.

Implicit Conversions

Conversion between types can normally be achieved automatically (implicitly) only if you can guarantee that the value is not changed in any way. This is why the previous code failed; by attempting a conversion from an int to a byte, you were potentially losing 3 bytes of data. The compiler won't let you do that unless you explicitly specify that's what you want to do. If you store the result in a long instead of a byte, however, you will have no problems:

```
byte value1 = 10;
byte value2 = 23;
long total = value1 + value2; // this will compile fine
Console.WriteLine(total);
```

Your program has compiled with no errors at this point because a long holds more bytes of data than a byte, so there is no risk of data being lost. In these circumstances, the compiler is happy to make the conversion for you without you needing to ask for it explicitly. As you would expect, you can perform implicit conversions only from a smaller integer type to a larger one, not from larger to smaller. You can also convert between integers and floating-point values; however, the rules are slightly different here. Though you can convert between types of the same size, such as int/uint to float and long/ulong to double, you can also convert from long/ulong to float. You might lose 4 bytes of data doing this, but it only means that the value of the float you receive will be less precise than if you had used a `double`; the compiler regards this as an acceptable possible error because the magnitude of the value is not affected. You can also assign an unsigned variable to a signed variable as long as the value limits of the unsigned type fit between the limits of the signed variable.

Nullable value types introduce additional considerations when you're implicitly converting value types:

➤ Nullable value types implicitly convert to other nullable value types following the conversion rules described for non-nullable types in the previous rules; that is, `int?` implicitly converts to `long?`, `float?`, `double?`, and `decimal?`.

➤ Non-nullable value types implicitly convert to nullable value types according to the conversion rules described in the preceding rules; that is, `int` implicitly converts to `long?`, `float?`, `double?`, and `decimal?`.

➤ Nullable value types do not implicitly convert to non-nullable value types; you must perform an explicit conversion as described in the next section. That's because there is a chance that a nullable value type will have the value `null`, which cannot be represented by a non-nullable type.

Explicit Conversions

Many conversions cannot be implicitly made between types, and the compiler returns an error if any are attempted. The following are some of the conversions that cannot be made implicitly:

➤ `int` to `short`—Data loss is possible.

➤ `int` to `uint`—Data loss is possible.

➤ `uint` to `int`—Data loss is possible.

➤ `float` to `int`—Everything is lost after the decimal point.

➤ Any numeric type to `char`—Data loss is possible.

➤ `decimal` to any other numeric type—The decimal type is internally structured differently from both integers and floating-point numbers.

➤ `int?` to `int`—The nullable type may have the value `null`.

However, you can explicitly carry out such conversions using *casts*. When you cast one type to another, you deliberately force the compiler to make the conversion. A cast looks like this:

```
long val = 30000;
int i = (int)val; // A valid cast. The maximum int is 2147483647
```

You indicate the type to which you are casting by placing its name in parentheses before the value to be converted.

Casting can be a dangerous operation to undertake. Even a simple cast from a `long` to an `int` can cause problems if the value of the original `long` is greater than the maximum value of an `int`:

```
long val = 3000000000;
int i = (int)val; // An invalid cast. The maximum int is 2147483647
```

In this case, you get neither an error nor the result you expect. If you run this code and output the value stored in `i`, this is what you get:

```
-1294967296
```

It is good practice to assume that an explicit cast does not return the results you expect. As shown earlier, C# provides a `checked` operator that you can use to test whether an operation causes an arithmetic overflow. You can use the `checked` operator to confirm that a cast is safe and to force the runtime to throw an overflow exception if it is not:

```
long val = 3000000000;
int i = checked((int)val);
```

Bearing in mind that all explicit casts are potentially unsafe, make sure you include code in your application to deal with possible failures of the casts. Chapter 10, "Errors and Exceptions," introduces structured exception handling using the `try` and `catch` statements.

Using casts, you can convert most primitive data types from one type to another; for example, in the following code, the value `0.5` is added to `price`, and the total is cast to an `int`:

```
double price = 25.30;
int approximatePrice = (int)(price + 0.5);
```

This gives the price rounded to the nearest dollar. However, in this conversion, data is lost—namely, everything after the decimal point. Therefore, such a conversion should never be used if you want to continue to do more calculations using this modified price value. However, it is useful if you want to output the approximate value of a completed or partially completed calculation—if you don't want to bother the user with a lot of figures after the decimal point.

This example shows what happens if you convert an unsigned integer into a `char`:

```
ushort c = 43;
char symbol = (char)c;
Console.WriteLine(symbol);
```

The output is the character that has an ASCII number of 43, which is the + sign. This will work for any kind of conversion you want between the numeric types (including `char`), such as converting a `decimal` into a `char`, or vice versa.

Converting between value types is not restricted to isolated variables, as you have seen. You can convert an array element of type `double` to a struct member variable of type `int`:

```
struct ItemDetails
{
  public string Description;
  public int ApproxPrice;
}
//...
double[] Prices = { 25.30, 26.20, 27.40, 30.00 };
ItemDetails id;
id.Description = "Hello there.";
id.ApproxPrice = (int)(Prices[0] + 0.5);
```

To convert a nullable type to a non-nullable type or another nullable type where data loss may occur, you must use an explicit cast. This is true even when converting between elements with the same basic underlying type—for example, `int?` to `int` or `float?` to `float`. This is because the nullable type may have the value `null`, which cannot be represented by the non-nullable type. As long as an explicit cast between two equivalent non-nullable types is possible, so is the explicit cast between nullable types. However, when casting from a nullable type to a non-nullable type and the variable has the value `null`, an `InvalidOperationException` is thrown. Here is an example:

```
int? a = null;
int b = (int)a; // Will throw exception
```

By using explicit casts and a bit of care and attention, you can convert any instance of a simple value type to almost any other. However, there are limitations on what you can do with explicit type conversions—as far as value types are concerned, you can only convert to and from the numeric and `char` types and `enum` types. You cannot directly cast Booleans to any other type or vice versa.

If you need to convert between numeric and string, you can use methods provided in the .NET class library. The `Object` class implements a `ToString` method, which has been overridden in all the .NET predefined types and which returns a string representation of the object:

```
int i = 10;
string s = i.ToString();
```

Similarly, if you need to parse a string to retrieve a numeric or Boolean value, you can use the `Parse` method supported by all the predefined value types:

```
string s = "100";
int i = int.Parse(s);
Console.WriteLine(i + 50); // Add 50 to prove it is really an int
```

Note that `Parse` registers an error by throwing an exception if it is unable to convert the string (for example, if you try to convert the string `Hello` to an integer). Again, exceptions are covered in Chapter 10. Instead of using the `Parse` method, you can also use `TryParse`, which doesn't throw an exception in case of an error, but returns `true` if it succeeds.

Boxing and Unboxing

Chapter 2 explains that all types—both the simple predefined types, such as `int` and `char`, and the complex types, such as classes and structs—derive from the `object` type. This means you can treat even literal values as though they are objects:

```
string s = 10.ToString();
```

However, you also saw that C# data types are divided into value types, which are allocated on the stack, and reference types, which are allocated on the managed heap. How does this work with the capability to call methods on an `int`, if the `int` is nothing more than a 4-byte value on the stack?

C# achieves this through a bit of magic called *boxing*. Boxing and its counterpart, *unboxing*, enable you to convert value types to reference types and then back to value types. I include this topic in the section on casting because this is essentially what you are doing—you are casting your value to the `object` type. Boxing is the term used to describe the transformation of a value type to a reference type. Basically, the runtime creates a temporary reference-type box for the object on the heap.

This conversion can occur implicitly, as in the preceding example, but you can also perform it explicitly:

```
int myIntNumber = 20;
object myObject = myIntNumber;
```

Unboxing is the term used to describe the reverse process, whereby the value of a previously boxed value type is cast back to a value type. Here, I use the term *cast* because this has to be done explicitly. The syntax is similar to explicit type conversions already described:

```
int myIntNumber = 20;
object myObject = myIntNumber; // Box the int
int mySecondNumber = (int)myObject; // Unbox it back into an int
```

A variable can be unboxed only if it has been boxed. If you execute the last line when `myObject` is not a boxed `int`, you get a runtime exception.

One word of warning: When unboxing, you have to be careful that the receiving value is of the same type as the value that was boxed. Even if the resulting type has enough room to store all the bytes in the value being unboxed, an `InvalidCastException` is thrown. You can avoid this by casting from the original type in the new type, as shown here:

```
int myIntNumber = 42;
object myObject = (object)myIntNumber;
long myLongNumber = (long)(int)myObject;
```

OPERATOR OVERLOADING

Instead of invoking methods, the code can become more readable using operators. Just compare these two code lines to add two vectors:

```
vect3 = vect1 + vect2;
vect3 = vect1.Add(vect2);
```

With predefined number types, you can use +, -, /, *, and % operators, and you can also concatenate strings with the + operator. Using such operators is not only possible with predefined types, but also with custom types as long as they make sense with the types. What would a + operator used with two `Person` objects do?

You can overload the following operators:

OPERATORS	DESCRIPTION
`+x, -x, !x, ~x, ++, --, true, false`	These are unary operators that can be overloaded.
`x + y, x - y, x * y, x / y, x % y, x & y, x	y, x ^ y, x << y, x >> y, x == y, x != y, x < y, x > y, x <= y, x >= y`	These are binary operators that can be overloaded.
`a[i], a?[i]`	Element access cannot be overloaded with an operator overload, but you can create an indexer, which is shown later in this chapter.
`(T)x`	Instead of using an operator overload, you can use the cast to create a user-defined conversion, which is shown later in this chapter as well.

> **NOTE** *You might wonder what the reason is for overloading the* `true` *and* `false` *operators. Conditional logical operators* `&&` *and* `||` *cannot be directly overloaded. To create a custom implementation for these operators, you can overload the* `true`, *the* `false`, *the* `&`, *and the* `|` *operators.*
>
> *Similarly, you can't explicitly overload compound conversion operators such as* `+=` *and* `-=`. *If you overload the binary operator, compound conversion is implicitly overloaded.*
>
> *Some operators need to be overloaded in pairs. If you overload* `==`, *you also must overload* `!=`. *If you overload* `<`, *then you must overload* `>`, *and if you overload* `<=`, *then you must overload* `>=`.

How Operators Work

To understand how to overload operators, it's useful to think about what happens when the compiler encounters an operator. Using the addition operator (+) as an example, suppose that the compiler processes the following lines of code:

```
int x = 1;
int y = 2;
long z = x + y;
```

The compiler identifies that it needs to add two integers and assign the result to a long. The expression x + y is just an intuitive and convenient syntax for calling a method that adds two numbers. The method takes two parameters, x and y, and returns their sum. Therefore, the compiler does the same thing it does for any method call: it looks for the best matching overload of the addition operator based on the parameter types—in this case, one that takes two integers. As with normal overloaded methods, the desired return type does not influence the compiler's choice as to which version of a method it calls. As it happens, the overload called in the example takes two int parameters and returns an int; this return value is subsequently converted to a long. This can result in an overflow if the two added int values don't fit into an int although a long is declared to write the result to.

The next lines cause the compiler to use a different overload of the addition operator:

```
double d1 = 4.0;
double d2 = d1 + x;
```

In this instance, the parameters are a double and an int, but there is no overload of the addition operator that takes this combination of parameters. Instead, the compiler identifies the best matching overload of the addition operator as being the version that takes two doubles as its parameters, and it implicitly casts the int to a double. Adding two doubles requires a different process from adding two integers. Floating-point numbers are stored as a mantissa and an exponent. Adding them involves bit-shifting the mantissa of one of the doubles so that the two exponents have the same value, adding the mantissas, and then shifting the mantissa of the result and adjusting its exponent to maintain the highest possible accuracy in the answer.

Now you are in a position to see what happens if the compiler finds something like this:

```
Vector vect1, vect2, vect3;
// initialize vect1 and vect2
vect3 = vect1 + vect2;
vect1 = vect1 * 2;
```

Here, Vector is the struct, which is defined in the following section. The compiler sees that it needs to add two Vector instances, vect1 and vect2, together. It looks for an overload of the addition operator, which takes two Vector instances as its parameters.

If the compiler finds an appropriate overload, it calls up the implementation of that operator. If it cannot find one, it checks whether there is any other overload for + that it can use as a best match—perhaps something with two parameters of other data types that can be implicitly converted to Vector instances. If the compiler cannot find a suitable overload, it raises a compilation error, just as it would if it could not find an appropriate overload for any other method call.

Operator Overloading with the Vector Type

This section demonstrates operator overloading through developing a struct named Vector that represents a three-dimensional vector. The 3D vector is just a set of three numbers (doubles) that tell you how far something is moving. The variables representing the numbers are called x, y, and z: the x tells you how far something moves east, y tells you how far it moves north, and z tells you how far it moves upward. Combine the three numbers and you get the total movement.

You can add or multiply vectors by other vectors or by numbers. Incidentally, in this context, we use the term *scalar*, which is math-speak for a simple number—in C# terms that is just a double. The significance of addition should be clear. If you move first by the vector (3.0, 3.0, 1.0) and then move by the vector (2.0, -4.0, -4.0), the total amount you have moved can be determined by adding the two vectors. Adding vectors means adding each component individually, so you get (5.0, -1.0, -3.0). In this context, mathematicians write c=a+b, where a and b are the vectors and c is the resulting vector. You want to be able to use the Vector struct the same way.

> **NOTE** *The fact that this example is developed as a struct rather than a class is not significant with operator overloading. Operator overloading works in the same way for structs, classes, and records.*

The following is the definition for `Vector`—containing the read-only public fields, constructors, and a `ToString` override so you can easily view the contents of a `Vector`. Operator overloads are added next (code file `OperatorOverloadingSample/Vector.cs`):

```
readonly struct Vector
{
  public Vector(double x, double y, double z) => (X, Y, Z) = (x, y, z);

  public Vector(Vector v) => (X, Y, Z) = (v.X, v.Y, v.Z);

  public readonly double X;
  public readonly double Y;
  public readonly double Z;
  public override string ToString() => $"( {X}, {Y}, {Z} )";
}
```

This example has two constructors that require specifying the initial value of the vector, either by passing in the values of each component or by supplying another `Vector` whose value can be copied. Constructors like the second one, which takes a single `Vector` argument, are often termed *copy constructors* because they effectively enable you to initialize a class or struct instance by copying another instance.

Here is the interesting part of the `Vector` struct—the operator overload that provides support for the addition operator:

```
public static Vector operator +(Vector left, Vector right) =>
  new Vector(left.X + right.X, left.Y + right.Y, left.Z + right.Z);
```

The operator overload is declared in much the same way as a static method, except that the `operator` keyword tells the compiler it is actually an operator overload you are defining. The `operator` keyword is followed by the actual symbol for the relevant operator, in this case the addition operator (+). The return type is whatever type you get when you use this operator. Adding two vectors results in a vector; therefore, the return type is also a `Vector`. For this particular override of the addition operator, the return type is the same as the containing class, but that is not necessarily the case, as you see later in this example. The two parameters are the things you are operating on. For binary operators (those that take two parameters), such as the addition and subtraction operators, the first parameter is the value on the left of the operator, and the second parameter is the value on the right.

The implementation of this operator returns a new `Vector` that is initialized using the X, Y, and Z fields from the `left` and `right` variables.

C# requires that all operator overloads be declared as `public` and `static`, which means they are associated with their class or struct, not with a particular instance. Because of this, the body of the operator overload has no access to nonstatic class members or the `this` identifier. This is fine because the parameters provide all the input data the operator needs to know to perform its task.

Now all you need to do is write some simple code to test the `Vector` struct (code file `OperatorOverloadingSample/Program.cs`):

```
Vector vect1, vect2, vect3;
vect1 = new(3.0, 3.0, 1.0);
vect2 = new(2.0, -4.0, -4.0);
vect3 = vect1 + vect2;
Console.WriteLine($"vect1 = {vect1}");
Console.WriteLine($"vect2 = {vect2}");
Console.WriteLine($"vect3 = {vect3}");
```

Compiling and running this code returns the following result:

```
vect1 = ( 3, 3, 1 )
vect2 = ( 2, -4, -4 )
vect3 = ( 5, -1, -3 )
```

Just by implementing the + operator, you can use the compound assignment operator +=. Let's add vect2 to the existing value of vect3:

```
vect3 += vect2;
Console.WriteLine($"vect3 = {vect3}");
```

This compiles and runs, resulting in the following:

```
vect3 = ( 7, -5, -7)
```

In addition to adding vectors, you can multiply and subtract them and compare their values. These operators can be implemented in the same way as the + operator. What might be more interesting is multiplying a vector by a double. With the following three operator overloads, a vector is multiplied by a vector, a vector is multiplied by a double, and a double is multiplied by a vector. You need to implement the different operators depending what's on the left and right sides, but you can reuse implementations. The operator overload where the vector is on the left and the double on the right just reuses the operator overload where the arguments are changed (code file OperatorOverloadingSample/Vector.cs):

```
public static Vector operator *(Vector left, Vector right) =>
  new Vector(left.X * right.X, left.Y * right.Y, left.Z * right.Z);

public static Vector operator *(double left, Vector right) =>
  new Vector(left * right.X, left * right.Y, left * right.Z);

public static Vector operator *(Vector left, double right) =>
  right * left;
```

The operators are used in the following code snippet. The int number used is converted to a double because this is the best match for the overload:

```
Console.WriteLine($"2 * vect3 = {2 * vect3}");
Console.WriteLine($"vect3 += vect2 gives {vect3 += vect2}");
Console.WriteLine($"vect3 = vect1 * 2 gives {vect3 = vect1 * 2}");
Console.WriteLine($"vect1 * vect3 = {vect1 * vect3}");
```

> **NOTE** *There's an important restriction on operator overloading. Because operator overloads are defined using a static member, you cannot add static members to an interface contract. This might change in a future C# version; interfaces just got an improvement with C# 8 and default interface methods. Some more improvements have already been discussed.*
>
> *In case you need operator overloads with generic types, you can create constraints on classes. The types can also be abstract classes and generic types. With generic types, you can implement operator overloads.*

COMPARING OBJECTS FOR EQUALITY

Comparing objects for equality has become easier with C# 9 and records. Records already have built-in functionality to compare the values of the type. Let's look at what's implemented with records (what you can override) and what you need to do with classes and structs.

To compare references, the object class defines the static method ReferenceEquals. This is not a comparison by value; instead it just compares the variables if they reference the same object in the heap. The functionality is the same for classes and records. Comparing two variables referencing the same object in the heap returns true. If the two variables reference different objects in the heap, the method returns false, even if the content of the two objects is the same. Using this method to compare two variables referencing structs, new objects are created to reference the value type (known as *boxing*) and thus always returns `false`. The compiler warns on comparing structs this way.

The default implementation of the `object` class `Equals` method just invokes `object.ReferenceEquals`. In case you need to compare the values for equality, you can use the built-in functionality of the record type or create a custom implementation with the class. To compare the values of two reference types, you need to consider what's automatically implemented by a record and what you can implement when comparing classes for equality:

➤ The object type defines the virtual method `bool Equals(object?)` that can be overridden.

➤ The interface `IEquatable<T>` defines the generic method `bool Equals(T? object)` that can be implemented.

➤ The operators `==` and `!=` can be overridden.

➤ Records also implement an `EqualityContract`, which is used with the comparison to not only compare the values, but also if the comparison is done with the same contract.

To compare references, the `Book` class implements the `IEquatable<Book>` interface with the `bool Equals(Book? other)` method. This method compares the `Title` and `Publisher` properties. Similar to the record type, the `Book` class specifies the `EqualityContract` property to also compare the type of the class. This way, comparing the `Title` and `Publisher` properties with an object of another type returns always `false`. The implementation for equality comparison is only done with this method. The overridden `Equals` method from the base class invokes this method, as well as the implementation for the operators `==` and `!=`. Implementing equality also requires overriding the `GetHashCode` method from the base class (code file `EqualitySample/Book.cs`):

```
class Book : IEquatable<Book>
{
  public Book(string title, string publisher)
  {
    Title = title;
    Publisher = publisher;
  }
  public string Title { get; }
  public string Publisher { get; }

  protected virtual Type EqualityContract { get; } = typeof(Book);

  public override string ToString() => Title;

  public override bool Equals(object? obj) =>
    this == obj as Book;

  public override int GetHashCode() =>
    Title.GetHashCode() ^ Publisher.GetHashCode();

  public virtual bool Equals(Book? other) =>
    this == other;

  public static bool operator ==(Book? left, Book? right) =>
    left?.Title == right?.Title && left?.Publisher == right?.Publisher &&
    left?.EqualityContract == right?.EqualityContract;

  public static bool operator !=(Book? left, Book? right) =>
    !(left == right);
}
```

> **NOTE** *Don't be tempted to overload the comparison operator by only calling the instance version of the* Equals *method inherited from* System.Object. *If you do so and then an attempt is made to evaluate* (objA == objB), *when* objA *happens to be* null, *you get an exception because the .NET runtime tries to evaluate* null.Equals(objB). *Working the other way around (overriding* Equals *to call the comparison operator) should be safe.*

> **NOTE** *To implement equality comparison, some work is needed. With the record type, this work is done from the compiler. If you use records within records, everything works out of the box. However, if you use classes as record members, only references are compared— unless you implement equality comparison.*

In the `Program.cs` file, two `Book` objects are created that have the same content. Because there are two different objects in the heap, `object.ReferenceEquals` returns `false`. Next, the `Equals` method from the `IEquatable<Book>` interface, the overloaded `object Equals`, and the operator `==` are used, and they all return `true` because of the implemented value comparison (code file `EqualitySample/Program.cs`):

```
Book book1 = new("Professional C#", "Wrox Press");
Book book2 = new("Professional C#", "Wrox Press");

if (!object.ReferenceEquals(book1, book2))
{
  Console.WriteLine("Not the same reference");
}

if (book1.Equals(book2))
{
  Console.WriteLine("The same object using the generic Equals method");
}

object book3 = book2;
if (book1.Equals(book3))
{
  Console.WriteLine("The same object using the overridden Equals method");
}

if (book1 == book2)
{
  Console.WriteLine("The same book using the == operator");
}
```

> **NOTE** *For struct types, similar functionality to classes applies; there are just a few important differences. Remember, you can't use* object.ReferenceEquals *with value types. Another difference is that the* object.Equals *method is already overridden to compare the values. For more functionality with equality, similar to what has been shown with the* Book *class, implement the* IEquality<T> *interface and override the* == *and* != *operators.*

IMPLEMENTING CUSTOM INDEXERS

Custom indexers cannot be implemented using the operator overloading syntax, but they can be implemented with a syntax that looks similar to properties.

With the following code snippet, an array is created, and the indexer is used to access array elements. The second code line uses the indexer to access the second element and pass 42 to it. The third line uses the indexer to access the third element and pass the value of the element to the variable x.

```
int[] arr1 = {1, 2, 3};
arr1[1] = 42;
int x = arr1[2];
```

> **NOTE** *Arrays are explained in Chapter 6.*

To create a custom indexer, first create a Person record with the properties FirstName, LastName, and Birthday (code file CustomIndexerSample/Person.cs):

```
public record Person(string FirstName, string LastName, DateTime Birthday)
{
  public override string ToString() => $"{FirstName} {LastName}";
}
```

The class PersonCollection defines a private array field that contains Person elements and a constructor where a number of Person objects can be passed (code file CustomIndexerSample/PersonCollection.cs):

```
public class PersonCollection
{
  private Person[] _people;

  public PersonCollection(params Person[] people) =>
    _people = people.ToArray();
}
```

For allowing indexer-syntax to be used to access the PersonCollection and return Person objects, you can create an indexer. The indexer looks very similar to a property because it also contains get and set accessors. What's different is the name. Specifying an indexer makes use of the this keyword. The brackets that follow the this keyword specify the type that is used with the index. An array offers indexers with the int type, so int types are used here to pass the information directly to the contained array _people. The use of the set and get accessors is similar to properties. The get accessor is invoked when a value is retrieved; the set accessor is invoked when a Person object is passed on the right side.

```
public Person this[int index]
{
  get => _people[index];
  set => _people[index] = value;
}
```

With indexers, any type can be used as the indexing type. With the sample application, the DateTime struct is used. This indexer is used to return every person with a specified birthday. Because multiple people can have the same birthday, not a single Person object is returned; instead, a list of people is returned with the interface IEnumerable<Person>. With the implementation of the indexer, the Where method is used. A lambda expression is passed with the argument. The Where method is defined in the namespace System.Linq:

```
public IEnumerable<Person> this[DateTime birthDay]
{
  get => _people.Where(p => p.Birthday == birthDay);
}
```

The indexer using the `DateTime` type lets you retrieve `Person` objects but doesn't allow you to set `Person` objects because there's a `get` accessor but no `set` accessor. A shorthand notation exists to create the same code with an expression-bodied member (the same syntax available with properties):

```
public IEnumerable<Person> this[DateTime birthDay] =>
  _people.Where(p => p.Birthday == birthDay);
```

With the top-level statements of the sample application, a `PersonCollection` object with four `Person` objects is created. With the first `WriteLine` method, the third element is accessed using the `get` accessor of the indexer with the `int` parameter. Within the `foreach` loop, the indexer with the `DateTime` parameter is used to pass a specified date (code file `CustomIndexerSample/Program.cs`):

```
Person p1 = new("Ayrton", "Senna", new DateTime(1960, 3, 21));
Person p2 = new("Ronnie", "Peterson", new DateTime(1944, 2, 14));
Person p3 = new("Jochen", "Rindt", new DateTime(1942, 4, 18));
Person p4 = new("Francois", "Cevert", new DateTime(1944, 2, 25));
PersonCollection coll = new(p1, p2, p3, p4);
Console.WriteLine(coll[2]);
foreach (var r in coll[new DateTime(1960, 3, 21)])
{
  Console.WriteLine(r);
}
Console.ReadLine();
```

When you run the program, the first `WriteLine` method writes `Jochen Rindt` to the console; the result of the `foreach` loop is `Ayrton Senna` because that person has the same birthday as is assigned within the second indexer.

USER-DEFINED CONVERSIONS

Earlier in this chapter (see the "Explicit Conversions" section), you learned that you can convert values between predefined data types through a process of casting. You also saw that C# allows two different types of casts: implicit and explicit. This section looks at these types of casts.

For an explicit cast, you explicitly mark the cast in your code by including the destination data type inside parentheses:

```
int i = 3;
long l = i; // implicit
short s = (short)i; // explicit
```

For the predefined data types, explicit casts are required where there is a risk that the cast might fail or some data might be lost. The following are some examples:

➤ When converting from an `int` to a `short`, the `short` might not be large enough to hold the value of the `int`.

➤ When converting from signed to unsigned data types, incorrect results are returned if the signed variable holds a negative value.

➤ When converting from floating-point to integer data types, the fractional part of the number will be lost.

➤ When converting from a nullable type to a non-nullable type, a value of `null` causes an exception.

By making the cast explicit in your code, C# forces you to affirm that you understand there is a risk of data loss, and therefore presumably you have written your code to take this into account.

Because C# allows you to define your own data types (structs and classes), it follows that you need the facility to support casts to and from those data types. The mechanism is to define a cast as a member operator of one of the relevant classes. Your cast operator must be marked as either `implicit` or `explicit` to indicate how you intend it to be used. The expectation is that you follow the same guidelines as for the predefined casts: if you know that the cast is always safe regardless of the value held by the source variable, then you define it as `implicit`. Conversely, if you know there is a risk of something going wrong for certain values—perhaps some loss of data or an exception being thrown—then you should define the cast as `explicit`.

> **NOTE** *You should define any custom casts you write as explicit if there are any source data values for which the cast will fail or if there is any risk of an exception being thrown.*

The syntax for defining a cast is similar to that for overloading operators discussed earlier in this chapter. This is not a coincidence—a cast is regarded as an operator whose effect is to convert from the source type to the destination type. To illustrate the syntax, the following is taken from an example `struct` named `Currency`, which is introduced in the next section, "Implementing User-Defined Casts":

```
public static implicit operator float (Currency value)
{
   // processing
}
```

The return type of the operator defines the target type of the cast operation, and the single parameter is the source object for the conversion. The cast defined here allows you to implicitly convert the value of a `Currency` into a `float`. Note that if a conversion has been declared as `implicit`, the compiler permits its use either implicitly or explicitly. If it has been declared as `explicit`, the compiler only permits it to be used explicitly. Similar to other operator overloads, casts must be declared as both `public` and `static`.

Implementing User-Defined Casts

This section illustrates the use of implicit and explicit user-defined casts in an example called `CastingSample`. In this example, you define a struct, `Currency`, which holds a positive USD ($) monetary value. C# provides the `decimal` type for this purpose, but it is possible you still will want to write your own struct or class to represent monetary values if you need to perform sophisticated financial processing and therefore want to implement specific methods on such a class.

> **NOTE** *The syntax for casting is the same for structs and classes. This example happens to be for a struct, but it would work just as well if you declared `Currency` as a class.*

Initially, the definition of the `Currency` struct is as follows (code file `CastingSample/Currency.cs`):

```
public readonly struct Currency
{
   public readonly uint Dollars;
   public readonly ushort Cents;
```

```
    public Currency(uint dollars, ushort cents) => (Dollars, Cents) = (dollars, cents);

    public override string ToString() => $"${Dollars}.{Cents,-2:00}";
}
```

The use of unsigned data types for the `Dollar` and `Cents` fields ensures that a `Currency` instance can hold only positive values. It is restricted this way to illustrate some points about explicit casts later. You might want to use a type like this to hold, for example, salary information for company employees (people's salaries tend not to be negative!).

Start by assuming that you want to be able to convert `Currency` instances to `float` values, where the integer part of the `float` represents the dollars. In other words, you want to be able to write code like this:

```
Currency balance = new(10, 50);
float f = balance; // We want f to be set to 10.5
```

To be able to do this, you need to define a cast. Hence, you add the following to your `Currency` definition:

```
public static implicit operator float (Currency value) =>
    value.Dollars + (value.Cents/100.0f);
```

The preceding cast is implicit. It is a sensible choice in this case because, as it should be clear from the definition of `Currency`, any value that can be stored in the `Currency` can also be stored in a `float`. There is no way that anything should ever go wrong in this cast.

> **NOTE** *There is a slight cheat here. In fact, when converting a* uint *to a* float, *there can be a loss in precision, but Microsoft has deemed this error sufficiently marginal to count the* uint-*to-*float *cast as implicit.*

However, if you have a `float` that you would like to be converted to a `Currency`, the conversion is not guaranteed to work. A `float` can store negative values, whereas `Currency` instances can't, and a `float` can store numbers of a far higher magnitude than can be stored in the `(uint)` `Dollar` field of `Currency`. Therefore, if a `float` contains an inappropriate value, converting it to a `Currency` could give unpredictable results. Because of this risk, the conversion from `float` to `Currency` should be defined as explicit. Here is the first attempt, which does not return quite the correct results, but it is instructive to examine why:

```
public static explicit operator Currency (float value)
{
    uint dollars = (uint)value;
    ushort cents = (ushort)((value-dollars)*100);
    return new Currency(dollars, cents);
}
```

The following code now successfully compiles:

```
float amount = 45.63f;
Currency amount2 = (Currency)amount;
```

However, the following code, if you tried it, would generate a compilation error because it attempts to use an explicit cast implicitly:

```
float amount = 45.63f;
Currency amount2 = amount; // wrong
```

By making the cast explicit, you warn the developer to be careful because data loss might occur. However, as you will soon see, this is not how you want your `Currency` struct to behave. Try writing a test harness and running the sample. Here is the `Main` method, which instantiates a `Currency` struct and attempts a few conversions. At the start of this code, you write out the value of `balance` in two different ways—this is needed to illustrate something later in the example (code file `CastingSample/Program.cs`):

```
try
{
  Currency balance = new(50,35);
  Console.WriteLine(balance);
  Console.WriteLine($"balance is {balance}"); // implicitly invokes ToString
  float balance2 = balance;
  Console.WriteLine($"After converting to float, = {balance2}");
  balance = (Currency) balance2;
  Console.WriteLine($"After converting back to Currency, = {balance}");
  Console.WriteLine("Now attempt to convert out of range value of " +
    "-$50.50 to a Currency:");

  checked
  {
    balance = (Currency) (-50.50);
    Console.WriteLine($"Result is {balance}");
  }
}
catch(Exception e)
{
  Console.WriteLine($"Exception occurred: {e.Message}");
}
```

Notice that the entire code is placed in a `try` block to catch any exceptions that occur during your casts. In addition, the lines that test converting an out-of-range value to `Currency` are placed in a `checked` block in an attempt to trap negative values. Running this code produces the following output:

```
50.35
Balance is $50.35
After converting to float, = 50.35
After converting back to Currency, = $50.34
Now attempt to convert out of range value of -$50.50 to a Currency:
Result is $4294967246.00
```

This output shows that the code did not quite work as expected. First, converting back from `float` to `Currency` gave a wrong result of $50.34 instead of $50.35. Second, no exception was generated when you tried to convert an obviously out-of-range value.

The first problem is caused by rounding errors. If a cast is used to convert from a `float` to a `uint`, the computer truncates the number rather than rounds it. The computer stores numbers in binary rather than decimal, and the fraction 0.35 cannot be exactly represented as a binary fraction (just as 1⁄3 cannot be represented exactly as a decimal fraction; it comes out as 0.3333 recurring). The computer ends up storing a value very slightly lower than 0.35 that can be represented exactly in binary format. Multiply by 100, and you get a number fractionally less than 35, which is truncated to 34 cents. Clearly, in this situation, such errors caused by truncation are serious, and the way to avoid them is to ensure that some intelligent rounding is performed in numerical conversions.

Luckily, Microsoft has written a class that does this: `System.Convert`. The `System.Convert` object contains a large number of static methods to perform various numerical conversions, and the one that we want is `Convert.ToUInt16`. Note that the extra care taken by the `System.Convert` methods comes at a performance cost. You should use them only when necessary.

Let's examine the second problem—why the expected overflow exception wasn't thrown. The issue here is that the place where the overflow really occurs isn't actually in the `Main` routine at all—it is inside the code for the cast operator, which is called from the `Main` method. The code in this method was not marked as `checked`.

The solution is to ensure that the cast itself is computed in a `checked` context, too. With both this change and the fix for the first problem, the revised code for the conversion looks like the following:

```
public static explicit operator Currency (float value)
{
  checked
  {
    uint dollars = (uint)value;
    ushort cents = Convert.ToUInt16((value-dollars)*100);
    return new Currency(dollars, cents);
  }
}
```

Note that you use `Convert.ToUInt16` to calculate the cents, as described earlier, but you do not use it for calculating the dollar part of the amount. `System.Convert` is not needed when calculating the dollar amount because truncating the `float` value is what you want there.

> **NOTE** *The* `System.Convert` *methods also carry out their own overflow checking. Hence, for the particular case we are considering, there is no need to place the call to* `Convert.ToUInt16` *inside the checked context. The checked context is still required, however, for the explicit casting of* `value` *to dollars.*

You won't look at the new results with this new `checked` cast just yet because you have some more modifications to make to the `CastingSample` example later in this section.

> **NOTE** *If you are defining a cast that will be used very often, and for which performance is at an absolute premium, you may prefer not to do any error checking. That is also a legitimate solution, provided that the behavior of your cast and the lack of error checking are very clearly documented.*

Casts Between Classes

The `Currency` example involves only classes that convert to or from `float`—one of the predefined data types. However, it is not necessary to involve any of the simple data types. It is perfectly legitimate to define casts to convert between instances of different structs or classes that you have defined. You need to be aware of a couple of restrictions, however:

➤ You cannot define a cast if one of the classes is derived from the other (these types of casts already exist, as you will see later).

➤ The cast must be defined inside the definition of either the source or the destination data type.

To illustrate these requirements, suppose that you have the class hierarchy shown in Figure 5-1.

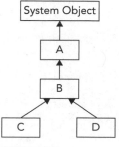

FIGURE 5-1

In other words, classes C and D are indirectly derived from A. In this case, the only legitimate user-defined cast between A, B, C, or D would be to convert between classes C and D, because these classes are not derived from each other. The code for this might look like the following (assuming you want the casts to be explicit, which is usually the case when defining casts between user-defined classes):

```
public static explicit operator D(C value)
{
   //...
}

public static explicit operator C(D value)
{
   //...
}
```

For each of these casts, you can choose where you place the definitions—inside the class definition of C or inside the class definition of D, but not anywhere else. C# requires you to put the definition of a cast inside either the source class (or struct) or the destination class (or struct). A side effect of this is that you cannot define a cast between two classes unless you have access to edit the source code for at least one of them. This is sensible because it prevents third parties from introducing casts into your classes.

After you have defined a cast inside one of the classes, you cannot also define the same cast inside the other class. Obviously, there should be only one cast for each conversion; otherwise, the compiler would not know which one to use.

Casts Between Base and Derived Classes

To see how these casts work, start by considering the case in which both the source and the destination are reference types and consider two classes, MyBase and MyDerived, where MyDerived is derived directly or indirectly from MyBase.

First, from MyDerived to MyBase, it is always possible (assuming the constructors are available) to write this:

```
MyDerived derivedObject = new MyDerived();
MyBase baseCopy = derivedObject;
```

Here, you are casting implicitly from MyDerived to MyBase. This works because of the rule that any reference to a type MyBase is allowed to refer to objects of class MyBase or anything derived from MyBase. In object-oriented programming, instances of a derived class are, in a real sense, instances of the base class, plus something extra. All the functions and fields defined on the base class are defined in the derived class, too.

Alternatively, you can write this:

```
MyBase derivedObject = new MyDerived();
MyBase baseObject = new MyBase();
MyDerived derivedCopy1 = (MyDerived) derivedObject; // OK
MyDerived derivedCopy2 = (MyDerived) baseObject; // Throws exception
```

This code is perfectly legal C# (in a syntactic sense, that is) and illustrates casting from a base class to a derived class. However, the final statement throws an exception when executed. When you perform the cast, the object being referred to is examined. Because a base class reference can, in principle, refer to a derived class instance, it is possible that this object is actually an instance of the derived class that you are attempting to cast to. If that is the case, the cast succeeds, and the derived reference is set to refer to the object. If, however, the object in question is not an instance of the derived class (or of any class derived from it), the cast fails, and an exception is thrown.

Notice that the casts that the compiler has supplied, which convert between base and derived class, do not actually do any data conversion on the object in question. All they do is set the new reference to refer to the object if it is legal for that conversion to occur. To that extent, these casts are very different in nature from the ones that you normally define yourself. For example, in the CastingSample example earlier, you defined casts that convert between a Currency struct and a float. In the float-to-Currency cast, you actually instantiated a new

`Currency` struct and initialized it with the required values. The predefined casts between base and derived classes do not do this. If you want to convert a `MyBase` instance into a real `MyDerived` object with values based on the contents of the `MyBase` instance, you cannot use the cast syntax to do this. The most sensible option is usually to define a derived class constructor that takes a base class instance as a parameter and have this constructor perform the relevant initializations:

```
class DerivedClass: BaseClass
{
  public DerivedClass(BaseClass base)
  {
    // initialize object from the Base instance
  }
  // ...
```

Boxing and Unboxing Casts

The previous discussion focused on casting between base and derived classes where both participants were reference types. Similar principles apply when casting value types, although in this case it is not possible to simply copy references—some copying of data must occur.

It is not, of course, possible to derive from structs or primitive value types. Casting between base and derived structs invariably means casting between a primitive type or a struct and `System.Object`. (Theoretically, it is possible to cast between a struct and `System.ValueType`, though it is hard to see why you would want to do this.)

The cast from any struct (or primitive type) to `object` is always available as an implicit cast—because it is a cast from a derived type to a base type—and is just the familiar process of boxing. Here's an example using the `Currency` struct:

```
Currency balance = new(40,0);
object baseCopy = balance;
```

When this implicit cast is executed, the contents of `balance` are copied onto the heap into a boxed object, and the `baseCopy` object reference is set to this object. What actually happens behind the scenes is this: when you originally defined the `Currency` struct, .NET implicitly supplied another (hidden) class, a boxed `Currency` class, which contains all the same fields as the `Currency` struct but is a reference type, stored on the heap. This happens whenever you define a value type, whether it is a `struct` or an `enum`, and similar boxed reference types exist corresponding to all the primitive value types of `int`, `double`, `uint`, and so on. It is not possible, or necessary, to gain direct programmatic access to any of these boxed classes in source code, but they are the objects that are working behind the scenes whenever a value type is cast to `object`. When you implicitly cast `Currency` to `object`, a boxed `Currency` instance is instantiated and initialized with all the data from the `Currency` struct. In the preceding code, it is this boxed `Currency` instance to which `baseCopy` refers. By these means, it is possible for casting from derived to base type to work syntactically in the same way for value types as for reference types.

Casting the other way is known as *unboxing*. Like casting between a base reference type and a derived reference type, it is an explicit cast because an exception is thrown if the object being cast is not of the correct type:

```
object derivedObject = new Currency(40,0);
object baseObject = new object();
Currency derivedCopy1 = (Currency)derivedObject; // OK
Currency derivedCopy2 = (Currency)baseObject; // Exception thrown
```

This code works in a way similar to the code presented earlier for reference types. Casting `derivedObject` to `Currency` works fine because `derivedObject` actually refers to a boxed `Currency` instance—the cast is performed by copying the fields out of the boxed `Currency` object into a new `Currency` struct. The second cast fails because `baseObject` does not refer to a boxed `Currency` object.

When using boxing and unboxing, it is important to understand that both processes actually copy the data into the new boxed or unboxed object. Hence, manipulations on the boxed object, for example, do not affect the contents of the original value type.

Multiple Casting

One thing you have to watch for when you are defining casts is that if the C# compiler is presented with a situation in which no direct cast is available to perform a requested conversion, it attempts to find a way of combining casts to do the conversion. For example, with the `Currency` struct, suppose the compiler encounters a few lines of code like this:

```
Currency balance = new(10,50);
long amount = (long)balance;
double amountD = balance;
```

You first initialize a `Currency` instance, and then you attempt to convert it to a `long`. The trouble is that you haven't defined the cast to do that. However, this code still compiles successfully. Here's what happens: the compiler realizes that you have defined an implicit cast to get from `Currency` to `float`, and the compiler already knows how to explicitly cast a `float` to a `long`. Hence, it compiles that line of code into IL code that converts `balance` first to a `float` and then converts that result to a `long`. The same thing happens in the final line of the code, when you convert `balance` to a `double`. However, because the cast from `Currency` to `float` and the predefined cast from `float` to `double` are both implicit, you can write this conversion in your code as an implicit cast. If you prefer, you could also specify the casting route explicitly:

```
Currency balance = new(10,50);
long amount = (long)(float)balance;
double amountD = (double)(float)balance;
```

However, in most cases, this would be seen as needlessly complicating your code. The following code, by contrast, produces a compilation error:

```
Currency balance = new(10,50);
long amount = balance;
```

The reason is that the best match for the conversion that the compiler can find is still to convert first to `float` and then to `long`. The conversion from `float` to `long` needs to be specified explicitly, though.

Not all of this by itself should give you too much trouble. The rules are, after all, fairly intuitive and designed to prevent any data loss from occurring without the developer knowing about it. However, the problem is that if you are not careful when you define your casts, it is possible for the compiler to select a path that leads to unexpected results. For example, suppose that it occurs to someone else in the group writing the `Currency` struct that it would be useful to be able to convert a `uint` containing the total number of cents in an amount into a `Currency` (cents, not dollars, because the idea is not to lose the fractions of a dollar). Therefore, this cast might be written to try to achieve this:

```
// Do not do this!
public static implicit operator Currency(uint value) =>
    new Currency(value/100u, (ushort)(value%100));
```

Note the u after the first 100 in this code ensures that `value/100u` is interpreted as a `uint`. If you had written `value/100`, the compiler would have interpreted this as an `int`, not a `uint`.

The comment `Do not do this!` is clearly noted in this code, and here is why: the following code snippet merely converts a `uint` containing `350` into a `Currency` and back again; but what do you think `bal2` will contain after executing this?

```
uint bal = 350;
Currency balance = bal;
uint bal2 = (uint)balance;
```

The answer is not `350` but `3`! Moreover, it all follows logically. You convert `350` implicitly to a `Currency`, giving the result `balance.Dollars = 3`, `balance.Cents = 50`. Then the compiler does its usual figuring out of the best path for the conversion back. `Balance` ends up being implicitly converted to a `float` (value `3.5`), and this is converted explicitly to a `uint` with value `3`. One way to fix this would be to create a user-defined cast to `uint`.

Of course, other instances exist in which converting to another data type and back again causes data loss. For example, converting a `float` containing 5.8 to an `int` and back to a `float` again loses the fractional part, giving you a result of 5, but there is a slight difference in principle between losing the fractional part of a number and dividing an integer by more than 100. `Currency` has suddenly become a rather dangerous class that does strange things to integers!

The problem is that there is a conflict between how your casts interpret integers. The casts between `Currency` and `float` interpret an integer value of 1 as corresponding to one dollar, but the latest `uint-to-Currency` cast interprets this value as one cent. This is an example of poor design. If you want your classes to be easy to use, you should ensure that all your casts behave in ways that are mutually compatible, in the sense that they intuitively give the same results. In this case, the solution is obviously to rewrite the `uint-to-Currency` cast so that it interprets an integer value of 1 as one dollar:

```
public static implicit operator Currency (uint value) =>
    new Currency(value, 0);
```

Incidentally, you might wonder whether this new cast is necessary at all. The answer is that it could be useful. Without this cast, the only way for the compiler to carry out a `uint-to-Currency` conversion would be via a `float`. Converting directly is a lot more efficient in this case, so having this extra cast provides performance benefits, though you need to ensure that it provides the same result as via a `float`, which you have now done. In other situations, you may also find that separately defining casts for different predefined data types enables more conversions to be implicit rather than explicit, though that is not the case here.

A good test of whether your casts are compatible is to ask whether a conversion will give the same results (other than perhaps a loss of accuracy as in `float-to-int` conversions) regardless of which path it takes. The `Currency` class provides a good example of this. Consider this code:

```
Currency balance = new(50, 35);
ulong bal = (ulong) balance;
```

At present, there is only one way that the compiler can achieve this conversion: by converting the `Currency` to a `float` implicitly and then to a `ulong` explicitly. The `float-to-ulong` conversion requires an explicit conversion, but that is fine because you have specified one here.

Suppose, however, that you then added another cast to convert implicitly from a `Currency` to a `uint`. You actually do this by modifying the `Currency` struct by adding the casts both to and from `uint` (code file `CastingSample/Currency.cs`):

```
public static implicit operator Currency(uint value) =>
    new Currency(value, 0);
public static implicit operator uint(Currency value) => value.Dollars;
```

Now the compiler has another possible route to convert from `Currency` to `ulong`: to convert from `Currency` to `uint` implicitly and then to `ulong` implicitly. Which of these two routes will it take? C# has some precise rules about the best route for the compiler when there are several possibilities. (The rules are not covered in this book, but if you are interested in the details, see the MSDN documentation.) The best answer is that you should design your casts so that all routes give the same answer (other than possible loss of precision), in which case it doesn't really matter which one the compiler picks. (As it happens in this case, the compiler picks the `Currency-to-uint-to-ulong` route in preference to `Currency-to-float-to-ulong`.)

To test casting the `Currency` to `uint`, add this test code to the `Main` method (code file `UserDefinedConversion/Program.cs`):

```
try
{
    Currency balance = new(50,35);
    Console.WriteLine(balance);
    Console.WriteLine($"balance is {balance}");
    uint balance3 = (uint) balance;
    Console.WriteLine($"Converting to uint gives {balance3}");
}
```

```
catch (Exception ex)
{
    Console.WriteLine($"Exception occurred: {ex.Message}");
}
```

Running the sample now gives you these results:

```
50
balance is $50.35
Converting to uint gives 50
```

The output shows that the conversion to uint has been successful, though, as expected, you have lost the cents part of the Currency in making this conversion.

However, the output also demonstrates one last potential problem that you need to be aware of when working with casts. The first line of output does not display the balance correctly, displaying 50 instead of 50.35.

So, what is going on? The problem here is that when you combine casts with method overloads, you get another source of unpredictability.

The WriteLine statement using the format string implicitly calls the Currency.ToString method, ensuring that the Currency is displayed as a string.

The first code line with WriteLine, however, simply passes a raw Currency struct to the WriteLine method. Now, WriteLine has many overloads, but none of them takes a Currency struct. Therefore, the compiler starts fishing around to see what it can cast the Currency to in order to make it match up with one of the overloads of WriteLine. As it happens, one of the WriteLine overloads is designed to display uints quickly and efficiently, and it takes a uint as a parameter—you have now supplied a cast that converts Currency implicitly to uint.

In fact, WriteLine has another overload that takes a float as a parameter and displays the value of that float. If you look closely at the output running the example previously where the cast to uint did not exist, you see that the first line of output displayed Currency as a float, using this overload. In that example, there wasn't a direct cast from Currency to uint, so the compiler picked Currency-to-float as its preferred way of matching up the available casts to the available WriteLine overloads. However, now that there is a direct cast to uint available in Currency, the compiler has opted for that route.

The upshot of this is that if you have a method call that takes several overloads and you attempt to pass it a parameter whose data type doesn't match any of the overloads exactly, then you are forcing the compiler to decide not only what casts to use to perform the data conversion, but also which overload, and hence which data conversion, to pick. The compiler always works logically and according to strict rules, but the results may not be what you expect. If there is any doubt, you are better off specifying which cast to use explicitly.

SUMMARY

This chapter looked at the standard operators provided by C#, described the mechanics of object equality, and examined how the compiler converts the standard data types from one to another. It also demonstrated how you can implement custom operator support on your data types using operator overloads. Finally, you looked at a special type of operator overload, the cast operator, which enables you to specify how instances of your types are converted to other data types.

The next chapter dives into arrays where the index operator has an important role.

6

Arrays

CODE DOWNLOADS FOR THIS CHAPTER

The source code for this chapter is available on the book page at `www.wiley.com`. Click the Downloads link. The code can also be found at `https://github.com/ProfessionalCSharp/ProfessionalCSharp2021` in the directory `1_CS/Arrays`.

The code for this chapter is divided into the following major examples:

- ➤ SimpleArrays
- ➤ SortingSample
- ➤ YieldSample
- ➤ SpanSample

➤ IndicesAndRanges

➤ ArrayPoolSample

➤ BitArraySample

All the projects have nullable reference types enabled.

MULTIPLE OBJECTS OF THE SAME TYPE

If you need to work with multiple objects of the same type, you can use collections (see Chapter 8, "Collections") and arrays. C# has a special notation to declare, initialize, and use arrays. Behind the scenes, the `Array` class comes into play, which offers several methods to sort and filter the elements inside the array. Using an enumerator, you can iterate through all the elements of the array.

> **NOTE** *For using multiple objects of different types, you can combine them using classes, structs, records, and tuples, which are covered in Chapter 3.*

SIMPLE ARRAYS

If you need to use multiple objects of the same type, you can use an array. An *array* is a data structure that contains a number of elements of the same type.

Array Declaration and Initialization

An array is declared by defining the type of elements inside the array, followed by empty brackets and a variable name. For example, an array containing integer elements is declared like this:

```
int[] myArray;
```

After declaring an array, memory must be allocated to hold all the elements of the array. An array is a reference type, so memory on the heap must be allocated. You do this by initializing the variable of the array using the `new` operator, with the type and the number of elements inside the array. Here, you specify the size of the array:

```
myArray = new int[4];
```

With this declaration and initialization, the variable `myArray` references four integer values that are allocated on the managed heap (see Figure 6-1).

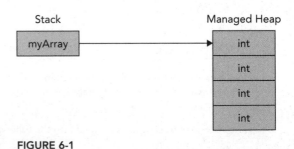

FIGURE 6-1

> **NOTE** *An array cannot be resized after its size is specified without copying all the elements. If you don't know how many elements should be in the array in advance, you can use a collection (see Chapter 8).*

Instead of using a separate line to declare and initialize an array, you can use a single line:

```
int[] myArray = new int[4];
```

You can also assign values to every array element using an array initializer. The following code samples all declare an array with the same content but with less code for you to write. The compiler can count the number of elements in the array by itself, which is why the array size is left out with the second line. The compiler also can map the values defined in the initializer list to the type used on the left side, so you also can remove the new operator left of the initializer. The code generated from the compiler is always the same:

```
int[] myArray1 = new int[4] {4, 7, 11, 2};
int[] myArray2 = new int[] {4, 7, 11, 2};
int[] myArray3 = {4, 7, 11, 2};
```

Accessing Array Elements

After an array is declared and initialized, you can access the array elements using an indexer. Arrays support only indexers that have parameters of type int.

With the indexer, you pass the element number to access the array. The indexer always starts with a value of 0 for the first element. Therefore, the highest number you can pass to the indexer is the number of elements minus one because the index starts at zero. In the following example, the array myArray is declared and initialized with four integer values. The elements can be accessed with indexer values 0, 1, 2, and 3.

```
int[] myArray = new int[] {4, 7, 11, 2};
int v1 = myArray[0]; // read first element
int v2 = myArray[1]; // read second element
myArray[3] = 44; // change fourth element
```

> **NOTE** *If you use a wrong indexer value that is bigger than the length of the array, an exception of type* IndexOutOfRangeException *is thrown.*

If you don't know the number of elements in the array, you can use the Length property, as shown in this for statement:

```
for (int i = 0; i < myArray.Length; i++)
{
  Console.WriteLine(myArray[i]);
}
```

Instead of using a for statement to iterate through all the elements of the array, you can also use the foreach statement:

```
foreach (var val in myArray)
{
  Console.WriteLine(val);
}
```

> **NOTE** *The* `foreach` *statement makes use of the* `IEnumerable` *and* `IEnumerator` *interfaces and traverses through the array from the first index to the last. This is discussed in detail later in this chapter.*

Using Reference Types

In addition to being able to declare arrays of predefined types, you also can declare arrays of custom types. Let's start with the following `Person` record using positional record syntax to declare the *init-only setter* properties `FirstName` and `LastName` (code file `SimpleArrays/Person.cs`):

```
public record Person(string FirstName, string LastName);
```

Declaring an array of two `Person` elements is similar to declaring an array of `int`:

```
Person[] myPersons = new Person[2];
```

However, be aware that if the elements in the array are reference types, memory must be allocated for every array element. If you use an item in the array for which no memory was allocated, a `NullReferenceException` is thrown.

> **NOTE** *For information about errors and exceptions, see Chapter 10, "Errors and Exceptions."*

You can allocate every element of the array by using an indexer starting from 0. When you create the second object, you make use of C# 9 *target-typed new* as the type (code file `SimpleArrays/Program.cs`):

```
myPersons[0] = new Person("Ayrton", "Senna");
myPersons[1] = new("Michael", "Schumacher");
```

Figure 6-2 shows the objects in the managed heap with the `Person` array. `myPersons` is a variable that is stored on the stack. This variable references an array of `Person` elements that is stored on the managed heap. This array has enough space for two references. Every item in the array references a `Person` object that is also stored in the managed heap.

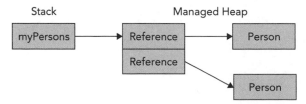

FIGURE 6-2

As with the `int` type, you can use an array initializer with custom types:

```
Person[] myPersons2 =
{
  new("Ayrton", "Senna"),
  new("Michael", "Schumacher")
};
```

MULTIDIMENSIONAL ARRAYS

Ordinary arrays (also known as *one-dimensional arrays*) are indexed by a single integer. A multidimensional array is indexed by two or more integers.

FIGURE 6-3

Figure 6-3 shows the mathematical notation for a two-dimensional array that has three rows and three columns. The first row has the values 1, 2, and 3, and the third row has the values 7, 8, and 9.

To declare this two-dimensional array with C#, you put a comma inside the brackets. The array is initialized by specifying the size of every dimension (also known as *rank*). Then the array elements can be accessed by using two integers with the indexer (code file `SimpleArrays/Program.cs`):

```
int[,] twodim = new int[3, 3];
twodim[0, 0] = 1;
twodim[0, 1] = 2;
twodim[0, 2] = 3;
twodim[1, 0] = 4;
twodim[1, 1] = 5;
twodim[1, 2] = 6;
twodim[2, 0] = 7;
twodim[2, 1] = 8;
twodim[2, 2] = 9;
```

> **NOTE** *After declaring an array, you cannot change the rank.*

You can also initialize the two-dimensional array by using an array indexer if you know the values for the elements in advance. To initialize the array, one outer curly bracket is used, and every row is initialized by using curly brackets inside the outer curly brackets:

```
int[,] twodim = {
  {1, 2, 3},
  {4, 5, 6},
  {7, 8, 9}
};
```

> **NOTE** *When using an array initializer, you must initialize every element of the array. It is not possible to defer the initialization of some values until later.*

By using two commas inside the brackets, you can declare a three-dimensional array by placing initializers for two-dimensional arrays inside brackets separated by commas:

```
int[,,] threedim = {
  { { 1, 2 }, { 3, 4 } },
  { { 5, 6 }, { 7, 8 } },
  { { 9, 10 }, { 11, 12 } }
};
Console.WriteLine(threedim[0, 1, 1]);
```

Using a `foreach` loop, you can iterate through all the items of a multidimensional array.

JAGGED ARRAYS

A two-dimensional array has a rectangular size (for example, 3 × 3 elements). A jagged array provides more flexibility in sizing the array. With a jagged array, every row can have a different size.

Figure 6-4 contrasts a two-dimensional array that has 3 × 3 elements with a jagged array. The jagged array shown contains three rows: the first row contains two elements, the second row contains six elements, and the third row contains three elements.

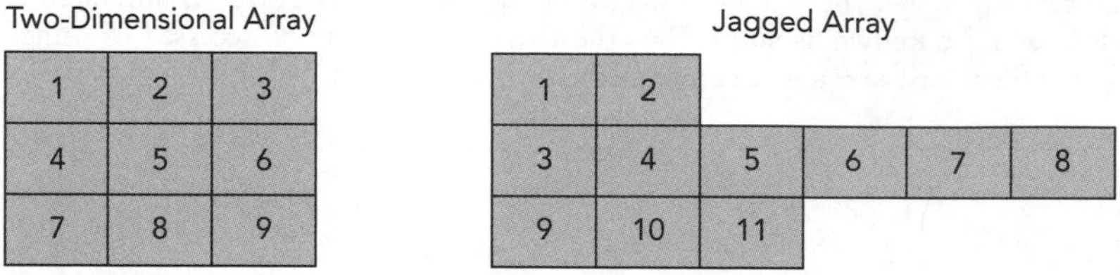

Two-Dimensional Array   Jagged Array

FIGURE 6-4

A jagged array is declared by placing one pair of opening and closing brackets after another. To initialize the jagged array, in the following code snippet an array initializer is used. The first array is initialized by items of arrays. Each of these items again is initialized with its own array initializer (code file `SimpleArrays/Program.cs`):

```
int[][] jagged =
{
  new[] { 1, 2 },
  new[] { 3, 4, 5, 6, 7, 8 },
  new[] { 9, 10, 11 }
};
```

You can iterate through all the elements of a jagged array with nested `for` loops. In the outer `for` loop, every row is iterated, and the inner `for` loop iterates through every element inside a row:

```
for (int row = 0; row < jagged.Length; row++)
{
  for (int element = 0; element < jagged[row].Length; element++)
  {
    Console.WriteLine($"row: {row}, element: {element}, " +
      $"value: {jagged[row][element]}");
  }
}
```

The output of the iteration displays the rows and every element within the rows:

```
row: 0, element: 0, value: 1
row: 0, element: 1, value: 2
row: 1, element: 0, value: 3
row: 1, element: 1, value: 4
row: 1, element: 2, value: 5
row: 1, element: 3, value: 6
row: 1, element: 4, value: 7
row: 1, element: 5, value: 8
row: 2, element: 0, value: 9
row: 2, element: 1, value: 10
row: 2, element: 2, value: 11
```

ARRAY CLASS

Declaring an array with brackets is a C# notation using the `Array` class. Using the C# syntax behind the scenes creates a new class that derives from the abstract base class `Array`. This makes it possible to use methods and properties that are defined with the `Array` class with every C# array. For example, you've already used the `Length` property or iterated through the array by using the `foreach` statement. By doing this, you are using the `GetEnumerator` method of the `Array` class.

Other properties implemented by the `Array` class are `LongLength`, for arrays in which the number of items doesn't fit within an integer, and `Rank`, to get the number of dimensions.

Let's take a look at other members of the `Array` class by getting into various features.

Creating Arrays

The `Array` class is abstract, so you cannot create an array by using a constructor. However, instead of using the C# syntax to create array instances, it is also possible to create arrays by using the static `CreateInstance` method. This is extremely useful if you don't know the type of elements in advance because the type can be passed to the `CreateInstance` method as a `Type` object.

The following example shows how to create an array of type `int` with a size of 5. The first argument of the `CreateInstance` method requires the type of the elements, and the second argument defines the size. You can set values with the `SetValue` method and read values with the `GetValue` method (code file `SimpleArrays/Program.cs`):

```
Array intArray1 = Array.CreateInstance(typeof(int), 5);
for (int i = 0; i < 5; i++)
{
   intArray1.SetValue(3 * i, i);
}

for (int i = 0; i < 5; i++)
{
   Console.WriteLine(intArray1.GetValue(i));
}
```

You can also cast the created array to an array declared as `int[]`:

```
int[] intArray2 = (int[])intArray1;
```

The `CreateInstance` method has many overloads to create multidimensional arrays and to create arrays that are not 0 based. The following example creates a two-dimensional array with 2 × 3 elements. The first dimension is 1 based; the second dimension is 10 based:

```
int[] lengths = { 2, 3 };
int[] lowerBounds = { 1, 10 };
Array racers = Array.CreateInstance(typeof(Person), lengths, lowerBounds);
```

Setting the elements of the array, the `SetValue` method accepts indices for every dimension:

```
racers.SetValue(new Person("Alain", "Prost"), 1, 10);
racers.SetValue(new Person("Emerson", "Fittipaldi"), 1, 11);
racers.SetValue(new Person("Ayrton", "Senna"), 1, 12);
racers.SetValue(new Person("Michael", "Schumacher"), 2, 10);
racers.SetValue(new Person("Fernando", "Alonso"), 2, 11);
racers.SetValue(new Person("Jenson", "Button"), 2, 12);
```

Although the array is not 0 based, you can assign it to a variable with the normal C# notation. You just have to take care not to cross the array boundaries:

```
Person[,] racers2 = (Person[,])racers;
Person first = racers2[1, 10];
Person last = racers2[2, 12];
```

Copying Arrays

Because arrays are reference types, assigning an array variable to another variable just gives you two variables referencing the same array. For copying arrays, the array implements the interface `ICloneable`. The `Clone` method that is defined with this interface creates a shallow copy of the array.

If the elements of the array are value types, as in the following code segment, all values are copied (see Figure 6-5):

```
int[] intArray1 = {1, 2};
int[] intArray2 = (int[])intArray1.Clone();
```

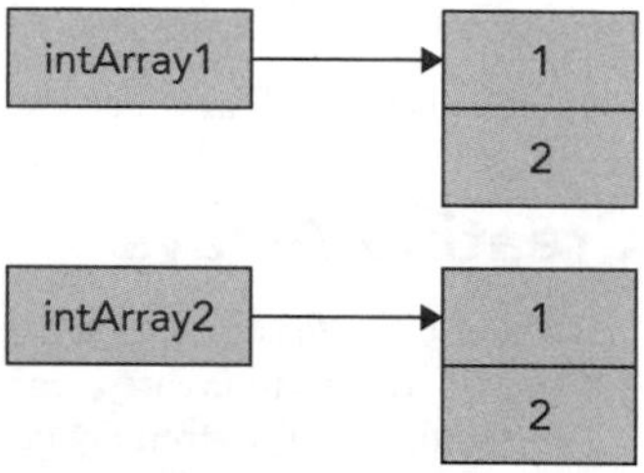

FIGURE 6-5

If the array contains reference types, only the references are copied, not the elements. Figure 6-6 shows the variables `beatles` and `beatlesClone`, where `beatlesClone` is created by calling the `Clone` method from `beatles`. The `Person` objects that are referenced are the same for `beatles` and `beatlesClone`. If you change a property of an element of `beatlesClone`, you change the same object of `beatles` (code file `SimpleArray/Program.cs`):

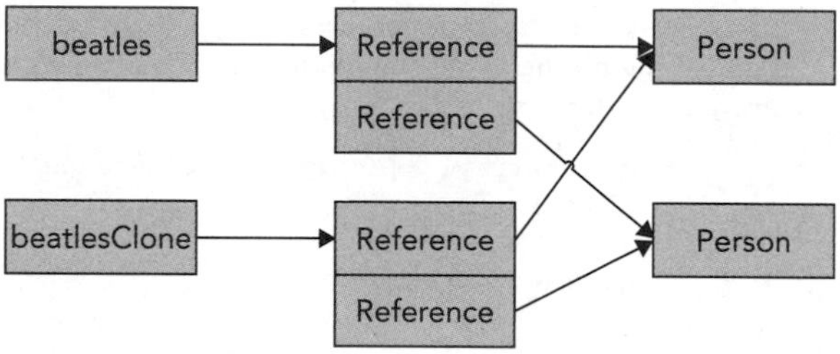

```
Person[] beatles = {
  new("John", "Lennon"),
  new("Paul", "McCartney")
};
Person[] beatlesClone = (Person[])beatles.Clone();
```

FIGURE 6-6

Instead of using the `Clone` method, you can use the `Array.Copy` method, which also creates a shallow copy. However, there's one important difference between `Clone` and `Copy`: `Clone` creates a new array; with `Copy` you have to pass an existing array with the same rank and enough elements.

> **NOTE** *If you need a deep copy of an array containing reference types, you have to iterate the array and create new objects.*

Sorting

The `Array` class uses the Quicksort algorithm to sort the elements in the array. The `Sort` method requires the interface `IComparable` to be implemented by the elements in the array. Simple types such as `System.String` and `System.Int32` implement `IComparable`, so you can sort elements containing these types.

With the sample program, the array `names` contains elements of type `string`, and this array can be sorted (code file `SortingSample/Program.cs`):

```
string[] names = {
  "Lady Gaga",
  "Shakira",
```

```
    "Beyonce",
    "Ava Max"
};
Array.Sort(names);
foreach (var name in names)
{
    Console.WriteLine(name);
}
```

The output of the application shows the sorted result of the array:

```
Ava Max
Beyonce
Lady Gaga
Shakira
```

If you are using custom classes with the array, you must implement the interface IComparable. This interface defines just one method, CompareTo, which must return 0 if the objects to compare are equal; a value smaller than 0 if the instance should go before the object from the parameter; and a value larger than 0 if the instance should go after the object from the parameter.

Change the Person record to implement the interface IComparable<Person>. The comparison is first done on the value of the LastName by using the Compare method of the String class. If the LastName has the same value, the FirstName is compared (code file SortingSample/Person.cs):

```
public record Person(string FirstName, string LastName) : IComparable<Person>
{
    public int CompareTo(Person? other)
    {
        if (other == null) return 1;
        int result = string.Compare(this.LastName, other.LastName);
        if (result == 0)
        {
            result = string.Compare(this.FirstName, other.FirstName);
        }
        return result;
    }
    //...
```

Now it is possible to sort an array of Person objects by the last name (code file SortingSample/Program.cs):

```
Person[] persons = {
    new("Damon", "Hill"),
    new("Niki", "Lauda"),
    new("Ayrton", "Senna"),
    new("Graham", "Hill")
};

Array.Sort(persons);
foreach (var p in persons)
{
    Console.WriteLine(p);
}
```

Using Array.Sort with Person objects, the output returns the names sorted by last name:

```
Damon Hill
Graham Hill
Niki Lauda
Ayrton Senna
```

If the `Person` object should be sorted differently than the implementation within the `Person` class, a comparer type can implement the interface `IComparer<T>`. This interface specifies the method `Compare`, which defines two arguments that should be compared. The return value is similar to the result of the `CompareTo` method that's defined with the `IComparable` interface.

With the sample code, the class `PersonComparer` implements the `IComparer<Person>` interface to sort `Person` objects either by `FirstName` or by `LastName`. The enumeration `PersonCompareType` defines the different sorting options that are available with `PersonComparer`: `FirstName` and `LastName`. How the compare should be done is defined with the constructor of the class `PersonComparer`, where a `PersonCompareType` value is set. The `Compare` method is implemented with a `switch` statement to compare either by `LastName` or by `FirstName` (code file `SortingSample/PersonComparer.cs`):

```
public enum PersonCompareType
{
  FirstName,
  LastName
}

public class PersonComparer : IComparer<Person>
{
  private PersonCompareType _compareType;
  public PersonComparer(PersonCompareType compareType) =>
    _compareType = compareType;

  public int Compare(Person? x, Person? y)
  {
    if (x is null && y is null) return 0;
    if (x is null) return 1;
    if (y is null) return -1;

    return _compareType switch
    {
      PersonCompareType.FirstName => x.FirstName.CompareTo(y.FirstName),
      PersonCompareType.LastName => x.LastName.CompareTo(y.LastName),
      _ => throw new ArgumentException("unexpected compare type")
    };
  }
}
```

Now you can pass a `PersonComparer` object to the second argument of the `Array.Sort` method. Here, the people are sorted by first name (code file `SortingSample/Program.cs`):

```
Array.Sort(persons, new PersonComparer(PersonCompareType.FirstName));
foreach (var p in persons)
{
  Console.WriteLine(p);
}
```

The `persons` array is now sorted by first name:

```
Ayrton Senna
Damon Hill
Graham Hill
Niki Lauda
```

> **NOTE** *The* `Array` *class also offers* `Sort` *methods that require a delegate as an argument. With this argument, you can pass a method to do the comparison of two objects rather than relying on the* `IComparable` *or* `IComparer` *interfaces. Chapter 7, "Delegates, Lambdas, and Events," discusses how to use delegates.*

ARRAYS AS PARAMETERS

Arrays can be passed as parameters to methods and returned from methods. To return an array, you just have to declare the array as the return type, as shown with the following method `GetPersons`:

```
static Person[] GetPersons() =>
  new Person[] {
    new Person("Damon", "Hill"),
    new Person("Niki", "Lauda"),
    new Person("Ayrton", "Senna"),
    new Person("Graham", "Hill")
  };
```

When passing arrays to a method, the array is declared with the parameter, as shown with the method `DisplayPersons`:

```
static void DisplayPersons(Person[] persons)
{
  //...
}
```

ENUMERATORS

By using the `foreach` statement, you can iterate elements of a collection (see Chapter 8) without needing to know the number of elements inside the collection. The `foreach` statement uses an enumerator. Figure 6-7 shows the relationship between the client invoking the `foreach` method and the collection. The array or collection implements the `IEnumerable` interface with the `GetEnumerator` method. The `GetEnumerator` method returns an enumerator implementing the `IEnumerator` interface. The interface `IEnumerator` is then used by the `foreach` statement to iterate through the collection.

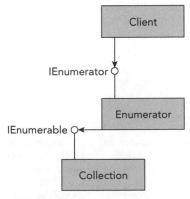

FIGURE 6-7

> **NOTE** *The* GetEnumerator *method is defined with the interface* IEnumerable. *The* foreach *statement doesn't really need this interface implemented in the collection class. It's enough to have a method with the name* GetEnumerator *that returns an object implementing the* IEnumerator *interface.*

IEnumerator Interface

The foreach statement uses the methods and properties of the IEnumerator interface to iterate all elements in a collection. For this, IEnumerator defines the property Current to return the element where the cursor is positioned and defines the method MoveNext to move to the next element of the collection. MoveNext returns true if there's an element and false if no more elements are available.

The generic version of the interface IEnumerator<T> derives from the interface IDisposable and thus defines a Dispose method to clean up resources allocated by the enumerator.

> **NOTE** *The* IEnumerator *interface also defines the* Reset *method for COM interoperability. Many .NET enumerators implement this by throwing an exception of type* NotSupported-Exception.

foreach Statement

The C# foreach statement is not resolved to a foreach statement in the IL code. Instead, the C# compiler converts the foreach statement to methods and properties of the IEnumerator interface. Here's a simple foreach statement to iterate all elements in the persons array and display them person by person:

```
foreach (var p in persons)
{
    Console.WriteLine(p);
}
```

The foreach statement is resolved to the following code fragment. First, the GetEnumerator method is invoked to get an enumerator for the array. Inside a while loop, as long as MoveNext returns true, the elements of the array are accessed using the Current property:

```
IEnumerator<Person> enumerator = persons.GetEnumerator();
while (enumerator.MoveNext())
{
    Person p = enumerator.Current;
    Console.WriteLine(p);
}
```

yield Statement

Using the foreach statement, it's easy to use the IEnumerable and IEnumerator interfaces—the compiler converts the code to use the members of these interfaces. To create classes implementing these interfaces, the compiler offers the yield statement. When you use yield return and yield break, the compiler generates a state machine to iterate through a collection implementing the members of these interfaces. yield return returns one element of a collection and moves the position to the next element; yield break stops the iteration. The iteration also ends when the method is completed, so a yield break is only needed to stop earlier.

The next example shows the implementation of a simple collection using the `yield return` statement. The class `HelloCollection` contains the method `GetEnumerator`. The implementation of the `GetEnumerator` method contains two `yield return` statements where the strings `Hello` and `World` are returned (code file `YieldSample/Program.cs`):

```
class HelloCollection
{
  public IEnumerator<string> GetEnumerator()
  {
    yield return "Hello";
    yield return "World";
  }
}
```

> **NOTE** *A method or property that contains* `yield` *statements is also known as an iterator block. An iterator block must be declared to return an* `IEnumerator` *or* `IEnumerable` *interface or the generic versions of these interfaces. This block may contain multiple* `yield` *return or* `yield break` *statements; a* `return` *statement is not allowed.*

Now it is possible to iterate through the collection using a `foreach` statement:

```
public void HelloWorld()
{
  HelloCollection helloCollection = new();
  foreach (string s in helloCollection)
  {
    Console.WriteLine(s);
  }
}
```

> **NOTE** *Remember that the* `yield` *statement produces an enumerator and not just a list filled with items. This enumerator is invoked by the* `foreach` *statement. As each item is accessed from the* `foreach`, *the enumerator is accessed. This makes it possible to iterate through huge amounts of data without reading all the data into memory in one turn.*

Different Ways to Iterate Through Collections

In a slightly larger and more realistic way than the Hello World example, you can use the `yield return` statement to iterate through a collection in different ways. The class `MusicTitles` enables iterating the titles in a default way with the `GetEnumerator` method, in reverse order with the `Reverse` method, and through a subset with the `Subset` method (code file `YieldSample/MusicTitles.cs`):

```
public class MusicTitles
{
  string[] names = {"Tubular Bells", "Hergest Ridge", "Ommadawn", "Platinum"};

  public IEnumerator<string> GetEnumerator()
  {
    for (int i = 0; i < 4; i++)
```

```
      {
        yield return names[i];
      }
    }

    public IEnumerable<string> Reverse()
    {
      for (int i = 3; i >= 0; i--)
      {
        yield return names[i];
      }
    }

    public IEnumerable<string> Subset(int index, int length)
    {
      for (int i = index; i < index + length; i++)
      {
        yield return names[i];
      }
    }
  }
}
```

> **NOTE** *The default iteration supported by a class is the* GetEnumerator *method, which is defined to return* IEnumerator. *Named iterations return* IEnumerable.

The client code to iterate through the string array first uses the GetEnumerator method, which you don't have to write in your code because it is used by default with the implementation of the foreach statement. Then the titles are iterated in reverse, and finally a subset is iterated by passing the index and number of items to iterate to the Subset method (code file YieldSample/Program.cs):

```
MusicTitles titles = new();
foreach (var title in titles)
{
  Console.WriteLine(title);
}
Console.WriteLine();

Console.WriteLine("reverse");
foreach (var title in titles.Reverse())
{
  Console.WriteLine(title);
}
Console.WriteLine();

Console.WriteLine("subset");
foreach (var title in titles.Subset(2, 2))
{
  Console.WriteLine(title);
}
```

USING SPAN WITH ARRAYS

For a fast way to access managed or unmanaged continuous memory, you can use the Span<T> struct. One example where Span<T> can be used is an array; the Span<T> struct holds continuous memory behind the scenes. Another example of a use for Span<T> is a long string.

Using Span<T>, you can directly access array elements. The elements of the array are not copied, but they can be used directly, which is faster than a copy.

In the following code snippet, first a simple int array is created and initialized. A Span<int> object is created, invoking the constructor and passing the array to the Span<int>. The Span<T> type offers an indexer, and thus the elements of the Span<T> can be accessed using this indexer. Here, the second element is changed to the value 11. Because the array arr1 is referenced from the span, the second element of the array is changed by changing the Span<T> element. Finally, the span is returned from this method because it is used within top-level statements to pass it on to the next methods that follow (code file SpanSample/Program.cs):

```
Span<int> IntroSpans()
{
  int[] arr1 = { 1, 4, 5, 11, 13, 18 };
  Span<int> span1 = new(arr1);
  span1[1] = 11;
  Console.WriteLine($"arr1[1] is changed via span1[1]: {arr1[1]}");
  return span1;
}
```

Creating Slices

A powerful feature of Span<T> is that you can use it to access parts, or *slices*, of an array. By using the slices, the array elements are not copied; they're directly accessed from the span.

The following code snippet shows two ways to create slices. With the first one, a constructor overload is used to pass the start and length of the array that should be used. With the variable span3 that references this newly created Span<int>, it's only possible to access three elements of the array arr2, starting with the fourth element. Another overload of the constructor exists where you can pass just the start of the slice. With this overload, the remains of the array are taken until the end. You can also create a slice from a Span<T> object, invoking the Slice method. Similar overloads exist here. With the variable span4, the previously created span1 is used to create a slice with four elements starting with the third element of span1 (code file SpanSample/Program.cs):

```
private static Span<int> CreateSlices(Span<int> span1)
{
  Console.WriteLine(nameof(CreateSlices));
  int[] arr2 = { 3, 5, 7, 9, 11, 13, 15 };
  Span<int> span2 = new(arr2);
  Span<int> span3 = new(arr2, start: 3, length: 3);
  Span<int> span4 = span1.Slice(start: 2, length: 4);

  DisplaySpan("content of span3", span3);
  DisplaySpan("content of span4", span4);
  Console.WriteLine();
  return span2;
}
```

You use the `DisplaySpan` method to display the contents of a span. The following code snippet makes use of the `ReadOnlySpan`. You can use this span type if you don't need to change the content that the span references, which is the case in the `DisplaySpan` method. `ReadOnlySpan<T>` is discussed later in this chapter in more detail:

```
private static void DisplaySpan(string title, ReadOnlySpan<int> span)
{
  Console.WriteLine(title);
  for (int i = 0; i < span.Length; i++)
  {
    Console.Write($"{span[i]}.");
  }
  Console.WriteLine();
}
```

When you run the application, the content of span3 and span4 is shown—a subset of the arr2 and arr1:

```
content of span3
9.11.13.
content of span4
6.8.10.12.
```

> **NOTE** `Span<T>` *is safe from crossing the boundaries. If you're creating spans that exceed the contained array length, an exception of type* `ArgumentOutOfRangeException` *is thrown. Read Chapter 10 for more information on exception handling.*

Changing Values Using Spans

You've seen how to directly change elements of the array that are referenced by the span using the indexer of the `Span<T>` type. There are more options as shown in the following code snippet.

You can invoke the `Clear` method, which fills a span containing `int` types with `0`; you can invoke the `Fill` method to fill the span with the value passed to the `Fill` method; and you can copy a `Span<T>` to another `Span<T>`. With the `CopyTo` method, if the destination span is not large enough, an exception of type `ArgumentException` is thrown. You can avoid this outcome by using the `TryCopyTo` method. This method doesn't throw an exception if the destination span is not large enough; instead, it returns `false` as being not successful with the copy (code file `SpanSample/Program.cs`):

```
private static void ChangeValues(Span<int> span1, Span<int> span2)
{
  Console.WriteLine(nameof(ChangeValues));
  Span<int> span4 = span1.Slice(start: 4);
  span4.Clear();
  DisplaySpan("content of span1", span1);
  Span<int> span5 = span2.Slice(start: 3, length: 3);
  span5.Fill(42);
  DisplaySpan("content of span2", span2);
  span5.CopyTo(span1);
  DisplaySpan("content of span1", span1);
```

```
        if (!span1.TryCopyTo(span4))
        {
          Console.WriteLine("Couldn't copy span1 to span4 because span4 is " +
            "too small");
          Console.WriteLine($"length of span4: {span4.Length}, length of " +
            $"span1: {span1.Length}");
        }
        Console.WriteLine();
      }
```

When you run the application, you can see the content of span1 where the last two numbers have been cleared using span4, the content of span2 where span5 was used to fill the value 42 with three elements, and again the content of span1 where the first three numbers have been copied over from span5. Copying span1 to span4 was not successful because span4 has just a length of 4, whereas span1 has a length of 6:

```
content of span1
2.11.6.8.0.0.
content of span2
3.5.7.42.42.42.15.
content of span1
42.42.42.8.0.0.
Couldn't copy span1 to span4 because span4 is too small
length of span4: 2, length of span1: 6
```

ReadOnly Spans

If you need only read-access to an array segment, you can use ReadOnlySpan<T> as was already shown in the DisplaySpan method. With ReadOnlySpan<T>, the indexer is read-only, and this type doesn't offer Clear and Fill methods. You can, however, invoke the CopyTo method to copy the content of the ReadOnlySpan<T> to a Span<T>.

The following code snippet creates readOnlySpan1 from an array with the constructor of ReadOnlySpan<T>. readOnlySpan2 and readOnlySpan3 are created by direct assignments from Span<int> and int []. Implicit cast operators are available with ReadOnlySpan<T> (code file SpanSample/Program.cs):

```
      void ReadonlySpan(Span<int> span1)
      {
        Console.WriteLine(nameof(ReadonlySpan));
        int[] arr = span1.ToArray();
        ReadOnlySpan<int> readOnlySpan1 = new(arr);
        DisplaySpan("readOnlySpan1", readOnlySpan1);

        ReadOnlySpan<int> readOnlySpan2 = span1;
        DisplaySpan("readOnlySpan2", readOnlySpan2);
        ReadOnlySpan<int> readOnlySpan3 = arr;
        DisplaySpan("readOnlySpan3", readOnlySpan3);
        Console.WriteLine();
      }
```

> **NOTE** *How to implement implicit cast operators is discussed in Chapter 5, "Operators and Casts." Read more information on spans in Chapter 13, "Managed and Unmanaged Memory."*

> **NOTE** *Previous editions of this book demonstrated the use of* `ArraySegment<T>`. *Although* `ArraySegment<T>` *is still available, it has some shortcomings, and you can use the more flexible* `Span<T>` *as a replacement. In case you're already using* `ArraySegment<T>`, *you can keep the code and interact with spans. The constructor of* `Span<T>` *also allows passing an* `ArraySegment<T>` *to create a* `Span<T>` *instance.*

INDICES AND RANGES

Starting with C# 8, indices and ranges based on the `Index` and `Range` types were included, along with the range and hat operators. Using the hat operator, you can access elements counting from the end.

Indices and the Hat Operator

Let's start with the following array, which consists of nine integer values (code file `IndicesAndRanges/Program.cs`):

```
int[] data = { 1, 2, 3, 4, 5, 6, 7, 8, 9 };
```

The traditional way to access the first and last elements of this array is to use the indexer implemented with the `Array` class, pass an integer value for the nth element starting with 0 for the first element, and use the length minus 1 for the last element:

```
int first1 = data[0];
int last1 = data[data.Length - 1];
Console.WriteLine($"first: {first1}, last: {last1}");
```

With the hat operator (`^`), you can use `^1` to access the last element, and the calculation based on the length is no longer necessary:

```
int last2 = data[^1];
Console.WriteLine(last2);
```

Behind the scenes, the `Index` struct type is used. An implicit cast from `int` to `Index` is implemented, so you can assign `int` values to the `Index` type. Using the hat operator, the compiler creates an `Index` that initializes the `IsFromEnd` property to `true`. Passing the `Index` to an indexer, the compiler converts the value to an `int`. If the `Index` starts from the end, calculation is done with either a `Length` or a `Count` property (depending on what property is available):

```
Index firstIndex = 0;
Index lastIndex = ^1;
int first3 = data[firstIndex];
int last3 = data[lastIndex];
Console.WriteLine($"first: {first3}, last: {last3}");
```

Ranges

To access a range of the array, the range operator (`..`) can be used with the underlying `Range` type. In the sample code, the `ShowRange` method is implemented to display the values of an array with a string output (code file `IndicesAndRanges/Program.cs`):

```
void ShowRange(string title, int[] data)
{
  Console.WriteLine(title);
  Console.WriteLine(string.Join(" ", data));
  Console.WriteLine();
}
```

By invoking this method with different values passed using the range operator, you can see the various forms of ranges. A range is defined with `..` embedded with an `Index` on the left and an `Index` on the right. Starting with `..` and omitting the `Index` from the left side just starts from the beginning. Omitting the `Index` from the right side, the range goes up to the end. Using `..` with the array just returns the complete array.

The `Index` on the left side specifies an inclusive value, whereas the `Index` on the right side is exclusive. With the end of the range, you need to specify the element following the last element you want to access. When the `Index` type was used before, you've seen that `^1` references the last value of the collection. When using the `Index` on the right side of a range, you must specify `^0` to address the element after the last element (remember the right side of the range is exclusive).

With the code sample, a full range is used (`..`), the first three elements are passed with `0..3`; the fourth to the sixth elements are passed with `3..6`; and counting from the end, the last three elements are passed with `^3..^0`:

```
ShowRange("full range", data[..]);
ShowRange("first three", data[0..3]);
ShowRange("fourth to sixth", data[3..6]);
ShowRange("last three", data[^3..^0]);
```

Behind the scenes, the `Range` struct type is used, and you can assign ranges to variables:

```
Range fullRange = ..;
Range firstThree = 0..3;
Range fourthToSixth = 3..6;
Range lastThree = ^3..^0;
```

The `Range` type specifies a constructor that passes two `Index` values for the start and the end, `End` and `Start` properties that return an `Index`, and a `GetOffsetAndLength` method that returns a tuple consisting of the offset and length of a range.

Efficiently Changing Array Content

Using a range of an array, the array elements are copied. Changing values within the range, the original values of the array do not change. However, as described in the section "Using Span with Arrays," a `Span` allows accessing a slice of an array directly. The `Span` type also supports indices and ranges, and you can change the content of an array by accessing a range of the `Span` type.

The following code snippet demonstrates accessing a slice of an array and changing the first element of the slice; the original value of the array didn't change because a copy was done. In the code lines that follow, a `Span` is created to access the array using the `AsSpan` method. With this `Span`, the range operator is used, which in turn invokes the `Slice` method of the `Span`. Changing values from this slice, the array is directly accessed and changed using an indexer on the slice (code file `IndicesAndRanges/Program.cs`):

```
var slice1 = data[3..5];
slice1[0] = 42;
Console.WriteLine($"value in array didn't change: {data[3]}, " +
  $"value from slice: {slice1[0]}");
```

```
var sliceToSpan = data.AsSpan()[3..5];
sliceToSpan[0] = 42;
Console.WriteLine($"value in array: {data[3]}, value from slice: {sliceToSpan[0]}");
```

Indices and Ranges with Custom Collections

To support indices and ranges with custom collections, not a lot of work is required. To support the hat operator, the MyCollection class implements an indexer and the Length property. To support ranges, you can either create a method that receives a Range type or—a simpler way—create a method with the name Slice that has two int parameters and can have the return type you need. The compiler converts the range to calculate the start and length (code file IndicesAndRanges/MyCollection.cs):

```
using System;
using System.Linq;

public class MyCollection
{
  private int[] _array = Enumerable.Range(1, 100).ToArray();

  public int Length => _array.Length;

  public int this[int index]
  {
    get => _array[index];
    set => _array[index] = value;
  }

  public int[] Slice(int start, int length)
  {
    var slice = new int[length];
    Array.Copy(_array, start, slice, 0, length);
    return slice;
  }
}
```

The collection is initialized. With just the few lines that have been implemented, the hat operator can be used with the indexer, and with the range operator, the compiler converts this to invoke the Slice method (code file IndicesAndRanges/Program.cs):

```
MyCollection coll = new();
int n = coll[^20];
Console.WriteLine($"Item from the collection: {n}");
ShowRange("Using custom collection", coll[45..^40]);
```

ARRAY POOLS

If you have an application where a lot of arrays are created and destroyed, the garbage collector has some work to do. To reduce the work of the garbage collector, you can use array pools with the ArrayPool class (from the namespace System.Buffers). ArrayPool manages a pool of arrays. Arrays can be rented from and returned to the pool. Memory is managed from the ArrayPool itself.

Creating the Array Pool

You can create an ArrayPool<T> by invoking the static Create method. For efficiency, the array pool manages memory in multiple buckets for arrays of similar sizes. With the Create method, you can define the maximum array length and the number of arrays within a bucket before another bucket is required:

```
ArrayPool<int> customPool = ArrayPool<int>.Create(
  maxArrayLength: 40000, maxArraysPerBucket: 10);
```

The default for the maxArrayLength is 1024 × 1024 bytes, and the default for maxArraysPerBucket is 50. The array pool uses multiple buckets for faster access to arrays when many arrays are used. Arrays of similar sizes are kept in the same bucket as long as possible, and the maximum number of arrays is not reached.

You can also use a predefined shared pool by accessing the Shared property of the ArrayPool<T> class:

```
ArrayPool<int> sharedPool = ArrayPool<int>.Shared;
```

Renting Memory from the Pool

Requesting memory from the pool happens by invoking the Rent method. The Rent method accepts the minimum array length that should be requested. If memory is already available in the pool, it is returned. If it is not available, memory is allocated for the pool and returned afterward. In the following code snippet, an array of 1024, 2048, 3096, and so on elements is requested in a for loop (code file ArrayPoolSample/Program.cs):

```
private static void UseSharedPool()
{
  for (int i = 0; i < 10; i++)
  {
    int arrayLenqth = (i + 1) << 10;
    int[] arr = ArrayPool<int>.Shared.Rent(arrayLength);
    Console.WriteLine($"requested an array of {arrayLength} " +
      $"and received {arr.Length}");
    //...
  }
}
```

The Rent method returns an array with at least the requested number of elements. The array returned could have more memory available. The shared pool keeps arrays with at least 16 elements. The element count of the managed arrays always doubles—for example, 16, 32, 64, 128, 256, 512, 1024, 2048, 4096, 8192 elements, and so on.

When you run the application, you can see that larger arrays are returned if the requested array size doesn't fit the arrays managed by the pool:

```
requested an array of 1024 and received 1024
requested an array of 2048 and received 2048
requested an array of 3072 and received 4096
requested an array of 4096 and received 4096
requested an array of 5120 and received 8192
requested an array of 6144 and received 8192
requested an array of 7168 and received 8192
requested an array of 8192 and received 8192
requested an array of 9216 and received 16384
requested an array of 10240 and received 16384
```

Returning Memory to the Pool

After you no longer need the array, you can return it to the pool. After the array is returned, you can later reuse it by renting it again.

You return the array to the pool by invoking the `Return` method of the array pool and passing the array to the `Return` method. With an optional parameter, you can specify whether the array should be cleared before it is returned to the pool. Without clearing it, the next one renting an array from the pool could read the data. By clearing the data, you avoid this, but you need more CPU time (code file: `ArrayPoolSample/Program.cs`):

```
ArrayPool<int>.Shared.Return(arr, clearArray: true);
```

> **NOTE** *Information about the garbage collector and how to get information about memory addresses is in Chapter 13.*

BITARRAY

If you need to work with an array of bits, you can use the `BitArray` type (from the namespace `System.Collections`). `BitArray` is a reference type that contains an array of `int`s, where for every 32 bits a new integer is used. `BitArray` defines `Count` and `Length` properties, an indexer, a `SetAll` method to set all the bits according to the parameters passed, a `Not` method to inverse the bits, as well as `And`, `Or`, and `Xor` methods for binary AND, binary OR, and exclusive OR.

> **NOTE** *Chapter 5 covers bitwise operators that can be used with number types such as* `byte`, `short`, `int`, *and* `long`. *The* `BitArray` *class has similar functionality but can be used with a different number of bits than the C# types.*

With the code sample, the extension method `GetBitsFormat` iterates through a `BitArray` and writes `1` or `0` to a `StringBuilder`, depending on whether the bit is set. For better readability, a separator character is added every four bits (code file `BitArraySample/BitArrayExtensions.cs`):

```
public static class BitArrayExtensions
{
  public static string GetBitsFormat(this BitArray bits)
  {
    StringBuilder sb = new();
    for (int i = bits.Length - 1; i >= 0; i--)
    {
      sb.Append(bits[i] ? 1 : 0);
      if (i != 0 && i % 4 == 0)
      {
        sb.Append("_");
      }
    }
    return sb.ToString();
  }
}
```

The following example demonstrates the `BitArray` class creating a bit array with nine bits, indexed from 0 to 8. The `SetAll` method sets all nine bits to `true`. Then the `Set` method changes bit 1 to `false`. Instead of the `Set` method, you can also use an indexer, as shown with index 5 and 7 (code file `BitArraySample/Program.cs`):

```
BitArray bits1 = new(9);
bits1.SetAll(true);
bits1.Set(1, false);
bits1[5] = false;
bits1[7] = false;
Console.Write("initialized: ");
Console.WriteLine(bits1.GetBitsFormat());
Console.WriteLine();
```

This is the displayed result of the initialized bits:

```
initialized: 1_0101_1101
```

The `Not` method generates the inverse of the bits of the `BitArray`:

```
Console.WriteLine($"NOT {bits1.FormatString()}");
bits1.Not();
Console.WriteLine($"  = {bits1.FormatString()}");
Console.WriteLine();
```

The result of `Not` is all bits inverted. If the bit were `true`, it is `false`; and if it were `false`, it is `true`:

```
NOT 1_0101_1101
  = 0_1010_0010
```

In the following example, a new `BitArray` is created. With the constructor, the variable `bits1` is used to initialize the array, so the new array has the same values. Then the values for bits 0, 1, and 4 are set to different values. Before the `Or` method is used, the bit arrays `bits1` and `bits2` are displayed. The `Or` method changes the values of `bits1`:

```
BitArray bits2 = new(bits1);
bits2[0] = true;
bits2[1] = false;
bits2[4] = true;
Console.WriteLine($"   {bits1.FormatString()}");
Console.WriteLine($"OR {bits2.FormatString()}");
bits1.Or(bits2);
Console.WriteLine($"=  {bits1.FormatString()}");
Console.WriteLine();
```

With the `Or` method, the set bits are taken from both input arrays. In the result, the bit is set if it was set with either the first or the second array:

```
   0_1010_0010
OR 0_1011_0001
=  0_1011_0011
```

Next, the `And` method is used to operate on `bits2` and `bits1`:

```
Console.WriteLine($"    {bits2.FormatString()}");
Console.WriteLine($"AND {bits1.FormatString()}");
bits2.And(bits1);
Console.WriteLine($"=   {bits2.FormatString()}");
Console.WriteLine();
```

The result of the And method only sets the bits where the bit was set in both input arrays:

```
    0_1011_0001
AND 0_1011_0011
=   0_1011_0001
```

Finally, the Xor method is used for an exclusive OR:

```
Console.WriteLine($"    {bits1.FormatString()} ");
Console.WriteLine($"XOR {bits2.FormatString()}");
bits1.Xor(bits2);
Console.WriteLine($"=   {bits1.FormatString()}");
Console.ReadLine();
```

With the Xor method, the resultant bit is set only if the bit was set either in the first or second input, but not both:

```
    0_1011_0011
XOR 0_1011_0001
=   0_0000_0010
```

SUMMARY

This chapter covered how to use the C# notation to create and use simple, multidimensional, and jagged arrays. The Array class is used behind the scenes of C# arrays, enabling you to invoke properties and methods of this class with array variables.

You saw how to sort elements in the array by using the IComparable and IComparer interfaces; and you learned how to create and use enumerators, the interfaces IEnumerable and IEnumerator, and the yield statement.

With the Span<T> type, you saw efficient ways to access a slice of the array. You also saw range and index enhancements with C#.

The last sections of this chapter showed you how to efficiently use arrays with the ArrayPool, as well as how to use the BitArray type to deal with an array of bits.

The next chapter gets into details of more important features of C#: delegates, lambdas, and events.

7

Delegates, Lambdas, and Events

WHAT'S IN THIS CHAPTER?

➤ Delegates

➤ Lambda expressions

➤ Closures

➤ Events

CODE DOWNLOADS FOR THIS CHAPTER

The source code for this chapter is available on the book page at www.wiley.com. Click the Downloads link. The code can also be found at https://github.com/ProfessionalCSharp/ProfessionalCSharp2021 in the directory 1_CS/Delegates.

The code for this chapter is divided into the following major examples:

➤ SimpleDelegates

➤ MulticastDelegates

➤ LambdaExpressions

➤ EventsSample

All the projects have nullable reference types enabled.

REFERENCING METHODS

Delegates are the .NET variant of addresses to methods. A delegate is an object-oriented type-safe pointer to one or multiple methods. Lambda expressions are directly related to delegates. When the parameter is a delegate type, you can use a lambda expression to implement a method that's referenced from the delegate.

This chapter explains the basics of delegates and lambda expressions, and it shows you how to implement methods called by delegates with lambda expressions. It also demonstrates how .NET uses delegates as the means of implementing events.

> **NOTE** *C# 9 also has the concept of a function pointer—a direct pointer to a managed or native method without the overhead of a delegate. Function pointers are explained in Chapter 13, "Managed and Unmanaged Memory."*

DELEGATES

In Chapter 4, "Object-Oriented Programming in C#," you read about using interfaces as contracts. If the parameter of a method has the type of an interface, with the implementation of the method any members of the interface can be used without being dependent on any interface implementation. Indeed, the implementation of the interface can be done independently of the method implementation. Similarly, a method can be declared to receive a parameter of a delegate type. The method receiving the delegate parameter can invoke the method that's referenced from the delegate. Similar to interfaces, the implementation of the method that's referenced by the delegate can be done independently of the method that's invoking the delegate.

The concept of passing delegates to methods can become clearer with some examples:

➤ **Tasks**—With tasks you can define a sequence of execution that should run in parallel with what currently is running in the main task. You can invoke the `Run` method of a `Task` and pass the address of a method via a delegate to invoke this method from the task. Tasks are explained in Chapter 11, "Tasks and Asynchronous Programming."

➤ **LINQ**—LINQ is implemented via extension methods that require a delegate as a parameter. Here you can pass functionality such as how to define the implementation to compare two values. LINQ is explained in detail in Chapter 9, "Language Integrated Query."

➤ **Events**—With events, you separate the producer that fires events and the subscribers that listen to events. The publisher and subscriber are decoupled. What's common between them is the contract of a delegate. Events are explained in detail later in this chapter.

Declaring Delegates

When you want to use a class in C#, you do so in two stages. First, you need to define the class—that is, you need to tell the compiler what fields and methods make up the class. Then (unless you are using only static methods), you instantiate an object of that class. With delegates, it is the same process. You start by declaring the delegates you want to use. Declaring delegates means telling the compiler what kind of method a delegate of that type will represent. Then, you have to create one or more instances of that delegate. Behind the scenes, a delegate type is a class, but there's specific syntax for delegates that hide details.

The syntax for declaring delegates looks like this:

```
delegate void IntMethodInvoker(int x);
```

This declares a delegate called IntMethodInvoker and indicates that each instance of this delegate can hold a reference to a method that takes one int parameter and returns void. The crucial point to understand about delegates is that they are type-safe. When you define the delegate, you have to provide full details about the signature and the return type of the method that it represents.

> **NOTE** *One good way to understand delegates is to think of a delegate as something that gives a name to a method signature and the return type.*

Suppose that you want to define a delegate called TwoLongsOp that represents a method that takes two longs as its parameters and returns a double. You could do so like this:

```
delegate double TwoLongsOp(long first, long second);
```

Or, to define a delegate that represents a method that takes no parameters and returns a string, you might write this (code file GetAStringDemo/Program.cs):

```
//...
delegate string GetAString();
```

The syntax is similar to that for a method definition, except there is no method body and the definition is prefixed with the keyword delegate. Because what you are doing here is basically defining a new class, you can define a delegate in any of the same places that you would define a class—that is to say, either inside another class, outside of any class, or in a namespace as a top-level object. Depending on how visible you want your definition to be and the scope of the delegate, you can apply any of the access modifiers that also apply to classes to define its visibility:

```
public delegate string GetAString();
```

> **NOTE** *Delegates are implemented as classes derived from the class* System.MulticastDelegate, *which is derived from the base class* System.Delegate. *The C# compiler is aware of this class and uses the delegate syntax to hide the details of the operations of this class.*

After you have defined a delegate, you can create an instance of it so that you can use it to store details about a particular method.

Using Delegates

The following code snippet demonstrates the use of a delegate. It is a rather long-winded way of calling the ToString method on an int (code file GetAStringDemo/Program.cs):

```
int x = 40;
GetAString firstStringMethod = new GetAString(x.ToString);
Console.WriteLine($"String is {firstStringMethod()}");
//...
```

This code instantiates a delegate of type GetAString and initializes it so it refers to the ToString method of the integer variable x. Delegates always take a one-parameter constructor, which is the address of a method. This method must match the signature and return type with which the delegate was defined. Because ToString is an instance method (as opposed to a static method), the instance needs to be supplied with the parameter.

The next line invokes the delegate to display the string. In any code, supplying the name of a delegate instance, followed by parentheses containing any parameters, has exactly the same effect as calling the method wrapped by the delegate.

In fact, supplying parentheses to the delegate instance is the same as calling the `Invoke` method of the delegate class. Because `firstStringMethod` is a variable of a delegate type, the C# compiler replaces `firstStringMethod` with `firstStringMethod.Invoke`:

```
firstStringMethod();
firstStringMethod.Invoke();
```

For less typing, at every place where a delegate instance is needed, you can just pass the name of the address. This is known by the term *delegate inference*. This C# feature works as long as the compiler can resolve the delegate instance to a specific type. The example initialized the variable `firstStringMethod` of type `GetAString` with a new instance of the delegate `GetAString`:

```
GetAString firstStringMethod = new GetAString(x.ToString);
```

You can write the same just by passing the method name with the variable x to the variable `firstStringMethod`:

```
GetAString firstStringMethod = x.ToString;
```

The code that is created by the C# compiler is the same. The compiler detects that a delegate type is required with `firstStringMethod`, so it creates an instance of the delegate type `GetAString` and passes the address of the method with the object x to the constructor.

> **NOTE** *Be aware that you can't add the parentheses to the method name as* x.ToString() *and pass it to the delegate variable. This would be an invocation of the method. The invocation of the* ToString *method returns a string object that can't be assigned to the delegate variable. You can only assign the address of a method to the delegate variable.*

Delegate inference can be used anywhere a delegate instance is required. Delegate inference can also be used with events because events are based on delegates (as you'll see later in this chapter).

One feature of delegates is that they are type-safe to the extent that they ensure that the signature of the method being called is correct. However, interestingly, they don't care what type of object the method is being called against or even whether the method is a static method or an instance method.

> **NOTE** *An instance of a given delegate can refer to any instance or static method on any object of any type provided that the signature of the method matches the signature of the delegate.*

To demonstrate this, the following example expands the previous code snippet so that it uses the `firstStringMethod` delegate to call a couple of other methods on another object—an instance method and a static method. For this, the `Currency` struct is defined. This type has its own overload of `ToString` and a static method with the same signature to `GetCurrencyUnit`. This way, the same delegate variable can be used to invoke these methods (code file `GetAStringDemo/Currency.cs`):

```
struct Currency
{
  public uint Dollars;
  public ushort Cents;
```

```
      public Currency(uint dollars, ushort cents)
      {
        Dollars = dollars;
        Cents = cents;
      }

      public override string ToString() => $"${Dollars}.{Cents,2:00}";

      public static string GetCurrencyUnit() => "Dollar";

      public static explicit operator Currency (float value)
      {
        checked
        {
          uint dollars = (uint)value;
          ushort cents = (ushort)((value - dollars) * 100);
          return new Currency(dollars, cents);
        }
      }

      public static implicit operator float (Currency value) =>
        value.Dollars + (value.Cents / 100.0f);

      public static implicit operator Currency (uint value) =>
        new Currency(value, 0);

      public static implicit operator uint (Currency value) =>
        value.Dollars;
    }
```

Now you can use the `GetAString` instance as follows (code file `GetAStringDemo/Program.cs`):

```
    private delegate string GetAString();

    //...
    var balance = new Currency(34, 50);

    // firstStringMethod references an instance method
    firstStringMethod = balance.ToString;
    Console.WriteLine($"String is {firstStringMethod()}");

    // firstStringMethod references a static method
    firstStringMethod = new GetAString(Currency.GetCurrencyUnit);
    Console.WriteLine($"String is {firstStringMethod()}");
```

This code shows how you can call a method via a delegate and subsequently reassign the delegate to refer to different methods on different instances of classes, even static methods or methods against instances of different types of class, provided that the signature of each method matches the delegate definition.

When you run the application, you get the output from the different methods that are referenced by the delegate:

```
    String is 40
    String is $34.50
    String is Dollar
```

Now that you've been introduced to the foundations of delegates, it's time to move onto something more useful and practical: passing delegates to methods.

Passing Delegates to Methods

This example defines a MathOperations class that uses a couple of static methods to perform two operations on doubles. Then you use delegates to invoke these methods. The MathOperations class looks like this (code file SimpleDelegates/MathOperations):

```
public static class MathOperations
{
  public static double MultiplyByTwo(double value) => value * 2;
  public static double Square(double value) => value * value;
}
```

You invoke these methods as follows (code file SimpleDelegates/Program.cs):

```
using System;

DoubleOp[] operations =
{
  MathOperations.MultiplyByTwo,
  MathOperations.Square
};

for (int i=0; i < operations.Length; i++)
{
  Console.WriteLine($"Using operations[{i}]");
  ProcessAndDisplayNumber(operations[i], 2.0);
  ProcessAndDisplayNumber(operations[i], 7.94);
  ProcessAndDisplayNumber(operations[i], 1.414);
  Console.WriteLine();
}

void ProcessAndDisplayNumber(DoubleOp action, double value)
{
  double result = action(value);
  Console.WriteLine($"Value is {value}, result of operation is {result}");
}

delegate double DoubleOp(double x);
```

In this code, you instantiate an array of DoubleOp delegates (remember that after you have defined a delegate class, you can basically instantiate instances just as you can with normal classes, so putting some into an array is no problem). Each element of the array is initialized to refer to a different operation implemented by the MathOperations class. Then, you loop through the array, applying each operation to three different values. This illustrates one way of using delegates—to group methods together into an array so that you can call several methods in a loop.

The key lines in this code are the ones in which you actually pass each delegate to the ProcessAndDisplayNumber method, such as this:

```
ProcessAndDisplayNumber(operations[i], 2.0);
```

This passes in the name of a delegate but without any parameters. Given that operations[i] is a delegate, syntactically the following is true:

➤ operations[i] means the delegate (that is, the method represented by the delegate).

➤ operations[i](2.0) means actually calling this method, passing in the value in parentheses.

The `ProcessAndDisplayNumber` method is defined to take a delegate as its first parameter:

```
void ProcessAndDisplayNumber(DoubleOp action, double value)
```
Then, within the implementation of this method, you call this:

```
double result = action(value);
```
This actually causes the method that is wrapped up by the `action` delegate instance to be called, and its return result is stored in `Result`. Running this example gives you the following:

```
Using operations[0]:
Value is 2, result of operation is 4
Value is 7.94, result of operation is 15.88
Value is 1.414, result of operation is 2.828

Using operations[1]:
Value is 2, result of operation is 4
Value is 7.94, result of operation is 63.043600000000005
Value is 1.414, result of operation is 1.9993959999999997
```

> **NOTE** *With the outcome you're seeing, you might expect different results with some of the multiplications, but if you round the results, they match. This is because of how* double *values are stored. Depending on the data you're working with, this might not be good enough—for example with financial data. Here you should use the* decimal *type instead.*

Action<T> and Func<T> Delegates

Instead of defining a new delegate type with every parameter and return type, you can use the `Action<T>` and `Func<T>` delegates. The generic `Action<T>` delegate is meant to reference a method with `void` return. This delegate class exists in different variants so that you can pass up to 16 different parameter types. The `Action` class without the generic parameter is for calling methods without parameters. `Action<in T>` is for calling a method with one parameter; `Action<in T1, in T2>` is for a method with two parameters; and `Action<in T1, in T2, in T3, in T4, in T5, in T6, in T7, in T8>` is for a method with eight parameters.

The `Func<T>` delegates can be used in a similar manner. `Func<T>` allows you to invoke methods with a return type. Similar to `Action<T>`, `Func<T>` is defined in different variants to pass up to 16 parameter types and a return type. `Func<out TResult>` is the delegate type to invoke a method with a return type and without parameters. `Func<in T, out TResult>` is for a method with one parameter, and `Func<in T1, in T2, in T3, in T4, out TResult>` is for a method with four parameters.

The example in the preceding section declared a delegate with a `double` parameter and a `double` return type:

```
delegate double DoubleOp(double x);
```

Instead of declaring the custom delegate `DoubleOp`, you can use the `Func<in T, out TResult>` delegate. You can declare a variable of the delegate type or, as shown here, an array of the delegate type:

```
Func<double, double>[] operations =
{
  MathOperations.MultiplyByTwo,
  MathOperations.Square
};
```
and use it with the `ProcessAndDisplayNumber` method as a parameter:

```
static void ProcessAndDisplayNumber(Func<double, double> action,
  double value)
```

```
  {
    double result = action(value);
    Console.WriteLine($"Value is {value}, result of operation is {result}");
  }
```

Multicast Delegates

So far, each of the delegates you have used wraps just one method call. Calling the delegate amounts to calling that method. If you want to call more than one method, you need to make an explicit call through a delegate more than once. However, it is possible for a delegate to wrap more than one method. Such a delegate is known as a *multicast delegate*. When a multicast delegate is called, it successively calls each method in order. For this to work, the delegate signature should return a void; otherwise, you would only get the result of the last method invoked by the delegate.

With a void return type, you can use the Action<double> delegate (code file MulticastDelegates/Program.cs):

```
Action<double> operations = MathOperations.MultiplyByTwo;
operations += MathOperations.Square;
```

In the earlier example, you wanted to store references to two methods, so you instantiated an array of delegates. Here, you simply add both operations into the same multicast delegate. Multicast delegates recognize the operators +, +=, and -=. Alternatively, you can expand the last two lines of the preceding code, as in this snippet:

```
Action<double> operation1 = MathOperations.MultiplyByTwo;
Action<double> operation2 = MathOperations.Square;
Action<double> operations = operation1 + operation2;
```

With the sample project MulticastDelegates, the MathOperations type from SimpleDelegates has been changed to return void and to display the results on the console (code file MulticastDelegates/MathOperations.cs):

```
public static class MathOperations
{
  public static void MultiplyByTwo(double value) =>
    Console.WriteLine($"Multiplying by 2: {value} gives {value * 2}");

  public static void Square(double value) =>
    Console.WriteLine($"Squaring: {value} gives {value * value}");
}
```

To accommodate this change, you also have to rewrite ProcessAndDisplayNumber (code file MulticastDelegates/Program.cs):

```
static void ProcessAndDisplayNumber(Action<double> action, double value)
{
  Console.WriteLine($"ProcessAndDisplayNumber called with value = {value}");
  action(value);
  Console.WriteLine();
}
```

Now you can try your multicast delegate:

```
Action<double> operations = MathOperations.MultiplyByTwo;
operations += MathOperations.Square;
ProcessAndDisplayNumber(operations, 2.0);
```

```
ProcessAndDisplayNumber(operations, 7.94);
ProcessAndDisplayNumber(operations, 1.414);
```

Each time `ProcessAndDisplayNumber` is called, it displays a message saying that it has been called. Then the following statement causes each of the method calls in the `action` delegate instance to be called in succession:

```
action(value);
```

Running the preceding code produces this result:

```
ProcessAndDisplayNumber called with value = 2
Multiplying by 2: 2 gives 4
Squaring: 2 gives 4

ProcessAndDisplayNumber called with value = 7.94
Multiplying by 2: 7.94 gives 15.88
Squaring: 7.94 gives 63.043600000000005

ProcessAndDisplayNumber called with value = 1.414
Multiplying by 2: 1.414 gives 2.828
Squaring: 1.414 gives 1.9993959999999997
```

If you are using multicast delegates, be aware that the order in which methods chained to the same delegate will be called is formally undefined. Therefore, avoid writing code that relies on such methods being called in any particular order.

Invoking multiple methods by one delegate might cause an even bigger problem. The multicast delegate contains a collection of delegates to invoke one after the other. If one of the methods invoked by a delegate throws an exception, the complete iteration stops. Consider the following `MulticastIteration` example. Here, the simple delegate `Action` is used. This delegate is meant to invoke the methods `One` and `Two`, which fulfill the parameter and return type requirements of the delegate. Be aware that method `One` throws an exception (code file `MulticastDelegatesUsingInvocationList/Program.cs`):

```
static void One()
{
  Console.WriteLine("One");
  throw new Exception("Error in One");
}

static void Two()
{
  Console.WriteLine("Two");
}
```

With the top-level statements, delegate `d1` is created to reference method `One`; next, the address of method `Two` is added to the same delegate. `d1` is invoked to call both methods. The exception is caught in a `try/catch` block:

```
Action d1 = One;
d1 += Two;
try
{
  d1();
}
catch (Exception)
{
  Console.WriteLine("Exception caught");
}
```

Only the first method is invoked by the delegate. Because the first method throws an exception, iterating the delegates stops here, and method `Two` is never invoked. The result might differ because the order of calling the methods is not defined:

```
One
Exception Caught
```

> **NOTE** *Errors and exceptions are explained in detail in Chapter 10, "Errors and Exceptions."*

In such a scenario, you can avoid the problem by iterating the list on your own. The `Delegate` class defines the method `GetInvocationList` that returns an array of `Delegate` objects. You can now use these delegates to invoke the methods associated with them directly, catch exceptions, and continue with the next iteration (code file `MulticastDelegatesUsingInvocationList/Program.cs`):

```
Action d1 = One;
d1 += Two;
Delegate[] delegates = d1.GetInvocationList();
foreach (Action d in delegates)
{
  try
  {
    d();
  }
  catch (Exception)
  {
    Console.WriteLine("Exception caught");
  }
}
```

When you run the application with the code changes, you can see that the iteration continues with the next method after the exception is caught:

```
One
Exception caught
Two
```

Anonymous Methods

Up to this point, a method must already exist for the delegate to work (that is, the delegate is defined with the same signature as the method(s) it will be used with). However, there is another way to use delegates—with *anonymous methods*. An anonymous method is a block of code that is used as the parameter for the delegate.

The syntax for defining a delegate with an anonymous method doesn't change. It's when the delegate is instantiated that things change. The following simple console application shows how using an anonymous method can work (code file `AnonymousMethods/Program.cs`):

```
string mid = ", middle part,";
Func<string, string> anonDel = delegate(string param)
{
  param += mid;
  param += " and this was added to the string.";
  return param;
};
Console.WriteLine(anonDel("Start of string"));
```

The delegate `Func<string, string>` takes a single string parameter and returns a string. `anonDel` is a variable of this delegate type. Instead of assigning the name of a method to this variable, a simple block of code is used, prefixed by the `delegate` keyword and followed by a string parameter.

As you can see, the block of code uses a method-level string variable, `mid`, which is defined outside of the anonymous method and adds it to the parameter that was passed in. The code then returns the string value. When the delegate is called, a string is passed in as the parameter, and the returned string is output to the console.

The benefit of using anonymous methods is that it reduces the amount of code you have to write. You don't need to define a method just to use it with a delegate. This becomes evident when you define the delegate for an event (events are discussed later in this chapter), and it helps reduce the complexity of the code, especially where several events are defined. With anonymous methods, the code does not perform faster. The compiler still defines a method; the method just has an automatically assigned name that you don't need to know.

You must follow a couple of rules when using anonymous methods. An anonymous method can't have a jump statement (`break`, `goto`, or `continue`) that has a target outside of the anonymous method. The reverse is also true: a jump statement outside the anonymous method cannot have a target inside the anonymous method.

If you have to write the same functionality more than once, don't use anonymous methods. In this case, instead of duplicating the code, write a named method. You have to write it only once and reference it by its name.

> **NOTE** *The syntax for anonymous methods was introduced with C# 2. With new programs, you really don't need this syntax anymore because lambda expressions (explained in the next section) offer the same—and more—functionality. However, you'll find the syntax for anonymous methods in many places in existing source code, which is why it's good to know it.*
>
> *Lambda expressions have been available since C# 3.*

LAMBDA EXPRESSIONS

One way lambda expressions are used is to assign code—using a lambda expression—to a parameter. You can use lambda expressions whenever you have a delegate parameter type. The previous example using anonymous methods is modified in the following snippet to use a lambda expression:

```
string mid = ", middle part,";
Func<string, string> lambda = param =>
{
  param += mid;
  param += " and this was added to the string.";
  return param;
};
Console.WriteLine(lambda("Start of string"));
```

The left side of the lambda operator, `=>`, lists the necessary parameters. The right side following the lambda operator defines the implementation of the method assigned to the variable `lambda`.

Parameters

With lambda expressions, there are several ways to define parameters. If there's only one parameter, just the name of the parameter is enough. The following lambda expression uses the parameter named s. Because the delegate type defines a `string` parameter, s is of type `string`. The implementation returns a formatted string that is finally written to the console when the delegate is invoked: `change uppercase TEST` (code file `LambdaExpressions/Program.cs`):

```
Func<string, string> oneParam = s => $"change uppercase {s.ToUpper()}";
Console.WriteLine(oneParam("test"));
```

If a delegate uses more than one parameter, you can combine the parameter names inside brackets. Here, the parameters x and y are of type double as defined by the Func<double, double, double> delegate:

```
Func<double, double, double> twoParams = (x, y) => x * y;
Console.WriteLine(twoParams(3, 2));
```

For convenience, you can add the parameter types to the variable names inside the brackets. If the compiler can't match an overloaded version, using parameter types can help resolve the matching delegate:

```
Func<double, double, double> twoParamsWithTypes =
  (double x, double y) => x * y;
Console.WriteLine(twoParamsWithTypes(4, 2));
```

Multiple Code Lines

If the lambda expression consists of a single statement, a method block with curly brackets and a return statement are not needed. There's an implicit return added by the compiler:

```
Func<double, double> square = x => x * x;
```

It's completely legal to add curly brackets, a return statement, and semicolons. Usually it's just easier to read without them:

```
Func<double, double> square = x =>
{
  return x * x;
};
```

However, if you need multiple statements in the implementation of the lambda expression, curly brackets and the return statement are required:

```
Func<string, string> lambda = param =>
{
  param += mid;
  param += " and this was added to the string.";
  return param;
};
```

Closures

With lambda expressions, you can access variables outside the block of the lambda expression. This is known as *closure*. Closures are a great feature, but they can also be dangerous if not used correctly.

In the following example, a lambda expression of type Func<int, int> requires one int parameter and returns an int. The parameter for the lambda expression is defined with the variable x. The implementation also accesses the variable someVal, which is outside the lambda expression. As long as you do not assume that the lambda expression creates a new method that is used later when f is invoked, this might not look confusing at all. Looking at this code block, the returned value calling f should be the value from x plus 5, but this might not be the case (code file LambdaExpressions/Program.cs):

```
int someVal = 5;
Func<int, int> f = x => x + someVal;
```

Assuming the variable someVal is later changed and then the lambda expression is invoked, the new value of someVal is used. The result of invoking f(3) is 10:

```
someVal = 7;
Console.WriteLine(f(3));
```

Similarly, when you're changing the value of a closure variable within the lambda expression, you can access the changed value outside of the lambda expression.

Now, you might wonder how it is possible at all to access variables outside of the lambda expression from within the lambda expression. To understand this, consider what the compiler does when you define a lambda expression. With the lambda expression x => x + someVal, the compiler creates an anonymous class that has a constructor to pass the outer variable. The constructor depends on how many variables you access from the outside. With this simple example, the constructor accepts an int. The anonymous class contains an anonymous method that has the implementation as defined by the lambda expression, with the parameters and return type:

```
public class AnonymousClass
{
  private int _someVal;
  public AnonymousClass(int someVal) => _someVal = someVal;

  public int AnonymousMethod(int x) => x + _someVal;
}
```

In case a value outside of the scope of the lambda expression needs to be returned, a reference type is used.

Using the lambda expression and invoking the method creates an instance of the anonymous class and passes the value of the variable from the time when the call is made.

> **NOTE** *In case you are using closures with multiple threads, you can get into concurrency conflicts. It's best to use only immutable types for closures. This way it's guaranteed the value can't change, and synchronization is not needed.*

> **NOTE** *You can use lambda expressions anywhere the type is a delegate. Another use of lambda expressions is when the type is* Expression *or* Expression<T>, *in which case the compiler creates an expression tree. This feature is discussed in Chapter 9.*

EVENTS

Events are based on delegates and offer a publish/subscribe mechanism to delegates. You can find events everywhere across the framework. In Windows applications, the Button class offers the Click event. This type of event is a delegate. A handler method that is invoked when the Click event is fired needs to be defined and to include parameters as defined by the delegate type.

> **NOTE** *See design guidelines for events in the Microsoft documentation:* https://docs .microsoft.com/en-us/dotnet/standard/design-guidelines/event.

In the code example shown in this section, events are used to connect the CarDealer and Consumer classes. The CarDealer class offers an event when a new car arrives. The Consumer class subscribes to the event to be informed when a new car arrives.

Event Publisher

You start with a `CarDealer` class that offers a subscription based on events. `CarDealer` defines the event named `NewCarCreated` of type `EventHandler<CarInfoEventArgs>` with the event keyword. Inside the method `CreateANewCar`, the event `NewCarCreated` is fired by invoking the method `RaiseNewCarCreated`. The implementation of this method verifies whether the delegate is not null and raises the event (code file `EventsSample/CarDealer.cs`):

```
public class CarInfoEventArgs: EventArgs
{
  public CarInfoEventArgs(string car) => Car = car;
  public string Car { get; }
}

public class CarDealer
{
  public event EventHandler<CarInfoEventArgs>? NewCarInfo;
  public void CreateANewCar(string car)
  {
    Console.WriteLine($"CarDealer, new car {car}");
    RaiseNewCarCreated(car);
  }

  private void RaiseNewCarCreated(string car) =>
    NewCarCreated?.Invoke(this, new CarInfoEventArgs(car));
}
```

The class `CarDealer` offers the event `NewCarCreated` of type `EventHandler<CarInfoEventArgs>`. As a convention, events typically use methods with two parameters; the first parameter is an object and contains the sender of the event, and the second parameter provides information about the event. The second parameter is different for various event types. You could create a specific delegate type such as

```
public delegate void NewCarCreatedHandler(object sender, CarInfoEventArgs e);
```

or use the generic type `EventHandler` as shown in the sample code. With `EventHandler<TEventArgs>`, the first parameter needs to be of type `object`, and the second parameter is of type `T`. `EventHandler<TEventArgs>` also defines a constraint on `T`; it must derive from the base class `EventArgs`, which is the case with `CarInfoEventArgs`.

```
public event EventHandler<CarInfoEventArgs> NewCarInfo;
```

The delegate `EventHandler<TEventArgs>` is defined as follows:

```
public delegate void EventHandler<TEventArgs>(object sender, TEventArgs e)
  where TEventArgs: EventArgs
```

Defining the event in one line is a C# shorthand notation. The compiler creates a variable of the delegate type `EventHandler<CarInfoEventArgs>` and adds methods to subscribe and unsubscribe from the delegate. The long form of the shorthand notation is shown next. This is similar to auto-properties and full properties. With events, the `add` and `remove` keywords are used to add and remove a handler to the delegate:

```
private EventHandler<CarInfoEventArgs>? _newCarCreated;
public event EventHandler<CarInfoEventArgs>? NewCarCreated
{
  add => _newCarCreated += value;
  remove => _newCarCreated -= value;
}
```

> **NOTE** *The long notation to define events is useful if more needs to be done than just adding and removing the event handler, such as adding synchronization for multiple thread access. The UWP, WPF, and WinUI controls make use of the long notation to add bubbling and tunneling functionality with the events.*

The class `CarDealer` fires the event by calling the `Invoke` method of the delegate. This invokes all the handlers that are subscribed to the event. Remember, as previously shown with multicast delegates, the order of the methods invoked is not guaranteed. To have more control over calling the handler methods, you can use the `Delegate` class method `GetInvocationList` to access every item in the delegate list and invoke each on its own, as shown earlier.

```
NewCarCreated?.Invoke(this, new CarInfoEventArgs(car));
```

Firing the event requires only a one-liner. Prior to C# 6, firing the event was more complex—checking the delegate for `null` (if no subscriber was registered) before invoking the method, which should have been done in a thread-safe manner. Now, checking for null is done using the `?.` operator.

Event Listener

The class `Consumer` is used as the event listener. This class subscribes to the event of the `CarDealer` and defines the method `NewCarIsHere` that in turn fulfills the requirements of the `EventHandler<CarInfoEventArgs>` delegate with parameters of type `object` and `CarInfoEventArgs` (code file `EventsSample/Consumer.cs`):

```csharp
public record Consumer(string Name)
{
  public void NewCarIsHere(object? sender, CarInfoEventArgs e) =>
    Console.WriteLine($"{Name}: car {e.Car} is new");
}
```

Now the event publisher and subscriber need to connect. You do this by using the `NewCarInfo` event of the `CarDealer` to create a subscription with `+=`. The consumer `sebastian` subscribes to the event, and after the car Williams is created, the consumer `max` subscribes. After the car Aston Martin is created, `sebastian` unsubscribes with `-=` (code file `EventsSample/Program.cs`):

```csharp
CarDealer dealer = new();
Consumer sebastian = new("Sebastian");
dealer.NewCarInfo += sebastian.NewCarIsHere;
dealer.NewCar("Williams");

Consumer max = new("Max");
dealer.NewCarInfo += max.NewCarIsHere;
dealer.NewCar("Aston Martin");
dealer.NewCarInfo -= sebastian.NewCarIsHere;
dealer.NewCar("Ferrari");
```

When you run the application, a Williams arrives, and Sebastian is informed. After that, Max registers for the subscription as well, and both Sebastian and Max are informed about the new Aston Martin. Then Sebastian unsubscribes, and only Max is informed about the Ferrari:

```
CarDealer, new car Williams
Sebastian: car Williams is new
CarDealer, new car Aston Martin
Sebastian: car Aston Martin is new
```

```
Max: car Aston Martin is new
CarDealer, new car Ferrari
Max: car Ferrari is new
```

SUMMARY

This chapter provided the basics of delegates, lambda expressions, and events. You learned how to declare a delegate and add methods to the delegate list; you learned how to implement methods called by delegates with lambda expressions; and you learned the process of declaring event handlers to respond to an event, as well as how to create a custom event and use the patterns for raising the event.

Using delegates and events in the design of a large application can reduce dependencies and the coupling of layers. This enables you to develop components that have a higher reusability factor.

Lambda expressions are C# language features based on delegates. With these, you can reduce the amount of code you need to write.

The next chapter covers the use of different forms of collections.

8

Collections

WHAT'S IN THIS CHAPTER?

- ➤ Understanding collection interfaces and types
- ➤ Working with lists, queues, and stacks
- ➤ Working with linked and sorted lists
- ➤ Using dictionaries and sets
- ➤ Evaluating performance
- ➤ Using immutable collections

CODE DOWNLOADS FOR THIS CHAPTER

The source code for this chapter is available on the book page at www.wiley.com. Click the Downloads link. The code can also be found at https://github.com/ProfessionalCSharp/ProfessionalCSharp2021 in the directory 1_CS/Collections.

The code for this chapter is divided into the following major examples:

- ➤ ListSamples
- ➤ QueueSample
- ➤ LinkedListSample
- ➤ SortedListSample
- ➤ DictionarySample
- ➤ SetSample
- ➤ ImmutableCollectionsSample

All the projects have nullable reference types enabled.

OVERVIEW

Chapter 6, "Arrays," covers arrays and the interfaces implemented by the `Array` class. The size of arrays is fixed. If the number of elements is dynamic, you should use a collection class instead of an array.

`List<T>` is a collection class that can be compared to arrays, but there are also other kinds of collections: queues, stacks, linked lists, dictionaries, and sets. The other collection classes have partly different APIs to access the elements in the collection and often a different internal structure for how the items are stored in memory. This chapter covers all of these collection classes and their differences, including performance differences.

COLLECTION INTERFACES AND TYPES

Most collection classes are in the `System.Collections` and `System.Collections.Generic` namespaces. Generic collection classes are located in the `System.Collections.Generic` namespace. Collection classes that are specialized for a specific type are located in the `System.Collections.Specialized` namespace. Thread-safe collection classes are in the `System.Collections.Concurrent` namespace. Immutable collection classes are in the `System.Collections.Immutable` namespace.

Of course, there are also other ways to group collection classes. Collections can be grouped into lists, collections, and dictionaries based on the interfaces that are implemented by the collection class.

> **NOTE** *You can read detailed information about the interfaces* `IEnumerable` *and* `IEnumerator` *in Chapter 6.*

The following table describes the most important interfaces implemented by collections and lists:

INTERFACE	DESCRIPTION
`IEnumerable<T>`	The interface `IEnumerable` is required by the `foreach` statement. This interface defines the method `GetEnumerator`, which returns an enumerator that implements the `IEnumerator` interface.
`ICollection<T>`	`ICollection<T>` is implemented by generic collection classes. With this you can get the number of items in the collection (`Count` property) and copy the collection to an array (`CopyTo` method). You can also add and remove items from the collection (`Add`, `Remove`, `Clear`).
`IList<T>`	The `IList<T>` interface is for lists where elements can be accessed from their position. This interface defines an indexer, as well as ways to insert or remove items from specific positions (`Insert`, `RemoveAt` methods). `IList<T>` derives from `ICollection<T>`.
`ISet<T>`	This interface is implemented by sets. Sets allow combining different sets into a union, getting the intersection of two sets, and checking whether two sets overlap. `ISet<T>` derives from `ICollection<T>`.

INTERFACE	DESCRIPTION
IDictionary<TKey, TValue>	The interface IDictionary<TKey, TValue> is implemented by generic collection classes that have a key and a value. With this interface, all the keys and values can be accessed, items can be accessed with an indexer of type TKey, and items can be added or removed.
ILookup<TKey, TValue>	Similar to the IDictionary<TKey, TValue> interface, lookups have keys and values. However, with lookups, the collection can contain multiple values with one key.
IComparer<T>	The interface IComparer<T> is implemented by a comparer and used to sort elements inside a collection with the Compare method.
IEqualityComparer<T>	IEqualityComparer<T> is implemented by a comparer that can be used for keys in a dictionary. With this interface, the objects can be compared for equality.

LISTS

For resizable lists, .NET offers the generic class List<T>. This class implements the IList, ICollection, IEnumerable, IList<T>, ICollection<T>, and IEnumerable<T> interfaces.

The following examples use the members of the record Racer as elements to be added to the collection to represent a Formula 1 racer. This type has five properties: Id, FirstName, LastName, Country, and the number of Wins as specified with the positional record constructor. An overloaded constructor allows you to specify only four values when initializing the object. The method ToString is overridden to return the name of the racer. The record Racer also implements the generic interface IComparable<T> for sorting racer elements and IFormattable to allow passing custom format strings (code file ListSamples/Racer.cs):

```
public record Racer(int ID, string FirstName, string LastName, string Country,
  int Wins) : IComparable<Racer>, IFormattable
{
  public Racer(int id, string firstName, string lastName, string country)
    : this(id, firstName, lastName, country, Wins: 0)
  { }

  public override string ToString() => $"{FirstName} {LastName}";

  public string ToString(string? format, IFormatProvider? formatProvider) =>
    format?.ToUpper() switch
    {
      null => ToString(),
      "N" => ToString(),
      "F" => FirstName,
      "L" => LastName,
      "W" => $"{ToString()}, Wins: {Wins}",
      "C" => Country,
      "A" => $"{ToString()}, Country: {Country}, Wins: {Wins}",
```

```
            _ => throw new FormatException(string.Format(formatProvider,
                "Format {0} is not supported", format))
        };

    public string? ToString(string format) => ToString(format, null);

    public int CompareTo(Racer? other)
    {
        int compare = LastName?.CompareTo(other?.LastName) ?? -1;
        if (compare == 0)
        {
            return FirstName?.CompareTo(other?.FirstName) ?? -1;
        }
        return compare;
    }
}
```

Creating Lists

You can create list objects by invoking the default constructor. With the generic class List<T>, you must specify the type for the values of the list with the declaration. The following code shows how to declare a List<T> with int and a list with Racer elements. ArrayList is a nongeneric list that accepts any Object type for its elements.

```
List<int> intList = new();
List<Racer> racers = new();
```

Using the default constructor creates an empty list. As soon as elements are added to the list, the capacity of the list is extended to allow 4 elements. If the fifth element is added, the list is resized to allow 8 elements. If 8 elements are not enough, the list is resized again to contain 16 elements. With every resize, the capacity of the list is doubled.

When the capacity of the list changes, the complete collection is reallocated to a new memory block. With the implementation of List<T>, an array of type T is used. With reallocation, a new array is created, and Array.Copy copies the elements from the old array to the new array. To save time, if you know the number of elements that should be in the list in advance, you can define the capacity with the constructor. The following example creates a collection with a capacity of 10 elements. If the capacity is not large enough for the elements added, the capacity is resized to 20 and then to 40 elements—doubled again:

```
List<int> intList = new(10);
```

You can get and set the capacity of a collection by using the Capacity property:

```
intList.Capacity = 20;
```

The capacity is not the same as the number of elements in the collection. The number of elements in the collection can be read with the Count property. Of course, the capacity is always larger or equal to the number of items. As long as no element was added to the list, the count is 0:

```
Console.WriteLine(intList.Count);
```

If you are finished adding elements to the list and don't want to add any more, you can get rid of the unneeded capacity by invoking the TrimExcess method; however, because the relocation takes time, TrimExcess has no effect if the item count is more than 90 percent of capacity:

```
intList.TrimExcess();
```

Collection Initializers

You can also assign values to collections using collection initializers. The syntax of collection initializers is similar to array initializers, which are explained in Chapter 6. With a collection initializer, values are assigned to the collection within curly brackets at the time the collection is initialized:

```
List<int> intList = new() {1, 2};
List<string> stringList = new() { "one", "two" };
```

> **NOTE** *Collection initializers are not reflected within the IL code of the compiled assembly. The compiler converts the collection initializer to invoke the* Add *method for every item from the initializer list.*

Adding Elements

You can add elements to the list with the Add method, shown in the following example. The generic instantiated type defines the parameter type of the Add method:

```
List<int> intList = new();
intList.Add(1);
intList.Add(2);
List<string> stringList = new();
stringList.Add("one");
stringList.Add("two");
```

The variable racers is defined as type List<Racer>. With the new operator, a new object of the same type is created. Because the class List<T> was instantiated with the concrete class Racer, now only Racer objects can be added with the Add method. In the following sample code, five Formula 1 racers are created and added to the collection. The first three are added using the collection initializer, and the last two are added by explicitly invoking the Add method (code file ListSamples/Program.cs):

```
Racer graham = new(7, "Graham", "Hill", "UK", 14);
Racer emerson = new(13, "Emerson", "Fittipaldi", "Brazil", 14);
Racer mario = new(16, "Mario", "Andretti", "USA", 12);
List<Racer> racers = new(20) {graham, emerson, mario};
racers.Add(new Racer(24, "Michael", "Schumacher", "Germany", 91));
racers.Add(new Racer(27, "Mika", "Hakkinen", "Finland", 20));
```

With the AddRange method of the List<T> class, you can add multiple elements to the collection at once. The method AddRange accepts an object of type IEnumerable<T>, so you can also pass an array as shown here (code file ListSamples/Program.cs):

```
racers.AddRange(new Racer[] {
  new(14, "Niki", "Lauda", "Austria", 25),
  new(21, "Alain", "Prost", "France", 51)});
```

> **NOTE** *The collection initializer can be used only during declaration of the collection. The* AddRange *method can be invoked after the collection is initialized. In case you get the data dynamically after creating the collection, you need to invoke* AddRange.

If you know some elements of the collection when instantiating the list, you can also pass any object that implements `IEnumerable<T>` to the constructor of the class. This is similar to the `AddRange` method (code file `ListSamples/Program.cs`):

```
List<Racer> racers = new(
  new Racer[] {
    new (12, "Jochen", "Rindt", "Austria", 6),
    new (22, "Ayrton", "Senna", "Brazil", 41) });
```

Inserting Elements

You can insert elements at a specified position with the `Insert` method (code file `ListSamples/Program.cs`):

```
racers.Insert(3, new Racer(6, "Phil", "Hill", "USA", 3));
```

The method `InsertRange` offers the capability to insert a number of elements, similar to the `AddRange` method shown earlier.

If the index set is larger than the number of elements in the collection, an exception of type `ArgumentOutOfRangeException` is thrown.

Accessing Elements

All classes that implement the `IList` and `IList<T>` interfaces offer an indexer, so you can access the elements by using an indexer and passing the item number. The first item can be accessed with an index value 0. By specifying `racers[3]`, for example, you access the fourth element of the list:

```
Racer r1 = racers[3];
```

When you use the `Count` property to get the number of elements, you can do a `for` loop to iterate through every item in the collection, and you can use the indexer to access every item (code file `ListSamples/Program.cs`):

```
for (int i = 0; i < racers.Count; i++)
{
  Console.WriteLine(racers[i]);
}
```

Because `List<T>` implements the interface `IEnumerable`, you can iterate through the items in the collection using the `foreach` statement as well (code file `ListSamples/Program.cs`):

```
foreach (var r in racers)
{
  Console.WriteLine(r);
}
```

> **NOTE** *Chapter 6 explains how the* `foreach` *statement is resolved by the compiler to make use of the* `IEnumerable` *and* `IEnumerator` *interfaces.*

Removing Elements

You can remove elements by index or by passing the item that should be removed. Here, the fourth element is removed from the collection:

```
racers.RemoveAt(3);
```

Instead of using the `RemoveAt` method, you can also directly pass a `Racer` object to the `Remove` method to remove this element. However, removing by index with the `RemoveAt` method is faster. The `Remove` method first searches in the collection to get the index of the item with the `IndexOf` method and then uses the index to remove the item. `IndexOf` first checks whether the item type implements the interface `IEquatable<T>`. If it does, the `Equals` method of this interface is invoked to find the item in the collection that is the same as the one passed to the method. If this interface is not implemented, the `Equals` method of the `Object` class is used to compare the items. The default implementation of the `Equals` method in the `Object` class does a bitwise comparison with value types, but compares only references with reference types.

> **NOTE** Chapter 5, "Operators and Casts," explains how you can override the `Equals` method.

In the following example, the racer referenced by the variable `graham` is removed from the collection (code file `ListSamples/Program.cs`):

```
if (!racers.Remove(graham))
{
  Console.WriteLine("object not found in collection");
}
```

The method `RemoveRange` removes a number of items from the collection. The first parameter specifies the index where the removal of items should begin; the second parameter specifies the number of items to be removed:

```
int index = 3;
int count = 5;
racers.RemoveRange(index, count);
```

To remove all items with some specific characteristics from the collection, you can use the `RemoveAll` method. This method uses the `Predicate<T>` parameter when searching for elements, which is discussed next. To remove all elements from the collection, use the `Clear` method defined with the `ICollection<T>` interface.

Searching

There are different ways to search for elements in the collection. You can get the index to the found item or a reference to the item itself. You can use methods such as `IndexOf`, `LastIndexOf`, `FindIndex`, `FindLastIndex`, `Find`, and `FindLast`. To just check whether an item exists, the `List<T>` class offers the `Exists` method.

The method `IndexOf` requires an object as a parameter and returns the index of the item if it is found inside the collection. If the item is not found, –1 is returned. Remember that `IndexOf` is using the `IEquatable<T>` interface to compare the elements (code file `ListSamples/Program.cs`):

```
int index1 = racers.IndexOf(mario);
```

With the `IndexOf` method, you can also specify that the complete collection should not be searched, and instead specify an index where the search should start and the number of elements that should be iterated for the comparison. To start from the end of the list to search for the index, you can use the `LastIndexOf` method.

Instead of searching a specific item with the `IndexOf` method, you can search for an item that has some specific characteristics that you can define with the `FindIndex` method. `FindIndex` requires a parameter of type `Predicate`:

```
public int FindIndex(Predicate<T> match);
```

The `Predicate<T>` type is a delegate that returns a Boolean value and requires type `T` as a parameter. If the predicate returns `true`, there's a match, and the element is found. If it returns `false`, the element is not found, and the search continues.

```
public delegate bool Predicate<T>(T obj);
```

With the `List<T>` class that is using `Racer` objects for type `T`, you can pass the address of a method that returns a `bool` and defines a parameter of type `Racer` to the `FindIndex` method. Finding the first racer of a specific country, you can use a lambda expression with a `Racer` parameter and a `bool` return as specified by the delegate. The following code uses a lambda expression that defines the implementation to search for an item where the `Country` property is set to `Finland`:

```
int index2 = racers.FindIndex(r => r.Country == "Finland");
```

Similar to the `IndexOf` method, with the `FindIndex` method you can also specify the index where the search should start and the count of items that should be iterated through. To do a search for an index beginning from the last element in the collection, you can use the `FindLastIndex` method.

The method `FindIndex` method returns the index of the found item. Instead of getting the index, you can also go directly to the item in the collection. The `Find` method requires a parameter of type `Predicate<T>`, much like the `FindIndex` method. The `Find` method in the following example searches for the first racer in the list who has the `FirstName` property set to `Niki`. Of course, you can also do a `FindLast` search to find the last item that fulfills the predicate.

```
Racer racer = racers.Find(r => r.FirstName == "Niki");
```

To get not only one but all the items that fulfill the requirements of a predicate, you can use the `FindAll` method. The `FindAll` method uses the same `Predicate<T>` delegate as the `Find` and `FindIndex` methods. The `FindAll` method does not stop when the first item is found; instead, the `FindAll` method iterates through every item in the collection and returns all items for which the predicate returns `true`.

With the `FindAll` method invoked in the next example, all `Racer` items are returned where the property `Wins` is set to more than 20. All racers who won more than 20 races are referenced from the `bigWinners` list:

```
List<Racer> bigWinners = racers.FindAll(r => r.Wins > 20);
```

Iterating through the variable `bigWinners` with a `foreach` statement gives the following result:

```
foreach (Racer r in bigWinners)
{
   Console.WriteLine($"{r:A}");
}
Michael Schumacher, Germany Wins: 91
Niki Lauda, Austria Wins: 25
Alain Prost, France Wins: 51
```

The result is not sorted, but the next section covers that.

Sorting

The `List<T>` class enables sorting its elements by using the `Sort` method. `Sort` uses the Quicksort algorithm whereby all elements are compared until the complete list is sorted. You can use several overloads of the `Sort` method. You can pass a delegate of type `Comparison<T>`, and an object implementing `IComparer<T>`. Using the `Sort` method without arguments is possible only if the elements in the collection implement the interface `IComparable`.

With the `IComparable<T>` implementation of the `Racer` type, the `Sort` method sorts racers by last name followed by first name:

```
racers.Sort();
```

If you need to do a sort other than the default supported by the item types, you need to use other techniques, such as passing an object that implements the `IComparer<T>` interface.

The class `RacerComparer` implements the interface `IComparer<T>` for `Racer` types. This class enables you to sort by the first name, last name, country, or number of wins. The kind of sort that should be done is defined with the inner enumeration type `CompareType`. The `CompareType` is set with the constructor of the class `RacerComparer`. The interface `IComparer<Racer>` defines the method `Compare`, which is required for sorting. In the implementation of this method, the `Compare` and `CompareTo` methods of the `string` and `int` types are used (code file `ListSamples/RacerComparer.cs`):

```
public class RacerComparer : IComparer<Racer>
{
  public enum CompareType
  {
    FirstName,
    LastName,
    Country,
    Wins
  }

  private CompareType _compareType;
  public RacerComparer(CompareType compareType) =>
    _compareType = compareType;

  public int Compare(Racer? x, Racer? y)
  {
    if (x is null && y is null) return 0;
    if (x is null) return -1;
    if (y is null) return 1;

    int CompareCountry(Racer x, Racer y)
    {
      int result = string.Compare(x.Country, y.Country);
      if (result == 0)
      {
        result = string.Compare(x.LastName, y.LastName);
      }
      return result;
    }

    return _compareType switch
    {
      CompareType.FirstName => string.Compare(x.FirstName, y.FirstName),
      CompareType.LastName => string.Compare(x.LastName, y.LastName),
      CompareType.Country => CompareCountry(x, y),
      CompareType.Wins => x.Wins.CompareTo(y.Wins),
      _ => throw new ArgumentException("Invalid Compare Type")
    };
  }
}
```

> **NOTE** *The* `Compare` *method returns 0 if the two elements passed to it are equal with the order. If a value less than 0 is returned, the first argument is less than the second. With a value larger than 0, the first argument is greater than the second. Passing* `null` *with an argument, the method shouldn't throw a* `NullReferenceException` *or* `ArgumentNullException`. *Instead,* `null` *should take its place before any other element; thus, –1 is returned if the first argument is* `null`, *and +1 if the second argument is* `null` *and 0 if both arguments are* `null`.

You can now use an instance of the `RacerComparer` class with the `Sort` method. Passing the enumeration `RacerComparer.CompareType.Country` sorts the collection by the property `Country`:

```
racers.Sort(new RacerComparer(RacerComparer.CompareType.Country));
```

Another way to do the sort is by using the overloaded `Sort` method, which requires a `Comparison<T>` delegate. `Comparison<T>` is a delegate to a method that has two parameters of type `T` and a return type `int`. If the parameter values are equal, the method must return 0. If the first parameter is less than the second, a value less than zero must be returned; otherwise, a value greater than zero is returned:

```
public delegate int Comparison<T>(T x, T y);
```

Now you can pass a lambda expression to the `Sort` method to do a sort by the number of wins. The two parameters are of type `Racer`, and in the implementation the `Wins` properties are compared by using the `int` method `CompareTo`. Also in the implementation, r2 and r1 are used in reverse order, so the number of wins is sorted in descending order. After the method has been invoked, the complete racer list is sorted based on the racer's number of wins:

```
racers.Sort((r1, r2) => r2.Wins.CompareTo(r1.Wins));
```

You can also reverse the order of a complete collection by invoking the `Reverse` method.

Read-Only Collections

After collections are created, they are read/write, of course; otherwise, you couldn't fill them with any values. However, after the collection is filled, you can create a read-only collection. The `List<T>` collection has the method `AsReadOnly` that returns an object of type `ReadOnlyCollection<T>`. The class `ReadOnlyCollection<T>` implements the same interfaces as `List<T>`, but all methods and properties that change the collection throw a `NotSupportedException`. Besides the interfaces of `List<T>`, `ReadOnlyCollection<T>` also implements the interfaces `IReadOnlyCollection<T>` and `IReadOnlyList<T>`. With the members of these interfaces, the collection cannot be changed.

Queues

A *queue* is a collection whose elements are processed according to first in, first out (FIFO) order, meaning the item that is put first in the queue is read first. Examples of queues are standing in line at the airport, a human resources queue to process employee applicants, print jobs waiting to be processed in a print queue, and a thread waiting for the CPU in a round-robin fashion. Sometimes the elements of a queue differ in their priority. For example, in the queue at the airport, business passengers are processed before economy passengers. In this case, multiple queues can be used, one queue for each priority. At the airport this is easily handled with separate check-in queues for business and economy passengers. The same is true for print queues and threads. You can have an array or a list of queues whereby one item in the array stands for a priority. Within every array item there's a queue where processing happens using the FIFO principle.

> **NOTE** *Later in this chapter, a different implementation with a linked list is used to define a list of priorities.*

A queue is implemented with the Queue<T> class. Internally, the Queue<T> class uses an array of type T, similar to the List<T> type. It implements the interfaces IEnumerable<T> and ICollection, but it doesn't implement ICollection<T> because this interface defines Add and Remove methods that shouldn't be available for queues.

The Queue<T> class does not implement the interface IList<T>, so you cannot access the queue using an indexer. The queue just allows you to add an item to the end of the queue (with the Enqueue method) and to get items from the head of the queue (with the Dequeue method).

Figure 8-1 shows the items of a queue. The Enqueue method adds items to one end of the queue; the items are read and removed at the other end of the queue with the Dequeue method. Invoking the Dequeue method once more removes the next item from the queue.

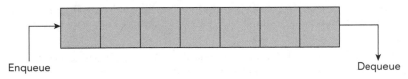

Enqueue   Dequeue

FIGURE 8-1

The following table describes the important methods of the Queue<T> class:

SELECTED QUEUE <T> MEMBERS	DESCRIPTION
Count	Returns the number of items in the queue.
Enqueue	Adds an item to the end of the queue.
Dequeue	Reads and removes an item from the head of the queue. If there are no more items in the queue when the Dequeue method is invoked, an exception of type InvalidOperationException is thrown.
Peek	Reads an item from the head of the queue but does not remove the item.
TrimExcess	Resizes the capacity of the queue. The Dequeue method removes items from the queue, but it doesn't resize the capacity of the queue. To get rid of the empty items at the beginning of the queue, use the TrimExcess method.

When creating queues, you can use constructors similar to those used with the List<T> type. The default constructor creates an empty queue, but you can also use a constructor to specify the capacity. With an overload of the constructor, you can also pass any other collection that implements the IEnumerable<T> interface that is copied to the queue.

The following example demonstrating the use of the `Queue<T>` class is a document management application. One task is used to add documents to the queue, and another task reads documents from the queue and processes them.

> **NOTE** *To make the queue sample more interesting, different tasks are used to work with the queue. One task writes messages to the queue, and another task reads messages from the queue. Reading and writing happens after a random time delay; you can monitor how the queue grows larger and smaller. Tasks are used in a simple way here, but you might want to read Chapter 11, "Tasks and Asynchronous Programming," before getting into this sample code.*

The items stored in the queue are of type `Document`. The record `Document` defines a title and content (code file `QueueSample/Document.cs`):

```
public record Document(string Title, string Content);
```

The `DocumentManager` class is a thin layer around the `Queue<T>` class. It defines how to handle documents: adding documents to the queue with the `AddDocument` method and getting documents from the queue with the `GetDocument` method.

Inside the `AddDocument` method, the document is added to the end of the queue using the `Enqueue` method. The first document from the queue is read with the `Dequeue` method inside `GetDocument`. Because multiple tasks can access the `DocumentManager` concurrently, access to the queue is locked with the `lock` statement. The `AddDocument` method returns the number of items in the queue to allow monitoring the queue size.

`IsDocumentAvailable` is a read-only Boolean property that returns `true` if there are documents in the queue and `false` if there are't (code file `QueueSample/DocumentManager.cs`):

```
public class DocumentManager
{
  private readonly object _syncQueue = new object();
  private readonly Queue<Document> _documentQueue = new();

  public int AddDocument(Document doc)
  {
    lock (_syncQueue)
    {
      _documentQueue.Enqueue(doc);
      return _documentQueue.Count;
    }
  }

  public Document GetDocument()
  {
    Document doc = null;
    lock (_syncQueue)
    {
      doc = _documentQueue.Dequeue();
    }
    return doc;
  }

  public bool IsDocumentAvailable => _documentQueue.Count > 0;
}
```

The class `ProcessDocuments` processes documents from the queue in a separate task. The only method that can be accessed from the outside is `Start`. In the `StartAsync` method, a new task is instantiated. A `ProcessDocuments` object is created to start the task, and the `RunAsync` method is defined as the start method of the task. With the `Task.Run` method, you can pass an `Action` delegate. Here, the `RunAsync` instance method of the `ProcessDocuments` class is invoked from the task.

With the `RunAsync` method of the `ProcessDocuments` class, a `do...while` loop is defined. Within this loop, the property `IsDocumentAvailable` is used to determine whether there is a document in the queue. If so, the document is taken from the `DocumentManager` and processed. If the task waits more than five seconds, waiting stops. Processing in this example is writing information only to the console. In a real application, the document could be written to a file, written to the database, or sent across the network (code file `QueueSample/ProcessDocuments.cs`):

```
public class ProcessDocuments
{
  public static Task StartAsync(DocumentManager dm) =>
    Task.Run(new ProcessDocuments(dm).RunAsync);

  protected ProcessDocuments(DocumentManager dm) =>
    _documentManager = dm ?? throw new ArgumentNullException(nameof(dm));

  private readonly DocumentManager _documentManager;

  protected async Task RunAsync()
  {
    Random random = new();
    Stopwatch stopwatch = new();
    stopwatch.Start();
    bool stop = false;
    do
    {
      if (stopwatch.Elapsed >= TimeSpan.FromSeconds(5))
      {
        stop = true;
      }
      if (_documentManager.IsDocumentAvailable)
      {
        stopwatch.Restart();
        Document doc = _documentManager.GetDocument();
        Console.WriteLine($"Processing document {doc.Title}");
      }
      // wait a random time before processing the next document
      await Task.Delay(random.Next(20));
    } while (!stop) ;
    Console.WriteLine("stopped reading documents");
  }
}
```

With the start of the application, a `DocumentManager` object is instantiated, and the document processing task is started. Then 1,000 documents are created and added to the `DocumentManager` (code file `QueueSample/Program.cs`):

```
DocumentManager dm = new();

Task processDocuments = ProcessDocuments.StartAsync(dm);
```

```
// Create documents and add them to the DocumentManager
Random random = new();
for (int i = 0; i < 1000; i++)
{
  var doc = new Document($"Doc {i}", "content");
  int queueSize = dm.AddDocument(doc);
  Console.WriteLine($"Added document {doc.Title}, queue size: {queueSize}");
  await Task.Delay(random.Next(20));
}
Console.WriteLine($"finished adding documents");
await processDocuments;
Console.WriteLine("bye!");
```

When you start the application, the documents are added to and removed from the queue, and you get output similar to the following:

```
Added document Doc 318, queue size: 6
Added document Doc 319, queue size: 7
Processing document Doc 313
Added document Doc 320, queue size: 7
Processing document Doc 314
Processing document Doc 315
Added document Doc 321, queue size: 7
Processing document Doc 316
```

A real-life scenario using the task described with the sample application might be an application that processes documents received with a Web API service.

STACKS

A stack is another container that is similar to the queue. You just use different methods to access the stack. The item that is added last to the stack is read first, so the stack is a last in, first out (LIFO) container.

Figure 8-2 shows the representation of a stack where the Push method adds an item to the stack, and the Pop method gets the item that was added last.

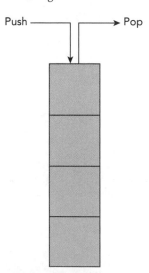

FIGURE 8-2

Similar to the `Queue<T>` class, the `Stack<T>` class implements the interfaces `IEnumerable<T>` and `ICollection`. Important members of the `Stack<T>` class are listed in the following table:

SELECTED STACK<T> MEMBERS	DESCRIPTION
Count	Returns the number of items in the stack.
Push	Adds an item on top of the stack.
Pop	Removes and returns an item from the top of the stack. If the stack is empty, an exception of type `InvalidOperationException` is thrown.
Peek	Returns an item from the top of the stack but does not remove the item.
Contains	Checks whether an item is in the stack and returns `true` if it is.

In this example, three items are added to the stack with the `Push` method. With the `foreach` method, all items are iterated using the `IEnumerable` interface. The enumerator of the stack does not remove the items; it just returns them item by item (code file `StackSample/Program.cs`):

```
Stack<char> alphabet = new();
alphabet.Push('A');
alphabet.Push('B');
alphabet.Push('C');
foreach (char item in alphabet)
{
   Console.Write(item);
}
Console.WriteLine();
```

Because the items are read in order from the last item added to the first, the following result is produced:

```
CBA
```

Reading the items with the enumerator does not change the state of the items. With the `Pop` method, every item that is read is also removed from the stack. This way, you can iterate the collection using a `while` loop and verify the `Count` property if items still exist:

```
Stack<char> alphabet = new();
alphabet.Push('A');
alphabet.Push('B');
alphabet.Push('C');
Console.Write("First iteration: ");
foreach (char item in alphabet)
{
   Console.Write(item);
}
Console.WriteLine();
Console.Write("Second iteration: ");
while (alphabet.Count > 0)
{
   Console.Write(alphabet.Pop());
}
Console.WriteLine();
```

The result gives CBA twice—once for each iteration. After the second iteration, the stack is empty because the second iteration used the `Pop` method:

```
First iteration: CBA
Second iteration: CBA
```

LINKED LISTS

`LinkedList<T>` is a doubly linked list, whereby one element references the next and the previous one, as shown in Figure 8-3. This way you can easily walk forward through the complete list by moving to the next element or backward by moving to the previous element.

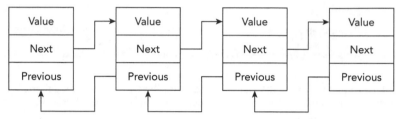

FIGURE 8-3

The advantage of a linked list is that if items are inserted anywhere in the list, the linked list is very fast. When an item is inserted, only the `Next` reference of the previous item and the `Previous` reference of the next item must be changed to reference the inserted item. With the `List<T>` class, when an element is inserted, all subsequent elements must be moved.

Of course, there's also a disadvantage with linked lists. Items of linked lists can be accessed only one after the other. It takes a long time to find an item that's somewhere in the middle or at the end of the list.

A linked list cannot just store the items inside the list; together with every item, the linked list must have information about the next and previous items. That's why the `LinkedList<T>` contains items of type `LinkedListNode<T>`. With the class `LinkedListNode<T>`, you can get to the next and previous items in the list. The `LinkedListNode<T>` class defines the properties `List`, `Next`, `Previous`, and `Value`. The `List` property returns the `LinkedList<T>` object that is associated with the node. `Next` and `Previous` are for iterating through the list and accessing the next or previous item. `Value` returns the item that is associated with the node. `Value` is of type `T`.

The `LinkedList<T>` class itself defines members to access the first (`First`) and last (`Last`) items of the list, to insert items at specific positions (`AddAfter`, `AddBefore`, `AddFirst`, `AddLast`), to remove items from specific positions (`Remove`, `RemoveFirst`, `RemoveLast`), and to find elements where the search starts from either the beginning (`Find`) or the end (`FindLast`) of the list.

With the sample application, a `Document` record is defined to put it into the LinkedList (code file `LinkedListSample/Program.cs`):

```
record Document(int Id, string Text);
```

The following code snippet creates a `LinkedList` and adds the first item to the start of the list using `AddFirst`. The `AddFirst` method returns a `LinkedListNode` object that's used with the next invocation to the list to add the document with an ID of 2 after the first object. The document with an ID of 3 is added last to the list using the `AddLast` method (which is also at that stage after the document with ID of 2). Using the `AddBefore` method, the document with an ID of 4 is added before the last one. After filling the list, the `LinkedList` is iterated using the `foreach` statement:

```
LinkedList<Document> list = new();
LinkedListNode<Document> first = list.AddFirst(new Document(1, "first"));
```

```
    list.AddAfter(first, new Document(2, "after first"));
    LinkedListNode<Document> last = list.AddLast(new Document(3, "Last"));
    Document doc4 = new(4, "before last");
    list.AddBefore(last, doc4);

    foreach (var item in list)
    {
      Console.WriteLine(item);
    }
```

Instead of using the `foreach` statement, you can easily iterate through all elements of the collection by accessing the `Next` property of every `LinkedListNode`:

```
    void IterateUsingNext(LinkedListNode<Document> start)
    {
      if (start.Value is null) return;
      LinkedListNode<Document>? current = start;
      do
      {
        Console.WriteLine(current.Value);
        current = current.Next;
      } while (current is not null);
    }
```

The method `IterateUsingNext` is invoked from the top-level statements passing the first object:

```
    if (list.First is not null)
    {
        IterateUsingNext(list.First);
    }
```

Running the application, you'll see two times the documents iterated. One iteration is shown here:

```
    Document { Id = 1, Text = first }
    Document { Id = 2, Text = after first }
    Document { Id = 4, Text = before last }
    Document { Id = 3, Text = Last }
```

Using the `Remove` method passing a `Document` object requires the `Remove` method to iterate through the collection until the `Document` can be found and removed:

```
    list.Remove(doc4);

    Console.WriteLine("after removal");
    foreach (var item in list)
    {
        Console.WriteLine(item);
    }
```

Later in this chapter, in the section "Performance," you'll see a table with the big-O notation where you can compare the performance of different collection classes based on the operations, so you can decide for the collection type to use more easily.

SORTED LIST

If the collection you need should be sorted based on a key, you can use `SortedList<TKey, TValue>`. This class sorts the elements based on a key. You can use any type for the value and also for the key.

The following example creates a sorted list for which both the key and the value are of type `string`. The default constructor creates an empty list, and then two books are added with the `Add` method. With overloaded constructors, you can define the capacity of the list and pass an object that implements the interface `IComparer<TKey>`, which is used to sort the elements in the list.

The first parameter of the `Add` method is the key (the book title); the second parameter is the value (the ISBN). Instead of using the `Add` method, you can use the indexer to add elements to the list. The indexer requires the key as index parameter. If a key already exists, the `Add` method throws an exception of type `ArgumentException`. If the same key is used with the indexer, the new value replaces the old value (code file `SortedListSample/Program.cs`):

```
SortedList<string, string> books = new();
books.Add("Front-end Development with ASP.NET Core", "978-1-119-18140-8");
books.Add("Beginning C# 7 Programming", "978-1-119-45866-1");

books["Enterprise Services"] = "978-0321246738";
books["Professional C# 7 and .NET Core 2.1"] = "978-1-119-44926-3";
```

> **NOTE** `SortedList<TKey, TValue>` *allows only one value per key. If you need multiple values per key, you can use* `Lookup<TKey, TElement>`.

You can iterate through the list using a `foreach` statement. Elements returned by the enumerator are of type `KeyValuePair<TKey, TValue>`, which contains both the key and the value. The key can be accessed with the `Key` property, and the value can be accessed with the `Value` property:

```
foreach (KeyValuePair<string, string> book in books)
{
  Console.WriteLine($"{book.Key}, {book.Value}");
}
```

The iteration displays book titles and ISBN numbers ordered by the key:

```
Beginning C# 7 Programming, 978-1-119-45866-1
Enterprise Services, 978-0321246738
Front-end Development with ASP.NET Core, 978-1-119-18140-8
Professional C# 7 and .NET Core 2.1, 978-1-119-44926-3
```

You can also access the values and keys by using the `Values` and `Keys` properties. The `Values` property returns `IList<TValue>`, and the `Keys` property returns `IList<TKey>`, so you can use these properties with a `foreach`:

```
foreach (string isbn in books.Values)
{
  Console.WriteLine(isbn);
}
foreach (string title in books.Keys)
{
  Console.WriteLine(title);
}
```

The first loop displays the values and next the keys:

```
978-1-119-45866-1
978-0321246738
978-1-119-18140-8
978-1-119-44926-3
Beginning C# 7 Programming
```

```
Enterprise Services
Front-end Development with ASP.NET Core
Professional C# 7 and .NET Core 2.1
```

If you try to access an element with an indexer and pass a key that does not exist, an exception of type `KeyNotFoundException` is thrown. To avoid that exception, you can use the method `ContainsKey`, which returns `true` if the key passed exists in the collection, or you can invoke the method `TryGetValue`, which tries to get the value but doesn't throw an exception if it isn't found:

```csharp
string title = "Professional C# 10";
if (!books.TryGetValue(title, out string isbn))
{
  Console.WriteLine($"{title} not found");
}
else
{
  Console.WriteLine($"{title} found: {isbn}");
}
```

DICTIONARIES

A dictionary represents a sophisticated data structure that enables you to access an element based on a key. Dictionaries are also known as *hash tables* or *maps*. The main feature of dictionaries is fast lookup based on keys. You can also add and remove items freely, as with `List<T>`, but without the performance overhead of having to shift subsequent items in memory.

Figure 8-4 shows a simplified representation of a dictionary. Here employee IDs such as `B4711` are the keys added to the dictionary. The key is transformed into a hash. With the hash, a number is created to associate an index with the values. The index then contains a link to the value. The figure is simplified because it is possible for a single index entry to be associated with multiple values, and the index can be stored in a hash table.

.NET offers several dictionary classes. The main class you use is `Dictionary<TKey, TValue>`.

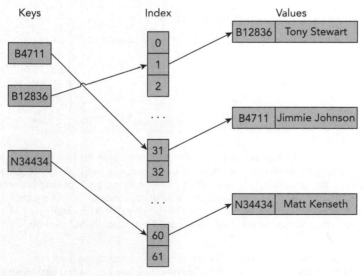

FIGURE 8-4

Dictionary Initializers

C# offers a syntax to initialize dictionaries at declaration with *dictionary initializers*. A dictionary with a key of `int` and a value of `string` can be initialized as follows:

```
Dictionary<int, string> dict = new()
{
  [3] = "three",
  [7] = "seven"
};
```

Here, two elements are added to the dictionary. The first element has a key of 3 and a string value `three`; the second element has a key of 7 and a string value `seven`. This initializer syntax is easily readable and is an adaptation of the collection initializer syntax shown earlier in this chapter.

Key Type

A type that is used as a key in the dictionary must override the method `GetHashCode` of the `Object` class. Whenever a dictionary class needs to determine where an item should be located, it calls the `GetHashCode` method. The `int` that is returned by `GetHashCode` is used by the dictionary to calculate an index of where to place the element. I won't go into this part of the algorithm; what you should know is that it involves prime numbers, so the capacity of a dictionary is a prime number.

The implementation of `GetHashCode` must satisfy the following requirements:

➤   The same object should always return the same value.

➤   Different objects can return the same value.

➤   It must not throw exceptions.

➤   It should use at least one instance field.

➤   The hash code should not change during the lifetime of the object.

Besides the requirements that must be satisfied by the `GetHashCode` implementation, it's also good practice to satisfy these requirements:

➤   It should execute as quickly as possible; it must be inexpensive to compute.

➤   The hash code value should be evenly distributed across the entire range of numbers that an `int` can store.

> **NOTE** *Good performance of the dictionary is based on a good implementation of the method* `GetHashCode`.

What's the reason for having hash code values evenly distributed across the range of integers? If two keys return hashes that have the same index, the dictionary class needs to start looking for the nearest available free location to store the second item—and it will have to do some searching to retrieve this item later. This is obviously going to hurt performance. In addition, if a lot of your keys tend to provide the same storage indexes for where they should be stored, this kind of clash becomes more likely. However, because of the way that Microsoft's part of the algorithm works, this risk is minimized when the calculated hash values are evenly distributed between `int.MinValue` and `int.MaxValue`.

Besides having an implementation of `GetHashCode`, the key type also must implement the `IEquatable<T>`. `Equals` method or override the `Equals` method from the `Object` class. Because different key objects may return the same hash code, the method `Equals` is used by the dictionary comparing keys. The dictionary examines whether two keys, such as A and B, are equal; it invokes `A.Equals(B)`. This means you must ensure that the following is always true: If `A.Equals(B)` is true, then `A.GetHashCode` and `B.GetHashCode` must always return the same hash code.

This may seem a fairly subtle point, but it is crucial. If you contrived some way of overriding these methods so that the preceding statement were not always true, a dictionary that uses instances of this class as its keys would not work properly. Instead, you'd find funny things happening. For example, you might place an object in the dictionary and then discover that you could never retrieve it, or you might try to retrieve an entry and have the wrong entry returned.

> **NOTE** *For this reason, the C# compiler displays a compilation warning if you supply an override for* `Equals` *but don't supply an override for* `GetHashCode`.

For `System.Object`, this condition is true because `Equals` simply compares references, and `GetHashCode` actually returns a hash that is based solely on the address of the object. This means that hash tables based on a key that doesn't override these methods will work correctly. However, the problem with this approach is that keys are regarded as equal only if they are the same object. That means when you place an object in the dictionary, you have to hang onto the reference to the key; you can't simply instantiate another key object later with the same value. If you don't override `Equals` and `GetHashCode`, the type is not very convenient to use in a dictionary as a key.

Incidentally, `System.String` implements the interface `IEquatable` and overloads `GetHashCode` appropriately. `Equals` provides value comparison, and `GetHashCode` returns a hash based on the value of the string. Strings can be used conveniently as keys in dictionaries.

Number types such as `Int32` also implement the interface `IEquatable` and overload `GetHashCode`. However, the hash code returned by these types simply maps to the value. If the number you would like to use as a key is not itself distributed around the possible values of an integer, using integers as keys doesn't fulfill the rule of evenly distributing key values to get the best performance. `Int32` is not meant to be used in a dictionary.

A C# 9 record is a class, but offers value semantics. With this, it also implements the `IEquatable` interface and overrides `GetHashCode`.

If you need to use a key type that does not implement `IEquatable` and does not override `GetHashCode` according to the key values you store in the dictionary, you can create a comparer implementing the interface `IEqualityComparer<T>`. This interface defines the methods `GetHashCode` and `Equals` with an argument of the object passed, so you can offer an implementation different from the object type itself. An overload of the `Dictionary<TKey, TValue>` constructor allows passing an object implementing `IEqualityComparer<T>`. If such an object is assigned to the dictionary, this class is used to generate the hash codes and compare the keys.

Dictionary Example

The dictionary example in this section is a program that sets up a dictionary of employees. The dictionary is indexed by `EmployeeId` objects, and each item stored in the dictionary is an `Employee` object that stores details of an employee.

The struct `EmployeeId` is implemented to define a key to be used in a dictionary. The members of the class are a prefix character and a number for the employee. Both of these variables are read-only and can be initialized only in the constructor to ensure that keys within the dictionary cannot change. The default implementation of the record's `GetHashCode` uses all of its fields to generate the hash code. When you have read-only variables, it is guaranteed that they can't be changed. The fields are filled within the constructor. The `ToString` method is overloaded to get a string representation of the employee ID. As required for a key type, `EmployeeId` implements the interface `IEquatable` and overloads the method `GetHashCode` (code file `DictionarySample/EmployeeId.cs`):

```csharp
public class EmployeeIdException : Exception
{
  public EmployeeIdException(string message) : base(message) { }
}

public struct EmployeeId : IEquatable<EmployeeId>
{
  private readonly char _prefix;
  private readonly int _number;
  public EmployeeId(string id)
  {
    if (id == null) throw new ArgumentNullException(nameof(id));
    _prefix = (id.ToUpper())[0];
    int last = id.Length > 7 ? 7 : id.Length;
    try
    {
      _number = int.Parse(id[1..last]);
    }
    catch (FormatException)
    {
      throw new EmployeeIdException("Invalid EmployeeId format");
    }
  }

  public override string ToString() => _prefix.ToString() +
    $"{_number,6:000000}";

  public override int GetHashCode() => (_number ^ _number << 16) * 0x15051505;

  public bool Equals(EmployeeId other) =>
    _prefix == other._prefix && _number == other._number;

  public override bool Equals(object obj) => Equals((EmployeeId)obj);

  public static bool operator ==(EmployeeId left, EmployeeId right) =>
    left.Equals(right);

  public static bool operator !=(EmployeeId left, EmployeeId right) =>
    !(left == right);
}
```

The `Equals` method that is defined by the `IEquatable<T>` interface compares the values of two `EmployeeId` objects and returns `true` if both values are the same. Instead of implementing the `Equals` method from the `IEquatable<T>` interface, you can also override the `Equals` method from the `Object` class:

```csharp
public bool Equals(EmployeeId other) =>
  _prefix == other._prefix && _number == other._number;
```

With the `_number` variable, a value from 1 to around 190,000 is expected for the employees. This doesn't fill the range of an integer. The algorithm used by `GetHashCode` shifts the number 16 bits to the left, then does an XOR (exclusive OR) with the original number, and finally multiplies the result by the hex value 15051505. The hash code is fairly evenly distributed across the range of an integer:

```csharp
public override int GetHashCode() => (number ^ number << 16) * 0x1505_1505;
```

The `Employee` type is a simple record with private fields for the name, salary, and ID of the employee. The constructor initializes all values, and the method `ToString` returns a string representation of an instance. The implementation of `ToString` uses a format string to create the string representation for performance reasons (code file `DictionarySample/Employee.cs`):

```
public record Employee
{
  private readonly string _name;
  private readonly decimal _salary;
  private readonly EmployeeId _id;
  public Employee(EmployeeId id, string name, decimal salary)
  {
    _id = id;
    _name = name;
    _salary = salary;
  }

  public override string ToString() =>
    $"{_id.ToString()}: {_name, -20} {_salary,12:C}";
}
```

In the `Program.cs` file, a new `Dictionary<TKey, TValue>` instance is created, where the key is of type `EmployeeId` and the value is of type `Employee`. The constructor allocates a capacity of 31 elements. Remember that capacity is based on prime numbers. However, when you assign a value that is not a prime number, you don't need to worry. The `Dictionary<TKey, TValue>` class itself takes the next prime number from a list of specially selected prime numbers that follows the integer passed to the constructor to allocate the capacity. After creating the employee objects and IDs, they are added to the newly created dictionary using the new dictionary initializer syntax. Of course, you can also invoke the `Add` method of the dictionary to add objects instead (code file `DictionarySample/Program.cs`):

```
EmployeeId idKyle = new("J18");
Employee kyle = new Employee(idKyle, "Kyle Bush", 138_000.00m );

EmployeeId idMartin = new("J19");
Employee martin = new(idMartin, "Martin Truex Jr", 73_000.00m);

EmployeeId idKevin = new("S4");
Employee kevin = new(idKevin, "Kevin Harvick", 116_000.00m);

EmployeeId idDenny = new EmployeeId("J11");
Employee denny = new Employee(idDenny, "Denny Hamlin", 127_000.00m);

EmployeeId idJoey = new("T22");
Employee joey = new(idJoey, "Joey Logano", 96_000.00m);

EmployeeId idKyleL = new ("C42");
Employee kyleL = new (idKyleL, "Kyle Larson", 80_000.00m);


Dictionary<EmployeeId, Employee> employees = new(31)
{
  [idKyle] = kyle,
  [idMartin] = martin,
  [idKevin] = kevin,
```

```
  [idDenny] = denny,
  [idJoey] = joey,
};

foreach (var employee in employees.Values)
{
  Console.WriteLine(employee);
}
//...
```

After the entries are added to the dictionary, employees are read from the dictionary inside a `while` loop. The user is asked to enter an employee number to store in the variable `userInput`, and the user can exit the application by pressing the key `x`. If the key is in the dictionary, it is examined with the `TryGetValue` method of the `Dictionary<TKey, TValue>` class. `TryGetValue` returns `true` if the key is found or `false` otherwise. If the value is found, the value associated with the key is stored in the employee variable. This value is written to the console.

> **NOTE** *You can also use an indexer of the* `Dictionary<TKey, TValue>` *class instead of* `TryGetValue` *to access a value stored in the dictionary. However, if the key is not found, the indexer throws an exception of type* `KeyNotFoundException`.

```
while (true)
{
  Console.Write("Enter employee id (X to exit)> ");
  string? userInput = Console.ReadLine();
  userInput = userInput?.ToUpper();
  if (userInput == null || userInput == "X") break;

  try
  {
    EmployeeId id = new(userInput);
    if (!employees.TryGetValue(id, out Employee? employee))
    {
      Console.WriteLine($"Employee with id {id} does not exist");
    }
    else
    {
      Console.WriteLine(employee);
    }
  }
  catch (EmployeeIdException ex)
  {
    Console.WriteLine(ex.Message);
  }
}
```

Running the application produces the following output:

```
J000018: Kyle Bush          $138.000,00
J000019: Martin Truex Jr     $73.000,00
S000004: Kevin Harvick      $116.000,00
```

```
J000011: Denny Hamlin        $127.000,00
T000022: Joey Logano          $96.000,00
Enter employee id (X to exit)> T22
T000022: Joey Logano          $96.000,00
Enter employee id (X to exit)> J18
J000018: Kyle Bush           $138.000,00
Enter employee id (X to exit)> X
```

Lookups

Dictionary<TKey, TValue> supports only one value per key. The class Lookup<TKey, TElement> resembles a Dictionary<TKey, TValue> but maps keys to a collection of values. This class is defined with the namespace System.Linq.

Lookup<TKey, TElement> cannot be created like the dictionary. Instead, you have to invoke the method ToLookup, which returns a Lookup<TKey, TElement> object. The method ToLookup is an extension method that is available with every class implementing IEnumerable<T>. In the following example, a list of Racer objects is filled. Because List<T> implements IEnumerable<T>, the ToLookup method can be invoked on the racers list. This method requires a delegate of type Func<TSource, TKey> that defines the selector of the key. Here, the racers are selected based on their country by using the lambda expression r => r.Country. The foreach loop accesses only the racers from Australia by using the indexer (code file LookupSample/Program.cs):

```
List<Racer> racers = new();
racers.Add(new Racer(26, "Jacques", "Villeneuve", "Canada", 11));
racers.Add(new Racer(18, "Alan", "Jones", "Australia", 12));
racers.Add(new Racer(11, "Jackie", "Stewart", "United Kingdom", 27));
racers.Add(new Racer(15, "James", "Hunt", "United Kingdom", 10));
racers.Add(new Racer(5, "Jack", "Brabham", "Australia", 14));

var lookupRacers = racers.ToLookup(r => r.Country);

foreach (Racer r in lookupRacers["Australia"])
{
  Console.WriteLine(r);
}
```

> **NOTE** *You can read more about extension methods in Chapter 9, "Language Integrated Query." Lambda expressions are explained in Chapter 7, "Delegates, Lambdas, and Events."*

The output shows the racers from Australia:

```
Alan Jones
Jack Brabham
```

Sorted Dictionaries

SortedDictionary<TKey, TValue> is a binary search tree in which the items are sorted based on the key. The key type must implement the interface IComparable<TKey>. If the key type is not sortable, you can also create a comparer implementing IComparer<TKey> and assign the comparer as a constructor argument of the sorted dictionary.

Earlier in this chapter you read about `SortedList<TKey, TValue>`. `SortedDictionary<TKey, TValue>` and `SortedList<TKey, TValue>` have similar functionality, but because `SortedList<TKey, TValue>` is implemented as a list that is based on an array, and `SortedDictionary<TKey, TValue>` is implemented as a tree, the classes have different characteristics:

➤ `SortedList<TKey, TValue>` uses less memory than `SortedDictionary<TKey, TValue>`.

➤ `SortedDictionary<TKey, TValue>` has faster insertion and removal of elements.

➤ When populating the collection with already sorted data, `SortedList<TKey, TValue>` is faster if capacity changes are not needed.

> **NOTE** `SortedList` *consumes less memory than* `SortedDictionary`. `SortedDictionary` *is faster with inserts and the removal of unsorted data.*

SETS

A collection that contains only distinct items is known by the term *set*. .NET Core includes two sets, `HashSet<T>` and `SortedSet<T>`, that both implement the interface `ISet<T>`. `HashSet<T>` contains a hash table of distinct items that is unordered; with `SortedSet<T>`, the list is ordered.

The `ISet<T>` interface offers methods to create a union of multiple sets, to create an intersection of sets, or to provide information if one set is a superset or subset of another.

In the following sample code, three new sets of type `string` are created and filled with Formula 1 cars. The `HashSet<T>` class implements the `ICollection<T>` interface. However, the `Add` method is implemented explicitly, and a different `Add` method is offered by the class, as you can see in the following code snippet. The `Add` method differs by the return type; a Boolean value is returned to provide the information if the element was added. If the element was already in the set, it is not added, and `false` is returned (code file `SetSample/Program.cs`):

```
HashSet<string> companyTeams = new()
{ "Ferrari", "McLaren", "Mercedes" };

HashSet<string> traditionalTeams = new() { "Ferrari", "McLaren" };

HashSet<string> privateTeams = new()
{ "Red Bull", "Toro Rosso", "Force India", "Sauber" };

if (privateTeams.Add("Williams"))
{
  Console.WriteLine("Williams added");
}

if (!companyTeams.Add("McLaren"))
{
  Console.WriteLine("McLaren was already in this set");
}
```

The result of these two `Add` methods is written to the console:

```
Williams added
McLaren was already in this set
```

The methods `IsSubsetOf` and `IsSupersetOf` compare a set with a collection that implements the `IEnumerable<T>` interface and returns a Boolean result. Here, `IsSubsetOf` verifies whether every element in `traditionalTeams` is contained in `companyTeams`, which is the case; `IsSupersetOf` verifies whether `traditionalTeams` has any additional elements compared to `companyTeams`:

```
if (traditionalTeams.IsSubsetOf(companyTeams))
{
  Console.WriteLine("traditionalTeams is subset of companyTeams");
}
if (companyTeams.IsSupersetOf(traditionalTeams))
{
  Console.WriteLine("companyTeams is a superset of traditionalTeams");
}
```

The output of this verification is shown here:

```
traditionalTeams is a subset of companyTeams
companyTeams is a superset of traditionalTeams
```

Williams is a traditional team as well, which is why this team is added to the `traditionalTeams` collection:

```
traditionalTeams.Add("Williams");
if (privateTeams.Overlaps(traditionalTeams))
{
  Console.WriteLine("At least one team is the same with traditional " +
    "and private teams");
}
```

Because there's an overlap, this is the result:

```
At least one team is the same with traditional and private teams.
```

The variable `allTeams` that references a new `SortedSet<string>` is filled with a union of `companyTeams`, `privateTeams`, and `traditionalTeams` by calling the `UnionWith` method:

```
SortedSet<string> allTeams = new(companyTeams);
allTeams.UnionWith(privateTeams);
allTeams.UnionWith(traditionalTeams);
Console.WriteLine();
Console.WriteLine("all teams");
foreach (var team in allTeams)
{
  Console.WriteLine(team);
}
```

Here, all teams are returned, but every team is listed just once because the set contains only unique values; and because the container is a `SortedSet<string>`, the result is ordered:

```
Ferrari
Force India
Lotus
McLaren
Mercedes
Red Bull
Sauber
Toro Rosso
Williams
```

The method `ExceptWith` removes all private teams from the `allTeams` set:

```
allTeams.ExceptWith(privateTeams);
Console.WriteLine();
Console.WriteLine("no private team left");
foreach (var team in allTeams)
{
    Console.WriteLine(team);
}
```

The remaining elements in the collection do not contain any private teams:

```
Ferrari
McLaren
Mercedes
```

PERFORMANCE

Many collection classes offer the same functionality as others; for example, `SortedList` offers nearly the same features as `SortedDictionary`. However, often there's a big difference in performance. Whereas one collection consumes less memory, the other collection class is faster with the retrieval of elements. The Microsoft documentation often provides performance hints about methods of the collection, giving you information about the time the operation requires in big-O notation:

➤ **O(1):** This means that the time this operation needs is constant no matter how many items are in the collection. For example, the `ArrayList` has an `Add` method with O(1) behavior. No matter how many elements are in the list, it always takes the same amount of time when adding a new element to the end of the list. The `Count` property provides the number of items, so it is easy to find the end of the list.

➤ **O(log n):** This means that the time needed for the operation increases with every element in the collection, but the increase of time for each element is not linear but logarithmic. `SortedDictionary<TKey, TValue>` has O(log n) behavior for inserting operations inside the collection; `SortedList<TKey, TValue>` has O(n) behavior for the same functionality. Here, `SortedDictionary<TKey, TValue>` is a lot faster because it is more efficient to insert elements into a tree structure than into a list.

➤ **O(n):** This means it takes the worst-case amount of time of n to perform an operation on the collection. The `Add` method of `ArrayList` can be an O(n) operation if a reallocation of the collection is required. Changing the capacity causes the list to be copied, and the time for the copy increases linearly with every element.

The following table lists collection classes and their performance for different actions such as adding, inserting, and removing items. With this table, you can select the best collection class for your purpose. The left column lists the collection class. The Add column gives timing information about adding items to the collection. The `List<T>` and the `HashSet<T>` classes define `Add` methods to add items to the collection. With other collection classes, use a different method to add elements to the collection; for example, the `Stack<T>` class defines a `Push` method, and the `Queue<T>` class defines an `Enqueue` method. You can find this information in the table as well.

If there are multiple big-O values in a cell, the reason is that if a collection needs to be resized, resizing takes a while. For example, with the `List<T>` class, adding items needs O(1). If the capacity of the collection is not large enough and the collection needs to be resized, the resize requires O(n) time. The larger the collection, the longer the resize operation takes. It's best to avoid resizes by setting the capacity of the collection when you create it to a value that can hold all the elements.

If the table cell contents is n/a, the operation is not applicable with this collection type.

COLLECTION	ADD	INSERT	REMOVE	ITEM	SORT	FIND
List<T>	O(1) or O(n) if the collection must be resized	O(n)	O(n)	O(1)	O (n log n), worst case O(n ^ 2)	O(n)
Stack<T>	Push, O(1), or O(n) if the stack must be resized	n/a	Pop, O(1)	n/a	n/a	n/a
Queue<T>	Enqueue, O(1), or O(n) if the queue must be resized	n/a	Dequeue, O(1)	n/a	n/a	n/a
HashSet<T>	O(1) or O(n) if the set must be resized	Add O(1) or O(n)	O(1)	n/a	n/a	n/a
SortedSet<T>	O(1) or O(n) if the set must be resized	Add O(1) or O(n)	O(1)	n/a	n/a	n/a
LinkedList<T>	AddLast O(1)	Add After O(1)	O(1)	n/a	n/a	O(n)
Dictionary <TKey, TValue>	O(1) or O(n)	n/a	O(1)	O(1)	n/a	n/a
SortedDictionary<TKey, TValue>	O(log n)	n/a	O(log n)	O(log n)	n/a	n/a
SortedList <TKey, TValue>	O(n) for unsorted data, O(log n) for end of list, O(n) if resize is needed	n/a	O(n)	O(log n) to read/write, O(log n) if the key is in the list, O(n) if the key is not in the list	n/a	n/a

IMMUTABLE COLLECTIONS

If an object can change its state, it is hard to use it from multiple simultaneously running tasks. Synchronization is necessary with these collections. If an object cannot change state, it's a lot easier to use it from multiple threads. An object that can't change is an immutable object. Collections that cannot be changed are immutable collections.

> **NOTE** *The topics of using multiple tasks and threads and programming with asynchronous methods are explained in detail in Chapter 11, "Tasks and Asynchronous Programming," and Chapter 17, "Parallel Programming."*

When you compare read-only collections like those discussed earlier in this chapter with immutable collections, there's a big difference: read-only collections make use of an interface to mutable collections. Using this interface, the collection cannot be changed. However, if someone still has a reference to the mutable collection, it still can be changed. With immutable collections, nobody can change this collection.

Let's start with a simple immutable string array using the class `ImmutableArray`. This class is defined in the `System.Collections.Immutable` namespace. You can create the array with the static `Create` method as shown. The `Create` method is overloaded where other variants of this method allow passing any number of elements. Notice that two different types are used here: the nongeneric `ImmutableArray` class with the static `Create` method and the generic `ImmutableArray` struct that is returned from the `Create` method. In the following code snippet, an empty array is created (code file `ImmutableCollectionSample/Program.cs`):

```
ImmutableArray<string> a1 = ImmutableArray.Create<string>();
```

An empty array is not very useful. The `ImmutableArray<T>` type offers an `Add` method to add elements. However, contrary to other collection classes, the `Add` method does not change the immutable collection itself. Instead, a new immutable collection is returned. So, after the call of the `Add` method, a1 is still an empty collection, and a2 is an immutable collection with one element. The `Add` method returns the new immutable collection:

```
ImmutableArray<string> a2 = a1.Add("Williams");
```

With this, it is possible to use this API in a fluent way and invoke one `Add` method after the other. The variable a3 now references an immutable collection containing four elements:

```
ImmutableArray<string> a3 =
    a2.Add("Ferrari").Add("Mercedes").Add("Red Bull Racing");
```

With each of these stages using the immutable array, the complete collections are not copied with every step. Instead, the immutable types make use of a shared state and copy the collection only when it's necessary.

However, it's even more efficient to first fill the collection and then make it an immutable array. When some manipulation needs to take place, you can again use a mutable collection. A builder class offered by the immutable types helps with that.

To see this in action, first an `Account` record is created that is put into the collection. This type itself is immutable and cannot be changed by using read-only auto properties (code file `ImmutableCollectionSample/Account.cs`):

```
public record Account(string Name, decimal Amount);
```

Next a `List<Account>` collection is created and filled with sample accounts (code file `ImmutableCollectionSample/Program.cs`):

```
List<Account> accounts = new()
{
  new("Scrooge McDuck", 667377678765m),
```

```
      new("Donald Duck", -200m),
      new("Ludwig von Drake", 20000m)
   };
```

From the accounts collection, an immutable collection can be created with the extension method `ToImmutableList`. This extension method is available as soon as the namespace `System.Collections.Immutable` is opened.

```
      ImmutableList<Account> immutableAccounts = accounts.ToImmutableList();
```

The variable `immutableAccounts` can be enumerated like other collections. It just cannot be changed:

```
      foreach (var account in immutableAccounts)
      {
         Console.WriteLine($"{account.Name} {account.Amount}");
      }
```

Instead of using the `foreach` statement to iterate immutable lists, you can use the `ForEach` method that is defined with `ImmutableList<T>`. This method requires an `Action<T>` delegate as parameter, and thus a lambda expression can be assigned:

```
      immutableAccounts.ForEach(a => Console.WriteLine($"{a.Name} {a.Amount}"));
```

When you work with these collections, methods like `Contains`, `FindAll`, `FindLast`, `IndexOf`, and others are available. Because these methods are like the methods from other collection classes discussed earlier in this chapter, they are not explicitly shown here.

In case you need to change the content for immutable collections, the collections offer methods such as `Add`, `AddRange`, `Remove`, `RemoveAt`, `RemoveRange`, `Replace`, and `Sort`. These methods are very different from normal collection classes because the immutable collection that is used to invoke the methods is never changed, but these methods return a new immutable collection.

Using Builders with Immutable Collections

Creating new immutable collections from existing ones can be done easily with the previously mentioned `Add`, `Remove`, and `Replace` methods. However, this is not very efficient if you need to do multiple changes that involve adding and removing many elements for the new collection. For creating new immutable collections that involve even more changes, you can create a builder.

Let's continue with the sample code and make multiple changes to the account objects in the collection. To do this, you can create a builder by invoking the `ToBuilder` method. This method returns a collection that you can change. In the sample code, all accounts with an amount larger than zero are removed. The original immutable collection is not changed. After the change with the builder is completed, a new immutable collection is created by invoking the `ToImmutable` method of the `Builder`. This collection is used next to output all overdrawn accounts (code file `ImmutableCollectionSample/Program.cs`):

```
      ImmutableList<Account>.Builder builder = immutableAccounts.ToBuilder();
      for (int i = builder.Count - 1; i >= 0; i--)
      {
         Account a = builder[i];
         if (a.Amount > 0)
         {
            builder.Remove(a);
         }
      }
      ImmutableList<Account> overdrawnAccounts = builder.ToImmutable();
      overdrawnAccounts.ForEach(a => Console.WriteLine(
         $"overdrawn: {a.Name} {a.Amount}"));
```

Other than removing elements with the `Remove` method, the `Builder` type offers the methods `Add`, `AddRange`, `Insert`, `RemoveAt`, `RemoveAll`, `Reverse`, and `Sort` to change the mutable collection. After finishing the mutable operations, invoke `ToImmutable` to get the immutable collection again.

Immutable Collection Types and Interfaces

Other than `ImmutableArray` and `ImmutableList`, the NuGet package `System.Collections.Immutable` offers some more immutable collection types as shown in the following table:

IMMUTABLE TYPE	DESCRIPTION
`ImmutableArray<T>`	`ImmutableArray<T>` is a struct that uses an array type internally but doesn't allow changes to the underlying type. This struct implements the interface `IImmutableList<T>`.
`ImmutableList<T>`	`ImmutableList<T>` uses a binary tree internally to map the objects and implements the interface `IImmutableList<T>`.
`ImmutableQueue<T>`	`ImmutableQueue<T>` implements the interface `IImmutableQueue<T>` that allows access to elements FIFO with `Enqueue`, `Dequeue`, and `Peek`.
`ImmutableStack<T>`	`ImmutableStack<T>` implements the interface `IImmutableStack<T>` that allows access to elements LIFO with `Push`, `Pop`, and `Peek`.
`ImmutableDictionary<TKey, TValue>`	`ImmutableDictionary<TKey, TValue>` is an immutable collection with unordered key/value pair elements implementing the interface `IImmutableDictionary<TKey, TValue>`.
`ImmutableSortedDictionary<TKey, TValue>`	`ImmutableSortedDictionary<TKey, TValue>` is an immutable collection with ordered key/value pair elements implementing the interface `IImmutableDictionary<TKey, TValue>`.
`ImmutableHashSet<T>`	`ImmutableHashSet<T>` is an immutable unordered hash set implementing the interface `IImmutableSet<T>`. This interface offers set functionality explained earlier in this chapter.
`ImmutableSortedSet<T>`	`ImmutableSortedSet<T>` is an immutable ordered set implementing the interface `IImmutableSet<T>`.

Like the normal collection classes, immutable collections implement interfaces as well—such as `IImmutableList<T>`, `IImmutableQueue<T>`, and `IImmutableStack<T>`. The big difference with these immutable interfaces is that all the methods that make a change in the collection return a new collection.

Using LINQ with Immutable Arrays

For using LINQ with immutable arrays, the class `ImmutableArrayExtensions` defines optimized versions for LINQ methods such as `Where`, `Aggregate`, `All`, `First`, `Last`, `Select`, and `SelectMany`. All that you need to use the optimized versions is to directly use the `ImmutableArray` type and open the `System.Linq` namespace.

The `Where` method defined with the `ImmutableArrayExtensions` type looks like this to extend the `ImmutableArray<T>` type:

```
public static IEnumerable<T> Where<T>(
    this ImmutableArray<T> immutableArray, Func<T, bool> predicate);
```

The normal LINQ extension method extends `IEnumerable<T>`. Because `ImmutableArray<T>` is a better match, the optimized version is used when you are invoking LINQ methods.

SUMMARY

This chapter took a look at working with different kinds of generic collections. Arrays are fixed in size, but you can use lists for dynamically growing collections. For accessing elements on a FIFO basis, there's a queue; and you can use a stack for LIFO operations. Linked lists allow for fast insertion and removal of elements but are slow for searching. With keys and values, you can use dictionaries, which are fast for searching and inserting elements. Sets are useful for unique items and can be ordered (`SortedSet<T>`) or not ordered (`HashSet<T>`).

Chapter 9 gives you details about working with arrays and collections by using LINQ syntax.

Language Integrated Query

WHAT'S IN THIS CHAPTER?

➤ Working with traditional queries across objects using List

➤ Using extension methods

➤ Getting to know LINQ query operators

➤ Working with Parallel LINQ

➤ Working with expression trees

CODE DOWNLOADS FOR THIS CHAPTER

The source code for this chapter is available on the book page at www.wiley.com. Click the Downloads link. The code can also be found at https://github.com/ProfessionalCSharp/ProfessionalCSharp2021 in the directory 1_CS/LINQ.

The code for this chapter is divided into the following major examples:

➤ LINQIntro

➤ EnumerableSample

➤ ParallelLINQ

➤ ExpressionTrees

All the sample projects have nullable reference types configured.

LINQ OVERVIEW

Language Integrated Query (LINQ) integrates query syntax inside the C# programming language, making it possible to access different data sources with the same syntax. LINQ accomplishes this by offering an abstraction layer.

This chapter describes the core principles of LINQ and the language extensions for C# that make the C# LINQ query possible.

> **NOTE** *For details about using LINQ across a database, read Chapter 21, "Entity Framework Core."*

This chapter starts with a simple LINQ query before diving into the full potential of LINQ. The C# language offers an integrated query language that is converted to method calls. This section shows you what the conversion looks like so you can use all the possibilities of LINQ.

Lists and Entities

The LINQ queries in this chapter are performed on a collection containing Formula 1 champions from 1950 to 2020. This data needs to be prepared with classes and lists within a .NET 5.0 library.

For the entities, the record type `Racer` is defined (as shown in the following code snippet). `Racer` defines several properties and an overloaded `ToString` method to display a racer in a string format. This class implements the interface `IFormattable` to support different variants of format strings, and the interface `IComparable<Racer>`, which can be used to sort a list of racers based on the `LastName`. For more advanced queries, the class `Racer` contains not only single-value properties such as `FirstName`, `LastName`, `Wins` `Country`, and `Starts`, but also properties that contain a collection, such as `Cars` and `Years`. The `Years` property lists all the years of the championship title. Some racers have won more than one title. The `Cars` property is used to list all the cars used by the driver during the title years (code file `DataLib/Racer.cs`):

```
public record Racer(string FirstName, string LastName, string Country,
  int Starts, int Wins, IEnumerable<int> Years, IEnumerable<string> Cars) :
  IComparable<Racer>, IFormattable
{
  public Racer(string FirstName, string LastName, string Country,
    int Starts, int Wins)
    : this(FirstName, LastName, Country, Starts, Wins, new int[] { },
      new string[] { })
  { }

  public override string ToString() => $"{FirstName} {LastName}";

  public int CompareTo(Racer? other) => LastName.CompareTo(other?.LastName);

  public string ToString(string format) => ToString(format, null);

  public string ToString(string? format, IFormatProvider? formatProvider) =>
    format switch
    {
      null => ToString(),
      "N" => ToString(),
      "F" => FirstName,
```

```
        "L" => LastName,
        "C" => Country,
        "S" => Starts.ToString(),
        "W" => Wins.ToString(),
        "A" => $"{FirstName} {LastName}, country: {Country}, starts: {Starts},
          wins: {Wins}",
        _ => throw new FormatException($"Format {format} not supported")
    };
  }
}
```

> **NOTE** *With the Formula 1 racing series, in every calendar year, a driver championship and a constructor championship take place. With the driver championship, the best driver is world champion. With the constructor championship, the best team wins the award. See* https://www.formula1.com *for details, current standings, and an archive going back to 1950.*

A second entity class is `Team`. This class just contains the team name and an array of years for constructor championships (code file `DataLib/Team.cs`):

```
public record Team
{
  public Team(string name, params int[] years)
  {
    Name = name;
    Years = years != null ? new List<int>(years) : new List<int>();
  }
  public string Name { get; }
  public IEnumerable<int> Years { get; }
}
```

The class `Formula1` returns a list of racers in the method `GetChampions`. The list is filled with all Formula 1 champions from the years 1950 to 2020 with the method `InitializeRacers` (code file `DataLib/Formula1.cs`):

```
public static class Formula1
{
  private static List<Racer> s_racers;
  public static IList<Racer> GetChampions() => s_racers ??= InitalizeRacers();

  private static List<Racer> InitializeRacers => new()
  {
    new ("Nino", "Farina", "Italy", 33, 5, new int[] { 1950 },
      new string[] { "Alfa Romeo" }),
    new ("Alberto", "Ascari", "Italy", 32, 10, new int[] { 1952, 1953 },
      new string[] { "Ferrari" }),
    new ("Juan Manuel", "Fangio", "Argentina", 51, 24,
      new int[] { 1951, 1954, 1955, 1956, 1957 },
      new string[] { "Alfa Romeo", "Maserati", "Mercedes", "Ferrari" }),
    new ("Mike", "Hawthorn", "UK", 45, 3, new int[] { 1958 },
      new string[] { "Ferrari" }),
    new ("Phil", "Hill", "USA", 48, 3, new int[] { 1961 },
      new string[] { "Ferrari" }),
    new ("John", "Surtees", "UK", 111, 6, new int[] { 1964 },
```

```
        new string[] { "Ferrari" }),
      new ("Jim", "Clark", "UK", 72, 25, new int[] { 1963, 1965 },
        new string[] { "Lotus" }),
      //...
    };
    //...
}
```

Where queries are done across multiple lists, the `GetConstructorChampions` method in the following code snippet returns the list of all constructor championships (these championships have been around since 1958):

```
private static List<Team> s_teams;
public static IList<Team> GetConstructorChampions() => s_teams ??= new()
{
  new ("Vanwall", 1958),
  new ("Cooper", 1959, 1960),
  new ("Ferrari", 1961, 1964, 1975, 1976, 1977, 1979, 1982, 1983, 1999,
      2000, 2001, 2002, 2003, 2004, 2007, 2008),
  new ("BRM", 1962),
  new ("Lotus", 1963, 1965, 1968, 1970, 1972, 1973, 1978),
  new ("Brabham", 1966, 1967),
  new ("Matra", 1969),
  new ("Tyrrell", 1971),
  new ("McLaren", 1974, 1984, 1985, 1988, 1989, 1990, 1991, 1998),
  new ("Williams", 1980, 1981, 1986, 1987, 1992, 1993, 1994, 1996, 1997),
  new ("Benetton", 1995),
  new ("Renault", 2005, 2006),
  new ("Brawn GP", 2009),
  new ("Red Bull Racing", 2010, 2011, 2012, 2013),
  new ("Mercedes", 2014, 2015, 2016, 2017, 2018, 2019, 2020)
};
```

LINQ Query

Using these prepared lists and objects from the previously created library, you can do a LINQ query—for example, a query to get all world champions from Brazil sorted by the highest number of wins. To accomplish this, you could use methods of the `List<T>` class—for example, the `FindAll` and `Sort` methods. However, with LINQ there's a simpler syntax (code file `LINQIntro/Program.cs`):

```
static void LinqQuery()
{
  var query = from r in Formula1.GetChampions()
              where r.Country == "Brazil"
              orderby r.Wins descending
              select r;

  foreach (Racer r in query)
  {
    Console.WriteLine($"{r:A}");
  }
}
```

The result of this query shows world champions from Brazil ordered by number of wins:

```
Ayrton Senna, country: Brazil, starts: 161, wins: 41
Nelson Piquet, country: Brazil, starts: 204, wins: 23
Emerson Fittipaldi, country: Brazil, starts: 143, wins: 14
```

The expression

```
from r in Formula1.GetChampions()
where r.Country == "Brazil"
orderby r.Wins descending
select r;
```

is a LINQ query. The clauses `from`, `where`, `orderby`, `descending`, and `select` are predefined keywords in this query.

The query expression must begin with a `from` clause and end with a `select` or `group` clause. In between, you can optionally use `where`, `orderby`, `join`, `let`, and additional `from` clauses.

> **NOTE** *The variable* query *just has the LINQ query assigned to it. The query is not performed by this assignment but rather as soon as the query is accessed using the* foreach *loop. This is discussed in more detail later in the section "Deferred Query Execution."*

Extension Methods

The compiler converts the LINQ query to method calls. At runtime, extension methods will be invoked. LINQ offers various extension methods for the `IEnumerable<T>` interface, so you can use the LINQ query across any collection that implements this interface. An extension method is defined as a static method whose first parameter defines the type it extends, and it is declared in a static class.

> **NOTE** *Extension methods are covered in Chapter 3, "Classes, Records, Structs, and Tuples."*

One of the classes that define LINQ extension methods is `Enumerable` in the namespace `System.Linq`. You just have to import the namespace to open the scope of the extension methods of this class. A sample implementation of the `Where` extension method is shown in the following code. The first parameter of the `Where` method that includes the `this` keyword is of type `IEnumerable<T>`. This enables the `Where` method to be used with every type that implements `IEnumerable<T>`. A few examples of types that implement this interface are arrays and `List<T>`. The second parameter is a `Func<T, bool>` delegate that references a method that returns a Boolean value and requires a parameter of type `T`. This predicate is invoked within the implementation to examine whether the item from the `IEnumerable<T>` source should be added into the destination collection. If the method is referenced by the delegate, the `yield return` statement returns the item from the source to the destination:

```
public static IEnumerable<TSource> Where<TSource>(
  this IEnumerable<TSource> source,
  Func<TSource, bool> predicate)
{
  foreach (TSource item in source)
  {
    if (predicate(item))
      yield return item;
  }
}
```

Because `Where` is implemented as a generic method, it works with any type that is contained in a collection. Any collection implementing `IEnumerable<T>` is supported.

Now it's possible to use the extension methods `Where`, `OrderByDescending`, and `Select` from the class `Enumerable`. Because each of these methods returns `IEnumerable<TSource>`, it is possible to invoke one method after the other by using the previous result. With the arguments of the extension methods, anonymous methods that define the implementation for the delegate parameters are used (code file `LINQIntro/Program.cs`):

```
static void ExtensionMethods()
{
  List<Racer> champions = new(Formula1.GetChampions());
  var brazilChampions =
    champions.Where(r => r.Country == "Brazil")
      .OrderByDescending(r => r.Wins)
      .Select(r => r);

  foreach (Racer r in brazilChampions)
  {
    Console.WriteLine($"{r:A}");
  }
}
```

Deferred Query Execution

During runtime, the query expression does not run immediately as it is defined. The query runs only when the items are iterated. The reason is that the extension method shown earlier makes use of the `yield return` statement to return the elements where the predicate is true. Because the `yield return` statement is used, the compiler creates an enumerator and returns the items as soon as they are accessed from the enumeration.

This has a very interesting and important effect. In the following example, a collection of `string` elements is created and filled with first names. Next, a query is defined to get all the names from the collection whose first letter is J. The collection should also be sorted. The iteration does not happen when the query is defined. Instead, the iteration happens with the `foreach` statement, where all items are iterated. Only one element of the collection fulfills the requirements of the `where` expression to start with the letter J: Juan. After the iteration is done and Juan is written to the console, four new names are added to the collection. Then the iteration is done again (code file `LINQIntro/Program.cs`):

```
void DeferredQuery()
{
  List<string> names = new() { "Nino", "Alberto", "Juan", "Mike", "Phil" };
  var namesWithJ = from n in names
                   where n.StartsWith("J")
                   orderby n
                   select n;

  Console.WriteLine("First iteration");
  foreach (string name in namesWithJ)
  {
    Console.WriteLine(name);
  }
  Console.WriteLine();

  names.Add("John");
  names.Add("Jim");
  names.Add("Jack");
  names.Add("Denny");
  Console.WriteLine("Second iteration");
```

```
    foreach (string name in namesWithJ)
    {
      Console.WriteLine(name);
    }
  }
```

Because the iteration does not happen when the query is defined, but does happen with every `foreach`, the output from the application changes:

```
First iteration
Juan
Second iteration
Jack
Jim
John
Juan
```

Of course, you also must be aware that the extension methods are invoked every time the query is used within an iteration. Most of the time, this is very practical because you can detect changes in the source data. However, sometimes this is impractical. You can change this behavior by invoking the extension methods `ToArray`, `ToList`, and the like. In the following example, you can see that `ToList` iterates through the collection immediately and returns a collection implementing `IList<string>`. The returned list is then iterated through twice; in between iterations, the data source gets new names:

```
List<string> names = new() { "Nino", "Alberto", "Juan", "Mike", "Phil" };
var namesWithJ = (from n in names
                  where n.StartsWith("J")
                  orderby n
                  select n).ToList();

Console.WriteLine("First iteration");
foreach (string name in namesWithJ)
{
  Console.WriteLine(name);
}
Console.WriteLine();

names.Add("John");
names.Add("Jim");
names.Add("Jack");
names.Add("Denny");

Console.WriteLine("Second iteration");
foreach (string name in namesWithJ)
{
  Console.WriteLine(name);
}
```

The result indicates that in between the iterations, the output stays the same although the collection values have changed:

```
First iteration
Juan
Second iteration
Juan
```

STANDARD QUERY OPERATORS

`Where`, `OrderByDescending`, and `Select` are only a few of the query operators defined by LINQ. The LINQ query defines a declarative syntax for the most common operators. There are many more query operators available with the `Enumerable` class.

The following table lists the standard query operators defined by the `Enumerable` class.

STANDARD QUERY OPERATORS	DESCRIPTION
`Where` `OfType<TResult>`	*Filtering operators* define a restriction to the elements returned. With the `Where` query operator, you can use a predicate; for example, a lambda expression that returns a bool. `OfType<TResult>` filters the elements based on the type and returns only the elements of the type `TResult`.
`Select` `SelectMany`	*Projection operators* are used to transform an object into a new object of a different type. `Select` and `SelectMany` define a projection to select values of the result based on a selector function.

`OrderBy`
`ThenBy`
`OrderByDescending`
`ThenByDescending`
`Reverse`
	Sorting operators change the order of elements returned. `OrderBy` sorts values in ascending order. `OrderByDescending` sorts values in descending order. `ThenBy` and `ThenByDescending` operators are used for a secondary sort if the first sort gives similar results. `Reverse` reverses the elements in the collection.

`Join` `GroupJoin`	*Join operators* are used to combine collections that might not be directly related to each other. With the `Join` operator, you can do a join of two collections based on key selector functions. This is similar to the JOIN you know from SQL. The `GroupJoin` operator joins two collections and groups the results.
`GroupBy` `ToLookup`	*Grouping operators* put the data into groups. The `GroupBy` operator groups elements with a common key. `ToLookup` groups the elements by creating a one-to-many dictionary.

`Any`
`All`
`Contains`
	Quantifier operators return a Boolean value if elements of the sequence satisfy a specific condition. `Any`, `All`, and `Contains` are quantifier operators. `Any` determines whether any element in the collection satisfies a predicate function. `All` determines whether all elements in the collection satisfy a predicate. `Contains` checks whether a specific element is in the collection.

`Take`
`Skip`
`TakeWhile`
`SkipWhile`
	Partitioning operators return a subset of the collection. `Take`, `Skip`, `TakeWhile`, and `SkipWhile` are partitioning operators. With these, you get a partial result. With `Take`, you have to specify the number of elements to take from the collection. `Skip` ignores the specified number of elements and takes the rest. `TakeWhile` takes the elements as long as a condition is true. `SkipWhile` skips the elements as long as the condition is true.

STANDARD QUERY OPERATORS	DESCRIPTION
Distinct Union Intersect Except Zip	*Set operators* return a collection set. `Distinct` removes duplicates from a collection. With the exception of `Distinct`, the other set operators require two collections. `Union` returns unique elements that appear in either of the two collections. `Intersect` returns elements that appear in both collections. `Except` returns elements that appear in just one collection. `Zip` combines two collections into one.
First FirstOrDefault Last LastOrDefault ElementAt ElementAtOrDefault Single SingleOrDefault	*Element operators* return just one element. `First` returns the first element that satisfies a condition. `FirstOrDefault` is similar to `First`, but it returns a default value of the type if the element is not found. `Last` returns the last element that satisfies a condition. With `ElementAt`, you specify the position of the element to return. `Single` returns only the one element that satisfies a condition. If more than one element satisfies the condition, an exception is thrown. All the `XXOrDefault` methods are similar to the methods that start with the same prefix, but they return the default value of the type if the element is not found.
Count Sum Min Max Average Aggregate	*Aggregate operators* compute a single value from a collection. With aggregate operators, you can get the sum of all values, the number of all elements, the element with the lowest or highest value, an average number, and so on.
ToArray AsEnumerable ToList ToDictionary Cast<TResult>	*Conversion operators* convert the collection to an array: `IEnumerable`, `IList`, `IDictionary`, and so on. The `Cast` method casts every item of the collection to the generic argument type.
Empty Range Repeat	*Generation* operators return a new sequence. The `Empty` operator returns an empty `IEnumerable`, `Range` returns `IEnumerable` containing a sequence of numbers, and `Repeat` returns `IEnumerable` with one repeated value.

The following sections provide examples demonstrating how to use these operators.

Filter

This section looks at some examples for a query. This sample application available with the code download offers passing command-line arguments for every different feature shown. With the Debug section in the Properties of Visual Studio, you can configure the command-line arguments as needed to run the different sections of the application. Using the command line with the installed SDK, you can invoke the commands using .NET CLI in this way:

```
> dotnet run -- filter simplefilter
```

which passes the arguments `filter simplefilter` to the application.

With the `where` clause, you can combine multiple expressions—for example, get only the racers from Brazil and Austria who won more than 15 races. The result type of the expression passed to the `where` clause just needs to be of type `bool` (code file `EnumerableSample/FilterSamples.cs`):

```
public static void SimpleFilter()
{
  var racers = from r in Formula1.GetChampions()
               where r.Wins > 15 &&
               (r.Country == "Brazil" || r.Country == "Austria")
               select r;

  foreach (var r in racers)
  {
    Console.WriteLine($"{r:A}");
  }
}
```

Starting the program with this LINQ query (`filter simplefilter`) returns Niki Lauda, Nelson Piquet, and Ayrton Senna, as shown here:

```
Niki Lauda, country: Austria, Starts: 173, Wins: 25
Nelson Piquet, country: Brazil, Starts: 204, Wins: 23
Ayrton Senna, country: Brazil, Starts: 161, Wins: 41
```

Not all queries can be done with the LINQ query syntax, and not all extension methods are mapped to LINQ query clauses. Advanced queries require using extension methods. To better understand complex queries with extension methods, it's good to see how simple queries are mapped. The following code uses the `Where` extension method instead of a LINQ query. The `Select` extension method would return the same object returned by the `Where` method, so it isn't needed here (code file `EnumerableSample/FilterSamples.cs`):

```
public static void FilterWithMethods()
{
  var racers = Formula1.GetChampions()
    .Where(r => r.Wins > 15 &&
      (r.Country == "Brazil" || r.Country == "Austria"));
  //...
}
```

Filter with Index

One scenario in which you can't use the LINQ query is an overload of the `Where` method. With an overload of the `Where` method, you can pass a second parameter that is the index. The index is a counter for every result returned from the filter. You can use the index within the expression to do some calculation based on the index. In the following example, the index is used within the code that is called by the `Where` extension method to return only racers whose last name starts with A if the index is even (code file `EnumerableSample/FilterSamples.cs`):

```
public static void FilteringWithIndex()
{
  var racers = Formula1.GetChampions()
    .Where((r, index) => r.LastName.StartsWith("A") && index % 2 != 0);
```

```
      foreach (var r in racers)
      {
        Console.WriteLine($"{r:A}");
      }
    }
```

The racers with last names beginning with the letter A are Alberto Ascari, Mario Andretti, and Fernando Alonso. Because Mario Andretti is positioned within an index that is odd, he is not in the result:

```
Alberto Ascari, Italy; starts: 32, wins: 13
Fernando Alonso, Spain; starts: 314, wins: 32
```

Type Filtering

For filtering based on a type, you can use the `OfType` extension method. Here the array data contains both `string` and `int` objects. When you use the extension method `OfType`, passing the string class to the generic parameter returns only the strings from the collection (code file `EnumerableSample/FilterSamples.cs`):

```
public static void TypeFilter()
{
  object[] data = { "one", 2, 3, "four", "five", 6 };
  var query = data.OfType<string>();

  foreach (var s in query)
  {
    Console.WriteLine(s);
  }
}
```

When you run this code, the strings one, four, and five are displayed:

```
one
four
five
```

Compound from

If you need to do a filter based on a member of the object that itself is a sequence, you can use a compound `from`. The `Racer` class defines a property `Cars`, where `Cars` is a string array. For a filter of all racers who were champions with a Ferrari, you can use the LINQ query shown next. The first `from` clause accesses the `Racer` objects returned from `Formula1.GetChampions`. The second `from` clause accesses the `Cars` property of the `Racer` class to return all cars of type `string`. Next the cars are used with the `where` clause to filter only the racers who were champions with a Ferrari (code file `EnumerableSample/CompoundFromSamples.cs`):

```
public static void CompoundFrom()
{
  var ferrariDrivers = from r in Formula1.GetChampions()
                       from c in r.Cars
                       where c == "Ferrari"
                       orderby r.LastName
                       select r.FirstName + " " + r.LastName;
  //...
}
```

If you are curious about the result of this query, following are all Formula 1 champions driving a Ferrari:

```
Alberto Ascari
Juan Manuel Fangio
```

```
Mike Hawthorn
Phil Hill
Niki Lauda
Kimi Räikkönen
Jody Scheckter
Michael Schumacher
John Surtees
```

The C# compiler converts a compound `from` clause with a LINQ query to the `SelectMany` extension method. You can use `SelectMany` to iterate a sequence of a sequence. The overload of the `SelectMany` method that is used with the example is shown here:

```
public static IEnumerable<TResult> SelectMany<TSource, TCollection, TResult> (
   this IEnumerable<TSource> source,
   Func<TSource,
   IEnumerable<TCollection>> collectionSelector,
   Func<TSource, TCollection, TResult> resultSelector);
```

The first parameter is the implicit parameter that receives the sequence of `Racer` objects from the `GetChampions` method. The second parameter is the `collectionSelector` delegate where the inner sequence is defined. With the lambda expression `r => r.Cars`, the collection of cars should be returned. The third parameter is a delegate that is now invoked for every car and receives the `Racer` and `Car` objects. The lambda expression creates an anonymous type with a `Racer` and a `Car` property. As a result of this `SelectMany` method, the hierarchy of racers and cars is flattened, and a collection of new objects of an anonymous type for every car is returned.

This new collection is passed to the `Where` method so that only the racers driving a Ferrari are filtered. Finally, the `OrderBy` and `Select` methods are invoked (code file `EnumerableSample/CompoundFromSamples.cs`):

```
public static void CompoundFromWithMethods()
{
  var ferrariDrivers = Formula1.GetChampions()
    .SelectMany(r => r.Cars, (r, c) => new { Racer = r, Car = c })
    .Where(r => r.Car == "Ferrari")
    .OrderBy(r => r.Racer.LastName)
    .Select(r => $"{r.Racer.FirstName} {r.Racer.LastName}");
  //...
}
```

Resolving the generic `SelectMany` method to the types that are used here, the types are resolved as follows. In this case, the source is of type `Racer`, the filtered collection is a `string` array, and, of course, the name of the anonymous type that is returned is not known and is shown here as `TResult`:

```
public static IEnumerable<TResult> SelectMany<Racer, string, TResult> (
   this IEnumerable<Racer> source,
   Func<Racer, IEnumerable<string>> collectionSelector,
   Func<Racer, string, TResult> resultSelector);
```

Because the query was just converted from a LINQ query to extension methods, the result is the same as before.

Sorting

To sort a sequence, the `orderby` clause was used already. This section reviews the earlier example, now with the `orderby descending` clause. Here the racers are sorted based on the number of wins as specified by the key selector in descending order (code file `EnumerableSample/SortingSamples.cs`):

```
public static void SortDescending()
{
  var racers = from r in Formula1.GetChampions()
```

```
                    where r.Country == "Brazil"
                    orderby r.Wins descending
                    select r;
      //...
  }
```

The `orderby` clause is resolved to the `OrderBy` method, and the `orderby descending` clause is resolved to the `OrderByDescending` method:

```
    public static void SortDescendingWithMethods()
    {
      var racers = Formula1.GetChampions()
        .Where(r => r.Country == "Brazil")
        .OrderByDescending(r => r.Wins)
        .Select(r => r);
      //...
    }
```

The `OrderBy` and `OrderByDescending` methods return `IOrderedEnumerable<TSource>`. This interface derives from the interface `IEnumerable<TSource>` but contains an additional method, `CreateOrderedEnumerable <TSource>`. This method is used for further ordering of the sequence. If two items are the same based on the key selector, ordering can continue with the `ThenBy` and `ThenByDescending` methods. These methods require an `IOrderedEnumerable<TSource>` to work on but return this interface as well. Therefore, you can add any number of `ThenBy` and `ThenByDescending` methods to sort the collection.

When using the LINQ query, you just add all the different keys (with commas) for sorting to the `orderby` clause. In the next example, the sort of all racers is done first based on country, next on last name, and finally on first name. The `Take` extension method that is added to the result of the LINQ query is used to return the first 10 results:

```
    public static void SortMultiple()
    {
      var racers = (from r in Formula1.GetChampions()
                    orderby r.Country, r.LastName, r.FirstName
                    select r).Take(10);
      //...
    }
```

The sorted result is shown here:

```
    Argentina: Fangio, Juan Manuel
    Australia: Brabham, Jack
    Australia: Jones, Alan
    Austria: Lauda, Niki
    Austria: Rindt, Jochen
    Brazil: Fittipaldi, Emerson
    Brazil: Piquet, Nelson
    Brazil: Senna, Ayrton
    Canada: Villeneuve, Jacques
    Finland: Hakkinen, Mika
```

Doing the same with extension methods makes use of the `OrderBy` and `ThenBy` methods:

```
    public static void SortMultipleWithMethods()
    {
      var racers = Formula1.GetChampions()
        .OrderBy(r => r.Country)
        .ThenBy(r => r.LastName)
```

```
      .ThenBy(r => r.FirstName)
      .Take(10);
   //...
}
```

Grouping

To group query results based on a key value, you can use the `group` clause. Now the Formula 1 champions should be grouped by country, and the number of champions within a country should be listed. The clause `group r by r.Country into g` groups all the racers based on the `Country` property and defines a new identifier `g` that you can use later to access the group result information. In the following example, the result from the `group` clause is ordered based on the extension method `Count` that is applied on the group result; and if the count is the same, the ordering is done based on the key. This is the country because this was the key used for grouping. The `where` clause filters the results based on groups that have at least two items, and the `select` clause creates an anonymous type with the `Country` and `Count` properties (code file `EnumerableSample/GroupSamples.cs`):

```csharp
public static void Grouping()
{
   var countries = from r in Formula1.GetChampions()
                   group r by r.Country into g
                   orderby g.Count() descending, g.Key
                   where g.Count() >= 2
                   select new
                   {
                     Country = g.Key,
                     Count = g.Count()
                   };

   foreach (var item in countries)
   {
     Console.WriteLine($"{item.Country, -10} {item.Count}");
   }
}
```

The result displays the collection of objects with the `Country` and `Count` properties:

```
UK 10
Brazil 3
Finland 3
Germany 3
Australia 2
Austria 2
Italy 2
USA 2
```

Doing the same with extension methods, the `groupby` clause is resolved to the `GroupBy` method. What's interesting with the declaration of the `GroupBy` method is that it returns an enumeration of objects implementing the `IGrouping` interface. The `IGrouping` interface defines the `Key` property, so you can access the key of the group after defining the call to this method:

```csharp
public static IEnumerable<IGrouping<TKey, TSource>> GroupBy<TSource, TKey>(
    this IEnumerable<TSource> source, Func<TSource, TKey> keySelector);
```

The `group r by r.Country into g` clause is resolved to `GroupBy(r => r.Country)` and returns the group sequence. The group sequence is first ordered by the `OrderByDescending` method, then by the `ThenBy` method. Next, the `Where` and `Select` methods that you already know are invoked (code file `EnumerableSample/GroupSamples.cs`):

```
public static void GroupingWithMethods()
{
  var countries = Formula1.GetChampions()
    .GroupBy(r => r.Country)
    .OrderByDescending(g => g.Count())
    .ThenBy(g => g.Key)
    .Where(g => g.Count() >= 2)
    .Select(g => new
    {
      Country = g.Key,
      Count = g.Count()
    });
  //...
}
```

Variables Within the LINQ Query

With the LINQ query as it is written for grouping, the `Count` method is called multiple times. You can change this by using the `let` clause. `let` allows defining variables within the LINQ query (code file `EnumerableSample/GroupSamples.cs`):

```
public static void GroupingWithVariables()
{
  var countries = from r in Formula1.GetChampions()
                  group r by r.Country into g
                  let count = g.Count()
                  orderby count descending, g.Key
                  where count >= 2
                  select new
                  {
                    Country = g.Key,
                    Count = count
                  };
  //...
}
```

> **NOTE** *Why is it a bad idea to invoke the* `Count` *method multiple times on a LINQ query? Of course, it's always faster to cache the result of a method instead of calling it multiple items. With the implementation of the extension method* `Count` *that's based on the* `IEnumerable` *interface, you should also think about how this method can be implemented. With the members of the* `IEnumerable` *interface, it's possible to iterate through all the elements and count the number of items in the list. The longer the list is, the longer it takes.*

Using the method syntax, the `Count` method was invoked multiple times as well. To define extra data to pass to the next method (what is really done by the `let` clause), you can use the `Select` method to create anonymous types. Here, an anonymous type with `Group` and `Count` properties is created. A collection of items with these properties is passed to the `OrderByDescending` method where the sort is based on the `Count` property of this anonymous type:

```
public static void GroupingWithAnonymousTypes()
{
  var countries = Formula1.GetChampions()
```

```
    .GroupBy(r => r.Country)
    .Select(g => new { Group = g, Count = g.Count() })
    .OrderByDescending(g => g.Count)
    .ThenBy(g => g.Group.Key)
    .Where(g => g.Count >= 2)
    .Select(g => new
    {
      Country = g.Group.Key,
      Count = g.Count
    });
  //...
}
```

Be aware of the number of interim objects created based on the `let` clause or `Select` method. When you query through large lists, the number of objects created that need to be garbage collected later on can have a huge impact on performance.

Grouping with Nested Objects

If the grouped objects should contain nested sequences, you can do that by changing the anonymous type created by the `select` clause. With this example, the returned countries should contain not only the properties for the name of the country and the number of racers, but also a sequence of the names of the racers. This sequence is assigned by using an inner `from`/`in` clause assigned to the `Racers` property. The inner `from` clause is using the `g` group to get all racers from the group, order them by last name, and create a new string based on the first and last name (code file `EnumerableSample/GroupSamples.cs`):

```
public static void GroupingAndNestedObjects()
{
  var countries = from r in Formula1.GetChampions()
                  group r by r.Country into g
                  let count = g.Count()
                  orderby count descending, g.Key
                  where count >= 2
                  select new
                  {
                    Country = g.Key,
                    Count = count,
                    Racers = from r1 in g
                             orderby r1.LastName
                             select r1.FirstName + " " + r1.LastName
                  };

  foreach (var item in countries)
  {
    Console.WriteLine($"{item.Country, -10} {item.Count}");
    foreach (var name in item.Racers)
    {
      Console.Write($"{name}; ");
    }
    Console.WriteLine();
  }
}
```

Using extension methods, the inner Racer objects are created using the group variable g of type IGrouping where the Key property is the key for the grouping—the country in this case—and the items of a group can be accessed using the Group property:

```
public static void GroupingAndNestedObjectsWithMethods()
{
  var countries = Formula1.GetChampions()
    .GroupBy(r => r.Country)
    .Select(g => new
    {
      Group = g,
      Key = g.Key,
      Count = g.Count()
    })
    .OrderByDescending(g => g.Count)
    .ThenBy(g => g.Key)
    .Where(g => g.Count >= 2)
    .Select(g => new
    {
      Country = g.Key,
      Count = g.Count,
      Racers = g.Group.OrderBy(r => r.LastName)
        .Select(r => r.FirstName + " " + r.LastName)
    });
  //...
}
```

The output now lists all champions from the selected countries:

```
UK         10
Jenson Button; Jim Clark; Lewis Hamilton; Mike Hawthorn; Graham Hill;
Damon Hill; James Hunt; Nigel Mansell; Jackie Stewart; John Surtees;
Brazil     3
Emerson Fittipaldi; Nelson Piquet; Ayrton Senna;
Finland    3
Mika Hakkinen; Kimi Raikkonen; Keke Rosberg;
Germany    3
Nico Rosberg; Michael Schumacher; Sebastian Vettel;
Australia  2
Jack Brabham; Alan Jones;
Austria    2
Niki Lauda; Jochen Rindt;
Italy      2
Alberto Ascari; Nino Farina;
USA        2
Mario Andretti; Phil Hill;
```

Inner Join

You can use the join clause to combine two sources based on specific criteria. First, however, let's get two lists that should be joined. With Formula 1, there are drivers and constructor champions. The drivers are returned from the method GetChampions, and the constructors are returned from the method GetConstructorChampions. It would be interesting to get a list that lists the driver and the constructor champions for each year.

To do this, the first two queries for the racers and the teams are defined (code file `EnumerableSample/JoinSamples.cs`):

```
public static void InnerJoin()
{
  var racers = from r in Formula1.GetChampions()
               from y in r.Years
               select new
               {
                 Year = y,
                 Name = r.FirstName + " " + r.LastName
               };

  var teams = from t in Formula1.GetConstructorChampions()
              from y in t.Years
              select new
              {
                Year = y,
                Name = t.Name
              };
  //...
}
```

Using these two queries, a join is done based on the year of the driver champion and the year of the team champion with the `join` clause. The `select` clause defines a new anonymous type containing `Year`, `Racer`, and `Team` properties:

```
var racersAndTeams = (from r in racers
                      join t in teams on r.Year equals t.Year
                      select new
                      {
                        r.Year,
                        Champion = r.Name,
                        Constructor = t.Name
                      }).Take(10);
Console.WriteLine("Year World Champion\t\t  Constructor Title");

foreach (var item in racersAndTeams)
{
  Console.WriteLine($"{item.Year}: {item.Champion,-20} {item.Constructor}");
}
```

Of course, you can also combine this to just one LINQ query, but that's a matter of taste:

```
var racersAndTeams =
  (from r in
   from r1 in Formula1.GetChampions()
   from yr in r1.Years
   select new
   {
     Year = yr,
     Name = r1.FirstName + " " + r1.LastName
   }
   join t in
     from t1 in Formula1.GetConstructorChampions()
     from yt in t1.Years
     select new
```

```
    {
      Year = yt,
      Name = t1.Name
    }
  on r.Year equals t.Year
  orderby t.Year
  select new
  {
    Year = r.Year,
    Racer = r.Name,
    Team = t.Name
  }).Take(10);
```

Using extension methods, the racers and teams can be joined by invoking the `Join` method, passing the teams with the first argument to join them with the racers, specifying the key selectors for the outer and inner collections, and defining the result selector with the last argument (code file `EnumerableSample/JoinSamples.cs`):

```
static void InnerJoinWithMethods()
{
  var racers = Formula1.GetChampions()
    .SelectMany(r => r.Years, (r1, year) =>
    new
    {
      Year = year,
      Name = $"{r1.FirstName} {r1.LastName}"
    });

  var teams = Formula1.GetConstructorChampions()
    .SelectMany(t => t.Years, (t, year) =>
    new
    {
      Year = year,
      Name = t.Name
    });

  var racersAndTeams = racers.Join(
    teams,
    r => r.Year,
    t => t.Year,
    (r, t) =>
      new
      {
        Year = r.Year,
        Champion = r.Name,
        Constructor = t.Name
      }).OrderBy(item => item.Year).Take(10);
  //...
}
```

The output displays data from the anonymous type for the first 10 years in which both a driver and constructor championship took place:

```
Year  World Champion    Constructor Title
1958: Mike Hawthorn     Vanwall
1959: Jack Brabham       Cooper
1960: Jack Brabham       Cooper
```

```
1961: Phil Hill        Ferrari
1962: Graham Hill      BRM
1963: Jim Clark        Lotus
1964: John Surtees     Ferrari
1965: Jim Clark        Lotus
1966: Jack Brabham     Brabham
1967: Denny Hulme      Brabham
```

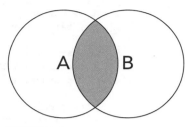

FIGURE 9-1

Figure 9-1 shows a graphical presentation of two collections combined with an inner join. Using an inner join, the results are matches with both collections.

Left Outer Join

The output from the previous join sample started with the year 1958—the first year when both the driver and constructor championships started. The driver championship had started earlier in the year 1950. With an inner join, results are returned only when matching records are found. To get a result with all the years included, you can use a left outer join. A *left outer join* returns all the elements in the left sequence even when no match is found in the right sequence.

The earlier LINQ query is changed to a left outer join. A left outer join is defined with the `join` clause together with the `DefaultIfEmpty` method. If the left side of the query (the racers) does not have a matching constructor champion, the default value for the right side is defined by the `DefaultIfEmpty` method (code file `EnumerableSample/JoinSamples.cs`):

```
public static void LeftOuterJoin()
{
  //...
  var racersAndTeams =
    (from r in racers
     join t in teams on r.Year equals t.Year into rt
     from t in rt.DefaultIfEmpty()
     orderby r.Year
     select new
     {
       Year = r.Year,
       Champion = r.Name,
       Constructor = t == null ? "no constructor championship" : t.Name
     }).Take(10);
  //...
}
```

When you do the same query with the extension methods, you use the `GroupJoin` method. The first three parameters are similar with `Join` and `GroupJoin`. The result of `GroupJoin` is different. Instead of a flat list that is returned from the `Join` method, `GroupJoin` returns a list where every matching item of the first list contains a list of matches from the second list. Using the following `SelectMany` method, the list is flattened again. In case no teams are available for a match, the `Constructors` property is assigned to the default value of the type, which is `null` with classes. Creating the anonymous type, the `Constructor` property gets the string "no constructor championship" assigned if the team is `null` (code file `EnumerableSample/JoinSamples.cs`):

```
public static void LeftOuterJoinWithMethods()
{
  //...
  var racersAndTeams =
    racers.GroupJoin(
      teams,
      r => r.Year,
```

```
      t => t.Year,
      (r, ts) => new
      {
        Year = r.Year,
        Champion = r.Name,
        Constructors = ts
      })
    .SelectMany(
      rt => rt.Constructors.DefaultIfEmpty(),
      (r, t) => new
      {
        Year = r.Year,
        Champion = r.Champion,
        Constructor = t?.Name ?? "no constructor championship"
      });
  //...
}
```

> **NOTE** *Other usages of the* `GroupJoin` *method are shown in the next section.*

When you run the application with this query, the output starts with the year 1950 as shown here:

```
Year Champion             Constructor Title
1950: Nino Farina          no constructor championship
1951: Juan Manuel Fangio   no constructor championship
1952: Alberto Ascari       no constructor championship
1953: Alberto Ascari       no constructor championship
1954: Juan Manuel Fangio   no constructor championship
1955: Juan Manuel Fangio   no constructor championship
1956: Juan Manuel Fangio   no constructor championship
1957: Juan Manuel Fangio   no constructor championship
1958: Mike Hawthorn        Vanwall
1959: Jack Brabham         Cooper
```

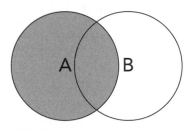

FIGURE 9-2

Figure 9-2 shows a graphical presentation of two collections combined with a left outer join. When you use a left outer join, the results are not just matches with both collections A and B but also include the left collection A.

Group Join

A left outer join makes use of a group join together with the `into` clause. It uses partly the same syntax as the group join. The group join just doesn't need the `DefaultIfEmpty` method.

With a group join, two independent sequences can be joined, whereby one sequence contains a list of items for one element of the other sequence.

The following example uses two independent sequences. One is the list of champions that you already know from previous examples. The second sequence is a collection of `Championship` types. The `Championship` type is shown in the next code snippet. This class contains the year of the championship and the racers with the first, second, and third positions of the year with the properties `Year`, `First`, `Second`, and `Third` (code file `DataLib/Championship.cs`):

```
public record Championship(int Year, string First, string Second,
  string Third);
```

The collection of championships is returned from the method `GetChampionships` as shown in the following code snippet (code file `DataLib/Formula1.cs`):

```
private static List<Championship> s_championships;
public static IEnumerable<Championship> GetChampionships() =>
  s_championships ??= new()
  {
    new (1950, "Nino Farina", "Juan Manuel Fangio", "Luigi Fagioli"),
    new (1951, "Juan Manuel Fangio", "Alberto Ascari", "Froilan Gonzalez"),
    //...
  };
```

The list of champions should be combined with the list of racers that are found within the first three positions in every year of championships, and for every world champion the results for every year should be displayed.

Because in the list of championships every item contains three racers, this list needs to be flattened first. One way to do this is by using a compound `from`. As there's no collection available with a property of a single item, but instead the three properties `First`, `Second`, and `Third` need to be combined and flattened, a new `List<T>` is created that is filled with information from these properties. For a newly created object, custom classes and anonymous types can be used as you've already seen several times. This time, you'll create a tuple. Tuples contain members of different types and can be created using tuple literals with parentheses as shown in the following code snippet. Here, the code creates a flat list of tuples containing the year, position in the championship, first name, and last name information from racers (code file `EnumerableSample/JoinSamples.cs`):

```
static void GroupJoin()
{
  var racers = from cs in Formula1.GetChampionships()
               from r in new List<
                 (int Year, int Position, string FirstName, string LastName)>()
               {
                 (cs.Year, Position: 1, FirstName: cs.First.FirstName(),
                  LastName: cs.First.LastName()),
                 (cs.Year, Position: 2, FirstName: cs.Second.FirstName(),
                  LastName: cs.Second.LastName()),
                 (cs.Year, Position: 3, FirstName: cs.Third.FirstName(),
                  LastName: cs.Third.LastName())
               }
               select r;
  //...
}
```

The extension methods `FirstName` and `LastName` just use the last blank character to split up the string (code file `EnumerableSample/StringExtensions.cs`):

```
public static class StringExtensions
{
  public static string FirstName(this string name) =>
    name.Substring(0, name.LastIndexOf(' '));

  public static string LastName(this string name) =>
    name.Substring(name.LastIndexOf(' ') + 1);
}
```

With a join clause, the racers from both lists can be combined. `Formula1.GetChampions` returns a list of `Racers`, and the `racers` variable returns the list of tuples that contains the year, the result, and the names of racers. It's not enough to compare the items from these two collections by using the last name. Sometimes a racer and his father can be found in the list (for example, Damon Hill and Graham Hill), so it's necessary to compare the items by both `FirstName` and `LastName`. You do this by creating a new tuple type for both lists. Using the `into` clause, the result from the second collection is put into the variable `yearResults`. `yearResults` is created for every racer in the first collection and contains the results of the matching first name and last name from the second collection. Finally, with the LINQ query, a new tuple type is created that contains the needed information (code file `EnumerableSample/JoinSamples.cs`):

```
static void GroupJoin()
{
  //...
  var q = (from r in Formula1.GetChampions()
          join r2 in racers on
          (
            r.FirstName,
            r.LastName
          )
          equals
          (
            r2.FirstName,
            r2.LastName
          )
          into yearResults
          select
          (
            r.FirstName,
            r.LastName,
            r.Wins,
            r.Starts,
            Results: yearResults
          ));

  foreach (var r in q)
  {
    Console.WriteLine($"{r.FirstName} {r.LastName}");
    foreach (var results in r.Results)
    {
      Console.WriteLine($"\t{results.Year} {results.Position}");
    }
  }
}
```

The last results from the `foreach` loop are shown next. Jenson Button has been among the top three for three years—in 2004 as third, 2009 as first, and 2011 as second; Sebastian Vettel was world champion four times, had the second position three times, and the third in 2015; and Nico Rosberg was world champion in 2016 and in the second position two times:

```
Jenson Button
        2004 3
        2009 1
        2011 2
Sebastian Vettel
        2009 2
        2010 1
        2011 1
        2012 1
        2013 1
        2015 3
        2017 2
        2018 2
```

```
Nico Rosberg
        2014 2
        2015 2
        2016 1
```

Using `GroupJoin` with extension methods, the syntax probably looks a bit easier to catch. First, the compound from is done with the `SelectMany` method. This part is not very different, and tuples are used again. The `GroupJoin` method is invoked by passing the racers with the first parameter to join the champions with the flattened racers, and the match for both collections with the second and third parameters. The fourth parameter receives the racer from the first collection and a collection of the second. These are the results containing the position and the year which are written to the `Results` tuple member (code file `EnumerableSample/Program.cs`):

```csharp
static void GroupJoinWithMethods()
{
  var racers = Formula1.GetChampionships()
    .SelectMany(cs => new List<(int Year, int Position, string FirstName,
      string LastName)>
    {
      (cs.Year, Position: 1, FirstName: cs.First.FirstName(),
        LastName: cs.First.LastName()),
      (cs.Year, Position: 2, FirstName: cs.Second.FirstName(),
        LastName: cs.Second.LastName()),
      (cs.Year, Position: 3, FirstName: cs.Third.FirstName(),
        LastName: cs.Third.LastName())
    });

  var q = Formula1.GetChampions()
    .GroupJoin(racers,
      r1 => (r1.FirstName, r1.LastName),
      r2 => (r2.FirstName, r2.LastName),
      (r1, r2s) => (r1.FirstName, r1.LastName, r1.Wins, r1.Starts,
        Results: r2s));
  //...
}
```

Set Operations

The extension methods `Distinct`, `Union`, `Intersect`, and `Except` are *set* operations. The following example creates a sequence of Formula 1 champions driving a Ferrari and another sequence of Formula 1 champions driving a McLaren and then determines whether any driver has been a champion driving both of these cars. Of course, that's where the `Intersect` extension method can help.

First, you need to get all champions driving a Ferrari. This uses a simple LINQ query with a compound from to access the property `Cars` that's returning a sequence of string objects:

```csharp
var ferrariDrivers = from r in Formula1.GetChampions()
                     from c in r.Cars
                     where c == "Ferrari"
                     orderby r.LastName
                     select r;
```

Now the same query with a different parameter of the `where` clause is needed to get all McLaren racers. It's not a good idea to write the same query again. Another option is to create a method in which you can pass the parameter car. In case the method wouldn't be needed in other places, you can create a local function. `racersByCar` is the name of a local function that is implemented as a lambda expression containing a LINQ query. The local function `racersByCar` is defined within the scope of the method `SetOperations`, and thus it can only be invoked within this method. The LINQ `Intersect` extension method is used to get all racers who won the championship with a Ferrari and a McLaren (code file `EnumerableSample/LinqSamples.cs`):

```
static void SetOperations()
{
  IEnumerable<Racer> racersByCar(string car) =>
    from r in Formula1.GetChampions()
    from c in r.Cars
    where c == car
    orderby r.LastName
    select r;

  Console.WriteLine("World champion with Ferrari and McLaren");
  foreach (var racer in racersByCar("Ferrari").Intersect(racersByCar("McLaren")))
  {
    Console.WriteLine(racer);
  }
}
```

The result is just one racer, Niki Lauda:

```
World champion with Ferrari and McLaren
Niki Lauda
```

> **NOTE** *The set operations compare the objects by invoking the* `GetHashCode` *and* `Equals` *methods of the entity class. For custom comparisons, you can also pass an object that implements the interface* `IEqualityComparer<T>`*. In the preceding example, the* `GetChampions` *method always returns the same objects, so the default comparison works. If that's not the case, the set methods offer overloads in which a comparison can be defined.*

Zip

The `Zip` method enables you to merge two related sequences into one with a predicate function.

First, two related sequences are created, both with the same filtering (country Italy) and ordering. For merging, this is important because item 1 from the first collection is merged with item 1 from the second collection, item 2 with item 2, and so on. In case the count of the two sequences is different, `Zip` stops when the end of the smaller collection is reached.

The items in the first collection have a `Name` property, and the items in the second collection have `LastName` and `Starts` properties.

Using the `Zip` method on the collection, `racerNames` requires the second collection `racerNamesAndStarts` as the first parameter. The second parameter is of type `Func<TFirst, TSecond, TResult>`. This parameter is implemented as a lambda expression and receives the elements of the first collection with the parameter `first`, and the elements of the second collection with the parameter `second`. The implementation creates and returns a string containing the `Name` property of the first element and the `Starts` property of the second element (code file `EnumerableSample/LinqSamples.cs`):

```
static void ZipOperation()
{
  var racerNames = from r in Formula1.GetChampions()
                   where r.Country == "Italy"
                   orderby r.Wins descending
```

```
            select new
            {
              Name = r.FirstName + " " + r.LastName
            };

    var racerNamesAndStarts = from r in Formula1.GetChampions()
                              where r.Country == "Italy"
                              orderby r.Wins descending
                              select new
                              {
                                r.LastName,
                                r.Starts
                              };

    var racers = racerNames.Zip(racerNamesAndStarts,
                (first, second) => first.Name + ", starts: " + second.Starts);

    foreach (var r in racers)
    {
      Console.WriteLine(r);
    }
}
```

The result of this merge is shown here:

```
Alberto Ascari, starts: 32
Nino Farina, starts: 33
```

Partitioning

Partitioning operations such as the extension methods Take and Skip can be used for easy paging—for example, to display just five racers on the first page, and continue with the next five on the following pages.

With the LINQ query shown here, the extension methods Skip and Take are added to the end of the query. The Skip method first ignores a number of items calculated based on the page size and the actual page number; the Take method then takes a number of items based on the page size (code file EnumerableSample/LinqSamples.cs):

```
public static void Partitioning()
{
  int pageSize = 5;
  int numberPages = (int)Math.Ceiling(Formula1.GetChampions().Count() /
    (double)pageSize);

  for (int page = 0; page < numberPages; page++)
  {
    Console.WriteLine($"Page {page}");

    var racers = (from r in Formula1.GetChampions()
                  orderby r.LastName, r.FirstName
                  select r.FirstName + " " + r.LastName)
                 .Skip(page * pageSize).Take(pageSize);

    foreach (var name in racers)
    {
      Console.WriteLine(name);
```

```
        }
      Console.WriteLine();
    }
  }
```

Here is the output of the first three pages:

```
Page 0
Fernando Alonso
Mario Andretti
Alberto Ascari
Jack Brabham
Jenson Button

Page 1
Jim Clark
Juan Manuel Fangio
Nino Farina
Emerson Fittipaldi
Mika Hakkinen

Page 2
Lewis Hamilton
Mike Hawthorn
Damon Hill
Graham Hill
Phil Hill
```

Paging can be extremely useful with Windows or web applications for showing the user only a part of the data.

> **NOTE** *This paging mechanism has an important behavior: Because the query is done with every page, changing the underlying data affects the results (for example when accessing a database). New objects are shown as paging continues. Depending on your scenario, this can be advantageous to your application. If this behavior is not what you need, you can do the paging not over the original data source but by using a cache that maps to the original data.*

With the `TakeWhile` and `SkipWhile` extension methods, you can also pass a predicate to retrieve or skip items based on the result of the predicate.

Aggregate Operators

The aggregate operators such as `Count`, `Sum`, `Min`, `Max`, `Average`, and `Aggregate` do not return a sequence; instead they return a single value.

The `Count` extension method returns the number of items in the collection. In the following example, the `Count` method is applied to the `Years` property of a `Racer` to filter the racers and return only those who won more than three championships. Because the same count is needed more than once in the same query, a variable `numberYears` is defined by using the `let` clause (code file EnumerableSample/LinqSamples.cs):

```
static void AggregateCount()
{
  var query = from r in Formula1.GetChampions()
              let numberYears = r.Years.Count()
              where numberYears >= 3
```

```
                              orderby numberYears descending, r.LastName
                              select new
                              {
                                Name = r.FirstName + " " + r.LastName,
                                TimesChampion = numberYears
                              };

                    foreach (var r in query)
                    {
                      Console.WriteLine($"{r.Name} {r.TimesChampion}");
                    }
                  }
```

The result is shown here:

```
Michael Schumacher 7
Lewis Hamilton 6
Juan Manuel Fangio 5
Alain Prost 4
Sebastian Vettel 4
Jack Brabham 3
Niki Lauda 3
Nelson Piquet 3
Ayrton Senna 3
Jackie Stewart 3
```

The Sum method summarizes all numbers of a sequence and returns the result. In the next example, Sum is used to calculate the sum of all race wins for a country. First the racers are grouped based on country; then, with the new anonymous type created, the Wins property is assigned to the sum of all wins from a single country (code file EnumerableSample/Program.cs):

```
static void AggregateSum()
{
  var countries = (from c in
                     from r in Formula1.GetChampions()
                     group r by r.Country into c
                     select new
                     {
                       Country = c.Key,
                       Wins = (from r1 in c
                                 select r1.Wins).Sum()
                     }
                     orderby c.Wins descending, c.Country
                     select c).Take(5);

  foreach (var country in countries)
  {
    Console.WriteLine($"{country.Country} {country.Wins}");
  }
}
```

The most successful countries based on the Formula 1 race champions are as follows:

```
UK 245
Germany 168
Brazil 78
France 51
Finland 46
```

The methods `Min`, `Max`, `Average`, and `Aggregate` are used in the same way as `Count` and `Sum`. `Min` returns the minimum number of the values in the collection, and `Max` returns the maximum number. `Average` calculates the average number. With the `Aggregate` method, you can pass a lambda expression that performs an aggregation of all the values.

Conversion Operators

In this chapter, you've already seen that query execution is deferred until the items are accessed. Using the query within an iteration, the query is executed. With a conversion operator, the query is executed immediately and the result is returned in an array, a list, or a dictionary.

In the next example, the `ToList` extension method is invoked to immediately execute the query and put the result into a `List<T>` (code file `EnumerableSample/LinqSamples.cs`):

```
static void ToList()
{
  List<Racer> racers = (from r in Formula1.GetChampions()
                        where r.Starts > 220
                        orderby r.Starts descending
                        select r).ToList();

  foreach (var racer in racers)
  {
    Console.WriteLine($"{racer} {racer:S}");
  }
}
```

The result of this query shows Jenson Button first:

```
Kimi Räikkönen 323
Fernando Alonso 314
Jenson Button 306
Michael Schumacher 287
Lewis Hamilton 260
Sebastian Vettel 250
```

It's not always that simple to get the returned objects into the list. For example, for fast access from a car to a racer within a collection class, you can use the new class `Lookup<TKey, TElement>`.

> **NOTE** *The* `Dictionary<TKey, TValue>` *class supports only a single value for a key. With the class* `Lookup<TKey, TElement>` *from the namespace* `System.Linq`, *you can have multiple values for a single key. These classes are covered in detail in Chapter 8, "Collections."*

In the following example when you use the compound `from` query, the sequence of racers and cars is flattened, and an anonymous type with the properties `Car` and `Racer` is created. With the lookup that is returned, the key should be of type `string` referencing the car, and the value should be of type `Racer`. To make this selection, you can pass a key and an element selector to one overload of the `ToLookup` method. The key selector references the `Car` property, and the element selector references the `Racer` property:

```
public static void ToLookup()
{
  var racers = (from r in Formula1.GetChampions()
                from c in r.Cars
```

```
                   select new
                   {
                     Car = c,
                     Racer = r
                   }).ToLookup(cr => cr.Car, cr => cr.Racer);

  foreach (var williamsRacer in racers["Williams"])
  {
    Console.WriteLine(williamsRacer);
  }
}
```

The result of all "Williams" champions accessed using the indexer of the `Lookup` class is shown here:

```
Alan Jones
Keke Rosberg
Nelson Piquet
Nigel Mansell
Alain Prost
Damon Hill
Jacques Villeneuve
```

In case you need to use a LINQ query over an untyped collection, such as the `ArrayList`, you can use the `Cast` method. In the following example, an `ArrayList` collection that is based on the `Object` type is filled with `Racer` objects. To make it possible to define a strongly typed query, you can use the `Cast` method:

```
public static void ConvertWithCast()
{
  var list = new System.Collections.ArrayList(Formula1.GetChampions()
    as System.Collections.ICollection);

  var query = from r in list.Cast<Racer>()
              where r.Country == "USA"
              orderby r.Wins descending
              select r;

  foreach (var racer in query)
  {
    Console.WriteLine($"{racer:A}");
  }
}
```

The results include the only Formula 1 champion from the United States:

```
Mario Andretti, country: USA, starts: 128, wins: 12
Phil Hill, country: USA, starts: 48, wins: 3
```

Generation Operators

The generation operators `Range`, `Empty`, and `Repeat` are not extension methods but normal static methods that return sequences. With LINQ to Objects, these methods are available with the `Enumerable` class.

Have you ever needed a range of numbers filled? Nothing is easier than using the `Range` method. This method receives the start value with the first parameter and the number of items with the second parameter:

```
static void GenerateRange()
{
```

```
var values = Enumerable.Range(1, 20);
foreach (var item in values)
{
  Console.Write($"{item} ", item);
}
Console.WriteLine();
}
```

> **NOTE** *The* `Range` *method does not return a collection filled with the values as defined. This method does a deferred query execution similar to the other methods. It returns a* `RangeEnumerator` *that simply does a* `yield` `return` *with the values incremented.*

Of course, the result now looks like this:

```
1 2 3 4 5 6 7 8 9 10 11 12 13 14 15 16 17 18 19 20
```

You can combine the result with other extension methods to get a different result—for example, using the `Select` extension method:

```
var values = Enumerable.Range(1, 20).Select(n => n * 3);
```

The `Empty` method returns an iterator that does not return values. This can be used for parameters that require a collection for which you can pass an empty collection.

The `Repeat` method returns an iterator that returns the same value a specific number of times.

PARALLEL LINQ

The class `ParallelEnumerable` in the `System.Linq` namespace splits the work of queries across multiple threads that run simultaneously on multiple processors. Although the `Enumerable` class defines extension methods to the `IEnumerable<T>` interface, most extension methods of the `ParallelEnumerable` class are extensions for the class `ParallelQuery<TSource>`. One important exception is the `AsParallel` method, which extends `IEnumerable<TSource>` and returns `ParallelQuery<TSource>`, so a normal collection class can be queried in a parallel manner.

Parallel Queries

To demonstrate Parallel LINQ (PLINQ), a large collection is needed. With small collections, you don't see any effect when the collection fits inside the CPU's cache. In the following code, a large `int` collection is filled with random values (code file `ParallelLinqSample/Program.cs`):

```
static IEnumerable<int> SampleData()
{
  const int arraySize = 500_00_000;
  var r = new Random();
  return Enumerable.Range(0, arraySize).Select(x => r.Next(140)).ToList();
}
```

Now you can use a LINQ query to filter the data, do some calculations, and get an average of the filtered data. The query defines a filter with the `where` clause to summarize only the items with values whose natural logarithm is less than four, and then the aggregation function `Average` is invoked. The only difference from the LINQ queries you've seen so far is the call to the `AsParallel` method:

```
static void LinqQuery(IEnumerable<int> data)
{
  var res = (from x in data.AsParallel()
             where Math.Log(x) < 4
             select x).Average();
  //...
}
```

Like the LINQ queries shown already, the compiler changes the syntax to invoke the methods `AsParallel`, `Where`, `Select`, and `Average`. `AsParallel` is defined with the `ParallelEnumerable` class to extend the `IEnumerable<T>` interface, so it can be called with a simple array. `AsParallel` returns `ParallelQuery<TSource>`. Because of the returned type, the `Where` method chosen by the compiler is `ParallelEnumerable.Where` instead of `Enumerable.Where`.

In the following code, the `Select` and `Average` methods are from `ParallelEnumerable` as well. In contrast to the implementation of the `Enumerable` class, with the `ParallelEnumerable` class, the query is *partitioned* so that multiple threads can work on the query. The collection can be split into multiple parts whereby different threads work on each part to filter the remaining items. After the partitioned work is completed, *merging* must occur to get the summary result of all parts:

```
static void ExtensionMethods(IEnumerable<int> data)
{
  var res = data.AsParallel()
    .Where(x => Math.Log(x) < 4)
    .Select(x => x).Average();
  //...
}
```

When you run this code, you can also start the task manager so you can confirm that all CPUs of your system are busy. If you remove the `AsParallel` method, multiple CPUs might not be used. Of course, if you don't have multiple CPUs on your system, then don't expect to see an improvement with the parallel version. On my system with 8 logical processors, the method runs 0.351 seconds with `AsParallel` and 1.23 seconds without.

> **NOTE** *You can customize parallel queries using extension methods such as* `WithExecutionMode`, `WithDegreeOfParallelism`, *and even custom partitioners. With* `WithExecutionMode` *you can pass a value of* `ParallelExecutionMode`, *which can be* `Default` *or* `ForceParallelism`. *By default, Parallel LINQ avoids parallelism with high overhead. With the method* `WithDegreeOfParallelism`, *you can pass an integer value to specify the maximum number of tasks that should run in parallel. This is useful if not all CPU cores should be used by the query. .NET contains specific partitioners that are used based on the collection types, e.g. for arrays, and the generic List type. You might have different requirements, or specific collection types with other layouts that could take advantage of partitioning of the data in other ways. Here you can write a custom partitioner deriving from the generic base classes* `OrderablePartitioner` *or* `Partitioner` *in the namespace* `System.Collections.Generic`.

Cancellation

.NET offers a standard way to cancel long-running tasks, and this is also true for Parallel LINQ. The classes needed for cancellation are defined in the `System.Threading` namespace.

To cancel a long-running query, you can add the method `WithCancellation` to the query and pass a `CancellationToken` to the parameter. The `CancellationToken` is created from the `CancellationTokenSource` instance that you create. The query is run in a separate thread where the exception of type `OperationCanceledException` is caught. This exception is fired if the query is canceled. From the main thread, the task can be canceled by invoking the `Cancel` method of the `CancellationTokenSource` (code file `ParallelLinqSample/Program.cs`):

```
public static void UseCancellation(IEnumerable<int> data)
{
  CancellationTokenSource cts = new();

  Task.Run(() =>
  {
    try
    {
      var res = (from x in data.AsParallel().WithCancellation(cts.Token)
                 where Math.Log(x) < 4
                 select x).Average();

      Console.WriteLine($"Query finished, sum: {res}");
    }
    catch (OperationCanceledException ex)
    {
      Console.WriteLine(ex.Message);
    }
  });
  Console.WriteLine("Query started");
  Console.Write("Cancel? ");
  string input = Console.ReadLine();
  if (input.ToLower().Equals("y"))
  {
    cts.Cancel();
  }
}
```

> **NOTE** *You can read more about cancellation and the* `CancellationToken` *in Chapter 17, "Parallel Programming."*

EXPRESSION TREES

With LINQ to Objects, the extension methods require a delegate type as parameter; this way, a lambda expression can be assigned to the parameter. Lambda expressions can also be assigned to parameters of type `Expression<T>`. The C# compiler defines different behavior for lambda expressions depending on the type. If the type is `Expression<T>`, the compiler creates an expression tree from the lambda expression and stores it in the assembly. The expression tree can be analyzed during runtime and optimized for querying against the data source.

Consider the following query:

```
var brazilRacers = from r in Formula1.GetChampions()
                   where r.Country == "Brazil"
                   orderby r.Wins descending
                   select r;
```

The preceding query expression uses the extension methods `Where`, `OrderByDescending`, and `Select`. The `Enumerable` class defines the `Where` extension method with the delegate type `Func<T, bool>` as a parameter predicate:

```
public static IEnumerable<TSource> Where<TSource>(
    this IEnumerable<TSource> source, Func<TSource, bool> predicate);
```

This way, the lambda expression is assigned to the predicate. Here, the lambda expression is similar to an anonymous method, as explained earlier:

```
Func<Racer, bool> predicate = r => r.Country == "Brazil";
```

The `Enumerable` class is not the only class for defining the `Where` extension method. The `Where` extension method is also defined by the class `Queryable<T>`. This class has a different definition of the `Where` extension method:

```
public static IQueryable<TSource> Where<TSource>(
    this IQueryable<TSource> source,
    Expression<Func<TSource, bool>> predicate);
```

Here, the lambda expression is assigned to the type `Expression<T>` (namespace `System.Linq.Expressions`) which behaves differently:

```
Expression<Func<Racer, bool>> predicate = r => r.Country == "Brazil";
```

Instead of using delegates, the compiler emits an expression tree to the assembly. The expression tree can be read during runtime. Expression trees are built from classes derived from the abstract base class `Expression`. The `Expression` class is not the same as `Expression<T>`. Some of the expression classes that inherit from `Expression` include `BinaryExpression`, `ConstantExpression`, `InvocationExpression`, `LambdaExpression`, `NewExpression`, `NewArrayExpression`, `TernaryExpression`, `UnaryExpression`, and more. The compiler creates an expression tree resulting from the lambda expression.

For example, the lambda expression `r.Country == "Brazil"` makes use of `ParameterExpression`, `MemberExpression`, `ConstantExpression`, and `MethodCallExpression` to create a tree and store the tree in the assembly. This tree is then used during runtime to create an optimized query to the underlying data source.

With the sample application, the method `DisplayTree` is implemented to display an expression tree graphically on the console. In the following example, an `Expression` object can be passed, and depending on the expression type, some information about the expression is written to the console. Depending on the type of the expression, `DisplayTree` is called recursively (code file `ExpressionTreeSample/Program.cs`):

```
static void DisplayTree(int indent, string message,
    Expression expression)
{
    string output = $"{string.Empty.PadLeft(indent, '>')} {message}" +
        $"! NodeType: {expression.NodeType}; Expr: {expression}";

    indent++;

    switch (expression.NodeType)
    {
        case ExpressionType.Lambda:
            Console.WriteLine(output);
            LambdaExpression lambdaExpr = (LambdaExpression)expression;
            foreach (var parameter in lambdaExpr.Parameters)
            {
                DisplayTree(indent, "Parameter", parameter);
            }
```

```
        DisplayTree(indent, "Body", lambdaExpr.Body);
        break;
    case ExpressionType.Constant:
        ConstantExpression constExpr = (ConstantExpression)expression;
        Console.WriteLine($"{output} Const Value: {constExpr.Value}");
        break;
    case ExpressionType.Parameter:
        ParameterExpression paramExpr = (ParameterExpression)expression;
        Console.WriteLine($"{output} Param Type: {paramExpr.Type.Name}");
        break;
    case ExpressionType.Equal:
    case ExpressionType.AndAlso:
    case ExpressionType.GreaterThan:
        BinaryExpression binExpr = (BinaryExpression)expression;
        if (binExpr.Method != null)
        {
            Console.WriteLine($"{output} Method: {binExpr.Method.Name}");
        }
        else
        {
            Console.WriteLine(output);
        }
        DisplayTree(indent, "Left", binExpr.Left);
        DisplayTree(indent, "Right", binExpr.Right);
        break;
    case ExpressionType.MemberAccess:
        MemberExpression memberExpr = (MemberExpression)expression;
        Console.WriteLine($"{output} Member Name: {memberExpr.Member.Name}, " +
            " Type: {memberExpr.Expression}");
        DisplayTree(indent, "Member Expr", memberExpr.Expression);
        break;
    default:
        Console.WriteLine();
        Console.WriteLine($"{expression.NodeType} {expression.Type.Name}");
        break;
    }
}
```

> **NOTE** The method `DisplayTree` does not deal with all expression types—only the types
> that are used with the following example expression.

The expression that is used for showing the tree is already well known. It's a lambda expression with a `Racer`
parameter, and the body of the expression takes racers from Brazil only if they have won more than six races.
This expression is passed to the `DisplayTree` method to see the tree:

```
Expression<Func<Racer, bool>> expression =
    r => r.Country == "Brazil" && r.Wins > 6;

DisplayTree(0, "Lambda", expression);
```

Looking at the tree result, you can see from the output that the lambda expression consists of a `Parameter` and an `AndAlso` node type. The `AndAlso` node type has an `Equal` node type to the left and a `GreaterThan` node type to the right. The `Equal` node type to the left of the `AndAlso` node type has a `MemberAccess` node type to the left and a `Constant` node type to the right, and so on:

```
Lambda! NodeType: Lambda; Expr: r => ((r.Country == "Brazil") AndAlso (r.Wins > 6))
> Parameter! NodeType: Parameter; Expr: r Param Type: Racer
> Body! NodeType: AndAlso; Expr: ((r.Country == "Brazil") AndAlso (r.Wins > 6))
>> Left! NodeType: Equal; Expr: (r.Country == "Brazil") Method: op_Equality
>>> Left! NodeType: MemberAccess; Expr: r.Country Member Name: Country, Type: String
>>>> Member Expr! NodeType: Parameter; Expr: r Param Type: Racer
>>> Right! NodeType: Constant; Expr: "Brazil" Const Value: Brazil
>> Right! NodeType: GreaterThan; Expr: (r.Wins > 6)
>>> Left! NodeType: MemberAccess; Expr: r.Wins Member Name: Wins, Type: Int32
>>>> Member Expr! NodeType: Parameter; Expr: r Param Type: Racer
>>> Right! NodeType: Constant; Expr: 6 Const Value: 6
```

Entity Framework Core (EF Core) is an example where the `Expression<T>` type is used. EF Core providers convert LINQ expression trees to SQL statements.

LINQ PROVIDERS

.NET includes several LINQ providers. A LINQ provider implements the standard query operators for a specific data source. LINQ providers might implement more extension methods than are defined by LINQ, but the standard operators must at least be implemented. LINQ to XML implements additional methods that are particularly useful with XML, such as the methods `Elements`, `Descendants`, and `Ancestors` defined by the class `Extensions` in the `System.Xml.Linq` namespace.

Implementation of the LINQ provider is selected based on the namespace and the type of the first parameter. The namespace of the class that implements the extension methods must be opened; otherwise, the extension class is not in scope. The parameter of the `Where` method defined by LINQ to Objects and the `Where` method defined by LINQ to Entities is different.

The `Where` method of LINQ to Objects is defined with the `Enumerable` class:

```
public static IEnumerable<TSource> Where<TSource>(
    this IEnumerable<TSource> source, Func<TSource, bool> predicate);
```

Inside the `System.Linq` namespace is another class that implements the operator `Where`. This implementation is used by LINQ to Entities. You can find the implementation in the class `Queryable`:

```
public static IQueryable<TSource> Where<TSource>(
    this IQueryable<TSource> source,
    Expression<Func<TSource, bool>> predicate);
```

Both of these classes are implemented in the `System.Core` assembly in the `System.Linq` namespace. How does the compiler select what method to use, and what's the magic in the `Expression` type? The lambda expression is the same regardless of whether it is passed with a `Func<TSource, bool>` parameter or an `Expression<Func<TSource, bool>>` parameter—only the compiler behaves differently. The selection is done based on the `source` parameter. The method that matches best based on its parameters is chosen by the compiler. Properties of Entity Framework Core contexts are of type `DbSet<TEntity>`. `DbSet<TEntity>` implements `IQueryable<TEntity>`, and thus Entity Framework Core uses the `Where` method of the `Queryable` class.

SUMMARY

This chapter described and demonstrated the LINQ query and the language constructs on which the query is based, such as extension methods and lambda expressions. You've looked at the various LINQ query operators—not only for filtering and ordering of data sources, but also for partitioning, grouping, doing conversions, joins, and so on.

With Parallel LINQ, you've seen how longer queries can easily be parallelized.

Another important concept of this chapter is the expression tree. Expression trees allow a program to build the tree at compile time, store it in the assembly, and then optimize it at runtime. You can read about its great advantages in Chapter 21.

The next chapter covers error handling—getting into the `try`, `catch`, and `throw` keywords.

10

Errors and Exceptions

WHAT'S IN THIS CHAPTER?

➤ Looking at the exception classes

➤ Using `try...catch...finally` to capture exceptions

➤ Filtering exceptions

➤ Creating user-defined exceptions

➤ Retrieving caller information

CODE DOWNLOADS FOR THIS CHAPTER

The source code for this chapter is available on the book page at www.wiley.com. Click the Downloads link. The code can also be found at `https://github.com/ProfessionalCSharp/ProfessionalCSharp2021` in the directory `1_CS/ErrorsAndExceptions`.

The code for this chapter is divided into the following major examples:

➤ SimpleExceptions

➤ ExceptionFilters

➤ RethrowExceptions

➤ SolicitColdCall

➤ CallerInformation

All the sample projects have nullable reference types configured.

HANDLING ERRORS

Errors happen, and they are not always caused by the person who coded the application. Sometimes your application generates an error because of an action that was initiated by the end user of the application, or it might be simply due to the environmental context in which your code is running. In any case, you should anticipate errors occurring in your applications and code accordingly.

.NET has enhanced the ways in which you deal with errors. C#'s mechanism for handling error conditions enables you to provide custom handling for each type of error condition and to separate the code that identifies errors from the code that handles them.

Your programs should be capable of handling any possible errors that might occur. For example, in the middle of some complex processing of your code, you might discover that it doesn't have permission to read a file; or, while it is sending network requests, the network might go down. In such exceptional situations, it is not enough for a method to simply return an appropriate error code—there might be 15 or 20 nested method calls, so what you really want the program to do is jump back up through all those calls to exit the task completely and take the appropriate counteractions. The C# language has very good facilities for handling this kind of situation through the mechanism known as *exception handling*.

This chapter covers catching and throwing exceptions in many different scenarios. You see exception types from different namespaces and their hierarchy, and you find out how to create custom exception types. You discover different ways to catch exceptions—for example, how to catch exceptions with the exact exception type or a base class. You also see how to deal with nested `try` blocks and how you could catch exceptions that way. For code that should be invoked no matter whether an exception occurs or the code continues with any error, you are introduced to creating `try`/`finally` code blocks.

By the end of this chapter, you will have a good grasp of advanced exception handling in your C# applications.

PREDEFINED EXCEPTION CLASSES

In C#, an exception is an object created (or *thrown*) when a particular exceptional error condition occurs. This object contains information that should help identify the problem. Although you can create your own exception classes (and you do so later), .NET includes many predefined exception classes. You can find all the .NET exceptions in the Microsoft documentation in the list of classes that derive from the `Exception` base class at `https://docs.microsoft.com/dotnet/api/system.exception`. This large list only shows the exceptions that directly derive from `Exception`. When you click every other base class, for example `https://docs.microsoft.com/en-us/dotnet/api/system.systemexception`, you see another large list of exception classes driving from `SystemException`.

Here some really important exception types are explained:

➤ When receiving arguments with a method, you should check the arguments to determine whether they contain values as expected. If this is not the case, you can throw an `ArgumentException` or an exception that derives from this exception class like `ArgumentNullException` and `ArgumentOutOfRangeException`.

➤ The `NotSupportedException` is thrown when a method is not supported—for example, from classes that implement interfaces but do not implement all the members of the interface. You should not invoke methods that throw this exception, so you should not handle this exception. This exception gives good information during development time to change your code.

➤ The `StackOverflowException` is thrown by the runtime when the area of memory allocated for the stack is full. A stack overflow can occur if a method continuously calls itself recursively. This is generally a fatal error because it prevents your application from doing anything apart from terminating (in which case it is unlikely that even the finally block will execute). Trying to handle errors like this yourself is usually pointless; instead, you should have the application gracefully exit.

➤ The `OverflowException` is thrown after an arithmetic calculation and the value does not fit into the variable type—in a checked context. Remember, you can create checked contexts with the checked keyword. Within the checked context, if you attempt to cast an `int` containing a value of –40 to an `uint`, an `OverflowException` is thrown. Creating checked contexts is covered in Chapter 5, "Operators and Casts."

➤ For exceptions with file I/O, the base class `IOException` is defined. `FileLoadException`, `FileNotFoundException`, `EndOfStreamException`, and `DriveNotFoundException` are some examples that derive from this base class.

➤ The `InvalidOperationException` is typically thrown if methods of a class are not invoked in the correct order, for example, an initialization call was missing.

➤ The `TaskCanceledException` is thrown on cancellation of tasks or timeouts.

> **NOTE** *Read the Microsoft documentation for methods you invoke. Every method that might throw exceptions has documentation in the section "Exceptions" of which exceptions can be thrown. For example, the documentation for* `GetStreamSync` *from the* `HttpClient` *class (*`https://docs.microsoft.com/en-us/dotnet/api/system.net.http`
`.httpclient.getstreamasync`*) lists* `ArgumentNullException`, `HttpRequestException`, *and* `TaskCanceledException`.

> **NOTE** *Looking at the hierarchy of the exception types, you might be wondering about the purpose of the base classes* `SystemException` *and* `ApplicationException`. *With the original design of .NET, it was planned to have* `SystemException` *as a base class for all exceptions thrown from the runtime, and* `ApplicationException` *as a base class for all application-defined exceptions. As it turned out,* `ApplicationException` *was rarely used as the base class for specific exceptions. Nowadays, it's okay to directly derive your custom exception from the* `Exception` *base class.*

CATCHING EXCEPTIONS

Given that .NET includes a selection of predefined base class exception objects, this section describes how you use them in your code to trap error conditions. In dealing with possible error conditions in C# code, you typically divide the relevant part of your program into blocks of three different types:

➤ `try` blocks encapsulate the code that forms part of the normal operation of your program and that might encounter some serious error conditions.

➤ `catch` blocks encapsulate the code dealing with the various error conditions that your code might have encountered by working through any of the code in the accompanying `try` block. This block could also be used for logging errors.

➤ `finally` blocks encapsulate the code that cleans up any resources or takes any other action that you normally want handled at the end of a `try` or `catch` block. It is important to understand that the `finally` block is executed whether an exception is thrown. Because the purpose of the `finally` block is to contain cleanup code that should always be executed, the compiler flags an error if you place a return statement inside a `finally` block. An example of using the `finally` block is closing any connections that were opened in the `try` block. Understand that the `finally` block is completely optional. If your application does not require any cleanup code (such as disposing of or closing any open objects), then there is no need for this block.

> **NOTE** `finally` *blocks are a great way to write some cleanup code. This block is executed in every case the* `try`/`finally` *block is left. It's executed on a successful return of the* `try` *block and also executed if an exception is thrown.*

The following steps outline how these blocks work together to trap error conditions:

1. The execution flow first enters the `try` block.

2. If no errors occur in the `try` block, execution proceeds normally through the block, and when the end of the `try` block is reached, the flow of execution jumps to the `finally` block if one is present (step 5). However, if an error does occur within the `try` block, execution jumps to a `catch` block (step 3).

3. The error condition is handled in the `catch` block.

4. At the end of the `catch` block, execution automatically transfers to the `finally` block if one is present.

5. The `finally` block is executed (if present).

The C# syntax used to bring all this about looks roughly like this:

```
try
{
  // code for normal execution
}
catch
{
  // error handling
}
finally
{
  // clean up
}
```

A few variations on this theme exist:

➤ You can omit the `finally` block because it is optional.

➤ You can also supply as many `catch` blocks as you want to handle specific types of errors. However, you don't want to get too carried away and have a huge number of `catch` blocks.

➤ You can define filters with catch blocks to catch the exception with the specific block only if the filter matches.

➤ You can omit the `catch` blocks altogether, in which case the syntax serves not to identify exceptions but to guarantee that code in the `finally` block will be executed when execution leaves the `try` block. This is useful if the `try` block contains several exit points. If you don't write a `catch` block, a `finally` block is required. You cannot use just a `try` block. What would a `try` block be good for without `try` or `finally`?

So far so good, but the question that has yet to be answered is this: if the code is running in the try block, how does it know when to switch to the catch block if an error occurs? If an error is detected, the code does something known as *throwing an exception*. In other words, it instantiates an exception object class and throws it:

```
throw new OverflowException();
```

Here, you have instantiated an exception object of the OverflowException class. As soon as the application encounters a throw statement inside a try block, it immediately looks for the catch block associated with that try block. If more than one catch block is associated with the try block, it identifies the correct catch block by checking which exception class the catch block is associated with. For example, when the OverflowException object is thrown, execution jumps to the following catch block:

```
catch (OverflowException ex)
{
  // exception handling here
}
```

In other words, the application looks for the catch block that indicates a matching exception class instance of the same class (or of a base class).

With this extra information, you can extend the try block with multiple catch blocks. Assume, for the sake of argument, that two possible serious errors can occur in the try block: an overflow and an array out of bounds. Assume also that your code contains two Boolean variables, Overflow and OutOfBounds, which indicate whether these conditions exist. You have already seen that a predefined exception class exists to indicate overflow (OverflowException); similarly, an IndexOutOfRangeException class exists to handle an array that is out of bounds.

Now your try block looks like this:

```
try
{
  // code for normal execution
  if (Overflow == true)
  {
    throw new OverflowException();
  }
  // more processing
  if (OutOfBounds == true)
  {
    throw new IndexOutOfRangeException();
  }
  // otherwise continue normal execution
}
catch (OverflowException ex)
{
  // error handling for the overflow error condition
}
catch (IndexOutOfRangeException ex)
{
  // error handling for the index out of range error condition
}
finally
{
  // clean up
}
```

This is because you can have throw statements that are nested in several method calls inside the try block, but the same try block continues to apply even as execution flow enters these other methods. If the application encounters a `throw` statement, it immediately goes back up through all the method calls on the stack, looking for the end of the containing `try` block and the start of the appropriate `catch` block. During this process, all the local variables in the intermediate method calls will correctly go out of scope. This makes the `try...catch` architecture well suited to the situation described at the beginning of this section, whereby the error occurs inside a method call that is nested inside 15 or 20 method calls, and processing must stop immediately.

As you can probably gather from this discussion, `try` blocks can play a significant role in controlling the flow of your code's execution. However, it is important to understand that exceptions are intended for exceptional conditions, hence their name. You wouldn't want to use them as a way of controlling when to exit a `do...while` loop.

Exceptions and Performance

Exception handling has a performance implication. In cases that are common, you shouldn't use exceptions to deal with errors. For example, when converting a string to a number, you can use the `Parse` method of the `int` type. This method throws a `FormatException` in case the `string` passed to this method can't be converted to a number, and it throws an `OverflowException` if a number can be converted but it doesn't fit into an `int`:

```
void NumberDemo1(string n)
{
    if (n is null) throw new ArgumentNullException(nameof(n));
    try
    {
        int i = int.Parse(n);
        Console.WriteLine($"converted: {i}");
    }
    catch (FormatException ex)
    {
        Console.WriteLine(ex.Message);
    }
    catch (OverflowException ex)
    {
        Console.WriteLine(ex.Message);
    }
}
```

If the method `NumberDemo1` is typically used only in a way to pass numbers in a string and receiving something other than a number is exceptional, it's okay to program it this way. However, in cases when it's normal for the program flow to expect strings that cannot be converted, you can use the `TryParse` method. This method doesn't throw an exception if the string cannot be converted to a number. Instead, `TryParse` returns `true` if parsing succeeds, and it returns `false` if parsing fails:

```
void NumberDemo2(string n)
{
    if (n is null) throw new ArgumentNullException(nameof(n));
    if (int.TryParse(n, out int result))
    {
        Console.WriteLine($"converted {result}");
    }
    else
    {
        Console.WriteLine("not a number");
    }
}
```

Implementing Multiple Catch Blocks

The easiest way to see how `try...catch...finally` blocks work in practice is with a couple of examples. The first example is called `SimpleExceptions`. It repeatedly asks the user to type a number and then displays it. However, for the sake of this example, imagine that the number must be between 0 and 5; otherwise, the program isn't able to process the number properly. Therefore, you throw an exception if the user types anything outside this range. The program then continues to ask for more numbers for processing until the user presses the Enter key without entering anything.

> **NOTE** *You should note that this code does not provide a good example of when to use exception handling, but it does show good practice on how to use exception handling. As their name suggests, exceptions are provided for other than normal circumstances. Users often type silly things, so this situation doesn't really count. Normally, your program handles incorrect user input by performing an instant check and asking the user to retype the input if it isn't valid. However, generating exceptional situations is difficult in a small example that you can read through in a few minutes, so I'm making do with this less-than-ideal one to demonstrate how exceptions work. The examples that follow present more realistic situations.*

The code for `SimpleExceptions` looks like this (code file `SimpleExceptions/Program.cs`):

```
while (true)
{
  try
  {
    Console.Write("Input a number between 0 and 5 " +
      "(or just hit return to exit)> ");
    string? userInput = Console.ReadLine();

    if (string.IsNullOrEmpty(userInput))
    {
      break;
    }

    int index = Convert.ToInt32(userInput);

    if (index < 0 || index > 5)
    {
      throw new IndexOutOfRangeException($"You typed in {userInput}");
    }
    Console.WriteLine($"Your number was {index}");
  }
  catch (IndexOutOfRangeException ex)
  {
    Console.WriteLine("Exception: " +
      $"Number should be between 0 and 5. {ex.Message}");
  }
  catch (Exception ex)
  {
    Console.WriteLine($"An exception was thrown. Exception type: {ex.GetType().Name} " +
      $"Message: {ex.Message}");
  }
```

```
      finally
      {
         Console.WriteLine("Thank you\n");
      }
   }
```

The core of this code is a while loop, which continually uses ReadLine to ask for user input. ReadLine returns a string, so your first task is to convert it to an int using the System.Convert.ToInt32 method. The System.Convert class contains various useful methods to perform data conversions, and it provides an alternative to the int.Parse method. In general, System.Convert contains methods to perform various type conversions. Recall that the C# compiler resolves int to instances of the System.Int32 base class.

> **NOTE** *It is also worth pointing out that the parameter passed to the* catch *block is scoped to that* catch *block—which is why you can use the same parameter name,* ex, *in successive* catch *blocks in the preceding code.*

In the preceding example, you also check for an empty string because it is your condition for exiting the while loop. Notice how the break statement breaks right out of the enclosing try block as well as the while loop because this is valid behavior. Of course, when execution breaks out of the try block, the Console.WriteLine statement in the finally block is executed. Although you just display a greeting here, more commonly you will be doing tasks such as closing file handles and calling the Dispose method of various objects to perform any cleanup. After the application leaves the finally block, it simply carries on executing into the next statement that it would have executed had the finally block not been present. In the case of this example, though, you iterate back to the start of the while loop and enter the try block again (unless the finally block was entered as a result of executing the break statement in the while loop, in which case you simply exit the while loop).

Next, you check for your exception condition:

```
   if (index < 0 || index > 5)
   {
      throw new IndexOutOfRangeException($"You typed in {userInput}");
   }
```

When throwing an exception, you need to specify what type of exception to throw. Although the class System.Exception is available, it is intended only as a base class. It is considered bad programming practice to throw an instance of this class as an exception because it conveys no information about the nature of the error condition. .NET contains many other exception classes that are derived from Exception. Each of these matches a particular type of exception condition, and you are free to define your own as well. The goal is to provide as much information as possible about the particular exception condition by throwing an instance of a class that matches the particular error condition. In the preceding example, System.IndexOutOfRangeException is the best choice for the circumstances. IndexOutOfRangeException has several constructor overloads. The one chosen in the example takes a string describing the error. Alternatively, you might choose to derive your own custom Exception object that describes the error condition in the context of your application.

Suppose that the user next types a number that is not between 0 and 5. The number is picked up by the if statement, and an IndexOutOfRangeException object is instantiated and thrown. At this point, the application immediately exits the try block and hunts for a catch block that handles IndexOutOfRangeException. The first catch block it encounters is this:

```
   catch (IndexOutOfRangeException ex)
   {
      Console.WriteLine($"Exception: Number should be between 0 and 5." +
         $"{ex.Message}");
   }
```

Because this `catch` block takes a parameter of the appropriate class, the `catch` block receives the exception instance and is executed. In this case, you display an error message and the `Exception.Message` property (which corresponds to the string passed to the `IndexOutOfRangeException`'s constructor). After executing this `catch` block, control then switches to the `finally` block, just as if no exception had occurred.

Notice that in the example you have also provided another `catch` block:

```
catch (Exception ex)
{
   Console.WriteLine($"An exception was thrown. Message was: {ex.Message}");
}
```

This `catch` block would also be capable of handling an `IndexOutOfRangeException` if it weren't for the fact that such exceptions will already have been caught by the previous `catch` block. A reference to a base class can also refer to any instances of classes derived from it, and all exceptions are derived from `Exception`. This `catch` block isn't executed because the application executes only the first suitable `catch` block it finds from the list of available `catch` blocks. This catch block isn't executed when an exception of type `IndexOutOfRangeException` is thrown. The application executes only the first suitable catch block it finds from the list of available catch blocks. This second catch block catches other exceptions derived from the `Exception` base class. Be aware that the three separate calls to methods within the `try` block (`Console.ReadLine`, `Console.Write`, and `Convert.ToInt32`) might throw other exceptions.

If the user types something that is not a number—say a or `hello`—the `Convert.ToInt32` method throws an exception of the class `System.FormatException` to indicate that the string passed into `ToInt32` is not in a format that can be converted to an `int`. When this happens, the application traces back through the method calls, looking for a handler that can handle this exception. Your first `catch` block (the one that takes an `IndexOutOfRangeException`) will not do. The application then looks at the second `catch` block. This one will do because `FormatException` is derived from `Exception`, so a `FormatException` instance can be passed in as a parameter here.

The structure of the example is fairly typical of a situation with multiple `catch` blocks. You start with `catch` blocks that are designed to trap specific error conditions. Then, you finish with more general blocks that cover any errors for which you have not written specific error handlers. Indeed, the order of the `catch` blocks is important. Had you written the previous two blocks in the opposite order, the code would not have compiled because the second `catch` block is unreachable (the `Exception` `catch` block would catch all exceptions). Therefore, the uppermost `catch` blocks should be the most granular options available, ending with the most general options.

Now that you have analyzed the code for the example, you can run it. The following output illustrates what happens with different inputs and demonstrates both the `IndexOutOfRangeException` and the `FormatException` being thrown:

```
Input a number between 0 and 5 (or just hit return to exit)> 4
Your number was 4
Thank you
Input a number between 0 and 5 (or just hit return to exit)> 0
Your number was 0
Thank you
Input a number between 0 and 5 (or just hit return to exit)> 10
Exception: Number should be between 0 and 5. You typed in 10
Thank you
Input a number between 0 and 5 (or just hit return to exit)> hello
An exception was thrown. Exception type: FormatException, Message: Input string was not
in a correct format.
Thank you
Input a number between 0 and 5 (or just hit return to exit)>
Thank you
```

Catching Exceptions from Other Code

The previous example demonstrates the handling of two exceptions. One of them, `IndexOutOfRangeException`, was thrown by your own code. The other, `FormatException`, was thrown from inside one of the base classes. It is common for code in a library to throw an exception if it detects that a problem has occurred or if one of the methods has been called inappropriately by being passed the wrong parameters. However, library code rarely attempts to catch exceptions; this is regarded as the responsibility of the client code.

Often, exceptions are thrown from the base class libraries while you are debugging. The process of debugging to some extent involves determining why exceptions have been thrown and removing the causes. Your aim should be to ensure that by the time the code is actually shipped, exceptions occur only in exceptional circumstances and, if possible, are handled appropriately in your code.

System.Exception Properties

The example illustrated the use of only the `Message` property of the exception object. However, a number of other properties are available in `System.Exception`, as shown in the following table:

PROPERTY	DESCRIPTION
Data	Enables you to add key/value statements to the exception that can be used to supply extra information about it.
HelpLink	A link to a help file that provides more information about the exception.
HResult	A numerical value that is assigned to the exception.
InnerException	If this exception was thrown inside a `catch` block, then `InnerException` contains the exception object that sent the code into that `catch` block.
Message	Text that describes the error condition.
Source	The name of the application or object that caused the exception.
StackTrace	Provides details about the method calls on the stack (to help track down the method that threw the exception).
TargetSite	A .NET reflection object that describes the method that threw the exception.

The property value for `StackTrace` is supplied automatically by the .NET runtime if a stack trace is available. `Source` will always be filled in by the .NET runtime as the name of the assembly in which the exception was raised (though you might want to modify the property in your code to give more specific information), whereas `Data`, `Message`, `HelpLink`, and `InnerException` must be filled in by the code that threw the exception, by setting these properties immediately before throwing the exception. For example, the code to throw an exception might look something like this:

```
if (ErrorCondition)
{
  ClassMyException myException = new("Help!!!!");
  myException.Source = "My Application Name";
  myException.HelpLink = "MyHelpFile.txt";
  myException.Data["ErrorDate"] = DateTime.Now;
  myException.Data.Add("AdditionalInfo", "Contact Bill from the Blue Team");
  throw myException;
}
```

Here, `ClassMyException` is the name of the particular exception class you are throwing. Note that it is common practice for the names of all exception classes to end with `Exception`. The string passed to the constructor sets the `Message` property. In addition, note that the `Data` property is assigned in two possible ways.

Exception Filters

With the many different exception types and the hierarchy of exceptions, the original plan with .NET was as soon as you need to handle errors differently, use a different exception type. With many technologies used with .NET, this turned out to not be a practical scenario. For example, using the Windows Runtime often results in COM exceptions, and you want to handle `COMException` differently based on the error code from this exception. To deal with this, C# 6 was enhanced to support exception filters. A `catch` block runs only if the filter returns `true`. You can have different `catch` blocks that act differently when catching different exception types. In some scenarios, it's useful to have the `catch` blocks act differently based on the content of an exception. When doing network calls, you get a network exception for many different scenarios—for example, if the server is not available or the data supplied do not match the expectations. It's good to react to these errors differently. Some exceptions can be recovered in different ways, whereas with others, the user might need some information.

The following code sample throws the exception of type `MyCustomException` and sets the `ErrorCode` property of this exception (code file `ExceptionFilters/Program.cs`):

```
public static void ThrowWithErrorCode(int code)
{
    throw new MyCustomException("Error in Foo") { ErrorCode = code };
}
```

In the following example, the `try` block safeguards the method invocation with two `catch` blocks. The first catch `block` uses the `when` keyword to filter only exceptions if the `ErrorCode` property equals `405`. The expression for the `when` clause needs to return a Boolean value. If the result is `true`, this `catch` block handles the exception. If it is `false`, other catches are looked for. When passing `405` to the method `ThrowWithErrorCode`, the filter returns `true`, and the first `catch` handles the exception. When passing another value, the filter returns `false`, and the second `catch` handles the exception. With filters, you can have multiple handlers to handle the same exception type.

Of course, you can also remove the second `catch` block and not handle the exception in that circumstance.

```
try
{
    ThrowWithErrorCode(405);
}
catch (MyCustomException ex) when (ex.ErrorCode == 405)
{
    Console.WriteLine($"Exception caught with filter {ex.Message} " +
        $"and {ex.ErrorCode}");
}
catch (MyCustomException ex)
{
    Console.WriteLine($"Exception caught {ex.Message} and {ex.ErrorCode}");
}
```

Rethrowing Exceptions

When you catch exceptions, it's common to rethrow exceptions, which means you can change the exception type while throwing the exception again. With this method, you can give the caller more information about what happened. The original exception might not have enough information about the context of what was going on. You can also log exception information and give the caller different information. For example, for a user running the application, exception information does not really help. A system administrator reading log files can react accordingly.

An issue with rethrowing exceptions is that the caller often needs to find out the reason for what happened with the earlier exception, and where it happened. Depending on how exceptions are thrown, stack trace information might be lost. For you to see the different options on rethrowing exceptions, the sample program RethrowExceptions shows the different options.

For this sample, two custom exception types are created. The first one, MyCustomException, defines the property ErrorCode in addition to the members of the base class Exception; the second one, AnotherCustomException, supports passing an inner exception (code file RethrowExceptions/MyCustomException.cs):

```csharp
public class MyCustomException : Exception
{
  public MyCustomException(string message)
    : base(message) { }

  public int ErrorCode { get; set; }
}

public class AnotherCustomException : Exception
{
  public AnotherCustomException(string message, Exception innerException)
    : base(message, innerException) { }
}
```

The method HandleAll invokes the methods HandleAndThrowAgain, HandleAndThrowWithInnerException, HandleAndRethrow, and HandleWithFilter. The exception that is thrown is caught to write the exception message as well as the stack trace to the console. To better find what line numbers are referenced from the stack trace, the #line preprocessor directive is used that restarts the line numbering. With this, the invocation of the methods using the delegate m is in line 114 (code file RethrowExceptions/Program.cs):

```csharp
#line 100
public static void HandleAll()
{
  Action[] methods =
  {
    HandleAndThrowAgain,
    HandleAndThrowWithInnerException,
    HandleAndRethrow,
    HandleWithFilter
  };

  foreach (var m in methods)
  {
    try
    {
      m(); // line 114
    }
    catch (Exception ex)
    {
      Console.WriteLine(ex.Message);
      Console.WriteLine(ex.StackTrace);
      if (ex.InnerException != null)
      {
        Console.WriteLine($"\tInner Exception{ex.InnerException.Message}");
        Console.WriteLine(ex.InnerException.StackTrace);
      }
```

```
        Console.WriteLine();
      }
    }
  }
```

The method `ThrowAnException` is the one to throw the first exception. This exception is thrown in line 8002. During development, it helps to know where this exception is thrown:

```
#line 8000
public static void ThrowAnException(string message)
{
  throw new MyCustomException(message); // line 8002
}
```

Naïvely Rethrowing the Exception

The method `HandleAndThrowAgain` does nothing more than log the exception to the console and throw it again using `throw ex`:

```
#line 4000
public static void HandleAndThrowAgain()
{
  try
  {
    ThrowAnException("test 1");
  }
  catch (Exception ex)
  {
    Console.WriteLine($"Log exception {ex.Message} and throw again");
    throw ex; // you shouldn't do that - line 4009
  }
}
```

After running the application, the following simplified output shows the stack trace (without the namespace and the full path to the code files):

```
Log exception test 1 and throw again
test 1
at Program.HandleAndThrowAgain() in Program.cs:line 4009
at Program.HandleAll() in Program.cs:line 114
```

The stack trace shows the call to the m method within the `HandleAll` method, which in turn invokes the `HandleAndThrowAgain` method. The information where the exception is thrown at first is completely lost in the call stack of the final catch. This makes it hard to find the original reason of an error. Usually it's not a good idea to just throw the same exception with `throw` passing the exception object. The C# compiler now gives you the warning `CA2200: re-throwing caught exception changes stack information`.

Changing the Exception

One useful scenario is to change the type of the exception and add information to the error. This is done in the method `HandleAndThrowWithInnerException`. After logging the error, a new exception of type `AnotherCustomException` is thrown to pass ex as the inner exception:

```
#line 3000
public static void HandleAndThrowWithInnerException()
{
  try
```

```
  {
    ThrowAnException("test 2"); // line 3004
  }
  catch (Exception ex)
  {
    Console.WriteLine($"Log exception {ex.Message} and throw again");
    throw new AnotherCustomException("throw with inner exception", ex); // 3009
  }
}
```

By checking the stack trace of the outer exception, you see line numbers 3009 and 114 similar to before. However, the inner exception gives the original reason of the error. It gives the line of the method that invoked the erroneous method (3004) and the line where the original (the inner) exception was thrown (8002):

```
Log exception test 2 and throw again
throw with inner exception
at Program.HandleAndThrowWithInnerException() in Program.cs:line 3009
at Program.HandleAll() in Program.cs:line 114
Inner Exception throw with inner exception
at Program.ThrowAnException(String message) in Program.cs:line 8002
at Program.HandleAndThrowWithInnerException() in Program.cs:line 3004
```

No information is lost this way.

> **NOTE** *When trying to find reasons for an error, take a look at whether an inner exception exists. This often gives helpful information.*

> **NOTE** *When catching exceptions, it's good practice to change the exception when rethrowing. For example, catching an* SqlException *can result in throwing a business-related exception such as* InvalidIsbnException.

Rethrowing the Exception

If the exception type should not be changed, the same exception can be rethrown just with the throw statement. Using throw without passing an exception object throws the current exception of the catch block and keeps the exception information:

```
#line 2000
public static void HandleAndRethrow()
{
  try
  {
    ThrowAnException("test 3");
  }
  catch (Exception ex)
  {
    Console.WriteLine($"Log exception {ex.Message} and rethrow");
    throw; // line 2009
  }
}
```

With this in place, the stack information is not lost. The exception was originally thrown in line 8002 and rethrown in line 2009. Line 114 contains the delegate m that invoked `HandleAndRethrow`:

```
Log exception test 3 and rethrow
test 3
   at Program.ThrowAnException(String message) in Program.cs:line 8002
   at Program.HandleAndRethrow() in Program.cs:line 2009
   at Program.HandleAll() in Program.cs:line 114
```

Using Filters to Add Functionality

When rethrowing exceptions using the `throw` statement, the call stack contains the address of the throw. When you use exception filters, it is possible not to change the call stack at all. Now add a `when` keyword that passes a filter method. This filter method named `Filter` logs the message and always returns `false`. That's why the `catch` block is never invoked:

```
#line 1000
public void HandleWithFilter()
{
  try
  {
    ThrowAnException("test 4"); // line 1004
  }
  catch (Exception ex) when(Filter(ex))
  {
    Console.WriteLine("block never invoked");
  }
}
#line 1500
public bool Filter(Exception ex)
{
  Console.WriteLine($"just log {ex.Message}");
  return false;
}
```

Now when you look at the stack trace, the exception originates in the `HandleAll` method in line 114 that in turn invokes `HandleWithFilter`, line 1004 contains the invocation to `ThrowAnException`, and line 8002 contains the line where the exception was thrown:

```
just log test 4
test 4
   at Program.ThrowAnException(String message) in Program.cs:line 8002
   at Program.HandleWithFilter() in Program.cs:line 1004
   at RethrowExceptions.Program.HandleAll() in Program.cs:line 114
```

> **NOTE** *The primary use of exception filters is to filter exceptions based on a value of the exception. Exception filters can also be used for other effects, such as writing log information without changing the call stack. However, exception filters should be fast running, so you should do only simple checks and avoid side effects. Logging is one of the excusable exceptions.*

What Happens If an Exception Isn't Handled?

Sometimes an exception might be thrown, but there is no `catch` block in your code that is able to handle that kind of exception. The `SimpleExceptions` example can serve to illustrate this. Suppose, for example, that you omitted the `FormatException` and catchall `catch` blocks, and you supplied only the block that traps an `IndexOutOfRangeException`. In that circumstance, what would happen if a `FormatException` were thrown?

The answer is that the .NET runtime would catch it. Later in this section, you learn how you can nest `try` blocks; and, in fact, there is already a nested `try` block behind the scenes in the example. The .NET runtime has effectively placed the entire program inside another huge `try` block—it does this for every .NET program. This `try` block has a `catch` handler that can catch any type of exception. If an exception occurs that your code does not handle, the execution flow simply passes right out of your program and is trapped by this `catch` block in the .NET runtime. However, the results of this probably will not be what you want because the execution of your code is terminated promptly. The user sees a dialog that complains that your code has not handled the exception and provides any details about the exception the .NET runtime was able to retrieve. At least the exception has been caught!

In general, if you are writing an executable, try to catch as many exceptions as you reasonably can and handle them in a sensible way. If you are writing a library, it is normally best to catch exceptions that you can handle in a useful way, or where you can add information to the context and throw other exception types as shown in the previous section. Assume that the calling code handles any errors it encounters.

USER-DEFINED EXCEPTION CLASSES

In the previous section, you already created a user-defined exception. You are now ready to look at a larger example that illustrates exceptions. This example, called `SolicitColdCall`, contains two nested `try` blocks and illustrates the practice of defining your own custom exception classes and throwing another exception from inside a `try` block.

This example assumes that a sales company wants to increase its customer base. The company's sales team is going to phone a list of people to invite them to become customers, a practice known in sales jargon as *cold-calling*. To this end, you have a text file available that contains the names of the people to be cold-called. The file should be in a well-defined format in which the first line contains the number of people in the file and each subsequent line contains the name of the next person. In other words, a correctly formatted file of names might look like this:

```
4
George Washington
Benedict Arnold
John Adams
Thomas Jefferson
```

This version of cold-calling is designed to display the name of the person on the screen (perhaps for the salesperson to read). That is why only the names, and not the phone numbers, of the individuals are contained in the file.

For this example, your program asks the user for the name of the file and then simply reads it in and displays the names of people. That sounds like a simple task, but even so, a couple of things can go wrong and require you to abandon the entire procedure:

➤   The user might type the name of a file that does not exist. This is caught as a `FileNotFound` exception.

➤   The file might not be in the correct format. There are two possible problems here. One, the first line of the file might not be an integer. Two, there might not be as many names in the file as the first line of the file indicates. In both cases, you want to trap this oddity as a custom exception that has been written especially for this purpose, `ColdCallFileFormatException`.

There is something else that can go wrong that doesn't cause you to abandon the entire process but does mean you need to abandon a person's name and move on to the next name in the file (and therefore trap it by an inner `try` block). Some people are spies working for rival sales companies, so you obviously do not want to let these people know what you are up to by accidentally phoning one of them. For simplicity, assume that you can identify who the spies are because their names begin with B. Such people should have been screened out when the data file was first prepared, but in case any have slipped through, you need to check each name in the file and throw a `SalesSpyFoundException` if you detect a sales spy. This, of course, is another custom exception object.

Finally, you implement this example by coding a class, `ColdCallFileReader`, which maintains the connection to the cold-call file and retrieves data from it. You code this class in a safe way, which means that its methods all throw exceptions if they are called inappropriately—for example, if a method that reads a file is called before the file has even been opened. For this purpose, you write another exception class: `UnexpectedException`.

Catching the User-Defined Exceptions

Start with the top-level statements of the `SolicitColdCall` sample, which catches your user-defined exceptions. Note that you need to call up file-handling classes in the `System.IO` namespace as well as the `System` namespace (code file `SolicitColdCall/Program.cs`):

```
Console.Write("Please type in the name of the file " +
  "containing the names of the people to be cold called > ");
string? fileName = Console.ReadLine();
if (fileName != null)
{
  ColdCallFileReaderLoop1(fileName);
  Console.WriteLine();
}
Console.ReadLine();

void ColdCallFileReaderLoop1(string fileName)
{
  ColdCallFileReader peopleToRing = new();
  try
  {
    peopleToRing.Open(fileName);
    for (int i = 0; i < peopleToRing.NPeopleToRing; i++)
    {
      peopleToRing.ProcessNextPerson();
    }
    Console.WriteLine("All callers processed correctly");
  }
  catch(FileNotFoundException)
  {
    Console.WriteLine($"The file {fileName} does not exist");
  }
  catch(ColdCallFileFormatException ex)
  {
    Console.WriteLine($"The file {fileName} appears to have been corrupted");
    Console.WriteLine($"Details of problem are: {ex.Message}");
    if (ex.InnerException != null)
    {
      Console.WriteLine($"Inner exception was: {ex.InnerException.Message}");
    }
  }
}
```

```
    catch(Exception ex)
    {
        Console.WriteLine($"Exception occurred:\n{ex.Message}");
    }
    finally
    {
        peopleToRing.Dispose();
    }
}
```

This code is a little more than just a loop to process people from the file. You start by asking the user for the name of the file. Then you instantiate an object of a class called `ColdCallFileReader`, which is defined shortly. The `ColdCallFileReader` class is the class that handles the file reading. Notice that you do this outside the initial `try` block—that's because the variables that you instantiate here need to be available in the subsequent `catch` and `finally` blocks, and if you declare them inside the `try` block, they would go out of scope at the closing curly brace of the `try` block, where the compiler would complain about it.

In the `try` block, you open the file (using the `ColdCallFileReader.Open` method) and loop over all the people in it. The `ColdCallFileReader.ProcessNextPerson` method reads in and displays the name of the next person in the file, and the `ColdCallFileReader.NPeopleToRing` property indicates how many people should be in the file (obtained by reading the file's first line). There are three `catch` blocks: one for `FileNotFoundException`, one for `ColdCallFileFormatException`, and one to trap any other .NET exceptions.

> **NOTE** *With the sample application, the object of type* `ColdCallFileReader` *is instantiated outside of the* `try` *block. It's a good practice to create constructors that can't fail and don't take a long processing time. In case you use such types, you can create an outer* try/catch *block or declare the variable outside the* `try` *block and instantiate it within the* `try` *block.*

In the case of a `FileNotFoundException`, you display a message to that effect. Notice that in this `catch` block, the exception instance is not actually used at all. This `catch` block is used to illustrate the user-friendliness of the application. Exception objects generally contain technical information that is useful for developers, but not the sort of stuff you want to show to end users. Therefore, in this case, you create a simpler message of your own.

For the `ColdCallFileFormatException` handler, you have done the opposite, specifying how to obtain fuller technical information, including details about the inner exception, if one is present.

Finally, if you catch any other generic exceptions, you display a user-friendly message, instead of letting any such exceptions fall through to the .NET runtime.

The `finally` block is there to clean up resources. In this case, that means closing any open file—performed by the `ColdCallFileReader.Dispose` method.

> **NOTE** C# *offers the* using *statement and the* using *declaration where the compiler itself creates a* try/finally *block calling the* `Dispose` *method in the* `finally` *block. The* using *keyword can be used with objects implementing the* `IDisposable` *interface. You can read the details of the* using *statement and declaration in Chapter 13, "Managed and Unmanaged Memory."*

Throwing the User-Defined Exceptions

Now take a look at the definition of the class that handles the file reading and (potentially) throws your user-defined exceptions: `ColdCallFileReader`. Because this class maintains an external file connection, you need to ensure that it is disposed of correctly in accordance with the principles outlined for the disposing of objects in Chapter 13. Therefore, you derive this class from `IDisposable`.

First, you declare some private fields (code file `SolicitColdCall/ColdCallFileReader.cs`):

```
public class ColdCallFileReader: IDisposable
{
  private FileStream? _fileStream;
  private StreamReader? _streamReader;
  private uint _nPeopleToRing;
  private bool _isDisposed = false;
  private bool _isOpen = false;
```

`FileStream` and `StreamReader`, both in the `System.IO` namespace, are the base classes that you use to read the file. `FileStream` enables you to connect to the file in the first place, whereas `StreamReader` is designed to read text files and implements a method, `ReadLine`, which reads a line of text from a file. You look at `StreamReader` more closely in Chapter 18, "Files and Streams," which discusses file handling in depth.

The `_isDisposed` field indicates whether the `Dispose` method has been called. `ColdCallFileReader` is implemented so that after `Dispose` has been called, it is not permitted to reopen connections and reuse the object. `_isOpen` is also used for error checking—in this case, checking whether the `StreamReader` actually connects to an open file.

The process of opening the file and reading in that first line—the one that tells you how many people are in the file—is handled by the `Open` method:

```
public void Open(string fileName)
{
  if (_isDisposed)
  {
    throw new ObjectDisposedException(nameof(ColdCallFileReader));
  }

  _fileStream = new(fileName, FileMode.Open);
  _streamReader = new(_fileStream);

  try
  {
    string? firstLine = _streamReader.ReadLine();
    if (firstLine != null)
    {
      _nPeopleToRing = uint.Parse(firstLine);
      _isOpen = true;
    }
  }
  catch (FormatException ex)
  {
    throw new ColdCallFileFormatException(
      $"First line isn't an integer {ex}");
  }
}
```

The first thing you do in this method (as with all other `ColdCallFileReader` methods) is check whether the client code has inappropriately called it after the object has been disposed of and, if so, throw a predefined `ObjectDisposedException` object. The `Open` method checks the `_isDisposed` field to determine whether `Dispose` has already been called. Because calling `Dispose` implies that the caller has now finished with this object, you regard it as an error to attempt to open a new file connection if `Dispose` has been called.

Next, the method contains a `try`/`catch` block. The purpose of this one is to catch any errors resulting from a file in which the first line does not contain an integer. If the method `uint.Parse` cannot parse the first line successfully, a `FormatException` can be thrown. If that problem arises, the exception is caught and converted to a more meaningful exception that indicates a problem with the format of the cold-call file. Note that `System.FormatException` is there to indicate format problems with basic data types, not with files, so it's not a particularly useful exception to pass back to the calling routine in this case. The new exception thrown will be trapped by the outermost `try` block. Because no cleanup is needed here, there is no need for a `finally` block. Other exceptions that can happen such as the `IOException` on calling the `ReadLine` method are not caught here and are forwarded to the next `try` block.

If everything is fine, you set the `_isOpen` field to `true` to indicate that there is now a valid file connection from which data can be read.

The `ProcessNextPerson` method also contains an inner `try` block:

```
public void ProcessNextPerson()
{
  if (_isDisposed)
  {
    throw new ObjectDisposedException(nameof(ColdCallFileReader));
  }

  if (!_isOpen)
  {
    throw new UnexpectedException(
      "Attempted to access coldcall file that is not open");
  }

  try
  {
    string? name = _streamReader?.ReadLine();
    if (name is null)
    {
      throw new ColdCallFileFormatException("Not enough names");
    }
    if (name[0] is 'B')
    {
      throw new SalesSpyFoundException(name);
    }
    Console.WriteLine(name);
  }
  catch(SalesSpyFoundException ex)
  {
    Console.WriteLine(ex.Message);
  }
  finally
  {
  }
}
```

Two possible problems can exist when reading the file in the `ProcessNextPerson` method (assuming there actually is an open file connection that is checked first). The first error that is handled is when `null` is returned from the `ReadLine` method. This method returns `null` if it has gone past the end of the file. Because the file contains the number of names at the start of the file, a `ColdCallFileFormatException` is thrown on a mismatch, and there are fewer names than there should be. This is then caught by the outer exception handler, which causes the execution to terminate.

With the second, the line is accessed. If it is discovered that the name is a sales spy, a `SalesSpyFoundException` is thrown. Because that exception has been caught here, inside the loop, it means that execution can subsequently continue in the `Main` method of the program, and the subsequent names in the file continue to be processed.

Again, you don't need a `finally` block here because there is no cleanup to do; however, this time an empty `finally` block is included just to show that you can do so, if you want.

The example is nearly finished. You have just two more members of `ColdCallFileReader` to look at: the `NPeopleToRing` property, which returns the number of people who are supposed to be in the file, and the `Dispose` method, which closes an open file. Notice that the `Dispose` method returns immediately if it has already been called—this is the recommended way of implementing it. It also confirms that there actually is a file stream to close before closing it. This example is shown here to illustrate defensive coding techniques:

```csharp
public uint NPeopleToRing
{
  get
  {
    if (_isDisposed)
    {
      throw new ObjectDisposedException("peopleToRing");
    }
    if (!_isOpen)
    {
      throw new UnexpectedException(
        "Attempted to access cold-call file that is not open");
    }
    return _nPeopleToRing;
  }
}

public void Dispose()
{
  if (_isDisposed)
  {
    return;
  }
  _isDisposed = true;
  _isOpen = false;

  _streamReader?.Dispose();
  _streamReader = null;
}
```

Defining the User-Defined Exception Classes

Finally, you need to define three of your own exception classes. Defining your own exception is quite easy because there are rarely any extra methods to add. It is just a case of implementing a constructor to ensure that the base class constructor is called correctly. Here is the full implementation of SalesSpyFoundException (code file SolicitColdCall/SalesSpyFoundException.cs):

```
public class SalesSpyFoundException: Exception
{
   public SalesSpyFoundException(string spyName)
     : base($"Sales spy found, with name {spyName}") { }

   public SalesSpyFoundException(string spyName, Exception innerException)
     : base($"Sales spy found with name {spyName}", innerException) {   }
}
```

Notice that it is derived from Exception, as you would expect for a custom exception. In fact, in practice, you would probably have added an intermediate class, something like ColdCallFileException, derived from Exception, and then derived both of your exception classes from this class. This ensures that the handling code has that extra-fine degree of control over which exception handler handles each exception. However, to keep the example simple, you will not do that.

You have done one bit of processing in SalesSpyFoundException. You have assumed that the message passed into its constructor is just the name of the spy found, so you turn this string into a more meaningful error message. You have also provided two constructors: one that simply takes a message, and one that also takes an inner exception as a parameter. When defining your own exception classes, it is best to include, at a minimum, at least these two constructors (although you will not actually be using the second SalesSpyFoundException constructor in this example).

The ColdCallFileFormatException follows the same principles as the previous exception, but you don't do any processing on the message (code file SolicitColdCall/ColdCallFileFormatException.cs):

```
public class ColdCallFileFormatException: Exception
{
   public ColdCallFileFormatException(string message)
     : base(message) {}

   public ColdCallFileFormatException(string message, Exception innerException)
     : base(message, innerException) {}
}
```

Finally, you have UnexpectedException, which looks much the same as ColdCallFileFormatException (code file SolicitColdCall/UnexpectedException.cs):

```
public class UnexpectedException: Exception
{
   public UnexpectedException(string message)
     : base(message) { }

   public UnexpectedException(string message, Exception innerException)
     : base(message, innerException) { }
}
```

Now you are ready to test the program. First, try the people.txt file. The contents are defined here:

```
4
George Washington
Benedict Arnold
```

```
John Adams
Thomas Jefferson
```

This has four names (which match the number given in the first line of the file), including one spy. Then try the following `people2.txt` file, which has an obvious formatting error:

```
49
George Washington
Benedict Arnold
John Adams
Thomas Jefferson
```

Finally, try the example, but specify the name of a file that does not exist, such as `people3.txt`. Running the program three times for the three filenames returns these results:

```
SolicitColdCall
Please type in the name of the file containing the names of the people to be cold
called > people.txt
George Washington
Sales spy found, with name Benedict Arnold
John Adams
Thomas Jefferson
All callers processed correctly

SolicitColdCall
Please type in the name of the file containing the names of the people to be cold
called > people2.txt
George Washington
Sales spy found, with name Benedict Arnold
John Adams
Thomas Jefferson
The file people2.txt appears to have been corrupted.
Details of the problem are: Not enough names

SolicitColdCall
Please type in the name of the file containing the names of the people to be cold
called > people3.txt
The file people3.txt does not exist.
```

This application has demonstrated a number of different ways in which you can handle the errors and exceptions that you might find in your own applications.

CALLER INFORMATION

When dealing with errors, it is often helpful to get information about the error where it occurred. Earlier in this chapter, the `#line` preprocessor directive was used to change the line numbering of the code to get better information with the call stack. A method can get caller information through optional parameters. You can use attributes to get the line numbers, filenames, and member names from within code. The attributes `CallerLineNumber`, `CallerFilePath`, and `CallerMemberName` defined within the namespace `System.Runtime.CompilerServices` are directly supported by the C# compiler, which sets these values.

The `Log` method from the following code snippet demonstrates how to use these attributes. With the implementation, the information is written to the console (code file `CallerInformation/Program.cs`):

```csharp
public void Log([CallerLineNumber] int line = -1,
    [CallerFilePath] string path = default,
    [CallerMemberName] string name = default)
```

```
  {
    Console.WriteLine($"Line {line}");
    Console.WriteLine(path);
    Console.WriteLine(name);
    Console.WriteLine();
  }
```

Let's invoke this method with some different scenarios. In the following `Main` method, the `Log` method is called by using an instance of the `Program` class, within the set accessor of the property, and within a lambda expression. Argument values are not assigned to the method, enabling the compiler to fill them in:

```
public static void Main()
{
  Program p = new();
  p.Log();
  p.SomeProperty = 33;
  Action a1 = () => p.Log();
  a1();
}

private int _someProperty;
public int SomeProperty
{
  get => _someProperty;
  set
  {
    Log();
    _someProperty = value;
  }
}
```

The result of the running program is shown next. Where the `Log` method was invoked, you can see the line numbers, the filename, and the caller member name. With the `Log` inside the `Main` method, the member name is `Main`. The invocation of the `Log` method inside the set accessor of the property `SomeProperty` shows `SomeProperty`. The `Log` method inside the lambda expression doesn't show the name of the generated method, but instead the name of the method where the lambda expression was invoked (`Main`), which is more useful, of course.

```
Line 9
C:\ProCSharp\ErrorsAndExceptions\CallerInformation\Program.cs
Main

Line 21
C:\ProCSharp\ErrorsAndExceptions\CallerInformation\Program.cs
SomeProperty

Line 11
C:\ProCSharp\ErrorsAndExceptions\CallerInformation\Program.cs
Main
```

Using the `Log` method within a constructor, the caller member name shows `ctor`. With a destructor, the caller member name is `Finalize`, as this is the method name generated.

> **NOTE** *The destructor and finalizer are covered in Chapter 13.*

> **NOTE** *A great use of the* `CallerMemberName` *attribute is with the implementation of the interface* `INotifyPropertyChanged`. *This interface requires the name of the property to be passed with the method implementation. You can see the implementation of this interface in Chapter 30, "Patterns with XAML Apps."*

SUMMARY

This chapter examined the rich mechanism C# provides for dealing with error conditions through exceptions. You are not limited to the generic error codes that could be output from your code; instead, you have the capability to go in and uniquely handle the most granular of error conditions. Sometimes these error conditions are provided to you through .NET itself; at other times, though, you might want to code your own error conditions as illustrated in this chapter. In either case, you have many ways to protect the workflow of your applications from unnecessary and dangerous faults.

Detailed information on logging errors is covered in Chapter 16, "Diagnostics and Metrics."

The next chapter goes into important keywords for asynchronous programming: `async` and `await`.

11

Tasks and Asynchronous Programming

WHAT'S IN THIS CHAPTER?

- ➤ The importance of asynchronous programming
- ➤ Using the `async` and `await` keywords with the task-based async pattern
- ➤ Creating and using tasks
- ➤ Foundations of asynchronous programming
- ➤ Error handling with asynchronous methods
- ➤ Cancellation of asynchronous methods
- ➤ Async streams
- ➤ Asynchronous programming with Windows apps

CODE DOWNLOADS FOR THIS CHAPTER

The source code for this chapter is available on the book page at www.wiley.com. Click the Downloads link. The code can also be found at https://github.com/ProfessionalCSharp/ProfessionalCSharp2021 in the directory 1_CS/Tasks.

The code for this chapter is divided into the following major examples:

- ➤ TaskBasedAsyncPattern
- ➤ TaskFoundations
- ➤ ErrorHandling
- ➤ AsyncStreams
- ➤ AsyncDesktopWindowsApp

All the sample projects have nullable reference types enabled.

WHY ASYNCHRONOUS PROGRAMMING IS IMPORTANT

Users find it annoying when an application does not immediately react to requests. As we scroll through a list, we have become accustomed to experiencing a delay because we've learned that behavior over several decades. We are accustomed to this behavior when using the mouse. However, with a touch UI, we often don't accept such a delay. An application with a touch UI needs to react immediately to requests. Otherwise, the user tries to redo the action, possibly by touching the screen more firmly.

Because asynchronous programming was hard to achieve with older versions of .NET, it was not always done when it should have been. One of the applications that blocked the UI thread fairly often is an older version of Visual Studio. With that version, opening a solution containing hundreds of projects meant you could take a long coffee break. Visual Studio 2017 offered the *Lightweight Solution Load* feature, which loads projects only as needed and with the selected project loaded first. Since Visual Studio 2015, the NuGet package manager is no longer implemented as a modal dialog. The new NuGet package manager can load information about packages asynchronously while you do other things at the same time. These are just a few examples of important changes built into Visual Studio related to asynchronous programming.

Many APIs with .NET offer both a synchronous and an asynchronous version. Because the synchronous version of the API was a lot easier to use, it was often used where it wasn't appropriate. With the Windows Runtime (WinRT), if an API call is expected to take longer than 40 milliseconds, only an asynchronous version is available. Since C# 5.0, programming asynchronously is as easy as programming in a synchronous manner, so there shouldn't be any barriers to using the asynchronous APIs, but of course there can be traps, which are covered in this chapter.

C# 8 introduced async streams that make it easy to consume async results continuously. This topic is covered in this chapter as well.

> **NOTE** *.NET offers different patterns for asynchronous programming. .NET 1.0 defined the async pattern. With this pattern,* BeginXX *and* EndXX *methods are offered. One example is the* WebRequest *class in the* System.Net *namespace with the* BeginGetResponse *and* EndGetResponse *methods. This pattern is based on the* IAsyncResult *interface and the* AsyncCallback *delegate. When using this pattern with the implementation of Windows applications, it is necessary to switch back to the user interface (UI) thread after the result is received.*
>
> *.NET 2.0 introduced the event-based async pattern. With this pattern, an event is used to receive the asynchronous result, and the method to invoke has the Async postfix. An example is the* WebClient *class (an abstraction of* WebRequest*) with the method* DownloadStringAsync *and the corresponding event* DownloadStringCompleted*. Using this pattern with Windows applications where a synchronization context is created, it's not necessary to switch to the UI thread manually. This is done from the event.*
>
> *With new applications, you can ignore the methods offered by these patterns. Instead, C# 5 introduced the task-based async pattern. This pattern is based on .NET 4 features, the task parallel library (TPL). With this pattern, an asynchronous method returns a* Task *(or other types offering the* GetAwaiter *method), and you can use the* await *keyword to wait for the result. Methods usually have the Async postfix with this pattern as well. A modern class for doing network requests for implementing this pattern is* HttpClient *with the* GetAsync *method.*
>
> *Both the* WebClient *and* WebRequest *classes offer the new pattern as well. To avoid a naming conflict with the older pattern,* WebClient *adds* Task *to the method name—for example,* DownloadStringTaskAsync*.*
>
> *With new clients, just ignore the* Begin/End *methods, and the events based on the async pattern with the classes that offer this functionality to support legacy applications.*

TASK-BASED ASYNC PATTERN

Let's start with using an implementation of the task-based async pattern. The `HttpClient` class (which is explained in more detail in Chapter 19, "Networking") among many other classes implements this pattern. Nearly all methods of this class are named with an `Async` postfix and return a `Task`. This is the declaration of one overload of the `GetAsync` method:

```
public Task<HttpResponseMessage> GetAsync(Uri? requestUri);
```

The sample application uses these namespaces besides the `System` namespace:

```
System.Net.Http

System.Threading.Tasks
```

With the sample application, a command-line argument can be passed to start the application. If a command-line argument is not set, the user is asked to enter a link to a website. After the `HttpClient` is instantiated, the `GetAsync` method is invoked. Using the `await` keyword, the calling thread is not blocked, but the result variable response is only filled as soon as the `Task` returned from the `GetAsync` method is completed (the task status will have the state `RunToCompletion`). When you use the `async` keyword, there's no need to specify an event handler or pass a completion delegate as was necessary with the older async patterns. The `HttpResponseMessage` has a `IsSuccessStatusCode` property that is used to verify if the response from the service was successful. With a successful return, the content is retrieved using the `ReadAsStringAsync` method. This method returns `Task<string>` that can be awaited as well. As soon as the result is available, the first 200 characters of the string HTML are written to the console (code file `TaskBasedAsyncPattern/Program.cs`):

```csharp
using System;
using System.Net.Http;
using System.Threading.Tasks;

string uri = (args.Length >= 1) ? args[0] : string.Empty;
if (string.IsNullOrEmpty(uri))
{
  Console.Write("enter an URL (e.g. https://csharp.christiannagel.com): ");
  uri = Console.ReadLine() ?? throw new InvalidOperationException();
}
using HttpClient httpClient = new();
try
{
  using HttpResponseMessage response = await httpClient.GetAsync(new Uri(uri));
  if (response.IsSuccessStatusCode)
  {
    string html = await response.Content.ReadAsStringAsync();
    Console.WriteLine(html[..200]);
  }
  else
  {
    Console.WriteLine($"Status code: {response.StatusCode}");
  }
}
catch (UriFormatException ex)
{
  Console.WriteLine($"Error parsing the Uri {ex.Message}");
}
```

```
catch (HttpRequestException ex)
{
    Console.WriteLine($"HTTP request exception: {ex.Message}");
}
catch (TaskCanceledException ex)
{
    Console.WriteLine($"Task canceled: {ex.Message}");
}
```

> **NOTE** *The* using *declaration that's used with the* HttpClient *and the* HttpResponseMessage *invokes the* Dispose *method at the end of the variable scope. This is explained in detail in Chapter 13, "Managed and Unmanaged Memory."*

To run the program and pass command-line arguments using the .NET CLI, you need to pass two dashes to distinguish the command-line arguments that are meant for the application from the arguments used for the .NET CLI and start the application this way:

```
> dotnet run -- https://csharp.christiannagel.com
```

Using top-level statements, the variable args is created automatically. Using await with the top-level statements, the generated Main method is defined with an async scope. When you write a custom Main method that uses await, it needs to be declared to return a Task:

```
public class Program
{
    static async Task Main(string[] args)
    {
        //...
    }
}
```

TASKS

The async and await keywords are compiler features. The compiler creates code by using functionality from the Task class, which you also can write yourself. This section gives information about the Task class and what the compiler does with the async and await keywords. It shows you an effortless way to create an asynchronous method and demonstrates how to invoke multiple asynchronous methods in parallel. You also see how you can change a class to offer the asynchronous pattern with the async and await keywords.

The sample application uses these namespaces besides the System namespace:

```
System.Collections.Generic

System.IO

System.Linq

System.Net

System.Runtime.CompilerServices

System.Threading

System.Threading.Tasks
```

> **NOTE** *This downloadable sample application makes use of command-line arguments, so you can easily verify each scenario. For example, using the .NET CLI, you can pass the* async *command-line parameter with this command:* dotnet run -- -async. *When using Visual Studio, you can also configure the application arguments in Debug Project Settings.*

To better understand what's going on, the TraceThreadAndTask method is created to write thread and task information to the console. Task.CurrentId returns the identifier of the task. Thread.CurrentThread.ManagedThreadId returns the identifier of the current thread (code file TaskFoundations/Program.cs):

```
public static void TraceThreadAndTask(string info)
{
  string taskInfo = Task.CurrentId == null ? "no task" : "task " +
    Task.CurrentId;

  Console.WriteLine($"{info} in thread {Thread.CurrentThread.ManagedThreadId} " +
    $"and {taskInfo}");
}
```

Creating Tasks

Let's start with the synchronous method Greeting, which takes a while before returning a string (code file TaskFoundations/Program.cs):

```
static string Greeting(string name)
{
  TraceThreadAndTask($"running {nameof(Greeting)}");
  Task.Delay(3000).Wait();
  return $"Hello, {name}";
}
```

To make such a method asynchronously, you define the method GreetingAsync. The task-based asynchronous pattern specifies that an asynchronous method is named with the Async suffix and returns a Task. GreetingAsync is defined to have the same input parameters as the Greeting method but returns Task<string>. Task<string> defines a task that returns a string in the future. A simple way to return a task is by using the Task.Run method. This method creates a new task and starts it. The generic version Task.Run<string>() creates a task that returns a string. Because the compiler already knows the return type from the implementation (Greeting returns a string), you can also simplify the implementation by using Task.Run():

```
static Task<string> GreetingAsync(string name) =>
  Task.Run(() =>
  {
    TraceThreadAndTask($"running {nameof(GreetingAsync)}");
    return Greeting(name);
  });
```

Calling an Asynchronous Method

You can call this asynchronous method GreetingAsync by using the await keyword on the task that is returned. The await keyword requires the method to be declared with the async modifier. The code within this method does not continue before the GreetingAsync method is completed. However, you can reuse the thread that started the `CallerWithAsync` method. This thread is not blocked (code file `TaskFoundations/Program.cs`):

```
private async static void CallerWithAsync()
{
  TraceThreadAndTask($"started {nameof(CallerWithAsync)}");
  string result = await GreetingAsync("Stephanie");
  Console.WriteLine(result);
  TraceThreadAndTask($"ended {nameof(CallerWithAsync)}");
}
```

When you run the application, you can see from the first output that there's no task. The `GreetingAsync` method is running in a task, and this task is using a different thread from the caller. The synchronous `Greeting` method then runs in this task. As the `Greeting` method returns, the `GreetingAsync` method returns, and the scope is back in the `CallerWithAsync` method after the await. Now, the `CallerWithAsync` method runs in a different thread than before. There's not a task anymore, but although the method started with thread 1, after the `await` thread 4 was used. The `await` made sure that the continuation happens after the task was completed, but it now uses a different thread. This behavior is different between Console applications and applications that have a synchronization context, which is described later in this chapter in the "Async with Windows Apps" section:

```
started CallerWithAsync in thread 1 and no task
running GreetingAsync in thread 4 and task 1
running Greeting in thread 4 and task 1
Hello, Stephanie
ended CallerWithAsync in thread 4 and no task
```

> **NOTE** *The* `async` *modifier can be used with methods that return* `void` *or return an object that offers the* `GetAwaiter` *method. .NET offers the* `Task` *and* `ValueTask` *types. With the Windows Runtime, you also can use* `IAsyncOperation`*. You should avoid using the* `async` *modifier with void methods; read more about this in the "Error Handling" section later in this chapter.*

The next section explains what's driving the `await` keyword. Behind the scenes, continuation tasks are used.

Using the Awaiter

You can use the `async` keyword with any object that offers the `GetAwaiter` method and returns an awaiter. An awaiter implements the interface `INotifyCompletion` with the method `OnCompleted`. This method is invoked when the task is completed. With the following code snippet, instead of using `await` on the task, the `GetAwaiter` method of the task is used. `GetAwaiter` from the `Task` class returns a `TaskAwaiter`. Using the `OnCompleted` method, a local function is assigned that is invoked when the task is completed (code file `TaskFoundations/Program.cs`):

```
private static void CallerWithAwaiter()
{
  TraceThreadAndTask($"starting {nameof(CallerWithAwaiter)}");
  TaskAwaiter<string> awaiter = GreetingAsync("Matthias").GetAwaiter();
  awaiter.OnCompleted(OnCompleteAwaiter);

  void OnCompleteAwaiter()
  {
    Console.WriteLine(awaiter.GetResult());
    TraceThreadAndTask($"ended {nameof(CallerWithAwaiter)}");
  }
}
```

When you run the application, you can see a result similar to the scenario in which you used the `await` keyword:

```
starting CallerWithAwaiter in thread 1 and no task
running GreetingAsync in thread 4 and task 1
running Greeting in thread 4 and task 1
Hello, Matthias
ended CallerWithAwaiter in thread 4 and no task
```

The compiler converts the `await` keyword by putting all the code that follows within the block of an `OnCompleted` method.

Continuation with Tasks

You can also handle continuation by using features of the `Task` object. `GreetingAsync` returns a `Task<string>` object. The `Task` object contains information about the task created and allows waiting for its completion. The `ContinueWith` method of the `Task` class defines the code that should be invoked as soon as the task is finished. The delegate assigned to the `ContinueWith` method receives the completed task with its argument, which allows accessing the result from the task using the `Result` property (code file `TaskFoundations/Program.cs`):

```
private static void CallerWithContinuationTask()
{
  TraceThreadAndTask("started CallerWithContinuationTask");

  var t1 = GreetingAsync("Stephanie");

  t1.ContinueWith(t =>
  {
    string result = t.Result;
    Console.WriteLine(result);

    TraceThreadAndTask("ended CallerWithContinuationTask");
  });
}
```

Synchronization Context

If you verify the thread that is used within the methods, you will find that in all three methods—`CallerWithAsync`, `CallerWithAwaiter`, and `CallerWithContinuationTask`—different threads are used during the lifetime of the methods. One thread is used to invoke the method `GreetingAsync`, and another thread takes action after the `await` keyword or within the code block in the `ContinueWith` method.

With a console application, usually this is not an issue. However, you have to ensure that at least one foreground thread is still running before all background tasks that should be completed are finished. The sample application invokes `Console.ReadLine` to keep the main thread running until the Return key is pressed.

With applications that are bound to a specific thread for some actions (for example, with WPF, UWP, and WinUI applications, UI elements can be accessed only from the UI thread). This is an issue.

Using the `async` and `await` keywords you don't have to do any special actions to access the UI thread after an `await` completion. By default, the generated code switches the thread to the thread that has the synchronization context. A WPF application sets a `DispatcherSynchronizationContext`, and a Windows Forms application sets a `WindowsFormsSynchronizationContext`. Windows apps use the `WinRTSynchronizationContext`. If the calling thread of the asynchronous method is assigned to the synchronization context, then with the continuous execution after the `await`, the same synchronization context is used by default. If the same synchronization context shouldn't be used, you must invoke the `Task` method `ConfigureAwait(continueOnCapturedContext: false)`. An example that illustrates this usefulness is a Windows app in which the code that follows the `await` is not using any UI elements. In this case, it is faster to avoid the switch to the synchronization context.

Using Multiple Asynchronous Methods

Within an asynchronous method, you can call multiple asynchronous methods. How you code this depends on whether the results from one asynchronous method are needed by another.

Calling Asynchronous Methods Sequentially

You can use the await keyword to call every asynchronous method. In cases where one method is dependent on the result of another method, this is useful. In the following code snippet, await is used with every invocation of GreetingAsync (code file TaskFoundations/Program.cs):

```
private async static void MultipleAsyncMethods()
{
  string s1 = await GreetingAsync("Stephanie");
  string s2 = await GreetingAsync("Matthias");
  Console.WriteLine($"Finished both methods.{Environment.NewLine} " +
    $"Result 1: {s1}{Environment.NewLine} Result 2: {s2}");
}
```

Using Combinators

If the asynchronous methods are not dependent on each other, it is a lot faster not to await on each separately; instead, assign the return of the asynchronous method to a Task variable. The GreetingAsync method returns Task<string>. Both these methods can now run in parallel. Combinators can help with this. A combinator accepts multiple parameters of the same type and returns a value of the same type. The passed parameters are "combined" to one. Task combinators accept multiple Task objects as parameters and return a Task.

The sample code invokes the Task.WhenAll combinator method that you can await to have both tasks finished (code file TaskFoundations/Program.cs):

```
private async static void MultipleAsyncMethodsWithCombinators1()
{
  Task<string> t1 = GreetingAsync("Stephanie");
  Task<string> t2 = GreetingAsync("Matthias");
  await Task.WhenAll(t1, t2);
  Console.WriteLine($"Finished both methods.{Environment.NewLine} " +
    $"Result 1: {t1.Result}{Environment.NewLine} Result 2: {t2.Result}");
}
```

The Task class defines the WhenAll and WhenAny combinators. The Task returned from the WhenAll method is completed as soon as all tasks passed to the method are completed; the Task returned from the WhenAny method is completed as soon as one of the tasks passed to the method is completed.

The WhenAll method of the Task type defines several overloads. If all the tasks return the same type, you can use an array of this type for the result of the await. The GreetingAsync method returns a Task<string>, and awaiting for this method results in a string. Therefore, you can use Task.WhenAll to return a string array:

```
private async static void MultipleAsyncMethodsWithCombinators2()
{
  Task<string> t1 = GreetingAsync("Stephanie");
  Task<string> t2 = GreetingAsync("Matthias");
  string[] result = await Task.WhenAll(t1, t2);
  Console.WriteLine($"Finished both methods.{Environment.NewLine} " +
    $"Result 1: {result[0]}{Environment.NewLine} Result 2: {result[1]}");
}
```

The WhenAll method is of practical use when the waiting task can continue only when all tasks it's waiting for are finished. The WhenAny method can be used when the calling task can do some work when any task it's waiting for is completed. It can use a result from the task to go on.

Using ValueTasks

Previous to C# 7, the await keyword required a Task to wait for. Since C# 7, any class implementing the GetAwaiter method can be used. A type that can be used with await is ValueTask. Task is a class, but ValueTask is a struct. This has a performance advantage because the ValueTask doesn't have an object on the heap.

What is the real overhead of a Task object compared to the asynchronous method call? A method that needs to be invoked asynchronously typically has a lot more overhead than an object on the heap. Most times, the overhead of a Task object on the heap can be ignored—but not always. For example, a method can have one path where data is retrieved from a service with an asynchronous API. With this data retrieval, the data is written to a local cache. When you invoke the method the second time, the data can be retrieved in a fast manner without needing to create a Task object.

The sample method GreetingValueTaskAsync does exactly this. In case the name is already found in the dictionary, the result is returned as a ValueTask. If the name isn't in the dictionary, the GreetingAsync method is invoked, which returns a Task. This task is awaited. The result received is used to return it in a ValueTask (code file TaskFoundations/Program.cs):

```csharp
private readonly static Dictionary<string, string> names = new Dictionary<string,
string>();

static async ValueTask<string> GreetingValueTaskAsync(string name)
{
  if (names.TryGetValue(name, out string result))
  {
    return result;
  }
  else
  {
    result = await GreetingAsync(name);
    names.Add(name, result);
    return result;
  }
}
```

The UseValueTask method invokes the method GreetingValueTaskAsync two times with the same name. The first time, the data is retrieved using the GreetingAsync method; the second time, data is found in the dictionary and returned from there:

```csharp
private static async void UseValueTask()
{
  string result = await GreetingValueTaskAsync("Katharina");
  Console.WriteLine(result);
  string result2 = await GreetingValueTaskAsync("Katharina");
  Console.WriteLine(result2);
}
```

If a method doesn't use the async modifier and a ValueTask needs to be returned, ValueTask objects can be created using the constructor passing the result or passing a Task object:

```csharp
static ValueTask<string> GreetingValueTask2Async(string name)
{
  if (names.TryGetValue(name, out string result))
  {
    return new ValueTask<string>(result);
  }
  else
  {
    Task<string> t1 = GreetingAsync(name);
```

```
            TaskAwaiter<string> awaiter = t1.GetAwaiter();
            awaiter.OnCompleted(OnCompletion);
            return new ValueTask<string>(t1);

            void OnCompletion()
            {
              names.Add(name, awaiter.GetResult());
            }
        }
    }
}
```

ERROR HANDLING

Chapter 10, "Errors and Exceptions," provides detailed coverage of errors and exception handling. However, in the context of asynchronous methods, you should be aware of some special handling of errors.

The code for the ErrorHandling example makes use of the System.Threading.Tasks namespace in addition to the System namespace.

Let's start with a simple method that throws an exception after a delay (code file ErrorHandling/Program.cs):

```
static async Task ThrowAfter(int ms, string message)
{
  await Task.Delay(ms);
  throw new Exception(message);
}
```

If you call the asynchronous method without awaiting it, you can put the asynchronous method within a try/catch block—and the exception will not be caught. That's because the method DontHandle that's shown in the following code snippet has already completed before the exception from ThrowAfter is thrown. You need to await the ThrowAfter method, as shown in the example that follows in the next section. Pay attention that the exception is not caught in this code snippet:

```
private static void DontHandle()
{
  try
  {
    ThrowAfter(200, "first");
    // exception is not caught because this method is finished
    // before the exception is thrown
  }
  catch (Exception ex)
  {
    Console.WriteLine(ex.Message);
  }
}
```

> **WARNING** *Asynchronous methods that return* void *cannot be awaited. The issue with this is that exceptions that are thrown from* async void *methods cannot be caught. That's why it is best to return a* Task *type from an asynchronous method. Handler methods or overridden base methods are exempted from this rule because you can't change the return type here. In cases where you need async void methods, it's best to handle exceptions directly within this method; otherwise, the exception can be missed.*

Handling Exceptions with Asynchronous Methods

A good way to deal with exceptions from asynchronous methods is to use `await` and put a `try`/`catch` statement around it, as shown in the following code snippet. The `HandleOnError` method releases the thread after calling the `ThrowAfter` method asynchronously, but it keeps the `Task` referenced to continue as soon as the task is completed. When that happens (which, in this case, is when the exception is thrown after two seconds), the `catch` matches and the code within the `catch` block is invoked (code file `ErrorHandling/Program.cs`):

```
private static async void HandleOnError()
{
  try
  {
    await ThrowAfter(2000, "first");
  }
  catch (Exception ex)
  {
    Console.WriteLine($"handled {ex.Message}");
  }
}
```

Handling Exceptions with Multiple Asynchronous Methods

What if two asynchronous methods are invoked and both throw exceptions? In the following example, first the `ThrowAfter` method is invoked, which throws an exception with the message `first` after two seconds. After this method is completed, the `ThrowAfter` method is invoked, throwing an exception after one second. Because the first call to `ThrowAfter` already throws an exception, the code within the `try` block does not continue to invoke the second method, instead landing within the `catch` block to deal with the first exception (code file `ErrorHandling/Program.cs`):

```
private static async void StartTwoTasks()
{
  try
  {
    await ThrowAfter(2000, "first");
    await ThrowAfter(1000, "second"); // the second call is not invoked
    // because the first method throws
    // an exception
  }
  catch (Exception ex)
  {
    Console.WriteLine($"handled {ex.Message}");
  }
}
```

Now start the two calls to `ThrowAfter` in parallel. The first method throws an exception after two seconds and the second one after one second. With `Task.WhenAll`, you wait until both tasks are completed, whether an exception is thrown or not. Therefore, after a wait of about two seconds, `Task.WhenAll` is completed, and the exception is caught with the `catch` statement. However, you only see the exception information from the first task that is passed to the `WhenAll` method. It's not the task that threw the exception first (which is the second task), but the first task in the list:

```
private async static void StartTwoTasksParallel()
{
  try
  {
```

```
      Task t1 = ThrowAfter(2000, "first");
      Task t2 = ThrowAfter(1000, "second");
      await Task.WhenAll(t1, t2);
   }
   catch (Exception ex)
   {
      // just display the exception information of the first task
      // that is awaited within WhenAll
      Console.WriteLine($"handled {ex.Message}");
   }
}
```

One way to get the exception information from all tasks is to declare the task variables t1 and t2 outside of the try block, so they can be accessed from within the catch block. Here you can check the status of the task to determine whether they are in a faulted state with the IsFaulted property. In case of an exception, the IsFaulted property returns true. The exception information itself can be accessed by using Exception.InnerException of the Task class. Another, and usually better, way to retrieve exception information from all tasks is demonstrated next.

Using AggregateException Information

To get the exception information from all failing tasks, you can write the result from Task.WhenAll to a Task variable. This task is then awaited until all tasks are completed. Otherwise, the exception would still be missed. As described in the preceding section, with the catch statement, only the exception of the first task can be retrieved. However, now you have access to the Exception property of the outer task. The Exception property is of type AggregateException. This exception type defines the property InnerExceptions (not only InnerException), which contains a list of all the exceptions that have been awaited for. Now you can easily iterate through all the exceptions (code file ErrorHandling/Program.cs):

```
private static async void ShowAggregatedException()
{
   Task taskResult = null;
   try
   {
      Task t1 = ThrowAfter(2000, "first");
      Task t2 = ThrowAfter(1000, "second");
      await (taskResult = Task.WhenAll(t1, t2));
   }
   catch (Exception ex)
   {
      Console.WriteLine($"handled {ex.Message}");
      foreach (var ex1 in taskResult.Exception.InnerExceptions)
      {
         Console.WriteLine($"inner exception {ex1.Message}");
      }
   }
}
```

CANCELLATION OF ASYNC METHODS

To cancel asynchronous operations, .NET includes a cancellation framework. The heart of this is the CancellationToken that's created from a CancellationTokenSource defined in the System.Threading namespace. To allow for cleanup of resources, a task should never be killed. To demonstrate how this can be done, the RunTaskAsync method receives a CancellationToken with a parameter. Within the implementation, the cancellation token is checked if cancellation is requested. If it is, the task has time for cleanup of some resources and exits by invoking the `ThrowIfCancellationRequested` method of the `CancellationToken`. In case cleanup is not required, you can immediately invoke `ThrowIfCancellationRequired`, which throws the `OperationCanceledException` if cancellation is required (code file `TaskCancellation/Program.cs`):

```
Task RunTaskAsync(CancellationToken cancellationToken) =>
  Task.Run(async () =>
  {
    while (true)
    {
      Console.Write(".");
      await Task.Delay(100);
      if (cancellationToken.IsCancellationRequested)
      {
        // do some cleanup
        Console.WriteLine("resource cleanup and good bye!");
        cancellationToken.ThrowIfCancellationRequested();
      }
    }
  });
```

The `Task.Delay` method offers an overload where you can pass the `CancellationToken` as well. This method throws an `OperationCanceledException` as well. If you use this overloaded `Task.Delay` method and need some resource cleanup in the code, you need to catch the `OperationCanceledException` to do the cleanup and re-throw the exception.

When you start the `RunTaskAsync` method, a `CancellationTokenSource` is created. Passing a `TimeSpan` to the constructor cancels the associated token after the specified time. If you have some other task that should do the cancellation, this task can invoke the `Cancel` method of the `CancellationTokenSource`. The `try`/`catch` block catches the previously mentioned `OperationCanceledException` when cancellation occurs.

```
CancellationTokenSource cancellation = new(TimeSpan.FromSeconds(5));

try
{
  await RunTaskAsync(cancellation.Token);
}
catch (OperationCanceledException ex)
{
  Console.WriteLine(ex.Message);
}
```

ASYNC STREAMS

A great enhancement since C# 8 is the support of async streams. Instead of getting just one result from an asynchronous method, a stream of async results can be received. Async streams is based on the interfaces `IAsyncDisposable`, `IAsyncEnumerable`, and `IAsyncEnumerator`, and updated implementations for the `foreach` and `yield` statements. `IAsyncDisposable` defines the `DisposeAsync` method for asynchronously disposing of resources. `IAsyncEnumerable` corresponds to the synchronous `IEnumerable` interface and defines the `GetAsyncEnumerator` method. `IAsyncEnumerator` corresponds to the synchronous `IEnumerator` interface and defines the `MoveNextAsync` method and the `Current` property. The `foreach` statement has been updated with the syntax `await foreach` to iterate through async streams. The `yield` statement has been modified to support returning `IAsyncEnumerable` and `IAsyncEnumerator`.

NOTE *Read Chapter 6, "Arrays," for information about how the* foreach *and* yield *statements make use of the synchronous iterator interfaces.*

To see async streams in action, a virtual device represented from the class ADevice returns random sensor data in an async stream. The sensor data is defined with the record SensorData. The device returns sensor data until it is canceled. Adding the attribute EnumeratorCancellation to the CancellationToken allows cancellation via an extension method shown later. Within the endless loop implementation, the yield return statement is used to return stream values for the IAsyncEnumerable interface (code file AsyncStreams/Program.cs):

```
public record SensorData(int Value1, int Value2);

public class ADevice
{
  private Random _random = new();
  public async IAsyncEnumerable<SensorData> GetSensorData(
    [EnumeratorCancellation] CancellationToken = default)
  {
    while(true)
    {
      await Task.Delay(250, cancellationToken);
      yield return new SensorData(_random.Next(20), _random.Next(20));
    }
  }
}
```

After defining a method that returns an async stream with the help of the yield return statement, let's use this from an await foreach. Here, the async stream is iterated, and the cancellation token is passed using the WithCancellation method to stop the stream after five seconds:

```
using System;
using System.Threading;
using System.Threading.Tasks;

CancellationTokenSource cancellation = new(TimeSpan.FromSeconds(5));

var aDevice = new ADevice();
try
{
  await foreach (var data in aDevice.GetSensorData().WithCancellation(cancellation.Token))
  {
    Console.WriteLine($"{data.Value1} {data.Value2}");
  }
}
catch (OperationCanceledException ex)
{
  Console.WriteLine(ex.Message);
}
```

NOTE *See Chapter 25, "Services," and Chapter 28, "SignalR," for information about how async streaming can be used to asynchronously stream data across the network.*

ASYNC WITH WINDOWS APPS

Using the `async` keyword with Windows apps works the same as what you've already seen in this chapter. However, you need to be aware that after calling `await` from the UI thread, when the asynchronous method returns, you're back in the UI thread by default. This makes it easy to update UI elements after the asynchronous method is completed.

> **NOTE** *The Windows apps sample code in this chapter uses the new technology WinUI to create a Windows application. Because this technology is so new, please check for updated readme files in the directory of the code samples for what you need to run this application. Using WPF or UWP instead is not a lot different, and you can change the code for these technologies easily.*

Let's create a WinUI Desktop application with Visual Studio. This app contains five buttons and a `TextBlock` element to demonstrate different scenarios (code file `AsyncWindowsApps/MainWindow.xaml`):

```
<StackPanel>
  <Button Content="Start Async" Click="OnStartAsync" Margin="4"/>
  <Button Content="Start Async with ConfigureAwait" Click="OnStartAsyncConfigureAwait"
    Margin="4"/>
  <Button Content="Start Async with Thread Switch"
    Click="OnStartAsyncWithThreadSwitch" Margin="4"/>
  <Button Content="Use IAsyncOperation" Click="OnIAsyncOperation" Margin="4"/>
  <Button Content="Deadlock" Click="OnStartDeadlock" Margin="4"/>
  <TextBlock x:Name="text1" Margin="4"/>
</StackPanel>
```

> **NOTE** *Programming WinUI apps is covered in detail in Chapters 29 through 32.*

In the `OnStartAsync` method, the thread ID of the UI thread is written to the `TextBlock` element. Next, the asynchronous method `Task.Delay`, which does not block the UI thread, is invoked, and after this method is completed, the thread ID is written to the `TextBlock` again (code file `AsyncWindowsDesktopApp/MainWindow.xaml.cs`):

```
private async void OnStartAsync(object sender, RoutedEventArgs e)
{
  text1.Text = $"UI thread: {GetThread()}";
  await Task.Delay(1000);
  text1.Text += $"\n after await: {GetThread()}";
}
```

For accessing the thread ID, WinUI can now use the `Thread` class. With older UWP versions, you need to use `Environment.CurrentManagedThreadId` instead:

```
private string GetThread() => $"thread: {Thread.CurrentThread.ManagedThreadId}";
```

When you run the application, you can see similar output in the text element. Contrary to console applications, with Windows apps defining a synchronization context, after the `await` you can see the same thread as before. This allows direct access to UI elements:

```
UI thread: thread 1
after await: thread 1
```

Configure Await

If you don't need access to UI elements, you can configure `await` not to use the synchronization context. The next code snippet demonstrates the configuration and also shows why you shouldn't access UI elements from a background thread.

With the method `OnStartAsyncConfigureAwait`, after writing the ID of the UI thread to the text information, the local function `AsyncFunction` is invoked. In this local function, the starting thread is written before the asynchronous method `Task.Delay` is invoked. Using the task returned from this method, the `ConfigureAwait` is invoked. With this method, the task is configured by passing the `continueOnCapturedContext` argument set to `false`. With this context configuration, you see that the thread after the await is not the UI thread anymore. Using a different thread to write the result to the `result` variable is okay. What you should never do is shown in the `try` block: accessing UI elements from a non-UI thread. The exception you get contains the `HRESULT` value as shown in the `when` clause. Just this exception is caught in the `catch`: the result is returned to the caller. With the caller, `ConfigureAwait` is invoked as well, but this time the `continueOnCapturedContext` is set to true. Here, both before and after the await, the method is running in the UI thread (code file `AsyncWindowsDesktopApp/MainWindow.xaml.cs`):

```csharp
private async void OnStartAsyncConfigureAwait(object sender, RoutedEventArgs e)
{
  text1.Text = $"UI thread: {GetThread()}";

  string s = await AsyncFunction().ConfigureAwait(
    continueOnCapturedContext: true);

  // after await, with continueOnCapturedContext true we are back in the UI thread
  text1.Text += $"\n{s}\nafter await: {GetThread()}";

  async Task<string> AsyncFunction()
  {
    string result = $"\nasync function: {GetThread()}\n";
    await Task.Delay(1000).ConfigureAwait(continueOnCapturedContext: false);
    result += $"\nasync function after await : {GetThread()};";

    try
    {
      text1.Text = "this is a call from the wrong thread";
      return "not reached";
    }
    catch (Exception ex) when (ex.HResult == -2147417842)
    {
      result += $"exception: {ex.Message}";
      return result;
      // we know it's the wrong thread
      // don't access UI elements from the previous try block
    }
  }
}
```

> **NOTE** *Exception handling and filtering is explained in Chapter 10.*

When you run the application, you can see output similar to the following. In the async local function after the `await`, a different thread is used. The text "`not reached`" is never written, because the exception is thrown:

```
UI thread: thread 1
async function: thread 1
async function after await: thread 5; exception: The application called an interface
that was marshalled for a different thread.
after await: thread 1
```

> **NOTE** *In later WinUI chapters in this book, data binding is used instead of directly accessing properties of UI elements. However, with WinUI, you also can't write properties that are bound to UI elements from a non-UI thread.*

Switch to the UI Thread

In some scenarios, there's no effortless way around using a background thread and accessing UI elements. Here, you can switch to the UI thread with the `DispatcherQueue` object that is returned from the `DispatcherQueue` property. The `DispatcherQueue` property is defined in the `DependencyObject` class. `DependencyObject` is a base class of UI elements. Invoking the `TryEnqueu` method of the `DispatcherQueue` object runs the passed lambda expression again in a UI thread (code file `AsyncWindowsDesktopApp/MainWindow.xaml.cs`):

```csharp
private async void OnStartAsyncWithThreadSwitch(object sender, RoutedEventArgs e)
{
  text1.Text = $"UI thread: {GetThread()}";

  string s = await AsyncFunction();

  text1.Text += $"\nafter await: {GetThread()}";

  async Task<string> AsyncFunction()
  {
    string result = $"\nasync function: {GetThread()}\n";
    await Task.Delay(1000).ConfigureAwait(continueOnCapturedContext: false);
    result += $"\nasync function after await : {GetThread()}";

    text1.DispatcherQueue.TryEnqueue(() =>
    {
      text1.Text +=
        $"\nasync function switch back to the UI thread: {GetThread()}";
    }
    return result;
  }
}
```

When you run the application, you can see the UI thread used when using `RunAsync`:

```
UI Thread: thread 1
async function switch back to the UI thread: thread 1
async function: thread 1
async function after await: thread 4
after await: thread 1
```

Using IAsyncOperation

Asynchronous methods are defined by the Windows Runtime not to return a `Task` or a `ValueTask`. `Task` and `ValueTask` are not part of the Windows Runtime. Instead, these methods return an object that implements the interface `IAsyncOperation`. `IAsyncOperation` does not define the method `GetAwaiter` as needed by the `await` keyword. However, an `IAsyncOperation` is automatically converted to a `Task` when you use the `await` keyword. You can also use the `AsTask` extension method to convert an `IAsyncOperation` object to a task.

With the example application, in the method `OnIAsyncOperation`, the `ShowAsync` method of the `MessageDialog` is invoked. This method returns an `IAsyncOperation`, and you can simply use the `await` keyword to get the result (code file `AsyncDesktopWindowsApp/MainWindow.xaml.cs`):

```csharp
private async void OnIAsyncOperation(object sender, RoutedEventArgs e)
{
  MessageDialog dlg = new("Select One, Two, Or Three", "Sample");

  dlg.Commands.Add(new UICommand("One", null, 1));
  dlg.Commands.Add(new UICommand("Two", null, 2));
  dlg.Commands.Add(new UICommand("Three", null, 3));

  IUICommand command = await dlg.ShowAsync();

  text1.Text = $"Command {command.Id} with the label {command.Label} invoked";
}
```

Avoid Blocking Scenarios

It's dangerous using `Wait` on a `Task` and the `async` keyword together. With applications using the synchronization context, this can easily result in a deadlock.

In the method `OnStartDeadlock`, the local function `DelayAsync` is invoked. `DelayAsync` waits on the completion of `Task.Delay` before continuing in the foreground thread. However, the caller invokes the `Wait` method on the task returned from `DelayAsync`. The `Wait` method blocks the calling thread until the task is completed. In this case, the `Wait` is invoked from the foreground thread, so the `Wait` blocks the foreground thread. The `await` on `Task.Delay` can never complete, because the foreground thread is not available. This is a classical deadlock scenario (code file `AsyncWindowsDesktopApp/MainWindow.xaml.cs`):

```csharp
private void OnStartDeadlock(object sender, RoutedEventArgs e)
{
  DelayAsync().Wait();
}

private async Task DelayAsync()
{
  await Task.Delay(1000);
}
```

> **WARNING** *Avoid using* Wait *and* await *together in applications using the synchronization context.*

SUMMARY

This chapter introduced the async and await keywords. In the examples provided, you've seen the advantages of the task-based asynchronous pattern compared to the asynchronous pattern and the event-based asynchronous pattern available with earlier editions of .NET.

You've also seen how easy it is to create asynchronous methods with the help of the Task class and learned how to use the async and await keywords to wait for these methods without blocking threads. You looked at the error-handling and cancelation aspects of asynchronous methods, and you've seen how async streams are supported with C#. For invoking asynchronous methods in parallel, you've seen the use of Task.WhenAll.

For more information on parallel programming and details about threads and tasks, see Chapter 17, "Parallel Programming."

The next chapter continues with core features of C# and .NET and gives detailed information on reflection, metadata, and source generators.

12

Reflection, Metadata, and Source Generators

WHAT'S IN THIS CHAPTER?

➤ Using custom attributes

➤ Inspecting the metadata at runtime using reflection

➤ Working with the dynamic type

➤ Creating dynamic objects with `ExpandoObject`

➤ Compiling code with source generators

CODE DOWNLOADS FOR THIS CHAPTER

The source code for this chapter is available on the book page at www.wiley.com. Click the Downloads link. The code can also be found at https://github.com/ProfessionalCSharp/ProfessionalCSharp2021 in the directory 1_CS/ReflectionAndSourceGenerators.

The code for this chapter is divided into the following major examples:

➤ LookupWhatsNew

➤ TypeView

➤ VectorClass

➤ WhatsNewAttributes

➤ Dynamic

➤ DynamicFileReader

➤ CodeGenerationSample

All the sample projects have nullable reference types enabled.

INSPECTING CODE AT RUNTIME AND DYNAMIC PROGRAMMING

This chapter focuses on custom attributes, reflection, dynamic programming, and source code generation during the build process with C# 9 source generators. Custom attributes are mechanisms that enable you to associate custom metadata with program elements. This metadata is created at compile time and embedded in an assembly. *Reflection* is a generic term that describes the capability to inspect and manipulate program elements at runtime. For example, reflection allows you to do the following:

➤ Enumerate the members of a type

➤ Instantiate a new object

➤ Execute the members of an object

➤ Find out information about a type

➤ Find out information about an assembly

➤ Inspect the custom attributes applied to a type

➤ Create and compile a new assembly

This list represents a great deal of functionality and encompasses some of the most powerful and complex capabilities provided by .NET. Because one chapter does not have the space to cover all the capabilities of reflection, I focus on those elements that you are likely to use most frequently.

To demonstrate custom attributes and reflection, in this chapter, you first develop an example based on a company that regularly ships upgrades of its software and wants to have details about these upgrades documented automatically. In the example, you define custom attributes that indicate the date when program elements were last modified and what changes were made. You then use reflection to develop an application that looks for these attributes in an assembly and can automatically display all the details about what upgrades have been made to the software since a given date.

Another example in this chapter considers an application that reads from or writes to a database and uses custom attributes as a way to mark which classes and properties correspond to which database tables and columns. By reading these attributes from the assembly at runtime, the program can automatically retrieve or write data to the appropriate location in the database without requiring specific logic for each table or column.

The second aspect of this chapter is dynamic programming, which has been a part of the C# language since version 4 when the `dynamic` type was added. Although C# is a statically typed language, the additions for dynamic programming give the C# language capabilities for calling script functions from within C#.

In this chapter, you look at the `dynamic` type and the rules for using it. You also see what an implementation of `DynamicObject` looks like and how you can use it. `ExpandoObject`, which is an implementation of `DynamicObject`, is also covered.

The third big aspect of this chapter is a C# 9 enhancement—source generators. With source generators, code can be created while you start the build process. The source code you write can be enhanced, and you can also use other data sources to create C# source code. In this chapter, you'll see source generators checking attributes. This results in generating code that's available during compile time instead of using reflection during runtime.

CUSTOM ATTRIBUTES

You have already seen in this book how you can define attributes on various items within your program. These attributes have been defined by Microsoft as part of .NET, and many of them receive special support from the C# compiler. This means that for those particular attributes, the compiler can customize the compilation process in specific ways—for example, laying out a struct in memory according to the details in the `StructLayout` attributes.

.NET also enables you to define attributes. By default, custom attributes don't have any effect on the compilation process because the compiler has no intrinsic awareness of them (later you'll see source generators where custom attributes can have an effect on the compilation process). These attributes are emitted as metadata in the compiled assembly when they are applied to program elements.

By itself, this metadata might be useful for documentation purposes, but what makes attributes really powerful is that by using reflection, your code can read this metadata and use it to make decisions at runtime. This means that the custom attributes that you define can directly affect how your code runs. For example, custom attributes can be used to enable declarative code access security checks for custom permission classes, to associate information with program elements that can then be used by testing tools, or when developing extensible frameworks that allow the loading of plug-ins or modules.

Writing Custom Attributes

To understand how to write custom attributes, it is useful to know what the compiler does when it encounters an element in your code that has a custom attribute applied to it. Suppose that you have a C# property declaration that looks like this:

```
[FieldName("SocialSecurityNumber")]
public string SocialSecurityNumber
{
  get {
   //...
```

When the C# compiler recognizes that this property has an attribute applied to it (FieldName), it first appends the string Attribute to this name, forming the combined name FieldNameAttribute. The compiler then searches all the namespaces in its search path (those namespaces that have been mentioned in a using directive) for a class with the specified name. Note that if you mark an item with an attribute whose name already ends in the string Attribute, the compiler does not add the string to the name a second time; it leaves the attribute name unchanged. Therefore, the preceding code is equivalent to this:

```
[FieldNameAttribute("SocialSecurityNumber")]
public string SocialSecurityNumber
{
  get {
   //...
```

The compiler expects to find a class with this name, and it expects this class to be derived directly or indirectly from System.Attribute. The compiler also expects that this class contains information governing the use of the attribute. In particular, the attribute class needs to specify the following:

➤ The types of program elements to which the attribute can be applied (classes, structs, properties, methods, and so on)

➤ Whether it is legal for the attribute to be applied more than once to the same program element

➤ Whether the attribute, when applied to a class or interface, is inherited by derived classes and interfaces

➤ The mandatory and optional parameters the attribute takes

If the compiler cannot find a corresponding attribute class or if it finds one but the way that you have used that attribute does not match the information in the attribute class, the compiler raises a compilation error. For example, if the attribute class indicates that the attribute can be applied only to classes, but you have applied it to a struct definition, a compilation error occurs.

Continuing with the example, assume that you have defined the FieldName attribute like this:

```
[AttributeUsage(AttributeTargets.Property,
  AllowMultiple=false, Inherited=false)]
```

```
public class FieldNameAttribute: Attribute
{
  private string _name;
  public FieldNameAttribute(string name) => _name = name;
}
```

The following sections discuss each element of this definition.

Specifying the AttributeUsage Attribute

The first thing to note is that the attribute class is marked with an attribute—the `System`
`.AttributeUsage` attribute. This is an attribute defined by Microsoft for which the C# compiler provides
special support. The primary purpose of `AttributeUsage` is to identify the types of program elements to which
your custom attribute can be applied. This information is provided by the first parameter of the `AttributeUs-`
`age` attribute. This parameter is mandatory, and it is of an enumerated type, `AttributeTargets`. In the previous example, you have indicated that the `FieldName` attribute can be applied only to properties, which is fine,
because that is exactly what you have applied it to in the earlier code fragment. The `AttributeTargets` enum
type defines members to apply attributes on the assembly, classes, constructors, fields, events, methods, interfaces,
structs, return values, and more.

Note that when applying the attribute to a program element, you place the attribute in square brackets immediately before the element. However, two values in the preceding list do not correspond to any program element:
`Assembly` and `Module`. An attribute can be applied to an assembly or a module as a whole, rather than to an element in your code; in this case the attribute can be placed anywhere in your source code, but it must be prefixed
with the `assembly` or `module` keyword:

```
[assembly:SomeAssemblyAttribute(Parameters)]
[module:SomeAssemblyAttribute(Parameters)]
```

When indicating the valid target elements of a custom attribute, you can combine these values using the bitwise
`OR` operator. For example, if you want to indicate that your `FieldName` attribute can be applied to both properties
and fields, you use the following:

```
[AttributeUsage(AttributeTargets.Property | AttributeTargets.Field,
  AllowMultiple=false, Inherited=false)]
public class FieldNameAttribute: Attribute
```

You can also use `AttributeTargets.All` to indicate that your attribute can be applied to all
types of program elements. The `AttributeUsage` attribute also contains two other parameters: `AllowMultiple`
and `Inherited`. These are specified using the syntax of `<ParameterName>=<ParameterValue>` instead of simply
specifying the values for these parameters. These parameters are optional—you can omit them.

The `AllowMultiple` parameter indicates whether an attribute can be applied more than once to the same item.
The fact that it is set to `false` indicates that the compiler should raise an error if it sees something like this:

```
[FieldName("SocialSecurityNumber")]
[FieldName("NationalInsuranceNumber")]
public string SocialSecurityNumber
{
  //...
```

If the `Inherited` parameter is set to `true`, an attribute applied to a class or interface is also automatically applied
to all derived classes or interfaces. If the attribute is applied to a method or property, it automatically applies to
any overrides of that method or property, and so on.

Specifying Attribute Parameters

This section demonstrates how you can specify the parameters that your custom attribute takes. When the compiler encounters a statement such as the following, it examines the parameters passed into the attribute—which is a string—and looks for a constructor for the attribute that takes exactly those parameters:

```
[FieldName("SocialSecurityNumber")]
public string SocialSecurityNumber
{
   //...
```

If the compiler finds an appropriate constructor, it emits the specified metadata to the assembly. If the compiler does not find an appropriate constructor, a compilation error occurs. As discussed later in this chapter, reflection involves reading metadata (attributes) from assemblies and instantiating the attribute classes they represent. Because of this, the compiler must ensure that an appropriate constructor exists that allows the runtime instantiation of the specified attribute.

In the example, you have supplied just one constructor for `FieldNameAttribute`, and this constructor takes one string parameter. Therefore, when applying the `FieldName` attribute to a property, you must supply one string as a parameter, as shown in the preceding code.

To allow a choice of what types of parameters should be supplied with an attribute, you can provide different constructor overloads, although normal practice is to supply just one constructor and use properties to define any other optional parameters, as explained next.

Specifying Optional Attribute Parameters

As demonstrated with the `AttributeUsage` attribute, an alternative syntax enables optional parameters to be added to an attribute. This syntax involves specifying the names and values of the optional parameters. It works through `public` properties or fields in the attribute class. For example, suppose that you modify the definition of the `SocialSecurityNumber` property as follows:

```
[FieldName("SocialSecurityNumber", Comment="This is the primary key field")]
public string SocialSecurityNumber { get; set; }
{
   //...
```

In this case, the compiler recognizes the `<ParameterName>=<ParameterValue>` syntax of the second parameter and does not attempt to match this parameter to a `FieldNameAttribute` constructor. Instead, it looks for a `public` property or field (although public fields are not considered good programming practice, so normally you will work with properties) of that name that it can use to set the value of this parameter. If you want the previous code to work, you have to add some code to `FieldNameAttribute`:

```
[AttributeUsage(AttributeTargets.Property,
   AllowMultiple=false, Inherited=false)]
public class FieldNameAttribute : Attribute
{
   public string Comment { get; set; }
   private string _fieldName;
   public FieldNameAttribute(string fieldName)
   {
     _fieldName = fieldName;
   }
   //...
}
```

Custom Attribute Example: WhatsNewAttributes

In this section, you start developing the example mentioned at the beginning of the chapter. WhatsNewAttributes provides for an attribute that indicates when a program element was last modified. This is a more ambitious code example than many of the others in that it consists of three separate projects:

➤ WhatsNewAttributes—This library contains the definitions of the attribute classes LastModifiedAttribute and SupportsWhatsNewAttribute.

➤ VectorClass—This library makes use of the custom attributes. Types and members are annotated with these attributes.

➤ LookUpWhatsNew—This executable reads the attributes with reflection.

The WhatsNewAttributes Library

This section starts with the core WhatsNewAttributes .NET library. The source code is contained in the file WhatsNewAttributes.cs, which is located in the WhatsNewAttributes project of the WhatsNewAttributes solution in the example code for this chapter.

The WhatsNewAttributes.cs file defines two attribute classes, LastModifiedAttribute and SupportsWhatsNewAttribute. You use the attribute LastModifiedAttribute to mark when an item was last modified. It takes two mandatory parameters (parameters that are passed to the constructor): the date of the modification and a string containing a description of the changes. One optional parameter named Issues (for which a public property exists) can be used to describe any outstanding issues for the item.

In practice, you would probably want this attribute to apply to anything. To keep the code simple, its usage is limited here to classes, methods, and constructors. You allow it to be applied more than once to the same item (AllowMultiple=true) because an item might be modified more than once, and each modification has to be marked with a separate attribute instance.

SupportsWhatsNew is a smaller class representing an attribute that doesn't take any parameters. The purpose of this assembly attribute is to mark an assembly for which you are maintaining documentation via the LastModifiedAttribute. This way, the program that examines this assembly later knows that the assembly it is reading is one on which you are actually using your automated documentation process. Here is the complete source code for this part of the example (code file ReflectionSamlpes/WhatsNewAttributes/WhatsNewAttributes.cs):

```
[AttributeUsage(AttributeTargets.Class | AttributeTargets.Method |
   AttributeTargets.Constructor | AttributeTargets.Property, AllowMultiple=true,
   Inherited=false)]
public class LastModifiedAttribute: Attribute
{
  private readonly DateTime _dateModified;
  private readonly string _changes;
  public LastModifiedAttribute(string dateModified, string changes)
  {
    _dateModified = DateTime.Parse(dateModified);
    _changes = changes;
  }

  public DateTime DateModified => _dateModified;

  public string Changes => _changes;

  public string Issues { get; set; }
}
```

```
[AttributeUsage(AttributeTargets.Assembly)]
public class SupportsWhatsNewAttribute: Attribute
{
}
```

Based on what has been discussed, this code should be fairly clear. Notice, however, that the properties `DateModified` and `Changes` are read-only. Using the expression syntax, the compiler creates `get` accessors. There is no need for `set` accessors because you are requiring these parameters to be set in the constructor as mandatory parameters. You need the `get` accessors so that you can read the values of these attributes.

The VectorClass Library

The `VectorClass` .NET library references the `WhatsNewAttributes` library. After adding the `using` directives, the global assembly attribute marks the assembly to support the `WhatsNew` attributes (code file `ReflectionSamples/VectorClass/Vector.cs`):

```
[assembly: SupportsWhatsNew]
```

Now for the code for the `Vector` class. Some `LastModified` attributes are added to the class to mark changes:

```
[LastModified("2020/12/19", "updated for C# 9 and .NET 5")]
[LastModified("2017/7/19", "updated for C# 7 and .NET Core 2")]
[LastModified("2015/6/6", "updated for C# 6 and .NET Core")]
[LastModified("2010/12/14", "IEnumerable interface implemented: " +
  "Vector can be treated as a collection")]
[LastModified("2010/2/10", "IFormattable interface implemented " +
  "Vector accepts N and VE format specifiers")]
public class Vector : IFormattable, IEnumerable<double>
{
  [LastModified("2020/12/19", "changed to use deconstruction syntax")]
  public Vector(double x, double y, double z) => (X, Y, Z) = (x, y, z);

  [LastModified("2017/7/19", "Reduced the number of code lines")]
  public Vector(Vector vector)
    : this (vector.X, vector.Y, vector.Z { }

  public double X { get; }
  public double Y { get; }
  public double Z { get; }

  //...
}
```

You also mark the contained `VectorEnumerator` class:

```
[LastModified("2015/6/6",
  "Changed to implement the generic interface IEnumerator<T>")]
[LastModified("2010/2/14",
  "Class created as part of collection support for Vector")]
private class VectorEnumerator : IEnumerator<double>
{
```

The version number for the library is defined in the `csproj` project file (project file `VectorClass/VectorClass.csproj`):

```
<PropertyGroup>
  <TargetFramework>net5.0</TargetFramework>
```

```
  <Nullable>enable</Nullable>
  <Version>5.2.0</Version>
</PropertyGroup>
```

That's as far as you can get with this example for now. You are unable to run anything yet because all you have are two libraries. After taking a look at reflection in the next section, you will develop the final part of the example, in which you look up and display these attributes.

USING REFLECTION

In this section, you take a closer look at the System.Type class, which enables you to access information concerning the definition of any data type. You also look at the System.Reflection.Assembly class, which you can use to access information about an assembly or to load that assembly into your program. Finally, you combine the code in this section with the code in the previous section to complete the WhatsNewAttributes example.

The System.Type Class

So far, you have used the Type class only to hold the reference to a type as follows:

```
Type t = typeof(double);
```

Although previously referred to as a class, Type is an abstract base class. Whenever you instantiate a Type object, you are actually instantiating a class derived from Type. Type has one derived class corresponding to each actual data type, though in general the derived classes simply provide different overloads of the various Type methods and properties that return the correct data for the corresponding data type. They do not typically add new methods or properties. In general, there are three common ways to obtain a Type reference that refers to any given type.

➤ You can use the C# typeof operator as shown in the preceding code. This operator takes the name of the type (not in quotation marks, however) as a parameter.

➤ You can use the GetType method, which all classes inherit from System.Object:

```
double d = 10;
Type t = d.GetType();
```

GetType is called against a variable, rather than taking the name of a type. Note, however, that the Type object returned is still associated with only that data type. It does not contain any information that relates to that instance of the type. The GetType method can be useful if you have a reference to an object but you are not sure what class that object is actually an instance of.

➤ You can call the static method of the Type class, GetType:

```
Type t = Type.GetType("System.Double");
```

Type is really the gateway to much of the reflection functionality. It implements a huge number of methods and properties—far too many to provide a comprehensive list here. However, the following sections should give you a good idea of the kinds of things you can do with the Type class. Note that the available properties are all read-only; you use Type to find out about the data type—you cannot use it to make any modifications to the type!

Type Properties

You can divide the properties implemented by `Type` into three categories. First, a number of properties retrieve the strings containing various names associated with the class, as shown in the following table:

PROPERTY	RETURNS
`Name`	The name of the data type
`FullName`	The fully qualified name of the data type (including the namespace name)
`Namespace`	The name of the namespace in which the data type is defined

Second, it is possible to retrieve references to further type objects that represent related classes, as shown in the following table:

PROPERTY	RETURNS TYPE REFERENCE CORRESPONDING TO
`BaseType`	The immediate base type of this type.
`UnderlyingSystemType`	The type to which this type maps in the .NET runtime (recall that certain .NET base types actually map to specific predefined types recognized by IL). This member is only available in the full Framework.

A number of Boolean properties indicate whether this type is, for example, a `class`, an `enum`, and so on. These properties include `IsAbstract`, `IsArray`, `IsClass`, `IsEnum`, `IsInterface`, `IsPointer`, `IsPrimitive` (one of the predefined primitive data types), `IsPublic`, `IsSealed`, and `IsValueType`. The following example uses a primitive data type:

```
Type intType = typeof(int);
Console.WriteLine(intType.IsAbstract); // writes false
Console.WriteLine(intType.IsClass); // writes false
Console.WriteLine(intType.IsEnum); // writes false
Console.WriteLine(intType.IsPrimitive); // writes true
Console.WriteLine(intType.IsValueType); // writes true
```

This example uses the `Vector` class:

```
Type vecType = typeof(Vector);
Console.WriteLine(vecType.IsAbstract); // writes false
Console.WriteLine(vecType.IsClass); // writes true
Console.WriteLine(vecType.IsEnum); // writes false
Console.WriteLine(vecType.IsPrimitive); // writes false
Console.WriteLine(vecType.IsValueType); // writes false
```

Finally, you can also retrieve a reference to the assembly in which the type is defined. This is returned as a reference to an instance of the `System.Reflection.Assembly` class, which is examined shortly:

```
Type t = typeof (Vector);
Assembly? containingAssembly = Assembly.GetAssembly(t);
```

Methods

Most of the methods of `System.Type` are used to obtain details about the members of the corresponding data type—the constructors, properties, methods, events, and so on. Quite a large number of methods exist, but they all follow the same pattern. For example, two methods retrieve details about the methods of the data type: `GetMethod` and `GetMethods`. `GetMethod` returns a reference to a `System.Reflection.MethodInfo` object, which contains details about a method. `GetMethods` returns an array of such references. As the names suggest, the difference is that `GetMethods` returns details about all the methods, whereas `GetMethod` returns details about just one method with a specified parameter list. Both methods have overloads that take an extra parameter, a `BindingFlags` enumerated value that indicates which members should be returned—for example, whether to return public members, instance members, static members, and so on. If you add binding flags, you need to include one of `Instance` or `Static` and one of `Private` or `Public`. Otherwise, you don't get anything.

For example, the simplest overload of `GetMethods` takes no parameters and returns details about all the public methods of the data type:

```
Type t = typeof(double);
foreach (MethodInfo nextMethod in t.GetMethods())
{
    Console.WriteLine(nextMethod.Name);
}
```

The member methods of `Type` that follow the same pattern are shown in the following table. Note that plural names return an array.

TYPE OF OBJECT RETURNED	METHOD(S)
ConstructorInfo	GetConstructor, GetConstructors
EventInfo	GetEvent, GetEvents
FieldInfo	GetField, GetFields
MemberInfo	GetMember, GetMembers, GetDefaultMembers
MethodInfo	GetMethod, GetMethods
PropertyInfo	GetProperty, GetProperties

The `GetMember` and `GetMembers` methods return details about any or all members of the data type, regardless of whether these members are constructors, properties, methods, and so on.

The TypeView Example

This section demonstrates some of the features of the `Type` class with a short example, `TypeView`, which you can use to list the members of a data type. The example demonstrates how to use `TypeView` for a `double`; however, you can swap this type with any other data type just by changing one line of the code in the example.

The result of running the application is this output to the console:

```
Analysis of type Double
Type Name: Double
Full Name: System.Double
Namespace: System
Base Type: ValueType
```

```
public methods
IsFinite IsInfinity IsNaN IsNegative IsNegativeInfinity IsNormal IsPositiveInfinity
IsSubnormal CompareTo Equals op_Equality op_Inequality op_LessThan op_GreaterThan
op_LessThanOrEqual op_GreaterThanOrEqual GetHashCode ToString TryFormat Parse TryParse
GetTypeCode GetType

public fields
MinValue MaxValue Epsilon NegativeInfinity PositiveInfinity NaN
```

The console displays the name, full name, and namespace of the data type as well as the name of the base type. Next, it simply iterates through all the public instance members of the data type, displaying for each member the declaring type, the type of member (method, field, and so on), and the name of the member. The *declaring type* is the name of the class that actually declares the type member (for example, System.Double if it is defined or overridden in System.Double, or the name of the relevant base type if the member is simply inherited from a base class).

TypeView does not display signatures of methods because you are retrieving details about all public instance members through MemberInfo objects, and information about parameters is not available through a MemberInfo object. To retrieve that information, you would need references to MethodInfo and other more specific objects, which means that you would need to obtain details about each type of member separately.

The sample code for TypeView makes use of these namespaces besides the System namespace: System.Collections.Generic, System.Linq, System.Reflection, System.Text.

TypeView displays details about all public instance members, but doubles only define fields and methods. The main program is defined with top-level statements. It uses a StringBuilder instance called OutputText to build the text to be displayed.

Using the typeof statement, a Type object is retrieved, and this is passed to the AnalyzeType method. Finally, the output is written to the console (code file ReflectionSamples/TypeView/Program.cs):

```
StringBuilder OutputText = new();

// modify this line to retrieve details of any other data type
Type t = typeof(double);
AnalyzeType(t);
Console.WriteLine($"Analysis of type {t.Name}");
Console.WriteLine(OutputText.ToString());
Console.ReadLine();
```

You implement the AnalyzeType method by calling various properties and methods of the Type object to get the information you need concerning the type names. Instead of invoking the methods GetConstructors, GetMethods, and so on, you could invoke the method GetMembers, which returns all the members of the type. The ShowMembers local function makes use of LINQ to select the Name property of the member (this is common with all member types) and to remove overloaded members using the Distinct method. AddToOutput is a helper method to write the text to the StringBuilder:

```
void AnalyzeType(Type t)
{
  TypeInfo typeInfo = t.GetTypeInfo();
  AddToOutput($"Type Name: {t.Name}");
  AddToOutput($"Full Name: {t.FullName}");
  AddToOutput($"Namespace: {t.Namespace}");
   Type? tBase = typeInfo.BaseType;

  if (tBase != null)
  {
    AddToOutput($"Base Type: {tBase.Name}");
  }
```

```
ShowMembers("constructors", t.GetConstructors());
ShowMembers("methods", t.GetMethods());
ShowMembers("properties", t.GetProperties());
ShowMembers("fields", t.GetFields());
ShowMembers("events", t.GetEvents());

void ShowMembers(string title, IList<MemberInfo> members)
{
  if (members.Count == 0) return;
  AddToOutput($"\npublic {title}:");
  var names = members.Select(m => m.Name).Distinct();
  AddToOutput(string.Join(" ", names));
}

void AddToOutput(string Text) =>
  OutputText.Append($"{Text}{Environment.NewLine}");
}
```

The Assembly Class

The `Assembly` class is defined in the `System.Reflection` namespace and provides access to the metadata for a given assembly. It also contains methods that enable you to load and even execute an assembly—assuming that the assembly is an executable. As with the `Type` class, `Assembly` contains too many methods and properties to cover here, so this section is confined to covering those methods and properties that you need to get started and that you use to complete the `WhatsNewAttributes` example.

To analyze the code of the current assembly, you can invoke the method `Assembly.GetExecutingAssembly`. For code defined in other assemblies, you need to load the corresponding assembly into the running process. You can do this with either the `static` members `Assembly.Load` or `Assembly.LoadFrom`. The difference between these methods is that `Load` takes the name of the assembly, and the runtime searches in a variety of locations in an attempt to locate the assembly. These locations include the local directory and the global assembly cache. `LoadFrom` takes the full path name of an assembly and does not attempt to find the assembly in any other location:

```
Assembly assembly1 = Assembly.Load("SomeAssembly");
Assembly assembly2 = Assembly.LoadFrom
  (@"C:\My Projects\Software\SomeOtherAssembly");
```

A number of other overloads of both methods exist, which supply additional security information. After you have loaded an assembly, you can use various properties on it to find out, for example, its full name:

```
string name = assembly1.FullName;
```

Getting Details About Types Defined in an Assembly

One nice feature of the `Assembly` class is that it enables you to obtain details about all the types that are defined in the corresponding assembly. You simply call the `Assembly.GetTypes` method, which returns an array of `System.Type` references containing details about all the types. You can then manipulate these `Type` references as explained in the previous section:

```
Type[] types = theAssembly.GetTypes();
foreach(Type definedType in types)
{
  DoSomethingWith(definedType);
}
```

Getting Details About Custom Attributes

The methods you use to find out which custom attributes are defined on an assembly or type depend on the type of object to which the attribute is attached. If you want to find out what custom attributes are attached to an assembly as a whole, you need to call a `static` method of the `Attribute` class, `GetCustomAttributes`, passing in a reference to the assembly:

> **NOTE** *You might have wondered why, when you defined custom attributes, you had to go to all the trouble of actually writing classes for them. The custom attributes genuinely exist as objects, and when an assembly is loaded, you can read in these attribute objects, examine their properties, and call their methods.*

```
Attribute[] definedAttributes = Attribute.GetCustomAttributes(assembly1);
// assembly1 is an Assembly object
```

`GetCustomAttributes`, which is used to get assembly attributes, has a few overloads. If you call it without specifying any parameters other than an assembly reference, it simply returns all the custom attributes defined for that assembly. You can also call `GetCustomAttributes` by specifying a second parameter, which is a `Type` object that indicates the attribute class in which you are interested. In this case, `GetCustomAttributes` returns an array consisting of all the attributes present that are of the specified type.

Note that all attributes are retrieved as plain `Attribute` references. If you want to call any of the methods or properties you defined for your custom attributes, you need to cast these references explicitly to the relevant custom attribute classes. You can obtain details about custom attributes that are attached to a given data type by calling another overload of `Assembly.GetCustomAttributes`, this time passing a `Type` reference that describes the type for which you want to retrieve any attached attributes. To obtain attributes that are attached to methods, constructors, fields, and so on, however, you need to call a `GetCustomAttributes` method that is a member of one of the classes `MethodInfo`, `ConstructorInfo`, `FieldInfo`, and so on.

If you expect only a single attribute of a given type, you can call the `GetCustomAttribute` method instead, which returns a single `Attribute` object. You use `GetCustomAttribute` in the `WhatsNewAttributes` example to find out whether the `SupportsWhatsNew` attribute is present in the assembly. To do this, you call `GetCustomAttribute`, passing in a reference to the `WhatsNewAttributes` assembly and the type of the `SupportsWhatsNewAttribute` attribute. If this attribute is present, you get an `Attribute` instance. If no instances of it are defined in the assembly, you get `null`. If two or more instances are found, `GetCustomAttribute` throws a `System.Reflection.AmbiguousMatchException`. This is what that call would look like:

```
Attribute supportsAttribute =
    Attribute.GetCustomAttributes(assembly1, typeof(SupportsWhatsNewAttribute));
```

Completing the WhatsNewAttributes Example

You now have enough information to complete the `WhatsNewAttributes` example by writing the source code for the final assembly in the sample—the `LookUpWhatsNew` assembly. This part of the application is a console application. However, it needs to reference the other assemblies of `WhatsNewAttributes` and `VectorClass`.

The `Program` class contains the main program entry point as well as the other methods. All the methods you define are in this class, which also has two static fields—`outputText`, which contains the text as you build it in preparation for writing it to the console window, and `backDateTo`, which stores the date you have selected. All modifications made since this date will be displayed. Normally, you would display a dialog inviting the user to pick this date, but for this example, you don't want to get sidetracked into that kind of code. For this reason, `backDateTo` is hard-coded to a value of 2019/2/1. You can easily change this date when you download the code (code file `ReflectionSamples/LookupWhatsNew/Program.cs`):

```
StringBuilder outputText = new(1000);
DateTime backDateTo = new(2019, 2, 1);

Assembly theAssembly = Assembly.Load(new AssemblyName("VectorClass"));
Attribute? supportsAttribute = theAssembly.GetCustomAttribute(
  typeof(SupportsWhatsNewAttribute));

AddToOutput($"Assembly: {theAssembly.FullName}");
if (supportsAttribute is null)
{
  Console.WriteLine("This assembly does not support WhatsNew attributes");
  return;
}
else
{
  AddToOutput("Defined Types:");
}

IEnumerable<Type> types = theAssembly.ExportedTypes;
foreach(Type definedType in types)
{
  DisplayTypeInfo(definedType);
}

Console.WriteLine($"What's New since {backDateTo:D}");
Console.WriteLine(outputText.ToString());
Console.ReadLine();

//...
```

With the top-level statements, first the `VectorClass` assembly is loaded. If the assembly is not annotated with the `SupportsWhatsNew` attribute, the program exits. Assuming that all is well, you use the `Assembly.ExportedTypes` property to get a collection of all the types defined in this assembly and then loop through them. For each one, you call a method, `DisplayTypeInfo`, which adds the relevant text, including details regarding any instances of `LastModifiedAttribute`, to the `outputText` field. Finally, you show the complete text to the console. The `DisplayTypeInfo` method looks like this (code file `ReflectionSamples/LookupWhatsNew/Program.cs`):

```
void DisplayTypeInfo(Type type)
{
  // make sure we only pick out classes
  if (!type.GetTypeInfo().IsClass)
  {
    return;
  }

  AddToOutput($"{Environment.NewLine}class {type.Name}");

  IEnumerable<LastModifiedAttribute> lastModifiedAttributes =
    type.GetTypeInfo().GetCustomAttributes()
    .OfType<LastModifiedAttribute>()
    .Where(a => a.DateModified >= backDateTo).ToArray();
```

```
    if (lastModifiedAttributes.Count() == 0)
    {
      AddToOutput($"\tNo changes to the class {type.Name}" +
        $"{Environment.NewLine}");
    }
    else
    {
      foreach (LastModifiedAttribute attribute in lastModifiedAttributes)
      {
        WriteAttributeInfo(attribute);
      }
    }

    AddToOutput("changes to methods of this class:");

    foreach (MethodInfo method in
      type.GetTypeInfo().DeclaredMembers.OfType<MethodInfo>())
    {
      IEnumerable<LastModifiedAttribute> attributesToMethods =
        method.GetCustomAttributes().OfType<LastModifiedAttribute>()
          .Where(a => a.DateModified >= backDateTo).ToArray();

      if (attributesToMethods.Count() > 0)
      {
        AddToOutput($"{method.ReturnType} {method.Name}()");
        foreach (Attribute attribute in attributesToMethods)
        {
          WriteAttributeInfo(attribute);
        }
      }
    }
  }
```

Notice that the first thing you do in this method is check whether the Type reference you have been passed actually represents a class. Because, to keep things simple, you have specified that the LastModified attribute can be applied only to classes or member methods, you would be wasting time by doing any processing if the item is not a class (it could be a class, delegate, or enum).

Next, you use the Type.GetTypeInfo().GetCustomAttributes() method to determine whether this class has any LastModifiedAttribute instances attached to it. If so, you add their details to the output text, using a helper method, WriteAttributeInfo.

Finally, you use the DeclaredMembers property of the TypeInfo type to iterate through all the member methods of this data type and then do the same with each method as you did for the class—check whether it has any LastModifiedAttribute instances attached to it; if so, you display them using WriteAttributeInfo.

The next bit of code shows the WriteAttributeInfo method, which is responsible for determining what text to display for a given LastModifiedAttribute instance. Note that this method is passed an Attribute reference, so it needs to cast this to a LastModifiedAttribute reference first. After it has done that, it uses the properties that you originally defined for this attribute to retrieve its parameters. It confirms that the date of the attribute is sufficiently recent before actually adding it to the text for display (code file ReflectionSamples/LookupWhatsNew/Program.cs):

```
    void WriteAttributeInfo(Attribute attribute)
    {
      if (attribute is LastModifiedAttribute lastModifiedAttribute)
      {
```

```
    AddToOutput($"\tmodified: {lastModifiedAttribute.DateModified:D}: " +
      $"{lastModifiedAttribute.Changes}");

    if (lastModifiedAttribute.Issues != null)
    {
      AddToOutput($"\tOutstanding issues: {lastModifiedAttribute.Issues}");
    }
  }
}
```

Finally, here is the helper `AddToOutput` method:

```
static void AddToOutput(string text) =>
  outputText.Append($"{Environment.NewLine}{text}");
```

Running this code produces the results shown here:

```
What's New since Friday, February 1, 2019

Assembly: VectorClass, Version=5.2.0.0, Culture=neutral, PublicKeyToken=null
Defined Types:

class Vector
        modified: Sunday, February 28, 2021: changed the LastModified dates
        modified: Saturday, December 19, 2020: updated for C# 9 and .NET 5
changes to methods of this class:
System.Boolean Equals()
        modified: Sunday, February 28, 2021: changed for nullability
System.String ToString()
        modified: Saturday, December 19, 2020: changed to use switch expression
        modified: Saturday, December 19, 2020: changed with nullability annotations
```

Note that when you list the types defined in the `VectorClass` assembly, you actually pick up two classes: `Vector` and the embedded `VectorEnumerator` class. In addition, note that because the `backDateTo` date of 2019/2/1 is hard-coded in this example, you actually pick up the attributes that are dated 2020/12/19 and 2021/2/28 but not those dated earlier.

USING DYNAMIC LANGUAGE EXTENSIONS FOR REFLECTION

Until now, you've used reflection for reading metadata. You can also use reflection to create instances dynamically from types that aren't known at compile time. The next sample shows creating an instance of the `Calculator` class without the compiler knowing of this type at compile time. The assembly `CalculatorLib` is loaded dynamically without adding a reference. During runtime, the `Calculator` object is instantiated, and a method is called. After you know how to use the Reflection API, you'll do the same using the C# `dynamic` keyword.

Creating the Calculator Library

The library that is loaded is a simple .NET library containing the type `Calculator` with implementations of the `Add` and `Subtract` methods. Because the methods are really simple, they are implemented using the expression syntax (code file `DynamicSamlpes/CalculatorLib/Calculator.cs`):

```
public class Calculator
{
  public double Add(double x, double y) => x + y;
  public double Subtract(double x, double y) => x - y;
}
```

After you compile the library, copy the generated DLL to the folder `c:/addins`. The client application doesn't add a fixed dependency to this library; it loads the file dynamically. Using the .NET CLI you can specify the output path with the `--output` option:

```
> dotnet build --output c:/addins.
```

Instantiating a Type Dynamically

For using reflection to create the `Calculator` instance dynamically, create a console project with the name `ClientApp`.

The constant `CalculatorTypeName` defines the name of the `Calculator` type, including the namespace. The start of the application requires a command-line argument with the path to the library and then invokes the methods `UsingReflection` and `UsingReflectionWithDynamic`, two variants doing reflection (code file `DynamicSamples/ClientApp/Program.cs`):

```
const string CalculatorTypeName = "CalculatorLib.Calculator";

if (args.Length != 1)
{
  ShowUsage();
  return;
}
UsingReflection(args[0]);
UsingReflectionWithDynamic(args[0]);

void ShowUsage()
{
  Console.WriteLine($"Usage: {nameof(ClientApp)} path");
  Console.WriteLine();
  Console.WriteLine("Copy CalculatorLib.dll to an addin directory");
  Console.WriteLine("and pass the absolute path of this directory " +
    "when starting the application to load the library");
}
```

Before using reflection to invoke a method, you need to instantiate the `Calculator` type. The method `GetCalculator` loads the assembly dynamically using the method `LoadFile` of the `Assembly` class and creates an instance of the `Calculator` type with the `CreateInstance` method:

```
object? GetCalculator(string addinPath)
{
  Assembly assembly = Assembly.LoadFile(addinPath);
  return assembly.CreateInstance(CalculatorTypeName);
}
```

The sample code for the `ClientApp` makes use of these namespaces: `System.Reflection` and `Microsoft.CSharp.RuntimeBinder`.

Invoking a Member with the Reflection API

The Reflection API is used to invoke the method `Add` of the `Calculator` instance. First, the calculator instance is retrieved with the helper method `GetCalculator`. If you would like to add a reference to the `CalculatorLib`, you could use `new Calculator` to create an instance. But here it's not that easy.

Invoking the method using reflection has the advantage that the type does not need to be available at compile time. You could add it at a later time just by copying the library in the specified directory. To invoke the member using reflection, the `Type` object of the instance is retrieved using `GetType`—a method of the base class `Object`. With the help of the extension method `GetMethod`, a `MethodInfo` object for the method `Add` is accessed.

The `MethodInfo` defines the `Invoke` method to call the method using any number of parameters. The first parameter of the `Invoke` method needs the instance of the type where the member is invoked. The second parameter is of type `object []` to pass all the parameters needed by the invocation. You're passing the values of the `x` and `y` variables here (code file `DynamicSamples/ClientApp/Program.cs`):

```
void UsingReflection(string addinPath)
{
  double x = 3;
  double y = 4;
  object calc = GetCalculator(addinPath)
    ?? throw new InvalidOperationException("GetCalculator returned null");

  object? result = calc.GetType().GetMethod("Add")
    ?.Invoke(calc, new object[] { x, y })
    ?? throw new InvalidOperationException("Add method not found");
  Console.WriteLine($"the result of {x} and {y} is {result}");
}
```

When you run the program, the calculator is invoked and writes the result to the console. Using the reflection APIs to get the type, get a method, call the `Invoke` method, and pass an object array to pass arguments requires some work. Let's take a look at how you can do this using the `dynamic` keyword.

Invoking a Member with the Dynamic Type

When you use reflection with the `dynamic` keyword, the object that is returned from the `GetCalculator` method is assigned to a variable of a `dynamic` type. The `GetCalculator` method doesn't change; it still returns an object. The result is returned to a variable that is of type `dynamic`. With this, the `Add` method is invoked, and two double values are passed to it (code file `DynamicSamples/ClientApp/Program.cs`):

```
void UsingReflectionWithDynamic(string addinPath)
{
  double x = 3;
  double y = 4;
  dynamic calc = GetCalculator(addinPath)
    ?? throw new InvalidOperationException("GetCalculator returned null");
  double result = calc.Add(x, y);
  Console.WriteLine($"the result of {x} and {y} is {result}");

  //...
}
```

The syntax is really simple; it looks like calling a method with strongly typed access. However, there's no IntelliSense, so it's easy to make typos. There's also no compile-time check. The compiler runs fine when you invoke the `Multiply` method. Just remember that you only defined `Add` and `Subtract` methods with the calculator.

```
try
{
  result = calc.Multiply(x, y);
}
catch (RuntimeBinderException ex)
{
  Console.WriteLine(ex);
}
```

When you run the application and invoke the `Multiply` method, you get a `RuntimeBinderException`:

```
Microsoft.CSharp.RuntimeBinder.RuntimeBinderException: 'CalculatorLib.Calculator'
    does not contain a definition for 'Multiply'
    at CallSite.Target(Closure , CallSite , Object , Double , Double )
    at System.Dynamic.UpdateDelegates.UpdateAndExecute3[T0,T1,T2,TRet](CallSite
    site, T0 arg0, T1 arg1, T2 arg2)
    at ClientApp.Program.UsingReflectionWithDynamic(String addinPath) in...
```

Using the `dynamic` type also has more overhead compared to accessing objects in a strongly typed manner. Therefore, the keyword is useful only in some specific scenarios such as reflection. You don't have a compiler check invoking the `InvokeMember` method of the `Type`; instead, a string is passed for the name of the member. Using the `dynamic` type, which has a simpler syntax, has a big advantage compared to using the Reflection API in such scenarios.

The `dynamic` type can also be used with COM integration and scripting environments as shown after discussing the `dynamic` keyword more in detail.

EXPANDOOBJECT

What if you want to create your own dynamic object? You can implement the interface `IDynamicMetaObjectProvider`. A class that's already implementing this interface is the base class `DynamicObject`. This class defines virtual methods that you can override. For example, `TrySetMember` is a method you can override to set a property. `TryInvokeMember` is a method you can override to invoke a method. An easier option is to use the `ExpandoObject` class. This class implements the interface `IDynamicMetaObjectProvider` and is ready to use without the need to derive from `ExpandoObject`. Indeed, you cannot derive from `ExpandoObject` because this class is `sealed`.

You can create a variable of type `dynamic` and assign an `ExpandoObject` to it. All the properties you set with this dynamic variable and all the methods you invoke get added to a dictionary within the `ExpandoObject` and are available as soon as you invoke them.

With the next code snippet, an `ExpandoObject` is instantiated and assigned to a variable of type dynamic. Because it's a dynamic, the compiler doesn't verify the members you invoke, such as setting properties (`FirstName` and `LastName`) and assigning a delegate to the name `GetNextDay`, which turns into a method with a `DateTime` parameter and a string return. It's also possible to create a deeper hierarchy. The `Friends` property is created, and a list of `Person` objects is assigned to it (code file `DynamicSamples/DynamicSample/Program.cs`):

```csharp
void UseExpando()
{
  dynamic expObj = new ExpandoObject();
  expObj.FirstName = "Daffy";
  expObj.LastName = "Duck";
  Console.WriteLine($"{expObj.FirstName} {expObj.LastName}");

  expObj.GetNextDay = new Func<DateTime, string>(day => day.AddDays(1).ToString("d"));

  Console.WriteLine($"next day: {expObj.GetNextDay(new DateTime(2021, 1, 3))}");

  expObj.Friends = new List<Person>();
  expObj.Friends.Add(new Person() { FirstName = "Bob", LastName = "Jones" });
  expObj.Friends.Add(new Person() { FirstName = "Robert", LastName = "Jones" });
  expObj.Friends.Add(new Person() { FirstName = "Bobby", LastName = "Jones" });
```

```
      foreach (dynamic friend in expObj.Friends)
      {
        Console.WriteLine($"{friend.FirstName} {friend.LastName}");
      }
    }
  }
```

The following is another example of using `dynamic` and `ExpandoObject`. Assume that the requirement is to develop a general-purpose comma-separated values (CSV) file parsing tool. You won't know from one execution to another what data will be in the file, only that the values will be comma-separated and the first line will contain the field names.

First, open the file and read in the stream. You can use a simple helper method to do this (code file `DynamicSamples/DynamicFileReader/DynamicFileHelper.cs`):

```
public static class DynamicFileHelper
{
  //...
  private static StreamReader? OpenFile(string fileName)
  {
    if (File.Exists(fileName))
    {
      return new StreamReader(fileName);
    }
    return null;
  }
}
```

This just opens the file and creates a new `StreamReader` to read the file contents.

Now you want to get the field names, which you can do easily by reading in the first line from the file and using the `Split` function to create a string array of field names:

```
string[] headerLine = reader.ReadLine()?.Split(',').Select(s => Trim()).ToArray();
```

Next is the interesting part. You read in the next line from the file, create a string array just like you did with the field names, and start creating your dynamic objects. Here's what the code looks like (code file `DynamicSamples/DynamicFileReader/DynamicFileHelper.cs`):

```
public static class DynamicFileHelper
{
  public static IEnumerable<dynamic> ParseFile(string fileName)
  {
    List<dynamic> retList = new();
    using StreamReader? reader = OpenFile(fileName);
    if (reader != null)
    {
      string[] headerLine = reader.ReadLine()?.Split(',').Select(
        s => s.Trim()).ToArray()
        ?? throw new InvalidOperationException("reader.ReadLine returned null");
      while (reader.Peek() > 0)
      {
        string[] dataLine = reader.ReadLine()?.Split(',')
          ?? throw new InvalidOperationException("reader.Readline returned null");
        dynamic dynamicEntity = new ExpandoObject();
        for (int i = 0; i < headerLine.Length; i++)
        {
          ((IDictionary<string, object>)dynamicEntity).Add(headerLine[i], dataLine[i]);
        }
```

```
        retList.Add(dynamicEntity);
      }
    }
    return retList;
  }
  //...
}
```

After you have the string array of field names and data elements, you create a new `ExpandoObject` and add the data to it. Notice that you cast the `ExpandoObject` to a `Dictionary` object. You use the field name as the key and the data as the value. Then you can add the new object to the `retList` object you created and return it to the code that called the method.

This is nice because you have a section of code that can handle any data you give it. The only requirements in this case are ensuring that the field names are the first line and that everything is comma-separated. This concept could be expanded to other file types or even to a `DataReader`.

The file `EmployeeList.txt` available in the download contains the following CSV data:

```
FirstName, LastName, City, State
Mario Andretti, Nazareth, Pennsylvania
Carlos, Reutemann, Santa Fe, Argentine
Sebastian, Vettel, Thurgovia, Switzerland
```

This file is read in the following code in `Program.cs` (code file DynamicSamples/DynamicFileReader/Program.cs)

```
var employeeList = DynamicFileHelper.ParseFile("EmployeeList.txt");
foreach (var employee in employeeList)
{
  Console.WriteLine($"{employee.FirstName} {employee.LastName} lives in " +
    $"{employee.City}, {employee.State}.");
}
Console.ReadLine();
```

and results in this output to the console:

```
Mario Andretti lives in Nazareth, Pennsylvania.
Carlos Reutemann lives in Santa Fe, Argentine.
Sebastian Vettel lives in Thurgovia, Switzerland.
```

SOURCE GENERATORS

A great extension of C# 9 is the new component *source generator*. This is not a C# syntax enhancement but an enhancement of the compilation process. During the compilation, C# source code can be generated and added to the project.

In this chapter, you've read about adding metadata to source code using attributes. Some of the attributes are known by the compiler, others are used by developer tools such as Visual Studio, and others are read during runtime—for example, from libraries. In this chapter, you've read about using reflection to read information dynamically.

Using reflection has some disadvantages, though. It takes extra overhead during runtime and also has issues with trimming code during the compilation process. As reflection is done during runtime, the compiler might trim methods and classes that are required with dynamic invocations. When using trimming of assemblies, you might need to configure methods and classes that should not be trimmed because of reflection.

> **NOTE** *Chapter 1, ".NET Applications and Tools," covered configuring trimming of applications.*

Instead of using reflection during runtime, you can use a source generator, which can read attributes during compile time and, because of the attributes, generate code that's also compiled during build time. The need for reflection can be reduced.

Attributes might not be the only source for source generators. A source generator can also use other sources, such as JSON or other files, to generate code.

Hello, World Source Generator

Let's start with the foundation of source generators—a simple generator that creates a method with a `HelloWorld` class and a `Hello` method. This method will be invoked from a .NET console application.

To implement a source generator, you need to create a .NET library. For the source generator to work with Visual Studio 2019, it needs to be a .NET Standard 2.0 library. The NuGet package `Microsoft.CodeAnalysis` needs to be added. To add support to use the C# compiler in the later sample, the `Microsoft.CodeAnalysis.CSharp.Workspaces` package needs to be added as well. The namespaces `Microsoft.CodeAnalysis`, `Microsoft.CodeAnalysis.Text`, `System.Collections.Generic`, and `System.Text` are used.

A source generator class needs to implement the interface `ISourceGenerator` and have the `Generator` attribute applied (source file `SourceGenerator/CodeGenerationSample/HelloWorldGenerator.cs`):

```
[Generator]
public class HelloWorldGenerator : ISourceGenerator
{
  //...
}
```

The interface `ISourceGenerator` defines the methods `Initialize` and `Execute`. `Initialize` is invoked before the code generation starts. The `Execute` method then does the main job of the generator. With the first sample, an implementation of the `Initialize` method is not required:

```
public void Initialize(GeneratorInitializationContext context)
{
  // No initialization required
}
```

With the implementation of the `Execute` method, a `StringBuilder` is initialized with a string containing the start of the source code: the namespace `CodeGenerationSample`, the class `HelloWorld`, and the `Hello` methods are generated. The method, class, and namespace are not closed yet because in the `Hello` method, code will be added that's using the `GeneratorExecutionContext` parameter:

```
public void Execute(GeneratorExecutionContext context)
{
  StringBuilder sourceBuilder = new(@"
using System;
namespace CodeGenerationSample
{
  public static class HelloWorld
```

```
{
  public static void Hello()
  {
    Console.WriteLine(""Hello from generated code!"");
    Console.WriteLine(""The following source files existed in the compilation:"");
");
  //...
```

The `GeneratorExecutionContext` is used to access syntax trees from the compilation. Here, the code where the source generator is used can be accessed to modify or extend it. With the first source code generator, just the file path of all the source files that are part of the compilation is written to the console:

```
public void Execute(GeneratorExecutionContext context)
{
  //...
  IEnumerable<SyntaxTree> syntaxTrees = context.Compilation.SyntaxTrees;

  foreach (SyntaxTree tree in syntaxTrees)
  {
    sourceBuilder.AppendLine($@"Console.WriteLine(@""source file:
{tree.FilePath}"");");
  }

  sourceBuilder.Append(@"
    }
  }
}");

  context.AddSource("helloWorld", SourceText.From(sourceBuilder.ToString(),
    Encoding.UTF8));
}
```

For using a source generator in a project, you need to add the `Analyzer` element and reference the library (project configuration file `SourceGenerator/SampleApp/SampleApp.csproj`):

```
<Project Sdk="Microsoft.NET.Sdk">

  <PropertyGroup>
    <OutputType>Exe</OutputType>
    <TargetFramework>net5.0</TargetFramework>
    <Nullable>enable</Nullable>
  </PropertyGroup>

  <ItemGroup>
    <Analyzer Include="c:\sourcegenerators\CodeGenerationSample.dll" />
  </ItemGroup>

</Project>
```

With this in place, you can add code to invoke the static `Hello` method of the `HelloWorld` class (code file `SampleApp/Program.cs`):

```
using System;
using SampleApp;

CodeGenerationSample.HelloWorld.Hello();
```

Running the application shows the hello message as well as the source code files that are available with the build within the source code generator. The directory names will differ on your system:

```
Hello from generated code!
The following source files existed in the compilation:
source file: C:\SampleApp\HelloControl.cs
source file: C:\SampleApp\Program.cs
source file:
C:\SampleApp\obj\Debug\net5.0\.NETCoreApp,Version=v5.0.AssemblyAttributes.cs
source file:
C:\CodeGenerationSample\SampleApp\obj\Debug\net5.0\SampleApp.AssemblyInfo.cs
```

Source Generators Using Partial Methods

Let's get into a more advanced scenario where a partial method is used from a source generator. With C# 9, the syntax for partial methods has been enhanced. As a reminder, the `partial` modifier with a class allows having the class to span multiple files. The compiler combines the partial classes from multiple files with the same name to one class. Before C# 9, partial methods had to be declared with the return type `void`. A partial method didn't need to have any implementation. Code generators often created partial methods, which have been invoked by the generated code. With your part of the implementation, you could then define an implementation of the partial method that's invoked by the generated code. With C# 9, partial methods can return a type. This partial method needs to have a private access modifier, and an implementation is required as well.

Chapter 5, "Operators and Casts," discusses that implementing equality for class types requires some boilerplate code: overriding the `object.Equals` method, implementing the `IEquality<T>` interface, and implementing the `==` and `!=` operators. When you use code generators, the `Book` class has the attribute `ImplementEquatable` applied and implements the partial method `IsTheSame` to compare for the values (code file `SourceGenerator/SampleApp/Book.cs`):

```csharp
using CodeGenerationSample;

namespace SampleApp
{
  [ImplementEquatable]
  public partial class Book
  {
    public Book(string title, string publisher)
    {
      Title = title;
      Publisher = publisher;
    }
    public string Title { get; }
    public string Publisher { get; }

    private static partial bool IsTheSame(Book? left, Book? right) =>
      left?.Title == right?.Title && left?.Publisher == right?.Publisher;

    public override int GetHashCode() =>
        Title.GetHashCode() ^ Publisher.GetHashCode();
  }
}
```

The `ImplementEquatable` attribute that's used by the `Book` class is one part of the source code that's generated from the source generator. The member field `attributeText` contains the complete content for the attribute. The following code will be injected (code file `SourceGenerator/CodeGenerationSample/EquatableGenerator.cs`):

```
private const string attributeText = @"
using System;
namespace CodeGenerationSample
{
  [AttributeUsage(AttributeTargets.Class, Inherited = false, AllowMultiple = false)]
  sealed class ImplementEquatableAttribute : Attribute
  {
    public ImplementEquatableAttribute() { }
  }
}
";
```

The new source generator `EquatableGenerator` implements the `Initialize` method to register the `SyntaxReceiver` type for syntax notifications. `RegisterForSyntaxNotifications` is a method of the `GeneratorInitializationContext` that requires a `SyntaxReceiverCreator` delegate as a parameter. This delegate just specifies that an object implementing `ISyntaxReceiver` needs to be returned:

```
[Generator]
public class EquatableGenerator : ISourceGenerator
{
  public void Initialize(GeneratorInitializationContext context)
  {
    context.RegisterForSyntaxNotifications(() => new SyntaxReceiver());
  }
  //...
}
```

The `SyntaxReceiver` class implements this interface with the implementation of the `OnVisitSyntaxNode` method. As the compiler visits the user's source code, this method is invoked for every syntax node. If the syntax node is a class with at least one attribute, it is added to the `CandidateClasses` collection. These classes might be expanded with an implementation for equality, as shown here:

```
internal class SyntaxReceiver : ISyntaxReceiver
{
  public List<ClassDeclarationSyntax> CandidateClasses { get; } = new();

  public void OnVisitSyntaxNode(SyntaxNode syntaxNode)
  {
    if (syntaxNode is ClassDeclarationSyntax classDeclarationSyntax
      && classDeclarationSyntax.AttributeLists.Count > 0)
    {
      CandidateClasses.Add(classDeclarationSyntax);
    }
  }
}
```

With the implementation of the `Execute` method, the source code for the attribute is retrieved from the `attributeText` variable and passed to the `GeneratorExecutionContext` with the `AddSource` method. To retrieve the syntax tree and get the symbol for comparison with the user source code, the compilation of this attribute is retrieved:

```
public void Execute(GeneratorExecutionContext context)
{
  context.AddSource("ImplementEquatableAttribute", SourceText.From(attributeText,
    Encoding.UTF8));
```

```
    if (!(context.SyntaxReceiver is SyntaxReceiver syntaxReceiver))
      return;

  CSharpParseOptions? options = (context.Compilation as CSharpCompilation)?.
    SyntaxTrees[0].Options as CSharpParseOptions;
  Compilation compilation = context.Compilation.AddSyntaxTrees(
    CSharpSyntaxTree.ParseText(SourceText.From(attributeText, Encoding.UTF8), options));

  INamedTypeSymbol? attributeSymbol = compilation.GetTypeByMetadataName(
    "CodeGenerationSample.ImplementEquatableAttribute");
  //...
}
```

Next, each candidate class stored within the `SyntaxReceiver` is verified if it has the `ImplementEquatableAttribute` applied. If a class has this attribute, the typed symbol is added to the `typedSymbols` collection. After the iteration of the candidates, the remaining candidates are iterated to add the source code for every one of these types. The source code is coming from the helper method `GetClassSource`:

```
public void Execute(GeneratorExecutionContext context)
{
  //...

  List<ITypeSymbol> typeSymbols = new();
  foreach (ClassDeclarationSyntax @class in syntaxReceiver.CandidateClasses)
  {
    SemanticModel model = compilation.GetSemanticModel(@class.SyntaxTree);

    INamedTypeSymbol? typeSymbol = model.GetDeclaredSymbol(@class);
    if (typeSymbol!.GetAttributes().Any(attr =>
      attr.AttributeClass!.Equals(attributeSymbol, SymbolEqualityComparer.Default)))
    {
      typeSymbols.Add(typeSymbol);
    }
  }

  foreach (INamedTypeSymbol typeSymbol in typeSymbols)
  {
    string classSource = GetClassSource(typeSymbol);
    context.AddSource(typeSymbol.Name, SourceText.From(classSource, Encoding.UTF8));
  }
}
```

The helper method `GetClassSources` receives the `ITypesSymbol` as a parameter to use the namespace name and the class name with the generated code. The implementation of the `IEquatable` interface and the operator overloads are returned:

```
private string GetClassSource(ITypeSymbol typeSymbol)
{
  string namespaceName = typeSymbol.ContainingNamespace.ToDisplayString();

  StringBuilder source = new($@"
using System;
```

```
namespace {namespaceName}
{{
  public partial class {typeSymbol.Name} : IEquatable<{typeSymbol.Name}>
  {{
    private static partial bool IsTheSame(
      {typeSymbol.Name}? left, {typeSymbol.Name}? right);

    public override bool Equals(object? obj) => this == obj as {typeSymbol.Name};

    public bool Equals({typeSymbol.Name}? other) => this == other;

    public static bool operator==({typeSymbol.Name}? left, {typeSymbol.Name}?
right)
      => IsTheSame(left, right);

    public static bool operator!=({typeSymbol.Name}? left, {typeSymbol.Name}?
right)
      => !(left == right);

  }}
}}
");
  return source.ToString();
}
```

With the source generator, two `Book` objects can now be instantiated and compared using the `==` operator (code file `SourceGenerator/SampleApp/Program.cs`):

```
Book b1 = new("Professional C#", "Wrox Press");
Book b2 = new("Professional C#", "Wrox Press");
if (b1 == b2)
{
  Console.WriteLine("the same book");
}
```

Instead of implementing the operators and the `IEquatable` interface every time equality is needed, you can now use a code generator. Many more scenarios are possible. You can create classes from CSV files and automatically implement interfaces such as `INotifyPropertyChanged`.

Future versions of .NET will reduce reflection code during runtime. With ASP.NET Core, controllers are dynamically searched for at the startup of the application. This increases the startup time. If code is instead generated, there's no need to do this at runtime, and the application can start up faster.

> **NOTE** *In this chapter, with the source generator, it was just possible to have a focus on the special features of the source generator. Now you might be interested in more information on accessing the different parts of the syntax tree in more detail. Source generators are based on the .NET Compiler Platform (Roslyn). A complete book could be written about this. Check the Microsoft documentation on the .NET Compiler Platform SDK at* `https://docs.microsoft.com/dotnet/csharp/roslyn-sdk/`.

SUMMARY

This chapter illustrated using the `Type` and `Assembly` classes, which are the primary entry points for accessing the extensive capabilities provided by reflection.

In addition, this chapter demonstrated a specific aspect of reflection that you are likely to use more often than any other—the inspection of custom attributes. You learned how to define and apply your own custom attributes and how to retrieve information about custom attributes at runtime.

The second focus of this chapter was working with a new C# 9 feature: source code generators. With a source generator, you can create source code from different sources, and this code is combined with the user's source code. A source generator can also access the syntax tree of the user's source code and change this accordingly. With `dotnet build`, the source generator gets triggered.

The next chapter gives details on freeing resources with the `IDisposable` interface, releasing native resources, and working with unsafe C# code.

13

Managed
and Unmanaged Memory

WHAT'S IN THIS CHAPTER?

➤ Allocating space on the stack and heap at runtime

➤ Garbage collection

➤ Releasing unmanaged resources using destructors and the `System.IDisposable` interface

➤ Understanding the syntax for using pointers in C#

➤ Using the `Span` type

➤ Using Platform Invoke to access native APIs on Windows and Linux

CODE DOWNLOADS FOR THIS CHAPTER

The source code for this chapter is available on the book page at www.wiley.com. Click the Downloads link. The code can also be found at https://github.com/ProfessionalCSharp/ProfessionalCSharp2021 in the directory 1_CS/Memory.

The code for this chapter is divided into the following major examples:

➤ PointerPlayground

➤ PointerPlayground2

➤ QuickArray

➤ SpanSample

➤ PlatformInvokeSample

All the projects have nullable reference types enabled.

MEMORY

Variables are stored on the stack. The data they reference can be on the stack (structs) or on the heap (classes). Structs also can be boxed so objects on the heap are created. The garbage collector needs to free up unmanaged objects that are no longer needed from the managed heap. When you use native APIs, you can allocate memory on the native heap. The garbage collector is not responsible for memory allocated on the native heap. You have to free this memory on your own. There's a lot to consider with regard to memory.

When you use a managed environment, you can easily be misled into not paying attention to memory management because the garbage collector (GC) deals with that anyway. A lot of work is done by the GC; it's very practical to know how it works, what the small and large object heaps are, and what data types are stored within the stack. Also, while the garbage collector deals with managed resources, what about unmanaged ones? You have to free them on your own. Probably your programs are fully managed programs, but what about the types defined with the .NET runtime and class libraries? For example, file types (discussed in Chapter 18, "Files and Streams") wrap a native file handle. This file handle needs to be released. To release this handle early, it's good to know the IDisposable interface, the using statement, and the using declaration that are explained in this chapter.

Other aspects are important as well. Although several language constructs make it easier to create immutable types, mutable objects have an advantage as well. The string class is an immutable type that's been available since .NET 1.0. Nowadays, people often have to deal with large strings, and the GC needs to clean up a lot of objects. Directly accessing the memory of the string and making changes makes a mutable—and in different scenarios, a more performant—program. The Span type makes this possible. With arrays (Chapter 6, "Arrays"), you've also seen the ArrayPool class that also can reduce the work of the GC.

This chapter starts with various aspects of memory management and memory access. A good understanding of memory management and knowledge of the pointer capabilities provided by C# will better enable you to integrate C# code with legacy code and perform efficient memory manipulation in performance-critical systems. This chapter covers ways to use the ref keyword for return types and local variables. This feature reduces the need for unsafe code and using pointers with C#. This chapter also discusses more details about using the Span type to access a different kind of memory, such as the managed heap, the native heap, and the stack.

MEMORY MANAGEMENT UNDER THE HOOD

One of the advantages of C# programming is that the programmer does not need to worry about detailed memory management; the garbage collector deals with the problem of memory cleanup on your behalf. As a result, you get something that approximates the efficiency of languages such as C++ without the complexity of having to handle memory management yourself as you do in C++. However, although you do not have to manage memory manually, it still pays to understand what is going on behind the scenes. Understanding how your program manages memory under the covers will help you increase the speed and performance of your applications. This section looks at what happens in the computer's memory when you allocate variables.

> **NOTE** *The precise details of many of the topics of this section are not presented here. This section serves as an abbreviated guide to the general processes rather than a statement of exact implementation.*

Value Data Types

Windows uses a system known as *virtual addressing* in which the mapping from the memory address seen by your program to the actual location in hardware memory is entirely managed by Windows. As a result, each process of a 32-bit application sees 4GB of available memory, regardless of how much hardware memory you actually have in your computer (with 64-bit applications on 64-bit processors this number is greater). This memory contains everything that is part of the program, including the executable code, any DLLs loaded by the code, and the contents of all variables used when the program runs. This 4GB of memory is known as the *virtual address space* or *virtual memory*. For convenience, this chapter uses the shorthand *memory*.

> **NOTE** *.NET applications are built as portable applications by default. A portable application runs on both 32- and 64-bit environments on Windows and on Linux as long as the .NET runtime is installed on the system. Not all APIs are available on all platforms, especially if you use native APIs. For this, you can specify platforms with your .NET application as explained in Chapter 1, ".NET Applications and Tools."*

Each memory location in the available 4GB is numbered starting from zero. To access a value stored at a particular location in memory, you need to supply the number that represents that memory location. In any compiled high-level language, the compiler converts human-readable variable names into memory addresses that the processor understands.

Somewhere inside a processor's virtual memory is an area known as the *stack*. The stack stores value data types that are not members of objects. In addition, when you call a method, the stack is used to hold a copy of any parameters passed to the method. To understand how the stack works, you need to understand the importance of variable scope in C#. If variable a goes into scope before variable b, then b always goes out of scope first. Consider the following code:

```
{
   int a;
   // do something
   {
      int b;
      // do something else
   }
}
```

First, the variable a is declared. Then, inside the inner code block, b is declared. Then the inner code block terminates, and b goes out of scope; then a goes out of scope. Therefore, the lifetime of b is entirely contained within the lifetime of a. The idea that you always deallocate variables in the reverse order of how you allocate them is crucial to the way the stack works.

Note that b is in a different block from code (defined by a different nesting of curly braces). For this reason, it is contained within a different scope. This is called *block scope* or *structure scope*.

You do not know exactly where in the address space the stack is—you don't need to know for C# development. A *stack pointer* (a variable maintained by the operating system) identifies the next free location on the stack. When your program first starts running, the stack pointer points to just past the end of the block of memory that is reserved for the stack. The stack fills downward, from high memory addresses to low addresses. As data is put on the stack, the stack pointer is adjusted accordingly, so it always points to just past the next free location. This is illustrated in Figure 13-1, which shows a stack pointer with a value of 800000 (0xC3500 in hex); the next free location is the address 799999.

The following code tells the compiler that you need space in memory to store an integer and a double, and these memory locations are referred to as nRacingCars and engineSize. The line that declares each variable indicates the point at which you start requiring access to this variable. The closing curly brace of the block in which the variables are declared identifies the point at which both variables go out of scope:

```
{
   int nRacingCars = 10;
   double engineSize = 3000.0;
   // do calculations;
}
```

Assuming that you use the stack shown in Figure 13-1, when the variable nRacingCars comes into scope and is assigned the value 10, this value is placed in locations 799996 through 799999—the 4 bytes just below the location pointed to by the stack pointer (4 bytes because that's how much memory is needed to store an int). To accommodate this, 4 is subtracted from the value of the stack pointer, so it now points to the location 799996, just after the new first free location (799995).

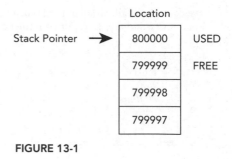

FIGURE 13-1

The next line of code declares the variable engineSize (a double) and initializes it to the value 3000.0. A double occupies 8 bytes, so the value 3000.0 is placed in locations 799988 through 799995 on the stack, and the stack pointer is decremented by 8 so that it again points to the location just after the next free location on the stack.

When engineSize goes out of scope, the runtime knows that it is no longer needed. Because of the way variable lifetimes are always nested, you can guarantee that whatever happened while engineSize was in scope, the stack pointer is now pointing to the location where engineSize is stored. To remove engineSize from the stack, the stack pointer is incremented by 8, and it now points to the location immediately after the end of engineSize. At this point in the code, you are at the closing curly brace, so nRacingCars also goes out of scope. The stack pointer is incremented by 4. When another variable comes into scope after engineSize and nRacingCars have been removed from the stack, it overwrites the memory descending from location 799999, where nRacingCars was stored.

If the compiler hits a line such as int i, j, then the order of variables coming into scope looks indeterminate. Both variables are declared at the same time and go out of scope at the same time. In this situation, it does not matter in what order the two variables are removed from memory. The compiler internally always ensures that the one that was put in memory first is removed last, thus preserving the rule that prohibits crossover of variable lifetimes.

Reference Data Types

Although the stack provides very high performance, it is not flexible enough to be used for all variables. The requirement that the lifetime of a variable must be nested is too restrictive for many purposes. Often, you need to use a method to allocate memory for storing data and keeping that data available long after that method has exited. This possibility exists whenever storage space is requested with the new operator—as is the case for all reference types. That is where the *managed heap* comes in.

If you have done any C++ coding that required low-level memory management, you are familiar with the heap. The managed heap is not quite the same as the native heap C++ uses, however; the managed heap works under the control of the garbage collector and provides significant benefits compared to traditional heaps.

The managed heap (or heap for short) is just another area of memory from the processor's available memory. The following code demonstrates how the heap works and how memory is allocated for reference data types:

```
void DoWork()
{
  Customer? arabel;
  arabel = new();
  Customer otherCustomer2 = new EnhancedCustomer();
}
```

This code assumes the existence of two classes, Customer and EnhancedCustomer. The EnhancedCustomer class extends the Customer class.

First, you declare a Customer reference called arabel. The space for this is allocated on the stack, but remember that this is only a reference rather than an actual Customer object. The arabel reference occupies 4 bytes, enough space to hold the address at which a Customer object will be stored. (You need 4 bytes to represent a memory address as an unsigned integer value between 0 and 4GB.)

The next line,

```
arabel = new Customer();
```

does several things. First, it allocates memory on the heap to store a `Customer` object (a real object, not just an address). Then it sets the value of the variable `arabel` to the address of the memory it has allocated to the new `Customer` object. (It also calls the appropriate `Customer` constructor to initialize the fields in the class instance, but you don't need to worry about that here.)

The `Customer` instance is not placed on the stack—it is placed on the heap. In this example, you don't know precisely how many bytes a `Customer` object occupies, but assume for the sake of argument that it is 32. These 32 bytes contain the instance fields of `Customer` as well as some information that .NET uses to identify and manage its class instances.

To find a storage location on the heap for the new `Customer` object, the .NET runtime looks through the heap and grabs the first adjacent unused block of 32 bytes. Again, for the sake of argument, assume that this happens to be at address `200000` and that the `arabel` reference occupied locations `799996` through `799999` on the stack. This means that before instantiating the `arabel` object, the memory content looks like Figure 13-2.

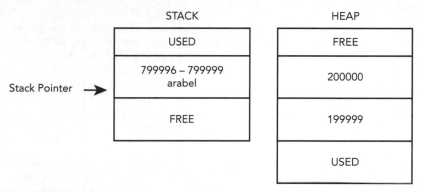

FIGURE 13-2

After allocating the new `Customer` object, the content of memory looks like Figure 13-3. Note that unlike the stack, memory in the heap is allocated upward, so the free space is above the used space.

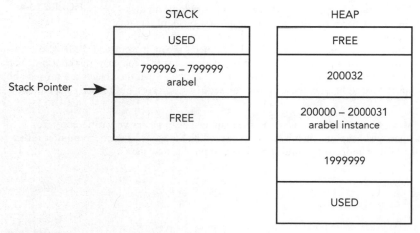

FIGURE 13-3

The next line of code both declares a `Customer` reference and instantiates a `Customer` object. In this instance, space on the stack for the `otherCustomer2` reference is allocated, and space for the `otherCustomer2` object is allocated on the heap in a single line of code:

```
Customer otherCustomer2 = new EnhancedCustomer();
```

This line allocates 4 bytes on the stack to hold the `otherCustomer2` reference, stored at locations `799992` through `799995`. The `otherCustomer2` object is allocated space on the heap starting at location `200032`.

It is clear from the example that the process of setting up a reference variable is more complex than for setting up a value variable, and there is performance overhead. In fact, the process is somewhat oversimplified here because the .NET runtime needs to maintain information about the state of the heap, and this information needs to be updated whenever new data is added to the heap. Despite this overhead, you now have a mechanism for allocating variables that is not constrained by the limitations of the stack. By assigning the value of one reference variable to another of the same type, you have two variables that reference the same object in memory. When a reference variable goes out of scope, it is removed from the stack as described in the previous section, but the data for a referenced object is still sitting on the heap. The data remains on the heap until either the program terminates or the garbage collector removes it, which happens only when the data is no longer referenced by any variables and the garbage collector runs.

The fact that data can remain in the heap for a long time is the power of reference data types, and you will see this feature used extensively in C# code. It means that you have a high degree of control over the lifetime of your data because it is guaranteed to exist in the heap as long as you are maintaining some reference to it.

Garbage Collection

The previous discussion and diagrams show the managed heap working very much like the stack, to the extent that successive objects are placed next to each other in memory. This means you can determine where to place the next object by using a heap pointer that indicates the next free memory location, which is adjusted as you add more objects to the heap. However, things are complicated by the fact that the lives of the heap-based objects are not coupled with the scope of the individual stack-based variables that reference them.

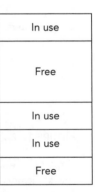

FIGURE 13-4

When the garbage collector runs, it removes all those objects from the heap that are no longer referenced. The GC finds all referenced objects from a root table of references and continues to a tree of referenced objects. Immediately after, the heap has objects scattered on it, which are mixed up with memory that has just been freed (see Figure 13-4).

If the managed heap stayed like this, allocating space for new objects would be an awkward process, with the runtime having to search through the heap for a block of memory big enough to store each new object. However, the garbage collector does not leave the heap in this state. As soon as the garbage collector has freed all the objects it can, it compacts the heap by moving all the remaining objects to form one continuous block of memory. This means that the heap can continue working just like the stack, as far as locating where to store new objects. Of course, when the objects are moved about, all the references to those objects need to be updated with the correct new addresses, but the garbage collector handles that, too.

This action of compacting by the garbage collector is where the managed heap works very differently from unmanaged heaps. With the managed heap, it is just a question of reading the value of the heap pointer rather than iterating through a linked list of addresses to find somewhere to put the new data.

> **NOTE** *Generally, the garbage collector runs when the .NET runtime determines that garbage collection is required. You can force the garbage collector to run at a certain point in your code by calling* System.GC.Collect. System.GC *is a .NET class that represents the garbage collector, and the* Collect *method initiates a garbage collection.*
>
> *Usually you shouldn't invoke* GC.Collect *programmatically because surviving objects move faster in the next generation (as described in the next section). However, this method has great usage during testing when you can see memory leaks where objects that should have been garbage collected are still alive. You also can see other scenarios where an object is garbage collected even if you still expect a reference to be available. Be aware that code can behave differently in debug and release builds. With release builds, more optimizations are taking place.*

When objects are created, they are placed within the managed heap. The first section of the heap is called the generation 0 section, or gen 0. As your new objects are created, they are moved into this section of the heap. Therefore, this is where the youngest objects reside.

Your objects remain there until the first collection of objects occurs through the garbage collection process. The objects that remain alive after this cleansing are compacted and then moved to the next section or generational part of the heap—the generation 1, or gen 1, section.

At this point, the generation 0 section is empty, and all new objects are again placed in this section. Older objects that survived the garbage collection process are further down in the generation 1 section. This movement of aged items actually occurs one more time. The next collection process that occurs is then repeated. This means that the items that survived the garbage collection process from the generation 1 section are moved to the generation 2 section, and the gen 0 items go to gen 1, again leaving gen 0 open for new objects.

> **NOTE** *Garbage collection occurs when you allocate an item that exceeds the capacity of the generation 0 section or when a* GC.Collect *is called.*

This process greatly improves the performance of your application. Typically, your youngest objects are the ones that can be collected, and a large number of objects that are associated with younger objects might be reclaimed as well. If these objects reside next to each other in the heap, then the garbage collection is faster. In addition, because related objects are residing next to each other, program execution is faster all around.

Another performance-related aspect of garbage collection in .NET is how the framework deals with larger objects that are added to the heap. In .NET, larger objects have their own managed heap, referred to as the *large object heap*. When objects greater than 85,000 bytes are utilized, they go to this special heap rather than the main heap. Your .NET application doesn't know the difference because this is all managed for you. Because compressing large items in the heap is expensive, it isn't done for the objects residing in the large object heap.

To improve garbage collection even more, collections in the generation 2 section and from the large object heap are done on a background thread. This means that application threads are only blocked for generation 0 and generation 1 collections, which reduces the overall pause time, especially for large-scale server apps. This feature is on by default for both servers and workstations.

Another optimization that helps in application performance is garbage collection balancing. This is specific to server garbage collection. Typically, a server has a pool of threads doing roughly the same thing. The memory allocation is similar across all the threads. For servers, there is one garbage collection heap per logical server. So, when one of the heaps runs out of memory and triggers a garbage collection, all of the other heaps most likely will benefit from the garbage collection as well. If a thread happens to use a lot more memory than other threads and it causes a garbage collection, the other threads may not be close to requiring the garbage collection, so it's not efficient. The GC balances the heaps—both the small object heap and the large object heap. This balancing process reduces unnecessary collection.

To take advantage of hardware with lots of memory, the GC class has added the `GCSettings.LatencyMode` property. Setting the property to one of the values in the `GCLatencyMode` enumeration gives a little control over how the GC performs collections. The following table shows the possible values for the `GCLatencyMode` that can be used:

MEMBER	DESCRIPTION
Batch	Disables the concurrency settings and sets the garbage collection for maximum throughput at the expense of responsiveness. This overrides the configuration setting.
Interactive	The default behavior on a workstation. This uses garbage collection concurrency and balances throughput and responsiveness.
LowLatency	Conservative garbage collection. Full collections occur only when there is memory pressure on the system. This setting should only be used for short periods of time to perform specific operations.
SustainedLowLatency	Does full blocking collections only when there is system memory pressure.
NoGCRegion	With `GCSettings`, this is a read-only property. You can set it within a code block by calling `GC.TryStartNoGCRegion` and `EndNoGCRegion`. By invoking `TryStartNoGCRegion`, you define the size of the memory that needs to be available, which the GC tries to reach. After a successful call to `TryStartNoGCRegion`, you define that the garbage collector should not run—until calling `EndNoGCRegion`.

The amount of time that the `LowLatency` or `NoGCRegion` settings are used should be kept to a minimum. The amount of memory being allocated should be as small as possible. An out-of-memory error could occur if you're not careful.

STRONG AND WEAK REFERENCES

The garbage collector cannot reclaim memory of an object that still has a reference—that is a strong reference. It can reclaim managed memory that is not referenced from the root table directly or indirectly. However, sometimes developers miss properly releasing a reference. Memory leaks can easily happen when not unsubscribing from events.

> **NOTE** *In case you have objects that reference each other but are not referenced from the root table—for example, object A references B, B references C, and C references A—the GC can destroy all these objects.*

When the class or struct is instantiated in the application code, it has a strong reference as long as there is any other code that references it. For example, if you have a class called `MyClass` and you create a reference to objects based on that class and call the variable `myClassVariable` as follows, as long as `myClassVariable` is in scope, there is a strong reference to the `MyClass` object:

```
MyClass? myClassVariable = new();
```

This means that the garbage collector cannot clean up the memory used by the `MyClass` object. Generally, this is a good thing because you might need to access the `MyClass` object. You might create a cache object that has references to several other objects, like this:

```
MyCache myCache = new();
myCache.Add(myClassVariable);
```

Now you've finished using the `myClassVariable`. It can go out of scope, or you assign `null`:

```
myClassVariable = null;
```

In case the garbage collector runs now, it can't release the memory that was referenced by the `myClassVariable` because the object is still referenced from the cache object. Such references can easily be missed, and you can avoid this by using the `WeakReference`.

A weak reference allows the object to be created and used, but if the garbage collector happens to run, it collects the object and frees up the memory. This is not something you would typically want to do because of potential bugs and performance issues, but there are certainly situations in which it makes sense. Weak references also don't make sense with small objects because weak references have an overhead of their own, and that might be bigger than the small object.

Weak references are created using the `WeakReference` class. With the constructor, you can pass a strong reference. The sample code creates a `DataObject` and passes the reference returned from the constructor. When using `WeakReference`, you can try to access the `Target` property. If the `Target` property doesn't return `null`, the object is still available. Assigning it to the variable `strongReference`, a strong reference to the object is created again, and it can't be garbage collected:

```
// Instantiate a weak reference to the DataObject object
WeakReference myWeakReference = new(new DataObject());
DataObject? strongReference = myWeakReference.Target as DataObject;
if (strongReference is not null)
{
  // use the strongReference
}
else
{
  // reference not available
}
```

> **NOTE** *The* `WeakReference` *class defines the* `IsAlive` *property. Accessing this property before creating a strong reference is not useful. In the time between accessing the* `IsAlive` *property and using the* `Target` *property, the object can be garbage collected. It's always necessary to check for* `null` *after accessing the* `Target` *property. A practical use of the* `IsAlive` *property is that a strong reference is currently not required, and you just want to check if the object is not alive anymore (e.g., to set a flag in a class or do some other cleanup).*

WORKING WITH UNMANAGED RESOURCES

The presence of the garbage collector means that you usually do not need to worry about objects you no longer need; you simply allow all references to those objects to go out of scope and let the garbage collector free memory as required. However, the garbage collector does not know how to free unmanaged resources (such as file handles, network connections, and database connections). When managed classes encapsulate direct or indirect references to unmanaged resources, you need to make special provisions to ensure that the unmanaged resources are released when an instance of the class is garbage collected.

When defining a class, you can use two mechanisms to automate the freeing of unmanaged resources. These mechanisms are often implemented together because each provides a slightly different approach:

➤   Declare a *destructor* (or finalizer) as a member of your class.

➤   Implement the `System.IDisposable` interface in your class.

The following sections discuss each of these mechanisms in turn and then look at how to implement the mechanisms together for best results.

Destructors or Finalizers

You have seen that constructors enable you to specify actions that must take place whenever an instance of a class is created. Conversely, destructors are called before an object is destroyed by the garbage collector. Given this behavior, a destructor would initially seem like a great place to put code to free unmanaged resources and perform a general cleanup. Unfortunately, things are not always so straightforward.

> **NOTE** *Although we talk about destructors in C#, in the underlying .NET architecture, these are known as* finalizers. *When you define a destructor in C#, what is emitted into the assembly by the compiler is actually a* Finalize *method. It doesn't affect any of your source code, but you need to be aware of it when examining generated Intermediate Language (IL) code.*

The syntax for a destructor will be familiar to C++ developers. It looks like a method, with the same name as the containing class, but prefixed with a tilde (~). It has no return type and takes no parameters or access modifiers. Here is an example:

```
class MyClass
{
  ~MyClass()
  {
    // Finalizer implementation
  }
}
```

When the C# compiler compiles a destructor, it implicitly translates the destructor code to the equivalent of an override of the `Finalize` method, which ensures that the `Finalize` method of the parent class is executed. The following example shows the C# code equivalent to the IL that the compiler would generate for the `~MyClass` destructor:

```
protected override void Finalize()
{
  try
  {
    // Finalizer implementation
  }
```

```
      finally
      {
        base.Finalize();
      }
  }
```

As shown, the code implemented in the ~MyClass destructor is wrapped in a try block contained in the Finalize method. A call to the parent's Finalize method is ensured by placing the call in a finally block. You can read about try and finally blocks in Chapter 10, "Errors and Exceptions."

Experienced C++ developers make extensive use of destructors, sometimes not only to clean up resources but also to provide debugging information or perform other tasks. C# destructors are used far less than their C++ equivalents. The problem with C# destructors as compared to their C++ counterparts is that they are nondeterministic. When a C++ object is destroyed, its destructor runs immediately. However, because of the way the garbage collector works when using C#, there is no way to know when an object's destructor will actually execute. The destructor runs when a finalizer starts. The finalizer is started with a garbage collection. Hence, you cannot place any code in the destructor that relies on being run at a certain time, and you should not rely on the destructor being called for different class instances in any particular order. When your object is holding scarce and critical resources that need to be freed as soon as possible, you do not want to wait for garbage collection.

Another problem with C# destructors is that the implementation of a destructor delays the final removal of an object from memory. Objects that do not have a destructor are removed from memory in one pass of the garbage collector, but objects that have destructors require two passes to be destroyed: the first pass calls the destructor without removing the object, and the second pass actually deletes the object. In addition, the runtime uses a single thread to execute the Finalize methods of all objects. If you use destructors frequently and use them to execute lengthy cleanup tasks, the impact on performance can be noticeable.

The IDisposable and IAsyncDiposable Interfaces

In C#, the recommended alternative to using a destructor is using the IDisposable or IAsyncDiposable interfaces. These interfaces define a pattern (with language-level support) that provides a deterministic mechanism for freeing unmanaged resources and avoids the garbage collector–related problems inherent with destructors. The IDisposable interface declares a single method named Dispose, which takes no parameters and returns void. Here is an implementation for MyClass:

```
class MyClass: IDisposable
{
  public void Dispose()
  {
    // implementation
  }
}
```

The IAsyncDisposable interface defines the DisposeAsync method that returns a ValueTask.

The implementation of Dispose should explicitly free all unmanaged resources used directly by an object and call Dispose on any encapsulated objects that also implement the IDisposable interface. In this way, the Dispose method provides precise control over when unmanaged resources are freed.

Suppose that you have a class named ResourceGobbler, which relies on the use of some external resource and implements IDisposable. If you want to instantiate an instance of this class, use it, and then dispose of it, you could do so like this:

```
ResourceGobbler theInstance = new();
// do your processing
theInstance.Dispose();
```

Unfortunately, this code fails to free the resources consumed by `theInstance` if an exception occurs during processing, so you should write the code as follows using a `try` block (as covered in detail in Chapter 10):

```
ResourceGobbler? theInstance = null;
try
{
  theInstance = new();
  // do your processing
}
finally
{
  theInstance?.Dispose();
}
```

The using Statement and the using Declaration

Using `try/finally` ensures that `Dispose` is always called on `theInstance` and that any resources consumed by it are always freed, even if an exception occurs during processing. However, if you always had to repeat such a construct, it would result in confusing code. C# offers a syntax that you can use to guarantee that `Dispose` or `DisposeAsync` is automatically called against an object that implements `IDisposable` or `IAsyncDisposable` when its reference goes out of scope. The syntax to do this involves the `using` keyword. The following code generates IL code equivalent to the `try` block just shown:

```
using (ResourceGobbler theInstance = new())
{
  // do your processing
}
```

> **NOTE** *The interface* `IDisposable` *or* `IAsyncDisposable` *is required to use an object with the* using *statement or the* using *declaration. There's one exception: because a value-only type (a* ref struct*) cannot implement any interface, with a* ref struct*, just the implementation of a* Dispose *method is required to use this type with the* using *statement or the* using *declaration.*

The `using` statement, followed in parentheses by a reference variable declaration and instantiation, causes that variable to be scoped to the accompanying statement block. In addition, when that variable goes out of scope, its `Dispose` method is called automatically, even if an exception occurs.

Since C# 8, a shorter form to release resources is available: the *using declaration*. With the `using` declaration, you don't write parentheses, and the curly brackets are not necessary. The compiler still creates code with `try/finally` to invoke the `Dispose` or `DisposeAsync` method. The resource is disposed when the variable goes out of scope. Typically, the variable goes out of scope when the method ends. As most methods are very short, disposing should often be done at the end of the method. That much indentation of code using many curly brackets can be reduced with the `using` declaration. With the `using` declaration, you can also add curly brackets to invoke the `Dipose` method earlier.

```
using ResourceGobbler theInstance = new();
// do your processing
```

There's another difference with the `using` statement and the `using` declaration. With the `using` declaration, a variable is always needed. The `using` statement can be used with the return of a method; you don't necessarily need to declare a variable if a variable is not needed to invoke members.

> **NOTE** *The* using *keyword has multiple uses with C#. The* using *directive is used to import namespaces. The* using *statement and* using *declaration can be used with objects implementing the* IDisposable *interface. The* Dispose *method is invoked with the end of the* using *scope.*

> **NOTE** *With several classes, both a* Close *and a* Dispose *method exist. If it is common to close a resource (such as a file and a database), both* Close *and* Dispose *have been implemented. Here, the* Close *method simply calls* Dispose. *This approach provides clarity in the use of these classes and supports the* using *statement. Newer types only implement the* Dispose *method as we're already used to it.*

Implementing IDisposable and a Destructor

The previous sections discussed two alternatives for freeing unmanaged resources used by the classes you create:

➤   The execution of a destructor is enforced by the runtime but is nondeterministic and places an unacceptable overhead on the runtime because of the way garbage collection works.

➤   The IDisposable interface provides a mechanism that enables users of a class to control when resources are freed but requires discipline to ensure that Dispose is called.

If you are creating a finalizer, you should also implement the IDisposable interface. You implement IDisposable on the assumption that most programmers will call Dispose correctly, but implement a destructor as a safety mechanism in case Dispose is not called. Here is an example of a dual implementation:

```
public class ResourceHolder: IDisposable
{
  private bool _isDisposed = false;
  public void Dispose()
  {
    Dispose(true);
    GC.SuppressFinalize(this);
  }

  protected virtual void Dispose(bool disposing)
  {
    if (!_isDisposed)
    {
      if (disposing)
      {
        // Cleanup managed objects by calling their
        // Dispose() methods.
      }
      // Cleanup unmanaged objects
      _isDisposed = true;
    }
  }
}
```

```
    ~ResourceHolder()
    {
      Dispose(false);
    }

    public void SomeMethod()
    {
      // Ensure object not already disposed before execution of any method
      if(_isDisposed)
      {
        throw new ObjectDisposedException(nameof(ResourceHolder));
      }
      // method implementation...
    }
  }
```

You can see from this code that there is a second `protected` overload of `Dispose` that takes one `bool` parameter—and this is the method that does all the cleaning up. `Dispose(bool)` is called by both the destructor and `IDisposable.Dispose`. The point of this approach is to ensure that all cleanup code is in one place.

The parameter passed to `Dispose(bool)` indicates whether `Dispose(bool)` has been invoked by the destructor or by `IDisposable.Dispose`. `Dispose(bool)` should not be invoked from anywhere else in your code. The idea is this:

➤ If a consumer calls `IDisposable.Dispose`, that consumer is indicating that all managed and unmanaged resources associated with that object should be cleaned up.

➤ If a destructor has been invoked, all resources still need to be cleaned up. However, in this case, you know that the destructor must have been called by the garbage collector, and you should not attempt to access other managed objects because you can no longer be certain of their state. In this situation, the best you can do is clean up the known unmanaged resources and hope that any referenced managed objects also have destructors that will perform their own cleaning up.

The `_isDisposed` member variable indicates whether the object has already been disposed of and ensures that you do not try to dispose of member variables more than once. It also enables you to test whether an object has been disposed of before executing any instance methods, as shown in `SomeMethod`. This simplistic approach is not thread-safe and depends on the caller ensuring that only one thread is calling the method concurrently. Requiring a consumer to enforce synchronization is a reasonable assumption and one that is used repeatedly throughout the .NET class libraries (in the `Collection` classes, for example). Threading and synchronization are discussed in Chapter 17, "Parallel Programming."

Finally, `IDisposable.Dispose` contains a call to the method `System.GC.SuppressFinalize`. `GC` is the class that represents the garbage collector, and the `SuppressFinalize` method tells the garbage collector that a class no longer needs to have its destructor called. Because your implementation of `Dispose` has already done all the cleanup required, there's nothing left for the destructor to do. Calling `SuppressFinalize` means that the garbage collector will treat that object as if it doesn't have a destructor at all.

IDisposable and Finalizer Rules

You've learned about finalizers, the `IDisposable` interface, the Dispose pattern, and some rules on using these constructs. Because releasing resources is such an important aspect with managed code, the rules are summarized in this list:

➤ If your class defines a member that implements `IDisposable`, the class should also implement `IDisposable`.

➤ Implementing `IDisposable` does not mean you should also implement a finalizer. Finalizers create additional overhead with both creating an object and releasing the memory of the object as an additional pass from the GC is needed. You should implement a finalizer only if needed—for example, to release native resources, a finalizer is really needed.

➤ If a finalizer is implemented, you should also implement the interface IDisposable. This way, the native resource can be released earlier, not only when the GC is finding out about the allocated resource that's available for releasing it.

➤ Within the finalization code implementation, don't access objects that might have been finalized already. The order of finalizers is not guaranteed.

➤ If an object you use implements the IDisposable interface, call the Dispose method when the object is no longer needed. In case you're using this object within a method, the using statement or using declaration comes in handy. In case the object is a member of the class, make the class implement IDisposable as well.

UNSAFE CODE

As you have just seen, C# is good at hiding much of the basic memory management from the developer, thanks to the garbage collector and the use of references. However, sometimes you will want direct access to memory. For example, you might want to access a function in an external (non-.NET) DLL that requires a pointer to be passed as a parameter (as many Windows API functions or native Linux functions do), or possibly for performance reasons. This section examines the C# facilities that provide direct access to the content of memory.

Accessing Memory Directly with Pointers

Although I am introducing *pointers* as if they are a new topic, in reality pointers are not new at all. You have been using references freely in your code, and a reference is simply a type-safe pointer. You have already seen how variables that represent objects and arrays actually store the memory address of where the corresponding data (the *referent*) is stored. A pointer is simply a variable that stores the address of something else in the same way as a reference. The *difference* is that C# does not allow you direct access to the address contained in a reference variable. With a reference, the variable is treated syntactically as if it stores the actual content of the referent.

C# references are designed to make the language simpler to use and to prevent you from inadvertently doing something that corrupts the contents of memory. With a pointer, however, the actual memory address is available to you. This gives you a lot of power to perform new kinds of operations. For example, you can add 4 bytes to the address to examine or even modify whatever data happens to be stored 4 bytes further in memory.

There are two main reasons for using pointers:

➤ **Backward compatibility**—Despite all the facilities provided by .NET, it is still possible to call native Windows and Linux API functions, and for some operations, this may be the only way to accomplish your task. These API functions are generally written in C++ or C and often require pointers as parameters. However, in many cases, it is possible to write the DllImport declaration in a way that avoids use of pointers—for example, by using the System.IntPtr class. Many features of .NET itself make use of native APIs.

➤ **Performance**—On those occasions when speed is of the utmost importance, pointers can provide a route to optimized performance. If you know what you are doing, you can ensure that data is accessed or manipulated in the most efficient way. However, be aware that more often than not, there are other areas of your code where you can likely make the necessary performance improvements without resorting to using pointers. Try using a code profiler to look for the bottlenecks in your code; Visual Studio includes a code profiler.

Low-level memory access has a price. The syntax for using pointers is more complex than that for reference types, and pointers are unquestionably more difficult to use correctly. You need good programming skills and an excellent ability to think carefully and logically about what your code is doing to use pointers successfully. Otherwise, it is easy to introduce subtle, difficult-to-find bugs into your program when using pointers. For example, it is easy to overwrite other variables, cause stack overflows, access areas of memory that don't store any variables, or even overwrite information about your code that is needed by the .NET runtime, thereby crashing your program.

Despite these issues, pointers remain a powerful and flexible tool in the writing of efficient code.

> **WARNING** *I strongly advise against using pointers unnecessarily because your code will not only be harder to write and debug, but it will also fail the memory type safety checks imposed by the CLR. An example where pointers are necessary is to invoke native APIs.*

Writing Unsafe Code with the unsafe Keyword

As a result of the risks associated with pointers, C# allows the use of pointers only in blocks of code that you have specifically marked for this purpose. The keyword to do this is `unsafe`. You can mark an individual method as being `unsafe` like this:

```
unsafe int GetSomeNumber()
{
    // code that can use pointers
}
```

Any method can be marked as `unsafe`, regardless of what other modifiers have been applied to it (for example, `static` methods or `virtual` methods). In the case of methods, the `unsafe` modifier applies to the method's parameters, allowing you to use pointers as parameters. You can also mark an entire class or struct as `unsafe`, which means that all its members are assumed unsafe:

```
unsafe class MyClass
{
    // any method in this class can now use pointers
}
```

Similarly, you can mark a member as `unsafe`:

```
class MyClass
{
    unsafe int* pX; // declaration of a pointer field in a class
}
```

Or you can mark a block of code within a method as `unsafe`:

```
void MyMethod()
{
    // code that doesn't use pointers
    unsafe
    {
        // unsafe code that uses pointers here
    }

    // more 'safe' code that doesn't use pointers
}
```

You cannot mark a local variable by itself as `unsafe`. If you want to use an unsafe local variable, you need to declare and use it inside a method or block that is unsafe. There is one more step before you can use pointers.

The C# compiler rejects unsafe code unless you tell it that your code includes unsafe blocks. You can configure unsafe code by setting the `AllowUnsafeBlocks` in the `csproj` project file, as shown here:

```
<PropertyGroup>
  <AllowUnsafeBlocks>True</AllowUnsafeBlocks>
</PropertyGroup>
```

Pointer Syntax

After you have marked a block of code as `unsafe`, you can declare a pointer using the following syntax:

```
int* pWidth, pHeight;
double* pResult;
byte*[] pFlags;
```

This code declares four variables: `pWidth` and `pHeight` are pointers to integers, `pResult` is a pointer to a `double`, and `pFlags` is an array of pointers to bytes. It is common practice to use the prefix `p` in front of names of pointer variables to indicate that they are pointers. When used in a variable declaration, the symbol `*` indicates that you are declaring a pointer (that is, something that stores the address of a variable of the specified type).

When you have declared variables of pointer types, you can use them in the same way as normal variables, but first you need to learn two more operators:

➤ `&` means take the address of, and it converts a value data type to a pointer—for example, `int` to `*int`. This operator is known as the address operator.

➤ `*` means get the content of this address and convert a pointer to a value data type—for example, `*float` to `float`. This operator is known as the *indirection* operator (or the *dereference* operator).

You can see from these definitions that `&` and `*` have opposite effects.

> **NOTE** *You might be wondering how it is possible to use the symbols `&` and `*` in this manner because these symbols also refer to the operators of bitwise AND (`&`) and multiplication (`*`). Actually, it is always possible for both you and the compiler to know what is meant in each case because with the pointer meanings, these symbols always appear as unary operators— they act on only one variable and appear in front of that variable in your code. By contrast, bitwise AND multiplication are binary operators—they require two operands.*

The following code shows examples of how to use these operators:

```
int x = 10;
int* pX, pY;
pX = &x;
pY = pX;
*pY = 20;
```

You start by declaring an integer, x, with the value 10 followed by two pointers to integers, pX and pY. You then set pX to point to x (that is, you set the content of pX to the address of x). Then you assign the value of pX to pY so that pY also points to x. Finally, in the statement `*pY = 20`, you assign the value 20 as the contents of the location pointed to by pY—in effect changing x to 20 because pY happens to point to x. Note that there is no particular connection between the variables pY and x. It is just that at the present time, pY happens to point to the memory location at which x is held.

To get a better understanding of what is going on, consider that the integer x is stored at memory locations `0x12F8C4` through `0x12F8C7` (1243332 to 1243335 in decimal) on the stack (there are four locations because an `int` occupies 4 bytes). Because the stack allocates memory downward, this means that the variables pX will be stored at locations `0x12F8C0` to `0x12F8C3`, and pY will end up at locations `0x12F8BC` to `0x12F8BF`. Note that pX and pY also occupy 4 bytes each. That is not because an `int` occupies 4 bytes, but because on a 32-bit application you need 4 bytes to store an address. With these addresses, after executing the previous code, the stack will look like Figure 13-5.

0x12F8C4-0x12F8C7	x=20 (=0x14)
0x12F8C0-0x12F8C3	pX=0x12F8C4
0x12F8BC-0x12F8BF	pY=012F8C4

FIGURE 13-5

> **NOTE** *Although this process is illustrated with integers, which are stored consecutively on the stack on a 32-bit processor, this does not happen for all data types. The reason is that 32-bit processors work best when retrieving data from memory in 4-byte chunks. Memory on such machines tends to be divided into 4-byte blocks, and each block is sometimes known under Windows as a DWORD because this was the name of a 32-bit unsigned `int` in pre-.NET days. It is most efficient to grab DWORDs from memory—storing data across DWORD boundaries normally results in a hardware performance hit. For this reason, the .NET runtime normally pads out data types so that the memory they occupy is a multiple of 4. For example, a short occupies 2 bytes, but if a short is placed on the stack, the stack pointer will still be decremented by 4, not 2, so the next variable to go on the stack will still start at a DWORD boundary.*

You can declare a pointer to any value type (that is, any of the predefined types `uint`, `int`, `byte`, and so on, or to a struct). However, it is not possible to declare a pointer to a class or an array; this is because doing so could cause problems for the garbage collector. To work properly, the garbage collector needs to know exactly what class instances have been created on the heap, and where they are; but if your code started manipulating classes using pointers, you could easily corrupt the information on the heap concerning classes that the .NET runtime maintains for the garbage collector. In this context, any data type that the garbage collector can access is known as a *managed type*. Pointers can only be declared as *unmanaged* types because the garbage collector cannot deal with them.

Casting Pointers to Integer Types

Because a pointer really stores an integer that represents an address, you won't be surprised to know that the address in any pointer can be converted to or from any integer type. Pointer-to-integer-type conversions must be explicit. Implicit conversions are not available for such conversions. For example, it is perfectly legitimate to write the following:

```
int x = 10;
int* pX, pY;
pX = &x;
pY = pX;
*pY = 20;
ulong y = (ulong)pX;
int* pD = (int*)y;
```

The address held in the pointer pX is cast to a `ulong` and stored in the variable y. You have then cast y back to an `int*` and store it in the new variable pD. Hence, now pD also points to the value of x.

The primary reason for casting a pointer value to an integer type is to display it. The interpolation string (and similarly `Console.Write`) does not have any overloads that can take pointers, but they do accept and display pointer values that have been cast to integer types:

```
WriteLine($"Address is {pX}"); // wrong -- will give a compilation error
WriteLine($"Address is {(ulong)pX}"); // OK
```

You can cast a pointer to any of the integer types. However, because an address occupies 4 bytes on 32-bit systems, casting a pointer to anything other than a `uint`, `long`, or `ulong` is almost certain to lead to overflow errors. (An `int` causes problems because its range is from roughly –2 billion to 2 billion, whereas an address runs from zero to about 4 billion.) If you are creating a 64-bit application, you need to cast the pointer to `ulong`.

It is also important to be aware that the `checked` keyword does not apply to conversions involving pointers. For such conversions, exceptions are not raised when overflows occur, even in a `checked` context. The .NET runtime assumes that if you are using pointers, you know what you are doing and are not worried about possible overflows.

Casting Between Pointer Types

You can also explicitly convert between pointers pointing to different types. For example, the following is perfectly legal code:

```
byte aByte = 8;
byte* pByte= &aByte;
double* pDouble = (double*)pByte;
```

However, if you try something like this, be careful. In this example, if you look at the `double` value pointed to by `pDouble`, you are actually looking up some memory that contains a `byte` (`aByte`), combined with some other memory, and treating it as if this area of memory contained a `double`, which does not give you a meaningful value. However, you might want to convert between types to implement the equivalent of a C union, or you might want to cast pointers from other types into pointers to `sbyte` to examine individual bytes of memory.

void Pointers

If you want to maintain a pointer but not specify to what type of data it points, you can declare it as a pointer to a void:

```
int x = 10;
int* pointerToInt = &x;
void* pointerToVoid;
pointerToVoid = (void*)pointerToInt;
```

The main use of this is if you need to call an API function that requires `void*` parameters. Within the C# language, there isn't a great deal that you can do using `void` pointers. In particular, the compiler flags an error if you attempt to de-reference a `void` pointer using the `*` operator. You can cast the `void*` into some other pointer type and then use it with other scenarios.

Pointer Arithmetic

It is possible to add or subtract integers to and from pointers. However, the compiler is quite clever about how it arranges this. For example, suppose that you have a pointer to an `int`, and you try to add 1 to its value. The compiler assumes that you actually mean you want to look at the memory location following the `int`, and hence it increases the value by 4 bytes—the size of an `int`. If it is a pointer to a `double`, adding 1 actually increases the value of the pointer by 8 bytes, the size of a `double`. Only if the pointer points to a `byte` or `sbyte` (1 byte each) does adding 1 to the value of the pointer actually change its value by 1.

You can use the operators +, -, +=, -=, ++, and -- with pointers, with the variable on the right side of these operators being a `long` or `ulong`.

> **NOTE** *You may not carry out arithmetic operations on void pointers. You need to cast the* void *pointer to other pointer types, and then you can perform pointer arithmetic.*

For example, assume the following definitions:

```
uint u = 3;
byte b = 8;
double d = 10.0;
uint* pUint= &u; // size of a uint is 4
byte* pByte = &b; // size of a byte is 1
double* pDouble = &d; // size of a double is 8
```

Next, assume the addresses to which these pointers point are as follows:

➤ pUint: 1243332

➤ pByte: 1243328

➤ pDouble: 1243320

Then execute this code:

```
++pUint; // adds (1*4) = 4 bytes to pUint
pByte -= 3; // subtracts (3*1) = 3 bytes from pByte
double* pDouble2 = pDouble + 4; // pDouble2 = pDouble + 32 bytes (4*8 bytes)
```

The pointers now contain this:

➤ pUint: 1243336

➤ pByte: 1243325

➤ pDouble2: 1243352

> **NOTE** *The general rule is that adding a number* x *to a pointer to type* T *with value* P *gives the result* P + X*(sizeof(T)). If successive values of a given type are stored in successive memory locations, pointer addition works very well, allowing you to move pointers between memory locations. If you are dealing with types such as* byte *or* char, *though, with sizes not in multiples of 4, successive values will not, by default, be stored in successive memory locations.*

You can also subtract one pointer from another pointer if both pointers point to the same data type. In this case, the result is a `long` whose value is given by the difference between the pointer values divided by the size of the type that they represent:

```
double* pD1 = (double*)1243324; // note that it is perfectly valid to
// initialize a pointer like this.
double* pD2 = (double*)1243300;
long L = pD1-pD2; // gives the result 3 (=24/sizeof(double))
```

The sizeof Operator

This section has been referring to the size of various data types. If you need to use the size of a type in your code, you can use the `sizeof` operator, which takes the name of a data type as a parameter and returns the number of bytes occupied by that type, as shown in this example:

```
int x = sizeof(double);
```

This sets x to the value 8.

The advantage of using `sizeof` is that you don't have to hard-code data type sizes in your code, which makes your code more portable. A `byte` (or `sbyte`) has the size of 1 byte, `sizeof(short)` returns 2, an `int` has the length of 4 bytes, and a `long` 8 bytes. You can also use `sizeof` for structs that you define yourself, although, in that case, the result depends on what fields are in the struct. You cannot use `sizeof` for classes.

Pointers to Structs: The Pointer Member Access Operator

Pointers to structs work in exactly the same way as pointers to the predefined value types. There is, however, one condition: the struct must not contain any reference types. This is due to the restriction mentioned earlier that pointers cannot point to any reference types. To avoid this, the compiler flags an error if you create a pointer to any struct that contains any reference types.

Suppose that you had a struct defined like this:

```
struct MyStruct
{
  public long X;
  public float F;
}
```

You could define a pointer to it as follows:

```
MyStruct* pStruct;
```

Then you could initialize it like this:

```
MyStruct myStruct = new();
pStruct = &myStruct;
```

It is also possible to access member values of a struct through the pointer:

```
(*pStruct).X = 4;
(*pStruct).F = 3.4f;
```

However, this syntax is a bit complex. For this reason, C# defines another operator that enables you to access members of structs through pointers using a simpler syntax. It is known as the *pointer member access operator*, and the symbol is a dash followed by a greater-than sign, so it looks like an arrow: `->`.

> **NOTE** *C++ developers will recognize the pointer member access operator because C++ also uses the symbol for this purpose.*

Using the pointer member access operator, the previous code can be rewritten like this:

```
pStruct->X = 4;
pStruct->F = 3.4f;
```

You can also directly set up pointers of the appropriate type to point to fields within a struct,

```
long* pL = &(myStruct.X);
float* pF = &(myStruct.F);
```

or,

```
long* pL = &(pStruct->X);
float* pF = &(pStruct->F);
```

Pointers to Class Members

As indicated earlier, it is not possible to create pointers to classes. That is because the garbage collector does not maintain any information about pointers—only about references—so creating pointers to classes could cause garbage collection not to work properly.

However, most classes contain value type members, and you might want to create pointers to them. This is possible, but it requires a special syntax. For example, suppose that you rewrite the struct from the previous example as a class:

```
class MyClass
{
  public long X;
  public float F;
}
```

Then you might want to create pointers to its fields, X and F, in the same way as you did earlier. Unfortunately, doing so produces a compilation error:

```
MyClass myObject = new();
long* pL = &(myObject.X); // wrong -- compilation error
float* pF = &(myObject.F); // wrong -- compilation error
```

Although X and F are unmanaged types, they are embedded in an object, which sits on the heap. During garbage collection, the garbage collector might move MyObject to a new location, which would leave pL and pF pointing to the wrong memory addresses. Because of this, the compiler does not let you assign addresses of members of managed types to pointers in this manner.

The solution is to use the fixed keyword, which tells the garbage collector that there may be pointers referencing members of certain objects, so those objects must not be moved. The syntax for using fixed looks like this when you want to declare only one pointer:

```
MyClass myObject = new();
fixed (long* pObject = &(myObject.X))
{
  // do something
}
```

You define and initialize the pointer variable in the brackets following the keyword fixed. This pointer variable (pObject in the example) is scoped to the fixed block identified by the curly braces. As a result, the garbage collector knows not to move the myObject object while the code inside the fixed block is executing.

If you want to declare more than one pointer, you can place multiple fixed statements before the same code block:

```
MyClass myObject = new();
fixed (long* pX = &(myObject.X))
fixed (float* pF = &(myObject.F))
```

```
{
  // do something
}
```

You can nest entire `fixed` blocks if you want to fix several pointers for different periods:

```
MyClass myObject = new();
fixed (long* pX = &(myObject.X))
{
  // do something with pX
  fixed (float* pF = &(myObject.F))
  {
    // do something else with pF
  }
}
```

You can also initialize several variables within the same `fixed` block, if they are of the same type:

```
MyClass myObject = new();
MyClass myObject2 = new();
fixed (long* pX = &(myObject.X), pX2 = &(myObject2.X))
{
  //...
}
```

In all these cases, it is immaterial whether the various pointers you are declaring point to fields in the same or different objects or to static fields not associated with any class instance.

Pointer Example: PointerPlayground

For understanding pointers, it's best to write a program using pointers and to use the debugger. The following code snippet is from an example named `PointerPlayground`. It does some simple pointer manipulation and displays the results, enabling you to see what is happening in memory and where variables are stored (code file `PointerPlayground/Program.cs`):

```
unsafe static void Main()
{
  int a = 10;
  short b = -1;
  byte c = 4;
  float d = 1.5F;
  int* pa = &a;
  short* pb = &b;
  byte* pc = &c;
  float* pd = &d;

  Console.WriteLine($"Address of a is 0x{(ulong)&a:X}, " +
    $"size is {sizeof(int)}, value is {a}");
  Console.WriteLine($"Address of b is 0x{(ulong)&b:X}, " +
    $"size is {sizeof(short)}, value is {b}");
  Console.WriteLine($"Address of c is 0x{(ulong)&c:X}, " +
    $"size is {sizeof(byte)}, value is {c}");
  Console.WriteLine($"Address of d is 0x{(ulong)&d:X}, " +
    $"size is {sizeof(float)}, value is {d}");
  Console.WriteLine($"Address of pa=&a is 0x{(ulong)&pa:X}, " +
    $"size is {sizeof(int*)}, value is 0x{(ulong)pa:X}");
```

```
Console.WriteLine($"Address of pb=&b is 0x{(ulong)&pb:X}, " +
    $"size is {sizeof(short*)}, value is 0x{(ulong)pb:X}");
Console.WriteLine($"Address of pc=&c is 0x{(ulong)&pc:X}, " +
    $"size is {sizeof(byte*)}, value is 0x{(ulong)pc:X}");
Console.WriteLine($"Address of pd=&d is 0x{(ulong)&pd:X}, " +
    $"size is {sizeof(float*)}, value is 0x{(ulong)pd:X}");

*pa = 20;
Console.WriteLine($"After setting *pa, a = {a}");
Console.WriteLine($"*pa = {*pa}");

pd = (float*)pa;
Console.WriteLine($"a treated as a float = {*pd}");

Console.ReadLine();
}
```

This code declares four value variables: int a, short b, byte c, float d. Also, it declares four pointers of these values: pa, pb, pc, and pd.

Next, you display the values of these variables as well as their sizes and addresses. Note that in taking the addresses of pa, pb, pc, and pd, you are effectively looking at a pointer *to* a pointer—an address of an address of a value. Also, in accordance with the usual practice when displaying addresses, you have used the {0:X} format specifier in the WriteLine commands to ensure that memory addresses are displayed in hexadecimal format.

Finally, you use the pointer pa to change the value of a to 20 and do some pointer casting to see what happens if you try to treat the content of a as if it were a float, with the same number of bytes but a different memory representation.

Compiling and running this code results in the following output:

```
Address of a is 0x565DD7E53C, size is 4, value is 10
Address of b is 0x565DD7E538, size is 2, value is -1
Address of c is 0x565DD7E534, size is 1, value is 4
Address of d is 0x565DD7E530, size is 4, value is 1.5
Address of pa=&a is 0x565DD7E528, size is 8, value is 0x565DD7E53C
Address of pb=&b is 0x565DD7E520, size is 8, value is 0x565DD7E538, diff -4
Address of pc=&c is 0x565DD7E518, size is 8, value is 0x565DD7E534, diff -4
Address of pd=&d is 0x565DD7E510, size is 8, value is 0x565DD7E530, diff -4
After setting *pa, a = 20
*pa = 20
a treated as a float = 2.8E-44
```

> **NOTE** *With the new .NET runtime, different addresses are shown every time you run the application.*

Checking through these results confirms the description of how the stack operates presented in the "Memory Management Under the Hood" section earlier in this chapter. It allocates successive variables moving downward in memory. Notice how it also confirms that blocks of memory on the stack are always allocated in multiples of 4 or 8 bytes. For example, b is a short (of size 2) and has the (hex) address 0x565DD7E538, indicating that the memory locations reserved for it are locations 0x565DD7E538 through 0x565DD7E53B. If the .NET runtime had been strictly packing up variables next to each other, b would have occupied just two locations, 0x565DD7E538 and 0x565DD7E539.

The next example illustrates pointer arithmetic, as well as pointers to structs and class members. This example is named `PointerPlayground2`. To start, you define a struct named `CurrencyStruct`, which represents a currency value as dollars and cents. You also define an equivalent class named `CurrencyClass` (code file `PointerPlayground2/Currency.cs`):

```csharp
internal struct CurrencyStruct
{
  public CurrencyStruct(long dollars, byte cents)
    => (Dollars, Cents) = (dollars, cents);

  public readonly long Dollars;
  public readonly byte Cents;
  public override string ToString() => $"$ {Dollars}.{Cents}";
}

internal class CurrencyClass
{
  public CurrencyClass(long dollars, byte cents)
    => (Dollars, Cents) = (dollars, cents);

  public readonly long Dollars = 0;
  public readonly byte Cents = 0;
  public override string ToString() => $"$ {Dollars}.{Cents}";
}
```

Now that you have your struct and class defined, you can apply some pointers to them. The following is the code for the new example. Because the code is fairly long, I'm going through it in pieces. You start by displaying the size of `CurrencyStruct`, creating a couple of `CurrencyStruct` instances and some `CurrencyStruct` pointers. You use the pAmount pointer to initialize the members of the amount1 `CurrencyStruct` and then display the addresses of your variables (code file `PointerPlayground2/Program.cs`):

```csharp
unsafe static void Main()
{
  Console.WriteLine($"Size of CurrencyStruct struct is " +
    $"{sizeof(CurrencyStruct)}");
  CurrencyStruct amount1 = new(10, 10), amount2 = new(20, 20);
  CurrencyStruct* pAmount = &amount1;
  long* pDollars = &(pAmount->Dollars);
  byte* pCents = &(pAmount->Cents);


  Console.WriteLine($"Address of amount1 is 0x{(ulong)&amount1:X}");
  Console.WriteLine($"Address of amount2 is 0x{(ulong)&amount2:X}");
  Console.WriteLine($"Address of pAmount is 0x{(ulong)&pAmount:X}");
  Console.WriteLine($"Value of pAmount is 0x{(ulong)pAmount:X}");
  Console.WriteLine($"Address of pDollars is 0x{(ulong)&pDollars:X}");
  Console.WriteLine($"Value of pDollars is 0x{(ulong)pDollars:X}");
  Console.WriteLine($"Address of pCents is 0x{(ulong)&pCents:X}");
  Console.WriteLine($"Value of pCents is 0x{(ulong)pCents:X}");

  // because Dollars are declared readonly in CurrencyStruct, you cannot change it
  // with a variable of type CurrencyStruct
  // pAmount->Dollars = 20;
  // but you can change it via a pointer referencing the memory address!
  *pDollars = 100;
```

```
Console.WriteLine($"amount1 contains {amount1}");
//...
}
```

Now you do some pointer manipulation that relies on your knowledge of how the stack works. Because of the order in which the variables were declared, you know that amount2 will be stored at an address immediately below amount1. The sizeof(CurrencyStruct) operator returns 16 (as demonstrated in the upcoming screen output), so CurrencyStruct occupies a multiple of 4 bytes. Therefore, after you decrement your currency pointer, it points to amount2:

```
--pAmount; // this should get it to point to amount2
Console.WriteLine($"amount2 has address 0x{(ulong)pAmount:X} " +
    $"and contains {*pAmount}");
```

Only you know that, because your knowledge of the stack means you can tell what the effect of decrementing pAmount will be. After you start doing pointer arithmetic, you will find that you can access all sorts of variables and memory locations that the compiler would usually stop you from accessing, hence the description of pointer arithmetic as unsafe.

Next, you do some pointer arithmetic on your pCents pointer. pCents currently points to amount1.Cents, but the aim here is to get it to point to amount2.Cents, again using pointer operations instead of directly telling the compiler that's what you want to do. To do this, you need to decrement the address that pCents contains by sizeof(Currency). The following WriteLine methods show the value of pCents with the new address, and the value that's referenced from pCents, which is the value for the Cents with amount2:

```
// do some clever casting to get pCents to point to cents
// inside amount2
CurrencyStruct* pTempCurrency = (CurrencyStruct*)pCents;
pCents = (byte*)( --pTempCurrency );
Console.WriteLine("Value of pCents is now 0x{(ulong)pCents:X}");
Console.WriteLine($"The value where pCents points to: {*pCents}");
```

Finally, you use the fixed keyword to create some pointers that point to the fields in a class instance and use these pointers to set the value of this instance. Notice that this is also the first time that you have been able to look at the address of an item stored on the heap, rather than the stack:

```
Console.WriteLine("\nNow with classes");
// now try it out with classes
CurrencyClass amount3 = new(30, 0);
fixed(long* pDollars2 = &(amount3.Dollars))
fixed(byte* pCents2 = &(amount3.Cents))
{
    Console.WriteLine($"amount3.Dollars has address 0x{(ulong)pDollars2:X}");
    Console.WriteLine($"amount3.Cents has address 0x{(ulong)pCents2:X}");
    *pDollars2 = -100;
    Console.WriteLine($"amount3 contains {amount3}");
}
```

Compiling and running this code gives output similar to this:

```
Size of CurrencyStruct struct is 16
Address of amount1 is 0x5E5657E2F0
Address of amount2 is 0x5E5657E2E0
Address of pAmount is 0x5E5657E2D8
Value of pAmount is 0x5E5657E2F0
Address of pDollars is 0x5E5657E2D0
Value of pDollars is 0x5E5657E2F0
```

```
Address of pCents is 0x5E5657E2C8
Value of pCents is 0x5E5657E2F8
amount1 contains $ 100.10
pAmount contains the new address 5E5657E2E0 and references this value $ 20.20
Value of pCents is now 0x5E5657E2E8
The value where pCents points to: 20

Now with classes
amount3.Dollars has address 0x1AF3BFFF988
amount3.Cents has address 0x1AF3BFFF990
amount3 contains $ -100.0
```

Notice that the size of the `CurrencyStruct` struct is 16—somewhat larger than you would expect given the size of its fields (a `long` and a `byte` should total 9 bytes).

Function Pointers

Function pointers are a new feature with C# 9. You've already learned about delegates that are type-safe pointers to methods. However, delegates are classes, and a delegate holds a list of methods, so there's some overhead associated with delegates. With function pointers, just the memory address is used to reference a method—in a type-safe manner. Type safety is similar to the type safety of delegates, and the `delegate` keyword is used here as well—a delegate combined with an asterisk: `delegate*`.

The following `Calc` method declares a parameter of type `delegate* managed<int, int, int>`. You use angle brackets to specify—similarly to the `Func` delegate—the parameter types and the return type. The method passed to the Calc method needs to have two `int` parameters and an `int` return. With the `managed` modifier, the method needs to be a .NET method. The `managed` modifier is optional, and you can remove it without any change in behavior (code file `PointerPlayground2/FunctionPointerSample.cs`):

```
public static void Calc(delegate* managed<int, int, int> func)
{
  int result = func(42, 11);
  Console.WriteLine($"function pointer result: {result}");
}
```

The `managed` modifier is optional, but the `unmanaged` modifier is required on declaring function pointers to unmanaged or native functions. With the unmanaged modifier you also can specify the calling convention such as `StdCall`. The calling convention specifies how the native function deals with parameters, in which order they are put on the stack, or if they are put on the stack at all. The convention specified here needs to match the implementation of the native method.

```
public static void CalcUnmanaged(delegate* unmanaged[Stdcall]<int, int, int> func)
{
  int result = func(42, 11);
  Console.WriteLine($"function pointer result: {result}");
}
```

Because function pointers are pointers in memory that can be misused, they need to be declared in classes with the `unsafe` keyword.

> **NOTE** *Read the section "Platform Invoke" later in this chapter for information on how to invoke unmanaged methods with P/Invoke.*

With the `Calc` method in place, you can declare a managed method that supports the parameter and return type requirements such as the `Add` method defined here:

```
static int Add(int x, int y) => x + y;
```

and invoke the `Calc` method passing the address of the `Add` method with the `&` operator:

```
FunctionPointerSample.Calc(&Add);
```

Using Pointers to Optimize Performance

Until now, all the examples have been designed to demonstrate the various things that you can do with pointers. You have played around with memory in a way that is probably interesting only to people who like to know what's happening under the hood, but that doesn't really help you write better code. Now you're going to apply your understanding of pointers and see an example of how judicious use of pointers has a significant performance benefit.

Creating Stack-Based Arrays

This section explores one of the main areas in which pointers can be useful: creating high-performance, low-overhead arrays on the stack. As discussed in Chapter 2, "Core C#," C# includes rich support for handling arrays. Chapter 6 gives more details on arrays. Although C# makes it easy to use both one-dimensional and rectangular or jagged multidimensional arrays, it suffers from the disadvantage that these arrays are actually objects; they are instances of `System.Array`. This means that the arrays are stored on the heap, with all the overhead that this involves. There may be occasions when you need to create a short-lived, high-performance array and don't want the overhead of reference objects. You can do this by using pointers, although this is easy only for one-dimensional arrays.

To create a high-performance array, you need to use a keyword: `stackalloc`. The `stackalloc` command instructs the .NET runtime to allocate an amount of memory on the stack. When you call `stackalloc`, you need to supply it with two pieces of information:

➤   The type of data you want to store

➤   The number of these data items you need to store

For example, to allocate enough memory to store 10 `decimal` data items, you can write the following:

```
decimal* pDecimals = stackalloc decimal[10];
```

This command simply allocates the stack memory; it does not attempt to initialize the memory to any default value. This is fine for the purpose of this example because you are creating a high-performance array, and initializing values unnecessarily would hurt performance. Your program can initialize the memory if necessary.

Remember, different than the heap, the variables stored on the stack are released when the method completes. This is also true for allocating an array on the stack, so allocating memory with `stackalloc` you don't need to release the memory on your own.

Similarly, to store 20 `double` data items, you write this:

```
double* pDoubles = stackalloc double[20];
```

Although this line of code specifies the number of variables to store as a constant, this can equally be a quantity evaluated at runtime. Therefore, you can write the previous example like this:

```
int size;
size = 20; // or some other value calculated at runtime
double* pDoubles = stackalloc double[size];
```

You can see from these code snippets that the syntax of stackalloc is slightly unusual. It is followed immediately by the name of the data type you want to store (which must be a value type) and then by the number of items you need space for, in square brackets. The number of bytes allocated is this number multiplied by sizeof(data type). The use of square brackets in the preceding code sample suggests an array, which is not too surprising. If you have allocated space for 20 doubles, then what you have is an array of 20 doubles. The simplest type of array that you can have is a block of memory that stores one element after another (see Figure 13-6).

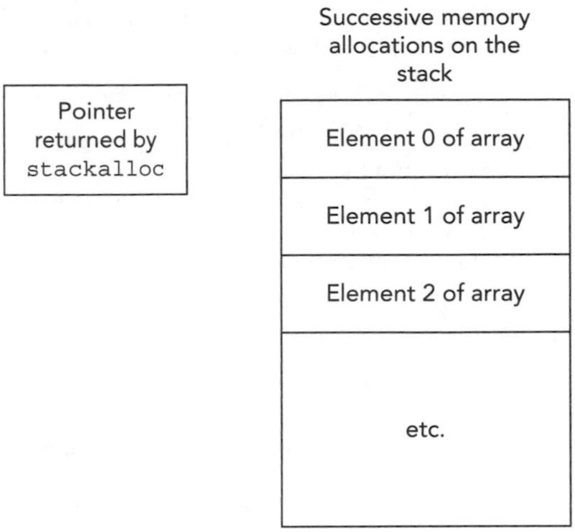

This diagram also shows the pointer returned by stackalloc, which is always a pointer to the allocated data type that points to the top of the newly allocated memory block. To use the memory block, you simply dereference the returned pointer. For example, to allocate space for 20 doubles and then set the first element (element 0 of the array) to the value 3.0, write this:

FIGURE 13-6

```
double* pDoubles = stackalloc double[20];
*pDoubles = 3.0;
```

To access the next element of the array, you use pointer arithmetic. As described earlier, if you add 1 to a pointer, its value will be increased by the size of whatever data type it points to. In this case, that's just enough to take you to the next free memory location in the block that you have allocated. Therefore, you can set the second element of the array (element number 1) to the value 8.4:

```
double* pDoubles = stackalloc double[20];
*pDoubles = 3.0;
*(pDoubles + 1) = 8.4;
```

By the same reasoning, you can access the element with index X of the array with the expression *(pDoubles+ X).

Effectively, you have a means by which you can access elements of your array, but for general-purpose use, this syntax is too complex. Fortunately, C# defines an alternative syntax using square brackets. C# gives a precise meaning to square brackets when they are applied to pointers; if the variable p is any pointer type and X is an integer, then the expression p[X] is always interpreted by the compiler as meaning *(p+X). This is true for all pointers, not only those initialized using stackalloc. With this shorthand notation, you now have a convenient syntax for accessing your array. In fact, it means that you have the same syntax for accessing one-dimensional, stack-based arrays as you do for accessing heap-based arrays that are represented by the System.Array class:

```
double* pDoubles = stackalloc double [20];
pDoubles[0] = 3.0; // pDoubles[0] is the same as *pDoubles
pDoubles[1] = 8.4; // pDoubles[1] is the same as *(pDoubles+1)
```

> **NOTE** *This idea of applying array syntax to pointers is not new. It has been a fundamental part of both the C and the C++ languages ever since those languages were invented. Indeed, C++ developers will recognize the stack-based arrays they can obtain using* stackalloc *as being essentially identical to classic stack-based C and C++ arrays. This syntax and the way it links pointers and arrays is one reason why the C language became popular in the 1970s and the main reason why the use of pointers became such a popular programming technique in C and C++.*

Although your high-performance array can be accessed in the same way as a normal C# array, a word of caution is in order. The following code in C# raises an exception:

```
double[] myDoubleArray = new double[20];
myDoubleArray[50] = 3.0;
```

The exception occurs because you are trying to access an array using an index that is out of bounds; the index is 50, whereas the maximum allowed value is 19. However, if you declare the equivalent array using stackalloc, there is no object wrapped around the array that can perform bounds checking. Hence, the following code does *not* raise an exception:

```
double* pDoubles = stackalloc double[20];
pDoubles[50] = 3.0;
```

In this code, you allocate enough memory to hold 20 doubles. Then you use the pDoubles variable to reference memory that is way outside the area of memory that you have allocated for the doubles. There is no knowing what data might be stored at that address. At best, you might have used some currently unused memory, but it is equally possible that you might have just overwritten some locations in the stack that were being used to store other variables or even the return address from the method currently being executed. Again, you see that the high performance to be gained from pointers comes at a cost; you need to be certain you know what you are doing, or you will get some very strange runtime bugs.

QuickArray Example

The discussion of pointers ends with a stackalloc example called QuickArray. In this example, the program simply asks users how many elements they want to be allocated for an array. The code then uses stackalloc to allocate an array of longs that size. The elements of this array are populated with the squares of the integers starting with 0, and the results are displayed on the console (code file QuickArray/Program.cs):

```
class Program
{
  unsafe public static void Main()
  {
    string? userInput;
    int size;
    do
    {
      Console.Write($"How big an array do you want? {Environment.NewLine}>");
      userInput = Console.ReadLine();
    } while (!int.TryParse(userInput, out size));

    long* pArray = stackalloc long[size];
    for (int i = 0; i < size; i++)
    {
      pArray[i] = i * i;
    }

    for (int i = 0; i < size; i++)
    {
      Console.WriteLine($"Element {i} = {*(pArray + i)}");
    }

    Console.ReadLine();
  }
}
```

Here is the output from the `QuickArray` example:

```
How big an array do you want?
> 15
Element 0 = 0
Element 1 = 1
Element 2 = 4
Element 3 = 9
Element 4 = 16
Element 5 = 25
Element 6 = 36
Element 7 = 49
Element 8 = 64
Element 9 = 81
Element 10 = 100
Element 11 = 121
Element 12 = 144
Element 13 = 169
Element 14 = 196
```

SPAN<T>

Chapter 3, "Classes, Records, Structs, and Tuples," includes creating reference types (classes) and value types (structs). Instances of classes are stored on the managed heap. The value of structs can be stored on the stack or, when boxing is used, on the managed heap. Now we have another kind: a type that can have its value only on the stack but never on the heap, which is sometimes called *ref-like types*. Boxing is not possible with these types. Such a type is declared with the `ref struct` keyword. Using `ref struct` gives some additional behaviors and restrictions. The restrictions are the following:

➤ They can't be added as array items.

➤ They can't be used as generic type arguments.

➤ They can't be boxed.

➤ They can't be static fields.

➤ They can only be instance fields of ref-like types.

`Span<T>` and `ReadOnlySpan<T>` are ref-like types covered in this section. These types are already covered in Chapter 6 with extension methods for arrays. Here, additional features are covered to reference data on the managed heap, the stack, and the native heap.

Spans Referencing the Managed Heap

A `Span` can reference memory on the managed heap, as you've seen in Chapter 6. In the following code snippet, an array is created, and with the extension method `AsSpan`, a new `Span` is created that references the memory of the array on the managed heap. After creating the `Span` referenced from the variable `span1`, a slice of the `Span` is created that is filled with the value `42`. Within comments in the following source code, you see the syntax using the `Slice` method of the `Span` type. The range operator is used to fulfill the same functionality. The next `Console.WriteLine` writes the values of the span `span1` to the console (code file `SpanSample/Program.cs`):

```
void SpanOnTheHeap()
{
  Console.WriteLine(nameof(SpanOnTheHeap));
  Span<int> span1 = (new int[] { 1, 5, 11, 71, 22, 19, 21, 33 }).AsSpan();
```

```
      // span1.Slice(start: 4, length: 3).Fill(42);
      span1[4..7].Fill(42);

      Console.WriteLine(string.Join(", ", span1.ToArray()));

      Console.WriteLine();
    }
```

When you run the application, you can see the output of span1 with the 42 filled within the slice of the span:

```
SpanOnTheHeap
1, 5, 11, 71, 42, 42, 42, 33
```

Spans Referencing the Stack

Span can be used to reference memory on the stack. Referencing a single variable on the stack is not as interesting as referencing a block of memory; that's why the following code snippet makes use of the stackalloc keyword. stackalloc returns a long*, which requires the method SpanOnTheStack to be declared unsafe. A constructor of the Span type allows passing a pointer with the additional parameter for the size. Next, the variable span1 is used with the indexer to fill every item (code file SpanSample/Program.cs):

```
unsafe void SpanOnTheStack()
{
  Console.WriteLine(nameof(SpanOnTheStack));

  long* lp = stackalloc long[20];
  Span<long> span1 = new(lp, 20);

  for (int i = 0; i < 20; i++)
  {
    span1[i] = i;
  }

  Console.WriteLine(string.Join(", ", span1.ToArray()));
  Console.WriteLine();
}
```

When you run the program, the following output shows the span with the initialized data on the stack:

```
SpanOnTheStack
0, 1, 2, 3, 4, 5, 6, 7, 8, 9, 10, 11, 12, 13, 14, 15, 16, 17, 18, 19
```

Spans Referencing the Native Heap

A great feature of spans is they can also reference memory on the native heap. Memory on the native heap usually is allocated from native APIs. In the following code snippet, the AllocHGlobal method of the Marshal class is used to allocate 100 bytes on the native heap. This class is defined in the System.Runtime.InteropServices namespace. The Marshal class returns a pointer with the IntPtr type. To directly access the int*, the ToPointer method of IntPtr is invoked. This is the pointer required by the constructor of the Span class. Writing int values to this memory, you need to pay attention how many bytes are needed. As an int contains 32 bits, the number of bytes is divided by 4 with a bit shift of two bits to get the number of int values that will fit in the memory. After this, the native memory is filled by invoking the Fill method of the Span. With a for loop, every item referenced from the Span is written to the console (code file SpanSample/Program.cs):

```
unsafe void SpanOnNativeMemory()
{
  Console.WriteLine(nameof(SpanOnNativeMemory));
  const int nbytes = 100;
```

```
    IntPtr p = Marshal.AllocHGlobal(nbytes);
    try
    {
      int* p2 = (int*)p.ToPointer();
      Span<int> span = new(p2, nbytes >> 2);
      span.Fill(42);

      int max = nbytes >> 2;
      for (int i = 0; i < max; i++)
      {
        Console.Write($"{span[i]} ");
      }
      Console.WriteLine();
    }
    finally
    {
      Marshal.FreeHGlobal(p);
    }
    Console.WriteLine();
}
```

When you run the application, the values stored in the native heap are written to the console:

```
SpanOnNativeMemory
42 42 42 42 42 42 42 42 42 42 42 42 42 42 42 42 42 42 42 42 42 42 42 42
```

> **NOTE** *For using* Span *to access native memory and the stack, unsafe code was needed because of the memory allocation and creation of the* Span *by passing a pointer. After the initialization, unsafe code is no longer required using the* Span. *Allocating native memory (as done with the* AllocHGlobal *method of the* Marshal *class), it's important to release this memory with* FreeHGlobal.

Span Extension Methods

For the Span type, extension methods are defined to make it easier to work with this type. The following code snippet demonstrates the use of the Overlaps, the Reverse, and the IndexOf methods. With the Overlaps method, it is checked if the span that is used to invoke this extension method overlaps the span passed with the argument. The Reverse method reverses the content of the span. The IndexOf method returns the index of the span passed with the argument (code file SpanSample/Program.cs):

```
void SpanExtensions()
{
  Console.WriteLine(nameof(SpanExtensions));
  Span<int> span1 = (new int[] { 1, 5, 11, 71, 22, 19, 21, 33 }).AsSpan();
  Span<int> span2 = span1[3..7];

  bool overlaps = span1.Overlaps(span2);
  Console.WriteLine($"span1 overlaps span2: {overlaps}");
  span1.Reverse();
  Console.WriteLine($"span1 reversed: {string.Join(", ", span1.ToArray())}");
  Console.WriteLine($"span2 (a slice) after reversing span1: " +
    $"{string.Join(", ", span2.ToArray())}");
  int index = span1.IndexOf(span2);
```

```
    Console.WriteLine($"index of span2 in span1: {index}");
    Console.WriteLine();
}
```

Running the program produces this output:

```
SpanExtensions
span1 overlaps span2: True
span1 reversed: 33, 21, 19, 22, 71, 11, 5, 1
span2 (a slice) after reversing span1: 22, 71, 11, 5
index of span2 in span1: 3
```

Other extension methods defined for the `Span` type are `StartsWith` to check if a span starts with the sequence of another span, `SequenceEqual` to compare the sequence of two spans, `SequenceCompareTo` for ordering of sequences, and `LastIndexOf` for returning the first matching index starting from the end of the span.

PLATFORM INVOKE

Not all the features of Windows or Linux API calls are available from .NET. This is true not only for old Windows API calls but also for very new features. Maybe you've written some DLLs that export unmanaged methods and you would like to use them from C# as well.

To reuse a native library, you can use platform invoke (P/Invoke). With P/Invoke, the CLR loads the library that includes the function that should be called and marshals the parameters.

To use the unmanaged function, first you must determine the name of the function and the parameters as they are exported. In the example, you use the `CreateHardLink` Windows API function to create a hard link to an existing file and the Linux `link` API function to do the same. With these API calls, you can have several filenames that reference the same file as long as the filenames are on the same hard disk. This API call is not available from .NET, so you must use platform invoke.

For Windows APIs, `https://pinvoke.net` has great information on mapping Windows APIs to .NET. This site lists many Windows APIs and how they can be represented with .NET. With Linux, the APIs are described with the manual pages accessible with the `man` command. `man link` shows the documentation on the link command, and `man 2 link` opens section 2 of the documentation to display the system calls. When you use this information from the manual pages, it's not too hard to map the APIs to .NET types.

> **NOTE** *To use Windows APIs from .NET, Microsoft has started the win32metadata project (`https://github.com/microsoft/win32metadata`) that's in its early stages at the time of this writing. This project makes use of the C# source generators to automatically generate `DllImport` declarations, and you just need to write the API method you want to invoke in a text file. For using these definitions, you just need to add a text file named `NativeMethods.txt` to the project, add the APIs you want to invoke (for example, `CreateHardLink`), add the NuGet package `Microsoft.Windows.CsWin32`, and import the namespace `Microsoft.Windows.Sdk`.*
>
> *You can read more about source generators in Chapter 12, "Reflection, Metadata, and Source Generators."*

Calling Native Windows APIs

To call a native function, you have to define a C# external method with the same number of arguments, and the argument types that are defined with the unmanaged method must have mapped types with managed code.

The Windows API call `CreateHardLink` has this definition in C++:

```
BOOL CreateHardLink(
   LPCTSTR lpFileName,
   LPCTSTR lpExistingFileName,
   LPSECURITY_ATTRIBUTES lpSecurityAttributes);
```

This definition must be mapped to .NET data types. The return type is a `BOOL` with unmanaged code; this simply maps to the `bool` data type. `LPCTSTR` defines a `long` pointer to a `const` string. The Windows API uses the Hungarian naming convention for the data type. `LP` is a `long` pointer, `C` is a `const`, and `STR` is a null-terminated string. The `T` marks the type as a generic type, and the type is resolved to either `LPCSTR` (an ANSI string) or `LPWSTR` (a wide Unicode string), depending on the compiler's settings to 32 or 64 bit. C strings map to the .NET type `String`. `LPSECURITY_ATTRIBUTES` is a long pointer to a struct of type `SECURITY_ATTRIBUTES`. You can create a .NET representation of `SECURITY_ATTRIBUTES` with a struct:

```
struct SECURITY_ATTRIBUTES
{
  uint nLength;
  unsafe void *lpSecurityDescriptor;
  bool bInheritHandle;
}
```

However, because passing NULL to this argument is allowed, mapping this type to the native int type `nint` is okay.

The C# declaration of the `CreateHardLink` method must be marked with the `extern` modifier because there's no implementation of this method within the C# code. The native implementation is in the DLL `kernel32.dll`, which is referenced with the attribute `[DllImport]`. The return type of the .NET declaration `CreateHardLink` is of type `bool`, and the native method `CreateHardLink` returns a `BOOL`, so some additional clarification is useful. Because there are different Boolean data types with C++ (for example, the native `bool` and the Windows-defined `BOOL`, which have different values), the attribute `[MarshalAs]` specifies to what native type the .NET type `bool` should map (code file `PInvokeSampleLib/Windows/WindowsNativeMethods.cs`):

```
[DllImport("kernel32.dll", SetLastError = true,
   EntryPoint = "CreateHardLinkW", CharSet = CharSet.Unicode)]
[return: MarshalAs(UnmanagedType.Bool)]
private static extern bool CreateHardLink(
   [In, MarshalAs(UnmanagedType.LPWStr)] string newFileName,
   [In, MarshalAs(UnmanagedType.LPWStr)] string existingFileName,
   nint securityAttributes);
```

The following table describes the settings that you can specify with the attribute `[DllImport]`. The `DllImportAttribute` class is defined in the `System.Runtime.InteropServices` namespace.

DLLIMPORT PROPERTY OR FIELD	DESCRIPTION
EntryPoint	You can give the C# declaration of the function a different name than the one it has with the unmanaged library. The name of the method in the unmanaged library is defined in the field `EntryPoint`.
CallingConvention	Depending on the compiler or compiler settings that were used to compile the unmanaged function, you can use different calling conventions. The calling convention defines how the parameters are handled and where to put them on the stack. You can define the calling convention by setting an enum value. The Windows API usually uses the `StdCall` calling convention on the Windows operating system, and it uses the `Cdecl` calling convention on Windows CE. Setting the value to `CallingConvention.Winapi` works for the Windows API.

DLLIMPORT PROPERTY OR FIELD	DESCRIPTION
CharSet	String parameters can be either ANSI or Unicode. With the CharSet setting, you can define how strings are managed. Possible values that are defined with the CharSet enumeration are Ansi, Unicode, and Auto. CharSet.Auto uses Unicode on the Windows NT platform, and ANSI on Microsoft's older operating systems.
SetLastError	If the unmanaged function sets an error by using the Windows API SetLastError, you can set the SetLastError field to true. This way, you can read the error number afterward by using Marshal.GetLastWin32Error. With .NET 6, new APIs are planned. The method GetLastWin32Error can be used with Windows and with Linux, although because of this naming, you probably wouldn't expect this API to be available on Linux. Because of the platform-independence of .NET, new API names are planned.

To use the Windows API CreateHardLink, the external method declaration with the DllImport attribute is declared with the private access modifier in the class WindowsNativeMethods. A method with the same name (CreateHardLink) but a different implementation is declared in the same class by using an internal access modifier. This method can be used within the library where the class is declared. The .NET implementation invokes the native method, checks for the error code that's retrieved with Marshal.GetLastWin32Error, and throws an exception in case of an error. To create an error message from this number, the Win32Exception class from the namespace System.ComponentModel is used. This class accepts an error number with the constructor and returns a localized error message. In case of an error, an exception of type IOException is thrown, which has an inner exception of type Win32Exception. The class WindowsNativeMethods has the attribute SupportedOSPlatform applied to give information to the programmer using this class that it's only available on the Windows platform (code file PInvokeSampleLib/Windows/WindowsNativeMethods.cs):

```
using System;
using System.IO;
using System.Runtime.InteropServices;
using System.Runtime.Versioning;

namespace PInvokeSample
{
  [SupportedOSPlatform("Windows")]
  internal static class WindowsNativeMethods
  {
    [DllImport("kernel32.dll", SetLastError = true,
      EntryPoint = "CreateHardLinkW", CharSet = CharSet.Unicode)]
    [return: MarshalAs(UnmanagedType.Bool)]
    private static extern bool CreateHardLink(
      [In, MarshalAs(UnmanagedType.LPWStr)] string newFileName,
      [In, MarshalAs(UnmanagedType.LPWStr)] string existingFileName,
      nint securityAttributes);

    internal static void CreateHardLink(string oldFileName,
                                        string newFileName)
    {
      if (!CreateHardLink(newFileName, oldFileName, IntPtr.Zero))
```

```
      {
        int errorCode = Marshal.GetLastWin32Error();
        throw new IOException($"CreateHardLink error: {errorCode}", errorCode);
      }
    }
  }
}
```

Calling Native Linux APIs

To invoke the link method running on the Linux operating system, the method `CreateHardLink` with the same signature and return type is defined. The Linux version of this method is defined in the class `LinuxNativeMethods`. The `CreateHardLink` method is implemented to invoke the `Link` method. The `Link` method is declared with the `extern` modifier and has the `DllImport` attribute applied. The native method is implemented in the shared library `libc`; the name of this shared library is passed to the `DllImport` constructor. In case of an error, the link method doesn't return the value 0. In this case, the `Marshal.GetLastWin32Error` method returns the error code. The possible error codes are defined with the enum `LinkErrors`, and error messages are defined in a dictionary (code file `PInvokeSampleLib/Linux/LinuxNativeMethods.cs`):

```csharp
using System.Collections.Generic;
using System.IO;
using System.Runtime.InteropServices;
using System.Runtime.Versioning;
using static PInvokeSample.LinuxNativeMethods.LinkErrors;

namespace PInvokeSample
{
  [SupportedOSPlatform("Linux")]
  internal static class LinuxNativeMethods
  {
    internal enum LinkErrors
    {
      EPERM = 1,
      ENOENT = 2,
      EIO = 5,
      EACCES = 13,
      EEXIST = 17,
      EXDEV = 18,
      ENOSPC = 28,
      EROFS = 30,
      EMLINK = 31
    }

    private static Dictionary<LinkErrors, string> _errorMessages = new()
    {
      { EPERM, "On GNU/Linux and GNU/Hurd systems and some others, you cannot " +
        "make links to directories.Many systems allow only privileged users to
do so." },
      { ENOENT, "The file named by oldname doesn't exist. You can't make a link " +
        "to a file that doesn't exist." },
      { EIO, "A hardware error occurred while trying to read or write to the " +
        "filesystem." },
      //...
    };
```

```
[DllImport("libc",
  EntryPoint = "Link",
  CallingConvention = CallingConvention.Cdecl,
  SetLastError = true)]
private static extern int Link(string oldpath, string newpath);

internal static void CreateHardLink(string oldFileName, string newFileName)
{
  int result = link(newFileName, oldFileName);
  if (result != 0)
    {
      int errorCode = Marshal.GetLastWin32Error();
      if (!_errorMessages.TryGetValue((LinkErrors)errorCode,
        out string? errorText))
      {
        errorText = "No error message defined";
      }
      throw new IOException(errorText, errorCode);
    }
}
```

The only `public` class offered by the `PInvokeSampleLib` library is `FileUtility`. Here, the implementation of the `CreateHardLink` method checks what operating system the application is running on with the help of the `OperatingSystem` class. Depending on the result, the parameters `oldFileName` and `newFileName` are forwarded to the corresponding method. Compared to the native method, the filename parameters are reversed. This is similar to other .NET classes such as `File.Copy` and also similar to the Linux `link` API (code file `PInvokeSampleLib/FileUtility.cs`):

```
public static class FileUtility
{
  public static void CreateHardLink(string oldFileName,
                                    string newFileName)
  {
    if (OperatingSystem.IsWindows())
    {
      WindowsNativeMethods.CreateHardLink(oldFileName, newFileName);
    }
    else if (OperatingSystem.IsLinux())
    {
      LinuxNativeMethods.CreateHardLink(oldFileName, newFileName);
    }
    else
    {
      throw new PlatformNotSupportedException();
    }
  }
}
```

Using the Library for Calling Native APIs

You can now use this class to easily create hard links. If the file passed with the first argument of the program does not exist, you get an exception with the message `The system cannot find the file specified`. If the file exists, you get a new filename that references the original file. You can easily verify this by changing text in one file; it shows up in the other file as well (code file `PInvokeSample/Program.cs`):

```
if (args.Length != 2)
{
  Console.WriteLine("usage: PInvokeSample existingfilename newfilename");
  return;
}
try
{
  FileUtility.CreateHardLink(args[0], args[1]);
}
catch (IOException ex)
{
  Console.WriteLine(ex.Message);
}
```

To run the application in a Linux environment, you can use the Windows Subsystem for Linux and run the application using the Windows terminal. With the Linux version of the application, if you specify a source file that does not exist, the following error message is shown:

```
The file named by oldname doesn't exist. You can't make a link to a file
that doesn't exist.
```

SUMMARY

Remember that to become a truly proficient C# programmer, you must have a solid understanding of how memory allocation and garbage collection work. This chapter described how the CLR manages and allocates memory on the heap and the stack. It also illustrated how to write classes that free unmanaged resources correctly and how to use pointers in C#. These are both advanced topics that are poorly understood and often implemented incorrectly by novice programmers. At a minimum, this chapter should have helped you understand how to release resources using the `IDisposable` interface and the `using` declaration.

You've also seen how to write code to invoke native methods of the Windows and Linux platforms. Many .NET APIs are built with native APIs behind, and you don't need to write your own `extern` declared methods. However, there are still many functions not covered from .NET, and you can use this technique to invoke these. You probably have some other C++ libraries that would be too hard to port to .NET, but now you can simply invoke these methods.

The first part of the book concludes with this chapter. The next chapter starts to dive into creating libraries and NuGet packages.

PART II
Libraries

14

Libraries, Assemblies, Packages, and NuGet

WHAT'S IN THIS CHAPTER?

➤ Differences between libraries, assemblies, packages

➤ Creating libraries

➤ Using .NET Standard

➤ Creating NuGet packages

➤ Supporting multiple platforms with NuGet packages

➤ Initializing libraries

CODE DOWNLOADS FOR THIS CHAPTER

The source code for this chapter is available on the book page at www.wiley.com. Click the Downloads link. The code can also be found at https://github.com/ProfessionalCSharp/ProfessionalCSharp2021 in the directory 2_Libs/Libraries.

The code for this chapter is divided into the following major examples:

➤ UsingLibs

➤ CreateNuGet

All the projects have nullable reference types enabled.

THE HELL OF LIBRARIES

Libraries make it possible for you to reuse code in multiple applications. With Windows, libraries have a long history, and architecture guidelines have taken different directions with newer technologies. Before .NET, dynamic link libraries (DLLs) could be shared between different applications. These DLLs have been installed in a shared directory. It wasn't possible to have multiple versions of these libraries on the same system, but they should have been upward compatible. Of course, this wasn't always the case. In addition, there were problems with application installations that did not pay attention to the guidelines and replaced a shared library with an older one. This was known as *DLL hell*.

.NET tried to solve this with *assemblies*. Assemblies are libraries that could be shared. In addition to normal DLLs, assemblies contain extensible metadata with information about the library and a version number, and it's possible to install multiple versions side by side in the *global assembly cache*. Microsoft tried to fix versioning issues, but this added another layer of complexity.

Let's assume you're using libraries A and B from your application X (see Figure 14-1). Application X references version 1.1 from library A and version 1.0 from library B. The issue is that library B references library A as well, but it references a different version—version 1.0. One process can have only one version of a library loaded. What version of the library A is loaded into the process? In this case, library B is used before library A, so version 1.0 wins. This is a big issue as soon as application X needs to use library A itself.

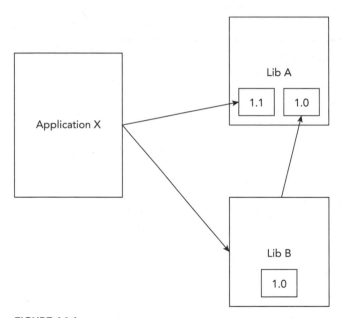

FIGURE 14-1

To avoid this issue, you could configure assembly redirects. You can define an assembly redirect for application X to load version 1.1 from library A. Library B then needs to use version 1.1 from library A as well. As long as library A is upward-compatible, this shouldn't be an issue.

Of course, compatibility doesn't always exist, and issues can be more complex. Publishers of components can create a publisher policy to define redirects with a policy that is delivered with the library itself. This redirect can be overridden by the application. There's a lot of complexity with this, which resulted in *assembly hell*.

> **NOTE** *With the new .NET, there's no global sharing of assemblies as it was with the .NET Framework. The Global Assembly Cache (GAC) is no longer used.*

NuGet packages add another abstraction layer to libraries. A NuGet package can contain multiple versions of one or more assemblies, along with other stuff, such as automatic configuration of assembly redirects.

Instead of waiting for new .NET Framework releases, you could add functionality via NuGet packages, which allowed for faster updates of the packages. NuGet packages are a great delivery vehicle. Some libraries, such as Entity Framework, switched to NuGet to allow for faster updates than the .NET Framework offered.

However, there are some issues with NuGet. Sometimes, a failure occurs when you add NuGet packages to projects. NuGet packages might not be compatible with the project. When adding packages is successful, sometimes the package makes some incorrect configuration with the project—for example, wrong binding redirects. This results in the feeling of NuGet package hell. The problems from DLLs moved to different abstraction layers and are indeed different. With newer NuGet versions and advancements in NuGet, Microsoft has tried to solve the issues with NuGet—and succeeded in many aspects.

Directions in the architecture of .NET Core also changed. With .NET Core, packages have been made more granular. For example, with the .NET Framework, the `Console` class is inside the `mscorlib` assembly, which is an assembly needed by every .NET Framework application. Of course, not every .NET application needs the `Console` class. With .NET Core, a separate package `System.Console` exists that contains the `Console` class and a few related classes. The goal was to make it easier to update and select what packages are really needed. With some beta versions of .NET Core 1.0, the project files contained a large list of packages, which didn't make development easier. Just before the release of .NET Core 1.0, Microsoft introduced meta-packages (or reference-packages). A meta-package doesn't include code; it includes a list of other packages. A target framework moniker such as net5.0 defines a list of packages and APIs that are readily available for the application without the need to add NuGet packages.

This chapter goes into the detail of assemblies and NuGet packages, explains how to share code using .NET Standard libraries, and also explains differences with Windows Runtime components.

ASSEMBLIES

An assembly is a library or executable that includes additional metadata. Using the new .NET, the application containing the `Main` method is created as a library with the file extension `.dll`. This DLL needs a hosting process to load this library, which you accomplish by using `dotnet run`, or just `dotnet` from a production environment. When you create stand-alone applications with .NET, different executables are created for every platform to load the library.

Let's take a look at a simple "Hello, World!" console application created in the directory `ConsoleApp`, using this command:

```
> dotnet new console -o ConsoleApp
```

After building the application, the DLL can be found in the `bin/debug/net5.0` directory. The `net5.0` directory depends on the target framework listed in the `csproj` project file.

> **NOTE** *You usually start the application using the dotnet bootstrapper (`dotnet ConsoleApp.dll`). On a Windows system, you'll also find the file `ConsoleApp.exe`. This is a Windows-specific file that can be used to start the application as well. It's just a bootstrapper to load the binary. On a Linux system, you'll find a similar bootstrapper that's Linux specific without the exe file extension.*

To read assemblies, you can install the .NET tool IL Disassembler (ildasm) using this:

```
> dotnet tool install dotnet-ildasm -g
```

After installing this tool, it can show metadata and IL code of assemblies. For easier reading of the result, the output is written to a text file with the -o option.

```
> dotnet ildasm ConsoleApp.dll -o output.txt
```

In the output, you'll find the section `.assembly "ConsoleApp"` that shows attribute values for the attributes `AssemblyCompany`, `AssemblyConfiguration`, `AssemblyFileVersion`, `AssemblyInformationalVersion`, `AssemblyProduct`, and `AssemblyTitle`.

> **NOTE** *In case you also have the .NET Framework SDK installed, you can find an older version of the ildasm tool with a graphical output. You can still use the old version of this tool with newer .NET libraries because the metadata information is still the same between .NET Framework and .NET libraries.*

You can configure assembly metadata that describes the application by using Visual Studio with Project Properties in the Package entry or by directly editing the project file (code file `ConsoleApp/ConsoleApp.csproj`):

```xml
<Project Sdk="Microsoft.NET.Sdk">

  <PropertyGroup>
    <OutputType>Exe</OutputType>
    <TargetFramework>net5.0</TargetFramework>
    <Nullable>enable</Nullable>
    <Version>5.0</Version>
    <AssemblyVersion>5.0</AssemblyVersion>
    <FileVersion>5.0</FileVersion>

    <Authors>Christian Nagel</Authors>
    <Company>CN innovation</Company>
    <Product>Sample App</Product>
    <Description>Sample App for Professional C#</Description>
    <Copyright>Copyright (c) CN innovation</Copyright>
    <PackageProjectUrl>
      https://github.com/ProfessionalCSharp
    </PackageProjectUrl>
    <RepositoryUrl>
      https://github.com/ProfessionalCSharp/ProfessionalCSharp2021
    </RepositoryUrl>
    <RepositoryType>git</RepositoryType>
    <PackageTags>Wrox Press, Sample, Libraries</PackageTags>

  </PropertyGroup>

</Project>
```

CREATING AND USING LIBRARIES

To use the same code with multiple projects, you create libraries. Using the .NET CLI, you can create generic class libraries, class libraries for WPF, Windows Forms, and Razor. Razor class libraries are covered in Chapter 26, "Razor Pages and MVC." When you create a class library with `dotnet new classlib`, by default, a library is created for .NET 5 and later versions, but you can also choose to select a different target framework. To make the correct choice, you have to ask, "With which application type and version of the framework should the library be shared?" There's another question you should ask: "Which APIs do I want to use in the library?" To answer both questions, it helps to understand parts of the history of .NET.

If you created a .NET Framework class library, this library could be used only with .NET Framework applications. When Silverlight (.NET applications running in a browser with the help of an add-in) came along, it was interesting to share code between Silverlight and WPF applications. Silverlight (code-named WPF-E, WPF Everywhere) offered limited functionality compared to the full .NET Framework. Microsoft defined the *Portable Class Library* to share code with these technologies. Later, Xamarin allowed creating mobile applications for Android and iOS and used this library type as well. Depending on the platform and version selection, different APIs are available. The more platforms and the older the version chosen, the fewer APIs are available. As more and more platforms have been added, this increased the complexity of the definitions and also increased complexity on using portable libraries from portable libraries.

.NET Standard provides a replacement for portable libraries. Instead of APIs defined in a matrix, .NET Standard has a simpler definition of the APIs available. With every version of the .NET Standard, additional APIs are added. APIs are never removed from the .NET Standard.

Starting with .NET 5.0, the .NET Standard is not further developed. From now on, you can create .NET 5.0 libraries, which can be used from .NET 5 upward. So, a .NET 6 and .NET 7 application can use the .NET 5 library. In case you create only new applications, you can skip the next section on .NET Standard. However, you probably still have to support or extend .NET Framework, UWP, Xamarin, and other application types probably for many years to come, in which case the .NET Standard is still relevant and important.

.NET Standard

The .NET Standard makes a linear definition of APIs available, which is different than the matrix definition with APIs that was available for portable libraries. Every version of the .NET Standard adds APIs, and APIs are never removed.

The higher the version of the .NET Standard, the more APIs you can use. However, the .NET Standard doesn't implement the APIs; it just defines the APIs that need to be implemented by a .NET platform. This can be compared to interfaces and concrete classes. An interface just defines a contract for members that need to be implemented by a class. Similarly, the .NET Standard specifies what APIs need to be available, and a .NET platform—supporting a specific version of the standard—needs to implement these APIs.

You can find which APIs are available for each standard version, as well as the differences between the standards, at `https://github.com/dotnet/standard/tree/master/docs/versions`.

Every version of the .NET Standard adds APIs to the standard:

➤ .NET Standard 1.1 added 2,414 APIs to .NET Standard 1.0.

➤ Version 1.2 added just 46 APIs.

➤ Version 1.3 added 3,314 APIs.

➤ Version 1.4 added only 18 Cryptography APIs.

➤ Version 1.5 mainly enhanced reflection support and added 242 APIs.

➤ Version 1.6 added more Cryptography APIs and enhanced regular expressions, with a total of 146 additional APIs.

➤ Version 2.0 added 19,507 APIs.

➤ Version 2.1 added enhancements requiring to update the runtime—for example, with support for default interface methods.

With .NET Standard 2.0, Microsoft made a big investment to make it easier to move legacy applications to .NET Core: 19,507 APIs have been added. Many of these APIs were not new. Some were already implemented with .NET Framework 4.6.1. For example, old APIs like `DataSet`, `DataTable`, and others have been available with the .NET Standard since version 2.0. This was a move to make it easier to bring legacy applications to the new .NET. A huge investment was needed for .NET Core, because .NET Core 2.0 implements the .NET Standard 2.0.

What APIs are not in the standard? Platform-specific APIs are not part of .NET Standard. For example, Windows Presentation Foundation (WPF) and Windows Forms define Windows-specific APIs that will not make it into the standard. You can, however, create WPF and Windows Forms applications and use .NET Standard libraries from there. You cannot create .NET Standard libraries that contain WPF or Windows Forms controls.

Let's discuss the platform support of .NET Standard. The Microsoft documentation at `https://docs.microsoft.com/en-us/dotnet/standard/net-standard` lists the details on what .NET Standard version supports which platform version. If you need to support .NET Framework 4.7.2 or up (including a check for the footnote on issues with .NET Framework 4.6.1), you can use .NET Standard 2.0 but not 2.1. With .NET Framework 4.6, you're restricted to .NET Standard 1.3. Using Windows 10 starting with version 10.0.16299, you can use .NET Standard 2.0. With the Mono platform, version 6.4 supports .NET Standard 2.1. .NET Standard 2.1 is also supported from .NET Core 3.0 and up.

> **NOTE** *To support the most platforms possible, you need to select a lower .NET Standard version. To have more APIs available, select a higher .NET Standard version.*

Creating a .NET Library

To create a .NET library, you can use the .NET Core CLI tools with the following command:

```
> dotnet new classlib -o SampleLib
```

By default, if you have .NET 5 installed, it creates a .NET 5 library. You can supply the option `--framework` and add `netstandard2.1` or `netstandard2.0` to create a .NET Standard library with the specific version. You can change the version number later on in the project file.

The project file created includes the `TargetFramework` element and specifies `net5.0`. To support nullable reference types, include the `Nullable` configuration (code file `UsingLibs/SampleLib/SampleLib.csproj`):

```
<Project Sdk="Microsoft.NET.Sdk">
  <PropertyGroup>
    <TargetFramework>net5.0</TargetFramework>
    <Nullable>enable</Nullable>
  </PropertyGroup>
</Project>
```

You can change the version of the target framework of the library by changing the value of the `TargetFramework` element. Later in this chapter, this configuration is enhanced to support multiple frameworks with one library.

Solution Files

When you work with multiple projects (for example, a console application and a library), it's helpful to work with solution files. With the newer versions of the .NET Core CLI tools, you can use solutions from the command line and from Visual Studio. For example,

```
> dotnet new sln
```

creates a solution file in the current directory. The solution is named after the directory name, but you can pass the option `--name` to specify a different name.

Using the `dotnet sln add` command, you can add existing projects to the solution file:

```
> dotnet sln add SampleLib/SampleLib.csproj
```

The project files are added to the solution file as shown in the following snippet (solution file `UsingLibs\UsingLibs.sln`):

```
Microsoft Visual Studio Solution File, Format Version 12.00
# Visual Studio 15
VisualStudioVersion = 15.0.26124.0
MinimumVisualStudioVersion = 15.0.26124.0
Project("{FAE04EC0-301F-11D3-BF4B-00C04F79EFBC}") = "SampleLib",
  "SampleLib\SampleLib.csproj", "{665E314C-584E-4B43-A14D-7C34BC4D75CD}"
EndProject
Project("{FAE04EC0-301F-11D3-BF4B-00C04F79EFBC}") = "ConsoleApp",
  "ConsoleApp\ConsoleApp.csproj", "{6709A473-93B4-4568-90F3-3A5F1D125D45}"
EndProject
Global
# ...
```

When you're using Visual Studio, you can select the solution in the Solution Explorer to add new projects. From the context menu, select Add and then select Existing Project to add existing projects.

Referencing Projects

You can reference a library by using the `dotnet add reference` command. The current directory just needs to be positioned in the directory of the project where the library should be added:

```
> dotnet add reference ..\SampleLib\SampleLib.csproj
```

The reference is added using a `ProjectReference` element in the `csproj` file (project file `UsingLibs/ConsoleApp/ConsoleApp.csproj`):

```
<Project Sdk="Microsoft.NET.Sdk">

  <ItemGroup>
    <ProjectReference Include="..\SampleLib\SampleLib.csproj" />
  </ItemGroup>

  <PropertyGroup>
    <OutputType>Exe</OutputType>
    <TargetFramework>5.0</TargetFramework>
    <Nullable>enable</Nullable>
  </PropertyGroup>

</Project>
```

Using the Solution Explorer in Visual Studio, you can add projects to other projects by selecting the Dependencies node and then selecting the Add Project Reference command from the Project menu.

Referencing NuGet Packages

If the library is already packaged within a NuGet package, the NuGet package can be directly referenced with the command `dotnet add package`:

```
> dotnet add package Microsoft.EntityFrameworkCore
```

Instead of adding a `ProjectReference` as before, this adds a `PackageReference`:

```xml
<Project Sdk="Microsoft.NET.Sdk">
  <ItemGroup>
    <ProjectReference Include="..\SampleLib\SampleLib.csproj" />
  </ItemGroup>
  <ItemGroup>
    <PackageReference Include="Microsoft.EntityFrameworkCore" Version="5.0.4" />
  </ItemGroup>
  <PropertyGroup>
    <OutputType>Exe</OutputType>
    <TargetFramework>net5.0</TargetFramework>
  </PropertyGroup>

</Project>
```

To request a specific version of the package, you can specify the `--version` option with the .NET CLI command. With Visual Studio, you can use the NuGet Package Manager (see Figure 14-2) to find packages and select a specific version of the package. With this tool, you also can get details on the package with links to the project and licensing information.

> **NOTE** *Not all the packages you find on* www.nuget.org *are useful with your application. You should check licensing information to make sure the license fits with your project needs. Also, you should check the package author. If it's an open source package, how active is the community behind it?*

NuGet Sources

Where are the packages coming from? www.nuget.org is a public server where Microsoft and third parties upload .NET packages. After the packages have been downloaded from the NuGet server for the first time, the packages are stored in the user profile. Thus, it becomes a lot faster to create another project with the same packages.

On Windows, the directory for the packages in the user profile is `%userprofile%\.nuget\packages`. Other temporary directories are used as well. To get all the information about these directories, it's best to install the NuGet command-line utility, which you can download from `https://dist.nuget.org/`.

To see the folders for the global packages, the HTTP cache, and the temp packages, you can use `nuget locals`:

```
> nuget locals all -list
```

In some companies, it's permissible to use only packages that have been approved and are stored in a local NuGet server. The default configuration for the NuGet server is in the file `NuGet.Config` in the directory `%appdata%/nuget`.

A default configuration looks similar to the following `NuGet.Config` file. Packages are loaded from `https://api.nuget.org`.

52555

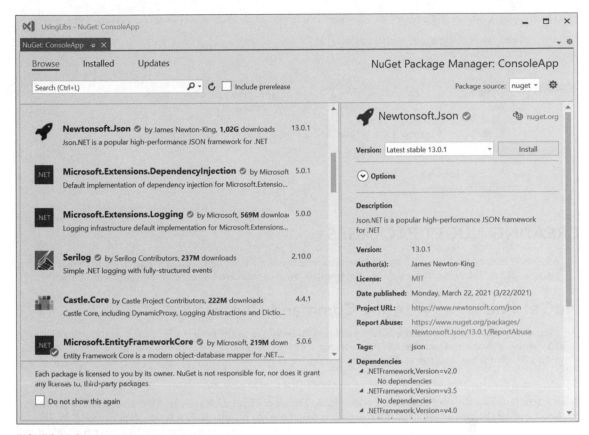

FIGURE 14-2

```xml
<?xml version="1.0" encoding="utf-8"?>
<configuration>
  <packageSources>
    <add key="nuget.org" value="https://api.nuget.org/v3/index.json"
        protocolVersion="3" />
  </packageSources>
</configuration>
```

You can change the defaults by adding and removing package sources. Instead of changing the defaults, you can create a NuGet configuration file for the project:

```
> dotnet new nugetconfig
```

Microsoft doesn't store packages from the daily build on the main NuGet server. To use daily builds of .NET Core NuGet packages, you need to configure other NuGet servers. For example, to use .NET 6 daily feeds, you can add the .NET 6 feed. The following commands also add a feed to a local directory:

```
> dotnet nuget add source -n dotnet6
  https://dnceng.pkgs.visualstudio.com/public/_packaging/dotnet6/nuget/v3/index.json
> dotnet nuget add source -n local c:\mypackages
```

The following NuGet file adds a local directory in addition to the public NuGet server and the .NET 6 feed:

```xml
<?xml version="1.0" encoding="utf-8"?>
<configuration>
  <packageSources>
    <clear />
    <add key="nuget" value="https://api.nuget.org/v3/index.json" />
    <add key="local packages" value="C:\mypackages" />
    <add key="dotnet6" value=
      "https://dnceng.pkgs.visualstudio.com/public/_packaging/dotnet6/nuget/v3/
    index.json"
    />
  </packageSources>
</configuration>
```

CREATING NUGET PACKAGES

After you created a library and an application where this library is referenced, it's time to create NuGet packages on your own. NuGet packages can be created easily by using the .NET Core CLI tools and Visual Studio.

NuGet Packages with the Command Line

Metadata information about the NuGet package can be added to the project file `csproj` as shown earlier in the "Assemblies" section. To create a NuGet package from the command line, you can use the `dotnet pack` command (started from the project directory):

```
> dotnet pack --configuration Release
```

Remember to set the configuration. By default, the Debug configuration is built. After a successful packaging, you can find the NuGet package in the directory `bin/Release` or related directories, depending on the selected configuration with the file extension `.nupkg`. A `.nupkg` file is a zip file that contains the binary with additional metadata. You can rename this file to a zip file to see its contents.

The package file includes the version number. The version number is taken from the `Version` value in the project file.

You can copy the generated NuGet package to a folder on your system or to a network share to make it available to your team. This command copies the package to a subfolder with the name of the package:

```
> nuget add bin\Release\SampleLib.5.0.1.nupkg -s c:\MyPackages
```

To use the folder `c:\MyPackages`, the `NuGet.config` file can be changed to include this package source as shown in the section "NuGet Sources." You also can reference the folder directly by using the `dotnet add package` command:

```
> dotnet add package SampleLib --source c:/MyPackages
```

By default, the latest released version of the package is referenced from the project where you add the package. With the option `--version`, you can specify the exact version to add.

To create prerelease packages, you just need to add a postfix to the version number—for example, `5.0.1-alpha`, `5.0.1-alpha.2`, `5.0.1-beta.1`, `5.0.1-beta.2`, `5.0.1-preview3`, `5.0.1-rc1`. Reverse alphabetical order is used to identify the newest version of the prerelease packages, so `beta` is newer than `alpha`, and `rc` is newer than `preview`. The same version number without a postfix is considered a release and thus a newer version. To add a prerelease package version to a project, you need to add the `--prerelease` option with `dotnet add package`.

Supporting Multiple Platforms

.NET 5 includes a lot more packages and APIs compared to what's available with .NET Standard 2.0. In case you want to offer new features for .NET 5+ clients but still want to support clients with .NET Standard 2.0 support, you can create a NuGet package containing multiple binaries with different version support.

To support multiple frameworks, in the project file, you can change the `TargetFramework` element to `TargetFrameworks`. All the *target framework monikers* for the target frameworks where binaries should be created are listed within.

> **NOTE** *The list of target framework monikers is shown at* https://docs.microsoft.com/dotnet/standard/frameworks.

The example adds the target framework monikers `net5.0` and `netstandard2.0`. With conditional settings, constants are defined with the element `DefineConstants`. You can use these constants with preprocessor directives to create different code between the different frameworks. The C# version is specified with the `LangVersion` element. Without this, the default C# versions based on the different frameworks would be used. With .NET 5, it's C# 9; with .NET Standard 2.0, it's C# 7.3. Changing the C# version to 9.0 doesn't mean you can use all the features with .NET Standard 2.0. For example, default interface members are not possible and can be used only for writing conditional C# code using the defined constant DOTNET50 (project file `CreateNuGet/SampleLib/SampleLib.csproj`):

```
<Project Sdk="Microsoft.NET.Sdk">
  <PropertyGroup>
    <TargetFrameworks>net5.0;netstandard2.0</TargetFrameworks>
    <Nullable>enable</Nullable>
    <LangVersion>9.0</LangVersion>
  </PropertyGroup>

  <PropertyGroup Condition="'$(TargetFramework)'=='netstandard2.0'">
    <DefineConstants>NETSTANDARD_20</DefineConstants>
  </PropertyGroup>

  <PropertyGroup Condition="'$(TargetFramework)'=='net5.0'">
    <DefineConstants>DOTNET50</DefineConstants>
  </PropertyGroup>

  <ItemGroup Condition="'$(TargetFramework)' == 'netstandard2.0'">
    <PackageReference Include="System.Text.Json" Version="5.0.1" />
  </ItemGroup>

</Project>
```

The project file also lists a conditional reference to the NuGet package `System.Text.Json`. This package is already referenced from the target framework moniker net5.0. It's not part of .NET Standard 2.0. Because this package also supports .NET Standard 2.0, it can be added to the project when building the library for .NET Standard 2.0. You can add conditional package references using the `--framework` option to specify the target framework moniker. This adds the package reference shown in the previous code snippet.

```
> dotnet add package --framework netstandard2.0 System.Text.Json
```

With the C# code, preprocessor directives are used to decide between .NET Standard 2.0 and .NET 5.0 code. The Show method returns different values depending on how the code was built. The JsonSerializer defined in the System.Text.Json namespace can now be used with both .NET versions. It's already part of .NET 5, and with .NET Standard 2.0, the library has been added (code file CreateNuGet/SampleLib/Demo.cs):

```csharp
using System.Text.Json;

namespace SampleLib
{
  public class Demo
  {
#if NETSTANDARD20
    private static string s_info = ".NET Standard 2.0";
#elif NET50
    private static string s_info = ".NET 5.0";
#else
    private static string s_info = "Unknown";
#endif

    public static string Show() => s_info;

    public string GetJson(Book book) =>
      JsonSerializer.Serialize(book);
  }
}
```

With this setup, you build the application with multiple target frameworks, and a DLL for every target framework is created. You can also build a library just for one of the specified target frameworks setting the --framework option. When you create a NuGet package, one package is created that contains all the libraries.

When creating the .NET console application, you can build the application for multiple target frameworks as well. Like the library before, with the console application, you configure multiple target frameworks. The console application will be built for .NET 5.0 and .NET Core 3.1 (project file CreateNuGet/ConsoleApp/ConsoleApp.csproj):

```xml
<TargetFrameworks>net5.0; netcoreapp3.1</TargetFrameworks>
```

An application cannot be built using the .NET Standard 2.0 target framework moniker. Remember, the .NET Standard doesn't contain an implementation of the APIs. If you're using .NET Core 3.1, .NET Standard 2.1 would be okay as well.

With the sample application, the same package is needed, but different assemblies from the package need to be selected. This is done automatically based on the project, and the package just needs to be added to the project. The complete project file for the console application is shown here (project file CreateNuGet/DotnetCaller/DotnetCaller.csproj):

```xml
<Project Sdk="Microsoft.NET.Sdk">
  <PropertyGroup>
    <OutputType>Exe</OutputType>
    <LangVersion>9.0</LangVersion>
    <Nullable>enable</Nullable>
    <TargetFrameworks>netcoreapp2.0;net47</TargetFrameworks>
  </PropertyGroup>
  <ItemGroup>
    <PackageReference Include="SampleLib" Version="5.0.1" />
  </ItemGroup>
</Project>
```

With the console application, because the language version is set to 9.0, top-level statements and target-typed new expressions can be used with .NET Core 3.1. The implementation of the console application does not need to be different between the two used frameworks:

```
using System;
using SampleLib;

Console.WriteLine(Demo.Show());
Book b = new() { Title = "Professional C#", Publisher = "Wrox Press"};
string json = Demo.GetJson(b);
Console.WriteLine(json);
```

Building the console application creates multiple binaries that contain references to different libraries. Running the application and setting the `--framework` to the two options shows two different results. This version:

```
> dotnet run --framework dotnetcoreapp3.1
```

results in the following output:

```
.NET Standard 2.0
{"Title":"Professional C#","Publisher":"Wrox Press"}
```

Running the .NET 5.0 version, as shown here:

```
> dotnet run --framework net5.0
```

results in this output:

```
.NET 5.0
{"Title":"Professional C#","Publisher":"Wrox Press"}
```

> **NOTE** *You've seen that NuGet packages can be installed and consumed from a folder. For small scenarios, this can be enough. For packages that should be publicly available, you can publish these on the* `https://www.nuget.org` *server. If you do not want to maintain your own NuGet server, for packages that should not be used publicly (or packages that are not yet ready to be used publicly), you can use GitHub Packages or Azure Artifacts with Azure DevOps services. To use NuGet packages with GitHub Packages, read* `https://docs.github.com/en/free-pro-team@latest/packages/guides/configuring-dotnet-cli-for-use-with-github-packages`. *Read this Azure Artifacts documentation on using Azure Artifacts:* `https://docs.microsoft.com/azure/devops/artifacts/`.

NuGet Packages with Visual Studio

Visual Studio 2019 allows you to create packages. In the Solution Explorer, when you select the project, you can open the context menu and select Pack to create a NuGet package. In the Project properties of the Package settings, you can also select to create a NuGet package on every build. This is probably overkill if you don't plan to distribute packages on every build. However, with this setting, you should configure the package metadata as well as the assembly and package version (see Figure 14-3).

You can use packages within Visual Studio by selecting Dependencies in Solution Explorer, opening the context menu, and selecting Manage NuGet Packages. This opens the NuGet Package Manager where you can select the package sources (including the packages from the local folder if you configured this via clicking on the Settings icon). You can browse the available packages, see the packages installed with the project, and check whether updates of packages are available.

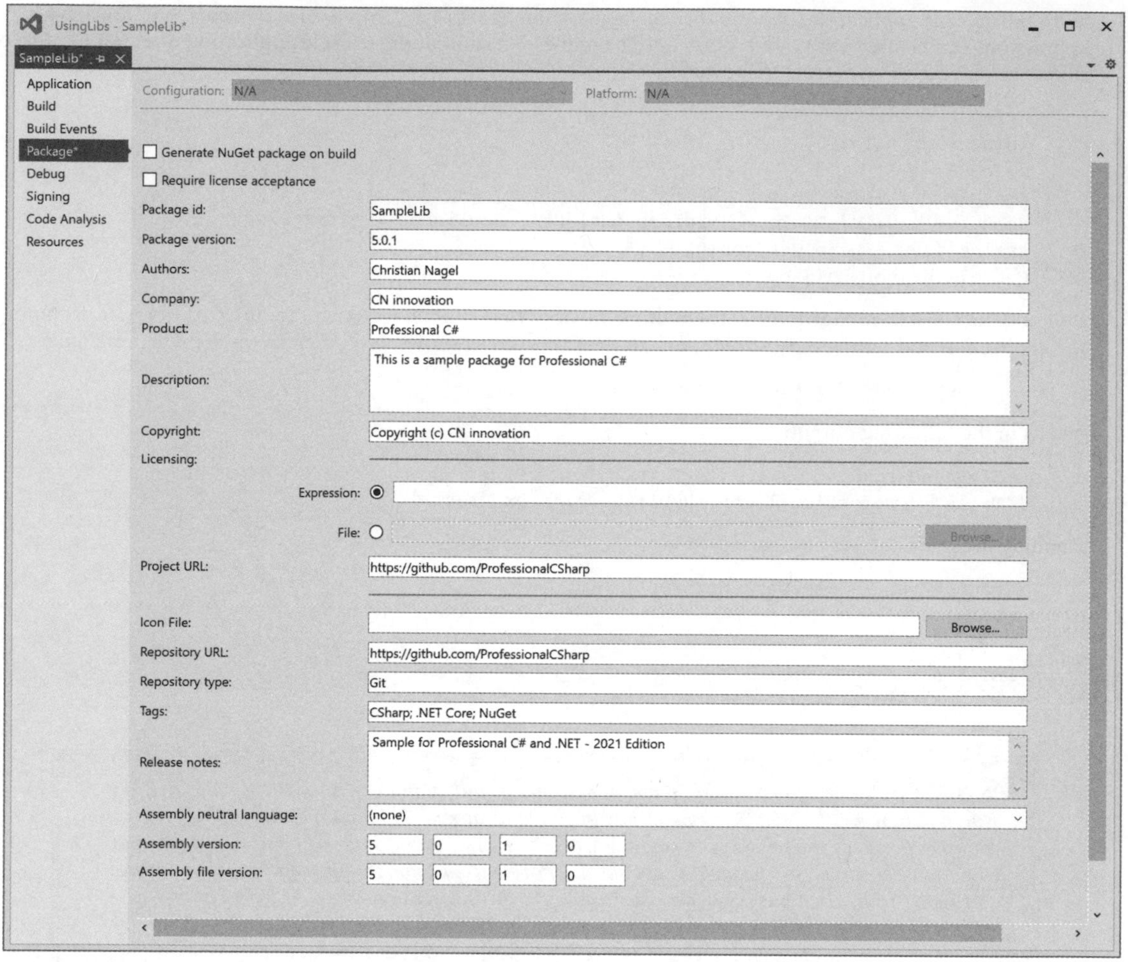

FIGURE 14-3

MODULE INITIALIZERS

In case you need initialization of a library that should be invoked before any class of the library is used, C# 9 has a new feature: *module initializers*. With a module initializer, the caller doesn't need to invoke any initialization method because it is called automatically before any type of the class is used. A module initializer needs to be a static method without arguments, a void return type, public or internal access modifiers, and the `ModuleInitializer` attribute applied. This attribute is defined in the namespace `System.Runtime.CompilerServices` and available only with .NET 5+ (code file `UsingLibs/SampleLib/Demo.cs`):

```
public class Demo
{
  //...
#if NET50
  [ModuleInitializer]
  internal static void Initializer()
```

```
    {
        Console.WriteLine("Module Initializer");
    }
#endif
}
```

Without using .NET 5, you can create a static constructor instead. However, a static constructor has more runtime overhead and requires that the class is used from the caller. The static constructor will be invoked before the first use of the class, no matter whether static or instance members are invoked. Another option is to define an `Initialize` method, but this needs to be explicitly invoked by the caller. Module initializers are not called automatically, no matter in which class they are specified.

SUMMARY

This chapter explained the differences between DLLs, assemblies, and NuGet packages. You've seen how to create and distribute libraries with NuGet packages.

The .NET Standard defines an API set that is implemented from different .NET platforms. You've seen how a .NET library can be used from .NET 5.0 and .NET Core 3.1 and how to create different binaries for different platforms with the necessary code differences.

The next chapter gets into the details of an important pattern: dependency injection. In Chapter 15, you will learn about another way of sharing code with different platforms by injecting platform-specific features.

15

Dependency Injection and Configuration

WHAT'S IN THIS CHAPTER?

- ➤ Understanding dependency injection
- ➤ Configuring the DI Container with the host class
- ➤ Managing the lifetime of services
- ➤ Disposing services
- ➤ Using options and configuration to initialize services
- ➤ Handling configuration with .NET applications
- ➤ Working with user secrets
- ➤ Using Azure App Configuration

CODE DOWNLOADS FOR THIS CHAPTER

The source code for this chapter is available on the book page at www.wiley.com. Click the Downloads link. The code can also be found at https://github.com/ProfessionalCSharp/ProfessionalCSharp2021 in the 2_Libs/DependencyInjectionAndConfiguration folder.

The code for this chapter is divided into the following major examples:

- ➤ WithDIContainer
- ➤ WithHost
- ➤ ServicesLifetime
- ➤ DIWithOptions
- ➤ DIWithConfiguration

➤ ConfigurationSample

➤ AzureAppConfigWebApp

All the projects have nullable reference types enabled.

WHAT IS DEPENDENCY INJECTION?

Faster development cycles demand unit tests and better updatability. Making some code changes should not result in errors where you don't expect them. Creating more modular applications where dependencies are reduced helps with that.

Dependency injection (DI) is a pattern where an object receives other objects it depends on—instead of creating it on its own. This reduces dependencies, because the receiving object doesn't need to know about the details of the object it receives; all it needs is a contract (usually a C# interface).

Dependency injection was introduced in Chapter 4, "Object-Oriented Programming in C#." This chapter enhances dependency injection using the container `Microsoft.Extensions.DependencyInjection` for having the management of dependencies in a central place of the application. This chapter starts with a small application for creating a dependency injection container with the `ServiceCollection` class, which is later changed to use the `Host` class that itself creates a DI container and shows various features of this DI container. The second part of this chapter shows the configuration of a .NET application, which is another feature of the `Host` class.

USING THE .NET DI CONTAINER

With a dependency injection container, you can have one place in your application where you define which contracts map to each specific implementation. You also can specify whether a service should be used as a singleton or a new instance should be created every time it's used.

With the next few samples, a greeting service (defined with the interface contract `IGreetingService` and implemented with the class `GreetingService`) is injected in the class `HomeController`. The interface defines the `Greet` method (code file `DI/WithDIContainer/IGreetingService.cs`):

```
public interface IGreetingService
{
  string Greet(string name);
}
```

The contract is implemented in the `GreetingService` class (code file `DepencencyInjectionSamples/WithDIContainer/GreetingService.cs`):

```
public class GreetingService : IGreetingService
{
  public string Greet(string name) => $"Hello, {name}";
}
```

Finally, the `IGreetingService` interface is injected using constructor injection in the class `HomeController` (code file `DepencencyInjectionSamples/WithDIContainer/HomeController.cs`):

```
public class HomeController
{
  private readonly IGreetingService _greetingService;
  public HomeController(IGreetingService greetingService) =>
    _greetingService = greetingService;
```

```
    public string Hello(string name) =>
      _greetingService.Greet(name).ToUpper();
}
```

Within the `Program` class, the `GetServiceProvider` method is defined. Here, a new `ServiceCollection` object is instantiated. `ServiceCollection` is defined in the namespace `Microsoft.Extensions.DependencyInjection` after you add the NuGet package `Microsoft.Extensions.DependencyInjection`. The extension methods `AddSingleton` and `AddTransient` are used to register the types that need to be known by the DI container. With the sample application, both the `GreetingService` and the `HomeController` are registered in the container, which makes it possible to retrieve the `HomeController` from the container.

The class `GreetingService` will be instantiated when the `IGreetingService` interface is requested. With the `HomeController`, an interface is not defined. Here, the `HomeController` is instantiated when `HomeController` is requested.

For the lifetime of `GreetingService`, the same instance is always returned when `IGreetingService` is requested. This is different with `HomeController`, where a new instance is always returned on every request to retrieve a `HomeController`. This information for the DI container is specified by using the `AddSingleton` and `AddTransient` methods. Later in this chapter, you can read more about the lifetime of services. Invoking the method `BuildServiceProvider` returns a `ServiceProvider` object that can then be used to access the services registered (code file `DI/WithDIContainer/Program.cs`):

```
static ServiceProvider GetServiceProvider()
{
  ServiceCollection = new();
  services.AddSingleton<IGreetingService, GreetingService>();
  services.AddTransient<HomeController>();
  return services.BuildServiceProvider();
}
```

> **NOTE** *If you add the same interface contract multiple times to the services collection, the last one added wins for getting the interface from the container. This makes it easy to replace contracts with different implementations if you need a changed functionality—for example, with services implemented by ASP.NET Core or Entity Framework Core.*
>
> *On the other hand, with the `ServiceCollection` class, you also have access not only to add but also to remove services and to retrieve a list of all services for a specific contract.*

Next, let's change the `Main` method to invoke the `RegisterServices` method for making the registration within the DI container and then to invoke the `GetRequiredService` method of the `ServiceProvider` to get a reference to a `HomeController` instance (code file `DI/WithDIContainer/Program.cs`):

```
using ServiceProvider container = GetServiceProvider();
var controller = container.GetRequiredService<HomeController>();
string result = controller.Hello("Stephanie");
Console.WriteLine(result);
```

> **NOTE** *With the* ServiceProvider *class, different overloads of* GetService *and* GetRequiredService *exist. The method that is directly implemented in the* ServiceProvider *class is* GetService *with a* Type *parameter. The generic method* GetService<T> *is an extension method that takes the generic type parameter and passes it to the* GetService *method.*
>
> *If the service is not available in the container,* GetService *returns* null. *The extension method* GetRequiredService *checks for a* null *result and throws an* InvalidOperationException *if the service is not found. If the service provider implements the interface* ISupportsRequiredService, *the extension method* GetRequiredService *invokes the* GetRequiredService *of the provider. The container of .NET Core does not implement this interface, but some third-party containers do.*

Let's examine how the different parts are connected when starting the application. When the application starts, on the request of the GetRequiredService method, the DI container creates an instance of the HomeController class. The HomeController constructor requires an object implementing IGreetingService. This interface is also registered with the container; for IGreetingService, a GreetingService object needs to be returned. The GreetingService class has a default constructor; thus, the container can create an instance and pass this instance to the constructor of the HomeController. This instance is used with the controller variable and used as before to invoke the Hello method.

What happens if not every dependency is registered with the DI container? In that case, the registration that maps IGreetingService to GreetingService is removed, and the container throws the InvalidOperationException. In case of the sample application, this error message shows up: Unable to resolve service for type 'WithDIContainer.IGreetingService' while attempting to activate 'WithDIContainer.HomeController'.

USING THE HOST CLASS

A class that offers out-of-the-box support for a dependency injection container is the Host class from the NuGet package Microsoft.Extensions.Hosting. This class not only offers creating the dependency injection container but also functionality for logging and configuration, which are features that practically all applications need.

> **NOTE** *Configuration using the* Host *class is covered in this chapter in the section "Configuration with .NET Applications." Logging is covered in Chapter 16, "Diagnostics and Metrics."*

Let's change the previous sample application to use the Host class. With the sample application, the HomeController, GreetingService, and IGreetingService types didn't change. When you use the Host class, a simplification is possible with the top-level statements in the file Program.cs. Instead of creating a new ServiceCollection, this is now a job of the CreateDefaultBuilder method of the Host class. The CreateDefaultBuilder method configures defaults for dependency injection, logging, and configuration. In the implementation of this method, a new ServiceCollection is created, and some commonly used interfaces are already registered. To configure more services, the CreateDefaultBuilder returns an IHostBuilder, and with this, the ConfigureServices method can be invoked to register additional services. One overload of the ConfigureServices method defines a ServiceCollection parameter that can be used to configure services as has been shown before in the `GetServiceProvider` method (code file `DepencencyInjectionSamples/WithHost/Program.cs`):

```
using var host = Host.CreateDefaultBuilder(args)
  .ConfigureServices(services =>
  {
    services.AddSingleton<IGreetingService, GreetingService>();
    services.AddTransient<HomeController>();
  }).Build();

var controller = host.Services.GetRequiredService<HomeController>();
string result = controller.Hello("Matthias");
Console.WriteLine(result);
```

> **NOTE** *You might think that adding extra source code when using the* `Host` *class makes it not worthwhile to use this feature. However, the* `CreateDefaultBuilder` *method also registers some commonly used services and configures defaults for logging and configuration. All of these topics are discussed later in this chapter and in Chapter 16.*

LIFETIME OF SERVICES

Registering a service as a singleton always returns the same instance; registering a service transient returns a new object every time the service is injected. There are more options available and more issues to think about. Let's start with another example showing this and implementing the `IDisposable` interface with the services, so you can see how disposing of service instances is handled by the container.

To easily differentiate between instances, every service instantiated will be given a different number. The number is created from a shared service. This shared service defines a simple interface `INumberService` to return a number (code file `DI/ServicesLifetime/INumberService.cs`):

```
public interface INumberService
{
  int GetNumber();
}
```

The implementation of `INumberService` always returns a new number in the `GetNumber` method. This service will be registered as singleton to have the number shared between the other services (code file `DI/ServicesLifetime/NumberService.cs`):

```
public class NumberService : INumberService
{
  private int _number = 0;
  public int GetNumber() => Interlocked.Increment(ref _number);
}
```

> **NOTE** *The* `Interlocked.Increment` *class offers a thread-safe increment. The* `Interlocked` *class is covered in Chapter 16.*

The other services that will be looked at are defined by the interface contracts ISeviceA, ISeviceB, and ISeviceC with the corresponding methods A, B, and C. The following code snippet shows the contract for ISeviceA (code file DI/ServicesLifetime/IServiceA.cs):

```
public interface IServiceA
{
  void A();
}
```

With the implementation of ServiceA, the constructor needs an injection of the INumberService. With this service, the number is retrieved to assign it to the private field _n. To see the lifetime of the objects when running the implementation, console output is written in the constructor, the method A, and the Dispose method. The ConfigurationA class is specified to pass configuration data to this service that will be used to show how the service is configured from the DI container (for example, transient or singleton) to display this on the console (code file DI/ServicesLifetime/ServiceA.cs):

```
public class ConfigurationA
{
  public string? Mode { get; set; }
}

public sealed class ServiceA : IServiceA, IDisposable
{
  private readonly int _n;
  private readonly string? _mode;
  public ServiceA(INumberService numberService,
    IOptions<ConfigurationA> options)
  {
     _mode = options.Value.Mode;
    _n = numberService.GetNumber();
    Console.WriteLine($"ctor {nameof(ServiceA)}, {_n}");
  }

  public void A() => Console.WriteLine($"{nameof(A)}, {_n}, mode: {_mode}");
  public void Dispose() =>
    Console.WriteLine($"disposing {nameof(ServiceA)}, {_n}");
}
```

The other service classes ServiceB and ServiceC are implemented similarly to ServiceA.

> **NOTE** *The* IDisposable *interface is explained in detail in Chapter 13, "Managed and Unmanaged Memory." The* IOptions *interface is explained later in this chapter in the section "Initialization of Services Using Options."*

In addition to the services, the controller ControllerX is implemented. ControllerX requires constructor injection of three services: IServiceA, IServiceB, and INumberService. With the method M, two of the injected services are invoked. Also, constructor and Dispose information is written to the console (code file DI/ServicesLifetime/ControllerX.cs):

```
public sealed class ControllerX : IDisposable
{
  private readonly IServiceA _serviceA;
  private readonly IServiceB _serviceB;
```

```
private readonly int _n;
private int _countm = 0;
public ControllerX(IServiceA serviceA, IServiceB serviceB,
  INumberService numberService)
{
  _n = numberService.GetNumber();
  Console.WriteLine($"ctor {nameof(ControllerX)}, {_n}");
  _serviceA = serviceA;
  _serviceB = serviceB;
}

public void M()
{
  Console.WriteLine($"invoked {nameof(M)} for the {++_countm}. time");
  _serviceA.A();
  _serviceB.B();
}

public void Dispose() =>
  Console.WriteLine($"disposing {nameof(ControllerX)}, {_n}");
}
```

Singleton and Transient Services

Let's start registering singleton and transient services. Here, the services `ServiceA`, `ServiceB`, `NumberService`, and the controller class `ControllerX` are registered. `NumberService` needs to be registered as singleton to have shared state. `ServiceA` is registered as singleton as well. `ServiceB` and `ControllerX` are registered as transient (code file `DI/ServicesLifetime/Program.cs`):

```
private static void SingletonAndTransient()
{
  Console.WriteLine(nameof(SingletonAndTransient));

  using var host = Host.CreateDefaultBuilder()
    .ConfigureServices(services =>
  {
    services.Configure<ConfigurationA>(config => config.Mode = "singleton");
    services.AddSingleton<IServiceA, ServiceA>();
    services.Configure<ConfigurationB>(config => config.Mode = "transient");

    services.AddTransient<IServiceB, ServiceB>();
    services.AddTransient<ControllerX>();
    services.AddSingleton<INumberService, NumberService>();
  }).Build();
  //...
}
```

`AddSingleton` and `AddTransient` are extension methods that make it easier to register services with the `Microsoft.Extensions.DependencyInjection` framework. Instead of using these helpful methods, you can register services with the `Add` method (which is itself invoked by the convenient extension methods). The `Add` method requires a `ServiceDescriptor` containing the service type, the implementation type, and the kind of the service. The kind of the service is specified using the `ServiceLifetime` enum type. `ServiceLifetime` defines the values `Singleton`, `Transient`, and `Scoped`:

```
services.Add(new ServiceDescriptor(typeof(ControllerX),
  typeof(ControllerX), ServiceLifetime.Transient));
```

> **NOTE** *The* `Add` *method of the* `ServiceCollection` *class is explicitly implemented for the interface* `IServiceCollection`. *With this, you can see the method only when using the interface* `IServiceCollection`, *not when you have a variable of the* `ServiceCollection` *type. Explicit interface implementation is covered in Chapter 4.*

The `GetRequiredService` method is invoked to get the `ControllerX` two times and invoke the method `M` before the `Host` instance is disposed of when the variable goes out of scope at the end of the method (code file `DI/ServicesLifetime/Program.cs`):

```
private static void SingletonAndTransient()
{
  //...
  Console.WriteLine($"requesting {nameof(ControllerX)}");

  ControllerX x = host.Services.GetRequiredService<ControllerX>();
  x.M();
  x.M();

  Console.WriteLine($"requesting {nameof(ControllerX)}");

  ControllerX x2 = host.Services.GetRequiredService<ControllerX>();
  x2.M();

  Console.WriteLine();
}
```

In order to run, the application is using the NuGet package `System.CommandLine.DragonFruit`. This library is based on `System.CommandLine` and gives an easy way to pass arguments to the `Main` method. This `Main` method is defined to receive a string that's stored in the variable `mode`, and thus the application can be started by passing `--mode singletonandtransient`:

```
static void Main(string mode)
{
  switch (mode)
  {
    case "singletonandtransient":
      SingletonAndTransient();
      break;
    case "scoped":
      UsingScoped();
      break;
    case "custom":
      CustomFactories();
      break;
    default:
      Usage();
      break;
  }
}
```

When you run the application, you can see when the `ControllerX` is requested and when `ServiceA` and `ServiceB` are instantiated, and the `NumberService` returns a new number every time the `GetNumber` method is invoked. When the `ControllerX` is requested the second time, the `ControllerX` is newly created and so is `ServiceB` because these types are registered as transient with the container. With `ServiceA`, the same instance is used as before, and no new instance is created:

```
SingletonAndTransient
requesting ControllerX
ctor ServiceA, 1
ctor ServiceB, 2
ctor ControllerX, 3
invoked M for the 1. time
A, 1, mode: singleton
B, 2, mode: transient
invoked M for the 2. time
A, 1, mode: singleton
B, 2, mode: transient
requesting ControllerX
ctor ServiceB, 4
ctor ControllerX, 5
invoked M for the 1. time
A, 1, mode: singleton
B, 4, mode: transient

disposing ControllerX, 5
disposing ServiceB, 4
disposing ControllerX, 3
disposing ServiceB, 2
disposing ServiceA, 1
```

Using Scoped Services

Services can also be registered within a scope. This is something between transient and singleton. With singleton, only a single instance is created. Transient creates a new instance every time the service is requested from the container. With scoped, the same instance is always returned from the same scope, but from a different scope, a different instance is returned. Scopes are by default defined with ASP.NET Core web applications. Here, the scope is an HTTP web request. With the scoped service, the same instance is returned as long as the request to the container is coming from the same HTTP request. With different HTTP requests, other instances are returned. This allows for easily sharing state inside an HTTP request.

With non-ASP.NET Core web applications, you need to create the scope for yourself to get the advantages of scoped services.

Let's start registering services with the local function `RegisterServices`. `ServiceA` is registered as a scoped service, `ServiceB` as singleton, and `ServiceC` as transient (code file `DI/ServicesLifetime/Program.cs`):

```
private static void UsingScoped()
{
  Console.WriteLine(nameof(UsingScoped));

  using var host = Host.CreateDefaultBuilder()
    .ConfigureServices(services =>
    {
      services.AddSingleton<INumberService, NumberService>();
      services.Configure<ConfigurationA>(config => config.Mode = "scoped");
      services.AddScoped<IServiceA, ServiceA>();
      services.Configure<ConfigurationB>(
        config => config.Mode = "singleton");
```

```
            services.AddSingleton<IServiceB, ServiceB>();
            services.Configure<ConfigurationC>(
              config => config.Mode = "transient");
            services.AddTransient<IServiceC, ServiceC>();
        }).Build();
      //...
  }
```

You can create a scope that invokes the `CreateScope` method of the `ServiceProvider`. This returns a scope object implementing the interface `IServiceScope`. From there you can access the `ServiceProvider` that belongs to this scope where you can request the services from the container. With the following code snippet, `ServiceA` and `ServiceC` are requested two times, whereas `ServiceB` is requested just once. Then the methods `A`, `B`, and `C` are invoked:

```
private static void UsingScoped()
{
  //...
  // the using statement is used here to end scope1 early
  using (IServiceScope scope1 = host.Services.CreateScope())
  {
    IServiceA a1 = scope1.ServiceProvider.GetRequiredService<IServiceA>();
    a1.A();
    IServiceA a2 = scope1.ServiceProvider.GetRequiredService<IServiceA>();
    a2.A();
    IServiceB b1 = scope1.ServiceProvider.GetRequiredService<IServiceB>();
    b1.B();
    IServiceC c1 = scope1.ServiceProvider.GetRequiredService<IServiceC>();
    c1.C();
    IServiceC c2 = scope1.ServiceProvider.GetRequiredService<IServiceC>();
    c2.C();
  }
  Console.WriteLine("end of scope1");
  //...
}
```

After the first scope is disposed of, another scope is created. With the second scope, again `ServiceA`, `ServiceB`, and `ServiceC` are requested, and methods are invoked:

```
private static void UsingScoped()
{
  //...
  using (IServiceScope scope2 = host.Services.CreateScope())
  {
    IServiceA a3 = scope2.ServiceProvider.GetRequiredService<IServiceA>();
    a3.A();
    IServiceB b2 = scope2.ServiceProvider.GetRequiredService<IServiceB>();
    b2.B();
    IServiceC c3 = scope2.ServiceProvider.GetRequiredService<IServiceC>();
    c3.C();
  }
  Console.WriteLine("end of scope2");
  Console.WriteLine();
}
```

When you run the application, you can see the services for the instances are created, methods are invoked, and services are automatically disposed of. As `ServiceA` is registered as transient, within the same scope, the same instance is used. `ServiceC` is registered as transient, so here an instance is created with every request to the container. At the end of the scope, the transient and scoped services are automatically disposed of, but `ServiceB` isn't. `ServiceB` is registered as singleton and thus needs to survive to the end of the scope:

```
UsingScoped
ctor ServiceA, 1
A, 1, mode: scoped
A, 1, mode: scoped
ctor ServiceB, 2
B, 2, mode: singleton
ctor ServiceC, 3
C, 3, mode: transient
ctor ServiceC, 4
C, 4, mode: transient
disposing ServiceC, 4
disposing ServiceC, 3
disposing ServiceA, 1
end of scope1
```

When you start the second scope, `ServiceA` and `ServiceB` are instantiated again. When you request `ServiceB`, the same object previously created is returned. At the end of the scope, `ServiceA` and `ServiceC` are disposed of again. `ServiceB` is disposed of after the root provider is disposed of:

```
ctor ServiceA, 5
A, 5, mode: scoped
B, 2, mode: singleton
ctor ServiceC, 6
C, 6, mode: transient
disposing ServiceC, 6
disposing ServiceA, 5
end of scope2

disposing ServiceB, 2
```

> **NOTE** *You don't need to invoke the* `Dispose` *method on services to release them. With services implementing the* `IDisposable` *interface, the container invokes the* `Dispose` *method. Transient and scoped services are disposed of when the scope is disposed of. Singleton services are disposed of when the root provider is disposed of.*
>
> *Service instances are disposed of in the reverse order that they were created. This is important when one service needs another one injected. For example, service A requires that service B is injected. Thus, service B is created first, followed by service A. For disposing of the services, service A is disposed of first. During the disposal of A, A can still access methods from service B.*

> **WARNING** *Disposing of transient services at the end of the scope might be too late for some scenarios. Transient services could be disposed of directly after use. However, this can be missed, and the registration of the service might have changed. There's also an issue that the garbage collector cannot release the memory of transient services registered because references are kept in the service container implementation (so it can be disposed of at the end of the scope). A good practice is to register disposable services as either scoped or singleton. Also remember that with non-ASP.NET Core applications, the scope needs to be created manually.*

Using Custom Factories

Instead of using the predefined methods to register transient, scoped, and singleton services, you can create a custom factory or pass an existing instance to the container. The next code snippet shows how you can do this.

You can pass a previously created instance to the container by using an overload of the `AddSingleton` method. Here, in the `RegisterServices` method, a `NumberService` object is created first and then passed to the `AddSingleton` method. Using the `GetService` method or injecting it in the constructor is not different from the code you've seen before. You just need to be aware that the container is not responsible for invoking the `Dispose` method in this case. With objects creating and passing to the container, it's your responsibility to dispose of these objects—if the objects need disposal at all.

You can also use a factory method to create the instance instead of letting the service be created from the container. If the service needs a custom initialization or defines constructors not supported by the DI container, this is a useful option. You can pass a delegate with an `IServiceProvider` parameter and return the service instance to the `AddSingleton`, `AddScoped`, and `AddTransient` methods. With the sample code, the local function named `CreateServiceBFactory` returns a `ServiceB` object. If the constructor of the service implementation needs other services, these can be retrieved using the passed `IServiceProvider` instance (code file `DI/ServicesLifetime/Program.cs`):

```
private static void CustomFactories()
{
  IServiceB CreateServiceBFactory(IServiceProvider provider) =>
    new ServiceB(provider.GetRequiredService<INumberService>(),
      provider.GetRequiredService<IOptions<ConfigurationB>>());

  Console.WriteLine(nameof(CustomFactories));

  using var host = Host.CreateDefaultBuilder()
    .ContigureServices(services =>
    {
      NumberService = new();

      services.AddSingleton<INumberService>(numberService);  // add existing
      services.Configure<ConfigurationB>(config => config.Mode = "factory");
      // use a factory
      services.AddTransient<IServiceB>(CreateServiceBFactory);
      services.Configure<ConfigurationA>(
        config => config.Mode = "singleton");
      services.AddSingleton<IServiceA, ServiceA>();
    }).Build();

  IServiceA a1 = host.Services.GetRequiredService<IServiceA>();
  IServiceA a2 = host.Services.GetRequiredService<IServiceA>();
  IServiceB b1 = host.Services.GetRequiredService<IServiceB>();
  IServiceB b2 = host.Services.GetRequiredService<IServiceB>();
  Console.WriteLine();
}
```

INITIALIZATION OF SERVICES USING OPTIONS

You've already seen that a service can be injected in another service. This can also be used to initialize a service with options. You cannot define a constructor with types not registered with the DI container because the container does not know how to initialize this. Services are needed. However, to pass options for a service, you can also use a service that is already available with .NET.

The sample code makes use of the previously used `GreetingService` with modifications to pass options. The configuration values needed by the service are defined with the class `GreetingServiceOptions`. The sample code requires a `string` parameter with the `From` property (code file DI/DIWithOptions/GreetingServiceOptions.cs):

```
public class GreetingServiceOptions
{
   public string? From { get; set; }
}
```

The options for the service can be passed by specifying a constructor with an `IOptions<T>` parameter. The previously defined class `GreetingServiceOptions` is the generic type used with `IOptions`. The value passed to the constructor is used to initialize the field `_from` (code file DI/DIWithOptions/GreetingService.cs):

```
public class GreetingService : IGreetingService
{
   public GreetingService(IOptions<GreetingServiceOptions> options) =>
     _from = options.Value.From;

   private readonly string? _from;

   public string Greet(string name) => $"Hello, {name}! Greetings from {_from}";
}
```

To make it easy to register the service with the DI container, the extension method `AddGreetingService` is defined. This method extends the `IServiceCollection` interface and allows passing the `GreetingServiceOptions` with a delegate. In the implementation, the `Configure` method is used to specify the configuration with the `IOptions` interface. The `Configure` method is an extension method for `IServiceCollection` defined in the `Microsoft.Extensions.Options` NuGet package (code file DI/DIWithOptions/GreetingServiceExtensions.cs):

```
public static class GreetingServiceExtensions
{
   public static IServiceCollection AddGreetingService(
     this IServiceCollection collection,
     Action<GreetingServiceOptions> setupAction)
   {
     if (collection == null)
       throw new ArgumentNullException(nameof(collection));
     if (setupAction == null)
       throw new ArgumentNullException(nameof(setupAction));

     collection.Configure(setupAction);
     return collection.AddTransient<IGreetingService, GreetingService>();
   }
}
```

The `HomeController` that's using the `GreetingService` with constructor injection doesn't require any changes compared to the previous sample (code file DI/DIWithOptions/HomeController.cs):

```
public class HomeController
{
   private readonly IGreetingService _greetingService;
   public HomeController(IGreetingService greetingService)
   {
     _greetingService = greetingService;
   }
   public string Hello(string name) => _greetingService.Greet(name);
}
```

You can now register the services with the helper method `AddGreetingService`. The configuration for the `GreetingService` is done here by passing the required options. What's also needed is a service that implements the `IOptions` interface. For this interface, a service implementation is already added from the `CreateDefaultBuilder` method. In case you don't use the `Host` class, you need to invoke the `AddOptions` method to register an implementation in the DI container (code file `DI/DIWithOptions/Program.cs`):

```
using var host = Host.CreateDefaultBuilder()
  .ConfigureServices(services =>
  {
    // services.AddOptions(); // already added from host
    services.AddGreetingService(options =>
    {
      options.From = "Christian";
    });
    services.AddSingleton<IGreetingService, GreetingService>();
    services.AddTransient<HomeController>();
  }).Build();
```

The service can now be used as before. The `HomeController` is retrieved from the container, and constructor injection is used in the `HomeController` where the `IGreetingService` is used:

```
var controller = host.Services.GetRequiredService<HomeController>();
string result = controller.Hello("Katharina");
Console.WriteLine(result);
```

When you run the application, now the options are used:

```
Hello, Katharina! Greetings from Christian
```

> **NOTE** *You can use* `IOptions`*-derived interfaces such as* `IOptionsSnapshot` *to update settings dynamically when the configuration is updated. How you do this with Azure App Configuration is explained later in this chapter.*

USING CONFIGURATION FILES

You can also use options as shown in the previous section when a service needs to be configured from a configuration file. However, there's a more direct way to do this; you can use the .NET configuration features in conjunction with an extension to the options. With the next sample, the services are unchanged and still use `IOptions<GreetingServiceOptions>` injected in the constructor. Now, the file `appsettings.json` is used to supply the option values. The `From` key defines a value that maps to the `From` property from the `GreetingServiceOptions` class (configuration file `DI/DIWithConfiguration/appsettings.json`):

```
{
  "GreetingService": {
    "From": "Matthias"
  }
}
```

The configuration file needs to be copied to the directory of the executable. You do this by adding the `CopyToOutputDirectory` element to the project file (project file `DI/DIWithConfiguration/DIWith Configuration.csproj`):

```
<ItemGroup>
  <None Update="appsettings.json">
    <CopyToOutputDirectory>PreserveNewest</CopyToOutputDirectory>
  </None>
</ItemGroup>
```

A new extension method that helps with registering the options of the `GreetingService`
class defines an `IConfiguration` parameter. With the implementation, an overload of the `Configure`
method is used where an object implementing the `IConfiguration` can be directly passed (code file
`DI/DIWithConfiguration/GreetingServiceExtensions.cs`):

```
public static class GreetingServiceExtensions
{
  public static IServiceCollection AddGreetingService(
    this IServiceCollection services, IConfiguration config)
  {
    if (services == null) throw new ArgumentNullException(nameof(services));
    if (config == null) throw new ArgumentNullException(nameof(config));

    services.Configure<GreetingServiceOptions>(config);
    return services.AddTransient<IGreetingService, GreetingService>();
  }
}
```

To inject the `IConfiguration` interface in a service, the `CreateDefaultBuilder` method configures this
interface in the DI container. To access this interface already with the configuration of the additional services,
the `ConfigureServices` method defines an overload where the `HttpBuilderContext` is supplied in addition
to the `IServiceCollection`. Using the `Configuration` property of the `HttpBuilderContext` returns the
`IConfiguration` interface that allows retrieving configured values. In the configuration file, for the service
configuration, the section named `GreetingService` is defined. Invoking the `GetSection` method returns an
`IConfigurationSection`. `IConfigurationSection` derives from `IConfiguration`, thus the returned value can
be passed to the `AddGreetingService` extension method (code file `DI/DIWithConfiguration/Program.cs`):

```
using var host = Host.CreateDefaultBuilder()
  .ConfigureServices((context, services) =>
  {
    var configuration = context.Configuration;
    services.AddGreetingService(
      configuration.GetSection("GreetingService"));
    services.AddSingleton<IGreetingService, GreetingService>();
    services.AddTransient<HomeController>();
  }).Build();

var controller = host.Services.GetRequiredService<HomeController>();
string result = controller.Hello("Katharina");
Console.WriteLine(result);
```

Running the application shows the following:

```
Hello, Katharina! Greetings from Matthias
```

This sample application retrieved configuration settings from `appsettings.json`. This filename is configured by
default with the `CreateDefaultBuilder` method of the `Host` class. This method configures more configuration
sources, which, of course, can also be changed as shown in the next section.

CONFIGURATION WITH .NET APPLICATIONS

The previous section shows how you can supply configuration values to services that are injected by the DI
container using the `IConfiguration` interface and the configuration file `appsettings.json`. This section covers
how .NET offers a flexible mechanism to get configuration values from different sources.

Using IConfiguration

The sample application uses configuration from `appsettings.json`, which specifies configuration values for a key; a section containing a key; a section named `ConnectionStrings`; and another section named `SomeTypedConfig`, which contains an inner section (configuration file `ConfigurationSample/appsettings.json`):

```
{
  "Key1": "value for Key1",
  "Section1": {
    "Key2": "value from appsettings.json"
  },
  "ConnectionStrings": {
    "BooksConnection": "this is the connection string to a database"
  },
  "SomeTypedConfig": {
    "Key3": "value for key 3",
    "Key4": "value for key 4",
    "InnerConfig": {
      "Key5": "value for key 5"
    }
  }
}
```

With the class `ConfigurationSampleService`, an object implementing `IConfiguration` is injected in the constructor (code file `ConfigurationSample/ConfigurationSampleService.cs`):

```
public class ConfigurationSampleService
{
  private readonly IConfiguration _configuration;

  public ConfigurationSampleService(IConfiguration configuration)
  {
    _configuration = configuration;
  }
  //...
}
```

To retrieve configuration values, different options are available. With the `GetValue` method, a key can be passed with the arguments of this method to retrieve the value. An indexer passing the key can be used as well. If a section is used with inner values, such as the section named Section1, the `GetSection` method can be used to retrieve the section, and from there on, the indexer can be used to access the inner values. `GetSection` returns `IConfigurationSection`, which in turn derives from `IConfiguration`. If the section is named `ConnectionStrings`, the extension method `GetConnectionString` can be used to pass a key within this section to retrieve connection strings. `GetConnectionString` is just an extension method that makes it convenient for using connection strings (code file `ConfigurationSample/ConfigurationSampleService.cs`):

```
public void ShowConfiguration()
{
  string value1 = _configuration.GetValue<string>("Key1");
  Console.WriteLine(value1);
  string value1b = _configuration["Key1"];
  Console.WriteLine(value1b);
  string value2 = _configuration.GetSection("Section1")["Key2"];
  Console.WriteLine(value2);
  string connectionString =
```

```
      _configuration.GetConnectionString("BooksConnection");
    Console.WriteLine(connectionString);
    Console.WriteLine();
  }
```

Reading Strongly Typed Values

With .NET configurations, classes can be used where the configuration values should be filled into (code file `ConfigurationSample/StronglyTypedConfig.cs`):

```
public class InnerConfig
{
  public string? Key5 { get; set; }
}

public class StronglyTypedConfig
{
  public string? Key3 { get; set; }
  public string? Key4 { get; set; }
  public InnerConfig? InnerConfig { get; set; }

  public override string ToString() =>
    $"values: {Key3} {Key4} {InnerConfig?.Key5}";
}
```

To bind the values from the configuration source, the `Get` extension method can be used. This method tries to fill matching keys to properties of the generic value type. Setting the `BinderOption` value `BindNonPublicProperties` to true also sets read-only values and not just read/write properties (code file `ConfigurationSample/ConfigurationSampleService.cs`):

```
public void ShowTypedConfiguration()
{
  Console.WriteLine(nameof(ShowTypedConfiguration));
  var section = _configuration.GetSection("SomeTypedConfig");
  var typedConfig = section.Get<StronglyTypedConfig>(
    binder => binder.BindNonPublicProperties = true);
  Console.WriteLine(typedConfig);
  Console.WriteLine();
}
```

Configuration Sources

When you use the `CreateDefaultBuilder` method of the `Host` class, you use these configuration sources:

- ➤ `appsettings.json`
- ➤ `appsettings.{environment-name}.json`
- ➤ Environment variables
- ➤ Command-line arguments
- ➤ User secrets in development-mode

The order is important. Every source coming later in the list can override settings from previous sources. The configuration sources are completely customizable. Other configuration providers are available in NuGet packages—for example, providers reading configuration values from XML or INI files.

The following code sample shows adding another JSON provider that's accessing the file `customconfig-urationfile.json`. You can separate any configuration data you like, such as all database connection strings to other configuration files. The extension method `AddJsonFile` references this file. The method `SetBasePath` that is invoked before `AddJsonFile` defines the directory where the file is searched. Setting the optional parameter to `true` doesn't throw an exception when the file does not exist (code file `ConfigurationSamples/Program.cs`):

```
using var host = Host.CreateDefaultBuilder(args)
  .ConfigureAppConfiguration(config =>
  {
    config.SetBasePath(Directory.GetCurrentDirectory());
    config.AddJsonFile("customconfigurationfile.json", optional: true);
  }).ConfigureServices(services =>
  {
    services.AddTransient<ConfigurationSampleService>();
    services.AddTransient<EnvironmentSampleService>();
  }).Build();
```

When you set configuration values with environment variables and command-line arguments, a colon indicates separate sections. The following statement invokes the application overriding values for `Key1` and `Key2` within the section `Section1`:

```
> dotnet run -- Key1="val1" Section1:Key2="val2"
```

> **NOTE** *If the JSON configuration file changes dynamically while the application is running, and new values should be retrieved from the application, you just have to set the* `reloadOnChange` *argument of the* `AddJsonFile` *method to* `true`*. This way, a file watcher is attached to be notified on changes, and the configuration values are updated. See Chapter 18, "Files and Streams," to learn how to create your own file watcher.*

Production and Development Settings

To differentiate between settings for development, production, and staging environments, the environmental variable `DOTNET_ENVIRONMENT` is used. The second configuration source that's in the list to search for configuration values is `appsettings.{environment-name}.json`. Configuration values that are different with production, staging, and development environments just need to be configured with `appsettings.Production.json`, `appsettings.Staging.json`, and `appsettings.Development.json`.

To set the environmental variable easily when running the application, you can configure launch settings in the `Properties` folder of the project and specify the `DOTNET_ENVIRONMENT` environment variable (configuration file `ConfigurationSample/Properties/launchsettings.json`):

```
{
  "profiles": {
    "ConfigurationSample": {
      "commandName": "Project",
      "environmentVariables": {
        "DOTNET_Environment": "Development"
      }
    }
  }
}
```

To check for the environment, the interface `IHostEnvironment` can be injected with a service. With this interface, the `EnvironmentName` property gives the name of the environment. Extension methods such as `IsDevelopment`, `IsStaging`, and `IsProduction` can be used to verify whether the application is running in a specific environment (code file `ConfigurationSample/EnvironmentSampleService.cs`):

```
public class EnvironmentSampleService
{
  private readonly IHostEnvironment _hostEnvironment;

  public EnvironmentSampleService(IHostEnvironment hostEnvironment)
  {
    _hostEnvironment = hostEnvironment;
  }

  public void ShowHostEnvironment()
  {
    Console.WriteLine(_hostEnvironment.EnvironmentName);
    if (_hostEnvironment.IsDevelopment())
    {
      Console.WriteLine("it's a development environment");
    }
  }
}
```

> **NOTE** *You can create custom environments to differentiate environments where you use simulated local services that are injected in the DI container—for example, to increase debugging speed by not accessing authentication or other services. For this, you can create extension methods to verify for the custom environment name. The implementation just needs to check for the value of the* EnvironmentName *property.*

User Secrets

Secrets shouldn't be stored within configuration files that are part of the source code repository. Open-source code repositories are continuously scanned for passwords and keys that could be used. Private-source code repositories also are not good places to keep the secrets. During development time, *user secrets* can be used. With user secrets, the configuration is stored in the user profile. Only the user who is allowed to access the user profile can get access to these configuration values. During production, you need to use a different environment instead. Here, depending on the environment, secrets can be stored in environmental variables or, better yet, in a service like the Azure Key Vault.

To work with user secrets, you can use the dotnet tool `user-secrets`. For example, the following:

```
> dotnet user-secrets init
```

adds a configuration specifying a `UserSecretsId` in the project file, such as this:

```
<UserSecretsId>7695182a-e84c-44c0-8644-4a531200ecff</UserSecretsId>
```

The ID is not a secret by itself. The ID can be a simple string. By default, a GUID is created. All applications where user secrets are used store the secrets in the user profile. To differentiate secrets from different applications, GUIDs are used. If you want to access the same secret configuration from multiple applications, use the same user secret ID with these applications.

To access user secrets from the application, the NuGet package `Microsoft.Extensions.Configuration.UserSecrets` needs to be added. The `Host` class method `CreateDefaultBuilder` configures user secrets if the application is running in the Development environment, and a user secret ID is specified in the project file. If you need user secrets in other scenarios, you can add the provider in the `ConfigureAppConfiguration` method calling `AddUserSecrets`.

To set a user secret via the command line, use the `set` command:

```
> dotnet user-secrets set Section1:Key2 "a secret"
```

To show all the application's secrets, use the `list` command:

```
> dotnet user-secrets list
```

AZURE APP CONFIGURATION

When publishing an ASP.NET Core web application to an Azure App Service, configuration values from the JSON configuration files can be retrieved and put into the configuration of the Azure App Service. This is a practical option; however, for many scenarios it's a better option to use Azure App Configuration. A solution often consists of multiple services that partially have the same configurations. Azure App Configuration allows one central place for the configuration, and all the applications within the solution can use the configuration. It also offers features such as having different configuration values for staging and production environments and using switches to turn features on or off based on different scenarios as needed.

To use Azure App Configuration from the application, another configuration provider needs to be configured.

With the solution, configuration during development and in production not only needs different configuration values but also different environments. When you use configuration for an application running in Microsoft Azure, you can use an identity that is defined with the Azure App Service to access the Azure App Configuration. This option is probably not available in your development environment.

In order to deal with that, you have different options. You already know that .NET configuration is flexible. During development time, you can use all the configuration locally and have secrets stored in user secrets.

At some point in time, you want to test and debug using your application as it's running locally while accessing configuration stored in Microsoft Azure. It's best to have different Azure subscriptions to separate your development and your production environment. If you are using Visual Studio Professional or Visual Studio Enterprise, every month you have a free amount of money you can spend on Azure resources. You can use your Azure development environment with your Visual Studio subscription.

Creating Azure App Configuration

Using the Azure Shell with the Bash environment, you can use the following Azure CLI commands to create a resource group and app configuration. Some keys and values used with the sample application are configured. Change the values for the resource group name (`rg`) and the location that best fits your location (`loc`):

```
rg=rg-procsharp
loc=westeurope
conf=ProCSharpConfig$Random
key1=AppConfigurationSample:Settings:Config1
val1="configuration value for key 1"
devval1="development value for key 1"
stagingval1="staging value for key 1"
prodval1="production value for key 1"
sentinelKey=AppConfigurationSample:Settings:Sentinel
sentinelValue=1
```

```
az group create --location $loc --name $rg
az appconfig create --location $loc --name $conf --resource-group $rg
az appconfig kv set -n $conf --key $key1 --value "$val1" --yes
az appconfig kv set -n $conf --key $key1 --label Development --value "$devval1" --yes
az appconfig kv set -n $conf --key $key1 --label Staging --value "$stagingval1" --yes
az appconfig kv set -n $conf --key $key1 --label Production --value "$prodval1" --yes
az appconfig kv set -n $conf --key $sentinelKey --value $sentinelValue --yes
```

> **NOTE** *Azure resources can be created and configured using the portal* (https://portal.azure.com), *the Azure CLI, PowerShell, and also an Azure SDK. Check Chapter 1, ".NET Applications and Tools" for different ways to create Microsoft Azure resources. You can open the Azure shell from the portal or by opening* https://shell.azure.com. *For the sample application, also check the readme file of the chapter samples for a Bash script to create the Azure resources.*

Using Azure App Configuration in the Development Environment

Let's explore a sample application using Azure App Configuration. An ASP.NET Core web application can be easily deployed with Azure App Services. With the sample application, you'll see the web application running locally and accessing the Azure App Configuration and also see it running when it's deployed to an Azure App Service and accessing the configuration. An empty web application can be created with `dotnet new web`. To use Azure App Configuration from an ASP.NET Core application, the NuGet package `Microsoft.Azure.AppConfiguration.AspNetCore` is added. This package has a dependency on `Microsoft.Extensions.Configuration.AzureAppConfiguration`, which would be enough for .NET applications. The ASP.NET Core package adds middleware functionality for dynamic configuration, as shown in the next section.

> **NOTE** *Read more information about the foundations of ASP.NET Core web applications in Chapter 24, "ASP.NET Core."*

To access Azure App Configuration, you use a *connection string* or an *endpoint*. The connection string includes a secret. Instead of using the connection string containing the secret, you can use the endpoint to your App Configuration resource and an account that is allowed to access the Azure resource when running the application. If you use the connection string with the secret, in the development environment, store the connection string with user secrets. With the sample application, an account is used that allows using the same code in the production environment.

The endpoint to the Azure App Configuration resource is shown using `az appconfig show`:

```
> az appconfig show --name $conf --query endpoint
```

This endpoint is added to the `appsettings.json` file with the key `AppConfigEndpoint`. Because a secret is not included, it's okay to have it in the source code repo.

To run the web application with a privileged user, add the environment variable `AZURE_USERNAME` and set it to your Azure username. To automatically do this on starting the application, change the file `launchsettings.json` in the `Properties` folder:

```
{
  "profiles": {
    "AzureAppConfigWebApp": {
      "commandName": "Project",
```

```
      "dotnetRunMessages": "true",
      "launchBrowser": true,
      "applicationUrl": "https://localhost:5001;http://localhost:5000",
      "environmentVariables": {
        "ASPNETCORE_ENVIRONMENT": "Development",
        "AZURE_USERNAME": "add your username here, e.g. name@outlook.com"
      }
    }
  }
}
```

Next, add the Azure App Configuration provider to the configuration of the `Host` class. With the web application, you can use `ConfigureAppConfiguration` of the `IWebHostBuilder` instead of the `ConfigureAppConfiguration` method of the `IHostBuilder` used before. The difference is that with the `IWebHostBuilder` version, you have access to the `WebHostBuilderContext` instead of the `HostBuilderContext`, which gives you more options. One overload of the `AddAzureAppConfiguration` method needs the connection string, including the secret. To use the account instead, you need the overload to pass the `AzureAppConfigurationOptions`. With the `options` variable, the `Connect` method can be used to pass the endpoint that's retrieved from the configuration and an instance of `DefaultAzureCredential` (code file `AzureAppConfigWebApp/Program.cs`):

```
public static IHostBuilder CreateHostBuilder(string[] args) =>
  Host.CreateDefaultBuilder(args)
    .ConfigureWebHostDefaults(webBuilder =>
    {
      webBuilder.ConfigureAppConfiguration((context, config) =>
      {
        // configuration is already needed from within setting up config
        var settings = config.Build();
        config.AddAzureAppConfiguration(options =>
        {
          DefaultAzureCredential credential = new();
          var endpoint = settings["AppConfigEndpoint"];

          options.Connect(new Uri(endpoint), credential);
        });
      });
      webBuilder.UseStartup<Startup>();
    });
```

> **NOTE** *The class* `DefaultAzureCredential` *has different ways to log in to Microsoft Azure. First, it tries to use* `EnvironmentalCredential`. *This credential class makes use of an environmental variable* `ACCOUNT_USERNAME` *that you can configure with the* `launchsettings.json` *file. If this fails, it uses* `ManagedIdentityCredential`. *When running the app in Azure, you can configure your App Service to run with a managed identity, which is then used to access Azure App Configuration. Next,* `SharedTokenCacheCredential` *is used. This uses a local token cache.* `VisualStdudioCredential` *is next. You can configure these credentials with Tools ⇨ Options ⇨ Azure Service Authentication. After this,* `VisualStudioCodeCredential` *and* `AzureCliCredential` *(credentials used with the Azure CLI) follow.* `InteractiveBrowserCredential` *(interactive log in via the browser) is the last option that's tried for a successful login, but only if the parameter* `includeInteractiveCredentials` *of the* `DefaultAzureCredential` *constructor is set to* `true`.

To inject the configured values, the `IndexAppSettings` class is defined. This will be used to fill the value for the key `AppConfigurationSample:Settings:Config1` (code file `AzureAppConfigWebApp/IndexAppSettings.cs`):

```csharp
public class IndexAppSettings
{
  public string? Config1 { get; set; }
}
```

In the code-behind of the Index Razor page, `IOptionsSnapshot` is injected to access the configuration value and fill the property `Config1` (code file `AzureAppConfigWebApp/Pages/Index.cshtml.cs`):

```csharp
public class IndexModel : PageModel
{
  private readonly ILogger<IndexModel> _logger;

  public IndexModel(IOptionsSnapshot<IndexAppSettings> options,
                    ILogger<IndexModel> logger)
  {
    _logger = logger;
    Config1 = options.Value.Config1 ?? "no value";
  }

  public string Config1 { get; }
  //...
}
```

> **NOTE** *The* `IOptions` *interface is explained earlier in this chapter in the section "Initialization of Services Using Options."* `IOptionsSnapshot` *derives from* `IOptions` *and allows changing configuration values dynamically as is shown in the next section.*

In the `Index` Razor page, the configuration value is shown accessing the `Config1` property (code file `AzureAppConfigWebApp/Pages/Index.cshtml`):

```html
<p>configuration value: @Model.Config1</p>
```

Dynamic Configuration

To avoid an application restart when a configuration value changes, the configuration can be set to reread configuration values after a sentinel value changes. This sentinel value needs to be set to a new value as soon as any other configuration for the application gets a new value.

To configure a refresh for all values when the sentinel value changes, you use an overload of the `AddAzureAppConfiguration` extension method to pass an action delegate. With the implementation of the lambda expression, the connection string for Azure App Configuration is now passed to the `Connect` method of the action delegate. Now it's also possible to invoke the `ConfigureRefresh` method. Passing a lambda expression with an `AzureAppConfigurationRefreshOptions` parameter, a configuration value can be registered that should be refreshed based on the setting passed to the `SetCacheExpiration` method. By default, the registered values are refreshed every 30 seconds. To reduce the invocations to the Azure App Configuration, the refresh is changed to refresh every five minutes. After the value is retrieved, and it is changed, all the other configuration values are retrieved as well because of the `refreshAll` parameter setting (code file `AzureAppConfigWebApp/Program.cs`):

```csharp
webBuilder.ConfigureAppConfiguration((context, config) =>
{
  // configuration is already needed from within setting up config
  var settings = config.Build();
```

```
config.AddAzureAppConfiguration(options =>
{
  DefaultAzureCredential credential = new();
  var endpoint = settings["AppConfigEndpoint"];
  options.Connect(new Uri(endpoint), credential)
    .ConfigureRefresh(refresh =>
    {
      refresh.Register(
        "AppConfigurationSample:Settings:Sentinel",
          refreshAll: true)
        .SetCacheExpiration(TimeSpan.FromMinutes(5));
    })
});
```

The ASP.NET Core middleware needs to be configured to check if the sentinel value was changed, and thus the refresh of the configuration values can be done automatically on every request. To configure the middleware, the `Startup` class is configured by invoking the `AddAzureAppConfiguration` method in the `ConfigureServices` method and by invoking the `UseAzureAppConfiguration` method in the `Configure` method.

For a test, you might lower the cache expiration time and change both the value for the key `AppConfigurationSample:Settings:Config1` as well as the sentinel value while the application is running. The new value will show up after the defined timespan.

Production and Staging Settings with Azure App Configuration

With the .NET configuration, you've seen different values based on the environment name (see the section "Production and Development Settings"). With Azure App Configuration, you can do this with a feature named *labels* in this service. On defining the configuration values for this service, labels named Production, Staging, and Development have been used. These labels are now used to map the different hosting environments.

Depending on the environment name, you can use label filters to filter the configuration. With the first `Select` method, no label filter is used. Here all the configuration values are retrieved. With the second `Select` method, configuration values are overridden based on the environment. This way, it's only necessary to add values for a specific environment when the values are different (code file `AzureAppConfigWebApp/Program.cs`):

```
config.AddAzureAppConfiguration(options =>
{
  DefaultAzureCredential credential = new();
  var endpoint = settings["AppConfigEndpoint"];
  options.Connect(new Uri(endpoint), credential)
    .Select(KeyFilter.Any, LabelFilter.Null)
    .Select(KeyFilter.Any, context.HostingEnvironment.EnvironmentName)
    .ConfigureRefresh(refresh =>
    {
      refresh.Register("AppConfigurationSample:Settings:Sentinel",
        refreshAll: true)
        .SetCacheExpiration(TimeSpan.FromMinutes(5));
    }));
```

Feature Flags

Feature flags is another feature of Azure App Configuration. With feature flags, you can enable or disable different parts at specific times or to a subset of users. New features (for example, preview features) of an application can be made available to a group of early adopters before the feature is available for all users. You can also implement a new feature with different user interface options and make this feature available to different groups of users. You can use telemetry information to find out how the different users find and use the new feature. Analysis of the information will tell you which version was most successful.

Azure App Configuration offers built-in feature flags based on a percentage of users, a specific time window, and user groups. You can also implement a custom feature filter that implements the interface `IFeatureFilter` in the namespace `Microsoft.FeatureManagement`.

To create the feature `FeatureX` with the previously defined Azure App Configuration, you can use the following Azure CLI command:

```
> az appconfig feature set --feature FeatureX -n $conf
```

The configuration of the feature is shown in the following:

```
> az appconfig feature show --feature FeatureX -n $conf
```

with a result like this:

```
{
    "conditions": {
      "client_filters": [
        {
          "name": "Microsoft.Percentage",
          "parameters": {
            "Value": 50
          }
        }
      ]
    },
    "description": "",
    "key": "FeatureX",
    "label": null,
    "lastModified": "2020-11-08T16:18:22+00:00",
    "locked": false,
    "state": "conditional"
}
```

To use feature flags with ASP.NET Core, you need to add the NuGet package `Microsoft.FeatureManagement.AspNetCore` to the project. The sample application has a percentage filter associated. With the percentage filter, a percentage can be configured for which the filter should return `true`. The DI container needs to be configured to add the implementation for feature management and to define the type of the filter that should be used (code file `AzureAppConfigWebApp/Startup.cs`):

```
services.AddFeatureManagement().AddFeatureFilter<PercentageFilter>();
```

In the code-behind file of the Razor page `FeatureSample`, the `IFeatureManager` is injected in the constructor. The `IsEnabledAsync` method passing `FeatureX` returns `true` or `false`. With the current configuration, 50 percent of the requests return `true`, and the feature can be used (code file `AzureAppConfigWebApp/FeatureSample.cshtml.cs`):

```
public class FeatureSampleModel : PageModel
{
  private readonly IFeatureManager _featureManager;
  public FeatureSampleModel(IFeatureManager featureManager)
  {
    _featureManager = featureManager;
  }

  public string? FeatureXText { get; private set; }
```

```
public async Task OnGetAsync()
{
  bool featureX = await _featureManager.IsEnabledAsync("FeatureX");
  string featureText = featureX ? "is" : "is not";
  FeatureXText = $"FeatureX {featureText} available";
}
}
```

> **NOTE** *With nonweb applications, the package* `Microsoft.FeatureManagement` *is enough to use features from .NET applications.* `Microsoft.FeatureManagement.AspNetCore` *adds classes for middleware and attributes for controllers as well as tag helpers. Tag helpers are covered in Chapter 26, "Razor Pages and MVC."*

Using the Azure Key Vault

To configure secrets in Microsoft Azure, the Azure Key Vault gives more security features. In the cloud, Hardware Security Modules (HSM), physical environments to safeguard and manage keys, can be used. With the Azure Key Vault, there's also a specific security role to monitor who accesses which keys.

To create an Azure Key Vault, you can use the Azure CLI with variables `rg` and `loc` as specified earlier:

```
> az keyvault create --resource-group $rg --location $loc
--enable-rbac-authorization --name procsharpkeyvault
```

To access the key vault, the Azure Key Vault provider can be used with the .NET configuration. An alternative option is to configure Azure App Configuration to access Azure Key Vault. This way the application can get all the settings via Azure App Configuration. This simplifies the setup. Behind the scenes, the Azure Key Vault is directly accessed from the application; thus, the identity used with the application needs to have access configured in Azure Key Vault to read the secret values.

Using the Fluent API of the `AzureAppConfigurationOptions`, `ConfigureKeyVault` is invoked to configure the credentials for the Key Vault. The Key Vault needs to be connected with the Azure App Configuration using a Key Vault reference configuration (code file `AzureAppConfigWebAppSample/Program.cs`):

```
webBuilder.ConfigureAppConfiguration((context, config) =>
{
  // configuration is already needed from within setting up config
  var settings = config.Build();
  config.AddAzureAppConfiguration(options =>
  {
    DefaultAzureCredential credential = new();
    var endpoint = settings["AppConfigEndpoint"];
    options.Connect(new Uri(endpoint), credential)
      .ConfigureRefresh(refresh =>
      {
        refresh.Register(
          "AppConfigurationSample:Settings:Sentinel",
            refreshAll: true)
          .SetCacheExpiration(TimeSpan.FromMinutes(5));
      })
```

```
        .ConfigureKeyVault(kv =>
        {
          kv.SetCredential(credential);
        });
      });
```

With this in place, configuration values can be retrieved from the Azure Key Vault as well.

> **NOTE** *Read Chapter 24 for information about how to deploy web apps to Azure App Services and how to configure managed identities.*

SUMMARY

This chapter covered various features of the `Host` class. The most important one is probably the dependency injection container that's hosted by this class. You've seen transient, scoped, and singleton services and how this DI container manages the lifetime.

This book contains several chapters where dependency injection has an important role. Chapter 21, "Entity Framework Core," shows how dependency injection is used with EF Core and how you can replace built-in functionality. Read Chapter 23, "Tests," for information on how dependency injection helps creating unit tests. Web applications (Chapters 24 through 28) have the dependency injection built in with the project templates. For Windows applications, read Chapter 30, "Patterns with XAML Apps," on how to use the DI container and the `Host` class.

The second part of this chapter covered flexible options to read configuration values from various sources. Besides environmental variables, the command line, JSON files, and user secrets, you've also seen how to read settings for the application from Azure App Configuration. For the application to read the configuration values no changes are needed. Only the setup of the `Host` class needs a change if more configuration sources are added.

The next chapter continues with features of the `Host` class that make use of logging. To see what the application is doing, also telemetry and metrics information is implemented.

16

Diagnostics and Metrics

WHAT'S IN THIS CHAPTER?

➤ Using the ILogger Interface

➤ Configuring Logging Providers

➤ Using OpenTelemetry with .NET Logging

➤ Adding Metric Counters

➤ Monitoring Metrics with .NET CLI

➤ Analyzing telemetry data with Visual Studio App Center

➤ Working with Application Insights

CODE DOWNLOADS FOR THIS CHAPTER

The source code for this chapter is available on the book page at www.wiley.com. Click the Downloads link. The code can also be found at https://github.com/ProfessionalCSharp/ProfessionalCSharp2021 in the directory 2_Libs/LoggingAndMetrics.

The code for this chapter is divided into the following major examples:

➤ LoggingSample

➤ OpenTelemetrySample

➤ MetricsSample

➤ WindowsAppAnalytics

➤ WebAppWithAppInsights

All the projects have nullable reference types enabled.

DIAGNOSTICS OVERVIEW

As release cycles for applications become faster and faster, it's becoming more and more important to learn how the application behaves while it's running in production. What exceptions are occurring? Knowing what features are used is also of interest. Do users find the new feature of the app? How long do they stay on the page? To answer these questions, you need real-time information on the application.

When you get information about the application, you need to differentiate logging, tracing, collecting metric data, and analyzing what users are doing. With logging, error information is recorded in centralized places. This information is used by system administrators to identify issues with applications.

Tracing helps to find out which method is called by which method. This information is useful for development and should be turned off when the application runs in production. Distributed tracing helps finding how services interact with each other to pinpoint failures and causes for performance issues. With .NET, the same technology can be used for logging and tracing using classes from the `System.Diagnostics` namespace. Analytics gives information about the users—where they reside, what operating system version they use, and what features they use in the application. This helps you find out if there are some issues with the application based on a location, hardware, or an operating system, and it also helps you understand what the users are doing. For example, you might be able to identify if users are having a hard time locating a new feature of the application.

This chapter explains how to get real-time information about your running application to identify any issues that it might have during production or to monitor resource usage to ensure that higher user loads can be accommodated. This is where the namespace `System.Diagnostics.Tracing` comes into play. This namespace offers classes for tracing using Event Tracing for Windows (ETW).

One way to deal with errors in your application, of course, is by throwing exceptions. However, an application might not fail with an exception, but it still doesn't behave as expected. The application might be running well on most systems but have a problem on a few. On the live system, you can change the log by starting a trace collector to get detailed live information about what's going on in the application. You can do this using ETW.

If there are problems with applications, the system administrator needs to be informed. The *Event Viewer* is a commonly used tool that not only the system administrator should be aware of but also the software developer. With the Event Viewer, you can interactively monitor problems with applications and add subscriptions to inform you about specific events that happen. ETW enables you to write information about the application.

Application Insights is a Microsoft Azure cloud service that enables you to monitor apps in the cloud. With just a few lines of code, you can get detailed information about how a web application or service is used.

Visual Studio App Center allows monitoring of Windows and Xamarin apps. After you've registered the app, you need just a few lines of code to receive useful information about the app.

OpenTelemetry (`https://opentelemetry.io`) is a new standard for observing and creating telemetry data in a vendor-neutral way. This becomes important if you create microservices with different technologies; with Open-Telemetry, logging, metrics, and distributed tracing information coming from multiple services developed using different technologies can be collected and analyzed.

This chapter explains these facilities and demonstrates how you can use them for your applications.

The .NET CLI tools used in this chapter to analyze tracing and metrics information are `dotnet trace` and `dotnet counters`. The tools are defined with the project, so you just need to restore the project local tools from a command prompt. Use this command while the current directory is set to the directory of the project:

```
> dotnet tool restore
```

Instead of installing the tools locally, you can install them globally with your user profile. To install the tools globally, run these .NET CLI commands:

```
> dotnet tool install dotnet-trace -g
> dotnet tool install dotnet-counters -g
```

To see the .NET CLI tools that are installed, use this:

```
> dotnet tool list -g
```

> **NOTE** *The sample application built in this chapter is using the* `HttpClient` *class, so you not only add your own logging and metrics information but also can see what logging and metrics information is offered from this class. You can read more information about using the* `HttpClient` *class and the HTTP client factory in Chapter 19, "Networking."*

LOGGING

Over the years, there have been several different logging and tracing facilities with .NET, and there are also many different third-party loggers. Trying to change an application from one logging technology to another one is not an easy task because the use of the ILogger API is spread everywhere in the source code. To make logging independent of any logging technology, you can use interfaces.

Since .NET Core 1.0, .NET has defined the generic `ILogger` interface in the namespace `Microsoft .Extensions.Logging`. This interface defines a `Log` method by passing a log level from the `LogLevel` enumeration, an event ID (using the struct `EventId`), generic state information, an `Exception` type to log exception information, and a formatter to define how the output should look with a string:

```
void Log<TState>(LogLevel logLevel, EventId eventId, TState state,
    Exception, Func<TState, Exception, string> formatter);
```

Other than the `Log` method, the `ILogger` interface also defines the `IsEnabled` method to check whether logging is currently enabled based on a `LogLevel` and the method `BeginScope` that returns a disposable scope for logging. That's practically all that's needed for logging. The `Log` method has many parameters that need to be filled. Extension methods for the `ILogger` interface exist with the `LoggerExtensions` class, such as `LogDebug`, `LogTrace`, `LogInformation`, `LogWarning`, `LogError`, `LogCritical`, and `BeginScope` with several overloads, which makes it easier to use by passing fewer arguments.

The log levels that are defined with the `LogLevel` enum include the following:

➤ `Trace` (level 0): Sensitive information can be written. This should not be enabled with production systems.

➤ `Debug` (level 1): Information useful just for debugging. There's no long-term value in keeping this information.

➤ `Information` (level 2): General flow of the application with long-time value.

➤ `Warning` (level 3): Abnormal or unexpected events happening in the application, but the execution of the application does not stop.

➤ `Error` (level 4): An error happened with the current activity, but it's not an application-wide issue.

➤ `Critical` (level 5): Unrecoverable issue in the application or the system.

Let's make use of the dependency injection and inject the `ILogger` interface in the class `NetworkService` as a generic parameter. The generic parameter defines the category of the logger. With the generic parameter, the category is made of the class name, including the namespace. In addition to the `ILogger` interface, the `HttpClient` is injected to make calls across the network and look at logging information offered by this class (code file `LoggingSample/NetworkService.cs`):

```
class NetworkService
{
  private readonly ILogger _logger;
  private readonly HttpClient _httpClient;
  public NetworkService(
    HttpClient,
    ILogger<NetworkService> logger)
  {
    _httpClient = httpClient;
    _logger = logger;
    _logger.LogTrace("ILogger injected into {0}", nameof(NetworkService));
  }
  //...
}
```

> **NOTE** *Instead of injecting the* `ILogger` *interface, you can also inject* `ILoggerFactory` *and create a logger from the factory. This is extremely practical if you have a hierarchy of service classes and want to inject the logger in a base class but create the category name with the name of the derived class.*
>
> *Later, in the section "Filtering," you can read how the category name can be used to filter the logs.*

The `ILogger` interface can simply be used for invoking an extension method such as `LogInformation` or `LogTrace`:

```
_logger.LogTrace("RunAsync started");
```

The extension methods offer overloads to pass additional parameters, exception information, and an event ID. For using the event ID, a list of event IDs is defined with the application (code file `LoggingSample/LoggingEvents.cs`):

```
class LoggingEvents
{
  public static EventId Injection { get; } =
    new EventId(2000, nameof(Injection));
  public static EventId Networking { get; } =
    new EventId(2002, nameof(Networking));
}
```

Next, `LogInformation` and `LogError` extension methods are used to show the start of the `NetworkRequestSampleAsync` method, when it's finished, and error information in case an exception is thrown (code file `LoggingSample/NetworkService.cs`):

```
class NetworkService
{
  //...

  public async Task NetworkRequestSampleAsync(Uri requestUri)
  {
```

```
    try
    {
      _logger.LogInformation(LoggingEvents.Networking,
        "NetworkRequestSampleAsync started with uri {0}",
        requestUri.AbsoluteUri);

      string result = await _httpClient.GetStringAsync(requestUri);
      Console.WriteLine($"{result[..50]}");
      _logger.LogInformation(LoggingEvents.Networking,
        "NetworkRequestSampleAsync completed, received {length} characters",
        result.Length);
    }
    catch (HttpRequestException ex)
    {
      _logger.LogError(LoggingEvents.Networking, ex,
        "Error in NetworkRequestSampleAsync, error message: {message}, " +
        "HResult: {error}", ex.Message, ex.HResult);
    }
  }
}
```

> **NOTE** *Passing the message to the* LogXX *methods, any number of objects can be supplied that are put into the format message string. This format string uses positional arguments to pass in the following objects, but neither positional numbers (as with the* String .Format *method) nor interpolated strings are used. Without the $ prefix to the strings, you can use string keywords with the curly bracket placeholders. These keywords can then be used for fast queries within log information, e.g., when using Azure Table Storage to store log information.*

The Runner class injects the ILogger interface in addition to the previously defined NetworkService class and writes debug and error messages (code file LoggingSample/NetworkService.cs):

```
class Runner
{
  private readonly ILogger _logger;
  private readonly NetworkService _networkService;
  public Runner(NetworkService networkService, ILogger<Runner> logger)
  {
    _networkService = networkService;
    _logger = logger;
  }

  public async Task RunAsync()
  {
    _logger.LogDebug("RunAsync started");
    bool exit = false;
    do
    {
      Console.Write("Please enter a URI or enter to exit: ");
      string? url = Console.ReadLine();
      if (string.IsNullOrEmpty(url))
```

```
      {
        exit = true;
      }
      else
      {
        try
        {
          Uri uri = new(url);
          await _networkService.NetworkRequestSampleAsync(uri);
        }
        catch (UriFormatException ex)
        {
          _logger.LogError(ex, ex.Message);
        }
      }
    } while (!exit);
  }
}
```

Next, logging providers need to be configured to make the log information available.

Configuring Providers

The `Host` class discussed in Chapter 15, "Dependency Injection and Configuration," preconfigures not only a DI container and configuration providers but also logging. Using the `CreateDefaultBuilder` method of the `Host` class configures these loggers:

➤ **Console:** This provider writes log information to the console.

➤ **Debug:** This provider writes log information to the `System.Diagnotics.Debug` class. With Visual Studio, this goes to the Output window. On Linux systems, depending on the distribution, debug log messages go to /var/log/messages or /var/log/syslog.

➤ **EventSource:** This provider logs with the name `Microsoft-Extensions-Logging`. On Windows, Event Tracing for Windows (ETW) is used.

➤ **EventLog:** This provider is configured only on Windows systems. It writes to the Windows EventLog. This is the only provider configured to write warnings and more critical messages, and it doesn't use the default logging configuration. The Windows EventLog should not be used to log verbose messaging.

Other than the configured providers, `CreateDefaultBuilder` uses the configuration from the configuration section named `Logging`.

For many applications, the default configuration using `CreateDefaultBuilder` will be fine, and you can add more providers as needed. With the sample application, the default logging configuration is not used, so you can better see what and how logging can be configured.

Logging configuration can be customized with the `IHostBuilder` extension method `ConfigureLogging`. With this method, an overloaded version with two parameters is used. Here, the `HostBuilderContext` is the first parameter. This context is used as the sample code is extended to access application configuration. The second parameter is of type `ILoggingBuilder`. With this, you can use extension methods from different providers to customize logging. First, the providers configured from the method `CreateDefaultBuilder` are removed by invoking the method `ClearProviders`. Then logging providers for the console, debug, event source, and event log (if running on Windows) are added (code file `LoggingSample/Program.cs`):

```
using var host = Host.CreateDefaultBuilder(args)
  .ConfigureLogging((context, logging) =>
```

```
  {
    logging.ClearProviders();

    bool isWindows = RuntimeInformation.IsOSPlatform(OSPlatform.Windows);

    logging.AddConsole();
    logging.AddDebug();
    logging.AddEventSourceLogger();

    if (isWindows)
    {
      logging.AddEventLog(); // EventLogLoggerProvider
    }

    //...
  })
  .ConfigureServices(services =>
  {
    services.AddHttpClient<NetworkService>(client =>
    {
    }).AddTypedClient<NetworkService>();
    services.AddScoped<Runner>();
  }).Build();
```

> **NOTE** *The* `ConfigureServices` *method of the* `Host` *class is covered in detail in Chapter 15.*

When you run the application with successful and unsuccessful results, you can see the following output on the console:

```
Please enter a URI or enter to exit: https://csharp.christiannagel.com
info: LoggingSample.NetworkService[2002]
      NetworkRequestSampleAsync started with uri
https://csharp.christiannagel.com/
info: System.Net.Http.HttpClient.NetworkService.LogicalHandler[100]
      Start processing HTTP request GET https://csharp.christiannagel.com/
info: System.Net.Http.HttpClient.NetworkService.ClientHandler[100]
      Sending HTTP request GET https://csharp.christiannagel.com/
info: System.Net.Http.HttpClient.NetworkService.ClientHandler[101]
      Received HTTP response headers after 692.1021ms - 200
info: System.Net.Http.HttpClient.NetworkService.LogicalHandler[101]
      End processing HTTP request after 707.6875ms - 200
<!DOCTYPE html>
<html lang="en">
<head>
<meta char
LoggingSample.NetworkService[2002]
      NetworkRequestSampleAsync completed, received 97126 character
Please enter a URI or enter to exit: info:
```

The log output and other console output may not arrive in the correct order because logging is written and flushed asynchronously to increase performance and reduce the logging overhead.

Passing an invalid hostname results in the error information as shown, including the call stack, because the exception object is passed to the `LogError` method:

```
fail: LoggingSample.Runner[0]
      Invalid URI: The format of the URI could not be determined.
      System.UriFormatException: Invalid URI: The format of the URI could not be
determined.
         at System.Uri.CreateThis(String uri, Boolean dontEscape, UriKind uriKind)
         at System.Uri..ctor(String uriString)
         at LoggingSample.Runner.RunAsync() in
C:\github\ProfessionalCSharp2021\02_Libs\
LoggingMetricsAndTelemetry\LoggingSample\LoggingSample\Runner.cs:line 35
Please enter a URI or enter to exit:
```

Filtering

You don't need all log messages at all times. While the application is running in the production environment, critical information and errors are of interest. While debugging the application, you might set up the configuration to show trace messages for specific trace sources to learn all the things going on in the application. You can define filters just for the logging needs you currently have.

Filtering is possible based on the logger provider and the log categories.

The following code snippet defines a filter for the `EventLogLoggerProvider` and the category name to filter only errors with the log level `Warning` and higher (code file `LoggingSample/Program.cs`):

```
bool isWindows = RuntimeInformation.IsOSPlatform(OSPlatform.Windows);
if (isWindows)
{
  logging.AddFilter<EventLogLoggerProvider>(level =>
    level >= LogLevel.Warning);
}
```

Configure Logging

You can configure filtering and logging using the .NET configuration. By default, when you use the `CreateDefaultBuilder` method from the `Host` class, configuration is retrieved from `appsettings.json`, `appsettings.{environmentname}.json`, environment variables, and command-line arguments, so you can override the configuration from the JSON files from command-line arguments. Read Chapter 15 for more information on the different configuration providers and how to add custom configuration providers.

To access the configuration for the logging providers, the `AddConfiguration` extension method is used with the `ILoggingBuilder` parameter. Configuration values are retrieved within the section `Logging` (code file `LoggingSample/Program.cs`):

```
logging.AddConfiguration(hostingContext.Configuration.GetSection("Logging"));
```

When you add the `LogLevel` entry to the `Logging` section, you can configure default levels for logging. By default, as specified with the `Default` key, `Information` messages and above are logged. An exception is for all log groups that start with `Microsoft`. Here, only the level `Warning` and above is logged. Another exception is for `Microsoft.Hosting.Lifetime`. Namely, `Information` and above messages are logged:

```
    "Logging": {
      "LogLevel": {
        "Default": "Information",
        "Microsoft": "Warning",
```

```
        "Microsoft.Hosting.Lifetime": "Information"
      }
    }
```

You can specify different configuration values for a provider. Here, for the `Console` provider (which matches the simple console), the `LogLevel` is configured to other values for the `LoggingSample` logging category:

```
{
  "Logging": {
    "Console": {
      "LogLevel": {
        "Default": "Information",
        "LoggingSample.NetworkService": "Warning",
        "LoggingSample.Runner": "Warning"
      }
    },
    "LogLevel": {
      "Default": "Warning",
      "Microsoft": "Information",
      "LoggingSample.NetworkService": "Warning"
    }
  }
}
```

Logging and Tracing with OpenTelemetry

To log messages with the OpenTelemetry standard, you need to configure a different logging provider by invoking the `ILoggerBuilder` extension method `AddOpenTelemetry` (NuGet package `OpenTelemetry`) and pass an exporter to the options of this method. The following code snippet adds the Console Exporter from the NuGet package `OpenTelemetry.Exporter.Console` to the Open Telemetry logging (code file `OpenTelemetrySample/Program.cs`):

```
.ConfigureLogging((hostingContext, logging) =>
{
  logging.ClearProviders();
  logging.AddFilter(level => level >= LogLevel.Trace);
  logging.AddOpenTelemetry(options => options.AddConsoleExporter());
  //...
})
```

With this small change to the logging configuration, the log output defined from the methods using the `ILogger` interface is shown with the OpenTelemetry format. The practical use of OpenTelemetry comes when using other exporters such as Jaeger or Prometheus to send the log information to open source or commercial backends. To do this, you just need to configure other exporters—for example, to Jaeger using the NuGet package `OpenTelemetry.Exporter.Jaeger`.

The log output shows empty values for `TraceId` and `SpanId`. These values are important when using distributed tracing. When you read about *tracer* and *span* with OpenTelemetry, .NET uses the terms and classes `ActivitySource` and `Activity`. The following code snippet creates an `ActivitySource` with the `Runner` class as a static internal member that's used to create activities (or spans) for the sample application. It's useful to specify one `ActivitySource` that's shared within the types of a library or a subcomponent. The `ActivitySource` allows enabling and disabling distributed tracing based on the name passed to the constructor (code file `OpenTelemetrySample/Runner.cs`):

```
class Runner
{
```

```
    internal readonly static ActivitySource ActivitySource =
      new("LoggingSample.DistributedTracing");
    //...
}
```

By using this `ActivitySource`, you can create nested activities. With the following code snippet, an activity is created within the `RunAsync` method with the name `Run`. You don't need to pass the activity to the log methods. Instead, the `StartActivity` method sets the static property `Activity.Current`, which is used by all the following log methods to show the IDs (and the logs nested within inner methods, such as the log invocations from the `NetworkService` class). A nested activity is started within the do/while loop (code file `OpenTelemetrySample/Runner.cs`):

```
public async Task RunAsync()
{
  using var activity = ActivitySource.StartActivity("Run");
  _logger.LogDebug("RunAsync started");
  bool exit = false;
  do
  {
    Console.Write("Please enter a URI or enter to exit: ");
    string? url = Console.ReadLine();
    using var urlActivity = ActivitySource.StartActivity(
      "Starting URL Request");
    if (string.IsNullOrEmpty(url))
    {
      exit = true;
    }
    else
    {
      try
      {
        Uri uri = new(url);
        await _networkSevice.NetworkRequestSampleAsync(uri);
      }
      catch (UriFormatException ex)
      {
        _logger.LogError(ex, ex.Message);
      }
    }
  } while (!exit);
}
```

If you create a library, you can use the `Activity` and `ActivitySource` classes without referencing any NuGet package from the OpenTelemetry libraries. The libraries should be independent of how the application collects log information.

Without specifying to collect information from the activity source, the method `ActivitySource.StartActivity` returns `null`. With the following code snippet, the OpenTelemetry SDK is used to configure collection of distributed trace information. The tracer provider builder (as mentioned, the tracer with OpenTelementry is the `ActivitySource`) is configured to collect distributed trace information from the source name that's passed to the `AddSource` method. This needs to be the same name that you passed to the `ActivitySource` constructor. This code requires the NuGet packages `OpenTelemetry` and `OpenTelemetry.Exporter.Console`. To log traces coming from ASP.NET Core, you can add the source with the name `Microsoft.AspNetCore`. The logs are written to the console exporter (code file `OpenTelemetrySample/Program.cs`):

```
using var tracerProvider = Sdk.CreateTracerProviderBuilder()
  .SetResourceBuilder(ResourceBuilder.CreateDefault()
    .AddService("OpenTelemetrySample"))
  .AddSource("LoggingSample.DistributedTracing")
  .AddConsoleExporter()
  .Build();
```

Remember, the console exporter is useful during development and testing. Other exporters such as Jaeger and Prometheus are useful in production environments.

More Logging Providers

On the NuGet server, many more logging providers are available. You can add `Serilog.Extensions.Logging` for easy logging to files. The NuGet package `Microsoft.Extensions.Logging.AzureAppServices` offers logging web applications hosted on Azure App Services to use the Azure App Service diagnostics logs including log live streaming. With the NuGet package `Microsoft.Extensions.Logging.ApplicationInsights`, `ILogger` events are forwarded to Application Insights. Application Insights is covered later in this chapter in the section "Application Insights."

METRICS

With metrics, you can measure actual counts of collected values to analyze issues with the application. You can do live monitoring, collect metrics information over time, and write the information to a file.

The .NET runtime offers metrics information to show CPU usage, heap size, number of objects and memory sizes for the different GC generations, assemblies loaded, and more. Libraries such as EF Core and ASP.NET Core hosting offer metrics data as well.

To read metrics information, you can either access this information in-proc or out-of-proc. In-proc, you can use the `EventListener` class to receive metrics information within the application. Out-of-proc, you can use platform-specific tools such as Event Tracing for Windows (ETW) on Windows systems or Linux Trace Toolkit Next Generation (LLTng) on Linux systems. There's also a platform-independent solution that doesn't give you events from the operating system; it gives you all the .NET-offered events from the .NET runtime and your application and doesn't require admin privileges.

With .NET, to receive metrics information out-of-proc, you can use the `EventPipe` class from the NuGet package `Microsoft.Diagnostics.NETCore.Client`. In this chapter, I use the .NET CLI with the counter tool, which itself is making use of the `EventPipe` class. You don't need to implement a monitoring tool on your own.

EventSource Class

So you can see metric information, the sample application offering logging information is enhanced with metrics. To offer metric information, you need to create a class that derives from the `EventSource` class, which is defined in the namespace `System.Diagnostics.Tracing`.

The class `MetricsSampleSource` derives from the base class `EventSource` and is annotated with the attribute `EventSource`. This attribute gives a name to allow this class as an event source for ETW. To allow instantiation only once, a public static `readonly` `Log` field and a private constructor are defined (code file `MetricsSample/MetricsSampleSource.cs`):

```
[EventSource(Name = "Wrox.ProCSharp.MetricsSample")]
internal class MetricsSampleSource : EventSource
{
  public static readonly MetricsSampleSource Log = new();
  private MetricsSampleSource()
    : base("Wrox.ProCSharp.MetricsSample") { }
  //...
}
```

Metric Counters

In the namespace `System.Diagnostics.Tracing`, four different counter types are defined—`EventCounter`, `IncrementingEventCounter`, `PollingCounter`, and `IncrementingPollingCounter`—that all derive from the base class `DiagnosticCounter`. The two `XXEventCounter` types are the easiest ones to use. You don't need to declare a variable for storing the counter; you just need to write or increment the metric values. With the `EventCounter` type, you write metrics information to invoke the method `WriteMetric`. The `IncrementingEventCounter` class defines the `Increment` method where you can specify a value that should be used for incrementing. With the `XXEventCounter` types, the values are reset depending on the refresh rate used. For example, say that the client application does a refresh once per second. Using the `IncrementingEventCounter` shows the values that have been incremented within the last second. With a refresh rate of 30 seconds, the incremented values within the last 30 seconds are shown.

In cases where you need more control, such as to show counter values since the start of the application, you can use the `XXPollingCounter` types. Polling counters are also required in case the values to show are retrieved from other sources, such as the `GC` class. For example, with the `System.Runtime` counts, to show the memory size of the objects in generation 0, a `PollingCounter` is used that retrieves the value using `GC.GetGenerationSize(0)`:

```
_gen0SizeCounter ??= new PollingCounter("gen-0-size", this,
  () => GC.GetGenerationSize(0))
  {
    DisplayName = "Gen 0 Size",
    DisplayUnits = "B"
  };
```

> **NOTE** *You can see the implementation of the .NET runtime event source at* https://github.com/dotnet/coreclr/blob/master/src/System.Private.CoreLib/src/System/Diagnostics/Eventing/RuntimeEventSource.cs.

With the sample application, this metrics information is offered:

➤ The number of requests based on the specified interval.

➤ The number of errors based on the specified interval.

➤ The time it takes to receive the HTTP request.

In the `MetricsSampleSource` class, to create only the counter types when monitoring is going on, the `OnEventCommand` method is overridden. This method is invoked on enabling, disabling, and updating of the event source. In case monitoring is turned on, the `DiagnosticCounter` derived types are instantiated: two `IncrementingEventCounter` and one `PollingCounter`. With the `PollingCounter`, a variable is declared that is accessed on polling the value. What's common with all the event types is to specify the name and the `EventSource` instance in the constructor. The properties `DisplayName` and `DisplayUnits` can be set with every `DiagnosticCounter`-derived type. With the constructor of the `PollingCounter`, a delegate that returns a `double` needs to be passed with the argument. Because several threads can access the counters simultaneously, this code needs to be thread-safe; that's why the `Interlocked` class from the `System.Threading` namespace is used. With the `XXEventCounter` types, the `DisplayRateTimeScale` specifies the rate at which the value should be retrieved. If you specify 10 seconds, for example, even if the refresh interval for displaying the values is set to 1 second, the values are just retrieved after 10 seconds (code file `MetricsSample/MetricsSampleSource.cs`):

```csharp
internal class MetricsSampleSource : EventSource
{
  //...
  private IncrementingEventCounter? _totalRequestsCounter;
  private IncrementingEventCounter? _errorCounter;
  private long _requestDuration;
  private PollingCounter? _requestDurationCounter;

  protected override void OnEventCommand(EventCommandEventArgs command)
  {
    if (command.Command == EventCommand.Enable)
    {
      _totalRequestsCounter ??= new IncrementingEventCounter("requests", this)
      {
        DisplayName = "Total requests",
        DisplayUnits = "Count",
        DisplayRateTimeScale = TimeSpan.FromSeconds(1)
      };
      _errorCounter ??= new IncrementingEventCounter("errors", this)
      {
        DisplayName = "Errors",
        DisplayUnits = "Count",
        DisplayRateTimeScale = TimeSpan.FromSeconds(1)
      };
      _requestDurationCounter ??= new PollingCounter(
        "request-duration", this, () => Interlocked.Read(ref _requestDuration))
      {
        DisplayName = "Request duration",
        DisplayUnits = "ms"
      };
    }
  }
  //...
}
```

Now just the counters need to be set. The first counter is set in the `RequestStart` method. The `IncrementingEventCounter`, `_totalRequestsCounter`, is incremented using the `Increment` method. To measure the time a request takes, a new `Stopwatch` (namespace `System.Diagnostics`) is created, started, and returned from this method. All this happens only if monitoring is enabled by checking the `IsEnabled` method from the base class:

```csharp
public Stopwatch? RequestStart()
{
  if (IsEnabled())
  {
    _totalRequestsCounter?.Increment();
```

```
        return Stopwatch.StartNew();
    }
    else
    {
        return default;
    }
}
```

The `RequestStop` method defines a parameter to receive the `Stopwatch` created earlier and sets the `ElapsedMilliseconds` with the backing field `_requestDuration`. This field is used by the `PollingCounter` to show the elapsed time. With the nonincrementing counters, the count is set directly. The tool to analyze the counts can calculate an average value based on the values set:

```
public void RequestStop(Stopwatch? stopwatch)
{
    if (stopwatch?.IsRunning == true)
    {
        stopwatch.Stop();
        Interlocked.Exchange(ref _requestDuration, stopwatch.ElapsedMilliseconds);
    }
}
```

> **NOTE** *When you use the* `EventCounter` *for the elapsed time of the request, if a refresh rate of one second is used, the count shows 0 if the value was not set within the last second. When you use the* `PollingCounter`, *you are in more control of the value shown. When you set the value on every request, the value shown is always the time of the last request.*

You can also implement the `Error` method to increment the `_errorCounter`:

```
public void Error()
{
    if (IsEnabled())
    {
        _errorCounter?.Increment();
    }
}
```

Using MetricsSampleSource

Next, the `NetworkService` class is updated to invoke the members of the `MetricsSample` class. With the following code snippet, the logging methods from before are removed for clarity, but they are still available with the downloadable source code. On the start of the request, the `RequestStart` method that returns a `Stopwatch` is invoked. This stopwatch is passed as an argument to the `RequestStop` method. In the case of an `HttpRequestException`, the `Error` method is invoked to increment the error count. To stop the stopwatch in every case, the code is wrapped into a `try/finally` block. Remember, if monitoring is not turned on, invoking the method `RequestStart` does not count metrics, and the `Stopwatch` returned is `null` (code file `MetricsSample/NetworkService.cs`):

```
public async Task NetworkRequestSampleAsync(Uri requestUri)
{
```

```csharp
    var stopWatch = MetricsSampleSource.Log.RequestStart();
    try
    {
      string result = await _httpClient.GetStringAsync(requestUri);
      MetricsSampleSource.Log.RequestStop(stopWatch);
      Console.WriteLine($"{result[..50]}");
    }
    catch (HttpRequestException ex)
    {
      MetricsSampleSource.Log.Error();
    }
    finally
    {
      MetricsSampleSource.Log.RequestStop(stopWatch);
    }
}
```

Monitoring Metrics with .NET CLI

Now that metrics information is in place, let's look at the information that can be accessed with `dotnet-counters`.

To see all the counters available with .NET, use this command:

```
dotnet counters list --runtime-version 5.0
```

The .NET 5 version of `dotnet counters` by default lists the counters available with .NET Core 3.1 (the LTS version). Some more metrics categories are available with .NET 5, which are shown by passing `5.0` to the `--runtime-version` option. The additional metrics categories are `System.Runtime`, `Microsoft .AspNetCore.Hosting`, `Microsoft-AspNetCore-Server-Kestrel`, and `System.Net.Http`.

To monitor the counters from the application, first start the application, and then get the process ID of the running application with the `ps` subcommand:

```
dotnet counters ps
```

This command shows the running .NET applications that can be monitored.

To monitor the running application with the counts offered by the application, use the `monitor` subcommand with the `-p` option to pass the process ID, followed by the category names that should be monitored. Only the category `System.Runtime` is monitored by default; you need to add all other categories that should be shown:

```
dotnet counters monitor -p 2711 Wrox.ProCSharp.MetricsSample
```

Be aware that the categories specified show up only when the counts are activated, so you might not see the `Wrox.ProCSharp.MetricsSample` category on start of monitoring. To use a different refresh interval—for example, to see updates after five seconds—use the option `--refresh-interval 5`. Figure 16-1 shows the output from `dotnet counters` with a running application.

Instead of live monitoring an application, you can create a file to record all counts. Start this command with `dotnet counters collect`. In addition to the options you've seen with the subcommand `monitor`, you can select to create a CSV or JON file with the `--format` option, and you can specify the name of the generated file with the `--name` option.

```
[System.Runtime]
    % Time in GC since last GC (%)                        0
    Allocation Rate (B / 1 sec)                     212.064
    CPU Usage (%)                                         0
    Exception Count (Count / 1 sec)                       0
    GC Fragmentation (%)                                NaN
    GC Heap Size (MB)                                     4
    Gen 0 GC Count (Count / 1 sec)                        0
    Gen 0 Size (B)                                        0
    Gen 1 GC Count (Count / 1 sec)                        0
    Gen 1 Size (B)                                        0
    Gen 2 GC Count (Count / 1 sec)                        0
    Gen 2 Size (B)                                        0
    IL Bytes Jitted (B)                             166.750
    LOH Size (B)                                          0
    Monitor Lock Contention Count (Count / 1 sec)         0
    Number of Active Timers                               2
    Number of Assemblies Loaded                          70
    Number of Methods Jitted                          2.192
    POH (Pinned Object Heap) Size (B)                     0
    ThreadPool Completed Work Item Count (Count / 1 sec) 12
    ThreadPool Queue Length                               0
    ThreadPool Thread Count                               4
    Working Set (MB)                                     48
[Wrox.ProCSharp.MetricsSample]
    Errors (Count / 1 sec)                                0
    Request duration (ms)                               523
    Total requests (Count / 1 sec)                        0
```

FIGURE 16-1

ANALYTICS WITH VISUAL STUDIO APP CENTER

Visual Studio App Center (`https://appcenter.ms`) is Microsoft's entry point to build Windows and mobile apps, distribute apps to beta testers, test apps, extend apps with push notifications, and get user analytics for apps.

You can get reports of users having issues with your apps—for example, you can find out about exceptions—and you can also find out the features users are using from your apps. For example, let's say you have added a new feature to your app. Are users finding the button to activate the feature?

> **NOTE** *Here are some examples of features that users had trouble finding from Microsoft's own products. The Xbox was the first device to offer a user interface with large tiles. The search feature was available directly below the tiles. Although this button was available where it seemed obvious the user would find it, users didn't see it. Microsoft moved the search functionality within a tile, and now users are able to find it.*
>
> *Another example is the physical search button that was available on the Windows Phone. This button was meant to be used to search within apps. Users complained about not having an option to search within email because they didn't think to press this physical button to search for emails. Microsoft changed the functionality. With a newer version, the physical search button was used only to search content from the Web, and the mail app had its own Search button.*
>
> *Windows 8 had a similar issue with search; users didn't use the search functionality from the charms bar to search within apps. Windows 8.1 changed the guideline to use search from the charms bar, and now the app contains its own search box. In Windows 10, there's also an auto suggest box to be used within the app that helps with searching.*

To enable app analytics, you first need to register with the Visual Studio App Center. Don't be afraid of high costs; crash reporting and analytics are available for free. Next, you need to create an app and copy the app secret from the web portal. Then you can create a new blank app (WinUI Desktop) with Visual Studio. To enable analytics, add the NuGet packages `Microsoft.AppCenter`, `Microsoft.AppCenter.Analytics`, and `Microsoft .AppCenter.Crashes` to the project.

With just a few API calls, you're ready to find out issues your users have. In the constructor of the `App` class, add `AppCenter.Start`, and add your previously copied app secret. To enable Analytics, you need to pass the type of the `Analytics` object as the second argument to the `Start` method (code file `WindowsAppAnalytics/ App.xaml.cs`):

```
public App()
{
  this.InitializeComponent();
  this.Suspending += OnSuspending;

  AppCenter.Start("84df09c4-d560-4c46-a44f-a5524c3abb7f",
    typeof(Analytics), typeof(Crashes));
}
```

> **NOTE** *Remember to add your app secret from your app configuration in the Visual Studio App Center to the* App *constructor.*

Now when you run the application, you see user information, when users start the application, locations, and user devices.

To get some more information from users, you need to create calls to `Analytics.TrackEvent`. All the possible events from the app are defined within the class `EventNames` (code file `WindowsAppAnalytics/EventNames.cs`):

```
public class EventNames
{
  public const string ButtonClicked = nameof(ButtonClicked);
  public const string PageNavigation = nameof(PageNavigation);
  public const string CreateMenu = nameof(CreateMenu);
}
```

The sample application contains controls to enable/disable analytics, enter some text, and click a button as shown in Figure 16-2. Events are collected when the `MainWindow` is activated. The `TrackEvent` method requires a string for the event name; this is taken from the `EventNames` class. The second argument of the `TrackEvent` method is optional. Here you can pass a dictionary of strings to track additional information. In the sample code, when the window is opened, the `PageNavigation` event contains information about the type of the page navigated to (code file `WindowsAppAnalytics/MainWindow.xaml.cs`):

```
public MainWindow()
{
  this.InitializeComponent();
  Analytics.TrackEvent(EventNames.PageNavigation,
    new Dictionary<string, string> { ["Page"] = nameof(MainWindow) });
}
```

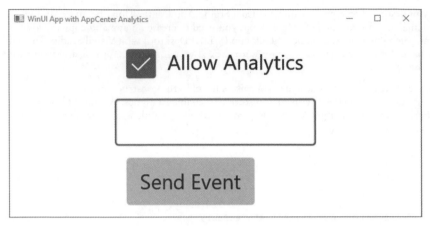

FIGURE 16-2

With the click of the button, `TrackEvent` tracks the `ButtonClick` event, with the information the user entered in the `TextBox` control:

```
private void OnButtonClick(object sender, RoutedEventArgs e)
{
  Analytics.TrackEvent(ButtonClicked,
    new Dictionary<string, string> { ["State"] = textState.Text });
}
```

Users might not agree to having information collected as the user wanders around the app. You can create a setting for the user where the user can enable/disable this functionality. If you set `Analytics.SetEnabledAsync(false)`, the Analytics APIs no longer reports data:

```
private async void OnAnalyticsChanged(object sender, RoutedEventArgs e)
{
  if (sender is CheckBox checkbox)
  {
    bool isChecked = checkbox?.IsChecked ?? true;
    await Analytics.SetEnabledAsync(isChecked);
  }
}
```

Visual Studio App Center has some limits in regard to analytics, as shown in this list:

➤ You can have only up to 200 distinct custom events daily.

➤ An event can have 20 properties (the rest are dropped).

➤ The event name is limited to 256 characters.

➤ Property keys and values are truncated after 128 characters.

When you run the application and monitor the Visual Studio App Center portal, you can see the events that occurred with the number of users (see Figure 16-3). When you click in the events, you can see the event count by user, the events per session, the details of the dictionary properties passed, and a log flow.

Apart from this information, Visual Studio App Center Analytics also gives you information about the following:

➤ Number of active users

➤ Daily sessions per user

➤ Session duration

➤ Top devices

➤ OS versions used

➤ Languages

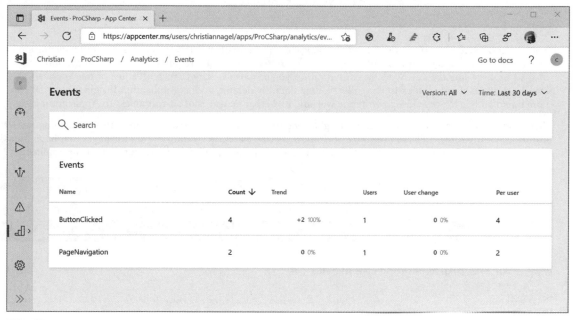

FIGURE 16-3

APPLICATION INSIGHTS

Visual Studio App Center Analytics information is based on Azure Application Insights. With your web or service applications, you can directly use Application Insights.

The sample web app with this chapter consists of an ASP.NET Core Razor web app that accesses a SQL Server database. Read Chapter 26, "Razor Pages and MVC," on creating Razor Pages and how to deploy the web application and the database to Microsoft Azure.

To use diagnostics and telemetry information with Application Insights, you add the NuGet package `Microsoft.ApplicationInsights.AspNetCore` to the project. If you just want to write log information to Application Insights, the NuGet package `Microsoft.Extensions.Logging.ApplicationInsights` can be enough. All that you need to do in the code is enable telemetry information by invoking the `AddApplicationInsightsTelemetry` method with the configuration of the DI container (code file `WebAppWithAppInsights/Startup.cs`):

```
public void ConfigureServices(IServiceCollection services)
{
  services.AddRazorPages();
  services.AddDbContext<BooksContext>(options =>
  {
    options.UseSqlServer(Configuration.GetConnectionString(
      "BooksConnection"));
  });
  services.AddApplicationInsightsTelemetry();
}
```

Without specifying any parameters with this method, the instrumentation key needs to be added to the configuration within the section `ApplicationInsights` and the key name `InstrumentationKey`:

```
{
  "ApplicationInsights": {
    "InstrumentationKey": "add your instrumentation key"
  }
}
```

The method `AddApplicationInsightsTelemetry` offers overloads where you can pass the instrumentation key, or with options the connection string. With some Azure regions you are required to use the connection string instead of just using the key. With the configuration you can also specify to turn off some of the Application Insights options if you don't want to collect all the data. By default, adding Application Insights to the DI container also adds a log provider to write the warning and error messages of all containers to Application Insights.

What data can you see with Application Insights? Figure 16-4 shows live metrics information: incoming requests, duration, failure rates, CPU and memory utilization, as well as telemetry information for pages that have been called. Figure 16-5 shows the application map. Here you see the different Azure resources that the application

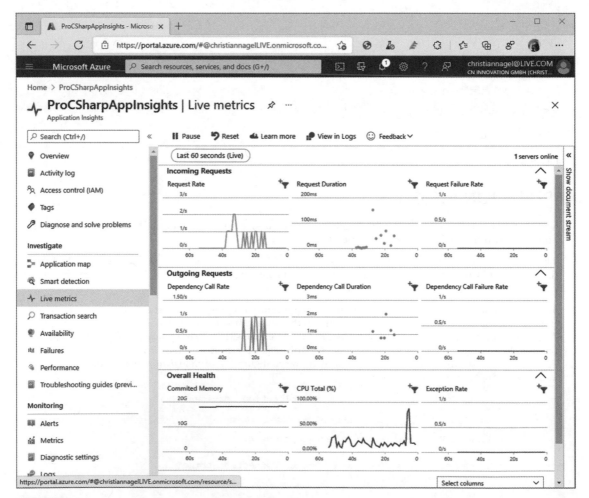

FIGURE 16-4

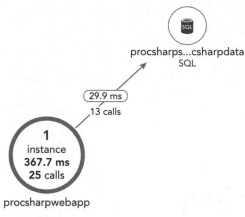

procsharps...csharpdata
SQL

29.9 ms
13 calls

1
instance
367.7 ms
25 calls

procsharpwebapp

FIGURE 16-5

interacts with. With the sample application, it's an Azure SQL database. The application map shows how many times resources have been invoked, the duration, and the error counts. In the case of errors, you can easily see common properties of the errors. Application Insights makes use of artificial intelligence to learn about the normal behavior and timings of the application to give you information about anomalies. You can specify alerts to inform you in different ways. To add information that's not automatically detected, you can inject the `TelemetryClient` in your Razor pages, controllers, or services, and report additional information invoking the `TrackEvent` method.

SUMMARY

In this chapter, you looked at logging and metrics facilities that can help you find intermittent problems in your applications. You should plan early and build these features into your applications; doing so will help you avoid many troubleshooting problems later.

With logging, you can write messages for debugging that help with analyzing the application, as well as exceptions and warnings that also help with running the application in production. You also have the flexibility to define different logging configurations based on the logging category as well as the logging providers.

You can use metrics to analyze counts reported from the runtime as well as different .NET libraries, and you can add your own counts as well.

With Visual Studio App Center Analytics, you've seen that many features come out of the box when you use this cloud service. You can easily get information from your users with just a few lines of code. If you add some more lines, you can find out if users don't use some new features of the app because they might have trouble finding them.

Application Insights is a great service for your Azure resources but can also be used from your on-premises environment to collect and analyze information about the application and quickly find issues.

The next chapter goes into the details of parallel programming with the `Task` and `Parallel` classes as well as synchronization objects that help you use multiple cores from the operating system. Issues that come up when you use multiple tasks are covered as well.

17

Parallel Programming

WHAT'S IN THIS CHAPTER?

- ➤ Understanding multithreading
- ➤ Working with the `Parallel` class
- ➤ Working with tasks
- ➤ Using the Cancellation framework
- ➤ Publish/subscribe with channels
- ➤ Working with timers
- ➤ Understanding threading issues
- ➤ Using the lock keyword
- ➤ Synchronizing with Monitor
- ➤ Synchronizing with mutexes
- ➤ Working with semaphores
- ➤ Using `ManualResetEvent`, `AutoResetEvent`, and `CountdownEvent`
- ➤ Working with `Barrier`
- ➤ Managing readers and writers with `ReaderWriterLockSlim`

CODE DOWNLOADS FOR THIS CHAPTER

The source code for this chapter is available on the book page at www.wiley.com. Click the Downloads link. The code can also be found at https://github.com/ProfessionalCSharp/ProfessionalCSharp2021 in the directory 2_Libs/Parallel.

The code for this chapter is divided into the following major examples:

- ➤ Parallel
- ➤ Task
- ➤ Cancellation
- ➤ ChannelSample
- ➤ Timer
- ➤ WinAppTimer
- ➤ ThreadingIssues
- ➤ SynchronizationSamples
- ➤ BarrierSample
- ➤ ReaderWriterLockSample
- ➤ LockAcrossAwait

Samples from this chapter make use of the `System.Threading`, `System.Threading.Tasks`, and `System.Linq` namespaces. All the projects have nullable reference types enabled.

OVERVIEW

There are several reasons for using multiple threads. Suppose you are making a network call from an application that might take some time. You don't want to stall the user interface and force the user to wait idly until the response is returned from the server. The user could perform some other actions in the meantime or even cancel the request that was sent to the server. Using threads can help.

For all activities that require a wait—for example, because of file, database, or network access—you can start a new thread to fulfill other activities at the same time. Even if you have only processing-intensive tasks to do, threading can help. Multiple threads of a single process can run on different CPUs, or, nowadays, on different cores of a multiple-core CPU, at the same time.

You must be aware of some issues when running multiple threads, however. Because they can run during the same time, you can easily get into problems if the threads access the same data. To avoid that, you must implement synchronization mechanisms.

.NET offers an abstraction mechanism for threads: tasks. Tasks allow building relations between tasks—for example, one task should continue when the first one is completed. You can also build a hierarchy consisting of multiple tasks.

Instead of using tasks, you can implement parallel activities using the `Parallel` class. You need to differentiate *data parallelism* where working with some data is processed simultaneously between different tasks, or *task parallelism* where different functions are executed simultaneously.

When creating parallel programs, you have a lot of different options. You should use the simplest option that fits your scenario. This chapter starts with the `Parallel` class, which offers easy parallelism. If this is all you need, just use this class. If you need more control, such as when you need to manage a relation between tasks or to define a method that returns a task, the `Task` class is the way to go.

This chapter also covers the data flow library, which might be the easiest one to use if you need actor-based programming to flow data through pipelines.

If you need even more control over parallelism, such as setting priorities, the `Thread` class might be the one to use.

> **NOTE** *The use of asynchronous methods with the async and await keywords is covered in Chapter 11, "Tasks and Asynchronous Programming."*
>
> *One variant of task parallelism is offered by Parallel LINQ, which is covered in Chapter 9, "Language Integrated Query."*

Creating a program that runs multiple tasks in parallel can lead to race conditions and deadlocks. You need to be aware of synchronization techniques.

It is best when you can avoid synchronization by not sharing data between threads. Of course, this is not always possible. If data sharing is necessary, you must use synchronization so that only one task at a time accesses and changes the shared state. If you don't pay attention to synchronization, race conditions and deadlocks can apply. A big issue with race conditions and deadlocks is that errors occur inconsistently and behave differently with release and debug builds. With a higher number of CPU cores, error numbers can increase. Such errors usually are hard to find. So, it's best to pay attention to synchronization from the beginning. In the section "Threading Issues," you'll see samples for race conditions and deadlocks.

Using multiple tasks is easy if the tasks don't access the same variables. You can avoid this situation to a certain degree, but at some point, you will find some data needs to be shared. When sharing data, you need to apply synchronization techniques. When threads access the same data and you don't apply synchronization, you are lucky when the problem pops up immediately. However, this is rarely the case. This chapter shows race conditions and deadlocks and how you can avoid them by applying synchronization mechanisms.

.NET offers several options for synchronization. You can use synchronization objects within a process or across processes. You can use them to synchronize one task or multiple tasks to access one or more resources. Synchronization objects can also be used to inform tasks that something completed. All these synchronization objects are covered in this chapter.

> **NOTE** *The need for synchronization can be partly avoided by using immutable data structures as much as possible. With immutable data structures, the data can be initialized but cannot be changed afterward. That's why synchronization is not needed with these types.*

Now that we're grounded in the basics of multithreading and tasks, let's start with the `Parallel` class—an uncomplicated way to add parallelism to your application.

PARALLEL CLASS

One great abstraction of threads is the `Parallel` class. With this class, both data and task parallelism are offered. This class is in the namespace `System.Threading.Tasks`.

The `Parallel` class defines static methods for a parallel `for` and `foreach`. With the C# statements `for` and `foreach`, the loop is run from one thread. The `Parallel` class uses multiple tasks and, thus, multiple threads for this job.

Whereas the `Parallel.For` and `Parallel.ForEach` methods invoke the same code during each iteration, `Parallel.Invoke` enables you to invoke different methods concurrently. `Parallel.Invoke` is for task parallelism, and `Parallel.ForEach` is for data parallelism.

Looping with the Parallel.For Method

The `Parallel.For` method is like the C# `for` loop statement for performing a task a number of times. With `Parallel.For`, the iterations run in parallel. The order of iteration is not defined.

> **NOTE** *This sample makes use of command-line arguments. To work through the different features, pass different arguments as shown on startup of the sample application or check the top-level statements. From Visual Studio, you can pass command-line arguments in the Debug options of the project properties. Using the* `dotnet` *command line, to pass the command-line argument* -p, *you can start the command* `dotnet run -- -p`.

To get the information about the thread and the task, the following `Log` method writes thread and task identifiers to the console (code file `ParallelSamples/ParallelSamples/Program.cs`):

```
public static void Log(string prefix) =>
   Console.WriteLine($"{prefix}, task: {Task.CurrentId}, " +
      $"thread: {Thread.CurrentThread.ManagedThreadId}");
```

Let's look at the `Parallel.For` method. With this method, the first two parameters define the start and end of the loop. The following example has the iterations from 0 to 9. The third parameter is an `Action<int>` delegate. The integer parameter is the iteration of the loop that is passed to the method referenced by the delegate. The return type of `Parallel.For` is the struct `ParallelLoopResult`, which provides information if the loop is completed:

```
public static void ParallelFor()
{
   ParallelLoopResult result =
      Parallel.For(0, 10, i =>
      {
         Log($"S {i}");
         Task.Delay(10).Wait();
         Log($"E {i}");
      });
   Console.WriteLine($"Is completed: {result.IsCompleted}");
}
```

In the body of `Parallel.For`, the index, task identifier, and thread identifier are written to the console. As shown in the following output, the order is not guaranteed. You will see different results if you run this program once more. This run of the program had the order 1-7-2-0-3 and so on with 10 tasks and 10 threads. A task does not necessarily map to one thread; a thread can be reused by different tasks.

```
S 1 task: 1, thread: 4
S 7 task: 8, thread: 10
S 2 task: 2, thread: 5
S 0 task: 3, thread: 1
S 3 task: 4, thread: 6
S 4 task: 5, thread: 7
S 5 task: 6, thread: 9
S 6 task: 7, thread: 8
S 8 task: 9, thread: 11
E 1 task: 1, thread: 4
E 6 task: 7, thread: 8
E 3 task: 4, thread: 6
```

```
E 8 task: 9, thread: 11
E 0 task: 3, thread: 1
E 5 task: 6, thread: 9
E 4 task: 5, thread: 7
E 2 task: 2, thread: 5
S 9 task: 10, thread: 12
E 7 task: 8, thread: 10
E 9 task: 10, thread: 12
Is completed: True
```

The delay within the parallel body waits for 10 milliseconds to have a better chance to create new threads. If you remove this line, you see fewer threads and tasks to be used.

What you can also see with the result is that every end log of a loop uses the same thread and task as the start log. Using `Task.Delay` with the `Wait` method blocks the current thread until the delay ends.

Change the previous example to now use the `await` keyword with the `Task.Delay` method (code file ParallelSamples/ParallelSamples/Program.cs):

```
public static void ParallelForWithAsync()
{
  ParallelLoopResult result =
    Parallel.For(0, 10, async i =>
    {
      Log($"S {i}");
      await Task.Delay(10);
      Log($"E {i}");
    });
  Console.WriteLine($"is completed: {result.IsCompleted}");
}
```

The result is in the following console output snippet. With the output after the `Thread.Delay` method, you can see the thread change. For example, loop iteration 1, which had thread ID 4 before the delay, has thread ID 7 after the delay. You can also see that tasks no longer exist—there are only threads—and here previous threads are reused. Another important aspect is that the `For` method of the `Parallel` class is completed without waiting for the delay. The `Parallel` class waits for the tasks it created, but it doesn't wait for other background activity. It is also possible that you won't see the output from the methods after the delay at all—if the main thread (which is a foreground thread) is finished, all the background threads are stopped.

```
S 3 task: 1, thread: 6
S 1 task: 6, thread: 4
S 2 task: 8, thread: 5
S 0 task: 4, thread: 1
S 7 task: 5, thread: 11
S 8 task: 2, thread: 10
S 4 task: 7, thread: 8
S 6 task: 9, thread: 9
S 5 task: 3, thread: 7
S 9 task: 1, thread: 6
Is completed: True
E 5 task: , thread: 11
E 8 task: , thread: 7
E 1 task: , thread: 7
E 4 task: , thread: 8
E 0 task: , thread: 6
E 6 task: , thread: 5
E 2 task: , thread: 10
```

```
E 9 task: , thread: 4
E 7 task: , thread: 11
E 3 task: , thread: 9
```

> **WARNING** *As demonstrated here, although using async features with .NET and C# is easy, it's still important to know what's happening behind the scenes, and you have to pay attention to some issues.*

Stopping Parallel.For Early

You can also break Parallel.For early without looping through all the iterations. A method overload of the For method accepts a third parameter of type Action<int, ParallelLoopState>. By defining a method with these parameters, you can influence the outcome of the loop by invoking the Break or Stop method of the ParallelLoopState.

Remember, the order of iterations is not defined (code file ParallelSamples/ParallelSamples/Program.cs):

```
public static void StopParallelForEarly()
{
  ParallelLoopResult result =
    Parallel.For(10, 40, (int i, ParallelLoopState pls) =>
    {
      Log($"S {i}");
      if (i > 12)
      {
        pls.Break();
        Log($"break now... {i}");
      }
      Task.Delay(10).Wait();
      Log($"E {i}");
    });
  Console.WriteLine($"Is completed: {result.IsCompleted}");
  Console.WriteLine($"lowest break iteration: {result.LowestBreakIteration}");
}
```

This run of the application demonstrates that the iteration breaks up with a value higher than 12, but other tasks can simultaneously run, and tasks with other values can run. All the tasks that have been started before the break can continue to the end. You can use the LowestBreakIteration property to ignore results from tasks that you do not need:

```
S 10 task: 1, thread: 1
S 22 task: 5, thread: 8
S 34 task: 9, thread: 11
break now 34 task: 9, thread: 11
S 13 task: 2, thread: 4
break now 13 task: 2, thread: 4
S 28 task: 7, thread: 9
break now 28 task: 7, thread: 9
S 16 task: 3, thread: 5
break now 16 task: 3, thread: 5
S 19 task: 4, thread: 6
break now 19 task: 4, thread: 6
S 31 task: 0, thread: 10
```

```
break now 31 task: 8, thread: 10
S 25 task: 6, thread: 7
break now 25 task: 6, thread: 7
break now 22 task: 5, thread: 8
E 28 task: 7, thread: 9
S 11 task: 10, thread: 12
E 10 task: 1, thread: 1
S 12 task: 1, thread: 1
E 31 task: 8, thread: 10
E 13 task: 2, thread: 4
E 34 task: 9, thread: 11
E 25 task: 6, thread: 7
E 19 task: 4, thread: 6
E 16 task: 3, thread: 5
E 22 task: 5, thread: 8
E 11 task: 10, thread: 12
E 12 task: 1, thread: 1
Is completed: False
lowest break iteration: 13
```

Parallel.For Initialization

Parallel.For might use several threads to do the loops. If you need an initialization that should be done with every thread, you can use the Parallel.For<TLocal> method. The generic version of the For method accepts—in addition to the from and to values—three delegate parameters. The first parameter is of type Func<TLocal>. Because the example here uses a string for TLocal, the method needs to be defined as Func<string>, a method returning a string. This method is invoked only once for each thread that is used to do the iterations.

The second delegate parameter defines the delegate for the body. In the example, the parameter is of type Func<int, ParallelLoopState, string, string>. The first parameter is the loop iteration; the second parameter, ParallelLoopState, enables stopping the loop, as shown earlier. With the third parameter, the body method receives the value that is returned from the init method. The body method also needs to return a value of the type that was defined with the generic For parameter.

The last parameter of the For method specifies a delegate, Action<TLocal>; in the example, a string is received. This method, a thread exit method, is called only once for each thread (code file ParallelSamples/ParallelSamples/Program.cs):

```csharp
public static void ParallelForWithInit()
{
  Parallel.For<string>(0, 10, () =>
  {
    // invoked once for each thread
    Log($"init thread");
    return $"t{Thread.CurrentThread.ManagedThreadId}";
  },
  (i, pls, str1) =>
  {
    // invoked for each member
    Log($"body i {i} str1 {str1}");
    Task.Delay(10).Wait();
    return $"i {i}";
  },
  (str1) =>
```

```
  {
    // final action on each thread
    Log($"finally {str1}");
  });
}
```

When you run the application with the option -pfi, you can see that the `init` method is called only once for each thread; the body of the loop receives the first string from the initialization and passes this string to the next iteration of the body with the same thread. Lastly, the final action is invoked once for each thread and receives the last result from everybody.

With this functionality, this method fits perfectly to accumulate a result of a huge data collection.

Looping with the Parallel.ForEach Method

`Parallel.ForEach` iterates through a collection implementing `IEnumerable` in a similar way to the `foreach` statement but in an asynchronous manner. Again, the order is not guaranteed (code file `ParallelSamples/ParallelSamples/Program.cs`):

```
public static void ParallelForEach()
{
  string[] data = {"zero", "one", "two", "three", "four", "five",
  "six", "seven", "eight", "nine", "ten", "eleven", "twelve"};
  ParallelLoopResult result =
    Parallel.ForEach<string>(data, s =>
    {
      Console.WriteLine(s);
    });
}
```

If you need to break up the loop, you can use an overload of the `ForEach` method with a `ParallelLoopState` parameter. You can do this in the same way you did earlier with the `For` method. An overload of the `ForEach` method can also be used to access an indexer to get the iteration number, as shown here:

```
Parallel.ForEach<string>(data, (s, pls, l) =>
{
  Console.WriteLine($"{s} {l}");
});
```

Invoking Multiple Methods with the Parallel.Invoke Method

If multiple tasks should run in parallel, you can use the `Parallel.Invoke` method, which offers the task parallelism pattern. `Parallel.Invoke` allows the passing of an array of `Action` delegates, whereby you can assign methods that should run. The example code passes the `Foo` and `Bar` methods to be invoked in parallel (code file `ParallelSamples/Program.cs`):

```
public static void ParallelInvoke()
{
  Parallel.Invoke(Foo, Bar, Foo, Bar, Foo, Bar);
}

public static void Foo() =>
  Console.WriteLine("foo");

public static void Bar() =>
  Console.WriteLine("bar");
```

When you run the application multiple times and invoke the `Parallel.Invoke` method, you'll see the order of invocations is not always the same.

The `Parallel` class is easy to use—for both task and data parallelism. If more control is needed and you don't want to wait until the action started with the `Parallel` class is completed, the `Task` class comes in handy. Of course, it's also possible to combine the `Task` and `Parallel` classes.

TASKS

For more control over the parallel actions, you can use the `Task` class from the namespace `System.Threading.Tasks`. A *task* represents some unit of work that should be done. This unit of work can run in a separate thread, and it is also possible to start a task in a synchronized manner, which results in a wait for the calling thread. With tasks, you have an abstraction layer but also a lot of control over the underlying threads.

Tasks provide much more flexibility in organizing the work you need to do. For example, you can define continuation work—what should be done after a task is complete. This can be differentiated based on whether the task was successful. You can also organize tasks in a hierarchy. For example, a parent task can create new children tasks. Optionally, this can create a dependency, so canceling a parent task also cancels its child tasks.

Starting Tasks

To start a task, you can use either `TaskFactory` or the constructor of the `Task` and the `Start` method. The `Task` constructor gives you more flexibility in creating the task.

When starting a task, an instance of the `Task` class can be created, and the code that should run can be assigned with an `Action` or `Action<object>` delegate, with either no parameters or one object parameter. In the following example, a method is defined with one parameter: `TaskMethod`. The implementation invokes the `Log` method where the ID of the task and the ID of the thread are written to the console, as well as information indicating whether the thread is coming from a thread pool and whether the thread is a background thread. Writing multiple messages to the console is synchronized by using the `lock` keyword with the `s_logLock` synchronization object (for synchronization, you can use any reference-type object). This way, parallel calls to `Log` can be done, and multiple writes to the console are not interleaving each other. Otherwise, the `title` could be written by one task, and the thread information that follows by another task (code file `ParallelSamples/TaskSamples/Program.cs`):

```
public static void TaskMethod(object? o)
{
  Log(o?.ToString() ?? string.Empty);
}

private static readonly object s_logLock = new();
public static void Log(string title)
{
  lock (s_logLock)
  {
    Console.WriteLine(title);
    Console.WriteLine($"Task id: {Task.CurrentId?.ToString() ?? "no task"}, " +
      $"thread: {Thread.CurrentThread.ManagedThreadId}");
    Console.WriteLine($"is pooled thread: " +
      $"{Thread.CurrentThread.IsThreadPoolThread}");
    Console.WriteLine($"is background thread: " +
      $"{Thread.CurrentThread.IsBackground}");
    Console.WriteLine();
  }
}
```

The following sections describe different ways to start a new task.

Tasks Using the Thread Pool

In this section, diverse ways are shown to start a task that uses a thread from the thread pool. The thread pool offers a pool of background threads. The thread pool manages threads on its own, increasing or decreasing the number of threads within the pool as needed. Threads from the pool are used to fulfill some actions and returned to the pool afterward.

The first way to create a task is with an instantiated `TaskFactory`, where the method `TaskMethod` is passed to the `StartNew` method, and the task is immediately started. The second approach uses the static `Factory` property of the `Task` class to get access to the `TaskFactory` and to invoke the `StartNew` method. This is similar to the first version in that it uses a factory, but there's less control over factory creation. The third approach uses the constructor of the `Task` class. When the `Task` object is instantiated, the task does not run immediately. Instead, it is given the status `Created`. The task is then started by calling the `Start` method of the `Task` class. The fourth approach calls the `Run` method of the `Task` that immediately starts the task. The `Run` method doesn't have an overloaded variant to pass an `Action<object>` delegate, but it's easy to simulate this by assigning a lambda expression of type `Action` and using the parameter within its implementation (code file `ParallelSamples/TaskSamples/Program.cs`):

```
public void TasksUsingThreadPool()
{
  TaskFactory tf = new();
  Task t1 = tf.StartNew(TaskMethod, "using a task factory");
  Task t2 = Task.Factory.StartNew(TaskMethod, "factory via a task");
  Task t3 = new(TaskMethod, "using a task constructor and Start");
  t3.Start();
  Task t4 = Task.Run(() => TaskMethod("using the Run method"));
}
```

The output returned with these variants is as follows. All these versions create a new task, and a thread from the thread pool is used. The output can differ any time you run it:

```
using a task factory
Task id: 1, thread: 4
is pooled thread: True
is background thread: True

factory via a task
Task id: 2, thread: 3
is pooled thread: True
is background thread: True

using a task constructor and Start
Task id: 3, thread: 5
is pooled thread: True
is background thread: True

using the Run method
Task id: 4, thread: 7
is pooled thread: True
is background thread: True
```

With both the `Task` constructor and the `StartNew` method of the `TaskFactory`, you can pass values from the enumeration `TaskCreationOptions`. Using this creation option, you can change how the task should behave differently, as is shown in the next sections.

Synchronous Tasks

A task does not necessarily need to use a thread from a thread pool—it can use other threads as well. Tasks can also run synchronously with the same thread as the calling thread. The following code snippet uses the method RunSynchronously of the Task class (code file ParallelSamples/TaskSamples/Program.cs):

```
private static void RunSynchronousTask()
{
  TaskMethod("just the main thread");
  Task t1 = new(TaskMethod, "run sync");
  t1.RunSynchronously();
}
```

Here, the TaskMethod is first called directly from the main thread before it is invoked from the newly created Task. As you can see from the following console output, the main thread doesn't have a task ID. It is not a pooled thread. Calling the method RunSynchronously uses the same thread as the calling thread but creates a task if one wasn't created previously:

```
just the main thread
Task id: no task, thread: 1
is pooled thread: False
is background thread: False

run sync
Task id: 1, thread: 1
is pooled thread: False
is background thread: False
```

Tasks Using a Separate Thread

If the code of a task should run for a longer time, you should use TaskCreationOptions.LongRunning to instruct the task scheduler to create a new thread rather than use a thread from the thread pool. This way, the thread doesn't need to be managed by the thread pool. When a thread is taken from the thread pool, the task scheduler can decide to wait for an already running task to be completed and use this thread instead of creating a new thread with the pool. With a long-running thread, the task scheduler knows immediately that it doesn't make sense to wait for this one. The following code snippet creates a long-running task (code file ParallelSamples/TaskSamples/Program.cs):

```
private static void LongRunningTask()
{
  Task t1 = new(TaskMethod, "long running", TaskCreationOptions.LongRunning);
  t1.Start();
}
```

Indeed, when you use the option TaskCreationOptions.LongRunning, a thread from the thread pool is not used. Instead, a new thread is created:

```
long running
Task id: 1, thread: 4
is pooled thread: False
is background thread: True
```

Results from Tasks

When a task is finished, it can write some state information to a shared object. Such a shared object must be thread-safe. Another option is to use a task that returns a result. Such a task is also known as *future* because it returns a result in the future. With early versions of the Task Parallel Library (TPL), the class had the name

Future as well. Now it is a generic version of the `Task` class. With this class, it is possible to define the type of the result that is returned with a task.

A method that is invoked by a task to return a result can be declared with any return type. The following example method `TaskWithResult` returns two int values with the help of a tuple. The input of the method can be void or of type `object`, as shown here (code file `ParallelSamples/TaskSamples/Program.cs`):

```
public static (int Result, int Remainder) TaskWithResult(object division)
{
    (int x, int y) = ((int x, int y))division;
    int result = x / y;
    int remainder = x % y;
    Console.WriteLine("task creates a result...");
    return (result, remainder);
}
```

> **NOTE** *Tuples allow you to combine multiple values into one. Tuples are explained in Chapter 3, "Classes, Records, Structs, and Tuples."*

When you define a task to invoke the method `TaskWithResult`, you use the generic class `Task<TResult>`. The generic parameter defines the return type. With the constructor, the method is passed to the `Func` delegate, and the second parameter defines the input value. Because this task needs two input values in the `object` parameter, a tuple is created as well. Next, the task is started. The `Result` property of the `Task` instance `t1` blocks and waits until the task is completed. Upon task completion, the `Result` property contains the result from the task:

```
public static void TaskWithResultDemo()
{
    Task<(int Result, int Remainder)> t1 = new(TaskWithResult, (8, 3));
    t1.Start();
    Console.WriteLine(t1.Result);
    t1.Wait();
    Console.WriteLine($"result from task: {t1.Result.Result} " +
        $"{t1.Result.Remainder}");
}
```

Continuation Tasks

With tasks, you can specify that after a task is finished, another specific task should start to run—for example, a new task that uses a result from the previous one or should do some cleanup if the previous task failed.

Whereas the task handler has either no parameter or one object parameter, the continuation handler has a parameter of type `Task`. Here, you can access information about the originating task (code file `ParallelSamples/TaskSamples/Program.cs`):

```
private static void DoOnFirst()
{
    Console.WriteLine($"doing some task {Task.CurrentId}");
    Task.Delay(3000).Wait();
}
```

```
private static void DoOnSecond(Task t)
{
  Console.WriteLine($"task {t.Id} finished");
  Console.WriteLine($"this task id {Task.CurrentId}");
  Console.WriteLine("do some cleanup");
  Task.Delay(3000).Wait();
}
```

A continuation task is defined by invoking the ContinueWith method on a task. You could also use TaskFactory for this. t1.OnContinueWith(DoOnSecond) means that a new task invoking the method DoOnSecond should be started as soon as the task t1 is finished. You can start multiple tasks when one task is finished, and a continuation task can have another continuation task, as this next example demonstrates (code file ParallelSamples/TaskSamples/Program.cs):

```
public static void ContinuationTasks()
{
  Task t1 = new(DoOnFirst);
  Task t2 = t1.ContinueWith(DoOnSecond);
  Task t3 = t1.ContinueWith(DoOnSecond);
  Task t4 = t2.ContinueWith(DoOnSecond);
  t1.Start();
}
```

So far, the continuation tasks have been started when the previous task was finished, regardless of the result. With values from TaskContinuationOptions, you can define that a continuation task should start only if the originating task was successful (or faulted). Some of the possible values are OnlyOnFaulted, NotOnFaulted, OnlyOnCanceled, NotOnCanceled, and OnlyOnRanToCompletion:

```
Task t5 = t1.ContinueWith(DoOnError, TaskContinuationOptions.OnlyOnFaulted);
```

Task Hierarchies

With task continuations, one task is started after another. Tasks can also form a hierarchy. When a task starts a new task, a parent/child hierarchy is started.

In the code snippet that follows, within the task of the parent, a new task object is created, and the task is started. The code for creating a child task is the same as that for a parent task. The only difference is that the task is created from within another task (code file ParallelSamples/TaskSamples/Program.cs):

```
public static void ParentAndChild()
{
  Task parent = new(ParentTask);
  parent.Start();
  Task.Delay(2000).Wait();
  Console.WriteLine(parent.Status);
  Task.Delay(4000).Wait();
  Console.WriteLine(parent.Status);
}

private static void ParentTask()
{
  Console.WriteLine($"task id {Task.CurrentId}");
  Task child = new(ChildTask);
  child.Start();
  Task.Delay(1000).Wait();
  Console.WriteLine("parent started child");
}
```

```
private static void ChildTask()
{
  Console.WriteLine("child");
  Task.Delay(5000).Wait();
  Console.WriteLine("child finished");
}
```

If the parent task is finished before the child task, the status of the parent task is shown as `WaitingFor-ChildrenToComplete`. The parent task is completed with the status `RanToCompletion` as soon as all children tasks are completed as well. Of course, this is not the case if the parent creates a task with the `TaskCreation-Option DetachedFromParent`.

Canceling a parent task also cancels the children. The cancellation framework is discussed later.

Returning Tasks from Methods

A method that returns a task with results is declared to return `Task<T>`—for example, a method that returns a task with a collection of strings:

```
public Task<IEnumerable<string>> TaskMethodAsync()
{
}
```

Methods that access the network or data are usually implemented in an asynchronous way to return a Task. The Task can then be used to retrieve the results (for example, by using the `async` keyword as explained in Chapter 11). If you have a synchronous path or need to implement an interface that is defined that way with synchronous code, there's no need to create a task for the sake of the result value. The `Task` class offers the ability to create a result with a completed task that is finished with the status `RanToCompletion` using the method `FromResult`:

```
return Task.FromResult<IEnumerable<string>>(
  new List<string>() { "one", "two" });
```

Waiting for Tasks

You've probably already seen the `WhenAll` and `WaitAll` methods of the `Task` class and wondered what the difference might be. Both methods wait for all tasks that are passed to them to complete. The `WaitAll` method blocks the calling task until all tasks that are waited for are completed. The `WhenAll` method returns a task that in turn allows you to use the `async` keyword to wait for the result, and it does not block the waiting task.

Although the `WhenAll` and `WaitAll` methods are finished when all the tasks you are waiting for are completed, you can wait for just one task of a list to be completed with `WhenAny` and `WaitAny`. Like the `WhenAll` and `WaitAll` methods, the `WaitAny` method blocks the calling task, whereas `WhenAny` returns a task that can be awaited.

A method that already has been used several times with several samples is the `Task.Delay` method. You can specify a number of milliseconds to wait before the task that is returned from this method is completed.

You can invoke the `Task.Yield` method to give up the CPU and thus allow other tasks to run. If no other task is waiting to run, the task calling `Task.Yield` continues immediately. Otherwise, it needs to wait until the CPU is scheduled again for the calling task.

Value Tasks

In case a method sometimes runs asynchronously, but not always, the `Task` class might be some overhead that's not needed. .NET now offers `ValueTask`, which is a struct compared to the `Task` that is a class; thus, the `ValueTask` doesn't have the overhead of an object in the heap. Usually when invoking asynchronous methods, such as making calls to an API server or a database, the overhead of the `Task` type can be ignored compared to the time needed for the work to be done. However, there are some cases where the overhead cannot be ignored, such as when a method is called thousands of times, and it rarely really needs a call across the network. This is a scenario where the `ValueTask` becomes handy.

Let's check out an example. The method `GetTheRealData` simulates a method that usually takes a long time, accessing data from the network or a database. Here, sample data is generated with the `Enumerable` class. The time and data are both retrieved, and a result in the form of a tuple is returned. This method returns a `Task` as we are used to (code file `ParallelSamples/ValueTaskSample/Program.cs`):

```
public static Task<(IEnumerable<string> data, DateTime retrievedTime)>
  GetTheRealData() =>
    Task.FromResult(
      (Enumerable.Range(0, 10)
        .Select(x => $"item {x}").AsEnumerable(), DateTime.Now));
```

The interesting part now follows in the method `GetSomeData`. This method is declared to return a `ValueTask`. With the implementation, first a check is done if cached data is not older than five seconds. If the cached data is not older, the cached data is directly returned and passed to the `ValueTask` constructor. This doesn't really need a background thread; the data can be directly returned. If the cache is older, the `GetTheRealData` method is invoked. This method needs a real task and could occur with some delay (code file `ParallelSamples/ValueTaskSample/Program.cs`):

```
private static DateTime _retrieved;
private static IEnumerable<string> _cachedData;
public static async ValueTask<IEnumerable<string>> GetSomeDataAsync()
{
  if (_retrieved >= DateTime.Now.AddSeconds(-5))
  {
    Console.WriteLine("data from the cache");
    return await new ValueTask<IEnumerable<string>>(_cachedData);
  }

  Console.WriteLine("data from the service");
  (_cachedData, _retrieved) = await GetTheRealData();
  return _cachedData;
}
```

> **NOTE** *The constructor of the* `ValueTask` *accepts type* `TResult` *for the data to be returned, or it accepts* `Task<TResult>` *to supply a* `Task` *returned from methods that do run asynchronously.*

The `Main` method includes a loop to invoke the `GetSomeDataAsync` method several times with a delay after every iteration (code file `ParallelSamples/ValueTaskSample/Program.cs`):

```
static async Task Main(string[] args)
{
  for (int i = 0; i < 20; i++)
  {
    IEnumerable<string> data = await GetSomeDataAsync();
    await Task.Delay(1000);
  }
  Console.ReadLine();
}
```

When you run the application, you can see that the data is returned from the cache, and after the cache is invalidated, the service is accessed first before the cache is used again.

```
data from the service
data from the cache
data from the cache
data from the cache
data from the cache
data from the service
data from the cache
data from the cache
data from the cache
data from the cache
data from the service
data from the cache
...
```

> **NOTE** *You haven't probably come across scenarios yet where you can't ignore the overhead from tasks compared to value tasks. However, having this core feature in .NET is one of the foundations of async streams, which is covered in Chapter 11.*

CANCELLATION FRAMEWORK

.NET includes a cancellation framework to enable the canceling of long-running tasks in a standard manner. Every blocking call should support this mechanism. Of course, not every blocking call currently implements this new technology, but more and more are doing so. Among the technologies that already offer this mechanism are tasks, concurrent collection classes, Parallel LINQ, and several synchronization mechanisms.

The cancellation framework is based on cooperative behavior; it is not forceful. A long-running task checks whether it is canceled and returns control accordingly.

A method that supports cancellation accepts a `CancellationToken` parameter. This class defines the property `IsCancellationRequested`, whereby a long operation can check to see whether it should abort. Other ways for a long operation to check for cancellation include using a `WaitHandle` property that is signaled when the token is canceled or using the `Register` method. The `Register` method accepts parameters of type `Action` and `ICancelableOperation`. The method that is referenced by the `Action` delegate is invoked when the token is canceled. This is like the `ICancelableOperation`, whereby the `Cancel` method of an object implementing this interface is invoked when the cancellation is done.

Cancellation of Parallel.For

This section starts with a simple example using the `Parallel.For` method. The `Parallel` class provides overloads for the `For` method, whereby you can pass a parameter of type `ParallelOptions`. With `ParallelOptions`, you can pass a `CancellationToken`. The `CancellationToken` is generated by creating a `CancellationTokenSource`. `CancellationTokenSource` implements the interface `ICancelableOperation` and can therefore be registered with the `CancellationToken` and allows cancellation with the `Cancel` method. The example doesn't call the `Cancel` method directly but uses a constructor overload to cancel the token after 500 milliseconds.

Within the implementation of the `For` loop, the `Parallel` class verifies the outcome of the `CancellationToken` and cancels the operation. Upon cancellation, the `For` method throws an exception of type `OperationCanceledException`, which is caught in the example. With the `CancellationToken`, it is possible to register for information when the cancellation is done. This is accomplished by calling the `Register` method and passing a delegate that is invoked on cancellation (code file `ParallelSamples/CancellationSamples/Program.cs`):

```
public static void CancelParallelFor()
{
  CancellationTokenSource cts = new(millisecondsDelay: 500);
  cts.Token.Register(() => Console.WriteLine("*** cancellation activated"));
  try
  {
    ParallelLoopResult result =
      Parallel.For(0, 100, new ParallelOptions
      {
        CancellationToken = cts.Token,
      },
      x =>
      {
        Console.WriteLine($"loop {x} started");
        int sum = 0;
        for (int i = 0; i < 100; i++)
        {
          Task.Delay(2).Wait();
          sum += i;
        }
        Console.WriteLine($"loop {x} finished");
      });
  }
  catch (OperationCanceledException ex)
  {
    Console.WriteLine(ex.Message);
  }
}
```

When you run the application, you get output like the following. Iteration 0, 50, 25, 75, and 1 were all started. This is on a system with a quad-core CPU. With the cancellation, all other iterations were canceled before starting. The iterations that were started are allowed to finish because cancellation is always done in a cooperative way to avoid the risk of resource leaks when iterations are canceled somewhere in between:

```
loop 36 started
loop 12 started
loop 72 started
loop 24 started
loop 48 started
loop 60 started
loop 0 started
loop 84 started
loop 96 started
*** cancellation activated
loop 12 finished
loop 60 finished
loop 36 finished
loop 72 finished
loop 96 finished
loop 84 finished
loop 24 finished
```

```
loop 48 finished
loop 0 finished
The operation was canceled.
```

Cancellation of Tasks

The same cancellation pattern is used with tasks. First, a new `CancellationTokenSource` is created. If you need just one cancellation token, you can use a default token by accessing `Task.Factory.CancellationToken`. Then, like the previous code, the task is canceled after 500 milliseconds. The task doing the major work within a loop receives the cancellation token via the `TaskFactory` object. The cancellation token is assigned to the `TaskFactory` by setting it in the constructor. This cancellation token is used by the task to check whether cancellation is requested by checking the `IsCancellationRequested` property of the `CancellationToken` (code file `ParallelSamples/CancellationSamples/Program.cs`):

```
public void CancelTask()
{
  CancellationTokenSource cts = new(millisecondsDelay: 500);
  cts.Token.Register(() => Console.WriteLine("*** task canceled"));
  Task t1 = Task.Run(() =>
  {
    Console.WriteLine("in task");
    for (int i = 0; i < 20; i++)
    {
      Task.Delay(100).Wait();
      CancellationToken token = cts.Token;
      if (token.IsCancellationRequested)
      {
        Console.WriteLine("cancelling was requested, " +
          "cancelling from within the task");
        token.ThrowIfCancellationRequested();
        break;
      }
      Console.WriteLine("in loop");
    }
    Console.WriteLine("task finished without cancellation");
  }, cts.Token);

  try
  {
    t1.Wait();
  }
  catch (AggregateException ex)
  {
    Console.WriteLine($"exception: {ex.GetType().Name}, {ex.Message}");
    foreach (var innerException in ex.InnerExcepstions)
    {
      Console.WriteLine($"inner exception: {ex.InnerException.GetType()}," +
        $"{ex.InnerException.Message}");
    }
  }
}
```

When you run the application, you can see that the task starts, runs for a few loops, and gets the cancellation request. The task is canceled and throws a `TaskCanceledException`, which is initiated from the method call `ThrowIfCancellationRequested`. With the caller waiting for the task, you can see that the exception

`AggregateException` is caught and contains the inner exception `TaskCanceledException`. This is used for a hierarchy of cancellations—for example, if you run a `Parallel.For` within a task that is canceled as well. The final status of the task is `Canceled`:

```
in task
in loop
in loop
in loop
in loop
*** task canceled
cancelling was requested, cancelling from within the task
exception: AggregateException, One or more errors occurred. (A task was canceled.)
inner exception: System.Threading.Tasks.TaskCanceledException, A task was canceled.
```

CHANNELS

In many applications, you have a producer/consumer scenario. One task produces data, and another task consumes and processes the data. In Chapter 11, you can read about a device simulation where a device streams sensor data, and this data is consumed using async streams. Here, you've seen syntax enhancements with C# as the `foreach` statement was extended with `await foreach`, and the `yield` statement was extended to support `IAsyncEnumerable<T>` and `IAsyncEnumerator<T>`.

With a producer/consumer scenario based on the data you deal with, there are different requirements. Is it necessary to deal with data in a fast pace? Is it okay to ignore data if processing is not fast enough, or is it required to process every item? Should data be ignored if it is already too old and new values can be retrieved? What's the optimal size of the buffer? Should the size of the buffer change dynamically?

Without requiring that you do a custom implementation, `System.Threading.Channels` offers great flexibility. A channel stores data written from a producer and allows reading data using a consumer. This library offers *unbounded channels*, which grow dynamically as needed until no more memory is available, and *bounded channels* with a fixed size.

Creating Bounded and Unbounded Channels

Let's look at a sample application before going into some of the features offered. The sample data that's written and read from the channel is a record (code file `ParallelSamples/ChannelSample/Program.cs`):

```
public record SomeData(string Text, int Number);
```

An unbounded channel is created with the class `Channel` invoking the static method `CreateUnbounded`. This method returns a class that derives from the abstract generic class `Channel<T>`. Optionally, you can pass settings with `UnboundedChannelOptions` to specify whether only a single writer or a single reader is used. Depending on the settings, different implementations are used regarding thread safety. Be aware that if you set both values to `true`, you cannot read and write concurrently. The `Channel<T>` class returned from the creation method defines a `Reader` and a `Writer` property that you can use to read from and write to the channel (code file `ParallelSamples/ChannelSample/Program.cs`):

```
Channel<SomeData> channel = Channel.CreateUnbounded<SomeData>(
    new UnboundedChannelOptions() { SingleReader = false, SingleWriter = true, });

Console.WriteLine("Using the unbounded channel");

var t1 = ChannelSample.WriteSomeDataAsync(channel.Writer);
var t2 = ChannelSample.ReadSomeDataAsync(channel.Reader);

await Task.WhenAll(t1, t2);
```

When you create a bounded channel, you specify the number of items the channel should hold by specifying the capacity with the constructor. In addition, you specify options with `BoundedChannelOptions`. Similarly to the unbounded channel, with the bounded channel you can specify whether just one reader or writer is used. Another option you specify is the `FullMode` property with one value of the `BoundedChannelFullMode` enum as discussed next:

```
Channel<SomeData> channel = Channel.CreateBounded<SomeData>(
  new BoundedChannelOptions(capacity: 10)
  {
    FullMode = BoundedChannelFullMode.Wait,
    SingleWriter = true
  });
```

What happens if you try to write to the channel, but the channel is already full? Of course, the unbounded channel cannot be full; it's resized until your application runs out of memory. With the bounded channel, there are different scenarios. You can write to the channel with the `TryWrite` method and the `WriteAsync` method. The `TryWrite` method returns `true` or `false`, depending on whether it's successful. With the default settings, the `TryWrite` method fails to write if the channel is at its capacity. The `WriteAsync` method just waits until some data is read and there's capacity available to write the data. The default setting with `BoundedChannelFullMode` is `Wait`.

Depending on the data you are dealing with, you might prefer other options. For example, if the producer writes new values that make the older data not that interesting anymore, you can decide to drop the oldest data that hasn't been read. You use the `DropOldest` enum value for this setting. You can also drop the newest data (`DropNewest`) or drop the data that's just written (`DropWrite`). In all these cases, `TryWrite` is successful (although the just written data can be dropped), and `WriteAsync` succeeds faster.

Writing to the Channel

With the sample application, the method `WriteSomeDataAsync` receives the generic `ChannelWriter` with its parameter and writes data to the channel using the `WriteAsync` method in a `for` loop. The `Complete` method informs the channel that no more data is going to be written. To implement a more natural experience with this sample code, a random time up to 50 milliseconds is used as a delay before every write is done in the loop (code file `ParallelSamples/ChannelSample/ChannelSample.cs`):

```
public static Task WriteSomeDataAsync(ChannelWriter<SomeData> writer) =>
  Task.Run(async () =>
  {
    for (int i = 0; i < 100; i++)
    {
      Random r = new();
      SomeData data = new($"text {i}", i);
      await Task.Delay(r.Next(50));
      await writer.WriteAsync(data);
      Console.WriteLine($"Written {data.Text}");
    }
    writer.Complete();
    Console.WriteLine("Writing completed");
  });
```

With the implementation of the method `WriteSomeDataWithTryWriteAsync`, the `TryWrite` method is used to write data to the channel. With this method, it needs to be checked whether the writing was successful. Remember, with a bounded channel, if the channel is at its capacity, with `BoundedChannelFullMode.Wait`, the `TryWrite` method fails to add the item and returns `false`:

```
public static Task WriteSomeDataWithTryWriteAsync(ChannelWriter<SomeData> writer) =>
  Task.Run(async () =>
  {
    for (int i = 0; i < 100; i++)
```

```
        {
            Random r = new();
            SomeData data = new($"text {i}", i);
            await Task.Delay(r.Next(50));
            if (!writer.TryWrite(data))
            {
                Console.WriteLine($"could not write {data.Number}, channel full");
            }
            else
            {
                Console.WriteLine($"Written {data.Text}");
            }
        }
        writer.Complete();
        Console.WriteLine("Writing completed");
    });
```

Reading from the Channel

With the implementation of the reader, a separate task is created to read from the channel. The `ReadAsync` method waits until some data can be retrieved. Before reading the data, a delay is used. The delay on reading the data is randomly larger than the delay on writing to the queue, which allows you to see that the capacity is filled over time, and items can be dropped (code file `ParallelSamples/ChannelSample/ChannelSample.cs`):

```
public static Task ReadSomeDataAsync(ChannelReader<SomeData> reader) =>
    Task.Run(async () =>
    {
        try
        {
            Console.WriteLine("Start reading...");
            Random r = new();
            while (true)
            {
                await Task.Delay(r.Next(80));
                var data = await reader.ReadAsync();
                Console.WriteLine($"read: {data.Text}, available items: {reader.Count}");
            }
        }
        catch (ChannelClosedException)
        {
            Console.WriteLine("channel closed");
        }
    });
```

Async Streaming with the Channel

Chapter 13, "Managed and Unmanaged Memory," covers async streaming. You can use this C# feature with channels as well. The `ChannelReader` method `ReadAllAsync` returns `IAsyncEnumerable<T>`, which allows using the `await foreach` statement to asynchronously iterate through all the items (code file `ParallelSamples/ChannelSample/ChannelSample.cs`):

```
public static Task ReadSomeDataUsingAsyncStreams(ChannelReader<SomeData> reader) =>
    Task.Run(async () =>
    {
```

```
    try
    {
      Console.WriteLine("Start reading...");
      Random r = new();
      await foreach (var data in reader.ReadAllAsync())
      {
        await Task.Delay(r.Next(80));
        Console.WriteLine($"read: {data.Text} available items: {reader.Count}");
      }
    }
    catch (ChannelClosedException)
    {
      Console.WriteLine("channel closed");
    }
  });
```

TIMERS

With a timer, you can do a repeat invocation of a method. Two timers will be covered in this section: the `Timer` class from the `System.Threading` namespace and the `DispatcherTimer` for XAML-based apps.

Using the Timer Class

When you use the `System.Threading.Timer` class, you can pass the method to be invoked as the first parameter in the constructor. This method must fulfill the requirements of the `TimerCallback` delegate, which defines a `void` return type and an `object` parameter. With the second parameter of the constructor, you can pass any object, which is then received with the object argument in the callback method. For example, you can pass an `Event` object to signal the caller. The third parameter specifies the time span during which the callback should be invoked the first time. With the last parameter, you specify the repeating interval for the callback. If the timer should fire only once, set the fourth parameter to the value -1.

If the time interval should be changed after creating the `Timer` object, you can pass new values with the `Change` method (code file `ParallelSamples/TimersSample/Program.cs`):

```
    private static void ThreadingTimer()
    {
      void TimeAction(object? o) =>
        Console.WriteLine($"System.Threading.Timer {DateTime.Now:T}");

      using Timer t1 = new(
        TimeAction,
        null,
        dueTime: TimeSpan.FromSeconds(2),
        period: TimeSpan.FromSeconds(3)))
      {
        Task.Delay(15000).Wait();
      }
    }
```

WinUI Dispatcher Timer

The `DispatcherTimer` from the namespace `Microsoft.UI.Xaml` (for WinUI apps) is a timer for XAML-based apps where the event handler is called within the UI thread; thus, it is possible to directly access user interface elements.

The sample application to demonstrate `DispatcherTimer` is a Windows app that shows the hand of a clock that switches every second. The following XAML code defines the commands that enable you to start and stop the clock (code file `ParallelSamples/WindowsAppTimer/MainWindow.xaml`):

```
<CommandBar IsOpen="True">
  <AppBarButton Icon="Play" Click="{x:Bind OnStartTimer}" Label="Play" />
  <AppBarButton Icon="Stop" Click="{x:Bind OnStopTimer}" Label="Stop" />
</CommandBar>
<Page.TopAppBar>
```

The hand of the clock is defined using the shape `Line`. To rotate the line, you use a `RotateTransform` element that is bound to the `TimerAngle` property:

```
<Canvas Width="300" Height="300" Grid.Row="1">
  <Ellipse Width="10" Height="10" Fill="Red" Canvas.Left="145" Canvas.Top="145" />
    <Line Canvas.Left="150" Canvas.Top="150" Fill="Green" StrokeThickness="3"
      Stroke="Blue" X1="0" Y1="0" X2="120" Y2="0" >
      <Line.RenderTransform>
        <RotateTransform CenterX="0" CenterY="0" Angle="{x:Bind TimerAngle, Mode=OneWay}"
            x:Name="rotate" />
      </Line.RenderTransform>
    </Line>
</Canvas>
```

> **NOTE** *WinUI applications and the interface* `INotifyPropertyChanged` *are introduced in Chapter 29, "Windows Apps." XAML shapes are explained in Chapter 31, "Styling Windows Apps."*

The `DispatcherTimer` object is created in the `MainWindow` class. In the constructor, the handler method `OnTick` is assigned to the `Tick` event, and the `Interval` is specified to be one second. The timer is started in the `OnTimer` method—the method that gets called when the user clicks the `Play` button in the `CommandBar`. When the tick event is fired, in the `OnTick` method, the property `TimerAngle` gets updated. This property fires the `PropertyChanged` event that's defined by the interface `INotifyPropertyChanged` to bring this update to the user interface (code file `ParallelSamples/WindowsAppTimer/MainPage.xaml.cs`):

```
public sealed partial class MainWindow : Window, INotifyPropertyChanged
{
  private DispatcherTimer _timer = new();

  public event PropertyChangedEventHandler? PropertyChanged;

  public MainWindow()
  {
    this.Title = "WinUI Dispatcher Timer App";
    this.InitializeComponent();
    _timer.Tick += OnTick;
    _timer.Interval = TimeSpan.FromSeconds(1);
  }

  private void OnStartTimer() => _timer.Start();

  private double _timerAngle;
  public double TimerAngle
```

```
    {
      get => _timerAngle;
      set
      {
        if (!EqualityComparer<double>.Default.Equals(_timerAngle, value))
        {
          _timerAngle = value;
          PropertyChanged?.Invoke(this, new PropertyChangedEventArgs(nameof(TimerAngle)));
        }
      }
    }

    private void OnTick(object? sender, object e) =>
      TimerAngle = (TimerAngle + 6) % 360;


    private void OnStopTimer() => _timer.Stop();
  }
```

When you run the application, the clock hand is shown (see Figure 17-1).

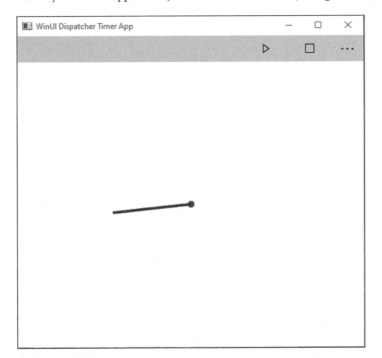

FIGURE 17-1

THREADING ISSUES

Programming with multiple threads is challenging. When starting multiple threads that access the same data, you can get intermittent problems that are hard to find. The problems are the same whether you use tasks, Parallel LINQ, or the Parallel class. To avoid getting into trouble, you must pay attention to synchronization issues and the problems that can occur with multiple threads. This section covers two in particular: race conditions and deadlocks.

A race condition results in inconsistent outcome of the application where results are invalid, and the issue only happens from time to time. Deadlocks happen when two threads block each other, and none of them can continue.

You can start the sample application `ThreadingIssues` with command-line arguments to simulate either race conditions or deadlocks.

Race Conditions

A race condition can occur if two or more threads access the same objects and access to the shared state is not synchronized. To demonstrate a race condition, the following example defines the class `StateObject` with an `int` field and the method `ChangeState`. In the implementation of `ChangeState`, the state variable is verified to determine whether it contains 5; if it does, the value is incremented. `Trace.Assert` is the next statement, which immediately verifies that state now contains the value 6.

After incrementing by 1 a variable that contains the value 5, you might assume that the variable now has the value 6; but this is not necessarily the case. For example, if one thread has just completed the `if (_state == 5)` statement, it might be preempted, with the scheduler running another thread. The second thread now goes into the `if` body and, because the state still has the value 5, the state is incremented by 1 to 6. The first thread is then scheduled again, and in the next statement, the state is incremented to 7. This is when the race condition occurs, and the assert message is shown (code file `SynchronizationSamples/ThreadingIssues/StateObject.cs`):

```
public class StateObject
{
  private int _state = 5;
  public void ChangeState(int loop)
  {
    if (_state == 5)
    {
      _state++;
      if (_state != 6)
      {
        Console.WriteLine($"Race condition occurred after {loop} loops");
        Trace.Fail("race condition");
      }
    }
    _state = 5;
  }
}
```

You can verify this by defining a method for a task. The method `RaceCondition` of the class `SampleTask` gets a `StateObject` as a parameter. Inside an endless `while` loop, the `ChangeState` method is invoked. The variable `i` is used just to show the loop number in the assert message (code file `SynchronizationSamples/ThreadingIssues/TaskWithRaceCondition.cs`):

```
public class TaskWithRaceCondition
{
  public void RaceCondition(object o)
  {
    if (o is not StateObject state)
      throw new ArgumentException("o must be a StateObject");
    else
    {
      Console.WriteLine("starting RaceCondition - when does the issue occur?");
```

```
          int i = 0;
          while (true)
          {
            if (!state.ChangeState(i++))
            {
              i = 0;
            }
          }
        }
      }
    }
```

In the method `RaceConditons`, a new `StateObject` is created that is shared among all the tasks. `Task` objects are created by invoking the `RaceCondition` method with the lambda expression that is passed to the `Run` method of the `Task`. The main thread then waits for user input. However, there's a good chance that the program will halt before reading user input because a race condition will happen (code file `SynchronizationSamples/Threading-Issues/Program.cs`):

```
public void RaceConditions()
{
  StateObject state = new();
  for (int i = 0; i < 2; i++)
  {
    Task.Run(() => new TaskWithRaceCondition().RaceCondition(state));
  }
}
```

When you start the program, you get race conditions. How long it takes until the first race condition happens depends on your system and whether you build the program as a release build or a debug build. With a release build, the problem happens more often because the code is optimized. If you have multiple CPUs in your system or dual-/quad-core CPUs, where multiple threads can run concurrently, the problem also occurs more often than with a single-core CPU. The problem occurs with a single-core CPU because thread scheduling is preemptive, but the problem doesn't occur that often.

In one run of the program on my system, I saw the first error after 18,205 loops; after resetting to continue looping, the next error manifested after 67,411 loops. You always get different results.

You can avoid the problem by locking the shared object. You do this inside the thread by locking the variable state, which is shared among the threads, with the `lock` statement, as shown in the following example. Only one thread can exist inside the lock block for the state object. Because this object is shared among all threads, a thread must wait at the lock if another thread has the lock for state. As soon as the lock is accepted, the thread owns the lock and gives it up at the end of the lock block. If every thread changing the object referenced with the state variable is using a lock, the race condition no longer occurs:

```
public class TaskWithRaceConditions
{
  public void RaceCondition(object o)
  {
    if (o is not StateObject state)
      throw new ArgumentException("o must be a StateObject");
    else
    {
      int i = 0;
      while (true)
      {
        lock (state) // no race condition with this lock
        {
```

```
        state.ChangeState(i++);
      }
    }
  }
 }
}
```

> **NOTE** *With the downloaded sample code, you need to uncomment the* lock *statements for solving the issues with race conditions.*

Instead of performing the lock when using the shared object, you can make the shared object thread-safe. In the following code, the ChangeState method contains a lock statement. Because you cannot lock the state variable itself (only reference types can be used for a lock), the variable _sync of type object is defined and used with the lock statement. If a lock is done using the same synchronization object every time the value state is changed, race conditions no longer happen:

```
public class StateObject
{
  private int _state = 5;
  private object _sync = new();
  public void ChangeState(int loop)
  {
    lock (_sync)
    {
      if (_state == 5)
      {
        _state++;
        if (_state != 6)
        {
          Console.WriteLine($"Race condition occurred after {loop} loops");
          Trace.Fail($"race condition at {loop}");
        }
      }
      _state = 5;
    }
  }
}
```

Deadlocks

Too much locking can get you in trouble as well. In a deadlock, at least two threads halt and wait for each other to release a lock. As both threads wait for each other, a deadlock occurs, and the threads wait endlessly.

To demonstrate deadlocks, the following code instantiates two objects of type StateObject and passes them with the constructor of the SampleTask class. Two tasks are created: one task running the method Deadlock1, and the other task running the method Deadlock2 (code file SynchronizationSamples/ThreadingIssues/Program.cs):

```
StateObject state1 = new();
StateObject state2 = new();
new Task(new SampleTask(state1, state2).Deadlock1).Start();
new Task(new SampleTask(state1, state2).Deadlock2).Start();
```

The methods `Deadlock1` and `Deadlock2` now change the state of two objects: `s1` and `s2`. That's why two locks are generated. `Deadlock1` first does a lock for `s1` and next for `s2`. `Deadlock2` first does a lock for `s2` and then for `s1`. Occasionally, the lock for `s1` in `Deadlock1` is resolved. Next, a thread switch occurs, and `Deadlock2` starts to run and gets the lock for `s2`. The second thread now waits for the lock of `s1`. Because it needs to wait, the thread scheduler schedules the first thread again, which now waits for `s2`. Both threads wait and don't release the lock as long as the lock block is not ended. This is a typical deadlock (code file `SynchronizationSamples/ThreadingIssues/TaskWithDeadlock.cs`):

```
public class TaskWithDeadlock
{
    public SampleTask(StateObject s1, StateObject s2) = (_s1, _s2) = (s1, s2);
    private readonly StateObject _s1;
    private readonly StateObject _s2;

    public void Deadlock1()
    {
      int i = 0;
      while (true)
      {
        lock (_s1)
        {
          lock (_s2)
          {
            _s1.ChangeState(i);
            _s2.ChangeState(i++);
            Console.WriteLine($"still running, {i}");
          }
        }
      }
    }

    public void Deadlock2()
    {
      int i = 0;
      while (true)
      {
        lock (_s2)
        {
          lock (_s1)
          {
            _s1.ChangeState(i);
            _s2.ChangeState(i++);
            Console.WriteLine($"still running, {i}");
          }
        }
      }
    }
}
```

As a result, the program runs some loops and soon becomes unresponsive. The message "still running" is written a few times to the console. Again, how soon the problem occurs depends on your system configuration, and the result will vary.

A deadlock problem is not always as obvious as it is here. One thread locks _s1 and then _s2; the other thread locks _s2 and then _s1. In this case, you just need to change the order so that both threads perform the locks in the same order. In a bigger application, the locks might be hidden deeply inside a method, thread 1 locks _s1 and _s2, thread 2 locks _s2 and _s3, and thread 3 locks _s3 and _s1.

You can prevent deadlocks by reducing the number of lock objects (for example, one lock object to synchronize access to state _s1 and _s2), by designing a good lock order in the initial architecture of the application, and by defining timeouts for the locks, as demonstrated in the next section.

INTERLOCKED

Instead of using the lock keyword for simple scenarios, there's a faster option. The Interlocked class is used to make simple statements for variables atomic. i++ is not thread-safe. It consists of getting a value from the memory, incrementing the value by 1, and storing the value back in memory. These operations can be interrupted by the thread scheduler. The Interlocked class provides methods for incrementing, decrementing, exchanging, and reading values in a thread-safe manner.

Using the Interlocked class is much faster than other synchronization techniques. However, you can use it only for simple synchronization issues.

For example, instead of performing incrementing inside a lock statement as shown here:

```
public int State
{
  get
  {
    lock (this)
    {
      return ++_state;
    }
  }
}
```

you can use Interlocked.Increment, which is faster:

```
public int State
{
  get => Interlocked.Increment(ref _state);
}
```

MONITOR

The C# compiler resolves the lock statement to use the Monitor class. The following lock statement

```
lock (obj)
{
  // synchronized region for obj
}
```

is resolved to invoke the Enter method, which waits until the thread gets the lock of the object. Only one thread at a time may be the owner of the object lock. As soon as the lock is resolved, the thread can enter the synchronized section. The Exit method of the Monitor class releases the lock. The compiler puts the Exit method into a finally handler of a try block so that the lock is also released if an exception is thrown:

```
Monitor.Enter(obj);
try
```

```
{
  // synchronized region for obj
}
finally
{
  Monitor.Exit(obj);
}
```

> **NOTE** *Chapter 10, "Errors and Exceptions," covers the* try/finally *block.*

The `Monitor` class has a big advantage over the `lock` statement of C#: you can add a timeout value for waiting to get the lock. Therefore, instead of endlessly waiting to get the lock, you can use the `TryEnter` method shown in the following example, passing a timeout value that defines the maximum amount of time to wait for the lock. If the lock for `obj` is acquired, `TryEnter` sets the Boolean `ref` parameter to `true` and performs synchronized access to the state guarded by the object `obj`. If `obj` is locked for more than 500 milliseconds by another thread, `TryEnter` sets the variable `_lockTaken` to `false`, and the thread does not wait any longer but is used to do something else. Maybe later, the thread can try to acquire the lock again.

```
bool _lockTaken = false;
Monitor.TryEnter(_obj, 500, ref _lockTaken);
if (_lockTaken)
{
  try
  {
    // acquired the lock
    // synchronized region for obj
  }
  finally
  {
    Monitor.Exit(obj);
  }
}
else
{
  // didn't get the lock, do something else
}
```

SPINLOCK

If the overhead on object-based lock objects (`Monitor`) would be too high because of garbage collection, you can use the `SpinLock` struct. `SpinLock` is designed with the idea that thread context switches are expensive operations, and for short locks it's faster to use CPU cycles (spin) for the wait. With this architecture, `SpinLock` is useful if you have many locks (for example, for every node in a list) and hold times are always extremely short. You should avoid holding more than one `SpinLock`, and don't call anything that might block.

Other than the architectural differences, `SpinLock` is similar in usage to the `Monitor` class. You acquire the lock with `Enter` or `TryEnter` and release the lock with `Exit`. `SpinLock` also offers two properties to provide information about whether it is currently locked: `IsHeld` and `IsHeldByCurrentThread`.

> **NOTE** *Be careful when passing* SpinLock *instances around. Because* SpinLock *is defined as a* struct, *assigning one variable to another creates a copy. Always pass* SpinLock *instances by reference.*

WAITHANDLE

WaitHandle is an abstract base class that you can use to wait for a signal to be set. You can wait for different things because WaitHandle is a base class and some classes are derived from it.

With WaitHandle, you can wait for one signal to occur (WaitOne), multiple objects that all must be signaled (WaitAll), or one of multiple objects (WaitAny). WaitAll and WaitAny are static members of the WaitHandle class and accept an array of WaitHandle parameters.

WaitHandle has a SafeWaitHandle property with which you can assign a native handle to an operating system resource and wait for that handle. For example, you can assign a SafeFileHandle to wait for a file I/O operation to complete.

The classes Mutex, EventWaitHandle, and Semaphore are derived from the base class WaitHandle, so you can use any of these with waits.

MUTEX

Mutex (mutual exclusion) is one of the classes that offers synchronization across multiple processes. It is similar to the Monitor class in that there is just one owner. That is, only one thread can get a lock on the mutex and access the synchronized code regions that are secured by the mutex.

With the constructor of the Mutex class, you can define whether the mutex should initially be owned by the calling thread, define a name for the mutex, and determine whether the mutex already exists. In the following example, the third parameter is defined as an out parameter to receive a Boolean value if the mutex was newly created. If the value returned is false, the mutex was already defined. The mutex might be defined in a different process because a mutex with a name is known to the operating system and is shared among different processes. If no name is assigned to the mutex, the mutex is unnamed and not shared among different processes.

```
using Mutex mutex = new(false, "ProCSharpMutex", out bool createdNew);
```

To open an existing mutex, you can also use the method Mutex.OpenExisting, which doesn't require the same .NET privileges as creating the mutex with the constructor.

Because the Mutex class derives from the base class WaitHandle, you can do a WaitOne to acquire the mutex lock and be the owner of the mutex during that time. The mutex is released by invoking the ReleaseMutex method:

```
if (mutex.WaitOne())
{
  try
  {
  // synchronized region
  }
  finally
  {
    mutex.ReleaseMutex();
  }
}
```

```
    else
    {
        // some problem happened while waiting
    }
```

Because a named mutex is known system-wide, you can use it to keep an application from being started twice. In the following console application, the constructor of the `Mutex` object is invoked. Then it is verified whether the mutex with the name `SingletonAppMutex` exists already. If it does, the application exits (code file `SynchronizationSamples/SingletonUsingMutex/Program.cs`):

```
Mutex mutex = new(false, "SingletonAppMutex", out bool mutexCreated);
if (!mutexCreated)
{
    Console.WriteLine("You can only start one instance of the application.");
    await Task.Delay(3000);
    Console.WriteLine("Exiting.");
    return;
}
Console.WriteLine("Application running");
Console.WriteLine("Press return to exit");
Console.ReadLine();
```

SEMAPHORE

A semaphore is similar to a mutex, but unlike the mutex, the semaphore can be used by multiple threads at once. A semaphore is a counting mutex, meaning that with a semaphore, you can define the number of threads that are allowed to access the resource guarded by the semaphore simultaneously. This is useful if you need to limit the number of threads that can access the available resources. For example, if a system has three physical I/O ports available, three threads can access them simultaneously, but a fourth thread needs to wait until the resource is released by one of the other threads.

.NET provides two classes with semaphore functionality: `Semaphore` and `SemaphoreSlim`. `Semaphore` can be named, can use system-wide resources, and allows synchronization between different processes. `SemaphoreSlim` is a lightweight version that is optimized for shorter wait times.

In the following example application, six tasks are created along with one semaphore with a count of three. In the constructor of the `Semaphore` class, you can define the count for the number of locks that can be acquired with the semaphore (the second parameter) and the number of locks that are free initially (the first parameter). If the first parameter has a lower value than the second parameter, the difference between the values defines the already allocated semaphore count. As with the mutex, you can also assign a name to the semaphore to share it among different processes. Here a `SemaphoreSlim` object is created that can be used only within the process. After the `SemaphoreSlim` object is created, six tasks are started, and they all wait for the same semaphore (code file `SynchronizationSamples/SemaphoreSample/Program.cs`):

```
int taskCount = 6;
int semaphoreCount = 3;
using SemaphoreSlim semaphore = new(semaphoreCount, semaphoreCount);
Task[] tasks = new Task[taskCount];
for (int i = 0; i < taskCount; i++)
{
    tasks[i] = Task.Run(() => TaskMain(semaphore));
}
Task.WaitAll(tasks);
Console.WriteLine("All tasks finished");
    //...
```

In the task's main method, `TaskMain`, the task does a `Wait` to lock the semaphore. Remember that the semaphore has a count of three, so three tasks can acquire the lock. Task 4 must wait, and here the timeout of 600 milliseconds is defined as the maximum wait time. If the lock cannot be acquired after the wait time has elapsed, the task writes a message to the console and repeats the wait in a loop. As soon as the lock is acquired, the thread writes a message to the console, sleeps for some time, and releases the lock. Again, with the release of the lock it is important that the resource be released in all cases. That's why the `Release` method of the `SemaphoreSlim` class is invoked in a `finally` handler (code file SynchronizationSamples/SemaphoreSample/Program.cs):

```
// ...
void TaskMain(SemaphoreSlim semaphore)
{
  bool isCompleted = false;
  while (!isCompleted)
  {
    if (semaphore.Wait(600))
    {
      try
      {
        Console.WriteLine($"Task {Task.CurrentId} locks the semaphore");
        Task.Delay(2000).Wait();
      }
      finally
      {
        Console.WriteLine($"Task {Task.CurrentId} releases the semaphore");
        semaphore.Release();
        isCompleted = true;
      }
    }
    else
    {
      Console.WriteLine($"Timeout for task {Task.CurrentId}; wait again");
    }
  }
}
```

When you run the application, you can indeed see that with three threads the lock is made immediately. The tasks with IDs 4, 5, and 6 must wait. The wait continues in the loop until one of the other threads releases the semaphore:

```
Task 3 locks the semaphore
Task 1 locks the semaphore
Task 2 locks the semaphore
Timeout for task 4; wait again
Timeout for task 5; wait again
Timeout for task 6; wait again
Timeout for task 4; wait again
Timeout for task 6; wait again
Timeout for task 4; wait again
Timeout for task 5; wait again
Timeout for task 6; wait again
Task 3 releases the semaphore
Task 1 releases the semaphore
Task 2 releases the semaphore
Task 4 locks the semaphore
Task 5 locks the semaphore
Task 6 locks the semaphore
```

```
Task 5 releases the semaphore
Task 6 releases the semaphore
Task 4 releases the semaphore
All tasks finished
```

EVENTS

Like mutex and semaphore objects, events are also system-wide synchronization resources. For using system events from managed code, .NET offers the classes `ManualResetEvent`, `AutoResetEvent`, `ManualResetEventSlim`, and `CountdownEvent` in the namespace `System.Threading`.

> **NOTE** *The* event *keyword from C# that is covered in Chapter 7, "Delegates, Lambdas, and Events," has nothing to do with the event classes from the namespace* System.Threading; *the* event *keyword is based on delegates. However, both event classes are .NET wrappers to the system-wide native event resource for synchronization.*

You can use events to inform other tasks that some data is present, that something is completed, and so on. An event can be signaled or not signaled. A task can wait for the event to be in a signaled state with the help of the `WaitHandle` class, discussed earlier.

A `ManualResetEventSlim` is signaled by invoking the `Set` method, and it's returned to a nonsignaled state with the `Reset` method. If multiple threads are waiting for an event to be signaled and the `Set` method is invoked, then all threads waiting are released. In addition, if a thread invokes the `WaitOne` method but the event is already signaled, the waiting thread can continue immediately.

An `AutoResetEvent` is also signaled by invoking the `Set` method, and you can set it back to a nonsignaled state with the `Reset` method. However, if a thread is waiting for an auto-reset event to be signaled, the event is automatically changed into a nonsignaled state when the wait state of the first thread is finished. This way, if multiple threads are waiting for the event to be set, only one thread is released from its wait state. It is not the thread that has been waiting the longest for the event to be signaled, but the thread waiting with the highest priority.

To demonstrate events with the `ManualResetEventSlim` class, the following class `Calculator` defines the method `Calculation`, which is the entry point for a task. With this method, the task receives input data for calculation and writes the result to the `Result` property. As soon as the result is completed (after a random amount of time), the event is signaled by invoking the `Set` method of the `ManualResetEventSlim` (code file `SynchronizationSamples/EventSample/Calculator.cs`):

```csharp
public class Calculator
{
  private ManualResetEventSlim _mEvent;
  public int Result { get; private set; }

  public Calculator(ManualResetEventSlim ev) => _mEvent = ev;

  public void Calculation(int x, int y)
  {
    Console.WriteLine($"Task {Task.CurrentId} starts calculation");
    Task.Delay(new Random().Next(3000)).Wait();
    Result = x + y;
```

```
      // signal the event-completed!
      Console.WriteLine($"Task {Task.CurrentId} is ready");
      _mEvent.Set();
   }
}
```

The top-level statements of the program defines arrays of four `ManualResetEventSlim` objects and four `Calculator` objects. Every `Calculator` is initialized in the constructor with a `ManualResetEventSlim` object, so every task gets its own event object to signal when it is completed. Now, the `Task` class is used to enable different tasks to run the calculation (code file SynchronizationSamples/EventSample/Program.cs):

```
const int taskCount = 4;
ManualResetEventSlim[] mEvents = new ManualResetEventSlim[taskCount];co
WaitHandle[] waitHandles = new WaitHandle[taskCount];
Calculator[] calcs = new Calculator[taskCount];

for (int i = 0; i < taskCount; i++)
{
  int i1 = i;
  mEvents[i] = new(false);
  waitHandles[i] = mEvents[i].WaitHandle;
  calcs[i] = new(mEvents[i]);
  Task.Run(() => calcs[i1].Calculation(i1 + 1, i1 + 3));
}
//...
```

The `WaitHandle` class is now used to wait for any one of the events in the array. `WaitAny` waits until any one of the events is signaled. In contrast to `ManualResetEvent`, `ManualResetEventSlim` does not derive from `WaitHandle`. That's why a separate collection of `WaitHandle` objects is kept, which is filled from the `WaitHandle` property of the `ManualResetEventSlim` class. `WaitAny` returns an index value that provides information about the event that was signaled. The returned value matches the index of the `WaitHandle` array that is passed to `WaitAny`. Using this index, information from the signaled event can be read:

```
for (int i = 0; i < taskCount; i++)
{
  int index = WaitHandle.WaitAny(waitHandles);
  if (index == WaitHandle.WaitTimeout)
  {
    Console.WriteLine("Timeout!!");
  }
  else
  {
    mEvents[index].Reset();
    Console.WriteLine($"finished task for {index}, result:
      {calcs[index].Result}");
  }
}
```

When you start the application, you can see the tasks doing the calculation and setting the event to inform the main thread that it can read the result. At random times, depending on whether the build is a debug or release build and on your hardware, you might see different orders and a different number of tasks performing calls:

```
Task 4 starts calculation
Task 1 starts calculation
Task 3 starts calculation
Task 2 starts calculation
```

```
Task 3 is ready
finished task for 3, result: 10
Task 4 is ready
finished task for 1, result: 6
Task 1 is ready
Task 2 is ready
finished task for 0, result: 4
finished task for 2, result: 8
```

In a scenario like this, to fork some work into multiple tasks and later join the result, the new CountdownEvent class can be useful. Instead of creating a separate event object for every task, you need to create only one. CountdownEvent defines an initial number for all the tasks that set the event, and after the count is reached, the CountdownEvent is signaled.

The Calculator class is modified to use the CountdownEvent instead of the ManualResetEvent. Rather than set the signal with the Set method, CountdownEvent defines the Signal method (code file SynchronizationSamples/EventSampleWithCountdownEvent/Calculator.cs):

```
public class Calculator
{
  private CountdownEvent _cEvent;
  public int Result { get; private set; }

  public Calculator(CountdownEvent ev) => _cEvent = ev;

  public void Calculation(int x, int y)
  {
    Console.WriteLine($"Task {Task.CurrentId} starts calculation");
    Task.Delay(new Random().Next(3000)).Wait();
    Result = x + y;
    // signal the event-completed!
    Console.WriteLine($"Task {Task.CurrentId} is ready");
    _cEvent.Signal();
  }
}
```

You can now simplify the top-level statements so that it's only necessary to wait for the single event. If you don't deal with the results separately as it was done before, this new edition might be all that's needed:

```
const int taskCount = 4;
CountdownEvent cEvent = new(taskCount);
Calculator[] calcs = new Calculator[taskCount];
for (int i = 0; i < taskCount; i++)
{
  calcs[i] = new(cEvent);
  int i1 = i;
  Task.Run(() => calcs[i1].Calculation, Tuple.Create(i1 + 1, i1 + 3));
}
cEvent.Wait();

Console.WriteLine("all finished");
for (int i = 0; i < taskCount; i++)
{
  Console.WriteLine($"task for {i}, result: {calcs[i].Result}");
}
```

BARRIER

For synchronization, the Barrier class is great for scenarios in which work is forked into multiple tasks and the work must be joined afterward. Barrier is used for participants that need to be synchronized. While the job is active, you can dynamically add participants—for example, child tasks that are created from a parent task. Participants can wait until the work is done by all the other participants before continuing.

The BarrierSample is somewhat complex, but it's worthwhile to demonstrate the features of the Barrier type. The sample creates multiple collections of two million random strings. Multiple tasks are used to iterate through the collection and count the number of strings, starting with a, b, c, and so on. The work is not only distributed between different tasks, but also within a task. After all tasks are iterated through the first collection of strings, the result is summarized, and the tasks continue later with the next collection.

The method FillData creates a collection and fills it with random strings (code file BarrierSample/Program.cs):

```
public static IEnumerable<string> FillData(int size)
{
  Random r = new();
  return Enumerable.Range(0, size).Select(x => GetString(r));
}

private static string GetString(Random r)
{
  StringBuilder sb = new(6);
  for (int i = 0; i < 6; i++)
  {
    sb.Append((char)(r.Next(26) + 97));
  }
  return sb.ToString();
}
```

A helper method to show information about a Barrier is defined with the method LogBarrierInformation:

```
private static void LogBarrierInformation(string info, Barrier barrier)
{
  Console.WriteLine($"Task {Task.CurrentId}: {info}. " +
    $"{barrier.ParticipantCount} current and " +
    $"{barrier.ParticipantsRemaining} remaining participants, " +
    $"phase {barrier.CurrentPhaseNumber}");
}
```

The CalculationInTask method defines the job performed by a task. With the parameters, the third parameter references the Barrier instance. The data that is used for the calculation is an array of IList<string>. The last parameter, a jagged int array, will be used to write the results as the task progresses.

The task makes the processing in a loop. With every loop, an array element of IList<string>[] is processed. After every loop is completed, the Task signals that it's ready by invoking the SignalAndWait method, and it waits until all the other tasks are ready with this processing as well. This loop continues until the task is fully finished. Then the task removes itself from the barrier by invoking the method RemoveParticipant (code file SynchronizationSamples/BarrierSample/Program.cs):

```
private static void CalculationInTask(int jobNumber, int partitionSize,
  Barrier, IList<string>[] coll, int loops, int[][] results)
{
  LogBarrierInformation("CalculationInTask started", barrier);

  for (int i = 0; i < loops; i++)
```

```
  {
    List<string> data = new(coll[i]);
    int start = jobNumber * partitionSize;
    int end = start + partitionSize;
    Console.WriteLine($"Task {Task.CurrentId} in loop {i}: partition " +
      $"from {start} to {end}");

    for (int j = start; j < end; j++)
    {
      char c = data[j][0];
      results[i][c - 97]++;
    }
    Console.WriteLine($"Calculation completed from task {Task.CurrentId} " +
      $"in loop {i}. {results[i][0]} times a, {results[i][25]} times z");

    LogBarrierInformation("sending signal and wait for all", barrier);
    barrier.SignalAndWait();
    LogBarrierInformation("waiting completed", barrier);
  }
  barrier.RemoveParticipant();
  LogBarrierInformation("finished task, removed participant", barrier);
}
```

With the `Main` method, a `Barrier` instance is created. In the constructor, you can specify the number of participants. In the example, this number is 3 (`numberTasks + 1`) because there are two created tasks, and the `Main` method is a participant as well. When you use `Task.Run`, two tasks are created to fork the iteration through the collection into two parts. After starting the tasks, using `SignalAndWait`, the main method signals its completion and waits until all remaining participants either signal their completion or remove themselves as participants from the barrier. As soon as all participants are ready with one iteration, the results from the tasks are zipped together with the `Zip` extension method. Then the next iteration is done to wait for the next results from the tasks (code file `SynchronizationSamples/BarrierSample/Program.cs`):

```
static void Main()
{
  const int numberTasks = 2;
  const int partitionSize = 1_000_000;
  const int loops = 5;
  Dictionary<int, int[][]> taskResults = new Dictionary<int, int[][]>();
  List<string> data = new List<string>[loops];
  for (int i = 0; i < loops; i++)
  {
    data[i] = new List(FillData(partitionSize * numberTasks);
  }

  using Barrier barrier = new(numberTasks + 1);
  LogBarrierInformation("initial participants in barrier", barrier);
  for (int i = 0; i < numberTasks; i++)
  {
    barrier.AddParticipant();
    int jobNumber = i;
    taskResults.Add(i, new int[loops][]);
    for (int loop = 0; loop < loops; loop++)
    {
      taskResult[i, loop] = new int[26];
    }
```

```
      Console.WriteLine("Main - starting task job {jobNumber}");
      Task.Run(() => CalculationInTask(jobNumber, partitionSize,
        barrier, data, loops, taskResults[jobNumber]));
    }

    for (int loop = 0; loop < 5; loop++)
    {
      LogBarrierInformation("main task, start signaling and wait", barrier);
      barrier.SignalAndWait();
      LogBarrierInformation("main task waiting completed", barrier);
      int[][] resultCollection1 = taskResults[0];
      int[][] resultCollection2 = taskResults[1];
      var resultCollection = resultCollection1[loop].Zip(
        resultCollection2[loop], (c1, c2) => c1 + c2);
      char ch = 'a';
      int sum = 0;
      foreach (var x in resultCollection)
      {
        Console.WriteLine($"{ch++}, count: {x}");
        sum += x;
      }
      LogBarrierInformation($"main task finished loop {loop}, sum: {sum}",
        barrier);
    }

  Console.WriteLine("finished all iterations");
  Console.ReadLine();
}
```

> **NOTE** *Jagged arrays are explained in Chapter 6, "Arrays." The* `Zip` *extension method is explained in Chapter 9.*

When you run the application, you can see output like the following. In the output, you can see that every call to `AddParticipant` increases the participant count as well as the remaining participant count. As soon as one participant invokes `SignalAndWait`, the remaining participant count is decremented. When the remaining participant count reaches 0, the wait of all participants ends, and the next phase begins:

```
Task : initial participants in barrier. 1 current and 1 remaining participants,
phase 0
Main - starting task job 0
Main - starting task job 1
Task : main task, start signaling and wait. 3 current and 3 remaining participants,
phase 0
Task 1: CalculationInTask started. 3 current and 2 remaining participants, phase 0
Task 2: CalculationInTask started. 3 current and 2 remaining participants, phase 0
Task 2 in loop 0: partition from 1000000 to 2000000
Task 1 in loop 0: partition from 0 to 1000000
Calculation completed from task 2 in loop 0. 38361 times a, 38581 times z
Task 2: sending signal and wait for all. 3 current and 2 remaining participants,
phase 0
Calculation completed from task 1 in loop 0. 38657 times a, 38643 times z
```

```
Task 1: sending signal and wait for all. 3 current and 1 remaining participants,
phase 0
Task 1: waiting completed. 3 current and 3 remaining participants, phase 1
Task : main task waiting completed. 3 current and 3 remaining participants, phase 1
```

READERWRITERLOCKSLIM

For a locking mechanism to allow multiple readers but only one writer for a resource, you can use the class ReaderWriterLockSlim. This class offers a locking functionality in which multiple readers can access the resource if no writer locked it, and only a single writer can lock the resource.

The ReaderWriterLockSlim class has blocking and nonblocking methods to acquire a read lock, such as EnterReadLock (blocking) and TryEnterReadLock (nonblocking), and to acquire a write lock with EnterWriteLock (blocking) and TryEnterWriteLock (nonblocking). If a task reads first and writes afterward, it can acquire an upgradable read lock with EnterUpgradableReadLock or TryEnterUpgradableReadLock. With this lock, the write lock can be acquired without releasing the read lock.

Several properties of this class offer information about the held locks, such as CurrentReadCount, WaitingReadCount, WaitingUpgradableReadCount, and WaitingWriteCount.

The following example creates a collection containing six items and a ReaderWriterLockSlim object. The method ReaderMethod acquires a read lock to read all items of the list and write them to the console. The method WriterMethod tries to acquire a write lock to change all values of the collection (code file SynchronizationSamples/ReaderWriterLockSample/ReaderWriter.cs):

```csharp
sealed class ReaderWriter : IDisposable
{
  private List<int> _items = new() { 0, 1, 2, 3, 4, 5 };
  private ReaderWriterLockSlim _rwl = new();

  public void ReaderMethod(object? reader)
  {
    try
    {
      _rwl.EnterReadLock();

      for (int i = 0; i < _items.Count; i++)
      {
        Console.WriteLine($"reader {reader}, loop: {i}, item: {_items[i]}");
        Task.Delay(40).Wait();
      }
    }
    finally
    {
      _rwl.ExitReadLock();
    }
  }

  public void WriterMethod(object? writer)
  {
    try
    {
      while (!_rwl.TryEnterWriteLock(50))
      {
        Console.WriteLine($"Writer {writer} waiting for the write lock");
```

```
        Console.WriteLine($"current reader count: {_rwl.CurrentReadCount}");
      }
      Console.WriteLine($"Writer {writer} acquired the lock");
      for (int i = 0; i < _items.Count; i++)
      {
        _items[i]++;
        Task.Delay(50).Wait();
      }
      Console.WriteLine($"Writer {writer} finished");
    }
    finally
    {
      _rwl.ExitWriteLock();
    }
  }

  private void Dispose(bool disposing)
  {
    if (!disposedValue)
    {
      if (disposing)
      {
        _rwl.Dispose();
      }
      disposedValue = true;
    }
  }

  void IDisposable.Dispose()
  {
    Dispose(disposing: true);
    GC.SuppressFinalize(this);
  }
}
```

With the top-level statements, six long-running tasks are created: two concurrent writers and four concurrent readers. To give the first writer a good chance to start before the readers, a short delay is used before starting the other tasks (code file SynchronizationSamples/ReaderWriterLockSample/Program.cs):

```
using ReaderWriter rw = new();
TaskFactory taskFactory = new(TaskCreationOptions.LongRunning,
  TaskContinuationOptions.None);
Task[] tasks = new Task[6];
tasks[0] = taskFactory.StartNew(rw.WriterMethod, 1);
await Task.Delay(5);
tasks[1] = taskFactory.StartNew(rw.ReaderMethod, 1);
tasks[2] = taskFactory.StartNew(rw.ReaderMethod, 2);
tasks[3] = taskFactory.StartNew(rw.WriterMethod, 2);
tasks[4] = taskFactory.StartNew(rw.ReaderMethod, 3);
tasks[5] = taskFactory.StartNew(rw.ReaderMethod, 4);

Task.WaitAll(tasks);
```

When you run the application, the following shows that the first writer gets the lock first. The second writer and all readers need to wait. Next, the second writer gets the lock, and after this is finished, the readers can start working. Running the application multiple times can show different results, but there's always only one writer or multiple readers running at any given time:

```
Writer 1 acquired the lock
Starting writer 2
Starting reader 2
Starting reader 3
Starting reader 1
Starting reader 4
Writer 2 waiting for the write lock, current readers: 0
Writer 2 waiting for the write lock, current readers: 0
Writer 2 waiting for the write lock, current readers: 0
Writer 2 waiting for the write lock, current readers: 0
Writer 2 waiting for the write lock, current readers: 0
Writer 1 finished
Writer 2 acquired the lock
Writer 2 finished
reader 3, loop: 0, item: 2
reader 1, loop: 0, item: 2
reader 2, loop: 0, item: 2
...
```

> **NOTE** *A group of collections that do not need locking are immutable collections defined in the namespace* `System.Collections.Immutable`. *These collection types are covered in Chapter 8, "Collections." Other thread-safe collections are collections from the namespace* `System.Collections.Concurrent`. *The* `BlockingCollection` *offers* `Add` *and* `TryAdd` *methods to add items. The* `Add` *method blocks, while the* `TryAdd` *method returns* `true` *or* `false` *depending on whether it was possible to add the item. To retrieve items from the collection, the* `Take` *method blocks while* `TryTake` *returns* `true` *or* `false` *to indicate whether it was successful taking an item from the collection. The* `BlockingCollection` *class can be used for a producer/consumer scenario. A more modern approach for a producer/consumer scenario is offered from channels, as shown in the section "Channels."*

LOCKS WITH AWAIT

In case you try to use the `lock` keyword while having the `async` keyword in the `lock` block, you get this compilation error: `cannot await in the body of a lock statement`. The reason is that after the `async` completes, the method might run in a different thread than before the `async` keyword. The `lock` keyword needs to release the lock in the same thread as the lock is acquired.

Such a code block results in compilation errors:

```
static async Task IncorrectLockAsync()
{
  lock (s_syncLock)
  {
    Console.WriteLine($"{nameof(IncorrectLockAsync)} started");
    await Task.Delay(500);  // compiler error: cannot await in the body
      // of a lock statement
    Console.WriteLine($"{nameof(IncorrectLockAsync)} ending");
  }
}
```

How can this be solved? You cannot use a Monitor for this, as the Monitor needs to release the lock from the same thread where it entered the lock. The lock keyword is based on Monitor.

While the Mutex object can be used for synchronization across different processes, it has the same issues: it grants a lock for a thread. Releasing the lock from a different thread is not possible. Instead, you can use the Semaphore— or the SemaphoreSlim class. Semaphores can release the semaphore from a different thread.

The following code snippet waits to acquire a semaphore using WaitAsync on a SemaphoreSlim object. The SemaphoreSlim object is initialized with a count of 1; thus, the wait on the semaphore is granted only once. In the finally code block, the semaphore is released by invoking the Release method (code file SynchronizationSamples/LockAcrossAwait/Program.cs):

```
private static SemaphoreSlim s_asyncLock = new(1);
static async Task LockWithSemaphore(string title)
{
  Console.WriteLine($"{title} waiting for lock");
  await s_asyncLock.WaitAsync();
  try
  {
    Console.WriteLine($"{title} {nameof(LockWithSemaphore)} started");
    await Task.Delay(500);
    Console.WriteLine($"{title} {nameof(LockWithSemaphore)} ending");
  }
  finally
  {
    s_asyncLock.Release();
  }
}
```

Let's try to invoke this method from multiple tasks concurrently. The method RunUseSemaphoreAsync starts six tasks to invoke the LockWithSemaphore method concurrently.

```
static async Task RunUseSemaphoreAsync()
{
  Console.WriteLine(nameof(RunUseSemaphoreAsync));
  string[] messages = { "one", "two", "three", "four", "five", "six" };
  Task[] tasks = new Task[messages.Length];

  for (int i = 0; i < messages.Length; i++)
  {
    string message = messages[i];

    tasks[i] = Task.Run(async () =>
    {
      await LockWithSemaphore(message);
    });
  }

  await Task.WhenAll(tasks);
  Console.WriteLine();
}
```

When you run the program, you can see that multiple tasks are started concurrently, but after the semaphore is locked, all other tasks need to wait until the semaphore is released again:

```
RunLockWithAwaitAsync
two waiting for lock
two LockWithSemaphore started
```

```
three waiting for lock
five waiting for lock
four waiting for lock
six waiting for lock
one waiting for lock
two LockWithSemaphore ending
three LockWithSemaphore started
three LockWithSemaphore ending
five LockWithSemaphore started
five LockWithSemaphore ending
four LockWithSemaphore started
four LockWithSemaphore ending
six LockWithSemaphore started
six LockWithSemaphore ending
one LockWithSemaphore started
one LockWithSemaphore ending
```

To make the use of the lock easier, you can create a class that implements the `IDisposable` interface to manage the resource. With this class, you can use the `using` statement in the same way as the `lock` statement is used to lock and release the semaphore.

The following code snippet implements the `AsyncSemaphore` class that allocates a `SemaphoreSlim` in the constructor, and on invoking the `WaitAsync` method on the `AsyncSemaphore`, the inner class `SemaphoreReleaser` is returned, which implements the interface `IDisposable`. On calling the `Dispose` method, the semaphore is released (code file SynchronizationSamples/LockAcrossAwait/AsyncSemaphore.cs):

```csharp
public sealed class AsyncSemaphore
{
  private class SemaphoreReleaser : IDisposable
  {
    private SemaphoreSlim _semaphore;

    public SemaphoreReleaser(SemaphoreSlim semaphore) =>
      _semaphore = semaphore;

    public void Dispose() => _semaphore.Release();
  }

  private SemaphoreSlim _semaphore;
  public AsyncSemaphore() =>
    _semaphore = new SemaphoreSlim(1);

  public async Task<IDisposable> WaitAsync()
  {
    await _semaphore.WaitAsync();
    return new SemaphoreReleaser(_semaphore) as IDisposable;
  }
}
```

Changing the implementation from the `LockWithSemaphore` method shown previously, now a `using` statement can be used where the semaphore is locked. Remember, the `using` statement creates a `catch`/`finally` block, and in the `finally` block, the `Dispose` method gets invoked (code file SynchronizationSamples/LockAcrossAwait/Program.cs):

```csharp
private static AsyncSemaphore s_asyncSemaphore = new AsyncSemaphore();
static async Task UseAsyncSemaphore(string title)
{
```

```
    using (await s_asyncSemaphore.WaitAsync())
    {
      Console.WriteLine($"{title} {nameof(LockWithSemaphore)} started");
      await Task.Delay(500);
      Console.WriteLine($"{title} {nameof(LockWithSemaphore)} ending");
    }
}
```

Using the `UseAsyncSemaphore` method similarly to the `LockWithSemaphore` method results in the same behavior. However, with a class written once, locking across `await` becomes simpler.

SUMMARY

This chapter explored how to code applications that use multiple tasks by using the `System.Threading.Tasks` namespace. Using multithreading in your applications takes careful planning. Too many threads can cause resource issues, but not enough threads can cause your application to be sluggish and perform poorly. With tasks, you get an abstraction to threads. This abstraction helps you avoid creating too many threads because threads are reused from a pool.

You've seen various ways to create multiple tasks, such as the `Parallel` class, which offers both task and data parallelism with `Parallel.Invoke`, `Parallel.ForEach`, and `Parallel.For`. With the `Task` class, you've seen how to gain more control over parallel programming. Tasks can run synchronously in the calling thread, using a thread from a thread pool, and a separate new thread can be created. Tasks also offer a hierarchical model that enables the creation of child tasks, also providing a way to cancel a complete hierarchy.

The cancellation framework offers a standard mechanism that can be consistently used with different classes to cancel a task early.

You've seen several synchronization objects that are available with .NET, and each has advantages and disadvantages. An easy synchronization can be done using the `lock` keyword. Behind the scenes, it's the `Monitor` type that allows setting timeouts, which is not possible with the `lock` keyword. For synchronization between processes, the `Mutex` object offers similar functionality. With the `Semaphore` object you've seen a synchronization object with a count—some tasks are allowed to run concurrently. To inform others of information that is ready, various kinds of event objects have been discussed, such as the `AutoResetEvent`, `ManualResetEvent`, and `CountdownEvent`. A straightforward way to have multiple readers and one writer is offered by the `ReaderWriterLock`. The `Barrier` type allows for more complex scenarios where multiple tasks can run concurrently until a synchronization point is reached. As soon as all tasks reach this point, all can continue concurrently to meet at the next synchronization point.

With `System.Threading.Channels`, you've seen a new flexible option for publish/subscribe communication using bounded and unbounded channels.

Here are some final guidelines regarding threading:

➤ Try to keep synchronization requirements to a minimum. Synchronization is complex and blocks threads. You can avoid it if you try to avoid sharing state. Of course, this is not always possible.

➤ Static members of a class should be thread-safe. Usually, this is the case with classes offered with .NET.

➤ Instance state does not need to be thread-safe. For best performance, synchronization is best used outside the class where it is needed, and not with every member of the class. Instance members of .NET classes usually are not thread-safe. In the Microsoft API documentation, you can find this information documented for every class of .NET in the "Thread Safety" section.

The next chapter gives information on another core .NET topic: files and streams.

18

Files and Streams

WHAT'S IN THIS CHAPTER?

- ➤ Exploring the directory structure
- ➤ Moving, copying, and deleting files and folders
- ➤ Reading and writing text in files
- ➤ Using streams to read and write files
- ➤ Using readers and writers to read and write files
- ➤ Compressing files
- ➤ Monitoring file changes
- ➤ Working with JSON serialization
- ➤ Using Windows Runtime streams

CODE DOWNLOADS FOR THIS CHAPTER

The source code for this chapter is available on the book page at www.wiley.com. Click the Downloads link. The code can also be found at https://github.com/ProfessionalCSharp/ProfessionalCSharp2021 in the directory 2_Libs/FilesAndStreams.

The code for this chapter is divided into the following major examples:

- ➤ FilesAndFolders
- ➤ StreamSamples
- ➤ ReaderWriterSamples
- ➤ CompressFileSample
- ➤ FileMonitor
- ➤ JsonSample
- ➤ WindowsAppEditor

The major namespaces used in this chapter are `System.IO`, `System.IO.Compression`, `System.Text`, and `System.Text.Json`. With the Windows app sample, `Winodws.Storage` and `Windows.Storage.Streams` are important namespaces. All projects have nullable reference types enabled.

OVERVIEW

When you're reading and writing to files and directories, you can use simple APIs, or you can use advanced ones that offer more features. Just use the simplest ones that fit your purpose. You also have to differentiate between .NET classes and the functionality offered from the Windows Runtime. From Universal Windows Platform (UWP) Windows apps, you don't have access to the file system in any directory; you have access only to specific directories. Alternatively, you can let the user pick files. This chapter covers all these options. You'll read and write files by using a simple API and get into more features by using streams. You'll use both .NET types and types from the Windows Runtime, and you'll mix both of these technologies to take advantage of .NET features with the Windows Runtime.

As you use streams, you also learn about compressing data and sharing data between different tasks using memory mapped files and pipes.

MANAGING THE FILE SYSTEM

Let's start with simple APIs from the `System.IO` namespace. The most important classes used to browse around the file system and perform operations such as moving, copying, and deleting files are:

➤ `FileSystemInfo`—This base class represents any file system object such as `FileInfo` and `DirectoryInfo`.

➤ `FileInfo` and `File`—These classes represent a file on the file system.

➤ `DirectoryInfo` and `Directory`—These classes represent a folder on the file system.

➤ `Path`—This class contains static members that you can use to manipulate pathnames.

➤ `DriveInfo`—This class has properties and methods that provide information about a selected drive.

> **NOTE** *Directories or folders? These terms are often used interchangeably. Directory is a classic term for a file system object. A directory contains files and other directories. A folder has its origin with Apple's Lisa and is a GUI object. Often it is associated with an icon to map to a directory.*

Notice in the previous list that two classes work with folders and two other classes work with files. Which one of these classes you use depends largely on how many operations you need in order to access that folder or file:

➤ `Directory` and `File` contain only static methods and are never instantiated. You use these classes by supplying the path to the appropriate file system object whenever you call a member method. If you want to do only one operation on a folder or file, using these classes is more efficient because it saves the overhead of creating a .NET object.

➤ `DirectoryInfo` and `FileInfo` implement roughly the same public methods as `Directory` and `File`, as well as some public properties and constructors, but they are stateful, and the members of these classes are not static. You need to instantiate these classes before each instance is associated with a particular folder or file. This means that these classes are more efficient if you are performing multiple operations using the same object. That's because they read the authentication and other information for the appropriate file system object on construction, and then they do not need to read that information again, no matter how many methods you call against each object (class instance). By comparison, the corresponding stateless classes need to check the details of the file or folder again with every method you call.

The next sample is a console application that accepts command-line arguments so you can easily start it with all the different features in action. Just check the downloaded source code for the arguments, or start the application without passing arguments to see the options you have.

Checking Drive Information

Before working with files and folders, let's check the drives of the system. You use the `DriveInfo` class, which can perform a scan of a system to provide a list of available drives and then dig in deeper to provide a lot of details about any of the drives.

The following code snippet invokes the static method `DriveInfo.GetDrives`. This method returns an array of `DriveInfo` objects. With this array, every drive that is ready is accessed to write information about the drive name, type, and format, and it also shows size information (code file `FilesAndFolders/Program.cs`):

```
void ShowDrives()
{
  DriveInfo[] drives = DriveInfo.GetDrives();
  foreach (DriveInfo drive in drives)
  {
    if (drive.IsReady)
    {
      Console.WriteLine($"Drive name: {drive.Name}");
      Console.WriteLine($"Format: {drive.DriveFormat}");
      Console.WriteLine($"Type: {drive.DriveType}");
      Console.WriteLine($"Root directory: {drive.RootDirectory}");
      Console.WriteLine($"Volume label: {drive.VolumeLabel}");
      Console.WriteLine($"Free space: {drive.TotalFreeSpace}");
      Console.WriteLine($"Available space: {drive.AvailableFreeSpace}");
      Console.WriteLine($"Total size: {drive.TotalSize}");
      Console.WriteLine();
    }
  }
}
```

When I run this program on my Windows system, which has only a solid-state disk (SSD), I see this information:

```
Drive name: C:\
Format: NTFS
Type: Fixed
Root directory: C:\
Volume label: Lokal Disk
Free space: 483677138944
Available space: 483677138944
Total size: 1022985498624
```

When I run the same application on the same system with Windows Subsystem for Linux (WSL-2) and the Ubuntu operating system, I see `Fixed` and `Ram` types. `Fixed` types use the `ext3` and `v9fs` formats; with the `Ram` types, you can see the `cgroupfs`, `cgroup2fs`, `devpts`, `proc`, `sysfs`, `temp`, `tmpfs`, and `binfmt_misc` formats. On Unix-based systems, a lot more functionality is available via file APIs, including information about processes and resource restrictions with control groups (cgroups).

Working with the Path Class

For accessing files and directories, the names of the files and directories need to be defined—including parent folders. When you combine multiple folders and files using string concatenation operators, you can easily miss a separator character or use one too many characters. The Path class can help with this because this class adds missing separator characters, and it also deals with different platform requirements on Windows- and Unix-based systems.

The Path class exposes some static methods that make operations on pathnames easier. For example, suppose that you want to display the full pathname for a file, ReadMe.txt, in the folder D:\Projects. You could find the path to the file using the following code:

```
Console.WriteLine(Path.Combine(@"D:\Projects", "ReadMe.txt"));
```

Path.Combine is the method of this class that you are likely to use most often, but Path also implements other methods that supply information about the path or the required format for it.

With the public fields VolumeSeparatorChar, DirectorySeparatorChar, AltDirectorySeparatorChar, and PathSeparator, you can get the platform-specific character that is used to separate drives, folders, and files, and the separator of multiple paths. With Windows, these characters are :, \, and /; with Linux, the special character for volumes and directories is /.

The Path class also helps with accessing the user-specific temp folder (GetTempPath) and creating temporary (GetTempFileName) and random filenames (GetRandomFileName). Make sure that the method GetTempFileName includes the folder, whereas GetRandomFileName just returns the filename without any folder.

The Environment class contains the SpecialFolder enumeration that defines a list of special folders—for example, Personal, MyDocuments, Recent, MyMusic, MyVideos, ApplicationData, LocalApplicationData, MyPictures, and more. Instead of using a hard-coded path, the following code iterates through all the enum values and shows the path to one special folder. You should use this API instead to be independent if a system is differently configured. However, be aware that depending on the operating system that is used, several of the special folders are not filled. The following code snippet iterates through all the defined special folders and shows the path (code file FilesAndFolders/Program.cs):

```
void ShowSpecialFolders()
{
  foreach (var specialFolder in Enum.GetNames(typeof(Environment.SpecialFolder)))
  {
    Environment.SpecialFolder folder =
      Enum.Parse<Environment.SpecialFolder>(specialFolder);

    string path = Environment.GetFolderPath(folder);
    Console.WriteLine($"{specialFolder}: {path}");
  }
}
```

This shows part of the output running the application in the WSL-2 subsystem with Ubuntu:

```
MyDocuments: /home/christian
Personal: /home/christian
LocalApplicationData: /home/christian/.local/share
CommonApplicationData: /usr/share
UserProfile: /home/christian
```

Creating Files and Folders

Now let's look at using the File, FileInfo, Directory, and DirectoryInfo classes. First, you use the WriteAllText method of the File class to create a file and write the string Hello, World!. Everything is done with a single API invocation (code file FilesAndFolders/Program.cs):

```
void CreateFile(string file)
{
  try
  {
    string path = Path.Combine(Environment.GetFolderPath(
      Environment.SpecialFolder.Personal), file);
    File.WriteAllText(path, "Hello, World!");
    Console.WriteLine($"created file {path}");
  }
  catch (ArgumentException)
  {
    Console.WriteLine("Invalid characters in the filename?");
  }
  catch (IOException ex)
  {
    Console.WriteLine(ex.Message);
  }
}
```

To copy a file, you can use either the `Copy` method of the `File` class or the `CopyTo` method of the `FileInfo` class:

```
FileInfo file = new(fileName1);
file.CopyTo(fileName2);
File.Copy(fileName1, fileName2);
```

With the `FileInfo` instance method, you need to write two code lines, whereas when you use the static `File` method, you need just one code line. If you need to perform additional actions on the file, the `FileInfo` class is faster. If you just need to do this one action on the file, you can reduce the code you need to write with the static method.

You can instantiate a `FileInfo` or `DirectoryInfo` class by passing to the constructor a string containing the path to the corresponding file system object. You have just seen the process for a file. For a folder, the code looks similar:

```
DirectoryInfo myFolder = new(directory);
```

If the path represents an object that does not exist, an exception is not thrown at construction; instead, it's thrown the first time you call a method that actually requires the corresponding file system object to be there. You can find out whether the object exists and is of the appropriate type by checking the `Exists` property, which is implemented by both of these classes:

```
FileInfo test = new(fileName);
Console.WriteLine(test.Exists);
```

Note that for this property to return `true`, the corresponding file system object must be of the appropriate type. In other words, if you instantiate a `FileInfo` object by supplying the path of a folder or you instantiate a `DirectoryInfo` object by giving it the path of a file, `Exists` has the value `false`. Most of the properties and methods of these objects return a value if possible—they won't necessarily throw an exception just because the wrong type of object has been called, unless they are asked to do something that is impossible. For example, the preceding code snippet might first display `false` (because `C:\Windows` is a directory), but it still displays the time the folder was created because a directory has that information. However, if you tried to open the directory as if it were a file, using the `FileInfo.Open` method, you'd get an exception.

You move and delete files or directories using the `MoveTo` and `Delete` methods of the `FileInfo` and `DirectoryInfo` classes. The equivalent methods on the `File` and `Directory` classes are `Move` and `Delete`. The `FileInfo` and `File` classes also implement the methods `CopyTo` and `Copy`, respectively. However, no methods exist to copy complete folders—you need to do that by copying each file and folder in the folder's hierarchy.

Using all of these methods is quite intuitive. You can find detailed descriptions in the Microsoft documentation.

Accessing and Modifying File Properties

Let's get some information about files. You can use both the `File` and `FileInfo` classes to access file information. The `File` class defines static methods, whereas the `FileInfo` class offers instance methods. The following code snippet shows how to use `FileInfo` to retrieve multiple pieces of information. If you instead used the `File` class, the access would be slower because every access would mean a check to determine whether the user is allowed to get this information. With the `FileInfo` class, the check happens only when calling the constructor.

The sample code creates a new `FileInfo` object and writes the result of the properties `Name`, `DirectoryName`, `IsReadOnly`, `Extension`, `Length`, `CreationTime`, `LastAccessTime`, and `Attributes` to the console (code file `FilesAndFolders/Program.cs`):

```
void FileInformation(string file)
{
  FileInfo fileInfo = new(file);
  if (!fileInfo.Exists)
  {
    Console.WriteLine("File not found.");
  }
  Console.WriteLine($"Name: {fileInfo.Name}");
  Console.WriteLine($"Directory: {fileInfo.DirectoryName}");
  Console.WriteLine($"Read only: {fileInfo.IsReadOnly}");
  Console.WriteLine($"Extension: {fileInfo.Extension}");
  Console.WriteLine($"Length: {fileInfo.Length}");
  Console.WriteLine($"Creation time: {fileInfo.CreationTime:F}");
  Console.WriteLine($"Access time: {fileInfo.LastAccessTime:F}");
  Console.WriteLine($"File attributes: {fileInfo.Attributes}");
}
```

The following statement passes the filename `./Program.cs` in command-line arguments:

```
> dotnet run -- fileinfo --file ./Program.cs
```

This results in the following output (on my machine):

```
Name: Program.cs
Directory: C:\FilesAndStreams\\FilesAndFolders
Read only: False
Extension: .cs
Length: 6773
Creation time: Friday, April 2, 2021 8:53:38 PM
Access time: Tuesday, April 6, 2021 9:47:07 PM
File attributes: Archive
```

A few of the properties of the `FileInfo` class cannot be set; they only define get accessors. It's not possible to set the filename, the file extension, and the length of the file. The creation time and last access time can be set. The method `ChangeFileProperties` writes the creation time of a file to the console and later changes the creation time to a date in the year 2035.

```
void ChangeFileProperties(string file)
{
  FileInfo = new(file);
  if (!fileInfo.Exists)
  {
    Console.WriteLine($"File {file} does not exist");
    return;
  }
```

```
       Console.WriteLine($"creation time: {fileInfo.CreationTime:F}");
       fileInfo.CreationTime = new DateTime(2035, 12, 24, 15, 0, 0);
       Console.WriteLine($"creation time: {fileInfo.CreationTime:F}");
   }
```

Running the program shows the initial creation time of the file as well as the creation time after it has been changed. Creating files in the future (at least specifying the creation time) is possible with this technique.

```
creation time: Sunday, December 20, 2015 9:41:49 AM
creation time: Wednesday, December 24, 2025 3:00:00 PM
```

To see the creation time of files with the command line on Windows, use `dir /T:C` on Windows.

> **NOTE** *There are some issues with the creation time on Linux, which are explained in the comment of the method* `SetCreationTime` *in the .NET source code:*
>
> *"Unix provides APIs to update the last access time* (`atime`) *and last modification time* (`mtime`). *There is no API to update the* `CreationTime`. *Some platforms (for example, Linux) don't store a creation time. On those platforms, the creation time is synthesized as the oldest of last status change time* (`ctime`) *and last modification time* (`mtime`). *We update the* `LastWriteTime` (`mtime`). *This triggers a metadata change for* `FileSystemWatcher` `NotifyFilters.CreationTime`. *Updating the* `mtime`, *causes the* `ctime` *to be set 'now.' So, on platforms that don't store a* `CreationTime`, `GetCreationTime` *returns the value that was previously set (when the value wasn't in the future)."*

> **NOTE** *Being able to manually modify these properties might seem strange at first, but it can be quite useful. For example, if you have a program that effectively modifies a file by simply reading it in, deleting it, and creating a new file with the new contents, you would probably want to modify the creation date to match the original creation date of the old file.*

Using File to Read and Write

With `File.ReadAllText` and `File.WriteAllText`, you can read and write a file using a single string. Instead of using one string, you can also use file operations that use a string for every line in a file as shown here. The method `ReadAllLines` returns a string array. `ReadLines` returns `IEnumerable<string>`, which allows you to iterate through all the lines where you can start looping through the file before the complete file was read (code file `FilesAndFolders/Program.cs`):

```
void ReadLineByLine(string file)
{
  IEnumerable<string> lines = File.ReadLines(file);
  int i = 1;
  foreach (var line in lines)
  {
    Console.WriteLine($"{i++}. {line}");
  }
}
```

For writing a string collection, you can use the method `File.WriteAllLines`. This method accepts a filename and an `IEnumerable<string>` type as parameter. To append strings to an existing file, you use `File.AppendAllLines`:

```
void WriteAFile()
{
  string fileName = Path.Combine(Environment.GetFolderPath(
    Environment.SpecialFolder.Personal), "movies.txt");
  string[] movies =
  {
    "Snow White And The Seven Dwarfs",
    "Gone With The Wind",
    "Casablanca",
    "The Bridge On The River Kwai",
    "Some Like It Hot"
  };

  File.WriteAllLines(fileName, movies);

  string[] moreMovies =
  {
    "Psycho",
    "Easy Rider",
    "Pulp Fiction",
    "Star Wars",
    "The Matrix"
  };
  File.AppendAllLines(fileName, moreMovies);
}
```

ITERATING FILES

To work with multiple files, you can use the `Directory` class. `Directory` defines the method `GetFiles` that returns a string array of all files in the directory. The method `GetDirectories` returns a string array of all directories.

All of these methods define overloads that allow passing a search pattern and a value of the `SearchOption` enumeration. `SearchOption` enables you to walk through all subdirectories or to stay in the top-level directory by using the value `AllDirectories` or `TopDirectoryOnly`. With this method you can pass simple expressions containing * for any number of characters and ? for single characters.

When you walk through a huge directory (or subdirectories), the methods `GetFiles` and `GetDirectories` need to have the complete result before the result is returned. An alternative is to use the methods `EnumerateFiles` and `EnumerateDirectories`. These methods offer the same parameters for the search pattern and options, but they immediately start returning a result with `IEnumerable<string>`.

Let's have a look at another example. Within a directory and all its subdirectories, all files that end with Copy are deleted in case another file exists with the same name and size. On Windows, you can simulate this easily by selecting all files in a folder by pressing Ctrl+A on the keyboard, pressing Ctrl+C on the keyboard for copy, and pressing Ctrl+V on the keyboard while the mouse is still in the same folder to paste. The new files have the `Copy` postfix applied.

The method `DeleteDuplicateFiles` iterates all files in the directory that is passed with the first argument, walking through all subdirectories using the option `SearchOption.AllDirectories`. Within the `foreach` statement, the current file in the iteration is compared to the file in the previous iteration. In cases where the filename is nearly the same and only - Copy is added, and if the size of the files is the same as well, the copied file is deleted by invoking `FileInfo.Delete` (code file `FilesAndFolders/Program.cs`):

```
void DeleteDuplicateFiles(string directory, bool checkOnly = true)
{
  IEnumerable<string> fileNames = Directory.EnumerateFiles(directory, "*",
    SearchOption.AllDirectories);
  string previousFileName = string.Empty;
  foreach (string fileName in fileNames)
  {
    string previousName = Path.GetFileNameWithoutExtension(previousFileName);
    int ix = previousFileName.LastIndexOf(" - Copy");
    if (!string.IsNullOrEmpty(previousFileName) &&
      previousName.EndsWith(" - Copy") &&
      fileName.StartsWith(previousFileName[..ix]))
    {
      FileInfo copiedFile = new(previousFileName);
      FileInfo originalFile = new(fileName);
      if (copiedFile.Length == originalFile.Length)
      {
        Console.WriteLine($"delete {copiedFile.FullName}");
        if (!checkOnly)
        {
          copiedFile.Delete();
        }
      }
    }
    previousFileName = fileName;
  }
}
```

WORKING WITH STREAMS

Now let's look at some powerful options that are available when you work with files: streams. The idea of a stream has been around for a long time. A stream is an object used to transfer data. The data can be transferred in one of two directions:

➤ If the data is being transferred from some outside source into your program, it is called *reading* from the stream.

➤ If the data is being transferred from your program to some outside source, it is called *writing* to the stream.

Often, the outside source will be a file, but that is not always the case. Other possibilities include the following:

➤ Reading data from or writing data to the network using some network protocol, where the intention is for this data to be picked up by or sent from another computer

➤ Reading from or writing to pipes, which allow one program to communicate with another on the local system

➤ Reading from or writing to an area of memory

Some streams allow only writing, other streams allow only reading, and yet others allow random access. Random access enables you to position a cursor at any given point within a stream—for example, to start reading from the start of the stream to later move to the end of the stream and continue with a position in the middle of the stream.

Of these examples, Microsoft has supplied a .NET class for writing to or reading from memory: the `System.IO.MemoryStream` object. The `System.Net.Sockets.NetworkStream` object handles network data. The `Stream` class does not make any assumptions of the nature of the data source. It can be file streams, memory streams, network streams, or any data source you can think of.

Some streams can also be chained. For example, the `DeflateStream` can be used to compress data. This stream can in turn write to the `FileStream`, `MemoryStream`, or `NetworkStream`. The `CryptoStream` enables you to encrypt data. It's also possible to chain the `DeflateStream` to the `CryptoStream` and write in turn to the `FileStream`.

> **NOTE** *Chapter 20, "Security," explains how you can use the* `CryptoStream`.

When you use streams, the outside source might even be a variable within your code. This might sound paradoxical, but the technique of using streams to transmit data between variables can be a useful trick for converting data between data types. The C language used something similar—the `sprintf` function—to convert between integer data types and strings or to format strings.

The advantage of having a separate object for the transfer of data, rather than using the `FileInfo` or `DirectoryInfo` classes to do this, is that separating the concept of transferring data from the particular data source makes it easier to swap data sources. Stream objects contain a lot of generic code that concerns the movement of data between outside sources and variables in your code. By keeping this code separate from any concept of a particular data source, you make it easier for this code to be reused in different circumstances.

Although it's not that easy to directly read from and write to streams, you can use readers and writers. This is another separation of concerns. Readers and writers can read from and write to streams. For example, the `StringReader` and `StringWriter` classes are part of the same inheritance tree as two classes that you use later to read and write text files. The classes will almost certainly share a substantial amount of code behind the scenes. Figure 18-1 illustrates the hierarchy of some stream-related classes in the `System.IO` namespace.

As far as reading and writing files goes, the classes that concern us most are the following:

➤ `FileStream`—This class is intended for reading and writing binary data in a file.

➤ `StreamReader` and `StreamWriter`—These classes are designed specifically for reading from and writing to streams offering APIs for text formats.

➤ `BinaryReader` and `BinaryWriter`—These classes are designed for reading from and writing to streams offering APIs for binary data.

The difference between using these classes and directly using the underlying stream objects is that a basic stream works in bytes. For example, suppose that as part of the process of saving some document you want to write the contents of a variable of type `long` to a binary file. Each `long` occupies 8 bytes, and if you use an ordinary binary stream, you would have to explicitly write each of those 8 bytes of memory.

In C# code, you would have to perform some bitwise operations to extract each of those 8 bytes from the `long` value. Using a `BinaryWriter` instance, you can encapsulate the entire operation in an overload of the `BinaryWriter.Write` method, which takes a `long` as a parameter and places those 8 bytes into the stream (and if the stream is directed to a file, into the file). A corresponding `BinaryReader.Read` method extracts 8 bytes from the stream and recovers the value of the `long`.

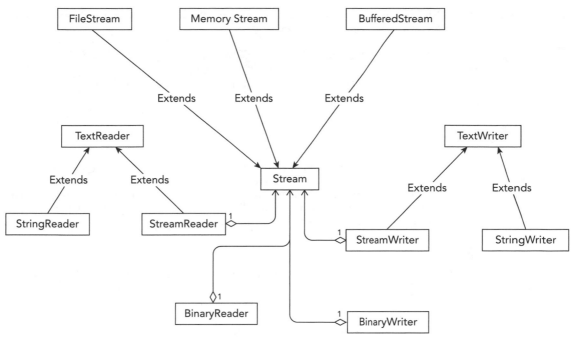

FIGURE 18-1

Working with File Streams

Let's get into programming streams reading and writing files. A `FileStream` instance is used to read data from or write data to a file. To construct a `FileStream`, you need four pieces of information:

➤ The *file* you want to access.

➤ The *mode*, which indicates how you want to open the file. For example, are you intending to create a new file or open an existing file? If you are opening an existing file, should any write operations be interpreted as overwriting the contents of the file or appending to the file?

➤ The *access*, which indicates how you want to access the file. For example, do you want to read from or write to the file or do both?

➤ The *share* access, which specifies whether you want exclusive access to the file. Alternatively, are you willing to have other streams access the file simultaneously? If so, should other streams have access to read the file, to write to it, or to do both?

The first piece of information is usually represented by a string that contains the full pathname of the file, and this chapter considers only those constructors that require a string here. Besides those, however, some additional constructors take a native Windows handle to a file instead. The remaining three pieces of information are represented by three .NET enums called `FileMode`, `FileAccess`, and `FileShare`. The values of these enumerations are listed in the following table and are self-explanatory:

ENUMERATION	VALUES
FileMode	Append, Create, CreateNew, Open, OpenOrCreate, or Truncate
FileAccess	Read, ReadWrite, or Write
FileShare	Delete, Inheritable, None, Read, ReadWrite, or Write

Note that in the case of `FileMode`, exceptions can be thrown if you request a mode that is inconsistent with the existing status of the file. `Append`, `Open`, and `Truncate` throw an exception if the file does not already exist, and `CreateNew` throws an exception if it does. `Create` and `OpenOrCreate` cope with either scenario, but `Create` deletes any existing file to replace it with a new, initially empty, one. The `FileAccess` and `FileShare` enumerations are bitwise flags, so values can be combined with the C# bitwise OR operator, |.

Creating a FileStream

There is a large number of constructors for the `FileStream`. The following sample uses one with four parameters (code file `StreamSamples/Program.cs`):

➤ The filename

➤ The `FileMode` enumeration with the `Open` value to open an existing file

➤ The `FileAccess` enumeration with the `Read` value to read the file

➤ The `FileShare` enumeration with a `Read` value to allow other programs to read but not change the file at the same time

```
void ReadFileUsingFileStream(string fileName)
{
  const int bufferSize = 4096;
  using FileStream stream = new(fileName, FileMode.Open, FileAccess.Read, FileShare
    .Read);
  ShowStreamInformation(stream);
  //...
}
```

Instead of using the constructor of the `FileStream` class to create a `FileStream` object, you can create a `FileStream` directly using the `File` class with the `OpenRead` method. The `OpenRead` method opens a file (similar to `FileMode.Open`), returns a stream that can be read (`FileAccess.Read`), and also allows other processes read access (`FileShare.Read`):

```
using FileStream stream = File.OpenRead(fileName);
```

Getting Stream Information

The `Stream` class defines the properties `CanRead`, `CanWrite`, `CanSeek`, and `CanTimeout` that you can read to get information about what can be done with a stream. For reading and writing streams, the timeout values `ReadTimeout` and `WriteTimeout` specify timeouts in milliseconds. Setting these values can be important in networking scenarios to make sure the user does not have to wait too long when reading or writing and the stream fails. The `Position` property returns the current position of the cursor in the stream. Every time some data is read from the stream, the position moves to the next byte that will be read. The sample code writes information about the stream to the console (code file `StreamSamples/Program.cs`):

```
void ShowStreamInformation(Stream stream)
{
  Console.WriteLine($"stream can read: {stream.CanRead}, " +
    $"can write: {stream.CanWrite}, can seek: {stream.CanSeek}, " +
    $"can timeout: {stream.CanTimeout}");
  Console.WriteLine($"length: {stream.Length}, position: {stream.Position}");
  if (stream.CanTimeout)
  {
    Console.WriteLine($"read timeout: {stream.ReadTimeout} " +
      $"write timeout: {stream.WriteTimeout} ");
  }
}
```

When you run the program with the file stream that has been opened, you get the following output. The position is currently 0 as read has not yet happened:

```
stream can read: True, can write: False, can seek: True, can timeout: False
length: 1113, position: 0
```

Analyzing Text File Encodings

With text files, the next step is to read the first bytes of the stream—the preamble. The *preamble* gives information about how the file is encoded (the text format used). This is also known as *byte order mark* (BOM).

You can read a stream by using ReadByte, which reads just a byte from the stream, or the Read method, which fills a byte array. With the GetEncoding sample method, an array of 5 bytes is created, and the byte array is filled from the Read method. The second and third parameters specify the offset within the byte array and the count of the number of bytes that are available to fill. The Read method returns the number of bytes read; the stream might be smaller than the buffer. In case no more characters are available to read, the Read method returns 0.

The sample code analyzes the first characters of the stream to return the detected encoding and positions the stream after the encoding characters (code file StreamSamples/Program.cs):

```
Encoding GetEncoding(Stream stream)
{
  if (!stream.CanSeek) throw new ArgumentException(
    "require a stream that can seek");

  Encoding = Encoding.ASCII;
  byte[] bom = new byte[5];
  int nRead = stream.Read(bom, offset: 0, count: 5);
  if (bom[0] == 0xff && bom[1] == 0xfe && bom[2] == 0 && bom[3] == 0)
  {
    Console.WriteLine("UTF-32");
    stream.Seek(4, SeekOrigin.Begin);
    return Encoding.UTF32;
  }
  else if (bom[0] == 0xff && bom[1] == 0xfe)
  {
    Console.WriteLine("UTF-16, little endian");
    stream.Seek(2, SeekOrigin.Begin);
    return Encoding.Unicode;
  }
  else if (bom[0] == 0xfe && bom[1] == 0xff)
  {
    Console.WriteLine("UTF-16, big endian");
    stream.Seek(2, SeekOrigin.Begin);
```

```
      return Encoding.BigEndianUnicode;
    }
    else if (bom[0] == 0xef && bom[1] == 0xbb && bom[2] == 0xbf)
    {
      Console.WriteLine("UTF-8");
      stream.Seek(3, SeekOrigin.Begin);
      return Encoding.UTF8;
    }
    stream.Seek(0, SeekOrigin.Begin);
    return encoding;
  }
```

The start of a file can begin with the characters FF and FE. The order of these bytes gives information about how the document is stored. Two-byte Unicode can be stored in little- or big-endian. (Endianness describes the order of bytes in memory.) With FF followed by FE, it's little-endian, and when FE is followed by FF, it's big-endian. This endianness goes back to mainframes by IBM that used big-endian for byte ordering, and PDP11 systems from Digital Equipment that used little-endian. Communicating across the network with computers that have different endianness requires changing the order of bytes on one side. Nowadays, the Intel CPU architecture uses little-endian, and the ARM architecture allows switching between little- and big-endian.

What's the other difference between these encodings? With ASCII, 7 bits are enough for every character. Originally based on the English alphabet, ASCII offers lowercase, uppercase, and control characters. Extended ASCII makes use of the eighth bit to allow switching to language-specific characters. Switching is not easy as it requires paying attention to the code map and also does not provide enough characters for some Asian languages. UTF-16 (Unicode Text Format) solves this by having 16 bits for every character. Because UTF-16 is still not enough for historical glyphs, UTF-32 uses 32 bits for every character. Although Windows NT 3.1 switched to UTF-16 for the default text encoding (from a Microsoft extension of ASCII before), nowadays the most-used text format is UTF-8. With the Web, UTF-8 turned out to be the most-used text format since 2007 (this superseded ASCII, which had been the most common character encoding before). UTF-8 uses a variable length for character definitions. One character is defined by using between 1 and 6 bytes. UTF-8 is detected by this character sequence at the beginning of a file: 0xEF, 0xBB, 0xBF.

Reading Streams

After opening the file and creating the stream, the file is read using the Read method. This is repeated until the method returns 0. A string is created using the Encoder created from the GetEncoding method defined earlier. Do not forget to close the stream using the Dispose method. If possible, use the using declaration—as is done with the following code sample—to dispose of the stream automatically (code file StreamSamples/Program.cs):

```
void ReadUsingFileStream(string fileName)
{
  const int BUFFERSIZE = 4096;
  using FileStream stream = new(fileName, FileMode.Open, FileAccess.Read, FileShare
.Read);

  ShowStreamInformation(stream);
  Encoding encoding = GetEncoding(stream);

  var buffer = new byte[BUFFERSIZE].AsSpan();

  bool completed = false;
  do
  {
    int nread = stream.Read(buffer);
    if (nread == 0) completed = true;
```

```
      if (nread < buffer.Length)
      {
        buffer[nread..].Clear();
      }

      string s = encoding.GetString(buffer[..nread]);
      Console.WriteLine($"read {nread} bytes");
      Console.WriteLine(s);
    } while (!completed);
  }
```

Writing Streams

How streams can be written is demonstrated by writing a simple string to a text file. To create a stream that can be written to, the `File.OpenWrite` method can be used. This time, a temporary filename is created with the help of members of the `Path` class. `GetTempPath` returns the path of the user's temp folder, `GetRandomFileName` returns a random filename, and finally the random filename extension is changed using `ChangeExtension` (code file `StreamSamples/Program.cs`):

```
void WriteTextFile()
{
  string tempFileName = Path.Combine(Path.GetTempPath(), Path.GetRandomFileName());
  string tempTextFileName = Path.ChangeExtension(tempFileName, "txt");
  using FileStream stream = File.OpenWrite(tempTextFileName);
  //...
```

When you're writing a UTF-8 file, the preamble needs to be written to the file. This can be done by sending the 3 bytes of the UTF-8 preamble to the stream with the `WriteByte` method:

```
stream.WriteByte(0xef);
stream.WriteByte(0xbb);
stream.WriteByte(0xbf);
```

There's an alternative for doing this. You don't need to remember the bytes to specify the encoding. The `Encoding` class already has this information. The `GetPreamble` method returns a byte array with the preamble for the file. This byte array is written using the `Write` method of the `Stream` class:

```
var preamble = Encoding.UTF8.GetPreamble().AsSpan();
stream.Write(preamble);
```

Now the content of the file can be written. As the `Write` method requires byte arrays to write, strings need to be converted. For converting a string to a byte array with UTF-8, `Encoding.UTF8.GetBytes` does the job before the byte array is written:

```
string hello = "Hello, World!";
var buffer = Encoding.UTF8.GetBytes(hello).AsSpan();
stream.Write(buffer);
Console.WriteLine($"file {stream.Name} written");
```

You can open the temporary file using an editor, and it will use the correct encoding.

Copying Streams

Now let's combine reading and writing from streams by copying the file content. With the next code snippet, the readable stream is opened with `File.OpenRead`, and the writeable stream is opened with `File.OpenWrite`. A buffer is read using the `Stream.Read` method and written with `Stream.Write`. The `Stream` methods have `Read` and `Write` overloads that can use the `Span<byte>`, which allows creating slices to reference the same memory underneath; thus, it is not necessary (contrary to the byte array overload) to pass the start position and size with the arguments for `Read` and `Write` (code file `StreamSamples/Program.cs`):

```
void CopyUsingStreams(string inputFile, string outputFile)
{
  const int BUFFERSIZE = 4096;
  using var inputStream = File.OpenRead(inputFile);
  using var outputStream = File.OpenWrite(outputFile);
  var buffer = new byte[BUFFERSIZE].AsSpan();
  bool completed = false;
  do
  {
    int nRead = inputStream.Read(buffer);
    if (nRead == 0) completed = true;
    outputStream.Write(buffer[..nRead]);
  } while (!completed);
}
```

> **NOTE** *The Span type is shown in detail in Chapter 13, "Managed and Unmanaged Memory."*

To copy a stream, it's not necessary to write the code to read and write a stream. Instead, you can use the `CopyTo` method of the `Stream` class, as shown here (code file `StreamSamples/Program.cs`):

```
void CopyUsingStreams2(string inputFile, string outputFile)
{
  using var inputStream = File.OpenRead(inputFile);
  using var outputStream = File.OpenWrite(outputFile);
  inputStream.CopyTo(outputStream);
}
```

Using Random Access to Streams

Random access to streams provides an advantage in that—even with large files—you can access a specific position within the file in a fast way.

To see random access in action, the following code snippet creates a large file. This code snippet creates the file `sampledata.data` with records that are all the same length and contain a number, a 20-character string, and a random date. The number of records that is passed to the method is created with the help of the `Enumerable.Range` method (defined with the `System.Linq` namespace). The `Select` method creates a tuple that contains `Number`, `Text`, and `Date` fields. Out of these records, a string with # pre- and postfix is created, with a fixed length for every value and a ; separator between each value. The `WriteAsync` method writes the record to the stream. The File and Stream APIs offer asynchronous APIs beside the synchronous ones. This sample makes use of the asynchronous APIs that allow the calling (code file `StreamSamples/Program.cs`):

```
string SampleDataFilePath = Path.Combine(Environment.GetFolderPath(
  Environment.SpecialFolder.ApplicationData), "samplefile.data");

public static async Task CreateSampleFileAsync(int count)
{
  FileStream stream = File.Create(SampleDataFilePath);
  using StreamWriter writer = new(stream);
```

```
      Random r = new();
      var records = Enumerable.Range(1, count).Select(x =>
      (
        Number: x,
        Text: $"Sample text {r.Next(200)}",
        Date: new DateTime(Math.Abs((long)((r.NextDouble() * 2 - 1) *
          DateTime.MaxValue.Ticks)))
      ));
      Console.WriteLine("Start writing records...");
      foreach (var rec in records)
      {
        string date = rec.Date.ToString("d", CultureInfo.InvariantCulture);
        string s =
          $"#{rec.Number,8};{rec.Text,-20};{date}#{Environment.NewLine}";
        await writer.WriteAsync(s);
      }
      Console.WriteLine($"Created the file {SampleDataFilePath}");
    }
```

> **NOTE** *The File and Stream APIs not only offer synchronous APIs but also APIs implementing the task-based async pattern (which is explained in Chapter 11, "Tasks and Asynchronous Programming"). This allows the calling thread to work on some other functionality instead of waiting for the I/O.*

> **NOTE** *Chapter 13 explains that every object implementing* IDisposable *should be disposed of. In the previous code snippet, it looks like* FileStream *is not disposed of. However, that's not the case. The* StreamWriter *takes control over the used resource and disposes of the stream when the* StreamWriter *is disposed of. To keep the stream opened for a longer period than the* StreamWriter *is alive, you can configure this with the constructor of the* StreamWriter. *In that case, you need to dispose of the stream explicitly.*

Now, let's position a cursor randomly within the stream to read different records. The user is asked to enter a record number that should be accessed. The byte in the stream that should be accessed is based on the record number and the record size. The Seek method of the Stream class now enables you to position the cursor within the stream. The second argument specifies whether the position is based on the beginning of the stream, the end of the stream, or the current position (code file StreamSamples/Program.cs):

```
async Task RandomAccessSampleAsync()
{
  const int RECORDSIZE = 44;
  try
  {
    using FileStream stream = File.OpenRead(SampleDataFilePath);
    var buffer = new byte[RECORDSIZE].AsMemory();

    do
    {
      try
```

```
    {
      Console.Write("record number (or 'bye' to end): ");
      string line = Console.ReadLine() ?? throw new InvalidOperationException();
      if (string.Equals(line, "bye", StringComparison.CurrentCultureIgnoreCase))
          break;

      if (int.TryParse(line, out int record))
      {
        stream.Seek((record - 1) * RECORDSIZE, SeekOrigin.Begin);
        int read = await stream.ReadAsync(buffer);
        string s = Encoding.UTF8.GetString(buffer.Span[0..read]);
        Console.WriteLine($"record: {s}");
      }
    }
    catch (Exception ex)
    {
      Console.WriteLine(ex.Message);
    }
  } while (true);
  Console.WriteLine("finished");
}
catch (FileNotFoundException)
{
  Console.WriteLine("Create the sample file using the option -sample first");
}
}
```

> **NOTE** *Contrary to the synchronous* Read *method of the* Stream *class where a* Span<byte>
> *parameter is offered with an overload, the* ReadAsync *method gives a* Memory<byte> *overload.*
> Span<T> *is a ref struct type and thus can only be stored on the stack. This is unsuitable for*
> *asynchronous methods, which is why the* Memory<byte> *type is offered with the asynchronous*
> *overloads.*

You can now try to create a file with 1.5 million records or more. A file this size is slow when you open it using Notepad, but it is extremely fast when you use random access. Depending on your system, the CPU, and the disk type, you might use higher or lower values for the tests.

> **NOTE** *If the records that should be accessed don't have a fixed size, it still can be useful to
> use random access for large files. One way to deal with this is to write the position of the
> records to the beginning of the file. Another option is to read a larger block where the record
> could be and find the record identifier and the record delimiters within the memory block.*

Using Buffered Streams

For performance reasons, when you read from or write to a file, the output is buffered. This means that if your program asks for the next bytes of a file stream and the stream passes the request on to the operating system (OS), then the OS will not connect to the file system and then locate and read the file off the disk just to get the additional bytes. Instead, the OS retrieves a large block of the file at one time and stores this block in an area of memory known as a *buffer*. Subsequent requests for data from the stream are satisfied from the buffer until the buffer runs out, at which point the OS grabs another block of data from the file.

Writing to files works in the same way. For files, this is done automatically by the OS, but you might have to write a stream class to read from some other device that is not buffered. If so, you can create a BufferedStream, which implements a buffer itself, and pass the stream that should be buffered to the constructor. Note, however, that BufferedStream is not designed for the situation in which an application frequently alternates between reading and writing data.

USING READERS AND WRITERS

Reading and writing text files using the FileStream class requires working with byte buffers and dealing with the encoding as described in the previous section. There's an easier way to do this: using readers and writers. You can use the StreamReader and StreamWriter classes to read and write to the FileStream, and you have an easier job not dealing with byte arrays and encodings.

That's because these classes work at a slightly higher level and are specifically geared to reading and writing text. The methods that they implement can automatically detect convenient points to stop reading text, based on the contents of the stream. In particular:

➤ These classes implement methods to read or write one line of text at a time: StreamReader.ReadLine and StreamWriter.WriteLine. In the case of reading, this means that the stream automatically determines where the next carriage return is and stops reading at that point. In the case of writing, it means that the stream automatically appends the carriage return–line feed combination to the text that it writes out. The NewLine property of the TextWriter base class allows to customize the newline character.

➤ By using the StreamReader and StreamWriter classes, you don't need to worry about the encoding used in the file.

The StreamReader Class

Let's convert the previous example to use the StreamReader to read a file. It looks a lot easier now. The constructor of the StreamReader receives the FileStream. You can check for the end of the file by using the EndOfStream property, and you read lines using the ReadLine method (code file ReaderWriterSamples/Program.cs):

```
void ReadFileUsingReader(string fileName)
{
    FileStream stream = new(fileName, FileMode.Open, FileAccess.Read, FileShare.Read);
    using StreamReader reader = new(stream);

    while (!reader.EndOfStream)
    {
        string? line = reader.ReadLine();
        Console.WriteLine(line);
    }
}
```

It's no longer necessary to deal with byte arrays and the encoding. However, be aware that the StreamReader by default uses the UTF-8 encoding. You can let the StreamReader use the encoding as it is defined by the preamble in the file by specifying a different constructor:

```
StreamReader reader = new(stream, detectEncodingFromByteOrderMarks: true);
```

You can also explicitly specify the encoding:

```
StreamReader reader = new(stream, Encoding.Unicode);
```

Other constructors enable you to set the buffer size to be used; the default is 1,024 bytes. Also, you can specify that the underlying stream should not be closed on closing the reader. By default, when the reader is closed (using the `Dispose` or `Close` method), the underlying stream is closed as well.

Instead of explicitly instantiating a new `StreamReader`, you can create a `StreamReader` by using the `OpenText` method of the `File` class (or by using the constructor of the `StreamReader`):

```
var reader = File.OpenText(fileName);
```

With the code snippet to read the file, the file was read line by line using the `ReadLine` method. The `StreamReader` also allows reading the complete file from the position of the cursor in the stream using `ReadToEnd`:

```
string content = reader.ReadToEnd();
```

The `StreamReader` also allows the content to read to a char array. This is similar to the `Read` method of the `Stream` class; it doesn't read to a byte array but instead to a char array. Remember, the char type uses two bytes. This is perfect for 16-bit Unicode, but is not as useful with UTF-8, where a single character can be between one and six bytes long:

```
int nChars = 100;
char[] charArray = new char[nChars];
int nCharsRead = reader.Read(charArray, 0, nChars);
```

The StreamWriter Class

The `StreamWriter` works in the same way as the `StreamReader`, except that you use `StreamWriter` only to write to a file (or to another stream). The following code snippet shows creating a `StreamWriter` that passes a `FileStream`. Then a passed string array is written to the stream (code file `ReaderWriterSamples/Program.cs`):

```
void WriteFileUsingWriter(string fileName, string[] lines)
{
  var outputStream = File.OpenWrite(fileName);
  using StreamWriter writer = new(outputStream, Encoding.UTF8);
  foreach (var line in lines)
  {
    writer.WriteLine(line);
  }
}
```

The `StreamWriter` is using the UTF-8 format by default to write the text content. But be aware that the preamble is written only if you pass the encoding to the constructor. Similarly to the constructor of the `StreamReader`, the `StreamWriter` allows specifying the buffer size and whether the underlying stream should not be closed on closing of the writer.

> **NOTE** *When opening existing files with* `File.OpenWrite` *or passing a filename to the constructor of the* `StreamWriter`, *you need to be aware of different behaviors:* `File.OpenWrite` *sets the current position of the stream to the start of the file, whereas using the* `StreamWriter` *constructor sets the current position to the end of the file.*

The `Write` method of the `StreamWriter` defines 19 overloads that allow passing strings and several .NET data types. When using the methods passing the .NET data types, remember that all these are changed to strings with the specified encoding. To write the data types in binary format, you can use the `BinaryWriter` that's shown next.

Reading and Writing Binary Files

To read and write binary files, one option is to directly use the stream types; in this case, it's good to use byte arrays for reading and writing. Another option is to use readers and writers defined for this scenario: `BinaryReader` and `BinaryWriter`. You use them similarly to the way you use `StreamReader` and `StreamWriter` except `BinaryReader` and `BinaryWriter` don't use any encoding. Files are written in binary format rather than text format.

Unlike the `Stream` type, `BinaryWriter` defines 20 overloads for the `Write` method. The overloads accept different types, as shown in the following code snippet that writes a `double`, an `int`, a `long`, and a `string` (code file `ReaderWriterSamples/Program.cs`):

```
public static void WriteFileUsingBinaryWriter(string binFile)
{
  var outputStream = File.Create(binFile);
  using var writer = new BinaryWriter(outputStream);
  double d = 47.47;
  int i = 42;
  long l = 987654321;
  string s = "sample";
  writer.Write(d);
  writer.Write(i);
  writer.Write(l);
  writer.Write(s);
}
```

To read the file again, you can use a `BinaryReader`. This class defines methods to read all the different types, such as `ReadDouble`, `ReadInt32`, `ReadInt64`, and `ReadString`, which are shown here:

```
public static void ReadFileUsingBinaryReader(string binFile)
{
  var inputStream = File.Open(binFile, FileMode.Open);
  using BinaryReader reader = new(inputStream))
  double d = reader.ReadDouble();
  int i = reader.ReadInt32();
  long l = reader.ReadInt64();
  string s = reader.ReadString();
  Console.WriteLine($"d: {d}, i: {i}, l: {l}, s: {s}");
}
```

The order for reading the file must match exactly the order in which it has been written. When creating your own binary format, you need to know what and how it is stored and read accordingly. The older Microsoft Word document format was using a binary file format, whereas the newer docx file extension is a ZIP file containing XML files. How ZIP files can be read and written is explained in the next section.

COMPRESSING FILES

.NET includes types to compress and decompress streams using different algorithms. You can use `DeflateStream`, `GZipStream`, and `BrotliStream` to compress and decompress streams; the `ZipArchive` class enables you to create and read ZIP files.

Both `DeflateStream` and `GZipStream` use the same algorithm for compression (in fact, `GZipStream` uses `DeflateStream` behind the scenes), but `GZipStream` adds a cyclic redundancy check to detect data corruption. Brotli is a relatively new open-source compression algorithm from Google. The speed of Brotli is similar to deflate, but it offers a better compression. Contrary to most other compression algorithms, it uses a dictionary for often-used words for better compression. Nowadays, this algorithm is supported by most modern browsers.

Using a ZIP file has the advantage that you can compress files to an archive (with `ZipArchive`), and you can open this archive directly with Windows Explorer; it's been built into Windows since 1998. You can't open a gzip archive with Windows Explorer; you need third-party tools for gzip.

> **NOTE** *The algorithm used by* `DeflateStream` *and* `GZipStream` *is the deflate algorithm. This algorithm is defined by RFC 1951 (*`https://tools.ietf.org/html/rfc1951`*). This algorithm is widely thought not to be covered by patents, which is why it is in widespread use.*
>
> *Brotli is available on GitHub at* `https://github.com/google/brotli` *and defined by RFC 7932 (*`https://tools.ietf.org/html/rfc7932`*). Brotli works great for compressing text files. You can try to compress a large text file with the deflate and Brotli algorithms, and you will see an impressive difference.*

Using the Deflate Stream

As explained earlier, a feature from streams is that you can chain them. To compress a stream, all you need to do is create `DeflateStream` and pass another stream (in this example, the `outputStream` to write a file) to the constructor, with the argument `CompressionMode.Compress` for compression. Writing to the `DeflateStream` either by using the `Write` method or by using other features, such as the `CopyTo` method as shown in the following code snippet, is all that's needed for file compression (code file `CompressFileSample/Program.cs`):

```
void CompressFile(string fileName, string compressedFileName)
{
  using FileStream inputStream = File.OpenRead(fileName);
  FileStream outputStream = File.OpenWrite(compressedFileName);
  using DeflateStream compressStream = new(outputStream, CompressionMode.Compress);
  inputStream.CopyTo(compressStream);
}
```

To decompress the deflate-compressed file again, the following code snippet opens the file using a `FileStream` and creates the `DeflateStream` object with `CompressionMode.Decompress` passing the file stream for decompression. The `Stream.CopyTo` method copies the decompressed stream to a `MemoryStream`. This code snippet then makes use of a `StreamReader` to read the data from the `MemoryStream` and write the output to the console. The `StreamReader` is configured to leave the assigned `MemoryStream` open (using the `leaveOpen` argument), so the `MemoryStream` could also be used after closing the reader:

```
void DecompressFile(string fileName)
{
  FileStream inputStream = File.OpenRead(fileName);
  using MemoryStream outputStream = new();
  using DeflateStream compressStream = new(inputStream, CompressionMode.Decompress);
  compressStream.CopyTo(outputStream);
  outputStream.Seek(0, SeekOrigin.Begin);
  using StreamReader reader = new(outputStream, Encoding.UTF8,
    detectEncodingFromByteOrderMarks: true, bufferSize: 4096,
    leaveOpen: true);
  string result = reader.ReadToEnd();
  Console.WriteLine(result);
  // because of leaveOpen set, you can use the outputStream after
  // the StreamReader is closed, and the StreamReader is closed on its own
}
```

Using Brotli

Using `BrotliStream`, compression with Brotli is like using deflate. You just need to instantiate the `BrotliStream` class (code file `CompressFileSample/Program.cs`):

```
void CompressFileWithBrotli(string fileName, string compressedFileName)
{
  using FileStream inputStream = File.OpenRead(fileName);
  FileStream outputStream = File.OpenWrite(compressedFileName);
  using BrotliStream compressStream = new(outputStream, CompressionMode.Compress);
  inputStream.CopyTo(compressStream);
}
```

Decompression works like this using `BrotliStream`:

```
void DecompressFileWithBrotli(string fileName)
{
  FileStream inputStream = File.OpenRead(fileName);
  using MemoryStream outputStream = new();
  using BrotliStream compressStream = new(inputStream, CompressionMode.Decompress);
  compressStream.CopyTo(outputStream);
  outputStream.Seek(0, SeekOrigin.Begin);
  using StreamReader reader = new(outputStream, Encoding.UTF8,
    detectEncodingFromByteOrderMarks: true, bufferSize: 4096,
    leaveOpen: true);
  string result = reader.ReadToEnd();
  Console.WriteLine(result);
}
```

Zipping Files

Today, the ZIP file format is the standard for many different file types. Word documents (`docx`) as well as NuGet packages are all stored as ZIP files. With .NET, it's easy to create a ZIP archive.

For creating a ZIP archive, you can create an object of `ZipArchive`. A `ZipArchive` contains multiple `ZipArchiveEntry` objects. The `ZipArchive` class is not a stream, but it uses a stream to read or write to (this is similar to the reader and writer classes discussed earlier). The following code snippet creates a `ZipArchive` that writes the compressed content to the file stream opened with `File.OpenWrite`. What's added to the ZIP archive is defined by the directory passed. `Directory.EnumerateFiles` enumerates all the files in the directory and creates a `ZipArchiveEntry` object for every file. Invoking the `Open` method creates a `Stream` object. With the `CopyTo` method of the `Stream` that is read, the file is compressed and written to the `ZipArchiveEntry` (code file `CompressFileSample/Program.cs`):

```
void CreateZipFile(string sourceDirectory, string zipFile)
{
  FileStream zipStream = File.Create(zipFile);
  using ZipArchive archive = new(zipStream, ZipArchiveMode.Create);

  IEnumerable<string> files = Directory.EnumerateFiles(
    sourceDirectory, "*", SearchOption.TopDirectoryOnly);
  foreach (var file in files)
  {
    ZipArchiveEntry entry = archive.CreateEntry(Path.GetFileName(file));
    using FileStream inputStream = File.OpenRead(file);
```

```
    using Stream outputStream = entry.Open();
    inputStream.CopyTo(outputStream);
  }
}
```

Instead of using streams with extracting entries from a ZIP archive, you can also use the `ExtractToFile` method.

WATCHING FILE CHANGES

With `FileSystemWatcher`, you can monitor file changes. Events are fired on creating, renaming, deleting, and changing files. This can be used in scenarios where you need to react to file changes—for example, with a server when a file is uploaded, or if a file is cached in memory and the cache needs to be invalidated when the file changes.

As `FileSystemWatcher` is easy to use, let's look at another sample. The sample code starts watching files with the method `WatchFiles`. Using the constructor of the `FileSystemWatcher`, you can supply the directory that should be watched. You can also provide a filter to access only specific files that match with the filter expression. When you set the property `IncludeSubdirectories`, you can define whether only the files in the specified directory should be watched or whether files in subdirectories should also be watched. With the `Created`, `Changed`, `Deleted`, and `Renamed` events, event handlers are supplied. All of these events are of type `FileSystemEventHandler` with the exception of the `Renamed` event that is of type `RenamedEventHandler`. `RenamedEventHandler` derives from `FileSystemEventHandler` and offers additional information about the event (code file `FileMonitor/Program.cs`):

```
FileSystemWatcher? _watcher;

if (args == null || args.Length != 1)
{
    Console.WriteLine("Enter the directory to watch markdown files: " +
      "FileMonitor [directory]");
    return;
}

WatchFiles(args[0], "*.md");
Console.WriteLine("Press enter to stop watching");
Console.ReadLine();
UnWatchFiles();

void WatchFiles(string path, string filter)
{
  _watcher = new(path, filter)
  {
    IncludeSubdirectories = true
  };
  _watcher.Created += OnFileChanged;
  _watcher.Changed += OnFileChanged;
  _watcher.Deleted += OnFileChanged;
  _watcher.Renamed += OnFileRenamed;
  _watcher.EnableRaisingEvents = true;
  Console.WriteLine("watching file changes...");
}
```

The information that is received with a file change is of type `FileSystemEventArgs`. It contains the name of the file that changed as well as the kind of change that is an enumeration of type `WatcherChangeTypes`:

```
    void OnFileChanged(object sender, FileSystemEventArgs e) =>
      Console.WriteLine($"file {e.Name} {e.ChangeType}");
```

On renaming the file, additional information is received with the `RenamedEventArgs` parameter. This type derives from `FileSystemEventArgs` and defines additional information about the original name of the file:

```
    void OnFileRenamed(object sender, RenamedEventArgs e) =>
      Console.WriteLine($"file {e.OldName} {e.ChangeType} to {e.Name}");
```

When you start the application by specifying a folder to watch and `*.md` as the filter, the following is the output after creating the file `sample1.md`, adding content, renaming it to `sample2.md`, and finally deleting it:

```
    watching file changes...
    Press enter to stop watching
    file sample1.md Created
    file sample1.md Changed
    file sample1.md Renamed to sample2.md
```

JSON SERIALIZATION

There are many ways to serialize and deserialize .NET objects. Binary (also known as *runtime serialization*), XML, and JSON serialization are built into the .NET base class library (BCL).

Binary serialization that serializes all fields has versioning issues. If names of private fields change (which can be in a base class), deserialization of content that was written with an older version might not work with new versions of the library. Microsoft recommends not using binary serialization with the built-in functionality.

> **WARNING** *Other than the versioning issues, the* `BinaryFormatter` *(used for binary serialization) is dangerous to use and not recommended for data processing. The* `Deserialize` *method is never safe with untrusted input. This also applies for the* `SoapFormatter`, `NetDataContractSerializer`, `LosFormatter`, *and* `ObjectStateFormatter`. *For more details, see* https://docs.microsoft.com/en-us/dotnet/standard/serialization/binaryformatter-security-guide.

To serialize objects into XML, classes from the namespace `System.Xml.Serialization` can be used. With the `XmlSerializer`, you can serialize .NET objects into XML and use attributes to influence the outcome of the XML result. LINQ to XML (`System.Xml.Linq`) offers an easy way to create XML elements. Windows Communication Foundation (WCF) and SOAP was based on XML. Microsoft Office files are ZIP files containing XML. .NET project files and XAML files that create user interfaces with WinUI are based on XML. .NET classes working with XML haven't been updated in the last years and don't support new features such as C# nominal records.

Nowadays, JSON serialization is more important. Most representational state transfer (REST) services use JSON to transfer data between the client and the server. Read Chapter 25, "Services," for information on how to implement services using REST.

> **NOTE** *While JSON is more important with new formats, XML still has many uses. For example, Office files are compressed ZIP files containing XML. .NET project files use XML. Creating user interfaces with WinUI is based on XAML, which is based on XML.*

Nowadays, JSON serialization is used more often. Not long ago, many of the Microsoft project templates used the `Newtonsoft.Json` library for JSON serialization. Now, with `System.Text.Json`, a new library was created by the .NET team. This library is faster and needs fewer object allocations because it is based on new techniques with the `Span` type. James Newton-King who developed `Newtonsoft.Json` is now working for Microsoft.

The sample application for JSON serialization is a console application using different options from the namespaces `System.Text.Json` and `System.Text.Json.Serialization`.

> **NOTE** *Other serialization options are shown in Chapter 25 and Chapter 28, "SignalR." In Chapter 25, gRPC Remote Procedure Calls (gRPC) services make use of serialization with Protocol Buffers (Protobuf). SignalR uses JSON by default, but you can easily configure to serialize with the binary format MessagePack.*

JSON Serialization

To serialize .NET objects in the JSON format, the records `Card`, `Category`, and `Item` are specified and contain `Title`, `Text`, and `Price` properties. A menu card (type `Card`) can contain a list of `Category` objects, and a `Category` contains a list of `Item` objects (code file `JsonSample/Program.cs`):

```
public record Item(string Title, string Text, decimal Price);
public record Category(string Title)
{
    public IList<Item> Items { get; init; } = new List<Item>();
}
public record Card(string Title)
{
    public IList<Category> Categories { get; init; } = new List<Category>();
}
```

In the `Program.cs` file, a `Card` is created that contains two categories and three items, and it is then serialized by invoking the `SerializeJson` method:

```
Category appetizers = new("Appetizers");
appetizers.Items.Add(new Item("Dungeness Crab Cocktail", "Classic cocktail sauce",
27M));
appetizers.Items.Add(new Item("Almond Crusted Scallops",
  "Almonds, Parmesan, chive beurre blanc", 19M));

Category dinner = new("Dinner");
dinner.Items.Add(new Item("Grilled King Salmon", "Lemon chive beurre blanc", 49M));

Card = new("The Restaurant");
card.Categories.Add(appetizers);
card.Categories.Add(dinner);

string json = SerializeJson(card);
DeserializeJson(json);
```

With the `JsonSerializer` class, you can invoke the `Serialize` method to create a JSON representation of the passed object. Optionally, you can configure the serialization passing configuration with the `JsonSerializerOptions`:

```
string SerializeJson(Card card)
{
```

```
Console.WriteLine(nameof(SerializeJson));
JsonSerializerOptions options = new()
{
  WriteIndented = true,
  PropertyNamingPolicy = JsonNamingPolicy.CamelCase,
  DictionaryKeyPolicy = JsonNamingPolicy.CamelCase,
  AllowTrailingCommas = true,
  // ReferenceHandler = ReferenceHandler.Preserve
};
string json = JsonSerializer.Serialize(card, options);
Console.WriteLine(json);
Console.WriteLine();
return json;
}
```

When you run the application, because the `PropertyNamingPolicy` was configured with
`JsonNamingPolicy.CamelCase`, contrary to the property names, the keys are shown with camelCase:

```
{
    "title": "The Restaurant",
    "categories": [
      {
        "title": "Appetizers",
        "items": [
          {
            "title": "Dungeon Crab Cocktail",
            "text": "Classic cocktail sauce",
            "price": 27
          },
          {
            "title": "Almond Crusted Scallops",
            "text": "Almonds, Parmesan, chive beurre blanc",
            "price": 19
          }
        ]
      },
      {
        "title": "Dinner",
        "items": [
          {
            "title": "Grilled King Salmon",
            "text": "Lemon chive buerre blanc",
            "price": 49
          }
        ]
      }
    ]
}
```

Other than supplying options, to influence JSON serialization, you can apply attributes to the model to be
serialized. With the `JsonIgnoreAttribute`, you can specify that this member should not be serialized. With
this attribute you can also specify a condition—for example, to only ignore it when the value is `null`
(`JsonIgnoreCondition.WhenWritingDefault`). The `JsonNumberHandlingAttribute` allows you to
specify that numbers should be serialized as JSON numbers (without quotes), or with quotes. With the
`JsonConverterAttribute`, you can specify to use a custom converter class with types or properties.

If you need to serialize an object graph with cyclic references, where objects reference other objects that already have been serialized, the `JsonSerializer` couldn't handle this scenario before .NET 5. Since .NET 5, you can configure the `ReferenceHandler` setting to `ReferenceHandler.Preserve`. This setting creates identifiers for every JSON object serialized; thus, the serializer knows what objects already have been serialized, and it can reference these objects by its ID. Use this setting only in scenarios where it is required based on your object tree. Many JSON serializers can't work with this result. The following snippet shows the result with this setting:

```
{
  "$id": "1",
  "title": "The Restaurant",
  "categories": {
    "$id": "2",
    "$values": [
      {
        "$id": "3",
        "title": "Appetizers",
        "items": {
          "$id": "4",
          "$values": [
            {
              "$id": "5",
              "title": "Dungeon Crab Cocktail",
              "text": "Classic cocktail sauce",
              "price": 27
            },
//...
```

JSON Deserialization

With the implementation of the method `DeserializeJson`, `JsonSerializer.Deserialize` is invoked to get the object tree out of the JSON string (code file `JsonSample/Program.cs`):

```
void DeserializeJson(string json)
{
    Console.WriteLine(nameof(DeserializeJson));
    JsonSerializerOptions options = new()
    {
        PropertyNameCaseInsensitive = true
    };
    Card? card = JsonSerializer.Deserialize<Card>(json, options);
    if (card is null)
    {
        Console.WriteLine("no card deserialized");
        return;
    }
    Console.WriteLine($"{card.Title}");
    foreach (var category in card.Categories)
    {
        Console.WriteLine($"\t{category.Title}");
        foreach (var item in category.Items)
        {
            Console.WriteLine($"\t\t{item.Title}");
        }
    }
    Console.WriteLine();
}
```

Using JsonDocument

With the `JsonDocument` class, you can access the document object model (DOM) of a JSON document. The static method `JsonDocument.Parse` returns a `JsonDocument` object. With this object you can access the JSON elements and arrays. The root element is accessed with the `JsonDocument` instance `document.RootElement`. The returned type is a `JsonElement`. This type offers many methods that return specific .NET types—if the data can be converted, for example, `GetBoolean`, `GetByte`, `GetDateTime`, `GetGuid`, `GetInt32`. Using `GetProperty` returns another `JsonElement`. The previously created JSON document contains the name `"categories"` that contains an array of items. With this JSON, using `GetProperty("categories")` allows to enumerate the array with the `EnumerateArray` method. For every array element, a `JsonElement` is returned. To access the different names and values of an element, you can use `EnumerateObject` (code file `JsonSample/Program.cs`):

```
void UseDom(string json)
{
  Console.WriteLine(nameof(UseDom));

  using JsonDocument document = JsonDocument.Parse(json);
  JsonElement titleElement = document.RootElement.GetProperty("title");
  Console.WriteLine(titleElement);
  foreach (JsonElement category in document.RootElement
    .GetProperty("categories").EnumerateArray())
  {
    foreach (JsonElement item in category.GetProperty("items").EnumerateArray())
    {
      foreach (JsonProperty property in item.EnumerateObject())
      {
        Console.WriteLine($"{property.Name} {property.Value}");
      }
      Console.WriteLine($"{item.GetProperty("title")}");
    }
  }
}
```

JSON Reader

A fast way to read through a JSON document and access all its tokens is by using the `Utf8JsonReader`. By invoking the `Read` method, you can access token by token. With the next code snippet, the `Read` method is used in a `while` loop. This method returns `true` as long as it's not the end of the stream. Using the reader in the current iteration, you can access the values with methods such as `GetString`, `GetInt32`, `GetDateTime`, and also JSON comments with `GetComment`. To see what kind of token was just read, you use the `TokenType` property. With the JSON previously generated, if the token type is a property name (`JsonTokenType.PropertyName`), and the name of the property is `"title"`, which is retrieved with the `GetString` method, the next token that's available on the next `Read` iteration is a `JsonTokenType.String`. `GetString` on this token returns the value of the title (code file `JsonSample/Program.cs`):

```
void UseReader(string json)
{
  bool isNextPrice = false;
  bool isNextTitle = false;
  string? title = default;
  byte[] data = Encoding.UTF8.GetBytes(json);
  Utf8JsonReader reader = new(data);
  while (reader.Read())
  {
```

```
      if (reader.TokenType == JsonTokenType.PropertyName && reader.GetString() == "title")
      {
        isNextTitle = true;
      }
      if (reader.TokenType == JsonTokenType.String && isNextTitle)
      {
        title = reader.GetString();
        isNextTitle = false;
      }
      if (reader.TokenType == JsonTokenType.PropertyName && reader.GetString() == "price")
      {
        isNextPrice = true;
      }
      if (reader.TokenType == JsonTokenType.Number && isNextPrice &&
        reader.TryGetDecimal(out decimal price))
      {
        Console.WriteLine($"{title}, price: {price:C}");
        isNextPrice = false;
      }
    }
    Console.WriteLine();
}
```

JSON Writer

Similar to using the `Utf8JsonReader` to read tokens, you can use the `Utf8Writer` to write tokens. The following code snippet creates a JSON document containing an array of `Book` objects that contain `Title` and `Subtitle` properties (code file `JsonSample/Program.cs`):

```
void UseWriter()
{
  using MemoryStream stream = new();

  JsonWriterOptions options = new()
  {
    Indented = true
  };
  using (Utf8JsonWriter writer = new(stream, options))
  {
    writer.WriteStartArray();
      writer.WriteStartObject();
        writer.WriteStartObject("Book");
          writer.WriteString("Title", "Professional C# and .NET");
          writer.WriteString("Subtitle", "2021 Edition");
        writer.WriteEndObject();
      writer.WriteEndObject();
      writer.WriteStartObject();
        writer.WriteStartObject("Book");
          writer.WriteString("Title", "Professional C# 7 and .NET Core 2");
          writer.WriteString("Subtitle", "2018 Edition");
        writer.WriteEndObject();
      writer.WriteEndObject();
    writer.WriteEndArray();
  }
  string json = Encoding.UTF8.GetString(stream.ToArray());
  Console.WriteLine(json);
```

```
        Console.WriteLine();
    }
```

This is the generated JSON from the previous code snippet:

```json
[
  {
    "Book": {
      "Title": "Professional C# and .NET",
      "Subtitle": "2021 Edition"
    }
  },
  {
    "Book": {
      "Title": "Professional C# 7 and .NET Core 2",
      "Subtitle": "2018 Edition"
    }
  }
]
```

USING FILES AND STREAMS WITH THE WINDOWS RUNTIME

With the Windows Runtime, you implement streams with native types. Although they are implemented with native code, they look like .NET types. However, there's a difference you need to be aware of: for streams, the Windows Runtime implements its own types in the namespace `Windows.Storage.Streams`. Here you can find classes such as `FileInputStream`, `FileOutputStream`, and `RandomAccessStreams`. All these classes are based on interfaces—for example, `IInputStream`, `IOutputStream`, and `IRandomAccessStream`. You'll also find the concept of readers and writers. Windows Runtime readers and writers are the types `DataReader` and `DataWriter`.

Let's look at what's different from the .NET streams you've seen so far and how .NET streams and types can map to these native types.

> **NOTE** *Because the WinUI framework is in an early stage, make sure to read the readme file associated with the downloadable sample code for information on how to build and start WinUI applications and for specifics with the samples.*

Windows App Editor

Let's create an editor starting with the WinUI Blank App Visual Studio template.

To add commands for opening and saving a file `AppBarButton`, elements are added to the window (code file `WinUIAppEditor/MainWindow.xaml`):

```xaml
<CommandBar IsOpen="True" Grid.Row="1" >
  <AppBarButton Icon="OpenFile" Label="Open" Click="{x:Bind OnOpen}" />
  <AppBarButton Icon="Save" Label="Save" Click="{x:Bind OnSave}" />
</CommandBar>
```

The `TextBox` added to the `Grid` will receive the contents of the file:

```xaml
<Grid Background="{ThemeResource ApplicationPageBackgroundThemeBrush}">
  <TextBox x:Name="text1" HorizontalTextAlignment="Left" AcceptsReturn="True" />
</Grid>
```

The OnOpen event handler first starts the dialog where the user can select a file. Remember, you used the OpenFileDialog earlier. With Windows apps, you can use pickers. To open files, FileOpenPicker is the preferred type. You can configure this picker to define the proposed start location for the user. You set the SuggestedStartLocation to PickerLocationId.DocumentsLibrary to open the user's documents folder. PickerLocationId is an enumeration that defines various special folders.

Next, the FileTypeFilter collection specifies the file types that should be listed for the user. Finally, the method PickSingleFileAsync returns the file selected from the user. To allow users to select multiple files, you can use the method PickMultipleFilesAsync instead. This method returns a StorageFile. StorageFile is defined in the namespace Windows.Storage. This class is the equivalent of the FileInfo class for opening, creating, copying, moving, and deleting files (code file WindowsAppEditor/MainWindow.xaml.cs):

```
public async void OnOpen()
{
  try
  {
    FileOpenPicker picker = new()
    {
      ViewMode = PickerViewMode.Thumbnail,
      SuggestedStartLocation = PickerLocationId.DocumentsLibrary
    };
    picker.FileTypeFilter.Add(".txt");
    picker.FileTypeFilter.Add(".md");

    StorageFile file = await picker.PickSingleFileAsync();
    //...
```

Now, open the file using OpenReadAsync. This method returns a stream that implements the interface IRandomAccessStreamWithContentType, which derives from the interfaces IRandomAccessStream, IInputStream, IOuputStream, IContentProvider, and IDisposable. IRandomAccessStream allows random access to a stream with the Seek method, and it gives information about the size of a stream. IInputStream defines the method ReadAsync to read from a stream. IOutputStream is the opposite; it defines the methods WriteAsync and FlushAsync. IContentTypeProvider defines the property ContentType that gives information about the content of the file. Remember the encodings of the text files? Now it would be possible to read the content of the stream invoking the method ReadAsync. However, the Windows Runtime also knows the reader's and writer's concepts that have already been discussed. A DataReader accepts an IInputStream with the constructor. The DataReader type defines methods to read primitive data types such as ReadInt16, ReadInt32, and ReadDateTime. You can read a byte array with ReadBytes, and a string with ReadString. The ReadString method requires the number of characters to read. The string is assigned to the Text property of the TextBox control to display the content:

```
    //...
    if (file != null)
    {
      IRandomAccessStreamWithContentType stream = await file.OpenReadAsync();
      using DataReader reader = new(stream);
      await reader.LoadAsync((uint)stream.Size);
      text1.Text = reader.ReadString((uint)stream.Size);
    }
  }
  catch (Exception ex)
  {
    MessageDialog dlg = new(ex.Message, "Error");
    await dlg.ShowAsync();
  }
```

> **NOTE** *Like the readers and the writers of the .NET base class library, the* DataReader *and* DataWriter *manage the stream that is passed with the constructor. On disposing of the reader or writer, the stream gets disposed of as well. With .NET classes, to keep the underlying stream open for a longer time, you can set the* leaveOpen *argument in the constructor. With the Windows Runtime types, you can detach the stream from the readers and writers by invoking the method* DetachStream.

On saving the document, the OnSave method is invoked. First, FileSavePicker is used to allow the user to select the document—similarly to FileOpenPicker. Next, the file is opened using OpenTransactedWriteAsync. The NTFS file system supports transactions; these are not covered directly from the base class libraries but are available with the Windows Runtime. OpenTransactedWriteAsync returns a StorageStreamTransaction object that implements the interface IStorageStreamTransaction. This object itself is not a stream (although the name might lead you to believe this), but it contains a stream that you can reference with the Stream property. This property returns an IRandomAccessStream stream. As you can create a DataReader, you can create a DataWriter to write primitive data types, including strings as in this example. The StoreAsync method finally writes the content from the buffer to the stream. The transaction needs to be committed by invoking the CommitAsync method before disposing of the writer:

```
public async void OnSave()
{
  try
  {
    FileSavePicker picker = new()
    {
      SuggestedStartLocation = PickerLocationId.DocumentsLibrary,
      SuggestedFileName = "New Document"
    };
    picker.FileTypeChoices.Add("Plain Text", new List<string>() { ".txt" });
    StorageFile file = await picker.PickSaveFileAsync();
    if (file != null)
    {
      using StorageStreamTransaction tx = await file.OpenTransactedWriteAsync();
      IRandomAccessStream stream = tx.Stream;
      stream.Seek(0);
      using DataWriter writer = new(stream);
      writer.WriteString(text1.Text);
      tx.Stream.Size = await writer.StoreAsync();
      await tx.CommitAsync();
    }
  }
  catch (Exception ex)
  {
    MessageDialog dlg = new(ex.Message, "Error");
    await dlg.ShowAsync();
  }
}
```

The DataWriter doesn't add the preamble defining the kind of Unicode file to the stream. You need to do that explicitly, as explained earlier in this chapter. The DataWriter just deals with the encoding of the file by setting the UnicodeEncoding and ByteOrder properties. The default setting is UnicodeEncoding.Utf8 and ByteOrder.BigEndian. Instead of working with the DataWriter, you can also take advantage of the features of StreamReader and StreamWriter as well as the .NET Stream class, as shown in the next section.

Mapping Windows Runtime Types to .NET Types

Let's start with reading the file. To convert a Windows Runtime stream to a .NET stream for reading, you can use the extension method AsStreamForRead. This method is defined in the namespace System.IO (that must be opened) in the assembly System.Runtime.WindowsRuntime. This method creates a new Stream object that manages the IInputStream. Now, you can use it as a normal .NET stream, as shown previously—for example, passing it to a StreamReader and using this reader to access the file (code file WindowsAppEditor/MainWindow.xaml.cs):

```csharp
public async void OnOpenDotnet()
{
  try
  {
    FileOpenPicker picker = new()
    {
      ViewMode = PickerViewMode.Thumbnail,
      SuggestedStartLocation = PickerLocationId.DocumentsLibrary
    };
    picker.FileTypeFilter.Add(".txt");
    picker.FileTypeFilter.Add(".md");

    StorageFile file = await picker.PickSingleFileAsync();
    if (file != null)
    {
      IRandomAccessStreamWithContentType wrtStream =
        await file.OpenReadAsync();
      Stream stream = wrtStream.AsStreamForRead();
      using StreamReader reader = new(stream);
      text1.Text = await reader.ReadToEndAsync();
    }
  }
  catch (Exception ex)
  {
    MessageDialog dlg = new(ex.Message, "Error");
    await dlg.ShowAsync();
  }
}
```

All the Windows Runtime stream types can easily be converted to .NET streams and the other way around. The following table lists the methods needed:

CONVERT FROM	CONVERT TO	METHOD
IRandomAccessStream	Stream	AsStream
IInputStream	Stream	AsStreamForRead
IOutputStream	Stream	AsStreamForWrite
Stream	IInputStream	AsInputStream
Stream	IOutputStream	AsOutputStream
Stream	IRandomAccessStream	AsRandomAccessStream

Now save the change to the file as well. The stream for writing is converted with the extension method `AsStreamForWrite`. Now, this stream can be written using the `StreamWriter` class. The code snippet also writes the preamble for the UTF-8 encoding to the file:

```csharp
public async void OnSaveDotnet()
{
  try
  {
    FileSavePicker picker = new()
    {
      SuggestedStartLocation = PickerLocationId.DocumentsLibrary,
      SuggestedFileName = "New Document"
    };
    picker.FileTypeChoices.Add("Plain Text", new List<string>() { ".txt" });
    StorageFile file = await picker.PickSaveFileAsync();
    if (file != null)
    {
      StorageStreamTransaction tx = await file.OpenTransactedWriteAsync();
      using var writer = new StreamWriter(tx.Stream.AsStreamForWrite());
      byte[] preamble = Encoding.UTF8.GetPreamble();
      await stream.WriteAsync(preamble, 0, preamble.Length);
      await writer.WriteAsync(text1.Text);
      await writer.FlushAsync();
      tx.Stream.Size = (ulong)stream.Length;
      await tx.CommitAsync();
    }
  }
  catch (Exception ex)
  {
    MessageDialog dlg = new(ex.Message, "Error");
    await dlg.ShowAsync();
  }
}
```

SUMMARY

In this chapter, you examined how to use the .NET classes with static and instance methods to access the file system from your C# code. For the file system, you used APIs to copy, move, create, and delete files and folders; and you used streams to read and write binary and text files.

You saw how to compress files using the deflate and the Brotli algorithm, and you created ZIP files. You used `FileSystemWatcher` to get information when files change.

In using the new `System.Text.Json` namespace and the new performant JSON serializer, you've seen easy ways to serialize and deserialize .NET objects into and from JSON. You've also seen other options to deal with JSON files, such as accessing the DOM with the `JsonDocument` and directly accessing the tokens from JSON with the `Utf8JsonReader` and `Utf8JsonWriter`.

Finally, you've seen how to map .NET streams to Windows Runtime streams to take advantage of .NET features within Windows apps.

The next chapter continues working with streams, sending streams across the network, and making use of `System.IO.Pipelines` for efficient communication across the network.

19

Networking

WHAT'S IN THIS CHAPTER?

➤ Manipulating IP addresses and performing DNS lookups

➤ Using socket programming

➤ Creating TCP and UDP clients and servers

➤ Using `HttpClient`

➤ Working with the `HttpClient` factory

CODE DOWNLOADS FOR THIS CHAPTER

The source code for this chapter is available on the book page at www.wiley.com. Click the Downloads link. The code can also be found at https://github.com/ProfessionalCSharp/ProfessionalCSharp2021 in the directory 2_Libs/Networking.

The code for this chapter is divided into the following major examples:

➤ Utilities

➤ Dns

➤ SocketServer

➤ SocketClient

➤ TcpServer

➤ TcpClientSample

➤ UdpReceiver

➤ UdpSender

➤ HttpServerSample

➤ HttpClientSample

Samples from this chapter use the `System.Net`, `System.Net.Sockets`, `System.Net.Http`, and `System.IO.Pipelines` namespaces. Important NuGet packages used are `Microsoft.Extensions.Http` and `Microsoft.Extensions.Hosting`. All the samples have nullable reference types enabled.

OVERVIEW

This chapter takes a practical approach to networking by mixing examples with a discussion of relevant theory and networking concepts as appropriate. This chapter is not a guide to computer networking but an introduction to using .NET for network communication.

This chapter shows you how to create both clients and servers using network protocols. It starts with utility classes such as `IPAddress`, `IPHostEntry`, and `Dns` before digging into programming with sockets. Here, sockets are used to show the functionality of communication via UDP and TCP.

After you learn the foundation of network programming, we move to higher-level APIs by using the `UdpClient` and `TcpClient` classes. These classes provide an abstraction layer to the `Socket` class in which you don't have full control over sockets, but using TCP and UDP communication is easier.

After this, we move to another abstraction layer: the HTTP protocol, which is the most used protocol in the Internet. The `HttpClient` class offers a modern asynchronous approach for creating HTTP requests. You'll use the `HttpClientFactory` class to manage `HttpClient` objects.

The two namespaces of most interest for networking are `System.Net` and `System.Net.Sockets`. The `System.Net` namespace is generally concerned with higher-level operations, such as downloading and uploading files and making web requests using HTTP and other protocols, whereas `System.Net.Sockets` contains classes to perform lower-level operations. You will find these classes useful when you want to work directly with sockets or protocols, such as with TCP/IP. The methods in these classes closely mimic the Windows socket (Winsock) API functions derived from the Berkeley sockets interface. You will also find that some of the objects in the chapter are found in the `System.IO` namespace.

WORKING WITH UTILITY CLASSES

On the Internet, you identify servers as well as clients by IP address or host name (also referred to as a Domain Name System [DNS] name). Generally speaking, the *host name* is the human-friendly name that you type in a web browser window, such as www.wrox.com or www.cninnovation.com. An *IP address* is the identifier that computers use to recognize each other. IP addresses are the identifiers used to ensure that web requests and responses reach the appropriate machines. It is even possible for a computer to have more than one IP address.

An IP address can be a 32-bit or 128-bit value, depending on whether Internet Protocol version 4 (IPv4) or Internet Protocol version 6 (IPv6) is used. An example of a 32-bit IP address is 192.168.1.100. Because there are now so many computers and other devices vying for a spot on the Internet, IPv6 was developed. IPv6 can potentially provide a maximum number of about 3×10^{38} unique addresses. .NET enables your applications to work with both IPv4 and IPv6.

For host names to work, you must first send a network request to translate the host name into an IP address—a task that's carried out by one or more DNS servers. A *DNS server* stores a table that maps host names to IP addresses for all the computers it knows about. For host names the DNS server doesn't know, it stores IP addresses of other DNS servers for lookups. Your local computer should always know about at least one DNS server. Network administrators configure this information when a computer is set up.

Before sending out a request, your computer first asks the DNS server to give it the IP address corresponding to the host name you have typed in. When it is armed with the correct IP address, the computer can address the request and send it over the network. All this work normally happens behind the scenes while the user is browsing the Web.

.NET supplies a number of classes that are able to assist with the process of looking up IP addresses and finding information about host computers.

URIs

`Uri` and `UriBuilder` are two classes in the `System` namespace. The `Uri` class represents a URI, and the `UriBuilder` class makes it easy to create a URI using the different parts of a URI.

> **NOTE** *Both uniform resource locators (URLs) and uniform resource identifiers (URIs) are used with web technologies. A URL references a web address. This is defined with RFC 1738 (*`https://tools.ietf.org/html/rfc1738`*). A URI is a superset of a URL and can identify anything, as defined by the Resource Description Framework (RDF); see* `https://www.w3.org/RDF/`*.*

The following code snippet demonstrates features of the `Uri` class. The constructor allows passing relative and absolute URLs. This class defines several read-only properties to access parts of a URL, such as the scheme, host name, port number, query strings, and segments of a URL (code file `Utilities/Program.cs`):

```
void UriSample(string uri)
{
  Uri page = new(uri);
  Console.WriteLine($"scheme: {page.Scheme}");
  Console.WriteLine($"host: {page.Host}, type: {page.HostNameType}, " +
    $"idn host: {page.IdnHost}");
  Console.WriteLine($"port: {page.Port}");
  Console.WriteLine($"path: {page.AbsolutePath}");
  Console.WriteLine($"query: {page.Query}");

  foreach (var segment in page.Segments)
  {
    Console.WriteLine($"segment: {segment}");
  }
}
```

When you run the application with the command `donet run -- uri --uri` and pass the URL and string that contains a path and a query string `https://www.amazon.com/Professional-NET-Core-Christian-Nagel/dp/1119449278/ref=sr_1_1?dchild=1&keywords=Professional+C%23`, you get the following output:

```
scheme: https
host: www.amazon.com, type: Dns, idn host: www.amazon.com
port: 443
path: /Professional-NET-Core-Christian-Nagel/dp/1119449278/ref=sr_1_1
query: ?dchild=1&keywords=Professional+C%23
segment: /
segment: Professional-NET-Core-Christian-Nagel/
segment: dp/
segment: 1119449278/
segment: ref=sr_1_1
```

Unlike the `Uri` class, the `UriBuilder` defines read-write properties, as shown in the following code snippet. You can create a `UriBuilder` instance, assign these properties, and get a URL returned from the `Uri` property:

```
void BuildUri()
{
  UriBuilder builder = new();
  builder.Scheme = "https";
  builder.Host = "www.cninnovation.com";
  builder.Port = 80;
  builder.Path = "training/MVC";
  Uri uri = builder.Uri;
  Console.WriteLine(uri);
}
```

Instead of using properties with the `UriBuilder`, this class also offers several overloads of the constructor where the parts of a URL can be passed as well.

IPAddress

`IPAddress` represents an IP address. The address itself is available as a byte array using the `GetAddressBytes` property and may be converted to a dotted decimal format with the `ToString` method. `IPAddress` also implements static `Parse` and `TryParse` methods that effectively perform the reverse conversion of `ToString`—converting from a dotted decimal string to an `IPAddress`. The code sample also accesses the `AddressFamily` property and converts an IPv4 address to IPv6, and vice versa (code file `Utilities/Program.cs`):

```
void IPAddressSample(string ipAddressString)
{
  if (!IPAddress.TryParse(ipAddressString, out IPAddress? address))
  {
    Console.WriteLine($"cannot parse {ipAddressString}");
    return;
  }
  byte[] bytes = address.GetAddressBytes();
  for (int i = 0; i < bytes.Length; i++)
  {
    Console.WriteLine($"byte {i}: {bytes[i]:X}");
  }
  Console.WriteLine($"family: {address.AddressFamily}, " +
    $"map to ipv6: {address.MapToIPv6()}, map to ipv4: {address.MapToIPv4()}");
  // ...
```

Passing the address 65.52.128.33 to the method results in this output:

```
byte 0: 41
byte 1: 34
byte 2: 80
byte 3: 21
family: InterNetwork, map to ipv6: ::ffff:65.52.128.33, map to ipv4: 65.52.128.3
3
```

The `IPAddress` class also defines static properties to create special addresses such as loopback, broadcast, and anycast:

```
void IPAddressSample(string ipAddressString)
{
  //...
  Console.WriteLine($"IPv4 loopback address: {IPAddress.Loopback}");
```

```
      Console.WriteLine($"IPv6 loopback address: {IPAddress.IPv6Loopback}");
      Console.WriteLine($"IPv4 broadcast address: {IPAddress.Broadcast}");
      Console.WriteLine($"IPv4 any address: {IPAddress.Any}");
      Console.WriteLine($"IPv6 any address: {IPAddress.IPv6Any}");
}
```

With a *loopback address*, the network hardware is bypassed. This is the IP address that represents the host name localhost.

The *broadcast address* is an address that addresses every node in a local network. Such an address is not available with IPv6 because this concept is not used with the newer version of the Internet Protocol. After the initial definition of IPv4, multicasting was added for IPv6. With multicasting, a group of nodes is addressed instead of all nodes. With IPv6, multicasting completely replaces broadcasting. Both broadcast and multicast are shown in code samples later in this chapter in the "Using UDP" section.

With an *anycast*, one-to-many routing is used as well, but the data stream is transmitted only to the node closest in the network. This is useful for load balancing. With IPv4, the Border Gateway rotocol (BGP) routing protocol is used to find the shortest path in the network; with IPv6, this feature is inherent.

When you run the application, you can see the following addresses for IPv4 and IPv6:

```
IPv4 loopback address: 127.0.0.1
IPv6 loopback address: ::1
IPv4 broadcast address: 255.255.255.255
IPv4 any address: 0.0.0.0
IPv6 any address: ::
```

IPHostEntry

The `IPHostEntry` class encapsulates information related to a particular host computer. This class makes the host name available via the `HostName` property (which returns a string), and the `AddressList` property returns an array of `IPAddress` objects. You are going to use the `IPHostEntry` class in the next example.

DNS

The `Dns` class can communicate with your default DNS server to retrieve IP addresses. The sample application is implemented as a console application that loops to ask the user for host names (you can add an IP address instead) to get an `IPHostEntry` via `Dns.GetHostEntryAsync`. From the `IPHostEntry`, the address list is accessed using the `AddressList` property. All the addresses of the host, as well as the `AddressFamily`, are written to the console (code file `DnsLookup/Program.cs`):

```
do
{
  Console.Write("Hostname:\t");
  string? hostname = Console.ReadLine();
  if (hostname is null ||
    hostname.Equals("exit", StringComparison.CurrentCultureIgnoreCase))
  {
    Console.WriteLine("bye!");
    return;
  }

  await OnLookupAsync(hostname);
  Console.WriteLine();
} while (true);
```

```
async Task OnLookupAsync(string hostname)
{
  try
  {
    IPHostEntry ipHost = await Dns.GetHostEntryAsync(hostname);
    Console.WriteLine($"Hostname: {ipHost.HostName}");
    foreach (IPAddress address in ipHost.AddressList)
    {
      Console.WriteLine($"Address Family: {address.AddressFamily}");
      Console.WriteLine($"Address: {address}");
    }
  }
  catch (SocketException ex)
  {
    Console.WriteLine(ex.Message);
  }
}
```

Run the application and enter a few host names to see output similar to what's shown in the following example. With the host name `www.wiley.com`, you can see that this host name defines multiple IP addresses. `portal.azure.com` returns with different host names and IP addresses depending on your region.

```
Hostname: www.cninnovation.com
Hostname: www.cninnovation.com
Address Family: InterNetwork, address: 65.52.128.33

Hostname: www.wiley.com
Hostname: 1x6jqndp2gdqp.cloudfront.net
Address Family: InterNetwork, address: 13.32.2.108
Address Family: InterNetwork, address: 194.232.104.139
Address Family: InterNetwork, address: 13.32.2.25
Address Family: InterNetwork, address: 13.32.2.54
Address Family: InterNetwork, address: 13.32.2.51

Hostname: portal.azure.com
Hostname: portal-prod-germanywestcentral-02.germanywestcentral.cloudapp.azure.com
Address Family: InterNetwork, address: 51.116.144.197

Hostname: exit
bye!
```

> **NOTE** *The* Dns *class is somewhat limited. For example, you can't define using a server that's different than the default DNS server. Also, the* Aliases *property of the* IPHostEntry *is not populated from the method* GetHostEntryAsync. *It's populated from the obsolete method* Resolve, *and this doesn't populate this property fully. For full use of DNS lookups, it's better to use a third-party library.*

Now it's time to move to a low-level API using the `Socket` class.

Configuring Sockets

No matter what networking API you use, they are all based on sockets. To configure sockets, you can use the `ServicePoint`. With the `ServicePointManager` class, you can get `ServicePoint` instances by invoking the static method `FindServicePoint` and passing a URI. Using this, you can specifically configure sockets for this address.

To configure all sockets, no matter which connection is used, you can use static methods of the `ServicePointManager` class, such as by invoking the method `SetTcpKeepAlive`. This method sets the keep-alive flag with the socket to stay informed when the connection is lost and to keep the connection open in case of inactivity. With TCP keep-alive, probe packets are sent where an acknowledge (ACK) message is expected. The sample code enables the keep-alive flag with a message sent every second (`keepAliveInterval`) and a timeout of 60 seconds (`keepAliveTime`). A default setting is two hours for the timeout and one second for the interval:

```
ServicePointManager.SetTcpKeepAlive(
    enabled: true, keepAliveTime: 600000, keepAliveInterval: 1000);
```

Other settings you can specify with the `ServicePointManager` include the following:

➤ `DefaultConnectionLimit` specifies the maximum number of concurrent connections allowed by the application. With non–ASP.NET Core applications, the default value is 2, so often there's the need to increase this limit.

➤ `EnableDnsRoundRobin` enables DNS round-robin. By default, if the DNS name is accessible using multiple IP addresses (as you've seen in the section DNS), always the first IP address is used. If you set this to `true`, one after another IP address is used with DNS lookups.

➤ The Nagle algorithm is used to reduce the sending of many small packages. Packages are sent only when the buffer is full. If the buffer is not full, the package is sent only when the receiver of the packages already acknowledged all packages that have been sent so far. If you need a faster response—for example, when the user enters some data that should be sent immediately—you can turn off this algorithm by setting `UseNagleAlgorithm` to `false`.

➤ If you define a custom implementation to check for certificates, you can define a handler method of the delegate type `RemoteCertificateValidationCallback` and set it with the `ServerCertificateValidationCallback` property.

USING SOCKETS

The HTTP protocol is based on TCP (there's an exception: the upcoming HTTP/3 protocol is based on the QUIC protocol, which is an enhancement of UDP), and thus the `HttpXX` classes offer an abstraction layer over the `TcpXX` classes. The `TcpXX` classes, however, give you more control. You can even get more control than offered by the `TcpXX` or `UdpXX` classes with the `Socket` class. With sockets, you can use different protocols, not only protocols based on TCP or UDP—for example, Internet Control Message Protocol (ICMP), Internet Datagram Protocol (IDP), and PARC Universal Packet Protocol (PUP). You can also create a protocol. What might be even more important is that you can have more control over TCP- or UDP-based protocols.

TCP Echo Sample Using Sockets

Let's start with a server that listens to incoming requests and returns the received data to the client. This application is based on the TCP Echo protocol as defined by RFC 862 (`https://tools.ietf.org/html/rfc862`).

This sample application makes use of the Host class defined in the package Microsoft.Extensions.Hosting to use the preconfigured dependency injection container, logging, and configuration options. You can supply the application configuration values in the configuration file appsettings.json and override the configuration values passing parameters from the command line. This sample also makes use of logging as supported by the Host class. Networking classes generate some logging output, as you can see with the samples from this chapter. You can configure the logging level in the application configuration file as well.

> **NOTE** *Read Chapter 15, "Dependency Injection and Configuration," for information on the* Host *class and using .NET configuration, and Chapter 16, "Diagnostics and Metrics," for more information on logging.*

With the application configuration file appsettings.json, logging levels and the port number and timeout for the socket server are configured (configuration file SocketServer/appsettings.json):

```json
{
  "Logging": {
    "Console": {
      "LogLevel": {
        "Default": "Trace",
        "EchoServer": "Trace"
      }
    },
    "LogLevel": {
      "Default": "Trace",
      "Microsoft": "Information",
      "EchoServer": "Warning"
    }
  },
  "Echoserver": {
    "Port": "8200",
    "Timeout": "5000"
  }
}
```

With the top-level statements, the dependency injection (DI) container is configured. The EchoService class is defined with the container. This class contains the major code for the application, the use of the Socket class. The configuration for this is retrieved from the EchoServer section, which is then accessed with the constructor of the EchoService class and passed via the DI container. After the Host class is configured, the socket listener is started by invoking the StartListenerAsync method of the EchoService class. In addition, the CancelKeyPress event of the Console class is assigned to react to the cancellation of the user to send a cancel via the CancellationToken (code file SocketServer/Program.cs):

```csharp
using var host = Host.CreateDefaultBuilder(args)
  .ConfigureServices((context, services) =>
  {
    var settings = context.Configuration;
    services.Configure<EchoServiceOptions>(settings.GetSection("Echoserver"));
    services.AddTransient<EchoServer>();
  })
  .Build();

var logger = host.Services.GetRequiredService<ILoggerFactory>()
```

```
    .CreateLogger("EchoServer");

CancellationTokenSource cancellationTokenSource = new();

Console.CancelKeyPress += (sender, e) =>
{
    logger.LogInformation("cancellation initiated by the user");
    cancellationTokenSource.Cancel();
};

var service = host.Services.GetRequiredService<EchoServer>();
await service.StartListenerAsync(cancellationTokenSource.Token);

Console.ReadLine();
```

> **NOTE** *Cancellation tokens are explained in Chapter 11, "Tasks and Asynchronous Programming."*

From the values configured with the application settings, the port and timeout values are assigned to fields of the `EchoServer` class (code file `SocketServer/EchoServer.cs`):

```
record EchoServiceOptions
{
  public int Port { get; init; }
  public int Timeout { get; init; }
}

class EchoServer
{
  private readonly int _port;
  private readonly ILogger _logger;
  private readonly int _timeout;
  public EchoServer(IOptions<EchoServiceOptions> options, ILogger<EchoServer> logger)
  {
    _port = options.Value.Port;
    _timeout = options.Value.Timeout;
    _logger = logger;
  }
  //...
}
```

Creating a Listener

In the `StartListenerAsync` method, a new `Socket` object is created. With the constructor of the `Socket` class, you can specify the communication type. The `AddressFamily` is a large enumeration that offers many different networks. Examples are *DECnet*, which was released in 1975 by Digital Equipment and used as main network communication between PDP-11 systems; Banyan VINES, which was used to connect client machines; and, of course, `InterNetwork` for IPv4 and `InterNetworkV6` for IPv6. As mentioned previously, you can use sockets for a large number of networking protocols. The second parameter, `SocketType`, specifies the kind of socket. Examples are `Stream` for TCP, `Dgram` for UDP, or `Raw` for raw sockets. The third parameter is an enumeration for the `ProtocolType`. Examples are `IP`, `Ucmp`, `Udp`, `IPv6`, and `Raw`. The settings you choose need to match. For example, if you use TCP with IPv4, the address family must be InterNetwork, the socket type Stream, and the protocol type Tcp. To create a UDP communication with IPv4, the address family needs to be set to InterNetwork, the socket type Dgram, and the protocol type Udp.

The listener socket returned from the constructor is bound to an IP address and port number. With the sample code, the listener is bound to all local IPv4 addresses, and the port number is specified with the argument. Calling the Listen method starts the listening mode of the socket. The socket can now accept incoming connection requests. Specifying the parameter with the Listen method defines the size of the backlog queue—how many clients can connect concurrently before their connection is dealt with (code file SocketServer/EchoServer.cs):

```
public async Task StartListenerAsync(CancellationToken cancellationToken = default)
{
  try
  {
    using Socket listener = new(AddressFamily.InterNetwork,
                                SocketType.Stream,
                                ProtocolType.Tcp);
    listener.ReceiveTimeout = _timeout;
    listener.SendTimeout = _timeout;

    listener.Bind(new IPEndPoint(IPAddress.Any, _port));
    listener.Listen(backlog: 15);

    _logger.LogTrace("EchoListener started on port {0}", _port);
    //...
}
```

Waiting for the client to connect happens in the AcceptAsync method of the Socket class. This method continues after the await as soon as a client connects. After a client connects, this method is invoked again to fulfill requests of other clients; this is why this method is called within a while loop. For the listening, a separate task, which can be canceled from the calling thread, is started. The task to read and write using the socket happens within the method ProcessClientJobAsync. This method receives the Socket instance that is bound to the client to read and write (code file SocketServer/EchoServer.cs):

```
public async Task StartListenerAsync(CancellationToken = default)
{
  //...
  while (true)
  {
    if (cancellationToken.IsCancellationRequested)
    {
      cancellationToken.ThrowIfCancellationRequested();
      break;
    }
    var socket = await listener.AcceptAsync();
    if (!socket.Connected)
    {
      _logger.LogWarning("Client not connected after accept");
      break;
    }

    _logger.LogInformation("client connected, local {0}, remote {1}",
    socket.LocalEndPoint, socket.RemoteEndPoint);

    Task _ = ProcessClientJobAsync(socket);
  }
}
```

```
        catch (SocketException ex)
        {
          _logger.LogError(ex, ex.Message);
        }
        catch (Exception ex)
        {
          _logger.LogError(ex, ex.Message);
          throw;
        }
      }
```

Communication with Pipelines

To communicate with the client, you can use receive and send methods of the `Socket` class using a memory buffer dealing with bytes. Another API that can be used with sockets is a `NetworkStream`. This class derives from the `Stream` base class, which allows reading and writing from the network and is mentioned in Chapter 18, "Files and Streams." You can also use readers and writers, which are also covered in Chapter 18. With all these options, you need to manage the size of the memory buffer, which can be quite complex if done efficiently, especially if the size of the data sent and received changes dynamically. You need to adapt the buffer sizes and repeat reading and combining the data if you receive more data than can fit into the buffer.

The NuGet package `System.IO.Pipelines` makes this job a lot easier. You don't need to allocate the buffer yourself; that's done using `PipeReader` and `PipeWriter` from the namespace `System.IO.Pipelines`. With the following implementation of the method `ProcessClientJobAsync`, the `PipeReader` and `PipeWriter` objects are created to pass the `NetworkStream` to the `Create` method. There's no need to create a memory buffer before invoking the `ReadAsync` method of the `PipeReader`. The `ReadAsync` method returns a `ReadResult`. This struct contains a reference to the allocated buffer (the `Buffer` property). This buffer is of type `ReadOnlySequence<byte>`. The buffer used by pipelines can be a list of multiple memory segments. `ReadOnlySequence<T>` contains an iterator that allows the program to walk through the segments. With the following code snippet, the segments are iterated with the `foreach` statement after the check that the sequence is not just a single segment (`IsSingleSegment` property). If you just enter data from the keyboard to send it to the server, usually you'll see just one segment. When passing the content of files, you can likely see multiple segments. With a single segment, the content can be accessed with the `FirstSpan` property of type `ReadOnlySpan<byte>`. With the echo service, the content read is encoded and returned to the caller with the `WriteAsync` method of the `PipeWriter`. Before continuing the read on the `PipeReader`, you need to advance the position of the reader by invoking the `AdvanceTo` method. This method needs a `SequencePosition` that's returned from the `GetPosition` method of the `ReadOnlySequence<T>` (code file `SocketServer/EchoServer.cs`):

```
    private async Task ProcessClientJobAsync(Socket socket,
      CancellationToken cancellationToken = default)
    {
      try
      {
        using NetworkStream stream = new(socket, ownsSocket: true);

        PipeReader reader = PipeReader.Create(stream);
        PipeWriter writer = PipeWriter.Create(stream);

        bool completed = false;
        do
        {
          ReadResult result = await reader.ReadAsync(cancellationToken);

          if (result.Buffer.Length == 0)
          {
            completed = true;
```

```
          _logger.LogInformation("received empty buffer, client closed");
        }
        ReadOnlySequence<byte> buffer = result.Buffer;
        if (buffer.IsSingleSegment)
        {
          string data = Encoding.UTF8.GetString(buffer.FirstSpan);
          _logger.LogTrace("received data {0} from the client {1}",
            data, socket.RemoteEndPoint);

          // send the data back
          await writer.WriteAsync(buffer.First, cancellationToken);
        }
        else
        {
          int segmentNumber = 0;
          foreach (var item in buffer)
          {
            segmentNumber++;
            string data = Encoding.UTF8.GetString(item.Span);
            _logger.LogTrace("received data {0} from the client {1} in the {2}. segment",
              data, socket.RemoteEndPoint, segmentNumber);

            // send the data back
            await writer.WriteAsync(item, cancellationToken);
          }
        }
        SequencePosition nextPosition = result.Buffer.GetPosition(
          result.Buffer.Length);
        reader.AdvanceTo(nextPosition);

    } while (!completed);
  }
  catch (SocketException ex)
  {
    _logger.LogError(ex, ex.Message);
  }
  catch (IOException ex) when ((ex.InnerException is
    SocketException socketException)
    && (socketException.ErrorCode is 10054))
  {
    logger.LogInformation("client {0} closed the connection",
      socket.RemoteEndPoint);
  }
  catch (Exception ex)
  {
    _logger.LogError(ex, "ex.Message with client {0}", socket.RemoteEndPoint);
    throw;
  }
  _logger.LogTrace("Closed stream and client socket {0}", socket.RemoteEndPoint);
}
```

> **NOTE** *Check Chapter 13, "Managed and Unmanaged Memory," for details on the* Span<T> *type.*

Implementing a Receiver

The receiver application SocketClient is implemented as a console application as well. Similar to the server, the startup code with top-level commands is done with the Host class to read configuration values. With the client, properties of the class EchoClientOptions are filled from the configuration file or command-line arguments (code file SocketClient/EchoClient.cs):

```
reccord EchoClientOptions
{
  public string? Hostname { get; init; }
  public int ServerPort { get; init; }
}

class EchoClient
{
  private readonly string _hostname;
  private readonly int _serverPort;
  private readonly ILogger _logger;
  public EchoClient(IOptions<EchoClientOptions> options, ILogger<EchoClient> logger)
  {
    _hostname = options.Value.Hostname ?? "localhost";
    _serverPort = options.Value.ServerPort;
    _logger = logger;
  }
  //...
}
```

The SendAndReceiveAsync method uses DNS name resolution to get the IPHostEntry from the hostname. This IPHostEntry is used to get an IPv4 address of the host. After the Socket instance is created (in the same way it was created for the server code), the address is used with the ConnectAsync method to make a connection to the server. With TCP, before sending data, a connection needs to be opened. Next, standard input and standard output from the Console class are redirected to the NetworkStream that's associated with the socket. All the data you enter with the console is sent to the echo server (code file SocketClient/EchoClient.cs):

```
public async Task SendAndReceiveAsync(CancellationToken cancellationToken)
{
  try
  {
    var addresses = await Dns.GetHostAddressesAsync(_hostname);
    IPAddress ipAddress = addresses.Where(
      address => address.AddressFamily == AddressFamily.InterNetwork).First();
    if (ipAddress is null)
    {
      _logger.LogWarning("no IPv4 address");
      return;
    }

    Socket clientSocket = new(AddressFamily.InterNetwork, SocketType.Stream,
      ProtocolType.Tcp);
    await clientSocket.ConnectAsync(ipAddress, _serverPort, cancellationToken);

    _logger.LogInformation("client connected to echo service");
    using NetworkStream stream = new(clientSocket, ownsSocket: true);

    Console.WriteLine("enter text that is streamed to the server and returned");
```

```
    // send the input to the network stream
    Stream consoleInput = Console.OpenStandardInput();
    Task sender = consoleInput.CopyToAsync(stream, cancellationToken);

    // receive the output from the network stream
    Stream consoleOutput = Console.OpenStandardOutput();
    Task receiver = stream.CopyToAsync(consoleOutput, cancellationToken);

    await Task.WhenAll(sender, receiver);
    _logger.LogInformation("sender and receiver completed");
  }
  catch (SocketException ex)
  {
    _logger.LogError(ex, ex.Message);
  }
  catch (OperationCanceledException ex)
  {
    _logger.LogInformation(ex.Message);
  }
 }
}
```

> **NOTE** *If you change the filtering of the address list to get an IPv6 address instead of an IPv4 address, you also need to change the* Socket *invocation to create a socket for the IPv6 address family.*

When you run both the client and server, you can see communication across TCP.

USING TCP CLASSES

The HTTP/1.1 and 2.0 protocols are based on the Transmission Control Protocol (TCP). With TCP, the client first needs to open a connection to the server before sending commands. This is the same behavior as you've seen with the previous sample opening a TCP connection with the Socket type. With the Socket class, you had to specify the address family, socket type, and protocol. This is abstracted by using TCP classes, as described in this section.

The TCP classes offer simple methods for connecting and sending data between two endpoints. An endpoint is the combination of an IP address and a port number. Existing protocols have well-defined port numbers—for example, HTTP uses port 80, whereas SMTP uses port 25. The Internet Assigned Numbers Authority, IANA (www.iana.org), assigns port numbers to these well-known services. Unless you are implementing a well-known service, you should select a port number higher than 1,024.

TCP traffic makes up the majority of traffic on the Internet today. It is often the protocol of choice because it offers guaranteed delivery, error correction, and buffering. The TcpClient class encapsulates a TCP connection and provides properties to regulate the connection, including buffering, buffer size, and timeouts. Reading and writing are accomplished by requesting a NetworkStream object via the GetStream method.

Creating a TCP Listener

The sample application is based on the Quote of the Day (QOTD) spec defined with RFC 865 (https://tools.ietf.org/html/rfc865). The QOTD service can be implemented with the TCP or UDP protocol. With TCP, as soon as the client connects, the server returns a random quote that should not be longer than 512 bytes. After the quote is sent, the server should close the connection.

Like the sample application for the Socket class, the Host class is used for configuration and logging functionality.

The QuoteServer class contains the code to read quotes from a file and returns a random quote as soon as a client connects. In the constructor, the port number and the filename containing the quotes are set. In the InitializeAsync method, the quotes file is read to fill the array referenced from the field _quotes (code file TcpServer/QuotesServer.cs):

```csharp
public class QuotesServerOptions
{
  public string? QuotesFile { get; set; }
  public int Port { get; set; }
}

public class QuotesServer
{
  private readonly int _port;
  private readonly ILogger _logger;
  private readonly string _quotesPath;
  private string[]? _quotes;
  private Random _random = new();

  public QuotesServer(IOptions<QuotesServerOptions> options, ILogger<QuotesServer> logger)
  {
    _port = options.Value.Port;
    _quotesPath = options.Value.QuotesFile ?? "quotes.txt";
    _logger = logger;
  }

  public async Task InitializeAsync(CancellationToken cancellationToken = default)
    => _quotes = await File.ReadAllLinesAsync(_quotesPath, cancellationToken);

  //...
}
```

When you use the TcpListener class to create a listener for the TCP protocol, you don't need to specify the address family, the socket type, and the protocol type; this configuration is clearly defined from the protocol supported with this class. You just need to specify the IP address and port number. After invoking the Start method, the socket is ready to receive connections. With an overload of the Start method, you can pass the size of the backlog queue, similarly to passing the Listen method with the socket sample. If you need full control of the socket that's used by the TcpListener class, you can access the Server property and access all the Socket members. Invoking the AcceptTcpClientAsync method returns a TcpClient object as soon as a client application opens a connection. The TcpClient class defines the Client property to access the underlying Socket type. You send the quote and close the connection as specified by the RFC with the invocation of the SendQuoteAsync method (code file TcpServer/QuotesServer.cs):

```csharp
public async Task RunServerAsync(CancellationToken cancellationToken = default)
{
  TcpListener listener = new(IPAddress.Any, _port);
  _logger.LogInformation("Quotes listener started on port {0}", _port);
  listener.Start();

  while (true)
  {
    cancellationToken.ThrowIfCancellationRequested();
    using TcpClient client = await listener.AcceptTcpClientAsync();
    _logger.LogInformation("Client connected with address and port: {0}",
```

```
          client.Client.RemoteEndPoint);
      var _ = SendQuoteAsync(client, cancellationToken);
    }
  }
```

In the `SendQuoteAsync` method, properties of the `TcpClient` class are used to change the settings of the underlying socket. The `LingerState` defines socket linger behavior to keep the socket open for the number of seconds set with the second argument of the constructor after the socket is closed to allow it to finish processing. Setting the `NoDelay` property to `true` turns off the Nagle algorithm. Remember, with the Nagle algorithm, messages are not sent if the buffer is not full and the receiver didn't acknowledge outstanding packages. With the QOTD service, changing the default behavior doesn't have an effect in this case because the connection is closed after sending just one message. Invoking the `GetStream` method of the `TcpClient` returns a `NetworkStream` that allows sending and receiving data. The `GetStream` method creates a `NetworkStream` that has the `ownsSocket` flag set to `true`. Disposing of the stream (which is done from the `using` declaration) also closes the socket. The `WriteAsync` method sends the quote to the client (code file `TcpServer/QuotesServer.cs`):

```csharp
private async Task SendQuoteAsync(TcpClient client,
  CancellationToken cancellationToken = default)
{
  try
  {
    client.LingerState = new LingerOption(true, 10);
    client.NoDelay = true;

    using var stream = client.GetStream(); // returns a stream that owns the socket
    var quote = GetRandomQuote();
    var buffer = Encoding.UTF8.GetBytes(quote).AsMemory();
    await stream.WriteAsync(buffer, cancellationToken);
  }
  catch (IOException ex)
  {
    _logger.LogError(ex, ex.Message);
  }
  catch (SocketException ex)
  {
    _logger.LogError(ex, ex.Message);
  }
}

private string GetRandomQuote()
{
  if (_quotes is null) throw new InvalidOperationException(
    $"Invoke InitializeAsync before calling {nameof(GetRandomQuote)}");
  return _quotes[_random.Next(_quotes.Length)];
}
```

Creating a TCP Client

The client application is implemented with the console application `TcpClientSample`. To create a TCP connection to the server, a new instance of the `TcpClient` class is created. With the `ConnectAsync` method, the name and port of the server need to be specified. After a successful connection, the content from the server is read using the `ReadAsync` method of the `NetworkStream` (code file `TcpClientSample/QuotesClient.cs`):

```csharp
public async Task SendAndReceiveAsync(CancellationToken cancellationToken = default)
{
  try
```

```
  {
    Memory<byte> buffer = new byte[4096].AsMemory();
    string? line;
    bool repeat = true;
    while (repeat)
    {
      Console.WriteLine(@"Press enter to read a quote, ""bye"" to exit");
      line = Console.ReadLine();
      if (line?.Equals("bye", StringComparison.CurrentCultureIgnoreCase) == true)
      {
        repeat = false;
      }
      else
      {
        TcpClient client = new();
        await client.ConnectAsync(_hostname, _serverPort, cancellationToken);
        using var stream = client.GetStream();
        int bytesRead = await stream.ReadAsync(buffer, cancellationToken);
        string quote = Encoding.UTF8.GetString(buffer.Span[..bytesRead]);
        buffer.Span[..bytesRead].Clear();
        Console.WriteLine(quote);
        Console.WriteLine();
      }
    };
  }
  catch (SocketException ex)
  {
    _logger.LogError(ex, ex.Message);
  }

  Console.WriteLine("so long, and thanks for all the fish");
}
```

When you run the server and the client, you can see quotes returned on the server:

```
Press enter to read a quote, "bye" to exit

"Nuclear-powered vacuum cleaners will probably be a reality within ten years.",
Alex Lewyt, Lewyt vacuum company, 1955

Press enter to read a quote, "bye" to exit

"Television won't be able to hold on to any market it captures after the first
six months.
People will soon get tired of staring at a plywood box every night.", Darryl Zanuck,
20th Century Fox, 1946

Press enter to read a quote, "bye" to exit
```

On the server, you can see log output in the console, including the ports used by the client:

```
info: QuotesServer[0]
      Quotes listener started on port 1700
info: QuotesServer[0]
      Client connected with address and port: 127.0.0.1:52788
info: QuotesServer[0]
      Client connected with address and port: 127.0.0.1:52789
```

> **NOTE** *Typical implementations of the QOTD client just open a connection, receive and print the quote, and end. With the implementation of the sample application, you can get quote after quote. Because the server closes the connection after every quote sent, a new socket is created with every request.*
>
> *As you'll read later in this chapter, with the HttpClient factory, a better practice would be to use the same socket for multiple requests. The underlying socket of the operating system stays open for 20 seconds before it's released. You can monitor the state of the sockets with the command* netstat -a.
>
> *Creating a QOTD server that does not close the connection to keep communicating with the same socket would make the implementation incompatible with existing clients and servers.*

USING UDP

The next protocol covered is the User Datagram Protocol (UDP). UDP is a simple protocol with little overhead. Before sending and receiving data with TCP, a connection needs to be made. This is not necessary with UDP; you just start sending or receiving. Of course, that means that UDP has less overhead than TCP, but it is also more unreliable. When you send data with UDP, you don't get information when this data is received. UDP is often used for situations in which the speed and performance requirements outweigh the reliability requirements—for example, video streaming. UDP also offers broadcasting messages to a group of nodes. In contrast, TCP offers features to confirm the delivery of data. TCP provides error correction and retransmission in the case of lost or corrupted packets. Last, but not least, TCP buffers incoming and outgoing data and guarantees that a sequence of packets scrambled in transmission is reassembled before delivery to the application. Even with the extra overhead, TCP is the most widely used protocol across the Internet because of its high reliability.

To demonstrate UDP, you create two console application projects that show various features of UDP: directly sending data to a host, broadcasting data to all hosts on the local network, and multicasting data to a group of nodes that belong to the same group.

Building a UDP Receiver

Start with the receiving application. The downloadable sample application uses command-line arguments where you can configure the port number and optional group address with appsettings.json or override it with command-line arguments. With the receiver, you can configure the port, an optional group address, and a Boolean flag if broadcast should be used (code file UdpReceiver/Receiver.cs):

```
public record ReceiverOptions
{
  public int Port { get; init; }
  public bool UseBroadcast { get; init; } = false;
  public string? GroupAddress { get; init; }
}

public class Receiver
{
  private readonly ILogger _logger;
  private readonly int _port;
  private readonly string? _groupAddress;
```

```
    private readonly bool _useBroadcast;
    public Receiver(IOptions<ReceiverOptions> options, ILogger<Receiver> logger)
    {
      _port = options.Value.Port;
      _groupAddress = options.Value.GroupAddress;
      _useBroadcast = options.Value.UseBroadcast;
      _logger = logger;
    }
    //...
}
```

The `RunAsync` method creates a `UdpClient` object with the port number that's received with the `ReceiverOptions` record. The `ReceiveAsync` method waits until some data arrives. This data can be found with the `UdpReceiveResult` with the `Buffer` property. After the data is encoded to a string, it's written to the console to continue the loop and wait for the next data to receive (code file `UdpReceiver/Receiver.cs`):

```
public async Task RunAsync()
{
    using UdpClient client = new(_port);
    client.EnableBroadcast = _useBroadcast;

    if (_groupAddress != null)
    {
      client.JoinMulticastGroup(IPAddress.Parse(_groupAddress));
        _logger.LogInformation("joining the multicast group {0}",
      IPAddress.Parse(_groupAddress));
    }

    bool completed = false;
    do
    {
      _logger.LogInformation("Waiting to receive data");
      UdpReceiveResult result = await client.ReceiveAsync();
      byte[] datagram = result.Buffer;
      string dataReceived = Encoding.UTF8.GetString(datagram);
      _logger.LogInformation("Received {0} from {1}", dataReceived, result.RemoteEndPoint);
      if (dataReceived.Equals("bye", StringComparison.CurrentCultureIgnoreCase))
      {
        completed = true;
      }
    } while (!completed);
    _logger.LogInformation("Receiver closing");

    if (_groupAddress != null)
    {
      client.DropMulticastGroup(IPAddress.Parse(_groupAddress));
    }
}
```

When you start the application, it waits for a sender to send data. The receiver ends the loop if it receives the string "bye." For the time being, ignore the multicast group because multicasting is discussed after you create the sender.

Creating a UDP Sender

The UDP sender application also enables you to configure it by passing command-line options. It has more options than the receiving application. Besides the port number with the Port element, the UseBroadcast option can be set to broadcast the message to all nodes in the local subnet, and a Group-Address setting can be used to send messages to all nodes that registered to a multicast group. The IPv6 setting allows using the IPv6 protocol instead of IPv4.

To send data, you need an IPEndPoint. Depending on the program arguments, you create this in different ways. With a broadcast, IPv4 defines the address 255.255.255.255 that is returned from IPAddress.Broadcast. There's no IPv6 address for broadcast because IPv6 doesn't support broadcasts. IPv6 replaces broadcasts with multicasts. Multicasts have been added to IPv4 as well.

When you're passing a host name, the host name is resolved using DNS lookup using the Dns class. The method GetHostEntryAsync returns an IPHostEntry where the IPAddress can be retrieved from the AddressList property. Depending on whether IPv4 or IPv6 is used, a different IPAddress is taken from this list. Depending on your network environment, only one of these address types might work. If a group address is passed to the method, the address is parsed using IPAddress.Parse (code file UdpSender/Sender.cs):

```csharp
private async Task<IPEndPoint?> GetReceiverIPEndPointAsync()
{
  IPEndPoint? endpoint = null;
  try
  {
    if (_useBroadcast)
    {
      endpoint = new IPEndPoint(IPAddress.Broadcast, _port);
    }
    else if (_hostName != null)
    {
      IPHostEntry hostEntry = await Dns.GetHostEntryAsync(_hostName);
      IPAddress? address = null;
      if (_useIpv6)
      {
        address = hostEntry.AddressList.Where(
          a => a.AddressFamily == AddressFamily.InterNetworkV6).FirstOrDefault();
      }
      else
      {
        address = hostEntry.AddressList.Where(
          a => a.AddressFamily == AddressFamily.InterNetwork).FirstOrDefault();
      }

      if (address == null)
      {
        Func<string> ipversion = () => _useIpv6 ? "IPv6" : "IPv4";
        _logger.LogWarning($"no {ipversion()} address for {_hostName}");
        return null;
      }
      endpoint = new IPEndPoint(address, _port);
    }
    else if (_groupAddress != null)
    {
      endpoint = new IPEndPoint(IPAddress.Parse(_groupAddress), _port);
    }
```

```
        else
        {
          throw new InvalidOperationException($"{nameof(_hostName)}, " +
            $"{nameof(_useBroadcast)}, or {nameof(_groupAddress)} must be set");
        }
      }
      catch (SocketException ex)
      {
        _logger.LogError(ex, ex.Message);
      }
      return endpoint;
    }
```

Now, regarding the UDP protocol, the most important part of the sender follows. After creating a `UdpClient` instance and converting a string to a byte array, data is sent using the `SendAsync` method. Note that neither the receiver needs to listen, nor the sender needs to connect. UDP is really simple. However, in a case in which the sender sends the data to nowhere—nobody receives the data—you also don't get any error messages (code file `UdpSender/Sender.cs`):

```
    public async Task RunAsync()
    {
      IPEndPoint? endpoint = await GetReceiverIPEndPointAsync();
      if (endpoint is null) return;

      try
      {
        string localhost = Dns.GetHostName();
        using UdpClient client = new();
        client.EnableBroadcast = _useBroadcast;
        if (_groupAddress != null)
        {
          client.JoinMulticastGroup(IPAddress.Parse(_groupAddress));
        }

        bool completed = false;
        do
        {
          Console.WriteLine(@$"{Environment.NewLine}Enter a message or ""bye"" to exit");
          string? input = Console.ReadLine();
          if (input is null) continue;
          Console.WriteLine();
          completed = input.Equals("bye", StringComparison.CurrentCultureIgnoreCase);

          byte[] datagram = Encoding.UTF8.GetBytes(input);
          int sent = await client.SendAsync(datagram, datagram.Length, endpoint);
          _logger.LogInformation("Sent datagram using local EP {0} to {1}"
            client.Client.LocalEndPoint, endpoint);
        } while (!completed);

        if (_groupAddress != null)
        {
          client.DropMulticastGroup(IPAddress.Parse(_groupAddress));
        }
      }
```

```
      catch (SocketException ex)
      {
        _logger.LogError(ex, ex.Message);
      }
  }
```

Now you can start the receiver and the sender. With the sender, you can see output similar to the one shown. The sender also successfully sends data when the receiver is not running:

```
Enter a message or "bye" to exit
message 1
info: Sender[0]
      Sent datagram using local EP 0.0.0.0:54446 to 127.0.0.1:8600

Enter a message or "bye" to exit
message 2

Enter a message or "bye" to exit
info: Sender[0]
      Sent datagram using local EP 0.0.0.0:54446 to 127.0.0.1:8600
```

The receiver shows the data received and the port and address where this message is coming from:

```
info: Receiver[0]
      Waiting to receive data
info: Receiver[0]
      Received message 1 from 127.0.0.1:54446
info: Receiver[0]
      Waiting to receive data
info: Receiver[0]
      Received message 2 from 127.0.0.1:54446
```

Without changing the configuration file, you can pass a different port number starting with the receiver:

```
> dotnet run -- UdpReceiver:Port=5400
```

and with the sender:

```
> dotnet run -- UdpSender:ReceiverPort=5400
```

You can enter data in the sender that will arrive in the receiver. If you stop the receiver, you can go on sending without detecting any error. You can also try to use a host name instead of localhost and run the receiver on a different system.

With the sender, you can set the `UdpSender:UseBroadcast=true` option to send a broadcast to all nodes listening to the specified port on the same network:

```
> dotnet run -- UdpSender:ReceiverPort=5400 UdpSender:UseBroadcast=true
```

With the output of the sender, you can see the message is sent to the IPv4 broadcast address:

```
info: Sender[0]
      Sent datagram using local EP 0.0.0.0:50695 to 255.255.255.255:5400
```

Be aware that broadcasts don't cross most routers, and of course, you can't use broadcasts on the Internet. This situation is different with multicasts, which are discussed next.

Using Multicasts

Broadcasts don't cross routers, but multicasts can. Multicasts have been invented to send messages to a group of systems—all nodes that belong to the same group. With IPv4, specific IP addresses are reserved for multicast use.

The addresses start with 224.0.0.0 and go to 239.255.255.253. Many of these addresses are reserved for specific protocols—for example, for routers—but 239.0.0.0/8 can be used privately within an organization. This is similar to IPv6, which has well-known IPv6 multicast addresses for different routing protocols. Addresses f::/16 are local within an organization; addresses ffxe::/16 have global scope and can be routed over public Internet.

For a sender or receiver to use multicasts, it must join a multicast group by invoking the JoinMulticastGroup method of the UdpClient:

```
client.JoinMulticastGroup(IPAddress.Parse(groupAddress));
```

To leave the group again, you can invoke the method DropMulticastGroup:

```
client.DropMulticastGroup(IPAddress.Parse(groupAddress));
```

When you start both the receiver and sender with the GroupAddress set, you can send messages to the group with the same IP address and port number:

```
> dotnet run -- UdpSender:ReceiverPort=5400 UdpSender:GroupAddress=230.0.0.1
> dotnet run -- UdpReceiver:Port=5400 UdpReceiver:GroupAddress=230.0.0.1
```

As with broadcasting, you can start multiple receivers and multiple senders. Depending on the quality of the network and the network load, the receivers will receive nearly all messages from each sender.

USING WEB SERVERS

Using Internet Information Services (IIS) on Windows and Apache or NGINX on Linux are great options for using a web server. A lightweight option with .NET is the Kestrel server. This server was created by the ASP.NET Core team and is available on Windows and Linux. When you use IIS and Apache or NGINX with ASP.NET Core, Kestrel is always used behind the scenes. From IIS, a request is forwarded to the Kestrel server.

To create an application hosting the Kestrel server, you can create an empty web application with the .NET CLI: dotnet new web.

Contrary to a simple console application, this project type has the SDK Microsoft.NET.Sdk.Web referenced. With this setting, not only are more build tools needed for web development available, but a reference to Microsoft.AspNetCore.App is included implicitly (configuration file HttpServerSample/HttpServerSample.csproj):

```
<Project Sdk="Microsoft.NET.Sdk.Web">

  <PropertyGroup>
    <TargetFramework>net5.0</TargetFramework>
    <Nullable>enable</Nullable>
  </PropertyGroup>

</Project>
```

The generated Program.cs file contains the Main method with the Host class to configure the dependency injection container, logging, and configuration. In addition to what you've used with the simple console applications, the extension method ConfigureWebHostDefaults, which is defined in the Microsoft.AspNetCore package, is used. Here the type to be used that contains startup methods is defined with the generic parameter of the method UseStartup. Typically, this class has the name Startup (code file HttpServerSample/Program.cs):

```
public class Program
{
  public static void Main(string[] args)
```

```
  {
    CreateHostBuilder(args).Build().Run();
  }

  public static IHostBuilder CreateHostBuilder(string[] args) =>
    Host.CreateDefaultBuilder(args)
      .ConfigureWebHostDefaults(webBuilder =>
      {
        webBuilder.UseStartup<Startup>();
      });
}
```

With a simple console application, you configured your services with the dependency injection container in the `ConfigureServices` extension method. With web applications, you configure the services in the `ConfigureServices` method of the `Startup` class. In addition, you configure middleware in the `Startup` class with the method `Configure`.

Configuring Kestrel

The `IWebHostBuilder` interface parameter of the `ConfigureWebHostDefaults` method allows configuring the hosting server and the HTTP and HTTP/2 options. The `ConfigureKestrel` extension method allows setting `KestrelServerOptions`—for example, limits on the HTTP protocol. `KestrelServerLimits` allows you to specify timeout values, maximum sizes for the headers and the body size, maximum number of concurrent connections, maximum number of connections upgraded to WebSockets, as well as HTTP/2 and HTTP/3 limits. An advantage of HTTP/2 is to have multiple concurrent streams using the same connection. You can limit the maximum number of concurrent streams with the `Http2Limits` type with the `MaxStreamsPerConnection` setting. The default
setting is 100.

In the following code snippet, the Kestrel server is configured to use ports 5020 and 5021, is set to return the HTTP Server header with every response, allows compression of HTTP headers, and specifies some limits (code file `HttpServerSample/Program.cs`):

```
public static IHostBuilder CreateHostBuilder(string[] args) =>
  Host.CreateDefaultBuilder(args)
    .ConfigureWebHostDefaults(webBuilder =>
    {
      webBuilder.UseStartup<Startup>()
        .ConfigureKestrel(kestrelOptions =>
        {
          kestrelOptions.AddServerHeader = true;
          kestrelOptions.AllowResponseHeaderCompression = true;
          kestrelOptions.Limits.Http2.MaxStreamsPerConnection = 10;
          kestrelOptions.Limits.MaxConcurrentConnections = 20;
        })
        .UseUrls("http://localhost:5020", "https://localhost:5021");
    });
```

> **NOTE** *With .NET 5, Kestrel by default is configured to support HTTP/1.1 and HTTP/2. To define a specific version, invoke one of the* `ListenXXX` *methods, such as* `ListenLocalhost`, *in the* `ConfigureKestrel` *method. With the* `Protocols` *property, you can specify one of the* `HttpProtocols` *enum values.*

> **NOTE** *One feature the Kestrel server does not support is Windows authentication. The Kestrel server supports authentication via OAuth 2.0 and OpenID Connect. If you need Windows authentication in your environment, you can use IIS and the Http.sys web server. With the* IWebBuilder, *you can invoke* UseHttpSys, *which changes the configuration to use Http.sys. This is only available on Windows.*

Startup

In the Startup class, the dependency injection container and middleware are configured. In the ConfigureServices method, the custom service classes GenerateHtml and Formula1 are registered. The GenerateHtml class is used to return HTML code. When an HTTP request is received, the application returns a response including HTTP header information. The Formula1 class is used with a web API to return Formula 1 champions in JSON format to the client (code file HttpServerSample/Startup.cs):

```
public class Startup
{
  public void ConfigureServices(IServiceCollection services)
  {
    services.AddScoped<GenerateHtml>();
    services.AddSingleton<Formula1>();
  }
  //...
}
```

The Configure method of the Startup class configures the middleware. Endpoints for the server are configured within the UseEndpoints method. The MapGet method maps HTTP GET requests. The first invocation of MapGet maps the link /api/racers and returns JSON information with the WriteAsJsonAsync method. The Formula1 class method that's injected with the Configure method defines the GetChampions method and returns a list of Formula 1 champions. The second invocation of MapGet maps the root path to invoke the GetHtmlContent method of the injected GenerateHtml class. This method receives the HttpRequest as a parameter to return HTML information showing the request (code file HttpServerSample/Startup.cs):

```
public class Startup
{
  public void Configure(IApplicationBuilder app, IWebHostEnvironment env,
    GenerateHtml generateHtml, Formula1 formula1)
  {
    if (env.IsDevelopment())
    {
      app.UseDeveloperExceptionPage();
    }

    app.UseRouting();

    app.UseEndpoints(endpoints =>
    {
      endpoints.MapGet("/api/racers", async context =>
      {
        await context.Response.WriteAsJsonAsync(formula1.GetChampions());
      });
```

```
endpoints.MapGet("/", async context =>
{
    string content = generateHtml.GetHtmlContent(context.Request);
    context.Response.ContentType = "text/html";
    await context.Response.WriteAsync(Encoding.UTF8.GetString(content));
});
});
}
//...
}
```

> **NOTE** *ASP.NET Core, including details on middleware, is covered in Chapter 24, "ASP.NET Core."*

> **NOTE** *The* `WriteAsJsonAsync` *method is implemented in the* `Microsoft.AspNetCore.Http.Extensions` *NuGet package and allows creating simple REST APIs. This makes use of the JSON serializer covered in Chapter 18. Read Chapter 25, "Services," for more information about REST APIs.*

HTTP Headers

The sample code returns an HTML file that is retrieved using the `GetHtmlContent` method. This method makes use of the `htmlFormat` format string with two placeholders in the heading and the body. The `GetHtmlContent` method fills in the placeholders using the `string.Format` method. To fill the HTML body, two helper methods are used that retrieve the header information from the request and all the property values of the `Request` object—`GetHeaderInfo` and `GetRequestInfo` (code file `HttpServerSample/GenerateHtml.cs`):

```
private static string s_htmlFormat =
    "<!DOCTYPE html><html><head><title>{0}</title></head>" +
    "<body>{1}</body></html>";

public string GetHtmlContent(HttpRequest request)
{
    string title = "Sample Listener using Kestrel";

    string content = $"<h1>Hello from the server</h1>" +
      $"<h2>Header Info</h2>" +
      $"{string.Join(' ', GetHeaderInfo(request.Headers))}" +
      $"<h2>Request Object Information</h2>" +
      $"{string.Join(' ', GetRequestInfo(request))}";

    return string.Format(s_htmlFormat, title, content);
}
```

The `GetHeaderInfo` method retrieves the keys and values from the `IHeaderDictionary` to return a `div` element that contains every key and value (code file `HttpServerSample/GenerateHtml.cs`):

```csharp
private IEnumerable<string> GetHeaderInfo(IHeaderDictionary headers)
{
  List<(string Key, string Value)> values = new();
  var keys = headers.Keys;
  foreach (var key in keys)
  {
    if (headers.TryGetValue(key, out var value))
    {
      values.Add((key, value));
    }
  }
  return values.Select(v => $"<div>{v.Key}: {v.Value}</div>");
}
```

The GetRequestInfo method makes use of reflection to get all the properties of the Request type and returns the property names as well as their values (code file HttpServerSample/GenerateHtml.cs):

```csharp
private IEnumerable<string> GetRequestInfo(HttpRequest request)
{
  var properties = request.GetType().GetProperties();
  List<(string Key, string Value)> values = new();
  foreach (var property in properties)
  {
    try
    {
      string? value = property.GetValue(request)?.ToString();
      if (value != null)
      {
        values.Add((property.Name, value));
      }
    }
    catch (TargetInvocationException ex)
    {
      _logger.LogInformation("{0}: {1}", property.Name, ex.Message);
      if (ex.InnerException != null)
      {
        _logger.LogInformation("\t{0}", ex.InnerException.Message);
      }
    }
  }
  return values.Select(v => $"<div>{v.Key}: {v.Value}</div>");
}
```

> **NOTE** *The* GetHeaderInfo *and* GetRequestInfo *methods make use of expression-bodied member functions, LINQ, and reflection. Expression-bodied member functions are explained in Chapter 3, "Classes, Records, Structs, and Tuples." Chapter 9, "Language Integrated Query," explains LINQ. Chapter 12, "Reflection, Metadata, and Source Generators," includes reflection as an important topic.*

Running the server and using a browser such as Microsoft Edge to access the server using a URL such as https://localhost:5021/ results in output as shown in Figure 19-1. Figure 19-2 shows the output from /api/racers with the Formula 1 champions.

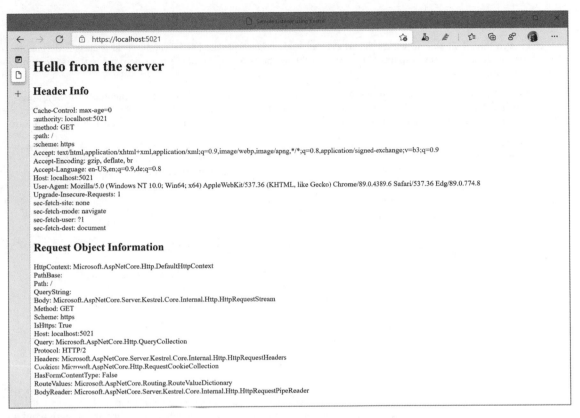

FIGURE 19-1

[{"firstName":"Nino","lastName":"Farina","country":"Italy","starts":33,"wins":5,"years":[1950],"cars":["Alfa Romeo"]},
{"firstName":"Alberto","lastName":"Ascari","country":"Italy","starts":32,"wins":13,"years":[1952,1953],"cars":["Ferrari"]},{"firstName":"Juan Manuel","lastName":"Fangio","country":"Argentina","starts":51,"wins":24,"years":[1951,1954,1955,1956,1957],"cars":["Alfa Romeo","Maserati","Mercedes","Ferrari"]},
{"firstName":"Mike","lastName":"Hawthorn","country":"UK","starts":45,"wins":3,"years":[1958],"cars":["Ferrari"]},
{"firstName":"Phil","lastName":"Hill","country":"USA","starts":48,"wins":3,"years":[1961],"cars":["Ferrari"]},
{"firstName":"John","lastName":"Surtees","country":"UK","starts":111,"wins":6,"years":[1964],"cars":["Ferrari"]},
{"firstName":"Jim","lastName":"Clark","country":"UK","starts":72,"wins":25,"years":[1963,1965],"cars":["Lotus"]},
{"firstName":"Jack","lastName":"Brabham","country":"Australia","starts":125,"wins":14,"years":[1959,1960,1966],"cars":["Cooper","Brabham"]},
{"firstName":"Denny","lastName":"Hulme","country":"New Zealand","starts":112,"wins":8,"years":[1967],"cars":["Brabham"]},
{"firstName":"Graham","lastName":"Hill","country":"UK","starts":176,"wins":14,"years":[1962,1968],"cars":["BRM","Lotus"]},
{"firstName":"Jochen","lastName":"Rindt","country":"Austria","starts":60,"wins":6,"years":[1970],"cars":["Lotus"]},
{"firstName":"Jackie","lastName":"Stewart","country":"UK","starts":99,"wins":27,"years":[1969,1971,1973],"cars":["Matra","Tyrrell"]},
{"firstName":"Emerson","lastName":"Fittipaldi","country":"Brazil","starts":143,"wins":14,"years":[1972,1974],"cars":["Lotus","McLaren"]},
{"firstName":"James","lastName":"Hunt","country":"UK","starts":91,"wins":10,"years":[1976],"cars":["McLaren"]},
{"firstName":"Mario","lastName":"Andretti","country":"USA","starts":128,"wins":12,"years":[1978],"cars":["Lotus"]},
{"firstName":"Jody","lastName":"Scheckter","country":"South Africa","starts":112,"wins":10,"years":[1979],"cars":["Ferrari"]},
{"firstName":"Alan","lastName":"Jones","country":"Australia","starts":115,"wins":12,"years":[1980],"cars":["Williams"]},
{"firstName":"Keke","lastName":"Rosberg","country":"Finland","starts":114,"wins":5,"years":[1982],"cars":["Williams"]},
{"firstName":"Niki","lastName":"Lauda","country":"Austria","starts":173,"wins":25,"years":[1975,1977,1984],"cars":["Ferrari","McLaren"]},
{"firstName":"Nelson","lastName":"Piquet","country":"Brazil","starts":204,"wins":23,"years":[1981,1983,1987],"cars":["Brabham","Williams"]},
{"firstName":"Ayrton","lastName":"Senna","country":"Brazil","starts":161,"wins":41,"years":[1988,1990,1991],"cars":["McLaren"]},
{"firstName":"Nigel","lastName":"Mansell","country":"UK","starts":187,"wins":31,"years":[1992],"cars":["Williams"]},
{"firstName":"Alain","lastName":"Prost","country":"France","starts":197,"wins":51,"years":[1985,1986,1989,1993],"cars":["McLaren","Williams"]},
{"firstName":"Damon","lastName":"Hill","country":"UK","starts":114,"wins":22,"years":[1996],"cars":["Williams"]},
{"firstName":"Jacques","lastName":"Villeneuve","country":"Canada","starts":165,"wins":11,"years":[1997],"cars":["Williams"]},
{"firstName":"Mika","lastName":"Hakkinen","country":"Finland","starts":160,"wins":20,"years":[1998,1999],"cars":["McLaren"]},
{"firstName":"Michael","lastName":"Schumacher","country":"Germany","starts":287,"wins":91,"years":[1994,1995,2000,2001,2002,2003,2004],"cars":["Benetton","Ferrari"]},{"firstName":"Fernando","lastName":"Alonso","country":"Spain","starts":314,"wins":32,"years":[2005,2006],"cars":["Renault"]},
{"firstName":"Kimi","lastName":"Räikkönen","country":"Finland","starts":330,"wins":21,"years":[2007],"cars":["Ferrari"]},
{"firstName":"Lewis","lastName":"Hamilton","country":"UK","starts":266,"wins":95,"years":[2008,2014,2015,2017,2018,2019,2020],"cars":["McLaren","Mercedes"]},
{"firstName":"Jenson","lastName":"Button","country":"UK","starts":306,"wins":16,"years":[2009],"cars":["Brawn GP"]},
{"firstName":"Sebastian","lastName":"Vettel","country":"Germany","starts":257,"wins":53,"years":[2010,2011,2012,2013],"cars":["Red Bull Racing"]},
{"firstName":"Nico","lastName":"Rosberg","country":"Germany","starts":207,"wins":24,"years":[2016],"cars":["Mercedes"]}]

FIGURE 19-2

THE HTTPCLIENT CLASS

Let's get to the client side so we can use the `HttpClient` class to make HTTP requests. This class is defined in the `System.Net.Http` namespace. The classes in the `System.Net.Http` namespace help make it easy to consume web services.

The `HttpClient` class derives from the `HttpMessageInvoker` class. This base class implements the `SendAsync` method. The `SendAsync` method is the workhorse of the `HttpClient` class. As you'll see later in this section, there are several derivatives of this method to use. As the name implies, the `SendAsync` method call is asynchronous.

The sample application makes use of the HttpClient factory from the NuGet package `Microsoft.Extensions.Http`. With the container configuration, the generic method `AddHttpClient` is invoked. The generic parameter is of type `HttpClientSamples` where the `HttpClient` object is injected. The `HttpClient` can be configured with the delegate parameter of the `AddHttpClient` method. Here, the `BaseAddress` property is specified (code file `HttpClientSample/Program.cs`):

```
IHostBuilder GetHostBuilder() =>
  Host.CreateDefaultBuilder()
  .ConfigureServices((context, services) =>
  {
    var httpClientSettings = context.Configuration.GetSection("HttpClient");
    services.Configure<HttpClientSamplesOptions>(httpClientSettings);
    services.AddHttpClient<HttpClientSamples>(httpClient =>
    {
      httpClient.BaseAddress = new Uri(httpClientSettings["Url"]);
    });
    //...
  });
```

The configuration file that's read with the setup of the DI container has the URL to the server created previously configured. When you run the client application, make sure to have this server running as well. You can also change the link in the configuration file to any other available server to see what's returned from there (configuration file `HttpClientSample/appsettings.json`):

```
{
  "HttpClient": {
    "Url": "https://localhost:5021",
    "InvalidUrl": "https://localhost1:5021"
  },
  "RateLimit": {
    "LimitCalls": 5
  }
}
```

With the constructor of the `HttpClientSamples` class, the `HttpClient` is injected along with the `HttpClientSamplesOptions` configuration that's coming from the configuration file via the configuration in the dependency injection container (code file `HttpClientSample/HttpClientSamples.cs`):

```
public record HttpClientSamplesOptions
{
    public string? Url { get; init; }
    public string? InvalidUrl { get; init; }
}

public class HttpClientSamples
{
  private readonly ILogger _logger;
```

```
private readonly HttpClient _httpClient;
private readonly string _url;
private readonly string _invalidUrl;

public HttpClientSamples(
  IOptions<HttpClientSamplesOptions> options,
  HttpClient httpClient,
  ILogger<HttpClientSamples> logger)
{
  _url = options.Value.Url ?? "https://localhost:5020";
  _invalidUrl = options.Value.InvalidUrl ?? "https://localhost1:5020";
  _httpClient = httpClient;
  _logger = logger;
}
//...
}
```

> **WARNING** *The* HttpClient *class implements the* IDisposable *interface. As a general guideline, objects implementing* IDisposable *should be disposed of after their use. This is also true for the* HttpClient *class. However, the* Dispose *method of the* HttpClient *does not immediately release the associated socket; it is released after a timeout. This timeout can take 20 seconds. With this timeout, using many* HttpClient *object instances can lead to the program running out of sockets. The solution: the* HttpClient *class is built for reuse. You can use this class with many requests and not create a new instance every time. Using the HttpClient factory takes away the need to create and dispose of* HttpClient *instances.*

Making an Asynchronous Get Request

Invoking the GetAsync makes an HTTP GET request to the server. Because the BaseAddress is already specified with the configuration of the HttpClient class that's injected with the HttpClientSamples class, only the relative address needs to be passed to the GetAsync method.

The call to GetAsync returns an HttpResponseMessage object. The HttpResponseMessage class represents a response including headers, status, and content. Checking the IsSuccessfulStatusCode property of the response tells you whether the request was successful. With a successful call, the content returned is retrieved as a string using the ReadAsStringAsync method (code file HttpClientSample/HttpClientSamples.cs):

```
public async Task SimpleGetRequestAsync()
{
  HttpResponseMessage response = await _httpClient.GetAsync("/");
  if (response.IsSuccessStatusCode)
  {
    Console.WriteLine($"Response Status Code: {(int)response.StatusCode} " +
      $"{response.ReasonPhrase}");
    string responseBodyAsText = await (response.Content?.ReadAsStringAsync()
      ?? Task.FromResult(string.Empty));
    Console.WriteLine($"Received payload of {responseBodyAsText.Length} characters");
    Console.WriteLine();
    Console.WriteLine(responseBodyAsText[0..50]);
  }
}
```

Executing this code with the command-line argument `simple` should produce the following output, including the log output from the source `System.Net.Http.HttpClient`:

```
info: System.Net.Http.HttpClient.HttpClientSamples.LogicalHandler[100]
      Start processing HTTP request GET https://localhost:5021/
info: System.Net.Http.HttpClient.HttpClientSamples.ClientHandler[100]
      Sending HTTP request GET https://localhost:5021/
info: System.Net.Http.HttpClient.HttpClientSamples.ClientHandler[101]
      Received HTTP response headers after 312.8412ms - 200
info: System.Net.Http.HttpClient.HttpClientSamples.LogicalHandler[101]
      End processing HTTP request after 328.6248ms - 200
Response Status Code: 200 OK
Received payload of 1008 characters

<!DOCTYPE html><html><head><title>Sample Listener
```

> **NOTE** *When checking for success, do not check the* `StatusCode` *property and compare it with 200 or* `HttpStatusCode.OK`. *200 is not the only success status code; all 2xx status codes indicate success. Instead, the* `IsSuccessStatusCode` *property returns a Boolean value if the call was successful or not. You can also throw an exception if a failure occurs, as shown in the next section.*

Throwing Exceptions from Errors

Invoking the `GetAsync` method of the `HttpClient` class by default doesn't generate an exception if the method fails. This could be easily changed by invoking the `EnsureSuccessStatusCode` method with the `HttpResponseMessage`. This method checks whether `IsSuccessStatusCode` is `false` and throws an exception otherwise (code file `HttpClientSample/HttpClientSamples.cs`):

```
public async Task ThrowExceptionAsync()
{
  try
  {
    HttpResponseMessage response = await _httpClient.GetAsync(_invalidUrl);
    response.EnsureSuccessStatusCode();

    Console.WriteLine($"Response Status Code: {(int)response.StatusCode} " +
      $"{response.ReasonPhrase}");
    string responseBodyAsText = await (response.Content?.ReadAsStringAsync()
      ?? Task.FromResult(string.Empty));
    Console.WriteLine($"Received payload of {responseBodyAsText.Length} characters");
    Console.WriteLine();
    Console.WriteLine(responseBodyAsText[..50]);
  }
  catch (HttpRequestException ex)
  {
    _logger.LogError(ex, ex.Message);
  }
}
```

Creating an HttpRequestMessage

The `GetAsync` method makes an HTTP GET request to the server. You can create POST requests with the `PostAsync` method and PUT requests with the `PutAsync` method. Chapter 25 shows details for how to invoke REST services using the `HttpClient`. All these methods are extension methods that invoke the `SendAsync` method and pass an `HttpRequestMessage` as shown in the following code snippet. When you use the `HttpRequestMessage`, you have more options—for example, using other HTTP methods such as HEAD and TRACE (method `UseHttpRequestMessageAsync` in the code file `HttpClientSample/HttpClientSamples.cs`):

```
HttpRequestMessage request = new(HttpMethod.Get, "/");
HttpResponseMessage response = await _httpClient.SendAsync(request);
```

> **NOTE** *The* `HttpRequestMessage` *specifies a version property that you can use to make requests with HTTP/2.0, passing* `new Version("2.0")`*. With the* `HttpClient` *class, you can set the property* `DefaultRequestVersion`*, which you can also configure with the HttpClient factory. By setting the* `DefaultVersionPolicy`*, you can specify to use exactly the specified version (*`RequestVersionExact`*) or communicate with the server on versions available (*`RequestVersionOrHigher` *or* `RequestVersionOrLower`*).*
>
> *HTTP/1.0 was specified in 1996 and was followed by 1.1 just a few years later. With 1.0, the connection was always closed after the server returned the data; with 1.1, a keep-alive header was added where the client was able to put their wish to keep the connection alive as the client might make more requests to receive not only the HTML code but also CSS and JavaScript files and images. After HTTP/1.1 was defined in 1999, it took 16 years until HTTP/2 was done in the year 2015.*
>
> *What are the advantages of version 2? HTTP/2 allows multiple concurrent requests on the same connection, header information is compressed, the client can define which of the resources is more important, and the server can send resources to the client via server push. HTTP/2 is supported in all modern browsers—with the exception of server push. Because server push is not used often, and when it is used, usually more data than needed is pushed to the client, the current plan is to remove this feature from Chromium-based browsers.*
>
> *HTTP/3 is currently a working draft (*`https://quicwg.org/base-drafts/draft-ietf-quic-http.html`*), but a lot of work is in progress to support this protocol with Windows, .NET, and the Kestrel server. HTTP/3 is based on the QUIC transport protocol instead of TCP. The original meaning of QUIC was QUICK UDP Internet Connections (see* `https://www.afasterweb.com/2019/04/30/some-quic-benefits-of-http/3/`*). QUIC solves some issues with TCP, which helps with faster connections and multiplexing. Read the paper at the previous link for more information. See* `https://github.com/dotnet/aspnetcore/issues/15271` *for the status of the HTTP/3 support of ASP.NET Core.*

Passing Headers

The `HttpRequestMessage` class has a property `Headers` where you can specify HTTP headers to be sent to the server. This can also be done directly with the `HttpClient` class.

An example of where an HTTP header might be needed is to specify accepted return formats where the server can decide to return specific formatted data. ASP.NET Core 5.0 Web APIs return JSON data by default. You can add XML serializers as described in Chapter 25. Then, you need to ask the server to return XML. This can be done by setting an `Accept` header to `"application/xml"`.

A generic way to set HTTP headers (besides the `Headers` property of the `HttpRequestMessage`) is the `DefaultRequestHeaders` property of the `HttpClient` class:

```
_httpClient.DefaultRequestHeaders.Add("Accept", "application/xml, */*");
```

Instead of setting this property before making the request to the server, you can also configure the headers with the `HttpClient` configuration in the DI container.

To pass multiple `Accept` values, you can use an overload of the `Add` method to pass multiple accepted formats:

```
_httpClient.DefaultRequestHeaders.Add("Accept", new[] { "application/xml", "*/*" });
```

Because the HTTP `Accept` header is commonly used, the `HttpClient` class also defines an `Accept` property to pass all the `Accept` headers (method `AddHttpHeadersAsync` in the code file `HttpClientSample/HttpClientSamples.cs`):

```
_httpClient.DefaultRequestHeaders.Accept.Add(
  new MediaTypeWithQualityHeaderValue("application/xml"));
_httpClient.DefaultRequestHeaders.Accept.Add(
  new MediaTypeWithQualityHeaderValue("*/*"));
```

The downloadable code sample defines the `ShowHeaders` method to display all the headers that are sent to the server and received from the server on the console (code file `HttpClientSample/Utilities.cs`):

```
static class Utilities
{
  public static void ShowHeaders(string title, HttpHeaders headers)
  {
    Console.WriteLine(title);
    foreach (var header in headers)
    {
      string value = string.Join(" ", header.Value);
      Console.WriteLine($"Header: {header.Key} Value: {value}");
    }
    Console.WriteLine();
  }
}
```

This method is invoked with the `AddHttpHeadersAsync` method (code file `HttpClientSample/HttpClientSamples.cs`):

```
public async Task AddHttpHeadersAsync()
{
  try
  {
    _httpClient.DefaultRequestHeaders.Accept.Add(
      new MediaTypeWithQualityHeaderValue("application/xml"));
    _httpClient.DefaultRequestHeaders.Accept.Add(
      new MediaTypeWithQualityHeaderValue("*/*"));
    Utilities.ShowHeaders("Request Headers:", _httpClient.DefaultRequestHeaders);

    HttpResponseMessage response = await _httpClient.GetAsync("/");
    response.EnsureSuccessStatusCode();

    Utilities.ShowHeaders("Response Headers:", response.Headers);
    Console.WriteLine();
  }
  catch (HttpRequestException ex)
  {
    Console.WriteLine($"{ex.Message}");
  }
}
```

When you run the application with the `headers` argument, you can see the headers sent and received. Remember with the Kestrel server created previously, it was turned on to return the Server header:

```
Request Headers:
Header: Accept Value: application/xml
Response Headers:
Header: Date Value: Mon, 01 Feb 2021 19:23:30 GMT
Header: Server Value: Kestrel
Header: Transfer-Encoding Value: chunked
```

Accessing the Content

The previous code snippets have shown you how to access the `Content` property to retrieve a string. The `Content` property in the response returns an `HttpContent` object. To get the data from the `HttpContent` object, you need to use one of the methods supplied. In the example, the `ReadAsStringAsync` method was used. It returns a string representation of the content. As the name implies, this is an async call. Instead of using the `async` keyword, the `Result` property could be used as well. Calling the `Result` property blocks the call until it's finished and then continues with execution.

Other methods to get the data from the `HttpContent` object are `ReadAsByteArrayAsync`, which returns a byte array of the data, and `ReadAsStreamAsync`, which returns a stream. You can also load the content into a memory buffer using `LoadIntoBufferAsync`.

> **NOTE** *Streams are explained in Chapter 18. Check Chapter 25 on receiving streams with the `HttpClient` class. For receiving large content, streams should be preferred to strings. Large strings are stored in the large object heap, which can lead to memory issues.*

Customizing Requests with HttpMessageHandler

The `HttpClient` class can take an `HttpMessageHandler` as a parameter to its constructor. This makes it possible for you to customize the request. You can pass an instance of a class derived from `DelegatingHandler`. There are numerous ways to influence the request—for example, for monitoring, making calls to other services, and so on. Chapter 27, "Blazor," covers an ASP.NET technology where you can run .NET code in a WebAssembly (WASM) in the browser. With Blazor WASM you can use the `HttpClient` class to make calls to services directly within the browser. However, the browser restricts what you can do, and you can't make network requests without the browser. Using Blazor WASM you can still use the `HttpClient` class. This is done using `HttpMessageHandler`, which in turn uses the Fetch API of the browser to make requests.

With the next code snippet, a `LimitCallsHandler` is defined to be used with the `HttpClient` factory. The method `AddHttpClient` returns an `IHttpClientBuilder`. With this you can use a fluent API to configure this factory. The generic parameter passed to the extension method `AddHttpMessageHandler` defines the type of the class that should be used with the `HttpMessageHandler`. In turn, the method `SetHandlerLifetime` is used to specify the lifetime of this handler (code file `HttpClientSample/Program.cs`):

```
services.Configure<LimitCallsHandlerOptions>(
  context.Configuration.GetSection("RateLimit"));
services.AddTransient<LimitCallsHandler>();
services.AddHttpClient<HttpClientSampleWithMessageHandler>(httpClient =>
{
  httpClient.BaseAddress = new Uri(httpClientSettings["Url"]);
}).AddHttpMessageHandler<LimitCallsHandler>()
  .SetHandlerLifetime(Timeout.InfiniteTimeSpan);

private HttpClient _httpClientWithMessageHandler;
public HttpClient HttpClientWithMessageHandler =>
```

```
_httpClientWithMessageHandler ?? (_httpClientWithMessageHandler =
  new HttpClient(new SampleMessageHandler("error")));
```

The purpose of this handler type, `LimitCallsHandler`, is to restrict the number of calls that can be done with the configured `HttpClient`. The number of calls allowed is specified with the `LimitCalls` property that's retrieved from the configuration file. The overridden method `SendAsync` is invoked by the `HttpClient`. With the implementation, the `SendAsync` method of the base class is invoked, but only as long as the limit is not reached. On reaching the limit, the HTTP status code `TooManyRequests` (429) is returned. This way, this error is not returned from the server but from the client handler (code file `HttpClientSample/LimitCallsHandler.cs`):

```csharp
public record LimitCallsHandlerOptions
{
  public int LimitCalls { get; init; }
}

public class LimitCallsHandler : DelegatingHandler
{
  private readonly ILogger _logger;
  private readonly int _limitCount;
  private int _numberCalls = 0;
  public LimitCallsHandler(IOptions<RateLimitHandlerOptions> options,
    ILogger<LimitCallsHandler> logger)
  {
    _limitCount = options.Value.LimitCalls;
    _logger = logger;
  }

  protected override Task<HttpResponseMessage> SendAsync(HttpRequestMessage request,
    CancellationToken cancellationToken)
  {
    if (_numberCalls >= _limitCount)
    {
      _logger.LogInformation("limit reached, returning too many requests");
      return Task.FromResult(new HttpResponseMessage(HttpStatusCode.TooManyRequests));
    }
    Interlocked.Increment(ref _numberCalls);
    _logger.LogTrace("SendAsync from within LimitCallsHandler");
    return base.SendAsync(request, cancellationToken);
  }
}
```

With the sample application, in the class `HttpClientSampleWithMessageHandler`, the `HttpClient` using the `LimitCallsHandler` is injected. Invoking the method `UseMessageHandlerAsync` multiple times, you can see the handler's limit in action, and the 429 error will be shown (code file `HttpClientSample/Program.cs`):

```csharp
var service = host.Services.GetRequiredService<HttpClientSampleWithMessageHandler>();
for (int i = 0; i < 10; i++)
{
  await service.UseMessageHandlerAsync();
}
```

HTTPCLIENT FACTORY

With the `HttpClientSample` application, you've already seen the `HttpClient` factory in action—configured with the DI container. The factory keeps a cache of `HttpMessageHandler` handler objects discussed in the previous section. The handler objects have a connection to the native operating system (OS) socket object. As more sockets are needed for communication, the factory creates new ones. If they are not used for some time, the factory disposes of the objects. The default lifetime of the handler objects is two minutes. If they are not used for two minutes, they are disposed of. You can change the lifetime of these objects by invoking the `SetHandlerLifetime` method, as shown in the next section.

Typed Clients

Using the generic version of the `AddHttpClient` method adds a *typed client*. A typed client is a class that has an `HttpClient` as a constructor parameter, and it's usually the preferred option on using the factory. The used overload of this method has an `Action<HttpClient>` parameter that allows you to configure the `HttpClient`—for example, on specifying the `BaseAddress` property as shown here (code file `HttpClientSample/Program.cs`):

```
IHostBuilder GetHostBuilder() =>
  Host.CreateDefaultBuilder()
    .ConfigureServices((context, services) =>
    {
      var httpClientSettings = context.Configuration.GetSection("HttpClient");
      services.Configure<HttpClientSamplesOptions>(httpClientSettings);
      services.AddHttpClient<HttpClientSamples>(httpClient =>
      {
        httpClient.BaseAddress = new Uri(httpClientSettings["Url"]);
      });
      services.Configure<LimitCallsHandlerOptions>(
        context.Configuration.GetSection("RateLimit"));
      services.AddTransient<LimitCallsHandler>();
      services.AddHttpClient<HttpClientSampleWithMessageHandler>(httpClient =>
      {
        httpClient.BaseAddress = new Uri(httpClientSettings["Url"]);
      }).AddHttpMessageHandler<LimitCallsHandler>()
        .SetHandlerLifetime(Timeout.InfiniteTimeSpan);
    });
```

Instead of using the generic parameter with the `AddHttpClient` method to register a typed client, you can also invoke the method `AddTypedClient` and supply the type with the generic parameter. This way you can add multiple types to use the same `HttpClient` configuration.

Named Clients

Using a typed client is one way to use the `HttpClient` factory. You can also define a name for the configured HTTP client and access HTTP clients from the pool using this name.

To specify a named client, several overloads exist with the `AddHttpClient` method. In the following sample code, a named client is specified with the name `racersClient`. This time for the configuration of the `HttpClient` object, the method `ConfigureHttpClient` is used instead of passing a delegate as an argument of the `AddHttpClient` method. With named clients, you also have the option to supply the configuration with the argument. Because the type where the named client should be used is not registered in the DI container on configuring the HTTP client, you need to register this type as well. In the sample application, the type using named clients is `NamedClientSample` (code file `HttpClientSample/Program.cs`):

```
services.AddHttpClient("racersClient")
  .ConfigureHttpClient(httpClient =>
  {
    httpClient.BaseAddress = new Uri(httpClientSettings["Url"]);
  });
services.AddTransient<NamedClientSample>();
```

To get a named client instance, you can inject the `IHttpClientFactory` with the constructor of the class where this instance is needed. By invoking the method `CreateClient` to pass the name, an object from the pool is returned. Then you can use this preconfigured client in the same way as before (code file `HttpClientSample/NamedClientSample.cs`):

```
class NamedClientSample
{
  private readonly ILogger _logger;
  private readonly HttpClient _httpClient;
  private readonly string _url;

  public NamedClientSample(
    IOptions<HttpClientSamplesOptions> options,
    IHttpClientFactory httpClientFactory,
    ILogger<HttpClientSamples> logger)
  {
    _logger = logger;
    _url = options.Value.InvalidUrl ?? "localhost:5052";
    _httpClient = httpClientFactory.CreateClient("racersClient");
  }
  //...
}
```

Resilient HTTP Requests

When accessing servers over the network, many parts can fail. Passing invalid data to the server that cannot be processed by the server is an error that cannot be recovered by redoing the request. However, there are many errors that might be only transient. The DNS server might not be accessible to resolve the server name. The wireless network itself might be temporarily unavailable while you're switching networks. A router can have issues that might be resolved in a moment. Some API services are restricted in the number of calls you are allowed to make in a second.

With many of the transient errors, it can be worthwhile to retry the call after a delay, and the issue might resolve silently for the user. You don't have to create loops to repeat the invocation with maximum retry counts and different delays because there are different options that don't change the logic of the main functionality where you invoke the service. With the `HttpClient` factory, you just need to add another NuGet package: `Microsoft.Extensions.Http.Polly`. `Microsoft.Extensions.Http.Polly` has a dependency on the Polly library. Polly is a .NET resiliency and transient-fault-handling library (https://github.com/App-vNext/Polly) that offers retry, circuit breakers, timeout, and fallback functionality that can be used in many scenarios. To use it with `HttpClients`, you can configure a retry policy based on an HTTP status code, as shown in the following code snippet. Here, the method `GetRetryPolicy` returns a policy that retries the invocation for a maximum of five attempts after 2, 4, 8, 16, and 32 seconds (code file `HttpClientSample/Program.cs`):

```
IAsyncPolicy<HttpResponseMessage> GetRetryPolicy()
  => HttpPolicyExtensions
    .HandleTransientHttpError()
    .OrResult(message => message.StatusCode == HttpStatusCode.TooManyRequests)
    .WaitAndRetryAsync(5, retryAttempt
      => TimeSpan.FromSeconds(Math.Pow(2, retryAttempt)));
```

This method returning the `IasyncPolicy` can be invoked as the argument of the method `AddPolicyHandler`. This method configures the policy of the typed client specified with the `AddHttpClient` method (code file `HttpClientSample/Program.cs`):

```
services.AddHttpClient<FaultHandlingSample>(httpClient =>
```

```
  {
    httpClient.BaseAddress = new Uri(httpClientSettings["InvalidUrl"]);
  }).AddPolicyHandler(GetRetryPolicy())
```

With the method `AddTransientHttpErrorPolicy`, a method is defined that is configured to handle predefined transient errors. You just need to specify different time intervals with this method to handle network failures, HTTP 5xx status codes, and HTTP 408 status codes (code file `HttpClientSample/Program.cs`):

```
  services.AddHttpClient<FaultHandlingSample>(httpClient =>
  {
    httpClient.BaseAddress = new Uri(httpClientSettings["InvalidUrl"]);
  }).AddTransientHttpErrorPolicy(
    policy => policy.WaitAndRetryAsync(
      new[] { TimeSpan.FromSeconds(1), TimeSpan.FromSeconds(3), TimeSpan.
FromSeconds(5) }));
```

With this in place, the code with the injected `HttpClient` object does not need any change to deal with these transient errors. Your exception handler is invoked only after the retries. Of course, enabling logging shows the retries. As the error still persists after the retries, the exception is thrown after the last retry:

```
info: System.Net.Http.HttpClient.FaultHandlingSample.LogicalHandler[100]
      Start processing HTTP request GET https://localhost1:5021/
info: System.Net.Http.HttpClient.FaultHandlingSample.ClientHandler[100]
      Sending HTTP request GET https://localhost1:5021/
info: System.Net.Http.HttpClient.FaultHandlingSample.ClientHandler[100]
      Sending HTTP request GET https://localhost1:5021/
info: System.Net.Http.HttpClient.FaultHandlingSample.ClientHandler[100]
      Sending HTTP request GET https://localhost1:5021/
info: System.Net.Http.HttpClient.FaultHandlingSample.ClientHandler[100]
      Sending HTTP request GET https://localhost1:5021/
fail: HttpClientSamples[0]
      No such host is known. (localhost1:5021)
```

SUMMARY

This chapter described the .NET classes available in the `System.Net` namespace for communication across networks. You have seen some of the .NET base classes that deal with opening client connections on the network and the Internet, as well as how to send requests to and receive responses from servers.

As a rule of thumb, when programming with classes in the `System.Net` namespace, you should always try to use the most specific class possible. For instance, using the `TcpClient` class instead of the `Socket` class isolates your code from many of the lower-level socket details. Moving one step higher, the `HttpClient` class is an easy way to use the HTTP protocol. Using the `HttpClient` factory, you don't need to instantiate and dispose of `HttpClient` objects. You've also seen how to use Polly to deal with transient errors that can be configured in a central place of the application.

This book covers much more networking than the core networking features you've seen in this chapter. Chapter 25 covers creating REST APIs with ASP.NET Core and Azure Functions, as well as gRPC for binary communication based on HTTP/2. In Chapter 28, "SignalR," you can read about real-time communication with SignalR to return information from the server to the client, which is based on WebSockets, as well as asynchronous streaming of data. WebSockets is a communication protocol which allows returning real-time information to the client.

In the next chapter, you'll learn about security. You can see the `CryptoStream` in action for encrypting streams, no matter whether they are used with files or networking. You'll also see features on authentication that are often an important part of using networking APIs.

20

Security

WHAT'S IN THIS CHAPTER?

➤ Working with authentication and authorization

➤ Creating and verifying signatures

➤ Implementing secure data exchange

➤ Using signing and hashing

➤ Handling web security

CODE DOWNLOADS FOR THIS CHAPTER

The source code for this chapter is available on the book page at www.wiley.com. Click the Downloads link. The code can also be found at https://github.com/ProfessionalCSharp/ ProfessionalCSharp2021 in the folder 2_Libs/Security. The code for this chapter is divided into the following major examples:

➤ IdentitySample

➤ WebAppWithADSample

➤ X509CertificateSample

➤ SigningDemo

➤ SecureTransfer

➤ ASPNETCoreMVCSecurity

Samples from this chapter mainly use the namespace System.Security.Cryptography. All the sample projects have *nullable reference types* enabled.

ELEMENTS OF SECURITY

Security has several key elements that you need to consider for making your applications secure. The primary one, of course, is the user of the application. Is the person authorized to access the application or someone posing as that person? How can this user be trusted? As you see in this chapter, ensuring the security of an application regarding the user is a two-part process. First, users need to be authenticated, and then they need to be authorized to verify that they are allowed to use the requested resources.

What about data that is stored or sent across the network? Is it possible for someone to access this data, for example, by using a network sniffer? Encryption of data is important in this regard. If you use HTTPS (which nearly all websites use today), keys are used to encrypt the data. You just need to install a certificate containing public and private keys on the server. If you use Microsoft Azure, encryption is done for the data in transit (sending it across), as well as for the data at rest (when data is stored). With many services, you can supply your own encryption key; otherwise, an encryption key is created from Azure.

This chapter explores the features available in .NET to help you manage security and demonstrates how .NET protects you from malicious code, how to administer security policies, and how to access the security subsystem programmatically.

You can also read about the issues you need to be aware of when making web applications secure.

VERIFYING USER INFORMATION

Two fundamental pillars of security are authentication and authorization. *Authentication* is the process of identifying the user, and *authorization* occurs afterward to verify that the identified user is allowed to access a specific resource. This section shows how to get information about users and get a token that in turn can be used to authenticate the user calling a REST service.

The sample application makes use of an Azure Active Directory. With an Azure subscription, you also have an Azure Active Directory. With an Azure subscription, you can use your default Azure Active Directory to run the first sample application. You can also create a new Azure Active Directory or modify the sample application slightly to access your on-premises directory services.

Working with the Microsoft Identity Platform

You can identify the user running the application by using an *identity*. The landscape of identities has become complex in recent years. Some years ago, we just had to deal with Windows users, users coming from the on-premises Active Directory, or local users on the Windows system. Today, this is a lot more complex; we have to deal with users from the Azure Active Directory (which also includes Office 365 users), identities from users on mobile devices, and users with accounts verified by Microsoft, Facebook, Google, Twitter, and other providers.

To make programming easier, Microsoft created the Microsoft identity platform. With this platform, we have users in Office 365 and Microsoft Azure who use Microsoft Azure Active Directory (AD). With Azure AD business-to-business (B2B), different organizations can share resources with other organizations using Azure AD. Azure AD business-to-consumer (B2C) is an extension of Azure AD in which users can register themselves to create a new account in the AD and keep their passwords managed from other providers using a Microsoft, Gmail, Facebook, or Twitter account—or any other account that uses OAuth or OpenID Connect.

Important parts of the Microsoft identity platform are users, resources, and policies. Users want to access a resource—for example, your web application—or use an application that's accessing your API. How the user should be allowed to access the resources is specified by a policy. Because users access resources from different networks using different devices, policies have become very complex. Microsoft identity supports complex and dynamic policies. These can be different, for example, if the user is on a trusted corporate network using a company laptop or the same user is accessing the same resource from a different network on a different device.

To authenticate the user, you can use the OpenID Connect authentication protocol. OpenID Connect extends the OAuth 2.0 authorization protocol. After getting an ID token from an authentication server, this token can be used to request an access token. With the access token, the user can access a resource that's secured by an authorization server.

Using Microsoft.Identity.Client

Let's create a simple console application that authenticates the user against the Azure AD and displays information about the user. The application references the NuGet packages `Microsoft.Extensions.Hosting` and `Microsoft.Identity.Client`. Before creating the application, you need to register it with Azure AD. When configuring the app registration, you need to define the name, the account types, and the redirect URI. With a client application, you can configure the link `http://localhost`, and you need to specify the same link with the client configuration. With the application configuration, you can also configure API permissions that the application is using (if the user grants the permissions). By default, the API permission `User.Read` is specified; this allows the application to sign in on behalf of the user and read the user's profile. `Openid` permissions with the names `email`, `offline_access`, `openid`, and `profile` are granted as well.

You can add additional permissions—for example, to use Microsoft Graph and to use your own APIs. (You can read about creating and using API permissions for your services in Chapter 25, "Services.") From the app registration, you need to copy the application (client) ID and the directory (tenant) ID. When using the Azure CLI, you can find the app ID by passing the name of the app with the `--display-name` argument and querying for the `appId` element in the array of applications returned, as shown here:

```
> az app list --display-name ProCSharpIdentityApp --query [].appId
```

The tenant ID is shown using az `account`, like so:

```
> az account show --query tenantId
```

You can use the command line, with the current directory of your project, to configure the user secrets `TenantId` and `ClientId`. With this setting, the configuration is read from the application while it's running in your development environment:

```
> dotnet user-secrets init
> dotnet user-secrets set TenantId <enter-your-tenant-id>
> dotnet user-secrets set ClientId <enter-your-client-id>
```

> **NOTE** *Configuration, user secrets, and dependency injection are covered in Chapter 15, "Dependency Injection and Configuration."*

With the following sample application, the `Runner` class is configured with the dependency injection container. To have the user secrets automatically configured with the DI container, you set the environmental variable `DOTNET_ENVIRONMENT` to `Development`. Because the dependency injection container is configured using the `CreateDefaultBuilder` method, the `IConfiguration` and `ILogger` interfaces can be injected with the constructor of the `Runner` class. The client ID and tenant ID are retrieved from the configuration. The `Init` method of the `Runner` class uses the `PublicClientApplicationBuilder` to create the `PublicClientApplication`, which can be used to log in and retrieve the ID and access tokens. The client ID is passed to the `Create` method, and the tenant ID is passed to the `WithAuthority` method.

To use Azure Active Directory, the cloud instance is specified with `AzureCloudInstance.AzurePublic`. For the U.S. government, Azure China, and the sovereign versions of Germany, different enum values need to be specified. The `WithRedirectUri` method needs to be configured with the link that's specified as a redirect URI with the app registration.

To help you identify issues and understand the communication going on, the Microsoft Identity platform offers rich logging information that you can enable using the `WithLogging` method (code file `IdentitySample/ Runner.cs`):

```csharp
using Microsoft.Extensions.Configuration;
using Microsoft.Extensions.Logging;
using System;
using System.Linq;
using System.Threading.Tasks;
using Id = Microsoft.Identity.Client;

//...

class Runner
{
  private readonly string _clientId;
  private readonly string _tenantId;
  private Id.IPublicClientApplication? _clientApp;
  private readonly ILogger _logger;

  public Runner(IConfiguration configuration, ILogger<Runner> logger)
  {
    _clientId = configuration["ClientId"]
      ?? throw new InvalidOperationException("Configure a ClientId");
    _tenantId = configuration["TenantId"]
      ?? throw new InvalidOperationException("Configure a TenantId");
    _logger = logger;
  }

  public void Init()
  {
    void LogCallback(Id.LogLevel level, string message, bool containsPii)
      => _logger.Log(level.ToLogLevel(), message);

    _clientApp = Id.PublicClientApplicationBuilder
      .Create(_clientId)
      .WithLogging(LogCallback, logLevel: Id.LogLevel.Verbose)
      .WithAuthority(Id.AzureCloudInstance.AzurePublic, _tenantId)
      .WithRedirectUri("http://localhost")
      .Build();
  }
  //...
}
```

To see logging information from Microsoft Identity, you can specify a callback method with the `WithLogging` method. This method is invoked with every log output. Microsoft Identity has its own logging implementation and `LogLevel` enum definition that are very different from Microsoft .NET logging. If you check the numbers used with the `Microsoft.Extensions.Logging.LogLevel` enum and the `Microsoft.Identity.Client` `.LogLevel` enum, they are ordered in the reverse direction. To not get into conflict with the two definitions when using both types, the alias ID in the sample application is defined to reference `Microsoft.Identity.Client`. With the extension method `ToLogLevel`, which is shown in the following code snippet, the log level from `Microsoft.Identity.Client` is converted to the log level from `Microsoft.Extensions.Logging`. As different values are used with these enum types, a simple `switch` expression is used to do the conversion. This extension method is invoked from the previously shown `LogCallback` method (code file `IdentitySample/Runner.cs`):

```csharp
internal static class IdentityLogLevelExtensions
{
```

```
    public static LogLevel ToLogLevel(this Id.LogLevel logLevel)
      => logLevel switch
      {
        Id.LogLevel.Error => LogLevel.Error,
        Id.LogLevel.Warning => LogLevel.Warning,
        Id.LogLevel.Info => LogLevel.Information,
        Id.LogLevel.Verbose => LogLevel.Trace,
        _ => throw new InvalidOperationException("unexpected log level")
      };
  }
```

With the `LogAsync` method that's shown next, first, a check is done by invoking the `GetAccountsAsync` method to see whether accounts are already cached. If they are, a silent authentication can be done without a need to ask the user for their login information by using the `AquireTokenSilent` method. If silent authentication does not return a token, login happens through an interactive login that invokes the `AquireTokenInteractive` method. The scopes required by the application (and also configured with the app registration) are specified in a string array and passed to the `AquireTokenXX` methods (code file `IdentitySample/Runner.cs`):

```
public async Task LoginAsync()
{
  if (_clientApp is null) throw new InvalidOperationException(
    "Invoke Init before calling this method");

  try
  {
    string[] scopes = { "user.read" };
    var accounts = await _clientApp.GetAccountsAsync();
    var firstAccount = accounts.FirstOrDefault();
    if (firstAccount is not null)
    {
      Id.AuthenticationResult result =
        await _clientApp.AcquireTokenSilent(scopes, firstAccount)
          .ExecuteAsync();
      ShowAuthenticationResult(result);
    }
    else
    {
      Id.AuthenticationResult result = await _clientApp.AcquireTokenInteractive(scopes)
        .ExecuteAsync();
      ShowAuthenticationResult(result);
    }
  }
  catch (Exception ex)
  {
    _logger.LogError(ex, ex.Message);
    throw;
  }
}
```

Besides offering `AquireTokenSilent` and `AquireTokenInteractive`, the `PublicClientApplication` also offers logins with other mechanisms. A login via username/password is done with `AquireTokenByUsernamePassword`. You can also use this class for Windows authentication and use `AquireTokenByIntegratedWindowsAuthentication`. Another option is to log in by using a device code: `AquireTokenWithDeviceCode`. This method can be used to log in on a device without a browser. When you invoke this method, a device code is returned. The user enters this code on a device with a browser. After the user successfully enters the code, access to the device is granted.

An ID token and access token are retrieved with just one call. The `ShowAuthenticationResult` method uses `AuthenticationResult` and shows token and account information (code file `IdentitySample/Runner.cs`):

```
private void ShowAuthenticationResult(Id.AuthenticationResult result)
{
    Console.WriteLine($"Id token: {result.IdToken[..20]}");
    Console.WriteLine($"Access token: {result.AccessToken[..20]}");
    Console.WriteLine($"Username: {result.Account.Username}");
    Console.WriteLine($"Environment: {result.Account.Environment}");
    Console.WriteLine($"Account Id: {result.Account.HomeAccountId}");
    foreach (var scope in result.Scopes)
    {
        Console.WriteLine($"scope: {scope}");
    }
}
```

Using Authentication and Authorization with a Web App

Now that you've seen how to authenticate a user in a console application, let's get into the .NET support for web applications.

> **NOTE** *This section makes use of ASP.NET Core and ASP.NET Core Razor Pages, which are covered in Chapter 24, "ASP.NET Core," and Chapter 26, "Razor Pages and MVC."*

When you create an ASP.NET Core application, you can create the code needed for authentication with a template. If you use `dotnet new` with the `--auth` option to specify `SingleOrg`, code is created to log in with Microsoft Azure Active Directory:

```
> dotnet new webapp --auth SingleOrg -o WebAppWithADSample
```

With this template, the `AddAuthentication` method is used to configure the DI container. `AddAuthentication` returns the authentication builder that is then used to invoke the method `AddMicrosoftIdentityWeb` to configure the Microsoft Identity platform for a web application.

Configuration values are retrieved from the section `AzureAd` with the configuration settings. After this, the `AddAuthorization` method configures the authorization. You'll change the implementation of this method later to define requirements for the user by accessing specific pages. With the MVC builder that follows the `AddMvcOptions` method—`AddMicrosoftIdentityUI`—user interfaces for logging in are used from the Microsoft Identity platform (code file `WebAppWithADSample/Startup.cs`):

```
public void ConfigureServices(IServiceCollection services)
{
    services.AddAuthentication(OpenIdConnectDefaults.AuthenticationScheme)
        .AddMicrosoftIdentityWebApp(Configuration.GetSection("AzureAd"));

    services.AddAuthorization(options =>
    {
        options.FallbackPolicy = options.DefaultPolicy;
    });
    services.AddRazorPages()
        .AddMvcOptions(options => {})
        .AddMicrosoftIdentityUI();
}
```

The configuration specified with the `AzureAd` section is added to the `appsettings.json` configuration file. You can add the domain, tenant ID, and client ID to this file. This time, because it's a web application, you need to register it with the redirect URI `https://localhost:5001/signin-oidc` when using the default port running this application locally with the Kestrel server. To run the application on a different URL, you then need to adapt this URI accordingly (config file `WebAppWithADSample/appsettings.json`):

```
{
  "AzureAd": {
    "Instance": "https://login.microsoftonline.com/",
    "Domain": "qualified.domain.name",
    "TenantId": "22222222-2222-2222-2222-222222222222",
    "ClientId": "11111111-1111-1111-11111111111111111",
    "CallbackPath": "/signin-oidc"
  }
}
```

With the configuration of the middleware, `UseAuthentication` and `UseAuthorization` are invoked to support authentication and authorization (code file `WebAppWithADSample/Startup.cs`):

```
public void Configure(IApplicationBuilder app, IWebHostEnvironment env)
{
  if (env.IsDevelopment())
  {
    app.UseDeveloperExceptionPage();
  }
  else
  {
    app.UseExceptionHandler("/Error");
    app.UseHsts();
  }

  app.UseHttpsRedirection();
  app.UseStaticFiles();

  app.UseRouting();

  app.UseAuthentication();
  app.UseAuthorization();

  app.UseEndpoints(endpoints =>
  {
    endpoints.MapRazorPages();
    endpoints.MapControllers();
  });
}
```

With the default policy configured, authentication is required. Without this policy, you can apply the `Authorize` attribute to classes and methods—for example, the class of a Razor page, an MVC controller, or an MVC action method. To override the authorization requirement, you can apply the `AllowAnonymous` attribute. In the following code snippet, the `Authorize` attribute is applied to the code-behind file of the Razor page `UserInfo`. Because the user is authorized, user information can be accessed. With the `OnGet` method that is invoked with an HTTP GET request to this page, user information is accessed; the name of the user and the claims delivered as part of the token are assigned to the properties `UserName` and `ClaimsInformation`. The property `ClaimsInformation` contains a generic `List` containing tuples (code file `WebAppWithADSample/Pages/UserInfo.cshtml.cs`):

```
[Authorize]
public class UserInfoModel : PageModel
```

```
    {
      public void OnGet()
      {
        UserName = User.Identity?.Name;

        foreach (var claim in User.Claims)
        {
          ClaimsInformation.Add((claim.Type,
            claim.Subject?.Name ?? string.Empty, claim.Value));
        }
      }

      public string? UserName { get; private set; }

      public List<(string Type, string Subject, string Value)> ClaimsInformation { get; } =
        new List<(string, string, string)>();
    }
```

When you use Razor syntax, values from the properties `UserName` and `ClaimsInformation` are shown in the user interface (code file `WebAppWithADSample/Pages/UserInfo.cshtml.cs`):

```
@page
@model WebAppWithADSample.Pages.UserInfoModel
@{
}

<h2>User: @Model.UserName</h2>

<table>
  @foreach (var claimsInfo in Model.ClaimsInformation)
  {
  <tr>
    <td>@claimsInfo.Type</td>
    <td>@claimsInfo.Subject</td>
    <td>@claimsInfo.Value</td>
  </tr>
  }
</table>
```

With the `AddAuthorization` method invoked in the `Startup` class, you can create policies that define specific requirements, such as a user belonging to a specific role defined in the Azure AD (`RequireRole` method), or that specific claims need to be available in a token (`RequireClaim` method) (code file `WebAppWithADSample/Startup.cs`):

```
services.AddAuthorization(options =>
{
  options.AddPolicy("Developers", policy =>
  {
    policy.RequireRole("DevGroup");
  });
  options.AddPolicy("Employees", policy =>
  {
    policy.RequireClaim("EmployeeNumber");
  });
  options.FallbackPolicy = options.DefaultPolicy;
});
```

After you set the `Policy` with the `Authorize` attribute, the requirements of the policy are now checked:

```
[Authorize(Policy="Developers")]
```

If the policy is not successful, the user receives an access denied message.

Now that you know more about user identities, tokens, and claims, let's step into another security-relevant topic: encryption of data.

ENCRYPTING DATA

Confidential data should be secured so that it cannot be read by unprivileged users. This is valid for both data that is sent across the network and stored data. You can encrypt such data with symmetric or asymmetric encryption keys.

With a symmetric key, you can use the same key for encryption and decryption. With asymmetric encryption, different keys are used for encryption and decryption: a public key and a private key. Something encrypted using a public key can be decrypted with the corresponding private key. This also works the other way around: something encrypted using a private key can be decrypted by using the corresponding public key but not the private key. It's practically impossible to calculate a private or public key from the other key.

Public and private keys are always created as a pair. The public key can be made available to everybody, and even put on a website, but the private key must be safely locked away. Following are some examples that demonstrate how public and private keys are used for encryption.

If Alice sends a message to Bob (see Figure 20-1) and she wants to ensure that no one other than Bob can read the message, she uses Bob's public key. The message is encrypted using Bob's public key. Bob opens the message and can decrypt it using his secretly stored private key. This key exchange guarantees that only Bob can read Alice's message.

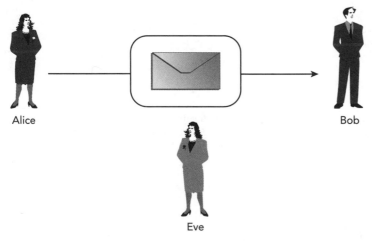

Alice

Bob

Eve

FIGURE 20-1

There is one problem, however: Bob can't be sure that the mail comes from Alice. Eve can use Bob's public key to encrypt messages sent to Bob and pretend to be Alice.

We can extend this principle using public/private keys. Let's start again with Alice sending a message to Bob. Before Alice encrypts the message using Bob's public key, she adds her signature and a hash of the message and encrypts this information using her own private key. Then she encrypts the complete mail using Bob's public key. Therefore, it is guaranteed that no one other than Bob can read the message. When Bob decrypts it, he detects an encrypted signature. The signature can be decrypted using Alice's public key. For Bob, it is not a problem to access Alice's public key because the key is public. After decrypting the signature, Bob can be sure that it was Alice who sent the message.

The encryption and decryption algorithms using symmetric keys are a lot faster than those using asymmetric keys. The problem with symmetric keys is that the keys must be exchanged in a safe manner. With network communication, one way to do this is by using asymmetric keys first for the key exchange and then symmetric keys for the encryption of the data that is sent across the wire.

In the following table, you'll find algorithms implemented by the .NET classes grouped into different categories with some information on the use and issues with different algorithms. The purpose of hash algorithms is to create a fixed-length hash value from binary strings of arbitrary length. These algorithms are used with digital signatures and for data integrity. If the same binary string is hashed again, the same hash result is returned. Also, if the binary string has been modified even a little, it is extremely unlikely that the hash result will be the same. *Symmetric key algorithms* use the same key for encryption and decryption of data. *Asymmetric algorithms* use a key pair: one key for encryption and another for decryption.

CATEGORY	ALGORITHM	DESCRIPTION
Hash	MD5	The Message Digest Algorithm 5 (MD5) was developed at RSA Laboratories. The algorithm should be used only with legacy applications; it can be broken on regular computers in less than a second.
	HMAC	Hash-based Message Authentication Code (HMAC) uses a hash function with a secret cryptography key and allows verifying data integrity and authenticity of a message.
	RIPEMD	RIPE Message Digest (RIPEMD) was developed by the EU project RACE Integrity Primitives Evaluation (RIPE). The original RIPEMD-128 is now considered insecure. RIPEMD-160 is the most commonly used algorithm of the RIPEMD family with 160-bit hash results. Specifications for RIPEMD-256 and RIPEMD-512 are available as well. These provide the same security but longer hash sizes. Bitcoin makes use of RIPEMD-160.
	SHA	The Secure Hash Algorithm (SHA) algorithms were designed by the National Security Agency (NSA). SHA-1 uses a 160-bit hash and is stronger than MD5 (128-bit) against brute-force attacks, but because of security issues, SHA1 has not been supported with HTTPS in browsers since 2017. Microsoft discontinued SHA-1 code signing for Windows Update in 2020. Git uses SHA-1 for data integrity against disk and DRAM corruption. The other SHA algorithms contain the hash size in the name. SHA512 is the strongest of these algorithms, with a hash size of 512 bits; it is also the slowest.
Symmetric	DES	Data Encryption Standard (DES) is now considered insecure because it uses only 56 bits for the key size and can be broken in less than 24 hours.

continues

(continued)

CATEGORY	ALGORITHM	DESCRIPTION
	Triple-DES	Triple-DES is the successor to DES and has a key length of 168 bits, but the effective security it provides is only 112-bit. It uses three iterations of DES.
	Rijndael AES	Today, Advanced Encryption Standard (AES) is the most-used symmetric algorithm. It has a key size of 128, 192, or 256 bits. Rijndael is the predecessor of AES. AES is an encryption standard adopted by the U.S. government.
Asymmetric	RSA	The Rivest, Shamir, Adleman (RSA) algorithm was the first one used for signing as well as encryption. This algorithm is widely used in e-commerce protocols.
	DSA	Digital Signature Algorithm (DSA) is a U.S. federal government standard for digital signatures as defined in Federal Information Processing Standards Publication (FIPS) PUB 186. A draft version available at the time of this writing indicates that DSA will no longer be approved for new digital signatures. The DSA algorithm is based on modular exponentiation and the discrete logarithm problem.
	ECDSA	Elliptic Curve DSA (ECDSA) uses elliptic curves instead of logarithms. These algorithms are more secure, with shorter key sizes. For example, having a key size of 1024 for DSA is similar in security to 160 bits for ECDSA. As a result, ECDSA is much faster.
	ECDH	Elliptic Curve Diffie-Hellman (ECDH) is based on elliptic curves similar to ECDSA. This algorithm allows you to exchange private keys in a secure way over an insecure channel.

With that many algorithms, you'll have a lot more classes available with .NET with which to implement these algorithms. .NET contains classes for encryption in the namespace `System.Security.Cryptography`. .NET implementations access OS system libraries. Keeping cryptography libraries safe is a high priority for all OS vendors. When the OS is updated, as the .NET classes invoke the libraries from the OS, .NET applications use the updated implementations. However, this dependency also means that .NET applications can use only those features the OS supports. To get the details, you can read `https://docs.microsoft.com/dotnet/standard/security/cross-platform-cryptography`.

To better navigate within the huge lists of classes, let's get into the object inheritance used by the .NET crypto classes. The most important abstract base classes, according to the algorithm categories in the preceding table, are `HashAlgorithm`, `SymmetricAlgorithm`, and `AsymmetricAlgorithm`.

Another list of abstract base classes, called *algorithm classes*, is derived from these base classes. For example, the classes `Aes`, `RSA`, and `ECDiffieHellman` are base classes representing specific algorithms. AES is a symmetric algorithm; thus, the `Aes` class derives from the base class `SymmetricAlgorithm`. RSA and Elliptic Curve Diffie-Hellman (ECDH) are asymmetric algorithms; thus, the `RSA` and `ECDiffieHellman` classes derive from the base class `AsymmetricAlgorithm`. All of these classes are abstract as well. Then you find another layer of classes with concrete algorithm implementations. `ECDiffieHellmanCng` and `ECDiffieHellmanOpenSsl` derive from `ECDiffieHellman`. Classes with the `Cng` prefix or postfix make use of the Cryptography Next Generation (CNG) Windows API. Classes with the `OpenSsl` postfix are based on the OpenSSL library available on Linux platforms.

To create applications that are platform-independent, you can use the `Create` method of an abstract base class. The implementation returned depends on the platform where the program runs. To take advantage of the platform-specific features, you need to use the platform-specific classes. The sample applications in this chapter are platform-independent.

The following sections include some examples that demonstrate how you can use these algorithms programmatically.

Getting an X.509 Certificate

To create a public/private key pair, you have different options. You can use the `Create` method of the `CngKey` class. This class is available only on Windows. If you use this class in a platform-independent application, the compiler gives you a warning. On Linux (including WSL-2), you can use the `ssh-keygen` and `openssl` utilities. In production environments, you might use certification services to create certificates with public and private keys. With Microsoft Azure, you can manage (and also create) your certificates with the Azure Key Vault. This Azure service was previously covered in Chapter 15. This chapter looks at it with regard to certificates. To create a new Azure Key Vault instance and certificates with the Azure CLI in your subscription, check the readme file that's part of the code samples. The download files contain scripts that you can start in the Bash shell.

This sample application uses the NuGet packages `Azure.Security.KeyVault.Certificates` to retrieve certificates:

➤ `Azure.Security.KeyVault.Secrets` to retrieve the private key of certificates

➤ `Azure.Identity` for authentication with Microsoft Azure with the same namespaces referenced

➤ The commonly used package `Microsoft.Extensions.Hosting`

The .NET library namespace used for the certificate class `X509Certificate2` is `System.Security.Cryptography.X509Certificates`. X.509 is a standard that defines the format for public key certificates. X.509 certificates are used with electronic signatures and TLS/SSL, which is the basis for HTTPS.

The sample application defines the class `KeyVaultService`, as shown in the following code snippet, which performs the communication with the Azure Key Vault using the Azure Key Vault API. The Azure Key Vault API uses .NET event sourcing for logging (which is covered in Chapter 16, "Diagnostics and Metrics") to offer metrics information. To see this information with `ILogger` providers, the event log provider is registered, invoking the method `AzureEventSourceListener`, and the values for the log levels are changed. The link to the Azure Key Vault is retrieved via the `VaultUri` settings that you can specify with the `appsettings.json` file or the user secrets, or it is passed using command-line parameters when starting the application (code file `X509CertificateSample/KeyVaultService.cs`):

```
static class EventLevelExtensions
{
  public static LogLevel ToLogLevel(this EventLevel eventLevel)
    => eventLevel switch
    {
      EventLevel.Critical => LogLevel.Critical,
      EventLevel.Error => LogLevel.Error,
      EventLevel.Warning => LogLevel.Warning,
      EventLevel.Informational => LogLevel.Information,
      EventLevel.Verbose => LogLevel.Trace,
      EventLevel.LogAlways => LogLevel.Critical,
      _ => throw new InvalidOperationException("Update for a new event level")
    };
}
```

```
class KeyVaultService : IDisposable
{
  private readonly string _vaultUri;
  private readonly ILogger _logger;
  private readonly DefaultAzureCredential _credential = new();
  private readonly AzureEventSourceListener _azureEventSourceListener;
  public KeyVaultService(IConfiguration configuration, ILogger<KeyVaultService> logger)
  {
    _vaultUri = configuration["VaultUri"];
    _logger = logger;
    _azureEventSourceListener = new AzureEventSourceListener((eventArgs, message)
      => _logger.Log(eventArgs.Level.ToLogLevel(), message), EventLevel.Verbose);
  }

  public void Dispose()
    => _azureEventSourceListener.Dispose();
  //...
}
```

For authentication with the Azure Key Vault, the source code makes use of the `DefaultAzureCredential` class. This class tries to use different accounts to connect with Microsoft Azure. One class used from `DefaultAzureCredential` is `VisualStudioCredential`, which uses the account specified with the `AZURE_USERNAME` environmental variable. As shown in the following code snippet, set this variable to the account that has access to reading certificates and secrets within the key vault to run the application in your local environment.

```
{
  "profiles": {
    "X509CertificateSample": {
      "commandName": "Project",
      "commandLineArgs": "KeyVaultUri={enter your Azure Key Vault URI",
      "environmentVariables": {
        "DOTNET_ENVIRONMENT": "Development",
        "AZURE_USERNAME": "{enter your azure username}"
      }
    }
  }
}
```

With the following code snippet, the certificate is retrieved using the `CertificateClient` class from the namespace `Azure.Security.KeyVault.Certificates`. With the method `GetCertificateAsync` passing the name of the certificate, the certificate—excluding the private key—is retrieved. The `Value` property of the `Response` contains the `KeyVaultCertificateWithPolicy` object. The public key is returned from the `Cer` property. To return an `X509Certificate2` object that includes both the public key and the private key, the private key is retrieved by invoking the `GetSecretAsync` method and passing the name and version of the secret. The name and version are taken from the URI parts of the `SecretId` property of the `KeyVaultCertificateWithPolicy` (code file X509CertificateSample/KeyVaultService.cs):

```
public async Task<X509Certificate2> GetCertificateAsync(string name)
{
  CertificateClientOptions options = new();
  options.Diagnostics.IsLoggingEnabled = true;
  options.Diagnostics.IsDistributedTracingEnabled = true;
  options.Diagnostics.IsLoggingContentEnabled = true;

  CertificateClient certClient = new(new Uri(_vaultUri), _credential, options);
  Response<KeyVaultCertificateWithPolicy> response =
```

```
       await certClient.GetCertificateAsync(name);
    byte[] publicKeyBytes = response.Value.Cer;
    Uri secretId = response.Value.SecretId;
    string secretName = secretId.Segments[2].Trim('/');
    string version = secretId.Segments[3].TrimEnd('/');

    SecretClient secretClient = new(new Uri(_vaultUri), _credential);
    Response<KeyVaultSecret> responseSecret =
        await secretClient.GetSecretAsync(secretName, version);
    KeyVaultSecret secret = responseSecret.Value;
    byte[] privateKeyBytes = Convert.FromBase64String(secret.Value);
    X509Certificate2 cert = new(privateKeyBytes);
    return cert;
}
```

Let's get into the top-level statements of the application. After the DI container is configured, the KeyVaultService is retrieved. Using this service, the certificate with the name AliceCert is retrieved, and some values such as the subject of the certificate, the key exchange algorithm, and valid dates are shown on the console (code file X509CertificateSample/Program.cs):

```
using var host = Host
    .CreateDefaultBuilder(args)
    .ConfigureServices(services =>
    {
        services.AddSingleton<KeyVaultService>();
    }).Build();

var service = host.Services.GetRequiredService<KeyVaultService>();
using var certificate = await service.GetCertificateAsync("AliceCert");

ShowCertificate(certificate);

void ShowCertificate(X509Certificate2 certificate)
{
    Console.WriteLine($"Subject: {certificate.Subject}");
    Console.WriteLine($"Not before: {certificate.NotBefore:D}");
    Console.WriteLine($"Not after: {certificate.NotAfter:D}");
    Console.WriteLine($"Has private key: {certificate.HasPrivateKey}");
    Console.WriteLine($"Key algorithm: {certificate.PublicKey.Key.KeyExchangeAlgorithm}");
    Console.WriteLine($"Key size: {certificate.PublicKey.Key.KeySize}");
}
```

When you run the application, you can see the logging communication with the Azure Key Vault, as well as information about the retrieved certificate.

.NET 6 will add methods to use the keys from the X509Certificate2 class with EC Diffie-Hellman types. The samples in the following sections create public/private pairs programmatically, but when .NET 6 is available, check the downloadable readme file of the chapter for links to samples with .NET 6.

Creating and Verifying a Signature

Now that you've seen how to create a public/private key pair using a certificate, let's get into verifying a signature with ECDSA algorithms.

With the following sample, Alice creates a signature that is encrypted with her private key. This signature can be verified with her public key. If the verification succeeds, it's guaranteed that the signature is from Alice because only she has the private key. See the following code snippet with `AliceRunner` to create the signature and `BobRunner` to verify the signature (code file `SigningDemo/Program.cs`):

```
using Microsoft.Extensions.DependencyInjection;
using Microsoft.Extensions.Hosting;

using var host = Host.CreateDefaultBuilder(args)
  .ConfigureServices(services =>
  {
    services.AddTransient<AliceRunner>();
    services.AddTransient<BobRunner>();
  })
  .Build();

var alice = host.Services.GetRequiredService<AliceRunner>();
var bob = host.Services.GetRequiredService<BobRunner>();
var keyAlice = alice.GetPublicKey();
var aliceData = alice.GetDocumentAndSignature();
bob.VerifySignature(aliceData.Data, aliceData.Sign, keyAlice);
```

Let's look at the main functionality in the `AliceRunner` class. In the constructor, which uses `ECDsa.Create`, an instance of the class implementing the ECDSA algorithms is returned. The method `ExportSubjectPublicKeyInfo` used in the method `GetPublicKey` returns the public key that can be used by other parties. In the method `GetDocumentsAndSignature`, Alice creates a string and a signature. The signature is created by invoking the method `SignData`. This method uses the private key for signing. The second argument of this method defines the name of the algorithm that should be used for signing. Here, `SHA512` is used. Both the document as well as the signature are returned from the method `GetDocumentsAndSignature` (code file `SigningDemo/AliceRunner.cs`):

```
class AliceRunner : IDisposable
{
  private readonly ILogger _logger;
  private ECDsa _signAlgorithm;
  public AliceRunner(ILogger<AliceRunner> logger)
  {
    _logger = logger;
    _signAlgorithm = ECDsa.Create();
    _logger.LogInformation($"Using this ECDsa class: {_signAlgorithm.GetType().Name}");
  }

  public void Dispose() => _signAlgorithm.Dispose();

  public byte[] GetPublicKey() => _signAlgorithm.ExportSubjectPublicKeyInfo();

  public (byte[] Data, byte[] Sign) GetDocumentAndSignature()
  {
    byte[] aliceData = Encoding.UTF8.GetBytes("I'm Alice");
    byte[] aliceDataSignature =
      _signAlgorithm.SignData(aliceData, HashAlgorithmName.SHA512);
    return (aliceData, aliceDataSignature);
  }
}
```

> **NOTE** *You can pass arguments to the* `ECDsa.Create` *methods to specify the algorithm used for the creation of the curve. The* `ECCurve` *struct defines* `NamedCurves` *that you can pass (for example,* `brainpoolP320r1`, `nistP521`*), but you can also specify your own configuration values to* `ECCurve` *to create an elliptic curve.*

Bob now needs to verify the signature. To do this, an instance of the ECDS algorithm class is created with the same parameters as used by Alice. The `VerifyData` method of the `ECDsa` class takes the data, the signature, and the hash algorithm. The algorithm needs to be the same as was used by Alice to create the signature. The public key from Alice needs to be imported with the `ImportSubjectPublicKeyInfo` method. `VerifyData` now uses this public key to determine whether the signature is from Alice. If this succeeds, it's guaranteed that the data has not been tampered with, and the signature was created using the private key that belongs to the public key received (code file `SigningDemo/BobRunner.cs`):

```
class BobRunner : IDisposable
{
  private readonly ILogger _logger;
  private ECDsa _signAlgorithm;
  public BobRunner(ILogger<AliceRunner> logger)
  {
    _logger = logger;
    _signAlgorithm = ECDsa.Create();
  }

  public void Dispose() => _signAlgorithm.Dispose();

  public byte[] GetPublicKey() => _signAlgorithm.ExportSubjectPublicKeyInfo();

  public void VerifySignature(byte[] data, byte[] signature, byte[] pubKey)
  {
    _signAlgorithm.ImportSubjectPublicKeyInfo(pubKey.AsSpan(), out int bytesRead);
    bool success = _signAlgorithm.VerifyData(data, signature, HashAlgorithmName.SHA512);

    _logger.LogInformation($"Signature is ok: {success}");
  }
}
```

When you run the application, you see a success result. While debugging, you can modify values from the data array to see that if you tamper with the data, `VerifyData` does not return success.

Implementing Secure Data Exchange

The next example helps explain public/private key principles, exchanging a secret between two parties, and communication with symmetric keys. A secret can be exchanged between two parties using the EC Diffie-Hellman algorithm. This algorithm allows exchanging a secret just by using public and private keys and exchanging the public key between two parties.

The following top-level statements show the main flow of the application. By using the `AliceRunner` and `BobRunner` classes, the public keys from Alice and Bob are retrieved. Alice then creates a secret message and uses the public key from Bob for the encryption. Bob reads the encrypted message using the public key from Alice (code file `SecureTransfer/Program.cs`):

```
using var host = Host
  .CreateDefaultBuilder(args)
  .ConfigureServices(services =>
  {
    services.AddTransient<AliceRunner>();
    services.AddTransient<BobRunner>();
  })
  .Build();
```

```
var alice = host.Services.GetRequiredService<AliceRunner>();
var bob = host.Services.GetRequiredService<BobRunner>();
var keyAlice = alice.GetPublicKey();
var keyBob = bob.GetPublicKey();
var message = await alice.GetSecretMessageAsync(keyBob);
await bob.ReadMessageAsync(message.Iv, message.EncryptedData, keyAlice);
```

In the constructor of the `AliceRunner` class, the static `Create` method of the `ECDiffieHellman` algorithm class is used to create an instance. Either `ECDiffieHellmanOpenSsl` or `ECDiffieHellmanCng` instances are created, depending on the platform where the application runs. Using the returned instance, the public key is retrieved from the `PublicKey` property. Instead of using byte arrays as with the `ECDsa` class, here an instance of the `ECDiffieHellmanPublicKey` is returned. `ECDiffieHellmanPublicKey` is an abstract base class, and concrete classes, which are determined by the platform, are returned here as well (code file `SecureTransfer/AliceRunner.cs`):

```
class AliceRunner : IDisposable
{
  private readonly ILogger _logger;
  private ECDiffieHellman _algorithm;
  public AliceRunner(ILogger<AliceRunner> logger)
  {
    _logger = logger;
    _algorithm = ECDiffieHellman.Create();
    _logger.LogInformation(
      $"Using this ECDiffieHellman class: {_algorithm.GetType().Name}");
  }

  public void Dispose() => _algorithm.Dispose();

  public ECDiffieHellmanPublicKey GetPublicKey() => _algorithm.PublicKey;
  //...
}
```

Alice's `ECDiffieHellman` instance contains the public and private keys from Alice. To encrypt the message that is sent to Bob, the public key from Bob is used to create a symmetric key. The method `DeriveKeyMaterial` makes use of Bob's public key to create the symmetric key. The returned symmetric key is used with the AES symmetric algorithm to encrypt the data. The `Aes` class requires the key and an initialization vector (IV). The IV is generated dynamically from the method `GenerateIV`. The symmetric key is exchanged with the help of the EC Diffie-Hellman algorithm, but the IV must also be exchanged. From a security standpoint, it is okay to transfer the IV unencrypted across the network, but the key exchange must be secured. The IV is part of the tuple that is returned from the `GetSecretMessageAsync`, along with the encrypted message. When you use the `Aes` object, an encryptor is created by invoking the `GetEncryptor` method. This encryptor is then used with a `CryptoStream`. The `CryptoStream` is configured to write into a `MemoryStream`. After the `CryptoStream` is flushed, the `MemoryStream` can be used to convert the data written to a byte array (code file `SecureTransfer/AliceRunner.cs`):

```
public async Task<(byte[] Iv, byte[] EncryptedData)> GetSecretMessageAsync(
  ECDiffieHellmanPublicKey otherPublicKey)
{
  string message = "secret message from Alice";
  _logger.LogInformation($"Alice sends message {message}");

  byte[] plainData = Encoding.UTF8.GetBytes(message);

  byte[] symmKey = _algorithm.DeriveKeyMaterial(otherPublicKey);
  _logger.LogInformation($"Alice creates this symmetric key with " +
    $"Bobs public key information: {Convert.ToBase64String(symmKey)}");
```

```
using Aes aes = Aes.Create();
_logger.LogInformation($"Using this Aes class: {aes.GetType().Name}");
aes.Key = symmKey;
aes.GenerateIV();
using ICryptoTransform encryptor = aes.CreateEncryptor();
using MemoryStream ms = new();
using (CryptoStream cs = new(ms, encryptor, CryptoStreamMode.Write))
{
   await cs.WriteAsync(plainData.AsMemory());
} // need to close the CryptoStream before using the MemoryStream
byte[] encryptedData = ms.ToArray();
_logger.LogInformation($"Alice: message is encrypted: " +
   $"{Convert.ToBase64String(encryptedData)}");
var returnData = (aes.IV, encrye ptedData);
aes.Clear();
return returnData;
}
```

> **NOTE** *Read more about streams in Chapter 18, "Files and Streams."*

The constructor and the GetPublicKey method look similar to the AliceRunner class; that's why they're not repeated with Bob. The ReadMessageAsync method shown in the following code snippet uses the public and private keys from Bob that have been created when creating the ECFiffieHellman instance, and the public key from Alice is used to create the symmetric key for the communication—again invoking DeriveKeyMaterial. Now the same symmetric key value as the one that was created from Alice is created—this is a property of the EC Diffie-Helman algorithm—without exchanging this key. This key is assigned to the Key property of the Aes instance. Here, the same IV that was created from Alice must be assigned to the IV property. Next, a decryptor is created invoking the method CreateDecryptor to decrypt the message. This decryptor is used with the CryptoStream class. The code is similar to the one from Alice, but now the message is decrypted (code file SecureTransfer/BobRunner.cs):

```
public async Task ReadMessageAsync(byte[] iv, byte[] encryptedData,
   ECDiffieHellmanPublicKey otherPublicKey)
{
   _logger.LogInformation("Bob receives encrypted data");
   byte[] symmKey = _algorithm.DeriveKeyMaterial(otherPublicKey);
   _logger.LogInformation($"Bob creates this symmetric key with " +
      $"Alice public key information: {Convert.ToBase64String(symmKey)}");

   Aes aes = Aes.Create();
   aes.Key = symmKey;
   aes.IV = iv;
   using ICryptoTransform decryptor = aes.CreateDecryptor();
   using MemoryStream ms = new();
   using (CryptoStream cs = new(ms, decryptor, CryptoStreamMode.Write))
   {
      await cs.WriteAsync(encryptedData.AsMemory());
   } // close the cryptostream before using the memorystream
   byte[] rawData = ms.ToArray();
   _logger.LogInformation($"Bob decrypts message to: {Encoding.UTF8.GetString(rawData)}");
   aes.Clear();
}
```

Running the application returns output like the following. The message from Alice is encrypted and then decrypted by Bob with the securely exchanged symmetric key.

```
info: AliceRunner[0]
      Using this ECDiffieHellman class: ECDiffieHellmanCng
info: AliceRunner[0]
      Alice sends message secret message from Alice
info: AliceRunner[0]
      Alice creates this symmetric key with Bobs public key information:
JAj1V/xZaaFQriVGsKWzBwWk0WpGSltC8O8ja6vqxX4=
info: AliceRunner[0]
      Using this Aes class: AesImplementation
info: AliceRunner[0]
      Alice: message is encrypted: ItD+jtDRlSyEIyNnT1BHMNXoRQG3xZzpClakd6Zy/js=
info: BobRunner[0]
      Bob receives encrypted data
info: BobRunn]
      Bob creates this symmetric key with Alice public key information:
JAj1V/xZaaFQriVGsKWzBwWk0WpGSltC8O8ja6vqxX4=
info: BobRunner[0]
      Bob decrypts message to: secret message from Alice
```

ENSURING WEB SECURITY

Web applications have some specific security issues you need to be aware of with applications that allow user input. User input cannot be trusted. Verifying input data on the client using JavaScript or built-in HTML5 features is only for the convenience of the user. Errors can be shown without making an extra network request to the server. However, the client cannot be trusted. HTTP requests can be intercepted, and the user (a hacker) can make different requests that bypass the HTML5 and JavaScript validation.

This section looks at common issues with web applications and what you need to be aware of to avoid issues. The sample application created is based on the ASP.NET Core MVC template; you can use `dotnet new mvc` or Visual Studio to create the foundation of this application.

Encoding

Never trust user input. Writing user information to a database and using this information to display on a website can be the cause of a typical hack. For example, a community website was showing the latest five new users on the home page. One of the new users managed to add a script to the username, and the script did a redirect to a malicious website. Because the user information was shown for every user coming to this site, every user was redirected.

The next example looks at how easy it is to simulate and avoid such a behavior. In the following code snippet, the `/echo` URL is mapped to an answer that returns the input from the user assigned to the x parameter that sends the response using `context.Response.WriteAsync` (code file `ASPNETCoreMVCSecurity/Startup.cs`):

```
endpoints.Map("/echo", async context =>
{
  string data = context.Request.Query["x"];
  await context.Response.WriteAsync(data);
});
```

Now it passes this request:

```
http://localhost:5001/echo?x=I'm a nice user
```

The string `I'm a nice user` is returned to the browser. This is not that bad, but users may try to hack the system. For example, users can input HTML code such as this:

```
http://localhost:5001/echo?x=<h1>Is this wanted?</h1>
```

The result shows the input string is formatted with the HTML `H1` tag. Users can do more bad things by entering JavaScript code:

```
localhost:5001/echo?x=<script>alert("this is bad");</script>
```

In most browsers, a pop-up window where the user entered text shows up.

If you try to avoid this issue by checking for `<script>` elements with the input and don't return anything in that case, you'll likely fail. Instead of using the `<script>` element, users can also use Unicode numbers for the angle brackets with the same result. Instead, encode the user input so that it can't be interpreted by the browser.

You can use the `HTMLEncoder` class from the namespace `System.Text.Encodings.Web` to encode user input:

```
endpoints.Map("/echoenc", async context =>
{
  string data = context.Request.Query["x"];
  await context.Response.WriteAsync(HtmlEncoder.Default.Encode(data));
});
```

When you use the `HtmlEncoder` class, the user can enter `<h1>` elements with the input `http://localhost:5001/echoenc?x=<h1>this gets converted</h1>`. As a result, `<h1>this gets converted</h1>` is shown in the browser. The `<` character is encoded to `&lt;` and thus displayed as text. The complete encoded string is as follows:

```
&lt;h1&gt;this gets converted&lt;/h1&gt;
```

Similarly, the script element is converted and doesn't run as a script in the browser.

> **NOTE** *You can use the* `HtmlEncoder` *class to allow specific inputs to go through. For example, you might allow the user to add* `<b>` *elements. You can create an encoder with accepted inputs using the* `HtmlEncoder.Create` *method. Today, a preferred method is to allow the user to include some formatting by using Markdown and converting Markdown to HTML. You can read my blog article about Markdown at* `https://csharp.christiannagel.com/2016/07/03/markdown/`.

The sample code has so far made use of ASP.NET Core functionality. When you directly return a string from an ASP.NET Core MVC controller or inside a view, encoding happens by default. You need to make an extra investment not to encode the result here.

Just returning a string with an ASP.NET Core controller results in an encoded string (code file `ASPNETCoreMVCSecurity/Controllers/HomeController.cs`):

```
public string Echo(string x) => x;
```

To send an unencoded string, the `Content` method of the `Controller` base class can be used, and you specify that the content is returned as `text/html`:

```
public IActionResult EchoUnencoded(string x) => Content(x, "text/html");
```

Let's go a step further by using Razor code in a view. Here, the `EchoWithView` method passes the input data from the user using `ViewBag.SampleData` to a view (code file `ASPNETCoreMVCSecurity/Controllers/HomeController.cs`):

```
public IActionResult EchoWithView(string x)
{
```

```
    ViewBag.SampleData = x;
    return View();
}
```

In the view, encoding happens by default when you pass the input data using the Razor expression @data. data is a local variable where the passed ViewBag information is assigned. For not making use of encoding, you can use the Html helper class with the method Raw (code file ASPNETCoreMVCSecurity/Views/Home/EchoWithView.cshtml):

```
@{
 string data = ViewBag.SampleData;
}
<div>
  this is encoded
</div>
<div>@data</div>

<br/>
<div>
  This is not encoded
</div>
<div>
  @Html.Raw(@data)
</div>
```

> **NOTE** *When explicitly sending unencoded data to the client, you need to make sure the input can be trusted—for example, using HTML converted from Markdown instead of directly returning user input.*

> **NOTE** *You can use the UrlEncoder class when using user input for URL strings similarly to how you use the HtmlEncoder class when using user input as HTML content.*

Preventing SQL Injection

Another common problem with web applications is SQL injection. As with HTML encoding, the issue can easily be avoided by using built-in functionality.

The following code snippet creates an SQL string that directly assigns the input parameter in the SqlSample controller method. With this, the user can enter ;SELECT * FROM Users, and the following information is shown to the user:

```
public IActionResult SqlSample(string id)
{
  string connectionString = GetConnectionString();
  SqlConnection sqlConnection = new(connectionString);
  SqlCommand command = sqlConnection.CreateCommand();
  // don't do this - string concatenation for SQL commands!
  command.CommandText = "SELECT * FROM Customers WHERE City = " + id;
  sqlConnection.Open();
  using (SqlDataReader reader =
    command.ExecuteReader(System.Data.CommandBehavior.CloseConnection))
  {
```

```
      StringBuilder sb = new();
      while (reader.Read())
      {
        for (int i = 0; i < reader.FieldCount; i++)
        {
          sb.Append(reader[i]);
        }
        sb.AppendLine();
      }
      ViewBag.Data = sb.ToString();
    }
  return View();
}
```

You should never use string concatenation with SQL statements. Instead, you can easily avoid this problem by using parameters or implicitly using Entity Framework Core parameters.

> **NOTE** *Entity Framework Core is covered in Chapter 21, "Entity Framework Core."*

Protecting Against Cross-Site Request Forgery

Cross-site request forgery (XSRF) is an attack in which a malicious website tries to simulate a user and enter data without the user knowing.

Let's get into an example where the user enters book information in a form. Book is a simple model class containing Title and Publisher properties. Within the HomeController, the EditBook method returns a view (code file ASPNETCoreMVCSecurity/Controllers/HomeController.cs):

```
public IActionResult EditBook() => View();
```

The view defines simple input data where the user can enter title and publisher information and pass this information to the server with an HTTP POST request (code file ASPNETCoreMVCSecurity/Views/EditBook.cshtml):

```
@{
    ViewData["Title"] = "EditBook";
}
<h2>Edit Book</h2>

<form asp-controller="Home" asp-action="EditBook" method="post">
  <label for="title">Title:</label>
  <input type="text" id="title" name="title" />
  <br />
  <label for="publisher">Publisher:</label>
  <input type="text" id="publisher" name="publisher" />
  <br />
  <input type="submit" value="Submit" />
</form>
```

With the HTTP POST request, the following EditBook method is invoked to display a view with the entered user data (code file ASPNETCoreMVCSecurity/Controllers/HomeController.cs):

```
[HttpPost]
public IActionResult EditBook(Book book) => View("EditBookResult", book);
```

When you run the application while opening the URL http://localhost:5001/Home/EditBook, book information can be entered, the submit button can be clicked, the information is received from the controller, and the book information is shown in the view result.

Meanwhile, a malicious website just needs to use the same link to post the data in its own form. Check the following code snippet with the form element that references the same URL as before. This form is hosted from a different website, `https://localhost:5002/dothis.html`. Here it's only a different port, but it could be a different domain name as well. The user doesn't need to enter anything with the form (the input elements are hidden and thus not shown to the user). The user just needs to click the submit button without knowing something different happens behind the scenes (code file `HackingSite/wwwroot/dothis.html`):

```
<h1>Click this for a win!</h1>

<!-- form has a redirect to the website being hacked -->
<form action="http://localhost:24897/Home/EditBook" method="post">
  <input type="hidden" value="bad book title" name="title"/>
  <input type="hidden" value="bad publisher" name="publisher"/>
  <input type="submit" value="Click Now!"/>
</form>
```

When you click this link, the malicious data is transmitted to the website on behalf of the user. If the user is authenticated with the book website and didn't sign out, the data is submitted on behalf of the user, and probably some ordering happened with a different delivery address.

To avoid this behavior, ASP.NET Core offers antiforgery tokens. Such a token needs to be created from the form that should be used from the user to enter valid data and is validated on receiving the data.

The Edit Book form is now changed to include this token with the HTML helper method `AntiForgeryToken` (code file `ASPNETCoreMVCSecurity/Views/EditBookSecure.cshtml`):

```
<form asp-controller="Home" asp-action="EditBookSecure" method="post">
  @Html.AntiForgeryToken()

  <label for="title">Title:</label>
  <input type="text" id="title" name="title" />
  <br />
  <label for="publisher">Publisher:</label>
  <input type="text" id="publisher" name="publisher "/>
  <br />
  <input type="submit" value="Submit "/>
</form>
```

When you run the application, you can see a hidden form field with the automatically generated token. When the data is retrieved, the token is validated using the `ValidateAntiForgeryToken` attribute (code file `ASPNETCoreMVCSecurity/Controllers/HomeController.cs`):

```
[HttpPost]
[ValidateAntiForgeryToken]
public IActionResult EditBookSecure(Book book) => View("EditBookResult", book);
```

When you run the malicious website now, a response is returned without accepting invalid data.

> **NOTE** *The Open Web Application Security Project (OWASP) foundation continuously analyzes security risks with web applications and publishes the OWASP top ten (*https:// owasp.org/www-project-top-ten/*). You can use OWASP Zed Attack Proxy (ZAP) (*https://www.zapproxy.org*) within GitHub actions (OWASP ZAP Full Scan) to analyze your web application and server to automatically scan it for issues. For a scan of the source code analysis tools for security, you can check the list of tools available at* https://owasp .org/www-community/Source_Code_Analysis_Tools.

SUMMARY

This chapter covered several aspects of security with .NET applications. Nowadays, we have a wide range of how users can be identified, and the Microsoft platform offers easy-to-use options. With web applications, you've seen the built-in functionality of ASP.NET Core to authenticate and authorize users with the Azure Active Directory.

A brief overview of cryptography demonstrated how the signing and encrypting of data enables the exchange of keys in a secure way. .NET offers both symmetric and asymmetric cryptography algorithms as well as hashing and signing. You've also seen how to create an X.509 certificate using the Azure Key Vault.

In many cases, you can work with security from higher abstraction levels. For example, when using HTTPS to access a web server, keys for encryption are exchanged behind the scenes. The `File` class offers an `Encrypt` method to easily encrypt files. Still, it's important to know what happens behind this functionality.

Regarding web applications, you've seen common issues with trusting user input that result in various attacks, including cross-site request forgery. You've seen how various issues can be avoided using encoding and antiforgery request tokens to avoid XSRF.

For more features on security, read Chapter 25 to authenticate users and client applications accessing REST services, and see Chapter 26 to authenticate and authorize users from a local database.

The next chapter, "Entity Framework Core," reads and writes data from the database, and this should be secured.

21

Entity Framework Core

WHAT'S IN THIS CHAPTER?

- ➤ Introducing Entity Framework Core
- ➤ Working with conventions, annotations, and the Fluent API
- ➤ Using queries, compiled queries, and global query filters
- ➤ Defining relationships with conventions, annotations, and the Fluent API
- ➤ Using table per hierarchy, table splitting, and owned entities
- ➤ Tracking objects
- ➤ Updating objects and object trees
- ➤ Handling conflicts with updates
- ➤ Using transactions
- ➤ Using migrations with the .NET CLI tools

CODE DOWNLOADS FOR THIS CHAPTER

The source code for this chapter is available on the book page at www.wiley.com. Click the Downloads link. The code can also be found at https://github.com/ProfessionalCSharp/ProfessionalCSharp2021 in the directory 2_Libs/EFCore. The code for this chapter is divided into the following major examples:

- ➤ Intro
- ➤ Models
- ➤ ScaffoldSample
- ➤ MigrationsSample
- ➤ Queries

➤ Relations

➤ LoadingRelatedData

➤ Tracking

➤ ConflictHandling-LastWins

➤ ConflictHandling-FirstWins

➤ Cosmos

Samples from this chapter mainly use the `Micrsooft.EntityFrameworkCore`, `Microsoft` `.EntityFrameworkCore.SqlServer`, and `Micrsoft.Extensions.Hosting` NuGet packages. All the sample projects have *nullable reference types* enabled.

INTRODUCING EF CORE

When you use ADO.NET directly, you can use a data reader such as `SqlDataReader` or `SqliteDataReader` to manually fill your objects with data from the database. With Entity Framework Core (EF Core), you don't need to write SQL statements because you get the mapping from relational data stores to classes and class hierarchies out of the box. With EF Core, you create a context that maps database tables to your model types, create new instances of your custom class, and update existing instances to add new records and update records in the database. EF Core offers an abstraction layer that makes a lot of the work of accessing a database easier.

Database Providers

With EF Core, you can use any database where an EF Core provider is available. Check the list of available providers in the Microsoft documentation at `https://docs.microsoft.com/ef/core/providers/`.

In this chapter, I mostly use Microsoft SQL Server. Microsoft SQL Server LocalDB is installed when you install Visual Studio. If you are using a Linux environment, you can install a Linux version of SQL Server. The easiest way to use a Linux version of Microsoft SQL Server is to run a Docker image. Check `https://hub.docker` `.com/_/microsoft-mssql-server` for information on how to pull and configure this Docker image to have SQL Server running inside a Linux container. If you're running a Windows environment, you can use this Docker image as well if you have Docker for Windows installed. After starting this Docker image, you need to use a connection string to access the running server.

You can also use an Azure SQL Database with the code samples. Just be sure to use a small database (which is enough for the samples), don't select the Core-based pricing model, and use database transaction units (DTUs) instead. This is a lot cheaper with small databases.

Creating an Azure SQL Database

To create an SQL database on Microsoft Azure, you can use the Azure CLI. You can use the Azure CLI directly from the Azure portal (`https://portal.azure.com`), click the Cloud Shell button, and select the Bash shell. You can also install the Azure CLI to your local system. Check `https://docs.microsoft.com/cli/azure/` `install-azure-cli` for download and installation instructions.

To create the database, a Bash script is available with the code download. You can also use the Azure CLI with these instructions as shown in the following script snippet:

1. First, variables are defined. With these variables, select the Azure region that best fits your location.

2. You create a resource group with the `az group create` command. The database server and the database will be added to this resource group.

3. Using `az sql server create` creates a new database server. You need to enable the firewall to allow access to this server with `az sql server firewall-rule create`. Using the IP address `0.0.0.0` allows access from Azure services. With the variable `clientip`, you need to add the IP address you use to access Azure services. You need to set this when setting the variable `clientip`.

4. Finally, using `az sql db create`, you create the Azure SQL database. Setting the option `--service-objective` to `Basic` creates a database with a maximum of 5 GB and a cheap option based on data transfer units. The connection string to this database needs to be configured with the sample applications, if you use this Azure service.

With the source code download, a Bash script is available that you can run from the Azure shell. Just make sure to enter your client's IP address, change the location to your nearest Azure region, and change the password. The commands use the \ line continuation character, which works with the Azure shell and the Windows Subsystem for Linux. Using the Windows command prompt, you can use ^ as the line continuation character. The following code uses the \ character (script file `createazuresql.sh`):

```
#! /bin/bash

# Prepare variables
rg=rg-procsharp
loc=westeurope
servername=procsharpserver$RANDOM
databasename=procsharp
clientip=enter your client-ip address

az group create --location $loc --name $rg
az sql server create --name $servername --resource-group $rg --location $loc \
--admin-user myadminuser --admin-password myadminpassword
az sql server firewall-rule create -g $rg -s $servername -n azurerule \
--start-ip-address 0.0.0.0 --end-ip-address 0.0.0.0
az sql server firewall-rule create -g $rg -s $servername -n clientiprule \
--start-ip-address $clientip --end-ip-address $clientp
az sql db create -g $rg -s $servername -n $databasename --service-objective Basic
```

To finally delete all the resources you created here, you can delete the resource group and all the resources associated with it:

```
> az group delete --name $rg
```

EF Core also supports NOSQL databases—just not relational ones. This is an important distinction to the previous Entity Framework that was available with the .NET Framework. In this chapter, you will use Azure Cosmos DB in the last section and see what's similar and what's different with relational databases.

Creating a Model

The sample application `Intro` for accessing the `Books` database is a .NET console app. Version 5 of EF Core supports using records, but there are some limits in particular with updates. For you to see in what scenarios you can use records and when to use classes (at least with .NET 5), the sample application can be built with records or classes. If you define the constant `USERECORDS` in the project configuration file, the compilation uses a `record`; otherwise, it uses a `class`.

The sample application defines a simple `Book` type with three properties. The `BookId` property maps to the primary key of the table, the `Title` property to the `Title` column, and the `Publisher` property to the `Publisher` column. With two properties, the `StringLength` attribute is applied to create an SQL Server column type `nvarchar(n)`. The application is using nullable reference types. With EF Core, this is used with conventions. The `Publisher` property is of type `string?`, which maps it to the database as not required and therefore allows null. The `Title` property is not nullable, and thus this is a required column. Creating a record type requires fewer code lines when using the positional records. The members of the primary constructor create init-only setters. To apply attributes to these properties, the `property` keyword needs to be used for applying the `StringLength` attribute. To assign an attribute to a field with an auto property, the `field` keyword is required. The class specifies a constructor with three parameters, and the last of these is optional. The `Book` class implements auto properties for all its members. With the class version, the property values can be changed after creating the object (code file `Intro/Book.cs`):

```
using System.ComponentModel.DataAnnotations;

#if USERECORDS

public record Book(
    [property: StringLength(50)] string Title,
    [property: StringLength(30)] string? Publisher = default,
    int BookId = 0);

#else

public class Book
{
    public Book(string title, string? publisher = default, int bookId = default)
    {
        Title = title;
        Publisher = publisher;
        BookId = bookId;
    }
    [StringLength(50)]
    public string Title { get; set; }
    [StringLength(30)]
    public string? Publisher { get; set; }
    public int BookId { get; set; }
}

#endif
```

Creating a Context

The association of the `Books` table with the database is created by the `BooksContext` class. This class derives from the base class `DbContext`, as shown in the following code snippet. The `BooksContext` class defines the `Books` property that is of type `DbSet<Book>`. This type allows creating queries and adding `Book` instances for storing book data in the database. The constructor specifies arguments of type `DbContextOptions`. This constructor is used when configuring the context with the dependency injection (DI) container. You specify the connection string to the database in the container configuration, as shown later in this chapter in the section "Configuring the Context with the DI Provider" (code file `Intro/BooksContext.cs`):

```
public class BooksContext : DbContext
{
    public BooksContext(DbContextOptions<BooksContext> options)
        : base(options) { }

    public DbSet<Book> Books => Set<Book>();
}
```

> **NOTE** *When creating a* DbContext *constructor to be used for dependency injection, you can also specify parameters that are registered with the DI container in addition to specifying the* DbContextOptions *parameter.*

> **NOTE** *In many samples (including samples from previous editions of this book), read-write properties are used with properties of type* DbSet. *With read-write properties, the property is assigned from the base class* DbContext. *Now because we have nullable enabled, the compiler gives a warning because the property is not initialized from the constructor of this class. The best fix for nullable reference types is to initialize this property by invoking the generic* Set *method of the base class and use a read-only property.*

If you're not using dependency injection, you can create a DbContext-derived class with a parameterless constructor (or just use the default constructor) instead of the constructor with DbOptions and override the OnConfiguring method to specify the database connection string:

```
public class BooksContext: DbContext
{
  public BooksContext() { }

  private const string ConnectionString =
    @"server=(localdb)\MSSQLLocalDb;database=ProCSharpBooks;" +
    @"trusted_connection=true";

  public DbSet<Book> Books => Set<Book>();

  protected override void OnConfiguring(DbContextOptionsBuilder optionsBuilder)
  {
    optionsBuilder.UseSqlServer(ConnectionString);
  }
}
```

The sample applications from this book all use the DI container. You've already seen advantages of the DI container in previous chapters and will see it in action in the following chapters as well.

Conventions, Annotations, and Fluent API

EF Core is using three concepts to define the model: conventions, annotations, and the Fluent API. With *conventions*, some things happen automatically, but be aware that conventions are based on the EF Core provider. With SQL Server, for example, if the property is of type int or Guid and has a name Id or {ClassName}Id, the property maps to a primary key. The .NET string type maps to the nvarchar(max) database type. Nullability definitions also define the mapping as mentioned in the previous section.

Conventions can be overridden using *annotations*—specifying attributes. The previous example used the StringLength attribute to map the Title property to a column type of nvarchar(50). You can use the Table and Column attributes to define the mapping from a type name to a corresponding table and a property name to a column.

There's also a convention for mapping .NET Types to table names. With EF Core, the property names of DbSet typed properties are used as default table names. Creating contexts is shown in the next section. Conventions do not exist for every annotation. To specify not nullable (required) columns, you can use the Required attribute. Before .NET 5, a convention with non-nullable reference types was not available. Annotations are more powerful than conventions because you can do more with them.

Instead of using annotations, you can also use a *Fluent API*, which means you handle configuration via code rather than attributes. With a Fluent API, you can use the return value of a method to invoke the next method. The Fluent API for EF Core is more powerful than the annotations are. The Fluent API is shown later in this chapter in the section "Creating a Model."

Configuring the Context with the DI Provider

The Host class first shown in Chapter 15, "Dependency Injection and Configuration," is used to create and configure the DI container, as shown with the following code snippet (code file Intro/Program.cs):

```
using var host = Host.CreateDefaultBuilder(args)
  .ConfigureServices((context, services) =>
  {
    var connectionString = context.Configuration.GetConnectionString
      ("BooksConnection");
    services.AddDbContext<BooksContext>(options =>
    {
      options.UseSqlServer(connectionString);
    });
    services.AddScoped<Runner>();
  })
  .Build();
```

The connection string is retrieved via configuration settings. The connection string used here references a localdb database. If you use other databases, you need to specify the corresponding connection string (configuration file Intro/appsettings.json):

```
{
  "ConnectionStrings": {
    "BooksConnection":
      "server=(localdb)\\mssqllocaldb;database=ProCSharpBooks;trusted_connection=true"
  }
}
```

With the Runner class, the DbContext is injected in the constructor (code file Intro/Runner.cs):

```
public class Runner
{
  private readonly BooksContext _booksContext;
  public Runner(BooksContext booksContext)
  {
    _booksContext = booksContext;
  }
  //...
}
```

After the Host class is configured, a new scope from the DI container is created to get a Runner instance returned with this scope. The Runner class is then used to invoke various methods using BooksContext to show different scenarios (code file Intro/Program.cs):

```
using var scope = host.Services.CreateScope();
var runner = scope.ServiceProvider.GetRequiredService<Runner>();
```

```
await runner.CreateTheDatabaseAsync();
await runner.AddBookAsync("Professional C# and .NET", "Wrox Press");
await runner.AddBooksAsync();
await runner.ReadBooksAsync();
await runner.QueryBooksAsync();
await runner.DeleteBooksAsync();
await runner.DeleteDatabaseAsync();
```

Creating the Database

The model and the context classes are defined. Now it's also possible to create the database programmatically. When you use the `Database` property of the `DbContext`, a `DatabaseFacade` is returned. You can use this to create and delete databases and to send SQL statements directly to the database. Invoking the method `EnsureCreatedAsync` makes sure that the database is created. If the database already exists, this method returns false. If the database does not exist, the database is created according to the definition of the context and the model, and true is returned (code file `Intro/Program.cs`):

```
public async Task CreateTheDatabaseAsync()
{
  bool created = await _booksContext.Database.EnsureCreatedAsync();
  string creationInfo = created ? "created" : "exists";
  Console.WriteLine($"database {creationInfo}");
}
```

When you run the program, if you already created the database earlier, the string `database exists` is written to the console. If you didn't create the database earlier, the database is created, followed by the string `database created`.

If you use Azure SQL Database, you need to create the database before starting the application. Invoking the method `EnsureCreatedAsync` here creates the schema with the Azure SQL Database.

> **NOTE** *Creating the database with* `Database.EnsureCreatedAsync` *doesn't give any support when the database schema changes. Another option is to create the database with migrations. Using migrations, you can upgrade or downgrade the database schema to any specific version. This can be done programmatically or by created SQL scripts. This feature is covered later in this chapter.*

Deleting the Database

Deleting the database is programmatically similar to creating it. You just need to invoke the method `EnsureDeletedAsync` of the `DatabaseFacade`:

```
public async Task DeleteDatabaseAsync()
{
  Console.Write("Delete the database? (y|n) ");
  string? input = Console.ReadLine();
  if (input?.ToLower() == "y")
  {
    bool deleted = await _booksContext.Database.EnsureDeletedAsync();
    string deletionInfo = deleted ? "deleted" : "not deleted";
```

```
        Console.WriteLine($"database {deletionInfo}");
    }
}
```

Just make sure you don't delete a database that should not be deleted. Pay attention to the connection string you use.

Writing to the Database

After the database and the `Books` table are created, you can fill the table with data. The `AddBookAsync` method is created to add a `Book` object to the database. `AddBookAsync` just adds the `Book` object to the context with the state *added*; it doesn't write it to the database. The object is written on invoking the method `SaveChangesAsync`. After writing the object, the `BookId` from the book variable is retrieved. This variable is changed from EF Core because in the database, this is an auto-increment key. This also works when using records because the created init-only set properties are behind-the-scenes properties with the get/set accessor, and the set accessor is annotated to be used only with the initialization (code file `Intro/Program.cs`):

```
public async Task AddBookAsync(string title, string publisher)
{
  Book book = new(title, publisher);
  await _booksContext.Books.AddAsync(book);
  int records = await _booksContext.SaveChangesAsync();
  Console.WriteLine($"{records} record added with {book.BookId}");

  Console.WriteLine();
}
```

For adding a list of books, you can use the `AddRange` method, as shown here:

```
public async Task AddBooksAsync()
{
  Book b1 = new("Professional C# 7 and .NET Core 2", "Wrox Press");
  Book b2 = new("Professional C# 6 and .NET Core 1.0", "Wrox Press");
  Book b3 = new("Professional C# 5 and .NET 4.5.1", "Wrox Press");
  Book b4 = new("Essential Algorithms", "Wiley");
  await _booksContext.Books.AddRangeAsync(b1, b2, b3, b4);
  int records = await _booksContext.SaveChangesAsync();
  Console.WriteLine($"{records} records added");

  Console.WriteLine();
}
```

> **NOTE** *To look at the database and see the schema and data, with Visual Studio, you can use SQL Server Object Explorer. For a multiplatform solution on Windows, macOS, and Linux, you can use Azure Data Studio. Check the readme file with the code downloads for a link to installation instructions.*

Reading from the Database

To read the data from C# code, you need to invoke `BooksContext` and access the `Books` property. With the `ToListAsync` method, a list is returned from a task so that it doesn't block the calling thread (code file `Intro/Program.cs`):

```
public async Task ReadBooksAsync(CancellationToken token = default)
{
  string query = _booksContext.Books.ToQueryString();
  Console.WriteLine(query);
  List<Book> books = await _booksContext.Books.ToListAsync(token);
  foreach (var b in books)
  {
    Console.WriteLine($"{b.Title} {b.Publisher}");
  }

  Console.WriteLine();
}
```

An easy way to see the generated query from the provider is to invoke the ToQueryString method:

```
SELECT [b].[BookId], [b].[Publisher], [b].[Title]
FROM [Books] AS [b]
```

Entity Framework offers a LINQ provider. With that, you can create LINQ queries to access the database. With the sample application, the method syntax is used as shown here:

```
public async Task QueryBooksAsync(CancellationToken token = default)
{
  await _booksContext.Books
    .Where(b => b.Publisher == "Wrox Press")
    .ForEachAsync(b =>
    {
      Console.WriteLine($"{b.Title} {b.Publisher}");
    }, token);

  Console.WriteLine();
}
```

This is the SQL query sent to the database:

```
SELECT [b].[BookId], [b].[Publisher], [b].[Title]
FROM [Books] AS [b]
WHERE [b].[Publisher] = N'Wrox Press'
```

> **NOTE** *LINQ is discussed in detail in Chapter 9, "Language Integrated Query."*

Updating with Classes

So far, the syntax using EF Core has been the same with classes and records. This changes now with updates. When using the Book class, you can change properties of these objects as needed and invoke SaveChangesAsync. In the following code sample, the Title property is changed. The SaveChangesAsync method verifies that the object has been modified, it is set to be in the modified state, and finally it is updated to the database with an SQL UPDATE statement. With the following code snippet, the object with key value 1 is retrieved from the database before being updated (code file Intro/Runner.cs):

```
public async Task UpdateBoookAsync()
{
  Book? book = await _booksContext.Books.FindAsync(1);
  if (book != null)
  {
```

```
      book.Title = "Professional C# and .NET - 2021 Edition";
      int records = await _booksContext.SaveChangesAsync();
      Console.WriteLine($"{records} record updated");
    }
    Console.WriteLine();
}
```

Updating with Records

Updating C# records is different than with classes when using EF Core 5. With records, you use the `with` expression to clone an existing record and change values. If you add this object to the context with the `Update` method (which sets the state to modified) and an object with the same ID is already tracked from the context, an exception of type `InvalidOperationException` is thrown. You can solve this by detaching the existing object from the context by setting the `State` property of `EntityEntry` to `EntityState.Detached`. This way, the newly created object can be attached and set to the modified state with the `Update` method (code file `Intro/Runner.cs`):

```
public async Task UpdateBookAsync()
{
  Book? book = await _booksContext.Books.FindAsync(1);

  if (book != null)
  {
    // detach the existing object from the context which allows to
    // attach it with the Update method
    _booksContext.Entry(book).State = EntityState.Detached;
    Book bookUpdate = book with { Title = "Professional C# and .NET - 2021 Edition" };
    _booksContext.Update(bookUpdate);
    int records = await _booksContext.SaveChangesAsync();
    Console.WriteLine($"{records} record updated");
  }
  Console.WriteLine();
}
```

> **NOTE** *Later in this chapter in the section "Saving Data," you can learn more about attaching and detaching objects from the context, why this is important for updates, and how you can query objects without attaching them to the context.*
>
> *The update behavior of EF Core might change after .NET 5. The* `with` *expression of records could be influenced by using a proxy to have a similar experience between updating records and updating classes. Check the source code in the GitHub repository for the book for updates and more information.*

Deleting Records

Finally, you need to clean up the database and delete all records. You do this by retrieving all records and invoking the `Remove` or `RemoveRange` method to set the state of the objects in the context to `deleted`. Invoking the `SaveChangesAsync` method now deletes the records from the database and invokes SQL `Delete` statements for every object (code file `Intro/Runner.cs`):

```
public async Task DeleteBooksAsync()
{
```

```
List<Book> books = await _booksContext.Books.ToListAsync();
_booksContext.Books.RemoveRange(books);
int records = await _booksContext.SaveChangesAsync();
Console.WriteLine($"{records} records deleted");

Console.WriteLine();
}
```

> **NOTE** *An object-relational mapping tool such as EF Core is not useful with all scenarios. Deleting all objects was not done efficiently with the sample code. Instead of sending a* DELETE *statement to the database for every record to delete, you can delete all records using a single SQL statement. EF Core is not that bad in such scenarios because rather than sending one statement after another to the database, multiple statements are combined into a batch statement. However, it's even better to just send one SQL statement in that case. This can be done using* context.Database.ExecuteSqlInterpolated *and* context.Database.ExecuteSqlRaw.

Now that you've seen how to add, query, update, and delete records, this chapter steps into features behind the scenes and gets into advanced scenarios using Entity Framework.

Logging and Metrics

You've already seen the ToQueryString method that returns a query string that's created from a provider so you can take a look at what SQL queries are sent to the database. There's more information available from EF Core. With a DbContextOptionsBuilder, you can invoke the LogTo method and supply a delegate with a method receiving a string parameter to define where log messages should be written to. You can supply the address of the Console.WriteLine method to have logs written to the console. You can access the DbContextOptionsBuilder from the AddDbContext method, where you configure the DI container, or on overriding the DbContext method OnConfiguring (if you don't use DI).

With DI configured, EF Core uses logging based on the ILogger and ILoggerFactory interfaces, as discussed in Chapter 16, "Diagnostics and Metrics." Besides the connection string to the database, you can configure the logging provider Console with the source Microsoft.EntityFramework and the log level in the configuration file appsettings.json.

```json
{
  "Logging": {
    "Console": {
      "LogLevel": {
        "Microsoft.EntityFramework": "Debug"
      }
    }
  },
  "ConnectionStrings": {
    "BooksConnection":
      "server=(localdb)\\mssqllocaldb;database=ProCSharpBooks;trusted_connection=true"
  }
}
```

Debug gives a detailed logging output, including objects created and disposed of. To see the SQL statements sent to the database, you just need to turn on the Information level. For more information on logging, read Chapter 16.

When you create a complex LINQ statement, it's often not that easy to find the generated SQL query in the log. To easily find out what query you've created that matches the generated SQL, you can invoke the `TagWith` method as an extension method of `IQueryable`. The string you specify with the `TagWith` method is shown as comments in the output log, which is associated with the SQL statement that's executed.

EF Core 5.0 has been updated not only to log information but also to allow you to see performance counts. To see the counts, first you need to get the process ID of the application. You can do this using `dotnet counters ps`. With this process ID, use `dotnet counters`, specify the `counters` category `Microsoft .EntityFrameworkCore`, and pass the process ID to the `-p` option:

```
> dotnet counters monitor Microsoft.EntityFrameworkCore -p 23480
```

EF Core shows the number of active `DbContexts`, failure counts for execution strategies and concurrency failures, queries done, queries with cache hits, and the number of `SaveChangesAsync`.

CREATING A MODEL

The first examples in this chapter mapped a single table. Now, let's get into a more complex example with a relationship between tables. In this section, you create a model with relations and use more features with model definitions, such as using Fluent APIs, using self-contained type configuration, mapping database columns to fields, and using shadow properties.

Creating a Relation

Let's start creating a model. The sample project defines a one-to-many relation using the `MenuCard` and `MenuItem` types. The `MenuCard` contains a list of `MenuItem` objects. This relation is simply defined by the `MenuItems` property of type `ICollection<MenuItem>` (code file `Models/MenuCard.cs`):

```
public class MenuCard
{
  public MenuCard(string title, int menuCardId = default)
    => (Title, MenuCardId) = (title, menuCardId);

  public int MenuCardId { get; set; }
  public string Title { get; set; }
  public ICollection<MenuItem> MenuItems { get; } = new List<MenuItem>();
  public override string ToString() => Title;
}
```

The relation can also be accessed in the other direction; a `MenuItem` can access the `MenuCard` using the `MenuCard` property. To create a required relationship between `MenuItem` and `MenuCard` (a `MenuItem` must be associated with a `MenuCard`), the property is declared to be not nullable. However, EF Core does not support supplying this relation with the constructor. To solve this dilemma, the field associated with the `MenuCard` property is declared to be nullable. With the constructor, this field is not initialized. In case the get accessor of the `MenuCard` property is accessed, if the field is still null, an `InvalidOperationException` is thrown. In retrieving a `MenuItem` from the database, EF Core needs to fill this relation. When creating a `MenuItem` programmatically, the `MenuCard` property can be initialized using a property initializer (code file `Models/MenuItem.cs`):

```
public class MenuItem
{
  public MenuItem(string text, int menuItemId = default) =>
    (Text, MenuItemId) = (text, menuItemId);
```

```
public int MenuItemId { get; set; }
public string Text { get; set; }
public decimal? Price { get; set; }
private MenuCard? _menuCard;
public MenuCard MenuCard
{
  get => _menuCard ?? throw new InvalidOperationException(
    $"{nameof(MenuCard)} not initialized");
  init => _menuCard = value;
}
public override string ToString() => Text;
}
```

The mapping to the database is done by the MenusContext class. This class is defined similarly to the previous context type; it just contains two properties to map the two object types: the properties MenuItems and MenuCards (code file MenusSamples/MenusContext.cs):

```
public class MenusContext: DbContext
{
  private const string ConnectionString = @"server=(localdb)\MSSQLLocalDb;" +
    "Database=MenuCards;Trusted_Connection=True";

  public DbSet<MenuItem> MenuItems { get; set; }
  public DbSet<MenuCard> MenuCards { get; set; }

  protected override void OnConfiguring(DbContextOptionsBuilder optionsBuilder)
  {
    base.OnConfiguring(optionsBuilder);
    optionsBuilder.UseSqlServer(ConnectionString);
  }
}
```

There are some parts in the creation code that would be useful to change. For example, the size of the Text and Title columns could be reduced in size from NVARCHAR(MAX). In addition, SQL Server defines a Money type that could be used for the Price column, and the schema name could be changed from dbo. Entity Framework gives you two options to make these changes from code: data annotations and the Fluent API, which are both discussed next.

Using the Fluent API for Mapping Definitions

In the previous sample code, conventions and annotations are used to specify the mapping of the model types to the database tables. You have more options with the Fluent API by overriding the OnModelCreating method of the DbContext-derived class. In the following code sample, the schema for the database definition is changed from the default dbo to mc to invoke the HasDefaultSchema method of the ModelBuilder class. You use the ModelBuilder API to specify the schema for the MenuItem class using the generic method Entity. The ToTable method maps the MenuItem class to the table MenuItems.

```
protected override void OnModelCreating(ModelBuilder modelBuilder)
{
  modelBuilder.HasDefaultSchema("mc");
  modelBuilder.Entity<MenuItem>().ToTable("MenuItems").HasKey(m => m.MenuItemId);
  modelBuilder.Entity<MenuItem>().Property(m => m.MenuItemId).ValueGeneratedOnAdd();
  modelBuilder.Entity<MenuItem>().Property(m => m.Text).HasMaxLength(50);
  modelBuilder.Entity<MenuItem>().Property(m => m.Price).HasColumnType("Money");
```

```
modelBuilder.Entity<MenuItem>().HasOne(m => m.MenuCard)
  .WithMany(c => c.MenuItems)
  .HasForeignKey("MenuCardId");

//...
}
```

> **NOTE** *The Fluent API gives you more options to configure the annotations, and annotations give you more options than conventions. You can use all these options in combination. Annotations override conventions, and the Fluent API overrides annotations.*
>
> *In scenarios where you can choose between the options, what should you select? Often, it's a matter of taste. Some developers prefer annotations as long as this option is possible with the things you need to configure; others always use the Fluent API. But there are other good reasons as well to choose one option over the other. For example, you can use entity types in a shared library, use the same classes to access the database, pass the data across an API, and use the same types with the client application. When you create microservices with a clearly defined use, this can be a good option to reduce the amount of code you need to write. Here, you can use the same annotations to map properties to the database and to validate user inputs on the client and with the API—for example, the string length with the StringLength attribute. In such a case, it's a good practice to avoid annotations that are specific for the database provider. You don't want to create a dependency on an EF Core library with a client application where you might not have access to this library or this version of the library. If you use a different application architecture with dedicated data transfer objects (DTO) to be sent across the network, and different types on the client (for example if you need a different technology for the client application such as Angular), selecting a mapping variant is just a matter of taste.*

Using Self-Contained Type Configuration

If you need to specify several different entity types, the implementation of the OnModelCreating method can grow large. To create easier-to-understand mappings, you can also create configuration classes for every data class. An entity type configuration class implements the generic interface IEntityTypeConfiguration.

With the sample application, a strongly typed list of column names that is used with the configuration of the mappings is defined with the class ColumnNames, as shown in the following code snippet. Instead of using strings when using these column names, IntelliSense can automatically complete the code you write, and the compiler warns of misspellings (code file Models/ColumnNames.cs):

```
internal class ColumnNames
{
    public const string LastUpdated = nameof(LastUpdated);
    public const string IsDeleted = nameof(IsDeleted);
    public const string MenuCardId = nameof(MenuCardId);
    public const string RestaurantId = nameof(RestaurantId);
}
```

To avoid writing the class name when specifying the constants, you use using static ColumnNames to import the names of the class members.

The class MenuCardConfiguration implements the Configure method of the IEntityTypeConfiguration interface and specifies the mapping of this class to the MenuCards table, constraints with the Title property, and a relation with the MenuItem class. One MenuCard references a list of MenuItem objects specified by the MenuItems property as specified with the HasMany method. To go back to the MenuCard from the MenuItem, you use the WithOne method. The MenuCard property of the MenuItem class references one MenuCard (code file Models/ MenuCardConfiguration.cs):

```
using Microsoft.EntityFrameworkCore;
using Microsoft.EntityFrameworkCore.Metadata.Builders;
using System;
using static ColumnNames;

internal class MenuCardConfiguration : IEntityTypeConfiguration<MenuCard>
{
  public void Configure(EntityTypeBuilder<MenuCard> builder)
  {
    builder.ToTable("MenuCards")
      .HasKey(c => c.MenuCardId);

    builder.Property(c => c.MenuCardId)
      .ValueGeneratedOnAdd();
    builder.Property(c => c.Title)
      .HasMaxLength(50);
    builder.HasMany(c => c.MenuItems)
      .WithOne(m => m.MenuCard);

    //...
  }
}
```

The MenuItem class is also configured with a specific configuration class. The Price property of type decimal maps to the SQL Server database type Money. When using annotations, you could use the DbType attribute to specify a database type. Another interesting aspect of the implementation is the use of the HasForeignKey method to map the relation to the MenuCard with the foreign key MenuCardId. Because the class MenuCard does not have a MenuCardId property, a lambda expression cannot be used to access this property; a string is required. The string that is used is strongly defined with the ColumnNames class. With this in place, a shadow property is created. Shadow properties are discussed later in the section "Working with Shadow Properties" (code file Models/MenuItemConfiguration.cs):

```
internal class MenuItemConfiguration : IEntityTypeConfiguration<MenuItem>
{
  public void Configure(EntityTypeBuilder<Menu> builder)
  {
    builder.ToTable("MenuItems")
      .HasKey(m => m.MenuItemId);
    builder.Property(m => m.MenuItemId)
      .ValueGeneratedOnAdd();
    builder.Property(m => m.Text)
      .HasMaxLength(50);
    builder.Property(m => m.Price)
      .HasColumnType("Money");

    builder.HasOne(m => m.MenuCard)
      .WithMany(c => c.MenuItems)
      .HasForeignKey(MenuCardId);

    //...
  }
}
```

To activate the configuration classes with the `OnModelCreating` method of the `DbContext`-derived class, you invoke the `ApplyConfiguration` method (code file `Models/MenusContext.cs`):

```
protected override void OnModelCreating(ModelBuilder modelBuilder)
{
  modelBuilder.HasDefaultSchema("mc")
    .ApplyConfiguration(new MenuCardConfiguration())
    .ApplyConfiguration(new MenuConfiguration());

  //...
}
```

Mapping to Fields

EF Core allows mapping table columns not only to properties but also to private fields. This makes it possible to create read-only properties and use private fields that are not accessible outside of the class.

Let's take a look at the `Restaurant` class in the following code snippet. This class contains a private field `_id` that is accessible only within the class. `Name` is a read-only property that accesses the field `_name` (code file `Models/Restaurant.cs`):

```
public class Restaurant
{
  public Restaurant(string name, int id = default) => (_name, _id) = (name, id);

  private int _id = default;
  private string _name;
  public string Name => _name;

  public override string ToString() => $"{Name}, {_id}";
}
```

The property `Name` can now be configured to map to the corresponding field with the `HasField` method. The `_bookId` doesn't have a corresponding property; thus, it is configured with an overload of the `Property` method where the name is assigned as a string. The method `HasColumnName` maps the field to the `Id` column in the database (code file `BooksSample/BooksContext.cs`):

```
internal class RestaurantConfiguration : IEntityTypeConfiguration<Restaurant>
{
  public void Configure(EntityTypeBuilder<Restaurant> builder)
  {
    builder.Property<int>("_id")
      .HasColumnName("Id")
      .IsRequired()
      .UsePropertyAccessMode(PropertyAccessMode.Field);

    builder.Property(r => r.Name)
      .HasField("_name")
      .UsePropertyAccessMode(PropertyAccessMode.FieldDuringConstruction)
      .HasMaxLength(30);

    builder.HasKey("_id");
  }
}
```

Working with Shadow Properties

Not only does EF Core allow mapping database columns to private fields, but it also lets you define a mapping that doesn't show up in the model at all. You can use shadow properties that can be retrieved with the entity in the context but are not available with the model.

The following code snippet defines the shadow properties IsDeleted, LastUpdated, RestaurantId, and MenuCardId with the MenuConfiguration. All these properties are not specified with the model type and are available only when using the EF Core context. The MenuCardId shadow property is created automatically because it's specified as a foreign key with the HasForeignKey method (code file Models/MenuConfiguration.cs):

```
internal class MenuConfiguration : IEntityTypeConfiguration<Menu>
{
  public void Configure(EntityTypeBuilder<Menu> builder)
  {
    //...

    builder.HasOne(m => m.MenuCard)
      .WithMany(c => c.MenuItems)
      .HasForeignKey(MenuCardId);

    // shadow properties
    builder.Property<bool>(IsDeleted);
    builder.Property<DateTime>(LastUpdated);
    builder.Property<Guid>(RestaurantId);
    // builder.Property<int>(MenuCardId); // created because of HasForeignKey
  }
}
```

You use the shadow property LastUpdated to write the actual time when the entity was updated last. You use the IsDeleted property to define a state in which the entity is deleted instead of truly deleting it. Sometimes, it can be useful not to delete the data on the request of the user; instead, you just mark it as deleted. This allows you to make an undo to recover the entity.

> **NOTE** *Because of the General Data Protection Regulation (GDPR),* https://en.wikipedia.org/wiki/General_Data_Protection_Regulation, *which is an EU law, you need to be careful to mark data as deleted but not delete it if the data is related to personal data.*

To update the shadow property LastUpdated automatically, the method SaveChangesAsync is overridden. If you're using the synchronous SaveChanges method to write changes to the database, you need to override this method as well. With the implementation, the actual state of the entities is checked. If the state is Added, Modified, or Deleted, the shadow property is updated with the current time. To manage the shadow property IsDeleted, deleted entities are changed to the Modified state, and the IsDeleted shadow property is set to true. Shadow properties don't have a property in the model that allows for accessing them; instead, you can use the CurrentValues indexer of the EntityEntry (code file Models/MenusContext.cs):

```
public override Task<int> SaveChangesAsync(CancellationToken cancellationToken = default)
{
```

```
ChangeTracker.DetectChanges();

foreach (var item in ChangeTracker.Entries<MenuItem>()
  .Where(e => e.State == EntityState.Added
  || e.State == EntityState.Modified
  || e.State == EntityState.Deleted))
{
  item.CurrentValues[LastUpdated] = DateTime.Now;

  if (item.State == EntityState.Deleted)
  {
    item.State = EntityState.Modified;
    item.CurrentValues[IsDeleted] = true;
  }
}
return base.SaveChangesAsync(cancellationToken);
}
```

> **NOTE** *The change tracker that is used with the sample code is shown in detail later in the section "Tracking Objects."*

> **NOTE** *When you have an* IsDeleted *property, it would be a good idea not to return entities where* IsDeleted *is set to true when using normal queries. You can do this with the EF Core feature global query filters, which is discussed later in this chapter.*

To show deleted entities, the `DeleteMenuItemAsync` method is defined to delete the entity with the ID that is passed to this method. Here, the `Remove` method is invoked by passing the entity object, and `SaveChangesAsync` is invoked (code file `Models/Runner.cs`):

```
public async Task DeleteMenuItemAsync(int id)
{
  MenuItem? menuItem = await _menusContext.MenuItems.FindAsync(id);
  if (menuItem is null) return;

  _menusContext.Remove(menuItem);
  int records = await _menusContext.SaveChangesAsync();
  Console.WriteLine($"{records} deleted");
}
```

Behind the scenes, the `IsDeleted` shadow property is set because of the change to the `SaveChangesAsync` method. To verify this, you can access the shadow property using the method `EF.Property` by passing the `IsDeleted` string. All the `Book` entities with this flag are shown in the `QueryDeletedMenusAsync` method:

```
public async Task QueryDeletedMenuItemsAsync()
{
  IEnumerable<MenuItem> deletedMenuItems =
    await _menusContext.MenuItems
      .Where(b => EF.Property<bool>(b, IsDeleted))
      .ToListAsync();
```

```
    foreach (var menuItem in deletedMenuItems)
    {
        Console.WriteLine($"deleted: {menuItem}");
    }
}
```

> **NOTE** EF *is a static class in the namespace* `Microsoft.EntityFrameworkCore` *that offers static methods that are useful when EF types are not available. In this section, you've seen the* `Property` *method that can be used to access shadow state. Later in this chapter, the* EF *class is used with compiled queries and* `EF.Functions`.

SCAFFOLDING A MODEL FROM THE DATABASE

Instead of creating the database from the model as you've seen with invoking the method `EnsureCreatedAsync`, you can create the model from the database. To do this, create a console application and add the NuGet package `Microsoft.EntityFrameworkCore.Design` to the packages referenced, and add the `dotnet-ef` tool to the project (unless you already have it registered with the global tools). To access Microsoft SQL Server, the package `Microsoft.EntityFrameworkCore.SqlServer` is needed as well (project file `ScaffoldSample/ScaffoldSample.csproj`):

```
<Project Sdk="Microsoft.NET.Sdk">

  <PropertyGroup>
    <OutputType>Exe</OutputType>
    <TargetFramework>net5.0</TargetFramework>
  </PropertyGroup>

  <ItemGroup>
    <PackageReference Include="Microsoft.EntityFrameworkCore.Design" Version="5.0.5">
      <PrivateAssets>all</PrivateAssets>
      <IncludeAssets>
        runtime; build; native; contentfiles; analyzers; buildtransitive
      </IncludeAssets>
    </PackageReference>
    <PackageReference Include="Microsoft.EntityFrameworkCore.SqlServer" Version="5.0.5"/>
  </ItemGroup>

</Project>
```

After the tools are installed, you can start the `dotnet ef` command and specify the connecting string to the database and the name of the EF Core provider:

```
> dotnet ef dbcontext scaffold
"server=(localdb)\MSSQLLocalDb;database=MenuCards;
trusted_connection=true" "Microsoft.EntityFrameworkCore.SqlServer"
```

The `dbcontext` command enables you to list `DbContext` objects from the project, as well as create `DBContext` objects. The command `scaffold` creates `DbContext`-derived classes as well as model classes. `dotnet ef dbcontext scaffold` needs two required arguments: the connection string to the database and the provider that should be used. With the statement shown earlier, the database `ProCSharpMenus` was accessed on `SQL Server` (localdb)\MSSQLLocalDb. The provider used was Microsoft.EntityFrameworkCore.SqlServer. This NuGet package needs to be added to the project.

After running this command, you can see the DbContext-derived classes as well as the model types generated. By default, the configuration of the model is done using the Fluent API. However, you can change it to use the data annotations supplying the --data-annotations option. The EF Core 5.0 design package has a dependency on the Humanizer library (https://humanizr.net) and supports pluralization with scaffolding. For example, if you have a table named People, the generated class has the name Person. You can disable pluralization with the option --no-pluralize. You can also influence the generated context class name, the tables to map, and the output directory. Just check the different available options using the option --help.

MIGRATIONS

So far, the database has been created with the EnsureCreatedAsync method, which is great for small applications. However, if you want to change the database schema after the database has been initially created, when using EnsureCreatedAsync you need to delete and re-create the database. There's another option: you can create the database with EF Core *migrations*. With EF Core migrations you can update the database schema programmatically. To support continuous integration (CI) and continuous delivery (CD), EF Core supports the concept of infrastructure as code (https://docs.microsoft.com/azure/devops/learn/what-is-infrastructure-as-code) with migrations, which gives you a great option for always supporting repeated deployments. You just need to think about who has the right to update the database schema. Usually, it's not the application that's running in production, and it's even bad from a security standpoint if the running application is allowed to change the schema. Instead, a different application should be in control to do this. You can also create SQL scripts for updating the database schema.

Implementing IDesignTimeDbContextFactory

With the sample application, the Book and BooksContext classes from before are used in a library with the name BooksLib. A console application that has a dependency on this library will do the migration. The console application also has a dependency on the NuGet package Microsoft.EntityFrameworkCore.Design.

Now the .NET CLI tools need to create the DbContext-derived class. You have three different options that you can implement to support the migration tools:

➤ Implement a default constructor with the DbContext-derived class and override the OnConfiguring method

➤ Use DI with a web-based project with a Program class and a CreateWebHostBuilder method

➤ Create a factory class that returns an instance of the context

Here, the DI container has been used with console applications, so I've implemented the third option. The factory class needs to implement the generic interface IDesignTimeDbContextFactory and return a context from the method CreateDbContext.

In the following code sample, the BooksContextFactory class implements the interface IDesignTimeDbContextFactory. The CreateDbContext method receives command-line arguments passed to the dotnet CLI for creating the migration. The connection string received via the parameters is passed to the DbContextOptionsBuilder to create options that in turn are passed as arguments to the constructor of the BooksContext (code file MigrationsApp/BooksContextFactory.cs):

```
using BooksLib;
using Microsoft.EntityFrameworkCore;
using Microsoft.EntityFrameworkCore.Design;
```

```
using System;

public class BooksContextFactory : IDesignTimeDbContextFactory<BooksContext>
{
  public BooksContext CreateDbContext(string[] args)
  {
    if (args.Length < 1)
    {
      Console.WriteLine($"please supply a connection string");
      Environment.Exit(-1);
      return null!;
    }
    else
    {
      string connectionString = args[0];
      DbContextOptionsBuilder<BooksContext> optionsBuilder = new();
      optionsBuilder.UseSqlServer(connectionString);
      return new BooksContext(optionsBuilder.Options);
    }
  }
}
```

> **NOTE** *If you used the* `CreateDbContext` *method before .NET 5, command-line arguments were not passed to this method. In that case, you needed to supply the connection string differently. With .NET 5, this has been fixed, and you can supply any options you need.*

Creating Migrations

With all this in place, you can create an initial migration. The following command—when started with the current directory set to the library—creates an initial migration named `InitBooks`. The startup project referenced with the option `--startup-project` contains the factory code with the connection string to the server:

```
> dotnet ef migrations add InitBooks --startup-project ../MigrationApp/MigrationApp.csproj
-- server=(localdb)\mssqllocaldb;database=ProCSharpBooks;trusted_connection=true
```

If your project contains multiple EF Core contexts, you need to supply the additional option `--context` and supply the name of the DB context class.

Running this command creates a `Migrations` folder with a snapshot to create the complete database schema based on the model (code file `BooksLib/Migration/BooksContextModelSnapshot.cs`):

```
[DbContext(typeof(BooksContext))]
partial class BooksContextModelSnapshot : ModelSnapshot
{
  protected override void BuildModel(ModelBuilder modelBuilder)
  {
#pragma warning disable 612, 618
    modelBuilder
      .HasAnnotation("Relational:MaxIdentifierLength", 128)
      .HasAnnotation("ProductVersion", "5.0.3")
      .HasAnnotation("SqlServer:ValueGenerationStrategy",
```

```
                SqlServerValueGenerationStrategy.IdentityColumn);

        modelBuilder.Entity("BooksLib.Book", b =>
        {
          b.Property<int>("BookId")
            .ValueGeneratedOnAdd()
            .HasColumnType("int")
            .HasAnnotation("SqlServer:ValueGenerationStrategy",
              SqlServerValueGenerationStrategy.IdentityColumn);

          b.Property<string>("Publisher")
            .HasMaxLength(30)
            .HasColumnType("nvarchar(30)");

          b.Property<string>("Title")
            .IsRequired()
            .HasMaxLength(50)
            .HasColumnType("nvarchar(50)");

          b.HasKey("BookId");

          b.ToTable("Books");
        });
#pragma warning restore 612, 618
      }
  }
```

For every migration, a migration class deriving from the base class `Migration` is created. This base class defines the `Up` and `Down` methods that allow applying the migration to this migration version or to step a level back (code file `BooksLib/<version>_InitBooks.cs`):

```
public partial class InitBooks : Migration
{
  protected override void Up(MigrationBuilder migrationBuilder)
  {
    migrationBuilder.CreateTable(
      name: "Books",
      columns: table => new
      {
        BookId = table.Column<int>(type: "int", nullable: false)
          .Annotation("SqlServer:Identity", "1, 1"),
        Title = table.Column<string>(type: "nvarchar(50)", maxLength: 50,
          nullable: false),
        Publisher = table.Column<string>(type: "nvarchar(30)", maxLength: 30,
          nullable: true)
      },
      constraints: table =>
      {
        table.PrimaryKey("PK_Books", x => x.BookId);
      });
  }
```

```
    protected override void Down(MigrationBuilder migrationBuilder)
    {
      migrationBuilder.DropTable(
        name: "Books");
    }
}
```

After making a change to a model, such as adding an optional Isbn property to the Book class (code file BooksLib/Book.cs), as shown here:

```
public class Book
{
  public Book(string title, string? publisher = default, int bookId = default)
  {
    Title = title;
    Publisher = publisher;
    BookId = bookId;
  }
  [StringLength(50)]
  public string Title { get; set; }
  [StringLength(30)]
  public string? Publisher { get; set; }
  public int BookId { get; set; }
  [StringLength(20)]
  public string? Isbn { get; set; }
}
```

you need a new migration:

```
> dotnet ef migrations add AddIsbn --startup-project ../MigrationApp/MigrationApp.csproj
-- server=(localdb)\mssqllocaldb;database=ProCSharpBooks;trusted_connection=true
```

With the new migration, that snapshot class is updated to show the current state, and a new Migration type is used to add and remove the Isbn column with the Up and Down methods (code file BooksLib/<version>_AddIsbn.cs):

```
public partial class AddIsbn : Migration
{
  protected override void Up(MigrationBuilder migrationBuilder)
  {
    migrationBuilder.AddColumn<string>(
      name: "Isbn",
      table: "Books",
      type: "nvarchar(20)",
      maxLength: 20,
      nullable: true);
  }

  protected override void Down(MigrationBuilder migrationBuilder)
  {
    migrationBuilder.DropColumn(
      name: "Isbn",
      table: "Books");
  }
}
```

> **NOTE** *Migrations are fully customizable. You can adapt the code to your own needs. With migrations, you might lose data. For example, with a migration, you might reduce the string length of a property. Because you forgot to limit a property with a previous version, the SQL datatype can be* nvarchar(max)*. If you limit this to* nvarchar(50)*, some data might be lost. When creating such a migration, you get a warning on the possible data loss. Whether you really lose data depends on whether the data stored in the database. You might know that the data length of the string is never larger than 50 characters, but is this also the case for the production database? You can customize the migration to check for the length of the data before the migration takes place and inform an administrator to take some actions before starting the migration. In any case, you should do a database backup before doing a migration if it's not just for testing purposes.*

> **NOTE** *With every change you're doing, you can create another migration. The new migration defines only the changes needed to get from the previous version to the new version. If a customer's database needs to be updated from any earlier version, the necessary migrations are invoked when migrating the database.*
>
> *During the development process, you might end up with many migrations that are not needed in production. You just need to keep the migrations for all the versions that might be running on the customer sites. To remove the migrations from development time, you can invoke* dotnet ef migrations remove *to remove the latest migration code. Then add new larger migrations that contain all the changes since the previous migration.*

Applying Migrations Programmatically

After you've configured the migrations, you can start the migration process of the database directly from the application. To do this, the console application is configured to use the dependency injection container to retrieve the DB context and then to invoke the `MigrateAsync` method of the `Database` property (code file `MigrationsApp/Program.cs`):

```
using BooksLib;
using Microsoft.EntityFrameworkCore;
using Microsoft.Extensions.Configuration;
using Microsoft.Extensions.DependencyInjection;
using Microsoft.Extensions.Hosting;

using var host = Host.CreateDefaultBuilder(args)
  .ConfigureServices((context, services) =>
  {
    var connectionString = context.Configuration.GetConnectionString("BooksConnection");
    services.AddDbContext<BooksContext>();
  })
  .Build();

using var scope = host.Services.CreateScope();
var context = scope.ServiceProvider.GetRequiredService<BooksContext>();
await context.Database.MigrateAsync();
```

If the database does not exist yet, the `Migrate` method creates the database—with the schemas defined by the model—as well as a `__EFMigrationsHistory` table that lists all the migrations that have been applied to the database. You cannot use the `EnsureCreated` method to create the database as was used earlier because this method does not apply the migration information to the database.

With an existing database, the database gets updated to the current version of the migration. Programmatically, you can get all the migrations available in the application with the `GetMigrations` method. To see all applied migrations, you can use the `GetAppliedMigrations` method. For all migrations that are missing in the database, use the `GetPendingMigrations` method.

Other Ways to Apply Migrations

Instead of applying migrations programmatically, you can apply migrations using the command line:

```
> dotnet ef database update --startup-project ../MigrationsConsoleApp
```

This command applies the latest migration to the database. You can also supply the name of the migration to this command to put the database into a specific version of the migration.

If you have a database administrator who needs to keep full control over the database and doesn't allow programmatic changes or changes from a tool such as the .NET Core CLI command line, you can create an SQL script and hand this over (or use it by yourself).

The following command line creates the SQL script `migrationsscript.sql` from the initial database creation up to the latest migration. You can also supply specific from/to values for the range of the migrations that should be applied in the script:

```
> dotnet ef migrations script --output migrationsscript.sql
--startup-project ..\MigrationsConsoleApp
```

WORKING WITH QUERIES

Now that I've defined the model and discussed migrations and scaffolding, let's examine queries in more detail. This section covers the following:

➤ Basic queries

➤ Asynchronous streams

➤ Raw SQL queries

➤ Compiled queries for better performance

➤ Global query filters

➤ `EF.Functions`

Basic Queries

You've already seen that accessing a context property of `DbSet` returns a list of all entities of the specified table. Let's look at some more queries and the outcome with SQL sent to the server.

Accessing the `Books` property retrieves all the `Book` records from the database (code file `BooksSample/QuerySamples.cs`):

```
private async Task QueryAllBooksAsync()
{
  Console.WriteLine(nameof(QueryAllBooksAsync));
```

```
using (var context = new BooksContext())
{
  List<Book> books = await context.Books.ToListAsync();
  foreach (var b in books)
  {
    Console.WriteLine(b);
  }
}
Console.WriteLine();
}
```

You can query for an object with a specific key with the `FindAsync` method. If the record is not found, this method returns `null` (code file `Queries/Runner.cs`):

```
public async Task FindByKeyAsync(int id)
{
  Console.WriteLine(nameof(FindByKeyAsync));
  MenuItem? menuItem = await _menusContext.MenuItems.FindAsync(id);
  Console.WriteLine(menuItem);
  Console.WriteLine();
}
```

This results in a `SELECT` SQL statement with `TOP(1)` and a `WHERE` clause:

```
SELECT TOP(1) [m].[MenuItemId], [m].[IsDeleted], [m].[LastUpdated], [m].[MenuCardId],
              [m].[Price], [m].[RestaurantId], [m].[Text]
FROM [mc].[MenuItems] AS [m]
WHERE [m].[MenuItemId] = @__p_0
```

Instead of using a `FindAsync` method, you can also use the `SingleAsync` or `SingleOrDefaultAsync` method. The difference between `SingleAsync` and `SingleOrDefaultAsync` is that `SingleAsync` throws an exception when no records are found, whereas `SingleOrDefaultAsync` returns null when no records are found. These methods also throw an exception if more than one record is found.

The following code snippet uses the method `SingleOrDefaultAsync` to ask for menu item text that should be available only once (code file `Queries/Runner.cs`):

```
MenuItem? menuItem = await _menusContext.MenuItems
  .TagWith("SingleOrDefault")
  .SingleOrDefaultAsync(m => m.Text == text);
```

The generated SQL statement asks for the `TOP(2)` records, which allows throwing an exception if two records are found:

```
SELECT TOP(2) [m].[MenuItemId], [m].[IsDeleted], [m].[LastUpdated], [m].[MenuCardId],
  [m].[Price], [m].[RestaurantId], [m].[Text]
FROM [mc].[MenuItems] AS [m]
WHERE [m].[Text] = @__title_0
```

The `FirstOrDefaultAsync` method doesn't throw an exception if multiple records fulfill the condition. In any case, only the first result is taken, or null is returned if no records are found (code file `Queries/Runner.cs`):

```
MenuItem? menuItem = await _menusContext.MenuItems
  .TagWith("FirstOrDefault")
  .FirstOrDefaultAsync(m => m.Text == title);
```

With `FirstOrDefaultAsync`, you use a `SELECT TOP(1)`:

```
SELECT TOP(1) [m].[MenuItemId], [m].[IsDeleted], [m].[LastUpdated], [m].[MenuCardId],
    [m].[Price], [m].[RestaurantId], [m].[Text]
FROM [mc].[MenuItems] AS [m]
WHERE [m].[Text] = @__title_0
```

The `Where` method returns all objects fulfilling the condition. It allows for simple filtering based on a condition. You can also use the `Contains` or `StartsWith` method within the `Where` expression (code file `Queries/Runner.cs`):

```
var menuItems = await _menusContext.MenuItems
    .Where(m => m.Text.Contains("menu"))
    .TagWith("Where")
    .ToListAsync();
```

The resulting SQL statement makes use of a simple `WHERE` in the SQL clause using a `LIKE` for the `Contains` method:

```
SELECT [m].[MenuItemId], [m].[IsDeleted], [m].[LastUpdated], [m].[MenuCardId],
    [m].[Price], [m].[RestaurantId], [m].[Text]
FROM [mc].[MenuItems] AS [m]
WHERE [m].[Text] LIKE N'%menu%'
```

Using the `Skip` and `Take` methods, you can implement paging functionality to skip some records and to take only a specific number of records. By invoking this multiple times, you can retrieve page by page (code file `Queries/Runner.cs`):

```
var menuItems = await _menusContext.MenuItems
    .OrderBy(m => m.MenuItemId)
    .Skip(skip)
    .Take(take)
    .TagWith("SkipAndTake")
    .ToListAsync();
```

The following SQL code shows how this translates to the `ORDER BY` and `OFFSET/FETCH` clause:

```
SELECT [m].[MenuItemId], [m].[IsDeleted], [m].[LastUpdated], [m].[MenuCardId],
    [m].[Price], [m].[RestaurantId], [m].[Text]
FROM [mc].[MenuItems] AS [m]
ORDER BY [m].[MenuItemId]
OFFSET @__p_0 ROWS FETCH NEXT @__p_1 ROWS ONLY
```

> **NOTE** *In Chapter 9, you can read about many more LINQ methods and LINQ clauses, which you can also use with EF Core. Just bear in mind that the implementation is different between LINQ to objects and LINQ to EF Core. With LINQ to EF Core, expression trees are used that allow creating an SQL query with the complete LINQ expression at runtime. With LINQ to objects, most of the LINQ queries are defined in the* `Enumerable` *class. LINQ with expression trees is implemented in the* `Queryable` *class, and many enhancements for EF Core, such as the* `Async` *variants, are implemented in the* `EntityFrameworkQueryable Extensions` *class. For more information about the expression tree, read Chapter 9.*

Asynchronous Streams

EF Core also supports asynchronous streams. The `DbSet` method `AsAsyncEnumerable` returns `IAsyncEnumerable`, which allows using `await foreach` to iterate through the result (code file `Queries/Runner.cs`):

```
public async Task GetAllMenusUsingAsyncStream()
{
  IAsyncEnumerable<MenuItem> menuItems = _menusContext.MenuItems.AsAsyncEnumerable();
  await foreach (var menuItem in menuItems)
  {
    Console.WriteLine(menuItem);
  }
}
```

While this just sends one SQL statement to the database server, not all objects are immediately materialized and tracked from the context. The caller using `IAsyncEnumerable` defines how the objects are materialized using `await foreach`. Depending on the result size and the size of the objects, this can return faster results and requires memory just as the objects are materialized.

Raw SQL Queries

EF Core also enables you to define raw SQL queries, which in turn return entity objects and track these objects. You just need to invoke the `FromSqlInterpolated` method of the `DbSet` object, as shown in the following code snippet (code file `Queries/Runner.cs`):

```
var menuItems = await _menusContext.MenuItems
  .FromSqlInterpolated(
    $"SELECT * FROM MenuItems WHERE LIKE '{term}%'")
  .TagWith("RawSQL")
  .ToListAsync();
```

The SQL query assigned to the `RawSql` method needs to return entity types that are part of the model, and data for all the properties of the model need to be returned.

The SQL string assigned to the `FromSqlInterpolated` method might look like SQL injection can happen as the string is defined. However, because of the argument type `FormattableString`, the expressions assigned within the string are used to create parameters for the SQL statement. Read Chapter 2, "Core C#," for more information on `FormattableString`.

The method `FromSqlInterpolated` throws an exception if you pass a normal string. To pass a normal string, you can use `FromSqlRaw`. This method supports named parameters with the SQL statement. You can pass parameters of type `SqlParameter` to a params array. Don't use string concatenation to create the SQL statement.

Compiled Queries

For queries that need to be done multiple times or when you need to start them faster as they are needed, you can prepare the compilation process for a query using a compiled query with the method `EF.CompileQuery`. This method offers different generic overloads where you can pass a different number of arguments. The first generic parameter of this method specifies a class deriving from `DbContext`. The query is compiled independent of the context, and you can pass different `DbContext` instances with every invocation of the precompiled query. With the other generic parameters, you can define the parameters and the return type you need with the query.

With the following code snippet, an extension method extends the `MenusContext` class and creates a compiled query passing a string parameter and returning a list of `MenuItem` objects. The compilation is taking place with the first invocation.

The first parameter that's needed when creating a compiled query is a class deriving from `DbContext`; with the following sample code it's the `MenusContext`. The extension method `MenusByText` extends the `MenusContext`; thus, this parameter is used as the first argument for the compiled query (code file `Queries/CompiledQueryExtensions.cs`):

```
using Microsoft.EntityFrameworkCore;
using System;
using System.Collections.Generic;
using System.Linq;

static class CompiledQueryExtensions
{
  private static Func<MenusContext, string, IEnumerable<MenuItem>>? s_menuItemsByText;

  private static Func<MenusContext, string, IEnumerable<MenuItem>>
    CompileMenusByTextQuery()
      => EF.CompileQuery((MenusContext context, string text)
        => context.MenuItems.Where(m => m.Text == text));

  public static IEnumerable<MenuItem> MenuItemsByText(this MenusContext menusContext,
    string text)
  {
    if (s_menuItemsByText is null)
    {
      s_menuItemsByText = CompileMenusByTextQuery();
    }
    return s_menuItemsByText(menusContext, text);
  }
  //...
}
```

The extension method is used with the following code snippet to invoke `MenusByText` using a `_menusContext` (code file `Queries/Runner.cs`):

```
var menuItems = _menusContext.MenusByText("menu 26");
foreach (var menuItem in menuItems)
{
  Console.WriteLine(menuItem);
}
```

Compiled queries support returning an asynchronous stream by using the `EF.CompileAsyncQuery` method. This method returns `IAsyncEnuerable<T>` (code file `Queries/CompiledQueryExtensions.cs`):

```
static class CompiledQueryExtensions
{
  //...
  private static Func<MenusContext, string, IAsyncEnumerable<MenuItem>>?
    s_menusByTextAsync;
  private static Func<MenusContext, string, IAsyncEnumerable<Menu>>
    CompileMenuItemsByTextAsyncQuery()
```

```
  => EF.CompileAsyncQuery((MenusContext context, string text)
    => context.MenuItems.Where(m => m.Text == text));

public static IAsyncEnumerable<Menu> MenuItemsByTextAsync(
  this MenusContext menusContext, string text)
{
  if (s_menuItemsByTextAsync is null)
  {
    s_menuItemsByTextAsync = CompileMenuItemsByTextAsyncQuery();
  }
  return s_menuItemsByTextAsync(menusContext, text);
}
}
```

This can be used with an `await foreach` (code file `Queries/Runner.cs`):

```
await foreach (var menuItem in _menusContext.MenuItemsByTextAsync("menu 26"))
{
  Console.WriteLine(menuItem);
}
```

Global Query Filters

Earlier in this chapter, you saw shadow state used with the `IsDeleted` column. Instead of specifying the WHERE clause with every query to filter out the records that have the `IsDeleted` property set to `true`, you can define a global query filter when creating the model. This is what the next code snippet does—globally checking for `IsDeleted`. Because `IsDeleted` is not mapped to the model and is just via shadow state, the value can be retrieved using `EF.Property` (code file `Queries/BooksContext.cs`):

```
protected override void OnModelCreating(ModelBuilder modelBuilder)
{
  base.OnModelCreating(modelBuilder);

  modelBuilder.Entity<Book>().HasQueryFilter(
    b => !EF.Property<bool>(b, IsDeleted));
  //...
}
```

With this query filter defined, the WHERE check for `IsDeleted` is added to every query used with this context.

> **NOTE** *Global query filters are also of practical use with multitenancy requirements. You can filter all queries for a context for a specific tenant ID. You just need to pass the tenant ID when constructing the context. With dependency injection, you need to specify a service that is injected with the constructor where the tenant ID can be retrieved in the query filter.*

> **NOTE** *Usually, the global query filter should be applied. With queries where you don't want the global query filter active, apply the method `IgnoreQueryFilters` with the query.*

EF.Functions

EF Core allows custom extension methods that can be implemented by providers. For this, the `EF` class defines the `Functions` property of type `DbFunctions` that can be extended using extension methods. The SQL Server provider offers methods for date calculations (for example `DateDiffDay`, `DateDiffHour`, `DateDiffMicrosecond`, `DateDiffMillisecond`, `DateFromParts`, and others).

The `Like` method is part of EF Core for relational database providers. The following code snippet enhances the query of the `Where` method by using `EF.Functions.Like` and supplying an expression that contains the parameter `textSegment`. The parameter `textSegment` is embedded within two `%` characters (code file Queries/Runner.cs):

```
public async Task UseEFCunctions(string textSegment)
{
  Console.WriteLine(nameof(UseEFCunctions));
  string likeExpression = $"%{textSegment}%";

  var menuItems = await _menusContext.MenuItems
    .Where(m => EF.Functions.Like(m.Text, likeExpression))
    .ToListAsync();
  foreach (var menuItem in menuItems)
  {
    Console.WriteLine(menuItem);
  }
  Console.WriteLine();
}
```

When you run the application, the method `Where` that contains `EF.Functions.Like` is translated to the SQL clause `WHERE` with `LIKE`:

```
SELECT [m].[MenuItemId], [m].[IsDeleted], [m].[LastUpdated], [m].[MenuCardId],
  [m].[Price], [m].[RestaurantId], [m].[Text]
FROM [mc].[MenuItems] AS [m]
WHERE [m].[Text] LIKE @__likeExpression_1
```

LOADING RELATED DATA

If a relation is configured to be required in the database, this does not necessarily mean it's required in the object model, and to fill related data, you need to be aware of this when loading relations. The available options are as follows:

➤ Eager loading

➤ Explicit loading

➤ Lazy loading

The sample application implements the data classes `Book`, `Chapter`, `Person`, and `Address`. A `Book` contains a `Chapters` property that contains a list of `Chapters` and an `Author` property of type `Person`. The `Author` class contains an `Address` property that references an `Address` object. With this sample, each of these classes uses separate tables. In a later sample in this chapter, in the section "Owned Entities," you see how to make objects that share a table.

Eager Loading Related Data

You can load related data immediately when a query is executed by invoking the `Include` method and specifying the relation. The following code snippet defines a query to retrieve books and uses the `Include` method to include the related author. The `Person` class used with the `Author` property contains another reference to the `Address`. Here, the `ThenInclude` method is used to include the address as well. The list of chapters is included using the `Include` method accessing the `Chapters` property of the `Book` type (code file `LoadedRelatedData/Runner.cs`):

```
public async Task EagerLoadingAsync()
{
  var books = await _booksContext.Books
    .Where(b => b.Publisher == "pub1")
    .Include(b => b.Author)
    .ThenInclude(a => a!.Address)
    .Include(b => b.Chapters)
    .ToListAsync();
  foreach (var book in books)
  {
    Console.WriteLine($"{book.Title} {book.Author?.FirstName} " +
      $"{book.Author?.Address?.Country}");
  }
}
```

Using this query containing `Include` and `ThenInclude` generates a single SQL statement joining the different tables:

```
SELECT [b].[BookId], [b].[AuthorId], [b].[Publisher], [b].[Title], [p].[PersonId],
  [p].[AddressId], [p].[FirstName], [p].[LastName], [a].[AddressId], [a].[City],
  [a].[Country], [c].[ChapterId], [c].[BookId], [c].[Title]
FROM [Books] AS [b]
INNER JOIN [People] AS [p] ON [b].[AuthorId] = [p].[PersonId]
INNER JOIN [Addresses] AS [a] ON [p].[AddressId] = [a].[AddressId]
LEFT JOIN [Chapters] AS [c] ON [b].[BookId] = [c].[BookId]
WHERE [b].[Publisher] = N'One'
ORDER BY [b].[BookId], [p].[PersonId], [a].[AddressId], [c].[ChapterId]
```

> **NOTE** *With EF Core 5, instead of combining several joins, you can enable split queries to create multiple queries. You can configure split queries either with the SQL Server options in the DI configuration to invoke the* `UseQuerySplittingBehavior` *method or by using the* `AsSplitQuery` *extension method with a query. With split queries, joins are still done with one-to-one relations, but with one-to-many relations instead of a join, multiple* SELECT *methods are sent to the server, which can improve the performance based on the complexity of the query.*

Eager Loading with Filtered Include

EF Core 5 allows filtering with the `Include` method to not load all related data. To use filtering with `Include`, specify a `Where` method within the lambda implementation to reference a collection, as is done with the include of chapters, as shown in the following code snippet (code file `LoadedRelatedData/Runner.cs`):

```
var books = await _booksContext.Books
```

```
.Where(b => b.Publisher == "pub2")
.Include(b => b.Author)
.ThenInclude(a => a!.Address)
.Include(b => b.Chapters!.Where(c => c.ChapterId > 5))
.ToListAsync();
```

When you run this code, the query is converted to an SQL query with a SELECT within the JOIN:

```
SELECT [b].[BookId], [b].[AuthorId], [b].[Publisher], [b].[Title], [p].[PersonId],
    [p].[AddressId], [p].[FirstName], [p].[LastName], [a].[AddressId], [a].[City],
    [a].[Country], [t].[ChapterId], [t].[BookId], [t].[Title]
FROM [Books] AS [b]
INNER JOIN [People] AS [p] ON [b].[AuthorId] = [p].[PersonId]
INNER JOIN [Addresses] AS [a] ON [p].[AddressId] = [a].[AddressId]
LEFT JOIN (
    SELECT [c].[ChapterId], [c].[BookId], [c].[Title]
    FROM [Chapters] AS [c]
    WHERE [c].[ChapterId] > 5
) AS [t] ON [b].[BookId] = [t].[BookId]
WHERE [b].[Publisher] = N'One'
ORDER BY [b].[BookId], [p].[PersonId], [a].[AddressId], [t].[ChapterId]
```

Explicit Loading Related Data

Instead of defining one query where all the needed related data is loaded, you can create a query to load just the Book objects from the Books table and leave all the relations empty. When needed, you make queries using *explicit loading* of related data.

Take a look at the following code snippet. The query requests all books with a specific publisher. If you try to access the Chapters and Author properties of the resulting book after starting the query, the values for these properties are null (if the related entities are not already loaded into the context). Relations are not loaded implicitly. EF Core supports explicit loading by using Entry methods of the context that return EntityEntry objects by passing an entity. The EntityEntry class defines Collection and Reference methods that allow explicit loading of relations. With a one-to-many relationship, you can use the Collection method to specify the collection, whereas a one-to-one relation needs the Reference method to specify the relation. Explicit loading then happens with the LoadAsync method (code file LoadingRelatedData/Runner.cs):

```
public async Task ExplicitLoadingAsync()
{
  var books = await _booksContext.Books
    .Where(b => b.Publisher == "pub1")
    .ToListAsync();

  foreach (var book in books)
  {
    Console.WriteLine(book.Title);
    var bookEntry = _booksContext.Entry(book);
    await bookEntry.Reference(b => b.Author).LoadAsync();
    Console.WriteLine($"{book.Author?.FirstName} {book.Author?.LastName}");

    await _booksContext.Entry(book.Author).Reference(a => a!.Address).LoadAsync();
    Console.WriteLine($"{book.Author!.Address!.Country}");

    await bookEntry.Collection(b => b.Chapters).LoadAsync();
```

```
      foreach (var chapter in book.Chapters)
      {
        Console.WriteLine(chapter.Title);
      }
    }
  }
}
```

The `NavigationEntry` class that implements the `LoadAsync` method also implements an `IsLoaded` property where you can check whether the relation is already loaded. You do not need to check for a loaded relation before invoking the `LoadAsync` method; this method already uses the `IsLoaded` property to check that the request to the SQL server is not done a second time.

When you run the application with the query for the books, the following `SELECT` statement is executed on SQL Server. This query only accesses the `Books` table:

```
SELECT [b].[BookId], [b].[AuthorId], [b].[Publisher], [b].[Title]
FROM [Books] AS [b]
WHERE [b].[Publisher] = N'pub1'
```

With the following `LoadAsync` method to retrieve the author for the book, the `SELECT` statement retrieves the chapters based on the `PersonId`:

```
SELECT [p].[PersonId], [p].[AddressId], [p].[FirstName], [p].[LastName]
FROM [People] AS [p]
WHERE [p].[PersonId] = @__p_0
```

After the `Person` object is materialized, the values from the `Addresses` table are retrieved using the `AddressId`:

```
SELECT [a].[AddressId], [a].[City], [a].[Country]
FROM [Addresses] AS [a]
WHERE [a].[AddressId] = @__p_0
```

With a fourth query, chapter information is retrieved from the `Chapters` table using the `BookId`:

```
SELECT [c].[ChapterId], [c].[BookId], [c].[Title]
FROM [Chapters] AS [c]
WHERE [c].[BookId] = @__p_0
```

Sending all these queries to the database repeats for every book. Because some books are written by the same author, a query to the author and address is not necessary for every book.

> **NOTE** *With explicit loading, you need to consider the number of requests that you make to the database server. If you know in advance what data you need, consider using eager loading instead. With explicit loading, the* DbContext *is required. If you send an object tree from an API server to the client, the client usually doesn't have the* DbContext *accessible and can't load related data without making requests to the API server. Programming services is covered in Chapter 25, "Services."*

Lazy Loading

Instead of using explicit loading to load related data, you have an easy programming option to access properties of data objects, and the relations are loaded like magic. This is easier to program than the explicit loading variant, but it still does the same number of queries. There are also some additional requirements: you need to reference the NuGet package `Microsoft.EntityFrameworkCore.Proxies`, and you need to configure proxies with the DI container. Invoke the method `UseLazyLoadingProxies` with the `options` argument. Change the parameter to turn it on or off (code file `LoadingRelatedData/Program.cs`):

```
using var host = Host.CreateDefaultBuilder(args)
  .ConfigureServices((context, services) =>
  {
    var connectionString = context.Configuration.GetConnectionString("BooksConnection");
    services.AddDbContext<BooksContext>(options =>
    {
      options.UseLazyLoadingProxies(true);
      options.UseSqlServer(connectionString);
    });
    services.AddScoped<Runner>();
  })
  .Build();
```

With lazy loading, there are some requirements for the entity types. The entity types cannot be `sealed`, and all the properties used for relations need to be declared `virtual`. The proxy creates a class that derives from your entity classes and overrides the `virtual` methods. With the implementation of the overridden methods, the same functionality you've seen with explicit loading is used; you just don't have to do this yourself (code file `LoadingRelatedData/Book.cs`):

```
public class Book
{
  public Book(string title, string? publisher = default, int bookId = default)
  {
    Title = title;
    Publisher = publisher;
    BookId = bookId;
  }
  [StringLength(50)]
  public string Title { get; set; }
  [StringLength(30)]
  public string? Publisher { get; set; }
  public int BookId { get; set; }

  // set accessor required for lazy loading
  public virtual ICollection<Chapter> Chapters { get; protected set; }
    = new HashSet<Chapter>();

  public int AuthorId { get; set; }
  [ForeignKey(nameof(AuthorId))]
  public virtual Person? Author { get; set; }
}
```

Making the queries is now a lot easier. In the following sample code, only a query to the `Books` table is done—without eager or explicit loading definitions—and then the properties `Chapters` and `Author` are used. When the properties are accessed for the first time, more queries to the database server are made to fill these properties (code file `LoadingRelatedData/Runner.cs`):

```
public async Task LazyLoadingAsync()
{
  Console.WriteLine(nameof(LazyLoadingAsync));
  var books = await _booksContext.Books
```

```
      .Where(b => b.Publisher == "pub1")
      .ToListAsync();

  foreach (var book in books)
  {
    Console.WriteLine(book.Title);
    Console.WriteLine($"{book.Author?.FirstName} {book.Author?.LastName}");

    Console.WriteLine($"{book.Author!.Address!.Country}");
    foreach (var chapter in book.Chapters)
    {
      Console.WriteLine(chapter.Title);
    }
  }
  Console.WriteLine();
}
```

> **NOTE** *While lazy loading seems to be the simplest option, queries are handled by accessing simple properties, which can take time. Also, the* DbContext *needs to be available. Without this, the properties stay empty.*

WORKING WITH RELATIONSHIPS

With the samples so far, you've seen one-to-one and one-to-many relations. With EF Core 5.0 you can also specify many-to-many relations. This section also covers table splitting, owned entities, and table per hierarchy.

Many-to-Many Relations

A new feature of EF Core 5.0 is the support of many-to-many relations. In the following code snippet, the Book class defines the Authors property of type ICollection<Person>. A book can be written by many authors (code file Relationships/Book.cs):

```
public class Book
{
  public Book(string title, string? publisher = default, int bookId = default)
  {
    Title = title;
    Publisher = publisher;
    BookId = bookId;
  }
  [StringLength(50)]
  public string Title { get; set; }
  [StringLength(30)]
  public string? Publisher { get; set; }
  public int BookId { get; set; }
  public DateTime? ReleaseDate { get; set; }

  public ICollection<Person> Authors = new HashSet<Person>();
}
```

On the other side of the relation, with the `Person` class, the `WrittenBooks` property defines a collection of `Book` objects (code file `Relationships/Person.cs`):

```
public class Person
{
  public Person(string firstName, string lastName, int personId = 0)
  {
    FirstName = firstName;
    LastName = lastName;
    PersonId = personId;
  }

  public int PersonId { get; private set; }

  public string FirstName { get; set; }
  public string LastName { get; set; }

  public ICollection<Book> WrittenBooks = new HashSet<Book>();

  //...
}
```

If you write the `WrittenBooks` and `Authors` properties with a `get` and `set` accessor (the `set` accessor doesn't need to be `public`), the relation is defined by conventions. Without the `set` accessor, Fluent API is needed to specify the relation. To seed the relation with data, the Fluent API is needed in any case. In the database, a many-to-many relation requires a joining or bridging table that contains the keys from both of the related tables. Before version 5, EF Core didn't support many-to-many relations directly, and you had to define two one-to-many relations using another class to map to the joining table. Now, a mapping type is automatically created in between. This mapping type uses a property-bag entity type, which uses the `Dictionary<string, object>` type definition to map the keys.

With the following code snippet, the mapping between the `WrittenBooks` property in the `Person` class and the `Authors` property in the `Book` class is defined using `HasMany` and `WithMany`. To fill the automatically used property-bag entity type with data, you use the `UsingEntity` method. `UsingEntity` can be used to rename the column and table names and to specify a custom class instead of using a property bag. With the code sample, data returned from the `GetBooksAuthors` is used to fill the table with initial data (code file `Relationships/ BooksContext.cs`):

```
public class BooksContext : DbContext
{
  public BooksContext(DbContextOptions<BooksContext> options)
    : base(options) { }

  protected override void OnModelCreating(ModelBuilder modelBuilder)
  {
    modelBuilder.HasDefaultSchema("books");

    modelBuilder.ApplyConfiguration<Person>(new PersonConfiguration());

    InitData data = new();
    modelBuilder.Entity<Book>()
      .HasMany(b => b.Authors)
      .WithMany(a => a.WrittenBooks)
      .UsingEntity(ba => ba.HasData(data.GetBooksAuthors()));
```

```
        modelBuilder.Entity<Person>().HasData(data.GetAuthors());
        modelBuilder.Entity<Book>().HasData(data.GetBooks());
    }

    public DbSet<Book> Books => Set<Book>();
    public DbSet<Person> People => Set<Person>();
}
```

The `GetBooksAuthors` method returns an object array to fill the property bag using anonymous types. The property names for the anonymous type are generated using the relation property name from one side of the relation and the key name property from the other side of the relation. `Person.WrittenBooks` combined with `Book.BookId` results in the anonymous type property name `WrittenBooksBookId`. Similarly, `Book.Authors` combined with `Person.PersonId` results in `AuthorsPersonId` (code file `Relationships/InitData.cs`):

```
public object[] GetBooksAuthors()
    => new object[]
    {
        new { WrittenBooksBookId = 1, AuthorsPersonId = 1 },
        new { WrittenBooksBookId = 1, AuthorsPersonId = 2 },
        new { WrittenBooksBookId = 2, AuthorsPersonId = 1 },
        //...
    };
```

With this mapping in place and with data filled in the database (the sample application makes use of migrations to create and fill the database), you can access the `Authors` property of the `Book` class to access information from the book authors. With the following code snippet, eager loading is used to fill the authors. Of course, you can also use explicit or lazy loading as discussed earlier (code file `Relationships/BooksContext.cs`):

```
public async Task GetBooksForAuthorAsync()
{
    var books = await _booksContext.Books
        .Where(b => b.Title.StartsWith("Professional C#"))
        .Include(b => b.Authors)
        .ToListAsync();
    foreach (var b in books)
    {
        Console.WriteLine(b.Title);
        foreach (var a in b.Authors)
        {
            Console.Write($"{a.FirstName} {a.LastName}");
        }
        Console.WriteLine();
    }
}
```

Table Splitting

Sometimes the number of database columns grows over time and you don't need to access all the columns every time. It's a good idea not to have all the properties within one entity class. With table splitting, you can split a table into multiple entity types. Using table splitting, each class that belongs to the same table needs a one-to-one relationship and defines its own primary key. However, because they share the same table, the primary key is shared, too.

Let's get into an example with the `MenuItem` class that represents information about a lunch menu, and `MenuDetails` contains information for the kitchen. The `MenuItem` class defines some properties for the menu, including the `Details` property. The `Details` property maps the relation to the `MenuDetails` class (code file `Relationships/Menus.cs`):

```
public class MenuItem
{
  public MenuItem(string title, int menuItemId = 0)
  {
    Title = title;
    MenuItemId = menuItemId;
  }
  public int MenuItemId { get; set; }
  public string Title { get; set; }
  public string? Subtitle { get; set; }
  public decimal Price { get; set; }
  public MenuDetails? Details { get; set; }
}
```

The `MenuDetails` class looks like it would map to its own table—with a primary key—and map to the `MenuItem` class with the `MenuItem` property (code file `Relationships/Menus.cs`):

```
public class MenuDetails
{
  public int MenuDetailsId { get; set; }
  public string? KitchenInfo { get; set; }
  public int MenusSold { get; set; }
  public MenuItem? MenuItem { get; set; }
}
```

Within the context, `MenuItems` and `MenuDetails` are two `DbSet` properties. In the `OnModelCreating` method, the `MenuItem` class is configured to a one-to-one relationship with `MenuDetails` using `HasOne` and `WithOne`. These APIs already have been discussed. Now you should put your attention to the invocation of the `ToTable` methods. Both `MenuItem` and `MenuDetails` map to the same table `MenuItems`. This makes the difference for table splitting (code file `Relationships/MenusContext.cs`):

```
public class MenusContext : DbContext
{
  public MenusContext(DbContextOptions<MenusContext> options)
    : base(options) { }

  protected override void OnModelCreating(ModelBuilder modelBuilder)
  {
    modelBuilder.HasDefaultSchema("ms");

    modelBuilder.Entity<MenuItem>()
      .HasOne<MenuDetails>(m => m.Details!)
      .WithOne(d => d.Menu!)
      .HasForeignKey<MenuDetails>(d => d.MenuDetailsId);
    modelBuilder.Entity<MenuItem>().ToTable("MenuItems");
    modelBuilder.Entity<MenuDetails>().ToTable("MenuItems");
  }

  public DbSet<MenuItem> MenuItems => Set<Menu>();
  public DbSet<MenuDetails> MenuDetails => Set<MenuDetails>();
}
```

> **NOTE** *EF Core 5 partially supports nullable reference types. When entity types are annotated, a convention is used to map to nullable columns. Many of the EF Core APIs are annotated, but not all are (at the time I'm writing this). When you use expressions with relations, nullable references result in a compiler warning. The EF Core team gives a guideline with two different contrary options for ways to deal with this. The first is to make the relation property (MenuDetails with the MenuItem class) not nullable, even if it could be null. If the entity type is used from EF Core only, this shouldn't be an issue. However, if the entity type is passed around and will be created in other ways, this can lead to issues—for example, NullReferenceException if the relation was not filled. The second option is to declare the reference as nullable (as was done with the sample code) and use the null forgiving operator ! within the arguments of the HasOne and WithOne methods to get rid of the compiler warning. With the sample code, the second option is used. With future EF Core versions, some enhancements are planned, including annotations for all the EF Core APIs.*

When you verify how the table was generated in the database, you can see with the following SQL statement that the `MenuItems` table includes the columns for both the `MenuItem` and `MenuDetails` classes, and only the primary key from the `MenuItem` class:

```
CREATE TABLE [dbo].[MenuItems](
  [MenuItemId] [int] IDENTITY(1,1) NOT NULL,
  [Price] [decimal](18, 2) NOT NULL,
  [Subtitle] [nvarchar](max) NULL,
  [Title] [nvarchar](max) NULL,
  [KitchenInfo] [nvarchar](max) NULL,
  [MenusSold] [int] NOT NULL,
CONSTRAINT [PK_MenuItems] PRIMARY KEY CLUSTERED
(
  [MenuItemId] ASC
)WITH (PAD_INDEX = OFF, STATISTICS_NORECOMPUTE = OFF, IGNORE_DUP_KEY = OFF,
  ALLOW_ROW_LOCKS = ON, ALLOW_PAGE_LOCKS = ON) ON [PRIMARY]
) ON [PRIMARY] TEXTIMAGE_ON [PRIMARY]
GO
```

Owned Entities

A different way to split a table into multiple entity types is with the feature known as *owned entities*. The owned entities don't need a primary key; they simply can be types owned within a normal entity. Entity types from owned entities can map to a single table—using the table splitting feature—or to different tables. When different tables are used, they share the same primary key.

Let's get into an example that shows both scenarios: using owned entities where part of the data is mapped to the same table and part is mapped to another table.

The following code snippet shows the main entity type, `Person`. This is the owner of owned entities with the primary key `PersonId`. This type contains two addresses: a `PrivateAddress` and a `BusinessAddress` (code file `Relations/Books/Person.cs`):

```
public class Person
{
  public int PersonId { get; set; }
  public string Name { get; set; }
```

```
public Address PrivateAddress { get; set; }
public Address? BusinessAddress { get; set; }
}
```

The Address is an owned entity—a type without its own primary key. This type has two string properties and a relation named Location of type Location. Location is another owned entity (code file Relations/Books/Address.cs):

```
public class Address
{
  public string? LineOne { get; set; }
  public string? LineTwo { get; set; }
  public Location? Location { get; set; }
}
```

Location contains Country and City properties, and as an owned entity, it also doesn't define a key (code file Relations/Books/Location.cs):

```
public class Location
{
  public string? Country { get; set; }
  public string? City { get; set; }
}
```

The most interesting part now comes with the context, where owned entities are defined in the PersonConfiguration class, as shown with the following code sample. When you customize the model for the Person class, the first invocation of OwnsOne specifies that the Person entity owns the entity referenced from the BusinessAddress property, which is an Address type. By default, column names based on the property name and type of the property are combined with an underscore separator. To change this default behavior, column names are configured with the HasColumnName method. The properties of the Location class are owned by the People table as well because another OwnsOne method is invoked with the builder of the BusinessAddress. With the PrivateAddress property of the Person, before invoking OwnsOne, the table PrivateAddresses is mapped. Instead of having the private address values stored with the People table, here another table is used (code file Relationships/Books/PersonConfiguration.cs):

```
internal class PersonConfiguration : IEntityTypeConfiguration<Person>
{
  public void Configure(EntityTypeBuilder<Person> builder)
  {
    builder.OwnsOne(p => p.BusinessAddress, builder =>
    {
      builder.Property(a => a!.LineOne).HasColumnName("AddressLineOne");
      builder.Property(a => a!.LineTwo).HasColumnName("AddressLineTwo");
      builder.OwnsOne(a => a!.Location, locationBuilder =>
      {
        locationBuilder.Property(l => l!.City).HasColumnName("BusinessCity");
        locationBuilder.Property(l => l!.Country).HasColumnName("BusinessCountry");
      });
    });

    builder.OwnsOne(p => p.PrivateAddress)
      .ToTable("PrivateAddresses")
      .OwnsOne(a => a!.Location, builder =>
      {
```

```
            builder.Property(a => a!.City).HasColumnName("City");
            builder.Property(a => a!.Country).HasColumnName("Country");
        });
    }
}
```

When creating the database, the `People` table contains columns from the owned entity types:

```
CREATE TABLE [dbo].[People](
    [PersonId] [int] IDENTITY(1,1) NOT NULL,
    [Name] [nvarchar](max) NULL,
    [CompanyAddress_LineOne] [nvarchar](max) NULL,
    [CompanyAddress_LineTwo] [nvarchar](max) NULL,
    [BusinessCity] [nvarchar](max) NULL,
    [BusinessCountry] [nvarchar](max) NULL,
CONSTRAINT [PK_People] PRIMARY KEY CLUSTERED
(
    [PersonId] ASC
)WITH (PAD_INDEX = OFF, STATISTICS_NORECOMPUTE = OFF, IGNORE_DUP_KEY = OFF,
    ALLOW_ROW_LOCKS = ON, ALLOW_PAGE_LOCKS = ON) ON [PRIMARY]
) ON [PRIMARY] TEXTIMAGE_ON [PRIMARY]
GO
```

The second table (`PrivateAddresses`) is created because of the `ToTable` mapping on the `PrivateAddress` property. The key for this table is the same as for the `People` table (`PersonId`):

```
CREATE TABLE [dbo].[Addr](
    [PersonId] [int] NOT NULL,
    [LineOne] [nvarchar](max) NULL,
    [LineTwo] [nvarchar](max) NULL,
    [Location_City] [nvarchar](max) NULL,
    [Location_Country] [nvarchar](max) NULL,
CONSTRAINT [PK_Addr] PRIMARY KEY CLUSTERED
(
    [PersonId] ASC
)WITH (PAD_INDEX = OFF, STATISTICS_NORECOMPUTE = OFF, IGNORE_DUP_KEY = OFF,
    ALLOW_ROW_LOCKS = ON, ALLOW_PAGE_LOCKS = ON) ON [PRIMARY]
) ON [PRIMARY] TEXTIMAGE_ON [PRIMARY]
GO
```

Table per Hierarchy

EF Core also supports the relationship type of table per hierarchy (TPH). With this relationship, multiple model classes that form a hierarchy are used to map to a single table. This relationship can be specified by using conventions and by using the Fluent API.

Let's start using conventions and the types `Payment`, `CashPayment`, and `CreditcardPayment` that form a hierarchy. `Payment` is a base class; `CashPayment` and `CreditcardPayment` derive from it.

With the implementation, the `Payment` class defines the primary key with the `PaymentId` property, a required `Name`, and an `Amount` property. The `Amount` property maps to a database column type `Money` (code file `Relations/Bank/Payments.cs`):

```
public abstract class Payment
{
    public Payment(string name, decimal amount, int paymentId = 0)
    {
```

```
      Name = name;
      Amount = amount;
      PaymentId = paymentId;
    }
    public int PaymentId { get; set; }
    [StringLength(20)]
    public string Name { get; set; }
    [Column(TypeName = "Money")]
    public decimal Amount { get; set; }
}
```

The class `CreditcardPayment` derives from `Payment` and adds a `CreditcardNumber` property (code file `Relations/Bank/Payments.cs`):

```
public class CreditcardPayment : Payment
{
  public CreditcardPayment(string name, decimal amount, int paymentId = 0)
    : base(name, amount, paymentId) { }
  public string? CreditcardNumber { get; set; }
}
```

Finally, the `CashPayment` class derives from `Payment` but doesn't declare any additional members (code file `Relations/Bank/Payments.cs`):

```
public class CashPayment : Payment
{
  public CashPayment(string name, decimal amount, int paymentId = 0)
    : base(name, amount, paymentId) { }
}
```

The EF Core context class, the `BankContext`, defines a `DbSet` property for the class to map to the `Payments` table. Here, the Fluent API is used to define the TPH mapping. The `HasDiscriminator` method specifies the name of the column to be used to differentiate the derived types that are returned. The method `HasValue` defines for the `CashPayment` class to have the value `cash` inside the `Type` column, and the mapping to the `CreditcardPayment` class is done with a value `creditcard` (code file `Relations/Bank/BankContext.cs`):

```
public class BankContext : DbContext
{
    public BankContext(DbContextOptions<BankContext> options)
        : base(options) {}

    public DbSet<Payment> Payments => Set<Payment>();

    protected override void OnModelCreating(ModelBuilder modelBuilder)
    {
        modelBuilder.HasDefaultSchema("bank");

        modelBuilder.Entity<Payment>()
            .HasDiscriminator<string>("Type")
            .HasValue<CashPayment>("cash")
            .HasValue<CreditcardPayment>("creditcard");

        modelBuilder.Entity<Payment>()
            .Property(p => p.Amount)
            .HasColumnType("Money");
    }
}
```

> **NOTE** *The sample application for TPH mapping uses the Fluent API. With conventions, the base class can't be abstract, and you need to define* DBSet *properties for every class of the hierarchy. By convention, the discriminator column is named* Discriminator.

The sample data created defines two CashPayment and one CreditcardPayment payments (code file Relations/Bank/BankRunner.cs):

```
public async Task AddSampleDataAsync()
{
  _bankContext.Payments.Add(new CashPayment("Donald", 0.5M));
  _bankContext.Payments.Add(new CashPayment("Scrooge", 20000M));
  _bankContext.Payments.Add(new CreditcardPayment("Gus Goose", 300M)
  {
    CreditcardNumber = "987654321"
  });
  await _bankContext.SaveChangesAsync();
}
```

When you run the application to create the database, just a single table—Payments—gets created. This table defines a Type column that maps a record from the table to the corresponding model type.

To query only specific types from the hierarchy, you can use the OfType extension method. In the following code snippet, you can see a query to return only payments of type CreditcardPayment (code file TPHWithConventions/Program.cs):

```
public async Task QuerySampleAsync()
{
  var creditcardPayments = await _bankContext.Payments
    .OfType<CreditcardPayment>()
    .ToListAsync();
  foreach (var payment in creditcardPayments)
  {
    Console.WriteLine($"{payment.Name}, {payment.Amount}");
  }
}
```

When you use the OfType method, EF Core creates a query with a WHERE clause to distinguish records only with a value of CreditcardPayment:

```
SELECT [p].[PaymentId], [p].[Amount], [p].[Discriminator], [p].[Name],
  [p].[CreditcardNumber]
FROM [Payments] AS [p]
WHERE [p].[Discriminator] = N'CreditcardPayment'
```

SAVING DATA

After creating the database with models and relations, you can write to it. The section "Introducing EF Core" showed you how to add, update, and delete records, but now let's examine various aspects of this in more detail.

With the sample application, this time the IDbContextFactory is used to create DbContexts. This allows having a shorter lifetime of the context and requires that you dispose of the context explicitly. This allows you to better simulate having multiple context objects as you have with web applications and services, where different context instances are used with every HTTP request. The `AddDbContextFactory` used in the following code snippet is new with EF Core 5.0 (code file `Tracking/Program.cs`):

```
using var host = Host.CreateDefaultBuilder(args)
  .ConfigureServices((context, services) =>
{
  var connectionString = context.Configuration.GetConnectionString("MenusConnection");
  services.AddDbContextFactory<MenusContext>(options =>
  {
    options.UseSqlServer(connectionString);
  });

  services.AddScoped<Runner>();
}).Build();
```

With the `Runner` class, the `IDbContextFactory` is injected. The variable `_menusContextFactory` can then be used to create new DbContexts (code file `Tracking/Runner.cs`):

```
private readonly IDbContextFactory<MenusContext> _menusContextFactory;
  public Runner(IDbContextFactory<MenusContext> menusContextFactory)
  => _menusContextFactory = menusContextFactory;
```

Adding Objects with Relations

The following code snippet writes a relationship: a `MenuCard` containing `MenuItem` objects. Here, the `MenuCard` and `MenuItem` objects are instantiated. The bidirectional associations are assigned. With the `MenuItem`, the `MenuCard` property is assigned to the `MenuCard`, and with the `MenuCard`, the `MenuItems` property is filled with `MenuItem` objects. The `MenuCard` instance is added to the context to invoke the `Add` method of the `MenuCards` property. When you add an object to the context, by default, all objects are added to the tree with the state added. Not only is the `MenuCard` saved, but the `MenuItem` objects are saved as well. Invoking `SaveChangesAsync` on the context now creates four records (code file `Tracking/Runner.cs`):

```
public async Task AddRecordsAsync()
{
  Console.WriteLine(nameof(AddRecordsAsync));
  using var context = _menusContextFactory.CreateDbContext();
  MenuCard soupCard = new("Soups");

  MenuItem[] soups = new[]
  {
    new MenuItem("Consommé Célestine (with shredded pancake)")
    {
      Price = 4.8m,
      MenuCard = soupCard
    },
    new MenuItem("Baked Potato Soup")
    {
      Price = 4.8m,
      MenuCard = soupCard
    },
    new MenuItem("Cheddar Broccoli Soup")
    {
      Price = 4.8m,
      MenuCard = soupCard
```

```
        }
    };

    foreach (var soup in soups)
    {
        soupCard.MenuItems.Add(soup);
    }

    context.MenuCards.Add(soupCard);

    ShowState(context);
    int records = await context.SaveChangesAsync();
    Console.WriteLine($"{records} added");
    Console.WriteLine();
}
```

The method ShowState that is invoked after adding the four objects to the context shows the state of all objects that are associated with the context. The DbContext class has a ChangeTracker associated that can be accessed using the ChangeTracker property. The Entries method of the ChangeTracker returns all the objects the change tracker knows about. With the foreach loop, every object, including its state, is written to the console (code file Tracking/Runner.cs):

```
private void ShowState(MenusContext context)
{
    foreach (EntityEntry entry in context.ChangeTracker.Entries())
    {
        Console.WriteLine($"type: {entry.Entity.GetType().Name}, " +
            $"state: {entry.State}, {entry.Entity}");
    }
    Console.WriteLine();
}
```

Run the application to see the Added state with these four objects:

```
type: MenuCard, state: Added, Soups
type: MenuItem, state: Added, Consommé Célestine (with shredded pancake)
type: MenuItem, state: Added, Baked Potato Soup
type: MenuItem, state: Added, Cheddar Broccoli Soup
```

Because of this state, the SaveChangesAsync method creates SQL Insert statements to write every object to the database.

Tracking Objects

You've seen that the context knows about added objects. However, the context also needs to know about changes. To know about changes, every object retrieved needs its state in the context. For seeing this in action, let's create two different queries that return the same object. The following code snippet defines two different queries where each query returns the same object with the menus as they are stored in the database. Only one object gets materialized; with the second query result, it is detected that the record returned has the same primary key value as an object already referenced from the context. Verifying whether the references of the variables m1 and m2 are the same results in returning the same object (code file Tracking/Runner.cs):

```
public async Task ObjectTrackingAsync()
{
    using var context = _menusContextFactory.CreateDbContext();
```

```
    Console.WriteLine(nameof(ObjectTrackingAsync));
    var m1 = await (from m in context.MenuItems
                    where m.Text.StartsWith("Con")
                    select m).FirstOrDefaultAsync();
    var m2 = await (from m in context.MenuItems
                    where m.Text.Contains("(")
                    select m).FirstOrDefaultAsync();
    if (object.ReferenceEquals(m1, m2))
    {
      Console.WriteLine("the same object");
    }
    else
    {
      Console.WriteLine("not the same");
    }
    ShowState(context);

    Console.WriteLine();
}
```

The first LINQ query results in an SQL SELECT statement with a LIKE comparison to compare for the string to start with the value Con:

```
SELECT TOP(1) [m].[MenuItemId], [m].[MenuCardId], [m].[Price], [m].[RestaurantId],
  [m].[Text]
FROM [mc].[MenuItems] AS [m]
WHERE [m].[Text] LIKE N'Con%'
```

With the second LINQ query, the database needs to be consulted as well. Here, a LIKE comparison is done to compare for a (in the middle of the text:

```
SELECT TOP(1) [m].[MenuItemId], [m].[MenuCardId], [m].[Price], [m].[RestaurantId],
  [m].[Text]
FROM [mc].[MenuItems] AS [m]
WHERE [m].[Text] LIKE N'%(%'
```

When you run the application, the same object is written to the console, and only one object is kept with the ChangeTracker. The state is Unchanged:

```
the same object
type: MenuItem, state: Unchanged, Consommé Célestine (with shredded pancake)
```

To not track the objects running queries from the database, you can invoke the AsNoTracking method with the DbSet:

```
var m1 = await (from m in context.MenuItems.AsNoTracking()
          where m.Text.StartsWith("Con")
          select m).FirstOrDefaultAsync();
```

With such a configuration, two queries are made to the database, two objects are materialized, and the state information is empty.

Instead of configuring the tracking behavior with the query, you can also configure the default tracking behavior setting the QueryTrackingBehavior property of the change tracker or configure it with UseTrackingBehavior with the options in the DI configuration.

> **NOTE** *Using the* NoTracking *configuration is useful when the context is used only to read records, but changes are not made. This reduces the overhead of the context as state information is not kept.*

Updating Objects

As objects are tracked, they can be updated easily, as shown in the following code snippet. First, a MenuItem object is retrieved. With this tracked object, the price is modified before the change is written to the database. In between all changes, state information is written to the console (code file Tracking/Runner.cs):

```
public async Task UpdateRecordsAsync()
{
  using var context = _menusContextFactory.CreateDbContext();
  MenuItem menuItem = await context.MenuItems
    .Skip(1)
    .FirstOrDefaultAsync();

  ShowState(context);
  menuItem.Price += 0.2m;
  ShowState(context);
  int records = await context.SaveChangesAsync();
  Console.WriteLine($"{records} updated");
  ShowState(context);
}
```

When you run the application, you can see that the state of the object is Unchanged after the record is loaded, Modified after the property value is changed, and Unchanged after saving is completed:

```
type: MenuItem, state: Unchanged, Baked Potato Soup
type: MenuItem, state: Modified, Baked Potato Soup
1 updated
type: MenuItem, state: Unchanged, Baked Potato Soup
```

When you access the entries from the change tracker, by default changes are automatically detected. You configure this by setting the AutoDetectChangesEnabled property of the ChangeTracker. To check manually to see whether changes have been made, you invoke the method DetectChanges. With the invocation of SaveChangesAsync, the state is changed back to Unchanged. You can do this manually by invoking the method AcceptAllChanges.

Updating Untracked Objects

DbContexts are usually very short-lived. Using EF Core with ASP.NET Core, with one HTTP request one object context is created to retrieve objects. When you receive an update from the client, the object must again be created on the server. This object is not associated with the object context. To update it in the database, the object needs to be associated with the DB context, and the state needs to be changed to create an INSERT, UPDATE, or DELETE statement.

Such a scenario is simulated with the next code snippet. The local function GetMenuItemAsync returns a MenuItem object that is disconnected from the context; the context is disposed of at the end of the local function. GetMenuItemAsync is invoked by the method UpdateRecordUntrackedAsync. This method changes the `MenuItem` object that is not associated with any context. After the change, the `MenuItem` object is passed to the local function `UpdateMenuAsync` to save it in the database within a new context. To mark this method as changed, the `Update` method attaches the object to the context and sets the state to `Modified`. Instead of using the `Update` method, you can use the `Attach` method and set the state via the `State` property of an `EntityEntry` object, as shown with the commented code (code file `Tracking/Runner.cs`):

```
public async Task UpdateRecordUntrackedAsync()
{
  Task<MenuItem> GetMenuItemAsync()
  {
    using var context = _menusContextFactory.CreateDbContext();
    return context.MenuItems
      .Skip(2)
      .FirstOrDefaultAsync();
  }

  async Task UpdateMenuAsync(MenuItem menuItem)
  {
    using var context = _menusContextFactory.CreateDbContext();
    ShowState(context);
    // EntityEntry<MenuItem> entry = context.MenuItems.Attach(m);
    // entry.State = EntityState.Modified;
    context.MenuItems.Update(menuItem);
    ShowState(context);
    await context.SaveChangesAsync();
  }

  var menuItem = await GetMenuItemsAsync();
  menuItem.Price += 0.7m;

  await UpdateMenuItemAsync(menuItem);
}
```

When you run the application with the `UpdateRecordTrackedAsync` method, you can see that the state is `Modified`. The object was detached at first, but because the state was explicitly updated, you can see the `Modified` state:

```
type: MenuItem, state: Modified, Cheddar Broccoli Soup
```

CONFLICT HANDLING

What if multiple users change the same record and then save the state? Who will win with the changes?

If multiple users accessing the same database work on different records, there's no conflict. All users can save their data without interfering with data edited by other users. If multiple users work on the same record, though, you need to give some thought to conflict resolution. You have different ways to deal with this. The easiest one is that *the last one wins*. The user saving the data last overwrites changes from the user that previously made changes.

EF Core also offers a way for letting the *first one win*. With this option, when saving a record, a verification is needed to see if the data that was originally read is still in the database. If this is the case, saving data can continue because no changes occurred between reading and writing. However, if the data changed, a conflict resolution needs to be done.

Let's get into these different options.

The Last One Wins

The default scenario is that the last one saving changes wins. To see multiple accesses to the database, the Intro sample with the `BooksContext` is extended with the new sample project `ConflictHandling-LastWins`.

For an easy simulation of two users, two DI scopes are created with two different `Runner` instances. The `Runner` object injects the `BooksContext` in the constructor. Because every `Runner` object is running in a different DI scope, two different `BooksContext` objects are created for every runner. The first user invokes `PrepareUpdateAsync` where a `Book` record is retrieved from the database. The same record is retrieved from the second user and invokes `PrepareUpdateAsync` as well. After this, both users invoke the `UpdateAsync` method where an updated `Book` object is written to the database. The winner is announced on reading the `Book` from the database after all the records have been written (code file `ConflictHandling-LastWins/Program.cs`):

```
using var user1Scope = host.Services.CreateScope();
using var user2Scope = host.Services.CreateScope();
var user1Runner = user1Scope.ServiceProvider.GetRequiredService<Runner>();
var user2Runner = user2Scope.ServiceProvider.GetRequiredService<Runner>();
int bookId = await user1Runner.PrepareUpdateAsync("user1");
await user2Runner.PrepareUpdateAsync("user2");
await user1Runner.UpdateAsync();
await user2Runner.UpdateAsync();

using var checkScope = host.Services.CreateScope();
var runner = checkScope.ServiceProvider.GetRequiredService<Runner>();
string updatedTitle = await runner.GetUpdatedTitleAsyc(bookId);
Console.Write("this is the winner: ");
Console.WriteLine(updatedTitle);
```

The `PrepareUpdateAsync` method behaves differently for the first and second users. With the first user, an `id` argument is not supplied to the method, so the last record is retrieved from the database and set to the selected book, and the `id` is returned. The second user uses this `id` to retrieve the same record from the database and writes it to its own instance of the `_selectedBook` field (code file `ConflictHandling-LastWins/Runner.cs`):

```
public async Task<int> PrepareUpdateAsync(string user, int id = 0)
{
  _user = user;
  if (id is 0)
  {
    _selectedBook = await _booksContext.Books.OrderBy(b => b.BookId).LastAsync();
    return _selectedBook.BookId;
  }
  _selectedBook = await _booksContext.Books.FindAsync(id);
  return id;
}
```

The `UpdateAsync` method makes a change to the selected book and uses the `BooksContext` to save the changes. Remember, this method is invoked two times for each of the two simulated users (code file `ConflictHandling-LastWins/Runner.cs`):

```
public async Task UpdateAsync()
{
  if (_selectedBook is null) throw new InvalidOperationException(
    "_selectedBook not set. Invoke PrepareUpdateAsync before UpdateAsync");
  _selectedBook.Title = $"Book updated from {_user}";
```

```
      int records = await _booksContext.SaveChangesAsync();
      if (records == 1)
      {
        Console.WriteLine($"Book {_selectedBook.BookId} updated from {_user}");
      }
    }
```

After the two users have been active, the book is retrieved again from the database by using the `FindAsync` method. This resolves which update was finally successful (code file `ConflictHandling-LastWins/Runner.cs`):

```
public async Task<string> GetUpdatedTitleAsyc(int id)
{
  var book = await _booksContext.Books.FindAsync(id);
  return $"{book.Title} with id {book.BookId}";
}
private static void CheckUpdate(int id)
{
  using (var context = new BooksContext())
  {
    Book book = context.Books.Find(id);
    Console.WriteLine($"updated: {book.Title}");
  }
}
```

What happens when you run the application? You see the first update is successful, and so is the second update. When updating a record, it is not verified whether any changes happened after reading the record, which is the case with this sample application. The second update just overwrites the data from the first update, as you can see with the application output:

```
database created
Book 100 updated from user1
Book 100 updated from user2
this is the winner: Book updated from user2 with id 100
```

The First One Wins

In the previous sample, you saw the default behavior when updating records. The last one wins. If you need a different behavior, such as the first user's changes being saved to the record, you need to make some changes. The sample project `ConflictHandling-FirstWins` uses the `Book` and `BooksContext` objects like before, but it deals with the first-one-wins scenario.

For conflict resolution, you need to specify the properties that should be verified if any change happened between reading and updating with a *concurrency token*. Based on the property you specify, the SQL `UPDATE` statement is modified to verify not only for the primary key but also all properties that are marked with the concurrency token. Adding many concurrency tokens to the entity type creates a huge `WHERE` clause with the `UPDATE` statement, which is not very efficient. Instead, you can add a property that is updated from SQL Server with every creation or updating of a record. You can define a property of type `byte[]` and mark it with the attribute `Timestamp`. This property is checked for changes, and the update fails if the record changed between reading the record to the context and trying to save it. If you don't want to have this property as a member of the class, you can use a shadow property.

In the following code snippet, the shadow property `Timestamp` of type `byte[]` is specified. The SQL Server data type where this is mapped to is of type `timestamp`. With SQL Server, this is all that's needed for an automatic update.

The `IsRowVersion` specifies for EF Core that the original value that's retrieved from the database is verified with the current value from the database. If this is no longer the same when updating, some other activity did an update of this record, and the new update will fail (code file `ConflictHandling-FirstWins/Books-Context.cs`):

```
protected override void OnModelCreating(ModelBuilder modelBuilder)
{
  var sampleBooks = GetSampleBooks();
  modelBuilder.Entity<Book>().HasData(sampleBooks);

  // shadow property
  modelBuilder.Entity<Book>().Property<byte[]>("Timestamp")
    .HasColumnType("timestamp")
    .IsRowVersion();
}
```

The `IsRowVersion` method is a combination of `ValueGeneratedOnAddOrUpdate` and `IsConcurrencyToken`. The properties marked with `IsConcurrencyToken` are verified for original and current values, and `ValueGeneratedOnAddOrUpdate` is the information to EF Core that the value gets updated from the database with add or update statements.

The process of the conflict-handling check is like what was done before. Both user 1 and user 2 invoke the `PrepareUpdateAsync` method, change the book title, and call the `UpdateAsync` method to make the change in the database.

The invocations from the top-level statements and the `PrepareUpdate` method are not repeated here; it's the same implementation as with the previous conflict handling sample. The `UpdateAsync` method is different. This method now needs to check for the exception of type `DbUpdateConcurrencyException` because such exceptions can happen when an update is made by another user. By invoking the `SaveChangesAsync` method now, with all the UPDATE statements created, you create WHERE clauses to check for all concurrency tokens. As the concurrency token is set on the timestamp, if any user changed any other column, the UPDATE fails. Within the handler of the `UIpdateConcurrencyException`, information about the failing records is shown (code file `ConflictHandling-FirstWins/Runner.cs`):

```
public async Task UpdateAsync()
{
  if (_selectedBook is null || _user is null)
    throw new InvalidOperationException(
      "_selectedBook not set. Invoke PrepareUpdateAsync before UpdateAsync");

  try
  {
    _selectedBook.Title = $"Book updated from {_user}";
    int records = await _booksContext.SaveChangesAsync();
    if (records == 1)
    {
      Console.WriteLine($"Book {_selectedBook.BookId} updated from {_user}");
    }
  }
  catch (DbUpdateConcurrencyException ex)
  {
    Console.WriteLine($"{_user}: update failed with {_selectedBook.Title}");
    Console.WriteLine($"error: {ex.Message}");
```

```
        foreach (var entry in ex.Entries)
        {
          if (entry.Entity is Book b)
          {
            PropertyEntry pe = entry.Property("TimeStamp");
            Console.WriteLine($"{b.Title} {BitConverter.ToString((byte[])pe.CurrentValue)}");
            ShowChanges(_selectedBook.BookId, _booksContext.Entry(_selectedBook));
          }
        }
      }
    }
```

With objects that are associated with the context, you can access the original values and the current values with a `PropertyEntry` object. The original values that were retrieved when reading the object from the database can be accessed with the `OriginalValue` property, and the current values can be accessed with the `CurrentValue` property. The `PropertyEntry` object can be accessed with the `Property` method of an `EntityEntry` as shown in the `ShowChanges` and `ShowChange` methods (code file `ConflictHandling-FirstWins/Runner.cs`):

```
private void ShowChanges(int id, EntityEntry entity)
{
  static void ShowChange(PropertyEntry propertyEntry, int id) =>
    Console.WriteLine($"id: {id}, current: {propertyEntry.CurrentValue}, " +
      $"original: {propertyEntry.OriginalValue}, " +
      $"modified: {propertyEntry.IsModified}");

  ShowChange(entity.Property("Title"), id);
  ShowChange(entity.Property("Publisher"), id);
}
```

When you run the application, you can see output such as the following. The timestamp values and book IDs differ with every run. The first user updates the book with the original title *sample book* to the new title *user 1 wins*. The `IsModified` property returns true for the `Title` property but false for the `Publisher` property because only the title changes. The original timestamp ends with 1.1.209; after the update to the database, the timestamp changes to 1.17.114. In the meantime, user 2 opens the same record; this book still has a timestamp of 1.1.209. User 2 updates this book, but here the update fails because the timestamp of this book does not match the timestamp from the database. Here, an exception of type `DbUpdateConcurrencyException` is thrown. In the exception handler, the reason for the exception is written to the console, as you can see in the program output:

```
Book 100 updated from user1
user2: update failed with Book updated from user2
error: Database operation expected to affect 1 row(s) but actually affected 0 row(s).
Data may have been modified or deleted since entities were loaded.
See http://go.microsoft.com/fwlink/?LinkId=527962 for information on understanding
and handling optimistic concurrency exceptions.
Book updated from user2 00-00-00-00-00-00-08-35
id: 100, current: Book updated from user2, original: title 100, modified: True
id: 100, current: sample, original: sample, modified: False
this is the winner: Book updated from user1 with id 100
```

When using concurrency tokens and handling the `DbConcurrencyException`, you can deal with concurrency conflicts as needed. You can, for example, automatically resolve concurrency issues. If different properties are changed, you can retrieve the changed record and merge the changes. If the property changed is a number where you do some calculations—for example, a point system—you can increment or decrement the values from both updates and just throw an exception if a limit is reached. You can also ask the user to resolve the concurrency issue by giving the user the information that's currently in the database and ask what changes they would like to make. Just don't ask too much from the user. It's likely that the only thing the user wants is to get rid of this rarely shown dialog, which means they might click OK or Cancel without reading the content. For rare conflicts, you can also write logs and inform the system administrator that an issue needs to be resolved.

USING TRANSACTIONS

With every access of the database, a transaction is involved, too. You can use transactions implicitly or create them explicitly with configurations as needed. The sample project used with this section demonstrates transactions in multiple ways. Here, the Menu, MenuCard, and MenuContext classes are used, as shown earlier with the Tracking project.

Using Implicit Transactions

An invocation of the SaveChangesAsync method automatically resolves to one transaction. If one part of the changes that need to be made fails—for example, because of a database constraint—all the changes already made are rolled back. This is demonstrated with the following code snippet. Here, the first MenuItem (m1) is created with valid data. A reference to an existing MenuCard is done by supplying the MenuCardId. After the update succeeds, the MenuCard property of the MenuItem m1 is filled automatically. However, the second MenuItem created, mInvalid, references an invalid menu card by supplying a MenuCardId that does not exist in the database. Because of the defined foreign key relation between MenuCard and MenuItem, adding this object will fail (code file Transactions/Runtime.cs):

```
public async Task AddTwoRecordsWithOneTxAsync()
{
  Console.WriteLine(nameof(AddTwoRecordsWithOneTxAsync));
  try
  {
    using var context = _menusContextFactory.CreateDbContext();
    var card = context.MenuCards.OrderBy(mc => mc.MenuCardId).First();
    MenuItem m1 = new("added")
    {
      MenuCardId = card.MenuCardId,
      Price = 99.99m
    };

    var notExistingCard = Guid.NewGuid();
    MenuItem mInvalid = new("invalid")
    {
      MenuCardId = notExistingCard,
      Price = 999.99m
    };
    context.MenuItems.AddRange(m1, mInvalid);
    int records = await context.SaveChangesAsync();
    Console.WriteLine($"{records} records added");
  }
  catch (DbUpdateException ex)
  {
    Console.WriteLine($"{ex.Message}");
    Console.WriteLine($"{ex.InnerException?.Message}");
```

```
    }
    Console.WriteLine();
  }
```

After running the application to invoke the method AddTwoRecordsWithOneTxAsync, you can verify the content of the database to see that not a single record was added. The exception message and the message of the inner exception give the details:

```
An exception occurred in the database while saving changes for context type
'MenusContext'.
Microsoft.EntityFrameworkCore.DbUpdateException: An error occurred while updating
the entries. See the inner exception for details.
---> Microsoft.Data.SqlClient.SqlException (0x80131904): The INSERT statement
conflicted with the FOREIGN KEY constraint "FK_MenuItems_MenuCards_MenuCardId".
The conflict occurred in database "ProCSharpTransactions", table "mc.MenuCards",
column 'MenuCardId'.
      The statement has been terminated.
```

If writing the first record to the database should be successful even if the second record write fails, you must invoke the SaveChangesAsync method multiple times.

Creating Explicit Transactions

Instead of using implicitly created transactions, you can also create them explicitly. This gives you the advantage of having the option to roll back in case some of your business logic fails, and you can combine multiple invocations of SaveChangesAsync within one transaction. To start a transaction that is associated with the DbContext-derived class, you need to invoke the BeginTransactionAsync method of the DatabaseFacade class that is returned from the Database property. The transaction returned implements the interface IDbContextTransaction. The SQL statements made with the associated DbContext are enlisted with the transaction. To commit or roll back, you must explicitly invoke the methods Commit or Rollback. In the sample code, Commit is done when the end of the DbContext scope is reached; Rollback is done in cases where an exception occurs (code file Transactions/Runner.cs):

```csharp
public async Task TwoSaveChangesWithOneTxAsync()
{
  Console.WriteLine(nameof(TwoSaveChangesWithOneTxAsync));
  using var context = _menusContextFactory.CreateDbContext();
  using var tx = await context.Database.BeginTransactionAsync();
  try
  {
    var card = context.MenuCards.First();
    MenuItem m1 = new("added with explicit tx")
    {
      MenuCardId = card.MenuCardId,
      Price = 99.99m
    };
    context.MenuItems.Add(m1);
    int records = await context.SaveChangesAsync();
    Console.WriteLine($"{records} records added");

    var notExistingCard = Guid.NewGuid();
    MenuItem mInvalid = new("invalid")
    {
      MenuCardId = notExistingCard,
```

```
      Price = 999.99m
    };
    context.MenuItems.Add(mInvalid);
    records = await context.SaveChangesAsync();

    Console.WriteLine($"{records} records added");
    tx.Commit();
  }
  catch (DbUpdateException ex)
  {
    Console.WriteLine($"{ex.Message}");
    Console.WriteLine($"{ex.InnerException?.Message}");
    Console.WriteLine("rolling back...");
    tx?.Rollback();
  }
  Console.WriteLine();
}
```

When you run the application, you can see that no records have been added, although the `SaveChangesAsync` method was invoked multiple times. The first return of `SaveChangesAsync` lists one record as being added, but this record is removed because of the `Rollback` later. Depending on the setting of the isolation level, the updated record can be seen only within the transaction before the rollback was done but not outside the transaction.

Using Ambient Transactions

An easy option to deal with transactions is to use ambient transactions from the `System.Transactions` namespace. An ambient transaction is a transaction set to the `Transaction.Current` property. Every resource that supports ambient transactions joins the transaction by enlisting to it. ADO.NET and EF Core with SQL Server supports ambient transactions and automatically enlists to this transaction. Every resource that enlisted to this transaction can fail it. If every resource sets the "happy bit," which means the transactional outcome for this resource is successful and the transaction-scope is successful as well, the transaction gets completed. If any resource that has enlisted did not grant success, when the scope is complete, the transaction rolls back.

You can create an ambient transaction by creating a new `TransactionScope`. Depending on the parameters used, this sets the `Transaction.Current` property to a transaction. With the `TransactionScopeOption` enum type, you can specify `Required`, `RequiresNew`, and `Suppress`:

➤ `Required` specifies a transaction is required. If one transaction is already set, this transaction is used. If no transaction is available, a new transaction is created.

➤ `RequiresNew` always creates a new transaction that is independent of a transaction that's already active.

➤ With the `Suppress` option, you specify that this scope should not have a transaction.

In the following code snippet, with `TransactionScopeOption.Required`, a new transaction will exist while the variable scope is active. With the second argument, `TransactionScopeAsyncFlowOption.Enabled`, you specify that the transaction flows across different threads, which is required in an asynchronous method. Otherwise, you need to run in the same thread when starting and completing the transaction, which is not the case when async methods are used without a synchronization context. When the root transaction scope is disposed of (with the sample code, the `scope` variable represents the root scope because this was the first ambient transaction created), the outcome of the transaction is resolved. The `scope` variable is disposed of at the end of the method `AmbientTransactionsAsync`. The scope itself must set the "happy bit," which is done by invoking the `Complete` method of the `TransactionScope`. This method is invoked at the end of the `try` code block. If any exception is thrown, the exception is aborted, no matter whether the database transactions would be successful. You can try this by using successful database operations and not invoking the `Complete` method. To see the outcome of the transaction, the `TransactionCompleted` event is fired. Within this handler, the status of the transaction is written to the console (code file `Transactions/Runner.cs`):

```
public async Task AmbientTransactionsAsync()
{
  Console.WriteLine(nameof(AmbientTransactionsAsync));

  using var scope = new TransactionScope(TransactionScopeOption.Required,
    TransactionScopeAsyncFlowOption.Enabled);

  if (Transaction.Current is null) throw new InvalidOperationException(
    "no ambient transaction available");
  Transaction.Current.TransactionCompleted += (sender, e) =>
  {
    var ti = e.Transaction?.TransactionInformation;
    Console.WriteLine($"transaction completed with status: " +
      $"{ti?.Status}, identifier: {ti?.LocalIdentifier}");
  };

  using var context = _menusContextFactory.CreateDbContext();
  try
  {
    var card = context.MenuCards.First();
    MenuItem m1 = new("added with explicit tx")
    {
      MenuCardId = card.MenuCardId,
      Price = 99.99m
    };
    context.MenuItems.Add(m1);
    int records = await context.SaveChangesAsync();
    Console.WriteLine($"{records} records added");

    var notExistingCard = Guid.NewGuid();
    MenuItem mInvalid = new("invalid")
    {
      MenuCardId = notExistingCard,
      Price = 999.99m
    };
    context.MenuItems.Add(mInvalid);
    records = await context.SaveChangesAsync();

    Console.WriteLine($"{records} records added");
    scope.Complete();
  }
  catch (DbUpdateException ex)
  {
    Console.WriteLine($"{ex.Message}");
    Console.WriteLine($"{ex.InnerException?.Message}");
  }
  Console.WriteLine();
}
```

USING AZURE COSMOS DB

Azure Cosmos DB (`https://azure.microsoft.com/services/cosmos-db/`) is a NoSQL database offering from Microsoft that allows storing various types of data. You can use Azure Cosmos DB for key-value, column-family, documents, and graph data. You can also use different APIs to access your data: SQL, Cassandra, MongoDB, and Gremlin. However, the API depends also on the data you store. For example, Gremlin is only used for graph data. EF Core supports only document-based storage with SQL.

No matter what APIs or kind of data you use, Azure Cosmos DB offers tunable throughput guarantees with a multimaster distribution model to write data concurrently—for example, in the United States and Asia. For small production workloads, a free tier is available.

To use the sample application, you need to create an SQL version of Azure Cosmos DB. You can use the free offering in Microsoft Azure or install a local emulator (`https://docs.microsoft.com/azure/cosmos-db/local-emulator`).

Although you can use EF Core to access your NoSQL database and don't need to learn a new API, there are some important differences. For example, you don't have tables with relations among them. Instead, you can group your documents within containers. In a container, you can store a lot of different document types because a container is not restricted to a particular schema for specific object types.

When creating a database, Azure allocates compute and storage resources, which are called *physical partitions*. Within a physical partition, logical partitions are used. A logical partition is limited to 20 GB. The number of logical partitions you can have is unlimited. If your storage needs exceed 20 GB, the data needs to be spread across multiple logical partitions. A transaction cannot span logical partitions. When working with documents, it's best to have one query within one partition. This increases performance and reduces cost. If your query spreads across multiple partitions, more RUs are needed. With a partition key, you can specify how to spread the data between logical partitions. See `https://docs.microsoft.com/azure/cosmos-db/partitioning-overview` for details.

Next, let's adapt a previous sample to store menu cards and menus to be used with Azure Cosmos DB.

The NuGet package needed to use the Azure Cosmos DB provider for EF Core is `Microsoft.EntityFrameworkCore.Cosmos`. To run the sample application locally, you need to supply the connection string to the Azure Cosmos DB database with the user secrets, as shown here:

```
{
  "ConnectionStrings": {
    "MenusConnection":
      "AccountEndpoint=... add the connection string to your Azure Cosmos account"
  }
}
```

To activate user secrets, you also need to enable the development environment by setting the `DOTNET_ENVIRONMENT` environment variable to `Development`. The `CreateDefaultBuilder` method of the `Host` class configures user secrets when this environment variable is set (configuration file `Cosmos/Properties/launchSettings.json`):

```
{
  "profiles": {
    "Cosmos": {
      "commandName": "Project",
      "environmentVariables": {
        "DOTNET_ENVIRONMENT": "Development"
      }
    }
  }
}
```

> **NOTE** *Read Chapter 15, "Dependency Injection and Configuration," for detailed information on configuration as well as how to configure secrets with Microsoft Azure App Configuration.*

Now the DI container needs can be configured. The connection string to the Azure Cosmos DB account is retrieved from the .NET configuration. Also, a restaurant identifier is retrieved from configuration. This restaurant identifier will be used as a partition key. Imagine multiple restaurants storing their menu cards within one database. The restaurant identifier is a good option for a partition key (code file Cosmos/Program.cs):

```
using var host = Host.CreateDefaultBuilder(args)
  .ConfigureServices((context, services) =>
  {
    var connectionString = context.Configuration.GetConnectionString("MenusConnection");
    var restaurantSettings = context.Configuration.GetSection("RestaurantConfiguration");

    services.Configure<RestaurantConfiguration>(restaurantSettings);
    services.AddDbContext<MenusContext>(options =>
    {
      options.UseCosmos(connectionString, "ProCSharpMenus1");
    });
    services.AddScoped<Runner>();
  })
  .Build();
```

The `MenuCard` class looks similar to the `MenuCard` class specified earlier. Here, the `RestaurantId` is defined as well. The partition key needs to be a string (code file Cosmos/MenuCard.cs):

```
public class MenuCard
{
  public MenuCard(string title, string restaurantId, Guid menuCardId = default)
    => (Title, RestaurantId, MenuCardId) = (title, restaurantId, menuCardId);

  public Guid MenuCardId { get; set; }
  public string Title { get; set; }
  public ICollection<MenuItem> MenuItems { get; internal set; } = new HashSet<MenuItem>();
  public string RestaurantId { get; set; }
  public bool IsActive { get; set; } = true;
  public override string ToString() => Title;
}
```

The `MenuItem` class that is used here can also be used with a relational database (code file Cosmos/MenuItem.cs):

```
public class MenuItem
{
  public MenuItem(string text, Guid menuItemId = default) =>
  (Text, MenuItemId) = (text, menuItemId);

  public Guid MenuItemId { get; set; }
  public string Text { get; set; }
```

```
    public decimal? Price { get; set; }
    public override string ToString() => Text;
  }
```

For storing documents, you now need to think about how the menu cards and the menus should be stored with the Azure Cosmos DB. Earlier in this chapter, you read about owned entities. You can use the OwnsOne method to add the properties of the Location and Address types to the columns of the People table. With document-based storage, this is even more important. You can also store a list of objects within one object; a hierarchy of JSON data is what is stored inside a document. As menu cards are usually the unit to read the menus and also change the menus, MenuItem objects can be combined with the MenuCard using OwnsMany.

The configuration of the MenusContext now has some specific Azure Cosmos DB configuration with the model. When you use the OwnsMany method, you include the MenuItem objects. A default container name is defined with the HasDefaultContainer method. Remember, with the relational database, the database schema name was specified. A partition key is defined with the method HasPartitionKey (code file Cosmos/MenusContext.cs):

```
internal class MenusContext : DbContext
{
  public MenusContext(DbContextOptions<MenusContext> options)
    : base(options) {}

  public DbSet<MenuCard> MenuCards => Set<MenuCard>();

  protected override void OnModelCreating(ModelBuilder modelBuilder)
  {
    modelBuilder.HasDefaultContainer("menucards");

    modelBuilder.Entity<MenuCard>().OwnsMany(c => c.MenuItems);
    modelBuilder.Entity<MenuCard>().HasKey(c => c.MenuCardId);

    modelBuilder.Entity<MenuCard>().HasPartitionKey(c => c.RestaurantId);
  }
}
```

With all this in place, the database can be created, and objects can be added, modified, and deleted as you are used to. The database is created with EnsureCreatedAsync. With the method AddMenuCardAsync, a card containing multiple menu items is created, added to the context, and saved (code file Cosmos/Runner.cs):

```
public async Task CreateDatabaseAsync()
{
  await _menusContext.Database.EnsureCreatedAsync();
}

public async Task AddMenuCardAsync()
{
  Console.WriteLine(nameof(AddMenuCardAsync));
  MenuCard soupCard = new("Soups", _restaurantId);

  MenuItem[] soups = new MenuItem[]
  {
    new("Consommé Célestine (with shredded pancake)")
    {
      Price = 4.8m
    },
```

```
        new("Baked Potato Soup")
        {
          Price = 4.8m
        },
        new("Cheddar Broccoli Soup")
        {
          Price = 4.8m
        }
    };

    foreach (var soup in soups)
    {
      soupCard.MenuItems.Add(soup);
    }

    _menusContext.MenuCards.Add(soupCard);

    int records = await _menusContext.SaveChangesAsync();
    Console.WriteLine($"{records} added");
    Console.WriteLine();
}
```

Looking into the storage explorer of the Azure Cosmos DB, you can see additional data that's added by the provider and the database. A `Discriminator` is added that contains the name of the class used. Remember, a container can have different types stored. The discriminator is used with queries. If a discriminator is not supplied with the object model, a shadow property is created automatically. With Cosmos DB, an identifier, which consists of the type and the key value, is created as well. Timestamp and entity tag (ETag) can be used for conflict handling; these can be accessed via shadow properties. Because of the `OwnsMany` model definition, the menu items are stored within the menu card:

```
{
    "MenuCardId": "bbe03556-4211-4694-ab73-6ba4af524d40",
    "Discriminator": "MenuCard",
    "IsActive": true,
    "RestaurantId": "FDCD4390-48AD-42F1-AC6A-596F56731795",
    "Title": "Soups",
    "id": "MenuCard|bbe03556-4211-4694-ab73-6ba4af524d40",
    "MenuItems": [
      {
        "MenuItemId": "bc6dabc3-6825-41a1-b45e-6c55a3ab0ada",
        "Price": 4.8,
        "Text": "Consommé Célestine (with shredded pancake)"
      },
      {
        "MenuItemId": "b46b5cca-1b40-4fdf-9fca-84bbf8461f7e",
        "Price": 4.8,
        "Text": "Baked Potato Soup"
      },
      {
        "MenuItemId": "6083da30-c405-4bb8-8f57-8f5c32b496da",
        "Price": 4.8,
        "Text": "Cheddar Broccoli Soup"
      }
    ],
    "_rid": "S+t-ALEbVnkBAAAAAAAAAA==",
```

```
  "_self": "dbs/S+t-AA==/colls/S+t-ALEbVnk=/docs/S+t-ALEbVnkBAAAAAAAAAA==/",
  "_etag": "\"af009326-0000-0d00-0000-6039f6180000\"",
  "_attachments": "attachments/",
  "_ts": 1614411288
}
```

The method `ShowCardsAsync` creates a query to retrieve the active documents with a title named `Soups` and includes the partition key with the query (code file `Cosmos/Runner.cs`):

```
public async Task ShowCardsAsync()
{
  var cards = await _menusContext.MenuCards
    .Where(c => c.IsActive)
    .Where(c => c.Title == "Soups")
    .WithPartitionKey(_restaurantId)
    .ToListAsync();
  foreach (var card in cards)
  {
    Console.WriteLine(card.Title);
    foreach (var menuItem in card.MenuItems)
    {
      Console.WriteLine(menuItem.Text);
    }
  }
}
```

The generated query adds the discriminator:

```
SELECT c
  FROM root c
  WHERE (((c["Discriminator"] = "MenuCard") AND c["IsActive"]) AND (c["Title"] = "Soups"))
```

As you've seen, there are similarities and important differences when using a NoSQL database and a relational database with EF Core. A couple of other differences you need to be aware of are that you can't create complex queries to access Azure Cosmos DB, and aggregate operators are not supported from this EF Core provider. Making counts is an expensive operation. To allow paging across the data with a NoSQL database, many applications just offer prev/next buttons, but don't give details on how many pages are available (at least not with exact values).

SUMMARY

This chapter introduced you to the rich features of the EF Core. You've learned how the `DbContext` keeps knowledge about entities retrieved and updated and how changes can be written to the database. You've also seen how migrations can be used to create and change the database schema from C# code. In terms of defining the schema, you've seen how the database mapping can be done using data annotations, and you've also seen the Fluent API that offers more features compared to the annotations and conventions.

You've seen possibilities for reacting to conflicts when multiple users work on the same record, as well as using transactions implicitly or explicitly for more transactional control.

This chapter also covered great features of EF Core, such as compiled queries, global query filters, table splitting, owned entities, many-to-many relations, and how to use a NoSQL database with EF Core.

The next chapter gets into globalization and localization features of .NET, using culture-specific date, time, and number formats, as well as resources to define text for different languages.

22

Localization

WHAT'S IN THIS CHAPTER?

➤   Formatting numbers and dates

➤   Using resources for localized content

➤   Localizing ASP.NET Core Web Applications

➤   Localizing WinUI apps

CODE DOWNLOADS FOR THIS CHAPTER

The source code for this chapter is available on the book page at www.wiley.com. Click the Downloads link. The code can also be found at https://github.com/ProfessionalCSharp/ProfessionalCSharp2021 in the directory 2_Libs/Localization.

The code for this chapter is divided into the following major examples:

➤   NumberAndDateFormatting

➤   SortingDemo

➤   CreateResource

➤   WinUICultureDemo

➤   ResourcesDemo

➤   ASPNETCoreLocalization

➤   WinUILocalization

Samples from this chapter mainly use the namespaces System.Globalization and System.Resources. All the sample projects have *nullable reference types* enabled.

GLOBAL MARKETS

NASA's Mars Climate Orbiter was lost on September 23, 1999, at a cost of $125 million, because one engineering team used metric units, whereas another used inches for the same key spacecraft operation. When writing applications for international distribution, different cultures and regions must be kept in mind.

Different cultures have diverging calendars and use different number and date formats, and sorting strings may lead to unexpected results because the order of A to Z is defined differently based on the culture. To make usable applications for global markets, you must globalize and localize them.

This chapter covers the globalization and localization of .NET applications. *Globalization* relates to internationalizing applications: preparing applications for international markets. With globalization, the application supports number and date formats that vary according to culture, calendars, and so on. *Localization* is about translating applications for specific cultures. For translations of strings, you can use resources such as .NET resources or WPF resource dictionaries.

.NET supports globalization and localization. To globalize an application, you can use classes from the namespace System.Globalization; to localize an application, you can use resources supported by the namespace System.Resources.

NAMESPACE SYSTEM.GLOBALIZATION

The System.Globalization namespace holds all the culture and region classes necessary to support different date formats, different number formats, and even different calendars that are represented in classes such as GregorianCalendar, HebrewCalendar, JapaneseCalendar, and so on. By using these classes, you can display different representations according to the user's locale.

This section looks at the following issues and considerations when using the System.Globalization namespace:

➤ Unicode issues

➤ Cultures and regions

➤ An example showing all cultures and their characteristics

➤ Sorting

Unicode Issues

A Unicode character has 16 bits, so there is room for 65,536 characters. Is this enough for all languages currently used in information technology? In the case of the Chinese language, for example, more than 80,000 characters are needed. Fortunately, Unicode has been designed to deal with this issue. With Unicode, you must differentiate between base characters and combining characters. You can add multiple combining characters to a base character to build a single display character or a text element.

Take, for example, the Icelandic character Ogonek. Ogonek can be created by using the base character 0x006F (Latin small letter o) and the combining characters 0x0328 (combining Ogonek) and 0x0304 (combining Macron), as shown in Figure 22-1. Combining characters are defined within ranges from 0x0300 to 0x0345. For American and European markets, predefined characters exist to facilitate dealing with special characters. The character Ogonek is also defined by the predefined character 0x01ED.

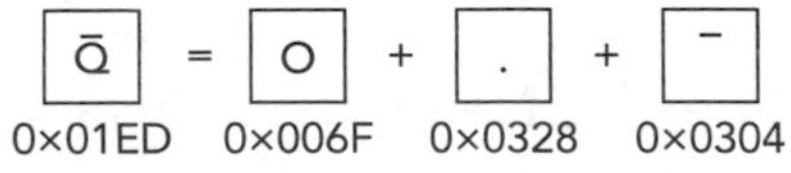

FIGURE 22-1

For Asian markets, where more than 80,000 characters are necessary for Chinese alone, such predefined characters do not exist. In Asian languages, you always have to deal with combining characters. The problem is getting the right number of display characters or text elements and getting to the base characters instead of the combined characters. The namespace `System.Globalization` offers the class `StringInfo`, which you can use to deal with this issue.

The following table lists the static methods of the class `StringInfo` that help in dealing with combined characters:

METHOD	DESCRIPTION
GetNextTextElement	Returns the first text element (base character and all combining characters) of a specified string
GetTextElementEnumerator	Returns a `TextElementEnumerator` object that allows iterating all text elements of a string
ParseCombiningCharacters	Returns an integer array referencing all base characters of a string

> **NOTE** *A single display character can contain multiple Unicode characters. To address this issue, when you write applications that support international markets, don't use the data type* `char`; *use* `string` *instead. A* `string` *can hold a text element that contains both base characters and combining characters, whereas a* `char` *cannot.*

Cultures and Regions

The world is divided into multiple cultures and regions, and applications must be aware of these cultural and regional differences. A culture is a set of preferences based on a user's language and cultural habits. RFC 4646 (http://www.ietf.org/rfc/rfc4646.txt) defines culture names that are used worldwide, depending on a language and a country or region. Some examples are en-AU, en-CA, en-GB, and en-US for the English language in Australia, Canada, the United Kingdom, and the United States, respectively.

Possibly the most important class in the `System.Globalization` namespace is `CultureInfo`. `CultureInfo` represents a culture and defines calendars, formatting of numbers and dates, and sorting strings used with the culture.

The class `RegionInfo` represents regional settings (such as the currency) and indicates whether the region uses the metric system. Some regions can use multiple languages. One example is the region of Spain, which has Basque (eu-ES), Catalan (ca-ES), Spanish (es-ES), and Galician (gl-ES) cultures. Just as one region can have multiple languages, one language can be spoken in different regions; for example, Spanish is spoken in Mexico, Spain, Guatemala, Argentina, and Peru, to name only a few countries.

Later in this chapter a sample application demonstrates these characteristics of cultures and regions.

Specific, Neutral, and Invariant Cultures

When using cultures with .NET, you must differentiate between three types: specific, neutral, and invariant cultures. A *specific culture* is associated with a real, existing culture defined with RFC 4646, as described in the preceding section. A specific culture can be mapped to a neutral culture. For example, de is the neutral culture of the specific cultures de-AT, de-DE, de-CH, and others. de is shorthand for the German language (Deutsch); AT, DE, and CH are shorthand for the countries Austria, Germany, and Switzerland, respectively.

When translating applications, it is typically not necessary to do translations for every region; not much difference exists between the German language in the countries Austria and Germany. Instead of using specific cultures, you can use a *neutral culture* to localize applications.

The *invariant culture* is independent of a real culture. When storing formatted numbers or dates in files or sending them across a network to a server, using a culture that is independent of any user settings is the best option.

Figure 22-2 shows how the culture types relate to each other.

Current Culture and Current UI Culture

When you set cultures, you need to differentiate between a culture for the user interface and a culture for the number and date formats. Cultures are associated with a thread, and with these two culture types, you can apply two culture settings to a thread. The CultureInfo class has the static properties CurrentCulture and CurrentUICulture. The property CurrentCulture is for setting the culture that is used with formatting and sort options, whereas the property CurrentUICulture is used for the language of the user interface.

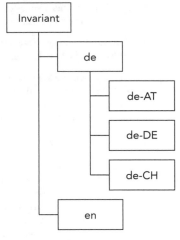

FIGURE 22-2

On Windows, the configured culture is used as the default culture of the running thread. On Linux, culture information comes from the ICU library (http://site.icu-project.org/), which is installed on Linux distributions. Be aware that not all Linux distributions have this library available. For example, an advantage of Alpine Linux is that it's very small, and the ICU is not installed by default. To deal with such issues, .NET implements the *Global Invariant Mode*. With this mode (which is enabled on Alpine Linux), all the cultures behave like the invariant culture. You can enable the invariant mode with a configuration in the project file:

```
<ItemGroup>
  <RuntimeHostConfigurationOption Include="System.Globalization.Invariant" Value="true"/>
</ItemGroup>
```

or by setting the environment variable DOTNET_SYSTEM_GLOBALIZATION_INVARIANT to true.

In many cases, you won't need to change the current culture; you can just use the culture configured from the user. In cases where you need to change the culture, you can easily do this programmatically by changing both cultures to, say, the Spanish culture, as shown in this code snippet (using the namespace System .Globalization):

```
CultureInfo ci = new("es-ES");
CultureInfo.CurrentCulture = ci;
CultureInfo.CurrentUICulture = ci;
```

Now that you know how to set the culture, the following sections discuss number and date formatting, which are influenced by the CurrentCulture setting.

Number Formatting

The number structures Int16, Int32, Int64, and so on, in the System namespace have an overloaded ToString method. You can use this method to create a different representation of the number, depending on the locale. For the Int32 structure, ToString is overloaded to pass a format string and an object implementing IFormatProvider.

The string specifies the format of the representation. The format can be a standard numeric formatting string or a picture numeric formatting string. For standard numeric formatting, strings are predefined where C specifies the currency notation, D creates a decimal output, E creates scientific output, F creates fixed-point output, G creates general output, N creates number output, and X creates hexadecimal output. With a picture numeric formatting string, it is possible to specify the number of digits, section and group separators, percent notation, and so on. The picture numeric format string ###,### means two three-digit blocks separated by a group separator.

The IFormatProvider interface is implemented by the NumberFormatInfo, DateTimeFormatInfo, and CultureInfo classes. This interface defines a single method, GetFormat, that returns a format object.

You can use NumberFormatInfo to define custom formats for numbers. With the default constructor of NumberFormatInfo, a culture-independent or invariant object is created. In using the properties of NumberFormatInfo, it is possible to change all the formatting options, such as a positive sign, a percent symbol, a number group separator, a currency symbol, and a lot more. A read-only, culture-independent NumberFormatInfo object is returned from the static property InvariantInfo. A NumberFormatInfo object in which the format values are based on the CultureInfo of the current thread is returned from the static property CurrentInfo.

To create the next example, you can start with a console application project. In this code, the first example shows a number displayed in the format of the current culture (here: U.S. English, the setting of the operating system). The second example uses the ToString method with the IFormatProvider argument. CultureInfo implements IFormatProvider, so create a CultureInfo object using the French culture. The third example changes the current culture. The culture is changed to German by using the property CurrentCulture of the CultureInfo instance (code file NumberAndDateFormatting\Program.cs):

```
void NumberFormatDemo()
{
    int val = 1234567890;

    // culture of the current thread
    string output = val.ToString("N");
    Console.WriteLine($"Current thread culture: {CultureInfo.CurrentCulture}: {output}");

    // use IFormatProvider
    output = val.ToString("N", new CultureInfo("fr-FR"));
    Console.WriteLine($"IFormatProvider with fr-FR culture {output}");

    // change the culture of the thread
    CultureInfo.CurrentCulture = new("de-DE");
    output = val.ToString("N");
    Console.WriteLine($"Changed culture of the thread to de-DE: {output}");
}
```

You can compare the following different output for U.S. English, French, and German, respectively, shown here:

```
Current thread culture: en-US: 1,234,567,890.00
IFormatProvider with fr-FR culture 1 234 567 890,000
Changed culture of the thread to de-DE: 1.234.567.890,000
```

Date Formatting

The same support for numbers is available for dates. With the string argument of the ToString method, you can specify a predefined format character or a custom format string for converting the date to a string. The class DateTimeFormatInfo specifies the possible values. With DateTimeFormatInfo, the case of the format strings has a different meaning. D defines a long date format; d defines a short date format. Other examples of possible formats are ddd for the abbreviated day of the week, dddd for the full day of the week, yyyy for the year, T for a long time, and t for a short time. With the IFormatProvider argument, you can specify the culture. Using an overloaded method without the `IFormatProvider` argument implies that the current culture is used (code file `NumberAndDateFormatting/Program.cs`):

```
void DateFormatDemo()
{
  DateTime d = new(2024, 09, 17);

  // current culture
  string output = d.ToString("D");
  Console.WriteLine($"Current thread culture: {CultureInfo.CurrentCulture}: {output}");

  // use IFormatProvider
  output = d.ToString("D", new CultureInfo("fr-FR"));
  Console.WriteLine($"IFormatProvider with fr-FR culture: {output}");

  CultureInfo.CurrentCulture = new("es-ES");
  output = d.ToString("D");
  Console.WriteLine($"Changed culture of the thread {CultureInfo.CurrentCulture}:"+
    $"{output}");
}
```

The output of this example program shows `ToLongDateString` with the current culture of the thread, a French version where a `CultureInfo` instance is passed to the `ToString` method, and a Spanish version where the `CurrentCulture` property of the thread is changed to es-ES:

```
Current thread culture: de-DE: Dienstag, 17. September 2024
IFormatProvider with fr-FR culture: mardi 17 septembre 2024
Changed culture of the thread es-ES: martes, 17 de septiembre de 2024
```

Cultures in Action

To see all cultures in action, you can use a sample WinUI app that lists all cultures and demonstrates different characteristics of culture properties. On the left side of the UI, a tree view is used to display all the cultures. On the right side is a user control that displays relevant information about the selected culture and region.

During initialization of the application, all available cultures are added to the `TreeView` control that is placed on the left side of the application. This initialization happens in a view model in the method `SetupCultures`, which is called in the constructor of the `CulturesViewModel` class (code file `WinUICultureDemo/CulturesViewModel.cs`):

```
public CulturesViewModel() => SetupCultures();
```

For the data that is shown in the user interface, the custom class `CultureData` is created. This class can be bound to a `TreeView` control because it has a property `SubCultures` that contains a list of `CultureData`. Therefore, the `TreeView` control enables walking through this tree. Other than the subcultures, `CultureData` contains the `CultureInfo` type and sample values for a number, a date, and a time. The number returns a string in the number format for the specific culture, and the date and time return strings in the specific culture formats as well. `CultureData` contains a `RegionInfo` class to display regions. With some neutral cultures (for example, English), creating a `RegionInfo` throws an exception because there are regions only with specific cultures. However, with other neutral cultures (for example, German), creating a `RegionInfo` succeeds and is mapped to a default region. The exception thrown here is handled (code file `WinUICultureDemo/CultureData.cs`):

```
public record CultureData(CultureInfo CultureInfo)
{
  public IList<CultureData> SubCultures { get; } = new List<CultureData>();
```

```
      double numberSample = 9876543.21;
      public string NumberSample => numberSample.ToString("N", CultureInfo);
      public string DateSample => DateTime.Today.ToString("D", CultureInfo);
      public string TimeSample => DateTime.Now.ToString("T", CultureInfo);

      private RegionInfo? _regionInfo;
      public RegionInfo? RegionInfo
      {
        get
        {
          try
          {
            return _regionInfo ??= new RegionInfo(CultureInfo.Name);
          }
          catch (ArgumentException)
          {
            // with some neutral cultures regions are not available
            return null;
          }
          return ri;
        }
      }
    }
```

In the method `SetupCultures`, you get all cultures from the static method `CultureInfo.GetCultures`. Passing `CultureTypes.AllCultures` to this method returns an unsorted array of all available cultures. The result is sorted by the name of the culture. With the result of the sorted cultures, a collection of `CultureData` objects is created, and the `CultureInfo` and `SubCultures` properties are assigned. With the result of this, a dictionary is created to enable fast access to the culture name.

For the data that should be shown in the UI, a list of `CultureData` objects is created that contains all the root cultures for the tree view after the `foreach` statement is completed. Root cultures can be verified to determine whether they have the invariant culture as their parent. The invariant culture has the locale identifier (LCID) `0x7f`. Every culture has a unique identifier that can be used for a fast verification. In the code snippet, root cultures are added to the `rootCultures` collection within the block of the `if` statement. If a culture has the invariant culture as its parent, it is a root culture.

If the culture does not have a parent culture, it is added to the root nodes of the tree. To find parent cultures, all cultures are remembered inside a dictionary. (See Chapter 8, "Collections," for more information about dictionaries.) If the culture iterated is not a root culture, it is added to the `SubCultures` collection of the parent culture. The parent culture can be quickly found by using the dictionary. In the last step, the root cultures are made available to the UI by assigning them to the `RootCultures` property (code file `WinUICultureDemo/CulturesViewModel.cs`):

```
    private void SetupCultures()
    {
      var cultureDataDict = CultureInfo.GetCultures(CultureTypes.AllCultures)
        .OrderBy(c => c.Name)
        .Select(c => new CultureData(c))
        .ToDictionary(c => c.CultureInfo.Name);

      List<CultureData> rootCultures = new();
      foreach (var cd in cultureDataDict.Values)
      {
        if (cd.CultureInfo.Parent.LCID == 0x7f)  // check for invariant culture
```

```
          {
            rootCultures.Add(cd);
          }
          else // add to parent culture
          {
            if (cultureDataDict.TryGetValue(cd.CultureInfo.Parent.Name,
              out CultureData? parentCultureData))
            {
              parentCultureData.SubCultures.Add(cd);
              continue;
            }

            // with the latest culture updates, some cultures don't have the
            // direct parent name in the list, take the next parent
            string parent = cd.CultureInfo.Parent.Name;
            int index = parent.IndexOf("-");
            if (index < 0)
            {
              // just add this culture to the root cultures
              rootCultures.Add(cd);
              continue;
            }
            string grandParent = parent[..index];
            if (cultureDataDict.TryGetValue(grandParent,
              out CultureData? grandParentCultureData))
            {
              grandParentCultureData.SubCultures.Add(cd);
            }
            else // parent also not found to the root cultures, add it directly
            {
              rootCultures.Add(cd);
            }
          }
        }

        foreach (var rootCulture in rootCultures.OrderBy(cd => cd.CultureInfo.EnglishName))
        {
          RootCultures.Add(rootCulture);
        }
      }

      public IList<CultureData> RootCultures { get; } = new List<CultureData>();
```

Now let's get into the XAML code for the display. A `TreeView` is used to display all the cultures. For the display of items inside the `TreeView`, an item template is used. This template uses a `TextBlock` that is bound to the `EnglishName` property of the `CultureInfo` class (code file `WinUICultureDemo/MainWindow.xaml`):

```xml
<TreeView x:Name="treeView1"
  Style="{StaticResource TreeViewStyle1}"
  ItemInvoked="{x:Bind OnSelectionChanged, Mode=OneTime}"
  SelectionMode="Single">
</TreeView>
```

In the code-behind file, the `TreeView` is initialized by accessing the `CultureData` objects from the view model. Using the `CultureData` objects, `TreeNode` objects are created for the `TreeView`. The `TreeNode` class defines a

`Data` property where the `CultureData` object is assigned. The `Add` method of the `TreeNode` allows adding child objects. Child objects are added by recursively invoking the local function `AddSubNodes` (code file `WinUICultureDemo/MainWindow.xaml.cs`):

```
private void OnActivated(object sender, WindowActivatedEventArgs args)
{
    void AddSubNodes(TreeViewNode parent)
    {
        if (parent.Content is CultureData cd && cd.SubCultures is not null)
        {
            foreach (var culture in cd.SubCultures)
            {
                TreeViewNode node = new()
                {
                    Content = culture
                };
                parent.Children.Add(node);

                foreach (var subCulture in culture.SubCultures)
                {
                    AddSubNodes(node);
                }
            }
        }
    }

    var rootNodes = ViewModel.RootCultures.Select(cd => new TreeViewNode
    {
        Content = cd
    });

    foreach (var node in rootNodes)
    {
        treeView1.RootNodes.Add(node);
        AddSubNodes(node);
    }
}
```

When the user selects a node inside the tree, the handler of the `SelectedItemChanged` event of the `TreeView` is called. In the following code snippet, the handler is implemented in the method `OnSelectionChanged`. With the implementation, the `SelectedCulture` property of the associated `ViewModel` is set to the selected `CultureData` object (code file `WinUICultureDemo/MainWindow.xaml.cs`):

```
private void OnSelectionChanged(TreeView sender, TreeViewItemInvokedEventArgs args)
{
    if (args.InvokedItem is TreeViewNode node && node.Content is CultureData cd)
    {
        ViewModel.SelectedCulture = cd;
    }
}
```

To display the values of the selected item, you use several `TextBlock` controls. These bind to the `CultureInfo` property of the `CultureData` class and in turn to properties of the `CultureInfo` type that is returned from `CultureInfo`, such as `Name`, `IsNeutralCulture`, `EnglishName`, `NativeName`, and so on. To convert a Boolean value, as returned from the `IsNeutralCulture` property, to a `Visibility` enumeration value, and to display calendar names, you use converters (XAML file `WinUICultureDemo/CultureDetailUC.xaml`):

```xml
<TextBlock Grid.Row="0" Grid.Column="0" Text="Culture Name:"/>
<TextBlock Grid.Row="0" Grid.Column="1"
  Text="{x:Bind CultureData.CultureInfo.Name, Mode=OneWay}"
  Width="100"/>
<TextBlock Grid.Row="0" Grid.Column="2" Text="Neutral Culture"
  Visibility="{x:Bind CultureData.CultureInfo.IsNeutralCulture, Mode=OneWay}"/>

<TextBlock Grid.Row="1" Grid.Column="0" Text="English Name:"/>
<TextBlock Grid.Row="1" Grid.Column="1" Grid.ColumnSpan="2"
  Text="{x:Bind CultureData.CultureInfo.EnglishName, Mode=OneWay}"/>

<TextBlock Grid.Row="2" Grid.Column="0" Text="Native Name:"/>
<TextBlock Grid.Row="2" Grid.Column="1" Grid.ColumnSpan="2"
  Text="{x:Bind CultureData.CultureInfo.NativeName}"/>

<TextBlock Grid.Row="3" Grid.Column="0" Text="Default Calendar:"/>
<TextBlock Grid.Row="3" Grid.Column="1" Grid.ColumnSpan="2"
  Text="{x:Bind CultureData.CultureInfo.Calendar, Mode=OneWay
  Converter={StaticResource calendarConverter}}"/>

<TextBlock Grid.Row="4" Grid.Column="0" Text="Optional Calendars:"/>
<ListBox Grid.Row="4" Grid.Column="1" Grid.ColumnSpan="2"
  ItemsSource="{x:Bind CultureData.CultureInfo.OptionalCalendars}">
  <ListBox.ItemTemplate>
    <DataTemplate>
      <TextBlock Text="{Binding
        Converter={StaticResource calendarConverter}}"/>
    </DataTemplate>
  </ListBox.ItemTemplate>
</ListBox>
```

To display the calendar text, you use an object that implements `IValueConverter`. Here is the implementation of the `Convert` method in the class `CalendarTypeToCalendarInformationConverter`. The implementation uses the class name and calendar type name to return a useful value for the calendar (code file `WinUICultureDemo/Converters/CalendarTypeToCalendarInformationConverter.cs`):

```csharp
public object? Convert(object? value, Type targetType, object? parameter,
  string? language)
{
  if (value is Calendar cal)
  {
    StringBuilder calText = new(50);
    calText.Append(cal.ToString());
    calText.Remove(0, 21);
    calText.Replace("Calendar", "");
    if (cal is GregorianCalendar gregCal)
    {
      calText.Append($" {gregCal.CalendarType}");
    }
    return calText.ToString();
  }
```

```
      else
      {
        return null;
      }
    }
```

The `CultureData` class contains properties to display sample information for number, date, and time formats. These properties are bound with the following `TextBlock` elements (XAML file `WinUICultureDemo/ CultureDetailUC.xaml`):

```
<TextBlock Grid.Row="0" Grid.Column="0" Text="Number"/>
<TextBlock Grid.Row="0" Grid.Column="1"
  Text="{x:Bind CultureData.NumberSample, Mode=OneWay}"/>
<TextBlock Grid.Row="1" Grid.Column="0" Text="Full Date"/>
<TextBlock Grid.Row="1" Grid.Column="1"
  Text="{x:Bind CultureData.DateSample, Mode=OneWay}"/>
<TextBlock Grid.Row="2" Grid.Column="0" Text="Time"/>
<TextBlock Grid.Row="2" Grid.Column="1"
  Text="{x:Bind CultureData.TimeSample, Mode=OneWay}"/>
```

The information about the region is shown with the last part of the XAML code. The complete area is hidden if the `RegionInfo` is not available. The `TextBlock` elements bind the `DisplayName`, `CurrencySymbol`, `ISOCurrencySymbol`, and `IsMetric` properties of the `RegionInfo` type:

```
<Grid Grid.Row="6" Grid.Column="0" Grid.ColumnSpan="3"
  Visibility="{x:Bind CultureData.RegionInfo, Mode=OneWay,
  Converter={StaticResource NullConverter}}">
  <!-- ... -->
  <TextBlock Grid.Row="0" Grid.Column="0" Text="Region Information"
    Style="{StaticResource SubheaderTextBlockStyle}"/>
  <TextBlock Grid.Row="0" Grid.Column="1" Grid.ColumnSpan="2"
    Text="{x:Bind CultureData.RegionInfo.DisplayName, Mode=OneWay}"/>

  <TextBlock Grid.Row="1" Grid.Column="0" Text="Currency"/>
  <TextBlock Grid.Row="1" Grid.Column="1"
    Text="{x:Bind CultureData.RegionInfo.CurrencySymbol, Mode=OneWay}"/>

  <TextBlock Grid.Row="1" Grid.Column="2"
    Text="{x:Bind CultureData.RegionInfo.ISOCurrencySymbol, Mode=OneWay}"/>

  <TextBlock Grid.Row="2" Grid.Column="1" Text="Is Metric"
    Visibility="{x:Bind CultureData.RegionInfo.IsMetric, Mode=OneWay}"/>
</Grid>
```

When you start the application, you can see all available cultures in the tree view, and selecting a culture lists its characteristics, as shown in Figure 22-3.

Sorting

Sorting strings varies according to the culture. With the Finnish language, some vowels with an accent are sorted after Z, whereas in many other countries accented vowels come right after nonaccented vowels. With Asian languages, sort order rules are based on phonetics, radical orders, and number of pen strokes. With an application, you might need to sort for a user or independent of a user to have sorted results on a server.

By default, sorting with .NET is culture-specific, but you can specify to do a culture-invariant sort.

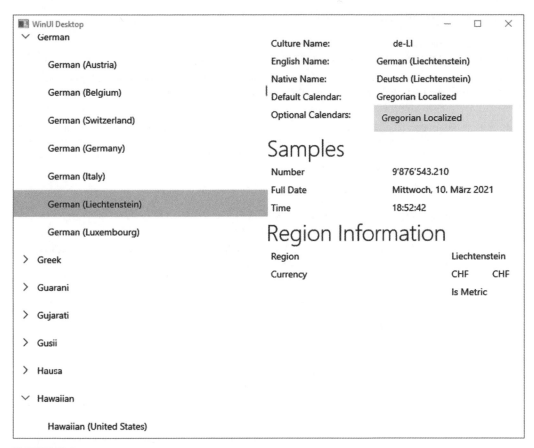

FIGURE 22-3

Let's get into a sample application to sort strings based on a specific culture and with an invariant culture.

The method `DisplayNames` shown here is used to display all elements of an array or a collection on the console (code file `SortingDemo/Program.cs`):

```
void DisplayNames(string title, IEnumerable<string> names)
{
  Console.WriteLine(title);
  Console.WriteLine(string.Join("-", names));
  Console.WriteLine();
}
```

In the `Main` method, after creating the array with countries from the European Union with native country names, the `CultureInfo.CurrentCulture` property is set to the Finnish culture so that the following `Array.Sort` uses the Finnish sort order. Calling the method `DisplayNames` displays all the countries on the console:

```
string[] countries = { "Österreich", "België", "България", "Hrvatska", "Česko",
    "Danmark", "Eesti", "Suomi", "France", "Deutschland", "Ελλάδα",
    "Magyarország", "Ireland", "Italia", "Latvija", "Lietuva", "Lëtzebuerg",
    "Malta", "Nederland", "Polska", "Portugal", "România", "Slovensko",
    "Slovenija", "España", "Sverige" };
```

```
CultureInfo.CurrentCulture = new CultureInfo("fi-FI");

Array.Sort(countries);
DisplayNames("Sorted using the Finnish culture", countries);
```

After the first display of the countries in the Finnish sort order, the array is sorted once again. If you want a sort that is independent of the users' culture, which would be useful when the sorted array is sent to a server or stored somewhere, you can use the invariant culture.

You can do this by passing a second argument to `Array.Sort`. The `Sort` method expects an object implementing `IComparer` with the second argument. The `Comparer` class from the `System.Collections` namespace implements `IComparer`. `Comparer.DefaultInvariant` returns a `Comparer` object that uses the invariant culture for comparing the array values for a culture-independent sort:

```
// sort using the invariant culture

Array.Sort(countries, Comparer.DefaultInvariant);
DisplayNames("Sorted using the invariant culture", countries);
```

The program output shows different sort results with the Finnish and culture-independent cultures—Österreich is positioned after Sverige with the Finnish culture and after Nederland with the invariant culture:

```
Sorted using the Finnish culture
België-Česko-Danmark-Deutschland-Eesti-España-France-Hrvatska-Ireland-Italia-Latvija-
Lëtzebuerg-Lietuva-Magyarország-Malta-Nederland-Polska-Portugal-România-Slovenija-
Slovensko-Suomi-Sverige-Österreich-Ελλάδα-България

Sorted using the invariant culture
België-Česko-Danmark-Deutschland-Eesti-España-France-Hrvatska-Ireland-Italia-Latvija-
Lëtzebuerg-Lietuva-Magyarország-Malta-Nederland-Österreich-Polska-Portugal-România-
Slovenija-Slovensko-Suomi-Sverige-Ελλάδα-България
```

> **NOTE** *If sorting a collection should be independent of a culture, the collection must be sorted with the invariant culture. This can be particularly useful when sending the sort result to a server or storing it inside a file. To display a sorted collection to the user, it's best to sort it with the user's culture.*

In addition to a locale-dependent formatting and measurement system, text and colors may differ depending on the culture. This is where resources come into play.

RESOURCES

You can put resources such as pictures or string tables into resource files or assemblies. Such resources can be very helpful when localizing applications, and .NET has built-in support to search for localized resources. A *satellite assembly* is an assembly that just contains localized resources. With an application, you can add multiple satellite assemblies for all the different languages supported by the application.

Resource files can be simple text-based files (which only support strings for the resources), binary files, or XML files. XML resource files usually have the `.resx` file extension. With WinUI and UWP applications, the `.resw` file extension is used with the same XML syntax.

Before you see how to use resources to localize applications, the following sections explain how you can create and read resources without looking at language aspects.

Resource Readers and Writers

`ResourceWriter` (from the `System.Resources` namespace) enables you to create binary resource files. The constructor of the writer requires a `Stream` that is created using the `File` class. You add resources by using the `AddResource` method (code file `CreateResource/Program.cs`):

```
private const string ResourceFile = "Demo.resources";
public static void CreateResource()
{
  FileStream stream = File.OpenWrite(ResourceFile);
  using var writer = new ResourceWriter(stream);
  writer.AddResource("Title", "Professional C#");
  writer.AddResource("Author", "Christian Nagel");
  writer.AddResource("Publisher", "Wrox Press");
}
```

To read the resources of a binary resource file, you can use `ResourceReader`. The `GetEnumerator` method of the reader returns an `IDictionaryEnumerator` that is used within the following `foreach` statement to access the key and value of the resource:

```
public static void ReadResource()
{
  FileStream stream = File.OpenRead(ResourceFile);
  using (var reader = new ResourceReader(stream))
  {
    foreach (DictionaryEntry resource in reader)
    {
      Console.WriteLine($"{resource.Key} {resource.Value}");
    }
  }
}
```

Running the application returns the keys and values that have been written to the binary resource file. To create XML-based `.resx` files, you can use the `ResXResourceWriter` class in the `System.Resources` namespace. At the time of this writing, this class is defined in the `System.Windows.Forms` assembly. The `.resw` files with UWP applications are based on `System.Windows.Forms` as well. The tool to convert resource files (`resgen`) is part of the .NET Framework SDK on the Windows platform. To solve some of the issues here, `msbuild` has built-in support to work with resource files on all platforms.

Using Resource Files with ResourceManager

With the default SDK definitions for project files, resource files are embedded in the assembly. You can customize this—for example, you can remove resources from the assembly by adding an `EmbeddedResource` element with the `Remove` attribute to an `ItemGroup` in the project file as shown:

```
<ItemGroup>
  <EmbeddedResource Remove="Resources\Messages.de.resx"/>
</ItemGroup>
```

The sample application uses embedded resources. To see how resource files can be loaded with the `ResourceManager` class, create a console application and name it `ResourcesDemo`.

Create a `Resources` folder and add a `Messages.resx` file to this folder. The `Messages.resx` file is filled with a key and value for U.S. English content—for example, the key `GoodMorning` and the value `Good Morning!`.

This will be the default language. You can add other language resource files with the naming convention to add the culture to the resource file, for example, `Messages.de.resx` for German languages. Translations that are different for regional languages—for example, languages for Switzerland—can be added to `Messages.de-CH.resx`. "Good Morning" translates to German "Guten Morgen" and to Swiss-German "Guata Morga."

The XML content of the file contains `data` elements with `name` attributes and `value` child elements (XML file `ResourcesDemo/Resources/Messages.resx`):

```
<data name="GoodMorning" xml:space="preserve">
  <value>Good Morning!</value>
</data>
```

When you add XML resource files to the project using a .NET SDK, by default, resource files are built using Embedded Resource. This adds the resource to the assembly. With localized versions of these files, after the build, you'll find subdirectories for the different languages—for example, `de` and `de-CH`. These subdirectories contain satellite assemblies. Satellite assemblies are assemblies that contain only binary resources and do not contain code. Depending on the culture setting for the user, resources from the satellite assemblies are retrieved.

To access the embedded resource, use the `ResourceManager` class from the `System.Resources` namespace. When you're instantiating the `ResourceManager`, one overload of the constructor needs the name of the resource and the assembly. The namespace of the application is `ResourcesDemo`; the resource file is in the folder `Resources`, which defines the subnamespace `Resources`, and it has the name `Messages.resx`. This defines the name `ResourcesDemo.Resources.Messages`. You can retrieve the assembly of the resource using the `GetTypeInfo` method of the `Program` type, which defines an `Assembly` property. When using resources from the current assembly, you also can use `Assembly.GetExecutingAssembly` to retrieve the current assembly. Using the resources instance, the `GetString` method returns the value of the key passed from the resource file. Passing a culture such as `de-CH` for the second argument looks for resources in the `de-CH` satellite assembly. If it's not found there, the neutral language for `de` is taken, the `de` resource file. If it's not found there, the default resource file without culture naming succeeds to return the value (code file `ResourcesDemo/Program.cs`):

```
ResourceManager resources = new("ResourcesDemo.Resources.Messages",
  typeof(Program).GetTypeInfo().Assembly);
string goodMorning = resources.GetString("GoodMorning", new CultureInfo("de-CH"));
Console.WriteLine(goodMorning);
```

Another overload of the `ResourceManager` constructor just requires the type of the class. This `ResourceManager` looks for a resource file named `Program.resx`:

```
ResourceManager programResources = new(typeof(Program));
Console.WriteLine(programResources.GetString("Resource1"));
```

LOCALIZATION WITH ASP.NET CORE

For localization of ASP.NET Core web applications, you can use the `CultureInfo` class and resources like those already discussed in this chapter, but there are some additional issues that you need to resolve. Setting the culture for the complete application doesn't fulfill usual needs because users are coming from different cultures. So, it's necessary to set the culture with every request to the server.

> **NOTE** *For using localization with ASP.NET Core, you need to know about both cultures and resources that are discussed in this chapter as well as creating ASP.NET Core applications. In case you haven't created ASP.NET Core web applications with .NET before, you should read Chapter 24, "ASP.NET Core," before continuing with this part of the chapter.*

How do you know about the culture of the user? There are different options. The browser sends preferred languages within the HTTP header with every request. This information from the browser can come from browser settings or when the browser itself checks the installed languages. Another option is to define URL parameters or use different domain names for different languages. You can use different domain names in some scenarios, such as www.cninnovation.com for an English version of the site and www.cninnovation.de for a German version. But what about www.cninnovation.ch? This should be offered both in German and French and probably Italian. URL parameters such as www.cninnovation.com/culture=de could help here. Using www.cninnovation.com/de works like the URL parameter by defining a specific route. https://docs .microsoft.com uses language routes such as https://docs.microsoft.com/de-AT. Another option is to allow the user to select the language and define a cookie to remember this option.

All these scenarios are supported out of the box by ASP.NET Core.

Registering Localization Services

To start seeing this in action, create a new ASP.NET Core Web App with Razor Pages. With the .NET CLI, the command is `dotnet new webapp`. The additional namespaces used with the ASP.NET Core sample are `Microsoft.AspNetCore.Localization`, `Microsoft.Extensions.Localization`, and `System .ComponentModel`.

Within the `Startup` class, you need to invoke the `AddLocalization` extension method to register services for localization (code file `ASPNETCoreLocalization/Startup.cs`):

```
public void ConfigureServices(IServiceCollection services)
{
  services.AddLocalization(options => options.ResourcesPath =
    "Resources");
  //...
  services.AddRazorPages();
}
```

The `AddLocalization` method registers services for the interfaces `IStringLocalizerFactory` and `IStringLocalizer`. With the registration code, the type `ResourceManagerStringLocalizerFactory` is registered as a singleton, and `StringLocalizer` is registered with transient lifetime. The class `ResourceManagerStringLocalizerFactory` is a factory for `ResourceManagerStringLocalizer`. This class in turn makes use of the `ResourceManager` class shown earlier for retrieving strings from resource files.

Configuring the Middleware

After localization is configured with the dependency injection container, you can configure localization with the middleware. Middleware functionality is invoked with every HTTP request and is configured in the `Configure` method of the `Startup` class. The `UseRequestLocalization` method defines an overload where you can pass `RequestLocalizationOptions`. Setting the `RequestLocalizationOptions` properties enables you to customize what cultures should be supported and to set the default culture. Here, the `DefaultRequestCulture` is set to en-US. The class `RequestCulture` is just a small wrapper around the culture for formatting—which is accessible via the `Culture` property—and the culture for using the resources (`UICulture` property). The sample code accepts en-US, en, de-AT, and de cultures for SupportedCultures and SupportedUICultures (code file ASPNETCoreLocalization/Startup.cs):

```
public void Configure(IApplicationBuilder app, IWebHostEnvironment env)
{
  //...

  CultureInfo[] supportedCultures = { new("en-US"), new("en"), new("de-AT"),
    new("de") };

  RequestLocalizationOptions localizationOptions = new()
  {
    DefaultRequestCulture = new RequestCulture(new CultureInfo("en-US")),
    SupportedCultures = supportedCultures,
    SupportedUICultures = supportedCultures
  };

  app.UseRequestLocalization(localizationOptions);

  app.UseHttpsRedirection();
  app.UseStaticFiles();

  app.UseRouting();

  app.UseAuthorization();

  app.UseEndpoints(endpoints =>
  {
    endpoints.MapRazorPages();
  });
}
```

With the RequestLocalizationOptions settings, you can configure RequestCultureProviders invoking the method AddInitialRequestCultureProvider and supplying classes that derive from the base class RequestCultureProvider. By default, three providers are configured that probably fulfill your needs: QueryStringRequestCultureProvider, CookieRequestCultureProvider, and AcceptLanguageHeaderRequestCultureProvider.

ASP.NET Core Culture Providers

Let's look at these culture providers in more detail. The QueryStringRequestCultureProvider uses the query string to retrieve the culture. By default, the query parameters culture and ui-culture are used with this provider, as shown with this URL: https://localhost:5001/?culture=de&ui-culture=en-US.

You can also change the query parameters by setting the QueryStringKey and UIQueryStringKey properties of the QueryStringRequestCultureProvider.

The CookieRequestCultureProvider defines the cookie named ASPNET_CULTURE (which can be set using the CookieName property). The values from this cookie are retrieved to set the culture. To create a cookie and send it to the client, you can use the static method MakeCookieValue to create a cookie from a RequestCulture and send it to the client. The CookieRequestCultureProvider uses the static method ParseCookieValue to get a RequestCulture.

With the third option for culture settings, you can use the HTTP header information that is sent by the browser. The HTTP header that is sent looks like this:

```
Accept-Language: en-us, de-at;q=0.8, it;q=0.7
```

The `AcceptLanguageHeaderRequestCultureProvider` uses this information to set the culture. You use up to three language values in the order defined by the quality value to find a first match with the supported cultures.

Using a Culture with ASP.NET Core

In a new Razor page (you can create this with `dotnet new page` or using Visual Studio), the request culture is accessed and used for date formatting. The request culture is automatically set with the current thread, but to get more information about it with ASP.NET Core, you can access the request culture using the `IRequestCultureFeature` contract. The `RequestCultureFeature` that implements the interface `IRequestCultureFeature` uses the first culture provider that matches the culture setting. If a URL defines a query string that matches the culture parameter, the `QueryStringRequestCultureProvider` is used to return the requested culture. If the URL does not match, but a cookie with the name `ASPNET_CULTURE` is received, the `CookieRequestCultureProvider` is used; otherwise, the `AcceptLanguageHeaderRequestCultureProvider` is used. With the following code snippet, the culture information is used to assign the `RequestCulture` property. Then, today's date is written to the `Today` property (code file `ASPNETCoreLocalization/Pages/RequestCulture.cshtml.cs`):

```
public class RequestCultureModel : PageModel
{
  public void OnGet()
  {
    var features = HttpContext.Features.ToList();
    var feature = HttpContext.Features.Get<IRequestCultureFeature>();
    RequestCulture requestCulture = feature.RequestCulture;
    RequestCulture = requestCulture.UICulture.ToString();
    Today = DateTime.Today.ToLongDateString();
  }
  public string? RequestCulture { get; private set; }
  public string? Today { get; private set; }
}
```

With the HTML and Razor code of the page, the `RequestCulture` and `Today` properties are accessed and shown to the user (code file `ASPNETCoreLocalization/Pages/RequestCulture.cshtml`):

```
@page
@model ASPNETCoreLocalization.Pages.RequestCultureModel

<h1>Show Request Culture</h1>
<div>@Model.RequestCulture</div>
<div>@Model.Today</div>
```

When you run the application, you can pass the culture and see the results, as shown in Figure 22-4. When you pass cultures that aren't supported with the URL request, you can see an output of the default culture.

Using Resources with ASP.NET Core

Let's add resource files to the ASP.NET Core application. The sample project adds the `Resources` folder and the file `Startup.resx` within it. In addition, `Pages` and `Models` subfolders are created. Within the `Pages` subfolder, you find resource files for pages, such as `UseResourceModel.resx`, with localized versions with the file extensions `resx.de` and `resx.de-AT`. In the `Models` subfolder, you find the resource files `Book.resx` and `Book.resx.de`. The name of the folder where the resources are found has been defined with the `ResourcePath` property of the `LocalizationOptions` class when invoking the `AddLocalization` method in the `Startup` class to configure the DI container, as shown earlier.

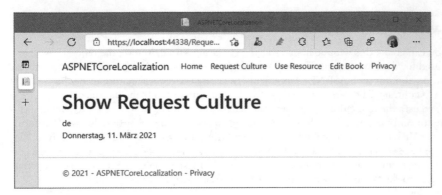

FIGURE 22-4

With the code-behind of the Razor page `UseResource`, `IStringLocalizer` is injected with two different generic parameters. The parameter `UseResourceModel` is used for resources only required with the page and retrieved from the corresponding resource files; the parameter `Startup` is used for shared resources. You can use any common class for shared resources. When you use `IStringLocalizer`, the indexer and the `GetString` method (both used with the sample code) can be used to access language-specific resource values (code file `ASPNETCoreLocalization/Pages/UseResource.cshtml.cs`):

```
public class UseResourceModel : PageModel
{
  private readonly IStringLocalizer _localizer;
  private readonly IStringLocalizer _sharedLocalizer;
  public UseResourceModel(IStringLocalizer<UseResourceModel> localizer,
    IStringLocalizer<Startup> sharedLocalizer)
  {
    _localizer = localizer;
    _sharedLocalizer = sharedLocalizer;
  }

  public void OnGet()
  {
    var feature = HttpContext.Features.Get<IRequestCultureFeature>();
    RequestCulture requestCulture = feature.RequestCulture;
    Message1 = _localizer["Message1"];
    Message2 = _localizer.GetString("Message2",
      feature.RequestCulture.Culture, feature.RequestCulture.UICulture);
    Message3 = _sharedLocalizer.GetString("SharedText");
  }

  public string? Message1 { get; private set; }
  public string? Message2 { get; private set; }
  public string? Message3 { get; private set; }
}
```

The resource for the key `Message1` is a simple string; the resource for `Message2` is defined with string format placeholders: `Using culture {0} and UI culture {1}`.

> **NOTE** *When you use formatted strings in resources, the syntax with interpolated strings cannot be used. The variables or expressions used with interpolated strings in the placeholders are not available from resources.*

When you add `?culture=de-AT` to the URL request (which uses the `QueryStringRequestCultureProvider`), you can see output as shown in Figure 22-5.

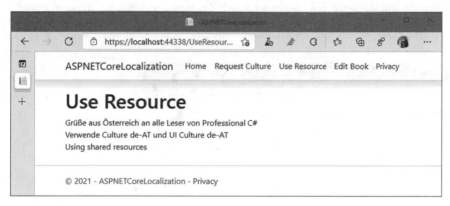

FIGURE 22-5

Localization with Data Annotations

Another way to retrieve resource values with ASP.NET Core is via applying annotations. To see the annotations in action, the `Book` record type is defined in the `Models` directory. This type has `DisplayName` attributes added to the properties `Title` and `Publisher` (code file `ASPNETCoreLocalization/Models/Book.cs`):

```
using System.ComponentModel;

namespace ASPNETCoreLocalization.Models
{
  public record Book(
    [property: DisplayName("BookTitle")] string Title,
    [property: DisplayName("Publisher")] string Publisher);
}
```

The resource file `Book.resx` together with localized versions contains resource values for the keys `BookTitle` and `Publisher`—the names specified with the `DisplayName` attribute. With the code-behind file of the `EditBook` Razor page, a new `Book` instance is created, and the `Book` property is set (code file `ASPNETCoreLocalization/Pages/EditBook.cshtml.cs`):

```
public class EditBookModel : PageModel
{
  public void OnGet()
  {
```

```
        Book = new Book("Professional C#", "Wrox Press");
    }

    public Book? Book { get; set; }
}
```

The Razor page shows edit fields for all the `Book` properties by using the HTML helper `EditorFor` (code file `ASPNETCoreLocalization/Pagesd/EditBook.cshtml`):

```
@page
@model ASPNETCoreLocalization.Pages.EditBookModel

@Html.EditorFor(model => model.Book)
```

When you run the application and access the link `/EditBook?culture=de-at`, resources are retrieved from both the controller and the view, as shown in Figure 22-6. Defining resources just for English (`Book.resx`) and German (`Book.de.resx`) returns values defined with the German culture passing the Austrian culture `de-at`.

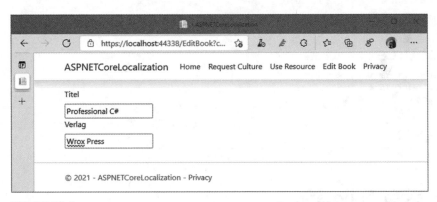

FIGURE 22-6

> **NOTE** *Don't forget to enable annotations for localization by invoking the method* `AddDataAnnotationsLocalization` *in the* `Startup` *class.*

LOCALIZATION WITH WINUI

Localization with WinUI is based on the concepts you've learned so far, but there are some differences. As part of the Project Reunion, resources are managed by MRT Core. MRT Core is the modern version of the Windows Resource Management System.

The concepts of cultures, regions, and resources are the same, but because Windows apps can be written with C# or C++ with XAML (many of the built-in Windows apps like the Windows Calculator are built with C++ and XAML), these concepts need to be available with all programming languages. Unlike the previous version of UWP apps, to manage resources, MRT Core is independent of the Windows 10 version. MRT offers more than just support localization of resources. Besides selecting resources based on the language, different resources can be used based on a theme, the device family, the scale, the layout direction, the contrast needs, and more.

The namespaces for resources are available with the `Microsoft.ApplicationModel.Resources` namespace. Let's get into an example so you can see localization with a WinUI Windows app in action. Create a small application using the Visual Studio project template Blank App, Packaged (WinUI in Desktop). Add two `TextBlock` controls and one `TextBox` control to the page.

With the `OnLaunched` method of the `App` class, a new `ResourceLoader` and a `ResourceManager` are created and passed to the constructor of the `MainWindow` class. If you need to access strings with your application, you just need to use the `ResourceLoader`. For more complex scenarios, instead use the `ResourceManager`. The sample application demonstrates using both of these types (code file `WinUILocalization/App.xaml.cs`):

```
protected override void OnLaunched(Microsoft.UI.Xaml.LaunchActivatedEventArgs args)
{
    ResourceLoader resourceLoader = new();
    ResourceManager resourceManager = new();
    m_window = new MainWindow(resourceLoader, resourceManager);
    m_window.Activate();
}
```

With the implementation, the default constructor of the `ResourceLoader` class is used. Using the default constructor, a resource with the name `Resources` is looked for. Other constructors allow passing a filename and a resource map. The resource map is discussed later in the section about using the `ResourceManager`. With the constructor of the `ResourceManager`, you can also pass a resource name. By default, the `ResourceManager` uses the root resource.

The resource files added to the project need to have the build action defined to `PRIResource`. In the project file, this is specified with the `PRIResource` element (project file `WinUILocalization/WinUILocalization.csproj`):

```
<ItemGroup>
    <PRIResource Include="Resources.lang-de-de.resw"/>
    <PRIResource Include="Resources.resw"/>
</ItemGroup>
```

Using the MRT ResourceLoader

Using the `ResourceLoader` is a simple task. With the `MainWindow`, the `ResourceLoader` is passed to the constructor (code file `WinUILocalization/MainWindow.xaml.cs`):

```
private readonly ResourceLoader _resourceLoader;
private readonly ResourceManager _resourceManager;
private readonly ResourceContext _resourceContext;
public MainWindow(ResourceLoader resourceLoader, ResourceManager resourceManager)
{
    _resourceLoader = resourceLoader;
    _resourceManager = resourceManager;
    //...
    this.InitializeComponent();
}
```

In the `OnGetResource` method, the `Text` property of the `textDate` field is filled with today's date using the current culture. The `_resourceLoader` variable retrieves the resource for the `Hello` key from the `Resources.resw` file (code file `WinUILocalization/MainWindow.xaml.cs`):

```
private void OnGetResource(object sender, RoutedEventArgs e)
{
```

```
      textDate.Text = DateTime.Today.ToString("D");
      textHello.Text = _resourceLoader.GetString("Hello");
  }
```

Using the MRT ResourceManager

The `ResourceManager` class offers more functionality. To access the resource, first the `ResourceMap` is retrieved using the `MainResourceMap` property. A resource map is a collection of resources—for example, resources with a specific language or resources from an app package. With the `ResourceMap` class, you can get the count of resources (`ResourceCount` property), access resources by index (`GetValueByIndex`), or access resources by value (`GetValue` or `TryGetValue`). The `TryGetValue` method returns null if the resource is not found. If the resource is found, `TryGetValue` returns a `ResourceCandidate` object. With this class, you can access binary resources (`ValueAsBytes`) or string resources (`ValueAsString`). You also can use the `ResourceCandidate` class to find out where the resource was coming from—from a string, a file path, or embedded data in the assembly. With the following code snippet, `TryGetValue` is used to access the resource `GoodMorning` from the file `Resources` (code file `WinUILocalization/MainWindow.xaml.cs`):

```
private void OnUseResourceManager(object sender, RoutedEventArgs e)
{
  ResourceMap map = _resourceManager.MainResourceMap;
  ResourceCandidate candidate = map.TryGetValue("Resources/GoodMorning");
  textGoodMorning.Text = candidate.ValueAsString;
}
```

Changing the Language with a ResourceContext

When you use the `ResourceManager`, you can create a `ResourceContext`, which allows looking for localized resources or resources based on device families or the layout. As shown in the following code snippet, you create resource contexts by invoking the method `CreateResourceContext` of the `ResourceManager`. The property `QualifierValues` returns a dictionary. Here you can define the qualifier name and the values that will be used to search for resources. To specify the language, you need to set languages for the key value language, or `lang`. In the sample code, the context is set to `de` for German resources. Examples of other key values you can use are `devicefamily`, `layoutdirection`, `scale`, and `theme` (code file `WinUILocalization/ MainWindow.xaml.cs`):

```
public MainWindow(ResourceLoader resourceLoader, ResourceManager resourceManager)
{
  _resourceLoader = resourceLoader;
  _resourceManager = resourceManager;
  _resourceContext = _resourceManager.CreateResourceContext();
  _resourceContext.QualifierValues["language"] = "de";

  this.InitializeComponent();
}
```

To use the localized resource, the resource context can be passed to the `TryGetValue` method of the `ResourceMap`:

```
private void OnUseContext(object sender, RoutedEventArgs e)
{
  ResourceMap map = _resourceManager.MainResourceMap;
  ResourceCandidate candidate = map.TryGetValue(
```

```
        "Resources/GoodEvening", _resourceContext);
      textGoodEvening.Text = candidate.ValueAsString;
    }
```

When you run the application, you can see the resources retrieved, as shown in Figure 22-7.

FIGURE 22-7

SUMMARY

This chapter demonstrated how to globalize and localize .NET applications. For the globalization of applications, you learned about using the namespace System.Globalization to format culture-dependent numbers and dates. Furthermore, you learned that sorting strings by default varies according to the culture, and you looked at using the invariant culture for a culture-independent sort.

Localizing an application is accomplished by using resources, which you can pack into files or satellite assemblies. The classes used with localization are in the namespace System.Resources.

You also learned how to localize ASP.NET Core, used special features for ASP.NET Core, and localized apps using WinUI with MRT.

The next chapter provides information about testing. You learn how to create unit tests with xUnit and use mocking libraries.

23

Tests

WHAT'S IN THIS CHAPTER?

➤   Performing unit tests with `xUnit.net`

➤   Determining code coverage

➤   Using a mocking library

➤   Performing integration testing with ASP.NET Core

CODE DOWNLOADS FOR THIS CHAPTER

The source code for this chapter is available on the book page at www.wiley.com. Click the Downloads link. The code can also be found at https://github.com/ProfessionalCSharp/ProfessionalCSharp2021 in the directory 2_Libs/Tests.

The code for this chapter is divided into the following major examples:

➤   UnitTestingSample

➤   MockingSample

➤   ASPNETCoreSample

All the samples have nullable reference types enabled.

OVERVIEW

Application development is becoming agile. When using waterfall process models to analyze the requirements, it's not unusual that you design the application architecture, do the implementation, and then find out as the solution is ready that you built an application that is not needed by the user. Software development becomes agile with faster release cycles and early participation of the end users. Just take a look at Windows 10: with millions of Windows insiders who give feedback to early builds, updates happen every few months or even weeks. There was one special week during the beta program of Windows 10 when Windows insiders received three builds of Windows 10 within one week. Windows 10 is a huge program, but Microsoft managed to change development in a big way. Also, if you participate in the open-source project of .NET, you can get nightly builds of NuGet packages. If you're adventurous, you might even write a book about an upcoming technology.

With such fast and continuous changes—and nightly builds that you are creating—you can't wait for insiders or end users to find all the issues. Windows 10 insiders wouldn't have been happy with Windows 10 crashing every few minutes. How often have you made a change in the implementation of a method only to find out something that doesn't seem related is not working anymore? You might have tried to avoid such issues by not changing the method and instead copying and changing the code to create a new method, which in turn creates a maintenance nightmare. It frequently happens that you fix a method in one place but miss the other ones with code duplicates.

You can avoid issues like these. Create tests for your methods, and let the tests run automatically. Using Visual Studio Enterprise, you can even run the tests with Live Unit Testing where the test runs while you're typing in the editor. Later, the test should run after you've checked in the source code. With continuous integration (CI) pipelines, load and security tests can run nightly so you can use CPU power that you don't need overnight.

Creating tests from the start increases the cost for the project from the beginning, but as the project progresses and during maintenance, creating tests has advantages and reduces the overall project cost.

This chapter has a focus on creating unit tests but also explains how to create integration tests with ASP.NET Core web applications. You'll also get references to create UI tests with XAML-based applications and to load tests with web applications.

A unit test should verify the functionality of the smallest testable parts of an application—for example, methods. When you pass different input values, a unit test should check all possible paths through a method.

UNIT TESTING

Writing unit tests helps with code maintenance. For example, when you're performing a code update, you want to be confident that the update isn't going to break something else. Having automatic unit tests in place helps to ensure that all functionality is retained after code changes are made.

The .NET CLI has built-in support to create and run unit tests. `dotnet new mstest` creates a unit test project with MSTest (https://github.com/microsoft/testfx). You can create a unit test with NUnit with `dotnet new nunit` (https://nunit.org/). `dotnet new xunit` creates a unit test project with xUnit.net (https://xunit.net/).

Because the .NET and ASP.NET Core teams make use of xUnit.net, in this book, the test projects are built with xUnit.net as well. However, if you prefer a different framework, it shouldn't be too hard to adapt. With other unit testing frameworks, you'll see different attributes to specify the tests and different methods for asserts, but the functionality is largely the same.

Creating Unit Tests

The following example tests a simple method in a class library named `UnitTestingSamples`. This is a .NET 5 class library. The class `DeepThought` contains the `TheAnswerToTheUltimateQuestionOfLifeTheUniverseAndEverything` method, which returns 42 as a result (code file `UnitTestingSamples/DeepThought.cs`):

```
public class DeepThought
{
   public int TheAnswerOfTheUltimateQuestionOfLifeTheUniverseAndEverything() => 42;
}
```

To ensure that nobody changes the method to return a wrong result (maybe someone who didn't read *The Hitchhiker's Guide to the Galaxy*), a unit test is created. To create a unit test project with xUnit, you can use the dotnet command

```
> dotnet new xunit
```

or you can add the project template xUnit Test Project from Visual Studio.

Before creating the first tests, it's a good idea to think about naming tests and test projects. Of course, you can use names as you like, but you can find a good guideline from the .NET Core team at

```
https://github.com/dotnet/aspnetcore/wiki/
Engineering-guidelines#unit-tests-and-functional-tests
```

Here's a summary of the guidelines:

➤ A test project has the name Tests appended to the name of the project—for example, for the project UnitTestingSamples, the test project has the name UnitTestingSamples.Tests.

➤ Test class names have the same class name as the class being tested, and the word Test is appended to the name. For example, the test class for UnitTestingSamples.DeepThought is UnitTestingSamples.DeepThoughtTest.

➤ Unit test method names have a descriptive name. For example, the name AddOrUpdateBookAsync_ThrowsForNull indicates a unit test to invoke the AddOrUpdateBookAsync method to check whether it throws an exception passing null.

The xUnit.net test project contains references to the NuGet packages Microsoft.NET.Test.Sdk, xunit, xunit.runner.visualstudio, and coverlet.collector. coverlet.collector is used to analyze the code coverage—the percentage of the source code lines that is covered by unit tests.

With xUnit.net, a test method is marked with the attribute Fact. The implementation of the test method creates an instance of DeepThought and invokes the method that is to be tested: TheAnswerToTheUltimateQuestionOfLifeTheUniverseAndEverything. The return value is compared with the value 42 using Assert.Equal. In case Assert.Equal fails, the test fails (code file UnitTestingSamples.UnitTestingSamples.Tests/DeepThoughtTest.cs):

```
public class DeepThoughtTest
{
  [Fact]
  public void ResultOfTheAnswerToTheUltimateQuestionOfLifeTheUniverseAndEverything()
  {
    // arrange
    int expected = 42;
    DeepThought dt = new();

    // act
    int actual =
      dt.TheAnswerToTheUltimateQuestionOfLifeTheUniverseAndEverything();

    // assert
    Assert.Equal(expected, actual);
  }
}
```

Unit tests are defined by three A's: arrange, act, and assert. First, everything is *arranged* for the unit test to start. In the first test, with the arrange phase, a variable `expected` is assigned the value that is expected from calling the method to test, and an instance of the `DeepThought` class is invoked. Now everything is ready to test the functionality. This happens with the *act* phase—the method is invoked. After completing the act phase, you need to verify whether the result is as expected. This is done in the *assert* phase using a method of the `Assert` class.

The `Assert` class is part of the `xUnit.net` framework in the `Xunit` namespace. This class offers several static methods that you can use with unit tests. Here you have many different options to check for valid results. `Assert.True` requires that the expression returns `true` to be successful. `Assert.False` is the opposite of that; the expression needs to return `false` to be successful. With `Assert.InRange`, the result must be within a specified range. `Assert.Null` and `Assert.NotNull` are used to check for results returning null. Results of collections can be checked with `Assert.Contains`, `Assert.DoesNotContain`, and `Assert.All`.

Running Unit Tests

To run unit tests, you can use the Test Explorer from Visual Studio or the .NET CLI:

```
> dotnet test
```

With the sample application, this results in this successful output:

```
Determining projects to restore...
Restored C:\procsharp\tests\UnitTestingSamples\UnitTestingSamples.csproj (in 94 ms).
Restored C:\procsharp\tests\UnitTestingSamples\UnitTestingSamples.Tests\
UnitTestingSamples.Tests.csproj (in 482 ms).
UnitTestingSamples -> C:\procsharp\tests\UnitTestingSamples\UnitTestingSamples\bin\Debug\
net5.0\UnitTestingSamples.dll
UnitTestingSamples.Tests -> C:\procsharp\tests\UnitTestingSamples\
UnitTestingSamples.Tests\bin\Debug\net5.0\UnitTestingSamples.Tests.dll
Test run for C:\procsharp\tests\UnitTestingSamples\UnitTestingSamples.Tests\
bin\Debug\net5.0\ UnitTestingSamples.Tests.dll (.NETCoreApp,Version=v5.0)
Microsoft (R) Test Execution Command Line Tool Version 16.9.0
Copyright (c) Microsoft Corporation.  All rights reserved.

Starting test execution, please wait...
A total of 1 test files matched the specified pattern.

Passed! - Failed:     0, Passed:     1, Skipped:     0, Total:     1,
Duration: 4 ms - UnitTestingSamples.Tests.dll (net5.0)
```

Of course, this was a simple scenario; the tests are not usually that simple. For example, methods can throw exceptions; they can have different paths for returning other values; and they can make use of other code (for example, database access code, or services that are invoked) that shouldn't be tested with the single unit test. Now let's look at a more involved scenario for unit testing.

Implementing Complex Methods

The `StringSample` class defines a constructor with a string parameter, the method `GetStringDemo`, and a field. The method `GetStringDemo` uses different paths depending on the `first` and `second` parameters and returns a string that results from these parameters (code file `UnitTestingSamples/StringSample.cs`):

```
public class StringSample
{
```

```
public StringSample(string init)
{
  if (init is null)
    throw new ArgumentNullException(nameof(init));

  _init = init;
}

private string _init;

public string GetStringDemo(string first, string second)
{
  if (first is null) throw new ArgumentNullException(nameof(first));
  if (string.IsNullOrEmpty(first))
    throw new ArgumentException("empty string is not allowed", first);
  if (second is null) throw new ArgumentNullException(nameof(second));
  if (second.Length > first.Length)
    throw new ArgumentOutOfRangeException(nameof(second),
      "must be shorter than first");

  int startIndex = first.IndexOf(second);
  if (startIndex < 0)
  {
    return $"{second} not found in {first}";
  }
  else if (startIndex < 5)
  {
    string result = first.Remove(startIndex, second.Length);
    return $"removed {second} from {first}: {result}";
  }
  else
  {
    return _init.ToUpperInvariant();
  }
}
}
}
```

> **NOTE** *When you're writing unit tests for complex methods, the unit test also sometimes gets complex. Here it is helpful to debug the unit test to find out what's going on. Debugging unit tests is straightforward with Visual Studio: just add breakpoints to the unit test code, and from the context menu of the Test Explorer, select Debug Selected Tests.*

Every possible execution route and check for exceptions should be covered by unit tests, as discussed next.

Expecting Exceptions

When invoking the constructor of the `StringSample` class and calling the method `GetStringDemo` with null, an `ArgumentNullException` is expected. You can easily check exceptions with testing code: apply the `ExpectedException` attribute to the test method as shown in the following example. This way, the test method succeeds with the exception (code file `UnitTestingSamples.Tests/StringSampleTest.cs`):

```
[Fact]
public void GetStringDemoExceptions()
```

```
  {
    StringSample sample = new(string.Empty);
    Assert.Throws<ArgumentNullException>(() => sample.GetStringDemo(null!, "a"));
    Assert.Throws<ArgumentNullException>(() => sample.GetStringDemo("a", null!));
    Assert.Throws<ArgumentException>(() =>
      sample.GetStringDemo(string.Empty, "a"));
  }
```

> **NOTE** *Although the library project has nullable reference types enabled and the parameters of the method are not annotated with nullable references, you should still check for receiving null values and throwing* ArgumentNullException. *If the calling application does not use C# 8 or later, the compiler does not result in compiler warnings passing null. Older compilers ignore the attributes created for nullable reference types, and the result would just be a* NullReferenceException *at locations it's probably not expected. Even with nullable reference types enabled, it's still a good practice to check for null with the method parameters.*

Testing All Code Paths

To test all code paths, you can create multiple tests, with each one taking a different route. The following test sample passes the strings a and b to the GetStringDemo method. Because the second string is not contained within the first string, the first path of the if statement applies. The result is checked accordingly (code file UnitTestingSamples.Tests/StringSampleTest.cs):

```
[Fact]
public void GetStringDemoBNotInA()
{
  // arrange
  string expected = "b not found in a";
  StringSample sample = new(string.Empty);

  // act
  string actual = sample.GetStringDemo("a", "b");

  // assert
  Assert.Equal(expected, actual);
}
```

You can also define a test method with parameters and use attributes passing different values. For this, the test method needs to have the attribute Theory instead of Fact applied. Data can be passed using multiple InlineData attributes that define the values, as shown in the following code snippet. With this in place, the test runner invokes the method GetStringDemoInlineData multiple times and passes values for every InlineData attribute:

```
[Theory]
[InlineData("", "a", "b", "b not found in a")]
[InlineData("", "longer string", "nger", "removed nger from longer string: lo string")]
[InlineData("init", "longer string", "string", "INIT")]
public void GetStringDemoInlineData(string init, string a, string b, string expected)
{
  StringSample sample = new(init);
```

```
        string actual = sample.GetStringDemo(a, b);
        Assert.Equal(expected, actual);
    }
```

Instead of using multiple `InlineData` attributes, you can also define a method that returns the values passed to the test method (such as the following `GetStringSampleData` method) and specify the method name with the `MemberData` attribute. This way you can use any source of data for the unit test:

```
    [Theory]
    [MemberData(nameof(GetStringSampleData))]
    public void GetStringDemoMemberData(string init, string a, string b, string expected)
    {
        StringSample sample = new(init);
        string actual = sample.GetStringDemo(a, b);
        Assert.Equal(expected, actual);
    }

    public static IEnumerable<object[]> GetStringSampleData() =>
        new[]
        {
            new object[] { "", "a", "b", "b not found in a" },
            new object[] { "", "longer string", "nger",
                "removed nger from longer string: lo string" },
            new object[] { "init", "longer string", "string", "INIT" }
        };
```

Code Coverage

To see what code is covered by unit tests and what code is still missing, you can use the `--collect` option of the `dotnet test` command. The NuGet package `coverlet.collector` is added to the project to collect code coverage in a platform-independent manner. In addition to the NuGet package, you need to add the .NET CLI tool `coverlet.console`. To install this tool with the test project, you can add a `tool-manifest` file and add the `coverlet.console` to the project tools (or instead add this tool as a global tool to your profile with the option -g). The second tool installed is the `dotnet-reportgenerator`, which gives you graphical output of the generated XML file from Coverlet:

```
    > dotnet new tool-manifest
    > dotnet tool install coverlet.console
    > dotnet tool install dotnet-reportgenerator-globaltool
```

With the collector and this tool in place, you can run the tests with the `--collect` option and pass the string `XPlat Code Coverage`, as shown in the next snippet. After running the unit tests with this option, results are found in the `TestResults` folder.

```
    > dotnet test --collect "XPlat Code Coverage"
```

To get an HTML view of the report, you can now use the report generator. With the -reports option, you specify the directory of the XML file that contains the collection information. The option -targetdir specifies the name of the directory where you want the HTML output. With the -reportTypes option, you can specify the output format:

```
    > dotnet tool run reportgenerator -reports:TestResults\{GUID}\coverage.cobertura.xml
    -targetdir:coveragereport -reportTypes:Html
```

When you open the HTML that's generated, you see a view similar to Figure 23-1.

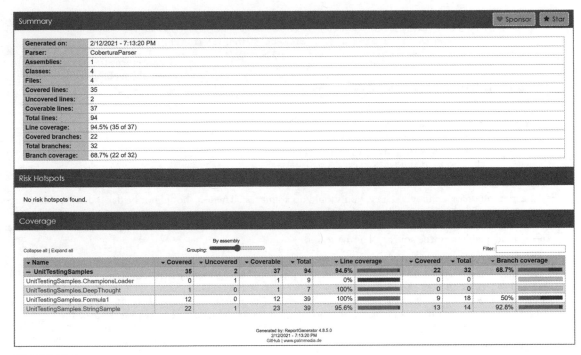

FIGURE 23-1

See the documentation at `https://github.com/coverlet-coverage/coverlet` and `https://github.com/Microsoft/vstest-docs/blob/master/docs/analyze.md` for more information on the different options you have with Coverlet and how to use this and other collectors with Visual Studio.

External Dependencies

Many methods are dependent on some functionality outside the application's control—for example, calling a web service or accessing a database. Maybe the service or database is not available during some test runs, which tests the availability of these external resources. Or worse, maybe the database or service returns different data over time, and it's hard to compare this with expected data. Such functionality outside the scope of what should be tested must be excluded from the unit test.

The following example is dependent on some outside functionality. The method `ChampionsByCountry` accesses an XML file from a web server that contains a list of Formula 1 world champions with `Firstname`, `Lastname`, `Wins`, and `Country` elements. This list is filtered by country, and it's numerically ordered using the value from the `Wins` element. The returned data is an `XElement` that contains converted XML code (code file `UnitTestingSamples/Formula1.cs`):

```
public XElement ChampionsByCountry(string country)
{
  XElement champions = XElement.Load(F1Addresses.RacersUrl);
  var q = from r in champions.Elements("Racer")
          where r.Element("Country").Value == country
          orderby int.Parse(r.Element("Wins").Value) descending
          select new XElement("Racer",
            new XAttribute("Name", r.Element("Firstname").Value + " " +
```

```
              r.Element("Lastname").Value),
          new XAttribute("Country", r.Element("Country").Value),
          new XAttribute("Wins", r.Element("Wins").Value));
      return new XElement("Racers", q.ToArray());
}
```

The link to the XML file is defined by the `F1Addresses` class (code file `UnitTestingSamples/`
`F1Addresses.cs`):

```
public class F1Addresses
{
  public const string RacersUrl =
    "http://www.cninnovation.com/downloads/Racers.xml";
}
```

For the method `ChampionsByCountry`, you should do a unit test. The test should not be dependent on the source
from the server. Server unavailability is one issue, but it can also be expected that the data on the server changes
over time to return new champions and other values. The test should ensure that filtering and ordering is done as
expected independent of the source from the server.

One way to create a unit test that is independent of the data source is to refactor the implementation of the
`ChampionsByCountry` method by using dependency injection. Here, a factory that returns an `XElement`
is created to replace the `XElement.Load` method. The interface `IChampionsLoader` is the only outside
requirement used from the `ChampionsByCountry` method. The interface `IChampionsLoader` defines the
method `LoadChampions` that can replace the aforementioned method (code file `UnitTestingSamples/`
`IChampionsLoader.cs`):

```
public interface IChampionsLoader
{
  XElement LoadChampions();
}
```

The class `ChampionsLoader` implements the interface `IChampionsLoader` by using the `XElement`
`.Load` method—the method that was used beforehand by the `ChampionsByCountry` method (code file
`UnitTestingSamples/ChampionsLoader.cs`):

```
public class ChampionsLoader: IChampionsLoader
{
  public XElement LoadChampions() => XElement.Load(F1Addresses.RacersUrl);
}
```

Now it's possible to change the implementation of the `ChampionsByCountry` method by using an interface
to load the champions instead of directly using `XElement.Load`. The `IChampionsLoader` is passed with
the constructor of the class `Formula1`, and this loader is then used by `ChampionsByCountry` (code file
`UnitTestingSamples/Formula1.cs`):

```
public class Formula1
{
  private readonly IChampionsLoader _loader;
  public Formula1(IChampionsLoader loader) => _loader = loader;

  public XElement ChampionsByCountry(string country)
  {
    var q = from r in _loader.LoadChampions().Elements("Racer")
            where r.Element("Country").Value == country
```

```
                    orderby int.Parse(r.Element("Wins").Value) descending
                    select new XElement("Racer",
                      new XAttribute("Name", r.Element("Firstname").Value + " " +
                        r.Element("Lastname").Value),
                      new XAttribute("Country", r.Element("Country").Value),
                      new XAttribute("Wins", r.Element("Wins").Value));
            return new XElement("Racers", q.ToArray());
        }
    }
```

With a typical implementation, a `ChampionsLoader` instance would be passed to the `Formula1` constructor to retrieve the racers from the server.

When you're creating the unit test, you can implement a custom method that returns sample Formula 1 champions, as shown in the method `Formula1SampleData` (code file `UnitTestingSamples.Tests/Formula1Test.cs`):

```
internal static string Formula1SampleData()
{
  return @"
<Racers>
  <Racer>
    <Firstname>Nelson</Firstname>
    <Lastname>Piquet</Lastname>
    <Country>Brazil</Country>
    <Starts>204</Starts>
    <Wins>23</Wins>
  </Racer>
  <Racer>
    <Firstname>Ayrton</Firstname>
    <Lastname>Senna</Lastname>
    <Country>Brazil</Country>
    <Starts>161</Starts>
    <Wins>41</Wins>
  </Racer>
  <Racer>
    <Firstname>Nigel</Firstname>
    <Lastname>Mansell</Lastname>
    <Country>England</Country>
    <Starts>187</Starts>
    <Wins>31</Wins>
  </Racer>
  //... more sample data
```

The method `Formula1VerificationData` returns sample test data that matches the expected result (code file `UnitTestingSamples.Tests/Formula1Test.cs`):

```
internal static XElement Formula1VerificationData()
{
  return XElement.Parse(@"
<Racers>
  <Racer Name=""Mika Hakkinen"" Country=""Finland"" Wins=""20""/>
  <Racer Name=""Kimi Raikkonen"" Country=""Finland"" Wins=""18""/>
</Racers>");
}
```

The loader of the test data implements the same interface—`IChampionsLoader`—as the `ChampionsLoader` class. This loader makes use of the sample data; it doesn't access the web server (code file `UnitTestingSamples.Tests/Formula1Test.cs`):

```
public class F1TestLoader: IChampionsLoader
{
  public XElement LoadChampions() => XElement.Parse(Formula1SampleData());
}
```

Now it's easy to create a unit test that makes use of the sample data (code file `UnitTestingSamples.Tests/Formula1Test.cs`):

```
[Fact]
public void ChampionsByCountryFilterFinland()
{
  Formula1 f1 = new Formula1(new F1TestLoader());
  XElement actual = f1.ChampionsByCountry("Finland");
  Assert.AreEqual(Formula1VerificationData().ToString(), actual.ToString());
}
```

Of course, a real test should do more than cover a case that passes `Finland` as a string, and two champions are returned with the test data. You should write other tests to pass a string with no matching result to return more than two champions and to result in a number sort order that is different from the alphanumeric sort order.

> **NOTE** *To test methods that don't use dependency injection and to replace the internally used dependencies with test classes, you can use Microsoft Fakes. Check* `https://docs` `.microsoft.com/en-us/visualstudio/test/isolating-code-under-test-` `with-microsoft-fakes` *for more information on Microsoft Fakes.*

USING A MOCKING LIBRARY

Let's get into a more complex example: creating a unit test for a client-side service library from an app using the MVVM pattern. Read Chapter 30, "Patterns with XAML Apps," for a complete picture of this app. The sample code for this chapter only includes a library used by this app. This service uses dependency injection to inject the repository defined by the interface `IBooksRepository`. The unit tests for testing the method `AddOrUpdateBookAsync` shouldn't test the repository; they test only the functionality within the method. For the repository, another unit test should be done. The following code snippet shows the implementation of the `BooksService` class (code file `MockingSamples/BooksLib/Services/BooksService.cs`):

```
public class BooksService: IBooksService
{
  private readonly ObservableCollection<Book> _books = new();
  private readonly IBooksRepository _booksRepository;
  public BooksService(IBooksRepository repository) =>
    _booksRepository = repository;

  public async Task LoadBooksAsync()
  {
    if (_books.Count > 0) return;
    IEnumerable<Book> books = await _booksRepository.GetItemsAsync();
```

```
    _books.Clear();
    foreach (var b in books)
    {
      _books.Add(b);
    }
  }

  public Book? GetBook(int bookId) =>
    _books.Where(b => b.BookId == bookId).SingleOrDefault();

  public async Task<Book> AddOrUpdateBookAsync(Book book)
  {
    if (book is null) throw new ArgumentNullException(nameof(book));

    Book? updated = null;
    if (book.BookId == 0)
    {
      updated = await _booksRepository.AddAsync(book);
      _books.Add(updated);
    }
    else
    {
      updated = await _booksRepository.UpdateAsync(book);
      if (updated is null) throw new InvalidOperationException();

      Book old = _books.Where(b => b.BookId == updated.BookId).Single();
      int ix = _books.IndexOf(old);
      _books.RemoveAt(ix);
      _books.Insert(ix, updated);
    }
    return updated;
  }

  public IEnumerable<Book> Books => _books;
}
```

Because the unit test for `AddOrUpdateBookAsync` shouldn't test the repository used for `IBooksRepository`, you need to implement a repository used for testing. To make this easy, you can use a mocking library that automatically fills in the blanks. A commonly used mocking library is Moq. With the unit testing project, the NuGet package `Moq` is added.

> **NOTE** *Instead of using the Moq framework, you also can implement an in-memory repository with sample data. You probably do this anyway to have sample data for the app during design time of the user interface.*

When you use `xUnit.net`, a new instance of the test class is created for every test run. In case you need common functionality for multiple tests, you can move this functionality to the constructor. If resources need to be released after each test run, you can implement the interface `IDisposable`.

Within the constructor of the `BooksServiceTest` class, a `Mock` object is instantiated with the generic parameter `IBooksRepository`. The `Mock` constructor creates an implementation for the interface. Because you need some results from the repository other than null to create useful tests, the `Setup` method defines which parameters can be passed, and the `ReturnsAsync` method defines the result that's returned from the method stub.

You access the mock object by using the `Object` property of the `Mock` class, and it is passed on to create an instance of the `BooksService` class. With these settings in place, you can implement the unit tests (code file `MockingSamples/BooksLib.Tests/Services/BooksServiceTest.cs`):

```csharp
public class BooksServiceTest : IDisposable
{
  private const string TestTitle = "Test Title";
  private const string UpdatedTestTitle = "Updated Test Title";
  public const string APublisher = "A Publisher";
  private BooksService _booksService;

  private Book _newBook = new Book
  {
    BookId = 0,
    Title = TestTitle,
    Publisher = APublisher
  };

  private Book _expectedBook = new Book
  {
    BookId = 1,
    Title = TestTitle,
    Publisher = APublisher
  };
  private Book _notInRepositoryBook = new Book
  {
    BookId = 42,
    Title = TestTitle,
    Publisher = APublisher
  };
  private Book _updatedBook = new Book
  {
    BookId = 1,
    Title = UpdatedTestTitle,
    Publisher = APublisher
  };

  public BooksServiceTest()
  {
    Mock<IBooksRepository> mock = new();
    mock.Setup(repository =>
      repository.AddAsync(_newBook)).ReturnsAsync(_expectedBook);
    mock.Setup(repository =>
      repository.UpdateAsync(_notInRepositoryBook)).ReturnsAsync(null as Book);
    mock.Setup(repository =>
      repository.UpdateAsync(_updatedBook)).ReturnsAsync(_updatedBook);

    _booksService = new BooksService(mock.Object);
  }
  //...
```

> **NOTE** *The* `IDisposable` *interface is explained in detail in Chapter 13, "Managed and Unmanaged Memory."*

The first unit test implemented—AddOrUpdateBookAsync_ThrowsForNull—verifies that an ArgumentNullException is thrown in case null is passed to the AddOrUpdateBookAsync method. The implementation just needs the _booksService member variable that is instantiated within the constructor, but it doesn't need the mocking setup. This code sample also shows that unit test methods can be implemented as asynchronous methods that return a Task (code file MockingSamples/BooksLib.Tests/Services/BooksServiceTest.cs):

```
[Fact]
public async Task AddOrUpdateBookAsync_ThrowsForNull()
{
  // arrange
  Book nullBook = null;
  // act and assert
  await Assert.ThrowsAsync<ArgumentNullException>(() =>
    _booksService.AddOrUpdateBookAsync(nullBook));
}
```

The unit test method AddOrUpdateBook_AddedBookReturnsFromRepository adds a new book (variable _newBook) to the service and expects the book _expectedBook to be returned. Within the implementation of the AddOrUpdateBookAsync method, the AddAsync method of the IBooksRepository is invoked; thus, the previously defined mock setup for this method applies. The result of this method should be that the Book returned is equal to the _expectedBook, and the _expectedBook also needs to be added to the books collection of the BooksService (code file MockingSamples/BooksLib.Tests/Services/BooksServiceTest.cs):

```
[Fact]
public async Task AddOrUpdateBook_AddedBookReturnsFromRepository()
{
  // arrange in constructor
  // act
  Book actualAdded = await _booksService.AddOrUpdateBookAsync(_newBook);

  // assert
  Assert.Equal(_expectedBook, actualAdded);
  Assert.Contains(_expectedBook, _booksService.Books);
}
```

The unit test AddOrUpdateBook_UpdateNotExistingBookThrows verifies that trying to update a book that does not exist in the service needs to result in an InvalidOperationException (code file MockingSamples/BooksLib.Tests/Services/BooksServiceTest.cs):

```
[Fact]
public async Task AddOrUpdateBook_UpdateNotExistingBookThrows()
{
  // arrange in constructor
  // act and assert
  await Assert.ThrowsAsync<InvalidOperationException>(() =>
    _booksService.AddOrUpdateBookAsync(_notInRepositoryBook));
}
```

The usual case to update a book is dealt with in the unit test AddOrUpdateBook_UpdateBook. Here, extra preparation is needed to first add the book to the service before updating it (code file MockingSamples/BooksLib.Tests/Services/BooksServiceTest.cs):

```
[Fact]
public async Task AddOrUpdateBook_UpdateBook()
```

```
{
  // arrange
  await _booksService.AddOrUpdateBookAsync(_newBook);

  // act
  Book updatedBook = await _booksService.AddOrUpdateBookAsync(_updatedBook);

  // assert
  Assert.Equal(_updatedBook, updatedBook);
  Assert.Contains(_updatedBook, _booksService.Books);
}
```

> **NOTE** *When you use the MVVM pattern with XAML-based applications and the MVC pattern with web-based applications, you reduce the complexity of the user interface and reduce the need for complex UI testing. However, there are still some scenarios that should be tested with the UI—for example, navigating through pages, drag and drop of elements, and more. This is where UI testing comes in. Appium supports testing XAML applications including UWP and Mobile MAUI applications. Check* https://appium.io *for more information about Appium. Visual Studio App Center (*https://appcenter.ms*) makes it easy to run UI tests of MAUI applications on hundreds of different Android and iOS devices. Check* https://github.com/ProfessionalCSharp/MoreSamples *and* https://csharp.christiannagel.com *for samples of using Appium to test the book's WinUI applications.*

ASP.NET CORE INTEGRATION TESTING

To test web applications, you can create unit tests that invoke methods of the controllers, repository, and utility classes. Tag helpers are simple methods in which the test can be covered by unit tests. Unit tests are used to test the functionality of the algorithms of the methods—in other words, the logic inside the methods.

To test not only small units but all the functionality together, you use *integration tests*. With integration tests, not only is a single method tested but all the functionality in combination is tested—for example, sending a request to open a page, including accessing functionality in the backend. You should have a lot more unit tests than integration tests. The Azure DevOps team has thousands of unit tests but only a few integration tests. If the same functionality could be covered either by unit or integration tests, you should choose unit tests.

ASP.NET Core offers the `WebApplicationFactory` class in the NuGet package and the namespace `Microsoft.AspNetCore.Mvc.Testing` to bootstrap an application in-memory for functional end-to-end testing.

To create an ASP.NET Core integration test, create an ASP.NET Core Web Application named `ASPNETCoreSample` with the Empty template. Running the application from the generated code returns the string `Hello World!`, and this will be tested from an integration test using `xUnit.net`.

> **NOTE** *ASP.NET Core is covered in detail in Chapters 24 to 28.*

The `xUnit.net` project `ASPNETCoreSample.IntegrationTest` needs a package reference to `Microsoft.AspNetCore.Mvc.Testing`. This package contains the `WebApplicationFactory` class to host and start the web application and to send requests. A reference to the web project `ASPNETCoreSample` is needed as well.

With xUnit.net, every time a test runs, the test class is newly instantiated, and the constructor is invoked. To share instances between multiple test methods, you use the generic interface IFixture as an annotation to the test class. The type generic defined with this interface is instantiated once for all test methods with the class. In the following code snippet, this is the WebApplicationFactory class. The generic parameter of the WebApplicationFactory is the entry point of the application, which can be the Startup or the Program class. Here, the Startup class is used to instantiate the web application to configure the dependency injection container and the middleware (code file ASPNETCoreSample/ASPNETCoreSample.IntegrationTest/AspNetCoreSampleTest.cs):

```
public class ASPNETCoreSampleTest
  : IClassFixture<WebApplicationFactory<ASPNETCoreSample.Startup>>
{
  private readonly WebApplicationFactory<ASPNETCoreSample.Startup> _factory;

  public ASPNETCoreSampleTest(WebApplicationFactory<ASPNETCoreSample.Startup> factory)
    => _factory = factory;
  //...
}
```

In the integration test, by using the _factory variable you create an HttpClient object that's configured by the factory. This client makes requests to the web application. This HttpClient is configured to follow redirects and to pass cookies received. With the implementation of the test class in the following code snippet, an HTTP GET request is done, and the response is compared with the Hello World! string that should be returned from the web application (code file ASPNETCoreSample/ASPNETCoreSample.IntegrationTest/AspNetCoreSampleTest.cs):

```
[Fact]
public async Task ReturnHelloWorld()
{
  // arrange
  var client = _factory.CreateClient();

  // act
  var response = await client.GetAsync("/");

  // assert
  response.EnsureSuccessStatusCode();
  string responseString = await response.Content.ReadAsStringAsync();
  Assert.Equal("Hello World!", responseString);
}
```

With the HttpClient class returned from the factory, you can create HTTP requests using verbs such as GET, POST, and PUT, and add HTTP header information. Read Chapter 19, "Networking," for more information on this class. When you use the factory with _factory.Server.CreateWebSocketClient, you can also use a WebSocketClient to create WebSocket requests. WebSockets are covered in Chapter 28, "SignalR."

> **NOTE** *With web applications, it is also a good practice to create performance and load tests. Does the application scale? How many users can the application support with one server? How many servers are needed to support a specific number of users? Which bottleneck is not that easy to scale? To answer these questions, performance and load tests can help. To create end-to-end tests nowadays, people often use Selenium or Playwright. Appium, which I mentioned earlier with testing desktop and mobile applications, is based on Selenium. The ASP.NET Core team switched after the release of .NET 5 from Selenium to Playwright. Read more about Selenium at* `https://www.selenium.dev/`. *Playwright is developed by Microsoft (*`https://playwright.dev/`*) with the source code available at* `https://github.com/microsoft/playwright`. *Check* `https://github.com/ProfessionalCSharp/MoreSamples` *and* `https://csharp.christiannagel.com` *for samples and articles using Playwright to test the web samples of the book.*

SUMMARY

Source code is not complete without unit tests. To test the functionality of your application, you should create unit tests. With unit tests, you're safe to make changes in your code without breaking other parts. You've seen how to create unit tests with xUnit.net and how to test for all the different paths. You've seen mock classes in place to get implementation for dependent contracts that you don't want to test.

With integration tests, you've seen how an ASP.NET Core web application can be loaded in memory and an HTTP client can be used from a test.

This was the last chapter of the second part of this book. The next part, "Web Applications and Services," is where you begin to dig into web applications and services with ASP.NET Core. In that part you will use Razor Pages, MVC, and Blazor for the user interface, and ASP.NET Core Web API, Azure Functions, GRPC, and SignalR for the services.

PART III

Web Applications and Services

24

ASP.NET Core

WHAT'S IN THIS CHAPTER?

➤ Understanding ASP.NET Core and web technologies

➤ Using static content

➤ Creating middleware components

➤ Working with endpoint routing

➤ Working with HTTP request and response

➤ Using sessions for state management

➤ Hosting web applications with Microsoft Azure

➤ Creating Docker images

CODE DOWNLOADS FOR THIS CHAPTER

The source code for this chapter is available on the book page at www.wiley.com. Click the Downloads link. The code can also be found at https://github.com/ProfessionalCSharp/ ProfessionalCSharp2021 in the directory 3_Web/ASPNETCore.

The code for this chapter is divided into the following major examples:

➤ SimpleHost

➤ WebSampleApp

Samples from this chapter mainly use the namespaces Microsoft.AspNetCore and System.Text (and subnamespaces). All the sample projects have *nullable reference types* enabled.

UNDERSTANDING WEB TECHNOLOGIES

After ASP.NET with the .NET Framework was released in 2002, ASP.NET Core (the first version released in 2016) was a complete rewrite that not only offers running this technology on Linux but also uses modern patterns (for example, dependency injection is built in) and offers new ways to create web applications. Razor Pages offer an easy way to create HTML pages mixed with C# code with support for dependency injection. From the outside, ASP.NET Core MVC looks similar to the previous MVC technology with ASP.NET, but inside it's very different. Blazor gives a full-stack .NET option. Instead of writing JavaScript code, you can write C# code that runs either on the server (Blazor Server) or on the client in a WebAssembly (Blazor WASM). Blazor is based on Razor Components that extend the functionality of Razor Pages.

This chapter covers the foundation of ASP.NET Core. Chapter 25, "Services," covers services where the Web API with ASP.NET Core plays an important part. For binary platform-independent communication, Chapter 25 also covers GRPC. Chapter 26, "Razor Pages and MVC," covers ASP.NET Razor Pages and MVC. Chapter 27, "Blazor," extends Razor Pages with Razor Components and covers full-stack .NET development with Blazor.

Before I get into the foundations of ASP.NET, I'll spend a few pages describing core web technologies that are important to know when creating web applications: HTML, CSS, JavaScript, scripting libraries, and WebAssembly.

HTML

HTML is the markup language that is interpreted by web browsers. It defines elements to display various headings, tables, lists, and input elements such as text and combo boxes.

HTML is a living standard that refers to modern web technologies (`https://html.spec.whatwg.org/`) and is continuously improving. It not only contains the semantic structure of web pages with the HTML elements but also styling with CSS, many JavaScript APIs such as the Fetch API, (`https://fetch.spec.whatwg.org/`), the Storage API (`https://storage.spec.whatwg.org/`), and others.

CSS

Whereas HTML defines the content of web pages, CSS defines the look. In the earlier days of HTML, for example, the list item tag `<li>` defined whether list elements should be displayed with a circle, a disc, or a square. Now, such information is completely removed from HTML and is instead put into a cascading style sheet (CSS).

With CSS styles, you can use flexible selectors to select HTML elements, and you can define styles for these elements. You can select an element via its ID or its name, and you can define CSS classes that can be referenced from within the HTML code. With newer versions of CSS, you can define quite complex rules for selecting specific HTML elements.

As of today, some web project templates make use of Bootstrap, which was originally developed by Twitter, but now a small team at GitHub maintains it (`https://github.com/twbs/bootstrap`). Bootstrap is a collection of CSS and HTML conventions, and you can easily adapt different looks and download ready-to-use templates. Visit `https://getbootstrap.com` for documentation and basic templates.

JavaScript and TypeScript

Not all platforms and browsers can use .NET code, but nearly every browser understands *JavaScript*. One common misconception about JavaScript is that it has something to do with Java. In fact, only the name is similar because Netscape (the originator of JavaScript) made an agreement with Sun (Sun invented Java) to be allowed to use Java in the name. Today, neither Netscape nor Sun exists. Sun was bought by Oracle, and now Oracle holds the trademark for Java.

Java and JavaScript (and C#) have the same roots—the C programming language. JavaScript is a functional programming language that is not object-oriented, although object-oriented capabilities have been added to it.

JavaScript enables accessing the *document object model* (DOM) from the HTML page, which makes it possible to change elements dynamically on the client.

ECMAScript is the standard that defines the current and upcoming features of the JavaScript language. Check `https://tc39.es/ecma262/` for the current state and future changes of the JavaScript language. New features are added every year, much like new features are added to C#.

Even though many browsers don't support the newest ECMAScript version, you can still write new ECMAScript code. Instead of writing JavaScript code, you can use *TypeScript*. The TypeScript syntax is based on ECMAScript, but it has some enhancements, such as strongly typed code and annotations. You'll find many similarities between C# and TypeScript. Because the TypeScript compiler transpiles (or compiles) to JavaScript, TypeScript can be used in every place where JavaScript is needed. For more information on TypeScript, check `https://www` `.typescriptlang.org`.

Scripting Libraries

In addition to the JavaScript programming language, you might need scripting libraries. Scripting libraries can be used on the client in combination with the server-side functionality of ASP.NET Core.

➤ jQuery (supported by the OpenJS Foundation `https://openjsf.org`) is a library that abstracts browser differences when accessing DOM elements and reacting to events. A few years ago, this library was used with nearly every website. Today, more options are available, and you can't expect to have jQuery available everywhere.

➤ Angular (`https://angular.io`) is a library from Google based on the MVC pattern for simplifying development and testing with single-page web applications. (Unlike ASP.NET MVC, Angular offers the MVC pattern with client-side code.)

➤ React (`https://reactjs.org`) is a library from Facebook that offers functionality to easily update user interfaces as data changes in the background.

ASP.NET Core templates for Visual Studio include templates for Angular and React. Visual Studio 2019 and Visual Studio Code support IntelliSense and debugging JavaScript and TypeScript code.

WebAssembly

WebAssembly is another standard with HTML technologies (`https://webassembly.org/`). WebAssembly allows writing binary code that's running in the browser so that not only JavaScript code but also the binary WASM code can run in the browser. The code is still running in the sandboxed environment of the browser, so it's safe to run this binary code on the client. The goal is to allow the creation of applications that need more CPU power to run in the browser, such as photo and video editing tools, CAD applications, and virtual reality and virtual machines (`https://webassembly.org/docs/use-cases/`).

Microsoft ported the .NET runtime to WASM code. This allows running .NET assemblies in the browser. This is used by Blazor, which is a library that can run Razor components either on the server or in the client within WebAssembly. This technology is covered in Chapter 27.

> **NOTE** *Styling web applications and writing JavaScript code is not covered in this book. You can read more about HTML and styles in* HTML and CSS: Design and Build Websites *by John Duckett (John Wiley & Sons, 2011), and you can get up to speed with* Beginning Java-Script, Fifth Edition, *by Jeremy McPeak and Paul Wilton (Wrox, 2015).*

CREATING AN ASP.NET CORE WEB PROJECT

Now that you have some background about web technologies, let's start by creating a simple console application and just a few lines of code to convert it to a web application. This first web app sample in this chapter answers HTTP requests and returns simple HTML code:

```
> dotnet new console -o SimpleHost
```

The SDK of the project file needs to be changed to `Microsoft.NET.Sdk.Web` to reference all of the NuGet packages needed by web applications (project configuration file `SimpleHost.csproj`):

```
<Project Sdk="Microsoft.NET.Sdk.Web">

  <PropertyGroup>
    <TargetFramework>net5.0</TargetFramework>
    <Nullable>enable</Nullable>
  </PropertyGroup>

</Project>
```

With the top-level statements of the application, the `Start` method of the `WebHost` class is invoked. This method has a parameter of `RequestDelegate`. `RequestDelegate` is a delegate that receives an `HttpContext` as parameter and returns a `Task`. The `HttpContext` can be used to read the request from the client and send a return. With the sample code, a response containing an HTML string is returned. The method `WaitForShutdownAsync` starts a task and keeps this task running until you use Ctrl+C or SIGTERM to stop the application (code file `SimpleHost/Program.cs`):

```
using Microsoft.AspNetCore;
using Microsoft.AspNetCore.Hosting;
using Microsoft.AspNetCore.Http;

await WebHost.Start(async context =>
{
  await context.Response.WriteAsync("<h1>A Simple Host!</h1>");
}).WaitForShutdownAsync();
```

With this in action, you can start the application with `dotnet run` and access it from a browser with the address `https://localhost:5001`. As soon as you request pages from the server, you'll also see log output in the console. ASP.NET Core hosting shows info-level log output with every request, such as the following:

```
info: Microsoft.AspNetCore.Hosting.Diagnostics[1]
      Request starting HTTP/2 GET https://localhost:5001/ - -
info: Microsoft.AspNetCore.Hosting.Diagnostics[2]
      Request finished HTTP/2 GET https://localhost:5001/ - - - 200 - - 31.4379ms
```

To see logging output when starting the application (which also shows the port numbers the Kestrel server is listening to), you can add an `appsettings.json` file that's read with the default configuration (config file `SimpleHost/appsettings.json`):

```
{
  "Logging": {
    "Console": {
      "LogLevel": {
        "Default": "Trace"
      }
    }
  }
}
```

With this simple web application, you can read the request coming in from the `HttpContext` and return different results based on the requests.

The `WebHost` class uses the `Host` class discussed in Chapter 15, "Dependency Injection and Configuration." The `Start` method of the `WebHost` class implicitly invokes the `CreateDefaultBuilder` of the `Host` class to configure several services, adds services for ASP.NET Core, and configures the Kestrel server. See Chapter 19, "Networking," for information on how to define a custom configuration of the Kestrel server.

You can change the configuration of the WebHost class using StartWith where an IApplicationBuilder can be used on further configuration. The IApplicationBuilder is shown later in this chapter when modifying middleware with ASP.NET Core. The Services property of the WebHost class can be used to register services with the DI container.

Host Server

Opening the project with Visual Studio creates the launchsetting.json file in the Properties folder. This file is also created when you create a web application using dotnet new web. With this file, you can specify environment variables that are used when starting the application, as well as URLs used by the Kestrel server. A profile to run IIS Express is configured in addition to the project command where the Kestrel server is started (configuration file SimpleHost/Properties/launchsettings.json):

```
{
  "iisSettings": {
    "windowsAuthentication": false,
    "anonymousAuthentication": true,
    "iisExpress": {
      "applicationUrl": "http://localhost:35246",
      "sslPort": 44397
    }
  },
  "profiles": {
    "IIS Express": {
      "commandName": "IISExpress",
      "launchBrowser": true,
      "environmentVariables": {
        "ASPNETCORE_ENVIRONMENT": "Development"
      }
    },
    "SimpleHost": {
      "commandName": "Project",
      "dotnetRunMessages": "true",
      "launchBrowser": true,
      "applicationUrl": "https://localhost:5001;http://localhost:5000",
      "environmentVariables": {
        "ASPNETCORE_ENVIRONMENT": "Development"
      }
    }
  }
}
```

> **NOTE** *When you use Visual Studio on Windows, Internet Information Services (IIS) Express is installed with Visual Studio. When you start the web app from Visual Studio, you can select between the different profiles configured in* launchsettings.json *to start the application via* IIS Express *or the* SimpleHost *profile. The profile with the same name as the application just starts the Kestrel server. When IIS is started, Kestrel is used behind the scenes. To support ASP.NET Core with IIS, a module is installed that forwards the request to the Kestrel server. This Kestrel functionality within IIS can run out of process or in process of the worker process. When you install the ASP.NET runtime on the server where IIS is hosted, make sure to install the Hosting Bundle that includes the IIS module (*https://dotnet.microsoft.com/download/dotnet/5.0*).*

Startup

Let's move into a more powerful web application. Creating an empty web application using `dotnet new web -o WebSampleApp` creates `Program.cs` with a `Main` method using the `Host` class, a `Startup.cs` file with the `Startup` class, `appsettings.json` from the configuration, and `launchsettings.json` to configure profiles and environment variables. Something that's different with the configuration of the `Host` class than what you've seen in earlier chapters is the use of the `ConfigureWebHostDefaults` method and the `UseStartup` method, as shown in the following code snippet. The method `ConfigureWebHostDefaults` configures the Kestrel server and adds IIS integration if it's running on the Windows platform, sets up the `IWebHostEnvironment` for static web assets, and configures some middleware modules. With the generic type parameter, the `UseStartup` method defines the class that should be used next for starting up the server; from the template generated, this is the `Startup` class (code file `WebSampleApp/Program.cs`):

```
public class Program
{
  public static void Main(string[] args)
  {
    CreateHostBuilder(args).Build().Run();
  }

  public static IHostBuilder CreateHostBuilder(string[] args) =>
    Host.CreateDefaultBuilder(args)
      .ConfigureWebHostDefaults(webBuilder =>
      {
        webBuilder.UseStartup<Startup>();
      });
}
```

With web applications, the dependency injection container usually is configured with the `Startup` class instead of the `Host` class. The `Startup` class has two important methods that are invoked dynamically from the ASP.NET Core runtime as shown in the following code snippet: `ConfigureServices` and `Configure`.

The `ConfigureServices` method is used to configure the dependency injection container (you can use the `ConfigureServices` method of the `Host` class in a similar way). This method has an `IServiceCollection` property that contains all the services already registered in the `Main` method, and it allows you to add additional services.

The `Configure` method is invoked dynamically to configure the ASP.NET Core middleware. Middleware is invoked with every HTTP request. The `Configure` method receives parameters via dependency injection. The parameters defined in the template are of type `IApplicationBuilder` and `IWebHostEnvironment`.

The interface `IWebHostEnvironment` allows you to access the name of the environment (`EnvironmentName`), the root path for the content (the directory of the sources), and the root path for the web content files (the subdirectory wwwroot). The default provider that accesses these directories is the `PhysicalFileProvider`. With a different provider, the content can be served from other sources—for example, from a database. Within the implementation of the `Configure` method, the `IWebHostEnvironment` is used to check whether the current environment is `Development` by invoking the extension method `IsDevelopment`. Exceptions are returned to the caller only in the development environment. Because of security issues, in the production environment, the user doesn't see detailed information on the exception.

The `IApplicationBuilder` interface is used to add middleware to the HTTP request pipeline. When you invoke the `Use` method of this interface, you can build the HTTP request pipeline to define what should be done in answer to a request. The `Use` method is implemented using a fluent API, and it again returns an `IApplicationBuilder`. With this, multiple middleware objects can easily be added to the pipeline. Several extension methods, such as UseRouting and UseEndpoints, make it easier to add middleware. Middleware will be added in several sections in this chapter. Later in this chapter, in the section "Creating Custom Middleware," you can create custom middleware and add it to the pipeline:

```
public class Startup
{
  public void ConfigureServices(IServiceCollection services)
  {
  }

  public void Configure(IApplicationBuilder app, IWebHostEnvironment env)
  {
    if (env.IsDevelopment())
    {
      app.UseDeveloperExceptionPage();
    }

    app.UseRouting();

    app.UseEndpoints(endpoints =>
    {
      endpoints.MapGet("/", async context =>
      {
        await context.Response.WriteAsync("Hello World!");
      });
    });
  }
}
```

Sample Application Preparations

The sample application contains an entry page where all the features shown by the application can easily be accessed using HTML links:

```
endpoints.MapGet("/", async context =>
{
  string[] lines = new[]
  {
    @"<ul>",
      @"<li><a href=""/hello.html"">Static Files</a> - requires " +
      @"UseStaticFiles</li>",
    @"<li>Request and Response",
      @"<ul>",
        @"<li><a href=""/RequestAndResponse"">Request and Response</a></li>",
        @"<li><a href=""/RequestAndResponse/header"">Header</a></li>",
        @"<li><a href=""/RequestAndResponse/add?x=38&y=4"">Add</a></li>",

        //...

      @"</ul>",
    @"</li>",
  @"</ul>"
  };
```

```
      StringBuilder sb = new();
      foreach (var line in lines)
      {
        sb.Append(line);
      }
      string html = sb.ToString().HtmlDocument("Web Sample App");

      await context.Response.WriteAsync(html);
    });
```

The `HTMLExtensions` class is defined to create some specific HTML and reduce the amount of HTML code needed. This class defines extension methods to create `div`, `span`, and `li` elements (code file `WebSampleApp/Extensions/HtmlExtensions.cs`):

```
public static class HtmlExtensions
{
  public static string Div(this string value) =>
    $"<div>{value}</div>";

  public static string Span(this string value) =>
    $"<span>{value}</span>";

  public static string Div(this string key, string value) =>
    $"{key.Span()}: {value.Span()}".Div();

  public static string Li(this string value) =>
    $@"<li>{value}</li>";

  public static string Li(this string value, string url) =>
    $@"<li><a href=""{url}"">{value}</a></li>";

  public static string Ul(this string value) =>
    $"<ul>{value}</ul>";

  public static string HtmlDocument(this string content, string title)
  {
    StringBuilder sb = new();
    sb.Append("<!DOCTYPE HTML>");
    sb.Append("<head><meta charset=\"utf-8\"><title>{title}</title></head>");
    sb.Append("<body>");
    sb.Append(content);
    sb.Append("</body>");
    return sb.ToString();
  }
}
```

ADDING CLIENT-SIDE CONTENT

Usually you don't want to just send simple strings to the client. By default, simple HTML files and other static content can't be sent. ASP.NET Core reduces the overhead as much as possible. Even static files are not returned from the server if you do not enable them.

To enable static files served from the web server, you can add the extension method `UseStaticFiles` to add the required middleware. This middleware checks whether the request matches an existing file (code file `WebSampleApp/Startup.cs`):

```
public void Configure(IApplicationBuilder app, IWebHostEnvironment env)
{
  /...
  app.UseStaticFiles();

  app.UseRouting();
  //...

}
```

The folder where you add static files is the `wwwroot` folder within the project. Let's add static content by adding a simple HTML file (code file `WebSampleApp/wwwroot/hello.html`), as shown here:

```
<!DOCTYPE html>
<html>
  <head>
    <meta charset="utf-8"/ >
    <title>ASP.NET Core Sample</title>
  </head>
  <body>
    <h1>Hello, ASP.NET with Static Files</h1>
  </body>
</html>
```

Now you make a request to the HTML file from the browser after starting the server—for example, `https://localhost:5001/Hello.html`. If you uncomment the extension method `UseStaticFiles`, the HTML file is not returned from the request.

The NuGet server is hosting NuGet packages containing .NET libraries. Most JavaScript libraries can be found on the Node server. These libraries are packaged with Node Package Manager (NPM), WebPack, Parcel, or other package managers. This topic is not covered here.

When using .NET, you can create a web application using Angular and an ASP.NET Core backend with the web API:

```
> dotnet new angular -o AngularSample
```

In the `ClientApp` subfolder, you'll find a file named `package.json`, which contains the configuration for NPM. You can create a similar project with the React JavaScript library for the frontend and ASP.NET Core with the backend; there's a similar folder structure with `package.json` for JavaScript libraries:

```
> dotnet new react -o ReactSample
```

This is a separate topic on its own. However, if you don't need to use a JavaScript library in a size similar to Angular or React and just want to use a few JavaScript and CSS files, the library manager can be all that you need. With this tool you can download JavaScript libraries from providers, select the files from the libraries you need, and copy them to your local source code.

To install the library manager as a global tool, use this:

```
> dotnet tool install microsoft.web.librarymanager.cli -g
```

Then you can use the `libman` command to get libraries. To initialize `libman` for the project, while in the project directory, invoke the following command:

```
> libman init
```

You'll be asked where to get the JavaScript libraries. By default, `cdnjs` is used. This creates the `libman.json` file as shown here:

```
{
  "version": "1.0",
  "defaultProvider": "cdnjs",
  "libraries": []
}
```

The providers you can use are `cdnjs` (https://cdnjs.com), `jsdlvr` (https://www.jsdelivr.com/), `unpkg` (https://unpkg.com/), and filesystem. `unpkg` is the content delivery network (CDN) service from Node that offers all the packages available on the Node server.

To get the files needed for jQuery, you can invoke the following command:

```
> libman install jquery
```

Within the libraries section, you'll find a reference to the library and the destination where the files should be copied to. You need to copy the files to the `wwwroot` directory where static files are served from the web application, as shown here:

```
{
  "version": "1.0",
  "defaultProvider": "cdnjs",
  "libraries": [
    {
      "library": "jquery@3.6.0",
      "destination": "wwwroot\\lib\\jquery"
    }
  ]
}
```

If you don't need the complete package content with your application, you can specify what files should be retrieved from the package with the `files` element, and you can change to get a specific library from a different CDN service with the `provider` element (config file `WebSampleApp/libman.json`):

```
{
  "version": "1.0",
  "defaultProvider": "cdnjs",
  "libraries": [
    {
      "provider": "unpkg",
      "library": "bootstrap@4.6.0",
      "files": [ "dist/css/bootstrap.css", "dist/js/bootstrap.js" ],
      "destination": "wwwroot/lib/bootstrap"
    },
    {
      "library": "jquery@3.6.0",
      "destination": "wwwroot/lib/jquery"
    }
  ]
}
```

CREATING CUSTOM MIDDLEWARE

When you invoke the `UseStaticFiles` extension method with the `IApplicationBuilder`, as shown in the previous section, middleware is implemented. This middleware checks the request if a physical file is available. If it is, this file is returned. Otherwise, the next middleware is invoked. Middleware is implemented as a pipeline—one middleware follows the next one. With middleware, authentication and authorization, session handling, caching, and more functionalities are implemented.

You can implement custom middleware functionality by invoking the Use method. The Use method is declared with this parameter and return type:

```
IApplicationBuilder Use(Func<RequestDelegate, RequestDelegate> middleware);
```

The Use method returns an IApplicationBuilder, so you can invoke the Use method with a fluent API. The parameter is a delegate with a RequestDelegate as a parameter and return type. RequestDelegate is a delegate that defines an HttpContext as a parameter returning a Task.

With the following invocation of the Use method, the variable next is a RequestDelegate parameter. This parameter references a lambda with the HttpContext parameter and returns a Task. With the implementation of the lambda, a custom header named CustomHeader1 is written to the HTTP response, and then the next middleware defined with the next variable is invoked (code file WebSampleApp/Startup.cs):

```
public void Configure(IApplicationBuilder app, IWebHostEnvironment env)
{
  if (env.IsDevelopment())
  {
    app.UseDeveloperExceptionPage();
  }

  app.Use(next => context =>
  {
    context.Response.Headers.Add("CustomHeader1", "custom header value");
    return next(context);
  });


  app.UseStaticFiles();
  //...
}
```

Instead of implementing the middleware as a parameter of the Use method, you can create a class such as the following HeaderMiddleware class. With a middleware class, the constructor receives the next middleware with the RequestDelegate parameter. Here you need to remember the next middleware reference to invoke it after the middleware's functionality is done. With the Invoke method, you implement the functionality of the middleware and invoke the next middleware forwarding the HttpContext. The sample code writes a custom HTTP header to the HTTP response similar to the previous middleware (code file WebSampleApp/Middleware/HeaderMiddleware.cs):

```
public class HeaderMiddleware
{
  private readonly RequestDelegate _next;

  public HeaderMiddleware(RequestDelegate next) => _next = next;

  public Task Invoke(HttpContext httpContext)
  {
    httpContext.Response.Headers.Add("CustomHeader2", "custom header value");
    return _next(httpContext);
  }
}
```

Implementing the middleware in a class has the advantage that you can add a lot more to the constructor—for example, other services that you might need from the middleware implementation or configuration settings, such as using the IOptions interface. IOptions is covered in Chapter 15.

To make it easy to register the middleware, an extension method for the `IApplicationBuilder` can be defined. The method `UseHeaderMiddleware` invokes the `UseMiddleware` method by passing the `HeaderMiddleware` as a generic parameter (code file `WebSampleApp/Middleware/HeaderMiddleware.cs`):

```
public static class HeaderMiddlewareExtensions
{
  public static IApplicationBuilder UseHeaderMiddleware(
    this IApplicationBuilder builder) =>
    builder.UseMiddleware<HeaderMiddleware>();
}
```

This middleware is added similar to the way all the other middleware is added. Because the middleware extension method `UseHeaderMiddleware` is added after `UseStaticFiles`, with static files this header information is not returned to the client (code file `WebSampleApp/Startup.cs`):

```
app.Use(next => context =>
{
  context.Response.Headers.Add("CustomHeader1", "custom header value");
  return next(context);
});

app.UseStaticFiles();

app.UseHeaderMiddleware();
```

When you run the application, you see the header returned to the client (using the browser's developer tools), and the heading shows up in every page, no matter which of the previously created links you use (see Figure 24-1).

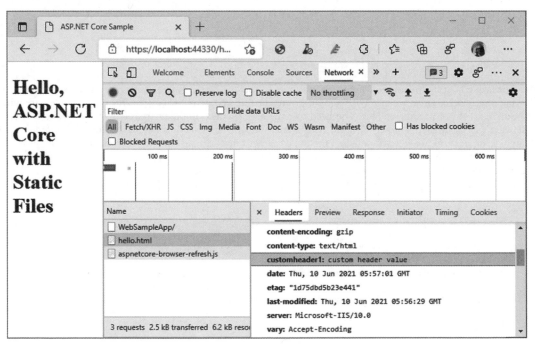

FIGURE 24-1

ENDPOINT ROUTING

How the links map to code is defined by endpoint routing. Endpoint routing is implemented as middleware, using the `UseRouting` method. The `UseRouting` method needs to be followed by the `UseEndpoints` method where the routes are defined. `UseRouting` uses the `EndpointRoutingMiddleware` where the routing decisions are made; it defines what route maps to which implementation. However, middleware specified before the routing can change the endpoint for a request. For example, if a request is denied because the user is not authenticated, the route is changed for this request—for example, to a page with unauthorized information.

To define routes, different technologies offer extension methods to the interface `IEndpointRouteBuilder`. With Razor Pages, the method `MapRazorPages` defines routing to link to Razor Pages in the Pages folder where the link maps the name of the Razor Page. With SignalR, the method `MapHub` maps a specified link to a class that derives from the `Hub` class. In the next four chapters, you'll learn about different routes using attribute-based routing with web APIs, and then route definitions with GRPC, Razor Pages, MVC routes, Blazor, and SignalR. In this chapter, you define custom routes without using these technologies.

Defining Routes

In the previous code samples, you saw how to define a route with the `Map` (or `MapGet`) method. Using the string `/` as an argument defined the response to the root path. `Map` is an extension method for the `IEndpointRouteBuilder` interface, which is the parameter type of the `UseEndpoints` method.

The following invocation of the `Map` method defines the route to the `/session` URL. If the URL matches this link, the `SessionSample` service is retrieved from the DI container, and the `SessionAsync` method is invoked (code file `WebSampleApp/Startup.cs`):

```
endpoints.Map("/session", async context =>
{
  var service = context.RequestServices.GetRequiredService<SessionSample>();
  await service.SessionAsync(context);
});
```

The following code snippet shows using a string pattern with a *route parameter*. The URI segment that follows `/randr/` maps to a route value with a key named `action`. Using a URI such as `/randr/header`, the parts of this URI can be retrieved using the `GetRouteValue` method of the `HttpContext` object. Because a `?` is added to the route parameter, the action is optional, and the URI `/randr` without following URI segments also matches this route definition. The `action` variable will be `null` in that case. With the `switch` expression used here, the `switch` path is designed using tuple pattern matching where both the route parameter and the HTTP method are used for the decision (code file `WebSampleApp/Startup.cs`):

```
endpoints.Map("/randr/{action?}", async context =>
{
  var service = context.RequestServices.GetRequiredService<RequestAndResponseSamples>();
  string? action = context.GetRouteValue("action")?.ToString();
  string method = context.Request.Method;
  string result = (action, method) switch
  {
    (null, "GET") => service.GetRequestInformation(context.Request),
    ("header", "GET") => service.GetHeaderInformation(context.Request),
    ("add", "GET") => service.QueryString(context.Request),
    ("content", "GET") => service.Content(context.Request),
    ("form", "GET" or "POST") => service.Form(context.Request),
    ("writecookie", "GET") => service.WriteCookie(context.Response),
    ("readcookie", "GET") => service.ReadCookie(context.Request),
```

```
    ("json", "GET") => service.GetJson(context.Response),
    _ => string.Empty
  };

  if (action is "json")
  {
    await context.Response.WriteAsync(result);
  }
  else
  {
    var doc = result.HtmlDocument("Request and Response Samples");
    await context.Response.WriteAsync(doc);
  }
});
```

Route Constraints

With the pattern parameter, you can specify constraints as defined in the following code snippet. Here, the two mandatory URI segments that follow the /add need to map to int values; otherwise, this Map method doesn't have a match for the route, and the following route definitions are checked for matches. The GetRouteValue returns a nullable object containing the string value, and you need to convert it to the type you need (code file WebSampleApp/Startup.cs):

```
endpoints.Map("/add/{x:int}/{y:int}", async context =>
{
  int x = int.Parse(context.GetRouteValue("x")?.ToString() ?? "0");
  int y = int.Parse(context.GetRouteValue("y")?.ToString() ?? "0");
  await context.Response.WriteAsync($"The result of {x} + {y} is {x + y}");
});
```

Besides int, you can pass several constraints such as bool, datetime, min, max, length, minlength, range, and others. Check the documentation for route constraint references at https://docs.microsoft.com/en-us/aspnet/core/fundamentals/routing?view=aspnetcore-5.0#route-constraint-reference.

REQUEST AND RESPONSE

With the HTTP protocol, the client sends an HTTP request to the server. This request is answered with an HTTP response.

The request consists of a header and, in many cases, body information to the server. The server uses the header information to know about the needs of the client and can send different results based on this information. Let's take a look at what information is sent by the client.

The method GetRequestInformation uses an HttpRequest object to access Scheme, Host, Path, QueryString, Method, and Protocol properties (code file WebSampleApp/Services/RequestAndResponseSamples.cs):

```
public string GetRequestInformation(HttpRequest request)
{
  StringBuilder sb = new();
  sb.Append("scheme".Div(request.Scheme));
  sb.Append("host".Div(request.Host.HasValue ? request.Host.Value :
    "no host"));
```

```
    sb.Append("path".Div(request.Path));
    sb.Append("query string".Div(request.QueryString.HasValue ?
      request.QueryString.Value : "no query string"));
    sb.Append("method".Div(request.Method));
    sb.Append("protocol".Div(request.Protocol));
    return sb.ToString();
  }
```

All the requests to demonstrate the sample code of this section are served passing the path /randr to the server, as specified in the Startup class. With the implementation of the RequestDelegate parameter, the RequestAndResponseSamples object is retrieved from the DI container, and the GetRequestInformation method is invoked. The result is then written to the HttpResponse object (code file WebSampleApp/Startup.cs):

```
endpoints.Map("/randr/{action?}", async context =>
{
  var service = context.RequestServices.GetRequiredService<RequestAndResponseSamples>();
  string? action = context.GetRouteValue("action")?.ToString();
  string method = context.Request.Method;
  string result = (action, method) switch
  {
    (null, "GET") => service.GetRequestInformation(context.Request),
    ("header", "GET") => service.GetHeaderInformation(context.Request),
    //...
  };
  await context.Response.WriteAsync(result);
});
```

Starting the program and accessing https://localhost:5001/randr/ results in the following information:

```
scheme: https
host: localhost:001
path: /randr
query string: no query string
method: GET
protocol: HTTP/2
```

When you add a query string, such as https://localhost:5001/randr?x=3&y=5, the query string accessing the property QueryString shows up:

```
query string: ?x=3&y=5
```

The following sections implement the different methods to show request headers, query strings, and more.

> **NOTE** *For HTML encoding the result, read Chapter 20, "Security."*

Request Headers

Let's take a look at what information the client sends within the HTTP header. To access the HTTP header information, the HttpRequest object defines the Headers property. This is of type IHeaderDictionary, and it contains a dictionary with the name of the header and a string array for the values. Using this information, the Div method created earlier is used to write div elements for the client (code file WebSampleApp/Services/RequestAndResponseSamples.cs):

```
public string GetHeaderInformation(HttpRequest request)
{
```

```
        StringBuilder sb = new();
        foreach (var header in request.Headers)
        {
          sb.Append(header.Key.Div(string.Join("; ", header.Value)));
        }
        return sb.ToString();
      }
```

The results you see depend on the HTTP version, browser, operating system, and configured languages that you're using. With Microsoft Edge running on Windows 10, you can see values as shown here:

```
:authority: localhost:5001
:method: GET
:path: /randr/header
:scheme: https
Accept: text/html,application/xhtml+xml,application/xml;q=0.9,image/webp,image/apng,*/*;
q=0.8,application/signed-exchange;v=b3;q=0.9
Accept-Encoding: gzip, deflate, br
Accept-Language: en-US,en;q=0.9,de;q=0.8
Cookie: color=red
Host: localhost:5001
Referer: https://localhost:5001/
User-Agent: Mozilla/5.0 (Windows NT 10.0; Win64; x64) AppleWebKit/537.36
(KHTML, like Gecko) Chrome/91.0.4435.0 Safari/537.36 Edg/91.0.825.0
Upgrade-Insecure-Requests: 1
sec-ch-ua: " Not;A Brand";v="99", "Microsoft Edge";v="91", "Chromium";v="91"
sec-ch-ua-mobile: ?0
sec-fetch-site: same-origin
sec-fetch-mode: navigate
sec-fetch-user: ?1
sec-fetch-dest: document
```

What can you get out of this header information?

With HTTP/2 the authority, method, path, and scheme headers are now prefixed with a :. Some headers used with HTTP/1.1, such as the Connection header, are no longer needed with HTTP/2.

The Accept header defines the Multipurpose Internet Mail Extensions (MIME) formats the browser accepts. MIME was originally used with email attachments but now has a more general-purpose use. The list is in order by the preferred formats. Depending on this information, you might decide to return data with different formats based on the client's needs. Edge prefers HTML followed by XHTML and XML followed by WEBP and APNG. With some of this information, a quantifier is also defined. The browsers used for the output all have *.* at the end of this list to accept all data returned.

The User-Agent header was used in ancient HTML times to differentiate the code to return to the client. Configuration files existed that list the capabilities of specific browsers. Because this often failed with newer browser versions and some browsers allow you to customize this string, this is no longer used. Just check the user agent string from the Edge browser that marks itself as Mozilla, AppleWebKit, Gecko, Chrome, Safari, and Edge. Instead of using the user-agent header, just check dynamically for the browser capabilities when working with JavaScript code.

The Accept-Language header information shows the languages the user has configured. You can use this information to return localized information. Localization is discussed in Chapter 22, "Localization."

The sec-fetch-xx header information belongs to the fetch metadata request headers of HTTP/2. sec-fetch-site is used with cross-origin resource sharing (CORS). sec-fetch-mode defines how the request was initiated. `sec-fetch-user` gives the information if the request was initiated by a user. `?1` is true, `?0` false. `sec-fetch-dest` defines the request destination to the server. With HTML code where the navigation was initiated, the value is `document`. Other values are `script`, `serviceworker`, `audio`, `image`, and others.

The header information that you've seen so far is what the browser sends for very simple sites. Usually, there will be more detail, such as cookies, authentication information, and custom information. To see all the information that is sent to and from a server, including the header information, you can use the browser's developer tools and start a network session; you'll see not only all the requests that are sent to the server but also header, body, parameters, cookies, and timing information, as shown in Figure 24-2.

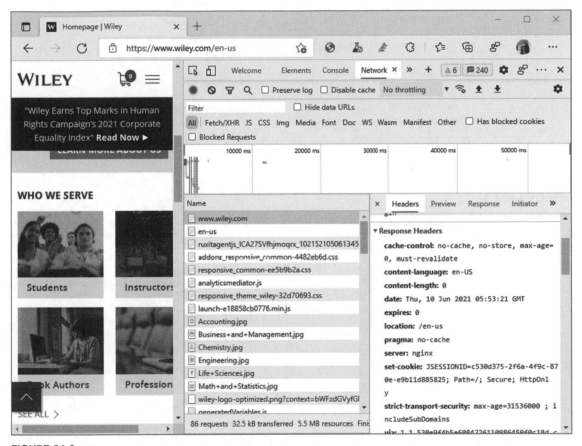

FIGURE 24-2

Query Parameters

The following `QueryParameters` method is used to retrieve parameters named x and y from the query string. If parsing the parameters to `int` values succeeds, a calculation is done. Depending on the input, different HTML code is returned (code file `WebSampleApp/Services/RequestAndResponseSamples.cs`):

```
public string QueryString(HttpRequest request)
{
    string xtext = request.Query["x"];
    string ytext = request.Query["y"];
```

```
    if (xtext == null || ytext == null)
    {
      return "x and y must be set".Div();
    }

    if (!int.TryParse(xtext, out int x))
    {
      return $"Error parsing {xtext}".Div();
    }

    if (!int.TryParse(ytext, out int y))
    {
      return $"Error parsing {ytext}".Div();
    }
    return $"{x} + {y} = {x + y}".Div();
}
```

The IQueryCollection returned from the Query string also enables you to access all the keys using the Keys property, and it offers a ContainsKey method to check whether a specified key is available.

Using the URL https://localhost:5001/randr/add?x=39&y=3 shows this result in the browser:

```
39 + 3 = 42
```

Form Data

Instead of passing data from the user to the server with a query string, you can use the form HTML element. This example uses an HTTP POST request instead of GET. With a POST request, the user data is passed with the body of the request instead of within the query string.

Using form data is defined with two requests. First, the form is sent to the client with a GET request, and then the user fills in the form and submits the data with a POST request. As shown in the following code snippet, the method Form invokes the GetForm or ShowForm method, depending on the HTTP method type (code file WebSampleApp/Services/RequestResponseSamples.cs):

```
public string Form(HttpRequest request) =>
  request.Method switch
  {
    "GET" => GetForm(),
    "POST" => ShowForm(request),
    _ => string.Empty
  };
```

The form is created with an input element named text1 and a Submit button. Clicking the Submit button invokes the form's action method with an HTTP method as defined with the method argument:

```
private static string GetForm() =>
  "<form method=\"post\" action=\"/randr/form\">" +
  "<input type=\"text\" name=\"text1\" />" +
  "<input type=\"submit\" value=\"Submit\ \"/>" +
  "</form>";
```

For reading the form data, the HttpRequest class defines a Form property. This property returns an IFormCollection object that contains all the data from the form that is sent to the server:

```
private string ShowForm(HttpRequest request)
{
```

```
StringBuilder sb = new();
if (request.HasFormContentType)
{
  IFormCollection coll = request.Form;
  foreach (var key in coll.Keys)
  {
    sb.Append(key.Div(HtmlEncoder.Default.Encode(coll[key])));
  }
  return sb.ToString();
}
else return "no form".Div();
}
```

Using the `/randr/form` link, the form is received with the GET request. When you click the Submit button, the form is sent with the POST request, and you can see the `text1` key for the form data.

Cookies

To remember user data between multiple requests, you can use cookies. Adding a cookie to the `HttpResponse` object sends the cookie within the HTTP header from the server to the client. By default, a cookie is temporary (not stored on the client), and the browser sends it back to the server if the URL is the same domain where the cookie was coming from. You can set the `Path` to restrict when the browser returns the cookie. In this case, the cookie is returned only when it comes from the same domain and the path `/randr` is used. When you set the `Expires` property, the cookie is a persistent cookie, which means it is stored on the client. When the expiration time passes, the cookie will be removed. However, there's no guarantee that the cookie isn't removed earlier (code file `WebSampleApp/Services/RequestResponseSamples.cs`):

```
public string WriteCookie(HttpResponse response)
{
  response.Cookies.Append("color", "red", new CookieOptions
  {
    Path = "/randr",
    Expires = DateTime.Now.AddDays(1)
  });
  return "cookie written".Div();
}
```

The cookie can be read again by reading the `HttpRequest` object. The `Cookies` property contains all the cookies that are returned by the browser:

```
public string ReadCookie(HttpRequest request)
{
  StringBuilder sb = new();
  IRequestCookieCollection cookies = request.Cookies;
  foreach (var key in cookies.Keys)
  {
    sb.Append(key.Div(cookies[key]));
  }
  return sb.ToString();
}
```

For testing cookies, you can also use the browser's developer tools. The tools show all the information about the cookies that are sent and received.

Sending JSON

The server returns more than HTML code; it also returns many kinds of data formats, such as CSS files, images, and videos. The client knows what kind of data it receives with the help of a MIME type in the response header.

The method `GetJson` creates a JSON string from an anonymous object with `Title`, `Publisher`, and `Author` properties. To serialize this object with JSON, the NuGet package `NewtonSoft.Json` is added, and the namespace `NewtonSoft.Json` imported. The MIME type for the JSON format is `application/json`. This is set via the `ContentType` property of the `HttpResponse` (code file `WebSampleApp/Services/RequestResponseSample.cs`):

```
public string GetJson(HttpResponse response)
{
  var b = new
  {
    Title = "Professional C# and .NET - 2021 Edition",
    Publisher = "Wiley",
    Author = "Christian Nagel"
  };
  string json = JsonSerializer.Serialize(b);
  response.ContentType = "application/json";
  return json;
}
```

This is the data returned to the client:

```
{"Title":"Professional C# and .NET 2021","Publisher":"Wiley",
  "Author":"Christian Nagel"}
```

> **NOTE** *JSON serialization is explained in Chapter 18, "Files and Streams." Sending/receiving JSON with REST APIs is covered in Chapter 25, "Services."*

SESSION STATE

A service that is implemented using middleware is *session state*. Session state enables temporarily remembering data from the client on the server. Session state itself is implemented as middleware.

Session state is initiated when a user first requests a page from a server. While the user keeps opening pages on the server, the session continues until a timeout (typically 10 minutes) occurs. To keep state on the server while the user navigates to a new page, state can be written to a session. When a timeout is reached, the session data is removed.

To identify a session, on the first request, a temporary cookie with a session identifier is created. This cookie is returned from the client with every request to the server until the browser is closed, and then the cookie is deleted. Session identifiers can also be sent in the URL string as an alternative to using cookies.

On the server side, session information can be stored in local memory. In a web farm, session state that is stored in local memory doesn't propagate between different systems. With a sticky session configuration, the user always returns to the same physical server, so the user has the state available on the server—unless the server fails. If the server is not configured to use sticky sessions, the client request can go to any server instance. With such a configuration, you can store session state within distributed memory or a database. Storing session state in distributed memory also helps with process recycling of the server process; recycling kills session state if you're using just a single server process.

To enable sessions, you need to configure middleware and the DI container. With the DI container, you need to register the `ISessionStore` interface that's used by the middleware.

The following code snippet shows the registration of the DI container. The `AddSession` method is an extension method that registers `ISessionStore` with the implementation class `DistributedSessionStore`. The class `DistributedSessionStore` needs an object implementing `IDistributedCache` with the constructor. This is registered with the extension method `AddDistributedMemoryCache`. With the options of the `AddSession` method, you can configure the idle timeout and the cookie options. The cookie is used to identify the session (code file `WebSampleApp/Startup.cs`):

```
public void ConfigureServices(IServiceCollection services)
{
  services.AddScoped<SampleService>();
  services.AddDistributedMemoryCache();
  services.AddSession(options =>
    options.IdleTimeout = TimeSpan.FromMinutes(10));
  //...
}
```

> **NOTE** *Instead of using* `AddDistributedMemoryCache` *to store the session, you can add the NuGet package* `Microsoft.Extensions.Caching.StackExchangeRedis` *and configure it to use a Redis server for the cache across different instances.*

The second part is to configure the middleware in the pipeline by calling the `UseSession` extension method. You need to invoke this method before any response is written where the session might be required—such as is done with the `UseHeaderMiddleware`—thus `UseSession` is called before the other methods. The code that uses session information is mapped to the `/Session` path (code file `WebSampleApp/Startup.cs`):

```
public void Configure(IApplicationBuilder app, ILoggerFactory loggerFactory)
{
  //...
  app.UseSession();
  app.UseHeaderMiddleware();
  //...
}
```

You can write session state using `Setxxx` methods, such as `SetString` and `SetInt32`. These methods are defined with the `ISession` interface that is returned from the `Session` property of the `HttpContext`. Session data is retrieved using `Getxxx` methods (code file `WebSampleApp/Services/SessionSample.cs`):

```
public class SessionSample
{
  private const string SessionVisits = nameof(SessionVisits);
  private const string SessionTimeCreated = nameof(SessionTimeCreated);
  public static async Task SessionAsync(HttpContext context)
  {
    int visits = context.Session.GetInt32(SessionVisits) ?? 0;
    string timeCreated = context.Session.GetString(SessionTimeCreated) ??
      string.Empty;
    if (string.IsNullOrEmpty(timeCreated))
    {
```

```
        timeCreated = DateTime.Now.ToString("t", CultureInfo.InvariantCulture);
        context.Session.SetString(SessionTimeCreated, timeCreated);
      }
      DateTime timeCreated2 = DateTime.Parse(timeCreated);
      context.Session.SetInt32(SessionVisits, ++visits);
      await context.Response.WriteAsync(
        $"Number of visits within this session: {visits} " +
        $"that was created at {timeCreated2:T}; " +
        $"current time: {DateTime.Now:T}");
    }
  }
```

> **NOTE** *The sample code uses an invariant culture to store the time when the session was created. The time shown to the user is using a specific culture. It's a good practice to use invariant cultures storing culture-specific data on the server. Information about invariant cultures and how to set cultures is explained in Chapter 22.*

HEALTH CHECKS

When you're running the web application in production, it's a good idea to implement health checks, which can automatically detect if there's an issue while the application is being monitored. Based on this, the routers can redirect to different service instances, the application can be restarted, or other actions can be triggered—for example, administrators can receive notifications.

When implementing health checks, you need to think about different scenarios. For example, the application might be *live* as soon as it responds to requests and might be *running* when the initialization is completed and the caches are filled. The application can be in a *healthy* state if every service used by the application can be reached and the database can be accessed. When the application is working partially, for example when not so important services cannot be reached, the state is *degraded*. If the application cannot be reached, it's *unhealthy*.

With ASP.NET Core, you can implement health checks with a simple method or a class that implements the interface IHealthCheck. With the sample application, the service class HealthSample is created to simulate healthy and unhealthy states. Invoking the method SetHealthy by passing a false value, the properties IsHealthy and IsReady return false. By setting a true value, the IsHealthy method immediately returns true. The IsReady property returns true after a delay of 10 seconds (code file WebSampleApp/Services/HealthSample.cs):

```
public class HealthSample : IDisposable
{
  private Timer? _timer;
  public void SetHealthy(bool healthy = true)
  {
    if (IsHealthy == healthy) return;

    _isReady = false;
    IsHealthy = healthy;

    if (IsHealthy)
    {
      if (_timer is not null)
      {
        _timer.Dispose();
```

```
      }
      _timer = new(o =>
      {
        _isReady = true;
      }, null, TimeSpan.FromSeconds(10), Timeout.InfiniteTimeSpan);
    }
  }

  public void Dispose() => _timer?.Dispose();

  public bool IsHealthy { get; set; } = false;

  private bool _isReady = false;
  public bool IsReady => IsHealthy && _isReady;
}
```

The class `CustomHealthCheck` implements the interface `IHealthCheck`. This interface defines the method `CheckHealthAsync` that needs to be implemented to return a `HealthCheckResult`. The `HealthCheckResult` can be `Healthy`, `Degraded`, and `Unhealthy`. With the health test, the `IsHealthy` property of the `HealthSample` is checked to return the corresponding state (code file `WebSampleApp/CustomHealthCheck.cs`):

```
public class CustomHealthCheck : IHealthCheck
{
  private readonly HealthSample _healthSample;
  public CustomHealthCheck(HealthSample healthSample) => _healthSample = healthSample;

  public Task<HealthCheckResult> CheckHealthAsync(HealthCheckContext context,
    CancellationToken cancellationToken = default)
  {
    if (_healthSample.IsLive) return Task.FromResult(
      HealthCheckResult.Healthy("healthy"));
    else return Task.FromResult(HealthCheckResult.Unhealthy("unhealthy"));
  }
}
```

The class `CustomReadyCheck` is implemented in a similar way. It just checks for the `IsReady` property of the `HealthSample` service.

To activate health checks, you need to register the service classes in the DI container and define routes for health checking, as shown in the following code snippet. The method `AddHealthChecks` registers a health check service class that derives from the abstract base class `HealthCheckService` and returns an `IHealthChecksBuilder` that can be used to add multiple health checks. The two health check types added are `CustomHealthCheck` and `CustomReadyCheck` using the `AddCheck` method. The first parameter of this method defines the name of the health check. With the second parameter, you can define what health status should be returned on failure. The third parameter defines tags that you can use to select specific health checks that should be used with a health link (code file `WebSampleApp/Startup.cs`):

```
public void ConfigureServices(IServiceCollection services)
{
  //...
  services.AddSingleton<HealthSample>();
  services.AddHealthChecks()
    .AddCheck<CustomHealthCheck>("livecheck",
      HealthStatus.Unhealthy, tags: new[] { "liveness" })
```

```
    .AddCheck<CustomReadyCheck>("readycheck",
      HealthStatus.Degraded, tags: new[] { "readiness" });
}
```

Instead of passing a type with the generic parameter of the `AddCheck` method, you can pass a delegate to the `AddCheck` and `AddCheckAsync` methods.

In the `Configure` method where the middleware is configured, you specify links for health checks with the endpoint configuration. With the following code snippet, the first invocation of the `MapHealthChecks` method defines a link where all health checks specified are tested. The `MapHealthChecks` method has an option to pass `HealthCheckOptions` with the second parameter. Here, the `Predicate` property is set and can be used to select health check definitions that are marked with the tag `liveness`. You can also specify which HTTP status codes should be returned based on the health information. The sample code just specifies the same configuration as the default configuration: 200 OK with healthy and degraded status and 503 service unavailable when the health check returned unhealthy. You can adapt this to your needs (code file `WebSampleApp/Startup.cs`):

```
app.UseEndpoints(endpoints =>
{
  endpoints.MapHealthChecks("/health/allchecks");
  endpoints.MapHealthChecks("/health/live", new HealthCheckOptions()
  {
    Predicate = reg => reg.Tags.Contains("liveness"),
    ResultStatusCodes = new Dictionary<HealthStatus, int>()
    {
      [HealthStatus.Healthy] = StatusCodes.Status200OK,
      [HealthStatus.Degraded] = StatusCodes.Status200OK,
      [HealthStatus.Unhealthy] = StatusCodes.Status503ServiceUnavailable
    }
  });
});
```

To implement health checks, ASP.NET Core includes functionality in the namespace `Microsoft.Extensions.Diagnostics.HealthChecks`.

The next health check maps to the link `/health/ready` and uses the readiness health check. This code sample shows that you can fully customize the output with the options by setting the `ResponseWriter` property. This property needs a delegate that receives the `HttpContext` and the `HealthReport` writer. You can use this writer to get every issue that was returned from the different health checks and return this information to the caller via the `HttpContext` (code file `WebSampleApp/Startup.cs`):

```
endpoints.MapHealthChecks("/health/ready", new HealthCheckOptions
{
  Predicate = reg => reg.Tags.Contains("readiness"),
  ResponseWriter = async (context, writer) =>
  {
    context.Response.StatusCode = writer.Status switch
    {
      HealthStatus.Healthy => StatusCodes.Status200OK,
      HealthStatus.Degraded => StatusCodes.Status503ServiceUnavailable,
      HealthStatus.Unhealthy => StatusCodes.Status503ServiceUnavailable,
      _ => StatusCodes.Status503ServiceUnavailable
    };

    if (writer.Status == HealthStatus.Healthy)
    {
```

```
        await context.Response.WriteAsync("ready");
      }
      else
      {
        await context.Response.WriteAsync(writer.Status.ToString());
        await context.Response.WriteAsync($"duration: {writer.TotalDuration}");
      }
    }
  });
```

With this health check in place, you can try the links to receive health check information. With the downloadable sample code, the link `sethealthy/?healthy=true` can be used to set the `HealthSample` service class to live and ready, passing false to unhealthy.

> **NOTE** *Instead of creating health check types for every scenario you need, you can use available NuGet packages with health-check classes such as* `Microsoft.Extensions.Diagnostics.HealthChecks.EntityFrameworkCore`, *which checks for accessibility of the database server connected to the EF Core context. With* `ASPNETCore.HealthChecks.*` *packages (these packages are not from Microsoft), health checks for SQL Server, Redis, Application Insights, MongoDB, CosmosDB, Azure KeyVault, and many other scenarios are available for use. Check the GitHub repo at* `https://github.com/xabaril/AspNetCore.Diagnostics.HealthChecks` *for more information.*

DEPLOYMENT

To publish the web application, from the Visual Studio Solution Explorer, you can select the Publish option in the context menu of the application. From there, you can directly publish the application to an on-premises IIS or a Microsoft Azure App Service. Using the `dotnet` CLI, you can use `dotnet publish` to prepare the files for publication (be sure the current directory of your command prompt is the directory of the project file). Use the option `-c Release` to prepare release code to publish. Read Chapter 1, ".NET Applications and Tools," to include the runtime with the publish package.

With Microsoft Azure, you can create an Azure App Service plan with Windows or Linux environments and a web app and publish the .NET application there. See the readme file with the chapter's downloadable code for a script and instructions to create an Azure App Service plan and a web app using the Azure CLI.

One great option to publish your application is to create a Docker image. With a Docker image, you have one file that you can publish into a registry (such as `hub.docker.com` or your private Azure Container Registry), and you can pull the image from an Azure Container Instance, a Kubernetes cluster, or an Azure App Service to run the image within a Docker container.

To create a Docker image from the application, you need to have a file named `Dockerfile` with the commands to create the image, and you need to have Docker Desktop installed. The following `Dockerfile` consists of multiple stages to create a Docker image. Every stage starts with a FROM command. The first FROM command creates a temporary image that is based on the image `mcr.microsoft.com/dotnet/aspnet:5.0`. This is Microsoft's prebuilt image containing the .NET 5 runtime and is optimized for production. With the Docker command EXPOSE, ports 80 and 443 are opened.

The next stage is based on a different image. `mcr.microsoft.com/dotnet/sdk:5.0` is the .NET 5.0 image that has the .NET SDK included. The new temporary image that's created is built using the `dotnet restore` command (to restore all packages from the NuGet server) and the `dotnet build` command (to build the binaries for the application). The third `FROM` continues with the second build image (`FROM build AS publish`) and invokes the `dotnet publish` command to create the files needed for publication. The fourth and last `FROM` uses the result of the first image (`FROM base as final`), copies the publish files from the publish image, and defines the entry point of the resulting image. When this image is started, the `dotnet` driver is used to load `WebSampleApp.dll` to start up the Kestrel server (Docker file `WebSampleApp/Dockerfile`):

```
FROM mcr.microsoft.com/dotnet/aspnet:5.0 AS base
WORKDIR /app
EXPOSE 80
EXPOSE 443

FROM mcr.microsoft.com/dotnet/sdk:5.0 AS build
WORKDIR /src
COPY ["WebSampleApp.csproj", "."]
RUN dotnet restore "./WebSampleApp.csproj"
COPY . .
WORKDIR "/src/."
RUN dotnet build "WebSampleApp.csproj" -c Release -o /app/build

FROM build AS publish
RUN dotnet publish "WebSampleApp.csproj" -c Release -o /app/publish

FROM base AS final
WORKDIR /app
COPY --from=publish /app/publish .
ENTRYPOINT ["dotnet", "WebSampleApp.dll"]
```

Using the Docker Desktop, you can build and publish the image using the Docker CLI with the current directory set to the location of the `Dockerfile`. The command `docker build` builds the image (you can see your images with `docker images`), `docker tag` tags the image with the prefix name of your container registry, and `docker push` pushes the image to the registry:

```
> docker build . -t WebSampleApp/v1.0
> docker tag WebSampleApp/v1.0 {linktoyourregistry}/WebSampleApp/v1.0
> docker push {linktoyourregistry}/WebSampleApp/v1.0
```

> **NOTE** *Check* www.docker.com *and* https://opencontainers.org *for more information about Docker. Also check the chapter's readme file with the downloadable source code for instructions and a script to create an Azure Container Registry and to publish the image stored from the registry to an Azure App Service.*

SUMMARY

In this chapter, you explored the foundation of ASP.NET Core and web applications. With this you learned how to register services with the DI container in the ASP.NET Core way, as well as configuring and creating custom middleware in the `Startup` class. Using endpoint routing, you configured routes to implement functionality based on requests from the client and to return HTTP responses including features such as cookies, form data, and storing session information.

You've seen how to implement health checking, which can be of great use when deploying Docker images and when you use many services that interact with each other.

The next chapter shows how you can use ASP.NET Core to deal with JSON request and responses with web APIs and also use GRPC for the binary communication with services.

25

Services

WHAT'S IN THIS CHAPTER?

➤ Overview of the ASP.NET Core web API

➤ Creating web API controllers

➤ Creating .NET clients calling REST APIs

➤ Using Entity Framework Core with services

➤ Handling authorization and authentication with REST Services

➤ Creating gRPC services and clients

➤ Streaming with gRPC

➤ Implementing Azure functions

CODE DOWNLOADS FOR THIS CHAPTER

The source code for this chapter is available on the book page at www.wiley.com. Click the Downloads link. The code can also be found at https://github.com/ProfessionalCSharp/ ProfessionalCSharp2021 in the directory 3_Web/Services.

The code for this chapter is divided into the following major examples:

➤ BooksApi

➤ BooksData

➤ BooksDataAndAuthentication

➤ GRPC

➤ AzureFunctions

All the sample projects have *nullable reference types* enabled.

UNDERSTANDING TODAY'S SERVICES

Once upon a time, Windows Communication Foundation (WCF) tried to offer all functionality needed by services. You could create services returning XML or binary data, asynchronous communication was offered by message queuing, and UDP could be used as well, and it was all based on SOAP standards. Everything was possible, and you could configure every option. The issue with that situation was that even seemingly simple scenarios often became quite complex.

Today, we are back to many different options. Microservices can be implemented with different technologies. You can use a request/reply pattern or a disconnected scenario to send messages to a queue and process the job asynchronously. Microservices can communicate via JSON serialization or can send messages in a binary format. There are many options you can choose from, and many options are covered here and in following chapters:

➤ Web APIs with ASP.NET Core can be used to implement a request/reply programming model based on the Representational State Transfer (REST) guidelines. Usually, JSON data is passed and returned, but you can pass other data as well—for example, a PNG image or XML data.

➤ gRPC Remote Procedure Calls (gRPC) was initially developed by Google and is a platform-independent technology that allows for binary communication based on HTTP/2. ASP.NET Core has built-in support for gRPC.

➤ Azure Functions give you a consumption-based offering where you pay only for the seconds you need CPU and memory. You can create a REST API with this technology as well, but you also can create functions that are triggered on events other than HTTP requests. The function can be started when messages arrive in a queue, when data is written to an Azure Cosmos DB, or when an event is published to an Azure Event Grid.

➤ SignalR gives an abstraction layer to WebSockets (but also works if WebSockets is not available) and offers communication from the server to the client, which is great for communication with a group of clients.

SignalR is covered in Chapter 28, "SignalR." All the other technologies mentioned are covered in this chapter.

REST SERVICES WITH ASP.NET CORE

REST is not a standard; it's a guideline. This guideline was defined by Roy Fielding in his 2000 PhD dissertation "Architectural Styles and the Design of Network-based Software Architectures" (`https://www.ics.uci.edu/~fielding/pubs/dissertation/fielding_dissertation.pdf`). REST is based on these principles:

➤ Client-server architecture

➤ Stateless communication, which allows for easy scaling of services

➤ Cacheable data so the client can keep data without the need to request it again

➤ A uniform interface to access resources

➤ A layered system that doesn't allow you to see beyond the immediate layer where the communication is taking place

➤ Code on demand (optional), which allows you to download code that the client can use with the received data

The uniform interface is central to the REST guidelines and covers resources that can be identified (for example, by using a URI), manipulation of resources is possible with representations (for example, JSON, XML), messages are self-describing, and a key concept is hypermedia as the engine of application state (HATEOAS). With

HATEOAS, information about what to do with a resource is returned with a response—for example, different links for deposit/withdraw/transfer/close on a balance.

Not all services require all REST principles; that's why Leonard Richardson defined different REST levels (https://www.martinfowler.com/articles/richardsonMaturityModel.html). Only REST level 3 supports all the guidelines, including HATEOAS. REST level 2 defines that a service supports different HTTP verbs (such as GET to read resources and POST to create new resources) and HTTP return codes (such as 201 for created). Microsoft Azure defines a level 2 REST API to create/update/read resources, such as resource groups, storage accounts, app services, and a lot more.

Let's start with creating a web API using ASP.NET Core by using the following command:

```
> dotnet new webapi -o BooksAPI
```

With .NET 5, this template creates a new project with an API implementing a weather forecast service based on random values (isn't there some randomness with published weather forecast information?). With the sample code, you'll get rid of the weather forecast and instead implement a service to create and read information about book chapters. Using a database and authorization will be addressed in later sections.

Defining a Model

First, you need a type that represents the data to return and change. To allow using the model both from the client and from the server, create a .NET 5 library Books.Shared that contains the BookChapter record (code file BooksApi/Books.Shared/BookChapter.cs):

```
using System;

namespace Books.Models
{
  public record BookChapter(Guid Id, int Number, string Title, int PageCount);
}
```

Creating a Service

Next, you create a service interface and class offering the functionality. The methods offered by the service are defined with the interface IBookChapterService—methods to retrieve, add, and update book chapters. The methods are defined asynchronously to allow for different implementations—for example, an implementation that calls another service (code file BooksApi/BooksApi/Services/IBookChapterService.cs):

```
public interface IBookChapterService
{
  Task AddAsync(BookChapter chapter);
  Task AddRangeAsync(IEnumerable<BookChapter> chapters);
  Task<IEnumerable<BookChapter>> GetAllAsync();
  Task<BookChapter?> FindAsync(Guid id);
  Task<BookChapter?> RemoveAsync(Guid id);
  Task<BookChapter?> UpdateAsync(BookChapter chapter);
}
```

The implementation of the service is defined by the class BookChapterService. The book chapters are kept in a collection class. Because multiple tasks from different client requests can access the collection concurrently, the type ConcurrentDictionary is used for the book chapters. This class is thread safe. The Add, Remove, and Update methods make use of the collection to add, remove, and update book chapters (code file BooksApi/BooksApi/Services/BookChaptersService.cs):

```
public class BookChapterService : IBookChapterService
{
```

```csharp
private readonly ConcurrentDictionary<Guid, BookChapter> _chapters = new();

private BookChapter GetInitializedId(BookChapter chapter)
{
  if (chapter.Id == Guid.Empty)
  {
    chapter = chapter with { Id = Guid.NewGuid() };
  }
  return chapter;
}

public Task AddAsync(BookChapter chapter)
{
  chapter = GetInitializedId(chapter);
  _chapters[chapter.Id] = chapter;
  return Task.CompletedTask;
}

public Task AddRangeAsync(IEnumerable<BookChapter> chapters)
{
  foreach (var c in chapters)
  {
    var chapter = GetInitializedId(c);
    _chapters[chapter.Id] = chapter;
  }
  return Task.CompletedTask;
}

public Task<BookChapter?> FindAsync(Guid id)
{
  _chapters.TryGetValue(id, out BookChapter? chapter);
  return Task.FromResult(chapter);
}

public Task<IEnumerable<BookChapter>> GetAllAsync() =>
  Task.FromResult<IEnumerable<BookChapter>>(_chapters.Values);

public Task<BookChapter?> RemoveAsync(Guid id)
{
  _chapters.TryRemove(id, out BookChapter? removed);
  return Task.FromResult(removed);
}

public async Task<BookChapter?> UpdateAsync(BookChapter chapter)
{
  var existingChapter = await FindAsync(chapter.Id);
  if (existingChapter is null) return null;
  _chapters[chapter.Id] = chapter;
  return chapter;
}
}
```

So that some sample chapters are available when you first access the service, the class `SampleChapters` fills the book chapter service with chapter information (code file `BooksApi/BooksApi/Services/SampleChapters.cs`):

```csharp
public class SampleChapters
{
```

```
    private readonly IBookChapterService _bookChaptersService;
    public SampleChapters(IBookChapterService bookChapterService) =>
      _bookChaptersService = bookChapterService;

    private string[] _sampleTitles = new[]
    {
      ".NET Application Architectures",
      "Core C#",
      "Classes, Structs, Tuples, and Records",
      "Object-Oriented Programming with C#",
      "Operators and Casts",
      "Arrays",
      "Delegates, Lambdas, and Events",
      "Collections",
      "ADO.NET and Transactions"
    };

    private int[] _chapterNumbers = { 1, 2, 3, 4, 5, 6, 7, 8, 25 };

    private int[] _pageCounts = { 35, 42, 33, 20, 24, 38, 20, 32, 44 };

    public void CreateSampleChapters()
    {
      List<BookChapter> chapters = new();
      for (int i = 0; i < 8; i++)
      {
        chapters.Add(new BookChapter(Guid.NewGuid(), _chapterNumbers[i],
          _sampleTitles[i], _pageCounts[i]));
      }
      _bookChaptersService.AddRangeAsync(chapters);
    }
  }
}
```

Let's get into the configuration of the DI container, which is shown with the following code snippet. From the ASP.NET Core web API template used, you can see the `AddControllers` extension method. This method registers several services to be used with API controllers, such as route handlers, pipeline filters, result handlers, and more. With the .NET 5 template, `AddSwaggerGen` is invoked as well. This method is defined in the NuGet package `Swashbuckle.AspNetCore`, which implements the OpenAPI standard (originally known as Swagger) to generate a description for the API services in the project. The description can be used to automatically create code for the client. With Swashbuckle, a website is generated where you can test the API. (See `https://openapis.org` for more information on this standard.) The `BookChapterService` and `SampleChapters` classes also are registered with the DI container, which allows the DI container to inject these types. `BookChapterService` is declared to be injected as singleton, which should keep state between invocations (code file `BooksApi/BooksApi/Startup.cs`):

```
public class Startup
{
  public Startup(IConfiguration configuration) => Configuration = configuration;

  public IConfiguration Configuration { get; }

  public void ConfigureServices(IServiceCollection services)
  {
    services.AddControllers();
    services.AddSwaggerGen(c =>
    {
      c.SwaggerDoc("v3", new OpenApiInfo { Title = "BooksApi", Version = "v3" });
```

```
    });

    services.AddSingleton<IBookChapterService, BookChapterService>();
    services.AddScoped<SampleChapters>();
  }
  //...
}
```

> **NOTE** *If you add C# documentation to the methods of the API (C# documentation is covered in Chapter 2, "Core C#"), after creating a documentation file, you can add this documentation to the OpenAPI description by invoking the method* `IncludeXmlComments` *with the options of* `AddSwaggerGen`.

The middleware is configured in the `Configure` method. If the application is running in the `Development` environment, OpenAPI information is shown by invoking the methods `UseSwagger` and `UseSwaggerUI` to configure the middleware for the OpenAPI definition and HTML page. In case you want other developers to use your API when the application is running in production, you can move these methods outside of the `IsDevelopment` check to invoke it from all environments. Showing exceptions on the client (`UseDeveloperExceptionPage`) should only ever be used in the `Development` environment. With the endpoint routing configuration, `MapControllers` is invoked to allow for attribute-based routing for the API controllers, as is shown in the next section. To fill the sample chapters, a route to `/init` is also defined, which uses an instance of the `SampleChapters` class to fill the chapter service with sample chapters (code file `BooksApi/BooksApi/Startup.cs`):

```
public void Configure(IApplicationBuilder app, IWebHostEnvironment env)
{
  if (env.IsDevelopment())
  {
    app.UseDeveloperExceptionPage();
    app.UseSwagger();
    app.UseSwaggerUI(c => c.SwaggerEndpoint("/swagger/v3/swagger.json", "BooksApi v3"));
  }

  app.UseHttpsRedirection();

  app.UseRouting();

  app.UseAuthorization();

  app.UseEndpoints(endpoints =>
  {
    endpoints.MapControllers();

    endpoints.MapGet("/init", async context =>
    {
      var sampleChapters = context.RequestServices.GetRequiredService<SampleChapters>();
      sampleChapters.CreateSampleChapters();
      await context.Response.WriteAsync("sample chapters initialized");
    });
  });
}
```

Creating a Controller

The `BookChaptersController` class that implements an API controller is shown in the next code snippet. A controller that's routed from the endpoint routing is a class with the `Controller` postfix. Optionally, a controller class can derive from the base class `ControllerBase`. The `ControllerBase` class offers some practical methods and properties, such as the `HttpContext`, `Request`, and `Response`. These properties are used to access the HTTP request and response as shown in the previous chapter. The base class also offers methods that can be used to directly return a result. The route to the controller is defined with the `Route` attribute. The route starts with `api` followed by the name of the controller—which is the name of the controller class without the `Controller` postfix. The `Produces` and `ApiController` attributes are of practical use for the `OpenApi` definition. The `Produces` attribute gives information about the type of data returned from the controller. The `ApiController` attribute defines some default behavior typical with API services. For example, with action method parameters, you don't need to specify the `FromBody` attribute because it is now a default (code file `BooksApi/BooksApi/Controllers/BookChaptersController.cs`):

```
[Produces("application/json")]
[Route("api/[controller]")]
[ApiController]
public class BookChaptersController : ControllerBase
{
  private readonly IBookChapterService _chapterService;

  public BookChaptersController(IBookChapterService chapterService) =>
    _chapterService = chapterService;
  //...
}
```

> **NOTE** *With an ASP.NET Core API controller, by default JSON information is returned. If you want to return XML, you must add an XML serializer to the DI container with the `IMvcBuilder` fluent API using the `AddXmlSerializerFormatter` method. You also must add the `Produces` attribute that the controller produces `application/xml`. This serializer requires a parameterless constructor; thus, a nominal record cannot be used in such a scenario. From the client application, you need to specify the accept header accordingly.*

Using the `HttpGet` attribute with the `GetBookChapters` method maps the HTTP GET request with the route specified with the controller class. The method `GetAllAsync` from the injected service returns `Task<IEnumerable <BookChapter>>` that's directly returned from this action method. The `ProducesResponseType` attribute specifies the HTTP status codes returned from an action method. This information is used by the OpenAPI description (code file `BooksApi/BooksApi/Controllers/BookChaptersController.cs`):

```
// GET api/bookchapters
[ProducesResponseType(StatusCodes.Status200OK)]
[HttpGet]
public Task<IEnumerable<BookChapter>> GetBookChapters() =>
 _chapterService.GetAllAsync();
```

To not return the complete list of books, you can specify a parameter with the `GetBookChapters` method similar to the `GetBookChapterById` method shown in the next code snippet. This method returns a single chapter based on the received `Guid` parameter. From the URL path, the `HttpGet` attribute specifies the same name in the route. The route specified with the action method is attached to the route defined with the class. In case the chapter is not found from the service, an HTTP 404 status code is returned using the `NotFound` method from the base class.

With a success, a 200 status code is returned from the `Ok` method. The method is declared to return an `ActionResult`, which is flexible in what to return—either the resource specified with the generic parameter (`BookChapter`) or just the error, such as 404 (code file `BooksApi/BooksApi/Controllers/BookChaptersController.cs`):

```
// GET api/bookchapters/guid
[ProducesResponseType(StatusCodes.Status200OK)]
[ProducesResponseType(StatusCodes.Status404NotFound)]
[HttpGet("{id}", Name = nameof(GetBookChapterById))]
public async Task<ActionResult<BookChapter>> GetBookChapterById(Guid id)
{
  BookChapter? chapter = await _chapterService.FindAsync(id);
  if (chapter is null)
  {
    return NotFound();
  }
  else
  {
    return Ok(chapter);
  }
}
```

On adding a new book chapter, the method `PostBookChapter` is added. This method receives a `BookChapter` as part of the HTTP body that is assigned to the method parameter after deserialization. In case the parameter `chapter` is null, a `BadRequest` (HTTP error 400) is returned. When adding the `BookChapter`, this method returns `CreatedAtRoute`. `CreatedAtRoute` returns the HTTP status 201 (Created) with the object serialized. The returned header information contains a link to the resource—that is, a link to the `GetBookChapterById` with the `id` set to the identifier of the newly created object (code file `BooksApi/BooksApi/Controllers/BookChaptersController.cs`):

```
// POST api/bookchapters
[ProducesResponseType(StatusCodes.Status400BadRequest)]
[ProducesResponseType(StatusCodes.Status201Created)]
[HttpPost]
public async Task<ActionResult> PostBookChapter(BookChapter chapter)
{
  if (chapter is null)
  {
    return BadRequest();
  }
  await _chapterService.AddAsync(chapter);
  return CreatedAtRoute(nameof(GetBookChapterById), new { id = chapter.Id }, chapter);
}
```

You update items using an HTTP PUT request. The `PutBookChapter` method updates an existing item from the collection. In case the object is not yet in the collection, `NotFound` is returned. If the object is found, it is updated, and a success result 204—no content with an empty body—is returned (code file `BooksApi/BooksApi/Controllers/BookChaptersController.cs`):

```
// PUT api/bookchapters/guid
[ProducesResponseType(StatusCodes.Status400BadRequest)]
[ProducesResponseType(StatusCodes.Status404NotFound)]
[ProducesResponseType(StatusCodes.Status204NoContent)]
[HttpPut("{id}")]
public async Task<ActionResult> PutBookChapter(Guid id, BookChapter chapter)
{
  if (chapter is null || id != chapter.Id)
  {
```

```
      return BadRequest();
    }
    var existingChapter = await _chapterService.FindAsync(id);

    var c = await _chapterService.UpdateAsync(chapter);
    if (c is null)
    {
      return NotFound();
    }
    else
    {
      return NoContent();
    }
  }
}
```

With the HTTP DELETE request, book chapters are simply removed from the dictionary (code file BooksApi/ BooksApi/Controllers/BookChaptersController.cs):

```
[ProducesResponseType(StatusCodes.Status200OK)]
[HttpDelete("{id}")]
public async Task<ActionResult> Delete(Guid id)
{
  await _chapterService.RemoveAsync(id);
  return Ok();
}
```

> **NOTE** *With the sample code, the* Delete *method deletes the book chapter if it's in the dictionary and does nothing if it's not there. An alternative version would be to return a 404 (not found) status code. The Microsoft REST API guidelines (*https://github.com/ Microsoft/api-guidelines/blob/master/Guidelines.md*) specify the* DELETE *request to be idempotent, so it should return the same result with multiple requests. With default implementations from the template accessing the database, 404 is returned if the data is not available. You need to decide for your scenario if you agree with the guidelines or need information if the resource is not found.*

With the controller and Swagger configuration in place, it is possible to do tests from the browser. You can see the OpenAPI definition at https://localhost:5001/swagger/v3/swagger.json. The Swagger graphical UI (see Figure 25-1) is shown at https://localhost:5001/swagger/index.html. With this page, you can run tests to your API from the browser.

Testing REST APIs

For a command-line interface, you can install the .NET tool microsoft.dotnet-httprepl (https://aka.ms/ http-repl-doc). The downloadable sample application has this tool defined as a local tool. You can install local tools with dotnet tool restore. When you run this tool, you can connect to a running service and send get, post, and put commands. Using the post command, you can submit the content of a JSON file as shown here:

```
> dotnet httprepl
(Disconnected)> connect https://localhost:5001
https://localhost:5001/> get api/BookChapters/
https://localhost:5001/> get api/BookChapters/ "e89837d9-4392-450c-902b-4e34fb72344c"
https://localhost:5001/> post api/BookChapters/ -f samplechapter.json
```

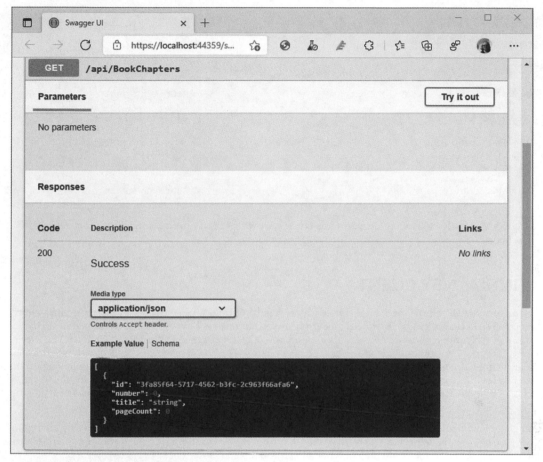

FIGURE 25-1

REST Results and Status Codes

The following table summarizes the results a service returns based on the HTTP methods:

HTTP METHOD	DESCRIPTION	REQUEST BODY	RESPONSE BODY
GET	Returns a resource	Empty	The resource
POST	Adds a resource	The resource to add	The resource
PUT	Updates a resource	The resource to update	None
DELETE	Deletes a resource	Empty	Empty

The following table shows important HTTP status codes as well as the `Controller` method with the instantiated object that returns the status code. To return any HTTP status code, you can return an `HttpStatusCodeResult` object that can be initialized with the status code you need.

HTTP STATUS CODE	CONTROLLER METHOD	TYPE
200 OK	Ok	OkResult
201 Created	CreatedAtRoute	CreatedAtRouteResult
204 No Content	NoContent	NoContentResult
400 Bad Request	BadRequest	BadRequestResult
401 Unauthorized	Unauthorized	UnauthorizedResult
404 Not Found	NotFound	NotFoundResult
Any status code		StatusCodeResult

All success status codes start with 2; error status codes start with 4. You can find a list of status codes in RFC 7231 at `https://tools.ietf.org/html/rfc7231#section-6.3`.

CREATING A .NET CLIENT

Using the browser to call the service is a simple way to handle testing. When creating JavaScript clients, you can use the Fetch API that is available with all modern browsers. In this book, a .NET client is created using the `HttpClient` API, and `HttpClient` objects are created using the `HttpClient` factory. Read Chapter 19, "Networking," for more information about the `HttpClient` factory. The NuGet packages needed with this console application are `Microsoft.Extensions.Hosting` (to use the `Host` class), `Microsoft.Extensions.Http` (to use the `HttpClient` factory), and `System.Net.Http.Json` (to use new .NET 5 extension methods for the `HttpClient` class for JSON serialization; using the JSON serializer is discussed in Chapter 18, "Files and Streams").

In the sample application, with the configuration of the DI container, the factory for the `HttpClient` (`AddHttpClient` method) is configured to use a typed client: the `BooksApiClient` class. The factory configuration sets the `BaseAddress` property to retrieve the URL from the service from a configuration or a hard-coded string if it's not found in the configuration (code file `BooksApi/BookServiceClient/Program.cs`):

```
using var host = Host.CreateDefaultBuilder(args)
  .ConfigureServices((context, services) =>
  {
    var bookApiSettings = context.Configuration.GetSection("BooksService");
    services.Configure<BooksApiClientOptions>(bookApiSettings);
    services.AddHttpClient<BooksApiClient>(config =>
    {
      var baseAddress = context.Configuration.GetSection("BooksService")["BaseAddress"] ??
        "https://localhost:5001";
      config.BaseAddress = new Uri(baseAddress);
    });
  }).Build();

Console.WriteLine("Client - press return to continue");
Console.ReadLine();

using var scope = host.Services.CreateScope();
```

```
var client = scope.ServiceProvider.GetRequiredService<BooksApiClient>();
await client.ReadChaptersAsync();
await client.ReadChapterAsync();
await client.ReadNotExistingChapterAsync();
await client.AddChapterAsync();
await client.UpdateChapterAsync();
await client.RemoveChapterAsync();
```

The `BooksApiClient` class uses `BooksApiClientOptions` to fill the link to the API. The `HttpClient` class is injected with the constructor (code file `BooksApi/BookServiceClient/BooksApiClient.cs`):

```csharp
public record BooksApiClientOptions
{
  public string? BooksApiUri { get; init; }
}

public class BooksApiClient
{
  private readonly HttpClient _httpClient;
  private readonly string _booksApiUri;
  private readonly ILogger _logger;
  private Guid? _chapterId;

  public BooksApiClient(HttpClient, IOptions<BooksApiClientOptions> options,
    ILogger<BooksApiClient> logger)
  {
    _httpClient = httpClient;
    _logger = logger;
    _booksApiUri = options.Value.BooksApiUri ?? "api/books";
  }
  //...
}
```

To have all the URLs needed in one place, they are configured with the .NET configuration (which you can override from command-line parameters and extend using the Azure App Configuration, as discussed in Chapter 15, "Dependency Injection and Configuration" (configuration file `BooksApi/BookServiceClient/appsettings.json`):

```json
{
  "BooksService": {
    "BaseAddress": "https://localhost:5001",
    "BooksApiUri": "api/BookChapters"
  },
  //...
}
```

Sending GET Requests

The server controller defines two methods with GET requests: one method that returns all chapters and the other that returns just a single chapter but requires the chapter's identifier with the URI. The method `ReadChaptersAsync` invokes the `GetFromJsonAsync` method using the `HttpClient` instance. This method returns a task with an array of book chapters that is shown on the console. The ID of the first chapter is remembered in the field `_firstChapterId` because this will be used in other methods that follow (code file `BooksApi/BookServiceClient/BooksApiClient.cs`):

```csharp
public async Task ReadChaptersAsync()
{
```

```
    Console.WriteLine(nameof(ReadChapterAsync));
    var chapters = await _httpClient.GetFromJsonAsync<IEnumerable<BookChapter>>(
      _booksApiUri);
    if (chapters is null) return;
    foreach (var chapter in chapters)
    {
      Console.WriteLine($"{chapter.Number} {chapter.Title}");
    }
    _chapterId = chapters.FirstOrDefault()?.Id;
    Console.WriteLine();
  }
```

The method `GetFromJsonAsync` is an extension method defined in the namespace `System.Net.Http.Json`, which does the following:

➤ It uses the `GetAsync` method of the `HttpClient` class to send a GET request.

➤ It throws an exception if the request is not successful, using the `EnsureSuccessStatusCode` method of the `HttpResponseMessage` class.

➤ It uses the `ReadAsStreamAsync` method of the `HttpContent` class to read the response stream.

> **NOTE** *The* `HttpContent` *class also offers the* `ReadAsStringAsync` *method to read a string from the HTTP response. However, this method should be used only with strings shorter than 85,000 bytes. When you get data from API services, you might get long strings (how long is the list returned?), which are put into the large object heap (LOH). The large object heap is handled differently from the garbage collector because of performance constraints. To avoid this issue, it's best to use streams that make use of a byte array buffer that is reused. Read Chapter 13, "Managed and Unmanaged Memory," for more information about the garbage collector and the LOH.*

When you run the application, you need to start both the service as well as the client app; remember to initialize the data by accessing the link `https://localhost:5001/init`. Invoking the `ReadChaptersAsync` method shows the status code 200 and the titles from the chapters (the logging output is simplified):

```
ReadChapterAsync
info: System.Net.Http.HttpClient.BooksApiClient.ClientHandler[100]
      Sending HTTP request GET https://localhost:5001/api/BookChapters
info: System.Net.Http.HttpClient.BooksApiClient.ClientHandler[101]
      Received HTTP response headers after 320.2596ms - 200
1 .NET Applications and Tools
2 Core C#
3 Classes, Structs, Tuples, and Records
4 Object-Oriented Programming with C#
5 Operators and Casts
6 Arrays
7 Delegates, Lambdas, and Events
8 Collections
25 Services
```

The method `ReadChapterAsync` shows the GET request to retrieve a single chapter. With this, the identifier of a chapter is added to the URI string (code file `BooksApi/BookServiceClient/BooksApiClient.cs`):

```
public async Task ReadChapterAsync()
{
```

```
Console.WriteLine(nameof(ReadChapterAsync));
if (_firstChapterId is not null)
{
  string uri = $"{_booksApiUri}/{_firstChapterId}";
  var chapter = await _httpClient.GetFromJsonAsync<BookChapter>(uri);
  if (chapter is not null)
  {
    Console.WriteLine($"{chapter.Number} {chapter.Title}");
  }
}
Console.WriteLine();
}
```

The result of the `ReadChapterAsync` method is shown here:

```
ReadChapterAsync
info: System.Net.Http.HttpClient.BooksApiClient.ClientHandler[100]
      Sending HTTP request GET https://localhost:5001/api/BookChapters/
44ecb858-86c6-4602-bd9c-e1357d6b5c4e
info: System.Net.Http.HttpClient.BooksApiClient.ClientHandler[101]
      Received HTTP response headers after 72.0244ms - 200
1 .NET Applications and Tools
```

What if a GET request is sent with a nonexistent chapter identifier? The method `ReadNotExistingChapterAsync` shows how to deal with this. Calling the `GetFromJsonAsync` method works as in the previous code snippet, but an identifier that does not exist is added to the URI. Remember from the implementation of the `GetFromJsonAsync` method implementation that the `EnsureSuccessStatusCode` method throws an exception. This exception is caught with a `try-catch` block looking for the `HttpRequestException` type. Here, an exception filter is also used to handle only exception code 404 (not found) (code file `BooksApi/BookServiceClient/BookChapterSampleRequest.cs`):

```
public async Task ReadNotExistingChapterAsync()
{
  Console.WriteLine(nameof(ReadNotExistingChapterAsync));
  string requestIdentifier = Guid.NewGuid().ToString();
  try
  {
    string uri = $"{_booksApiUri}/{requestIdentifier}";
    var chapter = await _httpClient.GetFromJsonAsync<BookChapter>(uri);
  }
  catch (HttpRequestException ex) when (ex.Message.Contains("404"))
  {
    _logger.LogError("book chapter with identifier {0} not found", requestIdentifier);
  }
  Console.WriteLine();
}
```

> **NOTE** *Handling exceptions and using exception filters is discussed in Chapter 10, "Errors and Exceptions."*

The result of the method shows the `NotFound` result from the service:

```
ReadNotExistingChapterAsync
info: System.Net.Http.HttpClient.BooksApiClient.ClientHandler[100]
      Sending HTTP request GET https://localhost:5001/api/BookChapters/
```

```
532eae52-1bed-4fc5-b8c0-ca7ec3b41eb8
info: System.Net.Http.HttpClient.BooksApiClient.ClientHandler[101]
      Received HTTP response headers after 37.3587ms - 404
fail: BookServiceClient.BooksApiClient[0]
      book chapter with identifier 532eae52-1bed-4fc5-b8c0-ca7ec3b41eb8 not found
```

Sending POST Requests

Let's send new objects to the service using the HTTP POST request. Unlike the GET request, with the POST request, a resource needs to be added to the HTTP body in application/json format. This is done from the extension method `PostAsJsonAsync`. After the POST request is sent, the status code and the location are shown in the console. With the implementation of the service controller, the header location is filled from the `CreatedAtRoute` method (code file `BooksApi/BookServiceClient/BooksApiClient.cs`):

```
public async Task AddChapterAsync()
{
  Console.WriteLine(nameof(AddChapterAsync));
  BookChapter chapter = new(Guid.NewGuid(), 25, "Services", 40);
  var response = await _httpClient.PostAsJsonAsync(_booksApiUri, chapter);
  Console.WriteLine($"status code: {response.StatusCode}");
  Console.WriteLine($"created at location: {response.Headers.Location?.AbsolutePath}");
  Console.WriteLine();
}
```

The result of the `AddChapterAsync` method shows a successful run to create the object:

```
AddChapterAsync
info: System.Net.Http.HttpClient.BooksApiClient.ClientHandler[100]
      Sending HTTP request POST https://localhost:5001/api/BookChapters
info: System.Net.Http.HttpClient.BooksApiClient.ClientHandler[101]
      Received HTTP response headers after 151.0361ms - 201
status code: Created
created at location: /api/BookChapters/7f0b05c1-2277-4c98-bb09-48f195480b9c
```

Sending PUT Requests

The HTTP PUT request—which is used for updating a record—is sent with the help of the `HttpClient` extension method `PutAsJsonAsync`. `PutAsJsonAsync` requires the URL to the service (including the identifier) in the first parameter, and the updated content with the second parameter. With the following code snippet, the chapter with the title ".NET Application Architectures" is updated to a new title (code file `BooksApi/BookServiceClient/BooksApiClient.cs`):

```
public async Task UpdateChapterAsync()
{
  Console.WriteLine(nameof(UpdateChapterAsync));

  var chapters = await _httpClient.GetFromJsonAsync<IEnumerable<BookChapter>>(
    _booksApiUri);
  if (chapters is null) return;
  var chapter = chapters.SingleOrDefault(
    c => c.Title == ".NET Application Architectures");
  if (chapter is not null)
  {
    string uri = $"{_booksApiUri}/{chapter.Id}";
    chapter = chapter with { Title = ".NET Applications and Tools" };
    var response = await _httpClient.PutAsJsonAsync(uri, chapter);
```

```
    if (response.IsSuccessStatusCode)
    {
      Console.WriteLine($"Status code: {response.StatusCode}");
      Console.WriteLine($"updated chapter {chapter.Title}");
    }
  }
  Console.WriteLine();
}
```

The console output of the UpdateChapterAsync method shows an HTTP NoContent result and the updated chapter title:

```
UpdateChapterAsync
info: System.Net.Http.HttpClient.BooksApiClient.ClientHandler[100]
      Sending HTTP request GET https://localhost:5001/api/BookChapters
info: System.Net.Http.HttpClient.BooksApiClient.ClientHandler[101]
      Received HTTP response headers after 35.1652ms - 200
info: System.Net.Http.HttpClient.BooksApiClient.ClientHandler[100]
      Sending HTTP request PUT https://localhost:5001/api/BookChapters/
40cfc158-38b5-43ff-8964-57a0bbf95903
info: System.Net.Http.HttpClient.BooksApiClient.ClientHandler[101]
      Received HTTP response headers after 7421.4237ms - 204
Status code: NoContent
Updated chapter .NET Applications and Tools
```

Sending DELETE Requests

The last request shown with the sample client is the HTTP DELETE request. When sending a DELETE request, JSON information is not needed; only the identifier needs to be passed. Instead of using an extension method, this time the DeleteAsync method from the HttpClient class is used directly to delete the resource (code file BooksApi/BookServiceClient/BooksApiClient.cs):

```
public async Task RemoveChapterAsync()
{
  Console.WriteLine(nameof(RemoveChapterAsync));
  var chapters = await _httpClient.GetFromJsonAsync<IEnumerable<BookChapter>>(
    _booksApiUri);
  if (chapters == null) return;

  var chapter = chapters.SingleOrDefault(c => c.Title == "ADO.NET and Transactions");
  if (chapter != null)
  {
    string uri = $"{_booksApiUri}/{chapter.Id}";
    var response = await _httpClient.DeleteAsync(uri);
    if (response.IsSuccessStatusCode)
    {
      Console.WriteLine($"removed chapter {chapter.Title}");
    }
  }
  Console.WriteLine();
}
```

When you run the application, the RemoveChapterAsync method first shows the status of the HTTP GET method because a GET request is done to retrieve all chapters. After this status information, the successful DELETE request is shown:

```
RemoveChapterAsync
info: System.Net.Http.HttpClient.BooksApiClient.ClientHandler[100]
```

```
        Sending HTTP request GET https://localhost:5001/api/BookChapters
info: System.Net.Http.HttpClient.BooksApiClient.ClientHandler[101]
        Received HTTP response headers after 36.4147ms - 200
https://localhost:5001/api/BookChapters/cefbfc7d-1b21-4851-94c0-1c4fe76d47e7
info: System.Net.Http.HttpClient.BooksApiClient.ClientHandler[100]
        Sending HTTP request DELETE https://localhost:5001/api/BookChapters/
cefbfc7d-1b21-4851-94c0-1c4fe76d47e7
info: System.Net.Http.HttpClient.BooksApiClient.ClientHandler[101]
        Received HTTP response headers after 34.8404ms - 200
removed chapter ADO.NET and Transactions
```

USING EF CORE WITH SERVICES

Chapter 21, "Entity Framework Core," introduces mapping objects to relations with Entity Framework Core (EF Core). A web API controller can easily use a DbContext. In the sample app, you don't need to change the controller at all; you just need to create and register a different repository for using EF Core. All the steps needed are described in this section.

Let's start with the code accessing the database in a new .NET 5 library named Books.Data. For using EF Core with SQL Server, the NuGet package Microsoft.EntityFrameworkCore.SqlServer needs to be added to the project that contains the services. The BookChapter record and the IBookChapterService interface were already defined earlier. With the new solution, the BookChapter record is defined in the shared library Books.Shared, which is used both from the client and from the server. The IBookChapter interface is defined in the Books.Data library, which is only used on the server.

The BooksContext class shown in the following code snippet defines the mapping of the BookChapter record to a database table. The Title column is restricted to a maximum of 120 characters as specified with the model definition. For the controller to not have a strong dependency on the context, the BooksContext class implements the interface IBookChapterService. Contrary to the previous implementation of this interface, now the members of the DbContext base class are used to write the data to the database (code file BooksData/Books.Data/Models/BooksContext.cs):

```csharp
public class BooksContext : DbContext, IBookChapterService, IDisposable
{
  public BooksContext(DbContextOptions<BooksContext> options)
    : base(options)
  {
    ChangeTracker.QueryTrackingBehavior = QueryTrackingBehavior.NoTracking;
  }

  public DbSet<BookChapter> Chapters => Set<BookChapter>();

  protected override void OnModelCreating(ModelBuilder modelBuilder)
  {
    modelBuilder.Entity<BookChapter>().Property(b => b.Title).HasMaxLength(120);
  }

  public async Task AddAsync(BookChapter chapter)
  {
    await Chapters.AddAsync(chapter);
    await SaveChangesAsync();
  }

  public async Task AddRangeAsync(IEnumerable<BookChapter> chapters)
  {
```

```
        await this.Chapters.AddRangeAsync(chapters);
        await SaveChangesAsync();
    }

    public async Task<IEnumerable<BookChapter>> GetAllAsync()
    {
      var chapters = await Chapters.ToListAsync();
      return chapters;
    }

    public async Task<BookChapter?> FindAsync(Guid id)
    {
      var chapter = await Chapters.FindAsync(id);
      return chapter;
    }

    public async Task<BookChapter?> RemoveAsync(Guid id)
    {
      var chapter = await Chapters.FindAsync(id);
      Chapters.Remove(chapter);
      await SaveChangesAsync();
      return chapter;
    }

    public async Task<BookChapter?> UpdateAsync(BookChapter chapter)
    {
      Chapters.Update(chapter);
      await SaveChangesAsync();
      return chapter;
    }
  }
}
```

With the DI container, EF Core and SQL Server need to be added to invoke the extension methods `AddDbContext` and `UseSqlServer`. When a service (or a controller in this case) requests the `IBookChapterService`, now an instance of the `BooksContext` class is returned. The `BooksContext` is added with the method `AddDbContext`. With the options of this method, the connection string is passed (code file `BooksData/BooksApi/Startup.cs`):

```
    public void ConfigureServices(IServiceCollection services)
    {
      services.AddDbContext<IBookChapterService, BooksContext>(options =>
      {
        var connectionString = Configuration.GetConnectionString("BooksConnection");
          options.UseSqlServer(connectionString);
      });
      services.AddControllers();
      //...
    }
```

The connection string itself is defined with the application settings in the host application project (configuration file `BooksData/BooksApi/appsettings.json`):

```
    "ConnectionStrings": {
      "BooksConnection": "server=(localdb)\\mssqllocaldb;database=APIBooksSample;
      trusted_connection=true;"
    }
```

To create and initialize the database with sample data, create a console application using the sample EF Core context class (referencing the `Books.Data` library) and use the sample implementation for the `SampleChapters` class used previously. The following code snippet shows the top-level statements of the initializer application where the DI container is configured. Using the `BooksContext`, the database is created. Then chapters from the `SampleChapters` class are used to fill the database (code file `BooksData/Books.Initializer/Program.cs`):

```
using Books.Data;
using Books.Services;
using Microsoft.EntityFrameworkCore;
using Microsoft.Extensions.Configuration;
using Microsoft.Extensions.DependencyInjection;
using Microsoft.Extensions.Hosting;

using var host = Host.CreateDefaultBuilder(args)
  .ConfigureServices((context, services) =>
  {
    string booksConnection = context.Configuration.GetConnectionString("BooksConnection");
    services.AddDbContext<BooksContext>(options =>
    {
      options.UseSqlServer(booksConnection);
    });

    services.AddTransient<SampleChapters>();
  })
  .Build();

using var scope = host.Services.CreateScope();
var booksContext = scope.ServiceProvider.GetRequiredService<BooksContext>();
await booksContext.Database.EnsureCreatedAsync();

var sampledata = scope.ServiceProvider.GetRequiredService<SampleChapters>();
var chapters = sampledata.GetSampleChapters();
await booksContext.Chapters.AddRangeAsync(chapters);
await booksContext.SaveChangesAsync();
```

> **NOTE** *EF Core also allows creating databases using migrations. Read Chapter 21 for information about how to implement migrations in the application.*

With the controller, no changes are required compared to the previous sample code. The controller class `BookChaptersController` injects the `IBookChapterService`. This sample solution contains a different implementation, but for the controller, the same contract is fulfilled, and now you can run both the client and the server using the database.

AUTHENTICATION AND AUTHORIZATION WITH AZURE AD B2C

Authentication and authorization are important parts of developing services. Not every user or every application should be allowed to write data to the database, and probably more users should be allowed to read the data.

Chapter 20, "Security," discusses authentication and authorization of ASP.NET Core web applications using the Azure Active Directory (AD). In this chapter, you use the Azure Active Directory Business-to-Consumer (B2C) to secure web APIs built with ASP.NET Core. The Azure Active Directory B2C includes all the features of an Azure Active Directory, but includes an extension app, which allows users to register with the AD, either using email and password or using their existing Twitter, Facebook, Google, Microsoft, or other OpenID Connect and OAuth accounts. You just need to register applications with the providers you would like to support.

After creating the Azure Active Directory B2C service, you can configure identity providers, as shown in Figure 25-2. With each identity provider you select, you need to configure a client ID and client secret. User attributes enable you to collect information from users, such as the name, email address, city, country, and other values (see Figure 25-3). In addition to the built-in user attributes, you can add custom attributes that you ask the user for when the user registers with the application or makes changes to their profile. To define what the user should be asked with the registration and what information should be sent to the API service, you create user flows. You can create different user flows for signing up and signing in, editing of the profile, and resetting the password. With a user flow, you define the identity providers used, the information that should be requested from the user, and what information should be sent to the application as claims within a token (see Figure 25-4). After creating the flow, you can change the layout of the dialog and test it directly from the portal (see Figure 25-5).

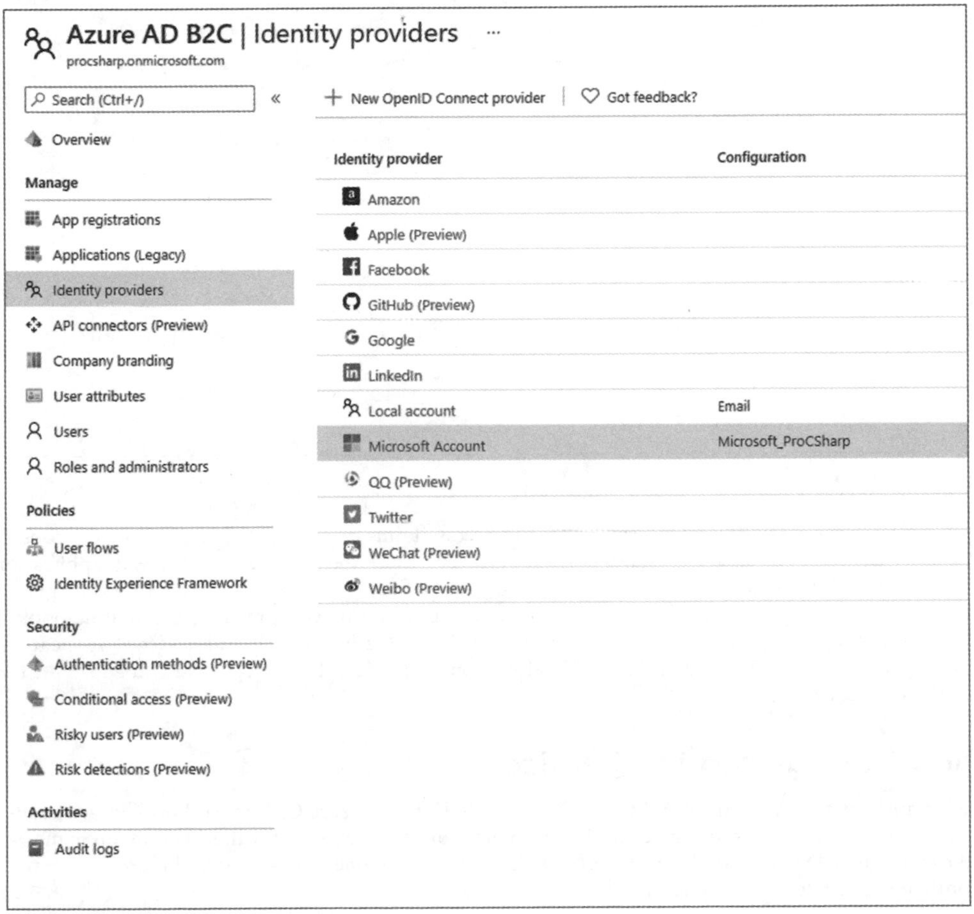

FIGURE 25-2

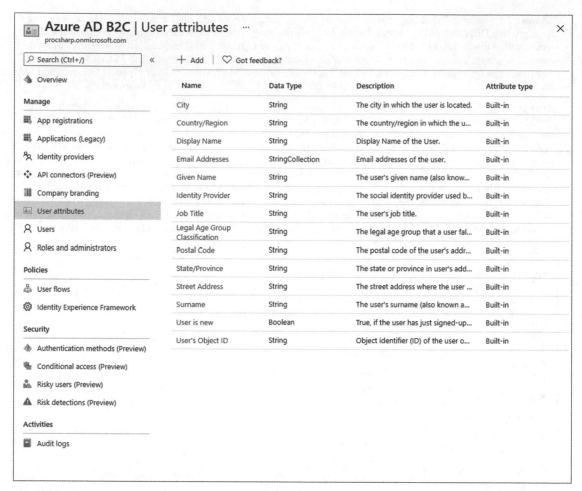

FIGURE 25-3

To allow the ASP.NET Core service to receive the token and access claims from the AD and to allow the console application to verify the user, you need to register these applications. With the service, register a web application, as shown in Figure 25-6. After registering the application, you can define scopes for the API. With the sample application, the scopes `Books.Read` and `Books.Write` are defined to differ between reading and writing book chapters. The client application needs to be registered as a public client/native (mobile and desktop) application. With the client application, you need to configure API permissions and select the `Books.Read` and `Books.Write` permissions that were previously created.

Creating and Configuring the Service

The service using authentication via the AD B2C can be created using the Azure CLI. Several options are available for configuration: `--client-id` for the client ID or application ID, `--domain` for the AD domain name, `--tenant-id` to pass the AD tenant ID, `--susi-policy-id` to pass the name of the flow, and more. You can change the configurations later in the code as well:

```
> dotnet new api --auth IndividualB2C -o BooksApi
```

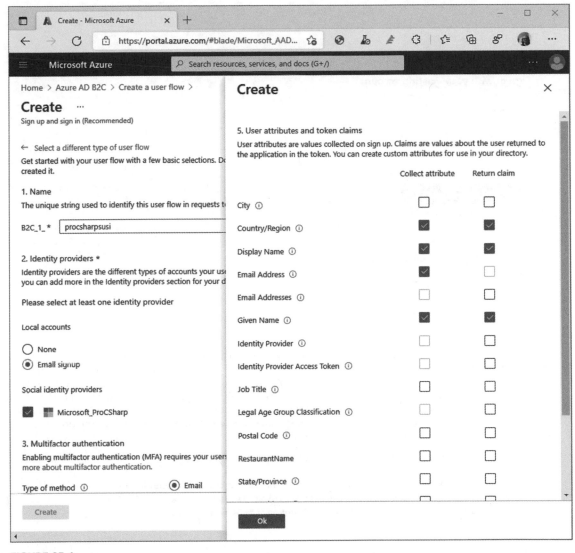

FIGURE 25-4

When you're changing the existing web API service, these NuGet packages need to be added: `Microsoft.Identity.Web`, `Microsoft.AspNetCore.Authentication.JwtBearer`, and `Microsoft.AspNetCore.Authentication.OpenIdConnect`.

With the configuration file `appsettings.json`, you need to specify the values for the `AzureADB2C` section. You get the values from the Azure AD B2C configuration (configuration file `BookDataWithAuthentication/BooksApi/appsettings.json`):

```
"AzureAdB2C": {
  "Instance": "https://login.microsoftonline.com/tfp/",
  "ClientId": "11111111-1111-1111-11111111111111111",
  "Domain": "qualified.domain.name",
  "SignUpSignInPolicyId": ""
},
```

FIGURE 25-5

The DI container needs some registration for the authentication. The method `AddAuthentication` registers the services needed for the authentication. For working with bearer tokens, the constant `JwtBearerDefaults` `.AuthenticationScheme` is used. The method `AddAuthentication` returns an `AuthenticationBuilder`. With this builder, the method `AddMicrosoftIdentityWebApi` is used. By default, this API uses the bearer scheme. The section where the configuration is read is configured with the `IConfigurationSection` argument. Setting the argument `subscribeToJwtBearerMiddlewareDiagnosticsEvents` to true adds logging information (code file `BookDataAndAuthentication/BooksApi/Startup.cs`):

```
public void ConfigureServices(IServiceCollection services)
{
  services.AddAuthentication(JwtBearerDefaults.AuthenticationScheme)
    .AddMicrosoftIdentityWebApi(Configuration.GetSection("AzureAdB2C"),
      subscribeToJwtBearerMiddlewareDiagnosticsEvents: true);

  //...
}
```

To authorize the clients as well as authenticate them, the `UseAuthorization` method needs to be added to the middleware configuration in the `Configure` method (code file `BookDataAndAuthentication/BooksApi/Startup.cs`):

```
public void Configure(IApplicationBuilder app, IWebHostEnvironment env)
{
  if (env.IsDevelopment())
  {
    app.UseDeveloperExceptionPage();
    app.UseSwagger();
    app.UseSwaggerUI(c => c.SwaggerEndpoint("/swagger/v1/swagger.json", "BooksApi v1"));
  }
```

```
    app.UseHttpsRedirection();

    app.UseRouting();

    app.UseAuthentication();
    app.UseAuthorization();

    app.UseEndpoints(endpoints =>
    {
      endpoints.MapControllers();
    });
  }
```

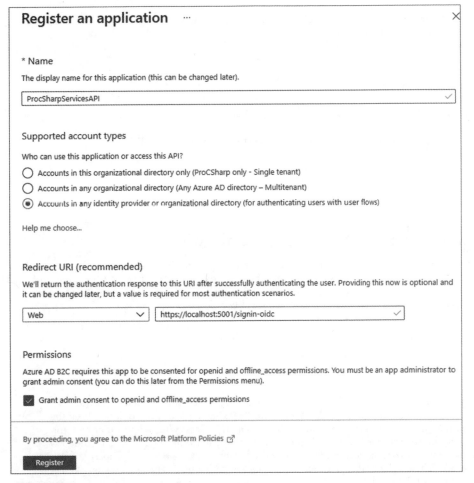

FIGURE 25-6

With the controller, you need to add the Authorize attribute not to allow anonymous invocations. To programmatically check for the scopes with different API calls, you can invoke the extension method VerifyUserHasAcceptedScope to check whether the received token has the scopes on the HttpContext. If the user is not authenticated, this method returns 401 (Unauthenticated). If the user is authenticated but the token does not have the required scope, it returns 403 (Forbidden) (code file `BookDataAndAuthentication/ BooksApi/Controllers/BookChaptersController.cs`):

```
[Produces("application/json")]
[Route("api/[controller]")]
[Authorize]
[ApiController]
public class BookChaptersController : ControllerBase
{
  private readonly IBookChapterService _chapterService;
  static readonly string[] readScopesRequired = { "Books.Read" };
  static readonly string[] writeScopesRequired = { "Books.Write" };

  public BookChaptersController(IBookChapterService chapterService)
  {
    _chapterService = chapterService;
  }

  // GET api/bookchapters/guid
  [HttpGet]
  public Task<IEnumerable<BookChapter>> GetBookChapters()
  {
    HttpContext.VerifyUserHasAnyAcceptedScope(readScopesRequired);

    return _chapterService.GetAllAsync();
  }
  //...
}
```

Adding Authentication to the Client Application

With the client application, the user needs to log in, and every invocation of the API service needs to have the access token header. The NuGet package needed with the client is `Microsoft.Identity.Client`. For authentication with the Azure AD, an `AzureAdB2C` configuration section is added to `appsettings.json` (config file `BookDataWithAuthentication/BookServiceClient/appsettings.json`):

```
"AzureAdB2C": {
  "ClientId": "11111111-1111-1111-11111111111111111",
  "TenantId": "qualified.domain.name",
  "SignUpSignInPolicyId": ""
},
```

To deal with the authentication of the user, the `ClientAuthentication` class is defined to use the `PublicClientApplicationBuilder` class to create an `IPublicClientApplication` object. Check the code download and read Chapter 20 for information about using this class. What's important here for accessing the API is to use the retrieved access token after logging in. With the `LoginAsync` method of the class `ClientAuthentication`, the access token is retrieved using the `AccessToken` property of the `AuthenticationResult`. The value is then written to the `_accessToken` field. The `GetAccesstokenAsync` method returns this access token value as shown in the following code snippet. In case the field `_accessToken` is `null` or the refresh parameter is `true`, another invocation to `LoginAsync` is done to retrieve the access token. This token is then returned from the method (code file `BookDataAndAuthentication/BookServiceClient/ ClientAuthentication.cs`):

```
private string? _accessToken;

public async ValueTask<string> GetAccesstokenAsync(bool refresh = false)
```

```
  {
    if (_accessToken is null || refresh)
    {
      await LoginAsync();
    }
    if (_accessToken is null)
    {
      throw new InvalidOperationException("No access token received!");
    }
    return _accessToken;
  }
```

The access token is used with a delegating handler `AuthenticationMessageHandler`, as shown in the following code snippet. To retrieve the token, the `ClientAuthentication` service is injected in the constructor. With the implementation of the overridden method `SendAsync`, the access token is retrieved from the authentication service and added to the request headers. Then the request is sent to the service by invoking the `SendAsync` method. In case an unauthorized or forbidden result is returned, the token is refreshed, and the request is repeated (code file `BookDataAndAuthentication/BookServiceClient/AuthenticationMessageHandler.cs`):

```
public class AuthenticationMessageHandler : DelegatingHandler
{
  private readonly ClientAuthentication _clientAuthentication;
  public AuthenticationMessageHandler(ClientAuthentication clientAuthentication)
  {
    _clientAuthentication = clientAuthentication;
  }

  protected override async Task<HttpResponseMessage> SendAsync(HttpRequestMessage request,
    CancellationToken cancellationToken)
  {
    string token = await _clientAuthentication.GetAccesstokenAsync();
    request.Headers.Authorization = new AuthenticationHeaderValue("Bearer", token);
    var response = await base.SendAsync(request, cancellationToken);
    if (response.StatusCode is HttpStatusCode.Unauthorized or HttpStatusCode.Forbidden)
    {
      token = await _clientAuthentication.GetAccesstokenAsync(refresh: true);
      request.Headers.Authorization = new AuthenticationHeaderValue("Bearer", token);
      response = await base.SendAsync(request, cancellationToken);
    }
    return response;
  }
}
```

With the configuration of the DI container, the `ClientAuthentication` service is registered as a singleton, and the `AuthenticationMessageHandler` is added as a handler for the `HttpClient` factory configuration for the typed client `BooksApiClient` (code file `BookDataAndAuthentication/BookServiceClient/Program.cs`):

```
using var host = Host.CreateDefaultBuilder(args)
  .ConfigureServices((context, services) =>
  {
    var clientAuthenticationSettings = context.Configuration.GetSection("AzureAdB2C");
    services.Configure<ClientAuthenticationOptions>(clientAuthenticationSettings);
    services.AddSingleton<ClientAuthentication>();
    var bookApiSettings = context.Configuration.GetSection("BooksService");
    services.Configure<BooksApiClientOptions>(bookApiSettings);
```

```
services.AddTransient<AuthenticationMessageHandler>();
services.AddHttpClient<BooksApiClient>(config =>
{
    var baseAddress = context.Configuration.GetSection("BooksService")["BaseAddress"]
      ?? "https://localhost:5001";
    config.BaseAddress = new Uri(baseAddress);
}).AddHttpMessageHandler<AuthenticationMessageHandler>();
}).Build();
```

With this in place, the user is authenticated on starting the application. The implementation of the `BooksApiClient` class can stay like before—with the message handler, every invocation of the `HttpClient` is injected to add the access token.

IMPLEMENTING AND USING SERVICES WITH GRPC

Sending JSON from a service is optimal with JavaScript clients. JavaScript objects can easily be created from a JSON tree. However, to reduce CPU time needed for the serialization, memory needs, and the bandwidth across the network (which also can decrease the cost), other options can be more useful. With the next solution, the same `Books.Shared` and `Books.Data` libraries are used, but the service and clients are implemented using gRPC.

Creating a gRPC Project

The .NET SDK has built-in support for gRPC. You can create a new gRPC service project with the .NET CLI:

```
> dotnet new grpc -o GRPCService
```

A gRPC project is an ASP.NET Core project with just a few additions. In the project file, you can see the NuGet package `Grpc.AspNetCore` referenced. This package has a dependency on `Google.Protobuf` and `Grpc.Tools`. Protocol buffers (Protobuf) are defined by Google for binary serialization (see `https://developers.google .com/protocol-buffers/`). The .NET SDK includes a Protobuf compiler that creates classes based on definition files referenced by the `Protobuf` element. Setting the `GrpcServices` attribute to `Server`, a stub for the server is created. This stub receives the binary message, invokes a method with the service, and returns a binary message to the caller (project file `GRPC/GRPCService/GRPCService.csproj`):

```
<Project Sdk="Microsoft.NET.Sdk.Web">

  <PropertyGroup>
    <TargetFramework>net5.0</TargetFramework>
    <Nullable>enable</Nullable>
  </PropertyGroup>

  <ItemGroup>
    <None Remove="Protos\sensor.proto" />
  </ItemGroup>

  <ItemGroup>
    <Protobuf Include="Protos\sensor.proto" GrpcServices="Server" />
    <Protobuf Include="Protos\books.proto" GrpcServices="Server" />
  </ItemGroup>

  <ItemGroup>
    <PackageReference Include="Grpc.AspNetCore" Version="2.34.0" />
  </ItemGroup>
```

```
<ItemGroup>
  <ProjectReference Include="..\Books.Data\Books.Data.csproj" />
</ItemGroup>

</Project>
```

With the template-generated code, the `Program.cs` file contains the `Main` method with the `Host` class to configure the `Startup` class; this code is not different compared to the ASP.NET Core projects you've seen so far, which is the reason it's not repeated here. With the `Startup` class, the `AddGrpc` method is used to configure the services used by gRPC in the DI container, as shown in the following code snippet. The `AddGrpc` method returns an `IGrpcServerBuilder`, which allows further configuration of the gRPC service. In addition, the EF Core context is configured as before (code file `GRPC/GRPCService/Startup.cs`):

```
public void ConfigureServices(IServiceCollection services)
{
  services.AddGrpc();
  services.AddDbContext<IBookChapterService, BooksContext>(options =>
  {
    string connectionString = _configuration.GetConnectionString("BooksConnection");
    options.UseSqlServer(connectionString);
  });
}
```

With the configuration of the endpoint routing in the middleware method `Configure`, `MapGrpcService` is used to map the `BooksService` and `SensorService` classes to endpoints (code file `GRPC/GRPCService/Startup.cs`):

```
app.UseEndpoints(endpoints =>
{
  endpoints.MapGrpcService<BooksService>();
  endpoints.MapGrpcService<SensorService>();

  endpoints.MapGet("/", async context =>
  {
    await context.Response.WriteAsync("Use a gRPC client!");
  });
});
```

Defining the Contract with Protobuf

Before implementing the service classes, the contracts need to be specified with a `.proto` file. With the sample application, `books.proto` in the following code segment defines the contracts for the service that uses the database to read and write book chapters. The `syntax` element defines the Protobuf version. The `package` element is used to prevent naming conflicts. If the `csharp_namespace` option is not specified, the package name defines the namespace of the generated C# classes. In the sample code, `csharp_namespace` is defined; thus, the generated namespace name is `GRPCService`. The `service` elements specify the operations offered from the service. The sample code defines the operations `GetBookChapters` and `AddBookChapter`. Each operation requires information about the message that is sent to the service and the message that is returned. `GetBookChapters` returns a message defined with the name `GetBookChapterResponse`. This operation doesn't require data to send to the service; thus, an `Empty` message is used. To make the `Empty` message available, the file `empty.proto` needs to be imported.

`GetBookChapterResponse` is defined with the `message` element. This element nests another `message` element: `Chapter`. Declaring a field with the `repeated` modifier, the field can be repeated any number of times (which is the case with any number of book chapters returned). The message `Chapter` specifies all the members that are needed to read and write book chapter records from the database. The numbers used with every field are unique tags for binary encoding. You can use Protobuf-specific data types such as `string`, `int32`. These types are platform-independent and map to C# data types such as `string` and `int` (proto file `GRPC/GRPCService/Protos/books.proto`):

```
syntax = "proto3";
package bookservice;
option csharp_namespace = "GRPCService";

import "google/protobuf/empty.proto";


// The book service definition.
service GRPCBooks {
  rpc GetBookChapters (google.protobuf.Empty) returns (GetBookChapterResponse);
  rpc AddBookChapter (AddBookChapterRequest) returns (AddBookChapterResponse);
}

message AddBookChapterRequest {
  Chapter Chapter = 1;
}

message AddBookChapterResponse {
  Chapter Chapter = 1;
}

message GetBookChapterResponse {
  repeated Chapter chapters = 1;
}

message Chapter {
  string id = 1;
  int32 number = 2;
  string title = 3;
  int32 pageCount = 4;
}
```

> **NOTE** *Protobuf is not the only option for serialization with gRPC. Another option is Microsoft's Bond framework (see* https://github.com/microsoft/bond*). Bond offers multiplatform and multilanguage support like gRPC and Protobuf. To use Bond with gRPC, see* https://microsoft.github.io/bond/manual/bond_over_grpc.html*. Although Bond is often used within Microsoft, gRPC with Protobuf has more support from the community.*

Implementing a gRPC Service

The Protobuf compiler creates classes for every message defined and classes for the services. Using the libraries to access the database, the `BookChapter` record is defined. With the gRPC service, the corresponding `Chapter` class is created by the Protobuf compiler. For an easy conversion between these two types, the application defines the extension methods `ToBookChapter` and `ToGRPCChapter` (code file `GRPC/GRPCService/Services/BooksService.cs`):

```
static class ChapterExtensions
{
  public static BookChapter ToBookChapter(this Chapter chapter) =>
```

```
      new BookChapter(
        Guid.Parse(chapter.Id),
        chapter.Number,
        chapter.Title,
        chapter.PageCount);

   public static Chapter ToGRPCChapter(this BookChapter chapter) =>
      new Chapter
      {
        Id = chapter.Id.ToString(),
        Number = chapter.Number,
        Title = chapter.Title,
        PageCount = chapter.PageCount
      };
}
```

Because of the service definition in the proto file, a static class GRPCBooks with an inner abstract base class is created: GRPCBooks.GRPCBooksBase. The name of the outer class comes from the name of the service, and the name Base is used as a postfix for the inner class. The class GRPCBooksBase defines the methods GetBookChapters and AddBookChapter that you need to override, as shown in the following code snippet. With the implementation of AddBookChapter, the injected IBookChapterService is used to add a book (after converting it from the gRPC class to the record) to the database. With the GetBookChapters, the database is queried for all the book chapters, and the chapters are converted and added to the response (code file GRPC/GRPCService/Services/BooksService.cs):

```
public class BooksService : GRPCBooks.GRPCBooksBase
{
  private readonly IBookChapterService _bookChapterService;
  private readonly ILogger _logger;
  public BooksService(ILogger<BooksService> logger,
    IBookChapterService bookChapterService)
  {
    _logger = logger;
    _bookChapterService = bookChapterService;
  }

  public override async Task<AddBookChapterResponse> AddBookChapter(
    AddBookChapterRequest request, ServerCallContext context)
  {
    var bookChapter = request.Chapter.ToBookChapter();
    await _bookChapterService.AddAsync(bookChapter);
    AddBookChapterResponse response = new()
    {
      Chapter = bookChapter.ToGRPCChapter()
    };
    return response;
  }

  public override async Task<GetBookChapterResponse> GetBookChapters(
    Empty request, ServerCallContext context)
  {
    var bookChapters = await _bookChapterService.GetAllAsync();
    GetBookChapterResponse response = new();
    response.Chapters.AddRange(bookChapters.Select(bc => bc.ToGRPCChapter()).ToArray());
    return response;
  }
}
```

Implementing a gRPC Client

To implement a gRPC client application, a .NET console application is used. For adding the NuGet packages and the definitions to create the client-side stub, with Visual Studio you can add a connected service to the gRPC service and reference the proto file. Without using Visual Studio, you need to add the NuGet packages `Google` `.Protobuf`, `Grpc.Net.ClientFactory`, and `Grpc.Tools`. To use the `Host` class with the client, the NuGet package `Microsoft.Extensions.Hosting` needs to be added as well. To create the client-side proxy, the proto file from the server is referenced using a `Protobuf` element with the `GrpcServices` attribute set to `Client`. This creates the stub for the client (project file GRPC/GRPC.BooksClient/GRPC.BooksClient.csproj):

```xml
<Project Sdk="Microsoft.NET.Sdk">
  <PropertyGroup>
    <OutputType>Exe</OutputType>
    <TargetFramework>net5.0</TargetFramework>
    <Nullable>enable</Nullable>
  </PropertyGroup>

  <ItemGroup>
    <PackageReference Include="Google.Protobuf" Version="3.15.6" />
    <PackageReference Include="Grpc.Net.ClientFactory" Version="2.36.0" />
    <PackageReference Include="Grpc.Tools" Version="2.36.4">
      <PrivateAssets>all</PrivateAssets>
      <IncludeAssets>runtime; build; native; contentfiles; analyzers;
        buildtransitive</IncludeAssets>
    </PackageReference>
    <PackageReference Include="Microsoft.Extensions.Hosting" Version="5.0.0" />
  </ItemGroup>

  <ItemGroup>
    <ProjectReference Include="..\Books.Shared\Books.Shared.csproj"/>
  </ItemGroup>

  <ItemGroup>
    <Protobuf Include="..\GRPCService\Protos\books.proto" GrpcServices="Client">
      <Link>Protos\books.proto</Link>
    </Protobuf>
  </ItemGroup>

  <ItemGroup>
    <None Update="appsettings.json">
      <CopyToOutputDirectory>PreserveNewest</CopyToOutputDirectory>
    </None>
  </ItemGroup>

</Project>
```

The stub that's created from the `books.proto` file has the name `GRPCBooks.GRPCBooksClient`. The NuGet package `Grpc.Net.ClientFactory` offers a similar factory as you've seen with the `HttpClient` factory. As you can see in the following code snippet, you can invoke the `AddGrpcClient` method and pass the generated stub class with the generic parameter. Using the options of type `GrpcClientFactoryOptions`, beside other configurations, you can specify the `Address` to the service. `GrpcChannelOptions` allow you to specify the maximum message size, the number of retry attempts, buffer sizes, and whether an `OperationCanceledException` should be thrown on cancelation (code file GRPC/GRPC.BooksClient/Program.cs):

```csharp
using GRPCService;
using Microsoft.Extensions.DependencyInjection;
```

```
using Microsoft.Extensions.Hosting;
using System;

using var host = Host.CreateDefaultBuilder(args)
  .ConfigureServices((context, services) =>
  {
    services.AddGrpcClient<GRPCBooks.GRPCBooksClient>(options =>
    {
      string grpcServiceUri = context.Configuration["GrpcServiceUri"]
        ?? "https://localhost:5001";
      options.Address = new Uri(grpcServiceUri);
      options.ChannelOptionsActions.Add(options =>
      {
        options.ThrowOperationCanceledOnCancellation = true;
      });
    });

    services.AddSingleton<Runner>();
  })
  .Build();

Console.WriteLine("press return to start");
Console.ReadLine();

var runner = host.Services.GetRequiredService<Runner>();
await runner.RunAsync();

Console.ReadLine();
```

The Runner class makes use of the gRPC client stub to invoke the service. The GRPCBooksGRPCBooksClient is injected in the constructor. Within the RunAsync method, the proxy methods AddBookChaptersAsync and GetBookChaptersAsync are invoked to send messages to the services and receive the results (code file GRPC/GRPC.BooksClient/Runner.cs):

```
public class Runner
{
  private readonly GRPCBooks.GRPCBooksClient _booksClient;
  private readonly ILogger _logger;
  public Runner(GRPCBooks.GRPCBooksClient booksClient, ILogger<Runner> logger)
  {
    _booksClient = booksClient;
    _logger = logger;
  }

  public async Task RunAsync()
  {
    CancellationTokenSource cts = new(10000); // cancel after 10 seconds

    try
    {
      BookChapter bookChapter = new(Guid.NewGuid(), 43, "A new GPRC chapter", 20);
      AddBookChapterRequest request = new()
      {
        Chapter = bookChapter.ToGRPCChapter()
      };
```

```
                var addBookResponse = await _booksClient.AddBookChapterAsync(request);
                Console.WriteLine($"added a new book");

                var getBookResponse = await _booksClient.GetBookChaptersAsync(new Empty());
                var bookChapters = getBookResponse.Chapters.Select(
                  c => c.ToBookChapter()).ToArray();
                foreach (var chapter in bookChapters)
                {
                    Console.WriteLine($"{chapter.Number}: {chapter.Title}");
                }
            }
            catch (Exception ex)
            {
                _logger.LogError(ex, ex.Message);
                throw;
            }
        }
    }
```

Streaming with gRPC

gRPC offers asynchronous streaming, as shown in the next sample. Instead of using a request/reply scenario, a stream of data can be sent from the client to the service or from the service to the client, or streams can be sent in both directions.

To implement streaming, the GRPCService is enhanced with a simulation of a device that continuously sends sensor data to the client. With the following sensor.proto file, a stream of SensorData messages is returned to the client after a message is received to invoke the GetSensorData operation. The data that is sent is defined with the message SensorData. This message includes two int32 values and a timestamp. For the timestamp value, google/protobuf/timestamp.proto needs to be imported. To pass a stream to the client, the rpc operation GetSensorData specifies to return a stream of SensorData messages with the stream modifier (proto file GRPC/GRPCSerivce/Protos/sensor.proto):

```
syntax = "proto3";
package sensing;
option csharp_namespace = "GRPCService";

import "google/protobuf/empty.proto";
import "google/protobuf/timestamp.proto";

service Sensor {
  rpc GetSensorData (google.protobuf.Empty) returns (stream SensorData);
}

message SensorData {
  google.protobuf.Timestamp timestamp = 1;
  int32 val1 = 2;
  int32 val2 = 3;
}
```

With this proto file, the method that needs to be overridden is declared with an IServerStreamWriter <SensorData> parameter. With this, the stream of data can be sent by invoking the WriteAsync method (code file GRPC/GRPCService/Services/SensorService.cs):

```
public override async Task GetSensorData(Empty request,
    IServerStreamWriter<SensorData> responseStream, ServerCallContext context)
```

```
{
  try
  {
    Random = new();

    while (!context.CancellationToken.IsCancellationRequested)
    {
      await Task.Delay(100, context.CancellationToken);
      SensorData data = new()
      {
        Timestamp = Timestamp.FromDateTime(DateTime.UtcNow),
        Val1 = random.Next(100),
        Val2 = random.Next(100)
      };
      Console.WriteLine($"returning data {data}");
      await responseStream.WriteAsync(data);
    }
  }
  catch (TaskCanceledException ex)
  {
    _logger.LogInformation(ex.Message);
  }
}
```

The client application is implemented in a similar way as before; the difference is the `sensor.proto` file. When a return stream is declared, the stub-created method returns an object of `AsyncServerStreamingCall<SensorData>`. This object can be used to access the `ResponseStream` and invoke the method `ReadAllAsync`. `ReadAllAsync` is an extension method for the `IAsyncStreamReader` and returns `IAsyncEnumerable`. This interface can be used with `await foreach` to asynchronously iterate through the stream (code file GRPC/GRPC.SensorClient/Runner.cs):

```
public async Task RunAsync()
{
  CancellationTokenSource cts = new(10000); // cancel after 10 seconds

  try
  {
    using var stream = _sensorClient.GetSensorData(new Empty());

    await foreach (var data in
      stream.ResponseStream.ReadAllAsync().WithCancellation(cts.Token))
    {
      Console.WriteLine($"data {data.Val1} {data.Val2} {data.Timestamp.ToDateTime():T}");
    }
  }
  catch (TaskCanceledException ex)
  {
    _logger.LogInformation(ex.Message);
  }
}
```

> **NOTE** *Streaming with* `IAsyncEnumerable` *is shown in Chapter 11, "Tasks and Asynchronous Programming."*

When you run both the service and the client application, a stream is returned to the client until the cancelation is requested after 10 seconds.

> **NOTE** *Besides gRPC, streaming is also supported with SignalR. SignalR is covered in Chapter 28, "SignalR."*

USING AZURE FUNCTIONS

When you create a REST API with ASP.NET Core, you can host it either with your own Windows server or with a Linux server, or you can use a platform-as-a-service (PaaS) offering and run it with Azure App Services—no matter whether you use Docker images or deploy the application directly. In all these cases, you have a virtual (or even physical) machine you pay for. Another option to create REST APIs is with Azure Functions. With this technology, you have consumption-based pricing as one option; you just pay for the seconds you need of the memory and CPU when the function is invoked. This consumption-based pricing is also known as the service offering *functions as a service* (FaaS) or by the term serverless. Of course, there's always a server in the backend, but the pricing model is different.

Azure Functions already had several iterations with Microsoft Azure. The first version is based on the .NET Framework. Versions 2 and 3 of Azure Functions are based on .NET Core 2.1 and 3—the long-term supported versions of .NET Core. Now the next generation is available. With the new generation, Azure Functions can run in an isolated process mode that allows you to run the function's code in a different process than the hosting environment: *out of process*. This way, you are independent of the runtime that's available on the hosting platform and can use .NET 5. At the time of this writing, there are some limits with this version because you don't have a Visual Studio template to create this Azure Function, and you cannot create the function app in the Azure portal. Instead, you can use the Azure CLI and the *Azure Functions Core Tools*. (See `https://docs.microsoft.com/en-us/azure/azure-functions/functions-run-local` for information on installing the Azure Functions Core Tools with Windows, macOS, and Linux.)

The sample application for the Azure Functions offers the same functionality as the ASP.NET Core web API and gRPC samples to read and create book chapters, using the same libraries as before. If you create the functionality of your applications independent of the hosting environment, you have the flexibility to choose and change technologies.

Creating an Azure Functions Project

To create an Azure Function, create a new folder `Books.Function`, and with the current directory set to this folder, use the Azure Functions command-line interface and specify `dotnetIsolated` with the `--worker-runtime` option and the `init` action:

```
> func init --worker-runtime dotnetIsolated
```

This creates a .NET 5 console application with a project file referencing the NuGet packages `Microsoft.Azure.Functions.Worker.Sdk` and `Microsoft.Azure.Functions.Worker`, configuration files `host.json` and `local.settings.json`, and the `Program` class using the .NET where the `Host` class is created. However, this time, instead of `CreateDefaultBuilder` to configure services, configuration, and logging, the method `ConfigureFunctionsWorkerDefaults` is invoked as shown in the following code snippet. With the sample application, the projects `Books.Shared` and `Books.Data` are referenced to use this existing functionality, and the EF Core context is configured with the `ConfigureServices` method as you've configured it previously. What's different is that the connection string is retrieved from an environment variable instead of by using the `IConfiguration` interface (code file `AzureFunctions/Books.Function/Program.cs`):

```
using Books.Data;
using Books.Services;
using Microsoft.EntityFrameworkCore;
using Microsoft.Extensions.DependencyInjection;
using Microsoft.Extensions.Hosting;
using System;

using var host = new HostBuilder()
  .ConfigureFunctionsWorkerDefaults()
  .ConfigureServices(services =>
  {
    string? connectionString = Environment.GetEnvironmentVariable("BooksConnection");
    if (connectionString is null)
      throw new InvalidOperationException("Configure the BooksConnection");

    services.AddDbContext<IBookChapterService, BooksContext>(options =>
    {
      options.UseSqlServer(connectionString);
    });
  })
  .Build();

await host.RunAsync();
```

The method `ConfigureFunctionsWorkerDefaults` customizes the JSON serializer to ignore casing, configures logging to integrate the `ILogger` with Azure Functions logging, configures Azure Function binding middleware, and adds gRPC support.

The file `local.settings.json` is used for the Azure Functions configuration values when you run this locally on your system. This file is not part of the Git repository and is not deployed to Microsoft Azure. The values configured within the `Values` section are put into environment variables from the Azure Functions host environment. Creating the Azure Function with the `dotnetIsolated` option specifies the `dotnet-isolated` worker runtime. Azure Functions require an Azure Storage account for storing the Azure Function as well as for logging. To run the Azure Function locally, a simulation environment is used instead of the real storage account. This is specified with the `UseDevelopmentStorage` setting. The `BooksConnection` needs to be added to reference your SQL Server database:

```
{
  "IsEncrypted": false,
  "Values": {
    "AzureWebJobsStorage": "UseDevelopmentStorage=true",
    "FUNCTIONS_WORKER_RUNTIME": "dotnet-isolated",
    "BooksConnection":
      "server=(localdb)\\mssqllocaldb;database=BooksDatabase;trusted_connection=true"
  }
}
```

You can customize the `Host` class to add custom middleware as you've read in the previous chapter (using the `IFunctionsWorkerApplicationBuilder` parameter of the `ConfigureFunctionsWorkerDefaults` method), configuration providers (for example the Azure App Configuration provider introduced in Chapter 15), and custom services for DI injection.

Adding HTTP Trigger Functions

To add a function to the project, you use `func new` by supplying the name of the template with the `--template` argument. With the sample application, the function will be triggered on HTTP requests; thus, the `Http Trigger` template is used:

```
> func new --name BooksService --authlevel anonymous --template "Http Trigger"
```

The class that's generated is defined as a static class with static methods. However, you can change that to an instance class to use constructor injection. With the following code snippet, the `IBookChapterService` is injected with the constructor (code file `AzureFunctions/Books.Function/BooksService.cs`):

```
public class BooksService
{
  private readonly IBookChapterService _bookChapterService;
  public BooksService(IBookChapterService bookChapterService)
  {
    if (bookChapterService is null)
      throw new ArgumentNullException(nameof(bookChapterService));
    _bookChapterService = bookChapterService;
  }
  //...
}
```

A function is declared with the `Function` attribute. The `HttpTrigger` attribute specified with the first parameter of the `GetChaptersAsync` method defines how the function is invoked. With the following declaration, the function is invoked on an HTTP GET request with the route `chapters`. With different trigger types, different parameter types are used. With the `HttpTrigger`, the parameter needs to be of type `HttpRequestData`. This type is used to read the request from the caller and to send a response. With the sample implementation, the `IBookChapterService` is used to get the chapter list, convert it to JSON with the `WriteAsJsonAsync` extension method (defined in the `Microsoft.Azure.Functions.Worker.Http` namespace), create the JSON data, and write it to the response body (code file `AzureFunctions/Books.Function/BooksService.cs`):

```
[Function("GetChapters")]
public async Task<HttpResponseData> GetChaptersAsync(
  [HttpTrigger(AuthorizationLevel.Anonymous, "get", Route = "chapters")]
    HttpRequestData req,
  FunctionContext executionContext)
{
  var logger = executionContext.GetLogger("BooksService");
  logger.LogInformation("Function GetChapters invoked.");

  var response = req.CreateResponse(HttpStatusCode.OK);
  var chapters = _bookChapterService.GetAllAsync();
  await response.WriteAsJsonAsync(chapters);
  return response;
}
```

The function `AddChapterAsync` is declared with an `HttpTrigger` for an HTTP POST request on the same route. Here, the HTTP body received is read using the `ReadFromJsonAsync` extension method, and with the help of the `IBookChapterService`, the book chapter is written to the database (code file `AzureFunctions/Books.Function/BooksService.cs`):

```
[Function("AddChapter")]
public async Task<HttpResponseData> AddChapterAsync(
  [HttpTrigger(AuthorizationLevel.Anonymous, "post", Route = "chapters")]
    HttpRequestData req,
  FunctionContext executionContext)
{
  var logger = executionContext.GetLogger("BooksService");
  logger.LogInformation("Function AddChapter invoked.");

  var chapter = await req.ReadFromJsonAsync<BookChapter>();
  if (chapter is null)
  {
```

```
        logger.LogError("invalid chapter received");
        return req.CreateResponse(HttpStatusCode.BadRequest);
    }
    var response = req.CreateResponse(HttpStatusCode.OK);
    await _bookChapterService.AddAsync(chapter);
    await response.WriteAsJsonAsync(chapter);
    return response;
}
```

To run the Azure Function on your local system, you can't start it from Visual Studio (at least at the time of this writing); you need to start it with the Azure Functions Core Tools, giving you the host environment:

```
> func start
```

By default, the Azure Function is available at port 7071. The URL to send the GET and POST requests is `http://localhost:7071/api/chapters`.

To debug from Visual Studio, you can start the function with the option `--dotnet-isolated-debug`. By setting this, the worker process waits until a debugger is attached.

To send HTTP requests, you can use `dotnet httprepl` (which is explained in Chapter 24, "ASP.NET Core") or customize the previously created client application.

MORE AZURE SERVICES

More can be done with Azure Functions beyond implementing them to be triggered on HTTP requests. They also can be triggered when a message arrives in a queue of an Azure Storage account, with queues and tokens from the Azure Service Bus, when data is changed in an Azure Cosmos database, on events from Azure Event Grid or the Azure Event hub, or with a timer trigger. For creating small services, it's not always necessary to react to network events, such as invocations from REST APIs or RPC calls. Communication can also be done asynchronously.

If your application now uses several APIs, you want to allow the client to use just one API layer that is then forwarded to the correct service with the correct version based on the request, and you want to implement throttling based on different subscriptions used by the client APIs, you might consider using Azure API management. This service gives you great options for these scenarios.

Check `https://github.com/ProfessionalCSharp/MoreSamples` for additional samples for these scenarios.

SUMMARY

This chapter described the features of the web API using ASP.NET Core. This technology offers an easy way to create REST services that can be called from any client—be it JavaScript or a .NET client. With a .NET client, you saw how to use the `HttpClient` class that sends requests using different HTTP verbs, including the use of the new JSON extension methods to deal with sending and receiving JSON data.

You've seen enhancements of the API sample to access a database with EF Core without big changes, and you've read about adding authentication and authorization both to the service and to the client application.

This chapter also covered communication in a platform-independent form using gRPC and streaming with gRPC.

Another option for implementing REST APIs is by using Azure Functions. With the advantage of a DI container, you could use the classes implemented earlier to offer the same functionality by using an Azure Function.

The next chapter covers creating user interfaces with ASP.NET Core using Razor Pages and MVC.

26

Razor Pages and MVC

WHAT'S IN THIS CHAPTER?

➤ Working with Razor Pages

➤ Using Razor syntax

➤ Routing with Razor Pages and MVC

➤ Implementing Razor Pages in a library

➤ Injecting services

➤ Using HTML Helpers

➤ Creating and using Tag Helpers

➤ Creating and using view components

➤ Differences between Razor Pages and ASP.NET Core MVC

CODE DOWNLOADS FOR THIS CHAPTER

The source code for this chapter is available on the book page at www.wiley.com. Click the Downloads link. The code can also be found at https://github.com/ProfessionalCSharp/ ProfessionalCSharp2021 in the directory 3_Web/RazorAndMVC.

The code for this chapter is divided into the following major examples:

➤ WebAppSample (Razor Pages web application)

➤ BooksViews (Razor Pages in a library)

➤ CustomTagHelpers

➤ EventViews (view components)

➤ MVCSample (ASP.NET Core MVC web application)

All the projects have nullable reference types enabled.

SETTING UP SERVICES FOR RAZOR PAGES AND MVC

Chapter 24, "ASP.NET Core," explains the foundation of ASP.NET Core with dependency injection and middleware and the features of HTTP requests and responses. This chapter makes use of dependency injection and middleware for Razor Pages and MVC to reduce the code needed for creating full-featured web applications.

Web pages built based on the *Model-View-Controller* (MVC) pattern (Figure 26-1) clearly separate models (entity objects representing data), views (the user interface, including HTML code), and functionality (controllers).

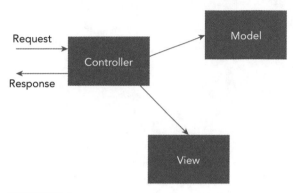

FIGURE 26-1

Razor Pages give you a simpler concept where you mix HTML code with C# within a single page, but you can also separate this using a code-behind file, which you probably already know from WPF or WinUI applications. Dependency injection is an important concept that's needed both with Razor Pages and MVC.

Creating Razor Pages Projects

Razor Pages were introduced with ASP.NET Core 2.0 to remove the complexity with MVC. Razor Pages offer an easier way to start creating web applications. In case you already have experience with MVC, many of the same features of MVC can be used with Razor Pages. You can also mix MVC projects with Razor Pages.

When you're using Visual Studio, you can create a Razor Pages application by using the project template Web Application. You use the command line to create the sample application with this:

```
> dotnet new webapp -o WebAppSample
```

With this template, the `Main` method uses the `Host` class in the same way as you saw in Chapter 24, "ASP.NET Core," with the empty web application. The configuration of the DI container is done in the `ConfigureServices` method of the `Startup` class. With Razor Pages, the extension method `AddRazorPages` is used to register all the services required; the most important are the Razor view engine and services to find and activate pages (code file `WebAppSample/Startup.cs`):

```
public void ConfigureServices(IServiceCollection services)
{
  services.AddRazorPages();
}
```

With the configuration of the middleware, static files are added by default (with web applications, you usually need static files such as CSS files and JavaScript files). With endpoint routing, routes for Razor Pages are added by invoking the method `MapRazorPages` (code file `WebAppSample/Startup.cs`):

```
public void Configure(IApplicationBuilder app, IWebHostEnvironment env)
{
  if (env.IsDevelopment())
```

```
  {
    app.UseDeveloperExceptionPage();
  }
  else
  {
    app.UseExceptionHandler("/Error");
    app.UseHsts();
  }

  app.UseHttpsRedirection();
  app.UseStaticFiles();

  app.UseRouting();

  app.UseAuthorization();

  app.UseEndpoints(endpoints =>
  {
    endpoints.MapRazorPages();
  });
}
```

With the default configuration, Razor Pages routing uses a Pages folder and subfolders and maps the URL to the .cshtml files in that folder. You can override settings by using the methods AddRazorOptions and AddRazorPageOptions. If you're accessing the URL /Hello, the page Pages/Hello.cshtml is searched. With the URL /Admin/User, the page Pages/Admin/User.cshtml is expected. If these pages are not found, search continues in the Views/Shared folder. When you set the property PageViewLocationFormats with the method AddRazorOptions, this behavior can be changed. Just by changing the folder Pages to a different folder, the AddRazorPagesOptions method can be used to set the RootDirectory property of the RazorPagesOptions.

Understanding Razor Syntax

Razor Pages (and also Razor views, as with MVC, and Razor components used with Blazor) use Razor syntax. With Razor syntax, you can mix HTML and C# code. Razor uses the @ character as a transition character to switch from HTML to C#.

An important distinction you need to make here is with statements that return a value and statements that don't. A value that is returned can be used directly with an *implicit Razor expression*. For example, ViewData["Title"] returns a string. The returned string is put directly between the HTML title tags as shown in the following code snippet. After this expression, Razor switches to HTML, and the following string before the title end element is simple HTML:

```
<title>@ViewData["Title"] - WebAppSample</title>
```

With the Razor syntax, the engine automatically detects the end of the C# code when it finds an HTML element. There are some cases in which the end of the C# code cannot be detected automatically. You can resolve this by using parentheses, as shown in the following example to mark a variable, and then the normal text continues. This is an *explicit Razor expression*:

```
<div>@(name), Stephanie</div>
```

When you're invoking methods that return void or specifying some other statements that don't return a value, you need a *Razor code block*. The following code block defines a string variable:

```
@{
  string name = "Angela";
}
```

You can now use the variable with an implicit Razor expression; you just use the transition character @ to access the variable:

```
<div>@name</div>
```

Another way to start a *Razor code block* is with the foreach statement:

```
@foreach(var item in list)
{
  <li>The item name is @item.</li>
}
```

With Razor, you can also use control structures with @if, else if, else, and @switch. Looping can be done with @for, @foreach, @while, and @do while.

> **NOTE** *Usually, text content is automatically detected with Razor—for example, Razor detects an opening angle bracket or parenthesis with a variable. There are a few cases in which this does not work. Here, you can explicitly use @: to define the start of text.*

Instead of importing namespaces with every Razor Page, you can import namespaces with the file _ViewImports.cshtml that's defined in the Pages folder with @using. To declare a namespace for the types defined in the folder, you can use @namespace (code file WebAppSample/Pages/_ViewImports.cshtml):

```
@using WebAppSample
@namespace WebAppSample.Pages
@addTagHelper *, Microsoft.AspNetCore.Mvc.TagHelpers
```

Tag helpers opened with @addTagHelper in this file are explained later in the section "Working with Tag Helpers."

RAZOR PAGES

Razor Pages have the file extension .cshtml and start with a @page directive. This is a simple Razor Page with HTML code:

```
@page
<h2>HTML Heading</h2>
```

You can create a Razor Page with dotnet new page and pass a name to the --name option:

```
> dotnet new page --name PageWithCodeBehind
> dotnet new page --name InlinePage --no-pagemodel
```

Razor Pages can be created with inline code (using the --no-pagemodel option). With this, C# methods can be declared in a @functions code block. Everything is in a single file. Without using the --no-pagemodel option, a code-behind file is generated, and C# methods are declared within a page-model class in the code-behind file with the .cshtml.cs file extension. By default, a code-behind file is used as shown with the Error page (code file WebAppSample/Pages/Error.cshtml):

```
@page
@model ErrorModel
@* ... *@
```

With a Razor Page, a class is created that derives from the base class `Microsoft.AspNetCore.Mvc.RazorPages.Page`. The `@model` directive uses a generic version of this base class and specifies the type of the model as the generic parameter. With this, the `Model` property of the generated class can be used to access data of the underlying code.

With the code-behind file, you can see the class declared with the `@model` directive deriving from the base class `PageModel` (code file `WebAppSample/Pages/Error.cshtml.cs`):

```
public class ErrorModel : PageModel
{
  //...
}
```

Other than using inline code with an `@functions` code block or using a code-behind file with a `PageModel`-derived class in the code-behind file, you have a third option: you can create a `PageModel`-derived class in the `@functions` code block. The model declaration is the same in this variant; you're just using one file instead of two files to implement the Razor Page. It's a matter of taste. By default, Visual Studio creates Razor Pages with code-behind files. Razor components that you'll create in the next chapter use inline code.

Layouts

Usually, many pages of web applications share some of the same content—for example, copyright information, a logo, and a main navigation structure. Using layout pages, you can share HTML code with different Razor Pages.

To use a layout, the Razor Page base class `PageModel` defines the `Layout` property. To specify default settings for Razor Pages, you use the `_ViewStart.cshtml` file. In the following code snippet, you can see the `Layout` property set to `_Layout` (code file `WebAppSample/Pages/_ViewStart.cshtml`):

```
@{
    Layout = "_Layout";
}
```

You can override this setting in specific pages to reference other layout files, or you can create other `_Layout.cshtml` files with changed content in other folders.

The layout page contains the HTML declaration, `html`, `head`, and `body` elements, and in the `body` `header` and `footer` elements. Of course, you can also use Razor syntax within this file. With the `.cshtml` file extension (and without a `@page` directive), the class used behind the scenes for the layout page is the `RazorPage` class.

The invocation of the method `RenderBody` is important with layout pages. This method is implemented with the base class and renders the content of the Razor Page.

```
<div class="container">
  <main role="main" class="pb-3">
    @RenderBody()
  </main>
</div>
```

After you know the details, let's recapitulate how this process works: based on the route, a Razor Page is selected. With the Razor Page, the `Layout` property is set (either within the page itself or with the default settings from `_ViewStart.csthml`). Based on this information, the page is processed, and a layout file is selected that's rendered. With the layout file, the `@RenderBody` method defines the position within the UI where the result of the Razor Page is rendered. Figure 26-2 shows the rendering of the `Index` page within the layout showing menu and footer information.

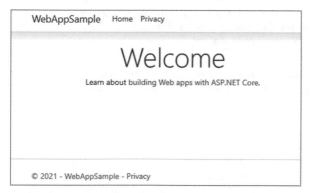

FIGURE 26-2

Passing Data Between Views

Often you need to pass information from one view to the other. Of course, you can create a service that shares state during a request (for example, registered as scoped within the DI container) and inject the service in the views. However, this is too much to do to share just simple data, such as a title that should be set with a Razor Page and shown within the layout. To do this, you use the ViewData property of the page. ViewData offers a dictionary where you can use a string as the key and pass and access the data using an indexer. The data can be any object.

The Index page sets ViewData with the Title index (code file WebAppSample/Pages/Index.cshtml):

```
@{
    ViewData["Title"] = "Home page";
}
```

With the layout, the value from the ViewData is retrieved to show it with the title element (code file WebAppSample/Pages/Shared/_Layout.cshtml):

```
<title>@ViewData["Title"] - WebAppSample</title>
```

Instead of using the ViewData property, you can use the ViewBag property. ViewBag accesses the same dictionary, but you can use property-like syntax:

```
ViewBag.Title = "Home page";
```

This looks like cleaner code, but IntelliSense doesn't offer you the property names. The ViewBag property is of type dynamic (see Chapter 12, "Reflection, Metadata, and Source Generators," for more information on dynamic), and thus the compiler does not complain if you use an incorrect string.

For information that should be read only once, you can use the TempData property. A TempData value can be read only once and is released after reading.

Render Sections

In case you want to put your page content in different parts of the layout, you can render sections. To do this, you invoke the RenderSectionAsync method in the layout page, as shown in the following code snippet. The layout has JavaScript files referenced that are useful for all the pages of the web application. With the section Scripts, additional JavaScript files useful only for specific pages can be referenced. If you don't want to require every page to have a Scripts section, the required argument is set to false (code file WebAppSample/Pages/Shared/_Layout.cshtml):

```
<body>
    <!-- -->
    <script src="~/lib/jquery/dist/jquery.min.js"></script>
```

```
    <script src="~/lib/bootstrap/dist/js/bootstrap.bundle.min.js"></script>
    <script src="~/js/site.js" asp-append-version="true"></script>
    @await RenderSectionAsync("Scripts", required: false)
</body>
```

Within the `head` element of the layout page, the section with the name `Keywords` is referenced. Within the head element, every page can add HTML keyword meta values (code file `WebAppSample/Pages/Shared/_Layout.cshtml`):

```
<head>
  <meta charset="utf-8" />
  <meta name="viewport" content="width=device-width, initial-scale=1.0" />
  <title>@ViewData["Title"] - WebAppSample</title>
  @await RenderSectionAsync("Keywords", required:false)
  <link rel="stylesheet" href="~/lib/bootstrap/dist/css/bootstrap.min.css" />
  <link rel="stylesheet" href="~/css/site.css" />
</head>
```

A Razor Page can now supply sections as shown in the following code snippet using the Razor directive `@section` and using the name of the section (code file `WebAppSample/Pages/Index.cshtml`):

```
@section Keywords {
  <meta name="keywords" content="C#, .NET, Azure">
}
```

Routing with Parameters

Routing with Razor Pages is defined with a simple convention: the filename of a Razor Page within the `Pages` folder is used with the URI. In addition to this, you can pass parameters to the page as shown with the following inline Razor Page. With Razor Pages depending on the HTTP verbs sent, you specify the methods `OnGet` and `OnPost`. The parameters that you specify with these methods are mapped from the request. Here, the `title` and `publisher` parameters are assigned to the `Title` and `Publisher` properties, which in turn are used with the HTML content with implicit Razor expressions accessing the properties (code file `WebAppSample/Pages/ShowBook.cshtml`):

```
@page

<div>
  <dl class="row">
    <dt class="col-sm-2">
      Title
    </dt>
    <dd class="col-sm-10">
      @Title
    </dd>
    <dt class="col-sm-2">
      Publisher
    </dt>
    <dd class="col-sm-10">
      @Publisher
    </dd>
  </dl>
</div>

@functions {
  private string? Title { get; set; }
```

```
    private string? Publisher { get; set; }
    public void OnGet(string? title, string? publisher) =>
      (Title, Publisher) = (title, publisher);
}
```

> **NOTE** *When implementing the methods for the HTTP GET and HTTP POST requests, you have many options; the methods just need to have the names* OnGet *and* OnPost *(or* OnGetAsync *and* OnPostAsync, *if asynchronous methods are used with the implementation). The parameters you specify map with the route definition. With the sample code here, the* OnGet *method is declared to return* void. *You can also declare to return other data types— for example, you can return a* string *if just a string should be returned. To return specific HTTP error codes together with content, you can declare the method to return an object implementing the interface* IActionResult. *Later in this chapter in the section "Model Binding," you declare methods to return* IAsyncResult.

Now you can pass the values with the URL string `https://localhost:5001/ShowBook ?title=ProCSharp&publisher=Wrox` to show it in the returned HTML page, as shown in Figure 26-3.

Title	ProCSharp
Publisher	Wrox

FIGURE 26-3

Instead of using parameters with the OnGet method, you can also access the RouteData property of the base class to access all the route values.

With the @page directive, you can create a *custom route* to map route values to parameter values. Using an @page directive such as **@page {title}** maps **ABook** from the URL `https://localhost:5001/ShowBook/ABook` to the **title** variable. The Calc page uses the @page directive `"{op}/{x}/{y}"`. With the URL `https://localhost:5001/Calc/add/38/4`, the op variable gets the value add, the x variable the value 38, and the y variable the value 4.

Optionally, you can also define constraints to the route. If you specify x to be of type int, with @page `"{op}/{x:int}/{y:int}"`, a URL where the value passed cannot be converted to int does not apply, and the next route that matches is searched.

The following code snippet uses a custom route with constraints where the parts of the URL that map to the x and y parameters need to be convertible to int and a constraint specifying a regular expression. With the regex constraint, the values of the route need to match one of add, sub, mul, and div to pass it to the op parameter. The Razor Page Calc uses the model CalcModel and accesses the Op, X, Y, and Result properties with Razor expressions (code file WebAppSample/Pages/Calc.cshtml):

```
@page "{op:regex(^[add|sub|mul|div])}/{x:int}/{y:int}"
@model WebAppSample.Pages.CalcModel

<h2>Calculation</h2>
<h4>The operation @Model.Op with @Model.X and @Model.Y results in @Model.Result</h4>
```

With the code-behind file, the CalcModel class receives the op, x, and y parameters with the OnGet method, does calculations depending on the value of the op variable, and passes the result to the Result property (code file WebAppSample/Pages/Calc.cshtml.cs):

```
public class CalcModel : PageModel
{
    public string Op { get; set; } = string.Empty;
    public int X { get; set; }
    public int Y { get; set; }
    public int Result { get; private set; }
    public void OnGet(string op, int x, int y)
```

```
    {
      Op = op;
      X = x;
      Y = y;
      Result = Op switch
      {
        "add" => X + Y,
        "sub" => X - Y,
        "mul" => X * Y,
        "div" => X / Y,
        _ => X + Y
      };
    }
  }
}
```

Calculation
The operation add with 17 and 25 results in 42

When you run the application, you can pass URLs such as `Calc/add/17/25` or `Calc/mul/8/4` to see the results (Figure 26-4).

FIGURE 26-4

Razor Libraries and Areas

Let's extend the sample solution to dig deeper with Razor Pages. Next, libraries are added to access a database. This solution consists of the web application created earlier with a .NET 5 library `BooksModel` and a Razor Class Library `BooksViews`. The `BooksModel` class just contains a `Book` record and a `BooksContext` to access the database. Read Chapter 21, "Entity Framework Core," for more information on accessing the database.

A Razor Class Library can be created with this .NET CLI command:

```
> dotnet new razorclasslib --support-pages-and-views -o BooksViews
```

Be sure to add the option `support-pages-and-views` for Razor Pages support. Without this option, the library is meant to host Razor components that are covered in the next chapter. Using this option adds the element `AddRazorSupportForMvc` to the project file.

When you use Razor class libraries with Razor Pages, to not get in conflicts with naming pages, you should use areas. Areas give you subfolders with URLs to reduce conflicts when you use pages from different categories in web applications.

Create

Book

Title

Professional C#

Publisher

Wrox Press

Create

Back to List

When you use areas, below the `Areas` folder you add a subfolder with the name of a category (such as `Admin` or `Books`) and then a `Pages` subfolder where you store your Razor Pages. The sample application defines `Index`, `Details`, `Create`, `Edit`, and `Delete` Razor Pages to read and write `Book` objects. By referencing the library from the application, the URL `https://localhost:5001/Books/Create` can be used to access the `Create` page in the `Books` area, as shown in Figure 26-5.

When using the Razor Class Library from the web application, all the pages from the library can be accessed from the application, but you can override specific pages just by creating the same folder structure in the web application and adding the Razor Pages to override in this folder.

FIGURE 26-5

Within the library, no layout is defined. Usually, it's more practical to use the same layout as defined by the web application. To use the same layout, you need to create the folder structure for the area and add a `_ViewStart.cshtml` file setting the `Layout` property of the Razor Pages within the view (code file `WebAppSample/Areas/Books/_ViewStart.cshtml`):

```
@{
  Layout = "~/Pages/Shared/_Layout.cshtml";
}
```

Injecting Services

With the code-behind file of a Razor page, you can inject services as you've seen it done with controllers and middleware types in the previous two chapters. In the next code snippet, in the `CreateModel` class, the EF Core context class `BooksContext` is injected in the constructor (code file `BooksViews/Areas/Books/Pages/Create.cshtml.cs`):

```
public class CreateModel : PageModel
{
  private readonly BookModels.BooksContext _context;

  public CreateModel(BookModels.BooksContext context)
  {
    _context = context;
  }
  //...
}
```

Instead of injecting the EF Core context, you can use the repository pattern and use an abstraction to the EF Core context that helps with becoming independent of the EF Core context and helps with testability as shown in Chapter 25, "Services."

To inject the service directly with the `.cshtml` file and not with code-behind file, you can use the `@inject` declaration. This kind of dependency injection is used with Razor components shown in Chapter 27, "Blazor."

Returning Results

When creating new books, first an HTTP GET request is done to get a form to fill out the data. As the data is filled out by the user, an HTTP POST request sends the book data with the HTTP body to the server.

If a GET request is sent from the client, the `OnGet` method in the `Create` page is invoked. Here, just the empty page is returned. With the implementation in the following code snippet, the `OnGet` method returns `IActionResult`. The `PageModel` base class defines several helper methods to return results. Examples are the `NotFound` method, which returns a `NotFoundResult` and an HTTP 404 status code, and the `Unauthorized` method, which returns an `UnauthorizedResult` with status code 401. With the `StatusCode` method, you have full control on the status code returned. The methods from the base class `PageModel` are similar to the methods of the `ControllerBase` class from Chapter 25. The `ControllerBase` class methods also are used with MVC, as you'll see later in this chapter in the section "ASP.NET Core MVC."

With the `Create` page, the `OnGet` method invokes the `Page` method to return the content of the Razor page with a status code 200 (code file `BooksView/Areas/Pages/Create.cshtml.cs`):

```
public IActionResult OnGet()
{
  return Page();
}
```

When sending a GET request, the user receives the form, can fill out the data, and submits the form by clicking the submit button (as shown in the following code snippet). This way, an HTTP POST request is sent, which is covered next (code file `BooksView/Areas/Pages/Create.cshtml`):

```
<form method="post">
  <!-- ... -->
  <input type="submit" value="Create" class="btn btn-primary" />
</form>
```

Model Binding

To access the data received with the POST request, the `BindProperty` attribute can be used. `BindProperty` uses a model binder (interface `IModelBinder`) to assign values from the form data to the type where the attribute is assigned to; in the following code snippet, the property `Book` of type `Book` is annotated with the `BindProperty` attribute. With the `OnPostAsync` method that is invoked with the POST request, the `Book` property received is used to add a new record to the EF Core context and write the new record to the database. With a success, an HTTP redirect request is sent to the browser, so the browser continues with a GET request to the `Index` page (code file `BooksView/Areas/Pages/Create.cshtml.cs`):

```
[BindProperty]
public Book? Book { get; set; }

public async Task<IActionResult> OnPostAsync()
{
  if (!ModelState.IsValid || Book is null)
  {
    return Page();
  }

  _context.Books.Add(Book);
  await _context.SaveChangesAsync();

  return RedirectToPage("./Index");
}
```

> **NOTE** *With the model type, you should make sure that the model type doesn't implement properties that should not be filled from a POST request. In case your model has such properties, an overposting attack could be done to fill these properties with a hacker's POST request. To avoid this, you can create a view-model type with only the properties that should be set and programmatically assign the model type to the values from the view-model type. Another option is to invoke the* `TryUpdateModelAsync` *(a method from the base class* `PageModel`*) instead of the* `BindProperty` *attribute. With an argument of this method, you can explicitly specify the properties that should be set.*

Working with HTML Helpers

Let's get into the user interface. Instead of just using HTML code with Razor syntax with expressions accessing the model, you can use HTML Helpers.

With a Razor page, the generated class contains an `Html` property of type `IHtmlHelper` or, if the `@model` directive is used, an `Html` property of the generic type `IHtmlHelper<Model>`. With this interface, several HTML Helpers are available that return HTML code. You can also create a custom HTML Helper by defining an extension method that extends the `IHtmlHelper` interface and returns a string.

With the `Index` page as shown in the following code snippet, the HTML Helpers `DisplayNameFor` and `DisplayFor` are used to generate HTML code. `DisplayNameFor` uses a lambda expression to define the property that should be used to access the property name. The name of the property is then returned with the HTML code. The `DisplayFor` method uses the same expression but returns the value of the property. The `DisplayNameFor` HTML Helper is used within the heading of the HTML table, the `DisplayFor` method within the `@foreach` iteration to show every value of the collection (code file `BooksView/Areas/Pages/Index.cshtml`):

```
<table class="table">
  <thead>
```

```
        <tr>
          <th>
            @Html.DisplayNameFor(model => model.Books![0].Title)
          </th>
          <th>
            @Html.DisplayNameFor(model => model.Books![0].Publisher)
          </th>
          <th></th>
        </tr>
      </thead>
      <tbody>
  @foreach (var item in Model.Books!) {
      <tr>
        <td>
          @Html.DisplayFor(modelItem => item.Title)
        </td>
        <td>
          @Html.DisplayFor(modelItem => item.Publisher)
        </td>
        <!-- ... -->
      </tr>
  }
    </tbody>
```

Displaying the name of the property is not useful in many cases. As shown with the following code snippet, with the model (or view-model type), you can use attributes such as the `DisplayName` attribute to specify a name that should be used for display (code file `BooksModels/Book.cs`):

```
public record Book(
    [property: MaxLength(50)]
    [property: DisplayName("Title")]
    string Title,

    [property:MaxLength(50)]
    [property:DisplayName("Publisher")]
    string Publisher,

    int BookId = 0);
```

> **NOTE** *With the* `DisplayName` *attribute, you can specify resources to be used to retrieve the name to display from a resource file. This allows for localization of the user interface. Read Chapter 22, "Localization," for more information.*

ASP.NET Core includes many HTML Helpers. Helpers that return simple HTML elements such as `BeginForm` (a form element), `CheckBox` (input type="checkbox"), `TextBox` (input type="text"), `DropDownList` (select with option), and helpers that return a complete form based on a model, such as `EditorForModel`.

Working with Tag Helpers

HTML Helpers have been available since early versions of ASP.NET MVC, the .NET Framework version of MVC. Tag Helpers are a newer construct, available with ASP.NET Core. Instead of using Razor syntax to activate the HTML Helpers, with Tag Helpers you write HTML syntax in your Razor Pages. Tag Helpers are still resolved on the server with server-side code; HTML and JavaScript syntax is returned to the client.

Tag Helpers can be implemented by adding attributes to existing HTML elements, and they can also replace existing elements or create new elements, as shown in this section and the next.

Let's get into an example using the anchor Tag Helper. With the following code snippet, the HTML element a is used to create a link within a Razor page. With this element, the attributes `asp-page`, `asp-route-id`, and `asp-area` are specified. What's behind the scenes is the `AnchorTagHelper` class with the properties `Page`, `Area`, and `RouteValues`. These properties are annotated with the attribute `HtmlAttributeName` using the values `"asp-page"`, `"asp-area"`, and `"asp-route-{value}"`. With the `asp-` prefix used, you can easily distinguish these server-side attribute names from HTML attribute names. When you use these attributes with the `AnchorTagHelper`, an `href` attribute is returned to the link of the corresponding Razor page including the `id` parameter (code file `BooksView/Areas/Books/Pages/Index.cshtml`):

```
<td>
  <a asp-page="./Edit" asp-route-id="@item.BookId" asp-area="Books">Edit</a> |
  <a asp-page="./Details" asp-route-id="@item.BookId" asp-area="Books">Details</a> |
  <a asp-page="./Delete" asp-route-id="@item.BookId" asp-area="Books">Delete</a>
</td>
```

Other examples of Tag Helpers are the `InputTagHelper` and the `LabelTagHelper` shown in the following code snippet. The `LabelTagHelper` is used with a `label` element and creates code for a display (and also using the annotations you've already seen with the HTML Helper), and the `InputTagHelper` is used with the input element. Both of these helpers map the `asp-for` attribute to the `For` property (code file `BooksView/Areas/Books/Pages/Create.cshtml`):

```
<label asp-for="Book!.Publisher" class="control-label"></label>
<input asp-for="Book!.Publisher" class="form-control" />
```

Not all Tag Helpers are that easily detectable by using the `asp-` prefix. The `EnvironmentTagHelper` uses the `environment` element. The content within the environment element is rendered only if the code is built for the specified environment. With the environment element, you can use the `include` and `exclude` attributes to include a list or exclude a list of environments. The following code snippet uses the `environment` element to either reference minified or full-size JavaScript files that help with debugging (code file `WebAppSample/Pages/Shared/_Layout.cshtml`):

```
<environment include="Development">
  <script src="~/lib/jquery/dist/jquery.js"></script>
  <script src="~/lib/bootstrap/dist/js/bootstrap.js"></script>
</environment>
<environment exclude="Development">
  <script src="~/lib/jquery/dist/jquery.min.js"></script>
  <script src="~/lib/bootstrap/dist/js/bootstrap.min.js"></script>
</environment>
```

The ASP.NET Core Tag Helpers are defined in the assembly `Microsoft.AspNetCore.Mvc.TagHelpers`. To allow Tag Helpers in Razor Pages, Tag Helpers need to be activated with the `@addTagHelper` directive. The following `@addTagHelper` directive opens all Tag Helpers specified by the * from the assembly `Microsoft.AspNetCore.Mvc.TagHelpers` (code file `WebAppSample/Areas/Books/_ViewImports.cshtml`):

```
@addTagHelper *, Microsoft.AspNetCore.Mvc.TagHelpers
```

Instead of the *, you can use the fully qualified class name of the Tag Helpers. Specifying the `@addTagHelper` directive in the `_ViewImports.cshtml` file enables Tag Helpers in all the Razor Pages of this directory and subdirectories. If Tag Helpers should just be enabled in specific pages, use this directive in these pages.

Validation of User Input

To validate user input on the client, you can use Tag Helpers. The `ValidationMessageTagHelper` attaches error messages to input fields (using the attribute `asp-validation-for`). This helper creates the HTML 5 attribute `data-valmsg-for`. The `ValidationSummaryTagHelper` (with the attribute `asp-validation-summary`) shows summary information with errors of the complete form (code file `BooksViews/Areas/Books/Pages/Edit.cshtml`):

```
<div asp-validation-summary="ModelOnly" class="text-danger"></div>
<div class="form-group">
  <label asp-for="Book!.Title" class="control-label"></label>
  <input asp-for="Book!.Title" class="form-control" />
  <span asp-validation-for="Book!.Title" class="text-danger"></span>
</div>
```

The validation controls make use of model annotations, such as the `Required` and `StringLength` attributes. With the attributes `CreditCard`, `EmailAddress`, `Phone`, and `Url`, you can use more attributes for input validation with typically used data. The `Range` attribute checks whether the input falls within the specified range. With the `RegularExpression`, you can specify a regular expression to check for the correct input. The validation Tag Helpers are based on the jQuery Validation plug-in (`https://jqueryvalidation.org/`). This library needs to be referenced from the web application.

Although validating the user input on the client enhances usability and reduces the network traffic, you also always need to verify the input with server-side code. With server-side code, you use the `ModelState` property of the `PageModel` class by checking the `IsValid` property: `ModelState.IsValid`. This verifies whether the received data that is bound is valid. Here, the same annotations that you added to the model (or the view model) apply.

Creating Custom Tag Helpers

Aside from using the predefined Tag Helpers, you can create a custom Tag Helper. The first custom Tag Helper converts Markdown code to HTML with the help of the NuGet package `Markdig`.

> **NOTE** *Markdown is a markup language that can be created with a text editor. Markdown is designed to be converted to HTML easily. Read my blog article "Using Markdown" for information about using Markdown with .NET at* `https://csharp.christiannagel.com/2016/07/03/markdown/`.

The Tag Helper `MarkdownTagHelper` is implemented in a .NET 5.0 library named `CustomTagHelpers`. This library references the NuGet package `Markdig` and has a FrameworkReference `Microsoft.AspNetCore.App`. With .NET 5 libraries, this `FrameworkReference` includes a reference to many ASP.NET Core packages.

The following code snippet shows the class declaration of the `MarkdownTagHelper`. A Tag Helper derives from the base class `TagHelper`. The attribute `HtmlTargetElement` specifies the element or attribute names that are used to specify the Tag Helper. This Tag Helper can be used either with the `markdown` element or with the `markdownfile` attribute that can be used within a `div` element. The `TagStructure` attribute allows configuration if the element needs self-closing (enumeration value `WithoutEndTag`) or allows an end tag or self-closing with `NormalOrSelfClosing` (code file `CustomTagHelpers/MarkdownTagHelper.cs`):

```
[HtmlTargetElement("markdown",
  TagStructure = TagStructure.NormalOrSelfClosing)]
[HtmlTargetElement(Attributes = "markdownfile")]
public class MarkdownTagHelper : TagHelper
{
  //...
}
```

Tag Helpers can make use of dependency injection. Because the `MarkdownTagHelper` needs the directory of the `wwwroot` files, and this directory is returned from the `IWebHostEnvironment` interface, this interface is injected in the constructor:

```
private readonly IWebHostEnvironment _env;
public MarkdownTagHelper(IWebHostEnvironment env) => _env = env;
```

Properties of a Tag Helper are automatically applied by the infrastructure when they are annotated with the `HtmlAttributeName` attribute. Here, the property `MarkdownFile` gets its value from the `markdownfile` attribute:

```
[HtmlAttributeName("markdownfile")]
public string? MarkdownFile { get; set; }
```

Next, let's get into the main functionality of this Tag Helper. Tag Helpers need to override one of the methods `Process` or `ProcessAsync`. The `ProcessAsync` method is used when async functionality is needed, whereas you can use the `Process` method if you invoke only synchronous methods. The following code snippet overrides the `ProcessAsync` method because the asynchronous method `GetChildContentAsync` is used within the implementation. With the implementation, the two different uses of the `MarkdownTagHelper` are considered. One use is to specify the `markdown` element where the content comes as a child of the element, and the other is the `markdownfile` attribute that references a markdown file.

If the attribute `markdownfile` is used, the `MarkdownFile` property is set; thus, the file specified with this property is read, and the content is written to the `markdown` variable. The directory of the file is retrieved via the `_env` variable of type `IHostingEnvironment`. This interface defines the `WebRootPath` property that returns the root path for the web files.

If the `MarkdownFile` property is not set, but instead the `markdown` element is used, the content of this element is read. The content of the element that is specified within Markdown can be accessed using the `TagHelperOutput`. To retrieve the content, the method `GetChildContentAsync` needs to be invoked, and after this method returns, the `GetContent` method needs to be invoked that finally returns the content as specified in the HTML page. Using the `Markdown` class of the Markdig library, the Markdown content is converted to HTML. This HTML code is then put into the content of the `TagHelperOutput` by invoking the `SetHtmlContent` method (code file `CustomTagHelpers/MarkdownTagHelper.cs`):

```
public override async Task ProcessAsync(TagHelperContext context,
  TagHelperOutput output)
{
  string markdown;
  if (MarkdownFile is not null)
  {
    string filename = Path.Combine(_env.WebRootPath, MarkdownFile);
    markdown = File.ReadAllText(filename);
  }
  else
  {
    markdown = (await output.GetChildContentAsync()).GetContent();
  }
  output.Content.SetHtmlContent(Markdown.ToHtml(markdown));
}
```

After creating the `MarkdownTagHelper` you can use it from a Razor page. The `@addTagHelper` adds all Tag Helpers from the library `CustomTagHelpers`. In the HTML code, the `markdown` element is used. This element contains a small segment of Markdown syntax with a heading 2, a link, and a list (code file `WebAppSample/Pages/UseMarkdown.cshtml`):

```
@page
@addTagHelper *, CustomTagHelpers
```

```
<h2>Markdown Sample</h2>

<markdown>
## This is simple Markdown

[C# Blog](https://csharp.christiannagel.com)


* one
* two
* three
</markdown>
```

When you run the application, the Markdown syntax gets converted to HTML output, as shown in Figure 26-6.

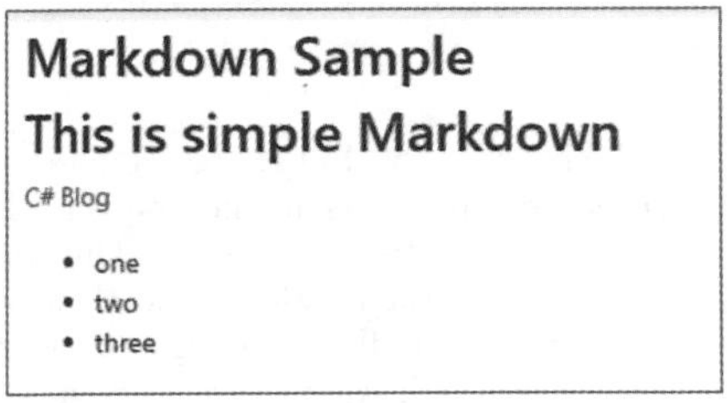

Now, the same functionality can be achieved by creating the file `Sample.md` (which contains the same Markdown content as shown earlier) and referencing the file from the `markdownfile` attribute (code file `WebAppSample/Pages/UseMarkdownAttribute.cshtml`):

```
<div markdownfile="Sample.md"></div>
```

With this in place, the property `MarkdownFile` of the `MarkdownTagHelper` is set, and thus the Markdown file is read.

Markdown Sample
This is simple Markdown

C# Blog

- one
- two
- three

FIGURE 26-6

Creating Elements with Tag Helpers

The next custom Tag Helper you build in this section extends the HTML `table` element to show a row for every item in a list and a column for every property. A model of data information is passed to the Tag Helper, and the Tag Helper creates `table`, `tr`, `th`, and `td` elements dynamically. This Tag Helper uses reflection to create the required information. Similar functionality like this can be implemented in view components as well, and the view helpers can be used with a Tag Helper. This section goes into detail about creating more complex Tag Helpers and using the `TagBuilder` class to dynamically create HTML elements.

> **NOTE** *Reflection is explained in Chapter 12.*

For this sample, the service class `MenusSamplesService` implements the method `CreateMenuItems` to return a list of `MenuItem` objects (code file `WebAppSample/Services/MenusSampleService.cs`):

```
public class MenuSamplesService
{
  private List<MenuItem>? _menuItems;

  public IEnumerable<MenuItem> GetMenuItems() =>
    _menuItems ??= CreateMenuItems();

  private List<MenuItem> CreateMenuItems()
  {
    DateTime today = DateTime.Today;
    return Enumerable.Range(1, 10).Select(i =>
      new MenuItem(i, $"menu {i}", 14.8, today.AddDays(i))).ToList();
  }
}
```

The Tag Helper class `TableTagHelper` is activated with the HTML `table` element. Unlike the previous helper with the `markup` element, this helper is used with a valid HTML element. The `HtmlTargetElement` specifies `table` to apply this helper and specifies the attribute `items`. This attribute is used to set the `Items` property as specified by the `HtmlAttributeName` attribute (code file `CustomTagHelpers/TableTagHelper.cs`):

```
[HtmlTargetElement("table", Attributes = ItemsAttributeName)]
public class TableTagHelper : TagHelper
{
  private const string ItemsAttributeName = "items";

  [HtmlAttributeName(ItemsAttributeName)]
  public IEnumerable<object> Items { get; set; }
  //...
}
```

The heart of the Tag Helper is in the method `Process`. This time the synchronous variant of this method can be used because no async method is used in the implementation. With the parameters of the `Process` method, you receive a `TagHelperContext`. This context contains both the attributes of the HTML element where the Tag Helper is applied and all child elements. With the `table` element specified when using the Tag Helper, rows and columns could already have been defined, and you could merge the result with the existing content. In the sample, this is ignored, and just the attributes are taken to put them in the result. The result needs to be written to the second parameter: the `TagHelperOutput` object. For creating HTML code, the `TagBuilder` type is used. The `TagBuilder` helps create HTML elements with attributes, and it deals with closing of elements. To add attributes to the `TagBuilder`, you use the method `MergeAttributes`. This method requires a dictionary of all attribute names and their values. This dictionary is created by using the LINQ extension method `ToDictionary`. With the `Where` method, all of the existing attributes—with the exception of the items attribute—of the table element are taken. The `items` attribute is used for defining items with the Tag Helper but is not needed later by the client:

```
public override void Process(TagHelperContext context, TagHelperOutput output)
{
  TagBuilder table = new("table");
  table.GenerateId(context.UniqueId, "id");
  var attributes = context.AllAttributes
    .Where(a => a.Name != ItemsAttributeName)
    .ToDictionary(a => a.Name);
  table.MergeAttributes(attributes);

  PropertyInfo[] properties = CreateHeading(table);
  //...
}
```

> **NOTE** *LINQ is explained in Chapter 9, "Language Integrated Query."*

Next, create the first row in the table by using the `CreateHeading` method. This first row contains a `tr` element as a child of the `table` element, and it contains `th` (table heading) elements for every property. To get all the property names, you invoke the `First` method to retrieve the first object of the collection. You access the properties of this instance using reflection, invoking the `GetProperties` method on the `Type` object, and writing the name of the property to the inner text of the `th` HTML element:

```
private PropertyInfo[] CreateHeading(TagBuilder table)
{
  if (Items is null) throw new InvalidOperationException("Items are empty");

  TagBuilder tr = new("tr");
```

```
    var heading = Items.First();
    PropertyInfo[] properties = heading.GetType().GetProperties();
    foreach (var prop in properties)
    {
      var th = new TagBuilder("th");
      th.InnerHtml.Append(prop.Name);
      tr.InnerHtml.AppendHtml(th);
    }
    table.InnerHtml.AppendHtml(tr);
    return properties;
}
```

The final part of the `Process` method iterates through all items of the collection and creates more rows (`tr`) for every item. With every property, a `td` element is added, and the value of the property is written as inner text. Last, the inner HTML code of the created `table` element is written to the output:

```
foreach (var item in Items)
{
  TagBuilder tr = new("tr");
  foreach (var prop in properties)
  {
    TagBuilder td = new("td");
    td.InnerHtml.Append(prop.GetValue(item).ToString());
    tr.InnerHtml.AppendHtml(td);
  }
  table.InnerHtml.AppendHtml(tr);
  }
  output.Content.Append(table.InnerHtml);
}
```

After you've created the Tag Helper, creating the view becomes very simple. With the code-behind file of the Razor page `UseTableTagHelper`, the service `MenuSampleService` is injected to receive the menus (code file `WebAppSample/Pages/UseTableTagHelper.cshtml.cs`):

```
public class UseTableTagHelperModel : PageModel
{
    public UseTableTagHelperModel(MenuSamplesService menuSampleService) =>
      MenuItems = menuSampleService.GetMenuItems();

    public IEnumerable<MenuItem> MenuItems { get; }
}
```

With the Razor page content, the Tag Helper needs to be activated by invoking `addTagHelper`. To create an instance of the `TableTagHelper`, the `items` attribute is added to the HTML table element (code file `WebAppSample/Pages/UseTableTagHelper.cshtml`):

```
@page
@addTagHelper *, CustomTagHelpers
@model WebAppSample.Pages.UseTableTagHelperModel

<table class="table" items="@Model.MenuItems"></table>
```

When you run the application, the table you see should look like the one shown in Figure 26-7. After you've created the Tag Helper, it is really easy to use. All the formatting that is defined using CSS still applies because all the attributes of the defined HTML table are still in the resulting HTML output.

Id	Text	Price	Date
1	menu 1	14,8	26/04/2021 00:00:00
2	menu 2	14,8	27/04/2021 00:00:00
3	menu 3	14,8	28/04/2021 00:00:00
4	menu 4	14,8	29/04/2021 00:00:00
5	menu 5	14,8	30/04/2021 00:00:00
6	menu 6	14,8	01/05/2021 00:00:00
7	menu 7	14,8	02/05/2021 00:00:00
8	menu 8	14,8	03/05/2021 00:00:00
9	menu 9	14,8	04/05/2021 00:00:00
10	menu 10	14,8	05/05/2021 00:00:00

FIGURE 26-7

With the `TableTagHelper`, there's still room for improvement. It just uses the name of the properties to display the title of the column. The values are shown with a default representation. How can you change this? The `TableTagHelper` can be implemented to access annotations from the model to retrieve attributes such as `DisplayName`, and the `DataType` attribute specifies that only the data part of `DateTime` should be displayed.

View Components

ASP.NET Core gives another option to create reusable views: *view components*. If you have a component with a complex user interface that should be usable across different web applications, you can add a view component to a library. Examples where view components are really useful are dynamic navigation of menus, a login panel, or a sidebar content in a blog.

With view components, the controller functionality is implemented in a class that derives from `ViewComponent` with a name that's postfixed with `ViewComponent` or has the attribute `ViewComponent` applied. The user interface is defined similarly to a view, but the method to invoke the view component is different.

The view component for the sample application is implemented in a Razor Class Library with support for Razor Pages and views. The following code snippet defines the class `EventListComponent` that derives from the base class `ViewComponent`. This class uses the `IEventsService` contract type that needs to be registered with the DI container. The `InvokeAsync` method is defined to be called from the page that shows the view component. This method can have any number and type of parameters. Instead of using an async method implementation, you can synchronously implement this method to return `IViewComponentResult` instead of `Task<IViewComponentResult>`. However, typically the async variant is the best to use—for example, for accessing a database. The `View` method used to return the `IViewComponentResult` is defined with the `ViewComponent` base class and returns a `ViewViewComponentResult`. `ViewViewComponentResult` receives a model with the constructor that can then be used by the Razor user interface (code file `EventViews/ViewComponents/EventListViewComponent.cs`):

```
[ViewComponent(Name ="EventList")]
public class EventListViewComponent : ViewComponent
{
  private readonly IEventsService _eventsService;
  public EventListViewComponent (IEventsService eventsService) =>
    _eventsService = eventsService;

  public Task<IViewComponentResult> InvokeAsync(DateTime from, DateTime to) =>
    Task.FromResult<IViewComponentResult>(
      View(EventsByDateRange(from, to)));

  private IEnumerable<Event> EventsByDateRange(DateTime from, DateTime to) =>
    _eventsService.Events.Where(e => e.Date >= from && e.Date <= to);
}
```

The library contains a default look for the view component that could be changed by the application using the view component. The default user interface needs to be stored with the name `default.cshtml` (a Razor view) in the folder `Views/Shared/Components/[viewcomponent]` or `Pages/Shared/Components/[viewcomponent]`. The `Views` folder works both with Razor Pages and Razor views. Razor views are discussed in the section "ASP.NET Core MVC." With the application using the view component, a different look can be created in the same directory structure of the web application or in the folder `Pages/Components/[viewcomponent]`. With the sample library, the view is stored in the folder `Views/Shared/Components/EventList`. The `default.cshtml` file is a simple Razor view (it doesn't have the `@page` directive) that has a model specified (with the `@model` directive). With Razor syntax, the `Model` property is used to access data from the `Event` type (code file `EventViews/Views/Shared/Components/EventList/default.cshtml`):

```
@using EventViews.Models
@model IEnumerable<Event>
```

```
<h5>Dates with the UI from the library</h5>
<table class="table">
  <thead>
    <tr>
      <td>Date</td>
      <td>Text</td>
    </tr>
  </thead>
  <tbody>
    @foreach (var ev in Model)
    {
      <tr>
        <td>@ev.Date.ToString("d")</td>
        <td>@ev.Text</td>
      </tr>
    }
  </tbody>
</table>
```

With the web application, the IEventsService interface is registered with an implementation of the FormulaEvents class. This class returns a list for Formula 1 race dates and is injected with the constructor of the view component implementation (code file WebAppSample/Startup.cs):

```
services.AddSingleton<IEventsService, Formula1Events>();
```

Using the view model becomes simple: you use a Tag Helper for view components. A simple Razor page is now used to ask the user for start and end dates, and as the information is posted, the view component is shown. After the user interface is shown with a GET request, the user fills out start and end dates. With a POST request, the dates match the binding with the DateSelectionViewModel. After the POST, the same page is returned to the client, but the value of the ShowEvents property switches to true to show the information from the view component (code file WebAppSample/Pages/UseViewComponent.cshtml.cs):

```
public class UseViewComponentModel : PageModel
{
  public bool ShowEvents { get; set; } = false;

  public IActionResult OnGet() => Page();

  [BindProperty]
  public DateSelectionViewModel DateSelection { get; set; } =
    new DateSelectionViewModel();

  public IActionResult OnPost()
  {
    ShowEvents = true;
    return Page();
  }
}

public class DateSelectionViewModel
{
  public DateTime From { get; set; } = DateTime.Today;
  public DateTime To { get; set; } = DateTime.Today.AddDays(20);
}
```

The Razor page adds Tag Helpers referencing the library where the view component is implemented. This enables Tag Helpers for view components. Label and input elements are used that map the From and To properties of the

`DateSelectionViewModel`. When the submit button is clicked, the POST request is sent to the server (code file `WebAppSample/Pages/UseViewComponent.cshtml`):

```
@page
@model WebAppSample.Pages.UseViewComponentModel

@addTagHelper *, EventViews

<h2>Formula 1 Calendar</h2>
<form method="post">
  <label asp-for="DateSelection.From" class="control-label"></label>
  <input asp-for="DateSelection.From" class="form-control" />
  <br />
  <label asp-for="DateSelection.To" class="control-label"></label>
  <input asp-for="DateSelection.To" class="form-control" />
  <input type="submit" value="submit" />
</form>
```

The last part of the Razor page is the view component that's shown if the `ShowEvents` property returns `true`. Tag Helpers for view components are prefixed with `vc` and are named after the name of the view component. The Tag Helper name uses a naming convention known as *lower kebab casing*. With the class name where parts have uppercase characters, the - is used. In addition, the `ViewComponent` postfix is removed. Thus, the class name `EventListViewComponent` changes to the Tag Helper name `event-list`. The parameter names of the `InvokeAsync` method are mapped by attributes of the Tag Helper (code file `WebAppSample/Pages/UseViewComponent.cshtml`):

```
@if (Model.ShowEvents)
{
<vc:event-list from="@Model.DateSelection.From" to="@Model.DateSelection.To" />
}
```

When you run the application, you can see the view component rendered as shown in Figure 26-8.

FIGURE 26-8

ASP.NET CORE MVC

After you know the ins and outs of Razor Pages, it's time to move on to ASP.NET Core MVC. Many things you've seen so far are the same with MVC, so I'm focusing on the differences. With ASP.NET Core MVC, you can use Razor syntax, HTML Helpers, Tag Helpers, view components, and more. MVC adds a controller and uses Razor views instead of Razor pages. Razor views are simpler than Razor pages. In principle, the code from the Razor page moves to the controller.

In this section, you create a sample application using ASP.NET Core MVC with user registration where the information is stored in a local database. You can create this application using this `dotnet` CLI command:

```
> dotnet new mvc --auth Individual -o MVCSample
```

> **NOTE** *A template that allows user registration is also available with Razor Pages. You just need to supply the template name* webapp *instead of* mvc.

MVC Bootstrapping

The first change to Razor Pages is the configuration of the DI container. The extension method `AddControllersWithViews` registers all services needed for controllers, views, and the Razor engine. The configuration of the EF Core context and the default identity comes from the `--auth` option. The `ApplicationDbContext` is an EF Core context that defines `DbSet` properties to store user information, roles of users, user claims, and login information. This context class can be extended in case you need some additional information (code file `MVCSample/Startup.cs`):

```
public void ConfigureServices(IServiceCollection services)
{
  services.AddDbContext<ApplicationDbContext>(options =>
    options.UseSqlite(
      Configuration.GetConnectionString("DefaultConnection")));
  services.AddDatabaseDeveloperPageExceptionFilter();

  services.AddDefaultIdentity<IdentityUser>(options =>
    options.SignIn.RequireConfirmedAccount = true)
      .AddEntityFrameworkStores<ApplicationDbContext>();
  services.AddControllersWithViews();
}
```

MVC Routing

An important change to Razor Pages is the endpoint routing configuration with the middleware in the `Configure` method. The method `MapControllerRoute` specifies the routing for MVC. With the web API in the previous chapter, you used attribute-based routing that you specified with the controller. With Razor Pages, routing is based on the name of a Razor page. With the `@page` directive, you can specify customizations to the route. With MVC you have a central place to specify all your routes. You can invoke `MapControllerRoute` multiple times with different route names where you can specify different patterns for the route. The controller and action terms need to be part of the pattern. The term *controller* references the name of a `Controller` class (without the `Controller` postfix), and `action` references the name of a method in the controller—an action method. With the pattern specified, `id` is optional (because of the `?`) and specifies the name of a method parameter. Using URI `Books/Details/42` maps to the `BooksController` with the `Details` action method and passes `42` for the `id` parameter. The pattern specifies default values for `controller` and `action` to be `Home` and `Index`. So by default with the URI `/`, the `Index` method of the `HomeController` is invoked without passing an argument value to the

`Index` method. You can just use the URI `Books`, which invokes the `Index` method in the `BooksController` class (code file `MVCSample/Startup.cs`):

```
public void Configure(IApplicationBuilder app, IWebHostEnvironment env)
{
  //...
  app.UseRouting();

  app.UseAuthentication();
  app.UseAuthorization();

  app.UseEndpoints(endpoints =>
  {
    endpoints.MapControllerRoute(
      name: "default",
      pattern: "{controller=Home}/{action=Index}/{id?}");
    endpoints.MapRazorPages();
  });
}
```

Similar to Razor Pages, you can also define constraints with a route, so it's possible to have a route with ASP.NET Core MVC that matches only when number values are passed.

Controllers

In the previous chapter, you created ASP.NET Core controllers to build web APIs. With ASP.NET Core MVC, it's the same controller; it just derives from the `Controller` base class instead of `ControllerBase`. The `Controller` class derives from `ControllerBase` but adds features used by MVC. The `Controller` base class implements methods to return different kinds of views, such as the `View`, `PartialView`, and `ViewComponent` methods, and `ViewData` and `TempData` properties. You've already used the `ViewData` property from a Razor Pages base class to pass data between different views. You can also pass data between controllers and views.

The following code snippet shows the implementation of the `HomeController` class. A controller needs to be located in the `Controller` subdirectory and named with a `Controller` postfix. Deriving from the `Controller` base class is optional. The `HomeController` implements the action methods `Index` and `Privacy`. Similar to the `OnGet` and `OnPost` method you looked at with Razor Pages, the action methods typically return `IActionResult` (but can return any data type). The `View` method that's used here searches for a view with a specific convention and returns the view to the caller (code file `MVCSample/Controllers/HomeController.cs`):

```
public class HomeController : Controller
{
  private readonly ILogger<HomeController> _logger;

  public HomeController(ILogger<HomeController> logger)
  {
    _logger = logger;
  }

  public IActionResult Index()
  {
    return View();
  }

  public IActionResult Privacy()
  {
```

```
      return View();
    }

    [ResponseCache(Duration = 0, Location = ResponseCacheLocation.None, NoStore = true)]
    public IActionResult Error()
    {
      return View(new ErrorViewModel
      {
        RequestId = Activity.Current?.Id ?? HttpContext.TraceIdentifier
      });
    }
  }
}
```

The convention that's used with ASP.NET Core MVC to look for views is to search in the `Views` folder for a folder with the same name as the controller—for example, `Views/Home`. Within this folder, if a view has the same name as the action method, this view is returned. If a view is not found in this folder, a view is searched for in the `Shared` folder. With the `Shared` folder, it's using the same fallback mechanism as you've seen with Razor Pages. To look for a different view name, you can pass the name of the view to the `View` method. In addition to the name, you can also supply a model to the view— any data object the view should work with. In addition to passing data with `ViewData`, you can pass data with a model.

Razor Views

Views used with ASP.NET Core MVC are Razor views, as shown with the `Privacy` view in the following code snippet. The same file extension and base class `RazorPage` is used with Razor views. In the code snippet, you can see the `ViewData` property of the `RazorPage` class to be used to set and get the value with the `Title` index (code file `MVCSample/Views/Home/Privacy.cshtml`):

```
@{
    ViewData["Title"] = "Privacy Policy";
}
<h1>@ViewData["Title"]</h1>
<p>Use this page to detail your site's privacy policy.</p>
```

Razor views don't have code-behind files. Usually there's not a lot of code needed with Razor views. The main functionality is within the controller—or, even better, with the services that are injected with the controller.

The `html` element as well as the `head` and `body` elements are not specified by the view. With MVC, you use a `_Layout` page in the `Shared` folder using the methods `RenderBody` and `RenderSection`, as you already learned with Razor Pages.

Strongly Typed Views

Razor views where a model is passed from the controller and the `@model` directive is used with the view are known by the name *strongly typed view*. With a strongly typed view, you have a `Model` property with the type that's defined by the `@model` directive.

With the following code snippet, the `Books` action method of the `HomeController` returns a list of `Book` objects (code file `MVCSample/Controllers/HomeController.cs`):

```
public IActionResult Books()
{
  IEnumerable<Book> books = Enumerable.Range(6, 12)
    .Select(i => new Book(i, $"Professional C# {i}", "Wrox Press")).ToArray();
  return View(books);
}
```

Because no different view name is specified with the Books method, a view with the name Books is searched in the folder Views/Home. This Razor view has the @model directive applied, as shown in the following code snippet, so the model can be used with the HTML Helpers (code file MVCSample/Views/Home/Books.cshtml):

```
@model IEnumerable<MVCSample.Controllers.Book>
@{
  ViewData["Title"] = "Books";
}

<h1>Books</h1>

<p>
  <a asp-action="Create">Create New</a>
</p>
<table class="table">
  <thead>
    <tr>
      <th>
        @Html.DisplayNameFor(model => model.Id)
      </th>
      <th>
        @Html.DisplayNameFor(model => model.Title)
      </th>
      <th>
        @Html.DisplayNameFor(model => model.Publisher)
      </th>
    </tr>
  </thead>
  <tbody>
    @foreach (var item in Model) {
      <tr>
        <td>
          @Html.DisplayFor(modelItem => item.Id)
        </td>
        <td>
          @Html.DisplayFor(modelItem => item.Title)
        </td>
        <td>
          @Html.DisplayFor(modelItem => item.Publisher)
        </td>
      </tr>
    }
  </tbody>
</table>
```

As you can see, it's the same technology used with MVC and Razor Pages.

Partial Views

Another type of view is the partial view. Behind the scenes, a partial view is a Razor view with the same base class; nothing is different. It's just used in a different way. A partial view doesn't have a layout assigned because it's only to be used within another Razor view (or Razor page). So, what's different from HTML or Tag Helpers? You use the .cshtml files with HTML and Razor syntax to implement the partial view. To use the partial view, you can use the HTML Helper PartialAsync or the partial Tag Helper, as shown here:

```
<partial name="MyPartial" />
```

A reason why the partial view is more important with MVC is that you can create a controller action method to return a partial view using the `PartialView` method of the `Controller` base class. This way, you can make an HTTP request from a browser client to load an HTML fragment and only update parts of the page. Using the partial HTML or Tag Helpers, the controller action method is not invoked.

Partial views use the same base class `RazorPage` and offer the same functionality. Strongly typed views use the same `@model` directive as you've seen with Razor Pages.

Identity UI

The sample application created has authentication and authorization for individual users turned on. When you start the application, you can register a new user and see the dialog shown in Figure 26-9. You can see other dialogs as well—for logging in the user, changing profile information, and more.

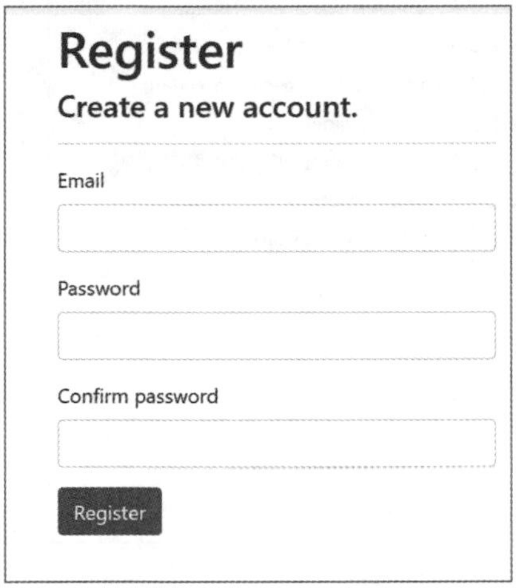

Register

Create a new account.

Email

Password

Confirm password

Register

FIGURE 26-9

Where are these dialogs coming from? With the application, you'll see an `Areas` folder with the subfolder `Identity` and the subfolder `Pages`. The only file within this folder is the file `_ViewStart.cshtml`:

```
@{
    Layout = "/Views/Shared/_Layout.cshtml";
}
```

All the user interfaces for the identity area are coming from the Razor Class Library `Microsoft.AspNetCore` `.Identity.UI`. This library defines Razor Pages for all the different dialogs used. The layout used with all these dialogs is coming from your web application.

As you learned in the section "Razor Libraries and Areas," you can override every Razor page of a Razor library. With Visual Studio, from the Solution Explorer you can select Add ➪ Add New Scaffolded Item and select Identity. When you click the Add button, you can see all the different dialogs you can override with your application, as shown in Figure 26-10. For all the pages you select, a copy of the Razor page, including the code-behind file, is created in your application, and you can change it as needed.

As you saw with the last step, MVC and Razor Pages mix very well.

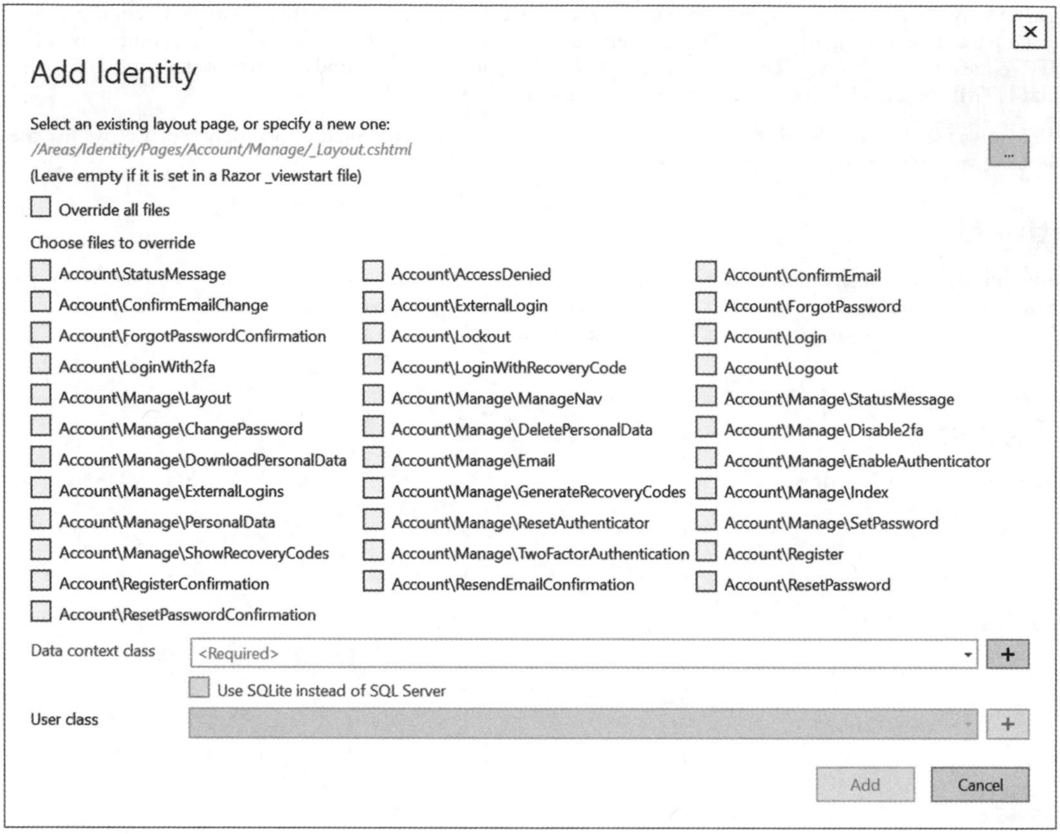

FIGURE 26-10

SUMMARY

In this chapter, you explored many features available with ASP.NET Core for Razor Pages as well as ASP.NET Core MVC. Razor syntax plays an important role with Razor Pages and views, and you can reuse and create UI components written with partial views, HTML Helpers, Tag Helpers, and view components.

You've seen how routing is done with Razor Pages and how this differs with ASP.NET Core MVC.

The next chapter dives into a new technology where Razor is used: Razor components. Razor components are based on the ideas of Razor Pages but are very different because you can't use Tag Helpers and HTML Helpers. With Razor components, you can run .NET code on the client within a WebAssembly using the Blazor technology.

27

Blazor

WHAT'S IN THIS CHAPTER?

➤ Getting to know Blazor Server and Blazor WebAssembly

➤ Understanding the layout with Blazor applications

➤ Navigating between Razor components

➤ Creating and using Razor components

➤ Injecting services

➤ Implementing event callbacks between components

➤ Using two-way binding

➤ Cascading parameters with component hierarchies

➤ Creating templated components

CODE DOWNLOADS FOR THIS CHAPTER

The source code for this chapter is available on the book page at www.wiley.com. Click the Downloads link. The code can also be found at https://github.com/ProfessionalCSharp/ ProfessionalCSharp2021 in the directory 3_Web/Blazor.

The code for this chapter is divided into the following major examples:

➤ Blazor.ServerSample

➤ Blazor.WASMSample

➤ Blazor.ComponentsSample

All the projects have *nullable reference types* enabled.

BLAZOR SERVER AND BLAZOR WEBASSEMBLY

Blazor is a new ASP.NET Core technology to create interactive web applications. With Blazor, you get full-stack .NET development without the need to write JavaScript code. The application can be built using HTML, C#, and CSS—both for the client and for the server.

You need to understand the difference between two options: Blazor Server and Blazor WebAssembly. Both options offer full-stack .NET development, and with both of these options, you're creating Razor components. Razor components are an extension of Razor Pages, which are covered in Chapter 26, "Razor Pages and MVC." With Blazor Server, Razor components run on the server. With Blazor WebAssembly, Razor components run on the client. To understand the differences and the advantages and disadvantages of these options, let's get into more details.

Blazor Server

With Blazor Server (see Figure 27-1), the client always needs to be connected to the server. You can write server-side C# code using Razor components. You directly work with HTML and C# on the server and make updates to HTML via data binding. Behind the scenes, HTML updates are sent to the client, and a Blazor client-side JavaScript library, which you don't need to deal with, updates the user interface. With Blazor Server, a connection (a *circuit*) between the client and the server stays open, and the client just needs to run HTML and JavaScript. To keep the connection open and to communicate between the client and the server, SignalR is used. SignalR offers an abstraction layer to WebSockets.

> **NOTE** *More information on SignalR and how you can use SignalR directly from .NET and JavaScript is covered in Chapter 28, "SignalR."*

FIGURE 27-1

When you use Blazor Server, the size of the code downloaded to the client is significantly smaller than with Blazor WebAssembly. With Blazor Server, you can use the server capabilities (for example, features discussed in the previous chapters), and tooling is much more mature. A disadvantage of Blazor Server is that the clients are always connected. There's no offline support. This way more continuous load is created on the server and on the network. What is the number of clients simultaneously connected to the server?

WebAssembly

Blazor WebAssembly is based on the WebAssembly (Wasm) standard (see `https://www.w3.org/TR/wasm-core-1/`). Wasm defines binary code that can run in the browser. All modern browsers support Wasm (see `https://caniuse.com/?search=webassembly`). That is, Internet Explorer (IE) does not support Wasm, but this shouldn't be an issue today because many websites no longer support IE. However, you need to be aware of what WebAssembly features are supported by the browser. WebAssembly is continuously enhanced with new features; check the roadmap for planned features for WebAssembly at `https://webassembly.org/roadmap/`.

Code to compile Wasm code can be written with many programming languages including C#, F#, C++, Rust, Go, Swift, and Pascal.

Goals defined by WebAssembly are to have fast-running code (near-native code performance), to be capable of running in a safe environment (the browser's sandbox), and to be portable. Use cases for WebAssembly are to create apps that have issues with JavaScript (such as video or image editing and CAD apps), run fat clients in the browser, and use it for language interpreters and virtual machines. Microsoft created a .NET runtime to run in the browser that's running binary Wasm code. The C# compiler creates IL code, and this IL code can run in the .NET runtime in the browser.

> **NOTE** *ASP.NET Core Blazor WebAssembly is one way to run WebAssembly code in the browser. Another option is the Uno Platform (*`https://platform.uno/`*), which allows you to run C# and XAML code with WinUI controls in the browser. See Chapters 29 through 31 for more information on WinUI.*

Blazor WebAssembly

When you use Blazor WebAssembly, you write Razor components similar to Blazor Server, but that's where the similarities end. Outside of the programming environment, Blazor WebAssembly is very different. Here, the .NET code runs on the client (Figure 27-2); you don't need a server at all because the files just need to be distributed to the client. Blazor WebAssembly can also be created to be a progressive web application (PWA), which can run without connection to a server (after the application is installed on the client).

FIGURE 27-2

Blazor WebAssembly is not making use of SignalR. Instead, the .NET runtime (Wasm binary) and the Blazor runtime are sent to the client along with the .NET DLLs (IL code) of your application. Now, you might think that the .NET runtime is huge. It's not as big as you might expect because it's a specific runtime built for WebAssembly and doesn't support all the features of the .NET runtime that's running locally on your system. Also, the binaries built for ASP.NET Core Blazor WebAssembly and from your application are trimmed. Trimming of the binaries means that code that's not used is trimmed from the binaries, and it plays an important role. Read Chapter 1, ".NET Applications and Tools," for information on trimming assemblies.

Blazor WebAssembly can be hosted with a static web app—for example, using an Azure Storage account or, even better, Azure Static Web Apps. Of course, usually a backend is needed as well. With Azure Static Web Apps, you can create a REST API service using Azure Functions, which is covered in Chapter 25, "Services."

To take full advantage of Blazor WebAssembly, it's still advantageous to use .NET on the server. Using .NET on the server allows you to prerender HTML code that is sent to the client, so the client can see the HTML code before the WebAssembly code is downloaded and runs.

Advantages of using Blazor WebAssembly compared to Blazor Server are that you can use the client capabilities and processing power and that the application can be installed as a PWA and can still run without the server available. Of course, there are disadvantages because more code needs to be downloaded to the client, and the development environment is not as mature as with the server side. Today debugging of client-side .NET Code works in most scenarios, but not in all.

CREATING A BLAZOR SERVER WEB APPLICATION

Let's start by creating a Blazor server web application using the .NET CLI with the following:

```
> dotnet new blazorserver -o Blazor.ServerSample
```

Of course, you can also use a Visual Studio template. With the generated code, the `Program.cs` file with the `Host` class configuration is the same as you've seen it in the previous chapters, but the configuration of the dependency injection container in the `Startup` class is different, as shown in the following code snippet. After adding Razor Pages with the extension method `AddRazorPages`, services needed for server-side Blazor are added with the extension method `AddServerSideBlazor`. `AddServerSideBlazor` returns an `IServerSideBlazorBuilder`, which allows configuring hub (`AddHubOptions`) and circuit (`AddCircuitOptions`) options. Hub options allow you to configure client timeouts, configure buffer sizes, and enable detailed errors. The generated template also registers a singleton for weather forecast information (code file `Blazor.ServerSample/Startup.cs`):

```
public void ConfigureServices(IServiceCollection services)
{
  services.AddRazorPages();
  services.AddServerSideBlazor();
  services.AddSingleton<WeatherForecastService>();
}
```

With the middleware, static files need to be configured to be sent to the client (`UseStaticFiles`). Endpoint routing specifies that Blazor takes over the default routing (`MapBlazorHub`); this configures the SignalR hub route used for the WebSocket communication from the client to the server. In case a route is not found, the fallback is set to _Host with `MapFallbackToPage` (code file `Blazor.ServerSample/Startup.cs`):

```
public void Configure(IApplicationBuilder app, IWebHostEnvironment env)
{
  //...
  app.UseHttpsRedirection();
  app.UseStaticFiles();

  app.UseRouting();

  app.UseEndpoints(endpoints =>
  {
    endpoints.MapBlazorHub();
    endpoints.MapFallbackToPage("/_Host");
  });
}
```

Blazor Server Startup

After the startup of ASP.NET Core with the DI container configuration and the middleware configuration, the next step to start Blazor Server is the `_Host.cshtml` Razor page. This file contains the `component` tag helper (which are discussed in Chapter 26), as shown in the following code snippet, which renders the Razor component `App`. With the `render-mode` options, you can specify the output of the Razor component. Setting this to `Static` just renders HTML, and Blazor code is not active. Using `Server` creates markers that are used by the Blazor communication to send the HTML and JavaScript output dynamically via SignalR. The default option is `ServerPrerendered`, where HTML is already prerendered on the server, and in addition to HTML, markers are sent to the client. With `ServerPrerendered`, the client sees the first HTML output faster. The markers are then used for dynamic updates (code file `Blazor.ServerSample/Pages/_Host.cshtml`):

```
<component type="typeof(App)" render-mode="ServerPrerendered"/>
```

With the `_Host` file, the HTML element `base` plays an important role in setting the base route for Blazor. This helper is used among other HTML header settings and includes style sheets used by all the Razor components (code file `Blazor.ServerSample/Pages/_Host.cshtml`):

```html
<head>
    <meta charset="utf-8" />
    <meta name="viewport" content="width=device-width, initial-scale=1.0" />
    <title>Blazor.ServerSample</title>
    <base href="~/" />
    <link rel="stylesheet" href="css/bootstrap/bootstrap.min.css" />
    <link href="css/site.css" rel="stylesheet" />
    <link href="Blazor.ServerSample.styles.css" rel="stylesheet" />
</head>
```

`App` is the first Razor component that comes into play with bootstrapping of the application. The complete generated `App` component is shown in the following code snippet. This component includes some other Razor components and a little HTML code. The `p` element is HTML; all the other elements are Razor components: `Router`, `Found`, `NotFound`, `RouteView`, and `LayoutView` (code file `Blazor.ServerSample/App.razor`):

```html
<Router AppAssembly="@typeof(Program).Assembly" PreferExactMatches="@true">
  <Found Context="routeData">
    <RouteView RouteData="@routeData" DefaultLayout="@typeof(MainLayout)" />
  </Found>
  <NotFound>
    <LayoutView Layout="@typeof(MainLayout)">
      <p>Sorry, there's nothing at this address.</p>
    </LayoutView>
  </NotFound>
</Router>
```

The `Router` component is responsible for the routing of Blazor apps. Chapter 26 covers creating routes with Razor pages and the `@page` directive. The `@page` directive is used with Razor components as well (but with Razor components, the `@page` directive is optional). If the Razor component includes a route, it is used by the `Router` component to add it to the possible route matches. If a match is found (using the `Found` component), the `RouteView` component is used to continue. If a match is not found (see the `NotFound` component), the `LayoutView` component is used. With the generated file, both the `RouteView` as well as the `LayoutView` use the same Razor component, `MainLayout`, to render the HTML layout. The `LayoutView` renders the child content within the associated layout specified by the `Layout` property. With the generated code, simple HTML code is shown if the URL does not have a matching route. With the `RouteView`, a default layout is specified, which can be overridden with the components if specific components should use a different layout. Next, the main responsibility of the `RouteView` is to activate a Razor component that matches the route and to pass route data to this component.

Blazor Layout

According to the definition of the `App` component, the `MainLayout` component as shown in the following code snippet is used for the default layout. This component inherits from the base class `LayoutComponentBase`. `LayoutComponentBase` defines the `Body` property of type `RenderFragment`. `RenderFragment` allows creating templated components as shown in detail in the section "Using Templated Components." With the `MainLayout`, the `Body` property is used to render the Razor component passed from the `RouteView`. Within the `MainLayout`, you can see another Razor component used: `NavMenu` is a component to show the navigation of the application.

Other than that, the `MainLayout` only contains HTML (code file `Blazor.ServerSample/Shared/MainLayout.razor`):

```
@inherits LayoutComponentBase

<div class="page">
  <div class="sidebar">
    <NavMenu />
  </div>

  <div class="main">
    <div class="top-row px-4">
      <a href="https://docs.microsoft.com/aspnet/" target="_blank">About</a>
    </div>

    <div class="content px-4">
      @Body
    </div>
  </div>
</div>
```

The `MainLayout` is stored in the folder `Shared`. Blazor makes use of the same mechanisms you've seen in the previous chapter. Components are searched first in the `Pages` folder, and if they can't be found there, the search continues in the `Shared` folder. This way you can override the application to use different `MainLayout.razor` layouts in different `Pages` and `Areas` folders.

Navigation

With the Razor component `NavMenu`, you can see some more Blazor features in action. As shown in the following code snippet, this component uses an HTML button where the `onclick` event is bound to the C# method `ToggleNavMenu`. With Blazor Server, as the user clicks the HTML button on the client, communication happens with the server where the `ToggleNavMenu` method runs on the server (code file `Blazor.ServerSample/Shared/NavMenu.razor`):

```
<div class="top-row pl-4 navbar navbar-dark">
  <a class="navbar-brand" href="">Blazor.ServerSample</a>
  <button class="navbar-toggler" @onclick="ToggleNavMenu">
    <span class="navbar-toggler-icon"></span>
  </button>
</div>
```

For mapping HTML element events to .NET methods, you just need to use the @ symbol as a prefix to the event name to bind the event to a .NET method. This is covered with more detail in the section "Two-Way Binding."

With Razor components, the C# code is defined within the `@code` section (which is different than the `@functions` section with Razor pages). With this code section, you can see the `ToggleNavMenu` that switches the value of the `collapseNavMenu` between true and false. The `NavMenuCssClass` returns different values, `collapse` or `null`, based on the value of the Boolean field (code file `Blazor.ServerSample/Shared/NavMenu.razor`):

```
@code {
  private bool collapseNavMenu = true;

  private string? NavMenuCssClass => collapseNavMenu ? "collapse" : null;
```

```
    private void ToggleNavMenu()
    {
      collapseNavMenu = !collapseNavMenu;
    }
  }
```

Binding in the other direction— from the C# code to HTML— is done with the `class` attribute of the first `div` element in the following code snippet. The HTML attribute `class` binds to the `NavMenuCssClass` string defined with the code segment. When an event occurs (such as the `click` event) and the C# source changes, the user interface gets updated. The `div` element also binds the `onclick` event to the `ToggleNavMenu` method, so you can either click the button or click the `div` element to invoke this method. The `NavMenu` component also contains `NavLink` components to create HTML links to Razor components that match the default route and the `counter` and `fetchdata` routes as specified by the `href` attributes. The `href` attributes are added to the anchor (a) elements that are rendered from `NavMenu` (code file `Blazor.ServerSample/Shared/NavMenu.razor`):

```
<div class="@NavMenuCssClass" @onclick="ToggleNavMenu">
  <ul class="nav flex-column">
    <li class="nav-item px-3">
      <NavLink class="nav-link" href="" Match="NavLinkMatch.All">
        <span class="oi oi-home" aria-hidden="true"></span> Home
      </NavLink>
    </li>
    <li class="nav-item px-3">
      <NavLink class="nav-link" href="counter">
        <span class="oi oi-plus" aria-hidden="true"></span> Counter
      </NavLink>
    </li>
    <li class="nav-item px-3">
      <NavLink class="nav-link" href="fetchdata">
        <span class="oi oi-list-rich" aria-hidden="true"></span> Fetch data
      </NavLink>
    </li>
  </ul>
</div>
```

The `NavLink` component not only creates an HTML anchor (a) element, but it also toggles the active CSS class. Setting the `Match` property to `NavLinkMatch.All` activates the class only if the link matches completely. With the default `NavLinkMatch.Prefix`, the CSS class is activated if the start of the link matches.

The Counter Component

Now that we've gone through the bootstrap, the layout, and the navigation, let's move on to components. The `Counter` component is one of the components created with the default template. There's not a big difference from the components `MainLayout` and `NavMenu`. The `Counter` component starts with a `@page` directive, which defines the link `/counter`. Razor components without a `@page` directive can only be used within other components. Because `Counter` has a `@page` directive with the link `/counter`, this component can be accessed by passing `/counter` with the URI. The `Counter` component also makes use of binding to connect the `onclick` event of the button to the .NET method `IncrementCount` and to retrieve the value of the `currentCount` field using `@currentCount` (code file `Blazor.ServerSample/Pages/Counter.razor`):

```
@page "/counter"

<h1>Counter</h1>
```

```
<p>Current count: @currentCount</p>

<button class="btn btn-primary" @onclick="IncrementCount">Click me</button>

@code {
  private int currentCount = 0;

  private void IncrementCount()
  {
    currentCount++;
  }
}
```

When you run the application, you can see the `Counter` component and click the button to increment the count. When you resize the application to make it smaller, the look changes because of the Bootstrap theme used. Making the application smaller, the toggle button discussed earlier in the section "Navigation" is visible (Figure 27-3), and you can show or hide the menus.

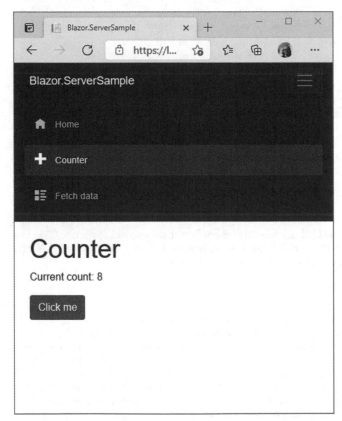

FIGURE 27-3

The FetchData Component

Another interesting component created with the default template is the `FetchData` component. This component injects the `WeatherForecastService` using the `@inject` directive. Remember, this service was registered into the

DI container at the start of the section "Creating a Blazor Server Web Application" (code file `Blazor`
`.ServerSample/Pages/FetchData.razor`):

```
@page "/fetchdata"

@using Blazor.ServerSample.Data
@inject WeatherForecastService ForecastService
<!-- ... -->
```

Within the code section, in the `OnInitializeAsync` method, the `GetForecastAsync` method is invoked, which
returns weather information for the next few days. With Razor components, on initialization the method
`OnInitializeAsync` is invoked (code file `Blazor.ServerSample/Pages/FetchData.razor`):

```
@code {
  private WeatherForecast[]? forecasts;

  protected override async Task OnInitializedAsync()
  {
    forecasts = await ForecastService.GetForecastAsync(DateTime.Now);
  }
}
```

> **NOTE** *The lifetime of Razor components is different than Razor Pages. As a parent compo-*
> *nent renders, you can override the following methods; they are invoked in the listed order:*
> `SetParametersAsync` *(sets the parameters),* `OnInitialized(Async)` *(override for your ini-*
> *tialization code),* `OnParametersSet(Async)` *(parameters are assigned),* `StateHasChanged`,
> `ShouldRender` *(returns true if rendering should be done), and* `OnAfterRender(Async)`
> *(invoked after rendering). Some of the methods have a synchronous as well an asynchronous*
> *version. The synchronous method is invoked before the asynchronous. If you invoke async*
> *APIs, override the async method. The* `OnInitialized(Async)` *methods are invoked only*
> *once when the component is initialized. The other methods are invoked every time the com-*
> *ponent is shown.*

With the following code snippet, the `WeatherForecast` array is used to display the information returned—using
Razor syntax mixed with HTML (`Blazor.ServerSample/Pages/FetchData.razor`):

```
@if (forecasts == null)
{
  <p><em>Loading...</em></p>
}
else
{
  <table class="table">
    <thead>
      <tr>
        <th>Date</th>
        <th>Temp. (C)</th>
        <th>Temp. (F)</th>
        <th>Summary</th>
      </tr>
    </thead>
    <tbody>
      @foreach (var forecast in forecasts)
```

```
            {
            <tr>
                <td>@forecast.Date.ToShortDateString()</td>
                <td>@forecast.TemperatureC</td>
                <td>@forecast.TemperatureF</td>
                <td>@forecast.Summary</td>
            </tr>
            }
        </tbody>
    </table>
    }
```

When you run the application, you can open the browser's developer tools to see WebSocket communication is used between client and server.

BLAZOR WEBASSEMBLY

Now that you understand the path through a Blazor Server project, let's get into the differences with Blazor WebAssembly. `dotnet new blazorwasm` creates a new Blazor WebAssembly project that you can publish to a server to publish files that need to be returned to the client. Let's add the `--hosted` and `--pwa` options to this:

```
> dotnet new blazorwasm --hosted --pwa -o Blazor.WasmSample
```

As a result of this command, three projects are created: a shared library containing code that can be used both from the API and from Blazor WebAssembly, an ASP.NET Core Web API project that not only hosts a Web API controller but also is used to contain all the Blazor WebAssembly files needed when publishing to send it to the client, and a project for Blazor WebAssembly.

The `Blazor.WasmSample.Server` project references both the `Blazor.WasmSample.Client` project as well as the `Blazor.WasmSample.Shared` project. This is an ASP.NET Core project hosting Razor Pages (covered in Chapter 26), an ASP.NET Core Web API (covered in Chapter 25), and the code to serve the Blazor client files for the client. When publishing, you need to create a publish package with this project that contains all the files you need to publish to the web server. A NuGet package added for the server-side part is `Microsoft.AspNetCore.Components.WebAssembly.Server`.

With the `Startup` class, you'll see some specific Blazor configurations with the configuration of the middleware. In development mode, `UseWebAssemblyDebugging`, middleware is added to allow debugging Blazor WebAssembly applications in Chromium-based browsers. Google Chrome and Microsoft Edge can be used for debugging. `UseBlazorFrameworkFiles` defines the path to be used for Blazor WebAssembly. With an overload of the method, you can supply a path. By default, the root path is used for Blazor. With the endpoint configuration, Razor Pages are mapped (the project contains an `Error.cshtml` Razor page that's returned if a server-side exception is returned as defined by the `UseExceptionHandler` method) with the invocation of `MapRazorPages`, and API controllers are mapped with the invocation of `MapControllers`. This project contains the `WeatherForecastController` to return weather information from the server. With this project, the fallback path is set to `index.html`. This file cannot be found on the server; it's part of the `Blazor.WasmSample.Client` project. The complete `wwwroot` directory is defined with the client project.

```
public void Configure(IApplicationBuilder app, IWebHostEnvironment env)
{
    if (env.IsDevelopment())
    {
        app.UseDeveloperExceptionPage();
        app.UseWebAssemblyDebugging();
    }
    else
```

```
    {
      app.UseExceptionHandler("/Error");
      app.UseHsts();
    }

    app.UseHttpsRedirection();
    app.UseBlazorFrameworkFiles();
    app.UseStaticFiles();

    app.UseRouting();

    app.UseEndpoints(endpoints =>
    {
      endpoints.MapRazorPages();
      endpoints.MapControllers();
      endpoints.MapFallbackToFile("index.html");
    });
  }
```

Blazor WebAssembly Startup

After the Blazor files are sent to the client, the bootstrap with Blazor WebAssembly is different from Blazor Server. The first difference is the index.html file that's used instead of the _Host Razor page. Razor Pages cannot be used on the client. index.html uses the base element for relative addresses and references style sheets similar to _Host. Other than that, the JavaScript file _framework/blazor.webassembly.js is referenced to load the Blazor WebAssembly.

With the Blazor.WasmSample.Client project, a Main method is available that's the start of the .NET code, as shown in the following code snippet. With the WebAssembly, the CreateDefaultBuilder method of the Host class cannot be used because some parts there are not available in the sandbox of the browser. However, the code is not that much different, and a ServiceCollection for the DI container is used as well. Here, the WebAssemblyHostBuilder with the CreateDefault method is used to create a WebAssemblyHostBuilder instance. This type can be used (similar to the HostBuilder class) to configure dependency injection, logging, and configuration. With the generated code, an HttpClient instance is registered in the DI container. This is important because when you're running in a WebAssembly, you're restricted to the sandbox of the browser, and you can't just create a new HttpClient instance and do HTTP requests. Instead, you are limited to using APIs offered by the browser. So that you still can use the HttpClient class with Blazor WebAssembly, System.Net.Http.BrowserHttpHandler is registered as a handler. This handler creates HTTP requests using the browser API. Because HttpClient is registered with the DI container, you can inject it and use it in the way you're accustomed to. The root component configured with the DI container is the App Razor component (code file Blazor.WasmSample.Client/Program.cs):

```
    public static async Task Main(string[] args)
    {
      var builder = WebAssemblyHostBuilder.CreateDefault(args);
      builder.RootComponents.Add<App>("#app");

      builder.Services.AddScoped(sp => new HttpClient
      {
        BaseAddress = new Uri(builder.HostEnvironment.BaseAddress)
      });

      await builder.Build().RunAsync();
    }
```

The App component, the NavMenu component, and the MainLayout component are exactly the same with Blazor WebAssembly as with Blazor Server.

Injecting HttpClient with Blazor WebAssembly

The Counter component you've seen with Blazor server is the same with Blazor WebAssembly. This code doesn't need any changes. With Blazor WebAssembly, the Counter component can run completely on the client. What's different is the FetchData component. With Blazor Server, functionality on the server can be directly accessed from the server because with Blazor Server the components run on the server. With Blazor WebAssembly, for getting the weather information from the server, an API can be accessed.

The following code snippet shows the injection of the HttpClient instance that's registered with the DI container using the @inject declaration. With this component, the namespace Blazor.WasmSample.Shared is also imported. The class WeatherForecast defined in the shared library can be used both with the API controller and the client application—.NET full-stack (code file Blazor.WasmSample/Pages/FetchData.razor):

```
@page "/fetchdata"
@using Blazor.WasmSample.Shared
@inject HttpClient Http
```

On initialization of the component, weather forecast information is retrieved by using the GetFromJsonAsync extension method (code file Blazor.WasmSample/Pages/FetchData.razor):

```
@code {
  private WeatherForecast[]? forecasts;

  protected override async Task OnInitializedAsync()
  {
    forecasts = await Http.GetFromJsonAsync<WeatherForecast[]>("WeatherForecast");
  }
}
```

When you run the application, you can open the browser developer tools and see the dotnet.wasm file downloaded, which is the .NET runtime in WebAssembly form. Figure 27-4 shows the weather information returned from the API and with the FetchData component.

> **NOTE** *With this implementation of the FetchData Razor component, the component is specific for Blazor WebAssembly. If you inject an EF Core context with a Razor component, this component can be used only with Blazor Server. However, you could inject a service that's independent from the client and the server—for example, use the IBooksService interface from the Razor component. For a Blazor WebAssembly project, you implement the IBooksService interface with a BooksApiClient implementation, which injects the HttpClient, and configure the BooksApiClient with the DI container of the Blazor WebAssembly project. For a Blazor Server project, you implement the IBooksService interface with a BooksDataClient implementation that injects the EF Core context. With the Blazor Server project, you configure the DI container to use the BooksDataClient implementation when IBooksService is requested. This way you can put the BooksComponent in a Razor Class Library and use the library both from Blazor WebAssembly and from Blazor Server.*

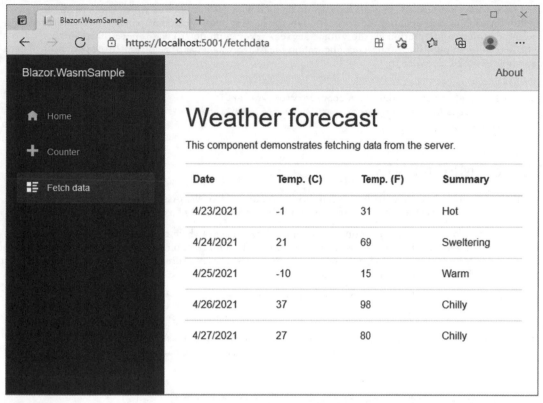

FIGURE 27-4

Working with Progressive Web Applications

Blazor WebAssembly can be configured to run as a PWA application. Using the `--pwa` option when creating the application adds the `service-worker.js` script. If this is enabled, an installation button is available with the browser so you can install the application locally. The application works without being connected to the server.

There are some caveats with PWAs. You should use this functionality only if the application works mainly with local data. Two major HTML APIs can be used to read and write data in the browser: local storage and IndexedDB. Local storage (`https://developer.mozilla.org/docs/Web/API/Window/localStorage`) allows storing and retrieving objects using a string index. The Indexed Database API (IndexedDB, `https://www.w3.org/TR/IndexedDB/`) supports storing data in tables, allows using transactions, and allows queries. The network might not be accessible when the application is used, and your APIs might not be accessible. When the network is available and a new version of the application is available, an update happens automatically. Be aware that the update only completes as the user closes the tab of the browser or the application. While the update is still in progress, the user runs an older version of the application. You cannot be sure which version the user is running, so you need to make sure you don't create breaking changes with your applications that break existing client versions.

Be aware that two versions of the `service-worker.js` scripts are created. In development mode, there's no implementation in this file. To avoid caching problems while developing, the application is not cached locally. Having an older version of the application would generate headaches with debugging. For publishing, the `service-worker.published.js` file is renamed to be used with the installation, which contains all the functionality for caching and updating the application on the local system. When the application is configured with `--pwa`, the project configuration file shows the `ServiceWorker` definition to use `service-worker` `.published.js` on publishing (project configuration file `Blazor.WasmSample.Client/Blazor` `.WasmSample.Client.csproj`):

```
<ItemGroup>
  <ServiceWorker Include="wwwroot\service-worker.js"
    PublishedContent="wwwroot\service-worker.published.js" />
</ItemGroup>
```

RAZOR COMPONENTS

Now that you know the differences between Blazor Server and Blazor WebAssembly, let's dig into Razor components. You can use these components with both Blazor Server and Blazor WebAssembly.

Although Razor components are built on the concept of Razor Pages (which are covered in Chapter 26), there are important differences. The `@page` directive can be used with both technologies. With Razor components, you cannot use HTML Helpers, Tag Helpers, and view components. These features use server-side functionality that is not available when the components run on the client.

To dig into the features of Razor components, a Blazor WebAssembly with a hosting API is created:

```
> dotnet new blazorwasm --hosted -o Blazor.ComponentsSample
```

In this section, you learn about passing parameters to components, injecting services, using event callbacks, programmatically updating the user interface, two-way binding, cascading parameters, templated components, and built-in components.

Understanding the Parameters of Components

The "The Counter Component" section earlier in this chapter described the `Counter` component and how you navigate to it. A component can also be contained in other components, and properties can be assigned to it.

The next code snippet shows the code block of the `Counter` component with an `Incrementor` property specified. With the `Parameter` attribute, this property can be assigned when using the component. Instead of incrementing the `currentCount` variable by 1, the value of the `Incrementor` property is now used to calculate the new value (code file `BlazorComponentsSample/Pages/Counter.razor`):

```
@code {
  private int currentCount = 0;

  [Parameter]
  public int Incrementor { get; set; } = 1;

  private void IncrementCount()
  {
    currentCount += Incrementor;
  }
}
```

The `Counter` component is now added to the `Index` component. When used within this component, the `Counter` component uses an `Incrementor` value of 3 (code file `BlazorComponentsSample/Pages/Index.razor`):

```
<Counter Incrementor="3" />
```

When you run the application now, you can see the Counter component to show up within the Index page (and also with the navigation of the application). In the Index component, an increment of 3 is done, while navigating to the Counter component uses the default increment of 1.

Injecting Services

When you run the application and use the Counter component (which is contained in the Index and Counter pages), the currentCount variable starts with 0 every time you open the page. When you open the pages, the component is newly initialized.

You can create a service to keep the state and share it with different components. The following CounterService class defines the Counter property for the state (code file BlazorComponentsSample/Services/CounterService.cs):

```
public class CounterService
{
  public int Counter { get; set; }
}
```

With the configuration of the DI container, the CounterService is registered as a singleton service as shown here (code file BlazorComponentsSample.Client/Program.cs):

```
public static async Task Main(string[] args)
{
  var builder = WebAssemblyHostBuilder.CreateDefault(args);
  builder.RootComponents.Add<App>("#app");

  builder.Services.AddScoped(sp => new HttpClient
  {
    BaseAddress = new Uri(builder.HostEnvironment.BaseAddress)
  });
  builder.Services.AddScoped<CounterService>();
  await builder.Build().RunAsync();
}
```

> **NOTE** *Blazor WebAssembly currently doesn't have a concept for DI scopes. Scopes behave like singleton services. Read Chapter 15, "Dependency Injection and Configuration," for information about the different modes for configuring services. With Blazor Server, the DI container is configured on the server side with ASP.NET Core and has the behavior you are used to with ASP.NET Core web applications.*

With the component, the CounterService is injected using the @inject directive. This directive creates a property of the specified type, and the CounterService can be used to access the Counter property with the IncrementCount method to read the value using binding, as shown in the following code snippet (code file BlazorComponentsSample/Pages/CounterWithService.razor):

```
@page "/counterwithservice"
@inject CounterService CounterService

<h1>Counter</h1>

<p>Current count: @CounterService.Counter</p>
```

```
<button class="btn btn-primary" @onclick="IncrementCount">Click me</button>

@code {
  [Parameter]
  public int Incrementor { get; set; } = 1;

  private void IncrementCount()
  {
    CounterService.Counter += Incrementor;
  }
}
```

When you use the application and switch to this component, then switch to other components, and then switch back, the state is kept.

Working with Event Callback

Razor components can publish events. To submit events to a parent component, you need to define a property of type `EventCallback`. As the following code snippet of the `TimerEvent` shows, an event is fired to the parent every time the `Elapsed` event of the .NET class `Timer` is fired. With the generic `EventCallback` type, you can specify information to pass to the parent component. The generic parameter needs to derive from the `EventArgs` base class. The custom `TimerEventArgs` class defines the `SignalTime` property of type `DateTime`. This value is assigned when firing the callback using the `InvokeAsync` method of the `EventCallback` class. The `TimerEvent` component defines `Start` and `Stop` methods to start and stop the timer (code file `BlazorComponentsSample/Pages/TimerEvent.razor`):

```
@using System.Timers
@implements IDisposable

<h4>Timer Event</h4>

@code {
  [Parameter]
  public int DelaySeconds { get; set; } = 10;

  [Parameter]
  public EventCallback<TimerEventArgs> OnTimerCallback { get; set; }

  public void Start() => timer?.Start();

  public void Stop() => timer?.Stop();

  private Timer? timer;
  protected override void OnInitialized()
  {
    timer = new()
    {
      Interval = 1000 * DelaySeconds
    };
    timer.Elapsed += async (sender, e) =>
    {
      await OnTimerCallback.InvokeAsync(new TimerEventArgs { SignalTime = e.SignalTime });
    };
```

```
    }

    public void Dipose() => timer?.Dispose();
}
```

You use the `TimerEvent` component from the `UseTimer` component. The number of seconds to specify with the timer is set by assigning a value to the `DelaySeconds` property. The `OnTimerCallback` is similarly assigned to the address of the `ShowTimer` method. The `TimerEvent` uses the `ref` keyword to map it to a variable. This allows using the `TimerEvent` component from the code to invoke methods (code file `BlazorComponentsSample/Pages/UseTimer.razor`):

```
<TimerEvent @ref="myTimer" DelaySeconds="3" OnTimerCallback="@ShowTimer" />
```

With the code declaration, the `ShowTimer` method is specified to receive a parameter of type `TimerEventArgs`—the parameter that was specified with the `EventCallback` parameter in the `TimerEvent` component. With the implementation of this method, the `message` and `timeMessage` fields are updated to show information from the event with the UI elements that bind to these fields (code file `BlazorComponentsSample/Pages/UseTimer.razor`):

```
@code {
  private TimerEvent? myTimer;
  private string timeMessage = string.Empty;
  private bool disableStartTimerButton = false;
  private bool disableStopTimerButton = true;

  string message = string.Empty;
  private void ShowTimer(TimerEventArgs e)
  {
    message += ".";
    timeMessage = e.SignalTime.ToLongTimeString();
  }
  //...
}
```

You've seen the `ref` keyword used with the HTML code where the `TimerEvent` component was referenced. Using this keyword requires that you declare a variable with the same name as the `ref` name of the type of the component. This variable will be filled when the component is created. With this, methods of the component can be invoked as shown in the following snippet by invoking the `Start` and `Stop` methods (code file `BlazorComponentsSample/Pages/UseTimer.razor`):

```
private TimerEvent? myTimer;
private void StartTimer()
{
  myTimer?.Start();
  DisableStartTimerButton();
}

private void StopTimer()
{
  myTimer?.Stop();
  DisableStartTimerButton(false);
}
```

When you run the application and click the `Start` button of the `UseTimer` component, you see the timer callback called to show dots and an update of the time, as shown with Figure 27-5.

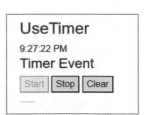

FIGURE 27-5

Programmatically Updating the UI

The user interface is automatically updated with events that are triggered by the user interface or with events specified with the EventCallback type. In case some functionality is triggered in the background, you need to inform the UI that the state has changed to start rendering again by invoking the method StateHasChanged.

The following code snippet uses a Timer object within a Razor component that updates the counter field with the Elapsed event. In the event handler, StateHasChanged is invoked to update the user interface. You can try to comment this method invocation to see that the user interface is not updated without this invocation. Another thing you can see with this code snippet is the expression syntax with binding. The onclick handler invoking the Start and Stop methods is implemented directly with the declaration (code file BlazorComponentsSample/Pages/Timer2.razor):

```
@page "/timer"
@using System.Timers
@implements IDisposable

<h4>Timer Event</h4>

<p>@counter</p>

<button @onclick="(() => timer.Start())">Start</button>

<button @onclick="(() => timer.Stop())">Stop</button>

@code {
  private int counter = 0;

  private Timer timer = new(1000);

  protected override void OnInitialized()
  {
    timer.Elapsed += (sender, e) =>
    {
      counter++;
      StateHasChanged();
    };
  }

  public void Dispose() => timer.Dispose();
}
```

Two-Way Binding

With previous code samples, you've seen binding from the source (a field) to the HTML DOM and from events to methods. Blazor also supports two-way binding with the @bind directive, as shown with the following code snippet. The following code snippet binds the text1 field to the value attribute of the input element (source to DOM) and the onchange event of the input element to update the text1 field (code file BlazorComponentsSample.Client/Pages/Binding.razor):

```
<input id="input1" @bind="text1" />
<div>@text1</div>
```

When you run the application, you can see the updated input value within the `div` element as soon as focus is lost. To use two-way binding for other events, you can specify the event by adding the `event` keyword to the `@bind` directive. The following code snippet binds the `text2` field to update with the `oninput` event; thus, the `text2` field changes with every single character change of the input element (code file `BlazorComponentsSample.Client/Pages/Binding.razor`):

```
<input id="input2" @bind-value="text2" @bind-value:event="oninput" />
<div>@text2</div>
```

Cascading Parameters

When you use the `Parameter` attribute, you can set values from a parent component to a child component. As the user interface grows, you might create a hierarchy of components—components that might be nested one within the other. Here, you can pass parameters from the outside to the inside, while components in between don't need to know anything about the parameters flowing from the outside to the inside. You can do this with cascading parameters.

With the inner components, you define properties that are annotated with the `CascadingParameter` attribute. The `Cascade3` component uses the `CascadingParameter` named `Value1` and displays the value (code file `BlazorComponentsSample.Client/Pages/Cascade3.razor`):

```
<h3>Cascade3</h3>

<div>@Value1</div>

@code {
  [CascadingParameter(Name = "Value1")]
  public string Value1 { get; set; } = string.Empty;
}
```

There's one component in between. The `Cascade2` component doesn't know anything about the `Value1` property and just nests the `Cascade3` component (code file `BlazorComponentsSample/Pages/Cascade2.razor`):

```
<h3>Cascade2</h3>
<Cascade3 />
```

To pass the value down through the complete tree, the `Cascade1` component uses the `CascadingValue` component. With this component, the `Value` is bound to the `SomeValue` property. The `Name` references `Value1`, the same name used with the `CascadingParameter` value with the inner component (code file `BlazorComponentsSample/Pages/Cascade1.razor`):

```
@page "/cascade"
<h3>Cascade1</h3>

<input type="text" @bind-value="SomeValue" @bind-value:event="oninput" />

<CascadingValue Value="@SomeValue" Name="Value1">
  <Cascade2 />
</CascadingValue>

@code {
  [Parameter]
  public string SomeValue { get; set; } = string.Empty;
}
```

When you run the application, you can see the value you enter with the outermost component is displayed with the innermost component. The matching between the CascadingValue component and the CascadingParameter attribute happens with the type and the name. Supplying the name is optional if you do not use multiple cascading parameters with the same type.

Using Templated Components

When you create nested components, you can supply the content of the nested component with the outer component and pass it to the nested inner component. Such components are known by the term *templated components*. Templated components specify one or more properties of type RenderFragment. With templated components, generic types can be useful, but this is not a requirement.

The following code snippet shows the templated component Repeater. With this component, you can supply a list of items with the property Items. The generic type used is TItem, as specified with the @typeparam at the beginning of the code. Two properties are of type RenderFragment. The HeaderTemplate property is used to show header information, and the ItemTemplate property specifies the look for every item and is invoked within the @foreach iteration (code file BlazorComponentsSample/Shared/Repeater.razor):

```
@typeparam TItem

<div>
  <div>@HeaderTemplate</div>
  @foreach (var item in Items ?? Array.Empty<TItem>())
  {
     <div>@ItemTemplate(item)</div>
  }
</div>

@code {
#nullable disable
  [Parameter]
  public RenderFragment HeaderTemplate { get; set; }
  [Parameter]
  public RenderFragment<TItem> ItemTemplate { get; set; }
#nullable restore
  [Parameter]
  public IEnumerable<TItem>? Items { get; set; }
}
```

When you use the Repeater component, the HeaderTemplate and ItemTemplate are used as child elements. Each of these elements defines the content to be used within the Repeater component. The TItem attribute specified with the Repeater element defines the generic type, the Book class. The Context attribute defines the content parameter for the iteration (code file BlazorComponentsSample/Pages/UseTemplate.razor):

```
@page "/template"
<h3>UseTemplate</h3>

<Repeater Items="@books" TItem="Book">
  <HeaderTemplate>
    <div class="bookstitle">The Books</div>
  </HeaderTemplate>
  <ItemTemplate Context="book">
    <div class="book">@book.Title</div>
  </ItemTemplate>
```

```
</Repeater>

@code {
  private IEnumerable<Book> books = Enumerable.Range(1, 10)
    .Select(i => new Book
    {
      Id = Guid.NewGuid(),
      Title = $"title {i}",
      Publisher = "Sample",
      ReleaseDate = DateTime.Today.AddDays(i)
    }).ToArray();
}
```

Using Built-in Components

Blazor includes several components that can be used with your application. Probably the most important ones are form components that you can use to create editable forms. The next sample defines a type for a form with annotations that can be used to validate the user input.

To see an edit form in action, define a model-type for all the data that should be filled out with the form, as shown with the following code snippet. With this model, annotations are used for input validation (code file `BlazorComponentsSample/Models/BookEditModel.cs`):

```
public class BookEditModel
{
  [StringLength(20, ErrorMessage = "Title is too long")]
  [Required]
  public string Title { get; set; } = string.Empty;

  public DateTime ReleaseDate { get; set; } = DateTime.Today;
  public string? Type { get; set; } = string.Empty;
}
```

To create an input formula, the `EditForm` component can be used as shown with the following code snippet. The `EditForm` component creates an `EditContext` as a cascading parameter. All the children of the `EditForm` component can access this context to register notifications and play a part in validation. Instead of assigning the `EditContext` directly with the `EditForm`, the `Model` property can be assigned to the model type (the `BookEditModel` with the sample), which in turn implicitly sets the `EditContext`. Child components used are the `DataAnnotationValidator` and the `ValidationSummary` components. The `DataAnnotationValidator` uses the annotations of the model (such as the `StringLength` and `Required` attributes) to validate the model. When you click the submit button of the form, the validation is invoked, and error messages are shown with the `ValidationSummary` component. Information on the errors is accessible with the `EditContext`, which is used both from the `DataAnnotationValidator` as well as the `ValidationSummary` components. If the validation is successful, the handler with the `OnValidSubmit` callback is invoked. With invalid inputs, you can implement a handler for `OnInvalidSubmit`. To read details of the validation, the `HandleValidSubmit` method can access the `EditContext` parameter. With the form, the components `InputText`, `InputSelect`, and `InputDate` are used to bind to properties of the model. These components generate HTML `input`, `select`, and `input type="date"` elements and access the `EditContext` (code file `BlazorComponentsSample/Pages/Editor.razor`):

```
<EditForm Model="@bookEditModel" OnValidSubmit="HandleValidSubmit">
  <DataAnnotationsValidator />
  <ValidationSummary />
  <p>
```

```
        <label>
          Title:
          <InputText @bind-Value="bookEditModel.Title" />
        </label>
      </p>
      <p>
        <label>
          Type:
          <InputSelect @bind-Value="bookEditModel.Type">
            <option value="Hardcover">Hardcover</option>
            <option value="Ebook">Ebook</option>
          </InputSelect>
        </label>
      </p>
      <p>
        <label>
          Release date:
          <InputDate @bind-Value="bookEditModel.ReleaseDate" />
        </label>
      </p>

      <button type="submit">Submit</button>
      <div>@validText</div>
    </EditForm>

    @code {
      private BookEditModel bookEditModel = new();
      private string validText = string.Empty;

      private void HandleValidSubmit(EditContext context)
      {
        validText = "Input is valid, ready to send it to the server";
      }
    }
```

Other built-in Razor components you can use in a form are `InputCheckbox`, `InputFile`, `InputNumber`, `InputRadio`, `InputRadioGroup`, and `InputTextArea`. For custom validation, you can write custom attributes for overriding the `ValidationAttribute` or write components that access the `EditContext` for validation similar to the `DataAnnotationValidator`.

For Blazor, you can find components from many third-party vendors, such as Telerik, Syncfusion, DevExpress, Mublazor, and others. Just look for available NuGet packages.

SUMMARY

This chapter introduced you to the newest way to create ASP.NET Core applications: Blazor. You've seen Blazor with server-side components and Blazor making use of WebAssembly to run .NET in the browser.

You've seen the features of Razor components, including passing parameters, injecting services, using events, two-way binding, and more.

The next chapter dives into SignalR, a technology for real-time communication. Blazor Server is based on SignalR. With Blazor WebAssembly, you can use SignalR to send notifications to a group of clients.

28

SignalR

CODE DOWNLOADS FOR THIS CHAPTER

The source code for this chapter is available on the book page at www.wiley.com. Click the Downloads link. The code can also be found at https://github.com/ProfessionalCSharp/ProfessionalCSharp2021 in the directory 3_Web/SignalR.

The code for this chapter is divided into the following major examples:

➤ SignalRSample/ChatServer

➤ SignalRSample/WinAppChatClient

➤ SignalRStreaming

The major namespace used is Microsoft.AspNetCore.SignalR. All the projects have nullable reference types enabled.

OVERVIEW

With .NET you can use events to get notifications. You can register an event handler method with an event, also known as *subscribing* to an event, and as soon as the event is fired from another place, your method gets invoked. Events cannot be used with web applications.

Previous chapters covered a lot about web applications and web services. What was common with these applications and services is that the request was always started from the client application. The client makes an HTTP request and receives a response.

What if the server has some news to tell? There's nothing like events that you can subscribe to, or is there? With the web technologies you've seen so far, this can be resolved by the client polling for new information. The client has to make a request to the server to ask whether new information is available. Depending on the request interval defined, this way of communication results in either a high load of requests on the network that just results in "no new information is available," or the actual information is already old by the time the client asks for it.

With clients behind a firewall, when using the HTTP protocol, there's no way for the server to initiate a connection to the client. The connection always needs to be started from the client side. Because HTTP connections are stateless and clients often can't connect to ports other than port 80 or 443, WebSockets can help. WebSockets are initiated with an HTTP request, but they're upgraded to a WebSocket connection where the connection stays open. When you use the WebSockets protocol, the server can send information to the client over the open connection as soon as the server has new information.

SignalR is an ASP.NET Core web technology that offers an easy abstraction over WebSockets. Using SignalR is a lot easier than programming using the sockets interface, and you get more features right out of the box.

CREATING A SIMPLE CHAT USING SIGNALR

SignalR is a technology based on WebSockets but can fall back to other options. If WebSockets are not available both on the client and on the server, polling is used from the client to continuously check for new data. Nowadays, all browsers and servers support WebSockets. However, they can be turned off, and you may have some issues when using proxies. If you deploy your web application with Azure App Services, WebSockets are turned off by default because you need more resources for WebSockets on the server to support the connection to the client that is kept open. With an Azure App Service, you need to explicitly enable WebSockets. Using proxies before your web application, you also need to think about support of WebSockets. For example, when you use Azure Front Door (https://azure.microsoft.com/services/frontdoor/) for load balancing and protection, this service does not support WebSockets (at the time of this writing).

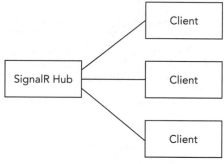

The first SignalR sample application is a chat application, which is easy to create with SignalR. With this application, multiple clients can be started to communicate with each other via the SignalR hub (see Figure 28-1). When one of the client applications sends a message, all the connected clients receive this message in turn.

The server application is started as an empty ASP.NET Core web application. One of the clients is created with HTML and JavaScript, and the other client application is a Windows app that uses WinUI.

FIGURE 28-1

Creating a Hub

The empty ASP.NET Core web project is named `ChatServer`. After you create the project, add a new class named `ChatHub` to the `Hubs` folder. The main functionality of SignalR is defined with the hub. The hub is indirectly invoked by the clients, and in turn the clients are called. The class `ChatHub` derives from the base class `Hub` to get the needed hub functionality. The method `Send` is defined to be invoked by the client applications sending a message to the other clients. You can use any method name with any number of parameters. The client code just needs to match the method name as well as the parameters. To send a message to the clients, the `Clients` property of the `Hub` class is used. The `Clients` property returns an object that implements the interface `IHubCallerClients`. This interface allows you to send messages to specific clients or to all connected clients. To return a message to just a single client, you can use the `Client` method to pass a connection identifier. The sample code sends a message to all clients using the `All` property. The `All` property returns an `IClientProxy`.

`IClientProxy` defines the method `SendAsync` to invoke a method within the client. The method invoked is the first parameter, which is the method name. The `SendAsync` method is overloaded to allow passing up to 10 arguments to the client method. In case you have more than 10, an overload allows passing an object array. With the sample code, the method name defined is `BroadcastMessage`, and two string parameters—the `name` and the `message`—are passed to this method (code file `SignalRSample/ChatServer/Hubs/ChatHub.cs`):

```
public class ChatHub: Hub
{
  public void Send(string name, string message) =>
    Clients.All.BroadcastMessage(
      HttpUtility.HtmlEncode(name),
      HttpUtility.HtmlEncode(message));
}
```

> **NOTE** *With the* `ChatHub` *class, before returning the data that is received from the client, it is HTML-encoded. Otherwise, the client could send HTML-formatted data or even JavaScript content—for example, to redirect all users receiving the data to another website. Read Chapter 20, "Security," for security issues with web applications.*

To use SignalR, the interfaces for SignalR need to be registered with the dependency injection container. You do this in the `ConfigureServices` method of the `Startup` class—invoking the `AddSignalR` extension method for the `IServiceCollection` interface (code file `SignalRSample/ChatServer/Startup.cs`):

```
public class Startup
{
  public void ConfigureServices(IServiceCollection services)
  {
    services.AddSignalR();
  }
  //...
}
```

With the configuration of the middleware in the `Configure` method, SignalR needs to be mapped with the endpoint configuration. When you use the `MapHub` extension method of the `IEndpointRouteBuilder`, you specify the class type for the hub (which needs to derive from the `Hub` class) and the link to use this route. With an overload of the method, you can also specify options for the underlying WebSockets (code file `SignalRSample/ChatServer/Startup.cs`):

```
app.UseEndpoints(endpoints =>
{
  endpoints.MapHub<ChatHub>("/chat");
  //...
  endpoints.Map("/", async context =>
  {
    StringBuilder sb = new();
    sb.Append("<h1>SignalR Sample</h1>");
    sb.Append("<div>Open <a href='/ChatWindow.html'>ChatWindow</a> " +
      "for communication</div>");
    await context.Response.WriteAsync(sb.ToString());
  });
});
```

> **NOTE** *For serving the HTML client from the same web server as the SignalR server, the extension method* UseStaticFiles *needs to be added to the middleware pipeline, and the folder* wwwroot *needs to be created.*

Creating a Client with HTML and JavaScript

The previous version of SignalR included a JavaScript library with jQuery extensions. At that time, nearly every website was using jQuery to access the DOM elements of the HTML page. The ASP.NET Core version of the SignalR library doesn't have a dependency on any other scripting library. All you need is a JavaScript file that you can retrieve from content delivery network (CDN) servers. With the sample application, libman is used to retrieve the JavaScript file and was introduced in Chapter 24, "ASP.NET Core."

To install libman as a tool for the project, you need to create a tool manifest file and add libman to the manifest file:

```
> dotnet new tool-manifest
> dotnet tool install microsoft.web.library.manager.cli
```

After this tool is installed, you can create a libman.json configuration file using libman init and add the JavaScript library with the libman install command. Be aware that the SignalR JavaScript library is not available at the libman-default CDN provider CDNJS, but it is available at the CDN server from Node (https://unpkg.com):

```
> dotnet libman init
> dotnet libman install @microsoft/signalr@latest --provider unpkg
  --destination wwwroot/lib/signalr --files dist/browser/signalr.js
  --files dist/browser/signalr.min.js
```

For the HTML client, two input fields and a button are defined to allow the user to enter a name and a message and then click a button to send the message to the SignalR server. The messages received will be displayed in the output element (code file SignalRSample/ChatServer/wwwroot/ChatWindow.html):

```
<label for="name">Name:</label>
<input type="text" id="name" />
<br />
<label for="message">Message:</label>
<input type="text" id="message" />
<br />
<input id="sendButton" type="button" value="send" />
<p />
<output id="output"></output>
```

The first script element references the JavaScript file from the SignalR library. Remember to use the minified file for production. When the DOM tree of the HTML file is loaded, a connection to the Chat server is created. When you use connection.on, you define what should happen when a message arrives from the SignalR server. The first parameter is the name of the method used when calling the proxy in the server except the casing changes from C# Pascal casing (BroadcaseMessage) to JavaScript camel casing (broadcastMessage). With the second parameter, a function is defined that has the same number of parameters as are sent from the server. When a message arrives, the content of the output element changes to include this message. After registering to receive this event, the connection to the SignalR server is started by invoking the start function. When the connection completes successfully, the then function defines what's next. Here, an event listener is assigned to the click event of the button to send the message to the SignalR server. The method that is invoked with the SignalR server is defined with the first parameter of the invoke function—send in the sample code—that's the same name as the method that is defined in the ChatHub (just the casing differs). Again, the same number of arguments are used (code file SignalRSample/ChatServer/wwwroot/ChatWindow.html):

```html
<script src="lib/signalr/dist/browser/signalr.min.js"></script>
<script>
  document.addEventListener("DOMContentLoaded", function () {
    const connection = new signalR.HubConnection('/chat');
    connection.on('broadcastMessage', (name, message) => {
      console.log(message);
      document.getElementById('output').innerHTML +=
        `message from ${name}: ${message}<br />`;
    });

    connection.start().then(function () {
      document.getElementById('sendButton')
        .addEventListener('click', function () {
          let name = document.getElementById('name').value;
          let message = document.getElementById('message').value;

          connection.invoke('send', name, message);
        });
      });
    });
</script>
```

When you run the application, you can open multiple browser windows—even using different browser applications—and you can enter names and messages for a chat (see Figure 28-2).

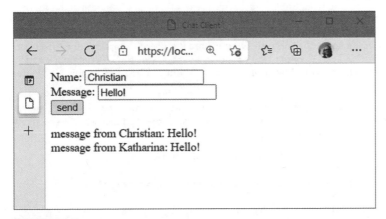

FIGURE 28-2

When you use the Microsoft Edge Developer Tools (press F12 while Microsoft Edge is open), you can use network monitoring to see the upgrade from the HTTP protocol to the WebSocket protocol, as shown in Figure 28-3.

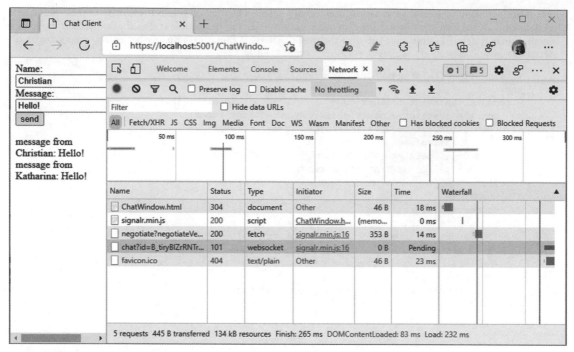

FIGURE 28-3

Creating SignalR .NET Clients

The sample .NET client application to use the SignalR server is a WinUI 3 app. The functionality is similar to the HTML/JavaScript application shown earlier. Check the readme file of the downloadable code to see what's needed to build the application. NuGet packages that need to be added are `Microsoft.AspNetCore.SignalR .Client` (the SignalR client library for .NET), `Microsoft.Extensions.Hosting` (for the DI container), and `Microsoft.Toolkit.Mvvm` (an MVVM library from Microsoft; see more about MVVM in Chapter 30, "Patterns with XAML Apps").

The user interface of the Windows application defines two `TextBoxes`, two `Buttons`, and one `ListBox` element to enter the name and message, to connect to the service hub, and to show a list of received messages, respectively (code file `SignalRSample/WinAppChatClient/Views/ChatUC.xaml`):

```
<TextBox Header="Name" Text="{x:Bind ViewModel.Name, Mode=TwoWay}"
  Grid.Row="0" Grid.Column="0" />
<TextBox Header="Message" Text="{x:Bind ViewModel.Message, Mode=TwoWay}"
  Grid.Row="1" Grid.Column="0" />
<StackPanel Orientation="Vertical" Grid.Column="1" Grid.RowSpan="2">
  <Button Content="Connect" Command="{x:Bind ViewModel.ConnectCommand}" />
  <Button Content="Send"
    Command="{x:Bind ViewModel.SendCommand, Mode=OneTime}" />
</StackPanel>
<ListBox ItemsSource="{x:Bind ViewModel.Messages, Mode=OneWay}" Grid.Row="2"
  Grid.ColumnSpan="2" Margin="12" />
```

With the `App` class of the application, the DI container is configured as shown in the following code snippet. Here, services are registered for showing a dialog (`DialogService`) to have a central place for the configuration for the service links (`UrlService`) and for the view models that are used with the application (code file `SignalRSample/WinAppChatClient/App.xaml.cs`):

```csharp
public App()
{
  this.InitializeComponent();
  _host = Host.CreateDefaultBuilder()
    .ConfigureServices(services =>
    {
      services.AddScoped<IDialogService, DialogService>();
      services.AddScoped<UrlService>();
      services.AddScoped<ChatViewModel>();
      services.AddScoped<GroupChatViewModel>();
    }).Build();
}

private IHost _host;

internal IServiceProvider Services => _host.Services;
```

The `UrlService` class that is registered with the DI container contains the URL addresses to the chat server. You need to change the `BaseUri` to the address that is shown when starting your SignalR server (code file `SignalRSample/WinAppChatClient/Services/UrlService.cs`):

```csharp
public class UrlService
{
  private string BaseUri = "https://localhost:5001/";
  public string ChatAddress => $"{BaseUri}/chat";
  public string GroupAddress => $"{BaseUri}/groupchat";
}
```

Within the code-behind file of the user control, the `ChatViewModel` is assigned to the `ViewModel` property using the DI container (code file `SignalRSample/WinAppChatClient/Views/ChatUC.xaml.cs`):

```csharp
public sealed partial class ChatUC : UserControl
{
  public ChatUC()
  {
    this.InitializeComponent();

    if (Application.Current is App app)
    {
      _scope = app.Services.CreateScope();
      ViewModel = _scope.ServiceProvider.GetRequiredService<ChatViewModel>();
    }
    else
    {
      throw new InvalidOperationException("Application.Current is not App");
    }
  }

  private readonly IServiceScope? _scope;
  public ChatViewModel ViewModel { get; private set; }
```

The hub-specific code is implemented in the class `ChatViewModel`. First, take a look at the bound properties and commands. The property `Name` is bound to enter the chat name and the `Message` property to enter the message. The `ConnectCommand` property maps to the `OnConnect` method to initiate the connection to the server; the `SendCommand` property maps to the `OnSendMessage` method to send a chat message (code file `SignalRSample/WinAppChatClient/ViewModels/ChatViewModel.cs`):

```
public sealed class ChatViewModel
{
  private readonly IDialogService _dialogService;
  private readonly UrlService _urlService;

  public ChatViewModel(IDialogService dialogService, UrlService urlService)
  {
    _dialogService = dialogService;
    _urlService = urlService;

    ConnectCommand = new RelayCommand(OnConnect);
    SendCommand = new RelayCommand(OnSendMessage);
  }

  public string Name { get; set; }
  public string Message { get; set; }

  public ObservableCollection<string> Messages { get; } =
    new ObservableCollection<string>();
  public RelayCommand SendCommand { get; }
  public RelayCommand ConnectCommand { get; }
  //...
}
```

The `OnConnect` method initiates the connection to the server. You can create a `HubConnection` with the `HubConnectionBuilder`. This builder uses a fluent API for its configuration. In the sample code, you can see the URL to the server first configured with the `WithUrl` method. After the configuration is done, the `Build` method of the `HubConnectionBuilder` creates a `HubConnection`. To register with messages that are returned from the server, the `On` method is invoked. The first parameter passed to the `On` method defines the method name that is called by the server; the second parameter defines a delegate to the method that is invoked. The method `OnMessageReceived` has the parameters specified with the generic parameter arguments of the `On` method: two strings. To finally initiate the connection, the `StartAsync` method on the `HubConnection` instance is invoked to connect to the SignalR server (code file `SignalRSample/WinAppChatClient/ViewModels/ChatViewModel.cs`):

```
private HubConnection _hubConnection;

public async void OnConnect()
{
  await CloseConnectionAsync();
  _hubConnection = new HubConnectionBuilder()
    .WithUrl(_urlService.ChatAddress)
    .Build();

  _hubConnection.Closed += HubConnectionClosed;
  _hubProxy.On<string, string>("BroadcastMessage", OnMessageReceived);

  try
  {
```

```
      await _hubConnection.StartAsync();
      await _dialogService.ShowMessageAsync("Client connected");
    }
    catch (Exception ex)
    {
      _dialogService.ShowMessage(ex.Message);
    }
  }
}
```

> **NOTE** *SignalR supports both JSON and the MessagePack protocol (see* https://msgpack
> .org). *When you use .NET clients, MessagePack has its advantages because it is more
> compact. To use MessagePack, add the NuGet package* Microsoft.AspNetCore
> .SignalR.Protocols.MessagePack *and invoke the* AddMessagePackProtocol *method
> with the configuration of the hub connection.*

Sending messages to SignalR requires only calls to the SendAsync method of the HubConnection. The first
parameter is the name of the method that should be invoked by the server; the following parameters are the
parameters of the method on the server (code file SignalRSample/WinAppChatClient/ViewModels/
ChatViewModel.cs):

```
Public async void OnSendMessage()
{
  try
  {
    _hubConnection.SendAsync("Send", Name, Message);
  }
  catch (Exception ex)
  {
    await _dialogService.ShowMessageAsync(ex.Message);
  }
}
```

When receiving a message, the OnMessageReceived method is invoked. The Messages property is an
ObservableCollection class to immediately update the user interface when a message arrives (code file
SignalRSample/WinAppChatClient/ViewModels/ChatViewModel.cs):

```
public async void OnMessageReceived(string name, string message)
{
  try
  {
    Messages.Add($"{name}: {message}");
  }
  catch (Exception ex)
  {
    await _dialogService.ShowMessageAsync(ex.Message);
  }
}
```

When you run the application, you can receive and send messages from the Windows app client, as shown in
Figure 28-4. You can also open the web page simultaneously and communicate between them.

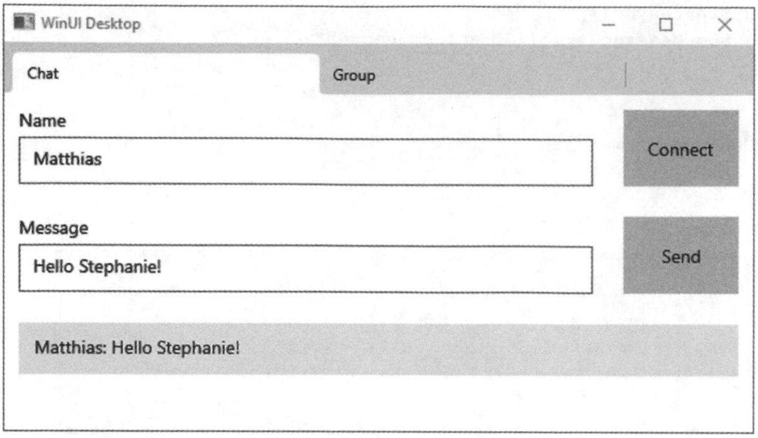

FIGURE 28-4

GROUPING CONNECTIONS

Usually, you don't want to communicate among all clients. Instead, you want to communicate among a group of clients. There's support out of the box for such a scenario with SignalR.

In this section, you add another chat hub with grouping functionality and have a look at other options that are possible using SignalR hubs. The Windows app client application is extended to enter groups and send a message to a selected group.

Extending the Hub with Groups

To support a group chat, you create the class GroupChatHub. With the previous hub, you saw how to use the SendAsync method to define the message that is sent to the clients. Instead of using this method, you can also create a custom interface, as shown in the following code snippet. This interface is used as a generic parameter with the base class Hub (code file SignalRSample/ChatServer/Hubs/GroupChatHub.cs):

```
public interface IGroupClient
{
   Task MessageToGroup(string groupName, string name, string message);
}

public class GroupChatHub: Hub<IGroupClient>
{
   //...
}
```

AddGroup and LeaveGroup are methods defined to be called by the client. When you register the group, the client sends a group name with the AddGroup method. The Hub class defines a Groups property where connections to groups can be registered. The Groups property of the generic Hub class returns IGroupManager. This interface defines two methods: AddToGroupAsync and RemoveFromGroupAsync. Both methods need a group name and a connection identifier to add or remove the specified connection to the group. The connection identifier is a unique identifier associated with a client connection. The client connection identifier—as well as other information about the client—can be accessed with the Context property of the Hub class. The following code snippet invokes the AddToGroupAsync method of the IGroupManager to register a group with the connection, and it invokes the

RemoveFromGroupAsync method to unregister a group (code file `SignalRSample/ChatServer/Hubs/GroupChatHub.cs`):

```
public Task AddGroup(string groupName) =>
    Groups.AddToGroupAsync(Context.ConnectionId, groupName);

public Task LeaveGroup(string groupName) =>
    Groups.RemoveFromGroupAsync(Context.ConnectionId, groupName);
```

> **NOTE** *The* Context *property of the* Hub *class returns an object of type* HubCallerContext. *With this class, not only can you access the connection identifier associated with the connection, but you can access other information about the client, such as the user, but only if the user is authorized.*

Invoking the Send method—this time with three parameters, including the group—sends information to all connections that are associated with the group. The Clients property is now used to invoke the Group method. The Group method accepts a group string to send the MessageToGroup message to all connections associated with the group name. With an overload of the Group method, you can add connection IDs that should be excluded. Because the Hub implements the interface IGroupClient, the Group method returns the IGroupClient. This way, the MessageToGroup method can be invoked using compile-time support (code file `SignalRSample/ChatServer/Hubs/GroupChatHub.cs`):

```
public Task Send(string group, string name, string message) =>
    Clients.Group(group).MessageToGroup(group, name, message);
```

Several other extension methods are defined to send information to a list of client connections. You've seen the Group method to send messages to a group of connections that's specified by a group name. With this method, you can exclude client connections. For example, the client who sent the message might not need to receive it. The Groups method accepts a list of group names where a message should be sent. You've already seen the All property to send a message to all connected clients. Methods to exclude sending the message to the caller are OthersInGroup and OthersInGroups. These methods send a message to one specific group excluding the caller, or a message to a list of groups excluding the caller.

You can also send messages to a customized group that's not based on the built-in grouping functionality. Here, it helps to override the methods OnConnectedAsync and OnDisconnectedAsync. The OnConnectedAsync method is invoked every time a client connects; the OnDisconnectedAsync method is invoked when a client disconnects. Within these methods, you can access the Context property of the Hub class to access client information as well as the client-associated connection ID. Here, you can write the connection information to a shared state to have your server scalable using multiple instances, accessing the same shared state. You can also select clients based on your own business logic. For example, your implementation can decide to send messages first to clients based on priorities.

```
public override Task OnConnectedAsync() =>
    base.OnConnectedAsync();

public override Task OnDisconnectedAsync(Exception exception) =>
    base.OnDisconnected(exception);
```

Extending the Windows Client App with Groups

After readying the grouping functionality with the hub, you can extend the Windows app client application. For the grouping features, another user control associated with the GroupChatViewModel class is defined.

The `GroupChatViewModel` class defines some more properties and commands compared to the `ChatViewModel` defined earlier. The `NewGroup` property defines the group the user registers to. The `SelectedGroup` property defines the group that is used with the continued communication, such as sending a message to the group or leaving the group. The `SelectedGroup` property needs change notification to update the user interface on changing this property; that's why the `INotifyPropertyChanged` interface is implemented with the `GroupChatViewModel` class, and the `set` accessor of the property `SelectedGroup` fires a notification. Commands to join and leave the group (the `EnterGroupCommand` and `LeaveGroupCommand` properties, respectively) are defined as well (code file `SignalRSample/WinAppChatClient/ViewModels/GroupChatViewModel.cs`):

```
public sealed class GroupChatViewModel
{
  private readonly IDialogService _dialogService;
  private readonly UrlService _urlService;

  public GroupChatViewModel(IDialogService dialogService,
    UrlService urlService)
  {
    _dialogService = dialogService;
    _urlService = urlService;

    ConnectCommand = new RelayCommand(OnConnect);
    SendCommand = new RelayCommand (OnSendMessage);
    EnterGroupCommand = new RelayCommand (OnEnterGroup);
    LeaveGroupCommand = new RelayCommand (OnLeaveGroup);
  }

  public string? Name { get; set; }
  public string? Message { get; set; }
  public string? NewGroup { get; set; }
  public string? SelectedGroup { get; set; }

  public ObservableCollection<string> Messages { get; } =
    new ObservableCollection<string>();
  public ObservableCollection<string> Groups { get; } =
    new ObservableCollection<string>();
  public ICommand SendCommand { get; }
  public ICommand ConnectCommand { get; }
  public ICommand EnterGroupCommand { get; }
  public ICommand LeaveGroupCommand { get; }
  //...
}
```

The handler methods for the `EnterGroupCommand` and `LeaveGroupCommand` commands are shown in the following code snippet. Here, the `AddGroup` and `RemoveGroup` methods are called within the group hub (code file `SignalRSample/WinAppChatClient/ViewModels/GroupChatViewModel.cs`):

```
public async void OnEnterGroup()
{
  try
  {
    if (NewGroup is not null)
    {
      await _hubConnection.InvokeAsync("AddGroup", NewGroup);
      Groups.Add(NewGroup);
```

```
        SelectedGroup = NewGroup;
      }
    }
    catch (Exception ex)
    {
      await _dialogService.ShowMessageAsync(ex.Message);
    }
  }

  public async void OnLeaveGroup()
  {
    try
    {
      if (SelectedGroup is not null)
      {
        await _hubConnection.InvokeAsync("LeaveGroup", SelectedGroup);
        Groups.Remove(SelectedGroup);
      }
    }
    catch (Exception ex)
    {
      _dialogService.ShowMessage(ex.Message);
    }
  }
```

Sending and receiving the messages is similar to the previous sample. The difference is that the group information is added now (code file `SignalRSample/WinAppChatClient/ViewModels/GroupChatViewModel.cs`):

```
  public async void OnSendMessage()
  {
    try
    {
      await _hubConnection.InvokeAsync("Send", SelectedGroup, Name, Message);
    }
    catch (Exception ex)
    {
      _dialogService.ShowMessage(ex.Message);
    }
  }

  public void OnMessageReceived(string group, string name, string message)
  {
    try
    {
        Messages.Add($"{group}-{name}: {message}");
    }
    catch (Exception ex)
    {
      await _dialogService.ShowMessageAsync(ex.Message);
    }
  }
```

When you run the application, you can send messages for all groups that have been joined and see received messages for all registered groups, as shown in Figure 28-5.

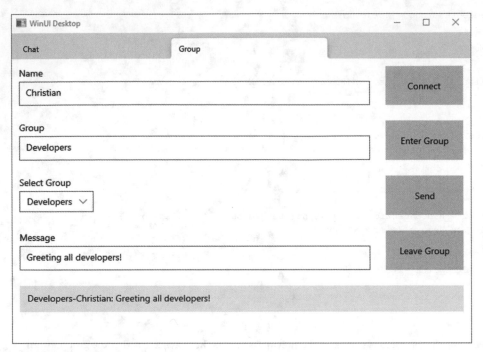

FIGURE 28-5

STREAMING WITH SIGNALR

SignalR supports streaming, including from the server to the client, from the client to the server, and simultaneously in both directions.

The sample application returns a stream of simulated sensor data to the client. To implement this, create a new empty ASP.NET Core web application and add the configuration of SignalR similar to the previous sample. The hub class `StreamingHub` is now declared to return `IAsyncEnumerable<SensorData>`. The hub passes 1,000 `SensorData` values to the client unless the client sends a cancellation that is received with the `cancellationtoken` (code file `SignalRStreaming/Hubs/StreamingHub.cs`):

```
public record SensorData(int Val1, int Val2, DateTime TimeStamp);

public class StreamingHub : Hub
{
  public async IAsyncEnumerable<SensorData> GetSensorData(
    [EnumeratorCancellation] CancellationToken cancellationToken)
  {
    Random r = new();
    for (int i = 0; i < 1000; i++)
    {
      yield return new SensorData(r.Next(20), r.Next(20), DateTime.Now);
      await Task.Delay(1000, cancellationToken);
    }
  }
}
```

> **NOTE** *Instead of using* `IAsyncEnumerable` *for streaming, a SignalR streaming hub can also return a* `ChannelReader` *or a* `ChannelWriter`—*depending on the direction of the stream— from the namespace* `System.Threading.Channels`. *Using* `IAsyncEnumerable` *is just the simpler option to implement with the help of C# extensions with the* `yield` *statement and* `await foreach`. *The foundation of async streams is covered in Chapter 11, "Tasks and Asynchronous Programming."*

This time, the client application is created with a .NET console application template. The creation and starting of the hub connection is done in the same way as before. Now, the `StreamAsync` method is used to invoke the `GetSensorData` method. This method returns `IAsyncEnumerable`, which can now be used with the `await foreach` statement. Passing the cancellation token to the service is done with the `WithCancellation` method; after 10 seconds, requesting the stream is canceled (code file `StreamingClient/Program.cs`):

```csharp
using Microsoft.AspNetCore.SignalR.Client;
using System;
using System.Threading;
using System.Threading.Tasks;

Console.WriteLine($"Wait for service - press return to start");
Console.ReadLine();

var connection = new HubConnectionBuilder()
  .WithUrl("https://localhost:5001/stream")
  .Build();

await connection.StartAsync();

CancellationTokenSource cts = new(10000);

try
{
  await foreach (var data in
    connection.StreamAsync<SensorData>("GetSensorData").WithCancellation(cts.Token))
  {
    Console.WriteLine(data);
  }
}
catch (OperationCanceledException)
{
  Console.WriteLine("Canceled!");
}

await connection.StopAsync();

Console.WriteLine("Completed");


public record SensorData(int Val1, int Val2, DateTime TimeStamp);
```

When you run both the service and the client application, the stream of sensor data is shown in the client application until the cancellation happens after 10 seconds.

> **NOTE** *Instead of invoking* `StreamAsync` *on the client, you can invoke the method* `StreamAsChannelAsync`. *This returns a* `ChannelReader`, *no matter whether you returned a* `ChannelReader` *or* `IAsyncEnumerable` *with the service.*

SUMMARY

This chapter described communicating with multiple clients with ASP.NET Core SignalR. SignalR offers an easy way to use the WebSocket technology to keep the network connection open to allow passing continuous information from the server to the client. With SignalR you can also send information to all connected clients or a group of clients. The sample application demonstrated how you can implement clients to register for groups, and the server returns information from groups.

With creating SignalR clients, you've seen using JavaScript as well as .NET clients. The API is similar for the different client libraries—just the naming of the hub methods differs.

You've seen how to implement streaming with SignalR using the `yield` statement to return `IAsyncEnumerable` and using `await foreach`.

The next chapter is the start of Part IV of the book and is the first chapter of several that cover how to use XAML to create Windows apps.

PART IV

Apps

29

Windows Apps

WHAT'S IN THIS CHAPTER?

- ➤ Introducing XAML
- ➤ Working with controls
- ➤ Working with compiled data binding
- ➤ Implementing navigation
- ➤ Using layout panels

CODE DOWNLOADS FOR THIS CHAPTER

The source code for this chapter is available on the book page at www.wiley.com. Click the Downloads link. The code can also be found at https://github.com/ProfessionalCSharp/ProfessionalCSharp2021 in the directory 4_Apps/Windows.

The code for this chapter is divided into the following major examples:

- ➤ XAMLIntro
- ➤ ControlsSamples
- ➤ DataBindingSamples
- ➤ NavigationControls
- ➤ LayoutSamples

All the projects have nullable reference types enabled.

INTRODUCING WINDOWS APPS

Many options are available for creating Windows applications. When the .NET Framework was first released in 2002, Windows Forms was *the* technology to create Windows applications. Since .NET Core 3.1, you can also create Windows Forms applications with the new .NET. The "old" .NET (.NET Framework 3.0) introduced Windows Presentation Foundation (WPF). With WPF, the user interface is created with eXtensible Application Markup Language (XAML), an XML syntax that allows flexible scaling. Silverlight (code name WPF-E or WPF Everywhere) was a technology that brought XAML syntax to the browser, and the Windows phone with a slimmed-down version of .NET. This technology needed an add-in with the browser. For some years, Silverlight was also the technology to create applications for Windows phones. The last version of Silverlight had the goal for more desktop support with the ability to control Microsoft Office (after more features had been integrated with HTML 5). With this, the Universal Windows Platform (UWP) became the successor of Silverlight to create XAML-based applications for Windows.

Compared to WPF, UWP offers modern XAML features not available with WPF. UWP applications run in a sandboxed environment where the user is in control of what the app can do. When installing UWP applications from the Microsoft Store, the user gets some guarantees about what the app might do and can uninstall the application again without keeping some files or registry keys on the system. With UWP, a slimmed-down version of .NET with the Windows Runtime (WinRT) is used.

Now we have a new technology for the user interface. Modern XAML syntax is used with rich desktop applications, and the desktop applications can take advantage of the newest C# language features with the latest version of .NET: WinUI. The controls are separated from the Windows 10 version. Instead of waiting for new Windows 10 versions to be available with the users before using new UI controls, the UI controls are part of the library and can be used with older Windows 10 versions.

WinUI gives you different options to create applications: packaged desktop applications, desktop applications that are not packaged, and UWP applications. Packaged desktop applications make use of MSIX. MSIX is the Windows app package format for deploying Windows apps (`https://docs.microsoft.com windows/msix`). With packaged desktop applications, two projects are created: one with the application code and one to create the deployment package. Applications deployed using MSIX run in a lightweight app container. When you use MSIX, the application is isolated from other apps and can be fully uninstalled without having bits left on your system. A UWP app container, also known as *native container*, supports better battery life (by suspending applications when they are not used) and explicit security control. With a native container, the user grants permissions defining what the application is allowed to do. Within the Microsoft Store, you can add not only applications using a native container but also applications using MSIX app containers. With MSIX containers, some users complain that your app needs full permissions to run.

At the time of this writing, WinUI supports only packaged desktop applications, but the other application types are on the WinUI roadmap. See the WinUI 3.0 feature roadmap for the current state of WinUI: `https://github .com/Microsoft/microsoft-ui-xaml/blob/master/docs/roadmap.md#winui-30-feature-roadmap`.

> **NOTE** *The GitHub repo of the previous edition of this book (*`https://github.com/ ProfessionalCSharp/ProfessionalCSharp7`*) includes UWP samples using the ink control and the map control and some other UWP features. At the time of this writing, WinUI does not have support for ink and maps. With the fast updates of WinUI, make sure to check the readme file of the book samples for updates and see* `https://github.com/ ProfessionalCSharp/MoreSamples` *for additional samples with WinUI—for example, with the ink and map controls.*

This chapter and the following chapters provide information on creating Windows applications with WinUI. Nearly all the topics discussed are possible with other XAML-based technologies as well. Practically the same syntax can be used with UWP applications.

When you compare WinUI with WPF, the XAML syntax looks nearly the same, but there are important differences. Besides having more modern controls with WinUI, controls have other properties (such as the `Header` property with the `TextBlock` element). WinUI offers compiled binding (in addition to the reflection-based binding that's also available with WPF). The class hierarchy of WinUI is simpler than the class hierarchy of WPF;

there are many similarities but with completely different implementations. Whereas WPF is developed with .NET, the WinUI controls have been built with C++.

Another user interface option that's making use of XAML is .NET Multi-Platform App UI (MAUI). This library is the successor of Xamarin.Forms. Here you have other controls and other control hierarchies offering renderers for Android and iOS.

> **NOTE** *The Project Reunion is a code name from Microsoft to combine all the desktop technologies under one umbrella. Instead of porting your existing C++/MFC and WPF applications to WinUI, you can use WinUI controls from all the desktop technologies and easily use new features in your existing applications.*

Windows Runtime

Before digging into the XAML syntax, you need to know about the Windows Runtime (WinRT). WinRT is the modern native API of the Windows platform, and WinUI (and UWP) applications make use of this runtime. It's built with C++ and a new generation of COM objects. Many applications available as part of the Windows operating system (for example, Calculator) are developed with C++ and XAML. You can check the source code of the Calculator at `https://github.com/Microsoft/Calculator` to see the XAML code and its C++ view models, and you can even add pull requests to enhance its functionality.

To use WinRT from .NET applications, C#/WinRT offers projection support for C#. With the projection support, native details of WinRT APIs are hidden and mapped to .NET data types.

With .NET, metadata is extensible with custom attributes and can be accessed using reflection. (Read more about this in Chapter 12, "Reflection, Metadata, and Dynamic Programming.") WinRT is using the same format for its metadata as .NET. Thus, you can open the `.winmd` files (metadata files for WinRT) using the `ildasm` command line to see the API calls with their parameters. You can find the Windows metadata files in the directory `%ProgramFiles(x86)%\Windows Kits\10\References\`.

Language projection maps Windows Runtime types to .NET types. For example, in the file `Windows.Foundation.FoundationContract.winmd`, you'll find the `IIterable` and `IIterator` interfaces in the namespace `Windows.Foundation.Collections`. These interfaces look similar to the .NET interfaces `IEnumerable` and `IEnumerator`. Indeed, they are automatically mapped with language projection.

Not all the interfaces of the contracts can be directly mapped. Chapter 18, "Files and Streams," shows files and streams with the Windows Runtime from the namespace `Windows.Storage.Streams`. To use the Windows streams with .NET streams, you can use extension methods such as `AsStream`, `AsStreamForRead`, and `AsStreamForWrite`.

To use WinRT, all that needs to be configured with .NET 5 is to use the correct target framework moniker. Instead of using `net5.0` as the target framework (as you've done so far with .NET console and ASP.NET Core applications), the target framework moniker `net5.0-windows10.0.19041.0` is used with WinUI applications. 19041.0 specifies the Windows 10 build version to use the C#/WinRT projection and thus the APIs available. Be aware that a new projection layer is not available with every Windows 10 update. Windows 10 version 20H2 with build number 19042 and version 21H1 with build 19043 only include minor updates without new APIs; thus, no new projections are required.

The following project file snippet shows the `TargetFramework` configuration of the sample applications (project file `XAMLIntro/HelloWindows/HelloWindows.csproj`):

```
<TargetFramework>net5.0-windows10.0.19041.0</TargetFramework>
```

> **NOTE** *See* `https://docs.microsoft.com/windows/uwp/csharp-winrt/` *for more information about the projection layer C#/WinRT with information on how you can write your own projections for native libraries.*

Hello, Windows

Let's start creating a new Windows app with Visual Studio. Search for *WinUI desktop application with the templates*. Make sure to check this chapter's readme file for updates. After you input the name and location, the next question asked is the target and minimum version supported. With every newer platform version, you get more features from the Windows Runtime. However, you need to pay attention to the version of Windows 10 that your users have. They can't install and run your Windows 10 app if the platform version is not supported. With WinUI 3.0, the user interface components are independent of the version of the Windows runtime and supports Windows 10 back to version 1809, which has the build number 17763. Version 1809 was released in November 2018.

With the target version you select, you specify the API version that can be used by the app. With the minimum version, you specify the build version where the app can be installed and run. If you set the target and minimum version to different values, you need to write adaptive code if you use APIs that are not available in the minimum version.

Application Manifest

You can change the build target and minimum version numbers with the project properties of the package project. Windows apps have another important configuration for the packaging: the file `Package.appxmanifest`. Opening this file with Visual Studio opens the Package Manifest Editor.

With the Application settings (see Figure 29-1), you can configure the display name of the application, the default language, supported rotations of the device, and automatic periodic tile updates.

On the Visual Assets tab, you can configure all the different icons of the application—tile images for different tile sizes, different device resolutions, a splash screen, and a package logo for the Windows Store.

Settings in the Capabilities tab allow you to select the capabilities needed by the app. Examples of such capabilities are Internet, Microphone, Bluetooth, Webcam, and others that allow the application access to these resources (if the user agrees to grant access). This is important with UWP-style applications that use the native app container. Packaged WinUI applications use the MSIX environment and thus require more privileges.

With the Declarations settings (see Figure 29-2), you can add features of the application that Windows needs to know about. For example, when sharing data from one app, Windows shows the apps that accept the shared data. For this, the app needs to be registered as a *share target*. Besides using the application as share target, examples of when you need to specify declarations are when the app should be activatable via a protocol or a file type extension, when communication should be done between app services, or when the app should communicate via app services.

The Content URIs tab allows for deep linking within the app. Here, you can specify URLs to open pages in the app. Finally, with the Packaging tab, you can configure the package name, version, and information about the publisher.

Application Startup

The entry point into the application, `HelloWindows.App`, is defined in the application manifest, as shown in the previous section. The `App` class derives from the `Application` base class and invokes the `InitializeComponent` method that's generated in the other part of the partial class to initialize the XAML code (code file `HelloWindows/App.xaml.cs`):

```
sealed partial class App : Application
{
```

```
public App()
{
  this.InitializeComponent();
}
//...
}
```

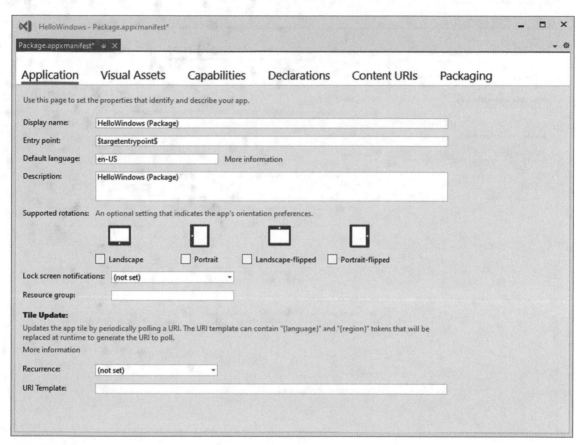

FIGURE 29-1

With the XAML code specified in `App.xaml`, you can see that XAML control resources from `Microsoft` `.UI.Xaml.Controls` are referenced. With this namespace, the default styles for the WinUI XAML controls are specified. How to customize the look of resources with resource dictionaries is covered in Chapter 31, "Styling Windows Apps."

With the C# `App` class, the `OnLaunched` method is overridden. This method is invoked when the application is started. As you learned from the application manifest, there are different ways to start the application. When reading information from the `LaunchActivatedEventArgs` parameter, you can find out how the application was started. The application can be started directly from the user or started when the user shares data from another application. With the default implementation, an instance of the `MainWindow` is created, and the `Activate` method is invoked (code file `XAMLIntro/HelloWindows/App.xaml.cs`):

```
protected override void OnLaunched(Microsoft.UI.Xaml.LaunchActivatedEventArgs args)
{
  m_window = new MainWindow();
```

```
    m_window.Activate();
}

private Window? m_window;
```

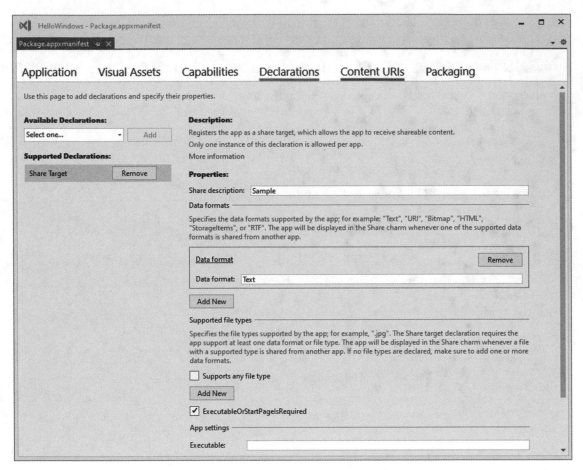

FIGURE 29-2

Main Window

Let's open the `MainWindow.xaml` file. The user interface is defined using XAML, a language that extends XML with some functionality that's discussed in detail in the section "Introducing XAML." As shown in the following code snippet, the root element is the `Window` that has some specialty with WinUI and is different from the other XAML elements. This class is not part of the hierarchy of the other XAML elements. The `Window` class doesn't have a base class and implements some interfaces important for WinRT. This means you don't have direct access to the properties available with all the framework elements. The custom class that's used in the code-behind is specified with the `x:Class` attribute: this is the `MainWindow` class. `MainWindow` derives from the `Window` class. The `xmlns` attributes used are similar to the way the C# `using` directive is used to import namespaces. With `xmlns`, you open types to be used with the XAML file. Similar to the `using` directive, you can create an alias. The alias `x` references types specified with `http://schemas.microsoft.com/winfx/2006/xaml`. The alias is then used as a prefix, as in x:Name to define a name for the Button element. The namespace that is opened by default and thus doesn't require a prefix when using the elements is http://schemas.microsoft.com/winfx/2006/xaml/ presentation. This is the namespace where the WinUI XAML controls are defined. You can open .NET namespaces and use .NET classes within XAML code by opening the .NET namespace with using as with xmlns: local="using:HelloWindows". This way, with the local prefix, simple .NET classes can be used within the XAML code, as shown in the next section. In the following code snippet, the StackPanel and Button controls are added as child elements of the Window element. With the StackPanel, the attributes Orientation, HorizontalAlignment, and VerticalAlignment are set. Using this XML syntax, the corresponding properties of the StackPanel class are set. With the Button control, the content is set to a simple string (which sets the Content property), and the Click attribute is set to the myButton_Click event handler. Click is an event in the Button control. Read Chapter 7, "Delegates, Lambdas, and Events," for details on C# events (code file XAMLIntro/HelloWindows/MainWindow.xaml):

```
<Window
  x:Class="HelloWindows.MainWindow"
  xmlns="http://schemas.microsoft.com/winfx/2006/xaml/presentation"
  xmlns:x="http://schemas.microsoft.com/winfx/2006/xaml"
  xmlns:local="using:HelloWindows"
  xmlns:d="http://schemas.microsoft.com/expression/blend/2008"
  xmlns:mc="http://schemas.openxmlformats.org/markup-compatibility/2006"
  mc:Ignorable="d">

  <StackPanel Orientation="Horizontal" HorizontalAlignment="Center"
    VerticalAlignment="Center">
    <Button x:Name="myButton" Click="myButton_Click">Click Me</Button>
  </StackPanel>
</Window>
```

In the code-behind file, the button can be accessed using the myButton variable. The x:Name attribute with the XAML file creates .NET variables. On clicking the button, the value of the Content property is changed with the myButton_Click event handler (code file XAMLIntro/HelloWindows/MainWindow.xaml.cs):

```
using Microsoft.UI.Xaml;

namespace HelloWindows
{
  public sealed partial class MainWindow : Window
  {
    public MainWindow()
    {
      this.InitializeComponent();
    }

    private void myButton_Click(object sender, RoutedEventArgs e)
    {
      myButton.Content = "Clicked";
    }
  }
}
```

After building and deploying the application, you can run it and click the button to see its content changes. Deployment of the application is automatically done from Visual Studio on a build when the Deploy configuration is set in the Configuration Manager (Build ⇨ Configuration Manager). If you don't deploy the app on build, you need to deploy it after build by using the Deploy option in the context menu when you select the project in Solution Explorer, or you can deploy all the projects in the solution with Visual Studio by selecting Build ⇨ Deploy Solution.

INTRODUCING XAML

When creating web applications with ASP.NET Core, you need to know HTML, CSS, and JavaScript in addition to knowing C#. When you create Windows apps, you need to know XAML besides C#. XAML is not only used to create Windows apps; it's also used with Windows Presentation Foundation (WPF), Windows Workflow Foundation (WF), and cross-platform apps with Xamarin.

Anything that can be done with XAML can also be done with C#. Every XAML element is represented with a class and thus can be accessed from C#. Why is there a need for XAML? XAML is typically used to describe objects and their properties, and this is possible in a deep hierarchy. For example, a `Page` contains a `Grid` control; the `Grid` control contains a `StackPanel` and other controls; and the `StackPanel` contains `Button` and `TextBox` controls. XAML makes it easy to describe such a hierarchy and assign properties of objects via XML attributes or elements.

XAML allows writing code in a declarative manner. Whereas C# is mainly an imperative programming language, XAML allows for declarative definitions. With an imperative programming language (like C#), the compiler compiles a C# for loop to a `for` loop with the Intermediate Language (IL) code. With a declarative programming language, you declare *what* should be done, but not *how* it should be done.

XAML is an XML syntax, but it defines several enhancements to XML. With these enhancements, XAML is still valid XML. The enhancements just have special meaning and special functionality. Examples for the enhancements are curly brackets within XML attributes. For XML, this is still just a string and thus valid XML. For XAML, this is a markup extension.

Before you can use XAML efficiently, you need to understand some important features of this programming language. These features are described in the following sections:

➤ **Dependency properties**—From the outside, dependency properties look like normal properties. However, they need less storage and implement change notification.

➤ **Routed events**—From the outside, routed events look like normal .NET events. However, you use custom event implementation with add and remove accessors to allow bubbling and tunneling. Events can tunnel from outer controls to inner controls and bubble from inner controls to outer controls.

➤ **Attached properties**—With attached properties, it is possible to add properties to other controls. For example, the `Button` control doesn't have a property to position it within a `Grid` control in a specific row and column. With XAML, it looks like it has such a property.

➤ **Markup extensions**—Writing XML attributes requires less coding compared to XML elements. However, XML attributes can only be strings; you can write much more powerful syntax with XML elements. To reduce the amount of code that needs to be written, markup extensions allow writing powerful syntax within attributes.

Mapping Elements to Classes

Behind every XAML element there's a class with properties, methods, and events. You can create UI elements either with C# code or using XAML. Let's get into an example. With the following code snippet, a `StackPanel` is defined that contains a `Button` control. With XML attributes, the `Button` has the `Content` property and the `Click` event assigned. The `Content` property just contains a simple string, whereas the `Click` event references the address of the method `OnButtonClick`. The XML attribute `x:Name` is used to declare a name to the `Button` control that can be used both from XAML and from the C# code-behind file (code file `XAMLIntro/Intro/MainWindow.xaml`):

```
<StackPanel x:Name="stackPanel1">
  <Button Content="Click Me!" x:Name="button1" Click="OnButtonClick" />
  <!-- ... -->
</StackPanel>
```

On top of the page, you can see the `Window` element with the XML attribute `x:Class`. This defines the name of the class where the XAML compiler generates partial code. With the code-behind file in Visual Studio, you can see the part of this class that you can modify (code file `XAMLIntro/Intro/MainWindow.xaml`):

```
<Window
  x:Class="XAMLIntro.MainWindow"
  <!-- ... -->
</Window>
```

The code-behind file contains part of the class `MainWindow` (the part that is not generated by the XAML compiler). In the constructor, the method `InitializeComponent` is invoked. The implementation of `InitializeComponent` is created by the XAML compiler. This method loads the XAML file and converts it to an object as specified with the root element in the XAML file. The `OnButtonClick` method is a handler for the `Click` event of the `Button` that was previously created in XAML code. The implementation just opens up a `MessageDialog` (code file `XAMLIntro/Intro/MainWindow.xaml.cs`):

```
public sealed partial class MainWindow : Window
{
  public MainPage()
  {
    this.InitializeComponent();
  }

  private async void OnButtonClick(object sender, RoutedEventArgs e)
  {
    await new MessageDialog("button 1 clicked").ShowAsync();
  }
}
```

Now let's create a new object from the `Button` class from C# code and add it to the existing `StackPanel`. In the following code snippet, the constructor of the `MainPage` was modified to create a new `Button`, set the `Content` property, and assign a lambda expression to the `Click` event. Finally, the newly created button is added to the `Children` of the `StackPanel` (code file `XAMLIntro/Intro/MainWindow.xaml.cs`):

```
public MainWindow()
{
  this.InitializeComponent();
  Button button2 = new()
  {
    Content = "created dynamically"
  };
  button2.Click += async (sender, e) =>
    await new MessageDialog("button 2 clicked").ShowAsync();
  stackPanel1.Children.Add(button2);
}
```

As you've seen, XAML is just another way to deal with objects, properties, and events. The next sections show you the advantages of XAML for user interfaces.

Using Custom .NET Classes with XAML

To use custom .NET classes within XAML code, you can use a simple plain old CLR object (POCO) class; there are no special requirements on the class definition. You just have to add the .NET namespace to the XAML declaration. To demonstrate this, a simple `Person` class with the `FirstName` and `LastName` properties is defined as shown here (code file `XAMLIntro/DataLib/Person.cs`):

```
public class Person
{
```

```
        public string? FirstName { get; set; }
        public string? LastName { get; set; }
        public override string ToString() => $"{FirstName} {LastName}";
    }
```

In XAML, an XML namespace alias named `datalib` is defined that maps to the .NET namespace `DataLib` in the assembly `DataLib`. With this alias in place, it's now possible to use all classes from this namespace by using the alias as a prefix for the elements.

In the XAML code, you add a `ListBox` that contains items of type `Person`. When you use XAML attributes, you set the values of the properties `FirstName` and `LastName`. When you run the application, the output of the `ToString` method is shown inside the `ListBox` (code file `XAMLIntro/Intro/MainWindow.xaml`):

```xml
<Window x:Class="XamlIntro.MainWindow"
    xmlns="http://schemas.microsoft.com/winfx/2006/xaml/presentation"
    xmlns:x="http://schemas.microsoft.com/winfx/2006/xaml"
    xmlns:local="using:XAMLIntro"
    xmlns:datalib="using:DataLib"
    xmlns:d="http://schemas.microsoft.com/expression/blend/2008"
    xmlns:mc="http://schemas.openxmlformats.org/markup-compatibility/2006"
    mc:Ignorable="d">

    <StackPanel x:Name="stackPanel1" >
      <Button Content="Click Me!" x:Name="button1" Click="OnButtonClick">
      <ListBox>
        <datalib:Person FirstName="Stephanie" LastName="Nagel" />
        <datalib:Person FirstName="Matthias" LastName="Nagel" />
        <datalib:Person FirstName="Katharina" LastName="Nagel" />
      </ListBox>
    </StackPanel>
</Window>
```

> **NOTE** *WPF and Xamarin use* `clr-namespace` *instead of* `using` *within the alias declaration. The reason is that XAML with WinUI and UWP is neither based on nor restricted to .NET. You can use native C++ with XAML as well, and thus* `clr` *(Common Language Runtime) would not be a good fit.*

Setting Properties as Attributes

With the previous XAML samples, properties of classes have been set by using XML attributes. To set properties from XAML, you can use XML attributes as long as the property type can be represented as a string or there is a conversion from a string to the property type. The following code snippet sets the `Content` and `Background` properties of the `Button` element with XML attributes:

```xml
<Button Content="Click Me!" Background="LightGoldenrodYellow" />
```

With the previous code snippet, the `Content` property is of type `object` and thus accepts a string. The `Background` property is of type `Brush`. A string is converted to a `SolidColorBrush` type that derives from `Brush`.

Using Properties as Elements

It's also always possible to use the element syntax to supply the value for properties. You can set the Background property of the Button class with the child element Button.Background. The following code snippet defines the Button with the same result as shown earlier with attributes:

```
<Button>
  Click Me!
  <Button.Background>
    <SolidColorBrush Color="LightGoldenrodYellow" />
  </Button.Background>
</Button>
```

Using elements instead of attributes allows you to apply more complex brushes to the Background property, such as a LinearGradientBrush, as shown in the following example (code file XAMLIntro/Intro/MainWindow.xaml):

```
<Button x:Name="button1" Click="OnButtonClick">
  Click Me!
  <Button.Background>
    <LinearGradientBrush StartPoint="0.5,0.0" EndPoint="0.5, 1.0">
      <GradientStop Offset="0" Color="Yellow" />
      <GradientStop Offset="0.3" Color="Orange" />
      <GradientStop Offset="0.7" Color="Red" />
      <GradientStop Offset="1" Color="DarkRed" />
    </LinearGradientBrush>
  </Button.Background>
</Button>
```

> **NOTE** *When you set the content in the sample, neither the* Content *attribute nor a* Button.Content *element is used to write the content; instead, the content is written directly as a child value to the* Button *element. That's possible because with a base class of the* Button *class (*ContentControl*), the* ContentProperty *attribute is applied with* [ContentProperty("Content")]. *This attribute marks the* Content *property as a* ContentProperty. *This way the direct child of the XAML element is applied to the* Content *property.*

Dependency Properties

XAML uses dependency properties for data binding, animations, property change notification, styling, and so forth. What's the reason for dependency properties? Let's assume you create a class with 100 properties of type int, and this class is instantiated 100 times on a single form. How much memory is needed? Because an int has a size of 4 bytes, the result is 4 × 100 × 100 = 40,000 bytes. Did you already have a look at the properties of a XAML element? Because of the huge inheritance hierarchy, a XAML element defines hundreds of properties. The property types are not simple int types; instead, they're a lot more complex. I think you can imagine that such properties could consume a huge amount of memory. However, you usually change only the values of a few of these properties, and most of the properties keep their default values that are common for all instances. This dilemma is solved with dependency properties. With dependency properties, object memory is not allocated for every property and every instance. Instead, the dependency property system manages a dictionary of all properties and allocates memory only if a value is changed. Otherwise, the default value is shared between all instances.

Dependency properties also have built-in support for change notification. With normal properties, you need to implement the interface `INotifyPropertyChanged` for change notification. How the interface `INotifyPropertyChanged` can be implemented is explained later in this chapter in the section "Working with Data Binding." Such a change mechanism is built-in with dependency properties. For data binding, the property of the UI element that is bound to the source of a .NET property must be a dependency property. Now, let's get into the details of dependency properties.

From the outside, a dependency property looks like a normal .NET property. However, with a normal .NET property, you usually also define the data member that is accessed by the `get` and `set` accessors of the property:

```
private int _value;
public int Value
{   ,
  get => _value;
  Set => _value = value;
}
```

Similar to normal properties, a dependency property has `get` and `set` accessors, but doesn't declare a data member. With dependency properties, the accessors invoke the methods `GetValue` and `SetValue` of the `DependencyObject`. This stipulates a requirement for dependency objects that they must be implemented in a class that derives from `DependencyObject` from the namespace `Microsoft.UI.Xaml`.

With a dependency property, the data member is kept inside an internal collection that is managed by the base class and allocates data only if the value changes. With unchanged values, the data can be shared between different instances or base classes. The `GetValue` and `SetValue` methods require a `DependencyProperty` argument. This argument is defined by a static member of the class that has the same name as the property appended to the term `Property`. With the property `Value`, the static member has the name `ValueProperty`. `DependencyProperty.Register` is a helper method that registers the property in the dependency property system. The following code snippet uses the `Register` method with four arguments to define the name of the property, the type of the property, the type of the owner—that is, the class `MyDependencyObject`—and the default value with the help of `PropertyMetadata` (code file XAMLIntro/DependencyObjectSample/MyDependencyObject.cs):

```
public class MyDependencyObject: DependencyObject
{
  public int Value
  {
    get => (int)GetValue(ValueProperty);
    set => SetValue(ValueProperty, value);
  }

  public static readonly DependencyProperty ValueProperty =
    DependencyProperty.Register("Value", typeof(int),
      typeof(MyDependencyObject), new PropertyMetadata(0));
}
```

Creating a Dependency Property

This section looks at an example that defines not one but three dependency properties. The class `MyDependencyObject` defines the dependency properties `Value`, `Minimum`, and `Maximum`. All of these properties are dependency properties that are registered with the method `DependencyProperty.Register`. The methods `GetValue` and `SetValue` are members of the base class `DependencyObject`. For the `Minimum` and `Maximum` properties, default values are defined that can be set with the `DependencyProperty.Register` method and a fourth argument to set the `PropertyMetadata`. When you use a constructor with one parameter, `PropertyMetadata`, the `Minimum` property is set to `0`, and the `Maximum` property is set to `100` (code file XAMLIntro/DependencyObjectSample/MyDependencyObject.cs):

```
public class MyDependencyObject: DependencyObject
{
```

```
public int Value
{
  get => (int)GetValue(ValueProperty);
  set => SetValue(ValueProperty, value);
}

public static readonly DependencyProperty ValueProperty =
  DependencyProperty.Register(nameof(Value), typeof(int),
    typeof(MyDependencyObject));

public int Minimum
{
  get => (int)GetValue(MinimumProperty);
  set => SetValue(MinimumProperty, value);
}

public static readonly DependencyProperty MinimumProperty =
  DependencyProperty.Register(nameof(Minimum), typeof(int),
    typeof(MyDependencyObject), new PropertyMetadata(0));

public int Maximum
{
  get => (int)GetValue(MaximumProperty);
  set => SetValue(MaximumProperty, value);
}

public static readonly DependencyProperty MaximumProperty =
  DependencyProperty.Register(nameof(Maximum), typeof(int),
    typeof(MyDependencyObject), new PropertyMetadata(100));
}
```

> **NOTE** *Within the implementation of the* get *and* set *property accessors, you should not do anything other than invoke the* GetValue *and* SetValue *methods. When you use the dependency properties, the property values can be accessed from the outside with the* GetValue *and* SetValue *methods, which is also done from WinUI; therefore, the strongly typed property accessors might not be invoked at all. They are just here for convenience, so you can use the normal property syntax from your custom code.*

Value Changed Callbacks and Events

To get some information on value changes, dependency properties also support value changed callbacks. You can add a DependencyPropertyChanged event handler to the DependencyProperty.Register method that is invoked when the property value changes. In the sample code, the handler method OnValueChanged is assigned to the PropertyChangedCallback of the PropertyMetadata object. In the OnValueChanged method, you can access the old and new values of the property with the DependencyPropertyChangedEventArgs argument (code file XAMLIntro/DependencyObjectSample/MyDependencyObject.cs):

```
public class MyDependencyObject: DependencyObject
{
  public int Value
  {
```

```
      get => (int)GetValue(ValueProperty);
      set => SetValue(ValueProperty, value);
    }

    public static readonly DependencyProperty ValueProperty =
      DependencyProperty.Register(nameof(Value), typeof(int),
        typeof(MyDependencyObject),
        new PropertyMetadata(0, OnValueChanged, CoerceValue));

    private static void OnValueChanged(DependencyObject obj,
      DependencyPropertyChangedEventArgs e)
    {
      int oldValue = (int)e.OldValue;
      int newValue = (int)e.NewValue;
      //...
    }
  }
```

Routed Events

Chapter 7 covers the .NET event model. With default implemented events, when an event is fired, the handler directly connected to the event is invoked. When you use UI technologies, there are different requirements for event handling. With some events, it should be possible to create a handler with a container control and react to events coming from children controls. Such an implementation is possible by creating a custom implementation for .NET events, as shown in Chapter 7 with add and remove accessors.

WinUI offers routed events. The sample app defines a UI consisting of a CheckBox that, if selected, stops the routing; a Button control with the Tapped event set to the OnTappedButton handler method; and a Grid with the Tapped event set to the OnTappedGrid handler. The Tapped event is one of the routed events with WinUI. This event can be fired with the mouse, touch, and pen devices (code file XAMLIntro/RoutedEvents/MainWindow.xaml):

```
<Grid Tapped="OnTappedGrid">
  <Grid.RowDefinitions>
    <RowDefinition Height="auto" />
    <RowDefinition Height="auto" />
    <RowDefinition />
  </Grid.RowDefinitions>
  <StackPanel Grid.Row="0" Orientation="Horizontal">
    <CheckBox x:Name="CheckStopRouting">Stop Routing</CheckBox>
    <Button Click="OnCleanStatus">Clean Status</Button>
  </StackPanel>
  <Button Grid.Row="1" Tapped="OnTappedButton">Tap me!</Button>
  <TextBlock Grid.Row="2" Margin="20" x:Name="textStatus" />
</Grid>
```

The OnTappedXX handler methods write status information to a TextBlock to show the handler method as well as the control that was the original source of the event (code file XAMLIntro/RoutedEvents/MainWindow.xaml.cs):

```
private void OnTappedButton(object sender, TappedRoutedEventArgs e)
{
  ShowStatus(nameof(OnTappedButton), e);
  e.Handled = CheckStopRouting.IsChecked == true;
}


private void OnTappedGrid(object sender, TappedRoutedEventArgs e)
```

```
  {
    ShowStatus(nameof(OnTappedGrid), e);
    e.Handled = CheckStopRouting.IsChecked == true;
  }

  private void ShowStatus(string status, RoutedEventArgs e)
  {
    textStatus.Text += $"{status} {e.OriginalSource.GetType().Name}";
    textStatus.Text += "\r\n";
  }

  private void OnCleanStatus(object sender, RoutedEventArgs e)
  {
    textStatus.Text = string.Empty;
  }
```

When you run the application and click outside the button but within the grid, you see the `OnTappedGrid` event handled with the `Grid` control as the originating source:

```
OnTappedGrid Grid
```

Click in the middle of the button to see that the event is routed. The first handler that is invoked is `OnTappedButton` followed by `OnTappedGrid`:

```
OnTappedButton TextBlock
OnTappedGrid TextBlock
```

What's also interesting is that the event source is not the `Button` but a `TextBlock`. The reason is that the button is styled using a `TextBlock` to contain the button text. If you click other positions within the button, you can also see `Grid` or `ContentPresenter` as the originating event source. The `Grid` and `ContentPresenter` are other controls the button is created from.

If you select the check box `CheckStopRouting` before clicking the button, you can see that the event is no longer routed because the `Handled` property of the event arguments is set to `true`:

```
OnTappedButton TextBlock
```

Within the Microsoft API documentation of the events, you can see whether an event type is routing within the remarks section of the documentation. With WinUI applications, tapped, drag and drop, key up and key down, pointer, focus, and manipulation events are routed events.

Attached Properties

Whereas dependency properties are properties available with a specific type, with an attached property, you can define properties for other types. Some container controls define attached properties for their children; for example, if the `RelativePanel` control is used, a `Below` property is available for its children. The `Grid` control defines `Row` and `Column` properties.

The following code snippet demonstrates how this looks in XAML. The `Button` class doesn't have the property `Grid.Row`, but it's attached from the `Grid`:

```
<Grid>
  <Grid.RowDefinitions>
    <RowDefinition />
    <RowDefinition />
  </Grid.RowDefinitions>
  <Button Content="First" Grid.Row="0" Background="Yellow" />
  <Button Content="Second" Grid.Row="1" Background="Blue" />
</Grid>
```

Attached properties are defined similarly to dependency properties, as shown in the next example. The class that defines the attached properties must derive from the base class `DependencyObject` and define a normal property, where the `get` and `set` accessors invoke the methods `GetValue` and `SetValue` of the base class. This is where the similarities end. Instead of invoking the method `Register` with the `DependencyProperty` class, now `RegisterAttached` is invoked, which registers an attached property that is available with every element (code file `XAMLIntro/AttachedProperty/MyAttachedProperyProvider.cs`):

```
public class MyAttachedPropertyProvider: DependencyObject
{
  public static readonly DependencyProperty MySampleProperty =
    DependencyProperty.RegisterAttached
      "MySample",
      typeof(string),
      typeof(MyAttachedPropertyProvider),
      new PropertyMetadata(string.Empty));

  public static void SetMySample(UIElement element, string value) =>
    element.SetValue(MySampleProperty, value);

  public static int GetMyProperty(UIElement element) =>
    (string)element.GetValue(MySampleProperty);
}
```

> **NOTE** *You might assume that* `Grid.Row` *can be added only to elements within a* `Grid`. *That's not the case. Attached properties can be added to any element. However, no one would use this property value. The* `Grid` *is aware of this property and reads it from its children elements to arrange them. It doesn't read it from children of children.*

In the XAML code, the attached property can now be attached to any elements. The second `Button` control, named `button2`, has the property `MyAttachedPropertyProvider.MySample` attached to it, and the value `42` assigned (code file `XAMLIntro/AttachedProperty/MainWindow.xaml`):

```
<Grid x:Name="grid1">
  <Grid.RowDefinitions>
    <RowDefinition Height="Auto"/>
    <RowDefinition Height="Auto"/>
    <RowDefinition Height="*"/>
  </Grid.RowDefinitions>
  <Button Grid.Row="0" x:Name="button1" Content="Button 1" />
  <Button Grid.Row="1" x:Name="button2" Content="Button 2"
    local:MyAttachedPropertyProvider.MySample="42" />
  <ListBox Grid.Row="2" x:Name="list1" />
</Grid>
```

When doing the same in code-behind, it is necessary to invoke the static method `SetMyProperty` of the class `MyAttachedPropertyProvider`. It's not possible to extend the class `Button` with a property. The method `SetProperty` gets a `UIElement` instance that should be extended by the property and the value. In the following code snippet, the property is attached to `button1`, and the value is set to `sample value` (code file `XAMLIntro/AttachedProperty/MainWindow.xaml.cs`):

```
public MainWindow()
{
  InitializeComponent();
```

```
      MyAttachedPropertyProvider.SetMySample(button1, "sample value");
      //...
  }
```

To read attached properties that are assigned to elements, you can use the `VisualTreeHelper` to iterate every element in the hierarchy and try to read its attached properties. The `VisualTreeHelper` is used to read the visual tree of the elements during runtime. The method `GetChildrenCount` returns the count of the child elements. To access a child, you can use the method `GetChild` and pass the index for an element with the second argument. This method then returns the element. The implementation of the `GetChildren` method returns elements only if they are of type `FrameworkElement` (or derived therefrom) and if the predicate passed with the `Func` argument returns `true` (code file XAMLIntro/AttachedProperty/MainWindow.xaml.cs):

```csharp
private IEnumerable<FrameworkElement> GetChildren(FrameworkElement element,
  Func<FrameworkElement, bool> pred)
{
  int childrenCount = VisualTreeHelper.GetChildrenCount(rootElement);
  for (int i = 0; i < childrenCount; i++)
  {
    var child = VisualTreeHelper.GetChild(rootElement, i) as FrameworkElement;
    if (child != null && pred(child))
    {
      yield return child;
    }
  }
}
```

The method `GetChildren` is now used from within the constructor of the page to add all elements with an attached property to the `ListBox` control (code file XAMLIntro/AttachedProperty/MainPage.xaml.cs):

```csharp
public MainWindow()
{
  InitializeComponent();
  MyAttachedPropertyProvider.SetMySample(button1, "sample value");
  foreach (var item in GetChildren(grid1, e =>
    MyAttachedPropertyProvider.GetMySample(e) != string.Empty))
  {
    list1.Items.Add(
      $"{item.Name}: {MyAttachedPropertyProvider.GetMySample(item)}");
  }
}
```

When you run the application, you see the two button controls in the `ListBox` with these values:

```
button1: sample value
button2: 42
```

> **NOTE** *Later in this chapter in the section "Implementing Layout Panels," you can see attached properties with many container controls, such as* `Canvas`, `Grid`, *and* `RelativePanel`.

Markup Extensions

With markup extensions, you can extend XAML with either element or attribute syntax. If an XML attribute contains curly brackets, that's a sign of a markup extension. Often markup extensions with attributes are used as shorthand notation instead of using elements.

One example of such a markup extension is `StaticResourceExtension`, which finds resources. Here's a resource of a linear gradient brush with the key `gradientBrush1` (code file `XAMLIntro/MarkupExtensions/MainWindow.xaml`):

```
<StackPanel.Resources>
  <LinearGradientBrush x:Key="gradientBrush1" StartPoint="0.5,0.0"
    EndPoint="0.5, 1.0">
    <GradientStop Offset="0" Color="Yellow" />
    <GradientStop Offset="0.3" Color="Orange" />
    <GradientStop Offset="0.7" Color="Red" />
    <GradientStop Offset="1" Color="DarkRed" />
  </LinearGradientBrush>
</StackPanel.Resources>
```

This resource can be referenced by using the `StaticResourceExtension` with attribute syntax to set the `Background` property of a `Button`. Attribute syntax is defined by curly brackets and the name of the extension class without the `Extension` suffix:

```
<Button Content="Test" Background="{StaticResource gradientBrush1}" />
```

Windows apps do not support all the markup extensions that have been available with WPF, but there are some. `StaticResource` and `ThemeResource` are discussed in Chapter 31, and the binding markup extensions `Binding` and `x:Bind` are discussed later in this chapter in the section "Working with Data Binding."

Custom Markup Extensions

Custom markup extensions allow you to add your own features within the curly brackets in XAML code. You can create custom binding, condition-based evaluation, or a simple calculator, as shown in the next sample.

The `Calculator` markup extension enables you to calculate two values using add, subtract, multiply, and divide operations. A markup extension is really simple: the class name contains the `Extension` postfix, and it derives from the base class `MarkupExtension` and overrides the method `ProvideValue`. With `ProvideValue`, the markup extension returns the value or object that is assigned to the property where the markup is defined. The type of the returned value is defined by the `MarkupExtensionReturnType` attribute. The following code snippet shows the implementation of the `Calculator` markup extension. This extension defines three properties that can be set: properties for `X`, `Y`, and the `Operation` that should be applied to `X` and `Y`. The operation is defined using an enum. In the implementation of the `ProvideValue` method, an operation is applied to `X` and `Y`, and the result is returned (code file `CustomMarkupExtension/CalculatorExtension.cs`):

```
public enum Operation
{
  Add,
  Subtract,
  Multiply,
  Divide
}

[MarkupExtensionReturnType(ReturnType = typeof(string))]
public class CalculatorExtension : MarkupExtension
{
  public double X { get; set; }
  public double Y { get; set; }
  public Operation Operation { get; set; }

  protected override object ProvideValue() =>
    (Operation switch
    {
```

```
        Operation.Add => X + Y,
        Operation.Subtract => X - Y,
        Operation.Multiply => X * Y,
        Operation.Divide => X / Y,
        _ => throw new InvalidOperationException()
    }).ToString();
}
```

Now, the `Calculator` markup extension can be used with the XML attribute syntax. Here, the markup extension is initialized for setting the properties. The return string is applied to the `Text` property of a `TextBlock` (code file `XAMLIntro/CustomMarkupExtension/MainWindow.xaml`):

```
<TextBlock Text="{local:Calculator Operation=Add, X=38, Y=4}" />
```

Using the markup extension syntax, the name `Extension` is not used. This postfix is automatically applied. This is, of course, different if the `CalculatorExtension` class is just used to instantiate it as child of the `Text` property and set the properties of the extension (code file `XAMLIntro/CustomMarkupExtension/MainWindow.xaml`):

```
<TextBlock>
  <TextBlock.Text>
    <local:CalculatorExtension Operation="Multiply" X="7" Y="6" />
  </TextBlock.Text>
</TextBlock>
```

When you run the application, the value `42` is returned from both operations used.

WORKING WITH CONTROLS

Because of the many controls available for Windows apps, it's good to know some specific base classes within the hierarchy of UI controls. Knowing these makes it easier to work with the WinUI controls and helps you understand what you can do with these types.

Let's get into the hierarchy of the UI classes with Windows apps.

➤ **DependencyObject**—This class is on top of the hierarchy for the Windows Runtime XAML elements. Every class that derives from `DependencyObject` can have dependency properties. You've already seen dependency properties with the introduction to XAML in this chapter.

➤ **UIElement**—This is the base class for elements with visual appearance. This class offers functionality for user interaction, such as pointer events (`PointerPressed`, `PointerMoved`, and so on), key handling events (`KeyDown`, `KeyUp`), focus events (`GotFocus`, `LostFocus`), pointer captures (`CapturePointer`, `PointerCanceled`, and so on), and drag and drop (`DragOver`, `Drop`, and so on). This class also offers the `Lights` property, a special feature for the fluent design, to highlight elements with a light effect. The `KeyboardAccelerators` property allows setting a key combination for fast access via the keyboard. This is often used from menus.

➤ **FrameworkElement**—The class `FrameworkElement` derives from `UIElement` and adds more features. Classes deriving from `FrameworkElement` can participate in the layout system. The properties `MinWidth`, `MinHeight`, `Height`, and `Width` are defined by the `FrameworkElement` class. Lifetime events are defined by `FrameworkElement` as well: `Loaded`, `SizeChanged`, and `Unloaded` are some of these events. Data binding features are another group of functionalities defined by the `FrameworkElement` class. This class defines the `DataContext`, `DataContextChanged`, `SetBinding`, and `GetBindingExpression` APIs.

➤ **Control**—The class `Control` derives from `FrameworkElement` and is the base class for UI controls—for example, `TextBox`, `Hub`, `DatePicker`, `SearchBox`, `UserControl`, and others. Controls typically have a default style with a `ControlTemplate` that is assigned to the `Template` property. The `Control` class defines overridable OnXX methods for the events defined by the base class UIElement. Some examples of these methods are OnDrop that can be used with drag and drop, OnKeyDown that is invoked before the KeyDown event occurs, and OnPointerPressed that is invoked before the PointerPressed event occurs. Controls define a TabIndex; properties for the foreground, background, and the border (Foreground, Background, BorderBrush, BorderThickness); and properties to enable it and use keyboard tabs to access it (IsTabStop, TabIndex).

➤ **ContentControl**—The class ContentControl derives from Control and enables you to have any content as a child of the control. Examples of ContentControl are AppBar, Frame, ButtonBase, GroupItem, and ToolTip controls. The ContentControl defines the Content property where any content can be assigned, a ContentTemplate property to assign a DataTemplate, a ContentTemplateSelector to dynamically assign a data template, and the ContentTransitions property for simple animations.

➤ **ItemsControl**—Contrary to the ContentControl, which can have only one content, the ItemsControl can view a content list. While the ContentControl defines the Content property to list its child item, the ItemsControl defines this with the Items property. Both ContentControl and ItemsControl derive from the base class Control. The ItemsControl can display a fixed number of items or items that are bound through a list. Controls that derive from ItemsControl are ListView, GridView, ListBox, Pivot, and Selector.

➤ **Panel**—Another class that can serve as a container of items is the Panel class. This class derives from the base class FrameworkElement. Panels are used to position and arrange child objects. Examples of classes that derive from Panel are Canvas, Grid, StackPanel, VariableSizedWrapGrid, VirtualizingPanel, ItemsStackPanel, ItemsWrapGrid, and RelativePanel. Panel controls are discussed later in the section "Implementing Layout Panels."

➤ **RangeBase**—This class derives from the Control class and is the base class for ProgressBar, ScrollBar, and Slider. RangeBase defines the Value property for the current value, Minimum and Maximum properties, and a ValueChanged event handler.

➤ **FlyoutBase**—This class directly derives from DependencyObject and enables you to show user interfaces on top of other elements—in other words, they "fly out."

> **NOTE** *Control templates are covered in detail in Chapter 31.*

Now that we've gone through the main categories and the hierarchy of the types, let's get into the details.

FrameworkElement-Derived UI Elements

Some elements aren't really controls, but they're still UI elements that are classes that derive from FrameworkElement. These classes don't allow a custom look by specifying a template. The following table presents the different categories of these classes and the description of their functionality:

CLASS	DESCRIPTION
Border Viewbox ContentPresenter ItemsPresenter	Presenters are classes that are not interactive, but they still offer a visual appearance. The `Border` class defines a border around a single control (which can be a `Grid` containing several other controls). The `Viewbox` enables you to stretch and scale the child element. The `ContentPresenter` is used within a `ControlTemplate`. It defines where the content of the control will be displayed. An `ItemsPresenter` is used to define the position of items within an `ItemsControl`. Control and item templates are discussed in Chapter 31.
TextBlock RichTextBlock	The `TextBlock` and `RichTextBlock` controls are used to display text. Text input is not possible with these controls; they are just used for display. The `TextBlock` control not only allows assigning simple text but also allows more complex text elements such as paragraphs and inline elements. The `RichTextBlock` supports overflow as well. Be aware that the `RichTextBlock` doesn't support working with rich text format (RTF). You need to use the `RichEditBox` instead.
Ellipse Polygon Polyline Path Rectangle	The `Shape` class derives from `FrameworkElement`. `Shape` itself is a base class for `Ellipse`, `Polygon`, `Polyline`, `Path`, `Rectangle`, and others. These classes are used to draw vectors to the screen. These classes are shown in Chapter 31.
Panel	The `Panel` class derives from `FrameworkElement`. Panels are used to organize the UI elements on the screen. The different panels available that derive from the `Panel` class are discussed later in this chapter in the section "Implementing Layout Panels."
Image	The `Image` control is used to display images. This control supports displaying images of these formats: JPEG, PNG, BMP, GIF, TIFF, JPEG XR, ICO, and SVG.
ParallaxView	The `ParallaxView` is a control that creates a parallax effect while scrolling.

continues

(continued)

CLASS	DESCRIPTION
WebView2	The WebView2 control uses the Chrome-based Microsoft Edge browser to display web pages with the WinUI application. If the browser is not installed on the client system, it can be distributed with the app using the WebView2 runtime (see https://developer.microsoft.com/microsoft-edge/webview2/).

Presenters

With the PresentersPage, some of the presenters controls are used—Border and Viewbox. The border is used to group two TextBox elements. Because the Border element can contain only one child, a StackPanel is used within the Border element. The Border specifies a Background, a BorderBrush, and a BorderThickness.

The two Viewbox controls in the following code snippet are used to stretch a Button control. The first Viewbox makes a stretch of mode Fill to completely fill the Button within the Viewbox, whereas the second Viewbox makes a stretch of mode Uniform. With Uniform, the aspect ratio is maintained (code file ControlsSamples/Views/PresentersPage.xaml):

```
<Border Background="LightSeaGreen" BorderBrush="DarkGreen" BorderThickness="12"
  Margin="12" Padding="8">
  <StackPanel Orientation="Vertical">
    <TextBox Header="Title" x:Name="Title" FontSize="34" />
    <TextBox Header="Publisher" x:Name="Publisher" FontSize="34" />
  </StackPanel>
</Border>
<Viewbox Grid.Row="1" Stretch="Fill" StretchDirection="Both">
  <Button Margin="4" FontSize="14">Button with fill stretch</Button>
</Viewbox>
<Viewbox Grid.Row="2" Stretch="Uniform" StretchDirection="Both">
  <Button Margin="4" FontSize="14">Button with uniform stretch</Button>
</Viewbox>
```

Figure 29-3 shows the presenters page from the running app. Here you can see how the TextBox controls are surrounded, and the buttons are shown in the two different Viewbox configurations.

> **NOTE** *Control-derived classes have an implicit border that you can customize with the* BorderThickness *and* BorderBrush *properties.*

Control-Derived Controls

Controls that directly derive from the base class Control belong to this category. The following table describes some of these controls:

CONTROL	DESCRIPTION
TextBox	This control is used to display simple, unformatted text. This control can be used for user input. The Text property contains the user input. PlaceholderText enables you to give the user information about what to enter in the input field. Usually, some information about the input text is shown nearby. This can be done directly using the Header property.
RichEditBox	Contrary to the TextBox control, the RichEditBox allows formatted text, hyperlinks, and images. The Text Object Model (TOM) is used from the Document property. You can use Microsoft Word to create RTF files that can be read into the RichEditBox.
PasswordBox	This control is used to enter a password. It has specific properties for password input, such as PasswordChar to define the character that should be displayed as the user enters the password. The password entered can be retrieved using the Password property. This control also has Header and PlaceholderText properties similar to the TextBox control.
ProgressRing	This control indicates that an operation is ongoing. It's displayed as a ring-shaped "spinner." Another control to display an ongoing operation is the ProgressBar, but this one belongs to the range controls.
DatePicker CalendarDatePicker CalendarView	The DatePicker and CalendarDatePicker controls are used to allow the user to select a date. The DatePicker is useful for date selection where the user knows the date, and showing a calendar is not helpful. The CalendarDatePicker uses the CalendarView internally. If a calendar should be visible all the time or you need to select multiple dates, you can use the CalendarView. Be aware there's also a DatePickerFlyout (a control that derives from Flyout) that allows the user to select a date in a new opened window.
TimePicker	The TimePicker allows the user to enter a time. As with to the DatePicker, you can use a TimePickerFlyout with the TimePicker.
AppBarSeparator	AppBarSeparator controls can be used as separators within a CommandBar.
ColorPicker	The ColorPicker allows the user to select a color.
Hub HubSection	The Hub control allows grouping content in a panning view. The content within this control is defined in multiple HubSection controls. The Hub control is used with many apps to lay out the main view of the app with "Hero" images. This control is discussed later in the section "Implementing Navigation."
UserControl	The UserControl is a control that can be used for reuse, and to simplify the XAML code with pages. User controls can be added to pages, and you'll use user controls in this and the next chapters.
Page	The Page class derives from UserControl, thus it is also a UserControl. Pages are used to navigate within a Frame. Navigation is discussed later in the section "Implementing Navigation," and in Chapter 30, "Patterns with XAML Apps," with the MVVM pattern.

continues

(continued)

CONTROL	DESCRIPTION
PersonPicture	`PersonPicture` is used to show the avatar image of a person. This control is used with the `ContactManager` and `Contact` APIs.
RatingControl	`RatingControl` is used to enter a star rating by the user.
SemanticZoom	The `SemanticZoom control` defines two views: one zoom-out view and one zoom-in view. This allows the user to quickly navigate into a large data set—for example, to display first characters in the zoom-out view. In the zoom-in view, the user is positioned at the data objects with the selected letter.
SplitView	The `SplitView` control has a pane and a content area. The pane can be opened and closed. When opening the pane, the content can be either partially behind the pane or moved to the right. The opened pane can be small (compact) or wide. The `SplitView` is used within the `NavigationView` control.
TwoPaneView	The `TwoPaneView` control helps with displays of two areas, such as list and details. With dual-screen devices, the `TwoPaneView` can split the user interface cleanly on the two screens. See `https://docs.microsoft.com/dual-screen/introduction` for dual-screen devices.
TreeView	The `TreeView` control shows a hierarchical list of nested items. See the sample from Chapter 22, "Localization," that displays a tree of nested cultures using the `TreeView` control.
MenuBar MenuBarItem	`MenuBar` is a new container to display menus in a horizontal row. `MenuBar` controls contain `MenuBarItem` controls that in turn contain `MenuFlyoutItem` controls.

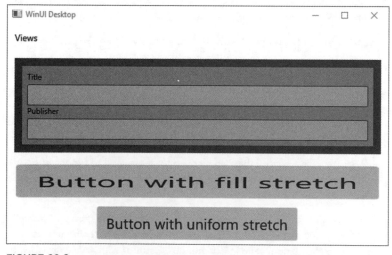

FIGURE 29-3

Using a TextBox

The first sample with `Control`-derived controls shows several `TextBox` controls. With the `TextBox` class, you can specify the `InputScope` property to a value of a large list of options such as `EmailNameOrAddress`, `CurrencyAmountAndSymbol`, or `Formula`. In case the app is used in tablet mode with an on-screen keyboard, the keyboard is adjusted to a different layout and shows keys as needed by the input field. The last `TextBox` in the sample code shows a multiline `TextBox`. To allow the user to press the Return key, the `AcceptsReturn` property is set. Also, the `TextWrapping` property is set to wrap the text if it doesn't fit on one line. The height of the `TextBox` is set to 150. In case the entered text doesn't fit with this size, a scrollbar is shown by using the attached property `ScrollViewer.VerticalScrollBarVisibility` (code file `ControlsSamples/Views/TextPage.xaml`):

```xml
<TextBox Header="Email" InputScope="EmailNameOrAddress"></TextBox>
<TextBox Header="Currency" InputScope="CurrencyAmountAndSymbol"></TextBox>
<TextBox Header="Alpha Numeric" InputScope="AlphanumericFullWidth"></TextBox>
<TextBox Header="Formula" InputScope="Formula"></TextBox>
<TextBox Header="Month" InputScope="DateMonthNumber"></TextBox>
<TextBox Header="Multiline" AcceptsReturn="True" TextWrapping="Wrap"
  Height="150" ScrollViewer.VerticalScrollBarVisibility="Auto" />
```

Figure 29-4 shows the result of the multiline `TextBox` with multiple lines that wrap and a scrollbar.

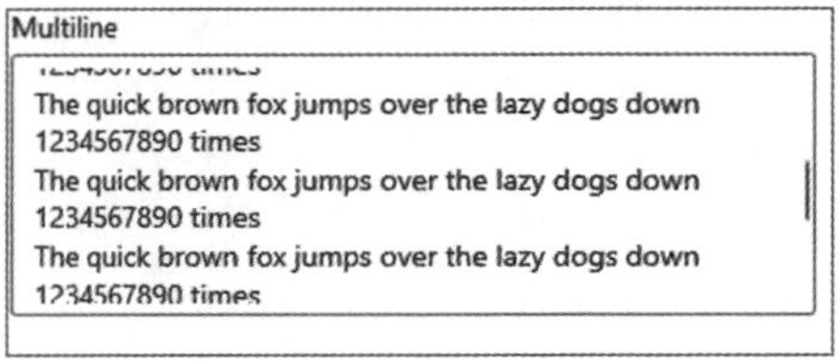

FIGURE 29-4

Selecting a Date

For selecting a date, multiple options are available. Let's look at the different options and at the special features of the `CalendarView` control.

With the following code snippet, the `CalendarView` is configured to allow multiple days to be selected. The first day of the week is set to Monday, the minimum day is set to the bound property `MinDate`, and the events `CalendarViewDayItemChanging` and `SelectedDatesChanged` are assigned to event handlers (code file `ControlsSamples/Views/DateSelectionPage.xaml`):

```xml
<CalendarView x:Name="CalendarView1" Margin="12" HorizontalAlignment="Center"
  SelectionMode="Multiple"
  FirstDayOfWeek="Monday"
  MinDate="{x:Bind MinDate, Mode=OneTime}"
  CalendarViewDayItemChanging="OnDayItemChanging"
  SelectedDatesChanged="OnDatesChanged" />
```

With the code-behind, the `MinDate` property is set to a predefined day. The user cannot use the calendar to go to a day before that (code file `ControlsSamples/Views/DateSelectionPage.xaml.cs`):

```csharp
public DateTimeOffset MinDate { get; } =
  DateTimeOffset.Parse("1/1/1965, new CultureInfo("en-US"));
```

With the `OnDayItemChanging` event handler, some days should be marked special. Days before today should be blocked out from a selection, and based on actual bookings, the day should be marked with colored lines.

To get the bookings, the method `GetBookings` is defined to return sample data. With a real app, you could get the data from a web API or a database. The `GetBookings` method just returns bookings for a number of days from now (`2`, `3`, `5`...) and the number of bookings in a day (`1`, `4`, `3`...) by returning a tuple (code file `ControlsSamples/Views/DateSelectionPage.xaml.cs`):

```csharp
private IEnumerable<(DateTimeOffset day, int bookings)> GetBookings()
{
  int[] bookingDays = { 2, 3, 5, 8, 12, 13, 18, 21, 23, 27 };
```

```
        int[] bookingsPerDay = { 1, 4, 3, 6, 4, 5, 1, 3, 1, 1 };

        for (int i = 0; i < 10; i++)
        {
          yield return (DateTimeOffset.Now.Date.AddDays(bookingDays[i]),
            bookingsPerDay[i]);
        }
      }
```

The `OnDayItemChanging` method is invoked when the items of the `CalendarView` are displayed. Every displayed day invokes this method. The method `OnDayItemChanging` is implemented using local functions. The main block of this method contains a `switch` statement to invoke different methods based on the data binding phases. The `CalendarView` control supports multiple phases to allow adapting the user interface in different iterations. The first phase is fast; after this phase, some information can already be displayed to the user. Every next phase follows later. With later phases, information might be retrieved from a web API, and this information will be updated as the data is available.

In the implementation of `OnDayItemChanging`, in the first phase, the local function `RegisterUpdateCallback` is invoked to register the next call to the `OnDayItemChanging` event handler. In the second phase, the dates are blacked out with the local function `SetBlackoutDates`. In the third phase, the bookings are retrieved (code file `ControlsSamples/Views/DateSelectionPage.xaml.cs`):

```
    private void OnDayItemChanging(CalendarView sender,
      CalendarViewDayItemChangingEventArgs args)
    {
      switch (args.Phase)
      {
        case 0:
          RegisterUpdateCallback();
          break;
        case 1:
          SetBlackoutDates();
          break;
        case 2:
          SetBookings();
          break;
        default:
          break;
      }

      // local functions...
    }
```

The local function `RegisterUpdateCallback` invokes the `RegisterUpdateCallback` of the `CalendarViewDayItemChangingEventArgs` argument passing the event handler method, so this method is invoked again (code file `ControlsSamples/Views/DateSelectionPage.xaml.cs`):

```
    void RegisterUpdateCallback() => args.RegisterUpdateCallback(OnDayItemChanging);
```

The local function `SetBlackoutDates` blacks out the dates before today, as well as all Saturdays and Sundays. The `CalendarViewDayItem` that is returned from the `args.Item` property defines an `IsBlackout` property (code file `ControlsSamples/Views/DateSelectionPage.xaml.cs`):

```
    async void SetBlackoutDates()
    {
      RegisterUpdateCallback();
      CalendarViewDayItem item = args.Item;
```

```
    await Task.Delay(500); // simulate a delay for an API call
    if (item.Date < DateTimeOffset.Now || item.Date.DayOfWeek == DayOfWeek.Saturday ||
        item.Date.DayOfWeek == DayOfWeek.Sunday)
    {
      args.Item.IsBlackout = true;
    }
  }
}
```

Finally, the `SetBookings` method retrieves the information about the bookings. The received date found in the `CalendarViewDayItem` is checked if it is also found in the bookings. If it is, a list of red or green colors (depending on the weekday) is added to the day item by invoking `SetDensityColors`. Finally, the `RegisterUpdateCallback` local function is invoked once again; otherwise, only the first day shown would be invoked with the third phase (code file `ControlsSamples/Views/DateSelectionPage.xaml.cs`):

```
void SetBookings()
{
  CalendarViewDayItem item = args.Item;
  await Task.Delay(3000); // simulate a delay for an API call
  var bookings = GetBookings().ToList();

  var booking = bookings.SingleOrDefault(b => b.day.Date == item.Date.Date);
  if (booking.bookings > 0)
  {
    List<Color> colors = new();
    for (int i = 0; i < booking.bookings; i++)
    {
      if (item.Date.DayOfWeek == DayOfWeek.Saturday ||
          item.Date.DayOfWeek == DayOfWeek.Sunday)
      {
        colors.Add(Colors.Red);
      }
      else
      {
        colors.Add(Colors.Green);
      }
    }

    item.SetDensityColors(colors);
  }
}
```

When a user selects a date, the `OnDatesChanged` method is invoked. With this method, all the dates selected are received in the `CalendarViewSelectedDatesChangedEventArgs`. The selected dates are written to the `currentDatesSelected` list, and the deselected dates are removed from the list again. Using a `string` `.Join`, all the selected dates are shown with the `MessageDialog` (code file `ControlsSamples/Views/DateSelectionPage.xaml.cs`):

```
private List<DateTimeOffset> currentDatesSelected = new List<DateTimeOffset>();

private async void OnDatesChanged(CalendarView sender,
  CalendarViewSelectedDatesChangedEventArgs args)
{
  currentDatesSelected.AddRange(args.AddedDates);
  args.RemovedDates.ToList().ForEach(date =>
    currentDatesSelected.Remove(date));
```

```
    string selectedDates = string.Join(", ",
      currentDatesSelected.Select(d => d.ToString("d")));

    await new MessageDialog($"dates selected: {selectedDates}").ShowAsync();
}
```

When you run the app, you can see the calendar, as shown in Figure 29-5; the previous days as well as Saturday/Sunday are blocked, and the information about bookings is shown with color lines.

When you click the month of the calendar, a complete year is shown. When you click the year on top, an epoch is visible (see Figure 29-6). This makes it easy to select dates far in the future.

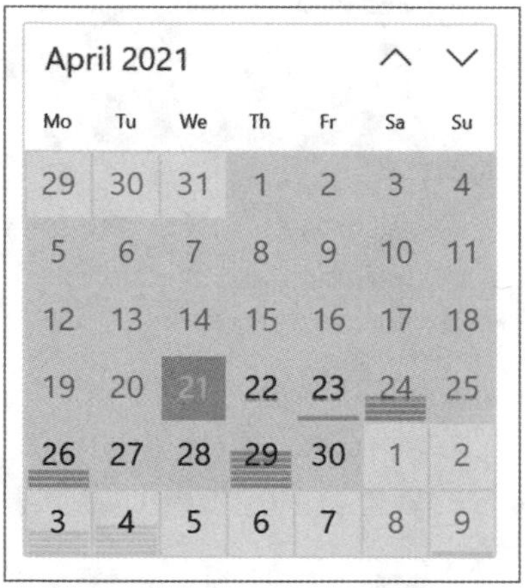

FIGURE 29-5

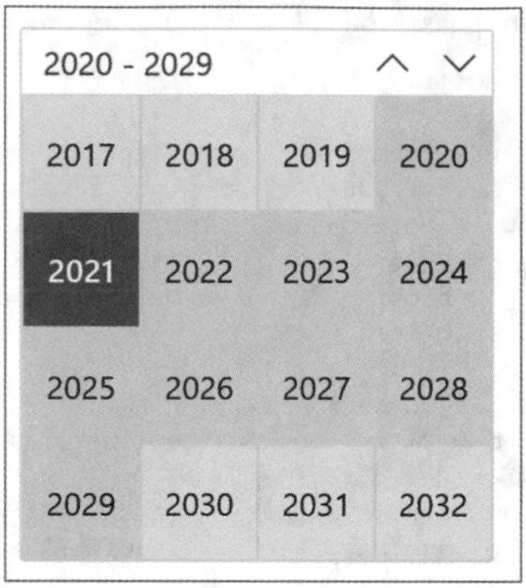

FIGURE 29-6

When using a `CalendarDatePicker`, you don't have as many features as with the `CalendarView`, but it doesn't occupy the space of the screen unless the user opens it to select a date. A `CalendarDatePicker` defines the `DateChanged` event; you can select only a single day (code file `ControlsSamples/Views/DateSelectionPage.xaml`):

```
<CalendarDatePicker x:Name="CalendarDatePicker1" Grid.Row="0" Grid.Column="1"
  DateChanged="OnDateChanged" Margin="12" />
```

With the `OnDateChanged` event handler, the `CalendarDatePickerDateChangedEventArgs` object are received that contain a `NewDate` property (code file `DateSelectionSample/MainPage.xaml.cs`):

```
private async void OnDateChanged(CalendarDatePicker sender,
  CalendarDatePickerDateChangedEventArgs args)
{
  await new MessageDialog($"date changed to {args.NewDate}").ShowAsync();
}
```

The XAML code for the `DatePicker` is similar. It doesn't just show a calendar to select the date but has a completely different view (code file `ControlsSamples/Views/DateSelectionPage.xaml`):

```
<DatePicker DateChanged="OnDateChanged1" x:Name="DatePicker1" Grid.Row="1"
  Margin="12" />
```

The event handler for the `DatePicker` receives object and `DatePickerValueChangedEventArgs` arguments (code file `ControlsSamples/Views/DateSelectionPage.xaml`):

```
private async void OnDateChanged1(object sender,
  DatePickerValueChangedEventArgs e)
```

```
    {
        await new MessageDialog($"date changed to {e.NewDate}").ShowAsync();
    }
```

Figure 29-7 shows the `DatePicker` when it's open. If the user knows the date without checking a calendar (for example, a birthday), it is a lot faster than scrolling through the years, the months, and the days.

17	December	2017
18	January	2018
19	February	2019
20	March	2020
21	April	2021
22	May	2022
23	June	2023
24	July	2024
25	August	2025
✓		✕

FIGURE 29-7

The last option for selecting a date is a flyout. Flyouts can be used with other controls. Here, a `Button` control is used, and the `Flyout` property of the button defines to use the `DatePickerFlyout`:

```
<Button Content="Select a Date" Grid.Row="1" Grid.Column="1" Margin="12">
    <Button.Flyout>
        <DatePickerFlyout x:Name="DatePickerFlyout1" DatePicked="OnDatePicked" />
    </Button.Flyout>
</Button>
```

Range Controls

Range controls such as `ScrollBar`, `ProgressBar`, and `Slider` derive from the common class `RangeBase`, as described in the following table.

CONTROL	DESCRIPTION
ScrollBar	This control contains a `Thumb` that enables the user to select a value. A scrollbar can be used, for example, if a document doesn't fit on the screen. Some controls contain scrollbars that are displayed if the content is too big.

continues

(continued)

CONTROL	DESCRIPTION
ProgressBar	This control indicates the progress of a lengthy operation.
Slider	This control enables users to select a range of values by moving a thumb.

Progress Bar

The sample application shows two `ProgressBar` controls. The second control has the `IsIndeterminate` property set to `True`. In case you don't know how long an activity takes, it's a good idea to use this property. If you think you know how long the action takes, you can set the current status value in the `ProgressBar` without setting the `IsIndeterminate` mode; the default is `False` (code file `ControlsSamples/Views/RangeControlsPage.xaml`):

```
<ProgressBar x:Name="progressBar1" Grid.Row="0" Margin="12" />
<ProgressBar IsIndeterminate="True" Grid.Row="1" Margin="12" />
```

On loading of the page, the `ShowProgress` method is invoked. Here, the current value of the first `ProgressBar` is set using a `DispatcherTimer`. The `DispatcherTimer` is configured to fire every second, and every second the `Value` property of the `ProgressBar` gets incremented (code file `ControlsSamples/Views/RangeControlsPage.xaml.cs`):

```
private void ShowProgress()
{
  DispatcherTimer timer = new();
  timer.Interval = TimeSpan.FromSeconds(1);
  int i = 0;
  timer.Tick += (sender, e) => progressBar1.Value = i++ % 100;
  timer.Start();
}
```

> **NOTE** *The* `DispatcherTimer` *class is explained in Chapter 17, "Parallel Programming."*

When you run the application, you can see two active `ProgressBar` controls. With the first one, you can see the status with an increasing value, whereas the second one shows progress with a bar that continuously moves (see Figure 29-8).

FIGURE 29-8

Slider

With the `Slider` control, you can specify `Minimum` and `Maximum` values and use the `Value` property to assign the current value. The code sample uses a `TextBox` to display the current value of the slider (code file `ControlsSamples/Views/RangeControlsPage.xaml`):

```
<Slider x:Name="slider" Minimum="10" Maximum="140" Value="60"
  Grid.Row="2" Margin="12" />
<TextBox Header="Slider Value" IsReadOnly="True"
  Text="{x:Bind slider.Value, Mode=OneWay}" Grid.Row="3" Margin="12" />
```

In Figure 29-9, you can see the `Slider` and the `TextBox`; notice how they correlate as the `TextBox` shows the actual value of the `Slider`.

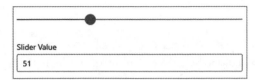

FIGURE 29-9

Content Controls

A `ContentControl` has a `Content` property and allows adding any single piece of content. Multiple content objects are not allowed as a direct child in the `Content` property, but you can add, for example, a `StackPanel`, which can have multiple controls as children.

CONTROL	DESCRIPTION
ScrollViewer	`ScrollViewer` is a `ContentControl` that can contain a single item and offers horizontal and vertical scrollbars. You can also use `ScrollViewer` with attached properties as has been shown previously with the `ParallaxViewSample`.
Frame	The `Frame` control is used for navigation between pages. This control is discussed later in the section "Implementing Navigation."
SelectorItem ComboBoxItem FlipViewItem GridViewItem ListBoxItem ListViewItem GroupItemPivotItem	These controls are `ContentControl` objects that belong as items to an `ItemsControl`. For example, the `ComboBox` control contains `ComboBoxItem` objects, the `ListBox` control contains `ListBoxItem` objects, and the `Pivot` control contains `PivotItem` objects. `GroupItem` objects are typically not used directly; they're used when you use an `ItemsControl`-derived control with a grouping configuration.
ToolTip	The `ToolTip` gives a pop-up window when the user hovers over a control to show a tooltip. Tooltips can be configured using the `ToolTipService.ToolTip` attached property. The tooltip can be more than text; it is a `ContentControl`.
TeachingTip	The `TeachingTip` is meant to give the user tips on how to do the work more effectively. By analyzing telemetry information and using machine learning, the application can learn what the users are doing and which features they might miss and should know about. This control supports rich content.
CommandBar	With the `CommandBar`, you can arrange `AppBarButton` controls and controls that belong to the command elements (such as `AppBarSeparator`). The `CommandBar` offers some layout features for these controls. With Windows 8, the `AppBar` was used instead of the `CommandBar`—that's why the buttons have these names. Now the `CommandBar` derives from the `AppBar`. However, you can also use other controls to lay out your commands if the layout from the `CommandBar` doesn't fit your requirements.

continues

(continued)

CONTROL	DESCRIPTION
ContentDialog	Using the `ContentDialog` opens a dialog box. You can customize this control with any XAML controls you need for your dialog.
SwipeControl	The `SwipeControl` allows contextual commands through touch interactions—for example, to open specific actions for items as the user swipes to the left or to the right.

> **NOTE** *See the next section, which includes a sample to fill the content of a* `ContentControl`—*with a* `Button`, *which itself is a* `ContentControl`.

Buttons

Button classes form a hierarchy. The `ButtonBase` class derives from `ContentControl`; thus, a button has a `Content` property and can contain any single content. The `ButtonBase` class also defines a `Command` property; thus, all buttons can have a command associated. The following table compares the different buttons.

CONTROL	DESCRIPTION
Button	The `Button` class is the most commonly used button. This class derives from `ButtonBase` (as all the other buttons do as well). `ButtonBase` is the base class of all buttons.
DropDownButton	The `DropDownButton` shows a chevron to indicate that a menu can be opened. With the content of the button, a `MenuFlyout` is usually used to display menus.
HyperlinkButton	The `HyperlinkButton` appears as a link. You can open web pages in the browser, open other apps, or navigate to other pages.
RepeatButton	The `RepeatButton` is a button where the `Click` event continuously fires while the user presses the button. With the normal `Button`, the `Click` event fires only once.
AppBarButton	The `AppBarButton` is used to activate commands in the app. You can add this button to the `CommandBar` and use an icon and a label to display information for the user.
AppBarToggleButton CheckBox RadioButton	`CheckBox`, `RadioButton`, and `AppBarToggleButton` derive from the base class `ToggleButton`. A `ToggleButton` can have three states: `Checked`, `Unchecked`, and `Indeterminate` represented by `bool?`. The `AppBarToggleButton` is a toggle button for the `CommandBar`.

Replacing the Content of the Button

A button is a `ContentControl` and can have any content. The following sample adds a `Grid` control to the button that contains an `Ellipse` and a `TextBlock`. The button also defines a `Click` event, to demonstrate it looks different, but it acts the same (code file `ControlsSample/Views/ButtonsPage.xaml`):

```
<Button Margin="12" Click="OnButtonClick">
  <Grid>
    <Ellipse Width="200" Height="90" Fill="red" />
    <TextBlock HorizontalAlignment="Center" VerticalAlignment="Center"
      Text="Click Me!" FontSize="24" />
  </Grid>
</Button>
```

In Figure 29-10, you can see the new look of the button. The `Content` property replaces the foreground, but the button still has the default background.

FIGURE 29-10

> **NOTE** *To replace the complete look of the button, including the background, and to make the button something other than a rectangle, you need to create a* ControlTemplate *for the button. How you do this is explained in Chapter 31.*

Linking with the HyperlinkButton

With the `HyperlinkButton` control, you can easily activate other apps. You can set the `NavigateUri` property to a URL, and clicking the button opens the default browser to open the web page.

```
<HyperlinkButton NavigateUri="https://csharp.christiannagel.com"
  Content="C# Infos" Grid.Column="1"
  Style="{StaticResource TextBlockButtonStyle}" FontSize="24" />
```

The `HyperlinkButton` by default looks like a link in the browser. With the `HyperlinkButton`, you can either set the `NavigateUri` or define a `Click` event, but you can't do both. As an action to a `Click` event, you can, for example, programmatically navigate to another page. Navigation is explained later in the section "Implementing Navigation."

You not only can assign `http://` or `https://` values to the `NavigateUri` property but also use `ms-appx://` to activate other apps.

Items Controls

Contrary to a `ContentControl`, an `ItemsControl` can contain a list of items. With an `ItemsControl`, you can either define items with the `Items` property or fill it using data binding and the `ItemsSource` property. You cannot use both. The following table describes the different Items controls.

CONTROL	DESCRIPTION
ItemsControl	The `ItemsControl` is the base class for all other items controls, and you can also use it directly to display a list of items.
Pivot	The `Pivot` control is a control for creating a tab-like behavior for the application. Read the section "Implementing Navigation" for more information on this control.
AutoSuggestBox	The `AutoSuggestBox` replaces the previous `SearchBox`. With the `AutoSuggestBox`, the user can enter text, and the control offers auto-completion.

continues

(continued)

CONTROL	DESCRIPTION
ListBox ComboBox FlipView	ListBox, ComboBox, and FlipView are three item controls that derive from the base class Selector. Selector derives from ItemsControl and adds the SelectedItem and SelectedValue properties to make it possible to select an item from the collection. The ListBox shows a list the user can select from. The ComboBox combines a TextBox and a drop-down list to allow the selection of a list while using less screen space. The FlipView control allows using touch interaction to flip through a list of items while only one item is shown.
ListView GridView	ListView and GridView derive from the base class ListViewBase, which derives from Selector—so these are the most powerful selectors. ListViewBase offers additional dragging and dropping of items and reordering of items, adds a header and a footer, and allows selecting multiple items. The ListView displays items vertically (but you can also create a template to have the list horizontally). The GridView displays items with rows and columns.

Flyouts

Flyouts are used to open a window above other UI elements—for example, a context menu. All flyouts derive from the base class FlyoutBase. The FlyoutBase class defines a Placement property that allows defining where the flyout should be positioned. It can be centered in the screen or positioned around the target element. The following table describes the flyouts.

CONTROL	DESCRIPTION
MenuFlyout	The MenuFlyout control is used to display a list of menu items.
Flyout	The Flyout control can contain one item that you can customize with XAML elements.
CommandBarFlyout	CommandBarFlyout is a specialized flyout that defines the layout for controls within app bars.

A different category of flyouts are flyouts of the MenuBar control. MenuFlyoutItem, MenuFlyoutSubItem, and MenuFlyoutSeparator derive from the base class MenuFlyoutItemBase.

WORKING WITH DATA BINDING

Data binding is an extremely important concept with XAML-based apps. Data binding gets data from .NET objects to the UI or the other way around. Simple objects can be bound to UI elements, a list of objects, and XAML elements. With data binding, the target can be any dependency property of a XAML element, and every property of a CLR object can be the source. Because XAML elements also offer .NET properties, every XAML element can be the source as well. Figure 29-11 shows the connection between the source and the target. The binding defines the connection.

Binding supports several binding modes between the target and source. With *one-way* binding, the source information goes to the target, but if the user changes information in the user interface, the source is not updated. For updates to the source, *two-way* binding is required.

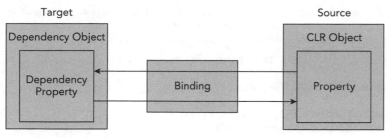

FIGURE 29-11

The following table shows the binding modes and their requirements:

BINDING MODE	DESCRIPTION
One-time	Binding goes from the source to the target and occurs only once when the application is started or the data context changes. Here, you get a snapshot of the data.
One-way	Binding goes from the source to the target. This is useful for read-only data because it is not possible to change the data from the user interface. To get updates to the user interface, the source must implement the interface INotifyPropertyChanged.
Two-way	The user can make changes to the data from the UI. Binding occurs in both directions— from the source to the target and from the target to the source. The source needs to implement read/write properties so that changes can be updated from the UI to the source.

> **NOTE** *WinUI supports two binding types: reflection-based binding using the* Binding *markup extension and compiled binding using the* x:Bind *markup extension. Be aware that the defaults with the binding modes differ between these binding types, so it's best to always specify the binding mode. This section has the main focus on the compiled binding.*

Data binding involves many facets besides the binding modes. This section provides binding to simple .NET objects and binding to lists. Using change notifications, the UI is updated with changes in the bound objects. This section also describes dynamically selecting data templates.

Let's start with the DataBindingSamples sample application. The app shows a list of books and allows the user to select a book to see the book details.

Change Notification with INotifyPropertyChanged

First, the model is created. To get updates to the user interface when property values change, the interface INotifyPropertyChanged needs to be implemented. For reusing this implementation, the ObservableObject class is created that implements this interface. The interface defines the PropertyChanged event handler. This event is fired from the method OnPropertyChanged. The method SetProperty is used to change a property value and to fire the PropertyChanged event. If the value to be set is not different from the current value, no event is fired, and the method just returns false. With different values, the property is set to the new value, and the PropertyChanged event is fired. This method makes use of the caller information feature from C# using the attribute `CallerMemberName`. When you define the parameter `propertyName` as an optional parameter with this attribute, the C# compiler passes the name of the property with this parameter, so it's not necessary to add a hard-coded string to the code (code file `DataBindingSamples/Models/ObservableObject.cs`):

```csharp
public abstract class ObservableObject : INotifyPropertyChanged
{
  public event PropertyChangedEventHandler? PropertyChanged;

  public virtual bool SetProperty<T>(ref T item, T value,
    [CallerMemberName] string? propertyName = null)
  {
    if (EqualityComparer<T>.Default.Equals(item, value)) return false;
    item = value;
    OnPropertyChanged(propertyName);
    return true;
  }

  protected virtual void OnPropertyChanged(string propertyName) =>
    PropertyChanged?.Invoke(this, new PropertyChangedEventArgs(propertyName));
}
```

> **NOTE** *Caller information is covered in Chapter 10, "Errors and Exceptions." The implementation of* `INotifyPropertyChanged` *is covered in more detail in Chapter 30, "Patterns with XAML Apps."*

The `Book` class derives from the base class `ObservableObject` and implements the properties `BookId`, `Title`, `Publisher`, and `Authors`. The `BookId` property is read-only; `Title` and `Publisher` make use of the change notification implementation from the base class; and the `Authors` property is a read-only property to return a list of authors (code file `DataBindingSamples/Models/Book.cs`):

```csharp
public class Book : ObservableObject
{
  public Book(int id, string title, string publisher, params string[] authors)
  {
    BookId = id;
    _title = title;
    _publisher = publisher;
    Authors = authors;
  }

  public int BookId { get; }

  private string _title;
  public string Title
  {
    get => _title;
    set => SetProperty(ref _title, value);
  }

  private string __publisher;
  public string Publisher
  {
```

```
      get => _publisher;
      set => SetProperty(ref _publisher, value);
    }

    public IEnumerable<string> Authors { get; }

    public override string ToString() => Title;
}
```

Creating a List of Books

The method GetSampleBooks returns a list of books that should be shown using the constructor of the Book class (code file DataBindingSamples/Services/SampleBooksService.cs):

```
public class SampleBooksService
{
  private List<Book> _books = new()
  {
    new(1, "Professional C# and .NET - 2021 Edition", "Wrox Press", "Christian Nagel"),
    new(2, "Professional C# 7 and .NET Core 2", "Wrox Press", "Christian Nagel"),
    new(3, "Professional C# 6 and .NET Core 1.0", "Wrox Press", "Christian Nagel"),
    new(4, "Professional C# 5.0 and .NET 4.5.1", "Wrox Press", "Christian Nagel",
      "Jay Glynn", "Morgan Skinner"),
    new(5, "Enterprise Services with the .NET Framework", "AWL", "Christian Nagel")
  };
  public IEnumerable<Book> GetSampleBooks() => _books;
}
```

Now, the BooksService class offers the methods RefreshBooks, GetBook, and AddBook, and the property Books. This property returns an ObservableCollection<Book> object. ObservableCollection is a generic class offering change notification by implementing the interface INotifyCollectionChanged (code file DataBindingSamples/Services/BooksService.cs):

```
public class BooksService
{
  private ObservableCollection<Book> _books = new();

  public void RefreshBooks()
  {
    _books.Clear();
    SampleBooksService sampleBooksService = new();
    var books = sampleBooksService.GetSampleBooks();
    foreach (var book in books)
    {
      _books.Add(book);
    }
  }

  public Book? GetBook(int bookId) =>
    _books.SingleOrDefault(b => b.BookId == bookId);

  public void AddBook(Book book) => _books.Add(book);

  public ObservableCollection<Book> Books => _books;
}
```

List Binding

Now you're ready to display a list of books. Any `ItemsSource`-derived control can be used to assign the `ItemsSource` property to binding to a list. The following code snippet uses the `ListView` control to bind the `ItemsSource` to the `Books` property. With the markup extension `x:Bind`, this first name specified is the source for the binding. The `Mode` parameter defines the binding mode. With `OneWay`, WinUI makes use of change notification to update the user interface when the source changes:

```
<ListView ItemsSource="{x:Bind Books, Mode=OneWay}" />
```

With the code-behind file, the `Books` property is specified to reference the `Books` property of the `BooksService` (code file `DataBindingSamples/MainPage.xaml.cs`):

```
public sealed partial class MainWindow : Window
{
  private BooksService _booksService = new();
  public MainPage()
  {
    this.InitializeComponent();
  }

  public ObservableCollection<Book> Books => _booksService.Books;
  //...
}
```

Binding Events to Methods

Without invoking the `RefreshBooks` method from the `BooksService`, the list stays empty. With the resources, two `XamlUICommand`s are defined that specify labels, icons, and keys. The `ExecuteRequested` properties binds to the methods `RefreshBooks` and `AddBooks` that are defined with the code-behind file (code file `DataBindingSamples/MainWindow.xaml`):

```
<Grid.Resources>
  <XamlUICommand x:Name="RefreshBooksCommand" Label="Refresh" Description="Refresh books"
    ExecuteRequested="{x:Bind RefreshBooks}">
    <XamlUICommand.IconSource>
      <SymbolIconSource Symbol="List" />
    </XamlUICommand.IconSource>
    <XamlUICommand.KeyboardAccelerators>
      <KeyboardAccelerator Key="R" Modifiers="Control" />
    </XamlUICommand.KeyboardAccelerators>
  </XamlUICommand>
  <XamlUICommand x:Name="AddBookCommand" Label="Add Book" Description="Add a book"
    ExecuteRequested="{x:Bind AddBook}">
    <XamlUICommand.IconSource>
      <SymbolIconSource Symbol="Add" />
    </XamlUICommand.IconSource>
    <XamlUICommand.KeyboardAccelerators>
      <KeyboardAccelerator Key="A" Modifiers="Control" />
    </XamlUICommand.KeyboardAccelerators>
  </XamlUICommand>
  <!-- ... -->
</Grid.Resources>
```

The `StandardUICommand` class defines a predefined set of commands, such as `Cut`, `Copy`, `Paste`, `Open` `Close`, `Play`, and a few others. With these commands you don't need to declare your own with `XamlUICommand`.

For the user interface, a `CommandBar` is created that lists two `AppBarButton` controls. With the `AppBarButton` controls, the `Command` property references commands using the `StaticResource` markup extension (code file `DataBindingSamples/MainWindow.xaml`):

```
<CommandBar Grid.Row="0" Grid.Column="0" Grid.ColumnSpan="2">
  <AppBarButton Command="{StaticResource RefreshBooksCommand}"/>
  <AppBarButton Command="{StaticResource AddBookCommand}"/>
</CommandBar>
```

The `AppBarButton` control defines `Label` and `Icon` properties and a `Click` event handler. As the `Command` property is specified, the values don't need to be specified.

Binding events to methods is possible if the method either has no arguments or has arguments as specified by the delegate type of the event. With the following code snippet, the methods `OnRefreshBooks` and `OnAddBook` are declared to return `void` without arguments (code file `DataBindingSamples/MainWindow.xaml.cs`):

```
public void RefreshBooks() => _booksService.RefreshBooks();

public void AddBook() =>
  _booksService.AddBook(new Book(GetNextBookId(),
    $"Professional C# and .NET - {GetNextYear()} Edition", "Wrox Press"));

private int GetNextBookId() => Books.Select(b => b.BookId).Max() + 1;
private int _year = 2021;
private int GetNextYear() => _year += 3;
```

> **NOTE** *Binding to methods is possible only with the* `x:Bind` *markup extension, not with the traditional* `Binding` *markup extension.*

Using Data Templates and the Data Template Selector

For creating a different look of the items, you can create a `DataTemplate`. The `DataTemplate` can be referenced using the key that is specified with the `x:Key` attribute. When you use the `x:DataType` attribute, you can use compiled binding within the data template. Compiled binding requires the type it binds to at compile time. To bind to the `Title` property, the type is defined with the `Book` class (code file `DataBindingSamples/MainWindow.xaml`):

```
<Page.Resources>
  <!-- ... -->
  <DataTemplate x:DataType="models:Book" x:Key="WroxTemplate">
    <Border Background="Red" Margin="4" Padding="4" BorderThickness="2"
      BorderBrush="DarkRed">
      <TextBlock Text="{x:Bind Title, Mode=OneWay}" Foreground="White"
        Width="300" />
    </Border>
  </DataTemplate>
  <!-- ... -->
</Page.Resources>
```

Data templates that should be used for items in an `ItemsControl` can be referenced using the `ItemTemplate` property of an `ItemsControl`. Instead of just using one `DataTemplate` for all the items in the list, now a `DataTemplateSelector` will be used to choose the `DataTemplate` dynamically based on the name of the publisher.

The `BookDataTemplateSelector` derives from the base class `DataTemplateSelector`. A data template selector needs to override the method `SelectTemplateCore` and return the selected `DataTemplate`. With the implementation of the `BookTemplateSelector`, two properties are specified: the `WroxTemplate` and the `DefaultTemplate`. In the `SelectTemplateCore` method, `Book` objects are received. You can use pattern matching using properties with the `switch` expression so that if the publisher is Wrox Press, the `WroxTemplate` is returned. In other cases, the `DefaultTemplate` is returned. You can extend the `switch` expression with more publishers (code file `DataBindingSamples/Utilities/BookTemplateSelector.cs`):

```
public class BookTemplateSelector : DataTemplateSelector
{
    public DataTemplate? WroxTemplate { get; set; }
    public DataTemplate? DefaultTemplate { get; set; }

    protected override DataTemplate? SelectTemplateCore(object item) =>
        item switch
        {
            Book { Publisher: "Wrox Press"} => WroxTemplate,
            Book => DefaultTemplate,
            _ => null
        };
}
```

Next, the data template selector needs to be instantiated and initialized. You do this in the XAML code. Here, the properties `WroxTemplate` and `DefaultTemplate` are assigned to reference the previously created `DataTemplate` templates (code file `DataBindingSamples/MainWindow.xaml`):

```
<Page.Resources>
  <!-- ... -->
  <DataTemplate x:DataType="models:Book" x:Key="WroxTemplate">
    <Border Background="Red" Margin="4" Padding="4" BorderThickness="2"
      BorderBrush="DarkRed">
      <TextBlock Text="{x:Bind Title, Mode=OneWay}" Foreground="White"
        Width="300" />
    </Border>
  </DataTemplate>
  <DataTemplate x:DataType="models:Book" x:Key="DefaultTemplate">
    <Border Background="LightBlue" Margin="4" Padding="4" BorderThickness="2"
      BorderBrush="DarkBlue">
      <TextBlock Text="{x:Bind Title, Mode=OneWay}" Foreground="Black"
        Width="300" />
    </Border>
  </DataTemplate>
  <utils:BookTemplateSelector x:Key="BookTemplateSelector"
    WroxTemplate="{StaticResource WroxTemplate}"
    DefaultTemplate="{StaticResource DefaultTemplate}" />
</Page.Resources>
```

To use the `BookTemplateSelector` with the items in the `ListView`, the `ItemTemplateSelector` property references the template using the key and the `StaticResource` markup extension:

```
<ListView ItemsSource="{x:Bind Books, Mode=OneWay}"
  ItemTemplateSelector="{StaticResource BookTemplateSelector}"
  Grid.Row="1" />
```

Show Lists and Details

To define the user interface with a list and a detail view, you use the `TwoPaneView` control. The `TwoPaneView` defines `Pane1` and `Pane2` properties. The content of `Pane1` is the `ListView`, and the content of `Pane2` is the user control that's defined next. Depending on the available size, `TwoPaneView` defines a wide and tall configuration.

As specified, with the wide configuration, the panes will be shown left-right; with a tall configuration, they are shown top-bottom (code file `DataBindingSamples/MainWindow.xaml`):

```xml
<TwoPaneView WideModeConfiguration="LeftRight" TallModeConfiguration="TopBottom"
  Grid.Row="1">
  <TwoPaneView.Pane1>
    <!-- ListView definition -->
  </TwoPaneView.Pane1>
  <TwoPaneView.Pane2>
    <views:BookUserControl x:Name="CurrentBook" Margin="4" />
  </TwoPaneView.Pane2>
</TwoPaneView>
```

Binding Simple Objects

Instead of just binding a list, the single book should be displayed in the second pane of the `TwoViewPane`. Compiled binding is used to bind to the `BookId`, `Title`, and `Publisher` properties of the `Book` property (code file `DataBindingSamples/Views/BookUserControl.xaml`):

```xml
<UserControl
    x:Class="DataBindingSamples.Views.BookUserControl"
    xmlns="http://schemas.microsoft.com/winfx/2006/xaml/presentation"
    xmlns:x="http://schemas.microsoft.com/winfx/2006/xaml"
    xmlns:local="using:DataBindingSamples.Views"
    xmlns:conv="using:DataBindingSamples.Converters"
    xmlns:d="http://schemas.microsoft.com/expression/blend/2008"
    xmlns:mc="http://schemas.openxmlformats.org/markup-compatibility/2006"
    mc:Ignorable="d"
    d:DesignHeight="300"
    d:DesignWidth="400">
    <!-- ... -->
    <StackPanel Orientation="Vertical" Grid.Row="1">
      <TextBox Header="BookId" IsReadOnly="True"
        Text="{x:Bind Book.BookId, Mode=OneWay}" />
      <TextBox Header="Title" Text="{x:Bind Book.Title, Mode=TwoWay}" />
      <TextBox Header="Publisher"
        Text="{x:Bind Book.Publisher, Mode=TwoWay}" />
      <!-- ... -->
    </StackPanel>
  </Grid>
</UserControl>
```

In the code-behind file, the `Book` property is defined as a dependency property. Change notification is needed for making updates when the values change; that's why a dependency property is used. It would also be possible to implement `INotifyPropertyChanged`, but because dependency properties are already available from the base class `DependencyObject`, dependency properties can be used easily (code file `DataBindingSamples/Views/BookUserControl.xaml.cs`):

```csharp
public Book Book
{
  get => (Book)GetValue(BookProperty);
  set => SetValue(BookProperty, value);
}

public static readonly DependencyProperty BookProperty =
  DependencyProperty.Register("Book", typeof(Book), typeof(BookUserControl),
    new PropertyMetadata(null));
```

The previous section showed the user control being referenced in the second pane of the `TwoViewPane`. What's missing is the binding in the `ListView` to show the currently selected item in the user control. As shown in the following code snippet, with the `ListView`, the `SelectedItem` property binds to the `Book` property of the user control. This time, `TwoWay` binding is needed to update the `UserControl` from the `ListView` (code file `DataBindingSamples/MainWindow.xaml`):

```
<ListView x:Name="BooksList" ItemsSource="{x:Bind Books, Mode=OneWay}"
    ItemTemplateSelector="{StaticResource BookTemplateSelector}"
    SelectedItem="{x:Bind CurrentBook.Book, Mode=TwoWay}" />
```

> **NOTE** *It would be also possible to create the binding the other way around—to bind the* `BookUserControl` *to the* `ListView`*. This way,* `OneWay` *binding would be enough—to take the updated values from the* `ListView` *to the* `BookUserControl`*. However, here the XAML compiler complains because it can't assign an* `object` *(coming from the* `ListView`*) to the strongly typed* `Book` *property of the* `BookUserControl`*. You could resolve this by creating a value converter as discussed next.*

Value Conversion

So far, the authors haven't been displayed in the user control. The reason is that the `Authors` property is a list. You can define an `ItemsControl` in the user control to display the `Authors` property. However, to display a simple comma-separated list of authors, it would be okay to use the `TextBlock`. You just need a converter to convert `IEnumerable<string>`—the type of the `Authors` property to a `string`.

A value converter is an implementation of the `IValueConverter` interface. This interface defines the methods `Convert` and `ConvertBack`. With two-way binding, both methods need to be implemented. Using one-way binding, the `Convert` method is enough. The class `CollectionToStringConverter` implements the `Convert` method by using the `string.Join` method to create a single string. A value converter also receives an object `parameter` that you can specify when using the value converter. Here, this parameter is used as a string separator (code file `DataBindingSamples/Converters/CollectionToStringConverter.cs`):

```
public class CollectionToStringConverter : IValueConverter
{
  public object Convert(object value, Type targetType, object parameter,
    string language)
  {
    IEnumerable<string> names = (IEnumerable<string>)value;
    return string.Join(parameter?.ToString() ?? ", ", names);
  }

  public object ConvertBack(object value, Type targetType, object parameter,
    string language)
  {
    throw new NotImplementedException();
  }
}
```

With the user control, the `CollectionToStringConverter` is instantiated in the resources section (code file `DataBindingSamples/Views/BookUserControl.xaml`):

```
<UserControl.Resources>
  <conv:CollectionToStringConverter x:Key="CollectionToStringConverter" />
</UserControl.Resources>
```

The converter can now be referenced from within the `x:Bind` markup extension using the `Converter` property. The `ConverterParameter` property specifies the string separator that is used within the `string.Join` method earlier (code file `DataBindingSamples/Views/BookUserControl.xaml`):

```
<TextBox Header="Authors" IsReadOnly="True"
  Text="{x:Bind Book.Authors, Mode=OneWay,
    Converter={StaticResource CollectionToStringConverter},
    ConverterParameter='; '}" />
```

When you run the app, the authors are now displayed, as shown in Figure 29-12.

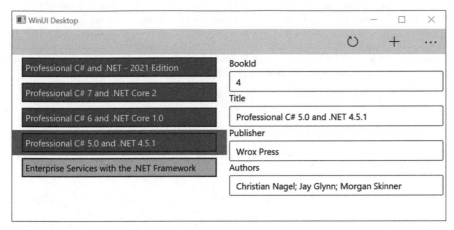

FIGURE 29-12

IMPLEMENTING NAVIGATION

If your application is composed of multiple pages, you need the ability to navigate between these pages. There are different application structures to navigate, such as using a hamburger button (see `https://blog.placeit.net/history-of-the-hamburger-icon/` for the origins and uses of this icon with three horizontal bars) to navigate to different root pages or to use different tabs and replace tab items.

If you need to provide a way for the user to navigate, the heart of the navigation is the `Frame` class. The `Frame` class enables the user to navigate to specific pages using the `Navigate` method and optionally pass parameters. The `Frame` class keeps a stack of the pages to which the user has navigated, which makes it possible to go back, go forward, limit the number of pages in the stack, and more.

In addition, you have different options for the main navigation of your application. In this section, you create a Windows application and use different pages to show the features of the `Hub`, `TabView`, and `NavigationView` controls. The sample application uses a `CommandBar` with `AppBarButton` controls and a `Frame`. In the code-behind file, the `Navigate` method of the `Frame` class is invoked. The parameter of this method requires the type of the page to navigate to (code file `NavigationControls/MainWindow.xaml.cs`):

```
private void OnNavigate(XamlUICommand sender, ExecuteRequestedEventArgs args)
{
  Type pageType = args.Parameter switch
  {
    "Hub" => typeof(HubPage),
    "Tab" => typeof(TabViewPage),
    "Navigation" => typeof(NavigationViewPage),
```

```
      _ => throw new InvalidOperationException()
    };

    MainFrame.Navigate(pageType);
}
```

The `Frame` class keeps a stack of pages that have been visited. The `GoBack` method makes it possible to navigate back within this stack (if the `CanGoBack` property returns true), and the `GoForward` method enables you to go forward one page after a back navigation. The `Frame` class also offers several events for navigation, such as `Navigating`, `Navigated`, `NavigationFailed`, and `NavigationStopped`.

The `Page` class defines methods that can be used on navigation. The method `OnNavigatedTo` is invoked when the page is navigated to. Within this page you can read how the navigation was done (`NavigationMode` property). You can also access parameters that are passed with the navigation. The method `OnNavigatingFrom` is the first method that is invoked when you navigate away from the page. Here, the navigation can be cancelled. The method `OnNavigatedFrom` is finally invoked when you navigate away from this page. Here, you should do some cleanup of resources that have been allocated with the `OnNavigatedTo` method.

Let's get into the functionality of the `Hub`, `TabView`, and `NavigationView`.

Hub

You can also allow the user to navigate between content within a single page using the `Hub` control. An example of when you might use this is if you want to show an image as an entry point (also known as a *hero* image) for the app and more information is shown as the user scrolls.

With the `Hub` control, you can define multiple sections. Each section has a header and content. You can also make the header clickable—for example, to navigate to a detail page. The following code sample defines a `Hub` control where you can click the headers of sections 2 and 3. When you click the section header, the method assigned with the `SectionHeaderClick` event of the `Hub` control is invoked. Each section consists of a header and some content. The content of the section is defined by a `DataTemplate` (code file `NavigationControls/Views/HubPage.xaml`):

```xml
<Hub SectionHeaderClick="{x:Bind OnHeaderClick}">
  <Hub.Header>
    <StackPanel Orientation="Horizontal">
      <TextBlock>Hub Header</TextBlock>
      <TextBlock Text="{x:Bind Info, Mode=TwoWay}" />
    </StackPanel>
  </Hub.Header>
  <HubSection Width="400" Background="LightBlue" Tag="Section 1">
    <HubSection.Header>
      <TextBlock>Section 1 Header</TextBlock>
    </HubSection.Header>
    <DataTemplate>
      <TextBlock>Section 1</TextBlock>
    </DataTemplate>
  </HubSection>
  <HubSection Width="300" Background="LightGreen" IsHeaderInteractive="True"
    Tag="Section 2">
    <HubSection.Header>
      <TextBlock>Section 2 Header</TextBlock>
    </HubSection.Header>
    <DataTemplate>
      <TextBlock>Section 2</TextBlock>
    </DataTemplate>
  </HubSection>
```

```
    <HubSection Width="300" Background="LightGoldenrodYellow"
      IsHeaderInteractive="True" Tag="Section 3">
      <HubSection.Header>
        <TextBlock>Section 3 Header</TextBlock>
      </HubSection.Header>
      <DataTemplate>
        <TextBlock>Section 3</TextBlock>
      </DataTemplate>
    </HubSection>
  </Hub>
```

When you click the header section, the `Info` dependency property is assigned the value of the `Tag` property. The `Info` property in turn is bound within the header of the `Hub` control (code file `NavigationControls/Views/HubPage.xaml.cs`):

```
public void OnHeaderClick(object sender, HubSectionHeaderClickEventArgs e)
{
  Info = e.Section.Tag as string;
}

public string Info
{
  get => (string)GetValue(InfoProperty);
  set => SetValue(InfoProperty, value);
}

public static readonly DependencyProperty InfoProperty =
  DependencyProperty.Register("Info", typeof(string), typeof(HubPage),
    new PropertyMetadata(string.Empty));
```

When you run the app, you can see multiple hub sections (see Figure 29-13) with a See More link in sections 2 and 3 because with these sections' `IsHeaderInteractive` is set to `true`. Of course, you can create a custom header template to have a different look for the header.

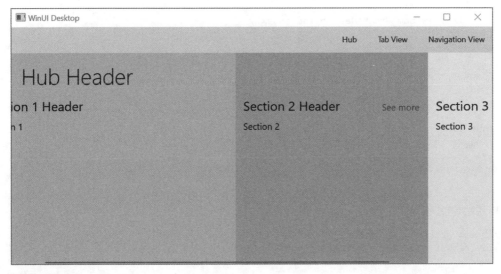

FIGURE 29-13

TabView

The `TabView` control enables you to show multiple tabs, like Visual Studio does for open files. You can define the tabs statically or dynamically. With the next sample application, tabs will be added dynamically from the C# code, and the XAML file just defines a `TabView` without contained tabs. The methods `OnTabAdd` and `OnTabClose` are invoked on adding and closing tables by setting the `AddTabButtonClick` and `TabCloseRequested` events (code file `NavigationControls/Views/TabViewPage.xaml`):

```
<TabView x:Name="tabView" AddTabButtonClick="OnAddTab" TabCloseRequested="OnTabClose" />
```

With the code-behind, on loading of the `TabViewPage`, three new tabs are created by invoking the `CreateNewTab` method. `CreateNewTab` creates a new `TabViewItem`, a new `Frame` object that's specified as the content of the `TabViewItem`, and it navigates to the `TabPage` using passing an argument to the `Navigate` method that's used as a parameter with the `TabPage`. When you add a new tab, the `OnTabAdd` method is invoked, which in turn creates a new tab with `CreateNewTab`. `OnTabClose` closes the tab (code file `NavigationControls/ Views/ TabViewPage.xaml.cs`):

```csharp
public sealed partial class TabViewPage : Page
{
  public TabViewPage()
  {
    this.InitializeComponent();
    this.Loaded += OnLoaded;
  }

  private int _tabNumber = 0;
  private void OnLoaded(object sender, RoutedEventArgs e)
  {
    for (int i = 1; i < 4; i++)
    {
      tabView.TabItems.Add(CreateNewTab(i));
      _tabNumber = i;
    }
  }

  private TabViewItem CreateNewTab(int index)
  {
    TabViewItem newItem = new()
    {
      Header = $"Header {index}",
      Tag = $"Tag{index}",
      IconSource = new SymbolIconSource() { Symbol = Symbol.Document }
    };
    Frame frame = new();
    frame.Navigate(typeof(TabPage), $"Content {index}");
    newItem.Content = frame;
    return newItem;
  }

  private void OnTabAdd(TabView sender, object args)
  {
    var newTabItem = CreateNewTab(++_tabNumber);
    tabView.TabItems.Add(newTabItem);
  }
```

```
        private void OnTabClose(TabView sender, TabViewTabCloseRequestedEventArgs args)
        {
          tabView.TabItems.Remove(args.Tab);
        }
    }
```

With the `TabPage` class, the `OnNavigatedTo` method is overridden to receive the parameter passed with the `Parameter` property of the `NavigationEventArgs` object (code file `NavigationControls/Views/TabPage.xaml.cs`):

```
protected override void OnNavigatedTo(NavigationEventArgs e)
{
  Text = e.Parameter?.ToString() ?? "No parameter";
}
```

When you run the application, you can see the `TabView` control with tabs that can be dynamically opened and closed (see Figure 29-14).

FIGURE 29-14

NavigationView

Windows 10 apps often use the `SplitView` control with a hamburger button. The hamburger button is used to open a list of menus. The menus are shown either just with an icon or with an icon and text if more space is available. For arranging the space for the content and the menus, the `SplitView` control comes into play. The `SplitView` offers space for a pane and content where the pane usually contains menu items. The pane can have a small and a large size, which can be configured depending on the available screen sizes.

The `NavigationView` control combines the `SplitView`, menus for typically vertical arrangement, and a hamburger button in one control.

Let's get into the features of the `NavigationView` and start with the following code snippet. Figure 29-15 highlights the different parts of the `NavigationView`. The first part defined in the `NavigationView` is the list of `MenuItems`. This list contains `NavigationViewItem` objects. Each of these items contains an `Icon`, a `Content`, and a `Tag`. The `Tag` can be used programmatically to use this information for navigation. With some of these items, a predefined icon is used. The `NavigationViewItem` tagged with `home` makes use of a `FontIcon` with the Unicode number E10F. To separate menu items, you can use the `NavigationViewItemSeparator`. With the `NavigationViewItemHeader`, you can specify a header content for a group of items. Pay attention not to cut this content when the pane is in compact mode. With the code snippet, the `NavigationViewItemHeader` is hidden if the pane is not fully open (code file `NavigationControls/Views/NavigationViewPage.xaml`):

```
<NavigationView x:Name="NavigationView1"
  Background="{ThemeResource ApplicationPageBackgroundThemeBrush}">
  <NavigationView.MenuItems>
    <NavigationViewItem Content="Home" Tag="home">
```

```
        <NavigationViewItem.Icon>
          <FontIcon Glyph="&#xE10F;"/>
        </NavigationViewItem.Icon>
      </NavigationViewItem>
      <NavigationViewItemSeparator/>
      <NavigationViewItemHeader Content="Main Tools"
        Visibility="{x:Bind NavigationView1.IsPaneOpen, Mode=OneWay}"/>
      <NavigationViewItem Icon="AllApps" Content="Apps" Tag="apps"/>
      <NavigationViewItem Icon="Video" Content="Games" Tag="games"/>
      <NavigationViewItem Icon="Audio" Content="Music" Tag="music"/>
    </NavigationView.MenuItems>

    <!-- ... -->

</NavigationView>
```

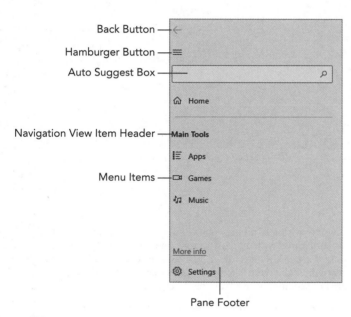

FIGURE 29-15

The `AutoSuggestBox` property of the `NavigationView` allows adding an `AutoSuggestBox` control to the navigation. This is shown on top of the menu items (code file `NavigationControls/Views/NavigationViewPage.xaml`):

```
<NavigationView.AutoSuggestBox>
  <AutoSuggestBox x:Name="autoSuggest" QueryIcon="Find"/>
</NavigationView.AutoSuggestBox>
```

With the `HeaderTemplate`, the top of the app can be customized. The code snippet defines a header template with a `Grid`, a `TextBlock`, and a `CommandBar` (code file `NavigationControls/Views/NavigationViewPage.xaml`):

```
<NavigationView.HeaderTemplate>
  <DataTemplate>
    <Grid Margin="8,8,0,0">
      <Grid.ColumnDefinitions>
```

```
        <ColumnDefinition Width="Auto"/>
        <ColumnDefinition/>
      </Grid.ColumnDefinitions>
      <TextBlock Style="{StaticResource TitleTextBlockStyle}"
        FontSize="28"
        VerticalAlignment="Center"
        Text="Welcome"/>
    <CommandBar Grid.Column="1"
      DefaultLabelPosition="Right"
      Background="{ThemeResource SystemControlBackgroundAltHighBrush}">
      <AppBarButton Label="Refresh" Icon="Refresh"/>
      <AppBarButton Label="Import" Icon="Import"/>
    </CommandBar>
  </Grid>
  </DataTemplate>
</NavigationView.HeaderTemplate>
```

The `PaneFooter` defines the lower part in the pane. Below the footer, by default a menu item for the Settings is shown; this menu, which is used by many apps, is included by default (code file `NavigationControls/Views/NavigationViewPage.xaml`):

```
<NavigationView.PaneFooter>
  <HyperlinkButton x:Name="MoreInfoBtn"
    Content="More info"
    Margin="12,0"/>
</NavigationView.PaneFooter>
```

Finally, the content of the `NavigationPane` is covered by a `Frame` control. This control is used to navigate to pages. The `NavigationPane` surrounds the page content (code file `NavigationControls/Views/NavigationViewPage.xaml`):

```
<Frame x:Name="ContentFrame" Margin="24">
  <Frame.ContentTransitions>
    <TransitionCollection>
      <NavigationThemeTransition/>
    </TransitionCollection>
  </Frame.ContentTransitions>
</Frame>
```

IMPLEMENTING LAYOUT PANELS

The `NavigationView` control discussed in the previous section is an important control to organize the layout of the user interface. With many new Windows 10 apps, you can see this control used for the main layout. There are several other controls that define a layout. This section demonstrates the `VariableSizedWrapGrid` for arranging multiple items in a grid that automatically wraps, the `RelativePanel` for arranging items relative to each other or relative to a parent, and adaptive triggers for rearranging the layout depending on the window size.

The `Canvas` panel enables you to explicitly position controls. This panel is great for arranging shapes. This is discussed in Chapter 31.

StackPanel

If you need to add multiple elements to a control that supports only one control, the easiest way is to use a `StackPanel`. The `StackPanel` is a simple panel that shows one element after the other. The orientation of the `StackPanel` can be horizontal or vertical.

In the following code snippet, the page contains a StackPanel with various controls organized vertically. The ListBox within the first ListBoxItem contains a StackPanel organized horizontally (code file LayoutSamples/Views/StackPanelPage.xaml):

```
<StackPanel Orientation="Vertical">
  <TextBox Text="TextBox" />
  <CheckBox Content="Checkbox" />
  <CheckBox Content="Checkbox" />
  <ListBox>
    <ListBoxItem>
      <StackPanel Orientation="Horizontal">
        <TextBlock Text="One A" />
        <TextBlock Text="One B" />
      </StackPanel>
    </ListBoxItem>
    <ListBoxItem Content="Two" />
  </ListBox>
  <Button Content="Button" />
</StackPanel>
```

Figure 29-16 shows the child controls of the StackPanel organized vertically.

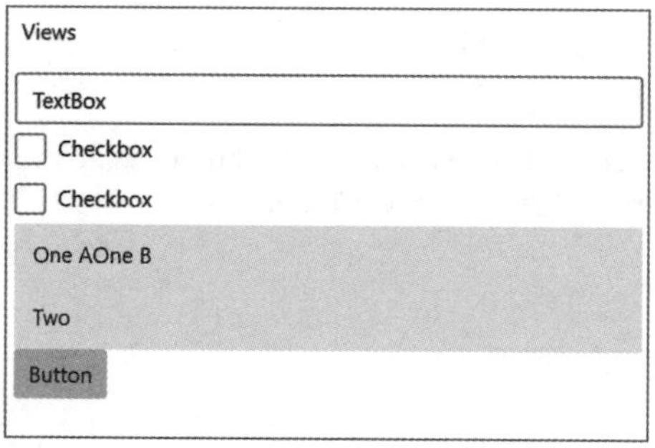

FIGURE 29-16

Grid

The Grid is an important panel. When you use the Grid, you can arrange your controls with rows and columns. For every column, you can specify a ColumnDefinition. For every row, you can specify a RowDefinition. The following example code lists two columns and three rows. With each column and row, you can specify the width or height. ColumnDefinition has a Width dependency property; RowDefinition has a Height dependency property. You can define the height and width in device-independent pixels, or you can set it to Auto to base the size on the content. The grid also allows *star sizing*, which means the space for the rows and columns is calculated according to the available space and relative to other rows and columns. When providing the available space for a column, you can set the Width property to *. To have the size doubled for another column, you specify 2*. The sample code, which defines two columns and three rows, uses star sizing for the columns (this is the default); the first row has a fixed size, and the second and third rows use star sizing. With the height calculation, the available height is reduced by the 200 pixels from the first row. The remaining area is divided between rows 2 and 3 in the relation 1.5:1.

The grid contains several Rectangle controls with different colors to make the cell sizes visible. Because the parent of these controls is a grid, you can set the attached properties Column, ColumnSpan, Row, and RowSpan (code file LayoutSamples/Views/GridPage.xaml):

```
<Grid>
  <Grid.ColumnDefinitions>
```

```
        <ColumnDefinition />
        <ColumnDefinition />
      </Grid.ColumnDefinitions>
      <Grid.RowDefinitions>
        <RowDefinition Height="200" />
        <RowDefinition Height="1.5*" />
        <RowDefinition Height="*" />
      </Grid.RowDefinitions>
      <Rectangle Fill="Blue" />
      <Rectangle Grid.Row="0" Grid.Column="1" Fill="Red" />
      <Rectangle Grid.Row="1" Grid.Column="0" Grid.ColumnSpan="2" Fill="Green" />
      <Rectangle Grid.Row="2" Grid.Column="0" Grid.ColumnSpan="2" Fill="Yellow" />
    </Grid>
```

Figure 29-17 shows the outcome of arranging rectangles in a grid.

FIGURE 29-17

VariableSizedWrapGrid

`VariableSizedWrapGrid` is a wrap grid that automatically wraps to the next row or column if the size available for the grid is not large enough. The second feature of this grid is an allowance for items with multiple rows or columns; that's why it's called *variable*.

The following code snippet creates a `VariableSizedWrappedGrid` with orientation `Horizontal`, a maximum number of 20 items in the row, and rows and columns that have a size of 50 (code file `LayoutSamples/Views/VariableSizedWrapGridSample.xaml`):

```
<VariableSizedWrapGrid x:Name="grid1" MaximumRowsOrColumns="20" ItemHeight="50"
  ItemWidth="50" Orientation="Horizontal" />
```

The `VariableSizedWrapGrid` is filled with 30 `Rectangle` and `TextBlock` elements that have random sizes and colors. Depending on the size, one to three rows or columns can be used within the grid. The size of the items is set using the attached properties `VariableSizedWrapGrid.ColumnSpan` and `VariableSizedWrapGrid.RowSpan` (code file `LayoutSamples/Views/VariableSizedWrapGridSample.xaml.cs`):

```
protected override void OnNavigatedTo(NavigationEventArgs e)
{
  base.OnNavigatedTo(e);
  Random r = new();
```

```
     Grid[] items =
       Enumerable.Range(0, 30).Select(i =>
       {
         byte[] colorBytes = new byte[3];
         r.NextBytes(colorBytes);
         Rectangle rect = new()
         {
           Height = r.Next(40, 150),
           Width = r.Next(40, 150),
           Fill = new SolidColorBrush(new Color
           {
             R = colorBytes[0],
             G = colorBytes[1],
             B = colorBytes[2],
             A = 255
           })
         };

         TextBlock textBlock = new()
         {
           Text = (i + 1).ToString(),
           HorizontalAlignment = HorizontalAlignment.Center,
           VerticalAlignment = VerticalAlignment.Center
         };
         Grid grid = new();
         grid.Children.Add(rect);
         grid.Children.Add(textBlock);
         return grid;
       }).ToArray();

     foreach (var item in items)
     {
       grid1.Children.Add(item);
       Rectangle? rect = item.Children.First() as Rectangle;
       if (rect is not null && rect.Width > 50)
       {
         int columnSpan = ((int)rect.Width / 50) + 1;
         VariableSizedWrapGrid.SetColumnSpan(item, columnSpan);
         int rowSpan = ((int)rect.Height / 50) + 1;
         VariableSizedWrapGrid.SetRowSpan(item, rowSpan);
       }
     }
```

When you run the application, you can see the rectangles and how they wrap for different window sizes, as shown in Figure 29-18.

RelativePanel

RelativePanel is a panel that allows one element to be positioned in relation to another element. If you've used the Grid control with definitions for rows and columns and you had to insert a row, you had to change all elements that were below the row that was inserted. The reason is that all rows and columns are indexed by numbers. This is not an issue with the RelativePanel, which enables you to place elements in relation to each other.

FIGURE 29-18

> **NOTE** *Compared to the* `RelativePanel`, *the* `Grid` *control still has its advantages with auto, star, and fixed sizing.*

The following code snippet aligns several `TextBlock` and `TextBox` controls, a `Button`, and a `Rectangle` within a `RelativePanel`. The `TextBox` elements are positioned to the right of the corresponding `TextBlock` elements; the `Button` is positioned relative to the bottom of the panel; and the `Rectangle` is aligned with the top with the first `TextBlock` and to the right of the first `TextBox` (code file `LayoutSamples/Views/RelativePanelPage.xaml`):

```
<RelativePanel>
  <TextBlock x:Name="FirstNameLabel" Text="First Name" Margin="8" />
  <TextBox x:Name="FirstNameText" RelativePanel.RightOf="FirstNameLabel"
    Margin="8" Width="150" />
  <TextBlock x:Name="LastNameLabel" Text="Last Name"
    RelativePanel.Below="FirstNameLabel" Margin="8" />
  <TextBox x:Name="LastNameText" RelativePanel.RightOf="LastNameLabel"
    Margin="8" RelativePanel.Below="FirstNameText" Width="150" />
  <Button Content="Save" RelativePanel.AlignHorizontalCenterWith="LastNameText"
    RelativePanel.AlignBottomWithPanel="True" Margin="8" />
  <Rectangle x:Name="Image" Fill="Violet" Width="150" Height="250"
    RelativePanel.AlignTopWith="FirstNameLabel"
    RelativePanel.RightOf="FirstNameText" Margin="8" />
</RelativePanel>
```

Figure 29-19 shows the alignment of the controls when you run the application.

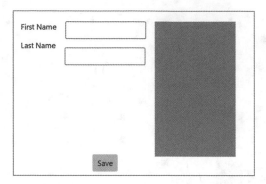

FIGURE 29-19

Adaptive Triggers

The RelativePanel is a great control for alignment. However, to support multiple screen sizes and rearrange the controls depending on the screen size, you can use adaptive triggers with the RelativePanel control. For example, on a small screen, the TextBox controls should be arranged below the TextBlock controls, but on a larger screen the TextBox controls should be arranged to the right of the TextBlock controls.

In the following code, the RelativePanel from before is changed to remove all RelativePanel attached properties that should not apply to all screen sizes, and an optional image is added (code file LayoutSamples/Views/AdaptiveRelativePanelPage.xaml):

```
<RelativePanel ScrollViewer.VerticalScrollBarVisibility="Auto" Margin="16">
  <TextBlock x:Name="FirstNameLabel" Text="First Name" Margin="8" />
  <TextBox x:Name="FirstNameText" Margin="8" Width="150" />
  <TextBlock x:Name="LastNameLabel" Text="Last Name" Margin="8" />
  <TextBox x:Name="LastNameText" Margin="8" Width="150" />
  <Button Content="Save" RelativePanel.AlignBottomWithPanel="True"
    Margin="8" />
  <Rectangle x:Name="Image" Fill="Violet" Width="150" Height="250"
    Margin="8" />
  <Rectangle x:Name="OptionalImage" RelativePanel.AlignRightWithPanel="True"
    Fill="Red" Width="350" Height="350" Margin="8" />
</RelativePanel>
```

When you use an adaptive trigger—with which the MinWindowWidth can be set to define when the trigger is fired—values for different properties are set to arrange the elements depending on the space available for the app. As the screen size gets smaller, the width needed by the app gets smaller as well. Moving elements below instead of beside reduces the width needed. Instead, the user can scroll down. With the smallest window width, the optional image is set to collapsed (code file LayoutSamples/Views/AdaptiveRelativePanelPage.xaml):

```
<VisualStateManager.VisualStateGroups>
  <VisualStateGroup>
    <VisualState x:Name="WideState">
      <VisualState.StateTriggers>
        <AdaptiveTrigger MinWindowWidth="1024" />
      </VisualState.StateTriggers>
      <VisualState.Setters>
```

```
                <Setter Target="FirstNameText.(RelativePanel.RightOf)"
                  Value="FirstNameLabel" />
                <Setter Target="LastNameLabel.(RelativePanel.Below)"
                  Value="FirstNameLabel" />
                <Setter Target="LastNameText.(RelativePanel.Below)"
                  Value="FirstNameText" />
                <Setter Target="LastNameText.(RelativePanel.RightOf)"
                  Value="LastNameLabel" />
                <Setter Target="Image.(RelativePanel.AlignTopWith)"
                  Value="FirstNameLabel" />
                <Setter Target="Image.(RelativePanel.RightOf)" Value="FirstNameText" />
              </VisualState.Setters>
            </VisualState>
            <VisualState x:Name="MediumState">
              <VisualState.StateTriggers>
                <AdaptiveTrigger MinWindowWidth="720" />
              </VisualState.StateTriggers>
              <VisualState.Setters>
                <Setter Target="FirstNameText.(RelativePanel.RightOf)"
                  Value="FirstNameLabel" />
                <Setter Target="LastNameLabel.(RelativePanel.Below)"
                  Value="FirstNameLabel" />
                <Setter Target="LastNameText.(RelativePanel.Below)"
                  Value="FirstNameText" />
                <Setter Target="LastNameText.(RelativePanel.RightOf)"
                  Value="LastNameLabel"/>
                <Setter Target="Image.(RelativePanel.Below)" Value="LastNameText" />
                <Setter Target="Image.(RelativePanel.AlignHorizontalCenterWith)"
                  Value="LastNameText" />
              </VisualState.Setters>
            </VisualState>
            <VisualState x:Name="NarrowState">
              <VisualState.StateTriggers>
                <AdaptiveTrigger MinWindowWidth="320" />
              </VisualState.StateTriggers>
              <VisualState.Setters>
                <Setter Target="FirstNameText.(RelativePanel.Below)"
                  Value="FirstNameLabel" />
                <Setter Target="LastNameLabel.(RelativePanel.Below)"
                  Value="FirstNameText" />
                <Setter Target="LastNameText.(RelativePanel.Below)"
                  Value="LastNameLabel"/>
                <Setter Target="Image.(RelativePanel.Below)" Value="LastNameText" />
                <Setter Target="OptionalImage.Visibility" Value="Collapsed" />
              </VisualState.Setters>
            </VisualState>
          </VisualStateGroup>
        </VisualStateManager.VisualStateGroups>
```

When you run the application, you'll see different snap points as you resize the application. The layout is rearranged, and controls move to other positions or are hidden depending on the available size. See the Figures 29-20 and 29-21 for different layout results.

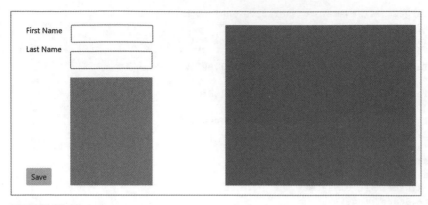

FIGURE 29-20

FIGURE 29-21

Deferred Loading

For a faster UI, you can delay creation of controls until they are needed. On small devices, some controls might not be needed at all, but with larger screens and faster systems they are needed. With previous versions of XAML applications, elements that have been added to the XAML code also have been instantiated. This is no longer the case with Windows 10. Here you can defer loading of controls until they are needed.

You can use deferred loading with adaptive triggers to load only some controls at a later time. One sample scenario where this is useful is when you have a smaller window that the user can resize to be larger. With the smaller window, some controls should not be visible, but they should be visible with the bigger size of the window. Another scenario where deferred loading can be useful is when some parts of the layout may take more time to load. Instead of making the user wait until he sees the completely loaded layout, you can use deferred loading.

To use deferred loading, you need to add the `x:Load` attribute with a value `False` to a control, as shown in the following code snippet with a `Grid` control. This control also needs to have a name assigned to it (code file `LayoutSamples/Views/DelayLoadingPage.xaml`):

```
<Grid x:Load="False" x:Name="deferGrid">
  <Grid.ColumnDefinitions>
```

```
    <ColumnDefinition />
    <ColumnDefinition />
  </Grid.ColumnDefinitions>
  <Grid.RowDefinitions>
    <RowDefinition />
    <RowDefinition />
  </Grid.RowDefinitions>
  <Rectangle Fill="Red" Grid.Row="0" Grid.Column="0" />
  <Rectangle Fill="Green" Grid.Row="0" Grid.Column="1" />
  <Rectangle Fill="Blue" Grid.Row="1" Grid.Column="0" />
  <Rectangle Fill="Yellow" Grid.Row="1" Grid.Column="1"/ >
</Grid>
```

To make this deferred control visible, all you need to do is invoke the `FindName` method to access the identifier of the control. This not only makes the control visible but also loads the XAML tree of the control before the control is made visible (code file `LayoutSamples/Views/DelayLoadingPage.xaml.cs`):

```
private void OnDeferLoad(object sender, RoutedEventArgs e)
{
  FindName(nameof(deferGrid));
}
```

> **NOTE** *The attribute* `x:Load` *has an overhead of about 600 bytes, so you should use it only on elements that need to be hidden. If this attribute is used on a container element, you pay the overhead only once with the element where the attribute is applied.*

SUMMARY

This chapter introduced many different aspects of programming Windows apps. You've seen the foundation of XAML and how it extends XML with attached properties and markup extensions. You've seen a hierarchy with many controls offered with WinUI and learned about the foundations of data binding.

You've seen how to deal with different screen sizes, options for laying out controls with different panels, and the categories and features of different controls.

The next chapter continues with XAML-based apps, the MVVM pattern, commands, and creating shareable view models.

30

Patterns with XAML Apps

WHAT'S IN THIS CHAPTER?

➤ Sharing code

➤ Creating models

➤ Creating repositories

➤ Creating view models

➤ Navigation between pages

➤ Using an event aggregator

CODE DOWNLOADS FOR THIS CHAPTER

The source code for this chapter is available on the book page at www.wiley.com. Click the Downloads link. The code can also be found at https://github.com/ProfessionalCSharp/ ProfessionalCSharp2021 in the directory 4_Apps/Patterns.

The code for this chapter contains these WinUI and library projects:

➤ BooksApp

➤ BooksLib

➤ GenericViewModels

All the projects have nullable reference types enabled.

WHY MVVM?

Dependency injection, as explained in Chapter 15, "Dependency Injection and Configuration," provides an easy way to create unit tests and gives you a way to build the major functionality of your application independent of a hosting technology. You've seen this in concrete examples in Chapter 25, "Services," where the same functionality has been used with ASP.NET Core Web APIs, gRPC, and Azure Functions.

Dependency injection plays an important part with XAML-based applications as well. Windows and mobile applications give you many options to use, and you shouldn't restrict your application development to one of these technologies. With XAML, you have older (WPF, Silverlight, Xamarin.Forms, UWP) and newer (WinUI, MAUI, Platform Uno) technologies. Some older technologies still have great support with .NET 5, such as WPF.

One project to support all Windows 10 platforms might not fit your needs. Can you write a program that supports Windows 10 only? Do you think about supporting devices such as the HoloLens or the Xbox? Windows 10X? What about supporting Android and iOS? Can .NET Multi-platform App UI (MAUI) support your needs? The goal should be to reuse as much code as possible to support the platforms needed and to have an easy switch from one technology to another.

With XAML-based applications, using dependency injection is helpful. The *Model-View-ViewModel (MVVM)* design pattern helps to separate the view from the functionality. With the view models you implement, you can inject services similar to what you've seen with the controllers with an ASP.NET Core technology. The MVVM design pattern was invented by John Gossman of the Expression Blend team as a great fit to XAML with advancements to the Model-View-Controller (MVC) and Model-View-Presenter (MVP) patterns because it uses data binding, a number-one feature of XAML.

With XAML-based applications, the XAML file and code-behind file are tightly coupled to each other. This makes it hard to reuse the code-behind and also hard to do unit testing. To solve this issue, the MVVM pattern allows for a better separation of the code from the user interface.

In principle, the MVVM pattern is not that hard to understand. However, when you're creating applications based on the MVVM pattern, you need to pay attention to a lot more needs; several patterns come into play for making applications work and making reuse possible, including dependency injection mechanisms for being independent of the implementation and communication between view models.

All this is covered in this chapter, and with this information not only can you use the same code with Windows apps and Windows desktop applications, but you can also use it for iOS and Android with the help of Xamarin. Forms and .NET MAUI. This chapter gives you a sample app that covers all the different aspects and patterns needed for a good separation to support different technologies.

DEFINING THE MVVM PATTERN

First, let's take a look at the MVC design pattern that is one of the origins of the MVVM pattern. The Model-View-Controller pattern separates the model, the view, and the controller (see Figure 30-1). The *model* defines the data that is shown in the view as well as the business rules about how the data can be changed and manipulated. The *controller* is the manager between the model and the view, it updates the model, and it sends data for display to the view. When a user request comes in, the controller takes action, uses the model, and updates the *view*.

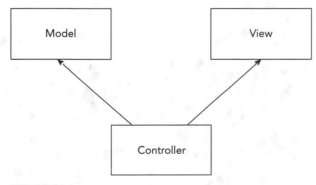

FIGURE 30-1

> **NOTE** *The MVC pattern is heavily used with ASP.NET Core MVC, which is covered in Chapter 26, "Razor Pages and MVC."*

With the Model-View-Presenter pattern (see Figure 30-2), the user interacts with the view. The presenter contains all the business logic for the view. The presenter can be decoupled from the view by using an interface to the view as a contract. This allows you to easily change the view implementation for unit tests. With MVP, the view and model are completely shielded from each other.

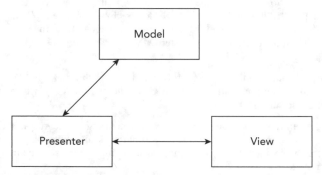

FIGURE 30-2

The main pattern used with XAML-based applications is the Model-View-ViewModel pattern (see Figure 30-3). This pattern takes advantage of the data-binding capabilities with XAML. With MVVM, the user interacts with the view. The view uses data binding to access information from the view model and invokes commands in the view model that are bound in the view as well. The view model doesn't have a direct dependency to the view. The view model itself uses the model to access data and gets change information from the model as well.

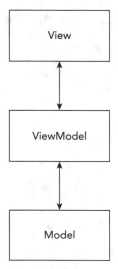

FIGURE 30-3

In the following sections of this chapter, you will see how to use this architecture with the application to create views, view models, models, and other patterns that are needed.

> **NOTE** *To reuse code with libraries, make sure to read Chapter 14, "Libraries, Assemblies, Packages, and NuGet."*

SAMPLE SOLUTION

The sample solution consists of a WinUI application for showing and editing a list of books. The solution uses these projects:

➤ **BooksApp**—A WinUI application project for the UI of a modern app. This application contains the views for the app with XAML code and platform-specific implementation of services.

➤ **BooksLib**—A .NET 5 library with models, view models, and services to create, read, and update books.

➤ **GenericViewModels**—A .NET 5 library with view model base classes that can be used across different projects.

This application uses the NuGet package `Microsoft.Toolkit.Mvvm`, which has core classes that are employed in applications using the MVVM pattern. Many other MVVM libraries are available for you to use as well, and you can easily create the core functionality needed for MVVM with your custom implementation. As we now have an MVVM library from Microsoft, this chapter makes use of it.

The user interface of the application will have two views: one view to show as a list of books and one view to show book details. When you select a book from the list, the detail is shown. It's also possible to add and edit books.

The `BooksLib` and `GenericViewModels` libraries can be used by multiple applications with XAML code—for example, with WinUI, Platform Uno, and .NET MAUI.

MODELS

Let's start defining the models, particularly the `Book` type. This is the type that will be shown and edited in the UI. To support data binding, the properties where values are updated from the user interface need a change notification implementation. The `BookId` property is only shown but not changed, so change notification is not needed with this property. The method `SetProperty` is defined by the base class `ObservableObject` that is defined in the namespace `Microsoft.Toolkit.Mvvm.ComponentModel` in the NuGet package `Microsoft.Toolkit.Mvvm` (code file `BooksLib/Models/Book.cs`):

```
public class Book: ObservableObject
{
  public Book(string? title = null, string? publisher = null, int id = 0)
  {
    BookId = id;
    _title = title ?? string.Empty;
    _publisher = publisher ?? string.Empty;
  }

  public int BookId { get; set; }
```

```
private string _title;
public string Title
{
  get => _title;
  set => SetProperty(ref _title, value);
}

private string _publisher;
public string Publisher
{
  get => _publisher;
  set => SetProperty(ref _publisher, value);
}

public override string ToString() => Title;
}
```

> **NOTE** *The* `ObservableObject` *class implements the interface* `INotifyPropertyChanged`.
> *This interface is used with data binding of XAML-based applications to notify the user*
> *interface that a change occurred in the data source. You need to specify* `OneWay` *or* `TwoWay`
> *binding to use* `INotifyPropertyChanged` *from the data sources with the* `Mode` *property of*
> *the binding markup extension.*

Next, you need a way to retrieve, update, and delete `Book` objects. You can read and write books from a database with EF Core or call a REST API or use RPC to access a service. The sample application just accesses books from the memory, but you can create an API service and a service class to call this API service. To make this easy, the contracts of the repository pattern are specified using the task-based async pattern where you can create a different implementation using the `HttpClient` class as covered in Chapter 25.

With the client application, it's best to be independent of the data store. For this, the repository design pattern was defined. The *repository* pattern is a mediator between the model and the data access layer; it can act as an in-memory collection of objects. It gives an abstraction of the data access layer and allows for easier unit tests.

The generic interface `IQueryRepository` defines methods for retrieving one item by ID or a list of items (code file `BooksLib/Services/IQueryRepository.cs`):

```
public interface IQueryRepository<T, in TKey>
  where T: class
{
  Task<T?> GetItemAsync(TKey id);
  Task<IEnumerable<T>> GetItemsAsync();
}
```

The generic interface `IUpdateRepository` defines methods to add, update, and delete items (code file `BooksLib/Services/IUpdateRepository.cs`):

```
public interface IUpdateRepository<T, in TKey>
  where T: class
{
  Task<T> AddAsync(T item);
  Task<T> UpdateAsync(T item);
  Task<bool> DeleteAsync(TKey id);
}
```

The IBooksRepository interface makes the previous two generic interfaces concrete by defining the type Book for the generic type T (code file BooksLib/Services/IBooksRepository.cs):

```
public interface IBooksRepository: IQueryRepository<Book, int>,
  IUpdateRepository<Book, int>
{
}
```

By using these interfaces, it's possible to change the repository. Create a sample repository BooksSampleRepository that implements the members of the interface IBooksRepository and contains a list of initial books (code file BooksLib/Services/BooksSampleRepository.cs):

```
public class BooksSampleRepository: IBooksRepository
{
  Private readonly List<Book> _books;
  public BooksSampleRepository() =>
    _books = GetSampleBooks();

  private List<Book> GetSampleBooks() =>
    new()
    {
      new("Professional C# and .NET - 2021 Edition", "Wrox Press", 1),
      new("Professional C# 7 and .NET Core 2", "Wrox Press", 2),
      new("Professional C# 6 and .NET Core 1.0", "Wrox Press", 3),
      new("Professional C# 5.0 and .NET 4.5.1", "Wrox Press", 4),
      new("Enterprise Services with the .NET Framework", "AWL", 5)
    };

  public Task<bool> DeleteAsync(int id)
  {
    Book? bookToDelete = _books.Find(b => b.BookId == id);
    if (bookToDelete is not null)
    {
      return Task.FromResult<bool>(_books.Remove(bookToDelete));
    }
    return Task.FromResult<bool>(false);
  }

  public Task<Book?> GetItemAsync(int id) =>
    Task.FromResult(_books.Find(b => b.BookId == id));

  public Task<IEnumerable<Book>> GetItemsAsync() =>
    Task.FromResult<IEnumerable<Book>>(_books);

  public Task<Book> UpdateAsync(Book item)
  {
    Book bookToUpdate = _books.Single(b => b.BookId == item.BookId);
    int ix = _books.IndexOf(bookToUpdate);
    _books[ix] = item;
    return Task.FromResult(_books[ix]);
  }

  public Task<Book> AddAsync(Book item)
  {
```

```
            item.BookId = _books.Select(b => b.BookId).Max() + 1;
            _books.Add(item);
            return Task.FromResult(item);
        }
    }
```

SERVICES

To get the books from the repository, you use a service, and you can use it across multiple view models that access the same data. Thus, the service is a good place to share data between view models.

The sample service for the books implements the generic interface IItemsService. This interface defines the Items property of a type ObservableCollection. ObservableCollection implements the interface INotifyCollectionChanged for notifications when the collection changes. The interface IItemsService also defines the SelectedItem property and change notification with the event SelectedItemChanged. Aside from that, the methods RefreshAsync, AddOrUpdateAsync, and DeleteAsync need to be implemented by the service class (code file GenericViewModels/Services/IItemsService.cs):

```
public interface IItemsService<T>
{
  Task RefreshAsync();

  Task<T> AddOrUpdateAsync(T item);

  Task DeleteAsync(T item);

  ObservableCollection<T> Items { get; }

  T? SelectedItem { get; set; }
  event EventHandler<T>? SelectedItemChanged;
}
```

The class BooksService derives from the base class ObservableObject and implements the generic interface IItemsService. The BooksService uses the previously created SampleBooksRepository but requires the functionality of this class offered by the IBooksRepository interface. The class is injected via the constructor and used on refreshing the books list, adding or updating books, and deleting books (code file BooksLib/Services/BooksService.cs):

```
public class BooksService : ObservableObject, IItemsService<Book>
{
  Private readonly ObservableCollection<Book> _books = new();
  private readonly IBooksRepository _booksRepository;

  public event EventHandler<Book>? SelectedItemChanged;

  public BooksService(IBooksRepository repository)
  {
    _booksRepository = repository;
  }

  public ObservableCollection<Book> Items => _books;

  private Book? _selectedItem;
  public Book? SelectedItem
  {
```

```
          get => _selectedItem;
          set
          {
            if (value is not null && SetProperty(ref _selectedItem, value))
            {
              SelectedItemChanged?.Invoke(this, _selectedItem);
            }
          }
        }

        public async Task<Book> AddOrUpdateAsync(Book book)
        {
          if (book.BookId == 0)
          {
            return await _booksRepository.AddAsync(book);
          }
          else
          {
            return await _booksRepository.UpdateAsync(book);
          }
        }

        public Task DeleteAsync(Book book) =>
          _booksRepository.DeleteAsync(book.BookId);

        public async Task RefreshAsync()
        {
          IEnumerable<Book> books = await _booksRepository.GetItemsAsync();
          _books.Clear();
          foreach (var book in books)
          {
            _books.Add(book);
          }
          SelectedItem = Items.FirstOrDefault();
        }
      }
```

Now that the service functionality is in place, let's move on to the view models.

VIEW MODELS

Every view or page has a view model. With the sample app, the BooksPage has the BooksViewModel associated. Later in the sample, you'll see that user controls can have their specific view models as well, but this is not always necessary. The BookDetailPage has the BookDetailViewModel associated. It's a UI design decision if the list of books and details can be implemented in the same page. That's a matter of the available screen size of the app: what can fit on the screen? With the sample application, a flexible approach was taken. If the size available for the app is large enough, the BooksPage shows the list and the details; if the size is not large enough, data will be shown in separate pages with navigation between.

There's a one-to-one mapping between page view and view model. In reality, there's a many-to-one mapping between view and view model because the same view can be implemented multiple times with different technologies—WinUI, WPF, Platform Uno, and others. This makes it important that the view model doesn't know anything about the view, but the view knows the view model. The view model is implemented in a .NET library, which allows using it from many technologies.

For common functionality of view models, it makes sense to create base classes. The `GenericViewModels` library contains a `ViewModelBase` class that implements features for progress information and for errors (code file `GenericViewModels/ViewModels/ViewModelBase.cs`):

```
public abstract class ViewModelBase : ObservableObject
{
  // functionality for progress information and
  // error information
}
```

The sample application shows a list of books and allows the user to select a book. Here, it is useful to define a generic base class for the view models with the properties `Items` and `SelectedItem`. The implementation of these properties makes use of the previously created service that implements the interface `IItemsService` (code file `GenericViewModels/ViewModels/MasterDetailViewModel.cs`):

```
public abstract class MasterDetailViewModel<TItemViewModel, TItem> :
  ViewModelBase
  where TItemViewModel : IItemViewModel<TItem>
  where IItem: class
{
private readonly IItemsService<TItem> _itemsService;

public MasterDetailViewModel(IItemsService<TItem> itemsService)
{
  _itemsService = itemsService;

  //...
}

public ObservableCollection<TItem> Items => _itemsService.Items;

protected TItem? _selectedItem;
public virtual TItem? SelectedItem
{
  get => _itemsService.SelectedItem;
  set
  {
    if (!EqualityComparer<TItem>.Default.Equals(
      _itemsService.SelectedItem, value))
    {
      _itemsService.SelectedItem = value;
      OnPropertyChanged();
    }
  }
}

//...
}
```

To display a single item in detail, the base class `ItemViewModel` defines an `Item` property (code file `GenericViewModels/ViewModels/ItemViewModel.cs`):

```
public abstract class ItemViewModel<T> : ViewModelBase, IItemViewModel<T>
{
  public ItemViewModel(T item) => _item = item;
```

```
    private T _item;
    public virtual T Item
    {
      get => _item;
      set => Set(ref _item, value);
    }
  }
```

More complex than the simple class `ItemViewModel` is the view model class `EditableItemViewModel`.
This class extends `ItemViewModel` by allowing editing, and thus it defines a read or edit mode. The property
`IsReadMode` is just the inverse of `IsEditMode`. The `EditableItemViewModel` makes use of the same service as
the `MasterDetailViewModel` class, the service that implements the interface `IItemsService`. This way, the
`EditableItemViewModel` and `MasterDetailViewModel` classes can share the same items and the same selection.
The view model class allows the user to cancel the input. For this, the item has a copied version with the
`EditItem` property (code file `GenericViewModels/ViewModels/EditableItemViewModel.cs`):

```
public abstract class EditableItemViewModel<TItem> : ItemViewModel<TItem>,
  IEditableObject
  where TItem : class
{
  private readonly IItemsService<TItem> _itemsService;

  public EditableItemViewModel(IItemsService<TItem> itemsService)
    : base(itemsService.SelectedItem ?? throw new InvalidOperationException())
  {
    _itemsService = itemsService;

    PropertyChanged += (sender, e) =>
    {
      if (e.PropertyName == nameof(Item))
      {
        OnPropertyChanged(nameof(EditItem));
      }
    };
    //...
  }

  //...
  private bool _isEditMode;
  public bool IsReadMode => !IsEditMode;
  public bool IsEditMode
  {
    get => _isEditMode;
    set
    {
      if (Set(ref _isEditMode, value))
      {
        OnPropertyChanged(nameof(IsReadMode));
        //...
      }
    }
  }

  private TItem? _editItem;
  public TItem? EditItem
```

```
    {
      get => _editItem ?? Item;
      set => Set(ref _editItem, value);
    }
    //...
}
```

IEditableObject

An interface that defines methods to change an object between different edit states is IEditableObject. This interface is defined in the namespace System.ComponentModel. IEditableObject defines the methods BeginEdit, CancelEdit, and EndEdit. BeginEdit is invoked to change the item from the read mode to the edit mode. CancelEdit cancels the edit and switches back to read mode. EndEdit is for a successful end of the edit mode and, thus, needs to save the data. The EditableItemViewModel class implements the methods of this interface by switching the edit mode, creating a copy of the item, and saving the state. This view model class is a generic one and doesn't know what should be done for copying and saving the item. Copying would be possible by using binary serialization. However, not all objects support binary serialization. Instead, the implementation is forwarded to the class that derives from EditableItemViewModel, similar to the save method OnSaveAsync. OnSaveAsync and CreateCopy are defined as abstract methods and thus need to be implemented by the derived class. Another method is defined to be invoked at the end of CancelEdit and EndEdit: OnEndEditAsync. This method can be implemented by a derived class, but it's not necessary to do. That's why the method is declared virtual with an empty body (code file GenericViewModels/ViewModels/EditableItemViewModel.cs):

```
public virtual void BeginEdit()
{
  IsEditMode = true;
  TItem itemCopy = CreateCopy(Item);
  if (itemCopy != null)
  {
    EditItem = itemCopy;
  }
}

public async virtual void CancelEdit()
{
  IsEditMode = false;
  EditItem = default;
  await _itemsService.RefreshAsync();
  await OnEndEditAsync();
}

public async virtual void EndEdit()
{
  using var _ = StartInProgress();
  await OnSaveAsync();
  EditItem = default;
  IsEditMode = false;
  await _itemsService.RefreshAsync();
  await OnEndEditAsync();
}

public abstract Task OnSaveAsync();
public abstract TItem CreateCopy(TItem item);
public virtual Task OnEndEditAsync() => Task.CompletedTask;
```

Concrete View Model Implementations

Let's move on to the concrete implementations of the view models. `BookDetailViewModel` derives from `EditableItemViewModel` and specifies `Book` as the generic parameter. With the base class already implementing the major functionality, this class can be simple. It injects the services for the interfaces `IItemsService` and `INavigationSerivce`. In the method `OnSaveAsync`, the request is forwarded to the `IItemsService`. The `OnSaveAsync` method also makes use of the interfaces `ILogger` and `IMessageService`. In the view model class, the `CreateCopy` method implements the creation of a copy of the book. This method is invoked by the base class (code file `BooksLib/ViewModels/BookDetailViewModel.cs`):

```
public class BookDetailViewModel : EditableItemViewModel<Book>
{
  private readonly IItemsService<Book> _itemsService;
  private readonly INavigationService _navigationService;
  private readonly IMessageService _messageService;
  private readonly ILogger _logger;

  public BookDetailViewModel(IItemsService<Book> itemsService,
    INavigationService navigationService, IMessageService messageService,
    ILogger<BookDetailViewModel> logger)
    : base(itemsService)
  {
    _itemsService = itemsService;
    _navigationService = navigationService;
    _messageService = messageService;
    _logger = logger;

    itemsService.SelectedItemChanged += (sender, book) =>
    {
      Item = book;
    };
  }

  public override Book CreateCopy(Book? item)
  {
    int id = item?.BookId ?? -1;
    string title = item?.Title ?? "enter a title";
    string publisher = item?.Publisher ?? "enter a publisher";
    return new Book(title, publisher, id);
  }

  public override async Task OnSaveAsync()
  {
    try
    {
      if (EditItem is null) return;
      await _itemsService.AddOrUpdateAsync(EditItem);
    }
    catch (Exception ex)
    {
      _logger.LogError("error {0} in {1}", ex.Message, nameof(OnSaveAsync));
      await _dialogService.ShowMessageAsync("Error saving the data");
    }
  }
  //...
}
```

> **NOTE** *The* `ILogger` *interface is explained in Chapter 16, "Diagnostics and Metrics." The interface* `IDialogService` *is discussed later in this chapter in the section "Opening Dialogs from View Models."*

The class `BooksViewModel` can be kept simple by inheriting the main functionality from `MasterDetailViewModel`. This class injects the `INavigationService` interface that will be discussed later, forwards the `IItemsService` interface to the base class, and overrides the `OnAdd` method that is invoked by the base class (code file `BooksLib/ViewModels/BooksViewModel.cs`):

```
public class BooksViewModel : MasterDetailViewModel<BookItemViewModel, Book>
{
  private readonly IItemsService<Book> _booksService;
  private readonly INavigationService _navigationService;

  public BooksViewModel(IItemsService<Book> booksService,
    INavigationService navigationService)
    : base(booksService)
  {
    _booksService = booksService ??
      throw new ArgumentNullException(nameof(booksService));
    _navigationService = navigationService ??
      throw new ArgumentNullException(nameof(navigationService));
    //...
  }

  public override void OnAdd()
  {
    Book newBook = new();
    Items.Add(newBook);
    SelectedItem = newBook;
  }

  //...
}
```

Commands

The view models offer commands that implement the interface `ICommand`. Commands allow a separation between the view and the command handler method via data binding. Commands also offer the functionality to enable or disable the command. The `ICommand` interface defines the methods `Execute` and `CanExecute` and the event `CanExecuteChanged`.

The class `RelayCommand` that implements this interface is implemented in the NuGet package `Microsoft .Toolkit.Mvvm` in the namespace `Microsoft.Toolkit.Mvvm.Input`.

The constructor of the `EditableItemViewModel` creates new `RelayCommand` objects and assigns the previously shown methods `BeginEdit`, `CancelEdit`, and `EndEdit` on execution of the commands. All these commands also check whether the command is available by using the `IsReadMode` and `IsEditMode` properties. When the `IsEditMode` property changes, the `CanExecuteChanged` event of the command is fired to update the command accordingly (code file `GenericViewModels/ViewModels/EditableItemViewModel.cs`):

```
public abstract class EditableItemViewModel<TItem> : ItemViewModel<TItem>,
  IEditableObject
```

```
    where TItem : class
{
  private readonly IItemsService<TItem> _itemsService;

  public EditableItemViewModel(IItemsService<TItem> itemsService)
  {
    _itemsService = itemsService;
    Item = _itemsService.SelectedItem;

    EditCommand = new RelayCommand(BeginEdit, () => IsReadMode);
    CancelCommand = new RelayCommand(CancelEdit, () => IsEditMode);
    SaveCommand = new RelayCommand(EndEdit, () => IsEditMode);
  }

  public RelayCommand EditCommand { get; }
  public RelayCommand CancelCommand { get; }
  public RelayCommand SaveCommand { get; }

  //...

  public bool IsEditMode
  {
    get => _isEditMode;
    set
    {
      if (Set(ref _isEditMode, value))
      {
        OnPropertyChanged(nameof(IsReadMode));
        CancelCommand.NotifyCanExecuteChanged();
        SaveCommand.NotifyCanExecuteChanged();
        EditCommand.NotifyCanExecuteChanged();
      }
    }
  }
  //...
}
```

From the XAML code, the commands are bound to the `Command` property of a `Button`. This is discussed when creating the views in the section "Views" in more detail (code file `BooksApp/Views/BookDetailUserControl.xaml`):

```
<AppBarButton Content="Edit" Icon="Edit"
  Command="{x:Bind ViewModel.EditCommand, Mode=OneTime}" />
<AppBarButton Content="Save" Icon="Save"
  Command="{x:Bind ViewModel.SaveCommand, Mode=OneTime}" />
```

Services, View Models, and Dependency Injection

View models and services inject services, and view models need to be created. For this, you can use a dependency injection container. The sample application makes use of `Microsoft.Extensions.DependencyInjection`, which is covered in detail in Chapter 15. `Microsoft.Toolkit.Mvvm` offers the `Ioc` class where this container is used by default.

The container is configured using `Ioc.Default.ConfigureServices` in the `RegisterServices` method of the `App` class. `RegisterServices` is invoked from the `OnLaunched` method (code file `BooksApp/App.xaml.cs`):

```
private void RegisterServices()
{
  Ioc.Default.ConfigureServices(
    new ServiceCollection()
      .AddSingleton<IBooksRepository, BooksSampleRepository>()
      .AddScoped<BooksViewModel>()
      .AddScoped<BookDetailViewModel>()
      .AddScoped<MainWindowViewModel>()
      .AddSingleton<IItemsService<Book>, BooksService>()
      .AddSingleton<IDialogService, WinUIDialogService>()
      .AddSingleton<INavigationService, WinUINavigationService>()
      .AddSingleton<WinUIInitializeNavigationService>()
      .AddLogging(builder =>
      {
        builder.AddDebug();
      }).BuildServiceProvider());
}
```

Now the view model needs to be associated with the view, which is done in the `BooksPage` by accessing the `AppServices` property of the `App` class and invoking the `GetService` method from the DI container. The container then instantiates the view model class with the required services as defined in the constructor of the view model class. The `BooksPage` contains a user control for the detail information of the book that needs a different view model. This view model is assigned by setting the property `ViewModel` of the `BookDetailUserControl` user control (code file `BooksApp/Views/BooksPage.xaml.cs`):

```
public sealed partial class BooksPage : Page
{
  public BooksPage()
  {
    this.InitializeComponent();
    BookDetailUC.ViewModel = Ioc.Default.GetRequiredService<BookDetailViewModel>();
  }

  public BooksViewModel ViewModel { get; } =
    Ioc.Default.GetRequiredService<BooksViewModel>();
}
```

With the `BookDetailPage`, the association to the view model happens similarly (code file `BooksApp/Views/BookDetailPage.xaml.cs`):

```
public sealed partial class BookDetailPage : Page
{
  public BookDetailPage()
  {
    this.InitializeComponent();
  }

  public BookDetailViewModel ViewModel { get; } =
    Ioc.Default.GetRequiredService<BookDetailViewModel>();
}
```

VIEWS

Now that you've been introduced to creating the view models and to connecting the views to the view models, it's time to get into the views.

The main view of the application is defined by the `MainWindow`. This window makes use of the `NavigationView` control that was introduced in the previous chapter. Usually, if you have only a small list of items for navigation, you shouldn't use this UI control. However, the sample application uses the control because it is assumed the application will grow to more than eight times its current size.

The `NavigationView` control assigns the `SelectionChanged` event to the `OnNavigationSelectionChanged` method of the `MainPageViewModel`. The `MainPageViewModel` is very different from the other view model types and will be discussed later in the section "Navigating Between Pages." One `NavigationViewItem` is defined to navigate to the `BooksPage` (code file `BooksApp/MainWindow.xaml`):

```xml
<NavigationView IsBackButtonVisible="Collapsed"
  SelectionChanged="{x:Bind ViewModel.OnNavigationSelectionChanged, Mode=OneTime}">
  <NavigationView.MenuItems>
    <NavigationViewItem Content="Books" Tag="books">
      <NavigationViewItem.Icon>
        <FontIcon FontFamily="Segoe MDL2 Assets" Glyph="&#xE82D;" />
      </NavigationViewItem.Icon>
    </NavigationViewItem>
  </NavigationView.MenuItems>

  <Frame x:Name="MainFrame" Margin="16">
    <Frame.ContentTransitions>
      <TransitionCollection>
        <NavigationThemeTransition/>
      </TransitionCollection>
    </Frame.ContentTransitions>
  </Frame>
</NavigationView>
```

Figure 30-4 shows the `NavigationView` of the running app with the navigation item set to the `BooksPage`.

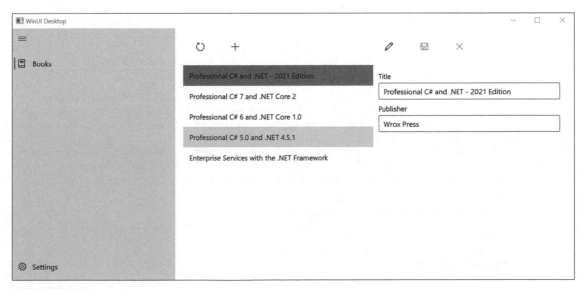

FIGURE 30-4

The BooksPage contains a ListView and binds the ItemsSource to the ItemsViewModel property of the BooksViewModel. Usually, you would bind it to the Items property of the BooksViewModel. However, the display of a single list item is not only used to show the value of the Book objects, but also contains buttons that are bound to commands. To implement such functionality, another view model can be used for the items (code file BooksApp/Views/BooksPage.xaml):

```xml
<StackPanel Orientation="Horizontal" Grid.Row="1">
  <AppBarButton Icon="Refresh" IsCompact="True"
    Command="{x:Bind ViewModel.RefreshCommand}"
    Label="Get Books" />
  <AppBarButton Icon="Add" IsCompact="True"
    Command="{x:Bind ViewModel.AddCommand}"
    Label="Add Book" />
</StackPanel>
<ListView ItemTemplate="{StaticResource BookItemTemplate}" Grid.Row="2"
  ItemsSource="{x:Bind ViewModel.ItemsViewModels, Mode=OneWay}"
  SelectedItem="{x:Bind ViewModel.SelectedItemViewModel, Mode=TwoWay}" />
<local:BookDetailUserControl x:Name="BookDetailUC" Visibility="Collapsed"
  Grid.Column="1" Grid.RowSpan="2" />
```

The BookDetailPage just contains a user control: the BookDetailUserControl. The BookDetailPage has the BookDetailViewModel associated, as you've seen previously. This view model is forwarded to the BookDetailUserControl by assigning the ViewModel property of the BookDetailPage to the ViewModel property of the BookDetailUserControl (code file BooksApp/Views/BookDetailPage.xaml):

```xml
<Grid Background="{ThemeResource ApplicationPageBackgroundThemeBrush}">
  <views:BookDetailUserControl ViewModel="{x:Bind ViewModel, Mode=OneTime}" />
</Grid>
```

The dependency property of the BookDetailUserControl is shown in the following code snippet. This mapping to the view model is then used for data binding in the XAML code (code file BooksApp/Views/BookDetailUserControl.xaml.cs):

```csharp
public BookDetailViewModel ViewModel
{
  get => (BookDetailViewModel)GetValue(ViewModelProperty);
  set => SetValue(ViewModelProperty, value);
}

public static readonly DependencyProperty ViewModelProperty =
  DependencyProperty.Register("ViewModel", typeof(BookDetailViewModel),
    typeof(BookDetailUserControl), new PropertyMetadata(null));
```

The user interface of the BookDetailUserControl makes use of two StackPanel elements. With the first StackPanel, the Command property of the AppBarButton controls is bound to the EditCommand, SaveCommand, and CancelCommand commands defined in the view model. The buttons will be automatically enabled or disabled depending on the state of the commands. With the second StackPanel, TextBox elements are used to display the Title and Publisher properties of the Book. For a read-only display, the IsReadOnly property is assigned to the IsReadMode property of the view model. When the view model is set to edit mode, the TextBox controls allow entering data (code file BooksApp/Views/BookDetailUserControl.xaml):

```xml
<StackPanel Orientation="Horizontal">
  <AppBarButton Content="Edit" Icon="Edit"
    Command="{x:Bind ViewModel.EditCommand, Mode=OneTime}" />
  <AppBarButton Content="Save" Icon="Save"
    Command="{x:Bind ViewModel.SaveCommand, Mode=OneTime}" />
  <AppBarButton Content="Cancel" Icon="Cancel"
```

```
                Command="{x:Bind ViewModel.CancelCommand, Mode=OneTime}" />
    </StackPanel>
    <StackPanel Orientation="Vertical" Grid.Row="1">
      <TextBox Header="Title"
               IsReadOnly="{x:Bind ViewModel.IsReadMode, Mode=OneWay}"
               Text="{x:Bind ViewModel.EditItem.Title, Mode=TwoWay,
               UpdateSourceTrigger=PropertyChanged}" />
      <TextBox Header="Publisher"
               IsReadOnly="{x:Bind ViewModel.IsReadMode, Mode=OneWay}"
               Text="{x:Bind ViewModel.EditItem.Publisher, Mode=TwoWay,
               UpdateSourceTrigger=PropertyChanged}" />
    </StackPanel>
```

Opening Dialogs from View Models

Sometimes it's necessary to show dialogs from actions within view models. As the view model is implemented in a .NET library, access to the `MessageDialog` class from WinUI is not possible without adding references to WinUI packages. This would hinder using this library from other technologies. You should avoid this situation anyway, because the `MessageDialog` is specific to UWP and WinUI. With WPF you use the `MessageBox` class instead. With `Xamarin.Forms`, you use `Page.DisplayAlert`.

What needs to be done is to define a contract that can be used by the view models and services. This contract is defined in the `BooksLib` library with the `IMessageService` interface (code file `BooksLib/Services/IDialogService.cs`):

```
public interface IDialogService
{
  Task ShowMessageAsync(string message);
}
```

In the `BookDetailViewModel`, the `IDialogService` is injected in the constructor and used on the `OnSaveAsync` method. The `ShowMessageAsync` method is invoked in the case of an exception (code file `BooksLib/ViewModels/BookDetailViewModel.cs`):

```
public override async Task OnSaveAsync()
{
  try
  {
    if (EditItem is null) throw new InvalidOperationException();
    await _itemsService.AddOrUpdateAsync(EditItem);
  }
  catch (Exception ex)
  {
    _logger.LogError("error {0} in {1}", ex.Message, nameof(OnSaveAsync));
    await _messageService.ShowMessageAsync("Error saving the data");
  }
}
```

Now just a specific implementation for WinUI is needed. The `ShowMessageAsync` method is implemented using the `MessageDialog` class. The `WinUIDialogService` is implemented in the WinUI BooksApp; that's why access to `MessageDialog` is now possible (code file `BooksApp/Services/WinUIDialogService.cs`):

```
public class WinUIDialogService : IDialogService
{
  public async Task ShowMessageAsync(string message) =>
    await new MessageDialog(message).ShowAsync();
}
```

With the dependency container configuration that was discussed earlier in the section "Services, View Models, and Dependency Injection," the `WinUIDialogService` is configured to be used when the `IDialogService` interface is requested. Creating .NET MAUI or WPF applications, different implementations need to be created that then need to be configured with the DI container of the application. The library where the `IDialogService` contract is used does not need to have knowledge about the implementation.

Navigating Between Pages

As with opening dialogs, navigating between pages is different among different technologies. With WinUI, the `Frame` class is used to navigate pages within the app. With WPF, it's again a `Frame` class, but it's a different one. With Xamarin.Forms, the `NavigationPage` is used for navigation. How the navigation is implemented with these technologies also differs. With UWP, you need a `Type` object to navigate to. With Xamarin.Forms, you need an object instance of the page. With Xamarin.Forms, the navigation methods are asynchronous, whereas they are synchronous with WinUI. For this, a common contract is needed again.

With the sample application, navigation to a page is needed, and you need a way to navigate back. Also, the current page needs to be accessed to know whether navigation needs to be done. For this, the interface `INavigationService` is defined. This interface is based on strings for navigation, which makes it possible to create implementations for the different platforms (code file `GenericViewModels/Services/INavigationService.cs`):

```
public interface INavigationService
{
  bool UseNavigation { get; set; }
  Task NavigateToAsync(string page);
  Task GoBackAsync();
  string CurrentPage { get; }
}
```

The `WinUINavigationService` needs a `Frame` assigned, so it can navigate for WinUI. When you define a property of a `Frame`, it's not possible to access it because from the outside, just the `INavigationService` interface is used. With the `INavigationService` interface, the `Frame` cannot be used to avoid a dependency on WinUI. What can be done in such a scenario is to create a service specific for WinUI that will be injected with the WinUI implementation of the `INavigationService`. Internally, when the `Pages` and `Frame` properties are accessed, this information is taken from the initialization service, as shown in the following code snippet (code file `BooksApp/Services/WinUINavigationService.cs`):

```
public class WinUINavigationService : INavigationService
{
  private readonly WinUIInitializeNavigationService _initializeNavigation;

  public WinUINavigationService(
    WinUIInitializeNavigationService initializeNavigation) =>
    _initializeNavigation = initializeNavigation;

  private Dictionary<string, Type>? _pages;
  private Dictionary<string, Type> Pages => _pages ??= _initializeNavigation.Pages;

  private Frame? _frame;
  private Frame Frame => _frame ??= _initializeNavigation.Frame;
  //...
}
```

The implementation of the `NavigateToAsync` method uses the `Frame` property to navigate to the page (code file `BooksApp/Services/WinUINavigationService.cs`):

```
public class UWPNavigationService : INavigationService
{
```

```
//...
public Task NavigateToAsync(string pageName)
{
  _currentPage = pageName;
  Frame.Navigate(Pages[pageName]);
  return Task.CompletedTask;
}
}
```

The only functionality the `WinUIInitializeNavigationService` offers is to initialize it with a `Frame` and a dictionary of pages and to retrieve this information (code file `BooksApp/Services/WinUIInitializeNavigationService.cs`):

```
public class WinUIInitializeNavigationService
{
  public void Initialize(Frame frame, Dictionary<string, Type> pages)
  {
    Frame = frame ?? throw new ArgumentNullException(nameof(frame));
    Pages = pages ?? throw new ArgumentNullException(nameof(pages));
  }
  private Frame? _frame;
  public Frame Frame => _frame ?? throw new InvalidOperationException(
    $"{nameof(WinUIInitializeNavigationService)} not initalized");

  private Dictionary<string, Type>? _pages;
  public Dictionary<string, Type> Pages => _pages ?? throw new InvalidOperationException(
    $"{nameof(WinUIInitializeNavigationService)} not initalized");
}
```

The `WinUIInitializeNavigationService` can now be initialized on a place where the `Frame` is available. With the WinUI sample application, this is in the `MainWindow`. Within the `NavigationView` control specified earlier, the `Frame` with the name `MainFrame` is specified. Now it would be possible to define the initialization within the code-behind file of the `MainWindow`, or in a WinUI-specific `MainPageViewModel`. For the sample application, the second option was chosen.

In the following code snippet, the `MainWindowViewModel` keeps a list of pages for the navigation and initializes the navigation service when the `SetNavigationFrame` is invoked (code file `BooksApp/ViewModels/MainWindowViewModel.cs`):

```
public class MainPageViewModel : ViewModelBase
{
  private readonly Dictionary<string, Type> _pages = new()
  {
    [PageNames.BooksPage] = typeof(BooksPage),
    [PageNames.BookDetailPage] = typeof(BookDetailPage)
  };

  private readonly INavigationService _navigationService;
  private readonly WinUIInitializeNavigationService _initializeNavigationService;
  public MainPageViewModel(INavigationService navigationService,
    WinUIInitializeNavigationService initializeNavigationService)
  {
    _navigationService = navigationService;
    _initializeNavigationService = initializeNavigationService;
  }
```

```
      public void SetNavigationFrame(Frame frame) =>
        _initializeNavigationService.Initialize(frame, _pages);

      //...
    }
```

With this view model in place, all that needs to be in the code-behind file of the `MainWindow` is the `ViewModel` property and the passing of the `MainFrame` to the navigation service via invocation of the method `SetNavigationFrame` (code file BooksApp/MainWindow.xaml.cs):

```
public sealed partial class MainWindow : Window
{
  public MainWindow()
  {
    this.InitializeComponent();
    ViewModel = Ioc.Default.GetRequiredService<MainPageViewModel>();
    ViewModel.SetNavigationFrame(MainFrame);
  }

  public MainPageViewModel ViewModel { get; }
}
```

The first navigation to the `BooksPage` happens in the `MainPageViewModel`. The method `OnNavigationSelectionChanged` is the handler for the `NavigationSelectionChanged` event of the `NavigationView` control. With the `Tag` set to `books`, navigation to the `BooksPage` is done using `INavigationService` (code file BooksApp/ViewModels/MainPageViewModel.cs):

```
public class MainPageViewModel : ViewModelBase
{
  //...
  public void OnNavigationSelectionChanged(NavigationView sender,
    NavigationViewSelectionChangedEventArgs args)
  {
    if (args.SelectedItem is NavigationViewItem navigationItem)
    {
      switch (navigationItem.Tag)
      {
        case "books":
          _navigationService.NavigateToAsync(PageNames.BooksPage);
          break;
        default:
          break;
      }
    }
  }
}
```

Navigation from the `BooksPage` is done directly from a shared view model. The navigation from the `BooksPage` to the `BooksDetailPage` happens when a list item is selected, and the `PropertyChanged` event fires. Navigation is also done only when the property `UseNavigation` is set to `true`. As previously mentioned, with WinUI, when the UI is large enough, navigation is not needed at this place because the detail information is then shown side by side with the list (code file BooksLib/ViewModels/BooksViewModel.cs):

```
public class BooksViewModel : MasterDetailViewModel<BookItemViewModel, Book>
{
  private readonly IItemsService<Book> _booksService;
  private readonly INavigationService _navigationService;
```

```
   public BooksViewModel(IItemsService<Book> booksService,
     INavigationService navigationService)
     : base(booksService)
   {
     _booksService = booksService ??
       throw new ArgumentNullException(nameof(booksService));
     _navigationService = navigationService ??
       throw new ArgumentNullException(nameof(navigationService));

     PropertyChanged += async (sender, e) =>
     {
       if (UseNavigation && e.PropertyName == nameof(SelectedItem) &&
         _navigationService.CurrentPage == PageNames.BooksPage)
       {
         await _navigationService.NavigateToAsync(PageNames.BookDetailPage);
       }
     };
   }

   public bool UseNavigation { get; set; }
   //...
 }
```

To inform the application about window size changes, you can use an event aggregator as discussed in the next section.

MESSAGING USING EVENTS

You can pass information between view models, views, and services by using stateful services that are configured with the DI container. In such services, you can also define events, so a subscriber can register to events while a publisher fires information. Instead of creating such custom services, you can use an event aggregator like the one available with `Microsoft.Toolkit.Mvvm`. With this framework, the `IMessenger` interface can be used to publish and subscribe messages. The `WeakReferenceManager` is one of the classes implementing this interface.

In case the books application is used on a mobile device with .NET MAUI, you might always navigate between the `BooksPage` and the `BookDetailPage` when clicking a book in the list. On the desktop, instead of using the `BookDetailPage`, a user control for the book details is set to visible in the `BooksPage`. If the window size of the application is not large enough, you can switch to use navigation to pages instead. To inform anyone who is interested about the window size, you can use an event aggregator.

For passing the information about the navigation from the main window to the view model, the `NavigationInfoEvent` is needed. This event information class uses a Boolean property to define whether navigation should be used (code file `BooksLib/Events/NavigationMessage.cs`):

```
public class NavigationInfo
{
  public bool UseNavigation { get; set; }
}

public class NavigationMessage : ValueChangedMessage<NavigationInfo>
{
  public NavigationMessage(NavigationInfo navigationInfo)
    : base(navigationInfo) {  }
}
```

The event is published when the size of the main window changes. With the `MainWindow` class, the `OnSizeChanged` event handler is registered to the `SizeChanged` event of the page. In the event handler, the `WeakReferenceMessenger` is accessed to send a `NavigationMessage` (code file `BooksApp/MainWindow.xaml.cs`):

```
public sealed partial class MainWindow : Window
{
  //...
  private void OnSizeChanged(object sender, SizeChangedEventArgs e)
  {
    double width = args.Size.Width;
    NavigationMessage navigation = new(new()
    {
      UseNavigation = width < 1024
    });
    WeakReferenceMessenger.Default.Send(navigation);
  }
}
```

In places where information about the window event size is needed, subscription to the event can be done by implementing the interface `IRecepient<TMessage>`. This interface defines the `Receive` method to receive the event information.

```
WeakReferenceMessenger.Default.Register<NavigationMessage>(this);
```

When you use the `Unregister` method, events can be unsubscribed. To avoid memory leaks when not unsubscribing, the `WeakReferenceMessenger` uses `WeakReference` objects. `Microsoft.Toolkit.Mvvm` also offers the faster `StrongReferenceManager`, but you need to make sure to unsubscribe.

SUMMARY

This chapter gave you an architectural guideline for creating XAML-based applications around the MVVM pattern. You've seen the separation of concerns (SoC) pattern by creating a model, view, and view model. Besides that, you've seen implementing change notification with the interface `INotifyPropertyChanged`, the repository pattern to separate the data access code, messaging between view models (that can also be used to communicate with views) by using events, and dependency injection with an IoC container.

The chapter also showed you a library of view models that can be used across applications. All this allows for code sharing while still using features of specific platforms. You can use platform-specific features with repository and service implementations, and contracts are available with all platforms.

The next chapter continues the discussion of XAML and is about styles and resources.

31

Styling Windows Apps

WHAT'S IN THIS CHAPTER?

➤ Styling Windows apps

➤ Creating a base drawing with shapes and geometry

➤ Scaling, rotating, and skewing with transformations

➤ Using brushes to fill backgrounds

➤ Working with styles, templates, and resources

➤ Creating animations

➤ Working with the VisualStateManager

CODE DOWNLOADS FOR THIS CHAPTER

The source code for this chapter is available on the book page at www.wiley.com. Click the Downloads link. The code can also be found at https://github.com/ProfessionalCSharp/ProfessionalCSharp2021 in the directory 4_Apps/Styles.

The code for this chapter is divided into the following major examples:

➤ Shapes

➤ Geometries

➤ Transformations

➤ Brushes

➤ Styles And Resources

➤ Templates

➤ Animation

➤ Transitions

➤ VisualStates

All the projects have nullable reference types enabled.

STYLING

With modern applications, developers have become a lot more concerned with having good-looking apps. When Windows Forms was the technology for creating desktop applications, the user interface didn't offer many options for styling the applications. Controls had a standard look that varied slightly based on the operating system version on which the application was running, but it was not easy to define a complete custom look.

This changed with Windows Presentation Foundation (WPF). WPF is based on DirectX and thus offers vector graphics that allow easy resizing of windows and controls. Controls are completely customizable and can have different looks. Styling of applications has become extremely important. An application can have any look. With a good design, the user can work with the application without the need to know how to use a Windows application. Instead, the user just needs to have domain knowledge. For example, the airport in Zurich created a WPF application where buttons look like airplanes. With the button, the user can get information about the position of the plane (the complete application looks like the airport). Colors of the buttons can have different meanings based on the configuration; they can show either the airline or on-time/delay information of the plane. This way, the user of the app easily sees which planes that are currently at the airport have small or big delays.

Having different looks for the app is even more important with modern Windows apps. With these apps, the device can be used by users who haven't used Windows applications before. With users who are knowledgeable of Windows applications, you should think about helping these users be more productive by having the typical process for how the user works easily accessible.

With its guidance on UI design with the Fluent Design System (`https://www.microsoft.com/design/fluent/`), Microsoft continuously evolves cross-platform UI design for applications, including web, Windows, iOS, Android, macOS, and other cross-platform applications. Many Microsoft applications use guidance from this design, and WinUI plays an important role (`https://microsoft.github.io/microsoft-ui-xaml/`).

This chapter starts with the core elements of XAML—*shapes* that enable you to draw lines, ellipses, and path elements. After that you're introduced to the foundation of shapes—*geometry* elements. You can use geometry elements to create fast vector-based drawings.

With *transformations*, you can scale and rotate any XAML element. With *brushes*, you can create solid color, gradient, or more advanced backgrounds. You see how to use brushes within *styles* and place styles within XAML *resources*.

Finally, with *templates* you can completely customize the look of controls, and you also learn how to create animations in this chapter.

SHAPES

Shapes are the core elements of XAML. With shapes, you can draw two-dimensional graphics using rectangles, lines, ellipses, paths, polygons, and polylines that are represented by classes derived from the abstract base class `Shape`. With WinUI, shapes are defined in the namespace `Microsoft.UI.Xaml.Shapes`.

The following XAML example draws a yellow face consisting of an ellipse for the face, two ellipses for the eyes, two ellipses for the pupils in the eyes, and a path for the mouth (code file `Shapes/MainWindow.xaml`):

```
<Canvas>
  <Ellipse Canvas.Left="10" Canvas.Top="10" Width="100" Height="100"
    Stroke="Blue" StrokeThickness="4" Fill="Yellow" />
  <Ellipse Canvas.Left="30" Canvas.Top="12" Width="60" Height="30">
    <Ellipse.Fill>
      <LinearGradientBrush StartPoint="0.5,0" EndPoint="0.5, 1">
        <GradientStop Offset="0.1" Color="DarkGreen" />
        <GradientStop Offset="0.7" Color="Transparent" />
      </LinearGradientBrush>
    </Ellipse.Fill>
```

```
      </Ellipse.Fill>
    </Ellipse>
    <Ellipse Canvas.Left="30" Canvas.Top="35" Width="25" Height="20"
      Stroke="Blue" StrokeThickness="3" Fill="White" />
    <Ellipse Canvas.Left="40" Canvas.Top="43" Width="6" Height="5"
      Fill="Black" />
    <Ellipse Canvas.Left="65" Canvas.Top="35" Width="25" Height="20"
      Stroke="Blue" StrokeThickness="3" Fill="White" />
    <Ellipse Canvas.Left="75" Canvas.Top="43" Width="6" Height="5"
      Fill="Black" />
    <Path Stroke="Blue" StrokeThickness="4"
      Data="M 40,74 Q 57,95 80,74" />
  </Canvas>
```

Figure 31-1 shows the result of the XAML code.

FIGURE 31-1

All these XAML elements can be accessed programmatically—even if they are buttons or shapes, such as lines or rectangles. Setting the `Name` or `x:Name` property with the `Path` element to `mouth` enables you to access this element programmatically with the variable name `mouth`:

```
<Path Name="mouth" Stroke="Blue" StrokeThickness="4"
  Data="M 40,74 Q 57,95 80,74 " />
```

With the next code changes, the mouth of the face is changed dynamically from the code-behind. A button with a click handler is added where the `SetMouth` method is invoked (code file `Shapes/MainWindow.xaml.cs`):

```
private void OnChangeShape() => SetMouth();
```

Using the code-behind, a geometrical shape can be created using figures and segments. First, you create a two-dimensional array of six points to define three points for the happy state and three points for the sad state (code file `Shapes/MainWindow.xaml.cs`):

```
private readonly Point[,] _mouthPoints = new Point[2, 3]
{
  { new(40, 74), new(57, 95), new(80, 74) },
  { new(40, 82), new(57, 65), new(80, 82) }
};
```

Next, you assign a new `PathGeometry` object to the `Data` property of the `Path`. The `PathGeometry` contains a `PathFigure` with the start point defined (setting the `StartPoint` property is the same as the letter `M` with path markup syntax discussed later in the section "Geometries Using Path Markup"). The `PathFigure` contains a `QuadraticBezierSegment` with two `Point` objects assigned to the properties `Point1` and `Point2` (the same as the letter `Q` with two points):

```
private bool _laugh = false;
public void SetMouth()
{
  int index = _laugh ? 0: 1;

  PathFigure figure = new() { StartPoint = _mouthPoints[index, 0] };
  figure.Segments = new PathSegmentCollection();
  QuadraticBezierSegment segment1 = new()
  {
    Point1 = _mouthPoints[index, 1];
    Point2 = _mouthPoints[index, 2];
  }

  figure.Segments.Add(segment1);
```

```
PathGeometry geometry = new();
geometry.Figures = new PathFigureCollection();
geometry.Figures.Add(figure);

mouth.Data = geometry;
_laugh = !_laugh;
}
```

Using segments and figures is explained in more detail in the next section. When you run the app, clicking the button switches between the laughing face and the sad face.

The following table describes the shapes available in the namespace `Microsoft.Ui.Xaml.Shapes`:

SHAPE CLASS	DESCRIPTION
Line	You can draw a line from the coordinates X1,Y1 to X2,Y2.
Rectangle	You draw a rectangle by specifying Width and Height for this class.
Ellipse	You can draw an ellipse.
Path	You can draw a series of lines and curves. The Data property is a Geometry type. You can do the drawing by using classes that derive from the base class Geometry, or you can use the path markup syntax to define geometry.
Polygon	You can draw a closed shape formed by connected lines. The polygon is defined by a series of Point objects assigned to the Points property.
Polyline	Like the Polygon class, you can draw connected lines with Polyline. The difference is that the polyline does not need to be a closed shape.

GEOMETRY

The previous sample showed that one of the shapes, Path, uses Geometry for its drawing. You can also use Geometry elements in other places, such as with a DrawingBrush.

In some ways, geometry elements are similar to shapes. Just as there are Line, Ellipse, and Rectangle shapes, there are also geometry elements for these drawings: LineGeometry, EllipseGeometry, and RectangleGeometry. There are also big differences between shapes and geometries. A Shape is a FrameworkElement that you can use with any class that supports UIElement as its children. FrameworkElement derives from UIElement. Shapes participate with the layout system and render themselves. The Geometry class can't render itself and has fewer features and less overhead than Shape. The Geometry class directly derives from DependencyObject.

The Path class uses Geometry for its drawing. The geometry can be set with the Data property of the Path. Simple geometry elements that can be set are EllipseGeometry for drawing an ellipse, LineGeometry for drawing a line, and RectangleGeometry for drawing a rectangle.

Geometries Using Segments

You can also create geometries by using segments. The geometry class PathGeometry uses segments for its drawing. The following code snippet uses the BezierSegment and LineSegment elements to build one red figure. Check the code download for the additional green figure. Figure 31-2 shows both figures. The first

`BezierSegment` draws a Bézier curve between the points 70,40, which is the starting point of the figure, and 150,63 with control points 90,37 and 130,46. The following `LineSegment` uses the ending point of the Bézier curve and draws a line to 120,110 (code file `Geometries/MainWindow.xaml`):

```
<Path Canvas.Left="0" Canvas.Top="0" Fill="Red" Stroke="Blue"
   StrokeThickness="2.5">
   <Path.Data>
      <GeometryGroup>
         <PathGeometry>
            <PathGeometry.Figures>
               <PathFigure StartPoint="70,40" IsClosed="True">
                  <PathFigure.Segments>
                     <BezierSegment Point1="90,37" Point2="130,46"
                        Point3="150,63" />
                     <LineSegment Point="120,110" />
                     <BezierSegment Point1="100,95" Point2="70,90"
                        Point3="45,91" />
                  </PathFigure.Segments>
               </PathFigure>
            </PathGeometry.Figures>
         </PathGeometry>
      </GeometryGroup>
   </Path.Data>
</Path>
```

Other than the `BezierSegment` and `LineSegment` elements, you can use `ArcSegment` to draw an elliptical arc between two points. With `PolyLineSegment`, you can define a set of lines, `PolyBezierSegment` consists of multiple Bézier curves, `QuadraticBezierSegment` creates a quadratic Bézier curve, and `PolyQuadraticBezierSegment` consists of multiple quadratic Bézier curves.

FIGURE 31-2

Geometries Using Path Markup

Earlier in this chapter, you saw a use of path markup with the `Path` shape. When you use path markup, behind the scenes a speedy drawing with `StreamGeometry` gets created. XAML for WinUI apps creates figures and segments. Programmatically, you can define a figure by creating lines, Bézier curves, and arcs. With XAML, you can use path markup syntax. You can use path markup with the `Data` property of the `Path` class. Special characters define how the points are connected. In the following example, `M` marks the start point, `L` is a line command to the point specified, and `Z` is the close command to close the figure. Figure 31-3 shows the result. The path markup syntax allows more commands such as horizontal lines (`H`), vertical lines (`V`), cubic Bézier curves (`C`), quadratic Bézier curves (`Q`), smooth cubic Bézier curves (`S`), smooth quadratic Bézier curves (`T`), and elliptical arcs (`A`) (code file `Geometries/MainWindow.xaml`):

FIGURE 31-3

```
<Path Canvas.Left="0" Canvas.Top="200" Fill="Yellow" Stroke="Blue"
   StrokeThickness="2.5"
   Data="M 120,5 L 128,80 L 220,50 L 160,130 L 190,220 L 100,150
      L 80,230 L 60,140 L0,110 L70,80 Z" StrokeLineJoin="Round">
</Path>
```

TRANSFORMATION

Because XAML is vector-based, you can resize every element. In the next example, the vector-based graphics are now scaled, rotated, and skewed. Hit testing (for example, with mouse moves and mouse clicks) works but without any need for manual position calculation.

Figure 31-4 shows a rectangle in several different forms. All the rectangles are positioned within a `StackPanel` element with horizontal orientation to have the rectangles one beside the other. The first rectangle has its original size and layout. The second one is resized, the third moved, the fourth rotated, the fifth skewed, the sixth transformed using a transformation group, and the seventh transformed using a matrix. The following sections get into the code samples of all these options.

FIGURE 31-4

Scaling

Adding the `ScaleTransform` element to the `RenderTransform` property of the `Rectangle` element, as shown here, scales the content of the complete rectangle by a factor of 0.5 in the X direction and 0.4 in the Y direction (code file `Transformations/MainWindow.xaml`):

```
<Rectangle Width="120" Height="60" Fill="Red" Margin="20">
  <Rectangle.RenderTransform>
    <ScaleTransform ScaleX="0.5" ScaleY="0.4" />
  </Rectangle.RenderTransform>
</Rectangle>
```

You can do more than transform simple shapes like rectangles; you can transform any XAML element as XAML defines vector graphics. In the following code, the `Canvas` element with the face shown earlier is put into a user control named `SmilingFace`, and this user control is shown first without transformation and then resized. You can see the result in Figure 31-5.

FIGURE 31-5

```
<local:SmilingFace />
<local:SmilingFace>
  <local:SmilingFace.RenderTransform>
    <ScaleTransform ScaleX="1.6" ScaleY="0.8" CenterY="180" />
  </local:SmilingFace.RenderTransform>
</local:SmilingFace>
```

Translating

For moving an element in the X or Y direction, you can use `TranslateTransform`. In the following snippet, the element moves to the left by assigning -90 to X, and in the direction downward by assigning 20 to Y (code file `Transformations/MainWindow.xaml`):

```
<Rectangle Width="120" Height="60" Fill="Green" Margin="20">
  <Rectangle.RenderTransform>
    <TranslateTransform X="-90" Y="20" />
  </Rectangle.RenderTransform>
</Rectangle>
```

Rotating

You can rotate an element by using `RotateTransform`. With `RotateTransform`, you set the angle of the rotation and the center of the rotation with `CenterX` and `CenterY` (code file `Transformations/MainWindow.xaml`):

```
<Rectangle Width="120" Height="60" Fill="Orange" Margin="20">
  <Rectangle.RenderTransform>
    <RotateTransform Angle="45" CenterX="10" CenterY="-80" />
  </Rectangle.RenderTransform>
</Rectangle>
```

Skewing

For skewing, you can use the `SkewTransform` element. With skewing you can assign angles for the x- and y-axes (code file `Transformations/MainWindow.xaml`):

```
<Rectangle Width="120" Height="60" Fill="LightBlue" Margin="20">
  <Rectangle.RenderTransform>
    <SkewTransform AngleX="20" AngleY="30" CenterX="40" CenterY="390" />
  </Rectangle.RenderTransform>
</Rectangle>
```

Transforming with Groups and Composite Transforms

An easy way to do multiple transformations at once is by using the `CompositeTransform` and `TransformationGroup` elements. The `TransformationGroup` element can have `SkewTransform`, `RotateTransform`, `TranslateTransform`, and `ScaleTransform` as its children (code file `Transformations/MainWindow.xaml`):

```
<Rectangle Width="120" Height="60" Fill="LightGreen" Margin="20">
  <Rectangle.RenderTransform>
    <TransformGroup>
      <SkewTransform AngleX="45" AngleY="20" CenterX="-390" CenterY="40" />
      <RotateTransform Angle="90" />
      <ScaleTransform ScaleX="0.5" ScaleY="1.2" />
    </TransformGroup>
  </Rectangle.RenderTransform>
</Rectangle>
```

Instead of using the `TransformGroup` to combine multiple transformations, you can use the class `CompositeTransform`. `CompositeTransform` defines properties to do multiple transformations at once—for example, `ScaleX` and `ScaleY` for scaling as well as `TranslateX` and `TranslateY` for moving an element.

Transforming Using a Matrix

Another option for defining multiple transformations at once is to specify a matrix. Here, you use `MatrixTransform`. `MatrixTransform` defines a `Matrix` property that has six values. Setting the values 1, 0, 0, 1, 0, 0 doesn't change the element. With the values 0.5, 1.4, 0.4, 0.5, –200, and 0, the element is resized, skewed, and translated (code file `Transformations/MainWindow.xaml`):

```
<Rectangle Width="120" Height="60" Fill="Gold" Margin="20">
  <Rectangle.RenderTransform>
    <MatrixTransform Matrix="0.5, 1.4, 0.4, 0.5, -200, 0" />
  </Rectangle.RenderTransform>
</Rectangle>
```

The class `MatrixTransform` defines the public fields `M11`, `M12`, `M21`, `M22`, `OffsetX`, and `OffsetY` that are set in that order if a string is assigned to the `Matrix` property. `MatrixTransform` implements an affine transformation, so only six of the nine matrix members need to be specified. The remaining matrix members have fixed values 0, 0, and 1. The `M11` and `M22` fields have a default value 1 and are used to scale in the X and Y directions. `M12` and `M21` have a default value 0 and are used to skew the control. `OffsetX` and `OffsetY` have a default value 0 and are used to move the control.

BRUSHES

This section demonstrates how to use XAML's brushes for drawing backgrounds and foregrounds. In this section, you learn about using solid color and linear gradient colors with brushes, you draw images with brushes, and you use the `AcrylicBrush`. Figure 31-6 shows ellipses and rectangles using different brushes. To easily see the type of the brush, `TextBlock` elements show the type of the brush.

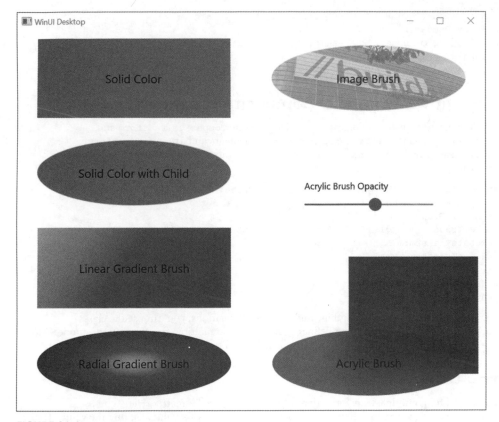

FIGURE 31-6

SolidColorBrush

The first button shown in Figure 31-6 uses the `SolidColorBrush`, which, as the name suggests, uses a solid color. The complete area is drawn with the same color.

Using a shape, you can define a solid color by setting the `Fill` attribute to a string that defines a solid color. The string is converted to a `SolidColorBrush` element with the help of the `BrushValueSerializer` (code file `Brushes/MainWindow.xaml`):

```
<Rectangle Fill="#FFC9659C" />
```

Of course, you will get the same effect by setting the `Fill` child element and adding a `SolidColorBrush` element as its content, as shown in the following code snippet. The first two shapes in the application use a hexadecimal value (alpha, red, green, and blue values) for the solid background color (code file `Brushes/MainWindow.xaml`):

```
<Ellipse>
  <Ellipse.Fill>
    <SolidColorBrush Color="#FFC9659C" />
  </Ellipse.Fill>
</Ellipse>
```

Gradient Brushes

For a smooth color change, you can use the `LinearGradientBrush`. This brush defines the `StartPoint` and `EndPoint` properties. With these, you can assign two-dimensional coordinates for the linear gradient. The default gradient is diagonal linear from `0,0` to `1,1`, from the upper-left corner of the object to the lower-right corner. By defining different values, the gradient can take different directions. For example, with a `StartPoint` of `0,0` and an `EndPoint` of `0,1`, you get a vertical gradient. The `StartPoint` value of `0,0` and `EndPoint` value of `1,0` creates a horizontal gradient.

With the content of this brush, you can define the color values at the specified offsets with the `GradientStop` element. Between the stops, the colors are smoothed (code file `Brushes/MainWindow.xaml`):

```
<Rectangle>
  <Rectangle.Fill>
    <LinearGradientBrush StartPoint="0,0" EndPoint="1,1">
      <GradientStop Offset="0" Color="LightGreen" />
      <GradientStop Offset="0.4" Color="Green" />
      <GradientStop Offset="1" Color="DarkGreen" />
    </LinearGradientBrush>
  </Rectangle.Fill>
</Rectangle>
```

WinUI also supports radial gradient brushes as shown with the following ellipse. With offsets from 0 to 1, the color is smoothed from the center to the outside. To change the center, you can set the property `GradientCenter`, which has a default value of `0.5,0.5`. (code file `Brushes/MainWindow.xaml`):

```
<Ellipse Grid.Row="3" Grid.Column="0">
  <Ellipse.Fill>
    <RadialGradientBrush>
      <GradientStop Offset="0" Color="LightGreen" />
      <GradientStop Offset="0.4" Color="Green" />
      <GradientStop Offset="1" Color="DarkGreen" />
    </RadialGradientBrush>
  </Ellipse.Fill>
</Ellipse>
```

ImageBrush

To load an image into a brush, you can use the `ImageBrush` element. With this element, the image defined by the `ImageSource` property is displayed. The image can be accessed from the file system or from a resource within the assembly. In the code example, the image is added from the file system (code file `Brushes/MainWindow.xaml`):

```
<Ellipse>
  <Ellipse.Fill>
    <ImageBrush ImageSource="msbuild.jpg" Opacity="0.5" />
  </Ellipse.Fill>
</Ellipse>
```

AcrylicBrush

The `AcrylicBrush` allows a transparency effect that lets other elements of the app or the host shine through.

Try the calculator that ships as part of Windows 10. The calculator has some slight transparency that lets other applications or the wallpaper image shine through to the app. This effect isn't applied to the main number buttons in the calculator, but the other elements of the calculator let the light of the background shine through.

You assign `AcrylicBrush` to any property where a brush is needed. With the following code snippet, the value for the `TintOpacity` is taken from the value of a slider with the application. This allows you to see the different effects of this brush based on the opacity when you move the slider in the app. The `TintColor` property specifies the main color of the brush. With the `BackgroundSource` property, you can select between `HostBackdrop` or `Backdrop`. When you use `Backdrop`, the colors from the app itself shine through. This is known as *in-app acrylic*. Elements that are overlaid from the controls using the brush shine through. With `HostBackdrop`, the colors from below the application are taken; this is *background acrylic*. Because acrylic UI effects require GPU power, this feature can shorten battery life. `AcrylicBrush` uses the solid color defined by the `FallbackColor` property when the system runs low on power. You also can configure the property `AlwaysUseFallback` to always use the fallback color. This setting can be triggered by user configuration to enhance the battery lifetime (code file `Brushes/MainWindow.xaml`):

```
<Ellipse Grid.Row="3" Grid.Column="1">
  <Ellipse.Fill>
    <AcrylicBrush BackgroundSource="Backdrop" TintColor="#FFFF0000"
      TintOpacity="{x:Bind acrylicOpacitySlider.Value, Mode=OneWay}"
      FallbackColor="Orange" />
  </Ellipse.Fill>
</Ellipse>
```

Figure 31-6 shows `AcrylicBrush` with a current `TintOpacity` setting of 0.4. The ellipse on the top is configured with `Backdrop`. Here, you can see that the background of the rectangle positioned underneath the ellipse shines through.

> **NOTE** *When should acrylic brushes be used? Acrylic adds texture and depth to the application. In-app navigation and commands look impressive with acrylic backgrounds. However, the primary app content should use solid backgrounds.*

STYLES AND RESOURCES

You can define the look and feel of the XAML elements by setting properties, such as `FontSize` and `Background`, with the `Button` element (code file `StylesAndResources/MainWindow.xaml`):

```
<Button Width="150" FontSize="12" Background="AliceBlue" Content="Click Me!" />
```

Instead of defining the look and feel with every element, you can define styles that are stored with resources. To completely customize the look of controls, you can use templates and add them to resources. Templates are covered in the section "Templates."

Styles

You can assign the `Style` property of a control to a `Style` element that has setters associated with it. A `Setter` element defines the `Property` and `Value` properties to set the specific properties and values for the target element. In the following example, the `Background`, `FontSize`, `FontWeight`, and `Margin` properties are set. The `Style` is set to the `TargetType` `Button` so that the properties of the `Button` can be directly accessed (code file `StylesAndResources/MainWindow.xaml`):

```xml
<Button Width="150" Content="Click Me!">
  <Button.Style>
    <Style TargetType="Button">
      <Setter Property="Background" Value="Yellow" />
      <Setter Property="FontSize" Value="14" />
      <Setter Property="FontWeight" Value="Bold" />
      <Setter Property="Margin" Value="4" />
    </Style>
  </Button.Style>
</Button>
```

Setting the `Style` directly with the `Button` element doesn't really help with style sharing. However, styles can be put into resources. You can use resources to assign styles to specific elements, assign a style to all elements of a type, or use a key for the style. To assign a style to all elements of a type, use the `TargetType` property of the `Style` and set it to the type. To define a style that needs to be referenced, `x:Key` must be set (code file `StylesAndResources/MainWindow.xaml`):

```xml
<Grid.Resources>
  <Style TargetType="Button">
    <Setter Property="Background" Value="LemonChiffon" />
    <Setter Property="FontSize" Value="18" />
    <Setter Property="Margin" Value="4" />
  </Style>
  <Style x:Key="ButtonStyle1" TargetType="Button">
    <Setter Property="Background" Value="Red" />
    <Setter Property="Foreground" Value="White" />
    <Setter Property="FontSize" Value="18" />
    <Setter Property="Margin" Value="8" />
  </Style>
</Grid.Resources>
```

In the sample application, the styles are defined within the `Grid` control using the `Resources` property.

In the following XAML code, the first button—which doesn't have a style defined with the element properties—gets the style that is defined for the `Button` type. With the next button, the `Style` property is set with the `StaticResource` markup extension to `{StaticResource ButtonStyle}`, whereas `ButtonStyle` specifies the key value of the style resource defined earlier, so this button has a red background and a white foreground. Specifying settings directly with the `Button` control overrides settings specified with the style (code file `StylesAndResources/MainWindow.xaml`):

```xml
<Button Width="200" Content="Default Button style" Margin="8" />
<Button Width="200" Content="Named style"
  Style="{StaticResource ButtonStyle1}" Margin="8" />
```

Rather than set the `Background` of a button to just a single value, you can set the value of the `Setter` with a child element. In case the brush is needed multiple times, you can use the `StaticResource` markup extension directly from a resource. The resource just needs to be defined before it's used as shown in the next code snippet. With the `BasedOn` property, a resource can take all the values from the based-on resource and overwrite the values that should be different. This code snippet defines the `FancyButtonStyle` that takes all the settings from the `ButtonStyle1` and just changes the value for the `Background` property. The brush for the `Background` property is retrieved from the sources specified with the key `GreenBrush` (code file `StylesAndResources/MainWindow.xaml`):

```xml
<LinearGradientBrush x:Key="GreenBrush" StartPoint="0,0" EndPoint="0,1">
  <GradientStop Offset="0.0" Color="LightCyan" />
```

```
    <GradientStop Offset="0.14" Color="Cyan" />
    <GradientStop Offset="0.7" Color="DarkCyan" />
</LinearGradientBrush>

<Style x:Key="FancyButtonStyle" TargetType="Button"
  BasedOn="{StaticResource ButtonStyle1}">
  <Setter Property="Background" Value="{StaticResource GreenBrush}" />
</Style>
```

This button has `FancyButtonStyle` applied:

```
<Button Width="200" Content="Style inheritance"
    Style="{StaticResource FancyButtonStyle}" />
```

Figure 31-7 shows the result of all these buttons after styling.

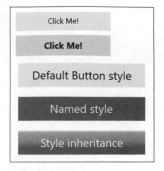

FIGURE 31-7

Resource Hierarchies

As you have seen with the styles sample, usually styles are stored within resources. The `FrameworkElement` base class defines the `Resourcces` property, so every class that derives from the `FrameworkElement` base class can specify resources.

Resources are searched hierarchically. If you define the resource with the root element, it applies to every child element. If the root element contains a `Grid`, the `Grid` contains a `StackPanel`, and you define the resource with the `StackPanel`, then the resource applies to every control within the `StackPanel`. If the `StackPanel` contains a `Button` and you define the resource just with the `Button`, then this style is valid only for the `Button`.

> **NOTE** *With hierarchies, you need to pay attention if you use the* `TargetType` *without a* `Key` *for styles. If you define a resource with the* `Canvas` *element and set the* `TargetType` *for the style to apply to* `TextBox` *elements, then the style applies to all* `TextBox` *elements within the* `Canvas`. *The style even applies to* `TextBox` *elements that are contained in a* `ListBox` *when the* `ListBox` *is in the* `Canvas`.

If you need the same style for more than one window, page, or user control, then you can define the style with the application. Creating a Windows app using Visual Studio, the file `App.xaml` is created for defining global resources of the application. The application styles are valid for every page or window of the application. Every element can access resources that are defined with the application. If resources are not found with the parent window, then the search for resources continues with the `Application`. You can define resources with resource dictionaries in separate files as shown with the resource `MyGradientBrush` (code file `StylesAndResources/Styles.xaml`):

```
<ResourceDictionary
  xmlns="http://schemas.microsoft.com/winfx/2006/xaml/presentation"
  xmlns:x="http://schemas.microsoft.com/winfx/2006/xaml"
  xmlns:local="using:StylesAndResources">
  <RadialGradientBrush x:Key="MyGradientBrush" x:Name="MyGradientBrush">
    <GradientStop Offset="0" Color="White" />
    <GradientStop Offset="0.6" Color="Orange" />
    <GradientStop Offset="1" Color="Red" />
  </RadialGradientBrush>
</ResourceDictionary>
```

This resource dictionary is referenced by setting the `MergedDictionaries` property of the `ResourceDictionary`, as shown in the following code snippet. When you reference the resource file from the `Application` class, the resource is available for every XAML element in the application (code file `StylesAndResources/App.xaml`):

```
<Application
  x:Class="StylesAndResources.App"
  xmlns="http://schemas.microsoft.com/winfx/2006/xaml/presentation"
  xmlns:x="http://schemas.microsoft.com/winfx/2006/xaml">
  <Application.Resources>
    <ResourceDictionary>
      <ResourceDictionary.MergedDictionaries>
        <XamlControlsResources xmlns="using:Microsoft.UI.Xaml.Controls" />
        <ResourceDictionary Source="Styles.xaml" />
      </ResourceDictionary.MergedDictionaries>
    </ResourceDictionary>
  </Application.Resources>
</Application>
```

Theme Resources

With Windows applications, default styles for light and dark themes are available that you can change dynamically. By specifying your custom styles, you can define styles for the different themes.

Theme resources can be defined in a resource dictionary within the `ThemeDictionaries` collection. The `ResourceDictionary` objects that are defined within the `ThemeDictionaries` collection need to have a key assigned that has the name of a theme—either `Light` or `Dark`. The sample code defines a button for the light theme that has a light background and dark foreground, and for the dark theme it defines a dark background and light foreground. The key `SampleButtonStyle` for the style is the same within both dictionaries (code file `StylesAndResources/UseThemesUserControl.xaml`):

```
<ResourceDictionary>
  <ResourceDictionary.ThemeDictionaries>
    <ResourceDictionary x:Key="Light">
      <Style TargetType="Button" x:Key="SampleButtonStyle">
        <Setter Property="Background" Value="Yellow" />
        <Setter Property="Foreground" Value="Black" />
      </Style>
    </ResourceDictionary>

    <ResourceDictionary x:Key="Dark">
      <Style TargetType="Button" x:Key="SampleButtonStyle">
        <Setter Property="Background" Value="Black" />
        <Setter Property="Foreground" Value="Yellow" />
      </Style>
    </ResourceDictionary>
  </ResourceDictionary.ThemeDictionaries>
</ResourceDictionary>
```

> **NOTE** *With the Windows app Fluent XAML Theme Editor (see Figure 31-8), which you can find in the Microsoft Store, you can easily create themes based on your color and border choices.*

FIGURE 31-8

You can set the default theme with the `RequestedTheme` property of a `FrameworkElement` to change the default theme. Different elements of a page can request different themes. The following code snippet changes the theme of a grid on the `Click` handler of a button (code file `StylesAndResources/UseThemesUserControl.xaml.cs`):

```
private void OnChangeTheme(object sender, RoutedEventArgs e)
{
  grid1.RequestedTheme = grid1.RequestedTheme == ElementTheme.Dark ?
    ElementTheme.Light : ElementTheme.Dark;
}
```

The `RequestedTheme` property is defined in the XAML element hierarchy. Every element can override the theme to be used for itself and its children. The following `Grid` element changes the default theme for the `Dark` theme. This is now the theme used for the `Grid` and all its children elements (code file `StylesAndResources/UseThemesUserControl.xaml`):

```
<Grid x:Name="grid1"
  Background="{ThemeResource ApplicationPageBackgroundThemeBrush}"
  RequestedTheme="Dark">
  <Button Style="{ThemeResource SampleButtonStyle}" Click="OnChangeTheme"
    Content="Change Theme" s/>
</Grid>
```

When you click the button, the theme is changed by setting the `RequestedTheme` property of a `FrameworkElement` (code file `StylesAndResources/UseThemesUserControl.xaml.cs`):

```
private void OnChangeTheme(object sender, RoutedEventArgs e)
{
  grid1.RequestedTheme = grid1.RequestedTheme == ElementTheme.Dark ?
    ElementTheme.Light : ElementTheme.Dark;
}
```

> **NOTE** *Using the* `ThemeResource` *markup extension is useful only in cases where the resource should look different based on the theme. If the resource should look the same, with all themes, keep using the* `StaticResource` *markup extension.*

TEMPLATES

A XAML `Button` control can contain any content. The content can be simple text, but you can also add a `Canvas` element, which can contain shapes; a `Grid`; or a video. In fact, you can do even more than that with a button! With template-based XAML controls, the functionality of controls is completely separate from their look and feel. A button has a default look, but you can completely customize that look.

Windows apps offer several template types that derive from the base class `FrameworkTemplate`.

TEMPLATE TYPE	DESCRIPTION
ControlTemplate	This enables you to specify the visual structure of a control and override its look.
ItemsPanelTemplate	For an `ItemsControl`, you can specify the layout of its items by assigning an `ItemsPanelTemplate`. Each `ItemsControl` has a default `ItemsPanelTemplate`. For the `MenuItem`, it is a `WrapPanel`. The `StatusBar` uses a `DockPanel`, and the `ListBox` uses a `VirtualizingStackPanel`.
DataTemplate	These are useful for graphical representations of objects. When styling a `ListBox`, by default the items of the `ListBox` are shown according to the output of the `ToString` method. By applying a `DataTemplate`, you can override this behavior and define a custom presentation of the items. `DataTemplates` are covered in Chapter 29, "Windows Apps."

Control Templates

Earlier in this chapter, I described how you can style the properties of a control. If setting simple properties of the controls doesn't give you the look you want, you can change the `Template` property. With the `Template` property, you can customize the complete look of the control. The next example demonstrates customizing buttons, and later in the chapter list views are customized step-by-step so you can see the intermediate results of the changes.

You customize the `Button` type in a separate resource dictionary file: `ControlTemplates.xaml`. In the following code sample, a style with the key name `RoundedGelButton` is defined. The style `RoundedGelButton` sets the properties `Background`, `Height`, `Foreground`, and `Margin`, and the `Template`. The `Template` is the most interesting aspect with this style. The `Template` specifies a `Grid` with just one row and one column.

Inside this cell, you can find an ellipse with the name `GelBackground`. This ellipse has a linear gradient brush for the stroke. The stroke that surrounds the rectangle is very thin because the `StrokeThickness` is set to 0.5.

The second ellipse, `GelShine`, is a small ellipse whose size is defined by the `Margin` property and so is visible within the first ellipse. The stroke is transparent, so there is no line surrounding the ellipse. This ellipse uses a linear gradient fill brush, which transitions from a light, partly transparent color to full transparency. This gives the ellipse a shimmering effect.

The `ContentPresenter` is the placeholder for the control's content, and it defines the place where the content should be positioned. In the code that follows, the content is placed in the first row of the `Grid`, as are the `Ellipse` elements. The `Content` property of the `ContentPresenter` defines what the content should be. The content is set to a `TemplateBinding` markup expression. `TemplateBinding` binds the template parent, which is the `Button` element in this case. `{TemplateBinding Content}` specifies that the value of the `Content` property of the `Button` control should be placed inside the placeholder as content (code file `Templates/Styles/ControlTemplates.xaml`):

```xaml
<ResourceDictionary
  xmlns="http://schemas.microsoft.com/winfx/2006/xaml/presentation"
  xmlns:x="http://schemas.microsoft.com/winfx/2006/xaml">

  <Style x:Key="RoundedGelButton" TargetType="Button">
    <Setter Property="Width" Value="100" />
    <Setter Property="Height" Value="100" />
    <Setter Property="Foreground" Value="White" />
    <Setter Property="Template">
      <Setter.Value>
        <ControlTemplate TargetType="Button">
          <Grid>
            <Ellipse Name="GelBackground" StrokeThickness="0.5" Fill="Black">
              <Ellipse.Stroke>
                <LinearGradientBrush StartPoint="0,0" EndPoint="0,1">
                  <GradientStop Offset="0" Color="#ff7e7e7e" />
                  <GradientStop Offset="1" Color="Black" />
                </LinearGradientBrush>
              </Ellipse.Stroke>
            </Ellipse>
            <Ellipse Margin="15,5,15,50">
              <Ellipse.Fill>
                <LinearGradientBrush StartPoint="0,0" EndPoint="0,1">
                  <GradientStop Offset="0" Color="#aaffffff" />
                  <GradientStop Offset="1" Color="Transparent" />
                </LinearGradientBrush>
              </Ellipse.Fill>
            </Ellipse>
            <ContentPresenter Name="GelButtonContent"
              VerticalAlignment="Center"
              HorizontalAlignment="Center"
              Content="{TemplateBinding Content}" />
          </Grid>
        </ControlTemplate>
      </Setter.Value>
    </Setter>
  </Style>
</ResourceDictionary>
```

From the `app.xaml` file, the resource dictionary is referenced as shown here (code file `Templates/App.xaml`):

```
<Application
  x:Class="Templates.App"
  xmlns="http://schemas.microsoft.com/winfx/2006/xaml/presentation"
  xmlns:x="http://schemas.microsoft.com/winfx/2006/xaml"
  xmlns:local="using:Templates">
  <Application.Resources>
    <ResourceDictionary>
      <ResourceDictionary.MergedDictionaries>
        <XamlControlsResources xmlns="using:Microsoft.UI.Xaml.Controls" />
        <ResourceDictionary Source="Styles/ControlTemplates.xaml" />
      </ResourceDictionary.MergedDictionaries>
    </ResourceDictionary>
  </Application.Resources>
</Application>
```

Now a `Button` control can be associated with the style. The new look of the button is shown in Figure 31-9 (code file `Templates/Views/ButtonTemplatesUsercontrol.xaml`):

FIGURE 31-9

```
<Button Style="{StaticResource RoundedGelButton}" Content="Click Me!" />
```

> **NOTE** *The* `TemplateBinding` *allows giving values to the template that are defined by the control. This can be used not only for the content but also for colors, stroke styles, and much more.*

Such a styled button now looks very fancy on the screen, but there's still a problem: there is no action if the button is clicked or touched or if the mouse moves over the button. This isn't the typical experience a user has with a button. However, there is a solution. With a template-styled button, you must have visual states or triggers that enable the button to have different looks in response to mouse moves and mouse clicks. First read the section "Animations" because the `VisualStateManager` makes use of animations; then read the section "Visual State Manager" to see how the button template is changed to react to clicks and mouse moves.

Instead of creating such a template from scratch, you can select a `Button` control either in the XAML designer or in the Document Explorer and select Edit Template from the context menu. Here, you can create an empty template or copy the predefined template. You use a copy of the template to take a look at how the predefined template looks.

Styling a ListView

Changing the style of a button or a label is a simple task, such as changing the style of an element that contains a list of elements. For example, how about changing a `ListView`? Again, this list control has behavior and a look. It can display a list of elements, and you can select one or more elements from the list. For the behavior, the `ListView` class defines methods, properties, and events. The look of the `ListView` is separate from its behavior. It has a default look, but you can change this look by creating a template.

To fill a `ListView` with some items, the class `CountryRepository` returns a list of a few countries that will be displayed. `Country` is a class with `Name` and `ImagePath` properties (code file `Templates/Models/CountryRepository.cs`):

```
public sealed class CountryRepository
{
  private static IEnumerable<Country>? s_countries;
```

```
public IEnumerable<Country> GetCountries() => s_countries ??= new List<Country>
{
  new() { Name = "Austria", ImagePath = "/Images/Austria.bmp" },
  new() { Name = "Germany", ImagePath = "/Images/Germany.bmp" },
  new() { Name = "Norway", ImagePath = "/Images/Norway.bmp" },
  new() { Name = "USA", ImagePath = "/Images/USA.bmp" }
};
}
```

Inside the code-behind file in the constructor of the StyledList class, a read-only property Countries is created and filled with the help of the GetCountries method of the CountryRepository (code file Templates/Views/StyledListUserControl.xaml.cs):

```
public ObservableCollection<Country> Countries { get; } =
  new ObservableCollection<Country>();

public StyledListUserControl()
{
  this.InitializeComponent();
  this.DataContext = this;
  var countries = new CountryRepository().GetCountries();
  foreach (var country in countries)
  {
    Countries.Add(country);
  }
}
```

Within the XAML code, the ListView named countryList1 is defined. countryList1 just uses the default style. The property ItemsSource is set to the Binding markup extension, which is used by data binding. From the code-behind, you have seen that the binding is done to an array of Country objects. Figure 31-10 shows the default look of the ListView. By default, only the names of the countries returned by the ToString method are displayed in a simple list (code file Templates/StyledListUserControl.xaml):

```
<Grid>
  <ListView ItemsSource="{x:Bind Countries}" Margin="10"
    x:Name="countryList1" />
</Grid>
```

Austria
Germany
Norway
USA

FIGURE 31-10

The look of the items in the ListView can be customized with a data template as has been shown in detail in Chapter 29. The sample code uses a data template that binds a TextBlock and an Image element to the Name and ImagePath properties (code file Templates/Styles/ListTemplates.xaml):

```
<DataTemplate x:Key="CountryDataTemplate">
  <Border Margin="4" BorderThickness="2" CornerRadius="6"
    BorderBrush="{StaticResource BorderBrush}"
    Background="{StaticResource BackgroundBrush}">
    <Border.BorderBrush>
    <Grid Margin="4">
      <Grid.RowDefinitions>
        <RowDefinition Height="auto" />
        <RowDefinition Height="auto" />
      </Grid.RowDefinitions>
      <Image Source="{Binding ImagePath, Mode=OneTime, FallbackValue=Name}" Width="120" />
      <TextBlock Text="{Binding Name, Mode=OneTime}" Grid.Row="1" Opacity="0.6"
        FontSize="16" VerticalAlignment="Bottom" HorizontalAlignment="Right" Margin="15"
        FontWeight="Bold" />
```

```
        </Grid>
      </Border>
    </DataTemplate>
```

Figure 31-11 shows the new look of the ListView.

Item Container Style

Every item of a ListView is placed into a container. The container can be customized with the ItemContainerStyle property of the ListView. The item container can define how the container for every item looks—for example, what foreground and background brushes should be used when the item is selected, pressed, and so on. For an easy view of the boundaries of the container, the Margin and Background properties are set in the following code snippet. The ListViewItemPresenter then presents the items. You can customize the focus brush, placeholder background, selected item foreground and background, and more with the presenter (code file Templates/Styles/ListTemplates.xaml):

```
<Style x:Key="ListViewItemStyle1" TargetType="ListViewItem">
  <Setter Property="Background" Value="Orange"/>
  <Setter Property="Margin" Value="5" />
  <Setter Property="Template">
    <Setter.Value>
      <ControlTemplate TargetType="ListViewItem">
        <ListViewItemPresenter />
      </ControlTemplate>
    </Setter.Value>
  </Setter>
</Style>
```

FIGURE 31-11

The style is associated with the ItemContainerStyle property of the ListView. Figure 31-12 shows the result of this style. This figure gives a good view of the boundaries of the items container (code file Templates/StyledListUserControl.xaml):

```
<ListView ItemsSource="{Binding Countries}" Margin="10"
  ItemContainerStyle="{StaticResource ListViewItemStyle1}"
  Style="{StaticResource ListViewStyle1}" MaxWidth="180" />
```

Items Panel

By default, the ListView arranges the items vertically. This is not the only way to arrange the items with this view; you can arrange them in other ways as well, such as horizontally. Arranging the items in an items control is the responsibility of the items panel.

The following code snippet defines a resource for an ItemsPanelTemplate, arranges the ItemsStackPanel horizontally instead of vertically, and gives a different background so you can easily see the boundaries of the items panel (code file Templates/Styles/ListTemplates.xaml):

```
<ItemsPanelTemplate x:Key="ItemsPanelTemplate1">
  <VirtualizingStackPanel Orientation="Horizontal" Background="Yellow"/>
</ItemsPanelTemplate>
```

FIGURE 31-12

The following ListView declaration uses the same Style and ItemContainerStyle as before but adds the resource for the ItemsPanel. Figure 31-13 shows the items now arranged horizontally (code file Templates/StyledListUserControl.xaml):

```
<ListView ItemsSource="{Binding Countries}" Margin="10"
  ItemContainerStyle="{StaticResource ListViewItemStyle1}"
```

```
        ItemTemplate="{StaticResource CountryDataTemplate}"
        ItemsPanel="{StaticResource ItemsPanelTemplate1}" />
```

FIGURE 31-13

To change the look of the complete control, you can also customize the Template property of the ListView—for example, to change the scrollbar behavior. Here, you can create a ControlTemplate for the target type ListView, similar to what you've seen with the customization of the Button control, and configure a ScrollViewer.

ANIMATIONS

When you use animations, you can make a smooth transition between images by using moving elements, color changes, transforms, and so on. XAML makes it easy to create animations. You can animate the value of most dependency properties. Different animation classes exist to animate the values of different properties, depending on their type.

The most important element of an animation is the timeline. This element defines how a value changes over time. Different kinds of timelines are available for changing different types of values. The base class for all timelines is Timeline. To animate a property of type double, you can use the class DoubleAnimation. The Int32Animation is the animation class for int values. You use PointAnimation to animate points and ColorAnimation to animate colors.

You can combine multiple timelines by using the Storyboard class. The Storyboard class itself is derived from the base class TimelineGroup, which derives from Timeline.

> **NOTE** *To see the animations without building and running the application, check the GIF files with the downloadable source code or directly check the links to the GIF files with the readme file of this chapter on GitHub.*

Timeline

A Timeline defines how a value changes over time. The following example animates the size of an ellipse. In the code that follows, DoubleAnimation timelines change scaling and translation of an ellipse; ColorAnimation changes the color of the fill brush. The Triggers property of the Ellipse class is set to an EventTrigger. The event trigger is fired when the ellipse is loaded. BeginStoryboard is a trigger action that begins the storyboard. With the storyboard, a DoubleAnimation element is used to animate the ScaleX, ScaleY, TranslateX, and TranslateY properties of the CompositeTransform class. The animation changes the horizontal scale to 5 and the vertical scale to 3 within ten seconds (code file Animation/SimpleAnimationControl.xaml):

```
<Ellipse x:Name="ellipse1" Width="100" Height="40"
  HorizontalAlignment="Left" VerticalAlignment="Top">
  <Ellipse.Fill>
    <SolidColorBrush Color="Green" />
```

```
      </Ellipse.Fill>
      <Ellipse.RenderTransform>
        <CompositeTransform ScaleX="1" ScaleY="1" TranslateX="0" TranslateY="0" />
      </Ellipse.RenderTransform>
      <Ellipse.Triggers>
        <EventTrigger>
          <BeginStoryboard>
            <Storyboard x:Name="MoveResizeStoryboard">
              <DoubleAnimation Duration="0:0:10" To="5"
                Storyboard.TargetName="ellipse1"
                Storyboard.TargetProperty=
                  "(UIElement.RenderTransform).(CompositeTransform.ScaleX)" />
              <DoubleAnimation Duration="0:0:10" To="3"
                Storyboard.TargetName="ellipse1"
                Storyboard.TargetProperty=
                  "(UIElement.RenderTransform).(CompositeTransform.ScaleY)" />
              <DoubleAnimation Duration="0:0:10" To="400"
                Storyboard.TargetName="ellipse1"
                Storyboard.TargetProperty=
                "(UIElement.RenderTransform).(CompositeTransform.TranslateX)" />
              <DoubleAnimation Duration="0:0:10" To="200"
                Storyboard.TargetName="ellipse1"
                Storyboard.TargetProperty=
                  "(UIElement.RenderTransform).(CompositeTransform.TranslateY)" />
              <ColorAnimation Duration="0:0:10" To="Red"
                Storyboard.TargetName="ellipse1"
                Storyboard.TargetProperty=
                  "(Ellipse.Fill).(SolidColorBrush.Color)" />
            </Storyboard>
          </BeginStoryboard>
        </EventTrigger>
      </Ellipse.Triggers>
    </Ellipse>
```

Animations are far more than the typical window-dressing animation that appears onscreen constantly and immediately. You can add animation to business applications that make the user interface feel more responsive. The look when a cursor moves over a button or when a button is clicked is defined by animations.

The following table describes what you can do with a timeline:

TIMELINE PROPERTIES	DESCRIPTION
AutoReverse	Use this property to specify whether the value that is animated should return, reversing the animation to its original value after the animation.
SpeedRatio	Use this property to transform the speed at which an animation moves. You can define the relation to the parent. The default value is 1; setting the ratio to a smaller value makes the animation move slower; setting the value greater than 1 makes it move faster.
BeginTime	Use this to specify the time span from the start of the trigger event until the moment the animation starts. You can specify days, hours, minutes, seconds, and fractions of seconds. This might not be real time, depending on the speed ratio. For example, if the speed ratio is set to 2 and the beginning time is set to six seconds, the animation will start after three seconds.

continues

(continued)

TIMELINE PROPERTIES	DESCRIPTION
Duration	Use this property to specify the length of time for one iteration of the animation.
RepeatBehavior	Assigning a RepeatBehavior struct to the RepeatBehavior property enables you to define how many times or for how long the animation should be repeated.
FillBehavior	This property is important if the parent timeline has a different duration. For example, if the parent timeline is shorter than the duration of the actual animation, setting FillBehavior to Stop means that the actual animation stops. If the parent timeline is longer than the duration of the actual animation, HoldEnd keeps the actual animation active before resetting it to its original value (if AutoReverse is set).

Depending on the type of the Timeline class, more properties may be available. For example, with DoubleAnimation, you can specify From and To properties for the start and end of the animation. An alternative is to specify the By property, whereby the animation starts with the current value of the Bound property and is incremented by the value specified by By.

Easing Functions

With the animations you've seen so far, the value changes in a linear way. In real life, a move never happens in a linear way. The move could start slowly and progressively get faster until reaching the highest speed, and then it slows down before reaching the end. When you let a ball fall against the ground, the ball bounces a few times before staying on the ground. Such nonlinear behavior can be created by using easing functions.

Animation classes have an EasingFunction property. This property accepts an object that derives from the base class EasingFunctionBase. With this type, an easing function object can define how the value should be animated over time. Several easing functions are available to create a nonlinear animation. Examples include ExponentialEase, which uses an exponential formula for animations; QuadraticEase, CubicEase, QuarticEase, and QuinticEase, with powers of 2, 3, 4, or 5; and PowerEase, with a power level that is configurable. Of special interest are SineEase, which uses a sinusoid curve; BounceEase, which creates a bouncing effect; and ElasticEase, which resembles animation values of a spring oscillating back and forth.

The following code snippet adds the BounceEase function to the DoubleAnimation. Adding different ease functions results in interesting animation effects:

```
<DoubleAnimation Storyboard.TargetProperty="(Ellipse.Width)"
  Duration="0:0:3" AutoReverse="True"
  FillBehavior=" RepeatBehavior="Forever"
  From="100" To="300">
  <DoubleAnimation.EasingFunction>
    <BounceEase EasingMode="EaseInOut" />
  </DoubleAnimation.EasingFunction>
</DoubleAnimation>
```

To see different easing animations in action, the next sample lets an ellipse move between two small rectangles. The Rectangle and Ellipse elements are defined within a Canvas, and the ellipse defines a TranslateTransform transformation to move the ellipse (code file Animation/EasingFunctions.xaml):

```
<Canvas Grid.Row="1">
  <Rectangle Fill="Blue" Width="10" Height="200" Canvas.Left="50"
    Canvas.Top="100" />
```

```
    <Rectangle Fill="Blue" Width="10" Height="200" Canvas.Left="550"
      Canvas.Top="100" />
    <Ellipse Fill="Red" Width="30" Height="30" Canvas.Left="60" Canvas.Top="185">
      <Ellipse.RenderTransform>
        <TranslateTransform x:Name="translate1" X="0" Y="0" />
      </Ellipse.RenderTransform>
    </Ellipse>
  </Canvas>
```

The user starts the animation by clicking a button. Before clicking the button, the user can select the easing function from the `ComboBox` `comboEasingFunctions` and an `EasingMode` enumeration value using radio buttons.

```
<StackPanel Orientation="Horizontal">
  <ComboBox x:Name="comboEasingFunctions" Margin="10" />
  <Button Click="OnStartAnimation" Margin="10">Start</Button>
  <Border BorderThickness="1" BorderBrush="Black" Margin="3">
    <StackPanel Orientation="Horizontal">
      <RadioButton x:Name="easingModeIn" GroupName="EasingMode" Content="In" />
      <RadioButton x:Name="easingModeOut" GroupName="EasingMode"
        Content="Out" IsChecked="True" />
      <RadioButton x:Name="easingModeInOut" GroupName="EasingMode"
        Content="InOut" />
    </StackPanel>
  </Border>
</StackPanel>
```

The list of easing functions that are shown in the `ComboBox` and activated with the animation is returned from the `EasingFunctionModels` property of the `EasingFunctionManager`. This manager converts the easing function to an `EasingFunctionModel` for display (code file `Animation/EasingFunctionsManager.cs`):

```
public class EasingFunctionsManager
{
  private readonly static List<EasingFunctionBase> s_easingFunctions = new()
  {
    new BackEase(),
    new SineEase(),
    new BounceEase(),
    new CircleEase(),
    new CubicEase(),
    new ElasticEase(),
    new ExponentialEase(),
    new PowerEase(),
    new QuadraticEase(),
    new QuinticEase()
  };

  public IEnumerable<EasingFunctionModel> EasingFunctionModels =>
    s_easingFunctions.Select(f => new EasingFunctionModel(f));
}
```

The class `EasingFunctionModel` defines a `ToString` method that returns the name of the class that defines the easing function. This name is shown in the combo box (code file `Animation/EasingFunctionModel.cs`):

```
public class EasingFunctionModel
{
  public EasingFunctionModel(EasingFunctionBase easingFunction) =>
    EasingFunction = easingFunction;
```

```
      public EasingFunctionBase EasingFunction { get; }

      public override string ToString() => EasingFunction.GetType().Name;
   }
```

The ComboBox is filled in the constructor of the code-behind file (code file Animation/
EasingFunctions.xaml.cs):

```
   private readonly EasingFunctionsManager _easingFunctions = new();
   private const int AnimationTimeSeconds = 6;

   public EasingFunctions()
   {
     InitializeComponent();
     foreach (var easingFunctionModel in _easingFunctions.EasingFunctionModels)
     {
       comboEasingFunctions.Items.Add(easingFunctionModel);
     }
   }
```

From the user interface, not only can you select the type of easing function that should be used for the animation,
but you also can select the easing mode. The base class of all easing functions (EasingFunctionBase) defines the
EasingMode property that can be a value of the EasingMode enumeration.

Clicking the button to start the animation invokes the OnStartAnimation method. This in turn invokes the
StartAnimation method. With this method, a Storyboard containing a DoubleAnimation is created programmatically. You've seen similar code earlier using XAML. The animation animates the X property of the
translate1 element (code file Animation/EasingFunctionsPage.xaml.cs):

```
   private void OnStartAnimation(object sender, RoutedEventArgs e)
   {
     if (comboEasingFunctions.SelectedItem is EasingFunctionModel easingFunctionModel)
     {
       EasingFunctionBase easingFunction = easingFunctionModel.EasingFunction;
       easingFunction.EasingMode = GetEasingMode();
       StartAnimation(easingFunction);
     }
   }

   private void StartAnimation(EasingFunctionBase easingFunction)
   {
     chartControl.Draw(easingFunction);

     Storyboard storyboard = new();
     DoubleAnimation ellipseMove = new();
     ellipseMove.EasingFunction = easingFunction;
     ellipseMove.Duration = new
       Duration(TimeSpan.FromSeconds(AnimationTimeSeconds));
     ellipseMove.From = 0;
     ellipseMove.To = 460;
     Storyboard.SetTarget(ellipseMove, translate1);
     Storyboard.SetTargetProperty(ellipseMove, "X");

     // start the animation in 0.5 seconds
     ellipseMove.BeginTime = TimeSpan.FromSeconds(0.5);

     // keep the position after the animation
     ellipseMove.FillBehavior = FillBehavior.HoldEnd;
     storyboard.Children.Add(ellipseMove);
```

```
    storyBoard.Begin();
}
```

Now you can run the application and see the ellipse move from the left to the right rectangle in different ways—with different easing functions. With some of the easing functions, such as BackEase, BounceEase, or ElasticEase, the difference is obvious. The difference is not as noticeable with some of the other easing functions. To better understand how the easing values behave, a line chart is created that shows a line with the value that is returned by the easing function based on time.

To display the line chart, you create a user control that defines a Canvas element. By default, the X direction goes from left to right and the Y direction from top to bottom. To change the Y direction to go from bottom to top, you define a transformation (code file Animation/EasingChartControl.xaml):

```
<Canvas x:Name="canvas1" Width="500" Height="500" Background="Yellow">
  <Canvas.RenderTransform>
    <TransformGroup>
      <ScaleTransform ScaleX="1" ScaleY="-1" />
      <TranslateTransform X="0" Y="500" />
    </TransformGroup>
  </Canvas.RenderTransform>
</Canvas>
```

In the code-behind file, the line chart is drawn using line segments. Line segments were previously discussed using XAML code in this chapter in the section "Geometries Using Segments." Here you see how they can be used from code. The Ease method of the easing function returns a value that is shown in the y-axis passing a normalized time value that is shown in the x-axis (code file Animation/EasingChartControl.xaml.cs):

```
private const double SamplingInterval = 0.01;

public void Draw(EasingFunctionBase easingFunction)
{
  canvas1.Children.Clear();
  var pathSegments = new PathSegmentCollection();
  for (double i = 0; i < 1; i += _samplingInterval)
  {
    double x = i * canvas1.Width;
    double y = easingFunction.Ease(i) * canvas1.Height;
    var segment = new LineSegment();
    segment.Point = new Point(x, y);
    pathSegments.Add(segment);
  }

  var p = new Path();
  p.Stroke = new SolidColorBrush(Colors.Black);
  p.StrokeThickness = 3;
  var figures = new PathFigureCollection();
  figures.Add(new PathFigure { Segments = pathSegments });
  p.Data = new PathGeometry { Figures = figures };
  canvas1.Children.Add(p);
}
```

The Draw method of the EasingChartControl is invoked on the start of the animation (code file Animation/EasingFunctions.xaml.cs):

```
private void StartAnimation(EasingFunctionBase easingFunction)
{
  // show the chart
  chartControl.Draw(easingFunction);
  //...
```

When you run the application, you can see in Figure 31-14 what it looks like to use `BounceEase` and `EaseOut`. Run the applications and check the downloadable .avi file for other selections.

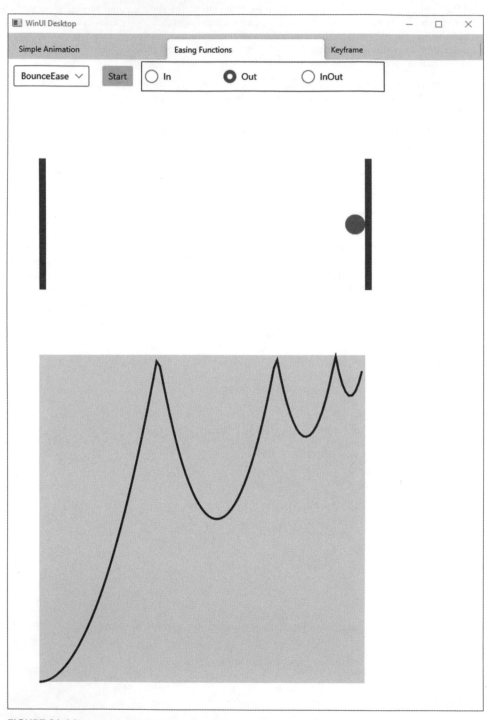

FIGURE 31-14

Keyframe Animations

With ease functions, you've seen how animations can be built in a nonlinear fashion. If you need one property to animate through several values for an animation, you can use *keyframe animations*. Like normal animations, keyframe animations are various animation types that exist to animate properties of different types.

`DoubleAnimationUsingKeyFrames` is the keyframe animation for double types. Other keyframe animation types are `Int32AnimationUsingKeyFrames`, `PointAnimationUsingKeyFrames`, `ColorAnimationUsingKeyFrames`, `SizeAnimationUsingKeyFrames`, and `ObjectAnimationUsingKeyFrames`.

The following example XAML code animates the position of an ellipse by animating the X and Y values of a `TranslateTransform` element. The animation starts when the ellipse is loaded by defining an `EventTrigger` to `RoutedEvent Ellipse.Loaded`. The event trigger starts a `Storyboard` with the `BeginStoryboard` element. The `Storyboard` contains two keyframe animations of type `DoubleAnimationUsingKeyFrame`. A keyframe animation consists of frame elements. The first keyframe animation uses a `LinearKeyFrame`, a `DiscreteDoubleKeyFrame`, and a `SplineDoubleKeyFrame`; the second animation is an `EasingDoubleKeyFrame`. The `LinearDoubleKeyFrame` makes a linear change of the value. The `KeyTime` property defines when in the animation the value of the `Value` property should be reached.

Here, the `LinearDoubleKeyFrame` has three seconds to move the property X to the value 30. `DiscreteDoubleKeyFrame` makes an immediate change to the new value after four seconds. `SplineDoubleKeyFrame` uses a Bézier curve whereby two control points are specified by the `KeySpline` property. `EasingDoubleKeyFrame` is a frame class that supports setting an easing function such as `BounceEase` to control the animation value (code file `Animation/KeyFrameAnimationPage.xaml`):

```xml
<Canvas>
  <Ellipse Fill="Red" Canvas.Left="20" Canvas.Top="20" Width="25" Height="25">
    <Ellipse.RenderTransform>
      <TranslateTransform X="50" Y="50" x:Name="ellipseMove" />
    </Ellipse.RenderTransform>
    <Ellipse.Triggers>
      <EventTrigger>
        <BeginStoryboard>
          <Storyboard>
            <DoubleAnimationUsingKeyFrames Storyboard.TargetProperty="X"
              Storyboard.TargetName="ellipseMove">
              <LinearDoubleKeyFrame KeyTime="0:0:2" Value="30" />
              <DiscreteDoubleKeyFrame KeyTime="0:0:4" Value="80" />
              <SplineDoubleKeyFrame KeySpline="0.5,0.0 0.9,0.0"
                KeyTime="0:0:10" Value="300" />
              <LinearDoubleKeyFrame KeyTime="0:0:20" Value="150" />
            </DoubleAnimationUsingKeyFrames>
            <DoubleAnimationUsingKeyFrames Storyboard.TargetProperty="Y"
              Storyboard.TargetName="ellipseMove">
              <SplineDoubleKeyFrame KeySpline="0.5,0.0 0.9,0.0"
                KeyTime="0:0:2" Value="50" />
              <EasingDoubleKeyFrame KeyTime="0:0:20" Value="300">
                <EasingDoubleKeyFrame.EasingFunction>
                  <BounceEase />
                </EasingDoubleKeyFrame.EasingFunction>
              </EasingDoubleKeyFrame>
            </DoubleAnimationUsingKeyFrames>
          </Storyboard>
        </BeginStoryboard>
      </EventTrigger>
    </Ellipse.Triggers>
  </Ellipse>
</Canvas>
```

Transitions

To make it easier for you to create animated user interfaces, UWP apps define transitions. Transitions make it easier to create compelling apps without the need to think about what makes a cool animation. Transitions pre-define animations for adding, removing, and rearranging items in a list; opening panels; changing the content of content controls; and more.

The following sample demonstrates several transitions to show them on the left side of a user control versus the right side, and it shows similar elements without transitions, which helps you see the differences. Of course, you need to start the application to see the difference because it is hard to demonstrate this in a book.

Reposition Transition

The first example makes use of the `RepositionThemeTransition` within the `Transitions` property of a `Button` element. A transition always needs to be defined within a `TransitionCollection` because such collections are never created automatically, and there's a misleading runtime error in case you don't use the `TransitionCollection`. The second button doesn't use a transition (code file `Transitions/RepositionUserControl.xaml`):

```
<Button Grid.Row="1" Click="OnReposition" Content="Reposition"
  x:Name="buttonReposition" Margin="10">
  <Button.Transitions>
    <TransitionCollection>
      <RepositionThemeTransition />
    </TransitionCollection>
  </Button.Transitions>
</Button>
<Button Grid.Row="1" Grid.Column="1" Click="OnReset" Content="Reset"
  x:Name="button2" Margin="10" />
```

The `RepositionThemeTransition` is a transition when a control changes its position. In the code-behind file, when the user clicks the button, the `Margin` property is changed, which also changes the position of the button.

```
private void OnReposition(object sender, RoutedEventArgs e)
{
  buttonReposition.Margin = new Thickness(100);
  button2.Margin = new Thickness(100);
}

private void OnReset(object sender, RoutedEventArgs e)
{
  buttonReposition.Margin = new Thickness(10);
  button2.Margin = new Thickness(10);
}
```

Pane Transition

The `PopupThemeTransition` and `PaneThemeTransition` are shown in the next user control. Here, the transitions are defined with the `ChildTransitions` property of the `Popup` control (code file `Transitions/PaneTransitionUserControl.xaml`):

```
<StackPanel Orientation="Horizontal" Grid.Row="2">
  <Popup x:Name="popup1" Width="200" Height="90" Margin="60">
    <Border Background="Red" Width="100" Height="60">
    </Border>
    <Popup.ChildTransitions>
      <TransitionCollection>
        <PopupThemeTransition />
```

```
          </TransitionCollection>
        </Popup.ChildTransitions>
      </Popup>
      <Popup x:Name="popup2" Width="200" Height="90" Margin="60">
        <Border Background="Red" Width="100" Height="60">
        </Border>
        <Popup.ChildTransitions>
          <TransitionCollection>
            <PaneThemeTransition />
          </TransitionCollection>
        </Popup.ChildTransitions>
      </Popup>
      <Popup x:Name="popup3" Margin="60" Width="200" Height="90">
        <Border Background="Green" Width="100" Height="60">
        </Border>
      </Popup>
    </StackPanel>
```

The code-behind file opens and closes the `Popup` controls by setting the `IsOpen` property. This in turn starts the transition (code file `Transitions\PaneTransitionUserControl.xaml`):

```
    private void OnShow(object sender, RoutedEventArgs e)
    {
      popup1.IsOpen = true;
      popup2.IsOpen = true;
      popup3.IsOpen = true;
    }

    private void OnHide(object sender, RoutedEventArgs e)
    {
      popup1.IsOpen = false;
      popup2.IsOpen = false;
      popup3.IsOpen = false;
    }
```

When you run the application, you can see that the `PopupThemeTransition` looks good for opening `Popup` and `Flyout` controls. The `PaneThemeTransition` opens the pop-up slowly from the right side. This transition can also be configured to open from other sides by setting properties and thus is best for panels, such as the settings bar, that move in from a side.

Transitions for Items

Adding and removing items from an item's control also defines a transition. The following `ItemsControl` uses the `EntranceThemeTransition` and `RepositionThemeTransition`. The `EntranceThemeTransition` is used when an item is added to the collection; the `RepositionThemeTransition` is used when items are rearranged—for example, by removing an item from the list (code file `Transitions/ListItemsUserControl.xaml`):

```
    <ItemsControl Grid.Row="1" x:Name="list1">
      <ItemsControl.ItemContainerTransitions>
        <TransitionCollection>
          <EntranceThemeTransition />
          <RepositionThemeTransition />
        </TransitionCollection>
      </ItemsControl.ItemContainerTransitions>
    </ItemsControl>
    <ItemsControl Grid.Row="1" Grid.Column="1" x:Name="list2" />
```

In the code-behind file, `Rectangle` objects are added and removed from the list control. As one of the `ItemsControl` objects doesn't have a transition associated, you can easily see the difference in behavior when you run the application (code file `Transitions/ListItemsUserControl.xaml.cs`):

```
private void OnAdd(object sender, RoutedEventArgs e)
{
  list1.Items.Add(CreateRectangle());
  list2.Items.Add(CreateRectangle());
}

private Rectangle CreateRectangle() =>
  new Rectangle
  {
    Width = 90,
    Height = 40,
    Margin = new Thickness(5),
    Fill = new SolidColorBrush { Color = Colors.Blue }
  };

private void OnRemove(object sender, RoutedEventArgs e)
{
  if (list1.Items.Count > 0)
  {
    list1.Items.RemoveAt(0);
    list2.Items.RemoveAt(0);
  }
}
```

> **NOTE** *With these transitions, you get an idea of how they reduce the work needed to animate the user interface. Be sure to check out more transitions available with UWP apps. You can see all the transitions by checking the derived classes from* `Transition` *in the Microsoft documentation.*

VISUAL STATE MANAGER

Earlier in this chapter in the section "Control Templates," you saw how to create control templates to customize the look of controls. Something was missing there. With the default template of a button, the button reacts to mouse moves and clicks and looks differently when the mouse moves over the button or the button is clicked. This change in the look of a control is handled with the help of visual states and animations, controlled by the `VisualStateManager`.

This section examines changing the button style to react to mouse moves and clicks, but it also describes how to create custom states to deal with changes of a complete page when several controls should switch to the disabled state—for example, when some background processing occurs.

With a XAML control, visual states, state groups, and states can be defined that specify animations for a state. State groups exist to allow having multiple states at once. For one group, only one state is allowed at one time. However, another state of another group can be active at the same time. Examples for this are the states and state groups with a button. The `Button` control defines the state groups `CommonStates` and `FocusStates`. States defined with `FocusStates` are `Focused`, `Unfocused`, and `PointerFocused`. The `CommonStates` group defines the states `Normal`, `Pressed`, `Disabled`, and `PointerOver`. With these options, multiple states can be active at the same time, but there is always only one state active within a state group. For example, a button can be in focus and in the normal state. It can also be in focus and pressed. You can also define custom states and state groups.

Let's get into concrete examples.

Predefined States with Control Templates

The custom control template created earlier to style the `Button` control is now enhanced by using visual states. An easy way to do this is by using Blend for Visual Studio. With Blend, you have a designer that allows creating and customizing states and recording the storyboard to define what should happen when one state switches to the other.

> **NOTE** *At the time of this writing, Blend for Visual Studio does not have support for WinUI. If this is still the case when you design your WinUI application, you can use Blend with UWP applications and copy the style to your WinUI application.*

The button template from before is changed to define visual states for the states `Pressed`, `Disabled`, and `PointerOver`. Within the states, a `Storyboard` defines a `ColorAnimation` to change the color of the `Fill` property of an ellipse (code file `VisualStates/MainPage.xaml`):

```
<Style x:Key="RoundedGelButton" TargetType="Button">
  <Setter Property="Width" Value="100" />
  <Setter Property="Height" Value="100" />
  <Setter Property="Foreground" Value="White" />
  <Setter Property="Template">
    <Setter.Value>
      <ControlTemplate TargetType="Button">
        <Grid>
          <VisualStateManager.VisualStateGroups>
            <VisualStateGroup x:Name="CommonStates">
              <VisualState x:Name="Normal"/>
              <VisualState x:Name="Pressed">
                <Storyboard>
                  <ColorAnimation Duration="0" To="#FFC8CE11"
                    Storyboard.TargetProperty=
                      "(Shape.Fill).(SolidColorBrush.Color)"
                    Storyboard.TargetName="GelBackground" />
                </Storyboard>
              </VisualState>
              <VisualState x:Name="Disabled">
                <Storyboard>
                  <ColorAnimation Duration="0" To="#FF606066"
                    Storyboard.TargetProperty=
                      "(Shape.Fill).(SolidColorBrush.Color)"
                    Storyboard.TargetName="GelBackground" />
                </Storyboard>
              </VisualState>
              <VisualState x:Name="PointerOver">
                <Storyboard>
                  <ColorAnimation Duration="0" To="#FF0F9D3A"
                    Storyboard.TargetProperty=
```

```
                           "(Shape.Fill).(SolidColorBrush.Color)"
                         Storyboard.TargetName="GelBackground" />
                </Storyboard>
              </VisualState>
            </VisualStateGroup>
          </VisualStateManager.VisualStateGroups>
          <Ellipse x:Name="GelBackground" StrokeThickness="0.5" Fill="Black">
              <Ellipse.Stroke>
              <LinearGradientBrush StartPoint="0,0" EndPoint="0,1">
                <GradientStop Offset="0" Color="#ff7e7e7e" />
                <GradientStop Offset="1" Color="Black" />
              </LinearGradientBrush>
            </Ellipse.Stroke>
          </Ellipse>
          <Ellipse Margin="15,5,15,50">
            <Ellipse.Fill>
              <LinearGradientBrush StartPoint="0,0" EndPoint="0,1">
                <GradientStop Offset="0" Color="#aaffffff" />
                <GradientStop Offset="1" Color="Transparent" />
              </LinearGradientBrush>
            </Ellipse.Fill>
          </Ellipse>
          <ContentPresenter x:Name="GelButtonContent"
            VerticalAlignment="Center"
            HorizontalAlignment="Center"
            Content="{TemplateBinding Content}" />
        </Grid>
      </ControlTemplate>
    </Setter.Value>
  </Setter>
</Style>
```

Now when you run the application, you can see the color changes based on moving and clicking the mouse.

Defining Custom States

You can define custom states by using the `VisualStateManager`, custom state groups by using `VisualStateGroup`, and states by using `VisualState`. The following code snippet creates the `Enabled` and `Disabled` states within the `CustomStates` group. The visual states are defined within the `Grid` of the main window. On changing the state, the `IsEnabled` property of a `Button` element is changed using a `DiscreteObjectKeyFrame` animation in no time (code file `VisualStates/MainPage.xaml`):

```
<VisualStateManager.VisualStateGroups>
  <VisualStateGroup x:Name="CustomStates">
    <VisualState x:Name="Enabled"/>
    <VisualState x:Name="Disabled">
      <Storyboard>
        <ObjectAnimationUsingKeyFrames
          Storyboard.TargetProperty="(Control.IsEnabled)"
          Storyboard.TargetName="button1">
          <DiscreteObjectKeyFrame KeyTime="0">
            <DiscreteObjectKeyFrame.Value>
              <x:Boolean>False</x:Boolean>
            </DiscreteObjectKeyFrame.Value>
          </DiscreteObjectKeyFrame>
```

```
        </ObjectAnimationUsingKeyFrames>
        <!-- another key frame animation for button2 -->
      </Storyboard>
    </VisualState>
  </VisualStateGroup>
</VisualStateManager.VisualStateGroups>
```

Setting Custom States

Now the states need to be set. You can do this easily by invoking the `GoToState` method of the `VisualStateManager` class. In the code-behind file, the `OnEnable` and `OnDisable` methods are `Click` event handlers for two buttons in the page (code file `VisualStates/MainWindow.xaml.cs`):

```
private void OnEnable(object sender, RoutedEventArgs e) =>
  VisualStateManager.GoToState(page1, "Enabled", useTransitions: true);

private void OnDisable(object sender, RoutedEventArgs e) =>
  VisualStateManager.GoToState(page1, "Disabled", useTransitions: true);
```

In a real application, you can change the state in a similar manner—for example, when a network call is invoked—and the user should not act on some of the controls within the page. The user should still be allowed to click a cancellation button. By changing the state, you can also show progress information.

SUMMARY

In this chapter, you toured many of the features of styling Windows apps. With XAML it is easy to separate the work of developers and designers. All UI features can be created with XAML, and the functionality can be created by using a code-behind file.

You have seen many shapes and geometry elements. Vector-based graphics enable XAML elements to be scaled, skewed, rotated, and translated.

Different kinds of brushes are available for painting the background and foreground of elements. You can use not only solid brushes and linear or radial gradient brushes but also acrylic brushes that offer transparent effects.

Styling and templates enable you to customize the look of controls; with the `VisualStateManager`, you can change properties of XAML elements dynamically. You can easily create animations by animating a property value from a XAML control.

This was the last of the WinUI chapters of this book. At the time of this writing, WinUI is still in its early stages, and many more features are coming. Check `https://csharp.christiannagel.com` and `https://github.com/ProfessionalCSharp/MoreSamples` for more features of WinUI and for information about how you can use XAML with mobile applications running on Android and iOS using .NET MAUI.

INDEX

D

O

OAuth 2.0, 544
Object class, 36, 139–141, 212–213
object orientation, 96
object-oriented programming (OOP), in C#
  generics, 115–118
  inheritance with classes, 96–104
  inheritance with records, 106–107
  modifiers, 104–106
  object orientation, 96
  using interfaces, 107–115
objects
  comparing for equality, 139–141
  multiple, of same type, 154
  tracking, 627–629
  updating, 629
  updating untracked, 629–630
ObservableObject class, 880
OfType method, 233, 236, 625
Ogonek character, 645
On method, 808
OnButtonClick method, 826–827
OnCompleted method, 293, 294
OnConfiguring method, 586
OnConnect method, 808
OnConnectedAsync method, 811
OnDatesChanged method, 845–846
OnDayItemChanging method, 844
OnDisconnectedAsync method, 811
one-dimensional arrays. *See* arrays
one-time binding mode, 853
OnEventCommand method, 430
one-way binding mode, 853
OnGet method, 758, 774–775
OnGetResource method, 665–666
OnInitializeAsync method, 787
OnMessageReceived method, 809
OnNavigatedTo method, 865
OnNavigationSelectionChanged method, 891–893
OnPost method, 758, 774–775
OnPropertyChanged method, 853–855
OnSave method, 517
OnSaveAsync method, 887–888
OnSendMessage method, 808
OnStartAsync method, 302
OnStartAsyncConfigureAwait method, 303
OnStartDeadlock method, 305
OnTabAdd method, 864–865
OnTabClose method, 864–865
OnTappedButton method, 832–833
OnTick, 462

OnTimer method, 462
OnVisitSyntaxNode method, 331
Open Web Application Security Project (OWASP), 580
OpenAPI, 718–719
OpenID Connect, 544, 560
OpenReadAsync method, 516–517
OpenTelemetry, 420, 427–429
OperatingSystem class, 371
OperationCanceledException, 300, 455
operators
  as, 123
  about, 120
  aggregate, 252–254
  binary, 127–131
  checked, 122–123
  compound assignment, 121
  conditional-expression (?:), 121–122
  conversion, 254–255
  defined, 63
  generation, 255–256
  how they work, 136–137
  indexer, 125
  is, 123
  nameof, 124–125
  null-coalescing (??), 125–126
  null-coalescing assignment, 126
  null-conditional, 126–127
  overloading, 136–139
  overloading with Vector type, 137–139
  sizeof, 124
  typeof, 124
  unchecked, 122–123
optional arguments, 70–71
OrderBy operator, 233, 237–239
OrderByDescending operator, 233, 237–239
otherCustomer2 object, 340
out of process, 748
out parameters, 85–86
outputText, 319
OverflowException, 265
Overlaps method, 367
overloading operators, 136–139
override modifier, 106
owned entities, 621–623
OwnsOne method, 641

P

Package Manifest Editor, 822
PackageReference, 384
Page control, 841